Here are some basic map concepts that will help you to get the most out of the maps in this textbook.

■ Always look at the scale, which allows you to determine the distance in miles or kilometers between locations on the map.

■ Examine the legend carefully. It explains the colors and symbols used on the map.

■ Note the locations of mountains, rivers, oceans, and other geographic features and consider how these would affect such human activities as agriculture, commerce, travel, and warfare.

■ Read the map caption thoroughly. It provides important information, sometimes not covered in the text itself.

■ Many of the maps showing premodern political boundaries and labels also carry a *spot map*. This smaller map identifies the contemporary, political boundaries of the area and allows you to gain a better understanding of the breadth of empires and the evolution of nations. In addition, an occasional *spot map* showing a detail of a larger map appears in the text.

www.wadsworth.com

www.wadsworth.com is the World Wide Web site for Wadsworth and is your direct source to dozens of on-line resources.

At *www.wadsworth.com* you can find out about supplements, demonstration software, and student resources. You can also send email to many of our authors and preview new publications and exciting new technologies.

www.wadsworth.com
Changing the way the world learns®

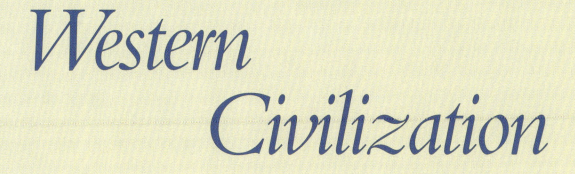

Western Civilization

A HISTORY OF EUROPEAN SOCIETY

Volume II: Since 1550

SECOND EDITION

Western Civilization

A HISTORY OF EUROPEAN SOCIETY

Volume II: Since 1550

SECOND EDITION

Steven C. Hause
Washington University–St. Louis

William Maltby
University of Missouri–St. Louis

THOMSON
WADSWORTH

Australia • Canada • Mexico • Singapore • Spain
United Kingdom • United States

THOMSON

WADSWORTH

Publisher: *Clark Baxter*
Senior Assistant Editor: *Julie Yardley*
Editorial Assistant: *Anne Gittinger*
Senior Technology Project Manager: *Melinda Newfarmer*
Marketing Manager: *Lori Grebe Cook*
Marketing Assistant: *Mary Ho*
Advertising Project Managers: *Brian Chaffee and Stacey Purviance*
Project Manager, Editorial Production: *Kimberly Adams*
Print/Media Buyer: *Barbara Britton*

Permissions Editor: *Sarah Harkrader*
Production Service: *Graphic World Inc.*
Text Designer: *Ellen Pettengell*
Art Editor: *Graphic World Inc.*
Copy Editor: *Graphic World Inc.*
Illustrator: *Graphic World Inc.*
Cover Designer: *Ellen Pettengell*
Cover Image: *National Trust/Art Resource, New York*
Cover Printer: *Quebecor World/Dubuque*
Compositor: *Graphic World Inc.*
Printer: *Quebecor World/Dubuque*

For more information about our products, contact us at:
Thomson Learning Academic Resource Center
1-800-423-0563

For permission to use material from this text or product, submit a request online at
http://www.thomsonrights.com.

Any additional questions about permissions can be submitted by email to thomsonrights@thomson.com.

Thomson Wadsworth
10 Davis Drive
Belmont, CA 94002-3098
USA

Asia
Thomson Learning
5 Shenton Way #01-01
UIC Building
Singapore 068808

Australia/New Zealand
Thomson Learning
102 Dodds Street
Southbank, Victoria 3006
Australia

Canada
Nelson
1120 Birchmount Road
Toronto, Ontario M1K 5G4

Canada
Europe/Middle East/Africa
Thomson Learning
High Holborn House
50/51 Bedford Row
London WC1R 4LR
United Kingdom

Latin America
Thomson Learning
Seneca, 53
Colonia Polanco
11560 Mexico D.F.
Mexico

Spain/Portugal
Paraninfo
Calle Magallanes, 25
28015 Madrid, Spain

Library of Congress Control Number: 2004107967

ISBN 0-534-62122-8

Contents in Brief

Contents in Detail

Chapter 19

THE POLITICAL EVOLUTION OF THE OLD REGIME, 1715–1789 448

Chapter 20

THE CULTURE OF OLD REGIME EUROPE 478

Chapter 32

THE AGE OF EUROPEAN UNION SINCE 1975 829

Maps

Documents

Tables

Preface

Every Western civilization textbook has an individual character. The special concern of this text is revealed in its subtitle, *A History of European Society.* The authors share an interest in the varieties of social history—of women, the family, and the daily lives of ordinary people—that have changed historical studies in recent years. We have tried to weave a synthesis of this contemporary social history scholarship throughout the text. We have sought to locate our social history in the traditional concerns of a Western civilization textbook, rooted in economic and political context and related to historical issues of differing cultures. War and technological developments—phenomena that influenced and were influenced by social and economic structures—are not treated in isolation but rather as phenomena with profound implications for everyday life. We have tried to provide insight into popular culture without sacrificing the traditional emphasis on the intellectual, scientific, and religious interests of the elite and without forgetting that popular culture and elite culture are often the same.

Our attempt to combine traditional breadth and a focus on social history has led us to integrate a large quantity of supporting materials and historical sources into the text. In addition to the maps, illustrations, and documents that usually serve this purpose, we have chosen to add a number of statistical tables and graphs needed to document social and economic history. These are closely integrated into the text so that their basic meaning is clear and their raw data can illuminate discussion.

Learning History through Narrative and Historical Analysis

Fundamentally, of course, the development of Western civilization is a story, and we tell it as a narrative. But unlike ancient bards and other storytellers, historians must also explain, analyze, and teach the characteristics of the different historical eras. The chapters into which the book is divided must explain why and how each historical era developed these characteristics.

Sometimes a chapter must focus on evaluating and explaining interactions, such as the events leading to a war or revolution; and sometimes a chapter must focus on showing what actually happened—telling the narrative story of important changes and developments. Both are skills that students of history will seek to develop as they refine their understanding of the past.

Guideposts. Most of the reviewers who helped guide our work agree that students can easily get lost in the wealth of information within a chapter. We share with our colleagues a keen desire that students learn to love history as much as we do. The sooner they spot both the forest and the trees in each chapter, the sooner real understanding begins to take root. To help our readers, we have added a **Chapter Outline** and **Focus Questions** at the beginning of each chapter and **Review Questions** at the end. We have also added a descriptive word or two—**topic heads**—at the beginning of appropriate paragraphs. We hope these unobtrusive guideposts will help students study, learn, and perform well on their exams by making it clear whenever the focus of a section shifts from one topic to the next. We have also included **pronunciation guides** following foreign terms and names to help students read and remember unfamiliar material. Acknowledging that pronunciations of foreign terms differ over time and that their sounds can be difficult to communicate in text, we nevertheless hope that by offering a starting point for the instructor to modify aurally as needed, we have given students an essential tool for participating in discussions.

The West in the World. The study of Western civilization inevitably, and increasingly, bears on changing notions of the idea of the West and the many points of contact between the West and the rest of the world. This edition opens with a discussion of the place of the West in a global, geographical context, and brief recurring essays throughout the text explore points of contact. However, we have also taken special care throughout the text to compare civilizations when doing so can help readers see the uniqueness and the similarities of major cultures. For example, a box in Chapter 1 discusses (and shows) the differences between the major monuments created for the rulers of Egypt and Mesopotamia.

Learning History through Primary Source Documents

For first-time readers, we want to bring to attention the documents that complement the narrative. Each chapter includes a broad range of letters, treaties, poems, broadsides, declarations, and other written sources—primary source documents similar to the material that most instructors use to supplement their courses. The purpose of such documents is to make the descriptions more vivid, to substantiate the analysis yet provoke questions, and to introduce readers to the raw materials of historical study. As often as possible, we have embedded with a document an illustration or two that illuminates the primary document. For example, in Chapter 2, images from artifacts of the period show Greek athletes performing events that a Pindar ode to the winner of the ancient Olympic games praises. For a comprehensive list, see page xxi.

Learning History through Tables

This edition is filled with numerous tables of historical data. Most of these tables illustrate the details of everyday life and help students to see the human faces hidden just behind each column of numbers. Until very recently, of course, the great majority of Europeans were illiterate and unable to leave behind a written record of their lives. By examining parish, municipal, and other records, we are able to piece together information such as wages and prices in ancient Rome, life expectancy in the Middle Ages, the incidence of abandoned children in major cities, and other telling details of everyday life.

For example, Table 18.3 in Chapter 18 shows that 45 percent of a worker's family income in late eighteenth-century Berlin was spent on bread, 12 percent was spent on other vegetable products, and 15 percent on meat and dairy products. The table clearly shows that for many centuries bread was the major source of nutrition for peasants and workers, rather than the side dish it has become today. The recurring bread riots discussed in the text reflect the real deprivation when the price of bread rose and ordinary people starved; the numbers make such a crisis starkly plain. For a comprehensive list, see page xxv.

Learning History through Art

Some of the richest views of history presented in Western civilization textbooks have come from seeing the art and architecture of the past. More recently, of course, television and the Internet have created a generation of visual learners. Without losing faith in the power of words, we have included more than 600 photographs in the book, most in full color. Each image bears directly on the discussion in the pages on which they appear. And those that are not embedded in a document or table include a caption of some length that complements the text. For example, an illustration in Chapter 18 shows a coach stop in a small eighteenth-century town. Students will enjoy the picture on their own—but many will also want to speculate on how long it will take to fix the broken wheel on one of the stagecoaches and to think further about the pace of transportation in eighteenth-century Europe.

Learning History through Maps

Geography and history are interrelated subjects, and maps are essential components of basic historical study. At the elementary level, it makes an enormous difference to the history of Europe that England is an island or that Germany and Poland have no natural barrier between them. At a more sophisticated level, a linguistic geography of central and eastern Europe shows the complexity of political conflicts in that region. All of the book's maps, more than 100, appear in full color, and most include such topographic features as mountains and rivers. These features make it clear, for example, how the mountainous terrain of the Peloponnesian Peninsula encouraged the development of independent city-states in ancient Greece. For a comprehensive list, see page xix.

Spot Maps. In addition, overlapped on maps of the ancient period through the eighteenth century are small maps showing contemporary political boundaries. For example, overlapped on the map of the ancient Middle East in Chapter 1 is a small spot map showing the political boundaries of the contemporary middle east—an area as important today as it was in ancient times.

Learning History through Timelines

One of the most common concerns of students who confront large amounts of historical material for the first time is an anxiety about dates. Dates are essential to constructing a sequence of events, and an understanding of change over time can come only with the help of the dates that mark time. Furthermore, a date can mark the aberration in a period, the event, invention, or discovery that heralds a development a hundred years later. Yet too many dates become a burden to readers. To address this problem, each chapter ends with a timeline to assist students in keeping events in their correct relationship without memorizing all of the dates in the text.

ACKNOWLEDGMENTS

We owe our gratitude to all those who helped us in the preparation of this second edition of *Western Civilization: A History of European Society.* We would like to thank all those at Wadsworth Publishing who have assisted us in producing this book: Clark Baxter, our editor and publisher who suggested the book and carried it into production; Julie Yardley, assistant editor, who put the supplement package together; Kim Adams, project manager; Lori Grebe Cook, marketing manager; and Melinda Newfarmer, technology project manager. We especially want to thank our reviewers: Kathryn Abbott, Western Kentucky University; William Abbott, Fairfield University; Gerald D. Anderson, North Dakota State University; Roz L. Ashby, Yavapai College; Robert Barnes, Arizona State University; David Bartley, Indiana Wesleyan University; Anthony Bedford, Modesto Junior College; Rodney E. Bell, University of South Dakota; Melissa Bonafont, Austin Texas Community College; Jerry Brookshire, Middle Tennessee State University; Richard Camp, California State University–Northridge; Marybeth Carlson, University of Dayton; Elizabeth Carney, Clemson University; Sherri Cole, Arizona Western College; Jeffrey Cox, University of Iowa; Kevin Cramer, Indiana University–Purdue University, Indianapolis; Frederic Crawford, Middle Tennessee State University; Philip B. Crow; Leslie Derfler, Florida Atlantic University; Linda S. Frey, University of Montana; Charlotte M. Gradie, Sacred Heart University; Sarah Gravelle, University of Detroit; Stephen Haliczer, Northern Illinois University; Barry Hankins, Baylor University; William Hartel, Marietta College; John A. Heitmann, University of Dayton; Mack Holt, George Mason University; David Hudson, California State University, Fresno; Frank Josserand, Southwest Texas State University; Gary Kates, Trinity University; Charles Killinger, Valencia Community College; Michael Kulikowski, University of Tennessee; Paul Leuschen, University of Arkansas; Eleanor Long, Hinds Community College; William Matheny, Liberty University; Olivia H. McIntyre, Eckerd College; David L. Longfellow, Baylor University; Bill Mackey, University of Alaska–Anchorage; Tom McMullen, Georgia Southern University; Paul L. Maier, Western Michigan University; Larry Marvin, St. Louis University; Carol Bresnahan Menning, University of Toledo; Jeffrey Merrick, University of Wisconsin–Milwaukee; Dennis Mihelich, Creighton University; Charles G. Nauert, Jr., University of Missouri–Columbia; Elizabeth Neumeyer, Kellogg Community College; Thomas C. Owen, Louisiana State University; William E. Painter, University of North Texas; Kathleen Paul, University of Southern Florida; Mark D. Potter, University of Wyoming; Dermot Quinn, Seton Hall University; Nancy Rachels, Hillsborough Community College; Elsa Rapp, Montgomery County Community College; Miriam Raub Vivian, California State University–Bakersfield; Richard R. Rivers, Macomb Community College; Kenneth W. Rock, Colorado State University; Karl A. Roider, Louisiana State University; Leonard Rosenband, Utah State University; Joyce E. Salisbury, University of Wisconsin–Green Bay; Claire A. Sanders, Texas Christian University; Jerry Sandvick, North Hennepin Community College; Thomas P. Schlunz, University of New Orleans; Donna Simpson, Wheeling Jesuit University; Elisabeth Sommer, Grand Valley State University; Ira Spar, Ramapo College of New Jersey; Jake W. Spidle, University of New Mexico; Roger D. Tate, Somerset Community College; Jackson Taylor, Jr., University of Mississippi; Timothy M. Teeter, Georgia Southern University; Lee Shai Weissbach, University of Louisville; Pamela West, Jefferson State Community College; Richard Weigel, Western Kentucky University; Richard S. Williams, Washington State University.

ABOUT THE AUTHORS

Steven C. Hause is Senior Scholar in the Humanities and Co-Director of European Studies at Washington University–St. Louis. He is also Professor of History Emeritus at the University of Missouri–St. Louis, where he held the Thomas Jefferson Professorship and won the Chancellor's Award for Excellence in Teaching (1996) and the Pierre Laclede Honors College Teacher of the Year Award (1989). He is the author and co-author of three previous books on the history of the women's rights movement in modern France, which have won four research prizes: *Women's Suffrage and Social Politics in the French Third Republic,* with Anne R. Kenney (Princeton University Press, 1984); *Hubertine Auclert, the French Suffragette* (Yale University Press, 1987); and *Feminisms of the Belle Epoque,* with Jennifer Waelti-Walters (University of Nebraska Press, 1994). His current research focuses on the Protestant minority in modern France. His essays have appeared in several journals, including *American Historical Review* and *French Historical Studies.*

William S. Maltby is Professor of History Emeritus at the University of Missouri–St. Louis, where he taught for more than 30 years. Among his publications are *The Black Legend in England: The Development of Anti-Spanish Sentiment, 1558–1660* (Duke University Press, 1971); *Alba: A Biography of Fernando Alvarez de Toledo, Third Duke of Alba, 1507–1582* (University of California Press, 1983); *The Reign of Charles V* (Palgrave Macmillan, 2002), and articles on various aspects of Early Modern European history. From 1977 to 1997, he also served as Executive Director of the Center for Reformation Research and as editor of several volumes and series of volumes on the history of the Reformation.

FOCUS QUESTIONS

● What major developments undermined the church's authority in the
  later Middle Ages?

● What major issues separated the reformers from those who remained
  Catholics?

● Why did a number of rulers and city
  governments support the Protestants?

● How did the reformations of the sixteenth century influence popular culture and the status of women?

Chapter 14

THE RELIGIOUS REFORMATIONS OF THE SIXTEENTH CENTURY

On April 17, 1521, a monk named Martin Luther appeared before Emperor Charles V and the princes of the Holy Roman Empire at the Diet of Worms. Four years earlier, he had attacked the church's practice of selling indulgences for cash. Although many churchmen agreed with him, the papacy condemned his position. In the controversy that followed, Luther began to attack other church doctrines and practices. After some delay, Pope Leo X condemned his teachings and ordered his books burned. The church then asked the Imperial Diet to declare Luther an outlaw. As Luther's prince, the Elector Frederick the Wise of Saxony demanded that "his" monk be per- mitted a hearing that, he hoped, would give Luther an opportunity to defend his views. Copies of Luther's writings were brought before the princes. An official of the Archbishop of Trier asked him if these were his books and if he was prepared to reject all or part of their contents. To everyone's amazement, Luther asked for time to consider. The next day, at 6:00 in the afternoon, he appeared again, and after a brief speech, answered in German: "I cannot and will not recant, because it is neither safe nor wise to act against conscience. Here I stand, I can do no other. God help me! Amen." Sweating and clearly shaken, Luther repeated his declaration in Latin and left the building. On the way home, an armed band of Frederick's men seized him and hurried him off to one of Frederick's castles to protect him from arrest.

For many, Luther's declaration marks the beginning of the Protestant Reformation. It was clearly one of the most dramatic moments in European history, but the movement it symbolizes had long been underway, and Luther's Reformation was but one of many. Taken together, the religious reformations of the sixteenth century shattered the unity of west- ern Christendom and changed the life of Europe forever.

Chapter 14 begins with the problems and conflicts that confronted the late medieval church and how they led to increasingly strident demands for reform. It then exam- ines the wide variety of religious movements that arose during the sixteenth century—Lutheran, Reformed, Calvinist, Anabaptist, and Anglican—before describing an equally important reformation within the Catholic Church. It concludes with the cultural and social consequences of religious change.

LATE MEDIEVAL DEMANDS FOR RELIGIOUS REFORM (C. 1300–1517)

The religious reformations of the sixteenth century grew out of a crisis that had been long in the making. For nearly 200 years, plague, war, and the perception of social collapse had raised the overall level of spiritual anxiety in European society while the growth of literacy narrowed the intellectual gap between the clergy and their flocks. Lay people (and many clergy) began to demand higher standards of spirituality than ever before. When the church, crippled by internal struggles of its own, failed to meet this revolution of rising expectations, calls for reform intensified. At the same time, the new assertiveness of the secular states brought their rulers into conflict with the church over rights, privileges, and revenues. The convergence of religious discontent with the interests of the state made the pressure for change irresistible.

The Conflicting Roles of the Medieval Church.
The condition of the church aroused strong feelings in medieval Europe not only because almost everyone was a believing Christian but because the church as an institution was more closely integrated with the secular world than it is today. The pope claimed responsibility not only for the spiritual welfare of western Christians but also for the administration and defense of the Papal States, a territory that embraced much of central Italy. At the local level, bishops, parishes, monasteries, and other ecclesiastical foundations probably controlled 20 percent of the arable land in Europe. In less-settled areas such as the north of England, the total may have approached 70 percent. Many Europeans therefore lived on estates held by the church or had regular business dealings with those who managed them. Such contacts often caused resentment and may at times have encouraged the appearance of corruption.

Social services, too, were the church's responsibility. Clerics commonly administered hospitals, the care of orphans, and the distribution of charity and controlled formal education from the grammar school to the university. In an age when inns were few and wretched, monasteries often served as hotels, offering food and lodging to travelers in return for nominal donations.

The church's many roles made it the most important institution in Europe, but practical responsibilities bred a certain worldliness. To meet them, the church often rewarded those in whom administrative skills were more developed than spirituality. Not everyone who became a priest or nun did so from the purest of motives. Because the church offered one of the few available routes to upward social mobility, ambition or family interest caused many to become clerics without an adequate religious vocation. Some had little choice. Parents often destined their sons for the priesthood at a tender age, while unmarriageable women or those who preferred a career other than that of wife and mother had only the convent as a refuge. For women of talent and ambition, the opportunity to govern an abbey or a charitable institution was a route to self-fulfillment and public service otherwise unavailable in medieval society. For an ambitious young man without an estate, or for a scholar who wished to pursue a career at the university, the church offered the only pathway to success.

Not all late medieval clerics, of course, had worldly motives. Extreme piety and asceticism existed in close proximity to spiritual indifference and corruption. For many people in an age of great spiritual need, the contrast may have been too painful to accept. In any case, the anticlericalism that had always been present in European life ran especially high in the fourteenth and fifteenth centuries. Although by no means universal—the ties between lay people and their parish priests often remained close—it was an underlying accompaniment to the events that convulsed the church throughout this period.

The Decline of Papal Authority

Papal authority was one of the first casualties of the conflict between church and state and of the growing confusion over the temporal and spiritual roles of the clergy. A series of scandals beginning around 1300 gravely weakened the ability of the popes either to govern the church or to institute effective reforms in the face of popular demand. In 1294, the saintly Celestine V resigned from the papacy in part because he feared that the exercise of its duties imperiled his soul. His successor, Boniface VIII, had no such concerns. A vigorous advocate of papal authority, Boniface came into conflict with both Edward I of England and Philip IV of France over the issue of clerical taxation. The two kings were at war with one another, and each sought to tax the clergy of their respective realms to pay for it. When the pope forbade the practice in the bull *Clericis Laicos,* Philip blocked the transmission of money from France to Rome. (A *bull* is a papal letter, sealed because of its importance with a round leaden seal, or *bulla.* It is named after the first word or words of its text.) Boniface backed down, but Philip was not content with partial victories. In 1301, he convicted the papal legate of treason and demanded that Boniface ratify the decision of the French courts. This he could not do without sacrificing papal jurisdiction over the French church. When Boniface issued the decree *Unam Sanctam,* a bold assertion of papal authority over the secular state, Philip had him kidnapped at Anagni in 1303. Physically mistreated by his captors and furious over this unprecedented assault on papal dignity, Boniface died shortly thereafter.

The Babylonian Captivity. After the brief pontificate of Benedict IX, French influence in the College of Cardinals secured the election of the bishop of Bordeaux, who became pope as Clement V (served 1305–1314). The Roman populace was outraged. Riot and disorder convinced Clement that Rome would be an unhealthy place for a Frenchman. He decided to establish himself at Avignon (Ah-vee-nyon), a papal territory in the south of France. The papacy would remain there for 73 years.

The stay of the popes at Avignon was called the **Babylonian Captivity,** because the church appeared to have been taken captive by the French as the biblical children of Israel had been held at Babylon. It was an international scandal for several reasons. The pope was living outside his diocese, and absenteeism had long been considered an abuse by reformers. Worse yet, the pope seemed to be a mere agent of the French monarchy. This was not quite true. The Avignon popes were more independent than they appeared to be at the time, but their support of France against England in the later stages of the Hundred Years' War reinforced negative impressions. They devoted their best efforts to

▼FIGURE 14.1 *The Papal Palace at Avignon.*
Contemporaries saw the magnificent palace built by the popes at Avignon as a symbol of clerical greed and worldliness. It is shown here from across the Rhône River with the ruined bridge of St. Benezet (the Pont d'Avignon of the nursery rhyme) in the foreground.

strengthening papal finances and to the construction of a magnificent palace complex at Avignon. Fiscal reforms backfired politically because most countries responded to it with legislation limiting papal jurisdiction and taxation within their borders. The palace was ostentatious and fostered the idea that the popes had no intention of returning to Rome. Most people came to believe that the popes were subservient to France as well as greedy and luxurious.

The Great Schism. Criticism mounted, and in 1377, Gregory XI returned the papacy to Rome. He died the following year, and his Italian successor, Urban VI, was elected amid rioting by the Roman mob and dissension among the cardinals. Urban quickly alienated those who had elected him by his erratic behavior and by his demands for an immediate reform of the papal court. Thirteen cardinals, twelve of whom were French, left Rome. Claiming that the election had been held under duress, they elected an antipope, Clement VII. The **Great Schism** (1378–1417) had begun.

The church now had two popes. England, the Holy Roman Empire, Hungary, and Poland supported Urban VI. France, Castile, Aragon, Naples, and Scotland supported Clement. International and dynastic issues were involved, and neither claimant would step down. For nearly 40 years, each side elected its own successors while papal administration deteriorated and the prestige of the papacy itself sank to levels not seen since before the Cluniac reforms.

The most promising solution was to convene a general council of the church. In 1409, the Council of Pisa elected Alexander V, who was generally accepted throughout Europe. However, the two prior claimants,

arguing that the council had been called illegally by the cardinals instead of by a pope, refused to quit. There were now three popes. Finally, in 1413, Alexander's successor, John XXIII, called the Council of Constance, which declared itself superior to any pope (see Document 14.1). John, who had in the meantime been found guilty of heresy, and the Avignon claimant Benedict XIII were deposed and Gregory XIII resigned. The Council then elected Martin V to succeed Gregory, thereby preserving the legitimacy of the Roman line, which has since been regarded as official.

Conciliarism and its Legacy. The Schism was over, but the papacy had been gravely weakened in both fact and theory. The actions of the council were supported by the work of three generations of thinkers who had come to believe that councils representing the entire body of the faithful had ultimate authority over the church and that the pope was little more than a symbol of unity. This position became known as **conciliarism.** Made plausible by more than a century of papal scandals, conciliarism became a formidable obstacle to the governance of the church. Fifteenth-century popes feared with some justification that they might be deposed for any controversial act, while councils, by their nature, found making everyday administrative decisions impossible. Legally, Pope Pius II resolved the issue in 1460, when he forbade appeals to a council without papal authorization in the bull *Execrabilis.* The memory of conciliarism nevertheless would inhibit papal efforts at reform for years to come.

The Possessionist Controversy. Conciliarism also served as a focus for criticisms of the papacy that had been simmering since the Babylonian Captivity. Other complaints against the papacy, some of which were adopted by the conciliarists, grew out of the **possessionist controversy.** By the end of the thirteenth century, the Franciscan order had split into two main factions: (1) the Observant or Spiritual Franciscans, who insisted on a literal interpretation of the Rule of St. Francis, which prohibited the order from owning property, and (2) the Conventuals, who believed that the work of the order could be done only if the brothers lived an orderly life in convents and possessed the material resources with which to perform their tasks. The whole issue spoke directly to the concerns of lay people who had long resented what they saw as the materialism and excessive fiscal demands of the clergy. After much argument, John XXII condemned the Observant position. Because the Franciscan Observants had no property, they tended to find lodging on their own and were therefore not subject to the discipline of a convent. This, he thought, could only breed scandal. The Observant Franciscans responded with written attacks on the validity of papal authority, many of which would be used by later critics of the church.

DOCUMENT 14.1

THE DECREE *SACROSANCTA*

By issuing the decree *Sacrosancta,* the Council of Constance (1414–1417) justified its deposition of three existing popes and the election of Martin V. Although repudiated by later popes, the decree helped end the Great Schism and provided a concise statement of the conciliarist position for future generations.

In the name of the Holy and indivisible Trinity; of the Father, Son, and Holy Ghost. Amen.

This holy synod of Constance, forming a general council for the extirpation of the present schism and the union and reformation, in head and members, of the church of God, legitimately assembled in the Holy Ghost, to the praise of Omnipotent God, in order that it may the more easily, safely, effectively, and freely bring about the union and reformation of the church of God, hereby determines, decrees, and declares what follows:

It first declares that this same council, legitimately assembled in the Holy Ghost, forming a general council and representing the Catholic Church militant, has its power immediately from Christ, and everyone, whatever his state or position, even if it be the Papal dignity itself, is bound to obey it in all those things which pertain to the faith and the healing of the said schism, and to the general reformation of the Church of God in head and members.

It further declares that anyone, whatever his condition, station or rank, even if it be the Papal, who shall contumaciously refuse to obey the mandates, decrees, ordinances or instructions which have been, or shall be issued by this holy council, or by any other general council, legitimately summoned, which concern, or in any way relate to the above mentioned subjects, shall, unless he repudiate his conduct, be subjected to condign penance and be suitably punished, having recourse, if necessary, to the other resources of the law.

From Council of Constance, "Sacrosancta," in Edward P. Cheyney, ed, *Pennsylvania Translations and Reprints*, vol. 3, no. 6 (Philadelphia: University of Pennsylvania Press, 1898).

Question: What was the purpose of this document?

The Struggle over the Forms of Piety

The issue of church governance became entangled in a growing dispute over the forms of piety. This conflict, which was about two different ways of living a Christian life, had been present implicitly in the reform movements of the twelfth century. The dominant form of piety that had emerged from the early Middle Ages was forged by the monastic tradition. It saw the clergy as heroic champions whose chief function was to serve as intermediaries between the laity and a God of judgment.

They did this primarily through the sacrament of communion (the Eucharist), which Catholics consider a sacrifice, and through oral prayers of intercession. This view, with its necessary emphasis on the public repetition of formulas, was challenged in the eleventh and twelfth centuries by Bernard of Clairvaux and other monastic theorists who sought a more personal experience of God through private devotions and mental prayer. The Franciscans adopted their views and eventually popularized them, although the process was lengthy and incomplete. The Observant Franciscans found mental prayer especially attractive because their interpretation of the Rule of St. Francis made corporate devotions difficult.

Abuses in Late Medieval Piety. To those who sought transformation of their inner life through personal contact with God, the older forms of piety were unacceptable. They came to believe that excessive emphasis on the sacraments and on oral prayer encouraged complacency as well as contractualism, the habit of making deals with God in return for special favors. The point is arguable, but in their critique of popular piety they were on firmer ground. Much late medieval piety was mechanistic and involved practices that would today be regarded as abuses. The sale of indulgences, the misuse of pilgrimages, and the proliferation of masses for the dead were all symptoms of the popular obsession with death and purgatory that followed in the wake of the bubonic plague. The sacraments of the church guaranteed salvation, but every sin committed in life carried with it a sentence to be served in purgatory. As the pains of purgatory were like those of hell, without the curse of eternal separation from God, much effort was spent in avoiding them. A mass said for the soul of the dead reduced the penalty by a specified number of years. Henry VII of England, who seems to have had a bad conscience, left money in his will for 10,000 masses. Many priests survived entirely on the proceeds from such bequests and had no other duties. An **indulgence** was a remission of the "temporal" or purgatorial punishment for sins that could be granted by the pope out of the church's "treasury of merits." Its price, too, was related to the number of years it subtracted from the buyer's term in purgatory, and an indulgence sometimes could be purchased in advance for sins not yet committed.

Clerical Ignorance. Such practices were deeply rooted in the rich and varied piety of the Middle Ages. If some religious were scandalized by them, other priests would not condemn genuine expressions of religious feeling, and still others no doubt accepted them out of ignorance. No systematic education had been established for parish priests, and thanks to absenteeism, many parishes were served by vicars or substitutes whose qualifications were minimal at best. However,

the church's critics did not reject pilgrimages, indulgences, the proper use of relics, or masses for the dead. They merely wished to ground these "works" in the faith and good intentions that would make them spiritually valid. They opposed simpleminded contractualism and "arithmetical" piety, but their concerns intensified their conflict with a church that remained immobilized by political and organizational difficulties.

Mysticism. Of those forms of piety that sought personal contact with God, the most ambitious was mysticism. The enormous popularity of mysticism in the later Middle Ages was in some respects a measure of the growing influence of women on religious life. Many of the great mystics were women. Others were men who became involved with the movement as confessors to convents of nuns. **Mysticism** may be defined as the effort to achieve spiritual union with God through ecstatic contemplation. Because the experience is highly personal, it had many variants, but most of them fell into two broad categories. The first, and probably the most common, was to experience visions or infusions of the Holy Spirit in the manner of St. Catherine of Siena (1347–1380) or Julian of Norwich (1342–c. 1416). The second, best typified by Meister Eckhardt (c. 1260–1328) and the Rhineland mystics, was influenced by the Neo-Platonic concept of ideas and aimed at a real union of the soul with God (see Document 14.2). They sought to penetrate the divine intelligence and perceive the universe as God perceives it. Both views were rooted firmly in the medieval tradition of interior piety, but Eckhardt and those like him were suspected of heresy because they seemed to deny the vital distinction between the Creator and the human soul.

The Modern Devotion. Neither form of experience was easy to achieve. Both involved a long process of mental and spiritual preparation that was described in an ever-growing literature. Manuals such as Walter Hilton's *Scale of Perfection* became extremely popular with lay people and were circulated in large numbers both before and after the invention of printing. Although mysticism was essentially private, it influenced the development of a powerful corporate movement known as the *Devotio Moderna*, or modern devotion. Its founder was Gerhard Groote (Ghro'-tuh, 1340–1384), who organized a community of religious women at Deventer in the Netherlands. These Sisters of the Common Life were laywomen, not nuns. They pledged themselves to a communal life informed by contemplation but directed toward service in the world. A parallel group for men, the Brethren of the Common Life, was founded shortly thereafter by Groote's disciple Florens Radewijns (Rah'-duh-vines). These two groups, together with the Augustinian Canons of the Windesheim Congregation, a fully monastic order also founded by Radewijns, formed the nucleus of a movement that spread rapidly through the Low Countries and western Germany. Catholic, but highly critical of the clergy, it emphasized charitable works, private devotion, and its own form of education. The goal of its adherents was the imitation of Christ. A book titled *The Imitation of Christ* by one of the Brethren, Thomas à Kempis, was a best seller until well into the twentieth century and did much to popularize a style of piety that was the opposite of contractualism.

Heresies and Other Movements

Other religious movements were less innocent, at least from the perspective of the church. Full-scale heresies emerged in England and Bohemia in response to the teachings of **John Wycliffe** (1330–1384) and **Jan Hus** (c. 1372–1415). Wycliffe was a successful teacher of theology at Oxford who became involved with politics during the 1370s. England was attempting to follow the French lead in restricting papal rights of appointment and taxation, and Wycliffe became the chief spokesman for the anticlerical views of Edward III's son, John of Gaunt. At first, Wycliffe restricted himself to the traditional arguments in favor of clerical poverty, but as his views began to attract criticism and as he began to realize that his personal ambitions would not be fulfilled, he drifted further into radicalism. In his last years, he rejected papal authority and declared that the Bible was the sole source of religious truth. Strongly influenced by St. Augustine and committed to an extreme form of philosophical realism, he supported predestination and ended by rejecting transubstantiation because it involved what he saw as the annihilation of the substance of the bread and wine. In his view, substance was by definition unchangeable, and the miracle of the mass was therefore an impossibility. This was heresy, as was his revival of the ancient Donatist idea that the value of the sacraments depended on the personal virtue of the priest who administered them.

The Lollards. Although John of Gaunt discretely withdrew his support, Wycliffe died before the church could bring him to trial. By this time, his ideas and the extraordinary violence of his attacks on the clergy had begun to attract popular attention. His followers, the Lollards, produced an English translation of the Bible and organized a march on London in 1413. Fearing that the egalitarian tendencies of the Lollards encouraged social disorder, Henry V suppressed the movement, but scattered communities preserved their traditions until the outbreak of the Protestant Reformation.

The Hussites. Because England and Bohemia were diplomatically aligned on the Great Schism, a number of Czech students left the University of Paris for Oxford after 1378. There they came in contact with the teachings of Wycliffe, and by 1400, his works were being openly

debated at Prague. Wycliffe's ideas became popular because they seemed to coincide with an already well-developed reform movement. Czech preachers had long attacked the morality of the clergy and now demanded a Czech translation of the Bible. Great resentment also existed over denying the communion to the laity in both kinds. Reserving both bread and wine for the priest while giving only bread to the laity had long been a common practice throughout Europe. The Bohemians saw it as an expression of clerical arrogance.

Although basically religious, these issues became hopelessly intertwined with the ethnic rivalry between Czechs and Germans that had troubled Bohemia for centuries. The kingdom of Bohemia had a large population of Germans who were often resented by their Slavic neighbors. Moreover, the church held nearly 40 percent of the land, and many of the leading churchmen were

FIGURE 14.2 *Jan Hus Defending His Views at the Council of Constance (1415).* In this nineteenth-century illustration, Hus defends himself before the committee of scholars appointed to look into the charges of heresy made against him. In fact, his condemnation was assured before he traveled to Constance.

German. To many, anticlericalism was therefore an expression of Czech national feeling as well as of frustrated piety. This association quickly drew the reform movement into the arena of imperial politics.

The University of Prague found itself at the center of these controversies. In 1409, King Vaclav expelled the German students and faculty and appointed Jan Hus, a Czech professor, as rector. Hus had been attracted to Wycliffe's writings by their anticlericalism, but he also saw their extreme philosophical realism as a weapon against the German theologians, most of whom were nominalists. He did not, however, reject transubstantiation and was in general more conservative than Wycliffe on every issue save that of papal authority. Hus did not think of himself as a heretic, and in 1415, he accepted an invitation to defend his views before the Council of Constance. The invitation had been orchestrated by Emperor Sigismund who offered him a safe conduct, but the promised guarantee was little more than a passport and Hus was burned at the stake on July 6.

The burning of Hus provoked a national outcry in Bohemia. Taking the communion chalice as their symbol, the Czechs broke with Rome and developed a liturgy in the Czech language. When their protector, Vaclav, died in 1419, he was succeeded as king by Sigismund. **The Hussites,** as they were now called, rose in armed revolt and resoundingly defeated the papal-imperial crusades against them in 1420, 1422, and 1431. Finally, in 1436, the Hussites secured a treaty that guaranteed them control over the Bohemian church and confirmed their earlier expropriation of church property.

Nominalism. Two intellectual movements contributed to the religious tensions and controversies of the later Middle Ages and threatened the church's authority in more subtle ways. Nominalism (see Chapter 9), which grew in popularity during the fourteenth and fifteenth centuries, tended to undermine the foundations of dogma by denying that religious teachings were susceptible to rational proof. Although never the dominant school in late medieval thought, it influenced many theologians, including Martin Luther.

Humanism. Humanism exerted an even stronger influence on religious issues. Humanists such as Erasmus criticized the moral shortcomings of the clergy and used their mastery of rhetoric to attack the scholastic philosophers. Their belief in the superiority of ancient over modern texts contributed to the idea that Scripture alone was the ultimate source of religious truth. Although many humanists, including Erasmus, remained within the old church, this concept of *sola scriptura* became central to the teachings of the reformers. Many of them, including **Huldrych Zwingli** (Hool'-drik Tsving'-lee, 1484–1531), Calvin, and Melanchthon had been trained as humanists. They used humanist methodology in their analysis of sacred texts. Humanist respect for antiquity may also have influenced the growing belief that the practices of the early church most closely approximated the intentions of Christ. They came to believe that subsequent developments, including the power of bishops and the rise of the papacy, were modern corruptions and therefore intolerable.

The Influence of Printing. After 1450, the invention of printing with moveable type (see Chapter 13) spread knowledge of these movements and criticisms to the farthest corners of Europe while encouraging the spread of literacy, especially in the towns. Handwritten books had been prohibitively expensive. Even the richest of collectors sometimes boasted of libraries that contained fewer than 200 volumes. Printing made books cheap as well as easily duplicated in large numbers. Even men and women of modest means could now learn to read, and scholars have estimated that by 1500, the literacy rate in some cities was nearly 50 percent. Religious and political tracts, the writings of the mystics, and popular sermons enjoyed great popularity.

THE PROTESTANT REFORMATIONS (1517–1555)

The reform movements that destroyed the unity of western Christendom in the sixteenth century must be seen as the products of a generalized dissatisfaction with the church. The development of printing, which made the writings of the reformers available to thousands of people, and the conjunction of religious reform with the political needs of certain states and cities transformed that dissatisfaction into the Protestant Reformations.

Martin Luther

The first and in many ways the most influential of these movements was the one created in Germany by Martin Luther (1483–1546). A monk of the Augustinian Observant order and professor of the New Testament at the University of Wittenberg in electoral Saxony,

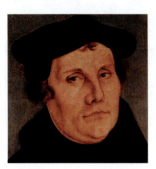

Martin Luther, 1529

Luther experienced a profound spiritual crisis that eventually brought him into open conflict with the church. Like many of his contemporaries, Luther was troubled by an overwhelming sense of sin and unworthiness for which the teachings of the church provided no relief. Neither the rigors of monastic life nor the sacrament of penance could provide him with assurance of salvation. In the course of his biblical studies, he gradually arrived at a solution. Based on his reading of Paul's Epistle to the Romans and on his growing admiration for the works of St. Augustine, he concluded that souls were not saved by religious ceremonies and good works and pious devotions but by faith alone. Human beings could never be righteous enough to merit God's forgiveness, but they could be saved if only they would believe and have faith in the righteousness of Christ. Like Augustine, he believed that faith came not from human effort but as an undeserved gift from God.

The Issue of Indulgences. Luther believed himself transformed by this insight. Even as he formulated it, he was confronted by the issue of indulgences. In 1517, a special indulgence was made available in the territories surrounding electoral Saxony. Its purpose was to raise money for the construction of St. Peter's basilica in Rome and to retire the debt incurred by Albrecht of Mainz in securing for himself through bribery the archbishoprics of Mainz and Magdeburg and the bishopric of Halberstadt. Albrecht had committed not only pluralism but also simony (the illegal purchase of church offices). To Luther, however, this was not the central issue. To him, as to many other clerics, the sale of indulgences was a symbol of the contractualism that beset medieval piety and blinded lay people to the true path of salvation. On October 31, 1517, he posted **Ninety-Five Theses** condemning this practice to the door of Wittenberg's Castle Church.

His action was in no way unusual. It was the traditional means by which a professor offered to debate all comers on a particular issue, and the positions taken by Luther were not heretical. The Council of Trent, called by Pope Pius III in 1542 as a means of renewing the Catholic Church, ultimately condemned the sale of indulgences. However, Luther's action unleashed a storm of controversy. Spread throughout Germany by the printing press, the theses were endorsed by advocates of reform and condemned by the pope, the Dominican order, the archbishop of Mainz, and the Fugger bank of Augsburg, which had loaned Albrecht the money for the elections.

Excommunication. In the debates that followed, Luther was forced to work out the broader implications of his teachings. At Leipzig in June 1519, he challenged the doctrinal authority of popes and councils and declared that Scripture took precedence over all other sources of religious truth. In 1520, he published three pamphlets that drew him at last into formal heresy. In his *Address to the Christian Nobility of the German Nation,* he encouraged the princes to demand reform (see Document 14.3). *On the Babylonian Captivity of the Church* abolished five of the church's seven sacraments and declared that the efficacy of baptism and communion depended on the faith of the recipient, not the ordination of the priest. He also rejected transubstantiation while arguing that Christ was nevertheless truly present in the Eucharist. *The Freedom of a Christian* summarized Luther's doctrine of salvation by faith alone. Luther had not intended to break with the church, but his extraordinary skill as a writer and propagandist ignited anticlerical and antipapal feeling throughout Germany. Compromise was now impossible, and he was excommunicated on January 31, 1521.

The Diet of Worms. The affair might have ended with Luther's trial and execution, but political considerations intervened. His own prince, Frederick "the Wise" of Saxony, arranged for him to defend his position before the **Imperial Diet of Worms,** held in the city of that name in April. Luther did not defend his teachings, but as we have seen, refused to retract them in dramatic terms. The newly elected Emperor **Charles V** was unimpressed. He placed Luther under the imperial ban, and Frederick was forced to protect his monk by hiding him in the Wartburg Castle for nearly a year. Luther used this enforced period of leisure to translate the New Testament into German.

Luther and the German Princes. Frederick's motives and those of the other princes and city magistrates who eventually supported Luther's reformation varied widely. Some were inspired by genuine religious feeling

DOCUMENT 14.3

MARTIN LUTHER'S ADDRESS TO THE GERMAN NOBILITY

Martin Luther's primary concerns were always spiritual and theological, but he knew how to appeal to other emotions as well. These extracts from his *Address to the Christian Nobility of the German Nation* are a relatively modest example of the rhetoric with which he attacked the authority of the Catholic Church.

What is the use in Christendom of those who are called "cardinals"? I will tell you. In Italy and Germany there are many rich convents, endowments, holdings, and benefices; and as the best way of getting these into the hands of Rome they created cardinals, and gave to them the bishoprics, convents, and prelacies, and thus destroyed the service of God. That is why Italy is almost a desert now. . . . Why? Because the cardinals must have the wealth. The Turk himself could not have so desolated Italy and so overthrown the worship of God.

Now that Italy is sucked dry, they come to Germany. They begin in a quiet way, but we shall soon have Germany brought into the same state as Italy. We have a few cardinals already. What the Romanists really mean to do, the "drunken" Germans are not to see until they have lost everything. . . .

Now this devilish state of things is not only open robbery and deceit and the prevailing of the gates of hell, but it is destroying the very life and soul of Christianity; therefore we are bound to use all our diligence to ward off this misery and destruction. If we want to fight Turks, let us begin here—we cannot find worse ones. If we rightly hang thieves and robbers, why do we leave the greed of Rome unpunished? For Rome is the greatest thief and robber that has ever appeared on earth, or ever will.

From Luther, Martin, "Address to the Nobility of the German Nation" (1520), in trans. Wace and Buckheim, B. J. Kidd, ed, *Documents Illustrative of the Continental Reformation*, No. 35 (Oxford, England: Oxford University Press, 1911).

Question: What criticism has Luther made against the church?

rejected Catholicism and established their own churches. They confiscated church property and appointed pastors or ministers, most of whom agreed with Luther, to replace the priests. Although Luther himself did not in any way control these state churches, they became known as **Lutheran** because they generally followed his teachings on the sacraments and salvation.

The Struggle with the Emperor. The Holy Roman Emperor objected to these developments on both political and religious grounds. Charles V (1500–1558; emperor from 1519) was a devout Catholic. He also supported the ideal of imperial unity, which was clearly threatened by anything that increased the power and revenues of the princes. Only 21 at

Charles V

the Diet of Worms, he had inherited an enormous accumulation of states, including Austria, Spain, the Netherlands, and much of Italy (see Chapter 15). In theory, only the Ottoman Empire could stand against him; in fact, he could do little to stop the spread of the Reformation. When he convinced the Imperial Diet to condemn the reforming states and cities in 1529, they issued a protest that earned them the name **Protestant.** In 1531, they formed the **Schmalkaldic League** in the town of that name and defended their Reformation with varying degrees of success for the remainder of Charles's reign. When the emperor abdicated and retired to a Spanish monastery in 1557, the Reformation was still intact. His power, although great, had not been equal to his responsibilities. Pressed on the Danube and in the Mediterranean by the Turks; forced to fight seven wars with France; and beset simultaneously by Protestant princes, urban revolutionaries, and popes who feared the extension of his influence in Italy, Charles failed utterly in his attempts to impose orthodoxy. The empire remained open to religious turmoil.

The Radical Reformation

Some of that turmoil began while Luther was still hidden in the Wartburg. The reformer had believed that once the gospel was freely preached, congregations would follow it without the direction of an institutional church. He discovered that not all of the pope's enemies shared his interpretation of the Bible. Movements arose that rejected what he saw as the basic insight of the Reformation: salvation by faith alone. To many ordinary men and women, this doctrine weak-

or, like Frederick, by a proprietary responsibility for "their" churches that transcended loyalty to a distant and non-German papacy. Others, especially in the towns, responded to the public enthusiasm generated by Luther's writings. Regardless of personal feelings, everyone understood the practical advantages of breaking with Rome. Revenues could be increased by confiscating church property and by ending ecclesiastical immunity to taxation. The control of church courts and ecclesiastical patronage were valuable prizes to those engaged in state building. By 1530, several of the more important German states and a number of towns had

FIGURE 14.3 *The Lutheran Sacraments.* This altar painting from the Lutheran church at Thorslunde, Denmark, is intended as a graphic lesson in theology. Infant baptism is shown at the left. In the center, two communicants receive the sacrament in both kinds (bread and wine), while the preacher at the right emphasizes the importance of God's word. Lutheran churches recognized only Baptism and Communion as sacraments. The Catholic Church recognized five more, which Luther rejected: Penance, Confirmation, Marriage, Ordination, and Extreme Unction.

Rejecting Luther's idea of salvation by faith, they saw baptism not only as a sacrament but as the heart of the redemptive process. Salvation, they said, was purely a reward for good works. Only a responsible adult, acting in complete freedom of will, could make the decision to follow Christ. The rite of baptism, preferably by immersion in a flowing stream, was the outward sign of that decision and committed the believer to a life without sin. He or she entered a "visible church of the saints" that must, by definition, be separate from the world around it. Most Anabaptists therefore became pacifists who would accept no civic responsibilities, refusing even to take an oath in court (see Document 14.4).

ened the ethical imperatives that lay at the heart of Christianity. They wanted a restoration of the primitive, apostolic church—a "gathered" community of Christians who lived by the letter of Scripture. Luther had not gone far enough. Luther in turn thought that they were *schwärmer,* or enthusiasts who wanted to return to the works righteousness of the medieval church. Faced with what he saw as a fundamental threat to reform, Luther turned to the state. In 1527, a system of visitations was instituted throughout Saxony that for all practical purposes placed temporal control of the church in the hands of the prince. It was to be the model for Lutheran Church discipline throughout Germany and Scandinavia, but it did not at first halt the spread of radicalism.

The Anti-Trinitarians.
Because these radical movements were often popular in origin or had coalesced around the teachings of an individual preacher, they varied widely in character. Perhaps the most radical were the **anti-Trinitarians,** who rejected the doctrine of the Trinity and argued for a piety based wholly on good works. Under the leadership of two Italian brothers, Laelio and Fausto Sozzini (Sotz-zee'-nee), anti-Trinitarianism found important converts among the Polish nobility but had little influence on western Europe.

The Anabaptists.
The most numerous radicals were the **Anabaptists,** a loosely affiliated group whose name derives from the practice of re-baptizing their converts.

Persecution of the Anabaptists.
Governmental authorities saw this rejection of civic responsibility as a threat to the political order. Hatred of the Anabaptists was one issue on which both Catholics and the followers of Luther could agree, and in 1529, an imperial edict made belief in adult baptism a capital offense. Hatred became something like panic when an atypically violent group of Anabaptists gained control of the German city of Münster and proclaimed it the New Jerusalem, complete with polygyny and communal sharing of property. They were eventually dislodged and their leaders executed, but the episode, although unparalleled elsewhere, convinced political and ecclesiastical leaders that their suspicions had been correct. They executed tens of thousands of Anabaptists throughout Germany and the Low Countries, and by 1550, the movement had dwindled to a remnant. A group of survivors, afterward known as **Mennonites,** were reorganized under the leadership of **Menno Simons.** Their moderation and emphasis on high ethical standards became a model for other dissenting groups.

Zwingli and the Reformed Movement in Switzerland

Meanwhile, another kind of reform had emerged in Switzerland. Zürich (Zuer'-ik), like other Swiss cantons, was a center of the mercenary industry. By 1518, a growing party of citizens had come to oppose what they

THE ANABAPTISTS REJECT CIVIC LIFE

In 1527, a group of Anabaptists met at Schleitheim on the Swiss–German border to clarify issues connected with their teachings. The result was the *Schleitheim Confession*, a document widely accepted by later Anabaptists. This excerpt demonstrates the Anabaptist belief that Christians must separate themselves from the life of a wicked world.

Fourth. We are agreed as follows on separation: A separation shall be made from the evil and the wickedness which the devil planted in the world; in this manner, simply that we should not have fellowship with them, the wicked, and not run with them in the multitude of their abominations. This is the way it is: Since all who do not walk in the obedience of faith and have not united themselves with God so that they wish to do his will, are a great abomination before God, it is not possible for anything to grow or issue from them except abominable things. For truly all creatures are in but two classes, good and bad, believing and unbelieving, darkness and light, the world and those who have come out of the world, God's temple and idols, Christ and Belial; and none can have part with the other.

To us then the command of the Lord is clear when He calls us to separate from the evil and thus He will be our God and we shall be his sons and daughters.

He further admonishes us to withdraw from Babylon and the earthly Egypt that we may not be partakers of the pain and suffering which the Lord will bring upon them.

From all this we should learn that everything which is not united with our God and Christ cannot be other than an abomination which we should shun and flee from. By this is meant all popish and anti-popish works and church services, meetings and church attendance, drinking houses, civic affairs, the commitments made in unbelief [oaths] and other things of that kind, which are highly regarded by the world and yet carried on in flat contradiction to the command of God.

Therefore there will also unquestionably fall from us the unChristian, devilish weapons of force—such as sword, armor and the like, and all their use for friends or against one's enemies.

From "The Schleitheim Confession," in Hans Hillerbrand, ed., *The Protestant Reformation* (New York: Harper Torchbooks, 1967, pp. 132–133).

Question: Why did the Anabaptists believe that they should separate themselves from society?

called the exchange of blood for money. The innovations of Gonsalvo de Córdoba had cost the Swiss their tactical advantage on the battlefield, and their casualties during the latter part of the Italian wars had been very heavy. Moreover, the trade had enriched a few contractors who were now thought to exert undue influence on local pol-

itics while compromising the city's neutrality through their relations with France and the papacy. One of the leading spokesmen for the antimercenary forces was Zwingli, a priest who had been a chaplain to the troops in Italy. He had received a good humanist education and, like Luther, was known for attacking indulgences and for sermons that relied heavily on the Scriptures. In 1519, the antimercenary party gained control of the Zürich city council and named Zwingli the people's priest of the city's main church, a post from which he was able to guide the process of reform.

Zwingli's Reformation. Zwingli's concept of reformation grew out of the democratic traditions of his native land. Believing that each congregation should determine its own policies under the guidance of the gospel, an idea reinforced by his humanist understanding of the early church, he saw no real distinction between church and state. Both entities elected representatives to determine policy. Both should be guided by the law of God. He therefore proceeded to reform the city step by step, providing guidance and advice on scripture but leaving the implementation of reforms to the city council.

Zwingli's Teachings. Like Luther, Zwingli was challenged at an early date by those who believed that his reforms were insufficiently thorough. In responding to such Anabaptist critics as Conrad Grebel (Gray'-bel) and Georg Blaurock, Zwingli developed teachings that differed from Luther's as well. When the Anabaptists asked how a child could be baptized if the efficacy of the sacrament depended on the faith of the recipient, Zwingli responded that the faith was that of the parent or guardian and that the sacrament was in effect a covenant to raise the child as a Christian. The rite was analogous to circumcision among the Jews. He also rejected Luther's doctrine of the Real Presence in communion and argued, after some hesitation, that for those with faith, Christ was present in spirit although not in body.

Zwingli's theologically original ideas appealed strongly to other reformers, especially in the cities of Switzerland and southwest Germany. Luther, however, rejected them at the **Marburg Colloquy** in 1529. The failure of this meeting marked the beginning of a separation between the Lutheran and Reformed traditions that persists to this day. It also coincided with the vote by the Imperial Diet to enforce the Edict of Worms against all non-Catholics. All those who protested against this measure were Protestants, but those who tended to agree with Zwingli became known as **Reformed** rather than Lutheran. In the meantime, the efforts of Zürich to export its reformation to other parts of Switzerland led to conflict with the rural cantons that wished to remain Catholic. Zwingli, who believed that his status as a minister did not exempt him from his duties as a citizen, died, sword in hand, at the battle of Kappel in 1531.

Calvin and Calvinism

Among those influenced by Zwingli's teachings was **John Calvin** (1509–1564). Calvin was born at Noyon in France, the son of a wealthy lawyer who for most of his career had been secretary to the local bishop. A bril-

liant student, Calvin was educated at Paris and at Orléans, where he earned a law degree. His interests eventually turned to humanism and then to theology. In 1534, he adopted the reformed faith. His conversion bore immediate fruit in *The Institutes of the Christian Religion,* a more or less systematic explanation of reformed teachings. The

John Calvin

first edition appeared in March 1536, and although Calvin continued to revise and expand it throughout his lifetime, this early effort contained the basic elements of his mature thought.

Calvin's Role in the Reformation.
Theologically, Calvin is best known for his uncompromising position on predestination, holding, like Zwingli, that God divides the elect from the reprobate by His own "dread decree" (see Document 14.5). Luther, like St. Augustine, believed that God predestines certain individuals to salvation but had stopped short of declaring that some are predestined to hell. To Calvin, this seemed illogical as well as a limitation on God's power. To select some is by definition to reject others. This doctrine of "double predestination," like many of his formulations on the sacraments and other issues, may be seen as refinements of ideas originally suggested by others, but Calvin was far more than a mere compiler. He made reformed doctrines more intelligible, educated a corps of pastors who spread his teachings to the farthest corners of Europe, and provided a model for the governance of Christian communities that would be influential for generations to come.

The Reformation in Geneva.
The unlikely vehicle for these achievements was the small city of Geneva. When Calvin arrived there in July 1536, the city was emerging from a period of political and religious turmoil. It had long been governed by a bishop whose appointment was controlled by the neighboring dukes of Savoy. Dissatisfaction with Savoyard influence led to the belated development of civic institutions and an alliance with the Swiss cantons of Bern and Fribourg. The bishop fled. The Bernese, who had accepted the Reformation

---

DOCUMENT 14.5

JOHN CALVIN ON PREDESTINATION

The importance of John Calvin's doctrine of predestination has probably been overstated. It was neither unique to him nor the center of his own theology, which emphasized what he called the knowledge of God. Nevertheless, the power of this summary statement from the *Institutes of the Christian Religion* indicates why Calvin's teachings on predestination made an indelible impression.

As Scripture, then, clearly shows, we say that God once established by his eternal and unchangeable plan those whom he long before determined once for all to receive into salvation and those whom, on the other hand, he would devote to destruction. We assert that, with respect to the elect, this plan was founded upon his freely given mercy, without regard to human worth; but by his just and irreprehensible judgment he has barred the door of life to those whom he has given over to damnation. Now among the elect we regard the call as a testimony of election. Then we hold justification [that is, acceptance by God] another sign of its manifestation, until they come into the glory in which the fulfillment of that election lies. But as the Lord seals his elect by call and justification, so, by shutting off the reprobate from knowledge of his name or from the sanctification of his Spirit, he, as it were, reveals by these marks what sort of judgment awaits them.

From Calvin, John, *Institutes of the Christian Religion,* vol. 2, ed. J. T. McNeill, trans. Ford Lewis Battles (Philadelphia: Westminster Press, 1960, p. 931).

Questions: According to Calvin, who is saved? What happens to those who are not saved?

---

while remaining nominally Catholic for diplomatic reasons, then dispatched a French refugee, Guillaume Farel, to convert the French-speaking Genevans. Farel was a fine preacher, but he realized that he was not the man to organize a church. When Calvin stopped at Geneva on his way from Ferrara to Strasburg, he prevailed upon the young scholar to stay and assist him in the task of reformation.

Calvin's first years in Geneva were full of turmoil. Although they had no love for the pope, the Genevans resisted Calvin's attempts to reform their morals. He established the kind of godly commonwealth he sought only with great difficulty. His opponents finally discredited themselves by supporting Miguel Servetus, an anti-Trinitarian executed by the Genevan city council as a heretic in 1553. This act, now regarded as an example of gross intolerance, was universally applauded by

Catholics and Protestants and secured Calvin's position in the city until his death.

Calvin's Geneva has been called a theocracy, but Calvin believed in the separation of church and state. Neither he nor any other Genevan pastor could hold public office, and the temporal affairs of the Genevan church were guided by an elected committee or a presbytery of laymen. The city continued to be governed by its two elected councils. These bodies were empowered, as in Zürich, to enforce conformity in faith and morals. A Consistory, composed of church elders and certain municipal officials, was responsible for defining both. Geneva soon became known as a center of the Reformed movement and as a refuge for those who were persecuted elsewhere. An academy was established to train pastors who were then dispatched to create missionary congregations in other parts of Europe. They were most successful in France, in the Netherlands, and in those countries such as Hungary, Bohemia, and Poland, where resistance to German culture inhibited the spread of Lutheranism. When the reformer died in 1564, Calvinism was already a major international movement.

The English Reformation

England's revolt against the papacy was an example of reformation imposed from the top. **Henry VIII** (reigned 1509–1547) and his chief minister, **Cardinal Thomas Wolsey** (c. 1475–1530), had little use for reformed doctrines. Henry had even earned the papal title "Defender of the Faith" for publishing an attack on Luther's view of the sacraments and would probably have been content to remain in the church had he not decided to divorce his queen, **Catherine of Aragon,** the daughter of Ferdinand and Isabella of Spain.

Henry VIII, 1537

The Divorce. Catherine had suffered a series of miscarriages and stillbirths. One child, Mary, survived, but Henry feared that without a male heir the succession would be endangered. He resolved to ask for a papal annulment and to marry **Anne Boleyn** (Bull'-in), a court lady with whom he had fallen in love. His re-

Cardinal Wolsey

quest posed serious difficulties for pope Clement VII. Emperor Charles V was Catherine's nephew. Charles vehemently opposed the divorce, and because his troops had recently sacked Rome (1527), albeit in the course of a mutiny, the pope was intimidated. Moreover, the basis of the request struck many canon lawyers as dubious. Catherine had originally been married to Henry's brother Arthur, who died before he could ascend the throne. To preserve the vital alliance with Catherine's father, Ferdinand of Aragon, Henry VII had quickly married her to his second son, but this had required a papal dispensation because marriage to the wife of one's brother is prohibited by Leviticus 18:16 and 20:21. Another biblical passage, Deuteronomy 25:5, specifically commands such marriages, but an annulment would involve repudiation of the earlier dispensation. Moreover, the fact that the marriage had endured for eighteen years raised what canon lawyers called "the impediment of public honesty."

Clement temporized. He appointed Cardinals Wolsey and Campeggio as legates to resolve the matter on the theory that their opinions would cancel each other out. Henry could not wait. In 1529, he deprived Wolsey of his secular offices and took **Thomas Cromwell** (1485–1540) and **Thomas Cranmer** (1489–1556) as his advisers. These two, a lawyer and a churchman, respectively, were sympathetic to reformed ideas and firm supporters of a strategy that would put pressure on the pope by attacking the privileges and immunities of the church in England.

The Reformation Parliament. This strategy was implemented primarily through the Reformation Parliament that sat from 1529 to 1536. Although Cromwell managed its proceedings to some extent, a consistent majority supported the crown throughout. Parliament passed a series of acts that restricted the dispatch of church revenues to Rome and placed the legal affairs of the clergy under royal jurisdiction. Finally, in 1532, Anne Boleyn became pregnant. To ensure the child's legitimacy, Cranmer married the couple in January 1533, and 2 months later he granted the king his divorce from Catherine. He was able to do so because William Warham, the Archbishop of Canterbury and a wily opponent of the divorce, had died at last (he was at least 98), permitting Henry to appoint Cranmer in his place. In September, Anne Boleyn gave birth to a daughter, Elizabeth, and in 1534, Parliament passed the **Act of Supremacy,** which declared that Henry was "the only supreme head of the Church in England."

Suppression of the Monasteries. From an economic point of view, the most important aspect of the English Reformation was Henry VIII's suppression of the monasteries. The monks were unpopular, except in the north, where monasteries dominated the economy, and Henry needed money. He had long since squandered the immense fortune left to him by his father. Beginning in 1536, Henry's government confiscated all monastic properties and dismissed the monks and nuns. Unlike priests, who retained their parishes if they accepted the Act of Supremacy, the dispossessed religious had to find places in the secular world. Vast sums flowed into the royal coffers, but unfortunately for his successors, Henry chose to sell off the monastic lands at bargain basement prices. By doing so, he enriched those who had supported him in the Reformation Parliament and satisfied his need for ready cash. His failure to incorporate these lands into the royal domain deprived the crown of renewable income that it would later need.

The Henrician Church.

Thomas More

Henry now ruled the English church. Although he closed the monasteries and convents and adopted Miles Coverdale's translation of the Bible into English, he changed little else. The clergy remained celibate (except Cranmer, who had been secretly married before his appointment as archbishop of Canterbury), and Henry reaffirmed the principles of Catholic theology in the Six Articles of 1539. Perhaps as a result, opposition was minimal. John Fisher, Bishop of Rochester, and Sir Thomas More, the great humanist who had been Henry's lord chancellor, were executed for their misgivings, but most of political England either supported the king or remained indifferent. The Lincolnshire rebellion and the northern revolt known as the Pilgrimage of Grace were localized reactions to Henry's proposed closing of the monasteries in 1536, and he suppressed them easily.

The Beginnings of the Anglican Church.

In 1536, Henry arranged the execution of Anne Boleyn on charges of adultery and had their marriage annulled. His third wife, Jane Seymour, gave him a male heir in 1537 but died in childbirth, and three subsequent wives failed to produce further children. Both Mary and Elizabeth were now officially illegitimate. When Henry died in 1547, Jane Seymour's son, age 10, ascended the throne as Edward VI (1547–1553) under the regency of his uncle, Edward Seymour, Duke of Somerset. Somerset was a convinced Protestant with close ties to Cranmer and the continental reformers. He and the young king, "that right godly imp," as the Protestants called him, lost little time in abolishing the Six Articles, encouraging clerical marriage, and imposing Cranmer's

FIGURE 14.4 *An Allegory of the English Reformation.* This image was intended as propaganda to support the succession of Edward VI, aged 10 and already tied to the Protestant cause. The dying Henry points to his son (who holds a scepter), as heir to his throne and Defender of the Faith (or Head of the Church of England) against the pope (forefront) who has been overcome. Against the pope's neck lies a Bible open to the words from Peter 1:24, "The word of the Lord endureth forever." On his chest are the words "All fleshe is grasse," and written along his arm is the word "Idolatry." At the bottom, monks flee.

Book of Common Prayer as the standard liturgy for English churches. An Order in Council abolished images in an act of official iconoclasm that destroyed centuries of English art.

In 1550, the equally Protestant Duke of Northumberland succeeded Somerset. He imposed a revised edition of the new liturgy and adopted the Forty-Two Articles, also written by Cranmer, as an official confession of faith. The articles proclaimed salvation by faith, reduced the sacraments to two, and denied transubstantiation, although not the Real Presence. The **Anglican,** or English state church, was now demonstrably Protestant and reflected not only the views but the masterful literary style of Thomas Cranmer.

The English Catholics.

Most of the English clergy accepted the new order. Although many lay people remained loyal to the old church, they found no effective way to express their views. Aside from a brief and unsuccessful rebellion in the west of England, little resistance emerged. In 1553, Edward died at the age of 16. His sister **Mary** assumed the crown and immediately restored Catholicism with the assent of Parliament, which demanded only that she not return the lands taken from the church.

Mary Tudor, 1554

Once again, clergy and laity accepted the religious reversal, but Mary's reign was a failure. Her marriage to Philip II of Spain aroused fears of Spanish-papal domination, even among those English who were still unfavorably disposed to Protestantism. Her persecution of the reformers, although hardly the bloodbath portrayed in John Foxe's *Books of Martyrs,* the great martyrology of the English reformation, deeply offended others and earned her the historical nickname "Bloody Mary." When her sister, **Elizabeth,** succeeded her in 1558, she was able to restore a moderate Protestantism leavened by virtual tolerance for all who would acknowledge the royal supremacy. The Elizabethan Settlement, as it is called, was the foundation on which modern **Anglicanism** would be built after years of effort and struggle.

Common Features of Protestantism. Although the reforming movements that opposed the medieval church varied widely in practice and doctrine, they shared several features in common. All rejected the authority of the pope. They claimed Scripture as the sole source of religious truth and repudiated the rulings of popes, councils, and the writings of the scholastics. They also rejected much of the church's sacramental system and, with it, the traditional role of the priest as an intermediary between God and the believer. For this reason, they insisted on publishing the Bible in the vernacular language of their own countries and abandoned the use of Latin in church services. Some, but not all, believed that salvation came through faith rather than as a reward for good deeds. Views on predestination, the precise nature of baptism and communion, and other theological issues caused bitter divisions, but in some respects, the day-to-day practice of the faith marked them off more clearly than anything else from those Europeans who remained Catholic. Most objected to the use of images, services for the dead, pilgrimages, and many other manifestations of medieval piety. By 1550, one could tell by walking into a church whether it had remained Catholic or adopted reform.

THE CATHOLIC REFORMATION (C. 1490–1564)

But not all reformations of the sixteenth century were anti-Catholic. The church transformed itself as well in a movement that has sometimes been called the *Counter-Reformation.* The term is unduly restrictive. Not all of the reforms undertaken by Catholics in the sixteenth century were a response to the challenge of Luther and his fellows, and some had preceded him by decades.

Reforms Before Luther. Cardinal Francisco Jiménez de Cisneros had begun to reform the church in Spain long before Luther nailed his Ninety-Five Theses to the church door. In France, Cardinal Georges d'Amboise (dam-bwaz) introduced similar reforms between 1501 and his death in 1510. Even Wolsey had attempted to reform the English monasteries during the 1520s. The impetus behind these reforms arguably came from the secular authorities and were largely directed toward the revival of monastic life. However, each of these cardinals received broad legatine authority from several popes, and monastic reform was a central issue in the late medieval church.

Monastic Reform and the Creation of New Orders. Moreover, the reform of existing orders and the creation of new ones were often undertaken without secular involvement. The Theatines, confirmed by the pope in 1524, grew out an association known as the Oratory of Divine Love whose origins date to 1494. The Barnabites (1533–1535), Somaschi (So-mahs'-kee, 1540), and the Capuchins (Ka-poo'-chins), an order of

FIGURE 14.5 *Cranmer Burned at the Stake.* Thomas Cranmer, Archbishop of Canterbury under Henry VIII and author of the Thirty-Nine Articles and the *Book of Common Prayer,* was England's most prominent Protestant clergyman. He was burnt at the stake on March 21, 1556, after the restoration of Catholicism by Queen Mary. Cranmer had at one point recanted his Protestant beliefs under interrogation but later reasserted his Protestant beliefs. He is shown here holding the hand that signed the recantation in the fire. Such executions aroused public disapproval and gravely weakened the Catholic cause.

reformed Franciscans, were all voluntary associations of churchmen pledged to the ideal of monastic reform. Maria Laurentia Longo (d. 1542) founded the female counterpart of the Capuchins, and in 1535, Angela Merici (Mare'-i-chee, c. 1473–1540) founded the **Ursulines,** an order that would play a decisive role in the education of Catholic women for centuries. None of these foundations was related in any way to the Protestant threat. Most popes regarded the proliferation of religious orders with suspicion. Their rivalries had long been a fruitful source of trouble, and most reform-minded clerics believed in consolidation rather than in new confirmations.

The Jesuits. Of all the religious orders founded or reformed during the sixteenth century, the Society of Jesus, or **Jesuits,** played the largest part in the struggle against Protestantism, but they had been created for other purposes. Their founder, **Ignatius of Loyola** (1491–1556), was originally inspired by the idea of converting the Muslims. After a long period of educational and religious development that produced *The Spiritual Exercises,* a manual of meditation that remains the foundation of Jesuit discipline, he and nine companions formed their order in 1534. Their asceticism, vigor, and vow of unconditional obedience to the pope led to their confirmation in 1540.

Although the order did little to convert the Muslims, it achieved moderate success in Asia under the leadership of **St. Francis Xavier** (Za'-vee-er, 1506–1552). In Europe, the Jesuits became the intellectual shock troops of the Counter-Reformation. Their high standards in recruitment and education made them natural leaders to reconvert areas of Europe that had deserted to Protestantism. Jesuit missions helped restore a Catholic majority in regions as diverse as Bavaria and Poland. An important means of achieving this was through education. Jesuit academies combining humanist educational principles with religious instruction spread through the subcontinent after 1555 and served much the same purpose for men that the Ursuline academies served for women.

Reforms Directed by the Papacy. The creation of new orders was essentially spontaneous, arising from reform-minded ele-

ments within the church, but the papacy itself was not idle. Reform remained difficult, if not impossible, until the ghost of conciliarism was laid to rest, and for this reason, the popes proceeded with great caution. Clement VII, besieged by the mutinous troops of Charles V and the demands of Henry VIII, accomplished little. Paul III (reigned 1534–1549) at first sought reconciliation by appointing a commission to investigate abuses within the church. Its report, a detailed analysis with recommendations for change, caused great embarrassment when the contents leaked to the public. Then an attempt to negotiate a settlement with the Lutherans broke down at the Regensburg Colloquy in 1541. These failures encouraged a policy of repression, and in 1542, the Roman Inquisition was revived under the direction of Gian Pietro Caraffa (John Pee-ay'-tro Kar-aff'-a), an implacable conservative and one of the founders of the Theatine order. Later, as Pope Paul IV (served 1555–1559), Caraffa would conduct a veritable reign of terror against those whom he regarded as corrupt or heretical. To protect the faithful from intellectual contamination, he also established the *Index Librorum Prohibitorum,* an ever-expanding list of books that Catholics were forbidden to read.

The Council of Trent. Repression alone could not solve the problems of the church. Despite the obvious danger to papal authority, Paul III decided to convene a general council at Trent in 1542. Sessions were held from 1543 to 1549, in 1551–1552, and in 1562–1563. Much disagreement arose over goals and the meetings

FIGURE 14.6 *The Final Session of the Council of Trent (Detail), 1563.* Attributed to Titian, this painting shows the conclusion of the great council whose decrees inspired the Catholic Church until the 1960s.

MAP 14.1. RELIGIOUS DIVISIONS IN EUROPE, 1560

Anglican	Roman Catholic
Calvinist	Lutheran
Calvinist influenced	Lutheran influenced
Holy Roman Empire boundary	+ Anabaptists

In 1560, Spain and Italy remained predominantly Catholic, but every other region had divided along confessional lines. This map shows the actual distribution of religious beliefs as opposed to the official religion imposed by governments. France and the Catholic principalities of Germany all had significant Protestant minorities, while Catholic populations survived with varying degrees of difficulty in Protestant lands.

were often sparsely attended, but the **Council of Trent** was a conspicuous success.

Theologically, Trent marked the triumph of Thomism, the theological system established by St. Thomas Aquinas. The Council specifically rejected Luther's ideas on justification, the sacraments, and the priesthood of all believers. It reasserted the medieval concept of the priestly office and the value of good works, and made efforts at the organizational level to correct most of the abuses that had been attacked by the reformers. These included not only the clerical sins of pluralism, absenteeism, nepotism, and simony but also such distortions of popular piety as the sale of indulgences and the misuse of images. The strengthening of ecclesiastical discipline was one of the council's greatest achievements.

Knowing that many of the church's problems arose from ignorance, the delegates ordered every diocese to establish a seminary for the education of its priests. To instruct the laity, they advocated the use of catechisms, or printed sets of questions and answers about the faith. At first, poverty prevented many bishops from carrying out all of these mandates, but the Council of Trent marked the beginning of the modern Catholic Church. Its institutional principles and the forms of piety that it established were not substantially modified until Vatican Council II in 1962–1965.

THE CONSEQUENCES OF REFORM

The impact of the sixteenth-century reformations has been the subject of much scholarly debate. The religious unity of western Christendom had clearly vanished forever. Religion became yet another source of conflict among European states and helped fuel the wars of the later sixteenth and early seventeenth century. Otherwise, cities and territorial states tended to benefit from reform, for Protestantism increased their control over church patronage and revenues. Even Catholic states exhibited more independence because the papacy became more cautious in its claims than it had been in the Middle Ages. Although hardly decisive, reform was therefore an important influence on the development of the modern state.

The Economics Effects of the Reformation. The economic consequences of the Reformation are far less clear. The idea that Protestantism somehow liberated acquisitive instincts and paved the way for the development of capitalism is highly suspect if for no other reason than that capitalism existed long before the Reformation and that the economic growth of such Protestant states as England and the Netherlands can be explained adequately in other ways. In some areas, notably England, the alienation of church property may have accelerated the capitalization of land that had begun in the years after the Black Death; in others, it served primarily to increase the domain revenues of the crown. In Denmark, for example, the crown held 40 percent of the arable land by 1620, primarily because, unlike Henry VIII, the Danish kings retained church lands confiscated during the Reformation.

The Status of Women. The reformers also sought to change the status of European women. Beginning with Luther and Zwingli, they rejected the ideal of clerical celibacy and declared that a Christian marriage was the ideal basis for a godly life. They specifically attacked medieval writings that either condemned women as temptresses or extolled virginity as the highest of female callings, and they drew attractive and sentimental portraits of the virtuous wife. A chief

A PROTESTANT VIEW OF MARRIAGE

The Money-Changer and His Wife (1539).

The city of Strasbourg in Alsace was an important center of the Reformation. Its reformer, Martin Bucer (Bootz'-er, 1491–1551), was more generous than most in his attitude toward women. Here, he argues that under certain circumstances a woman may leave her adulterous or abusive spouse and be free to remarry. Although rejected by Catholic authorities, a number of reformed cities accepted his viewpoint and passed laws accordingly.

For the Holy Spirit says that there is neither male nor female in Christ. In all things that pertain to salvation one should have as much regard for woman as for man. For though she is bound to keep her place, to put herself under the authority of her husband, just as the church does in relation to Christ, yet her subjection does not cancel the right of an honest woman, in accordance with the laws of God, to have recourse to and demand, by legitimate means, deliverance from a husband who hates her. For the Lord has certainly not made married woman subservient to have her polluted and tormented by the extortions and injuries of her husband, but rather so that she may receive discipline from him, as if from her master and savior, like the church from Christ. A wife is not so subject to her husband that she is bound to suffer anything he may impose upon her. Being free, she is joined to him in holy marriage that she may be loved, nourished, and maintained by him, as if she were his own flesh, just as the church is maintained by Christ. . . . Again, though a wife may be something less than her husband and subject to him, in order that they be rightly joined, the Holy Spirit has declared, through its apostle, that man and woman are equal before God in things pertaining to the alliance and mutual confederation of marriage. This is the meaning of the apostle's saying that a wife has power over the body of her husband, just as a husband has power over the body of his wife (1 Corinthians 7). . . . Hence, if wives feel that their association and cohabitation with their husbands is injurious to salvation as well of one as of the other, owing to the hardening and hatred on the part of their husbands, let them have recourse to the civil authority, which is enjoined by the Lord to help the afflicted.*

From Bucer, Martin, "De Regno Christi," book 2, chap. 34, in Julia O'Faolain and Lauro Martines, *Not in God's Image: Women in History from the Greeks to the Victorians* (New York: HarperCollins, 1973, pp. 200–201).

Question: According to Bucer, what is the proper relationship between husband and wife?

---

virtue of that ideal woman was her willingness to submit to male authority, but the attachment of the reformers to traditional social hierarchies should not be misinterpreted. The **companionate marriage** in which wife and husband offered each other mutual support was the Reformation ideal (see Document 14.6). If women were subordinate, it was, as Calvin said, because women "by the very order of nature are bound to obey." To him, other reformers, and Catholic theologians, the traditionally ordered family was both part and symbol of a divinely established hierarchy. To disrupt that hierarchy risked chaos.

The Reformation's endorsement of women may have been qualified, but it increased the status of wife and mother and placed new demands upon men, who were encouraged to treat their wives with consideration. As early as the 1520s, some German towns permitted women to divorce husbands who were guilty of gross abuse. The reformers also encouraged female literacy, at least in the vernacular, because they wanted women to read the Scriptures. The impact of these prescriptions on the lives of real women may be questioned. On the negative side, the Protestant emphasis on marriage narrowed a woman's career choices to one. Catholic Europe continued to offer productive lives to women who chose not to marry, but Protestant women could rarely escape the dominance of men. If they did, it was through widowhood or divorce, and Protestant societies offered no institutional support for the unmarried. St. Teresa of Avila

(Ah'-vee-la), Angelique Arnauld (Ar-nawd'), Madame Acarie (Ah-ca-ree), Jeanne de Chantal (Shan-tal), and the other great female figures of post-Tridentine Catholicism had few Protestant counterparts.

The Attack on Popular Culture.
From the standpoint of the reformers, whether Catholic or Protestant, such issues were of secondary importance. Their primary concern was the salvation of souls and the transformation of popular piety. They made heroic efforts to catechize or otherwise educate the laity in most parts of Europe, and after about 1570, an increasing tendency was seen toward clerical interference in lay morals. Catholic church courts and Protestant consistories sought to eliminate such evils as brawling, public drunkenness, and sexual misbehavior. Inevitably the churchmen were forced to condemn the occasions on which such activity arose. The celebration of holidays and popular festivals came under scrutiny, as did public performances of every kind from street jugglers to those of Shakespeare and his troop of actors. Dancing aroused special concern. No one worried about the stately measures trod by courtiers, but the rowdy and often sexually explicit dances of the peasants seemed, after years of familiarity, to induce shock.

Civil authorities supported this attack on popular culture for practical reasons. The celebration of holidays and popular festivals encouraged disorder. When accompanied as they usually were by heavy drinking, public amusements could lead to violence and even riots. Moreover, like street theater, most celebrations con-

tained seditious skits or pageants. They mocked the privileged classes, satirized the great, and delighted in the reversal of social and gender roles. The triumph of a Lord of Misrule, the costumed figure in street celebrations who mocked accepted standards, for even a day made magistrates nervous, and prudence demanded that such activities be regulated or prohibited outright. Popular beliefs and practices were attacked with equal vigor. The authorities rarely took action against academic magic, astrology, or alchemy—sciences that, although dubious, were widely accepted by the wealthy and educated—but they no longer tolerated folk magic. In some cases, official suspicion extended even to the traditional remedies used by midwives and village "wise women."

The Witch-Craze of 1550–1650.
The epidemic of witch hunting that convulsed Europe in the late sixteenth and early seventeenth centuries may have been related to these concerns. In the century after 1550, Protestant and Catholic governments in virtually every part of Europe executed more than 60,000 people for being witches or Satanists. Medieval thinkers such as Thomas Aquinas had denied the power of witches, but a later age thought differently. Magistrates and learned men built theories of a vast satanic plot around their imperfect knowledge of folk beliefs. Their ideas crystallized in manuals for witch hunters, the most famous of which, the *Malleus Maleficarum* (Hammer of Witches) went through twenty-nine editions between 1495 and 1669. Its authors, like most people in early modern Europe, believed that in a providential world there could be no accidents; evil required an explanation. Otherwise unexplained disasters were caused by witches who gained extraordinary powers through worshipping the devil and used those powers to injure their neighbors. The community could be protected only by burning witches alive.

In this case, ordinary people shared the concerns of the intellectual elite. Accusations of witchcraft tended to multiply in waves of hysteria that convulsed entire regions. Many of those denounced were no doubt guilty of trying to cast spells or some other unsavory act, but the victims fit a profile that suggests a generalized hostility toward women and perhaps that the persecutions were in part a means of exerting social control. The great majority of those burned were single women, old and poor, who lived at the margins of their communities. The rest, whether male or female, tended to be people whose assertive or uncooperative behavior had aroused hostility.

FIGURE 14.7 *Peasant Dance (c. 1567), Pieter Brueghel the Elder.* Religious reformers of all faiths objected to popular festivals of the kind portrayed here with its evident lack of restraint. Everyone in the village appears to be more or less drunk, perhaps especially the young couple kissing. Those who can still navigate, dance to the music of a bagpipe. An old man pulls a young woman forward, and in the background, another man urges a housewife to join the dance.

The trials subsided after 1650, but not before other traditional beliefs had been discredited by their association with witchcraft. Some of these involved "white" magic, the normally harmless spells and preparations used to ensure good harvests or to cure disease. Others were "errors," or what the Inquisition called *propositions*. This was a broad category that included everything from the popular notion that premarital sex was no sin to alternative cosmologies devised by imaginative peasants. Post-Tridentine Catholicism, no less than its Protestant rivals, discouraged uncontrolled speculation and was deeply suspicious of those forms of piety that lacked ecclesiastical sanction. Popular beliefs about the Virgin Mary, the saints, and miracles were scrutinized, while lay people claiming to have religious visions were ridiculed and sometimes prosecuted.

The efforts of the reformers, in other words, bore modest fruit. Drunkenness proved ineradicable, but some evidence is available that interpersonal violence decreased and that behavior in general became somewhat more sedate. Although lay morals and religious knowledge improved slowly if at all, the forms of piety were transformed in some cases beyond recognition.

Many ideas and practices vanished so completely that historians of popular culture can recover their memory only with great difficulty. Devotion based on personal contact with God through mental prayer became common in virtually all communions. Catholics abandoned the sale of indulgences and consciously sought to limit such abuses as the misuse of pilgrimages and relics. Protestants abandoned all three, together with Latin, vigils, the cult of the saints, masses for the dead, and mandatory fasts. By 1600, the religious landscape of Europe had been transformed, and much of the richness, vitality, and cohesion of peasant life had been lost.

CONCLUSION

After 1300, the Western church found itself under attack by the increasingly aggressive monarchies of the day and by those who demanded higher standards of piety in the face of plague and social disorder. Internal conflicts led to a series of scandals that undermined the authority of the popes and strengthened anticlerical sentiment. New spiritual and intellectual movements undermined traditional faith. Between 1517 and 1555, a series of religious movements emerged to challenge the medieval church: Lutheran, Reformed, Anabaptist, Calvinist, Anglican, and others. Several of them gained political support as both states and city governments used them to seize the church's wealth and increase their independence. Collectively, these movements are known as the Protestant Reformation, but their beliefs and organization differed widely, and they were rarely able to cooperate with one another. At the same time, the Catholic Church reformed itself from within, partially in response to the Protestant challenge, but largely because a majority of those who remained loyal to the old church demanded reforms as well. Together, the reformations of the sixteenth century gave birth to two distinct systems of Christian thought and practice, both of which opposed many aspects of medieval piety and popular culture. In so doing, they obliterated much of the medieval past and created a religious division in Western society that continues to this day.

Review Questions

- Why did late medieval popes find it difficult to respond to demands for reform?
- How did the rise of mysticism, nominalism, and humanism influence the coming of the Reformation?
- Why was Emperor Charles V unable to halt the growth of Protestantism in the Holy Roman Empire?
- What reforms did the Catholic Church introduce during the sixteenth century?

For Further Study

Readings

Dickens, A. G., *The Counter Reformation* (New York: Norton, 1979). Still the most accessible survey of Catholic reform. Profusely illustrated.

Dickens, A. G., *The English Reformation,* 2nd ed. (University Park: Pennsylvania State University Press, 1991). A readable, clear, and balanced presentation.

Kittelson, James M., *Luther the Reformer: The Story of the Man and His Career* (Minneapolis: Augsburg, 1986). A readable and sympathetic biography.

McGrath, Alister E., *A Life of John Calvin: A Study in the Shaping of Western Culture* (Cambridge, MA: Blackwell, 1990). Probably the most accessible of the works on Calvin.

Oakley, Francis, *The Western Church in the Later Middle Ages* (Ithaca, NY: Cornell, 1979). The best survey of the late medieval church and its difficulties.

InfoTrac College Edition

For additional reading, go to your online research library at *http://infotrac.thomsonlearning.com.*

Using Key Terms, enter the search terms:

Reformation	*Counter-Reformation*
Martin and *Luther* not *King*	*John Calvin*

Web Site

http://www.fordham.edu/halsall/mod/modsbook02.html
Internet Modern History Sourcebook. Look under Reformation.

THE LATE MEDIEVAL CHURCH AND THE REFORMATION

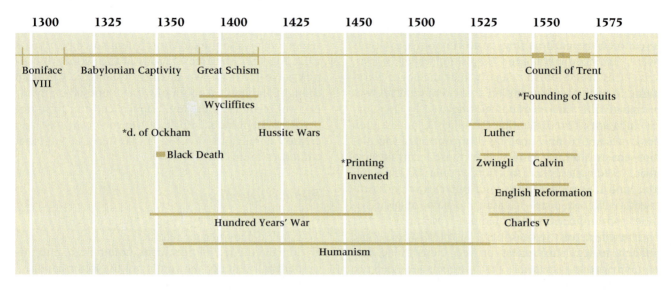

| 1300 | 1325 | 1350 | 1400 | 1425 | 1450 | 1500 | 1525 | 1550 | 1575 |

Boniface VIII

Babylonian Captivity

Great Schism

Council of Trent

Wycliffites

*Founding of Jesuits

*d. of Ockham

Hussite Wars

Luther

Black Death

Zwingli   Calvin

*Printing Invented

English Reformation

Hundred Years' War

Charles V

Humanism

Visit the Western Civilization Companion Web Site for resources specific to this textbook:
http://history.wadsworth.com/hause02/

The CD in the back of this book and the Western Civilization Resource Center at *http://history.wadsworth.com/western/* offer a variety of tools to help you succeed in this course, including access to quizzes; images; documents; interactive simulations, maps, and timelines; movie explorations; and a wealth of other sources.

Chapter 15

OVERSEAS CONQUEST AND RELIGIOUS WAR TO 1648

FOCUS QUESTIONS

- Why did Spain and Portugal embark upon the development of overseas empires?
- What caused the Revolt of the Netherlands, and how did the revolt come to involve France and England?
- What were the most important causes of the Thirty Years' War, and why did the conflict prove difficult to resolve?
- What were the major causes of the English Civil War?

*I*n the spring of 1519, **Hernán Cortés,** age 33, left Cuba without the governor's permission to conquer an empire. He brought with him 600 men, 16 horses, 14 artillery pieces, and 13 muskets. After 2 years of peril and privation, he succeeded. The Aztec Empire and all of central Mexico fell to the Spanish. Cortés had conquered a nation larger than his native Spain. Years later, Bernal Díaz del Castillo, one of his soldiers, wrote *The True History of the Conquest of New Spain* to explain how it all happened. Why would men come 4,000 miles from their homes to undertake such an improbable project? The answer, he said, was, "We came to serve God and also to get rich." It would be hard to imagine a better answer.

The voyages of exploration and conquest undertaken by Europeans in the late fifteenth and early sixteenth centuries had no real parallel in any other civilization. They arose from the expansion and consolidation of the European monarchies and from the desire to convert non-Christians to the faith. These same impulses brought nearly a century of war and suffering to Europe while visiting untold misery on the inhabitants of distant lands.

The first half of Chapter 15 tells of Europe's confrontation with a broader world: the overseas voyages undertaken by Europeans in the fifteenth and sixteenth century and the first great colonial empires they established. It then examines another conflict with non-Europeans: the struggle between the Ottoman Empire and the empire of Charles V. The second half of the chapter deals with a century of fratricidal struggles within Europe itself: the French Wars of Religion, the Revolt of the Netherlands, The Thirty Years' War, and the civil war in England. They, too, arose from a mixture of motives that Bernal Díaz would have understood.

THE FIRST EUROPEAN VOYAGES OVERSEAS

The process of overseas exploration began appropriately enough in Portugal, the first modern monarchy and a center of the fourteenth-century revolution in shipbuilding. The Portuguese state had been effectively consolidated by John I in 1385. Like other medieval rulers, he and his descendants hoped to maximize domain revenue by increasing taxable commerce. The gold and ivory of Africa were a tempting goal, but that trade was dominated by Moroccan intermediaries who shipped products from the African heartland by camel caravan and sold them to Europeans through such ports as Ceuta and Tangier. The Portuguese knew that enormous profits could be realized by sailing directly to the source of these commodities and bypassing the middlemen, who were in any case Muslims and their traditional enemies.

The Portuguese Voyages. These considerations, and a desire to find new converts for the church, inspired **Prince Henry "the Navigator"** (1394–1460) to establish a center for navigational development on the windswept bluffs of Sagres at the far southwestern tip of Europe. While Henry's cosmographers and mathematicians worked steadily to improve the quality of charts and navigational techniques, his captains sailed ever further along the African coast, returning with growing quantities of gold, ivory, pepper, and slaves. The enslavement of Africans was part of the expansionist enterprise from the start. The Portuguese ships were fast, handy caravels that combined the best features of northern and Mediterranean construction. Their instruments were improved versions of the compass, the quadrant, and the astrolabe. The compass had been introduced to the Mediterranean in the twelfth or thirteenth century, probably by the Arabs. The quadrant and the astrolabe permitted sailors to find their latitude based on the elevation of the sun above the horizon.

Before the death of Prince Henry, the Portuguese adopted the idea of sailing around the tip of Africa to India as their primary goal. By so doing they hoped to bypass the Italian–Arab monopoly and gain direct access to the spice trade. In May 1498, **Vasco da Gama** reached Calicut on the coast of India after a 2-year voyage. His arrival disturbed political and commercial relationships that had endured for centuries. Indian and Arab merchants found the newcomers rude and barbaric and their trade goods of little interest. Although the voyages of da Gama and Cabral made a profit, only the judicious use of force could secure a major Portuguese share in the trade. After 1508, **Alfonso de Albuquerque** (1453–1515) tried to gain control of the

Vasco da Gama (c. 1469–1525)

Indian Ocean by seizing its major ports. Aden and Ormuz eluded him, but Goa became the chief Portuguese base in India and the capture of Malacca (1511) opened the way to China. A Portuguese settlement was established there at Macao in 1556. The Portuguese initiated trade with Japan in 1543, and for 75 years thereafter, ships from Macao on the Chinese mainland brought luxury goods to Nagasaki in return for silver.

These achievements earned Portugal a modest place in Asian commerce. The Portuguese may have been the first people of any race to trade on a truly worldwide basis, but the total volume of spices exported to Europe did not immediately increase as a result of their activities. Furthermore, the Arab and Gujarati merchants of the Indian Ocean remained formidable competitors for more than a century.

Columbus and the Opening of America. Meanwhile, the Spanish, by sailing west, had reached America. Isabella of Castile and Ferdinand of Aragon regarded the expansion of their Portuguese rivals with dismay and believed, as Prince Henry had done, that they were obligated by morality and the requirements of dynastic prestige to spread the Catholic faith. When **Christopher Columbus,** a Genoese mariner, proposed to reach Asia by sailing across the Atlantic, they were prepared to listen. Columbus had offered the same project to the Portuguese in 1484 and was turned down. They apparently found him both demanding and ignorant. A self-educated man, Columbus ac-

FIGURE 15.1 *Christopher Columbus (1451–1506).* A fine contemporary portrait by an anonymous Spanish painter.

cepted only those theories that supported his own and underestimated the circumference of the globe by nearly 7,000 miles. The Portuguese cosmographers believed in the more accurate calculations of Eratosthenes. Because neither they nor he knew of America, they assumed that he would perish in the Atlantic several thousand miles from his goal. Columbus's first reception in Spain was no better, but he eventually gained the support of the queen and Ferdinand's treasurer, who found ways to finance the voyage with little risk to the crown.

In August 1492, Columbus set sail in the ship *Santa Maria*, accompanied by two small caravels, the *Pinta* and the *Niña*. Their combined crews totaled about ninety men. Columbus sailed southwest to the Canary Islands and then westward across the Atlantic, taking advantage of winds and currents that he could not fully have understood. Despite the season, he encountered no hurricanes, and on October 12, he sighted what he believed to be an island off the coast of Japan. It was one of the Bahamas.

Columbus made three more voyages before his death in 1506, insisting until the end that he had found the western passage to Asia. The realization that it was a continent whose existence had only been suspected by Europeans was left to others. One of them, a Florentine navigator named Amerigo Vespucci (1454–1512), gave it his name. The true dimensions of the "New World" became clearer in 1513, when Vasco Núñez de Balboa crossed the Isthmus of Panama on foot and became the first European to look upon the Pacific.

The achievement of Columbus has been somewhat diminished by his own failure to grasp its significance and by the fact that others had no doubt preceded him. The Vikings visited Newfoundland and may have explored the North American coast as far south as Cape Cod. Portuguese and Basque fishermen had almost certainly landed there in the course of their annual expeditions to the Grand Banks, but being fishermen, they kept their discoveries secret to discourage competitors and these early contacts came to nothing.

The voyage of Columbus, however, set off a frenzy of exploration and conquest. In the Treaty of Tordesillas (1494), the Spanish and Portuguese agreed to a line of demarcation established in the mid-Atlantic by the pope. Lands "discovered" to the east of that line belonged to Portugal; those to the west belonged to Spain. The inhabitants of those lands were not consulted. This left Brazil, Africa, and the route to India in Portuguese hands, but a line of demarcation in the Pacific was not defined. Much of Asia remained in dispute.

Magellan's Voyage. To establish a Spanish presence there, an expedition was dispatched in 1515 to reach the Moluccas by sailing west around the southern tip of South America. Its leader was **Fernando Magellan,** a Portuguese sailor in Spanish pay. Magellan crossed the Pacific only to be killed in the Moluccas by natives unimpressed with the benefits of Spanish sovereignty. His navigator, Sebastian del Cano, became the first captain to circumnavigate the globe when he brought the expedition's only remaining ship back to Spain with fifteen survivors in 1522. The broad outlines of the world were now apparent.

Ferdinand Magellan (c. 1480–1521)

THE TOOLS OF EXPLORATION

Improved ships and better navigational techniques made it possible for Europeans to embark on overseas explorations. Chapter 12 described the evolution of shipbuilding in the later Middle Ages. Navigation at sea depends on knowing the ship's direction and its position on the globe. The compass, which enabled mariners to find their direction at sea, had been known for centuries. Latitude, or the ship's distance from the equator, could be calculated with an astrolabe or with a cross-staff. Longitude, or east–west distance, was more difficult. Until the invention of accurate chronometers in the eighteenth century, it could only be estimated by a process known as dead reckoning.

▶ *A Portuguese Caravel of the Fifteenth Century.* Although rarely more than 70 or 80 feet in length, these vessels were extremely seaworthy and formed the mainstay of Portugal's explorations along the coasts of Africa and in the Atlantic. This one is lateen rigged for better performance to windward, but some of them carried square sails as well, usually on the foremast. The Spanish used caravels, too. This one probably resembles Columbus's *Niña*, before she was fitted with square sails for the trip across the Atlantic.

THE FIRST COLONIAL EMPIRES: PORTUGAL AND SPAIN

The Portuguese Colonies. Conquest and the imposition of European government accompanied exploration from the beginning. The Portuguese made no effort to impose their direct rule on large native populations, in part because they lacked the manpower to do so and in part because the primary purpose of Portuguese expansion was trade. Instead, they established a series of merchant colonies to collect goods from the African, Indian, or Asian interior for transshipment to Portugal in return for cash or European commodities. These colonies were rarely more than towns protected by a Portuguese garrison and governed by Portuguese law. They were not, for the most part, self-sustaining. To prosper, they had to maintain diplomatic and commercial relations with their neighbors while retaining the option of force, either for self-protection or to obtain a favorable market share in regional trade. Because Portugal's population was small, there was no question of large-scale immigration. Governors from Albuquerque onward sought to maintain colonial populations and to solidify Portuguese control by encouraging intermarriage with native peoples.

Communication between these far-flung stations and the mother country was maintained by the largest ships of the age, the thousand-ton carracks built especially for the *Carreira da India* (road to India). The voyage around the tip of Africa took months and caused dreadful mortality among crews, but profit to the crown made it all seem worthwhile. To discourage smuggling, everything had to be shipped to and from a central point—the Guinea Mines House at Lagos, near Sagres—where royal officials could inspect the cargoes of spice and silks and assess the one-third share owed to the king. In return, the monarchy provided military and naval protection for the colonies and for the convoys that served them. Colonial governors, although appointed by the crown, enjoyed the freedom that comes from being far from home. Corruption flourished, but Portuguese rule was rarely harsh.

The Astrolabe. Astrolabes have been used by astronomers since the sixth century. They are complex instruments that consist of a movable map of the stars, a series of lines indicating celestial coordinates, and a straight rule known as an *alidade.* The navigator points the alidade at the sun to determine his latitude, or distance from the equator. The astrolabe was simplified for navigational use in the fifteenth century and weighted to keep it vertical on a pitching ship, but it never achieved perfect accuracy and was difficult to use.

The Cross-staff. Cross-staffs became common in the early 1500s. They were simpler, easier to use, and more accurate than an astrolabe. The mariner figures latitude by moving a sliding crosspiece along a marked staff. When the bottom of the crosspiece is on the horizon and its upper edge is on the sun, he can read his latitude in the markings on the staff. He risks eye damage because he has to look into the sun, but the cross-staff could fix latitude to within about 1 degree of accuracy, while the astrolabe sometimes erred by as much as 5 degrees. A degree equals 60 nautical miles, or about 69 land miles.

Where controlling large tracts of land became necessary, as in Brazil, the Portuguese established captaincies that were in fact proprietary colonies. Captains-general would be appointed in return for their promise to settle and develop grants of land given to them by the crown. The model had first been used in the settlement of Madeira, a group of Atlantic islands settled by Portugal in the 1420s. Both Brazil and Madeira evolved into societies based largely on sugar plantations worked by African slaves.

The Spanish Conquests. The first Spanish attempts at colonization resembled the Portuguese experience in Brazil. Columbus had set a bad example by trying to enslave the native population of Hispaniola, the island now occupied by Haiti and the Dominican Republic. Spanish settlers made similar efforts at Cuba and elsewhere in the Caribbean without success. The Indians died of disease and overwork, fled to the mainland, or were killed while trying to resist. The Spanish then imported African slaves to work in the mines and sugar cane fields. In the meantime, the conquest of Mexico and Peru had changed the basic nature of Spanish colonial enterprise. Both regions contained populous, highly developed civilizations. For the first time, Europeans sought to impose their rule on societies as complex and populous as their own.

The various nations of central Mexico were grouped into political units that resembled city-states. Their combined population almost certainly exceeded that of Spain. By the fifteenth century, most of these peoples had become either subjects or tributaries of the warlike **Aztecs** whose capital, Tenochtitlán, was a vast city built in the midst of a lake where Mexico City now stands. Hernán Cortés could not have conquered this great empire in

Hernán Cortés

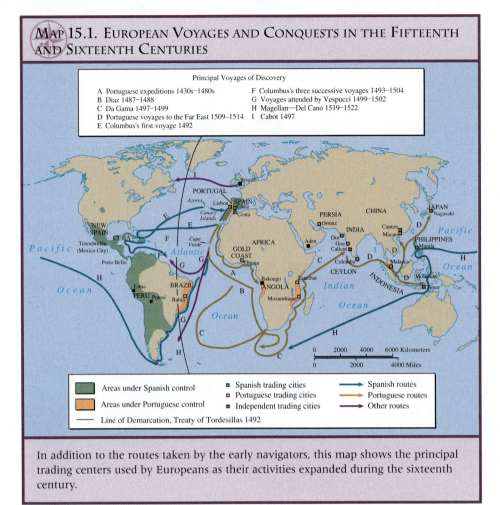

MAP 15.1. EUROPEAN VOYAGES AND CONQUESTS IN THE FIFTEENTH AND SIXTEENTH CENTURIES

Principal Voyages of Discovery

A Portuguese expeditions 1430s–1480s
B Diaz 1487–1488
C Da Gama 1497–1499
D Portuguese voyages to the Far East 1509–1514
E Columbus's first voyage 1492
F Columbus's three successive voyages 1493–1504
G Voyages attended by Vespucci 1499–1502
H Magellan—Del Cano 1519–1522
I Cabot 1497

Areas under Spanish control
Areas under Portuguese control
Line of Demarcation, Treaty of Tordesillas 1492
Spanish trading cities
Portuguese trading cities
Independent trading cities
Spanish routes
Portuguese routes
Other routes

In addition to the routes taken by the early navigators, this map shows the principal trading centers used by Europeans as their activities expanded during the sixteenth century.

1521 without the assistance of the Aztecs' many native enemies, but his success left Spain with the problem of governing millions whose culture was wholly unlike that of Europeans.

The problem was compounded in Peru a decade later. In 1530, **Francisco Pizarro** landed at Tumbez on the Pacific coast with 180 men and set about the destruction of the **Inca Empire.** The Incas were the ruling dynasty of the Quechua people. From their capital at Cuzco they controlled a region nearly 2,000 miles in length by means of an elaborate system of roads and military supply depots. More tightly organized than the Mexicans, Quechua society was based on communal landholding and a system of forced labor that supported both the rulers and a complex religious establishment that did not, unlike that of the Aztecs, demand human sacrifice. Pizarro had the good

Francisco Pizarro

fortune to arrive in the midst of a dynastic dispute that divided the Indians and virtually paralyzed resistance. By 1533, the Spanish, now numbering about 600, had seized the capital and a vast golden treasure, but they soon began to fight among themselves. Pizarro was murdered in one of a series of civil wars that ended only in 1548.

The Imposition of Royal Government. The rapid conquest of two great empires forced the Spanish crown to confront basic issues of morality and governance. Tension between conquerors and the crown had begun with Columbus. His enslavement of the Indians and high-handed treatment of his own men led to his replacement as governor of Hispaniola. Officials sent from Spain executed Balboa for his misbehavior in Darien. To regularize the situation, the *encomienda* system, an institution that had been used to settle Muslim regions during the Spanish Reconquest of the Middle Ages, was introduced after the conquests of Mexico and Peru. *Conquistadores* (kon-kees-ta-dor'-es; conquerors) were to provide protection and religious instruction for a fixed number of Indians in return for a portion of their labor. The system failed. The Spanish conquistadores were for the most part desperadoes, members of a large class of otherwise unemployable military adventurers that had survived the wars of Granada or of Italy. They had braved great dangers to win what they thought of as a New World and had no intention of allowing priests and bureaucrats to deprive them of their rewards.

Efforts to Protect the Indians. In the meantime, the Indians of the mainland had begun to die in enormous numbers, like those of the islands before them. Although many were killed while trying to defend themselves, most fell victim to European diseases for which they had developed no immunities. Smallpox was probably the worst. Estimates of mortality by the end of the sixteenth century range as high as 90 percent, and although all figures from this period are open

THE HAZARDS OF A LONG VOYAGE

The Straits of Magellan.

This passage, now called the Straits of Magellan and running between the southern tip of the South American mainland and the island of Tierra del Fuego, connects the Atlantic and Pacific Oceans. Its regular 100-mile-per-hour gusting winds must have terrified sailors.

This extract is taken from a firsthand account of Fernando Magellan's voyage around the world by Antonio Pigafetta, but similar conditions might be expected on any sea journey if it lasted long enough. The disease described is scurvy, which results from a deficiency of vitamin C. It was a serious problem even on transatlantic voyages. The cause was not understood until the eighteenth century, but captains could usually predict the first date of its appearance in a ship's company with some accuracy.

Wednesday, November 28, we debauched from that strait [since named after Magellan], engulfing ourselves in the Pacific Sea. We were three months and twenty days without getting any kind of fresh food. We ate biscuit, which was no longer biscuit, but powder of biscuits swarming with worms, for they had eaten the good. It stank strongly of the urine of rats. We drank yellow water that had been putrid for many days. We also ate some ox hides that covered the top of the mainyard to prevent the yard from chafing the shrouds, and which had become exceedingly hard because of the sun, rain, and wind. We left them in the sea for four or five days, and then placed them on top of the embers and so ate them; and we often ate sawdust from boards. Rats were sold for one-half ducat a piece, and even then we could not get them. But above all the other misfortunes the following was the worst. The gums of both the lower and upper teeth of some of our men swelled so that they could not eat under any circumstances and therefore died. Nineteen men died from that sickness. . . . Twenty-five or thirty men fell sick.

From Pigafetta, Antonio, *Magellan's Voyage around the World*, ed. and trans. J. A. Robertson (Cleveland: 1902).

Question: What would cause someone to go on a long sea voyage that presented such conditions and risks?

---

to question, the conquest clearly was responsible for the greatest demographic catastrophe in historical times (see Table 15.1).

Given the state of medical knowledge, little could be done to control the epidemics, but church and state alike were determined to do something about the conquistadores. The Dominican friar **Bartolomé de Las Casas** (1474–1566) launched a vigorous propaganda campaign on behalf of the Indians that ended in a series of debates at the University of Salamanca. Basing his arguments on Aristotle, he declared that the Indians were "rational beings" and therefore could not be enslaved. Las Casas won his point. In 1542 and 1543, Emperor Charles V (1500–1558) issued the so-called New Laws, forbidding Indian slavery and abolishing the encomienda system.

The Spanish Colonial System. The edicts for the protection of the Indians met with powerful resistance (see Document 15.2), and not until the reign of **Philip II** (1556–1598) did Spain implement the system of governance that would last throughout the colonial era. Mexico and Peru became kingdoms ruled by viceroys who were the personal representatives of the king. Like the Portuguese, the Spanish tried to limit access to its colonial trade. No foreigners could participate, and all

FIGURE 15.2 *A Sugar Mill.* European demand for sugar encouraged the colonization of Brazil and the Caribbean Islands. It also created an insatiable demand for African slaves to work the sugar plantations. In this open-air mill, slaves fed the cane into the ox-powered grinder to the right. The juice was then placed in the boiling vats (center), where it was reduced into molasses for shipment.

goods had to be shipped and received through the *Casa de Contratación,* a vast government customs house in Sevilla. From the middle of the sixteenth century, French and English adventurers sought to break this monopoly and eventually became a threat to Spanish shipping in both Caribbean and European waters. By this time, massive silver deposits had been discovered at Potosí in what is now Bolivia (1545) and at Zacatecas in Mexico (1548). Bullion shipments from the New World soon accounted for more than 20 percent of the empire's revenues, and a system of convoys, or *flotas,* was established for their protection.

The Cultural Legacy of the Conquests. The European conquests had a disastrous effect on Native Americans. The extermination of millions of people was largely unintentional, but the Spanish in particular saw American culture as a barrier to conversion and tried to destroy it. They leveled temples and built churches on the ruins. They destroyed cities and rebuilt them along Spanish lines, while extensive intermarriage between Spaniards and Americans tended to weaken the cultural identity of the latter. Religious instruction sought not only to instill Catholicism but also to obliterate traditional beliefs. This campaign against memory was remarkably successful, although many of the old ways survived as folklore or as superficially Christianized myths.

Biological Exchange. The term **biological exchange** refers to the transfer of new life forms among cultures. The introduction of European and African diseases to the New World provides a terrifying example,

but it was not fully reciprocal. Aside from a strain of syphilis endemic to the Americas, Europeans suffered few medical effects from the conquests as long as they remained in Europe. Those who came to America or visited Africa in search of slaves often died of yellow fever and other African diseases for which they had no immunity. Europeans also resisted American foods such as tomatoes, potatoes, maize, and bell peppers until the eighteenth century. Until then, biological exchange remained largely a one-way street. The colonists brought horses, cattle, and hogs to regions that lacked native sources of animal power or animal protein, but the value of these benefits has been questioned by modern ecologists and by vegetarians. Sugar, a Middle Eastern plant formerly cultivated in small quantities, became available for mass consumption in Europe when huge sugar plantations were established in the Caribbean and Brazil. The widespread availability of sugar was no

FIGURE 15.3 *An Illustration from the Works of Las Casas.* The Dominican friar, Bartolomé de Las Casas, worked tirelessly to improve the treatment of the Indians under Spanish rule. His *Very Brief Account of the Destruction of the Indies* (written 1542) provided a catalogue of atrocities that eventually helped inspire legal reform. It also provided Spain's many enemies with a propaganda tool of great value. In fact, Spanish behavior was probably little worse than that of other colonizing nations, all of whom saw indigenous peoples as a resource to exploit. In this illustration from a French edition of Las Casas's work, the Spanish roast an Indian alive over a slow fire. In the background, another has his hands cut off as a warning to others.

TABLE 15.1 POPULATION DECLINE IN CENTRAL MEXICO

Little agreement exists on the size of Mexico's pre-Columbian population. These figures are more conservative than most but reflect a stunning rate of mortality.

REGION	POPULATION 1530—1535	POPULATION IN 1568
Basin of Mexico (excluding Mexico City)	589,070–743,337	294,535–297,335
Mexico City	218,546–273,183	109,273
Morelos	460,797–614,396	153,599
Southern Hidalgo	257,442–321,802	128,721
Tlaxcala	140,000–165,000	140,000–165,000
West Puebla		
Above 2000 meters	160,664–200,830	80,332
Below 2000 meters	152,412–190,515	38,103
Total	1,978,931–2,509,063	944,563–972,363

Source: Adapted from William T. Sanders, "The Population of the Central Mexican Symbiotic Region, the Basin of Mexico, and the Teotihuacán Valley in the Sixteenth Century," in William M. Denevan, ed., *The Native Population of the Americas in 1492*, 2nd ed. (Madison: University of Wisconsin Press, 1992, p. 128).

Questions: Did all cities decrease in population? If not, which didn't? Why did Tlaxcala's population not decrease? What could explain the difference in the amount of decreased population in the two areas of West Puebla?

DOCUMENT 15.2

PROCLAMATION OF THE NEW LAWS IN PERU

In 1544, a new viceroy, Blasco Nuñez Vela, introduced the New Laws to Peru. The popular outrage recounted here by Francisco López de Gómara led to a serious but unsuccessful revolt under the leadership of Gonzalo Pizarro, the conqueror's brother.

Blasco Nuñez entered Trujillo amid great gloom on the part of the Spaniards; he publicly proclaimed the New Laws, regulating Indian tributes, freeing the Indians, and forbidding their use as carriers against their will and without pay. He told them, however, that if they had reason to complain of the ordinances they should take their case to the emperor; and that he would write to the king that he had been badly informed to order those laws.

When the citizens perceived the severity behind his soft words, they began to curse. [Some] said that they were ill-requited for their labor and services if in their declining years they were to have no one to serve them; these showed their teeth, decayed from eating roasted corn in the conquest of Peru; others displayed many wounds, bruises, and great lizard bites; the conquerors complained that after wasting their estates and shedding their blood in gaining Peru for the emperor, he was depriving them of the few vassals he had given them.

The priests and friars also declared that they could not support themselves nor serve their churches if they were deprived of their Indian towns; the one who spoke most shamelessly against the viceroy and even against the king was Fray Pedro Muñoz of the Mercedarian Order, saying . . . that the New Laws smelled of calculation rather than of saintliness, for the king was taking away the slaves that he had sold without returning the money received from them. . . . There was bad blood between this friar and the viceroy because the latter had stabbed the friar one evening in Málaga when the viceroy was corregidor there.

From López de Gómara, Francisco. "Historia de las Indias," trans. B. Keen. In *Latin American Civilization*, vol. 1 (Boston: Houghton Mifflin, 1974, pp. 142–143).

Question: What did the New Laws do, and how did the Spanish populace respond?

---

doubt bad for European teeth. It certainly allowed the large-scale distillation of gin and other spirits in the seventeenth century, a process that requires vast amounts of sugar. Both ranching and sugar planting had a destructive effect on native American ecologies.

Demographically, few Americans traveled to Europe and survived. Europeans and Africans emigrated (willingly or unwillingly) in great numbers to create a racially diverse population in the Americas. Africa and most of Asia remained demographically unchanged, because the permanent European presence there was comparatively small and because Asians and Europeans shared the same disease pool and therefore the same immunities. The world population of Africans and African

Americans may actually have increased despite the terrible mortality of the slave trade. The descendants of those who survived the slave ships became more numerous in the Americas, although the wretched conditions imposed by slavery kept their rate of growth far below that of Caucasians. Meanwhile, the cassava, a starchy South American root, became the staple food of West Africa and permitted a substantial increase among the populations that had eluded the slavers.

The Economic and Political Legacy of the Conquests. America's entry into the world market increased the overall volume of world trade, and its massive exports of gold and silver increased the European money supply. Early modern rulers began to think that it was better to increase revenues by seizing new territory and by expanding trade than by exploiting their existing subjects more efficiently. The idea, although popular with their subjects, was based in part on an illusion. Trade and colonies provided additional pretexts for war. Their protection demanded the establishment of fortresses and the maintenance of expensive deep-sea navies. During the sixteenth and early seventeenth centuries, the cost and intensity of European warfare reached new heights, and it was obvious well before

1600 that even if the primary cause of these conflicts was rarely colonial rivalry, their scope was becoming global.

A Clash of Empires: The Ottoman Challenge and Emperor Charles V (1526–1558)

The wars that plagued sixteenth-century and early seventeenth-century Europe were for the most part a continuation of old dynastic rivalries, complicated after 1560 by rebellion and civil war in nearly all of the major states. These struggles were pursued with unparalleled vigor even though most Europeans believed, or

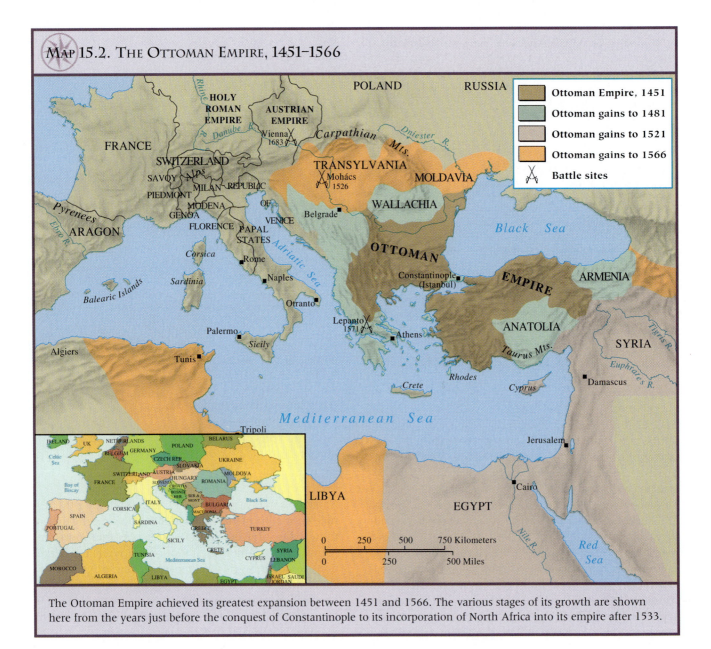

MAP 15.2. THE OTTOMAN EMPIRE, 1451–1566

Ottoman Empire, 1451
Ottoman gains to 1481
Ottoman gains to 1521
Ottoman gains to 1566
Battle sites

The Ottoman Empire achieved its greatest expansion between 1451 and 1566. The various stages of its growth are shown here from the years just before the conquest of Constantinople to its incorporation of North Africa into its empire after 1533.

FIGURE 15.4 *A Turkish Janissary.* The Janissaries, for the most part were Christian boys who had been enslaved, converted to Islam, and trained as soldiers. They formed the elite core of the Turkish army and often rose to positions of great wealth and power. The drawing is by Gentile Bellini (c. 1429–1507).

claimed to believe, that the survival of Christendom was threatened by Ottoman expansion.

The structure of the Ottoman state forced the sultans to maintain a program of conquest even after the fall of Constantinople. Their personal survival often depended on its success. Because the sultans practiced polygyny on a grand scale, inheritance was by a form of natural selection. Each of the sultan's legitimate sons was given a provincial governorship at age 14. Those who showed promise acquired more offices and more military support until, when the sultan died, one of them was in a position to seize power and murder his surviving brothers. The role of the military in securing and maintaining the succession meant that its loyalty had to be maintained at all times. The most important component of the army was the Janissaries, an infantry composed of men who were technically slaves of the sultan. Male children were taken as tribute from conquered areas, converted to Islam, and raised as soldiers. Originally, the Janissaries were forbidden to marry, but they were not immune to the attractions of wealth and power. Like the Praetorian Guard of ancient Rome, they could overthrow a sultan if their ambitions were not achieved. War

gave them booty, governorships, and new recruits. It was wise to keep them as busy as possible.

Turkish Offensives in Europe. The Turks first became a serious threat to western Europe in the reign of Süleyman I "the Magnificent" (1520–1566). In 1522, his fleet drove the Knights of St. John from their stronghold at Rhodes, thereby permitting unimpeded communications between Constantinople and Egypt. After defeating the Hungarians at Mohács in 1526, Süleyman controlled the central Hungarian plain. The Austrian Hapsburgs continued to rule a narrow strip of northwestern Hungary, but Transylvania under its *voivod* János Zapolya (d. 1540) became a Turkish tributary, Calvinist in religion, and bitterly hostile to the Catholic west. Then, in 1529 and again in 1532, Süleyman besieged Vienna. He failed on both occasions, largely because Vienna was beyond the effective limits of Ottoman logistics. But the effort made a profound impression. The Turk was at the gates.

In retrospect, the attacks on Vienna probably were intended only to prevent a Hapsburg reconquest of Hungary. They were not repeated until 1689. In 1533, the Turks launched a new offensive at sea. Fleets under the command of Khair ed-Din, a Christian convert to Islam known as Barbarossa for his flaming red beard, ravaged the coasts of Italy, Sicily, and Spain and threatened Christian commerce throughout the Mediterranean.

The Empire of Charles V. The brunt of these struggles ultimately fell on the Spanish Empire. In 1517, Charles of Hapsburg (1500–1558) ascended the thrones of Castile and Aragon to become Charles I, first king of a united Spain. He was the son of Juana "la Loca" (the Crazy), daughter of Ferdinand and Isabella, and Philip "the Handsome" (d. 1506), son of the emperor Maximilian I and Mary of Burgundy. His mother lived until 1555, but she was thought to be insane and had been excluded from the succession. From her, Charles inherited Castile and its possessions in the New World. From Ferdinand, he inherited Aragon and much of Italy, including Naples, Sicily, and Sardinia. With the death of his grandfather Maximilian in 1519, he gained the Hapsburg lands in Austria and Germany and the remaining inheritance of the dukes of Burgundy, including the seventeen provinces of the Netherlands. In 1519, he was elected Holy Roman Emperor as Charles V.

The Wars of Charles V. The massive accumulation of states and resources embroiled the young emperor in endless conflict. Although he had placed the Austrian lands under the rule of his brother Ferdinand, Charles defended Vienna in person against the Turks. Because Turkish naval efforts were directed primarily against his possessions in Spain and Italy, he thought it necessary to invade Tunis in 1535 and Algiers in 1541. Francis I of

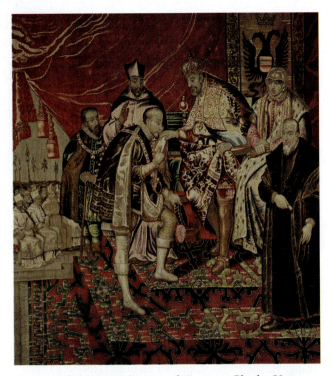

FIGURE 15.5 *The Abdication of Emperor Charles V.* Worn out by physical ailments and a lifetime of struggle, the emperor astonished the world by abdicating his offices and retiring to a Spanish monastery. In this French tapestry, woven between 1630 and 1640, Charles begins the process by resigning as ruler of the Netherlands in favor of his son Philip II (seen here kissing the emperor's hand). Charles abdicated as king of Spain in the following year and was succeeded as emperor by his brother Ferdinand I in 1558. Charles died on September 21, 1558. The ceremony shown here took place at Brussels on October 25, 1555.

France fought seven wars with him in 30 years to make good his own claim to Naples, Sicily, and Milan. This Hapsburg–Valois rivalry (named after the families of the two rulers) was in some ways a continuation of the Italian wars at the beginning of the century, but it was fought on three fronts: northern Italy, the Netherlands, and the Pyrenees. As a devout Catholic, the emperor also tried in 1546–1547 and again in 1552–1555 to bring the German Protestants to heel but received no help from the papacy. Paul III, fearing imperial domination of Italy, allied himself with the Most Christian King of France, who was in turn the ally of the major Protestant princes and of the Turks.

The empire of Charles V was multinational, but in time its center of gravity shifted toward Spain. Charles, born in the Low Countries and whose native tongue was French, became increasingly dependent on the revenues of Castile. Spanish soldiers, trained in the Italian wars, became the core of his army. Castilian administrators produced results, not endless complaints about the violation of traditional rights or procedures,

and by 1545, his secretary, his chief military adviser, and his confessor were Spanish. Sick and exhausted, Charles began to abdicate from his various offices in 1555. In 1557, he retired to the remote monastery of Yuste in Spanish Extremadura, where he died in 1558. His son, Philip II (reigned 1556–1598), was Spanish to his fingertips. His father's abdication left him Italy, the Netherlands, and the Spanish Empire, while the Hapsburg lands in central Europe were given to Charles's brother Ferdinand, who was elected emperor in 1558.

The war between France and Spain came to an end in 1559 with the treaty of Cateau-Cambrésis, but the underlying rivalry remained. Both sides were simply exhausted. Although Philip was forced to repudiate his father's debts, the predictability of Castilian revenues and a dramatic increase in wealth from the American mines soon restored Spanish credit. The policies of the new king would be those of the late emperor: the containment of Islam and of Protestantism and the neutralization of France.

THE CRISIS OF THE EARLY MODERN STATE (1560–1660)

The wars and rebellions of the later sixteenth century must be understood in this context. The cost of war had continued to grow, forcing states to increase their claims upon the resources of their subjects. By midcentury, nobles, cities, and their elected representatives had begun to resist those claims with unprecedented vigor, especially in France and the Netherlands. They began to reassert ancient privileges to counter demands for more money or for greater royal authority. This heightened resistance was based in part on economics. A series of bad harvests attributed to the "Little Ice Age," a period of cold, wet weather that lasted from the 1550s to after 1650, worked together with monetary inflation to keep trade and land revenues stagnant. Real wealth was not increasing in proportion to the demands made upon it. Although the European elite continued to prosper by comparison with the poor, they grew ever more jealous of their prerogatives.

The controversies that arose in the wake of the Reformation made matters worse. Outside the Iberian Peninsula, the populations of most states were now bitterly divided along confessional as well as economic lines. Because nearly everyone believed that religious tolerance was incompatible with political order, each group sought to impose its views on the others. This attitude was shared by many who were not fanatics. In a society that had always expressed political and economic grievances in religious language, the absence of a common faith made demonizing opponents easy.

Reaching compromise on any issue became difficult, if not impossible.

In the light of these struggles, it appeared that the evolution of the monarchies, for all its success, had not resolved certain basic issues of sovereignty. The relationship of the crown to other elements of the governing elite remained open to question in France, England, and the Netherlands. In the Holy Roman Empire, the role of the emperor was imperfectly defined, and many of the empire's constituent principalities engaged in internal disputes. Underlying everything was the problem of dynastic continuity. The success of the early modern state still depended to an extraordinary degree on the character and abilities of its ruler. Could its basic institutions continue to function if the prince were a child or an incompetent? Some even doubted that they could survive the accession of a woman.

The French Wars of Religion and the Revolt of the Netherlands

The peace of Cateau-Cambrésis was sealed by the marriage of Isabel of Valois, daughter of Henry II of France, to Philip II of Spain. The celebrations included a tournament in which the athletic, although middle-aged, Henry died when a splinter from his opponent's lance entered the eye socket of his helmet. The new king, Francis II, was a sickly child of 15. The establishment of a regency under the leadership of the **Guise** (Geeze) family marked the beginning of a series of conflicts known as the **Wars of Religion** that lasted until 1598. The Guise came from Lorraine, a duchy technically independent of France, and were not related to the royal family. Their ascendancy threatened the **Bourbons,** a clan descended from Louis IX and headed by the brothers Antoine, King of Navarre, and Louis, Prince of Condé. It was also a threat to Henry's widow, **Catherine de Médicis** (May'-dee-see, 1519–1589), who hoped to retain power on behalf of her son, Francis, and his three brothers. Yet another faction, headed by Anne de Montmorency, constable of France, sought, like Catherine, to play the Guise against the Bourbons for their own advantage.

At one level, the Wars of Religion were an old-fashioned struggle between court factions for control of the crown, but the Guise were also devout Catholics who intensified Henry II's policy of persecuting Protestants. Most French Protestants, or **Huguenots** (Hue-ge-noze), were followers of John Calvin. In 1559, they numbered no more than 5 or 10 percent of the population, but their geographical and social distribution made them a formidable minority. Heavily concentrated in the south and west, Calvinism appealed most to rural nobles and to the artisans of the towns, two groups with a long history of political, regional, and economic grievances. The nobles were for the most part trained in the profession of arms; unhappy artisans could easily disrupt trade and city governments.

Searching for allies, the Bourbons found the Huguenots and converted to Protestantism. The conflict was now both religious and to a degree regional, as the Catholics of Paris and the northeast rallied to the house of Guise, who in turn were secretly allied with Philip II of Spain. Francis II died in 1560, shortly after Condé and the Huguenots tried unsuccessfully to kidnap him at Amboise. He was succeeded by his brother, Charles IX (reigned 1560–1574), who was closely controlled by Catherine de Médicis, but the wars went on. Although the Huguenots were not at first successful on the battlefield, they gained limited religious toleration in 1570.

Causes of the Netherlands Revolt. Meanwhile, the Netherlands had begun their long rebellion against the king of Spain. The seventeen provinces of the Low Countries were now the richest part of Europe, an urbanized region devoted to trade and intensive agriculture. Although divided by language (Dutch or Flemish was spoken in the north and west, French or Walloon—a French dialect—in the south and east), they shared a common artistic and intellectual tradition and an easy-going tolerance for foreigners and heretics. A majority of the population remained Catholic, but Lutherans and Calvinists flourished in the major cities. Government was decentralized and, from the Spanish point of view, woefully inefficient. Philip II was represented by a regent, his half-sister Margaret of Parma (1522–1586), who presided over the privy council and the councils of finance and state. Seventeen provincial estates, all of which were represented in the States General, controlled taxes and legislation. A virulent localism based on the defense of historical privilege made agreement possible only on rare occasions. Taxes were often defeated by squabbles over who should pay the largest share—nobles or townspeople. No common legal code existed, and the nobles controlled a host of independent legal jurisdictions whose administration of justice was often corrupt.

None of this was acceptable to Philip II. He was determined to reorganize the government, reform the legal system, and root out heresy by reforming the church along the lines suggested by the Council of Trent. All of these proposals struck directly at the wealth and power of the Netherlandish nobles. Philip's plan to reorganize the governing councils weakened their authority, while legal reform would have eliminated the feudal courts from which many of the nobles drew large revenues. Although his reform of the church sought to increase the number of bishops, the king was determined to end the purchase of ecclesiastical offices and to appoint only clerics whose education and spirituality met the high standards imposed by the Council of Trent. The ancient

FIGURE 15.6 *French Catholics Massacre Protestants.* This engraving by Franz Hogenberg, dated 1567, illustrates a massacre of French Protestants (Huguenots) by Catholics during the Wars of Religion. A number of such incidents culminated in the St. Bartholomew's Day massacre of 1572 in which thousands of Protestants lost their lives. Engravings of this kind were widely distributed as a kind of news release that described important events for a largely illiterate population.

custom by which nobles invested in church offices for the support of their younger sons was at an end.

Four years of accelerating protest by leading members of the aristocracy accomplished nothing. Finally, in 1566, a wave of iconoclasm brought matters to a head. The Protestants, acting in opposition to Philip's plan for ecclesiastical reform and encouraged by members of the higher nobility, removed the images from churches across the country. In some areas, iconoclasm was accompanied by rioting and violence. Although the regent's government was able to restore order, Philip responded in shock and anger. In 1567, he dispatched his leading general, the Duke of **Alba** (or Alva, 1507–1582), to put down what he saw as rebellion. Although Alba was at first successful, the harshness of his government alienated virtually every segment of opinion. When he attempted to introduce a perpetual tax in 1572, most of the major cities declared their allegiance to **William "the Silent," Prince of Orange** (1533–1584), the man who had emerged as leader of the revolt.

The Huguenot Alliance. Although William was not yet a convert to Protestantism, he attempted to form an alliance with the French Huguenots, who, under the leadership of **Gaspard de Coligny** (Gahss-par de Ko-lee-nyee), had gained new influence with Charles IX. The situation was doubly perilous for Spain because Philip II, while maintaining Alba in the Netherlands, had renewed his father's struggles with the Turk. The Mediterranean war culminated in the great naval victory of **Lepanto** (October 7, 1571), but Philip's treasury was once again exhausted. French intervention in the Netherlands was averted only by the **Massacre of St. Bartholomew** (August 23–24, 1572) in which more than 5,000 Protestants, Coligny included, were killed by Catholic mobs. The massacre revived the French civil wars and permitted Alba to retake many of the rebellious towns, but the duke was recalled in 1573 and his successors were unable to bring the revolt under control. Margaret's son, Alessandro Farnese, Duke of Parma (1545–1592), finally was able to impose Spanish rule on the ten southern provinces in 1585.

Founding of the United Netherlands. By this time, the seven northern provinces had organized into an independent republic with William of Orange as *stadtholder,* or chief executive. The United Netherlands was Dutch in language and culture. Enriched by trade, secure in its control of the sea, and defended by the heavily fortified "water line" of three broad rivers—the Rhine, the Maas, and the Waal—the new republic was almost invulnerable to Spanish attack. It was also Protestant. The government was dominated by Calvinists, and William converted to Protestantism before he was assassinated by a Spanish agent in 1584. Refugees from Spanish rule, most of them French-speaking Calvinists, poured into the north, while a number of Dutch Catholics headed south into what is now Belgium.

English Intervention. These developments critically altered the balance of power in northern Europe. Philip II was still determined to recover his lost provinces and to assist the Catholics of France in their battle against the Huguenots. The English, restored to Protestantism by **Elizabeth I** (ruled 1558–1603), were equally determined to prevent a concentration of Spanish power on the coasts of the North Sea. When Parma took Antwerp, the largest and richest city in the Netherlands in 1584, they sent an expeditionary force to support the Dutch.

Although a prosperous land of about 3.5 million people, Elizabethan England was no match for the Spanish Empire. It had the core of a fine navy but no army worthy of the name. Perpetual taxes were unknown, and the improvidence of Henry VIII had left his daughter with meager revenues from the royal domain. In the

FIGURE 15.7 *Elizabeth I.* An engraving based on three portraits of Elizabeth made at the beginning, middle, and end of her long reign. From left to right, by Hans Holbein, F. Zucchero, and Marc Garrard the Elder.

the house of Guise, Mary had been driven from Scotland in 1568 by a coalition of Protestants inspired by the Calvinist reformer John Knox and led by her kinsman the earl of Moray. Elizabeth offered her refuge but held her under house arrest for 19 years before ordering her execution in 1587. Mary was killed not only because she had plotted against Elizabeth but also because the English queen was convinced that war with Spain was inevitable. Elizabeth wanted no rival to encourage the hopes of Philip II or of her own Catholic subjects. These fears, too, were realistic, because for more than 20 years, Elizabeth had pursued a course of intermittent hostility toward Spain. She had encouraged her subjects, notably Sir John Hawkins and Sir Francis Drake, to raid Spanish colonies in the Caribbean and in 1586 sent an English force to assist the Dutch. From the Spanish point of view, the execution of Mary was the last straw. Philip responded by sending a fleet to invade England. The great **Spanish Armada** of 1588 failed, but the disaster did not end the war. Philip rebuilt his navy and tried again without success in 1595, while Drake and the aged Hawkins made another vain attempt on Havana and Cartagena de Indias in the same year.

event of war, funds had to be sought from Parliament, and Parliament continually tried to interfere with the queen's policies. It was especially incensed at her refusal to marry, in part because its members thought a woman incapable of governing on her own and in part because it feared disorder if she died without an heir.

The Spanish Armada. Parliament need not have worried about Elizabeth's ability, but this last concern, at least, was real. Catholics everywhere had rejected Henry VIII's divorce. To them, Elizabeth was illegitimate, and **Mary Stuart, Queen of Scots** (1542–1587), was the true queen of England. A devout Catholic, descended from Henry VII and connected on her mother's side to

◄FIGURE 15.8
The Spanish Armada, 1588. This painting by an unknown artist shows a critical moment in the defeat of the Spanish Armada. The Spanish fleet had anchored off Gravelines on the Flemish coast to support an invasion of England by the duke of Parma. The English sent fireships (center) into the anchorage, forcing them to scatter and to abandon the invasion.

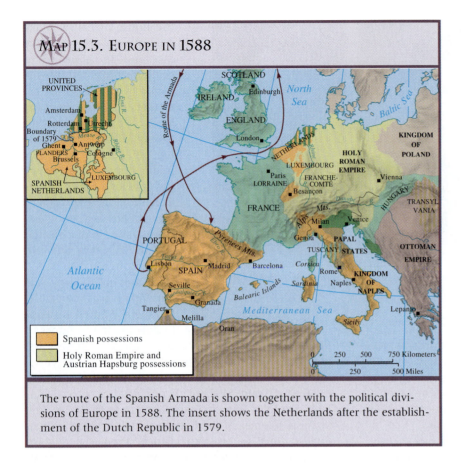

MAP 15.3. EUROPE IN 1588

Spanish possessions

Holy Roman Empire and
Austrian Hapsburg possessions

The route of the Spanish Armada is shown together with the political divisions of Europe in 1588. The insert shows the Netherlands after the establishment of the Dutch Republic in 1579.

southwest. In some respects, it created a state within a state, but the ordeal of France was over.

The Thirty Years' War

The resolution of the French wars and the death of Philip II in 1598 marked the end of a political cycle. The Netherlands continued to fight on under the leadership of William's son, Maurice of Nassau (1567–1625), a capable general who added the eastern Netherlands to the Dutch Republic. Spain and the Netherlands concluded a 10 years' truce in 1608, but it was a truce, not a treaty. Although Spain was financially exhausted, it still refused to recognize the Dutch state. War was expected to break out again when the truce expired in 1618. The war, when it came, was much more than a resumption of the Dutch Revolt. It involved all of the European states and turned central Europe into a battleground from 1618 to 1648.

The End of the Wars of Religion in France. By this time, the Spanish were at war in France as well. In 1589, the Bourbon leader Henry of Navarre emerged from the "War of the Three Henrys" as the only surviving candidate for the throne. The other two Henrys, Henry of Guise and Henry III, the last surviving son of Catherine de Médicis, had been assassinated by each other's supporters. Philip thought that if France were controlled by Huguenots, the Spanish Netherlands would be crushed between two Protestant enemies, and he sent Parma and his army into France. This expedition, too, was a costly failure, but Henry's interests turned out to be more political than religious. He converted to Catholicism in the interest of peace and ascended the throne as Henry IV (reigned 1589–1610). To protect the Huguenots, he issued the **Edict of Nantes** (Nahnt, 1598), which granted them freedom of worship and special judicial rights in a limited number of towns, most in the

Henry IV (Navarre) of France

The Bohemian War. The first phase of the Thirty Years' War began with a struggle for the crown of Bohemia. In 1555, the Peace of Augsburg had established the principle *cuius regio, eius religio;* that is, princes within the empire had the right to determine the religious beliefs of their subjects. Calvinists, however, were excluded from its provisions, and issues regarding the disposition of church properties and the conversion of bishops were left in dispute. Since then, two electoral principalities, the Palatinate and Brandenburg, had turned Calvinist, and several bishops had converted to Protestantism while retaining possession of their endowed lands. Violent quarrels arose over these issues, and by 1610, the empire was divided into two armed camps: the Protestant Union and the Catholic League.

The Bohemian controversy arose because Matthias, King of Bohemia in 1618, was also Holy Roman Emperor, a Catholic Hapsburg, and uncle of the future emperor **Ferdinand II** of Austria (1578–1637). Matthias was determined to preserve Bohemia for the faith and for his family, and in 1617, he secured the election of Ferdinand as his successor to the throne of Bohemia. Most of the Bohemian gentry and lesser nobility opposed this election. They were, for the most part, Calvinists or Hussites and feared persecution from the devout Ferdinand and his Jesuit advisers. On May

23, 1618, an assembly of Bohemians threw three of the Hapsburg's regents from a window of the Hradschin palace, appointed a provisional government, and began to raise an army.

The "Defenestration of Prague" was an act of war. Revolt spread to the hereditary lands, threatening not only Bohemia but also the basic integrity of the Hapsburg state. Worse yet, the King of Bohemia was an elector of the empire. If the Bohemians elected a Protestant, the Protestants would have a majority of electors just as a new imperial election appeared imminent. Matthias was in poor health and Ferdinand hoped to succeed him as king of Bohemia as well as emperor. Ferdinand needed time to muster support, but in June 1619, he invaded Bohemia with the army of the Catholic League, drawn largely from his ally, Bavaria. The Bohemians responded by offering the crown to a Calvinist prince, Frederick V (1596–1632), elector palatine and son-in-law of James I of England.

Frederick accepted, after the death of Matthias and the election of Ferdinand as emperor on August 28. It was a tragic mistake. He was supported by only a part of the Protestant Union. James I refused to help, and a diversionary attack on Hungary by Bethlen Gabor (1580–1629), the Calvinist prince of Transylvania, was eventually contained by the Hapsburgs. Finally, on November 8, 1620, Frederick and his Protestant allies were soundly defeated at the White Mountain near Prague. Frederick's cause was now hopeless. The Spanish truce with the Netherlands had expired, and the Palatinate lay squarely across the route by which Spanish troops and supplies were sent to the Low Countries. While Frederick's forces fought to preserve his claim to Bohemia, a Spanish army invaded his ancestral lands.

The Danish and Swedish Interventions. A second phase of the war began in 1625, when Christian IV of Denmark (1577–1648) emerged briefly as the champion of Protestantism. Christian's Lutheranism was reinforced by his territorial ambitions in north Germany, but he was no match for the imperial generals. By 1629, he was out of the war. His place was taken by the formidable **Gustav Adolph** of Sweden (1594–1632). Since the reign of Erik XIV (ruled 1560–1568), Swedish policy had aimed at control of the Baltic. Wars with Russia and Poland had taught Gustav the art of war and given him all of Livonia, a territory roughly equal to present-day Estonia, Latvia, and Lithuania. He now sought to defend his fellow Protestants and to establish Swedish control over Mecklenburg and Pomerania on the north German coast. His brilliant campaigns, financed in part by France, came to an end when he died victorious on the battlefield at Lützen on November 16, 1632.

The Final Phase. The last phase of the war (1535–1648) continued the Franco-Swedish alliance, but with France acting openly as the leader of the anti-imperial forces. Henry IV had died at the hands of an assassin in 1610, leaving the queen, Marie de Médicis, as regent for the 9-year-old Louis XIII (1601–1643). Her regency was unpopular, but the disasters of 1560 were not repeated. Louis seized power from his mother in 1617 and, after 1624, entrusted much of his government to Armand de Plessis, Cardinal Duke of **Richelieu** (Reeshel-you, 1585–1642). One of the ablest statesmen of the age, Richelieu was alarmed by the Spanish–Imperial alliance and returned to the policies of Francis I in the hope of preventing the encirclement of France by the Hapsburgs. He pursued the war through surrogates until the death of Gustav Adolph forced him into the open. The Spanish were by this time

FIGURE 15.9 *The Defenestration of Prague.* In 1618, Bohemian Protestants threw two Austrian Catholic imperial regents and their secretary out of windows of the Hradschin palace in Prague, thereby setting off the first phase of the Thirty Years' War. The act intentionally copied the beginning of the Hussite revolt 200 years before. Then, the victims had been tossed from the window of Prague's town hall and landed on a mass of upthrust pikes with fatal results. In 1618, victims fell 60 feet but were uninjured. Catholic accounts stated the men were carried to the ground by angels; Protestants contended that they escaped death by landing on a pile of manure.

MAP 15.4. THE THIRTY YEARS' WAR

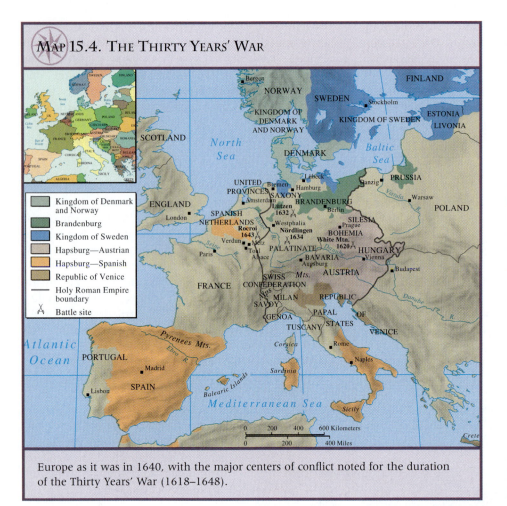

Kingdom of Denmark and Norway
Brandenburg
Kingdom of Sweden
Hapsburg—Austrian
Hapsburg—Spanish
Republic of Venice
Holy Roman Empire boundary
Battle site

Europe as it was in 1640, with the major centers of conflict noted for the duration of the Thirty Years' War (1618–1648).

cape. As the son of Mary Queen of Scots, James was already King of Scotland when he inherited the English crown from Elizabeth in 1602. Scotland was poor. England, like Denmark and Sweden, was a "domain" state: the regular revenues of the crown came not from taxes, which could be levied only by Parliament, but from the royal domain. This was not necessarily a disadvantage. The Danish monarch held more than 40 percent of the arable land in Denmark and derived vast revenues from the sound tolls levied on every ship passing from the North Sea into the Baltic. The Swedish royal estate derived great wealth from export duties on copper and iron, the country's major exports. Both countries therefore exerted a political and military influence wholly disproportionate to their size.

The Financial Problem. England had no comparable sources of revenue. The failure of Henry VIII to retain monastic lands taken at the time of the Reformation left the crown without sufficient property to "live of its own." Even import and export duties, although technically part of the domain, had to be authorized by Parliament. The resulting poverty, already evident under Elizabeth, restricted the crown's ability to reward its supporters. Worse, it forced her Stuart successors to seek wealth in ways that profoundly offended their subjects (see Document 15.4). Charles in particular resorted to arbitrary fines, *quo warranto* proceedings that led to the confiscation of properties held since before the days of written titles, and the abuse of wardships. He extended ship money (a tax for the protection of the coasts) to the inland counties and then spent it for purposes other than the navy. All of these measures struck directly at property rights and aroused a firestorm of opposition.

King Charles I of England

in irreversible decline, and their defeat by the French at Rocroi (1643) marked the end of their military power. A Franco-Swedish force ravaged Bavaria in 1648, and peace was at last concluded on October 24 of that year.

The Peace of Westphalia. The Treaties of Westphalia brought the Thirty Years' War to an end, leaving France the dominant power in Europe. The Netherlands, which had fought Spain in a series of bitter actions on land and sea, was at last recognized as an independent state, and the German principalities, many of which had been devastated, were restored to the boundaries of 1618. Bohemia reverted to the Hapsburgs, but imperial authority as a whole was weakened, except in the Hapsburg lands of southeastern Europe. It was a meager return for three decades of unparalleled violence.

The English Civil War

England did not participate in the Thirty Years' War because the early Stuart monarchs, **James I** (ruled 1603–1625) and **Charles I** (1625–1649), were caught in a political dilemma from which they could not es-

Much of this opposition was at first centered in the legal profession where such jurists as Sir Edward Coke (Cook, 1552–1634) revived the common law as a protection against royal prerogatives, but in the end, Parliament proved to be the crown's most formidable adversary. Between 1540 and 1640, the wealth and numbers of the landholding gentry, the professions, and the merchant community had increased enormously. These elements of the English elite dominated the House of Commons, which took the lead in opposing royal policies. The Stuarts feared their disaffection and would have preferred to rule without calling Parliament. Except for relatively short periods, this was impossible. Even the smallest of crises forced the crown to seek relief through parliamentary taxation.

The Unpopularity of the Stuarts.

The growing resentment in Parliament might have been better managed had it not been for the personalities of the Stuart kings. Neither James nor Charles inspired great loyalty. James was awkward, personally dirty, and a homosexual at a time when homosexuality was universally condemned. His son was arrogant and generally distrusted, and most people thought that the court as a whole was morally and financially corrupt. Although James, who annoyed his subjects with treatises on everything from the evils of tobacco to witchcraft, wrote eloquently in support of the divine right of kings, his own behavior and the devious policies of his son continually undermined the legitimacy of his family's rule.

The Religious Question.

The religious question was more serious. Elizabeth, not wishing "to make windows into men's souls," had established a church that was Protestant but relatively tolerant. Some of her subjects had retained a fondness for the ideas and liturgical practices of the old church; others, known as **Puritans,** followed Calvin with varying degrees of rigor. James I accepted Calvinist doctrines. He commissioned the **King James Bible** of 1611, the translation used by English-speaking Protestants for more than 300 years, and established Protestant colonists in northern Ireland. Although he rejected all demands to abolish bishops in favor of a more democratic form of church governance, he managed to avoid an open breach with the Puritans as they grew more powerful over the course of his reign.

Charles I, however, supported the anti-Puritan reforms of Archbishop William Laud (1573–1645). Laud was what might today be called a High-Church Anglican. He rejected papal authority and clerical celibacy, but his understanding of communion, baptism, and justification (the means by which believers are saved) seemed Catholic to the Puritans, as did his fondness for elaborate church rituals. Queen Henriette Marie (1609–1669), however, heard Mass regularly as an open Roman Catholic. She was the sister of Louis

---

THE DEFENSE OF LIBERTY AGAINST TYRANTS

In both France and the Netherlands, the Protestants had to justify their revolt against the monarchy. One of the most important theorists to do so was Philippe du Plessis-Mornay, a councilor to Henry of Navarre, the leader of the Bourbon faction who later became Henry IV. Plessis-Mornay based his argument on an early version of the social contract theory, which argued that all rulers received their power from the people. His ideas would have a powerful impact on the political thinkers of the Enlightenment and on the framers of the United States Constitution. This is an excerpt from his treatise, *Vindiciae contra tyrannos.*

Thus, at the beginning all kings were elected. And even those who seem today to come to the throne by succession must first be inaugurated by the people. Furthermore, even if a people has customarily chosen its kings from a particular family because of its outstanding merits, that decision is not so unconditional that if the established line degenerates, the people may not select another.

We have shown . . . that kings receive their royal status from the people; that the whole people is greater than the king and is above him; that the king in his kingdom, the emperor in his empire, are supreme only as ministers and agents, while the people is the true proprietor. It follows, therefore, that a tyrant who commits felony against the people who is, as it were, the owner of his fief; that he commits lèse majesté *[treason] against the kingdom or the empire; and that he is no better than any other rebel since he violates the same laws, although as king, he merits even graver punishment. And so . . . he may be either deposed by his superior or punished under the* lex Julia *[the Roman law on treason] for acts against the public majesty. But the superior here is the whole people or those who represent it. . . . And if things have gone so far that the tyrant cannot be expelled without resort to force, they may call the people to arms, recruit an army, and use force, strategy, and all the engines of war against him who is the declared enemy of the country and the commonwealth.*

From Philippe du Plessis-Mornay, "Vindiciae contra tyrannos," in *Constitutionalism and Resistance in the 16th Century,* trans. and ed. Julian H. Franklin (New York: Macmillan, 1969).

Question: How would a king react to this document?

XIII of France and a strong personality who exerted great influence over her husband. The Puritans suspected that Charles meant to restore Catholicism. They thought that their faith, as well as liberty and property, was at risk.

The Outbreak of the Revolt.

Twenty years of increasingly bitter conflict between Parliament and the crown led to civil war in 1642. The Scots rebelled in

DOCUMENT 15.4

THE ENGLISH PETITION OF RIGHT, 1628

The 1628 Petition of Right summarized Parliament's grievances against Charles I, who was trying to solve his financial problems through illegal and arbitrary means. The objections are based largely on perceived violations of the Magna Carta, also known as the Great Charter. The following are excerpts from a much longer document.

And where also, by the statute called the Great Charter of the Liberties of England, it is declared and enacted that no freeman may be taken or imprisoned, or be disseised [dispossessed] of his freehold or liberties or his free customs, or be outlawed or exiled or in any manner destroyed, but by the lawful judgment of his peers or by the law of the land. . . .

They do therefore humbly pray your most excellent majesty that no man hereafter be compelled to make or yield any gift, loan, benevolence, tax, or such like charge without common consent by act of parliament; and that none be called to make answer, or take such oath, or to give attendance, or be confined, or otherwise molested or disquieted concerning the same, or for refusal thereof; and that no freeman, in any such manner as is before mentioned, be imprisoned or detained; and that your majesty would be pleased to remove the said soldiers and mariners [who had been quartered in the counties to enforce the king's measures]; and that the foresaid commissions for proceeding by martial law may be revoked and annulled; and that hereafter no commissions of like nature may issue forth . . . lest by colour of them any of your majesty's subjects be destroyed or put to death, contrary to the laws and franchise of the land.

From Journals of the House of Lords, vol. 3.

Question: What abuses does this document address?

1638, when Charles, in his capacity as king of Scotland, tried to introduce the English *Book of Common Prayer* at Edinburgh. To pay for the Scottish war, he summoned what is called the Long Parliament because it met from 1640 to 1660. In response to his call for money, the Commons impeached Archbishop Laud and Charles's chief minister, Thomas Wentworth, Earl of Strafford. They then abolished the prerogative courts of Star Chamber and High Commission. When Charles failed in his attempt to impeach the parliamentary leaders, he fled from London. Parliament decided to raise an army in its own defense.

The Execution of Charles I.

After 3 years of hard fighting, Parliament's army defeated the royalists at Naseby (June 14, 1645), but serious divisions had appeared in the parliamentary ranks. Independents, who favored a congregational form of church government, now dominated the army. The Parliament they served was controlled by Presbyterians, who believed in a church governed by presbyters or elders rather than bishops. The Independents refused to disband without guaranteed freedom of conscience and the removal of certain Presbyterians from Parliament. The Scots, fearing a threat to the Presbyterian Church order they had just reestablished after a lapse of 30 years, became alarmed. Charles sought to capitalize on these strains by accepting the abolition of the Scottish episcopate in return for Presbyterian support, but Parliament's New Model Army, as it was called, defeated the Scots and their English allies at Preston (August 17–20, 1648). The victors now believed that compromise was impossible. In December, the army captured Charles and purged the Commons of its Presbyterian members. A court appointed by the Rump, as the remnant of Parliament was now called, sentenced the king to death. He was beheaded at Whitehall on January 30, 1649.

Cromwell's Protectorate.

For all practical purposes, the army now governed England. A republican constitution had been established, but real power lay in the hands of **Oliver Cromwell** (1599–1658), the most successful of the parliamentary generals. In 1653, Parliament named him Lord Protector of the Commonwealth of England, Scotland, and Ireland. A radical Protestant and Independent, Cromwell attempted to reform English society along Puritan lines while following a vigorous policy abroad. After subduing the Scots, he fought a naval war with the Dutch (1552–1554) and started another with Spain in 1656. The Irish Catholics, who had massacred thousands of Protestants in 1641, were ruthlessly suppressed.

Oliver Cromwell

Cromwell had refused to accept the crown when it was offered to him in 1657, but when he died in the following year, he left the Protectorate to his son Richard. Richard's rule was brief and troubled. He was forced to resign after only 9 months, and a Convention Parliament restored Charles II (1630–1685), son of Charles I, on May 8, 1660. The English had tired of Puritanism and military rule.

Charles II of England

The Price of Conflict

The Organization and Conduct of War. The wars and revolutions of the century after 1560 caused extensive disruption in almost every part of Europe, largely because of the way they were organized and fought. Armies had become vastly larger and more expensive in the course of the sixteenth century, and the wars themselves became almost interminable. Given their political objectives, it could not have been otherwise. The French Wars of Religion were a struggle between two, and at times three, irreconcilable segments of the country's elite. Most of the battles involved cavalry actions that resulted in a clear victory for one side or the other but that could not end the war. Only the total destruction of the losers could have prevented them from trying again. Neither battles nor massacres like that of St. Bartholomew could accomplish this.

In the Netherlands, the primary goal of both sides was to take and hold land or, conversely, to deny it to the enemy. After 1572, the war became a series of sieges that, thanks to the defensive value of the bastion trace, lasted months and often years. Both sides tended to avoid battles because their troops were, in the short term at least, irreplaceable. Sixteenth-century tactics demanded professional soldiers. The recruitment, training, and movement of replacements to the war zone took months, and positions under constant enemy pressure could not be left even partially defenseless.

If the war in the Netherlands was virtually static, the situation in Germany during the Thirty Years' War was too fluid. Central Europe had become a kind of power vacuum into which unpredictable forces were drawn. Bloody battles were fought only to see the victor confronted with yet another set of enemies. It is hard to imagine what, other than sheer exhaustion, might have ended the struggle. War, as Michael Roberts has said, "eternalized itself." No early modern state could afford this. Even the wealthiest European monarchies lacked the ability to recruit and maintain full-scale standing armies. They relied instead on a core of subject troops (or, as in the French Wars of Religion, troops personally and ideologically committed to a cause), supplemented by a far larger number of mercenaries. The latter were usually recruited by contractors who commanded them in the field. If the mercenaries were not paid, they left; if they stayed, they had little incentive to risk their lives unnecessarily. Their employers had little control over their actions, and even subject troops were capable of mutiny if they were left too long unpaid.

War, in other words, had become an even more chaotic business than usual. *Rank* in the modern sense meant little because officers sometimes refused to obey the orders of those who might have been their inferiors in civilian life. There were no uniforms, and weapons were not for the most part standardized. Logistics were a nightmare. The armies of the period might number anywhere from 30,000 to 100,000 combatants. They housed their troops in makeshift field shelters or quartered them on the civilian populations of the war zones, which meant that civilians might be forced to provide food and housing for months on end. The close contact between soldiers and civilians bred hostility and led to chronic breakdowns in military discipline. To complicate matters further, camp followers numbered at least three and often six for each combatant. These women and children were the support troops who made shelter, foraged for food, and nursed the sick and wounded. No army could function without them, but together with the men they made up a society that lived by its own rules with little concern for civilian norms.

The system reached a peak of absurdity during the Thirty Years' War when contractors such as the imperial general Albrecht von Wallenstein (1583–1634) offered recruits a month's pay—which they had to give back to pay for their arms and equipment—and then marched them so far from their homes that they could not easily return. From that point onward, they were expected to live off the land by looting farms and villages. Such practices account for much of the dislocation caused by the German wars. It was safer for a man's family to join him in the army than to be robbed, raped, or killed by marauding soldiers at home (see Document 15.5). Entire villages were depopulated only to reconstitute themselves wherever they found themselves when the war ended.

The Decline of Spain. When a state tried to provide adequately for its troops, the costs quickly became prohibitive and could lead to social breakdown. The fate of Spain is an example. During the 1570s, Philip II spent 140 percent of his annual revenues on warfare. The uncovered balance was provided by loans, often at high rates, from Italian or Dutch bankers. Not even the import of American silver could long sustain this kind of expenditure, and in time the economy of Castile virtually collapsed (see Table 15.2). The other Spanish kingdoms were exempt from most forms of taxation, but in Castile, taxes increased to the point that peasants had to leave the land and take refuge in the cities where the church periodically distributed grain and oil to the poor. Commerce and industry were virtually destroyed. Declining production not only reduced tax collection but increased the country's dependence on imports, which in turn lowered the value of Spanish money and worsened an inflation that had been fueled for years by silver from the Indies. When Philip II died in 1598, the population of Castile had been shrinking for nearly a decade.

To make matters worse, economic decline actually raised the costs of war by increasing the interest in government loans. Unfavorable exchange rates raised the cost of goods and services that Spain had to purchase in Germany or the Netherlands. Troops were often poorly supplied or left without pay for as much as 3 years at a time. This provoked mutinies, which prolonged the wars and raised costs even higher. Similar problems arose in other countries but were far more serious in Spain, because the military effort lasted for more than a century and a half. From the wars of Granada to the Peace of Westphalia, the Castilian economy had no opportunity to recover.

Philip III (1598–1645) and his minister, the shrewd but lethargic Duke of Lerma, tried to provide Spain with a much-needed respite from war but could not restrain the king's viceroys who launched military campaigns on their own without royal approval. When Philip IV's chief minister, the energetic Count-Duke of **Olivares** (1587–1645), tried to spread the burdens of taxation and recruitment to other Spanish realms, he faced rebellion. Portugal, which had been annexed by Philip II in 1580 after its king died without heirs, declared independence in 1640. Catalonia, on the other side of the peninsula, rebelled in the same year. The government of Olivares lacked the resources to stop them, and Portugal remains free to this day. Catalonia returned to the Spanish fold in 1652, after France emerged as a greater threat to its liberties than Castile.

The Condition of Europe. Spain may have been a special case, but the condition of Europe as a whole after a century of war and rebellion was grim. Most of the German states were a shambles, and the emperor's role had much diminished outside his hereditary lands. Although Cromwellian England briefly tapped the country's wealth in the service of the state, the restoration of Charles II revived many of the old conflicts between crown and Parliament and once again limited the king's wealth and ability to govern. France, the richest of all European states, proved more resilient, but when the 4-year-old Louis XIV ascended the throne under a regency in 1643, a series of aristocratic rebellions known as the Fronde (1648–1652) revealed that the foundations of the monarchy remained insecure.

Eastern Europe was no better. Russia had not yet emerged from its "Time of Troubles," the period of anarchy that followed the death of Ivan the Terrible in 1584. Military intervention by Poland and Sweden complicated a series of revolts led by boyars trying to reverse Ivan's policies of centralization. After 1613, the Romanov Dynasty restored a measure of stability in Moscow but faced challenges from the Old Believers, a movement that rejected all innovation in the Russian church, and from the **Cossacks,** the descendants of peasants who had fled serfdom in Poland and Russia in the sixteenth century. Establishing themselves on the Ukrainian steppes (the great plains north of the Black Sea) the Cossacks became fierce horsemen who served as a buffer against the Turks and Tartars of central Asia but violently resisted tsarist control. At midcentury, only the Dutch Republic appeared strong and stable. For Europe's monarchies it seemed that the years of turmoil had done little to resolve the problem of sovereignty.

Intellectual Achievement. Surprisingly, this age of troubles was in many places a time of intellectual, literary, and artistic achievement. A distinction must be made between those regions that were combat zones, those that remained peaceful

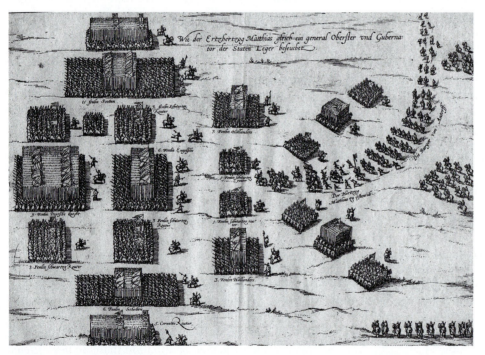

FIGURE 15.10 *Spanish Military Formations.* From the 1530s until the middle of the Thirty Years' War, the Spanish infantry was arguably the best in Europe. It used a formation based on a pike square surrounded by men armed with arquebuses, a kind of light matchlock firearm. This engraving by Franz Hogenberg (1578) shows several such formations. Some of the skirmishers shown outside the formation are *arquebusiers* who try to draw the enemy into battle. Others carry muskets, a heavier weapon whose longer range and greater firepower made it more effective against personal armor.

SOLDIERS LOOT A GERMAN FARM

The novel *Simplicissimus* by Hans von Grimmelshausen (c. 1622–1674) was based in part on the author's own experiences in the Thirty Years' War. In these passages from the beginning of the book, the title character, Simplicissimus, who is not as simple as he appears, describes the sack of his parent's farm. Like the hero, people took to the roads or joined the armies to avoid such horrors.

The first thing these troopers did in the blackened room of my Dad was to stable their mounts. Thereafter, each fell to his appointed task, fraught in every case with ruin and destruction. For although some began to slaughter, cook, and roast, as if for a merry banquet, others stormed through the house from top to bottom, ransacking even the privy, as though they thought the Golden Fleece might be hidden there. Some packed great bundles of cloth, apparel, and household goods, as if to set up a stall for a jumble sale, but what they had no use for they smashed and destroyed. Some thrust their swords into the hay and straw as if they had not enough sheep and pigs to slaughter. Others emptied the feather-beds and pillows of their down, filling them instead with meat and other provender, as if that would make them more comfortable to sleep on. Others again smashed stoves and windows as if to herald an everlasting summer. They flattened copper and pewter utensils and packed up the bent and useless pieces; chests, tables,

chairs, and benches they burnt, though in the yard they could have found many cords of firewood. Finally, they broke every dish and saucepan, either because they preferred their food roasted or because they intended to have no more than a single meal there.

And now they began to unscrew the flints from their pistols and to jam the peasant's thumbs into them, and to torture the poor lads as if they had been witches. Indeed, one of the captives had already been pushed into the bread oven and a fire lit under him, although he had confessed nothing. They put a sling around the head of another, twisting it tight with a piece of wood until the blood spurted from his mouth, nose, and ears. In short, each had his own device for torturing peasants, and each peasant received his individual torture. . . . Of the captured women, girls, and maidservants I have nothing in particular to tell, for the warriors would not let me see what they did with them. But this I do know: that from time to time one could hear pitiful screams coming from different parts of the house, and I don't suppose my Mum and Ursula fared any better than the others.

From Grimmelshausen, H. J. C. von, *Adventures of a Simpleton*, trans. W. Wallich (New York: Ungar, 1963, pp. 8–9).

Question: What would cause soldiers to behave this way?

---

but that were forced to assume heavy financial burdens, and those that were virtually untouched by the fighting. Even the most devastated regions experienced peace for at least a portion of the century between 1560 and 1660; their recovery was sometimes rapid.

Art. Painting, sculpture, and architecture continued to flourish, especially in Italy and Spain. Inspired by the Catholic Reformation, artists modified the artistic conventions of the Renaissance to express emotion and religious fervor in new ways. Using color, texture, and dramatic lighting, painters tried to create a dramatic effect far removed from the serene classicism of the Renaissance. Baroque sculpture, like that of the Hellenistic age, expresses strong emotion through dramatic postures and flowing drapery. Architects placed their buildings like stage sets for maximum impact. Sculptors and painters produced interior spaces so rich and detailed that they resemble the contemporary vision of heaven. Art historians call this style **Baroque.** In the Protestant north, Dutch artists created a very different style of painting that will be discussed in Chapter 16.

TABLE 15.2 CROWN INCOME AND DEBT IN CASTILE

These figures (in millions of ducats) provide an idea of the financial burdens that war imposed on the Castilian economy. During most of this period, nonmilitary costs rarely rose above 10 percent of the annual budget.

YEAR	REVENUE	DEBT	INTEREST ON DEBT
1515	1.5	12	0.8
1560	5.3	35	2.0
1575	6.0	50	3.8
1598	9.7	85	4.6
1623	15.0	112	5.6
1667	36.0	130	9.1

Source: C. Wilson and G. Parker, eds., *An Introduction to the Sources of European Economic History* (Ithaca, NY: Cornell University Press, 1977, p. 49).

Questions: How much does the interest on debt increase during the 152 years? Why was the increase of interest on the debt detrimental?

FIGURE 15.11 *View of St. Peter's, Rome.* Baroque architects and artists sought to create a sense of drama. St. Peter's, the cathedral church of Rome and seat of the Papacy, was completed in the early 1500s. Later architects built a portico around the plaza in front of the cathedral, not only to enclose the square but to focus the visitor's eye on the facade of the church. Popes have traditionally appeared on the balcony over the main entrance to address the faithful on holidays and other important occasions. The intended effect was something like a stage set. This eighteenth-century drawing shows how it looked to an earlier generation.

Literature and Theater. In some cases, the experience of war produced literary masterpieces. The age of the religious wars was not a golden one for France, but it produced the elegant and skeptical essays of **Michel de Montaigne** (Me-shel de Mon-ten-y, 1533–1592), an antidote to sectarian madness. In Germany, the wreckage of the Thirty Years' War was nearly complete, but it was wryly chronicled in Grimmelshausen's *Simplicissimus. Don Quixote* (Kee-hoe'-tay), one of the greatest of all literary classics, was written by **Miguel de Cervantes** (Me-gell de Ther-van'-tes, 1547–1616), who had lost an arm at the battle of Lepanto. It is, at least in part, a satire on his countrymen's fantastic dreams of glory. The age also gave birth to at least one classic of epic poetry. In *Paradise Lost,* Cromwell's Latin secretary, **John Milton** (1608–1674), created a Puritan epic to rival the vision of Dante.

John Milton

Theater flourished in Spain and England. In the time of Elizabeth I, London boasted several theaters that welcomed patrons from every class of society. Among the many authors who wrote, produced, and acted in these plays, **William Shakespeare** (1564–1616) is by far the most famous. His dramas and comedies had an impact on the development of the English language comparable to that of the King James Bible and the *Book of Common Prayer.* Puritan opposition closed the theaters until the restoration of Charles II in 1660. By the 1590s, nearly every city in the Spanish Empire boasted its own playhouse, and traveling theater companies had become common. Like Shakespeare, **Lope de Vega** (Lo'-pay de Vay'-ga, 1562–1635) and his contemporaries wrote for a popular audience. Lope produced no fewer than 1,500 plays, of which perhaps 500 survive. In later years, royal patronage helped to create a more refined theatrical tradition that dealt in heroic themes. The works of **Calderón de la Barca** (1600–1681), who best exemplifies this genre, are still produced as well.

William Shakespeare

Political Theory. Political turmoil gave birth to political theory. The challenge of governing a vast empire filled with people who had no prior experience of European ways produced an entire school of Spanish political theorists, most of whom were associated with the University of Salamanca. Between 1530 and 1570, they worked not only to justify the conquests but to create an imperial government based on divine and natural law in opposition to the ideas of Machiavelli. As social and economic problems multiplied in Spain itself after 1590, another group of theorists known as *arbitristas* proposed reforms that strongly influenced the views of Olivares and Philip IV.

The English Civil War overturned accepted conventions of government and produced a host of books and pamphlets on every political issue. Thomas Hobbes (1588–1679) argued that political salvation lay in *Leviathan,* an autocratic superstate, while *Oceana* by James Harrington (1611–1677) reflected the republican ideals of the Commonwealth. Both works powerfully influenced the thinking of a later age.

CONCLUSION

The age of the Renaissance and Reformation marked the beginning of European conquests overseas. Their purpose in the first instance was to expand the resources available to the emerging monarchies of western Europe. The conquests were therefore an extension of the state-building process, but a religious motive was evident, too, which at times recalled the Christian triumphalism of the Crusades. To say that European expansion overseas changed the world is an understatement. Although it laid the foundations for a world market and added much to Europe's store of wealth and knowledge, it did so at a terrible cost in human misery. In Europe itself, the rivalries that encouraged overseas exploration fueled the imperial struggles of the early sixteenth century and the so-called Religious Wars of 1559–1648. The growing cost of warfare stretched the resources of princes to the breaking point. This led to massive unrest as subjects sought to recover rights and privileges lost to rulers who were desperate to pay for security. Both the subsequent revolts and the international conflict that helped sustain them were complicated by religious issues that made them extremely difficult to resolve. In the end, the wars of what has been called the Iron Age brought much of Europe to the brink of political and economic ruin.

Review Questions

- What were the most important consequences of Spanish and Portuguese expansion?
- How and why did the Ottoman Empire come into conflict with that of Charles V?
- What were the major causes of the French Wars of Religion, and why did Henry IV emerge victorious?
- What characteristics of sixteenth- and seventeenth-century warfare caused its destructive effect on the economies and political structure of states?

For Further Study

Readings

Holt, Mack, *The French Wars of Religion* (Cambridge University Press, 1995). A clear, up-to-date account.

Hughes, Ann, *The Causes of the English Civil War* (New York: St. Martin's, 1991). Clear and brief.

Parker, Geoffrey, *The Dutch Revolt* (Ithaca, NY: Cornell University Press, 1977). The best treatment of its subject.

Parry, J. H., *The Age of Reconnaissance. Discovery, Exploration and Settlement, 1450 to 1650* (London: Weidenfeld and Nicholson, 1963). Still the best survey of the subject.

Wedgewood, C. V., *The Thirty Years' War* (London: Cape, 1938). Old, but still the most readable and accessible account for the nonspecialist.

InfoTrac College Edition

For additional reading, go to your online research library at *http://infotrac.thomsonlearning.com*.

Using Key Terms, enter the search terms:

F. Magellan	*Vasco da Gama*
Elizabeth I	*Thirty Years' War*

Using Subject Guide, enter the search terms:
Christopher Columbus

Web Sites

http://www.fordham.edu/halsall/mod/modsbook.html
Internet Modern History Sourcebook. Contains a good section on the Early Modern World System

http://www.british-civil-wars.co.uk
British Civil Wars, Commonwealth and Protectorate. Biographies, timelines, military analysis, and links to sources and related subjects.

Visit the Western Civilization Companion Web Site for resources specific to this textbook:
http://history.wadsworth.com/hause02/

The CD in the back of this book and the Western Civilization Resource Center at *http://history.wadsworth.com/western/* offer a variety of tools to help you succeed in this course, including access to quizzes; images; documents; interactive simulations, maps, and timelines; movie explorations; and a wealth of other sources.

Chapter 15

OVERSEAS CONQUEST AND RELIGIOUS WAR

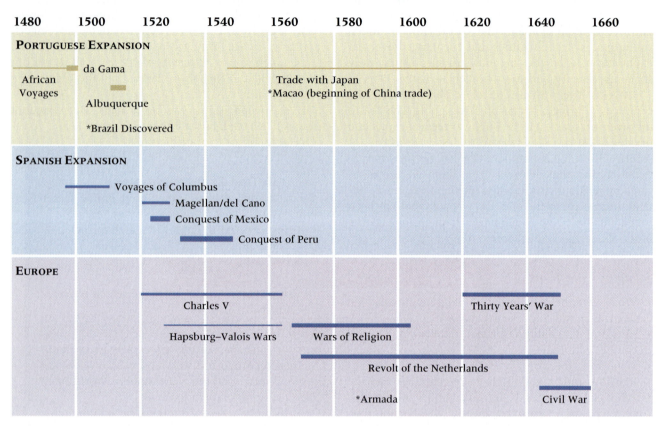

1480	1500	1520	1540	1560	1580	1600	1620	1640	1660

PORTUGUESE EXPANSION

da Gama

African Voyages

Albuquerque

*Brazil Discovered

Trade with Japan
*Macao (beginning of China trade)

SPANISH EXPANSION

Voyages of Columbus

Magellan/del Cano

Conquest of Mexico

Conquest of Peru

EUROPE

Charles V

Hapsburg–Valois Wars

Wars of Religion

Thirty Years' War

Revolt of the Netherlands

*Armada

Civil War

Chapter 16

PREINDUSTRIAL EUROPE: SCIENCE, ECONOMY, AND POLITICAL REORGANIZATION

FOCUS QUESTIONS

- How do the assumptions and methods of modern science differ from those of ancient and medieval science?
- What specific reforms in the conduct of war and government reflected the ideals of "absolutism"?
- Why did England emerge as a major power after the revolution of 1688?
- What were the most important social consequences of economic growth in the later seventeenth century?

The Anglo-Dutch wars of 1652–1653, 1665–1666, and 1672–1673 were among the bloodiest conflicts ever fought at sea. When asked why England attacked another Protestant power, the English General-at-Sea, George Monck, answered with characteristic bluntness: "What we want is more of the trade the Dutch now have." Economic competition had surpassed religion as the driving force in international affairs. The seventeenth century saw the emergence of England, France, and the Netherlands as imperial powers. After a brief "Golden Age," the Netherlands declined, leaving France and England as dominant powers. Both countries reorganized their military and governmental systems. In France, Louis XIV created an absolutist model for a host of other states, from Spain to Austria. In England, Parliament at last wrested power from the king and developed the financial system that would eventually pay for the Industrial Revolution. For this reason, the period from the late sixteenth to early eighteenth century is often called the Preindustrial Age, but the new wealth generated by imperial and commercial expansion did not benefit everyone. Even in England, the poor grew poorer as the middle class expanded and the rich grew even richer.

Chapter 16 begins with the Scientific Revolution that weakened the hold of religion on the mind of Europe's upper classes and produced discoveries that made the Industrial Revolution possible. It then looks briefly at French, English, and Dutch expansion overseas and describes the society of the Netherlands in its Golden Age. In the aftermath of the Religious Wars that ended in 1648, the monarchies of Europe reorganized. The methods of Louis XIV and his imitators are described, together with the very different approach to war and government developed by England. This chapter concludes with economic and social change in the later seventeenth century.

THE SCIENTIFIC REVOLUTION (1530–1727)

The Scientific Revolution of the late sixteenth and seventeenth centuries has no parallel among modern intellectual movements. Like the thought of ancient Greece, it changed not only ideas but also the process by which ideas are formulated. The Renaissance and the Reformation, for all their importance, had been rooted in traditional patterns of thought. They could be understood without re-ordering the concepts that had permeated Western thinking for more than 2,000 years. The development of modern science, although in some ways an outgrowth of these earlier movements, asked questions that had not been asked before, and by so doing created a whole new way of looking at the universe. Modern science and the scientific method with which it is associated may be the one body of European ideas that has had a transforming effect on virtually every non-Western culture.

Ancient and Medieval Science. In 1500, the basic assumptions of science had changed little since the days of Pliny (23–79 CE). The ancients believed in a universe organized according to rational principles and therefore open to human observation and deduction. Deduction in this case meant the logic of Aristotle, which was rooted firmly in language and the meaning of words. Ancient science therefore tended to be qualitative rather than quantitative. With few exceptions, it required neither measurement nor the construction of mathematical models. Accurate observation provided clues to the nature or essential quality of the object being observed. Reason could then determine the relationship of that object to other objects in the natural world.

This was important because the ancients believed that all parts of the universe were interrelated and that nothing could be studied in isolation. Today, this idea is called holistic or organic. It was stated expressly by Aristotle and, metaphorically, in the popular image of the individual human being as a microcosm or little world whose parts corresponded to those of the universe as a whole. It formed the basis not only of academic science but also of the applied sciences of the day: medicine, natural magic, astrology, and alchemy. The last three were partially inspired by the Hermetic tradition, a body of occult literature that supposedly derived from ancient Egypt. The church regarded the Hermetic arts with suspicion because they thought their practitioners tried to interfere with Providence, but its theoretical assumptions did not conflict with those of Aristotle. Many, if not most, of the early scientists were as interested in astrology or alchemy as they were in physics and made no real distinction between the occult and what would today be regarded as more legitimate disciplines.

Whatever their interests, ancient and medieval scientists agreed that the world was composed of the four elements—earth, air, fire, and water—and that the elements corresponded to the four humors that governed the body (blood, phlegm, yellow bile, and black bile) as well as to the signs of the zodiac. **Magic,** "the chief power of all the sciences," sought to understand these and other relationships between natural objects and to manipulate them to achieve useful results. **Alchemy** sought to change "base" metals into gold and to discover the sovereign cure for all diseases. The causes of natural phenomena were of academic but little practical interest and generally explained teleologically. That is, virtually everyone believed that the world had been created for a purpose and that the behavior of natural objects would necessarily be directed to that end. This preconception, together with the tendency to describe objects in qualitative terms, ensured that causation, too, would usually be explained in terms of the nature or qualities of the objects involved. Such ideas reflected the Christian view that divine providence governs the world.

Modern Scientific Method. Ideas of this kind are now found largely in the pages of supermarket tabloids, but they were once universally accepted by learned people. They provided a rational, comprehensive, and comforting vision of what might otherwise have been a terrifying universe. They have little in common with the principles of modern science, which substitutes measurement for qualitative description and attempts to express physical relationships in quantitative, mathematical terms. Because its vision of the world is mechanical instead of holistic and providential, modern science concentrates heavily on the causes of physical and biological reactions and tries to reject teleological and qualitative explanations. It is more likely to ask "how?" or "why?" than "what?" and has few compunctions about isolating a given problem to study it. Correspondences based on qualitative or symbolic relationships of the sort studied by magicians are ignored.

Methodologically, modern science seeks to create a hypothesis by reasoning logically from accurate observations. If possible, the hypothesis is then tested by experiment, and a mathematical model is constructed that will be both explanatory and predictive. The scientist can then formulate general laws of physical behavior without becoming entangled in the emotional overtones of language. The scientific model of the universe therefore tends to be mechanistic rather than holistic, mythological, or poetic. It is not necessarily godless, but its predictability does away with the need for divine intervention on a regular basis.

The Origins of Modern Scientific Thought

An intellectual shift of this magnitude did not occur quickly. Its roots are found in several traditions that co-existed uneasily in late medieval and Renaissance thought: the Aristotelian, the experimentalist, and the humanistic. During the sixteenth century, a process of fusion began as thinkers adopted elements of each in their attempts to solve an ever-growing list of problems. The problems arose mainly from the perception that old, accepted answers, however logical and comforting they may have been, did not square with observed reality. The answers, and the accumulation of methods by which they were achieved, laid the groundwork of modern science.

The Aristotelian tradition contributed a rigorous concern for accurate observation and a logical method for the construction of hypotheses. In the wake of nominalist criticism, many Aristotelians, especially in the Italian universities, had turned their attention to the physical sciences, often with impressive results. Their tradition remained vital in some places until the eighteenth century. Experimentalism derived ultimately from a radical offshoot of the Observant Franciscans. Believing (heretically) that God's kingdom would be established on Earth, some of them used experiment in an effort to understand the natural world. **Sir Francis Bacon** (1561–1626), the Lord Chancellor of England under James I, revived and popularized the idea of experiment without the religious overtones. Like his predecessors, he accomplished little because his hypotheses were faulty, but the elegance of his prose inspired a host of followers. His contemporary **Galileo Galilei** (1564–1642) used experiment to greater effect, although many of his best demonstrations were designed but never performed. The humanist tradition contributed classical texts that reintroduced half-forgotten ideas, including the physics of Archimedes and the heliocentric theories of Eratosthenes and Aristarchus of Samos. It also encouraged quantification by reviving the numerological theories of Pythagoras.

Sir Francis Bacon

Copernicus.

The thinkers of the sixteenth and seventeenth centuries were interested in nearly everything, but they achieved their greatest breakthroughs in astronomy and physics. The Middle Ages had accepted the ancient Ptolemaic theory that the Earth was the center of the universe and that the sun and the planets revolved around it in circular orbits. The problem lay in explaining why planets sometimes appear to move backward in their orbits (retrograde movement) and why they vary in brilliance. It seemed obvious that they must at some times be farther away from Earth than at others. But this was impossible, because if their orbits were circular, they would always be equidistant from the Earth around which they revolved. Ptolemy solved these problems only by using an elaborate system of mathematical fictions known as epicycles. Among the many scholars who found this incompatible with reason or observable reality was the Polish humanist and mathematician **Nicolaus Copernicus** (1473–1543). As a humanist, Copernicus knew that a minority of ancients had believed that the Earth circled the sun; as a mathematician he decided to construct a mathematical model to prove their theories. His hypothesis, complete with mathematical proofs, reached print shortly after his death. The **Copernican theory** that the Earth and planets revolved around the sun aroused opposition from those who believed it contrary to the Bible. Mathematicians and astronomers tended to support it, but no one regarded it as a perfect model of the universe. Copernicus had retained the idea of circular orbits, largely because he believed that the circle was the perfect geometrical figure and that God would not have created an imperfect universe. He therefore reduced the number of epicycles but did not eliminate them.

Nicolaus Copernicus

Kepler. A more plausible model of the cosmos was devised by **Johannes Kepler** (1571–1630), court astrologer to the emperor Rudolph II. Kepler's views combined mysticism, numerology, and solid observation. He believed that the Earth had a soul, but as a follower of Pythagoras, he thought that the universe was organized on geometrical principles. The Copernican epicycles offended his notions of mathematical harmony. He wanted to believe in circular orbits, but when he posited eccentric circles that did not center on the sun, he was left with a minute discrepancy in his mathematical formulas. It was a terrible dilemma: the circle may have been the perfect geometric figure, but he could not accept a universe founded on imperfect mathematics. In the end, he decided that planetary orbits had to be elliptical. This solution, which proved to be correct, was not generally accepted until long after his death, but Kepler did not mind. Like the number

Johannes Kepler

GALILEO ON SCIENTIFIC PROOF

In this excerpt from *The Assayer*, Galileo attacks an opponent for arguing in the traditional manner by compiling lists of authorities who support his position. It not only shows the gulf that separated scientific thinking from that of the traditionalists but also provides some indication of how Galileo made enemies with his pen.

Sarsi goes on to say that since this experiment of Aristotle's has failed to convince us, many other great men have also written things of the same sort. But it is news to me that any man would actually put the testimony of writers ahead of what experience shows him. To adduce more witnesses serves no purposes, Sarsi, for we have never denied that such things have been written and

believed. We did say they are false, but so far as authority is concerned yours alone is as effective as an army's in rendering the events true or false. You take your stand on the authority of many poets against our experiments. I reply that if those poets could be present at our experiments they would change their views, and without disgrace they could say they had been writing hyperbolically—or even admit they had been wrong. . . .

I cannot but be astonished that Sarsi would persist in trying to prove by means of witnesses something that I may see for myself at any time by means of experiment.

From Galilei, Galileo, "The Assayer," trans. and ed. Stillman Drake. *Discoveries and Opinions of Galileo* (New York: Doubleday, 1957, pp. 270–271).

Question: What earlier intellectual movement inspired Sarsi's form of argument, and how did it differ from Galileo's?

mystic he was, he continued searching for other, more elusive cosmic harmonies that could be described in musical as well as mathematical terms.

Galileo. Meanwhile, Galileo rejected the theory of elliptical orbits but provided important evidence that the planets rotated around the sun. A professor at the University of Padua, Galileo was perhaps the first thinker to use something like the modern scientific method. He quarreled with the Aristotelians over their indifference to mathematical proofs and denounced

their teleological obsession with final causes, but like them he was a careful observer. Unlike them, he tried to verify his hypotheses through experimentation. From the Platonists and Pythagoreans, he adopted the view that the universe followed mathematical laws and expressed his theories in mathematical formulae that were intended to be predictive. His vision, however, was mechanistic, not mystical or organic.

The invention of the telescope inspired Galileo's exploration of the planets. The Aristotelians had discovered the basic principles of optics, and eyeglasses were

FIGURE 16.1 *Galileo before the Holy Office of the Vatican.* In 1633, Galileo was condemned by the papal Inquisition for publishing a defense of the Copernican system in his *Dialogue on the Two World Chief World Systems: Ptolemaic and Copernican.* By this time, many churchmen accepted Copernicanism, but Galileo had offended many, including his one-time friend, Pope Urban VIII. He had ignored the pope's request to present the Copernican theory as a hypothesis and then had Simplicio, the foolish character in the dialogue, present the pope's ideas as his own. This reconstruction of the scene, including a good likeness of Galileo at the center, was painted by J. N. Robert-Fleury (1797–1890).

introduced early in the sixteenth century. By 1608, Dutch and Flemish lens grinders were combining two lenses at fixed distances from one another to create the first telescopes. Using a perfected version of the telescope that he had built himself, Galileo turned it on the heavens. The results created a sensation. His discovery of the moons of Jupiter and the phases of Venus seemed to support the Copernican theory, whereas his study of sunspots raised the unsettling possibility that the sun rotated on its axis like the planets.

Perhaps because he was not interested in astrology, Galileo ignored the problems of planetary motion that obsessed Kepler. Instead, he concentrated on the mechanics of motion. Kepler had established the position of the planets with his Rudolphine Tables of 1627, but he had been unable to explain either the causes of their motion or what kept them in their orbits. The issue had perplexed the ancients because they believed that rest was the normal state of any object. The Aristotelians had argued that an object remains at rest unless a force is applied against it and that the velocity of that object is proportionate to the force exerted in moving it. As a result, it was hard to explain why a projectile continued to move after the impetus behind it had ceased. Galileo turned the problem on its head by proving that a body in motion will move forever unless it is slowed or deflected by an external force and that the application of uniform force results in acceleration instead of motion at a constant rate. Movement, therefore, is as natural a state as rest. Once it had been set in motion by its Creator, the universe could, in theory, go on forever without further intervention.

The Trial of Galileo.

It was a profoundly disturbing vision. To Galileo, God was the Great Craftsman who created the world as a self-sustaining and predictable machine. To those who saw the universe as an organic entity upon which God still imposed His will, such a view was not only frightening but also blasphemous. In 1632, Galileo published his *Dialogue on the Two Chief World Systems: Ptolemaic and Copernican* in Italian rather than in Latin so that it could be more widely read. It brought him before the papal Inquisition in what has become one of the most famous trials in history. The indictment of Galileo was in some respects a mistake. Many Catholics, including the Jesuits, shared his views. Others agreed with him that there was no real conflict between science and religion. In the end, his ideas were condemned not only because he defended the Copernican system and because his ideas undermined a worldview that had prevailed for nearly 2,000 years but because he had personally offended the pope. Yet the importance of this celebrated trial should not be exaggerated. Galileo's condemnation forced him to retire to his country villa; it did not prevent him or any other Italian from proceeding with research along the lines he

had suggested. Galileo was arrogant and bad-tempered with patrons and opponents alike. He was also a brilliant writer and publicist (see Document 16.1). Had his ability to attract enemies not equaled his genius, the episode might never have occurred.

Vacuums and Gases.

Galileo's vision of the universe as a kind of giant machine eventually triumphed, and the church would not again mount a frontal attack

René Descartes

against it. **René Descartes** (Day-kart, 1596–1650), the most influential philosopher of his day, based his thought on a radical separation between mind and matter that precluded holistic thinking and encouraged the analysis of nature as a kind of machine that could be understood through the application of mathematical principles. His efforts inspired others, such as Pierre Gassendi (1592–1655), who attempted to revive the atomic theories of the Epicureans. To do so, he was forced to posit the existence of a vacuum. The possibility of nothingness had been denied by virtually everyone from Aristotle to Descartes, but the results of barometric experiments by Evangelista Torricelli (Tor-ri- chel'-lee, 1608–1647) and by Blaise Pascal (1623–1662) could be explained in no other way. In 1650, Otto von Guericke (fon Gear'-i-kee, 1602–1686) ended the debate by constructing an air pump with which a vacuum could be created. These efforts in turn inspired Robert Boyle (1627–1691) to formulate his laws about the behavior of gases.

Isaac Newton.

In astronomy and physics, the scientific movement culminated in the work of **Isaac Newton** (1642–1727). A professor at Cambridge and a member of the Royal Society, Newton was in some respects an odd character who spent at least as much time on alchemy and other occult speculations as he did on mathematics and physics. In spite of this, he formulated the laws of planetary motion and of gravity, thereby completing the work begun by Kepler and Galileo and establishing a cosmology that dominated Western thought until the publication of Einstein's theories in 1904.

In his *Principia*, or *Mathematical Principles of Natural Philosophy*, presented to the Royal Society in 1686, Newton formulated three laws of motion: (1) every object remains either at rest or in motion along a straight line until it is deflected or resisted by another force (the law of inertia), (2) the rate of change in the motion of an object is proportionate to the force acting on it, and (3) to every action there is an equal and opposite reaction. These formulations accounted not only for the

FIGURE 16.2 An Experiment with a Bird in the Air Pump *(1768)*. Scientific studies became a fad with members of the upper and middle classes. Here a disheveled "scientific gentlemen" demonstrates an air pump. He has placed a bird inside a vacuum chamber and pumped the air out of it, causing the bird to die. One woman averts her eyes, while a young girl stares in appropriate horror. Painting by Joseph Wright of Derby.

behavior of moving objects on Earth but also for the continuing movement of the planets. He then perfected Kepler's theories by demonstrating how the planets move through a vacuum in elliptical orbits under the influence of a force centered on the sun. That force was gravity, which he defined as the attractive force between two objects (see Document 16.2). It is directly proportionate to the product of their masses and inversely proportionate to the square of the distances between them. To many, these theories explained the mysteries of a universe that acted like clockwork—smooth, mechanical, and eternal. Newton, who was a deeply religious man, would not have been pleased at the use to which his ideas would soon be put by the philosophers of the eighteenth-century Enlightenment.

The Anatomical Revolution. Mechanistic views would also triumph in medicine, but the process by which they did so was more convoluted than it had been in physics. Physicians moved from mechanism to magic and back again in the course of the sixteenth century. The works of the ancient Greek anatomist Galen had long been known through Arabic commentaries and translations. Galen's views were mechanistic in the sense that he was careful to relate the form of organs to their function and had little use for magic or for alchemical cures. The recovery and translation

of original Galenic texts by the humanists popularized his teachings, and by the early sixteenth century, his influence dominated academic medicine.

Paracelsus and the Chemical Philosophy. In response, a Swiss physician and alchemist who called himself **Paracelsus** (Par-a-sel'-sus, 1493–1541) launched a frontal attack on the entire medical establishment. Declaring that "wise women" and barbers cured more patients than all of the Galenists put together, he proposed a medical philosophy based on natural magic and alchemy. All natural phenomena were chemical interactions between the four elements and what he called the three principles: sulfur, mercury, and salt—the combustible, gaseous, and solid components of matter. Because the human body was a microcosm of the universe and because diseases were produced by chemical forces acting on particular organs of the body, sickness could be cured with chemical antidotes.

This chemical philosophy was widely accepted. Its hermetic and Neo-Platonic overtones recommended it to many scholars, although those who practiced it may have killed fewer patients than their Galenist opponents. Paracelsus believed in administering drugs in small, carefully measured doses. He rejected bleeding, purges, and the treatment of wounds with poultices whose vile ingredients almost guaranteed the onset of infection. As a result, the bodies of his patients had a fighting chance to heal themselves, and he was credited with miraculous cures.

The Triumph of the Anatomists. The war between the Galenists and the Paracelsians raged throughout the midsixteenth century. In the end, the Galenists won. Their theories, although virtually useless for the treatment of disease, produced new insights, whereas those of Paracelsus did not. **Andreas Vesalius** (1514–1564) was shocked to discover that Galen's dissections had been carried out primarily on animals. Using Galenic principles, he retraced the master's steps using human cadavers and in 1543 published his *De humani corporis fabrica (On the Structure of the Human Body)*. Although

NEWTON ON GRAVITY

In the *Principia*, or *Mathematical Principles of Natural Philosophy*, Sir Isaac Newton describes his revolutionary concept of gravity and, in the process, sets forth some of his thoughts on scientific method. Note that he does not claim to understand how gravity is actually produced. That discovery was not made until the twentieth century. *Induction* is the process of reasoning from a particular phenomenon to a general principle. *Deduction* reasons from the general to the particular.

Hitherto, we have explained the phenomena of the heavens and of our sea by the power of gravity, but have not yet assigned the cause of this power. This is certain, that it must proceed from a cause that penetrates to the very centers of the sun and planets, without suffering the least diminution of its force; that operates not according to the quantity of the surfaces of the particles upon which it acts (as mechanical causes used to do) but according to the quantity of solid matter which they contain, and propagates its virtue on all sides to immense distances, decreasing always in the duplicate portion of the distances. . . .

Hitherto I have not been able to discover the cause of those properties of gravity from the phenomena, and I frame no hypothesis; for whatever is not deduced from phenomena is to be called an hypothesis; and hypothesis, whether metaphysical or physical, whether of occult qualities or mechanical, have no place in experimental philosophy. In this philosophy particular propositions are inferred from the phenomena, and afterward rendered general by induction. Thus it was the impenetrability, the mobility, and the impulsive force of bodies, and the laws of motion and gravitation were discovered. And to us it is enough that gravity does really exist, and acts according to the laws that we have explained, and abundantly serves to account for all the motions of the celestial bodies, and of our sea.

From Newton, Isaac, *The Mathematical Principles of Natural Philosophy*, book 3, vol. 2, trans. Andrew Motte (London: 1803, p. 310).

Question: Does Newton support inductive or deductive reasoning in scientific matters?

William Harvey

not without error, it was a vast improvement over earlier anatomy texts and a work of art in its own right that inspired others to correct and improve his work. The long debate over the circulation of the blood, culminating in the explanation published by **William Harvey** in 1628 (see Document 16.3), was also a Galenist enterprise that owed little or nothing to the chemical tradition.

By the time microscopes were invented in Holland at the beginning of the seventeenth century, the anatomists had seized the initiative. The new device strengthened their position by allowing them to examine small structures such as capillaries. Blood corpuscles were described for the first time, and bacteria were identified, although a full-fledged germ theory would not be verified until the nineteenth century. These discoveries made sustaining the ancient metaphor of the human body as a microcosm of the universe even more difficult.

The body was beginning to look more like a machine within a machine.

The Triumph of Science as an Intellectual System. By this time, interest in scientific inquiry had assumed the proportions of a fad. All over Europe, men of leisure and education were examining the physical world and developing theories about it. Many, including Boyle and Pascal, were also gifted writers whose work inspired others to emulate them. Science was becoming a movement, and it was only a matter of time until that movement was institutionalized. The English Royal Society and the French Academie des Sciences were founded in the 1660s, the latter under the patronage of **Louis XIV's** minister, **Jean Baptiste Colbert** (Zhan Bahp-teest Kole-bare', 1619–1683). Colbert, like England's King Charles II, was quick to perceive the possible connection between the new science and improved technologies for war, agriculture, and manufacturing. Not all of the work performed was useful, and much of it remained tied to the earlier vision of an organic, providential universe, but mechanistic and mathematical views gained ground steadily throughout the century.

As Galileo had explained to the Inquisition, there was no inherent conflict between science and religion. Few

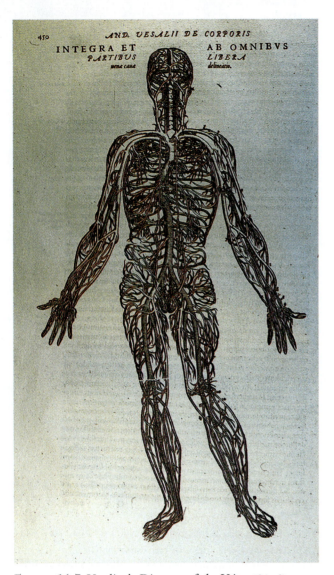

FIGURE 16.3 *Vesalius's Diagram of the Veins.* This diagram is from Andreas Vesalius's (1514–1564) *De humani corporis fabrica.* The venous system was especially important to physicians because drawing blood was the primary treatment for many ailments. As impressive as these drawings are, they contain anatomical errors. Vesalius did not understand the circulation of the blood and based some of his ideas on the dissection of animals (see the arrangement of veins at the base of the neck, which is not found in humans). However, his work, with its magnificent illustrations, is still a remarkable monument to the anatomical revolution.

people in seventeenth-century Europe abandoned their belief in God, but for the educated, science offered a new and exciting perspective on the universe. The Scientific Revolution increased the secularizing tendencies that had begun in the Renaissance and would reach a peak of sorts in the eighteenth-century Enlightenment. More concretely, it produced a body of knowledge that would prove useful in developing new technologies during the Industrial Revolution.

THE EXPANSION OF THE NORTHERN POWERS: FRANCE, ENGLAND, AND THE NETHERLANDS (1560–1660)

In the years when Galileo and others transformed European thought, seafarers from France, England, and the Netherlands continued the work of mapping the globe and exploiting its economic resources. The centralized, closely controlled empires created by the Iberian powers had been resented from the first by northern Europeans, who wished to engage in the American trade. French pirates and privateers became active in the Caribbean after the 1530s and sacked Havana in 1556. In 1565, the Spanish massacred a colony of French Protestants near the present site of St. Augustine, Florida. Neither of these failures inhibited French, English, and Dutch captains from trying to enter the Caribbean market. The Englishman John Hawkins (1532–1595) tried to break the Spanish–Portuguese monopoly by introducing cargoes of slaves in 1562 and again in 1567, but he was caught by the incoming Spanish fleet in 1567 and barely escaped with

Sir Francis Drake

his life. One of his surviving captains, Francis Drake (c. 1543–1596), raided Panama in 1572–1573 and attacked Spanish shipping in the Pacific when he circumnavigated the globe in 1577–1579.

The First English Colonies in North America.
To many in England, these efforts, however inspiring, were no substitute for the establishment of permanent English colonies. Commercial interests and the growing political and religious rivalry with Spain demanded nothing less. The first English settlement in North America was planted on Roanoke Island, North Carolina, in 1585 but disappeared before it could be reinforced. Subsequent efforts at Jamestown (1607) and Plymouth (1620) were more successful. The Spanish claimed sovereignty over North America but lacked the resources to settle it or to protect it against interlopers. The Native American population was, by comparison with that of Mexico or Peru, small, scattered, and politically disunited. Obstacles to settlement were relatively easy to overcome, and by 1650, the English had established themselves at various locations along the entire Atlantic seaboard from Newfoundland to the Carolinas.

WILLIAM HARVEY ON THE CIRCULATION OF BLOOD

The English physician William Harvey (1578–1657) first described the circulation of blood. His predecessors, including Galen and Vesalius, knew that blood moved within the body but did not understand the role of the heart as a kind of pump and did not know that the same blood moves from the heart through the arteries and then returns to the heart by way of the veins. In this passage from his treatise, "On the Motion of the Heart and Blood in Animals," Harvey summarizes the most important points of his argument.

But lest anyone should say that we give them words only, and make mere specious assertions without any foundation, and desire to innovate without sufficient cause, three points present themselves for confirmation, which being stated, I conceive that the truth I contend for will follow necessarily, and appear as a thing obvious to all. First, the blood is incessantly transmitted by the action of the heart from the vena cava [a large vein that feeds the right side of the heart] to the arteries in such quantity that it *cannot be supplied from the ingesta [digested food], and in such matter that the whole must quickly pass through the organ; Second, the blood under the influence of the arterial pulse enters and is expelled in a continuous, equable, and incessant stream through every part and member of the body, in much larger quantity than were sufficient for nutrition, or than the whole mass of fluids can supply. Third, the veins in like matter return this blood incessantly to the heart from parts and members of the body. These points proved, I conceive it will be manifest that the blood circulates, revolves, propelled and then returning, from the heart to the extremities, from the extremities to the heart, and thus that it performs a kind of circular motion.*

From Harvey, William, "On the Motion of the Heart and Blood in Animals, 1628," Chapter IX, in *The Works of William Harvey,* trans. Robert Willis (London: 1847).

Question: Why was this discovery important to the practice of medicine?

From the standpoint of global politics and immediate gain, these North American colonies were something of a disappointment. They produced no precious metals and offered England few strategic advantages. With the notable exception of tobacco from Virginia and Maryland, they had little of value to export and quickly became self-sufficient in everything but luxury items. In the meantime, the French had established themselves in the St. Lawrence valley and were developing an important trade in furs from the North American interior. English competition in the form of the Hudson's Bay Company did not emerge until 1670.

French and English Colonies in the Caribbean.
Expansion in the Caribbean remained a primary goal. The English established a colony on the uninhabited island of Barbados in 1624 and introduced sugar in 1640. By 1660, its sugar exports made Barbados the most valuable of the English colonies and its position windward of the Spanish Main made it virtually invulnerable to Spanish attacks. (The sailing ships of the day could sail into the wind only with great difficulty.) The French established sugar colonies of equal wealth on the nearby islands of Guadeloupe and Martinique. By this time, Spanish power was in decline. In 1656, an English fleet seized Jamaica. Eight years later, the French West India Company took possession of some settlements that had been established years before by French buccaneers in the western part of Hispaniola

and laid the foundations of St. Domingue, the rich slave colony that would one day become Haiti.

The French and English Colonial Systems.
The French and English, like the Spanish and Portuguese, wanted their colonial systems to be self-contained and closed to outsiders. In practice, this was as difficult to achieve, as it had been for their rivals. Both France and England governed their possessions on the proprietary model. They made huge grants of land to wealthy speculators and allowed them to serve as governors as long as they populated them with colonists. Neither country developed anything like the elaborate colonial bureaucracy of Spain. Royal authority tended to be correspondingly weak. Distance, the limitations of sailing ship technology, and the perishability of certain cargoes, notably slaves, encouraged smuggling and made it difficult to suppress. Planters and merchants of any nationality had nothing to gain from dealing exclusively with their own countrymen when others might offer better prices or more rapid delivery. Cargoes could always be landed secretly in remote coves, but much illegal activity was conducted in the open, for governors were under enormous pressure from their subjects to look the other way.

The Dutch in America.
Almost from the beginning, the chief beneficiaries of this illegal trade were the Dutch, whose maritime activities increased during their

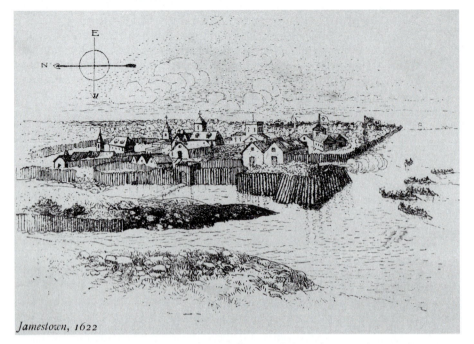

Jamestown, 1622

FIGURE 16.4 *Jamestown, the First Permanent English Colony in America.* The first colonies in North America were little more than agricultural villages. The English colony at Jamestown in Virginia is shown as it was in 1622, 15 years after its foundation. Note the wooden palisade that protected the town from potential attacks by both Indians and the Spanish.

revolt against Spain. The Dutch had some 98,000 ships registered by 1598, but ships and trained seamen were not enough. They needed bases from which to conduct their operations. Between 1621 and 1640, the newly formed Dutch West India Company seized Curaçao, St. Eustatius, St. Maarten, and Saba in the Caribbean and established a colony called New Amsterdam on the present site of New York. From 1624 to 1654, the Dutch controlled much of the Brazilian coast, and in 1637, they captured the African fortress and slave-trading station of Elmina from the Portuguese. Brazil and New Amsterdam were expensive ventures. The Dutch, like the Portuguese, lacked the manpower to impose their rule on large geographical areas, and when the English seized New Amsterdam in 1664, the West India Company settled down to a more modest—and in the end more profitable—career as a trading company based in Curaçao and St. Eustatius.

The Dutch East India Company. Only in the East did the Dutch manage to establish something like regional hegemony. Dutch traders first appeared in East Indian waters in 1595. Bypassing India, they sailed directly to the Spice Islands (Indonesia), rounding the Cape of Good Hope and running due east in the so-called roaring forties before turning north to Java or Sumatra. The fast but dangerous trip brought them directly to the sources of the Portuguese and Indian spice trade. To improve efficiency and minimize competition, the Dutch traders organized in 1602 into the East India Company.

Under the governor-generalship of **Jan Pieterszoon Coen** (Yan Pee'-ter-sone Koon, 1587–1629), the company's forces destroyed the Javan town of Djakarta and rebuilt it as Batavia, center of Dutch enterprise in the East. Local rulers were forced to restrict their trading activities to rice and other local necessities, and European competition was violently discouraged. English traders especially had been active in Asian waters since 1591. They had formed their own East India Company on Christmas Day in 1600 but lacked the ships and capital to match the Dutch. Coen expelled most of them from the region by 1620. His successors attacked the Portuguese colonies, seizing Malacca in 1641 and the Indian bases shortly thereafter, but Goa survived a Dutch blockade and remained in Portuguese hands until 1961. The Japanese trade fell into Dutch hands when the Portuguese were expelled in 1637, and for two centuries, a Dutch trading station in Nagasaki harbor provided that country's only contact with the West.

By 1650, the Dutch had become the dominant force in Europe's Asian trade. More than 100 Dutch ships sailed regularly to the East, exchanging German arms, armor, linens, and glass for spices and finished silks. Even the surviving Portuguese colonies were now forced to deal largely through Dutch intermediaries. The major exception was Macao, which continued to export Chinese silks to Spain via Manila. This monopoly was successfully challenged in the eighteenth century by the revived British East India Company and to a lesser degree by the French, but the Dutch remained in control of Indonesia until the outbreak of World War II. Like the Portuguese in Asia, however, they lacked the manpower to impose their government or culture on native peoples outside the major trading centers. They, too, tried to maintain direct control of a few strategically situated towns and relied on sea power, diplomacy, and the judicious use of force to protect their trade with native rulers.

FIGURE 16.5 *New Amsterdam.* The Dutch colony at New Amsterdam is shown as it appeared in a Dutch map of 1656. It was located at the lower end of Manhattan Island and eventually grew into the city of New York.

THE GOLDEN AGE IN THE NETHERLANDS (1598–1679)

Long-distance trade made the Netherlands an island of wealth and culture amidst the turmoil of the early seventeenth century. A century before, the city of Antwerp had dominated the economy of the region. Its merchants traded in wool from Spain and England, finished cloth from the towns of Brabant and Flanders, wine from the Iberian Peninsula, and a variety of products exported from Germany to England and Scandinavia. The city's prosperity, however, did not survive the Revolt of the Netherlands. Antwerp is located at the head of navigation on the Scheldt, a broad estuary whose western approaches are controlled by the Zeeland (Zay'-land) towns of Vlissingen (Flushing) and Middelburg. When the Zeelanders joined the Dutch revolt, they cut off Antwerp from the sea and destroyed its prosperity.

The Rise of Amsterdam. Amsterdam took its place. Set in the marshes where the Amstel River meets the IJ (eye), an inlet of the Zuider Zee (Zye'-der Zay), the city was virtually impregnable to attack by sea or land. Already the center of the Baltic trade, it grew enormously after 1585, when southern refugees poured in, bringing their capital with them. When Maurice of Nassau took the lands east of the Ijssel River from

Spain between 1591 and 1597, contact with Germany improved and Amsterdam replaced Antwerp as the conduit through which goods flowed from the German interior to the Atlantic and North Sea. The repeated failure of Spanish and Sicilian harvests in the same years made Amsterdam a dominant force in the Mediterranean trade as well. Dutch merchants had established themselves in the Baltic ports of Riga (Ree'-guh) and Gdansk (Danzig) at an early date. The Amsterdam exchange determined the price of wheat, and vast quantities were shipped southward in Dutch ships, together with timber, Swedish iron, and other northern products.

Shipbuilding, always a major industry in the ports of Holland and Zeeland, expanded with the growth of the carrying trade. Economies of scale, better access to Baltic naval stores, and the presence of a skilled maritime population enabled the Dutch to charge lower shipping rates than their competitors. With the founding of the East and West India companies, this advantage became global. The axis of the spice trade shifted from Lisbon to Amsterdam, and Dutch skippers took advantage of the delays occasioned by the flota system and by a general shortage of Iberian shipping to intrude on the commerce of the Americas. The profits from

FIGURE 16.6 *The Return of the Dutch Fleet to Amsterdam, 1599.* This painting by Andries van Eertvert (1590–1652) commemorates the return of one of the first Dutch trading voyages to the East Indies. Its success helped inspire the founding of the East India Company in 1602.

FIGURE 16.7 **The Dam at Amsterdam,** *1669, Jan van Kessel.* Much of Holland's overseas trade passed through the great city of Amsterdam. The Dam, shown here, is its central square. The palace of the stadtholders, now the Royal Palace, is on the left. The New Church, the largest of Amsterdam's Reformed churches, can be seen at right.

FIGURE 16.8 *Rembrandt van Rijn,* **Self-Portrait as a Young Man.** This is probably one of Rembrandt's many portrayals of himself in different guises and attitudes. Rembrandt is now regarded as the greatest Dutch painter of the Golden Age. In his own day, however, he often struggled to find commissions. This portrait shows his unequalled mastery of chiaroscuro as well as his ability to get to the heart of a subject's personality.

these sources generated investment capital, and Amsterdam soon became Europe's banking center as well as its commercial hub.

In these years, the modern city with its canals and high, narrow townhouses took shape. For all its wealth and beauty, however, Amsterdam was never more than the largest of several towns that supported and at times competed with each other in a variety of markets. The Dutch republic was overwhelmingly urban. A network of canals linked its cities and provided cheap, efficient transportation. Agriculturally, although a few large estates remained, most of the land was divided into relatively small plots and cultivated intensively to grow produce and dairy products for the nearby towns. Most peasants were independent farmers and relatively prosperous. Pockets of urban misery existed, but a real industrial proletariat existed only in the cloth towns of Haarlem and Leiden. Dutch society was therefore resolutely middle class. It valued hard work, thrift, and cleanliness; ostentation was suspect.

Dutch Art. A series of extraordinary painters provide a vivid picture of Dutch life in the seventeenth century. Jan Vermeer (1632–1675) portrayed bright, spotless interiors and virtuous housewives at work in an idealized vision of domesticity that was central to Dutch notions of the good life. Rembrandt van Rijn (van Rine, 1606–1669), Frans Hals (c. 1581–1666), and a host of others left brilliant portraits of city magistrates, corporate directors, and everyday drunks as well as grand illustrations of historical events. Masters like Ruisdael and van Goyen painted the brooding skies and placid

landscapes of the Netherlands, and dozens of still lifes by other painters dwell lovingly on food, flowers, and other everyday objects.

Government and Politics. The political and the social structure of the republic rested on the values of the late medieval city, preserved tenaciously through the long struggle against Spanish regalism. Each town elected a council, which in turn elected representatives to the Provincial Estates. The States General was elected by the provinces. The stadtholder was not a king or even a permanent officer, but a kind of "first citizen" elected to conduct war on land in times of crisis. He was almost always, however, a descendent of William of Orange. Five admiralties, each of which was nominally independent, conducted war at sea, supplementing its own warships with heavily armed vessels leased from the East and West India companies.

Local privilege dominated the system at every level, and conflict among the various components of the body politic was normally intense. Fortunately, the leadership of the councils, states, directorships, and committees formed a kind of interlocking directorship. A great merchant, banker, or rentier might hold several elected offices in the course of a lifetime, as well as directorships in one or more of the chartered companies. The Dutch republic was an oligarchy, not a democracy, but the existence of a well-defined group of prominent citizens facilitated communication, dampened local rivalries, and helped ensure a measure of continuity in what might otherwise have been a fragmented and overly decentralized system.

National policy therefore remained consistent. It encouraged trade, even with enemies, and supported freedom of the seas long before **Hugo Grotius** (Gro'-she-us, 1583–1645), attorney general of Holland, publicized the modern concept of international law. Although aggressive in its pursuit of new markets and the protection of old ones, Dutch foreign policy was otherwise defensive.

Tension between the governing elite and the stadtholders of the House of Orange dominated internal politics. At times, the struggle took the form of religious antagonism between extreme Calvinists, who tended to be Orangists supported by the artisan class, and the more relaxed Arminians, who rejected predestination and were supported by the great merchants. Class feeling played a major part in these struggles, but by comparison with other countries, both sides remained committed to religious toleration. The government actively encouraged Jewish settlement and protected Catholics from harassment. Holland became a refuge for the persecuted, many of whom, such as Descartes and the philosopher **Baruch Spinoza** (1632–1677), a Sephardic Jew, added luster to its intellectual life. Spinoza was among the first to offend Jews and Christians alike by arguing that God was in everything (an idea known as pantheism) but lacked the capacity to act in history and had no special interest in man. The Dutch republic was an oasis of tolerance as well as prosperity.

THE REORGANIZATION OF WAR AND GOVERNMENT (1648–1715)

Most seventeenth-century states were not as fortunate as the Dutch. Between 1560 and 1648, France, Spain, England, and the German principalities all suffered in varying degrees from military stalemate and political disintegration. Public order, perhaps even dynastic survival, depended on the reorganization of war and government. The restructuring of virtually every European state after 1648 has been called the triumph of **absolutism** (see Document 16.4). The term is in some ways misleading. No government before the Industrial Revolution could exert absolute control over the lives of its subjects. To do so even approximately requires modern transport and communications. But if by *absolutism* one means the theoretical subordination of all other elements of a country's power structure to the crown, the word is at least partially descriptive. The

DOCUMENT 16.4

ABSOLUTISM IN THEORY

Jacques-Bénigne Bossuet (Jhahk Bay'-neen-yee Bo-sue-ay, 1627–1704), Bishop of Meaux (Mo), was court preacher to Louis XIV and tutor to his son. In this passage, which reveals something of his power as a preacher, he argues the case for royal absolutism on both practical and religious grounds.

The royal power is absolute. . . . The prince need render account of his acts to no one. . . . Without this absolute authority the king could neither do good nor repress evil. It is necessary that his power be such that no one can escape him, and finally, the only protection of individuals against the public authority should be their innocence. This confirms the teaching of St. Paul: "Wilt thou not be afraid of the power? Do that which is good" [Rom. 13:3].

God is infinite, God is all. The prince, as prince, is not regarded as a private person: He is a public personage, all the state is in him. As all perfection and all strength are united in God, so all power of individuals is united in the person of the prince. What grandeur that a single man should embody so much!

Behold an immense people united in a single person; behold this holy power, paternal and absolute; behold the secret cause which governs the whole body of the state, contained in a single head: you see the image of God in the king, and you have the idea of royal majesty. God is holiness itself, goodness itself, and power itself. In these things lies the majesty of God. In the image of these things lies the majesty of the prince.

From Bossuet, Jacques-Bénigne, "Politics Drawn from the Very Words of Holy Scripture," in J. H. Robinson, ed., *Readings in European History*, vol. 2 (Boston: Ginn, 1906).

Question: Why would this view of the world soon be questioned by those who had accepted the Scientific Revolution?

Spain of Philip II met this definition in the sixteenth century; after 1660, the model for all other states was the France of Louis XIV.

The France of Louis XIV

Louis XIV (ruled 1643–1715) came to the throne as a child of 4. To the end of his life he harbored childhood memories of the Frondes and was determined to avoid further challenges from the French aristocracy at all costs. He knew that

Louis XIV of France

their influence derived from the networks of patronage that had long dominated rural life and used the fact that such networks are ultimately dependent on favors to destroy them as independent bases of power. As king of a country in which perpetual taxation had long been established, Louis had more favors to hand out than anyone else. He developed the tactic of forcing aristocrats to remain at court as a condition of receiving the titles, grants, monopolies, offices, and commissions upon which their influence was based. By doing so, he bound them to himself while cutting them off from their influence in the countryside.

The Court of Versailles. This was the real purpose behind the construction of **Versailles** (Vare-sigh), a palace large enough to house the entire court while separating it from the mobs of Paris, 12 miles away. Louis adopted the sun as his personal symbol and developed an elaborate ritual centered around his own person to occupy his courtiers. Every royal action was accompanied by great ceremony, and proud aristocrats contended for the honor of emptying the king's chamber pot or handing him his shirt. The world of Versailles was cramped, artificial, and riddled with intrigue, but it was a world controlled in every particular by a king who knew what was happening under his own roof. To stay was to sacrifice one's independence; to leave was to lose all hope of honor or profit. By 1670, the French nobility had been fully domesticated.

Royal Administration. The centralization implied by Versailles extended to the royal administration, although in this case, Louis followed precedents established by Henry IV and Richelieu. Richelieu in particular had worked to replace the old system of governing through councils with ministries, in which one man was responsible to the crown for each of the major functions of government. He had also brought royal authority to the provinces by introducing *intendants*, commissioners who supervised the collection of taxes and served as a constant check on local authorities. Louis expanded and perfected this system. Intendancies transcended provincial borders, further weakening the ties of local privilege. The ministers of war, finance, foreign affairs, and even of roads and bridges reported directly to the king, who, unlike his father, served as his own prime minister. Louis may have been the Sun King, surrounded by ritual and devoted to the pleasures of the bed, the table, and the hunt, but he was a hard worker. He devoted at least 6 hours a day, 7 days a week to public business. Significantly, Louis usually drew his ministers from the *nobles de la robe,* the great legal dynasties of the French towns, not from the old nobility.

The Organization of War. Because war was the primary function of the early modern state and accounted for the vast majority of its expenditures, Louis XIV made every effort to bring the military under control. He instituted a series of reforms under the guidance of the war ministers Michel Le Tellier (Meeshel Le Tell-yay, 1603–1685) and Le Tellier's son, the Marquis de Louvois (Loovwa, 1639–1691). A tableau of ranks, comparable to that used by most modern armies, established a hierarchy of command that in theory superseded civilian titles. The cost of quartering troops was allocated to entire provinces instead of to specific towns, and like military justice, financial

FIGURE 16.9 *Palace of Versailles.* This color engraving by Pierre Denis Martin shows the palace of Louis XIV as it looked in the eighteenth century. It was like a great city, inhabited by thousands of courtiers, officials, and servants, as well as a giant stage set that proclaimed the glory of the king. The vast gardens are in the distance.

arrangements for the army were placed under the control of the intendants.

On the battlefield, the French army abandoned the old combination of pike and shot in favor of volleys of musket fire from ranks that were rarely more than three deep. Based on the innovations of Gustav Adolph, this tactic required regular drills and marching in step, practices that had first been introduced by Maurice of Nassau but generally ignored by other armies. To improve discipline and unit cohesion, barracks, uniforms, and standardized muskets had all been adopted by 1691. Combined with the scientific principles of siege warfare perfected by Sébastian le Prestre de Vauban (Say'-bas-tyan Le Pre-tr de Vo-ban, 1633–1707), the reforms of Le Tellier and Louvois created what might be called the first modern army. Louis gave it ample opportunity to prove itself.

The Wars of Louis XIV.

In the early years of his reign, Louis pursued an aggressive and, in the best French tradition, anti-Hapsburg, foreign policy. His invasion of the Spanish Netherlands in 1667–1668 brought him into conflict with the Dutch republic, which he tried to destroy in a bitter war that lasted from 1672 to 1679. Faced with almost certain destruction, the Dutch overthrew their government and made William of Orange (later **William III of England,** lived 1650–1702) stadtholder. Holland saved itself by flooding the countryside, and William's diplomacy brought Spain, Sweden, Brandenburg, and the Holy Roman Empire into the war. France fought them all to a standstill, but the alliance was a precursor of things to come.

Emboldened by the favorable terms he had negotiated at the Peace of Nijmegen (1679), Louis then tried to annex all territories that had ever belonged to France, whether in the Netherlands, Italy, the Pyrenees, or the Rhineland. Hostility to the Holy Roman Empire made him the only Christian prince to oppose the liberation of Hungary from the Turks (1682–1699), although it was at last achieved with the assistance of **Eugene of Savoy** (1663–1736), a prince who had been raised at his court and who became one of his most formidable enemies as the Hapsburg Empire's leading general. At the same time, Louis's revocation of the Edict of Nantes and expulsion of the Huguenots in 1685 further alienated Europe's Protestants.

The basic issue at stake in the wars of Louis XIV was not, however, religion but rather the control of property in Europe and overseas. Louis's enemies believed that he aimed at nothing less than French hegemony, and by 1689, nearly all of Europe had turned against him. For the rest of his life, he followed a basically defensive policy, but it was too late. In the War of the League of Augsburg (1689–1697), Louis fought a powerful Anglo-Dutch coalition while France suffered through one of the worst economic depressions in its

MAP 16.1. THE WARS OF LOUIS XIV

- France in 1630
- Acquisitions to 1659 (minority of Louis XIV)
- Acquisitions to 1679
- Acquisitions to 1697 (Treaty of Ryswick)

Most of Louis's wars were fought to secure his frontiers with the Spanish Netherlands and the Holy Roman Empire. Each of them provoked the other European powers into forming coalitions that severely limited his gains.

history. In the **War of the Spanish Succession** (1701–1714), an allied army commanded by an Englishman, John Churchill, Duke of **Marlborough** (Mall'-bur-ruh, 1650–1722), consistently defeated his forces. This war and its predecessor were true world wars in that they involved conflict at sea and on distant continents. Not even France could sustain such burdens indefinitely, and when the Sun King died in 1715, the country was in a severe, if temporary, decline.

The power of Louis XIV was not unlimited. Within France, local privilege still thwarted his intentions, and parlements acting as appellate courts sometimes rejected his edicts on legal grounds. Law and custom frustrated his efforts to solve basic problems of finance. Until the French Revolution of 1789, the provinces continued to pay different taxes at different rates, based largely on agreements negotiated when they became part of the kingdom in the Middle Ages. Financial administration, although no worse than in many early modern states, remained primitive. The French kings borrowed against future tax revenues, which they then farmed out to their creditors for collection. This kind of **tax-farming** by private individuals was not only inefficient but also woefully corrupt and left no room for the sophisticated financial practices being devised by Louis's Dutch and English rivals.

France as a Model for Other Princes

The Hapsburgs. Despite these shortcomings and the uneven success of Louis's foreign policy, the France of Louis XIV became a model for other princes. From Spain to the Urals, they copied his court etiquette, his system of military and administrative organization, and even the architectural style of Versailles, which became the pattern for dozens of palaces and country estates. The last Hapsburg king of Spain, Charles II "the Bewitched," died childless in 1700, and the final war of Louis's reign was waged to place a member of his own Bourbon dynasty on the Spanish throne. The new ruler, Louis's grandson Philip V (reigned 1700–1746), began a process of reform that by 1788 had created a near replica of French administration.

After 1555, the eastern Hapsburgs devoted most of their efforts to building a multiethnic empire based on Austria and Bohemia. The victory of Eugene of Savoy over the Turks in 1683 enabled them to annex most of Hungary 1699. The Austrian archduke Charles (1685–1740), although he failed to gain Spanish support as the rival of Philip V in the War of the Spanish Succession, took the Spanish Netherlands as a consolation prize at the Peace of Utrecht in 1713. This territory, present-day Belgium, was also incorporated into the Austrian Empire. After his election as emperor in 1711, Charles, now known as Charles VI, began to reform the far-flung Austrian administration on French lines.

Most of the German princes followed suit, although it could be argued that Frederick Wilhelm I of Prussia (1688–1740) had already carried reform beyond anything achieved by Louis XIV. Set without geographical defenses in the midst of the northern German plain, Brandenburg-Prussia had been devastated in the Thirty Years' War and remained vulnerable to the shifts of central European politics. A veteran of the War of the Spanish Succession, Frederick Wilhelm resolved to turn his kingdom into a military power of the first rank and ended by making its administration subservient to the army. After 1723, his government became little more than a branch of the *kriegskommisariat*, or war ministry, but his reforms laid the groundwork for Prussia's emergence as a major power.

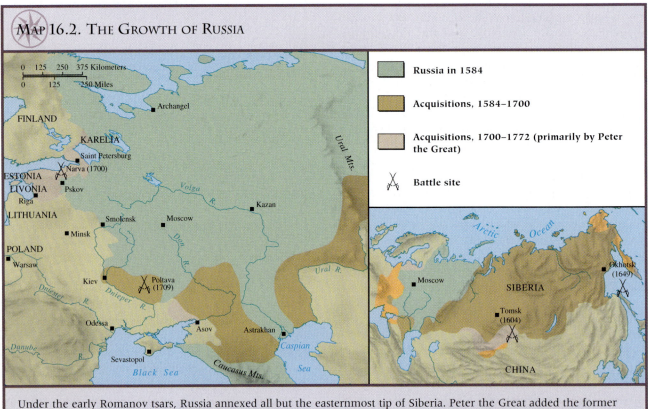

MAP 16.2. THE GROWTH OF RUSSIA

- Russia in 1584
- Acquisitions, 1584–1700
- Acquisitions, 1700–1772 (primarily by Peter the Great)
- ⚔ Battle site

Under the early Romanov tsars, Russia annexed all but the easternmost tip of Siberia. Peter the Great added the former Swedish provinces of Karelia, Estonia, and Livonia. When Peter died in 1725, Russia extended from the Baltic Sea to the Pacific Ocean.

FIGURE 16.10 *Peter the Great.* One of the tsar's greatest achievements was the construction of the city of St. Petersburg, built on pilings sunk into marshy ground near the mouth of the river Neva. He is shown here in an enamel in 1723 in front of the St. Paul and St. Peter Fortress and Trinity Square in his new capital.

Russia under Peter the Great. Perhaps the most spectacular efforts at reform were undertaken by Peter I "the Great" of Russia (1672–1725). Like Louis XIV, he had survived a turbulent regency in his youth and came to the throne determined to place his monarchy on a firmer basis. Peter realized that to do so he would have to copy western models, and he spent 1697–1698 traveling incognito to France, England, and the Netherlands as part of what he called the Grand Embassy. When he returned, he immediately began to institute reforms that, although western in inspiration, were carefully adapted to Russian conditions.

Using knowledge acquired firsthand in the shipyards of Holland and England, Peter supervised the building of a navy that could control the Baltic. He destroyed the *streltsy,* or palace guard, that formed the core of the Russian army and had long been a fruitful source of plots against the tsars and replaced it by an army organized on the French model. Peter, however, raised his troops through conscription for life, a method suggested by Louvois that could not be implemented in the less autocratic atmosphere of France. The new forces served him well. In the Great Northern War (1700–1720), he broke the power of Sweden and established Russian control over Estonia, Karelia, and Livonia. To consolidate his gains and to provide Russia with an all-weather port, he built the modern city of St. Petersburg near the mouth of the Neva River and made it his capital.

Internally, Peter established a series of colleges or boards to supervise the work of thirteen new governmental departments and divided the country into fifty provinces, each with its own governor appointed by himself. He created a table of ranks for civilian officials and opened state service for the first time to men of middle-class origin. To compensate the hereditary nobility for its loss of state positions, Peter abandoned the distinction between *pomest'e* and hereditary lands and introduced primogeniture. In some cases, he resorted to large-scale distributions of land and serfs. The condition of the latter predictably worsened, and peasant rebellions during the eighteenth century were put down with memorable savagery.

The Emergence of England as a World Power

The system created by Peter the Great was more autocratic than its western models—and more permanent. It lasted without major modifications into the nineteenth century. The situation in England was very different. Although **Charles II** (1660–1685) reclaimed his father's throne in 1660, the fundamental issue of sovereignty had not been resolved. Like his predecessors, Charles did not like to call Parliament into session, and the taxpaying gentry proved as unwilling as ever to provide adequate support for the crown. Shrewd, affable, and personally popular, the new king avoided open confrontations with his subjects, but poverty limited his freedom of action. For a time he even accepted a pension from Louis XIV, who hoped for English support against the Dutch. For this reason, England did not for some time develop the administrative structures that were being adopted on the continent.

The Creation of a New English Navy. Only in the creation of a modern navy could the English keep pace. Before 1660, England, like other countries, had possessed a handful of fighting ships supplemented in time of war by contracting with private owners who provided both ships and crews for the duration of hostilities. No permanent officer corps existed, and men who owed their positions to civilian rank or to military experience on land typically commanded the fleets. Administration was minimal, often temporary, and usually corrupt. The success of 1588 and the remarkable performance of the Commonwealth navies showed that such fleets could do well if properly motivated. But the system as a whole was analogous to military contracting on land: at best inefficient and at worst uncontrollable.

Both Charles II and his brother James, Duke of York (1633–1701), had a deep interest in naval affairs, and their unswerving support of secretary of the Admiralty **Samuel Pepys** (Peeps, 1633–1703) enabled him to introduce reforms that, in effect, created the English navy. Pepys, who is probably best known today for his famous diary, created a permanent corps of naval officers who attained their rank by the passage of formal examinations. To ensure their availability when needed, the navy kept them on half-pay when not at sea. He improved provisioning and repair facilities and increased the number of royal ships under the command of a reformed Admiralty. By the end of the century, even tactics had been changed to permit better control of battle fleets.

The Glorious Revolution.

But a reformed fleet was in itself no guarantor of world-power status. As Louis XIV's minister of finance and related matters, Colbert had introduced similar measures in France only to have his plans abandoned during the fiscal crisis of the 1690s. Great ships, like great armies, need a consistent supply of money. Ironically, England achieved this only by overthrowing the men who had made the naval reforms possible. When Charles II died in 1685, his brother ascended the throne as James II. A convert to Roman Catholicism, James instituted policies that alienated virtually every segment of the English elite, and in the fall of 1688, they deposed him in favor of his daughter Mary and her husband, William of Orange. As stadtholder of the Netherlands and King of England, William III brought the island nation into the Grand Alliance against Louis XIV.

The Glorious Revolution, as it is called, changed the basis of English politics. By overthrowing one king and effectively appointing another, Parliament and those it represented had at last resolved the issue of sovereignty. Parliament and not the king would rule England. Under William and again under his sister-in-law Anne (reigned 1702–1714), Parliament showed an unprecedented willingness to open its purse and support massive outlays for war, knowing that a weakened monarchy could not use the money to subvert the freedoms of its subjects.

England's Economic Growth.

The wealth that underwrote England's command of the sea and financed the campaigns of Marlborough on land came from nearly a century of unparalleled economic growth. England's growing commercial strength was based in part on geographical advantage. Faced with the implacable hostility of Louis XIV, the Dutch had to spend much of their wealth defending their borders on land. England, an island, was spared this expense. Moreover, with their deep-water ports and location to windward of the continent, the English could disrupt Dutch trade and steal their markets by blocking access via the English Channel. The Anglo-Dutch wars of 1652–1653, 1665–1666, and 1672–1673 were fought over this issue. Dutch seamen acquitted themselves well, but the cost of battles in which more than 100 ships might be engaged on each side, together with the need to provide convoys for trading vessels even in peacetime, gradually eroded their competitive advantage (see Document 16.5).

English Finances.

Even favorable geography could not have given England a decisive lead had it not been for a system of credit and finance that became the envy of Europe. The revolution of 1688 paved the way for the land tax of 1692 and the extension of excise taxes to a wide range of consumer goods. England acquired the benefits of permanent taxation for the first time in its history. The Bank of England, established in 1694, then stabilized English finances by underwriting government war loans. In the eighteenth century, it became the first of Europe's central banks, allowing private bankers to draw on its reserve in periods of financial crisis.

TABLE 16.1 ENGLISH TRADE BALANCES

The most active phase of the War of the Spanish Succession lasted from 1701 to 1711. During that period, the English lost 1,061 merchant ships to enemy raiders, with the worst year being 1702. At the same time, the English balance of trade (surplus of exports over imports) increased enormously, owing primarily to increased exports of cloth and grain to Portugal, Holland, Germany, and Russia and to decreased imports from France and Spain. Because the increase in trade more than compensated for the subsidies sent to the continent for war, the British were, in mercantilist terms, net beneficiaries of the war. The extra-European trade balance in the table to the right refers to trade with non-European partners.

Question: How did the policies described in Document 16.5 contribute to the results shown in this table?

Year	Extra-European Trade Balance	Overall Trade Balance
1699–1701	£489,000	£974,000
1702	233,000	971,000
1703	515,000	1,745,000
1704	968,000	1,519,000
1706	836,000	2,705,000
1707	672,000	2,024,000
1708	630,000	2,022,000
1709	271,000	2,111,000
1710	825,000	2,486,000
1711	969,000	2,731,000

Adapted from Jones, D. W., *War and Economy in the Age of William III and Marlborough* (Oxford: Basil Blackwell, 1988, p. 220).

DOCUMENT 16.5

HELVETIUS ON DUTCH TRADE IN DECLINE

The problem of maintaining Dutch trade reached a crisis during the War of the Spanish Succession (1702–1713) when war closed many of traditional markets. The following memo was presented to the French Foreign Minister in 1706 by Adrianus Engelhard Helvetius, a Swiss-born physician who dealt in medical supplies and made several visits to the Netherlands as a French spy during the War of the Spanish Succession. At the time he wrote, England and the Netherlands were firm allies.

The commerce of the United Provinces in Europe has never been in worse condition than it is today. During the course of earlier wars, although Dutch vessels were also open to the attacks of privateers, at least they could take refuge in the Atlantic and in the Mediterranean ports under Spanish rule, which are now closed to them. Furthermore, even when they were completely barred from the trade of France, they still continued to ply both the Baltic trades, which they continue to enjoy, and the trades of Spain, the kingdoms of Naples and Sicily, and Spanish Flanders, which now they have good reason to miss. Not only is the market greatly reduced for their cloth, both of their own manufacture as well as that made in India and the Baltic, and for their other wares, spices, salt fish, etc., but they are also deprived of the profitable return trade in wool, wine, and necessary commodities. . . .

As a result, there are frequent bankruptcies, word of which scares people and discourages them from entrusting money to the merchants, whose own funds are limited, as they are in the habit of doing in peacetime. This decline even effects the domestic commerce of the country, which is suffering badly, especially thanks to the cunning manipulations of the English, who take advantage of the opportunity to raise themselves upon the ruins of their allies.

The English, a people as fierce as they are capable, being convinced that the States General need their help so badly that they would not dare dispute anything with them, follow the maxim of making the Dutch pay their auxiliary troops, even when they are engaged in battle. They supply them with goods of every kind, sending cloth and Indian fabrics which are forbidden in England, butter, tallow, even manufactured candles, grain, etc., and in this they manage to make a profit on the support of troops for which they ought to be paying themselves.

From Helvetius, "Mémoire sur l'état présent du Gouvernment des Provinces Unis," in M. van der Bijl, ed., *Bijdragen en Mededeldingen van het Historisch Genootschap* 80 (1966, pp. 171–180); trans. Herbert H. Rowen, *The Low Countries in Early Modern Times. A Documentary History* (New York: Harper Row, 1972, pp. 226–227).

Question: What does Helvetius see as the primary reasons for Dutch decline?

Credit, backed by reliable taxation, paid for the fleet, Marlborough's armies, and the large subsidies that England paid to its continental allies. England, which became Great Britain when it merged with Scotland in 1707, was therefore able to expand its empire and protect its markets more easily than the Dutch, whose war fleet declined after 1673 and whose decentralized institutions blocked the formation of more effective credit mechanisms. English trade, which had been expanding steadily throughout the seventeenth century, became a flood during the War of the Spanish Succession when the British navy swept the seas of all rivals. In time, the enormous wealth derived largely from overseas markets would provide the capital for the Industrial Revolution and further strengthen English claims to great power status.

ECONOMIC AND SOCIAL CHANGE IN THE 1600s

Mercantilism. The economic policy that underlay these developments is called **mercantilism.** Mercantilism was not really a theory but rather a set of assumptions that had long been implicit in the rivalries between states and in the beginnings of European expansion overseas. Accepted by nearly everyone, these assumptions were applied with unusual consistency by Colbert as Louis XIV's Minister of Finance. Modern economists normally define a nation's wealth as the total value of its goods and services. Mercantilists defined wealth as a nation's store of gold and silver. This was in part because cash paid for war and therefore could be translated directly into power and prestige. Because they defined wealth in monetary terms and because economic growth rates are typically slow in preindustrial societies, mercantilist theory saw the world's wealth, for all practical purposes, as a fixed quantity. Economic and military policy was therefore a zero-sum game, the purpose of which was to acquire a surplus of gold and silver at the expense of one's neighbors. The mercantilists tried to achieve this by ensuring that exports exceeded imports. A country should become as self-sufficient as possible while encouraging the development of trades that might find an external market for their products.

The Importance of Overseas Empire. To Colbert and his contemporaries in other lands, this meant protection of the home market through tariffs and the

FIGURE 16.11 *Jean Baptiste Colbert (1619–1683).* Perhaps the most gifted minister of Louis XIV, Colbert was the architect of the king's mercantilist policies and the creator of the French navy. He also supported the sciences and founded the French Royal Academy.

development of an overseas empire that could produce commodities unavailable in the mother country. Ideally, an empire should have varied components: tropical colonies to produce dyewoods, sugar, cotton, indigo, and chocolate and northern colonies to produce timber, furs, and naval stores. The colonies would produce these raw materials in return for manufactured goods from home. Every effort was made to subsidize the manufacture of luxury items that could be shipped to the colonists or sold to unwary foreigners for cash.

To protect trade and colonies, a fighting navy was essential, for the line between war and commerce was necessarily blurred. The goal of both was wealth and power, and trade was "war by other means." War, in the mercantilist view, was the normal state of things, whereas peace was an aberration, a temporary lull between periods of hostility. The European game of annexations and sieges was therefore extended to every corner of the globe. Conflicts with parochial names like the War of the League of Augsburg and the War of the Spanish Succession were actually the first world wars in history.

The Redistribution of Wealth. Expanded trade did not, however, create universal prosperity. It increased the number of professionals and created job opportunities for a growing middle class of bookkeepers, accountants, and small tradesmen, but it also concentrated immense wealth in the hands of a few. In England, some of these investors were merchants and bankers, whereas others were great landholders who invested in trade. The aristocratic prejudice against commerce largely vanished in the seventeenth century, in part because the composition of the titled nobility had changed. Families remained who could trace their ancestry to the remote feudal past, but many more had been ennobled for their services to the monarchy in more recent times. Their immediate ancestors had been lawyers or servants of the crown, and they continued to maintain close ties with the urban world from which they had come. This was as true in France or Germany as it was in England. It had always been the case in Italy, and even in Spain the fabled prohibition against *hidalgos* (literally, "sons of somebody") engaging in trade was largely ignored.

It could hardly have been otherwise. Those who turned their back on new sources of wealth eventually lost both power and status. Commerce, even if it were conducted at one remove by investing with urban bankers and merchants, had become for many aristocrats the primary source of new capital. They committed much of this new wealth to ostentation in an effort to maintain their social position and to ensure access to the royal court, but much of it was also reinvested.

Social Stratification. Capital accumulated by trade would later provide the massive sums needed for the Industrial Revolution, but it did nothing to halt the growth of rural poverty and may actually have increased it by accelerating the capitalization of land, a process that had been underway since the fourteenth century. One effect of increased trade was therefore to intensify social polarization. In the seventeenth and eighteenth centuries, the rich grew richer while the poor grew poorer.

The degradation of peasant life was most obvious in those regions that provided agricultural produce for the world market. The growing European demand for grain encouraged Russian, Polish, and Prussian landholders to impose or extend the institution of serfdom. Production for export was best achieved on huge estates whose labor force could be minutely controlled. Left to their own devices, peasants would diversify crops and develop other economic strategies to enhance their own security. To landholders, this diversion of effort prevented them from maximizing their profits. Serfdom, like New World slavery, was therefore a way to "industrialize" agriculture, but by limiting peasant survival strategies, it dramatically reduced rural standards of living while enriching those who were already wealthy.

Social stratification was almost as great in England, the center of commercial growth. The condition of English peasants may have improved for a time after the Black Death, but it declined steadily after the mid-fifteenth century. The rich were better able than the poor to invest in land, develop it, and profit from the cultivation of cash crops. Smallholders found it increasingly difficult to compete. Royal policy compounded the problem by supporting the retention of feudal ties while permitting the enclosure of common lands. This was the process, described in Chapter 12, by which landholders appropriated land previously shared by the inhabitants of an entire village.

TABLE 16.2 ENGLISH WAGES AND PRICES, 1541–1702

A comparison between wages and prices shows that while the former doubled between 1541 and 1702, the price of ordinary food items tripled. The result was a severe decline in the living standards of laboring families. It should be noted, however, that most contemporaries thought English workers were far more prosperous than their counterparts in France or the Netherlands, and richer still than the peasants of central and eastern Europe.

LABOR	1541–1582	1583–1642	1643–1702
Weekly Wages			
Farmhand	3s. 3d.	4s. 10d.	6s. 4¾d.
Mason	4s. 10d.	6s. 5¾d.	9s. 10¾d.
Carpenter	5s.	6s. 2¾d.	10s. 2¾d.
Prices			
Wheat (quarter)*	13s. 10½d.	36s. 9d.	41s. 11½d
Barley (quarter)	8s. 5¾d.	19s. 9¾d.	22s. 2½d.
Oatmeal (quarter)	20s. 4¾d.	37s. 9¼d.	52s. 11d.
Chicken (1)	1d.	3d.	1s. 4d.
Goose (1)	4d.	1s. 4d.	3s.
Beer (barrel)	2s.		10s.

*A quarter, the standard measure for grains, equaled one-quarter of a hundredweight, or 25 pounds.
2 pence (d.) = 1 shilling (s.).
Figures adapted from Burnett, John, *A History of the Cost of Living* (Harmondsworth, UK: Pelican Books, 1969, pp. 71, 80–81).

Question: Try to calculate on a percentage basis how much wages rose between 1541 and 1702 and how much food prices rose during the same period. (*Hint:* To get the percent increase, convert monies in a given row to pence, then divide the total pence in the first column by the total pence in the last column.)

TABLE 16.3 ENGLISH INCOMES, 1688

In 1688, Gregory King (1648–1722) published his estimates of population and incomes in England. He believed that the number of merchants, shopkeepers, and artisans had increased but that the incomes of poor people had declined. The income figures are in millions of pounds sterling.

CLASS	NUMBER OF FAMILIES	INCOME	% OF FAMILIES	% OF INCOME
Nobility, gentry, officials	53,000	9.816	4	23
Merchants and traders	10,000	2.400	1	5
Freeholders and farmers	330,000	16.960	24	39
Shopkeepers and artisans	100,000	4.200	7	10
Military officers and clergy	19,000	1.120	2	2
Laborers, servants, paupers, seamen, common soldiers, etc.	849,000	9.010	62	21
Total	1,361,000	43.506	100	100

From King, Gregory, "Natural and Political Observations," in G. E. Barnett, ed., *Two Tracts by Gregory King* (Baltimore: Johns Hopkins, 1936, p. 31).

Question: In what ways do you think these figures might differ from those in a modern industrial country such as the United States?

Deprived of the marginal income that enabled them to survive, thousands of peasants surrendered their properties and left their homes with little more than the clothes on their backs.

Unemployment and Migration to the Cities.
Most found it difficult, if not impossible, to find work. The shift toward grazing reduced the demand for agricultural labor, while population growth after the midfifteenth century depressed wages. The situation worsened throughout the sixteenth and seventeenth centuries. Increased criminal activity and a growing population of "sturdy beggars" alarmed the authorities, but poor laws, based on the assumption that poverty and homelessness were the results of deliberate choice, accomplished nothing. Neither migration to America nor the expansion of urban employment fully relieved the pressure. Eighteenth-century London may have

been the commercial center of the world, but its slums became as enormous as its wealth. Unable to find work, England's dispossessed became a vast urban proletariat whose squalid, gin-soaked existence was immortalized in the drawings of William Hogarth (1697–1764) and in the novels of Henry Fielding (1707–1754).

In some regions, capitalization of the land encouraged social stratification without a major increase in trade. Spanish peasants, faced from the 1580s with heavy taxation and declining yields, borrowed money from urban investors to improve their land. When they found themselves unable to redeem their *censos* (a form of bond), the holders foreclosed and seized their property. By 1650, the population of Madrid had swelled to more than 100,000 as displaced peasants sought charity from the city's many religious houses and from an increasingly hard-pressed government. Lawyers, speculators, and officials amassed large estates but provided only inefficient absentee ownership.

The Costly Freedom of the French Peasant.
Although the French crown resisted the consolidation of properties common to virtually every other part of Europe, prosperity in the countryside remained elusive. Since the fifteenth century, French courts had generally supported peasant rights against those of the landowning nobility. The reasons were largely political—supporting the claims of peasants tended to break up concentrations of aristocratic power in the countryside—but by 1700, French peasants had become the freest in Europe.

FIGURE 16.12 *Peasants in Front of Their House, Le Nain (Early 1600s).* Economic growth did not affect all segments of the population equally. The gap between rich and poor increased in many parts of Europe. These French peasants, shown before their ramshackle house, have not benefitted from the changes in the economy.

Unfortunately, the wars of Louis XIV made them among the most heavily taxed. They had exchanged their oppressive landholders for a no less demanding king. At the same time, the increase of private ownership in an age of demographic growth led inevitably to the subdivision of properties. Partible inheritance remained the norm in France, and although more than half of the rural population owned a plot of land at century's end, it was rarely big enough to support a family. Thousands of peasants were forced into the labor market to pay their taxes at a time when wages had already begun to decline. Terrible famines in the 1690s showed that freedom in itself offered little protection against hunger.

Attitudes toward the Poor.
The growth of poverty did not go unnoticed by the more fortunate. Although in retrospect it seems obvious that it was caused by changes in economic relationships that had been aggravated by endemic warfare and the meager harvests of the Little Ice Age, contemporaries drew other conclusions. The attitude toward the poor began to change.

In medieval theory, if not always in practice, the poor were specially favored by God and entitled to charity. Begging symbolized the apostolic poverty of the friars, and the church regarded the giving of alms, whether to the church or to the poor, as a good work and a mark of piety. In the more conservative Catholic regions of southern Europe, this view persisted into modern times, but in the north, it had been replaced by fear and apprehension well before the Reformation.

The city of Augsburg adopted punitive measures against beggars and the homeless in 1459. Paris followed in 1473. In 1495, an ordinance of Henry VII of England condemned vagrants to three days in the stocks, following which they were to be whipped and returned to their place of origin. It was to be a model for later English poor laws. Charles VIII of France in the following year decreed that beggars be sent to row in the galleys. In the decades to come, such humanists as Erasmus, More, and Juan Luis Vives wrote against begging, while religious reformers like Luther, Calvin, and Zwingli agreed that there was no virtue in poverty.

To Protestant theologians, work performed in a Christian spirit was sanctifying. One of the more enlightened approaches to poverty involved the establishment of workhouses in which vagrants and petty criminals could rehabilitate themselves through labor. The Amsterdam *rasphuis* (rahsp'-house), founded at the beginning of the seventeenth century, was a model institution.

Inmates worked 12 to 14 hours a day turning logs of Brazil wood into sawdust so that the powder could be incorporated into dyes. The monotony of their day was enlivened by sermons and floggings. The city established a similar institution for poor women, who spun endless yards of thread to be sold by the city government. The idea behind all of these measures was that the poor were willfully lazy and that they could be reformed only if subjected to rigorous discipline.

The Rise of Gentility. Hostility to the poor was encouraged by their frightening numbers and by the many popular revolts that had occurred between the Black Death and the Great Peasants' War of 1524–1525. Virtually everyone understood that economic polarization posed a threat to the social order. What they did not understand was that the effects of polarization were being augmented by a redefinition of elite values that, consciously or not, dehumanized the poor in the eyes of their "betters."

The European elite had always justified their privilege by claiming some form of superiority. The knights of the first feudal age had taken pride in their strength and courage. In the absence of an immediate threat to society, their descendants had declared such qualities hereditary and enhanced them by cultivating chivalric courtesy. The early modern elite retained a self-proclaimed monopoly of these virtues and merged them with others that reflected the values of Renaissance humanism and of the late medieval urban life from which it had emerged. Refinement of taste and intellect became the new hallmarks of status.

Much of this gentility derived from a common education. Minimal acquaintance with the classics and an appreciation for classic aesthetics was essential. The gentleman or gentlewoman valued harmony, symmetry, and balance. Classical standards were reflected not only in the high-minded dramas of Racine or Calderón but in the architecture of Andrea Palladio (1518–1580). Baroque art and architecture, with its rich decoration and extravagant visual harmonies, gradually gave way to a more restrained style based on what was thought to have been the taste of ancient Rome. This Palladian interpretation of Roman aesthetics became the model for hundreds of palaces, country houses, and churches and persisted well into the nineteenth century. Its influence may be seen in the reconstruction of London by Sir Christopher Wren (1632–1723) after the great fire of 1666.

As the seventeenth century wore on, "reason," too, became important in the sense that those who wished to be thought "gentle" rejected superstition and extreme religiosity in favor of a more detached, "scientific" view of the world. The new science encouraged people to believe that the divine order was rational rather than providential or based on frequent interventions by a wrathful deity. A growing faith in the possibility of a rationally ordered society accompanied the growth of absolutism, while holistic, magical, or apocalyptic visions—and sometimes the display of emotion itself—became the province of the poor and ignorant.

Manners and Deportment. Manners and deportment were an even more important mark of status. Those who wished to be taken seriously adopted models of carriage, speech, and gesture based equally on courtly models and on the precepts of the classical rhetoricians. The stage, with its abundance of noble characters, provided instruction for those who lacked access to polite society. Table manners improved with the introduction of the fork, and books were written as guides to correct behavior. In time, the natural movements of ordinary people came to seem crude and loutish.

Clothing. Clothing, too, mirrored the growing separation between the classes as the fashions of the rich became ever more elaborate and expensive. Men in particular cultivated the art of magnificence with lace collars, massive wigs, and brocaded waistcoats that were sometimes trimmed in gold. To be seen in one's own hair was unacceptable even on the battlefield.

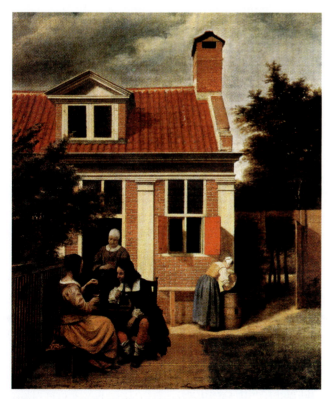

FIGURE 16.13 *A Country Cottage, 1665.* The size and prosperity of the middle class increased in both England and the Netherlands during the seventeenth century. This modest but elegant Dutch cottage was painted with its genteel inhabitants by Pieter de Hooch. Order and cleanliness have obviously become important values.

FIGURE 16.14 *The Triumph of Elegance.* Elegance, education, and taste replaced military values as the major claim to status. This painting by Dirck van Delen (1605–1671) shows ladies and gentlemen dancing sedately in an elegant room. Their elaborate ruffled collars were a very expensive status symbol and aroused the anger of moralists who periodically sought to ban the fashion.

Chimneys and glazed windows became common in the homes of town dwellers and in those of the richer peasants, while inventories of household goods began to show a steady increase in chairs, tables, and linens.

CONCLUSION

The political troubles of the late sixteenth and early seventeenth centuries did not preclude extraordinary developments in other areas. The Scientific Revolution changed the way Europeans thought about the physical universe. England, France, and above all, the Netherlands challenged the Iberian powers and created substantial empires of their own. In the process, they greatly expanded Europe's presence in world markets and accumulated capital in unprecedented amounts. The Netherlands emerged, however briefly, as a major power and a center of high culture. Eventually, states that had been nearly shattered by a century of war and revolution began to reconstruct themselves, reforming their governmental institutions, curbing the power of the local elite, and gaining control over the armies and navies whose independence had threatened to engulf them. The model for many of these changes was the France of Louis XIV, but the rise of England as an economic and naval power would have an even greater influence on the age to come.

Ordinary people tried to imitate the dress and bearing of the upper classes, but education, good manners, and a suit that cost as much as a middle class family's annual income were hard to counterfeit. "Presumption" of this sort was met with ridicule and often with violence, for upper-class men still carried swords or weighted canes and used them freely on those they regarded as inferior, but another mark of gentility, the idea of comfort, adapted more easily to the lives of ordinary people.

Domestic Comfort and Elegance. Magnificence in domestic architecture grew during the sixteenth century. The French royal palace known as the Louvre, the great chateaux built along the river Loire in the time of Francis I, and the country houses of Tudor England were legitimate ancestors of Versailles. But like Versailles, they subordinated comfort to grandeur. Their furniture, like that of the medieval castle, remained minimal. The great houses of the later seventeenth century were no less ostentatious, but their owners packed them with furnishings in the modern manner. Chairs, tables, carpets, and whatnots proliferated. Although rooms were still set aside for ceremonial and social functions, they were supplemented by sitting rooms and other cozy spaces for the private enjoyment of the owner's family. The sheer luxury of these interiors could not be matched by ordinary households, and tens of thousands of Europeans continued to huddle in wretched cottages, but the general level of domestic comfort rose steadily after about 1650.

Review Questions

- What did earlier intellectual movements contribute to the Scientific Revolution?
- How did the Dutch and English organize their first empires, and what accounts for the difference?
- How did the armies and navies of 1700 differ from those of 1648?
- What was the purpose of such palaces as Versailles?

For Further Study

Readings

Black, Jeremy, *European Warfare, 1660–1815* (New Haven, CT: Yale University Press, 1994). A clear, concise analysis of warfare as it developed in the seventeenth and eighteenth centuries.

Braudel, Fernand, *Civilization and Capitalism, 15th–18th Centuries*, 3 vols. trans. S. Reynolds (New York: Harper and Row, 1981–1984). Long, but filled with ideas and information on the development of the economy and material life in preindustrial Europe.

Schama, Simon, *The Embarrassment of Riches: An Interpretation of Dutch Culture in the Golden Age* (New York: Knopf, 1987). An insightful, beautifully illustrated portrait of Dutch culture at its peak.

Westfall, Richard S., *The Life of Isaac Newton* (Cambridge: Cambridge University Press, 1993). A good, recent biography of a complex figure.

Wolf, John B., *Louis XIV* (New York: W.W. Norton, 1968). A readable biography.

InfoTrac College Edition

For additional reading, go to your online research library at *http://infotrac.thomsonlearning.com*.

Using Key Terms, enter the search terms:

Copernicus	*Galileo* not *Jupiter*
Isaac Newton	*Mercantilism*
Louis XIV	*Peter the Great*

Web Site

http://es.rice.edu/ES/humsoc/Galileo
The Galileo Project. A cleverly designed site produced by Rice University covering nearly every aspect of Galileo's life and work.

EUROPE, 1600–1715

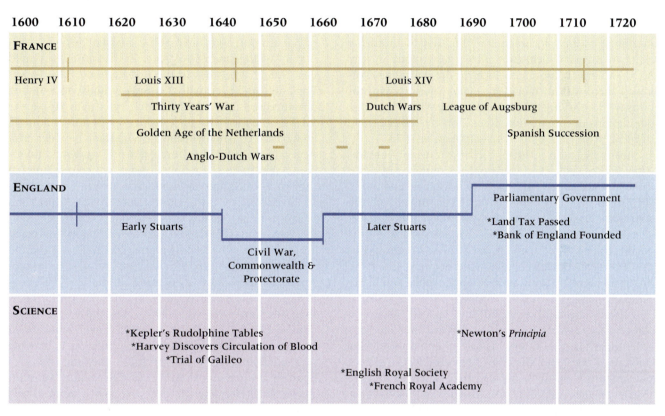

Visit the Western Civilization Companion Web Site for resources specific to this textbook:
http://history.wadsworth.com/hause02/

The CD in the back of this book and the Western Civilization Resource Center at *http://history.wadsworth.com/western/* offer a variety of tools to help you succeed in this course, including access to quizzes; images; documents; interactive simulations, maps, and timelines; movie explorations; and a wealth of other sources.

The West in the World

EUROPE AND THE WORLD (1400–1700)

The relative isolation of Europe ended after 1400. Europeans embarked on a series of explorations and conquests that revealed continents previously unknown to them and involved them in the commerce of the entire world. The Portuguese led the way with their exploration of the African coast. They did not penetrate the African interior, but they established trading stations from which they could import gold, ivory, and African slaves. By 1496, the Portuguese had found the sea route to India, and with it, a way to bypass the Arab–Italian monopoly of the spice trade. In 1500, they established a claim to Brazil, which grew into a vast colony on the South American continent. In Asia, the Portuguese followed their African model by establishing trading stations without trying to impose direct rule over the large populations of the interior. They soon established trade relations with China and reached Japan in 1543.

Meanwhile, the Spanish had encountered America. After the first voyage of Christopher Columbus in 1492, they quickly seized the Caribbean Islands and then, within 50 years, conquered the great empires of the Aztecs and Incas, societies whose existence they had not suspected in 1492. The Spanish conquests brought great wealth to Spain and made it, for a time, the greatest of the European powers. The conquerors established the Spanish language, the Roman Catholic faith, and many other elements of European culture throughout much of South and Central America, but they virtually destroyed Native American societies in the process. Epidemic diseases for which the Americans had no immunities killed millions, while Spain made a conscious effort to uproot native cultures in the belief that they posed an obstacle to conversion. The desire to gain converts for Catholic Christianity was an important component of Portuguese activity as well. The Jesuits, sailing on Portuguese ships, established missions in India, China, and Japan but had little or no impact on these societies as a whole. Their observations, however, did much to improve European knowledge of the Asian world.

Spanish and Portuguese success aroused the envy of other Europeans. By 1600, the French, Dutch, and English had begun to create empires of their own. All three founded colonies in the Caribbean and in North America, a vast region whose native population was far smaller and more politically fragmented than that of Mexico or Peru. In North America they began to settle the accessible regions near the coasts while driving Native Americans into the interior. By 1667, the English had overwhelmed the Dutch colonies in what is now New York and Delaware, but the French had established themselves on the St. Lawrence River in Canada and began to explore the Mississippi valley. Like Brazil, English and French colonies in the Caribbean and the English colonies in southern North America depended on slave labor. Between 1400 and 1800, almost 10 million Africans were taken from their homes by Europeans and sold in The New World.

The English and Dutch also contested Portugal's monopoly of the trade with Asia. Both countries created East India Companies in the first decade of the 1600s. England—and eventually France—established a trading presence in India, but the Dutch eventually drove the English and the Portuguese from what is now Indonesia and gained control over most of the trade between East Asia and Europe. The Dutch did not, however, dominate Asian trade as a whole, most of which remained in the hands of Chinese and Indian merchants.

Europe realized large profits from these ventures and began to import a host of new products, including coffee, tea, and tobacco. Sugar consumption increased enormously owing to new plantations in Brazil and the Caribbean, but Europeans were slower to accept American foods such as potatoes, tomatoes, chili peppers, and maize (corn). Most did not come into common use until the mid-1700s, and maize, the staple crop of Central and North America, never found favor except as a feed crop for animals. Cultural borrowing remained limited, if one excludes the imposition of Spanish culture on the Americas. Europeans found little to admire in the cultures they encountered, and would not make a sustained effort to understand them until much later.

Asians remained equally uninterested in Europe. India under the Mughal Empire (founded in 1526) and China under the Ming Dynasty (which replaced the Mongol Yuan Dynasty in 1368) were powerful, wealthy, and economically self-sufficient. Whenever possible, they ignored Europeans, whom they regarded as ignorant barbarians. That was about to change. In the 1700s, European wars would expand to include the new colonies and sometimes their Asian and African allies. People who had scarcely heard of Europe found themselves fighting and dying on every continent for European causes they did not understand.

EUROPE AND THE WORLD (1400–1700)

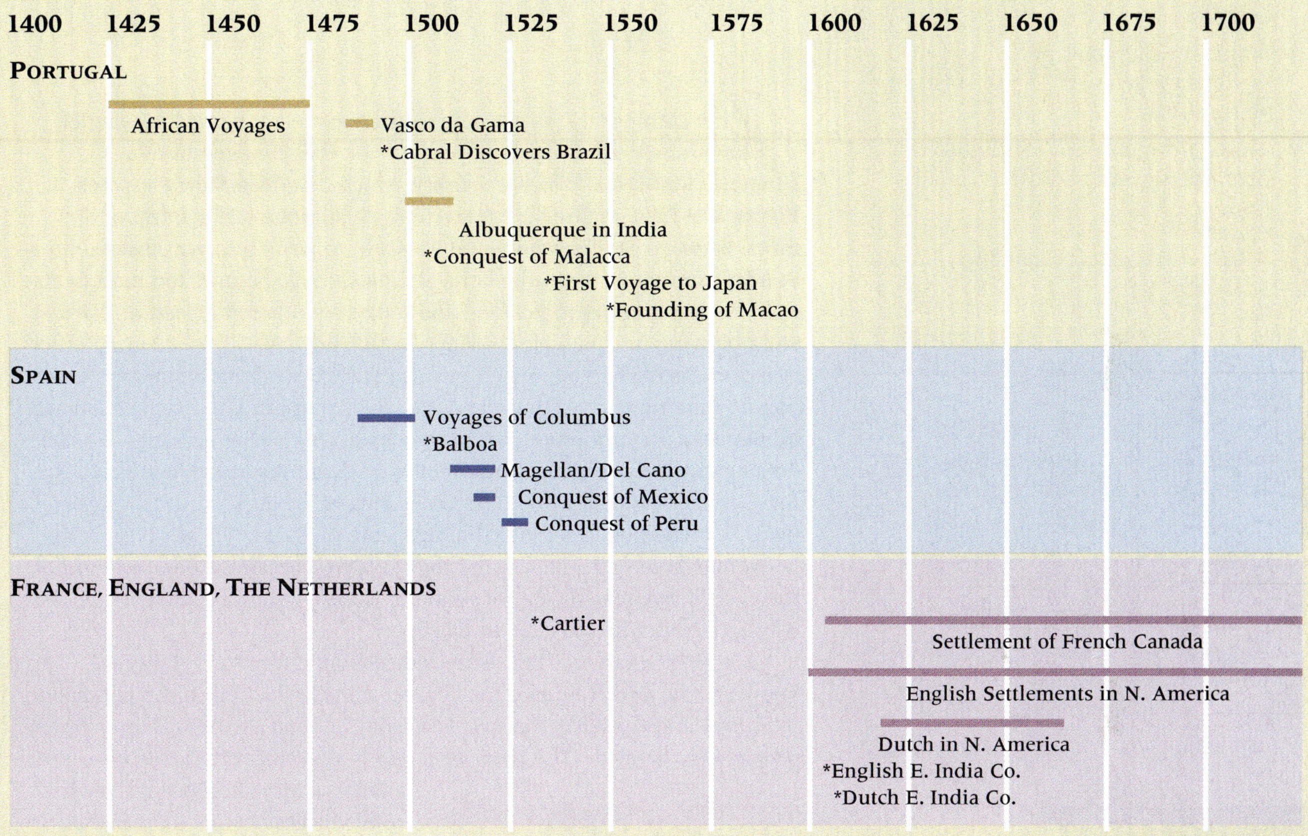

| 1400 | 1425 | 1450 | 1475 | 1500 | 1525 | 1550 | 1575 | 1600 | 1625 | 1650 | 1675 | 1700 |

PORTUGAL

African Voyages

Vasco da Gama
*Cabral Discovers Brazil

Albuquerque in India
*Conquest of Malacca
*First Voyage to Japan
*Founding of Macao

SPAIN

Voyages of Columbus
*Balboa
Magellan/Del Cano
Conquest of Mexico
Conquest of Peru

FRANCE, ENGLAND, THE NETHERLANDS

*Cartier

Settlement of French Canada

English Settlements in N. America

Dutch in N. America
*English E. India Co.
*Dutch E. India Co.

FOCUS QUESTIONS

- To what extent was the economy of the eighteenth century rural and agricultural?
- How did the primary social classes of the eighteenth century relate to the agricultural economy?
- How much variation existed within social classes, such as the peasantry or the aristocracy?
- What was the place of the urban economy in the eighteenth century?

Chapter 17

THE SOCIAL AND ECONOMIC STRUCTURE OF THE OLD REGIME

*I*n the spring of 1790, a young Russian aristocrat named Alexander Radishchev (Rod'-ih-shef), read a book that changed his life: Lawrence Sterne's *Sentimental Journey,* which described Sterne's travels in France and Italy. Radishchev undertook an arduous carriage trip of 400 miles, between St. Petersburg and Moscow, to write his own *Journey.* On a Sunday afternoon, when the bone-jarring carriage became too hard to endure, Radishchev began walking and soon encountered a peasant, hard at work plowing his small plot of land. Radishchev (who worked in an office as a customs official) expressed surprise at such work on a Sunday: "Have you no time to work during the week, then, and can you not have any rest on Sundays, in the hottest part of the day at that?" The peasant—a serf belonging to the local noble—answered with some surprise, "In a week, sir, there are six days, and we go six times a week to work on the master's fields. . . . The holidays [and] the nights are ours. If a fellow isn't too lazy, he won't starve to death." Radishchev's *Journey* became a denunciation of the evils of the near-slavery of serfdom, earning him a death sentence that was later commuted to exile to Siberia.

Chapter 17 examines the social and economic structure of this era, known as the **Old Regime.** The chapter starts by looking at the population of Europe and considers the social categories, then called *estates,* into which people were divided. (The term *social class* is a product of nineteenth-century analysis.) Most Europeans lived in rural villages, so this chapter then surveys the rural economy, including **preindustrial** manufacturing. This leads to a detailed examination of three major social categories: the aristocracy, the peasantry, and town dwellers. The urban economy leads to a discussion of national economies, covering mercantilism (the dominant economic philosophy of the Old Regime) and the global economy.

THE POPULATION OF EUROPE IN THE EIGHTEENTH CENTURY

Historians do not know with certainty how many people lived in Europe in 1680, or even in 1780. Governments did not yet record births and deaths (churches usually documented them), and they did not conduct a regular **census.** The first modern census in England was required by a law of 1800 and conducted in 1801. Isolated census data exist for the eighteenth century, such as a Swedish census of 1750 and the Spanish census of 1768–1769, but most population figures are estimates based on fragmentary records, local case studies, and demographic analysis.

Population Estimates. The best estimate is that Europe at the start of the eighteenth century had a total population of 120 to 130 million people (see Table 17.1)—less than one-seventh of the count at the end of the twentieth century. Spain, the richest world power of the sixteenth century, had a population of 9.2 mil-

lion in 1769. A good estimate of the population of Great Britain (England, Scotland, and Wales) at the beginning of the eighteenth century is 6.4 million—less than the population of London today. The strength of France during the Old Regime can be seen in its estimated population of 19.3 million in 1700. In all countries, most people lived in small villages and on isolated farms (see Table 17.2). Even in a city-state such as the republic of Venice, more than 80 percent of the population was rural. In France, one of the most developed countries of the Old Regime, the figure was more than 75 percent.

THE ECONOMIC STRUCTURES OF THE EIGHTEENTH-CENTURY RURAL WORLD

Open-Field Agriculture. Most Europeans lived, as their ancestors had, in small villages surrounded by open fields. The land was parceled for farming in many ways, but the general pattern was consistent: peasants and small farmers inhabited and worked land that belonged to aristocrats, the state, or the church. A typical village left some woodland standing (for gathering food and fuel), set aside some of the worst soil as wasteland (for grazing livestock), maintained some land as commonly owned, and left most of the land unfenced in **open fields.** Enclosed, or fenced in, fields were rare, but in

TABLE 17.1 ESTIMATED POPULATION OF EUROPE IN 1700

COUNTRY	POPULATION (IN MILLIONS)
France	19.3
European Russia	17.0
German states	13.5
Bavaria	2.4
Saxony (Dresden)	2.0
Prussia	1.6
Italian states	13.0
Two Sicilies	3.0
Papal states	2.0
Venice	1.8
Piedmont	1.7
Austrian Empire	11.0
Poland	9.0
Spain	7.5
Great Britain	6.4
Ottoman Empire	6.4
Ireland	2.5
Portugal	2.0
Holland	1.9
Sweden and Finland	1.5

Source: Mitchell, B. R., ed., *European Historical Statistics, 1750–1970* (London: Macmillan, 1975, pp. 17ff); and Babuscio, Jack, and Dunn, Richard M., eds., *European Political Facts, 1648–1789* (London: Macmillan, 1984, pp. 335ff).

Question: What do these data suggest about political and military power?

TABLE 17.2 THE RURAL AND URBAN POPULATIONS OF WESTERN EUROPE IN THE EIGHTEENTH CENTURY

AREA	1650	1700	1750	1800
Rural (in millions)	61.4	66.7	76.2	98.3
(as percentage)	91.0%	90.1%	89.9%	89.0%
Urban (in millions)	6.4	7.3	8.6	12.2
(as percentage)	9.0%	9.9%	10.1%	11.0%

Urban population based on towns of 10,000 or greater.

Sources: Based on data from Grigg, David B., *The Transformation of Agriculture in the West* (Oxford: Cambridge University Press, p. 65); and de Vries, Jan, *European Urbanization, 1500–1800* (Cambridge, MA: Harvard University Press, 1984).

Question: Do the data in the table prove that Europe was a rural civilization in the eighteenth century, or are other data and considerations needed?

VARIETIES OF AGRICULTURE IN THE EIGHTEENTH CENTURY

The vast majority of the population of Europe was engaged in agriculture in the eighteenth century, but many different systems of land use were practiced. The first figure shows how land was divided in long strips in a typical village in central Europe. The second figure, in contrast, shows the alternative system of enclosing land within boundaries. In strip farming, the strips might be reassigned (by the owner or by the village) on a regular basis and the land that a family worked might be spread around the community. Under the enclosed land system, the land more often had a single owner and was farmed by the same family each year. The following extract, a contract for sharecropping, shows that even within one of these systems there could be various arrangements for working the land.

Land Owned by the Church

Land Owned by Three Noble Families

Land Owned by a Wealthy Merchant

Land Owned by 250 Peasant Families

Open-Field Farming. Distribution by open strips.

some regions of western Europe—such as southwestern England, Brittany, and the Netherlands—the land was already subdivided by fences, stone walls, or hedgerows. **Enclosure** had occurred in some places to assist livestock farming and in others where peasants had been fortunate enough to acquire their own land. In most of Europe, however, the arable land was still farmed in the open-field system. From the midlands of England to eastern Europe (especially the German states and Russia), open fields were divided into long rectangular strips of approximately one acre each, defined by grass pathways between them (see *Varieties of Agriculture in the Eighteenth Century*). A peasant family usually worked several strips scattered around the community, plus a kitchen garden near home. This was an inefficient system but one that allowed the bad and good fields to be shared more equitably. In other regions of Europe (such as Spain, southern France, and Italy), the open fields were divided into small, irregular plots of land that peasant families farmed year after year.

Grains and Crop Rotation. Whatever system of land tenure was used, most plow land was planted with the grains on which the world lived—wheat, rye, barley, and oats. These crops were usually rotated annually, and each field laid fallow (unseeded) on a regular basis, normally every third year. Leaving a field unplanted conserved moisture, checked the spread of plant disease, and could help with the replacement of nitrates in the soil—important considerations because chemical fertilizers were unknown and animal manure was scarce. Fallow fields had the secondary advantage of providing additional pastureland for grazing.

Enclosed-Field Farming. Distribution by plot enclosed by hedgerows.

An Eighteenth-Century Sharecropping Contract

This list summarizes the chief points of a contract negotiated in southern France in 1779 on behalf of a great landowner. It was an agreement "at half fruits"—a 50/50 sharing of the crop between a marquis and the father and son who farmed his land. A study of this contract has estimated that this land would yield a harvest of 100 setiers *(set'-ee-a)* of wheat. Thus, the peasant sharecroppers paid (1) 20 setiers off the top to the marquis; then (2) 10 setiers of wheat as the price of cutting and flailing the wheat, leaving a harvest of 70 setiers. They then paid (3) 35 setiers as "half fruits" and (4) 20 setiers for seed. The result was 55 setiers to the marquis, 15 setiers for the peasant family. A family of five ate 20 setiers of wheat per year.

1. The lease shall be for one year, at "half fruits" and under the following conditions.
2. The lessees will furnish the seed.
3. Before the division of the harvest, the marquis will receive twenty setiers of wheat off the top.
4. The lessees will deliver the wheat already cut and flailed, at no cost to the marquis.
5. The lessees must use the "three field" system of planting— $\frac{1}{3}$ of the land planted to wheat, $\frac{1}{3}$ to some other grain, and $\frac{1}{3}$ left unplanted.
6. If the lessees do not leave $\frac{1}{3}$ of the land fallow, they forfeit the entire harvest.
7. All livestock will be held in common with profits and losses equally shared.
8. If there is a shortage of hay and straw for the livestock, the lessees must pay half of the cost of buying forage.
9. The lessees must maintain the land, including making drains for water, cutting brush, pruning vines . . . etc.
10. In addition to sharing the crop, the lessees must pay a rent of 72 chickens, 36 capons, and 600 eggs.
11. The lessees must raise pigs, geese, ducks, and turkeys, to be divided evenly; they must purchase the young animals to raise at their own expense.
12. The lessees must make their own ploughs and pay for the blacksmith work themselves.

Source: Forster, Robert, and Forster, Elborg, eds., *European Society in the Eighteenth Century* (New York: Harper & Row, 1969).

Question: Judging from this contract, do sharecroppers seem to have a stronger or weaker position compared to other peasants?

Tull, Townshend, and the Science of Agriculture. Scientific **agronomy**—the study of field-crop production and soil management—was in its infancy in the Old Regime, but noteworthy changes were appearing. In Britain, the improvements suggested by the studies of Jethro Tull and the Viscount Charles Townshend significantly increased eighteenth-century harvests. Tull, a gentleman farmer and scientist in Berkshire, England, introduced a new system of plowing and hoeing to pulverize the soil, and in 1701, he invented a seed drill that increased yields and decreased labor. (A seed drill prepared a hole in the soil for a seed, in contrast to the traditional method of seeding by "broadcasting" seeds, or throwing them over a field.) Tull summarized his ideas in an influential book in 1731, *Horse-Hoeing Husbandry,* a pioneering study of plant nutrition. Townshend advocated a planting system that eliminated the need for summer fallowing of plow land, and his **Norfolk,** or **four-course, system** rotated plantings of a root crop (such as turnips), barley, clover, and wheat. Townshend championed the choice of turnips as the root crop so vigorously (because they both enriched the nitrogen content of the soil, thereby improving subsequent harvests, and they provided good fodder for sheep or cattle) that he became known as "Turnip Townshend." Ideas such as these, circulated by a growing periodical press, raised crop yields to the extent that England fed an increasing population and still exported grain in the early eighteenth century.

Weakness of European Agriculture. Most European agriculture was not so successful, and peasant families faced a struggle to survive. Their primary concern was a harvest large enough to pay their obligations to the landowning aristocracy, to the royal tax collector, and to the church (a compulsory tithe), then to provide seed grain for the next year and to have sufficient food left over to sustain life for another year. The yield per acre was higher in western Europe than in eastern Europe, which explains much of the comparative prosperity and strength of the west. Each grain sown in Russia and Poland yielded an average harvest of four grains in 1700, whereas Spanish and Italian peasants harvested six grains and English and Dutch farmers averaged more than nine grains (see Table 17.3). By the late eighteenth century, harvests had improved in all regions, but an acre of land in western Europe still produced twice as much food as an acre in eastern Europe.

The Peasant Economy. Peasants typically supplemented their meager stock of grains with the produce of a small garden and the luxury of some livestock, such as a few pigs or chickens. Surplus grain might be sold, but it was more often bartered—a money economy was not yet the rule in the rural world, and little cash circulated there even in the nineteenth century—

at the nearest market town to acquire necessities that could not be produced at home. Even when livestock were slaughtered, peasants rarely ate the entire animal. They generally sold the choicer cuts of pork and kept the fatty remnants for soups, stews, or bacon (which is cut from pork bellies). More prosperous peasants might smoke or cure a ham or might prepare sausages; celebrations such as weddings, of course, might be wonderful events because the entire animal could be eaten.

The Family Economy. The margin of survival in the rural world of the Old Regime was often very slim—millions of Europeans struggled to obtain adequate nutrition, a situation known as a **subsistence economy.** Survival required all members of a peasant family to work, and to work from an early age, in the collective family effort, known as the **family economy.** The family economy was characterized by all members of the family working together, or in close proximity, as in sharing the multiple chores of farm life. At harvest time, for example, when it was urgently important to bring in the crops, women worked in the field alongside men. A recent study of women and gender in early modern Europe found that women performed 38 percent of the harvest labor (measured in hours) in Yorkshire, England. The labor of every family member, including children, was needed if the family were to survive. As an old poem recalls: "Man, to the Plow / Wife, to the Cow / Girl, to the Yarn / Boy, to the Barn / And your Rent will be netted."

Women and the Family Economy. Historians understand the role of women in the family economy in a comprehensive perspective that includes both productive activities (such as work in agriculture or in hand-

TABLE 17.3 THE COMPARATIVE SUCCESS OF EIGHTEENTH-CENTURY EUROPEAN AGRICULTURE IN DIFFERENT REGIONS

Generally, the sowing (planting) of one seed will yield one stalk grown. One stalk can carry a range of grains, and the following totals include wheat, barley, oats, and rye combined. Thus, in England and the Lowlands, for example, 1 seed grain sown produced 9.3 grains for use, generally on one stalk.

REGION	1650–1699	1750–1799
	Ratio of Grains Harvested to Seed Grain Sown	
England and Lowlands	9.3:1	10.1:1
France, Spain, Italy	6.2:1	7.0:1
Germany, Scandinavia	4.1:1	5.1:1
Russia, Poland, and East	3.8:1	4.7:1

Sources: Griff, David, *The Transformation of Agriculture in the West* (Oxford: Blackwell, 1992, p. 34); Slicher van Bath, B. H., "Agriculture in the Vital Revolution," in E. E. Rich and C. H. Wilson, eds., *The Economic Organization of Early Modern Europe,* vol. 5 of *The Cambridge Economic History of Europe* (Cambridge: Cambridge University Press, 1977, p. 81).

Questions: Do these data help clarify the comparative strengths of Western Europe and Eastern Europe? of eighteenth century France and Germany? To what extent is a table of population an approximation of military might?

FIGURE 17.1 *Family Labor in the Farm Economy.* Although work in rural family economy was often assigned based on sex, there was plenty for everyone. The labor of women, as well as that of men, was essential to bring in the harvest, as this painting by George Stubbs illustrates.

craft manufacture) and reproductive activities (not only in the literal sense of childbearing but also in nurturing family members of all ages, especially children and the elderly). Men typically held most of trade and craft jobs that required training, and women held a disproportionately large share of the unskilled jobs (although they succeeded well in the skilled jobs, such as lace-making or silk-thread work, that were open to them). Agricultural work was especially based on such a **sexual division of labor,** with men found behind the plough or swinging the scythe and women sowing seeds and taking responsibility for chores near the house, such as tending chickens, making beer, or milking cows. In the production of textiles, women did most of the spinning and men were more likely to be weavers. Working women were thus essential to the family economy long before industrialization and urbanization transformed families and work. A study of peasant women in eighteenth-century Belgium, for example, has found that 45 percent of all married women were listed in government records as farmers and 27 percent were recorded as spinners; only 6 percent were listed without an occupation. Unmarried adults were at a disadvantage in this rural economy, and widows were often the poorest members of a rural community.

Cottage Industry and Protoindustrialization.

Home production was an essential feature of this rural economy and meant more than churning butter or making cheese at home. Domestic manufacturing often included making all of a family's clothing, so many peasants learned to spin yarn, weave cloth, or sew clothing. This part-time textile production sometimes led to the sale of excess household products, and in some textile regions, domestic manufacturing evolved into a system of production known as **cottage industry,** in which a peasant family purposely made goods for sale instead of for use in the home. In regions where cottage industry grew in volume into a handcraft form of industrial manufacture—usually because entrepreneurs negotiated agreements with peasants to buy all of their output—historians have examined this economy as a preliminary stage of industrialization, called **protoindustrialization.** The entrepreneur might provide raw materials and pay peasant spinners to produce homespun threads; the yarn could then be delivered to a peasant weaver who also worked at home. This **"putting out" system** of textile manufacture stimulated later industrialization by developing manufacturing skills, marketing networks, and a class of prosperous provincial entrepreneurs. By some estimates, 10 percent of the rural population of Old Regime Europe was engaged in cottage industry.

The Village.

The rural community of peasant families was typically a village of fifty to a few hundred people. In parts of Europe, these villages had corporate structures

FIGURE 17.2 *Industry.* The textile industry began in rural cottages, not great factories. There, girls and women spun fibers into threads, then men (sometimes women) wove them into cloth, and women (sometimes men) sewed them into garments. During the Old Regime, an increasing pattern developed of some peasants devoting themselves entirely to textile work, converting their homes into a handcraft workshop. This illustration (a painting by Gillis Rombouts) shows a Dutch weaver's cottage in Haarlem. The sexual division of labor is clear in this case: the weaver is at the loom, and the weaver's wife spins thread while watching their infant child.

with inherited rules and regulations. These might regulate weights and measures, or they might regulate morality and behavior, such as the control of stray dogs or mandatory church attendance. Village assemblies, led by elders or by the heads of the households controlling most of the land, often held powers such as assigning land use (as they did in most German states and in Russia), dictating farming methods and crop rotation, settling disputes, collecting taxes, and even arranging marriages. Women were usually excluded from participation, although widows were sometimes accepted. Recent research has identified some exceptionally democratic villages in which women participated with full rights.

CORPORATIVE SOCIETY AND THE *STÄNDESTAAT* IN THE EIGHTEENTH CENTURY

Corporative Society and Equality before the Law. Europeans of the Old Regime lived in highly stratified societies, and the strata were usually defined in the law. This meant different laws, and different rights or privileges, applied to each group established by law. It also meant that the only equality before the law might come within one's social group: there was no equality in the law of peasant and aristocrat, or of shopkeeper and priest.

Corporative Society. The division of the population into such groups is known as **corporative society** (because the people were divided into legal bodies, *corpus* in Latin), or by its German name, the *Ständestaat* (Stehn'-duh-staht). Corporative society was a legacy of the Middle Ages. In much of western Europe, the legal basis for it had disappeared, whereas eastern Europe remained caste-ridden. Everywhere, hierarchical ideas provided the foundations of society. The structure of corporative society resembled a pyramid. Most of the population (peasants and laborers) formed the base of the pyramid, and a few privileged people (aristocrats and wealthy town dwellers) sat at the top, with a monarch at the pinnacle. Everyone was born to a position in the hierarchy, a position that, according to most churches, was divinely ordained, and little social mobility was evident from one order to another.

Estates. In two-thirds of Europe (France, Savoy, part of Switzerland, Denmark, the German states, Austria, Bohemia, Hungary, the Danubian provinces, Poland, and Russia), law and custom divided people into **estates** (often referred to by their name in French, *états* [ay-taah']). Historians have mostly studied corporative society in France, where the population was divided into three estates. The clergy, approximately 1 to 2 percent of the nation, comprised the first estate. The aristocracy, less than 1 percent of the population, formed the second estate. The remaining 97 percent of France, from the wealthiest bankers to the poorest vagabonds, collectively made up the **third estate.** In central Europe, the Ständestaat often contained four orders, or *Stände* (Stehn'-duh), because Scandinavian and German law divided what the French called the third estate into two parts, an order of town dwellers and another of peasants. The constitutions of the Old Regime, such as the Swedish Constitution of 1720, retained the ideal of corporative society. German jurisprudence perpetuated this division of the population throughout the eighteenth century. A fifty-volume compendium published in the 1740s reiterated the principles of the Ständestaat, and they were embodied in subsequent legal reforms, such as the Frederician (Fred'-er-ee-shun)

TABLE 17.4 THE SOCIAL STRUCTURE OF ENGLAND IN THE OLD REGIME

In the last years of the seventeenth century, Gregory King examined the tax rolls to determine the relative size and wealth of various social groups. We based our table on his original statistical calculations.

Question: The social groups shown in this table are grouped in an urban–rural distinction. What other groupings might be informative?

English Social Group	Individuals on Tax Rolls	Population (with families)	Percentage of England
Aristocracy	4,560	57,000	1.0
Nobility (peers)	160	6,400	0.1
Landowning gentry	172,000	1,036,000	18.8
Small farmers	550,000	2,050,000	37.2
Rural poor	400,000	1,300,000	23.6
Rural total	726,560	3,143,000	57.0
Merchants	10,000	64,000	1.2
Educated professions	25,000	145,000	2.7
Law	10,000	70,000	1.3
Clergy	10,020	52,520	0.9
Government service	10,000	70,000	1.3
Urban trades	110,000	465,000	8.5
Skilled artisans	60,000	240,000	4.4
Shopkeepers	50,000	225,000	4.1
Laborers	360,000	1,275,000	23.2
Vagrants and others	0	30,000	0.5
Urban total	525,020	2,101,520	38.3
Military officers	9,000	36,000	0.7
Soldiers and sailors	85,000	220,000	4.0
Military total	94,000	256,000	4.7

MAP 17.1. URBAN EUROPE IN 1750

Europe remained a rural civilization in the eighteenth century. Cities were fewer in number and smaller in size, chiefly concentrated in western and southern Europe—west of the Elbe–Trieste line.

lived in farming towns, but they were not part of an urban estate. But everywhere peasants were the majority. In England, 65 percent of the population lived by farming; in France and Sweden, 75 percent of the population were peasants; in Poland, 85 percent.

Variations of Rights and Duties. The rights and duties of people in each estate also varied from country to country, with the most striking differences evident between eastern and western Europe. Historians frequently express this division of Europe by an imaginary line called the **Elbe–Trieste** (El'-buh–Tree'-est) **line,** running from the mouth of the Elbe River on the North Sea to the Adriatic Sea at the city of Trieste. West of the Elbe–Trieste line (including Scandinavia), peasants could own farmland. French peasants, for example, owned between 30 and 40 percent of the arable land, although it was often of the poorest quality. East of the Elbe River, peasants lived in a form of legal servitude called **serfdom.** Millions of serfs were deprived of legal and civil rights, including the right to own land. Even states that permitted peasant land ownership, however, saw little of it. Swedish peasants accounted for 75 percent of the population but owned only 31 percent of the land; the king and the aristocracy, less than 5 percent of the population, owned 69 percent of the land in 1700. Sweden, however, was far ahead of most of Europe in peasant land ownership. In Bohemia, one of the richest provinces of the Hapsburg Empire, the monarch owned 5 percent of the land and the nobility owned 68.5 percent, whereas peasants owned less than 1 percent.

Code in Prussia. Thus, when eighteenth-century reformers began to demand equality before the law (see Chapter 20), they were attacking the fundamental structure of corporative society.

Variations in the Social Structure. The society of the Old Regime was more complicated than these legal categories suggest. In England, the legal distinctions among social groups were mostly abolished during the seventeenth century. The English aristocracy remained a privileged and dominant elite, but a new stratification based on nonlanded wealth was also emerging (see Table 17.4). In contrast, Russian fundamental laws perpetuated a rigid corporative society, and eighteenth-century reforms only tightened the system. In central Europe, yet another pattern developed where reformers known as *cameralists* refined the definitions of social categories. Austrian tax laws adopted in 1763, for example, divided the population into twenty-four distinct categories.

The composition and condition of each estate varied across Europe. The Polish aristocracy included 10 percent of the population, compared with 1 percent in France; this meant that the Polish aristocracy included barefoot farmers who lived in simple homes with earthen floors. Only 1 percent of Poles lived in towns of 10,000, compared with more than 15 percent of people in England and Wales. Sometimes, as in Spain, peasants

The Aristocracy: Varieties of the Privileged Elite

The Aristocracy. The pinnacle of the social structure in rural communities was the **aristocracy,** a small group of people who enjoyed a life of comparative ease. The aristocracy was defined by birth to aristocratic parents, marriage to an aristocratic spouse, or being named an aristocrat by the monarch. In most

The Social and Economic Structure of the Old Regime 403

countries, aristocrats formed a separate legal caste of approximately 1 percent of the population (see Table 17.5), bound by different laws and traditions that gave them special privileges, such as tax exemptions and the right to unpaid labor by the peasantry. Aristocratic status was typically shown by the **aristocratic particule** within a family name; this was usually the word *of* (*de* in French, *di* in Italian, *von* in German) inserted into a name, such as Madame de Sévigné (Say'-veen-yay).

The Nobility.
The **nobility** was a tiny elite at the top of the aristocracy, defined by the highest hereditary titles (such as duke or count) that a monarch could award. The monarch granted noble status to a family through a document called a **patent of nobility.** In each generation, the eldest son would bear the title of nobility and other males in the family might bear lesser titles. The nobility was a very small caste that dominated the highest positions in the military and government; its members often possessed fabulous wealth derived from ownership of the land (see Table 17.6). There were a total of fifty-two dukes in France in 1723, and old noble families were shocked at this large number because there had only been seventeen ducal families a century earlier. The entire no-

ble caste of *grandees* in Spain numbered only 528 titles in 1700. Pretenders might succeed in using an undeserved aristocratic particule in their name, but rarely a title. In Venice, a Golden Book recorded the names of the nobility; in the German states, an annual publication (the *Almanac of Gotha*) kept watch on aristocratic pedigrees.

Variations within the Aristocracy.
The aristocracy was a small class, but it was not homogeneous. The provincial aristocracy, living on inherited lands in the rural world, encompassed a great range of social and economic conditions. At the bottom, the aristocracy might include an elite with less land and wealth, known as the **gentry,** although in some countries, such as Britain, the landowning gentry did not possess aristocratic titles. Although the gentry enjoyed a comfortable existence, it was far removed from the wealth of great nobles. The Spanish, for example, distinguished between *grandees* (a term for the greatest nobles, such as the dukes of Alba) who possessed immense estates and national influence, locally important aristocrats (called *caballeros* [cah-ba-yair'-ose]) who owned enough land to live as a privileged elite, and a comparatively poor gentry (called *hidalgos*) who were said to have more titles than shirts. Such distinctions existed across Europe. In the east, a few families of grand **seigneurs** (sayn'-your) owned most of the land (and the serfs on it) while thousands of aristocrats owned little or nothing. The Polish aristocracy, known collectively as the *szlachta* (shlock'-tuh) included 700,000 to 1 million people, but only 30 to 40 magnate families possessed the wealth and power normally associated with the nobility. Part of the szlachta worked on the estates of great nobles as bailiffs, stewards, or tenant farmers; most of this caste lived as small farmers on rented land, and many were so poor that they were known as the *golota,* a barefoot aristocracy.

Variations within the Nobility.
There were variations even within the tiny nobility. Gradations of status depended on the length of time that a family had been noble, the means by which it had acquired its title, and the wealth and political influence that the family held. The highest nobles often emphasized the length of time their family had been noble. British history provides a good example. The leading figure in early eighteenth-century English politics, Sir Robert Walpole, was not born to a noble title, but for his accomplishments he was ennobled as the first Earl of Orford in 1742. One of Walpole's leading opponents, however, was the fourth duke and eighth Earl of Bedford, heir to a pedigree nearly 300 years old and a title that originated with the third son of King Henry IV, born in 1389. Thus, the Earl of Bedford was unlikely to consider the Earl of Orford his equal. And

---

TABLE 17.5 THE SIZE OF THE EUROPEAN ARISTOCRACY IN THE EIGHTEENTH CENTURY

In the eighteenth century, Saxony, in today's Germany, was part of the Holy Roman Empire. Savoy, spreading across today's France and Italy, was the most important Italian state of the eighteenth century.

REGION	DATE	NUMBER OF ARISTOCRATS	AS % OF POPULATION
France	1789	n.a.	0.5
Saxony *(Germany)*	c. 1700	n.a.	0.6
Brittany *(France)*	1750	14,000	0.6
Luxembourg	1766	1,500	0.7
Venice	1797	1,090	0.8
Prussia	1700s	n.a.	1.0
Savoy *(France and Italy)*	1702	3,400	1.1
Spain	1797	402,000	3.8
Poland	1700s	700,000 to 1,000,000	10.0

Source: Adapted from data in Dewald, Jonathan, *The European Nobility, 1400–1800* (Cambridge: Cambridge University Press, 1996, pp. 22–24).

Question: What conclusion do the variations in the column "Percentage of Population" suggest?

TABLE 17.6 THE FINANCES OF THE COUNTS AND COUNTESSES OF TAVANNES IN THE EIGHTEENTH CENTURY

This table gives us a snapshot of the financial records of a French noble family. Only partial records have survived, and the table uses mixed years for some figures; still, it gives us significant information about relative incomes and expenses. The unit of measure is the *livre* (leev'-reh), which had approximately the same value as an English shilling (one-twentieth of the pound sterling).

INCOME	AMOUNT
Income from land owned by the count	
Rent for lands in region #1 (annual average, 1696–1730)	1500+
Rent for lands in region #2 (annual average, 1699–1726)	3,500+
Rent for lands in region #3 (annual average, 1698–1723)	8,700+
Income from sale of wood from forest in region #3 (1788)	40,000+
Gross revenue from all land (after paying upkeep and wages; 1788)	86,269
Income from pensions given by the king	
Total pensions for 1754	46,900
Pension as commander of royal forces in Burgundy	26,250
Income from seigneurial dues (obligations paid by peasants)	
Total dues received in 1788	26,986
Income from the inheritance of the countess (1725)	
Income from four houses in Paris (value = 200,000)	10,000
Income from investments (value = 367,938)	8,698
Total capital inherited in 1725	803,924

Expenses

Wages paid to the count's staff (1780–1786)

Annual wages for the count's agent in Paris	800
Annual wages for a forest warden in Burgundy	200
Annual wages for a gardener or a maid in Burgundy	70
Annual wages for a chef in Paris	945
Annual wages for a coachman in Paris	720

Personal Expenses

Total personal expenses in 1788	62,000
Expenses for clothing, jewelry, and gifts in 1788	20,000
Expenses for the theater in 1788	2,000
Monthly expenses for Roquefort cheese (January 1784)	32
Monthly expenses for cognac (January 1784)	30
Monthly expenses for cayenne coffee (January 1784)	30

Source: Data from Forster, Robert, *The House of Saulx-Tavannes: Versailles and Burgundy, 1700–1830* (Baltimore: Johns Hopkins University Press, 1971).

Questions: What conclusions about the eighteenth-century class system can you draw from the data? Given this limited evidence, what is a reasonable guess of the count's income in the 1780s? What does the gap between the count's income and his staff's income suggest about the gap between classes? How does the count's monthly payment for cheese compare with his gardener's yearly wage? Notice the count's different sources of income. Do you think his coachman's income is as diversified, or would you guess that it comes solely from his wages?

---

both of them yielded precedence to the Earl of Norfolk, whose title dated back to the year 1070, shortly after the Norman Conquest of England. In other parts of western Europe, one of the distinctions frequently made separated a **"nobility of the sword"** composed of families ennobled for centuries as a result of military service to the monarch from a **"nobility of the robe"** composed of families more recently ennobled through service to the government. In central and eastern Europe, important distinctions rested on the number of **serfs** an aristocrat owned (see *Serfdom in Russia*).

The Court Aristocracy. Many of the fine distinctions within the aristocracy were simply matters of pride within a caste that paid excruciating attention to

comparative status, but some had larger implications. The aristocratic competition for precedence involved real issues of power and wealth. Only the top 5 percent (perhaps less) of the aristocracy could hope to be presented at court and meet the royal family; fewer still were invited to live at the royal court, hunting with King Louis XV of France in the royal forests, sharing the evening *tabagerie* (a smoking and drinking session) with King Frederick William I of Prussia, or enjoying the life of lavish dinners and balls. Yet a position at court—in a group known as the **court aristocracy**—was often the route to political office, military command, or perhaps a pension providing a lifetime income. Most provincial nobles lacked the opportunities for such advancement.

FIGURE 17.3 *Aristocratic Life.* Although the aristocracy was a diverse social group ranging from the immensely rich to impoverished families who lived much like peasants, aristocrats commonly presented an image of the idleness of fortunate people who need not work to survive. No image better captures the enjoyment of aristocratic frivolity than J. H. Fragonard's *The Swing,* shown here.

The Privileged Status of the Aristocracy

Wealth of the Nobility. The wealth and power of the high nobility present one of the most vivid images of the inequality of the corporative society of the Old Regime. Some aristocrats enjoyed dizzying wealth and a life of luxury. In the Austrian Netherlands (now Belgium), the duke of Arenberg had an annual income eighteen times the income of the richest merchant. In Poland, Prince Radziwill kept 10,000 retainers in his service. In England, the top 400 noble families each owned estates of 10,000 to 50,000 acres. In Russia, Empress Catherine the Great gave one of her discarded lovers a gift of 37,000 serfs, and Prince Menshikov owned 100,000 serfs. In Bohemia, 100 noble families owned one-third of the entire province, and the poorer members of this group owned land encompassing thirty villages. In Spain, the Count of Altamira owned the commercial city of Valencia.

Noble Wealth and Social Inequality. Such wealth produced breathtaking inequality. The Count of Tavannes in France paid a gardener or a maid on his provincial estates 70 livres (leev′) per year, and the valued chef at his Paris residence earned 945 livres per year; yet the count lavished 20,000 livres on clothing and jewelry. The count's monthly expenditure on coffee and cognac totaled nearly a year's wages for a servant, and his budget for theater tickets would have cost the total yearly earnings of twenty-eight servants. Sustaining a life of such luxury led many lesser nobles into ruinous debt. Extravagance and debt became so typical of the nobility (including royalty) in the eighteenth century that some countries, such as Spain, made arresting aristocrats for their debts illegal.

Noble State Service. In addition to enormous wealth, nobles held great power. They dominated offices of the state, both in the government and in the military. In some countries, notably Sweden, Prussia, and Russia, the concept of aristocratic service to the throne had led to an arrangement in which the aristocracy accepted compulsory **state service** and received in return a legal monopoly over certain positions. The eighteenth-century Russian Charter of the Nobility, for example, stated: "The title and privileges of the nobility . . . are acquired by service and work useful to the Empire." Therefore, it continued, whenever the emperor "needs the service of the nobility for the general well being, every nobleman is then obligated . . . to perform fully his duty." In return for this compulsory service, the Charter of the Nobility recognized the right of nobles to buy and sell villages, excluded nobles from some taxes that fell on commoners, gave nobles a monopoly of some positions, and spared nobles some of the punishments (such as flogging) specified in Russian law. In much of Europe, only aristocrats could become army officers.

Noble Political Power. Nobles universally dominated the highest positions in government. At the beginning of the eighteenth century, the chief minister of the king of France was a marquis, the prime minister of the king of Prussia was a count, the head of the state council of the Hapsburg Empire was a count, the chief minister of the tsar of Russia was a prince, and the chief adviser to the king of Spain was a cardinal. For the century before the French Revolution of 1789, the chief ministers of the kings of France were (in order) a marquis, a cardinal, a duke, a duke, a cardinal, a marquis, a count, a minor aristocrat, a duke, a duke, and a count. Principal advisers of the king of England during that period included a dozen earls, five viscounts, two dukes, one marquess, and four other lords.

Noble Privileges in the Law. In addition to personal wealth and powerful offices, aristocrats of the Old Regime usually held a privileged position in the law, exceptional rights on their landed estates, and great power over the people who lived on their land. In most countries, nobles were governed by substantially different laws than the rest of the population. Some countries had a separate legal code for aristocrats, some had legal charters detailing noble privileges, and some simply adopted laws granting special treatment. Legal privileges took many forms. Exemption from the laws that applied to commoners was one of the most cherished. Aristocrats were exempted from most taxes that fell on peasants or town dwellers, and they tenaciously defended their exemptions, even as the monarchy faced bankruptcy. In Hungary, the Magyar nobles were free from all direct taxes such as those on land or income; they guarded this privilege by giving regular contributions to the throne, but nobles controlled the process and the amount themselves. Aristocrats were exempt from the *corvée* (cor-vay'), a labor tax by which peasants were obliged to maintain roads and bridges. Penal codes usually exempted nobles from corporal punishment, such as flogging and branding.

Variations of Aristocratic Privilege. Aristocratic privilege varied significantly from country to country. In Britain and the Netherlands, seventeenth-century revolutions made aristocrats and commoners equal before the law and allowed neither tax exemptions nor a monopoly on offices (allowing the occasional commoner to become prime minister of England, as William Pitt did in 1756). Yet important privileges persisted there, too. English nobles held hereditary control of the upper house of Parliament, the House of Lords, and the right to be tried only by a jury of their peers.

Feudal Rights of the Aristocracy. The core of aristocratic privilege was found on their provincial estates. An aristocrat, as lord of the manor, held traditional **manorial rights** over the land and its inhabitants. These rights are variously known as **feudal rights,** because many had survived from the feudal system of the Middle Ages, or **seigneurial rights,** because the lord of the manor was known as the seigneur. Manorial rights increased significantly as one passed from western Europe to eastern Europe, where peasants remained in the virtual slavery of **serfdom.** But even in regions where serfdom no longer existed, aristocratic landowners were often entitled to **feudal dues** (payments in money or in kind), to unpaid labor by peasants in the seigneurial fields, or to both. Thus, peasants might be expected to harvest an aristocrat's crops before they could harvest their own and then to pay a percentage of their own crops to the same aristocrat.

Aristocratic Authority. Seigneurial rights in many countries (particularly in central and eastern Europe) also included the powers of local governance. The seigneur provided or oversaw the functions of the police, the judiciary, and civil government on his lands; a noble might thereby preside over the arrest, trial, and punishment of a peasant. Many aristocrats thus governed their provincial estates as self-sufficient, miniature kingdoms. A study of the Old Regime manors of Bohemia shows this vividly. Only the noble landowner was legally a citizen of the larger state (the Austrian Empire). The residents of the noble's villages and farmlands were

FIGURE 17.4 *The Corvée.* The highway system of eighteenth-century Europe required a great deal of labor to maintain. In most of central and eastern Europe, where serfdom survived, monarchs expected great landowners to require roadwork as part of the robot (obligatory labor) owed by serfs. In France, where serfdom had largely disappeared, peasants were required to pay a tax in labor, called the *corvée* (cor-vay'), like the roadwork shown here. Note the well-dressed aristocrats on horseback in contrast to peasants and their working horses. Note that peasant women (lower left) have prepared food and drink. Note that even more elaborate roadwork on a large bridge is going on in the background.

completely under his jurisdiction. Peasants farmed their fields for him. He conscripted them for the corvée, selected them for service in the Austrian army, and collected their taxes for the Hapsburg government. The same lord arrested draft evaders or tax delinquents and punished them, and peasants could not appeal his justice.

Variations within the Peasantry: Serfdom

Servitude in Europe. Most Europeans during the Old Regime were peasant farmers, but this peasantry, like the aristocracy, was not a homogeneous class. The foremost difference distinguished free peasants from those legally bound by virtual slavery. Outright slavery no longer existed in most of Europe by 1700, although European governments allowed slavery in their overseas colonies. Portugal (the only country to import African slaves into Europe), the Ottoman Empire, and the Danubian provinces (where 200,000 gypsies were enslaved) were exceptions.

Serfdom. Multitudes of European peasants still lived in the virtual slavery known as *serfdom,* a medieval institution that had survived into the Old Regime (and would last into the nineteenth century in parts of Europe). Serfdom was not slavery, but it resembled slavery in several ways. Serfs could not own land. They were bound to the soil, meaning that they could not choose to migrate from the land they farmed. In addition, serfs might be sold, given away, or gambled away. Entire villages could be abolished and relocated. Serfs might be subjected to corporal punishment such as flogging. One Russian count ordered the whipping of all serfs who did not attend church, and the penalty for missing Easter Communion was 5,000 lashes. A Russian decree of 1767 summarized this situation simply: serfs "owe their landlords proper submission and absolute obedience in all matters." The distinction between serfdom and slavery was noteworthy. Unlike slaves, serfs were not chattel property (property other than real estate). Serfs were rarely sold without including the land that they farmed or without their families. Serfs enjoyed a few traditional legal rights. They could make a legal appeal to a village council or a seigneurial court. They could not press charges or give evidence against nobles or their bailiffs, so their legal rights protected them within the peasant community but not against their lords.

Extent of Serfdom. Serfdom survived in some portions of western Europe and became more common as one traveled east. East of the Elbe River, serfdom was the dominant social institution. In parts of France and the western German states, vestigial serfdom still restricted hundreds of thousands of people. In Prussia and Poland, approximately 20 percent of the peasants were free and 80 percent serfs. In Hungary, only 2 percent of the peasants were free; in Denmark and in the Slavic provinces of the Austrian Empire (Bohemia and Silesia), perhaps 1 percent; in Russia, less than 1 percent. Thus, the Russian gentry typically owned hundreds of serfs and Russian grand seigneurs owned thousands (see *Serfdom in Russia*).

Varieties of Serfdom. Variations did exist within serfdom. In Russia, a peasant family typically belonged to a noble landowner, but 40 percent of the serfs were state serfs farming the imperial domains. These state serfs had been created by Peter the Great when he seized lands belonging to the Russian Orthodox Church. Those who labored for the nobility experienced conditions as diverse as did their seigneurs; more than 30 percent of landowners held small farms with fewer than 10 serfs, whereas 16 percent of the Russian nobility owned estates large enough to encompass an entire village of 100 or more serfs. The great nobility possessed so many souls that many served as house serfs, domestic servants whose life differed significantly from their counterparts who labored in the fields.

The Burdens of Serfdom. The basic legal obligation of serfs was compulsory, unpaid labor in the fields of landowners. This obligatory labor, called *robot* (row-baht') in much of central and eastern Europe, was defined by law but varied from region to region. In Prussia, serfs owed the Junker aristocrats 2 or 3 days of unpaid labor every week and more during the harvest. Junkers, however, needed more labor than their serfs provided and therefore hired some free peasants. The feudal labor laws of Bohemia specified 3 days per week of robot, plus harvest labor "at the will" of a noble. A law of 1775 defined a day of labor as 8 hours during the winter, 12 hours during the spring and summer, and 14 hours during the harvest. Russian serfs commonly worked 6 days per week for a landowner (see *Serfdom in Russia*). In some regions, however, a different system applied: serfs farmed an allotment of land and gave the landowners a large percentage of the harvest.

A study of the serfs in the Baltic provinces of Russia reveals how these obligations added up. A family of eight able-bodied peasants (including women) owed their master the following: two field workers for 3 days per week, every week of the year; 10 to 12 days of miscellaneous labor such as livestock herding; four trips, totaling about 56 days of labor, carting goods for the seigneur; 42 days of postal-relay services; and 24 days of spinning flax. In addition to such labor, European peasant families owed feudal payments in kind, such as grain, sheep, wool, chickens, and eggs. Even then they could not keep their remaining production. They had to guard 20 to 25 percent of a harvest as seed for the following year. Peasants also usually owed a compulsory tithe to an established church—approximately 10 percent of a harvest—and taxes to the government, which

SERFDOM IN RUSSIA

A Traveler Observes the Life of Russian Serfs

One of the difficulties facing social historians is that the surviving records of the past were (by definition) written by literate, educated people. The illiterate masses could not record the conditions of their lives for posterity. Historians must therefore rely on the indirect evidence provided by observers (and their deductions from other sources). Alexander Radishchev (1749–1802) was a Russian writer who opposed serfdom and wrote about it, resulting in his exile to Siberia. The following excerpt is Radishchev's description of his meeting with a serf, as published in his *A Voyage from St. Petersburg to Moscow* (1790).

The corduroy road tortured my body; I climbed out of the carriage and [walked]. A few steps from the road I saw a peasant ploughing a field. The weather was hot. . . . It was now Sunday. . . . The peasant was ploughing very carefully. The field, of course, was not part of his master's land.

He turned the plow with astonishing ease.

"God help you," I said, walking up to the ploughman.

"Thank you sir," the ploughman said to me, shaking the earth off the ploughshare. . . .

"You must be a Dissenter, since you plough on a Sunday."

"No, sir, I make the true sign of the cross," he said, showing me the three fingers together. "And God is merciful and does not bid us starve to death, so long as we have strength and a family."

"Have you no time to work during the week, then, and can you not have any rest on Sundays, in the hottest part of the day, at that?"

"In a week, sir, there are six days, and we go six times a week to work on the master's fields; in the evening, if the weather is good, we haul to the master's house the hay that is left in the woods. . . . God grant that it rains this evening. If you have peasants of your own, sir, they are praying to God for the same thing."

". . . But how do you manage to get food enough, if you have only the holidays free?"

"Not only the holidays: the nights are ours, too. If a fellow isn't lazy, he won't starve to death."

Radishchev, Alexander, *A Journey from St. Petersburg to Moscow* (Cambridge: Harvard University Press, 1958).

Threshing-Floor. *Alexey Venetsianov (1821–1822).* Serfs did not own the land that they farmed. Typically, however, the wealthy owners allowed the village (usually the village elders) to assign and reassign land within the community. Serfs worked together as a community for many of the chores of the farming year, such as threshing grain (separating the seed from a harvested plant). In this painting of a communal threshing-floor, the Russian painter Alexey Venetsianov shows the tired but pleased reactions of serfs after producing the pile of grain about to be loaded in the center background. Note that this task, like most in the peasant world, required men and women to work together.

TABLE 17.7 OWNERSHIP OF SERFS BY RUSSIAN ARISTOCRATS

CATEGORY	SERFS OWNED	% OF ARISTOCRACY
Grand Seigneur	1,000	16 combined
Gentry	101–1,000	
Impoverished	21–100	25
Poor Aristocracy	<20	59

Source: Data from Pipes, Richard, *Russia under the Old Regime* (New York: Penguin, 1974, p. 178).

frequently took between 30 and 40 percent of the crop. Studies have found that serfs owed 73 percent of their produce in Bohemia, 75 percent in eastern France, 83 percent in Silesia, and 86 percent in parts of Galicia. Such figures changed from year to year, but the burden remained crushing.

Variations within the Peasantry: Free Peasants

The free **peasants** of western and central Europe had been escaping from the burdens of serfdom since the fourteenth century. The beginnings of a money economy reduced the importance of feudal services by enabling some peasants to commute robot or corvée with cash. To increase revenues from import and export tariffs, some governments had encouraged a shift to livestock production by allowing aristocrats to enclose their own, and sometimes their tenants', lands. As a result, the capitalization of land was far advanced in the west by 1700, although most families still owed at least some feudal obligations to the landowning aristocracy. Whereas eastern serfs were fortunate to keep 25 percent of their harvest, free peasants could expect to keep more than half. Two different studies of Old Regime France have found that peasants owed between 33 and 40 percent of their total production in feudal dues, taxes, and tithes.

Varieties of Peasant Land Tenure. The condition of free peasants varied according to the forms of **land tenure.** The most prosperous peasants were landowners themselves. Studies of the French free peasantry found that nearly 4 million peasants owned some land and their own home in the eighteenth century, although most families owned so little land that they could not afford to market any of their harvest. Although most free peasants were landless, one group of them found relatively comfortable lives. The most successful of the landless French peasants were usually **tenant farmers,** about 10 to 20 percent of the landless population. Tenant farmers rented land, typically for a long term—such as 9 years—for a fixed money payment, and they then made the best profit that they could after paying the rent. Such long-term contracts

FIGURE 17.5 *The Home of a Successful Peasant Family.* Eighteenth-century peasant homes often had only one room, which was used for all purposes, including housing animals. This Breton family from a village near Morbihan possesses considerable wealth in its horses, cattle, and pigs. Note the limited furnishings and the absence of windows. Also note that most of the people and all of seats are clustered near to the hearth. A basket of food hangs from the rafters: why would it be there? Note the darkness of the image (like the cottage it depicts): is this a good metaphor for peasant life in the eighteenth century?

protected peasant families from eviction after a single bad harvest, and many aristocrats discovered the advantages of short-term contracts, which were typical in Spain. Other tenant farmers managed the rented lands but did not labor in the fields themselves, or they became wealthy by trading in grain or other commodities.

The Poorer Peasantry. The other 80 to 90 percent of landless peasants were not as fortunate as the tenant farmers. The most secure group was usually **sharecroppers,** often called *métayers* (may-tay'-yay). They produced most of the grain marketed in France by farming the estates of great landowners under contracts negotiated as free peasants. The sharecropping contract (see *Varieties of Agriculture in the Eighteenth Century*) typically provided leased land in return for a large share of its yield. Sharecropping contracts provided these peasant families with the means of survival, but little more. Below the sharecroppers was a lower class of agricultural laborers. Some worked for wages, others, called **cotters** in many countries, worked for the use of a cottage. Some found only seasonal employment (working to harvest grapes in the autumn, for example), in some cases living as migrant laborers, traveling with the changing harvests. Thus, the peasantry included a range of conditions that saw some peasants employed as laborers (or even domestic servants) by other peasants.

THE URBAN POPULATION OF THE OLD REGIME

Market Towns and Small Cities. Urban Europe in the eighteenth century ranged from rural market towns of 2,000 people to great administrative and commercial capital cities of 500,000. Important regional towns—such as Heidelberg, Helsinki, and Liverpool—often had populations below 10,000. A population of 100,000 constituted a great city, and only a few capitals reached that level in the early eighteenth century (see *Urban Europe in the Eighteenth Century*). Berlin had 55,000 people in 1700. St. Petersburg reached 68,000 in 1730. Buda and Pest were then separate towns with a combined total of 17,000 people. Many cities, such as Geneva, with a population of 28,000 in 1750, were so small that residents could easily walk their full width for an evening stroll.

Capital Cities. The largest city in Europe sat on its southeastern edge: Constantinople, seat of the vast Ottoman Empire, had an estimated 700,000 persons. The two dominant cities in the development of modern European civilization, London and Paris, both exceeded 500,000 people, but no other cities rivaled them. Rome was smaller than it had been under the Caesars, with a population of 135,000 in 1700, growing only to

Urban Europe in the Eighteenth Century

London in the Early Eighteenth Century. Most great cities—like Constantinople, London, and Paris—were located on water because it provided the least expensive and most reliable method of moving goods (from stones for building to grain for bread) into and out of the city. This oil painting of London's Westminster Bridge by Canaletto dramatizes the use of the Thames River. The Westminster Bridge was one of the most important projects in the rebuilding of London after the Great Fire of 1666. Seventeenth-century London had been served only by an ancient ferry service across the Thames at this point. The bridge is clearly a modern construction because it does not have housing built onto the bridge (as London Bridge did until 1761).

Feeding a Great City. All cities, from London and Paris with populations of 500,000 to important central European cities with populations closer to 50,000 (such as Berlin at 72,000 in 1730, or Munich at 38,000 in 1780, or Dresden at 62,000 in 1800), faced a daunting task of feeding the urban population. All were dependent on food transported from the countryside, and shortages in this importation produced numerous "bread riots" during the eighteenth century. To handle the difficult logistics of food distribution, cities created great food markets in the center of town, such as Les Halles in Paris or Covent Garden in London. This oil painting by Angelo Marie Costa depicts the market square in Naples during the mideighteenth century. Note the large amount of space devoted to stalls and the crowds of people at them.

TABLE 17.8 THE GREAT CITIES OF EUROPE IN 1700

This table shows all European cities with a population of 70,000 or more in 1700

CITY	POPULATION	CITY	POPULATION
Constantinople (Turkey)	700,000	Milan (Italy)	125,000
London (England)	575,000	Vienna (Austria)	114,000
Paris (France)	500,000	Palermo (Italy)	100,000
Naples (Italy)	300,000	Lyons (France)	97,000
Amsterdam (Netherlands)	200,000	Marseilles (France)	90,000
Lisbon (Portugal)	180,000	Brussels (Belgium)	80,000
Madrid (Spain)	140,000	Florence (Italy)	72,000
Venice (Italy)	138,000	Seville (Spain)	72,000
Rome (Italy)	135,000	Granada (Spain)	70,000
Moscow (Russia)	130,000	Hamburg (Germany)	70,000

170,000 at the century's end. Such large cities were the centers of Western civilization, but they did not yet make it an urban civilization. If one defines urban as beginning at a population of 10,000 people, Europe was only 9.4 percent urban at the end of the eighteenth century; if the definition is expanded to included towns of 5,000 people, Europe was 12.1 percent urban. Even if one counts small farming towns of 2,000 people (which were different from manufacturing and commercial towns), Europe was still less than 25 percent urban, although some regions were about 33 percent urban.

Chartered Cities and the Bourgeoisie.
In legal terms, cities and towns of the Old Regime were corporate entities (hence the terms *incorporated* and *unincorporated* for towns). Towns held legal charters, often centuries old, from the government. Charters specified the rights of town dwellers—collectively called the **bourgeoisie** (boor-zwa-zee'; from the French term *bourg* for "town") or **burghers** (from the similar German term)—rights that the rural population did not enjoy. As in the Middle Ages, an old German saying held true: "City air makes one free." The urban population thus formed a clearly defined estate, lacking many of the privileges of the aristocracy but freed from the obligations on the peasantry. Hence, they came to be seen as a **"middle" class.** As a group, they possessed significant nonlanded wealth, although they did not rival the wealth of landed nobles. Studies of wills probated during the Old Regime have shown that nobles possessed more than two-thirds of the wealth. A study of England in the 1740s has shown that the landowning aristocracy and upper gentry (a total of less than 3 percent of population) owned 95 percent of the national wealth.

Cities and Population Migration.
Many countries, particularly those east of the Elbe–Trieste line, prohibited peasants from migrating to the towns and obtaining urban freedoms. Bavarian law, Austrian law, and the Prussian legal code, for example, all bound German peasants to stay on the soil. Even in western Europe, some town charters restricted residence and citizenship, usually to people who showed a means of support. Cities needed migration, however. Conditions were generally so unhealthy that the death rate exceeded the birthrate. Cities could maintain their size or grow only by attracting rural immigrants. Thus, restrictions on population mobility began to disappear during the Old Regime. London grew rapidly in the eighteenth century, yet it recorded more deaths than births in every year of the century until 1790; in 1741, burials outnumbered baptisms by two to one.

THE SOCIAL AND ECONOMIC STRUCTURE OF URBAN EUROPE IN THE EIGHTEENTH CENTURY

The Variety of Eighteenth Century Towns.
The towns of the eighteenth century varied in their function as well as their size. Capital cities formed a special category of large cities where government and finance were centered, and the population was so huge that it was a challenge just to feed them. The next rank of major cities was usually manufacturing centers (such as Lyons and Granada) or great port cities (such as Marseilles, Hamburg, and Liverpool). Important regional towns similarly varied, serving as centers of administration (both governmental and religious) and manufacturing.

Cities and Manufacturing.
European towns were not yet characterized by the heavy industry or mass production associated with modern urban life. Economic historians have estimated that in 1750 Britain had attained only 10 percent of the industrialization that it would reach by 1900; France, the Italian states, and the German states were only at 7 to 9 percent. Manufacturing in the eighteenth century chiefly meant textiles. Combined **textile manufacturing** (wool, cotton, linen, and silk) accounted for 28 percent of all British manufacturing, whereas combined heavy industries (mining, metalworking, and construction) accounted for only 22 percent. Textiles similarly provided the traditional basis of urban prosperity in many regions of continental Europe, such as northeastern France, Flanders, and the city-states of northern Italy.

The Urban Occupational Structure.
The occupational structure of towns varied with the town's function. A study of Bayeux, a provincial administrative town in Normandy, found a working adult male population of 1,200. Their employment shows how an administrative town was different from the image of towns as manufacturing centers. Slightly more than 10 percent of the men of Bayeux were in the educated professions, mostly lawyers and officials or people trained in medical arts—physicians, surgeons, and apothecaries. An additional 1 percent of the men were tax collectors (an independent occupation) for the monarch or the regional nobility. The prosperous great merchants (not shopkeepers) who traded in regional agricultural or manufactured goods constituted nearly 3 percent of the male population. At the opposite end of Bayeux's social spectrum, urban laborers accounted for 10 percent of the population—a low number that shows that this was not a manufacturing town. Between the two extremes, approximately 75 percent of the male population was engaged in trades. Most of them worked in the production or distribution of food (grocers, butchers, and bakers), clothing (tailors, cobblers, and wig makers), and housing (hoteliers and innkeepers or the building trades). The remainder of the population practiced other trades characteristic of urban life: coopers, goldsmiths, clock makers, saddlers, cabinetmakers, drapers, and dozens of other crafts whose practitioners were called *artisans*.

The Upper Bourgeoisie.
At the pinnacle of the urban social structure sat the wealthy **patrician class** of the big cities and great manufacturing towns—an upper bourgeoisie of banking and finance, of manufacturing

FIGURE 17.6 *The Rising Middle Class.* The wealthy middle class of businessmen, merchants, manufacturers, and bankers became increasingly influential in the eighteenth century despite being largely excluded from aristocratic circles and institutions. In this painting, a prosperous British merchant flaunts his wealth: his docks and warehouses outside the window, his country estate in the painting, his gold on the table, his richly dressed family, and his servant.

and commerce. This urban oligarchy lacked the hereditary titles and privileges of the aristocracy. They were not yet as wealthy as nobles, and they held much less political power. But many families possessed enough wealth to live nobly and aspired to aristocratic status. A few members of this urban elite might enter the aristocracy through state service, and some families married into the aristocracy by providing lavish dowries to daughters who married nobles in debt. This wealthy class lived handsomely, but they represented only a small percentage of urban population, just as aristocrats did in the rural world.

Guilds and Artisans. The typical town dweller in the Old Regime was an **artisan,** and the dominant feature of an artisan's life was the **guild**—yet another corporation with a royal charter (usually providing monopoly control of some craft). Guilds had developed in Europe in the late Middle Ages (between the twelfth and fifteenth centuries) for the purpose of organizing craft production. They received statutes or charters specifying their rights from the monarch, making them corpora-

tions like the towns themselves. Guild charters were still being reaffirmed by monarchs in the late eighteenth century, as the king of Saxony did in 1780. These corporate charters gave the guilds monopolistic control of manufacturing in their respective trades. Thus, only a member of the coopers' guild could make barrels. Such monopolies extended to all manufacturing for sale or for exchange, but not for home use, and this naturally caused some tension between urban guilds and rural domestic manufacturing. The men of an urban tailors' guild, for example, could fight against the sale of any goods produced by women who worked as seamstresses in the surrounding countryside. Guilds used their charters to regulate trade. They restricted access to, or training in, each occupation; defined the standards of quality; and regulated the right to sell goods.

Apprentices, Journeymen, and Masters. Membership in a guild involved three stages of development: work as an **apprentice,** when one learned the basic skills of a trade; as a **journeyman,** when one developed these skills as a paid employee; and (for a few) as **master** of a craft, when one obtained the full privilege of practicing it, including the right to train apprentices and hire journeymen. Children became apprentices, learning a trade from a master, at an early age (see Document 17.1). A study of the guilds of Venice, for example, shows that apprentice goldsmiths began at age 7, weavers at 12; by age 18, one was too old to apprentice in most crafts. A child had to meet many requirements of the guild (such as proof of legitimate birth or practice of Christianity) and pay fees to both the guild and the master before becoming an apprentice. The children of masters had additional advantages. Guild regulations usually required masters to accept the children of other guild members as apprentices, to house them in their homes, and to provide them with adequate training and experience in a trade. Apprentices, in turn, were obliged to serve their masters for a fixed period of years (typically 3 or 4, but often more) without pay. Upon completion of their training, apprentices became journeymen and were expected to leave the town of their training and journey to work for wages with masters in other towns. The journeyman carried papers identifying him and his experience, signed by each of the masters for whom he had worked. Only after several years of such travels could a craftsman hope for acceptance as the master of a trade.

Masters and the Role of Women. Master craftsmen were important figures in a town. They controlled the guilds and therefore most of the occupations. Masters were expected to marry and to lead respectable lives. They usually maintained their workroom, shop, and residence in the same building. Women were generally excluded from an independent role in a guild, but they were an integral part of the craftsman's family

A CONTRACT OF APPRENTICESHIP IN THE GUNSMITHING TRADE, 1704

Contracts of apprenticeship could be negotiated through the appropriate guild or with a master craftsman. The following contract, from a small town in south central France, was negotiated by the widow of a craftsman (a master glove maker) to apprentice her son to a master in another craft (gunsmithing).

Were present Antoinette Faugeyron, widow of Jean Haste, master glovemaker, who of her own free will has apprenticed her son, Jean Haste, present here, to Claude Serre, gunsmith of this town, also present here, who accepts him in order to teach him well and conscientiously, as much as is in his power, the art of gunsmithing, which consists in the filing and forging of gunplates. [Serre] promises to teach him the secrets necessary to that effect. The said apprenticeship has been contracted for two years, beginning today and to be finished on the same day at the end of the said two years, during which time the said Serre shall feed and lodge the said apprentice and furnish him all the tools necessary to the said trade, and the said Faugeyron shall furnish his clothes and do his laundry, and all the work done by the said apprentice during the said time shall belong to the said Serre. The said apprentice shall not leave without a legitimate excuse, in which case the said Serre can take another [apprentice] at the expense of the said Faugeyron; conversely, the said Serre cannot dismiss the said apprentice without a legitimate excuse, and in this case the latter can learn another trade at the expense of the said Serre. Also, the present apprenticeship has been contracted at the price of thirty livres, half to be paid in cash now and half after the end of one year (by the widow Haste).

Question: Does it seem that each of the parties to this contract obtained a fair agreement?

FIGURE 17.7 *Domestic Servants.* By the late eighteenth century, domestic service was becoming the primary source of employment for women in many places. In this scene by Jean-Baptiste Chardin (1699–1779), a laundress tackles the arduous weekly chore of scrubbing bed linens by hand.

rity in the homes of their employers. For unmarried women, domestic service was often the only respectable employment available.

NATIONAL ECONOMIES OF THE EIGHTEENTH CENTURY: THE DOCTRINE OF MERCANTILISM

Economic Theory. *Economics* is an ancient word whose derivation goes back to Aristotle's Oikonomia, but economics as a field of study and theory is a recent development. In the eighteenth century, economics in the modern sense formed a small part of the study called *moral philosophy*. The first university professorship in political economy was created at the University of Naples in 1754, and the field of political economy (the precursor of modern economics) chiefly prospered in Scotland under the leadership of theorists such as Adam Smith, the most important founder of modern capitalism.

Mercantilism. Despite the limited study of political economics in the Old Regime, governments followed a well-developed economic philosophy known as the *mercantile system*. The doctrine of **mercantilism** did not stress the predominant feature of the economy of the Old Regime (agriculture) or the greatest form of wealth of that world (land). Instead, the mercantile system chiefly concerned manufactures, trade, wealth in gold and silver, and the role of the state in encouraging these.

economy. The wife of a master usually handled sales in the shop, kept the accounts for her husband's business, and managed the household. If a master died, his widow had the right to keep their shop, to hire the journeymen to work in it, and to manage the business.

Servants and Laborers. The lower rungs of the urban social structure were domestic servants and the laboring poor. At the beginning of the eighteenth century, domestic service was already becoming one of the largest sources of employment for the unskilled. Studies have found that 7 percent of the population of Ypres (Belgium), 15 percent of Münster (western Germany), and 20 percent of London were working as domestic servants. They lacked the independence and economic prospects of artisans, but they escaped from the poverty of unskilled labor while finding some comfort and secu-

The basic principle of mercantilism was a concept called **autarky**—the idea that a state should be self-sufficient in producing manufactured goods, should import as few foreign goods as possible, and should retain as much gold as possible. Simultaneously, the state sought export markets for its own goods. To achieve a favorable balance of trade and the consequent accumulation of wealth in gold required **government regulation** of the economy.

Mercantilist Monopolies. An important aspect of the mercantilist regulation of the economy was state support for manufactures and commerce. This meant that **monopolies,** not free trade, often seemed to serve the state's interests. Many governments of the Old Regime chartered monopolies with exclusive trading rights on the models of the British East India Company and the Dutch East India Company. During the 1720s alone, the Austrians chartered the Ostend Company to control trade with the Indies, the French merged several trading monopolies as the French Indies Company, and the Spanish gave the Chartered Company of Guipuzcoa (Caracas) a monopoly of the American trade. The shareholders in these mercantilist monopolies usually became rich. The Ostend Company, for example, paid its investors 137 percent interest in its first 7 years (nearly 20 percent per annum) while serving the emperor's interests by reviving the port of Ostend, stimulating Belgian business, and bringing Austria closer to self-sufficiency.

The mercantilist practice of creating chartered companies with protected privileges applied to much manufacturing in Europe. The French monarchy, for example, held a state monopoly in tapestries and porcelain, high-quality manufactures that could be profitably traded abroad. Prussia created a state tobacco monopoly, and Russia held a state salt monopoly. Many countries followed the Dutch example by chartering a national bank similar to the Bank of Amsterdam (1609). These banks served many important functions, such as supplying the mint with metals for coinage or providing the trading monopolies with credit. Parliament chartered the Bank of England in 1694 and gave it the privilege of printing paper money in 1718. The French created a Banque Royale in 1717; the Prussians, a Bank of Prussia in 1765.

Mercantilism and Government Regulation. Mercantilism encouraged manufacturing through direct aid and the state regulation of business. Direct aid might include subsidies, interest-free loans, or bonuses to manufacturers. Regulation took the form of explicit legislation. The French monarchy, for example, regulated mines, iron works, glass factories, and paper mills. French law specified what type and quality of raw materials could be used, which equipment and manufacturing processes must be employed, and standards of quality for the finished product. The French then sent factory inspectors to visit manufacturing sites and guarantee compliance with the law. A decree of 1740 explained that this procedure would maintain the quality of French manufactures and protect French trade from "the negligence and bad faith of the manufacturers and merchants." The most common mercantilist laws were **tariffs** and Navigation Acts. Tariffs placed taxes on goods entering a country to discourage imports (which produced an unfavorable balance of trade and drained gold from a country) and to protect domestic manufactures from foreign competition. Peter the Great of Russia, for example, levied heavy taxes on imported goods in 1724, even though Russians relied on European manufactures and luxury goods. In 1767, Charles Townshend, the British chancellor of the exchequer (minister of finance), drafted one of the most famous tariffs of the Old Regime: a high tax on glass, lead, paints, paper, and tea imported into Britain's American colonies, which led to the Boston Tea Party. While governments imposed such restrictions on imports, they simultaneously controlled trade through Navigation Acts requiring that goods shipped into (or out of) a country be carried only on ships of that country or that goods shipped into a country's colonies must depart from a port in the mother country.

The Physiocrats and Capitalism. Mercantilism was not unchallenged. Governments in the early eighteenth century were generally pleased with the successes of mercantilism (Britain and France both had very favorable balances of trade), but by midcentury, mercantilist policies were drawing increasing criticism. A group of theorists called the **Physiocrats** began to suggest major changes in economic policy, and their ideas supplanted the mercantile system with the basic doctrines of capitalism. The Physiocrats, led by French theorist François Quesnay, believed in limiting the powers of government, especially the power to intervene in economic activities. Quesnay and others proposed the abolition of monopolies and special privileges, the replacement of these policies by open competition in an unregulated marketplace, and the substitution of free trade for tariffs. The physiocratic school did not win great influence with the monarchical governments of the eighteenth century, but it opened the debate that ended mercantilism.

Adam Smith and Capitalism. Adam Smith, a Scottish economist who held the professorship of moral philosophy at Glasgow, adopted many of the ideas of the Physiocrats in writing his *Inquiry into the Nature and Causes of the Wealth of Nations* (1776), the cornerstone of the emerging field of political economy. Smith did not use the word **capitalism** to describe his ideas (and that term started to gain acceptance only in the late nineteenth century), but *The Wealth of Nations* became the most important founding work of a new school of economic thought. That doctrine, based on freedom of trade (without tariffs or monopolies) and the freedom of entrepreneurs (who possessed the capital, the source of the name capitalism) to develop business with government intervention and controls. Because the emphasis was on freedom, Smith's thought was long called **liberal economics** or **laissez-faire** (lay-zay-fair') **liberalism** (meaning allow the individual to act), although its roots remained in the physiocratic critique of mercantilism.

GLOBAL ECONOMIES OF THE EIGHTEENTH CENTURY: SLAVERY AND THE TRIANGULAR TRADE

Global Trade. European world trade grew and changed significantly during the Old Regime. In the seventeenth century, global trade chiefly linked Europe to India and the Far East, as the chartering of the great East Indies companies indicates. This trade had originally concentrated on the Spice Islands because great fortunes could be made by bringing pepper and other aromatic spices back to Europe, but the largest Asian trade evolved into competition for mainland markets such as India. During the seventeenth century, trade with the Indies might reward shareholders with more than 100 percent profits on their investment. By the eighteenth century, however, the focus of European global trade had turned to Africa and the Americas, where the profits had become larger.

Slavery and Eighteenth Century Trade. The profits of eighteenth-century trade, and much of Europe's prosperity, depended on slavery. The most profitable exploitation of slavery was a system called **triangular trade,** which began in the 1690s. The corners of this triangle were in Europe, Africa, and the Americas. British merchants were the most adept at the triangular trade, but it was practiced by slave traders from many countries. These slavers began their commerce by taking European manufactured goods (particularly textiles) to the western coast of Africa. These goods were sold or bartered for African slaves, who were offered for sale by local African rulers, by rivals who had taken them prisoner, or by Muslim slave traders. In the second leg of the triangular trade, a ship filled with slaves made the Atlantic crossing to European colonies in the Americas. The British, for example, brought slaves to Caribbean colonies (where 85 percent of the population lived in slavery) such as Jamaica and Barbados or to the mainland colonies in North America (where 20 percent of the population lived in slavery). African slaves were then sold to plantation owners, and the revenue was used to buy the agricultural goods (chiefly tobacco in North America and sugar in the Caribbean), which slave labor had produced. On the third leg of the triangle, these goods were returned to England, where they were sold at huge profits.

The Slave Trade. All European states with American colonies (including Holland and Denmark), and a few states without colonies (notably Prussia), participated in the slave trade. The French triangular trade sent textiles, jewelry, and hardware to West Africa; then shipped slaves to St. Domingue (Haiti), Guadeloupe, and Martinique in the Caribbean; and finally brought sugar and coffee back to France. The French amplified the British system by re-exporting sugar to the rest of continental Europe.

Sugar and Slavery. Sugar was the commodity on which the Caribbean slave economy rested. Sugar cane was not cultivated in Europe, and sugar was not yet extracted from beets. Slave-produced sugar from America sustained a growing European love of sweets. The European addiction to sugar cost humanity dearly: during the century from 1690 to 1790, one African died for every ton of sugar shipped to Europe. When the consumption of Caribbean sugar reached its peak in 1801, the cost had become one dead slave to provide the sugar for every 250 consumers in Britain.

Size of the Slave Trade. The scale of the slave trade was immense (see Table 17.9). The British Board of Trade estimated in 1709 that British colonies needed 25,000 additional slaves each year—4,000 for Barbados, 5,000 for North America, and 12,000 for Jamaica. When Britain obtained the *Asiento,* the contract for supplying slaves to Spanish America, in 1713, English slave traders brought an additional 5,000 slaves for Spanish colonies. The French delivered only 4,000 slaves per year in the early eighteenth century, but that figure rose to an average of 37,000 slaves per year by the 1780s. Britain and France alone sold approximately 3.5 million African slaves in the Americas during the eighteenth century. An average of 10 to 20 percent of the slaves died during an Atlantic crossing (50 to 75 percent on voyages when scurvy or amebic dysentery broke out on the ship), so the number of African slaves initially taken was closer to 4 million. Adding the Portuguese, Dutch, Danish, and Prussian slave trade, the grand total probably surpasses 5 million Africans. The demand for slaves was so high because the average life expectancy of a Caribbean slave was 7 years after arrival.

The Antislavery Movement. During the eighteenth century, signs were evident that this economy would also change. Moral revulsion with slavery began to create antislavery opinion, both in Europe and in the Americas. An American, Samuel Sewall, published an antislavery tract, *The Selling of Joseph,* as early as 1700. Two Portuguese Jesuits who served in Brazil, Jorge Benci and Giovanni Andreoni, published works in Europe attacking slavery. By 1727, the Religious Society of Friends (widely known as the Quakers) had begun an **abolitionist** (to abolish slavery) crusade. The

REGION	TOTAL POPULATION	SLAVE POPULATION	% IN SLAVERY
Spanish colonies	12,144,000	290,000	2.4
Mainland	12,000,000	240,000	2.0
Caribbean	144,000	50,000	34.7
British colonies	2,600,000	878,000	33.8
Mainland	2,100,000	450,000	21.4
Caribbean	500,000	428,000	85.6
Portuguese Brazil	2,000,000	700,000	35.0
French Caribbean	430,000	379,000	88.1
Dutch Caribbean	90,000	75,000	83.3
Danish Caribbean	25,000	18,000	35.0
Total, Mainland colonies	16,100,000	1,390,000	8.6
Total, Caribbean Islands	1,189,000	950,000	79.9

Source: Adapted from data in Blackburn, Robin, *The Overthrow of Colonial Slavery, 1776–1848* (London: Verso, 1988, p. 5).

Question: Why was the percentage of slaves so much higher on the Caribbean islands than on the mainland?

Gathering the Cane. Europeans developed a growing addiction to sugar—much of it to make coffee, tea, and chocolate palatable beverages—in the seventeenth and eighteenth centuries. The European craving for sugar built the slave economy of the West Indies. This engraving shows the tall sugar cane plant, the overseer with his whip (to discipline donkeys and slaves alike), male slaves cutting the cane, and female slaves gathering the heavy stalks.

moral arguments against slavery made slow progress because they faced powerful economic arguments that slavery was essential for both the colonial and the home economies. The Portuguese example illustrates both the progress and its slowness. Royal decrees abolished the slavery of American Indians (1755) and Asians (1758), then freed any African slave brought into Portugal (1761), and finally emancipated all African slaves held in Portugal (1773). But these decrees permitted the continuance of the slave trade and the perpetuation of African slavery in the Portuguese colony of Brazil, where it continued until 1888.

Slave Resistance and Rebellion. The greatest opposition to slavery naturally came from the slaves themselves, and all European governments faced slave rebellions in their colonies. One historian has calculated that the British colonies in North America experienced more than 200 slave rebellions before 1865. Slaves rebelled in New York City in 1712 and were stopped only by the arrival of the British army; anxiety about rebellion remained so high that in 1741, thirty-one slaves were executed in New York in fear that they were preparing

another rebellion. In a revolt of 1739 known as Cato's Conspiracy, 80 African slaves in South Carolina rebelled and sought to march to the Spanish colony of Florida. The Dutch faced a major rebellion, known as the Berbice Slave Rebellion, on their colony of Guyana in 1762; there the slaves won their initial battle with the Dutch militia and held out until larger forces arrived. The Danes put down slave rebellions on the island of St. John (in the Virgin Islands today) in 1733 with a ferocity that shocked European opinion: runaway slaves were tortured with red-hot pincers three times (at three different locations so that more people could watch), unless they were granted clemency and merely had a leg cut off; generous masters even pardoned their slaves with a sentence of 150 lashes and the amputation of one ear. The ferocity of European colonialists did not curtail slave rebellion. The French colony of St. Domingue lived with armed bands of runaway slaves known as *maroons* who fought a running war with plantation owners. One maroon, François Macandal, led a 6-year guerilla war in the 1750s; the French burnt him at the stake in 1758, but his example inspired the greatest slave rebellion of the century in 1791 (see Chapter 21).

CONCLUSION

Although some signs of change were appearing in the eighteenth century—such as the growing size of cities, the increasing importance of urban manufacturing, and the strengthening of the bourgeoisie—the social and economic structure of the Old Regime had not shifted greatly from previous centuries. Agriculture dominated the economy, and ownership of the land consequently shaped the social structure. Strong, old institutions such as the monarchy and the church held much of the land, but the largest share of the wealth of Europe was still held by a small elite of hereditary nobles who owned the land. The majority of the population (90 percent in some regions) worked the land without owning it. These realities sometimes obscure great social variations, not merely between aristocrats and peasants but also within each estate, including the aristocracy, although it typically constituted 2 percent of the population. Within this traditional society and economy, however, the elements of vast economic change and great political protest were already present.

Review Questions

- Why was agriculture important in the eighteenth-century economy?
- How would you describe the social structure of eighteenth-century Europe?
- What were the variations within the aristocracy, the peasantry, and the bourgeoisie?
- What were the economic theories of the eighteenth century?

For Further Study

Readings

Blum, J., *The End of the Old Order in Rural Europe* (Princeton: Princeton University Press, 1978). Detailed, comprehensive study of serfdom and the old rural order.

Clapham, J. H., et al., *The Cambridge Economic History of Europe*, 10 vols. (Cambridge, Cambridge University Press, 1941–1989). The elaborate economic history reference compiled by dozens of experts.

Dewald, Jonathan, *The European Nobility, 1400–1800* (Cambridge: Cambridge University Press, 1996). Excellent, succinct introduction to the wealth, privilege, life, and culture and the aristocracy during the Old Regime.

Heckscher, E., *Mercantilism*, 2 vols. (New York: Macmillan, 1955). The standard work on precapitalist economics in Europe.

Mitchell, B. R., *European Historical Statistics, 1750–1870* (London: Macmillan, 1975). An indispensable source for social and economic data such as statistics on population, labor, agriculture, and industry.

Mitchell, B. R., *British Historical Statistics* (Cambridge: Cambridge University Press, 1994) A broader range of statistical tables for Britain.

Wiesner, Merry E., *Women and Gender in Early Modern Europe*, 2nd ed. (Cambridge: Cambridge University Press, 2000). Excellent synthesis of the growing scholarship on women.

InfoTrac College Edition

For additional reading, go to your online research library at *http://infotrac.thomsonlearning.com*.

Using Key Terms, enter the search terms:
slave trade	*mercantilism*
aristocracy	*guilds*

Web Sites

http://edina.ac.uk/statacc/   The Statistical Accounts of Scotland, hosted by Edinburgh University. Provides a remarkable range of data on Scottish demography, agriculture, and economics in the 1790s.

http://dpls.dacc.wisc.edu/slavedata/index.html   The slave trade in the eighteenth century. A very rich collection of data on the slave trade hosted by the University of Wisconsin.

Visit the Western Civilization Companion Web Site for resources specific to this textbook:
http://history.wadsworth.com/hause02/

 The CD in the back of this book and the Western Civilization Resource Center at *http://history.wadsworth.com/western/* offer a variety of tools to help you succeed in this course, including access to quizzes; images; documents; interactive simulations, maps, and timelines; movie explorations; and a wealth of other sources.

THE SOCIAL AND ECONOMIC STRUCTURE OF THE OLD REGIME

1690	1700	1710	1720	1730	1740	1750	1760	1770	1780	1790	1800

POPULATION

Population of Europe Estimated at 150 Million
Sweden Conducts First Census of Population
1768–1769: Spain Conducts First Census
of Population
Britain Conducts First Census (1801)

AGRICULTURE

1701: Jethro Tull Introduces Seed Drill to Replace Broadcasting of Seeds
1730s: Townshend Introduces New Crop Rotation and Reliance on Turnip
1731: Jethro Tull's Book Introduces Effective New Method of Plowing
1740s: Aristocracy and Gentry Own 95 Percent of Wealth of England
1750: Majority of Population Lives in Rural World
Polish Population 99 Percent Rural
French Population 75 Percent Rural
English Population 65 Percent in Agriculture
1767: Russian Decree Reiterates Serfdom
1771: Savoy Abolishes Serfdom
1775: Austrian Law Defines Serfdom
1783: Baden Abolishes Serfdom
1787: Denmark Abolishes
Serfdom

URBAN EUROPE

1700: Constantinople Largest City in Europe (700,000), London and Paris More Than 500,000
1741: Deaths Outnumber Births in London by 2:1
1750: Industrialization of England Estimated at 10 Percent of
1900 Level
1750: 28 Percent of English Manufacturing in Textiles
1780: Guild Charters Reaffirmed in
German States

ECONOMIC SYSTEMS

Mercantilism Inherited as Dominant Economic System of Seventeenth and Eighteenth Centuries: Self-Sufficiency Protected by Tariffs
1690s: "Triangular Trade" Links Europe, Africa, and North America in Commercial Cycle of Heavy Slave Trading
1694: Parliament Charters the Bank of England
1713: Britain Acquires the *Asiento*, the Contract for Supplying Slaves to Spanish America
1717: France Charters Banque Royale
1718: Parliament Allows the Bank of England to Print and Circulate Paper Money
1720s: Austria Charters the Ostend Company with Monopoly of Trade in Indies
France Charters the French Indies Company with Monopoly of Trade in Indies
Spain Charters Chartered Company of Guipuzcoa with Monopoly of American Trade
1724: Peter the Great of Russia Introduces High Tariffs
1754: First University Professorship in Political Economy
1767: Britain Adopts High Townshend Tariffs
1768: Quesnay Publishes *La Physiocratie*,
Criticizing Mercantilism
1776: Adam Smith, *Wealth of Nations*

FOCUS QUESTIONS

- What difference does it make if distances seemed greater or travel slower in the eighteenth century?
- What explains the life expectancy of Europeans in the eighteenth century?
- What was the "biological Old Regime," and how did it affect daily life?
- What differences in disease and its treatment are most important in understanding life in the eighteenth century?
- What are the implications of the typical diet of the eighteenth century for daily life?
- What explains the different attitudes to stages of the life cycle in the eighteenth century?

Chapter 18

DAILY LIFE IN THE OLD REGIME

*I*n the autumn of 1705, Johann Sebastian Bach, then 20 years old and a recently appointed organist at a church in Thuringia in eastern Germany, learned that one of the most admired organ masters of the age, Dietrich Buxtehude, would soon perform a memorial concert in Lübeck in far northern Germany. To hear good music, Bach took a 4-week leave from his post and walked the 200 miles to Lübeck and then walked back. The miles that Bach walked are a good measure of how different daily life was in the eighteenth century.

Chapter 18 shows how the basic conditions of life in the eighteen century had changed little since the agricultural revolution of Neolithic times. It begins by exploring the basic relationships between people and their environment, such as Bach's walk to Lübeck. This chapter then examines the life of ordinary people beginning with its most striking feature—low life expectancy. The factors that help to explain that high level of mortality—collectively known as the **"biological Old Regime"**—are then discussed, specifically inadequate diet and the prevalence of epidemic disease. Finally, the **life cycle** of those who survived during the Old Regime is considered, including such topics as the dangers of childbirth; the understanding of childhood; and attitudes toward marriage, family, sexuality, and reproduction.

People and Their Environment: Population Density, Travel, and Communication

Population Density. Most of the people who lived in Europe during the Old Regime never saw a great city or even a town of 25,000 people. Most people stayed within a few miles of their home village and the neighboring market town. Studies of birth and death records show that more than 90 percent of the population of the eighteenth century died in the same region where they were born, passing their lives amid relatively few people. Powerful countries and great cities of the eighteenth century were small by twentieth-century standards (see Tables 17.1 and 17.2). Great Britain numbered an estimated 6.4 million people in 1700 (less than the state of Georgia today), and Vienna held 114,000 inhabitants (roughly the population of Fullerton, California, or Tallahassee, Florida). People at the start of the twenty-first century are also accustomed to life in densely concentrated populations. New York City has a population density of more than 55,000 people per square mile, and Maryland has a population density of nearly 500 people per square mile. The eighteenth century did not know such crowding: Great Britain had a population density of fifty-five people per square mile; Sweden, six (see Table 18.1).

Travel in the Eighteenth Century. Life in a rural world of sparse population was also shaped by the difficulty of travel and communication. The upper classes enjoyed a life of relative mobility that included such pleasures as owning homes in both town and country or taking a "grand tour" of historic cities in Europe. Journeymen who sought experience in their trade, agricultural laborers who were obliged to migrate with seasonal harvests, and peasants who were conscripted into the army were all exceptions in a world of limited mobility. Geographical obstacles, poor roads, weather, and bandits made travel slow and risky. For most people, the pace of travel was walking beside a mule or ox-drawn cart. Only well-to-do people traveled on horseback and even fewer in horse-drawn carriages (see *Travel and Communication in the Eighteenth Century*). Bach's remarkable walk to hear good music was not unique: after Napoleon Bonaparte graduated from a French military school in 1784, he walked 125 miles to Paris.

Difficulties of Travel. Travelers were at the mercy of the weather, which often rendered roads impassable because of flooding, mud, or snow. The upkeep of roads and bridges varied greatly. Governments maintained a few **post roads** (for postal service), but the upkeep of other roads depended on conscription of local labor. An

TABLE 18.1 European Population Density

Population density is measured by the number of people per square mile.

Country	Population Density in 1700	Population Density in the 1990s
Austrian Netherlands (Belgium)	153	853
Dutch republic (Netherlands)	119	959
Italian states (Italy)	112	499
German states (Germany)	98	588
France	92	275
Great Britain	55	616
Spain	38	201
Sweden	6	50

Source: Babuscio, Jack, and Dunn, Richard M., eds., *European Political Facts, 1648–1789* (London: Macmillian, 1984, pp. 335–353); and *The World Almanac and Book of Facts 1995* (Mahwah, NJ: World Almanac Books, 1994, pp. 740–839).

Question: What differences in life would be expected from the low population density figures for 1700?

English law of 1691, for example, simply required each parish to maintain the local roads and bridges; if upkeep was poor, the government fined the parish. Brigands also hindered travel. These **bandits** might become heroes to the peasants who protected them as rebels against authority and as benefactors of the poor, much as Robin Hood is regarded in English folklore, but they made travel risky for the few who could afford it.

Travel by Water. The fastest travel, for both people and goods, was often by water. Most cities had grown along rivers and coasts. Paris received the grain that sustained it by barges on the Seine; the timber that heated the city was floated down the river. The great transportation projects of the Old Regime were canals connecting these rivers. Travel on the open seas was normally fast, but it depended on fair weather. A voyager might be in England 4 hours after leaving France or trapped in port for days. If oceanic travel were involved, delays could reach remarkable lengths. In 1747, the electors of Portsmouth, England, selected Captain Edward Legge of the Royal Navy to represent them in Parliament; Legge, whose command had taken him to

TRAVEL AND COMMUNICATION IN THE EIGHTEENTH CENTURY

Coach Travel. Horse-drawn carriages and coaches remained the primary form of public transportation in Europe before the railroad age of the midnineteenth century. Postal service, business, and government all relied on a network of highways, stables, and coaching inns. Travel was slow, uncomfortable, and unpredictable. In this illustration, travelers in the Pyrenees wait at a coaching station and hotel in southern France while a wheel is repaired. Note the people in the background: most people travel on foot, although they may have a donkey to carry heavy goods.

the Americas, had died 87 days before this election, but the news had not yet arrived in Portsmouth.

Speed of Communication. Travel and communication were agonizingly slow by twenty-first-century standards. In 1734, the coach trip between Edinburgh and London (372 miles) took 12 days; the royal mail along that route required 48 hours of constant travel by relay riders. In 1765, it still took more than 2 weeks for the coach trip between Paris and Toulouse in southwestern France (see Table 18.2 in *Travel and Communication in the Eighteenth Century*). The commercial leaders of Venice could send messages to Rome (more than 250 miles) in 3 to 4 days, if conditions were favorable; messages to Moscow (more than 1,200 miles) required about 4 weeks (see Table 18.3). When King Louis XV of France died in 1774, this urgent news was rushed to the capitals of Europe via the fastest couriers: it arrived in Vienna and Rome 3 days later; Berlin, 4 days; and St. Petersburg, 6 days.

LIFE EXPECTANCY IN THE OLD REGIME

Eighteenth-Century Life-Expectancy Data. The living conditions of the average person during the Old Regime hold little appeal for people accustomed to twenty-first-century comforts. A famous writer of the mideighteenth century, Samuel Johnson, described the life of the masses as "little to be enjoyed and much to be endured." The most dramatic illustration of Johnson's point is **life-expectancy** data. Although the figures vary by social class or region, their message is grim. For everyone born during the Old Regime, the average age at death was close to 30. Demographic studies of northern France at the end of the seventeenth century found that the average age at death was 20. Data for Sweden in 1755 give an average life expectancy of 33. A comprehensive study of villages in southern England found a range between ages 35 and 45. These numbers are somewhat misleading

TABLE 18.2 THE SPEED OF COACH TRAVEL IN THE 1760s			
DATE	ROUTE	DAYS	KILOMETERS PER DAY
1760	London to Manchester	3	108
1760–1761	London to Leeds	3–4	76–101
1761	London to York	3–4	81–108
1766	London to Liverpool	2–3	112–169
1765	Paris to Angers	6½	49
1765	Paris to Rennes	8	43
1765	Paris to Toulouse	15½	44
1765	Paris to Lyons	5	94
1765	Paris to Strasbourg	11½	42

Sources: Szostak, Rick, *The Role of Transportation in the Industrial Revolution: A Comparison of England and France* (Montreal: McGill-Queen's, 1991, pp. 70–71); Jackman, W. T., *The Development of Modern Transportation in England* (Cambridge: Cambridge University Press, 1916, pp. 685–687); and Arbellot, G., "La Grande Mutation des Routes de France au milieu du XVIIIe siecle," in *Annales*, vol. 28 (1973): 790.

Question: Basing your answer on the table's data, which country had the better roads?

TABLE 18.3 AVERAGE SPEED OF A LETTER FROM VENICE IN 1700	
DESTINATION	TIME (DAYS)
Genoa or Rome	3–4
Munich or Vienna	5–6
Paris or Antwerp	7–8
London, Copenhagen, Lisbon, or Warsaw	10–11
Constantinople	17–21
Moscow	24–28

Source: Calculated from maps in Braudel, Fernand, *The Mediterranean and the Mediterranean World in the Age of Philip II* (New York: Harper, 1972, 1:366).

Question: What factors might explain such delays?

because they do not account for infant mortality, but they contain many truths about life in the past.

Implications of Short Life Expectancy. Short life expectancy meant that few people knew their grandparents. Research on a village in central England found that a population of 400 included only one instance of three generations alive in the same family. A study of Russian demography found more shocking results; between 20 and 30 percent of all serfs younger than age 15 had already lost both parents. Similarly, when the French philosopher Denis Diderot in 1759 returned to the village of his birth at age 46, he found that not a single person whom he knew from childhood had survived. Life expectancy was significantly higher for the rich than for the poor. Those who could afford fuel for winter fires, warm clothing, a superior diet, or multiple residences reduced many risks. The rich lived an estimated 10 years longer than the average in most regions and 17 years longer than the poor.

DISEASE AND THE BIOLOGICAL OLD REGIME

Infant Mortality and Life Expectancy. Life expectancy averages were low because **infant mortality** (death before age 1) was high, and death rates remained high throughout childhood. The study of northern France found that one-third of all children died each year and only a little more than half reached age 15. However, for those who survived infancy, life expectancy rose significantly. In a few healthier regions, especially where agriculture was strong, the people who lived through the terrors of childhood disease could expect to live nearly 50 more years.

The Biological Old Regime. The explanation for the shocking death rates and life expectancy figures of the Old Regime has been called the biological Old Regime, which suggests the natural restrictions created by chronic undernourishment, periodic famine, and unchecked disease. The first fact of existence in the eighteenth century was the probability of death from an infectious disease. Natural catastrophes (such as the Lisbon earthquake of 1755, which killed 30,000 people) or the human violence of wartime (such as the battle of Blenheim in 1704, which took more than 50,000 casualties in a single day) were terrible, but more people died from diseases. People who had the good fortune to survive natural and human catastrophe rarely died from heart disease or cancer, the great killers of the early twenty-first century. An examination of the 1740 death records for Edinburgh, for example, finds that the leading causes of death that year were tuberculosis and smallpox, which accounted for nearly half of all deaths (see Table 18.4).

Pandemic and Endemic Disease.
Some diseases were **pandemic**. The germs that spread them circulated throughout Europe at all times. The bacteria that attacked the lungs and caused tuberculosis (called *consumption* in the eighteenth century) were one such universal risk. Other diseases were **endemic**. They were a constant threat, but only in certain regions. Malaria, a febrile disease transmitted by mosquitoes, was endemic to warmer regions, especially where swamps or marshes were found. Rome and Venice were still in malarial regions in 1750; when Napoleon's army marched into Italy in 1796, his soldiers began to die from malaria before a single shot had been fired.

Epidemic Disease.
The most frightening diseases have always been **epidemic diseases**—waves of infection that periodically passed through a region. The worst epidemic disease of the Old Regime was **smallpox.** An epidemic of 1707 killed 36 percent of the pop-

ulation of Iceland. London lost 3,000 people to smallpox in 1710, then experienced five more epidemics between 1719 and 1746. An epidemic decimated Berlin in 1740, and another killed 6 percent of the population of Rome in 1746. Social historians have estimated that 95 percent of the population contracted smallpox, and 15 percent of all deaths in the eighteenth century can be attributed to it. Those who survived smallpox were immune thereafter, so it chiefly killed the young, accounting for one-third of all childhood deaths and as much as two-thirds of infant deaths (see Table 18.5). In the 80 years between 1695 and 1775, smallpox killed a queen of England, a king of Austria, a king of Spain, a tsar of Russia, a queen of Sweden, and a king of France. Smallpox ravaged the Hapsburgs, the royal family of Austria, and completely changed the history of their dynasty (see *The Conquest of Smallpox, Scourge of the Eighteenth Century*). Between 1654 and 1763, the disease killed nine immediate members of the royal family, causing the succession to the throne to shift four times. The death of Joseph I in 1711 cost the Hapsburgs their claim to the throne of Spain, which would have gone to his younger brother Charles. When Charles accepted the Austrian throne, the Spanish crown (which he could not hold simultaneously) passed to a branch of the French royal family. The accession of Charles to the Austrian throne also meant that his daughter, Maria Theresa, would ultimately inherit it—an event that led to years of war.

Mary Montagu and the Conquest of Smallpox.
Although smallpox was the greatest scourge of the eighteenth century, signs of a healthier future were evident. The Chinese and the Turks had already learned the benefits of intentionally infecting children with a mild case of smallpox to make them immune to the dis-

---

TABLE 18.4 LEADING EPIDEMICS: CAUSES OF DEATH IN THE EIGHTEENTH CENTURY COMPARED WITH THOSE OF THE PRESENT DAY

___	Deaths in Edinburgh in 1740			___	Deaths in the United States in 2000	
RANK	CAUSE	PERCENTAGE		RANK	CAUSE	PERCENTAGE
1	Consumption (tuberculosis)	22.4		1	Heart disease	31.0
2	Smallpox	22.1		2	Cancer	23.2
3	Fevers (including typhus and typhoid)	13.0		3	Stroke	6.8
4	"Old Age"	8.2		4	Respiratory diseases	4.8
5	Measles	8.1		5	Accidents	4.2

Source: Data for 1740 from Post, John D., *Food Shortage, Climatic Variability, and Epidemic Disease in Pre-industrial Europe* (Ithaca, NY: Cornell University Press, 1988, p. 241); data for the United States from *The Time Almanac: 2002* (Boston: Information Please, 2003, p. 132).

Question: Why don't "heart disease" and "cancer" appear as leading causes of death in 1740?

ease. A prominent English woman, Lady Mary Wortley Montagu (Mont'-ah-gew), followed her diplomat husband to Constantinople and observed the Turkish method of inoculating the young in 1717. She exposed her son to the treatment, and when it succeeded, she became the first European champion of the procedure (see *The Conquest of Smallpox, Scourge of the Eighteenth Century*). **Inoculation** (performed by opening a vein and introducing the disease) won acceptance very slowly because many social conservatives and religious leaders opposed it and popular opinion was suspicious of intentionally contracting a dangerous disease. Royal patronage was important in changing opinion. The Empress Maria Theresa had her entire family inoculated after she saw four of her children die of smallpox. Catherine the Great followed suit in 1768. But inoculation killed some people, and many feared it. The French outlawed the procedure in 1762, and the Vatican taught acceptance of the disease as a "visitation of divine will." Nonetheless, the death of Louis XV led to the inoculation of his three sons.

Edward Jenner and Smallpox Vaccination.
The second great step in the conquest of smallpox came from an English physician, Edward Jenner, who discovered the procedure of **vaccination.** Jenner had observed the similarities between smallpox and cowpox (a similar, but milder disease in cattle) and noted the apparent smallpox immunity of dairymaids who had contracted cowpox on their hands from milking cows. In 1796, Jenner used Mary Montagu's Turkish technique of inoculation on an 8-year-old boy, infecting him with cowpox from the hands of a dairymaid. This form of inoculation, dubbed vaccination (from the Latin *vacca,* meaning "cow"), quickly won converts in London and the support of some churches and government. Vaccination significantly changed daily life in the nineteenth century.

Typhus and Typhoid.
Whereas smallpox devastated all levels of society, some epidemic diseases chiefly killed the poor. **Typhus** (tie'-fus), spread by the bite of body lice, was common in squalid urban housing, jails, and army camps. **Typhoid** (tie'-foyd) **fever**, transmitted by contaminated food or water, was equally common in the unsanitary homes that peasants shared with their animals.

Bubonic Plague.
The most famous epidemic disease in European history was the **bubonic plague,** the Black Death that killed millions of people in the fourteenth century. The plague, introduced by fleas borne on rodents, no longer ravaged Europe, but it killed tens of thousands in the eighteenth century and evoked a special cultural terror. Between 1708 and 1713, the plague spread from Poland across central and northern Europe. Half the city of Danzig died, and the death rate was only slightly lower in Prague, Copenhagen, and Stockholm. Another epidemic spread from Russia in 1719. It reached the port of Marseilles in 1720, and 40,000 people perished. In 1771, Russia experienced another epidemic, which killed 57,000 people in Moscow alone.

Public Health before the Germ Theory

The Miasma Theory and Public Health.
Ignorance and poverty compounded the dangers of the biological Old Regime. The **germ theory** of disease transmission—that invisible microorganisms such as bacteria and viruses spread diseases—had been suggested centuries earlier, but governments, scientists, and churches dismissed this theory until the late nineteenth century. Instead, the dominant theory was the **miasma** (my-as'-muh) **theory** of contagion, holding that diseases spring from rotting matter in the earth. Acceptance of the miasma theory perpetuated dangerous conditions. Europeans did not understand the dangers of unsanitary housing, including royal palaces. Louis XIV's palace at Versailles was perhaps the greatest architectural ornament of an epoch, but human excrement accumulated in the corners and corridors of Versailles, just as it accumulated in heaps of dung alongside peasant cottages. One of the keenest observers of that age, the Duke de Saint-Simon, noted that even the royal apartments at Versailles opened out "over the privies and other dark and evil smelling places."

Cleanliness of Cities.
The great cities of Europe were filthy. Few had more than rudimentary sewer systems. Gradually, enlightened monarchs realized that they must clean their capitals, as King Charles III (Don Carlos) ordered for Madrid in 1761. This Spanish decree required all households to install piping on their property to carry solid waste to a sewage pit, ordered the construction of tiled channels in the streets to carry liquid wastes, and committed the state to clean public places. Such public policies significantly improved urban sanitation, but they were partial steps and the Spanish decree recognized this: "until such time as it be possible to construct the underground sewage system." The worst sanitation was often found in public institutions. The standard French army barracks of the eighteenth century had rooms measuring 16 feet by 8 feet; each room accommodated thirteen to fifteen soldiers, sharing four or five beds and innumerable diseases. Prisons were worse yet.

Weather and Health.
Another dangerous characteristic of Old Regime housing was a lack of sufficient heat. During the eighteenth century, the climatic condition known as the **Little Ice Age** persisted, with average

THE CONQUEST OF SMALLPOX, SCOURGE OF THE EIGHTEENTH CENTURY

Edward Jenner (1749–1823). Jenner was an English physician who had studied in London in the 1770s under John Hunter, one of the greatest medical scientists of the century, before beginning his practice in Gloustershire. His observation of the immunity of dairymaids to smallpox and his inference that they had acquired immunity from the cowpox transmitted to their hands by milking cows led him to conduct a famous expiriment (which would be totally unacceptable by today's medical precautions about using human subjects). In 1796, Jenner vaccinated an 8-year-old boy, James Phipps, with matter drawn from the cowpox scores on the hand of a milkmaid. Several weeks later, Jenner innoculated Phipps with smallpox, but the boy did not contract the disease. Jenner announced his success in a scholarly paper in 1798, and his method of vaccination soon proved so valuable at preventing smallpox that a grateful Parliament voted him a grant of £10,000 in 1803, then another grant of £20,000 in 1806. (These grants were worth approximately $150,000—an incredible fortune in 1800.)

TABLE 18.5 DEATH RATES IN FRENCH SMALLPOX EPIDEMICS, BY AGE GROUPS

AGE GROUP	PERCENTAGE OF THE DEAD WHO DIED OF SMALLPOX
Adult (age 20+)	3.7
Youth (age 10–19)	5.5
Child (age 3–9)	14.1
Infant (age 0–2)	66.8

Source: Adapted from data in Darmon, Pierre, *La Variole, les nobles, et les princes* (Paris: Editions Complexe, 1989, p. 34).

Question: Why are adult death rates so much lower than those for infants and children?

---

temperatures a few degrees lower than the twentieth century experienced. Winters were longer and harder; summers and growing seasons were shorter. Glaciers advanced in the north, and timberlines receded on mountains. In European homes, the heat provided by open fires was so inadequate that even nobles saw their inkwells and wine freeze in severe weather. Among the urban poor, where many families occupied unheated rooms in the basement or attic, the chief source of warmth was body heat generated by the entire family sleeping together. Some town dwellers tried heating their garrets by burning coal, charcoal, or peat in open braziers, without chimneys or ventilation, creating a grim duel between freezing cold and poisonous air. Peasants found warmth by bringing their livestock in-

doors and sleeping with the animals, exacerbating the spread of disease.

Religion and Disease. In a world lacking a scientific explanation of epidemic disease, religious teaching exercised great influence over public health standards. Churches offered solace to the afflicted, but they also offered another explanation of disease: it was the scourge of God. This theory of disease, like the miasma theory, contributed to inattention to public health. Many churches organized religious processions and ceremonies of expiation in hopes of divine cures. Unfortunately, such public assemblies often spread disease by bringing healthy people into contact with the infected. Processions and ceremonies also prevented effec-

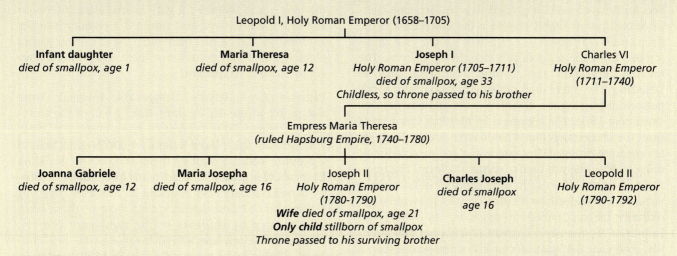

Leopold I, Holy Roman Emperor (1658–1705)

| **Infant daughter** *died of smallpox, age 1* | **Maria Theresa** *died of smallpox, age 12* | **Joseph I** *Holy Roman Emperor (1705–1711) died of smallpox, age 33 Childless, so throne passed to his brother* | **Charles VI** *Holy Roman Emperor (1711–1740)* |

Empress Maria Theresa
(ruled Hapsburg Empire, 1740–1780)

| **Joanna Gabriele** *died of smallpox, age 12* | **Maria Josepha** *died of smallpox, age 16* | **Joseph II** *Holy Roman Emperor (1780–1790)* **Wife** *died of smallpox, age 21* **Only child** *stillborn of smallpox Throne passed to his surviving brother* | **Charles Joseph** *died of smallpox age 16* | **Leopold II** *Holy Roman Emperor (1790–1792)* |

The Effects of Smallpox on the Austrian Royal Succession. Note the possible implications of smallpox: the two most important rulers of eighteenth-century Austria (Maria Theresa and Joseph II) may never have ruled if Joseph I had not died young of smallpox.

◄ *Mary Wortley Montagu.* Mary Wortley Montagu (1689–1762) was one of the most remarkable and important women of the eighteenth century. She was a precocious youth who insisted on learning Latin, the route to intellectual respectability normally reserved for men. When her father, the Earl of Kingston, arranged a marriage for her in the manner of the age, Mary refused and eloped with a member of Parliament, Edward Montagu, 30 years her senior. When he was named ambassador to the Ottoman Empire in 1716, Mary accompanied him to Constantinople, as her costume in this portrait suggests. There she observed the Turkish practice of inoculating children with a small amount of smallpox to prevent a full case of the disease—a practice that gave the Turks much better smallpox rates than the rest of Europe had. Mary Montagu daringly had her young son inoculated. Upon her return to Europe, Mary campaigned for the adoption of Turkish practices, thus beginning the conquest of the worst scourge of the century. Mary Montagu's later life included a career as a poet and author, hosting a literary salon in London, and a scandalous life of independence in Italy.

tive measures because they persuaded churches to oppose quarantines. Churches were not alone; merchants in most towns joined them in fighting quarantines.

Medicine and the Biological Old Regime

Availability of Medical Care. Most Europeans during the Old Regime never received medical attention from trained physicians. Few doctors were found in rural areas. Peasants relied on folk medicine, consulted unlicensed healers, or allowed illness to run its course. Many town dwellers received their medical advice from **apothecaries** (druggists). The propertied classes could consult trained physicians, although this was often a mixed blessing. Many medical doctors

were quacks, and even the educated ones often had minimal training. The best medical training in Europe was found at the University of Leiden in Holland, where Hermann Boerhaave pioneered clinical instruction at bedsides, and similar programs were created at the College of Physicians in Edinburgh in 1681 and in Vienna in 1745. Yet Jean-Paul Marat, one of the leaders of the French Revolution, received a medical degree at Edinburgh after staying there for a few weeks during the summer of 1774.

Eighteenth-Century Medicine. Medical science practiced curative medicine, following traditions that seem barbaric to people of later centuries. The **pharmacopeia** of medicinal preparations still favored ingredients such as unicorn's horn (ivory was usually used), crushed lice, incinerated toad, or ground shoe leather. One cherished medication, highly praised in the first edition of the *Encyclopedia Britannica* (1771), was usnea, the moss scraped from the scalp of prisoners hung in irons. The medical profession also favored treatments such as **bleeding** (the intentional drawing of blood from a sick person) or purging the ill with emetics and enemas (see Document 18.1). The argument for bleeding was derived from the observation that if blood were drawn, the body temperature dropped. Because fevers accompanied most diseases, bleeding was used to reduce the fever. This treatment often hastened death. King Louis XV of France was virtually bled to death by his physicians in 1774, although officially he succumbed to smallpox. As Baron von Leibniz, a distinguished German philosopher and scientist, observed, "[A] great doctor kills more people than a great general." The treatment given to King Charles II of England in 1685, as he died of an apparent embolism (a clot in an artery), shows the state of learned medicine. A team of a dozen physicians first drew a pint of blood from his right arm. They then cut open his right shoulder and cupped it with a vacuum jar to draw more blood. Charles then received an emetic to induce vomiting, followed by a purgative, then a second purgative. Next came an enema of antimony and herbs, which was followed by a sec-

ond enema and a third purgative. Physicians then shaved the king's head, blistered it with heated glass, intentionally broke the blisters, and smeared a powder into the wounds (to "strengthen his brain"). Next came a plaster of pitch and pigeon excrement. Death was probably a relief to the tortured patient.

Eighteenth-Century Hospitals. Hospitals were also scarce in the Old Regime. Nearly half of the counties of England did not contain a single hospital in 1710, and by 1800, there were still only 4,000 hospital beds in the entire country, half of them in London. Avoiding hospitals was generally safer in any case. These institutions had typically been founded by monastic orders as refuges for the destitute sick, and most of them were still operated by churches in the eighteenth century. There were a few specialized hospitals (the first children's clinic was founded at London in 1779), and most hospitals typically mixed together poor patients with a variety of diseases that spread inside the hospital. Patients received a minimal diet and rudimentary care but little medical treatment.

Eighteenth-Century Surgery. The history of surgery is even more frightening. In many regions, surgeons were still members of the barbers' guild. Because eighteenth-century physicians did not believe in the

FIGURE 18.1 *The Interior of a Pharmacy.* This eighteenth-century print depicts an apothecary's shop (a druggist) in Bologna, Italy. A large staff locates the correct ingredients while a pharmacist (behind the counter at center) grinds them by hand with a mortar and pestle. Often, a doctor would set up his office inside the apothecary's shop and write prescriptions for customers who would then buy the preparations—an efficient and profitable arrangement for both men.

FIGURE 18.2 *An Eighteenth-Century Leg Amputation.* This vivid painting depicts one of the horrors of medicine in the long age before the discovery of anesthetics in the nineteenth century. Leg amputations were surprisingly common in the eighteenth century because surgeons could not rejoin severed arteries that resulted from battle, horse-riding and road accidents, and severe fractures. Surgeons were cherished for the speed with which they could cut a limb. In this illustration, six men are needed to hold the patient still while the surgeon saws off the leg, and the anguish of the patient is evident. Note the bench of carpenter-shop tools in the foreground, the class of students in the background (indicating that this surgery is affiliated with a medical school), and the nonsterile dress of the medical staff, typical of a scene before the germ theory of disease transmission led to antiseptic conditions.

A NOVELIST SATIRIZES THE MEDICAL PRACTICE OF BLEEDING

A French physician applies leeches to a patient's neck.

Alain-René Lesage (1668–1747) was a Breton writer who showed his finest skills in his satires. He depicted human shortcomings and sufferings with a remarkable good humor, which suggests how people of the Old Regime coped with the difficulties of life. Lesage's masterpiece is the picaresque romance *Gil Blas* (1715). The protagonist (Blas) holds many different jobs that enable him to observe life. The following excerpt describes how a doctor bleeds a priest (one of Blas's employers) to death.

I served the priest Sédillo for three months. He fell ill; a fever came on, and this aggravated his gout. For the first time in his life, he called in a physician. . . . I went for Doctor Sangrado and brought him to the house. He was a tall, withered, wan man, who for forty years at least kept Clotho [the mythological figure who cut the thread of life] busy with her shears. This learned physician had a grave appearance . . . , but his jargon sounded great to the ears of the uninformed.

After having studied my master's symptoms, he said to him solemnly: "Common practitioners in this case would doubtless prescribe the traditional routine of salts, diuretics, purgatives . . . pernicious drugs invented by quacks. All chemical preparations seem made only to injure. I use simpler and more efficacious means. What is your usual diet?"

"I generally live on soups," replied the Canon, "and eat my meat with rich gravy."

"Soups and rich meats!" cried the doctor in surprise. "I am no longer surprised to find you ill. Luxurious living is like poisoned bait: it is a trap set by sensuality, a trap to cut short the days of wretched man. You must renounce pampering your appetite: the most boring food is the best for health. . . . "

"And do you drink wine?" he added.

"Yes," said the canon, "but diluted with water."

"Oh! It doesn't matter how you dilute it," replied the physician. "This is licentiousness with a vengeance! A frightful diet! You ought to have been dead years ago! How old are you?"

"I am entering my 69th year," replied the canon.

"Just as I said," responded the physician, "a premature old age is always the result of intemperance. If you had only drunk pure water all your life, and had been content with simple food . . . you would not now be tormented."

The licentiate promised to obey the doctor in all things. . . .

Doctor Sangrado then sent me for a surgeon whom he named, and ordered him to take from my master about 18 ounces of blood by way of a beginning. He then said to the surgeon, "Come back in three hours and do the same thing again; start over again tomorrow. It is a mistake to think that blood is necessary to preserve life. You can never bleed a patient too much."

The good canon, imagining that so great a doctor could not argue wrongly, allowed himself to be bled without resistance. When the doctor had ordered these frequent and copious bleedings, he said that we must also make the canon continually drink warm water. We heated the kettles in a hurry and . . . we began with pouring down two or three pints in as many swallows. An hour later we set upon him again; then, returning to the attack time after time, we fairly poured a deluge of water into his poor stomach. The surgeon, on the other hand, seconding our efforts by the quantity of blood he drew off, reduced the old canon to death's door in less than two days. . . .

[After learning of a possible inheritance], I promised to pray for his soul after his death. This event happened anon, for the surgeon having bled him once more, the poor old man, already much weakened, expired almost immediately. As he was breathing his last, the physician appeared and looked rather foolish in spite of the habit he had of dispatching his patients. . . . He coolly observed as he left that the patient had not been bled enough and had not drunk enough water. The medical executioner—I mean the surgeon—seeing that his job was done, followed the doctor, both remarking that they had said he would not recover, the very first day they saw him.

Question: What elements of modern medicine might be satirized as analagous practices?

germ theory of disease transmission, surgeons often cut people in squalid surroundings with no thought for basic cleanliness of their hands or their instruments. Without **antisepsis,** gangrene (then called *hospital putrefaction*) was a common result of surgery. No general **anesthetics** were available, so surgeons operated on a fully conscious patient. In these circumstances, opium became a favorite medication of well-to-do patients. It was typically taken as a tincture with alcohol known as **laudanum,** and it was available from apothecaries

FOOD CONSUMPTION IN THE EIGHTEENTH CENTURY

Historians use many sources to discover diets in the past. For the eighteenth century, there are good aggregate data, such as the amount of grain that an entire region consumed, which can be broken down to a per-capita basis. There are also many surviving records of institutions such as schools, armies, and prisons that show daily rations. Data such as the budget of a single family is rarer, but the surviving records (such as the budget of a Berlin family shown here) are very evocative. Note the percentage of income spent on food, for example, and calculate how much money that would be for modern workers.

Questions: Are these data convincing illustrations of the limited food supplies of the Eighteenth century? What other records might be helpful in making this point?

TABLE 18.6 GRAIN CONSUMPTION IN THE EIGHTEENTH CENTURY

The highest rate of grain consumption during the Old Regime was usually associated with the lowest standards of living. High rates indicate severely unbalanced diets; low rates are found in prosperous regions where other foods were more available.

REGION	PERIOD	PER-CAPITA DAILY GRAIN CONSUMPTION (IN POUNDS)
Holland	1798	0.7
France	c. 1700	1.3–1.4
England	1700s	1.4
Hanover	c. 1750	1.4
France	1775–1780	1.4–1.7
East Prussia	1750–1800	2.8[a]
Burgundy	1700s	3.1
Flanders	1710	3.2[b]

Source: Condensed from data in van Bach, B. H. Slicher, "Agriculture and the Vital Revolution," in *The Cambridge Economic History of Europe*, M. M. Postan and others, eds. (Cambridge: Cambridge University Press, 1977, 5:84).
[a]For people older than age 12 years.
[b]Includes grain for beer.

without a prescription. Laudanum drugged the patient; it often addicted survivors to opium, but it reduced suffering. Many famous figures of the eighteenth and nineteenth centuries died, as did the artist Sir Joshua Reynolds in 1792, "all but speechless from laudanum."

SUBSISTENCE DIET AND THE BIOLOGICAL OLD REGIME

Diet and Malnutrition. The second critical feature of the biological Old Regime was a dangerously inadequate food supply. In all regions of Europe, much of the population lived with chronic undernourishment, dreading the possibility of famine. A **subsistence diet** (one that barely met the minimum needed to sustain life) weakened the immune system, making people more vulnerable to contracting diseases and less able to withstand their ravages. Diet was thus a major factor in the Old Regime's high mortality rates and short life expectancies.

A Diet of Bread. Most of Europe lived chiefly on starches (see *Food Consumption in the Eighteenth Century*). The biblical description of bread as "the staff of life" was true, and most people obtained 50 to 75 percent of their total calories from some form of bread (it might have been converted to porridge or gruel). Interruptions of the grain supply—such as frozen rivers preventing transportation or poor weather lowering the harvest—meant suffering and death. In good times, a peasant family ate several pounds of bread a day, up to 3 pounds per capita; in lean times, they might share 1 pound of bread. A study of the food supply in Belgium has shown that the nation consumed a per-capita average of 1.25 pounds of cereal grains per day. A study of eastern Prussia has shown that the adult population

TABLE 18.7 FOOD IN THE BUDGET OF A BERLIN WORKER'S FAMILY	
EXPENSE	PERCENTAGE
Food	
Bread	45
Other vegetable products	12
Animal products (meat and dairy)	15
Beverages	2
Total food	74
Nonfood	
Housing	14
Heating, lighting	7
Clothing, other expenses	6
Total Nonfood	27

NOTE: Figures exceed 100 percent because of rounding.

Source: From data in Braudel, Fernand, *The Structures of Everyday Life* (New York: Harper and Row, 1981, p. 132).

TABLE 18.8 THE DIET IN AN AMSTERDAM PRISON, 1781

John Howard was an English reformer who toured European prisons in the 1770s and 1780s to compare the conditions in them. He praised Dutch prisons for having the best conditions, and he reported that adult male prisoners who worked a full shift received two meals per day and a third meal on Wednesday, following the menu below.

TIME	MEAL
Daily breakfast	1.5 pounds of bread, with butter
Daily beverage ration	4 pints of weak beer
Monday noon	Peas with salt and vinegar
Tuesday noon	Boiled peas
Wednesday noon	Gruel of oats or barley boiled in milk
Wednesday evening	Gruel of oats or barley boiled in milk
Thursday noon	Fish with milk or butter
Friday noon	Boiled peas
Saturday noon	Gruel of oats or barley boiled in milk
Sunday dinner	0.5 pound of beef or pork with beans

lived on nearly 3 pounds of grain per day. Peasant labors there received their entire annual wages in starches; the quantity ranged from 32 bushels of grain (1694) to 25 bushels of grain and 1 of peas (1760).

Wheat and Cheaper Grains. Bread made from wheat was costly because wheat yielded few grains harvested per grain sown. As a result, peasants lived on coarser, but bountiful, grains. Their heavy, dark bread normally came from rye and barley. In some poor areas, such as Scotland, oats were the staple grain. To save valuable fuel, many villages built communal ovens and baked bread in large loaves once a month, or even once a season. This created a hard bread that had to be broken with a hammer and soaked in liquid before it could be eaten. For variety, cereals could be mixed with liquid (usually water) without baking to create gruel, or the same ingredients could be used to make beer, which was virtually a liquid bread.

Variety in the Diet. Supplements to the monotonous diet of starches varied from region to region, but meat was a rarity. In a world without canning or refrigeration, meat was consumed only when livestock were slaughtered, in a salted or smoked form of preservation, or in a rancid condition. Successful peasants might have a little smoked bacon, dried sausage, or even an aged ham hanging from the rafters, but it was not the central part of the diet. A study of the food supply in Rome in the 1750s has shown that the average daily consumption of meat amounted to slightly more than 2 ounces per capita. For the lower classes, that meant a few ounces of sausage or dried meat per week. In that same decade, Romans consumed bread at an average varying between 1 and 2 pounds per day. Fruits and fresh vegetables were seasonal and typically limited to those regions where they were cultivated. A fresh orange was thus a luxury to most Europeans, and a fresh pineapple was rare and expensive. Occasional dairy products plus some cooking fats and oils (chiefly lard in northern Europe and olive oil in the south) brought urban diets close to 2,500 calories per day in good times. A study of Parisian workers in 1780 found that adult males engaged in physical labor averaged 2,000 calories per day, mostly from bread. (Figures of 3,500 to 4,000 calories are common today among males doing physical labor.) Urban workers often spent more than half of their wages for food, even when they just ate bread. A study of Berlin at the end of the eighteenth century showed that a working-class family might spend more than 70 percent of its income on food (see Table 18.7 in *Food Consumption in the Eighteenth Century*). Peasants ate only the few vegetables grown in kitchen gardens that they could afford to keep out of grain production.

Traditional Beverages: Wine, Beer, and Milk.

Beverages varied regionally. In many places, the water was unhealthy to drink and peasants avoided it without knowing the scientific explanation of their fears. Southern Europe produced and consumed large quantities of wine, and beer could be made anywhere that grain was grown. In 1777, King Frederick the Great of Prussia urged his people to drink beer, stating that he had been raised on it and believed that a nation "nourished on beer" could be "depended on to endure hardships." Such beers were often dark, thick, and heavy. When Benjamin Franklin arrived in England, he called the beer "as black as bull's blood and as thick as mustard." Wine and beer were consumed as staples of the diet, and peasants and urban workers alike derived many of their calories and carbohydrates from them, partly because few nonalcoholic choices were available. The consumption of milk depended on the local economy.

New Beverages: Coffee, Tea, and Chocolate.

Beverages infused in water (coffee, tea, and cocoa) became popular in European cities when global trading made them affordable and the availability of sugar made them palatable. The Spanish introduced the drinking of chocolate (which was exclusively a beverage until the nineteenth century), but it long remained a costly drink. Coffee drinking was brought to Europe from the Middle East, and it became a great vogue after 1650, producing numerous urban **coffeehouses.** But infused beverages never replaced wine and beer in the diet. Some governments feared that coffeehouses were centers of subversion and restricted them more than the taverns. Others worried about the economic implications of expensive imports. English coffee imports, for example, sextupled between 1700 and 1785, leading the government to tax tea and coffee. The king of Sweden issued an edict denouncing coffee in 1746, and when that failed to control the national addiction, he decreed total prohibition in 1756. Coffee smuggling produced such criminal problems, however, that the

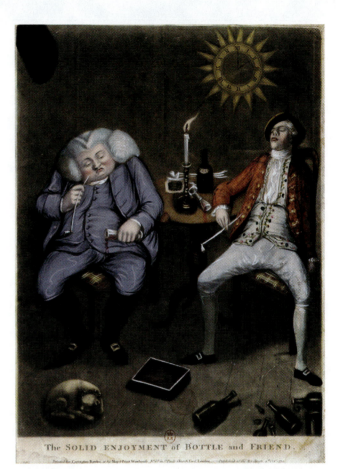

FIGURE 18.3 *Alcoholism in Eighteenth-Century Europe.* Europeans consumed enormous amounts of alcohol in the eighteenth century. Inebriation was widely accepted in society, alcohol was plentiful and cheap, medical knowledge of the dangers of alcohol was limited (indeed, physicians often prescribed alcohol), and drinking water was often more dangerous. In this scene, two friends have drunk themselves into a stupor, apparently consuming the contents of several bottles seen on the floor. Both of them have spilled their glasses, and one has already passed out. The first anti-alcohol society still remained more than 50 years in the future.

king legalized the drink again in 1766 and collected a heavy excise tax on it.

Beverages: Alcohol.

The popularity of infused beverages did not curtail the remarkable rate of alcohol consumption in the eighteenth century. Europeans had learned the method of distillation of alcohol from the Arabs in the late Middle Ages, but alcohol long remained a scarce commodity, more common in medications than in taverns. By the eighteenth century, however, cheap distilled alcohol had become widely available. The English drank an enormous amount of gin: only a steep gin tax in 1736 and vigorous enforcement of a Tippling Act of 1751 reduced consumption from 8.5 to 2.1 million gallons of gin per year during the 1750s.

FIGURE 18.4 *An Early London Coffeehouse.* The coffeehouse became extremely popular in eighteenth-century Europe. In addition to the stimulating beverage itself, the coffee shop offered many people a public meeting place where they might read newspapers, conduct business, or discuss issues of the day. The coffee shop was more respectable than the café or pub because it did not sell alcoholic beverages, so it won the approval of the hard-working urban middle classes and even the upper classes, as seen from the dress in this image of an English coffee shop in 1705.

The Columbian Exchange and the European Diet

The Columbian Exchange. The most important changes in the European diet of the Old Regime resulted from the gradual adoption of foods found in the Americas. In a reciprocal **Columbian exchange** of plants and animals unknown on the other continent, Europe and America both acquired new foods. No Italian tomato sauce or French fried potato existed before the Columbian exchange because the tomato and potato were plants native to the Americas and unknown in Europe. Similarly, the Columbian exchange introduced maize (American corn), peanuts, many peppers and beans, and cacao to Europe. The Americas had no wheat fields, grapevines, or melon patches and no horses, sheep, cattle, pigs, goats, or burros. In the second stage of this exchange, European plants established in the Americas began to flourish and yield exportation to Europe. The most historic example of this was the establishment of the sugar cane plantations in the Caribbean, where slave labor made sugar commonly available in Europe for the first time, but at a horrific human price.

The Potato. Europe's first benefit from the Columbian exchange came from the potato, which changed diets in the eighteenth century. The Spanish imported the potato in the sixteenth century after finding the Incas cultivating it in Peru, but Europeans initially refused to eat it because folk wisdom considered tubers dangerous. Churches opposed the potato because the Bible did not mention it. Potatoes, however, offer the tremendous advantage of yielding more calories per acre than grains do. In much of northern Europe, especially in western Ireland and northern Germany, short and rainy summer seasons severely limited the crops that could be grown and the population that could be supported. Irish peasants discovered that just one acre of potatoes, planted in soil that was poor for grains, could support a full family. German peasants learned that they could grow potatoes in their fallow fields during crop rotation, then discovered 1 acre of potatoes could feed as many people as 4 acres of the rye that they traditionally planted.

Peasants soon found another of the advantages of the potato: it could be left in the ground all winter without harvesting it. Ripe grain must be harvested and stored, becoming an easy target for civilian tax collectors or military requisitioners. Potatoes could be left in the ground until the day they were eaten, thereby providing peasants with much greater security. The steady growth of German population compared with France during the eighteenth and nineteenth centuries (with tremendous historic implications) is partly the result of this peasant decision and the educational work of agronomists such as Antoine Parmentier, who showed its merits in his *Treatise on the Uses of the Potato.* Just as the potato changed the history of Germany and Ireland, the introduction of maize changed other regions. Historians of the Balkans credit the nutritional advantages of maize with the population increase and better health that facilitated the Serbian and Greek struggles for independence.

Famine in the Old Regime

Frequency of Famine. Even after the introduction of the potato and maize, much of Europe lived on a subsistence diet. In bad times, the result was catastrophic. Famines, usually the result of two consecutive bad harvests, produced starvation. In such times, peasants ate their seed grain or harvested unripe grain and roasted it, prolonging both life and famine. They

THE COLUMBIAN EXCHANGE

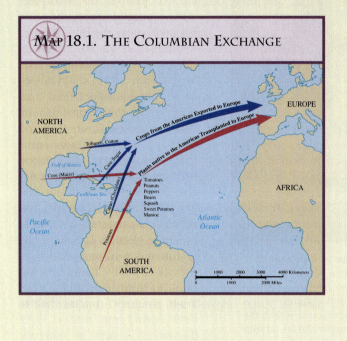

MAP 18.1. THE COLUMBIAN EXCHANGE

Foods introduced to Europe by the Columbia exchange.

Starches
Potatoes
Sweet potatoes
Wild rice
Cassava
Amaranth

Vegetables
Tomatoes
Bell peppers
Chili peppers
Pumpkins
Lima beans
Avocados
Zucchini squash

Nuts
Peanuts
Walnuts
Pecans

Cashews
Pinion pine nuts
Brazil nuts

Fruit and Berries
Pineapples
Papayas
Currants
Strawberries
Raspberries
Blueberries
Blackberries
Cranberries

Flavorings
Allspice
Vanilla
Maple syrup
Annatto

turned to making bread from ground chestnuts or acorns. They ate grass and weeds, cats and dogs, rodents, and even human flesh. Such disasters were not rare. The records of Tuscany show that the 300 years between 1450 and 1750 included 100 years of famine and 16 years of bountiful harvests. Agriculture was more successful in England, but the period between 1660 and 1740 saw one bad harvest in every 4 years. France, an agriculturally fortunate country, experienced 16 years of national famine during the eighteenth century, plus local famines.

Weather and Famine. The worst famine of the Old Regime, and one of the most deadly events in European history, occurred in Finland in 1696–1697. The extreme cold weather of the Little Ice Age produced a Finnish summer too short for grain to ripen. Between one-fourth and one-third of the entire nation died before that famine passed—a death rate that equaled the horrors of the bubonic plague. The weather produced other famines in that decade. In northern Europe, excess rain caused crops to rot in the field before ripening. In Mediterranean Europe, especially in central Spain, a drought followed by an onslaught of grasshoppers produced a similar catastrophe. Hunger also followed seasonal fluctuations. In lean years, the previous year's grain might be consumed before July, when the new

grain could be harvested. Late spring and early summer were consequently dangerous times when the food supply had political significance. Winter posed special threats for city dwellers. If the rivers and canals froze, the barges that supplied the cities could not move and the water-powered mills could not grind flour.

Food Pensions. Food supplies were such a concern in the Old Regime that marriage contracts and wills commonly provided food pensions. These pensions were intended to protect a wife or aged relatives by guaranteeing an annual supply of food. An examination of these pensions in southern France has shown that most of the food to be provided was in cereal grains. The typical form was a lifetime annuity intended to provide a supplement; the average grain given in wills provided fewer than 1,400 calories per day.

Diet, Disease, and Appearance

Diet and Height in the Eighteenth Century. Malnutrition, famine, and disease were manifested in human appearance. A diet so reliant on starches meant that people were short compared with later standards. For example, the average adult male of the eighteenth century stood slightly above 5 feet tall. Napoleon, ridiculed today for being so short, was as tall as most of his soldiers. Meticulous records kept for Napoleon's Army of Italy in the late 1790s (a victorious army) reveal that conscripts averaged 5 feet, 2 inches in height. Many famous figures of the era had similar heights: the notorious Marquis de Sade stood 5 feet, 3 inches. Conversely, many people known for their height were not tall by later standards. A French diplomat, Prince Talleyrand, appears in letters and memoirs to have had an advantage in negotiations because he "loomed over" other statesmen. Talleyrand stood 5 feet, 8 inches. The kings of Prussia recruited peasants considered to be "giants" to serve in the royal guards at Potsdam; a height of 6 feet defined a giant. Extreme height did occur in some families, such as the Russian royal family, the Romanovs: Peter the Great stood 6 feet, 7 inches. For the masses, diet limited their height. The superior diet of the aristocracy made them taller than peasants, just as it gave them a greater life expectancy; aristocrats explained such differences by their natural superiority as a caste.

Disease and Appearance. Just as diet shaped appearance, so did disease. Vitamin and mineral deficiencies led to a variety of afflictions, such as rickets and scrofula. Rickets marked people with bone deformities; scrofula produced hard tumors on the body, especially under the chin. The most widespread effect of disease came from smallpox. As its name indicates, the disease often left pockmarks on its victims, the result of scratching the sores, which itched terribly. Because 95 percent of the population contracted smallpox, pockmarked faces were common.

The noted Anglo-Irish dramatist Oliver Goldsmith described this in 1760:

> Lo, the smallpox with horrid glare
> Leveled its terrors at the fair;
> And, rifling every youthful grace,
> Left but the remnant of a face.

Disease and Fashion. Smallpox and diseases that discolored the skin such as jaundice, which left a yellow complexion, explain the eighteenth-century popularity of heavy makeup and artificial "beauty marks" (which could cover a pockmark) in the fashions of the wealthy. Other fashion trends of the age originated in poor public health. The vogue for wigs and powdered hair for men and women alike derived in part from infestation by lice. Head lice could be controlled by shaving the head and wearing a wig.

Dental Disease and Appearance. Dental disease marked people with missing or dark, rotting teeth. The absence of sugar in the diet delayed tooth decay, but oral hygiene scarcely existed because people did not know that bacteria caused their intense toothaches. Medical wisdom held that the pain came from a worm

FIGURE 18.5 At the Dentist. This eighteenth-century Italian painting vividly depicts one of the widespread nightmares of the age, the need to see a dentist. Dental hygiene was generally terrible and tooth decay almost universal, especially as sugar consumption rose sharply. Broken teeth, rotting teeth, and the ubiquitous toothache ultimately drove people to the dentist. But there was still no anesthesia, so teeth were extracted by simple force from fully conscious people, as this woman has just experienced.

that bored into teeth. Anton van Leeuwenhoek, the Dutch naturalist who invented the microscope, had seen bacteria in dental tartar in the late seventeenth century, and Pierre Fauchard, a French physician considered the founder of modern dentistry, had denounced the worm theory, but their science did not persuade their colleagues. For brave urban dwellers, barber-surgeons offered the painful process of extraction (without anesthesia). A simple, but excruciating, method involved inserting a whole peppercorn into a large cavity; the pepper expanded until the tooth shattered, facilitating extraction. More often, dental surgeons gripped the patient's head with their knees and used tongs to shake the tooth loose. Whether or not one faced such dreadful pain, dental disease left most people with only a partial set of teeth by their forties.

THE LIFE CYCLE

Birth

Pregnancy and Childbirth in the Eighteenth Century. Social historians also use another set of perspectives to examine the history of daily life: an examination of the **life cycle** from birth to old age (see Table 18.9). Few experiences better illustrate the perils of the Old Regime than the process of entering it. Pregnancy and birth were extremely dangerous for mother and child. Malnutrition and poor prenatal care caused a high rate of miscarriages, stillbirths, and deformities. Childbirth was still an experience without anesthesia or antisepsis. The greatest menace to the mother was **puerperal fever (childbed fever),** an acute infection of the genital tract resulting from the absence of aseptic methods. This disease swept Europe, particularly the few "laying-in" hospitals for women. An epidemic of puerperal fever in 1773 was so severe that folk memories in northern Italy recalled that not a single pregnant woman survived. Common diseases, such as rickets (from vitamin deficiency), made deliveries difficult and caused bone deformities in babies. No adequate treatment was available for hemorrhaging, which could cause death by bleeding or slower death by gangrene. Few ways existed to lower the risks of difficult deliveries. Surgical birth by a cesarean section gave the mother one chance in a thousand of surviving. Attempts to deliver a baby by using large forceps saved many lives but often produced horrifying injuries to the newborn or hemorrhaging in the mother. A delicate balance thus existed between the deep pride in bearing children and a deep fear of doing so. One of the most noted women of letters in early modern Europe, Madame de Sévigné, advised her daughter of two rules for survival: "Don't get pregnant and don't catch smallpox."

Attitudes to Childbirth. The established churches and the medical profession typically preached acceptance of the pain of childbirth by teaching that it represented the divine will. The explanation lay in the Bible. For "the sin of Eve" in succumbing to Satan and being "the devil's gateway" to Adam, God punished all women with the words: "I will greatly multiply thy sorrow and thy conception; in sorrow thou shalt bring forth children" (Gen. 3:16). Even when the means to diminish the pain of childbirth became available, this argument sustained opposition to it.

Infancy and Childhood

Infant Mortality. Statistics show that surviving the first year of infancy was more difficult than surviving birth. All across Europe, between 20 and 30 percent of the babies born died before their first birthday (see Table 18.10). An additional one-fourth of all children did not live to age 8, meaning that approximately half of the population died in infancy or early childhood. A noted scientist of the 1760s, Michael Lomonosev, calculated that half of the infants born in Russia died before age 3. So frightful was this toll that many families did not name a child until his or her first birthday; others gave a cherished family name to more than one child in the hope that one of them would carry it to adulthood. Johann Sebastian Bach fathered twenty children in two marriages and reckoned himself fortunate that ten lived into adulthood. The greatest histo-

TABLE 18.9 A COMPARISON OF LIFE CYCLES

LIFE CYCLE CHARACTERISTIC	SWEDEN, 1778–1782	UNITED STATES (1990 CENSUS)
Annual birthrate	34.5 per 1,000 population	14.4 per 1,000 population
Fertility rate	145.2 births per 1,000 women	69.2 births per 1,000 women
Infant mortality (age 0–1)	211.6 deaths per 1,000 live births	7.2 deaths per 1,000 live births
Life expectancy at birth		
Male	36 years	73.8 years
Female	39 years	79.5 years
Life expectancy at age 1		
Male	44 years longer (45 total years)	73.3 years longer (74.3 total)
Female	46 years longer (47 total years)	79.0 years longer (80.0 total)
Life expectancy at age 50		
Male	19 years longer (69 total years)	27.9 years longer (77.9 total)
Female	20 years longer (70 total years)	31.9 years longer (81.9 total)
Population distribution	ages 0–14 = 31.9%	ages 0–14 = 28.7%
	ages 15–64 = 63.2%	ages 15–64 = 58.6%
	ages 65+ = 4.9%	ages 65+ = 12.7%
Annual death rate	25.9 deaths per 1,000 population	8.6 deaths per 1,000 population

Source: Swedish data from Cipolla, Carlo M., *Before the Industrial Revolution* (New York: Norton, 1976, pp. 286–287); U.S. data from *Time Almanac: 2001* (Boston: passim) and *New York Times Almanac: 2000* (New York: Penguin, passim).

Question: Which contrasts between 1780 and 1990 seem the most important?

TABLE 18.10 INFANT MORTALITY IN THE EIGHTEENTH CENTURY

Percentages represent deaths before the first birthday; they do not include stillbirths.

COUNTRY	PERIOD	PERCENTAGE OF DEATHS BEFORE AGE 1
England	pre-1750	18.7
	1740–1790	16.1
	1780–1820	12.2
France	pre-1750	25.2
	1740–1790	21.3
	1780–1820	19.5
German states	pre-1750	15.4
	1740–1790	38.8
	1780–1820	23.6
Spain	pre-1750	28.1
	1740–1790	27.3
	1780–1820	22.0
Sweden	pre-1750	n.a.
	1740–1790	22.5
	1780–1820	18.7
United States	1995	0.8

Source: European data from Flinn, Michael W., *The European Demographic System, 1500–1820* (Baltimore: Johns Hopkins University Press, 1971, p. 92); U.S. data from *The World Almanac and Book of Facts, 1997* (Mahwah, NJ: World Almanac Books, 1996, p. 962).

n.a. = Not available.

Question: What might explain the difference between England's infant mortality rate in 1820 and the rate in the German states?

rian of the century, Edward Gibbon, was the only child of seven in his family to survive infancy.

Childhood Diseases. Newborns were acutely vulnerable to the biological Old Regime. Intestinal infections killed many in the first months. Unheated housing claimed more. Epidemic diseases killed more infants and young children than adults because some diseases, such as measles and smallpox, left surviving adults immune to them. The dangers of childhood touched all social classes. Madame de Montespan, the mistress of King Louis XIV of France, had seven children with him; three were born crippled or deformed, three others died in childhood, and one reached adulthood in good health.

Infanticide. Eighteenth-century parents commonly killed unwanted infants (daughters more often than sons). **Infanticide**—frequently by smothering the baby, usually by abandoning an infant to the elements—has a long history in Western culture. The mythical founders of Rome who were depicted on many emblems of that city, Romulus and Remus, were abandoned infants raised by a wolf; the newborn Moses was abandoned to his fate on the Nile. Infanticide did not constitute murder in eighteenth-century British law (it was manslaughter) if done by the mother before the baby reached age 1. In France, however, where infanticide was more common, Louis XIV ordered capital punishment for it, although few mothers were ever executed. The frequency of infanticide provoked instructions that all priests read the law in church in 1707 and again in 1731. A study of police records has found that more than 10 percent of all women arrested in Paris in the eighteenth century were nonetheless charged with infanticide. In central and eastern Europe, many midwives were also **"killing nurses"** who murdered babies for parents.

Child Abandonment. A slightly more humane reaction to unwanted babies was to abandon them in public places in the hope that someone else would care for them. That happened so often that cities established hospitals for **foundlings.** The practice had begun at Rome in the late Middle Ages when Pope Innocent III found that he could seldom cross the Tiber River without seeing babies thrown into it. Paris established its foundling hospital in 1670. Thomas Coram opened the foundling hospital at London in 1739 because he could not endure the frequency with which he saw dying babies lying in the gutters and dead ones thrown onto heaps of dung. The London Foundling Hospital could scarcely handle all of the city's abandoned babies. In 1758, 2,300 foundlings (younger than 1 year of age) were found abandoned in the streets of London. Abandonment increased in periods of famine and when the illegitimate birthrate rose (as it did during the eighteenth century). French data show that the famine of 1693–1694 doubled the abandonment of children at Paris and tripled it at Lyon. Abandonments in Paris grew to an annual average of 5,000 in the late eighteenth century, with a peak of 7,676 foundlings in 1772, which is a rate of twenty-one babies abandoned every day. Studies of foundlings in Italy have shown that 11 to 15 percent of all babies born at Milan between 1700 and 1729 were abandoned each year; at Venice, the figures ranged between 8 and 9 percent in 1756–1787.

Foundling Homes and Hospitals. The abandonment of children at this rate overwhelmed the ability of church or state to help. With 390,000 abandonments at the Foundling Hospital of Paris between 1640 and 1789—with 30 abandonments on the single night of April 20, 1720—the prospects for these children were bleak. Finances were inadequate, partly because churches feared that fine facilities might encourage illicit sexuality, so the conditions in foundling homes

FIGURE 18.6 *Abandoned Babies.* One of the most common forms of population control in the eighteenth century was the abandonment of newborns. Because so many babies were left at churches and public buildings and a shocking number were left to die outdoors, governments created foundling homes in some cities and tried ingenious solutions such as seen in this Italian print. A hospital has constructed a revolving door in the wall so that it is accessible from the street. Women, such as the one shown could simply walk up to the revolving door, deposit an unwanted infant, and rotate the child to the inside, without ever being seen by or speaking with anyone.

stayed grim. Whereas 50 percent of the general population survived childhood, only 10 percent of abandoned children reached age 10. The infant (before age 1) death rates for foundling homes in the late eighteenth century were 90 percent in Dublin, 80 percent in Paris, and only 52 percent in London (where infants were farmed out to wet nurses). Of 37,600 children admitted to the Foundling Hospital of Moscow between 1766 and 1786, more than 30,000 died there. The prospects of the survivors were poor, but one noteworthy exception was Jean d'Alembert, a mathematician and co-editor of the *Encyclopédie,* who was discovered in a pine box at a Parisian church in 1717.

Wet-Nursing. Young children were often separated from their parents for long periods. Immediately after birth, many were sent to **wet nurses,** foster mothers whose occupation was the breast-feeding of infants. The studies of France show that more than 95 percent of the babies born in Paris in 1780 were nursed commercially, 75 percent going to wet nurses in the provinces. Because breast-feeding normally lasted 12 to 18 months, only

wealthy parents (who could hire a live-in wet nurse) or the poorest might see their infant children with any frequency. The great French novelist Honoré de Balzac was born in 1799 and immediately dispatched to a wet nurse; he bitterly remembered his infancy as being "neglected by my family for three years." Infant care by rural wet nurses was not universal. It was most common in towns and cities, especially in social classes that could afford the service. The poor usually fed infants gruel—flour mixed in milk, or bread crumbs in water—by dipping a finger into it and letting the baby suck the finger. Upper-class families in England, France, and northern Italy chose wet-nursing; fewer did so in central Europe. Every king of France, starting with Louis IX (Saint Louis), was nurtured by a succession of royal nurses; but mothers in the Hapsburg royal family, including the empress Maria Theresa, were expected to nurse their own children.

Childhood Separation. Separation from parents often remained a feature of life for young children after their weaning. Both Catholicism, which perceived early childhood as an age of innocence, and Protestantism, which held children to be marked by original sin, advocated the separation of the child from the corrupt world of adults. This meant the segregation of children from many parental activities as well as the segregation of boys and girls. Extreme cases existed among the aristocracy and the wealthy. The Marquis de Lafayette, the hero of the American Revolution, lost his father in infancy; his mother left him at the family's provincial estate while she resided in Paris and visited him during a brief vacation once a year. Balzac went straight from his wet nurse to a Catholic boarding school, where the Oratorian Brothers allowed him no vacations and his mother visited him twice in 6 years.

Parent–Child Relationships. Family structures were changing in early modern times, but most children grew up in patriarchal families. Modern parent–child relationships, with more emphasis on affection than on discipline, were beginning to appear. However, most children still lived with the emotional detachment of both parents and the stern discipline of a father whose authority had the sanction of law. The Russian novelist Sergei Aksakov recalled that, when his mother had rocked her infant daughter to sleep in the 1780s, relatives rebuked her for showing "such exaggerated love," which they considered contrary to good parenting and "a crime against God." Children in many countries heard the words of Martin Luther repeated: "I would rather have a dead son than a disobedient one."

From Childhood to Adulthood. Childhood had not yet become the distinct and separate phase of life that it later became. In many ways, children passed directly from a few years of infancy into treatment as virtual adults. Middle- and upper-class boys of the eighteenth century made a direct transition from wearing the gowns and frocks of infancy into wearing the pants and panoply (such as swords) of adulthood. This rite of passage, when boys went from the care of women to the care of men, normally happened at approximately age 7. European traditions and laws varied, but in most economic, legal, and religious ways, boys became adults between 7 and 14. Peasant children became members of the household economy almost immediately, assuming such duties as tending to chickens or hoeing the kitchen garden. In the towns, a child seeking to learn a craft and enter a guild might begin with an apprenticeship (with another family) as early as age 7. Children of the elite were turned over to tutors or governesses, or they were sent away to receive their education at boarding schools. Children of all classes began to become adults by law at age 7. In English law, 7 was the adult age at which a child could be flogged or executed; the Spanish Inquisition withheld adult interrogation until age 13. Twelve was the most common adult age at which children could consent to marriage or to sexual relations.

The Double Standard. Tradition and law treated girls differently than boys. In the Roman law tradition, prevalent across southern Europe and influential in most countries, girls never became adults in the legal sense of obtaining rights in their own name. Instead, a patriarchal social order expected fathers to exercise the rights of their daughters until they married; women's legal rights then passed to their husbands. Most legal systems contained other double standards for young men and women. The earliest age for sexual consent was typically younger for a girl than for a boy, although standards of respectable behavior were much stricter for young women than for young men. Economic considerations also created double standards: a family might send a daughter to the convent, for example, instead of providing her with a dowry.

Marriage and the Family

Age at Marriage. Despite the early ages at which children entered the adult world, marriage was normally postponed until later in life. Royal or noble children might sometimes be married in childhood for political or economic reasons, but most of the population married at significantly older ages than those common in the twenty-first century. A study of seventeenth-century marriages in southern England has found that the average age of men at a first marriage was nearly 27; their brides averaged 23.6 years of age. Research on England in the eighteenth century shows that the age at marriage rose further. In rural Europe, men married at 27 to 28 years of age and women married at ages 25 to 26. Many variations were hidden within such averages. The most notable is the unique situation of firstborn sons. They would inherit the property, which would make marriage economically feasible and earlier marriage to perpetuate the family line desirable.

FIGURE 18.7 *The London Foundling Home.* This print suggests the size of the problem of abandoned children in the eighteenth century by showing the size of the girls's dining hall in the London Foundling Home in 1777. This institution was chartered, through the efforts of Thomas Coram, in 1739 "for the maintenance and education of exposed and deserted young children." The problem remained so severe that in 1756 the institution was required to accept all abandoned children up to 12 months of age, for which purpose a basket was hung outside the hospital. During the next 4 years, 14,934 infants were left at the home. The clean look of this print does not show the terrible death rate at such institutions. Of those 15,000 children, barely 4,000 lived long enough to be sent out as apprentices. Nearly three-fourths of these girls must have died by age 12 or 13.

Late Marriages. Most people had to postpone marriage until they could afford it. This typically meant waiting until they could acquire the property or position that would support a family. Younger sons often could not marry before age 30. The average age at first marriage of all males among the nobility of Milan was 33.4 years from 1700 to 1749; their wives averaged 21.2 years of age. Daughters might not marry until they had

ARRANGED MARRIAGES AND MARRIAGE CONTRACTS

Richard Brinsley Sheridan (1751–1816) was an Irish dramatist who wrote comedies of manners for the London stage. One of his greatest plays, *The Rivals* (1775), made fun of the tradition of arranged marriages. In it, a wealthy aristocratic father, Sir Anthony Absolute, arranges a suitable marriage for his son, Captain Jack Absolute (who is in love with a beautiful young woman), without consulting him. In the following scene, Captain Absolute tries to refuse the marriage and Sir Anthony tries first to bribe him and then to coerce him.

Absolute: Now, Jack, I am sensible that the income of your commission, and what I have hitherto allowed you, is but a small pittance for a lad of your spirit.

Captain Jack: Sir, you are very good.

Absolute: And it is my wish, while yet I live, to have my boy make some figure in the world. I have resolved, therefore, to fix you at once in a noble independence.

Captain Jack: Sir, your kindness overpowers me—such generosity makes the gratitude of reason more lively than the sensations even of filial affection.

Absolute: I am glad you are so sensible of my attention— and you shall be master of a large estate in a few weeks.

Captain Jack: Let my future life, sir, speak my gratitude; I cannot express the sense I have of your munificence. —Yet, sir, I presume you would not wish me to quit the army?

Absolute: Oh, that shall be as your wife chooses.

Captain Jack: My wife, sir!

Absolute: Ay, ay, settle that between you—settle that between you.

Captain Jack: A wife, sir, did you say?

Absolute: Ay, a wife—why, did I not mention her before?

Captain Jack: Not a word of her sir.

Absolute: Odd, so! I mus'n't forget her though. —Yes, Jack, the independence I was talking of is by marriage—the fortune is saddled with a wife—but I suppose that makes no difference.

Captain Jack: Sir! Sir! You amaze me!

Absolute: Why, what the devil's the matter with you, fool? Just now you were all gratitude and duty.

Captain Jack: I was, sir—you talked of independence and a fortune, but not a word of a wife!

Absolute: Why—what difference does that make? Odds life, sir! If you had an estate, you must take it with the live stock on it, as it stands!

Captain Jack: If my happiness is to be the price, I must beg leave to decline the purchase. Pray, sir, who is the lady?

Absolute: What's that to you, sir? Come, give me your promise to love, and to marry her directly.

Captain Jack: Sure, sir, this is not very reasonable. . . . You must excuse me, sir, if I tell you, once for all, that in this point I cannot obey you. . . .

Absolute: Sir, I won't hear a word—not one word! . . .

Captain Jack: What, sir, promise to link myself to some mass of ugliness!

Absolute: Zounds! Sirrah! The lady shall be as ugly as I choose: she shall have a hump on each shoulder; she shall be as crooked as the crescent; her one eye shall roll like the bull's in Cox's Museum; she shall have a skin like a mummy, and the beard of a Jew—she shall be all this, sirrah!

Yet I will make you ogle her all day, and sit up all night to write sonnets on her beauty.

Sheridan, Richard, The Rivals. London: 1775.

---

accumulated a **dowry**—land or money for the well-to-do, household goods in the lower classes—that would favor the economic circumstances of a family. Given the constraints of a limited life expectancy and a meager income, many people experienced marriage for only a few years, and others never married. A study of marriage patterns in eighteenth-century England suggests that 25 percent of the younger sons in well-to-do families never married. Another historian has estimated that fully 10 percent of the population of Europe was composed of unmarried adult women. For the middle class of Geneva in 1700, 26 percent of the women who died after age 50 had never married; the study of the Milanese nobility found that 35 percent of the women never married.

Arranged Marriages. The pattern of selecting a mate changed somewhat during the eighteenth century. Earlier habits in which parents arranged marriages for children (especially if property was involved) were changing, and a prospective couple often claimed the right to veto their parents' arrangement. Although propertied families often insisted on **arranged marriages** (see Document 18.2), it became more common during the eighteenth century for men and women to select their own partners, contingent upon parental vetoes. Marriages based on the interests of the entire family line and those based on an economic alliance yielded with increasing frequency to marriages based on romantic attachment. However, marriage contracts remained common.

Family Structure. After a long scholarly debate, historians now agree that Western civilization had no single pattern of **family structure** but rather a variety of arrangements. The most common pattern was not a large family of more than two generations living together; instead, the most common arrangement was the **nuclear family** in which parents and their children lived together. Extended families, characterized by co-residence with grandparents or other kin—known by many names, such as the *ganze hauz* in German tradition or the *zadruga* in eastern Europe—were atypical. A study of British families has found that 70 percent were composed of two generations, 24 percent were single-generation families, and only 6 percent fit the extended-family pattern. Studies of southern and eastern Europe have found more complex, **extended families.** In Russia, 60 percent of peasant families fit this multigenerational pattern; in parts of Italy, 74 percent.

Family Size. **Family size** also varied widely. Everywhere except France (where smaller families first became the norm), the average number of children born per family usually ranged between five and seven. Yet such averages hide many large families. For example, Brissot de Warville, a leader of the French Revolution, was born to a family of innkeepers who had seventeen children, seven of whom survived infancy; Mayer and Gutele Rothschild, whose sons created the House of Rothschild banks, had twenty children, ten of whom survived. The founder of Methodism, John Wesley, was the fifteenth of nineteen children. Households might also contain other people, such as servants, apprentices, and lodgers. Studies of eighteenth-century families in different regions have found that between 13 and 50 percent of them contained servants. A survey of London in the 1690s estimated that 20 percent of the population lodged with nonrelatives.

The Patriarchal Family. One of the foremost characteristics of the early modern family was **patriarchal authority.** This trait was diminishing somewhat in western Europe in the eighteenth century, but it remained strong. A father exercised authority over the children; a husband exercised authority over his wife. A woman vowed to obey her husband in the wedding ceremony, following the Christian tradition based on the words of Saint Paul: "Wives, submit yourself unto your own husbands, as unto the Lord." The idea of masculine authority in marriage was deeply embedded in popular culture. As a character in a play by Henry Fielding says to his wife, "Your person is mine. I bought it lawfully in church." The civil law in most countries enforced such patriarchy. In the greatest summary of English law, Sir William Blackstone's *Commentaries on the Law of England* (1765–1769), this was stated bluntly: "The husband and wife are one, and the husband is that one." A compilation of Prussian law under Frederick the Great, the Frederician Code of 1750, was similar: "The husband is master of his own household, and head of his family. And as the wife enters into it of her own accord, she is in some measure subject to his power" (see Document 18.3).

Divorce. Few ways of dissolving a marriage existed in the eighteenth century. In Catholic countries, the church considered marriage a sacrament and neither civil marriage by the state nor legal divorce existed. The church permitted a few annulments, exclusively for the upper classes. Protestant countries accepted the principle of divorce on the grounds of adultery or desertion, but divorces remained rare, even when legalized. Geneva, the home of Calvinism, recorded an average of one divorce per year during the eighteenth century. Divorce became possible in Britain in the late seventeenth century, but it required an individual act of Parliament for each divorce. Between 1670 and 1750, a total of 17 parliamentary divorces were granted in Britain, although the number rose to 114 between 1750 and 1799. Almost all divorces were granted to men of

FIGURE 18.8 *The Family.* Attitudes toward the family were beginning to change in the eighteenth century, as indicated by the increasing habit of the wealthy to commission paintings of the entire family. Note the symbolism of this painting: the wife sits at the center of the family, with the husband somewhat in the background of family matters. The father relates to his eldest son and heir, who is treated separately from the other children, and the father is turned slightly away from his younger children. In the background, the record of the family in busts and paintings is entirely of the men who were head of the family.

THE HUSBAND IN THE LAW

The Frederician Code, adopted in Prussia under Frederick the Great, was one of the greatest efforts to reorganize a legal system during the eighteenth century. It was chiefly the work of the minister of justice, Samuel von Cocceji. He relied on the principles of Roman law but also drew ideas from Germanic customary law and from the "enlightened" philosophy of the eighteenth century. The following excerpt states the legal rights of a husband; a similar section specified the rights and privileges of the wife, without curtailing the authority of husband.

1. As the domestic society, or family, is formed by the union of the husband and wife, we are to begin with enumerating the advantages and rights which result from this union.

2. The husband is by nature the head of his family. To be convinced of this, it is sufficient to consider, that the wife leaves her family to join herself to that of her husband; that she enters into his household, and into the habitation of which he is the master, with intention to have children by him to perpetuate the family.

3. Hence it follows, judging by the sole light of reason, that the husband is master of his own household, and head of his family. And as the wife enters into it of her own accord, she is in some measure subject to his power; whence flow several rights and privileges, which belong to the husband with regard to his wife.

For, (1) the husband has the liberty of prescribing laws and rules in his household, which the wife is to observe.

(2) If the wife be defective in her duty to her husband, and refuse to be subject, he is authorized to reduce her to her duty in a reasonable manner.

(3) The wife is bound, according to her quality, to assist her husband, to take upon her the care of the household affairs, according to his condition.

(4) The husband has the power over the wife's body, and she cannot refuse him the conjugal duty.

(5) As the husband and wife have promised not to leave each other during their lives, but to share the good and evil which may happen to them; the wife cannot, under pretext, for example, that her husband has lost his reason, leave him, without obtaining permission from the judge.

(6) For the same reason, the wife is obliged to follow her husband when he changes his habitation; unless, (a) it has been stipulated by the contract of marriage, or otherwise, that she shall not be bound to follow him if he should incline to settle elsewhere; or (b) unless it were for a crime that the husband changed his habitation, as if he had been banished from his country.

Source: Bell, Susan G., and Offen, Karen M., eds., *Women, the Family, and Freedom: The Debate in Documents*, vol. 1 (Stanford, CA: Stanford University Press, 1983).

Question: In what ways does this legal code maintain a patriarchal society?

---

prominent social position who wished to marry again, normally to produce heirs.

Separation and Wife Sale. Where arranged marriages were still common, the alternative to divorce was separation. The civil laws in many countries provided for contracts of separation, by which the maintenance of both partners was guaranteed. Simpler alternatives to divorce evolved in the lower classes, such as desertion or bigamy. The most extraordinary method, practiced in parts of England well into the nineteenth century, was the custom of **wife sale.** Such sales were generally by mutual consent of both husband and wife, but they nonetheless resembled cattle sales. Although the Old Regime was fundamentally an era of indissoluble, lifelong marriage, this did not mean a couple lived together for long periods. Given an average age at marriage in the midtwenties and an average age at death (for people who reached the midtwenties) in the

midforties, the typical marriage lasted for approximately 20 years.

Sexuality and Reproduction

Sexual Ignorance. Ignorance about human sexuality was widespread during the Old Regime, and remarkable theories still circulated about human reproduction, many of them restatements of sex manuals inherited from the ancient world. Medical science held that the loss of 1 ounce of semen debilitated a man's body the same way that the loss of 40 ounces of blood would and that a woman's menstruation could turn meat rancid. Consequently, physicians advised people to avoid all sex during the summer because a man's body would become dried out. Similarly, people were taught to avoid sex during menstruation because a child conceived then would be born diseased.

Religion and Sexuality. There were other disincentives to sexual activity. The strongest came from Christian moral injunctions. A Christian tradition regarding sex as unclean and chastity as a spiritual ideal dated from St. Paul and St. Jerome. Only marital intercourse was permissible, and then only for procreation; other sexual activity was understood to be a violation of the Seventh Commandment forbidding adultery. Good Christians were expected to practice chastity during pregnancy (when conception was impossible), on Sundays, and during the 40 days of Lent.

Sexual Disincentives. In addition to the disincentives of medical advice and Christian teaching, poor health, uncleanliness, fears of pregnancy or venereal disease, and repressive laws also restricted behavior. Laws varied regionally, but most sexual practices were against the law. Ecclesiastical courts in Catholic countries tried priests and laity alike for sexual offenses; secular courts acted in a similar manner in Protestant countries. A study of the archdiocesan tribunal at Cambrai (France) has found that 38 percent of the moral offenses involved unmarried sex, 32 percent adultery, and 11 percent incest. Punishments ranged from death (for incest between father and daughter) to providing a dowry (for seducing a virgin). Bestiality merited burning to death, for both the human and the animal. Pornography (broadly defined) often led to imprisonment, as it did for Denis Diderot. Common sentences were flogging, subjecting to public pillory, or being paraded through the streets with a shaved head.

Homosexuality. Homosexuality was universally illegal before the French Revolution (which legalized consenting adult relationships in 1791). Assessing its frequency is difficult. It had been a crime in England for centuries, normally punished by the pillory, and a public execution for homosexuality took place as late as 1772. Yet homosexuality was relatively open in England in the eighteenth century, and gentlemen's clubs of homosexuals existed with impunity in London, although periodic arrests of sodomites (the term *homosexual* was not coined until the late nineteenth century) occurred, such as the police campaign of 1707. King Frederick William I of Prussia was horrified to discover that both of his sons—the future Frederick the Great and Prince Henry, whom the Continental Congress briefly considered as a constitutional king for the United States—were homosexuals. The double standard of the time obscures the extent of **lesbianism** in the eighteenth century even more, but high society enjoyed widespread rumors about many prominent figures such as Queen Anne of England. Contemporary works such as Mary Wollstonecraft's *Mary: A Fiction,* Diderot's *La Religieuse,* and Fielding's *The Female Husband* indicate that the subject was much discussed.

Sexual Permissiveness. As the partial tolerance of homosexuality suggests, the eighteenth century was a period of comparatively relaxed sexual restrictions, especially compared with the more repressive sixteenth and seventeenth centuries. Some historians even describe the Old Regime as a period of sexual revolution. In Protestant countries, strict moral Puritanism weakened, and Catholicism repudiated its own version of Puritanism—Jansenism. In all countries, the ruling classes set an example of permissiveness. Most monarchs (who married for reasons of state, not for love) kept lovers, gently called *favorites.* Louis XV kept a small personal brothel, and Catherine the Great had an equally long list of favorites. Augustus the Strong, king of Poland and elector of Saxony, fathered at least 365 children, only one of them legitimate.

The Sexual Double Standard. The double standard remained a feature of the relaxed sexual standards. Tribunals assessing sex crimes typically gave harsher sentences to women, particularly for adultery. Women at the highest levels of society might act with some freedom if the legitimacy of heirs were certain. But European culture attached a value to female virginity and chastity and still associated a man's honor with the chastity of his female relations.

Venereal Disease. One of the foremost disincentives associated with eighteenth-century sexuality was the circulation of the venereal diseases (VDs) syphilis and gonorrhea. These diseases, commonly called the *pox,* were rampant in the ruling classes and found in most of the royal families of Europe. Louis XIV, Louis XV, and Napoleon all had VD. Syphilis was not as fatal as it had been in the fifteenth and sixteenth centuries, when epidemics of it swept Europe, but it remained a debilitating disease. Gonorrhea was pandemic in urban Europe. The famous Venetian lover Giovanni Casanova contracted eleven cases of VD during his life, although he survived until age 73. James Boswell, the distinguished British writer, caught gonorrhea seventeen times. Physicians could provide only limited help; their favored cure was treatment with mercury, a dangerous poison.

Prostitution. Prostitution was one of the chief sources of the spread of VDs. It was illegal but generally tolerated in public brothels. The open prostitution of the Middle Ages, with municipally operated (and even church-operated) brothels, no longer existed. However, large numbers of prostitutes were found in all cities. King Frederick I of Prussia tried to end prostitution in Berlin by closing all brothels in 1690, causing an increase of prostitution practiced in taverns. When the Prussian government decided to tolerate brothels again, a survey of 1765 found that Berlin contained nearly 9,000 prostitutes in a population of approximately 120,000 people. The Parisian

FIGURE 18.9 *The Arrest of Prostitutes.* Prostitution, both on the streets and in brothels, remained widespread in eighteenth-century Europe, with large numbers of prostitutes found in all cities. A survey of 1765 found that Berlin, with a population of 120,000 people, supported nearly 9,000 prostitutes—an astonishing rate of one prostitute per thirteen or fourteen people. Most governments outlawed prostitution but generally tolerated it and conducted only occasional campaigns against the prostitutes. In this French engraving from 1759, police in Paris are rounding up prostitutes and removing them from the city. Many will be sent to the French colony of Louisiana.

police estimated an even higher number of prostitutes there—between 20,000 and 30,000, or one of every eight women of marriageable age. Even in the shadow of the Vatican, 2 percent of all adult women were officially registered prostitutes.

Antiprostitution Efforts. Draconian measures did not eliminate prostitution. The Austrian government sought to end it in Vienna in the 1720s with harsh treatment of prostitutes. After the failure of punishments such as being put in the pillory or being made to sweep the streets with shaved heads, the government staged a public decapitation of a prostitute in 1723. Yet the empress Maria Theresa soon created a Chastity Commission to study the subject anew. Governments chose to control prostitution by limiting it to certain districts and keeping it off the streets or by registering prostitutes, thereby permitting some public health control and taxation. Governments were mostly concerned about the spread of disease (particularly to military garrisons) more than the condition of the women (typically domestic servants who had been seduced or girls from the country who could not find employment) driven by economic necessity to prostitute themselves.

Illegitimate Births. Another subject of social concern about eighteenth-century sexuality was the general increase in illegitimate births (see Table 18.11). **Illegitimacy** had been relatively uncommon, particu-

larly in rural areas, in the seventeenth century. The rate for rural France had been only 1 percent of all births. During the eighteenth century, and particularly after 1760, both illegitimate births and premarital conceptions increased significantly. The illegitimacy rate remained high because the practice of birth control was limited both by Christian moral injunctions and by slight knowledge of effective procedures. Tertullian had established the theological view of birth control in the third century, asserting that "to prevent a child being born is to commit homicide in advance." Religious opposition to birth control continued in the eighteenth century, even in Protestant Europe: it was the divine will that people "be fruitful and multiply." Despite Christian teaching, a significant percentage of the English upper classes and the general population of France practiced some forms of birth control in the eighteenth century, and both populations experienced a decline in their fertility rate compared with the rest of Europe. France had a birthrate of 40 per 1,000 population in the mideighteenth century, falling to 33 per 1,000 at the end of the century—30 per 1,000 in some areas. Many people clearly had found economic advantages in smaller families and had chosen to put economic factors above religious ones.

Birth Control. Judging the extent to which knowledge about birth control circulated is difficult. Christianity offered one traditional method: abstinence. *Coitus interruptus* was practiced, but its extent is unknown. The French philosopher Jean-Jacques Rousseau in his Discourse of 1753 discussed (with disapproval) that method of birth control ("cheating nature"), as well as many forms of nonreproductive sex, such as oral and manual sex. (Rousseau also fathered five illegitimate children and abandoned them to foundling homes.) Those who practiced birth control used such methods. Condoms (made from animal membranes) had been virtually unknown in the seventeenth century but were available in late eighteenth-century London and Paris, although they were chiefly used for protection against VD, not for family planning. Knowledge about female means of control, such as douching, also began to circulate during that period.

TABLE 18.11 PREMARITAL CONCEPTION AND ILLEGITIMATE BIRTH

COUNTRY	PERIOD	PERCENTAGE OF PREMARITAL CONCEPTIONS	PERCENTAGE OF ILLEGITIMATE BIRTHS
England	pre-1750	19.7	2.6
	1740–1790	37.3	4.3
	1780–1820	34.5	5.9
France	pre-1750	6.2	2.9
	1740–1790	10.1	4.1
	1780–1820	13.7	4.7
German states	pre-1750	13.8	2.5
	1740–1790	18.5	3.9
	1780–1820	23.8	11.9
Spain	pre-1750	n.a.	5.4
	1740–1790	n.a.	5.1
	1780–1820	n.a.	6.5
United States	1940	n.a.	3.5
	1960	n.a.	5.3
	1980	n.a.	18.4

Sources: Data for the Old Regime from Flinn, Michael W., *The European Demographic System, 1500–1820* (Baltimore: Johns Hopkins University Press, 1971, p. 82); data for the United States from *Information Please Almanac Atlas and Yearbook 1989* (Boston: Houghton Mifflin Co., 1989, p. 788).

n.a. = Not available.

Question: Why is the rate of illegitimate births in the United States in 1980 so much higher than that in eighteenth-century Europe?

Abortion. Abortion was also used to terminate unwanted pregnancies during the Old Regime. A Christian tradition received from Aristotle and passed onward by Roman law held that a soul was implanted in the fetus at the time of "animation" or "the quickening." Although all abortions were illegal, both moral law and criminal law distinguished between those before and after "ensoulment." The means of attempting abortions were crude and dangerous. Folk knowledge circulated about supposed abortifacient drugs and vegetal or mineral poisons, however, and the learned reference work of the century, the French *Encyclopédie*, discussed them in detail.

Old Age

The Elderly Population. Statistical averages showing the low life expectancies of the Old Regime should not produce the mistaken conclusion that older people were rare in the eighteenth century. Twenty percent of all newborns reached the age of 50, and 10 percent lived until age 70. French demographic studies have found that in the 1740s, 17 percent of men and 19 percent of women would reach age 60; by the 1770s, this had risen to 24 percent for men and 25 percent for women. The aged clearly represented a significant group in society. Once someone had survived to the age of 50, his or her life expectancy was not greatly different than it would be in the twenty-first century.

Accomplishment by the Elderly. Thus, a large proportion of the powerful and famous individuals who are remembered from the eighteenth century had life spans typical of twentieth-century leaders. King Louis XIV of France lived to be age 77 (1638–1715); his successor, Louis XV, died at age 64 (1710–1774). The three Hanoverian kings of eighteenth-century England (George I, George II, and George III) died at an average age of 75 (67, 77, and 82, respectively). Empress Catherine II of Russia and King Frederick II of Prussia earned their appellation, "the Great," partly because they lived long enough to achieve greatness—Catherine died at age 67, Frederick at age 74. And the eight popes of the eighteenth century, who were typically elected at an advanced age, died at an average age of nearly 78; four lived into their eighties. Similar life spans characterized many of the famous cultural figures of the Old Regime. Christopher Wren and Anton van Leeuwenhoek both lived into their nineties; Goethe, Goya, Kant, and Newton all lived into their eighties.

CONCLUSION

By focusing on the most basic issues of daily life (such as health and diet) and the most universal experiences of life (such as birth, marriage, and aging), social historians are able to portray historical continuity and change especially well. Life in eighteenth-century Europe was in many ways like it had been for centuries. The biological Old Regime closely resembled the conditions of life in ancient Greece and Rome; the dread horsemen of plague and famine defined life in much the same ways. Yet there were signs of historic change, too. The slow acceptance of inoculation against smallpox or the foods of the Columbian exchange pointed toward a modern Europe with vastly lower levels of disease and higher standards of nutrition. The name that historians attach to the eighteenth century in Europe, the Old Regime, is taken from political history, which links the eighteenth century to a vanished old order of monarchy and aristocracy. Just as two centuries were required for the political evolution of modern Europe, the evolution of daily life and the conquest of the biological Old Regime would take generations. But life in Europe was far from static, as the shifting attitudes toward arranged marriages or large families show.

Review Questions

- How would you describe the nature of the life expectancy in eighteenth-century Europe?
- How would you describe the concept of the biological Old Regime?
- What was the importance of the Columbian exchange?
- What were eighteenth-century European attitudes toward marriage and the family?

For Further Study

Readings

Braudel, Fernand, *Civilization and Capitalism, 15th–18th Century,* 3 vols., especially vol. 1, *The Structures of Everyday Life* (New York: Harper, 1985). One of the founding masterworks of modern social history.

Flinn, M. W., *The European Demographic System, 1500–1820* (Baltimore: Johns Hopkins, 1981). The best introduction to population question during the Old Regime.

Kiple, Kenneth F., and Kriemhild, C. Ornelas, eds., *The Cambridge World History of Food,* 2 vols. (Cambridge: Cambridge University Press, 2000). A comprehensive and erudite encyclopedia of the history of food.

Kohn, George C., ed., *Encyclopedia of Plague and Pestilence* (New York: Facts on File, 1995). A convenient guide to the history of epidemic disease.

McNeill, William, *Plagues and Peoples* (New York: Doubleday, 1977). Although this covers many centuries and continents, it is a pioneering work that put the history of disease at the forefront of social history.

Stearns, Peter, ed., *Encyclopedia of European Social History from 1350 to 2000,* 5 vols. (New York: Scribners, 2001). A gold mine of essays by distinguished scholars, covering all aspects of daily life in the past.

Stone, Lawrence, *The Family, Sex, and Marriage in England, 1500–1800* (New York: Harper, 1977). A pioneering work covering many aspects of daily life that has prompted much debate and further study.

InfoTrac College Edition

For additional reading, go to your online research library at *http://infotrac.thomsonlearning.com.*

Using Key Terms, enter the search term:
Columbian Exchange

Using the Subject Guide, enter the search terms:
smallpox   *bubonic plague*

Web Sites

http://www.mic.ki.se/HistDis.html   A comprehensive site maintained by the Karolinska Institutet in Stockholm with dozens of links to other sites with materials on the history of disease.

http://www.nlm.nih.gov   A valuable site maintained by the National Library of Medicine, whose Library Services include many materials on the history of medicine.

Visit the Western Civilization Companion Web Site for resources specific to this textbook:
http://history.wadsworth.com/hause02/

The CD in the back of this book and the Western Civilization Resource Center at *http://history. wadsworth.com/western/* offer a variety of tools to help you succeed in this course, including access to quizzes; images; documents; interactive simulations, maps, and timelines; movie explorations; and a wealth of other sources.

DAILY LIFE IN THE EIGHTEENTH CENTURY

1690	1700	1710	1720	1730	1740	1750	1760	1770	1780	1790	1800

1690: King of Prussia Closes Brothels

1691: English Law Requires Communities to Repair Local Roads

1669-1967: Terrible Winter of the "Little Ice Age"

1700: Smallpox Kills Heir to Throne of Britain

1708: Bubonic Plague Spreads from Poland Across Northern Europe

1709: Famine in France Produces Great Wave of Child Abandonment

1710: Smallpox Epidemic Kills 3,000 in London

1711: Smallpox Kills Emperor Joseph I of Austria

1718: Mary Montagu Learns Turkish Method of Smallpox Inoculation

1719: Wave of Five Smallpox Epidemics in 20 Years Begins in London

1719: Epidemic of Bubonic Plague Spreads from Russia Westward

1720: Bubonic Plague Kills 40,000 People in Marseilles

1723: Austrian Stages Public Execution of Prostitutes

1736: British Adopt Gin Tax to Control Heavy Drinking

1739: Coram Founds Foundling Hospital in London

1740: Smallpox Epidemic Decimates Berlin

1746: Smallpox Epidemic Kills 6 Percent of Rome

1746: Swedish Royal Edict Bans Coffee Drinking

1747: Margraf Discovers Sugar in Beetroots

1750: Frederician Code Restates Patriarchy

1751: British Tippling Act to Control Drinking

1753: British Marriage Act

1757: Parmentier Introduces Potato to France

1761: King Carlos Orders Cleaning of Madrid to Control Disease

1762: French Outlaw Inoculation

1765: Blackstone's *Commentaries* Restates Patriarchy

1765: Prussia Relegalizes Prostitution

1768: Catherine II Has Russian Royal Family Inoculated for Smallpox

1771: Bubonic Plague Kills 57,000 in Moscow

1772: Last Execution for Homosexuality in Britain

1774: Smallpox Kills Louis XV

1777: Prussian Edict Encourages Beer Drinking

1779: Pope Pius VI Orders Draining of Pontine Marshes

1779: First Children's Hospital Opens in London

1784: Rhône-Rhine Canal

1791: Homosexuality Legalized in France

FOCUS QUESTIONS

- How did the forms of monarchy differ in the eighteenth century?
- How did basic institutions of parliamentary government develop in eighteenth-century England?
- What were the problems confronting the French monarchy in the eighteenth century?
- How well does eighteenth-century Austria illustrate the concept of "enlightened despotism"?
- What explains the expansion of Prussia in the eighteenth century?
- What were the basic characteristics of government in eighteenth-century Russia?

Chapter 19

THE POLITICAL EVOLUTION OF THE OLD REGIME, 1715–1789

The Christmas season of 1740 found the 23-year-old Maria Theresa Hapsburg hoping that her fourth pregnancy in 4 years would produce the son she wanted so deeply. Married at age 18 in 1736, Maria Theresa had given birth to three daughters, but her oldest daughter died in June of 1740 and her father, Emperor Charles VI of Austria, died in October. Death would visit her family and her nation often. The death of Charles VI meant that Maria Theresa inherited the throne of Austria and all of the far-flung Hapsburg dominions. Charles VI had spent years working to guarantee the European acceptance of Maria Theresa's inheritance and had won the support of all neighboring rulers. But, on December 23, 1740, 2 months after Charles's death, one of the rulers who had promised to defend Maria Theresa—Frederick II (the Great) of Prussia—sent his armies into Austria. He launched a quarter-century of intermittent war among the German states that ultimately stretched from the Great Lakes of North America to the princely states of India.

Chapter 19 examines European politics during this last age of monarchical domination. It looks at the varieties of monarchy that emerged during the late seventeenth century—from **limited monarchies** (restricted by constitutions, parliaments, or aristocracies) to **autocratic monarchies** (with few restraints on despotic powers). In most of them, royal advisers slowly became **cabinets of ministers** led by a **prime minister;** in some, **parliaments** began to gain control over this **cabinet system.** In England, under the Hanoverian kings, the monarch was severely limited by the strength of Parliament and the restrictions of the **unwritten constitution.** In France, the Bourbon monarchy weakened after the death of Louis XIV, as the costs of war and an inadequate system of taxation produced a financial crisis that helped precipitate the French Revolution. Autocratic Prussia, meanwhile, emerged as a great power in the eighteenth century owing to the strength of its army, although Frederick the Great tried to balance **despotism** and **militarism** with ideas of enlightened reform. Austria, however, is a better illustration of **enlightened despotism,** partly in the reign of Maria Theresa, but chiefly under Joseph II, the most advanced of eighteenth-century autocrats. Chapter 19 concludes with a discussion of Russia, where the monarch had despotic power and few restraints.

THE STRUCTURES OF GOVERNMENT: MONARCHY

The basic political characteristic of the Old Regime was—as it had been for more than 1,000 years—a monarchical government. In the strictest sense, *monarchy* meant the rule of a single person who held **sovereignty** (supreme power) over a state. The power of monarchs was often challenged by the nobility, disputed by provinces, or attacked in open rebellions. But the concept of monarchy was almost universally accepted at the beginning of the eighteenth century. Even the skeptical intellectuals of that era still supported it, and only a few small states, such as the city-state of Genoa in northern Italy, sustained governments without monarchs, usually called *republics*.

Absolutism. The forms of monarchy varied significantly, but **absolutism** remained the predominant form of European monarchy. Most monarchs wanted such power and aspired to emulate the absolute monarchs of the seventeenth century, King Gustav Adolph of Sweden and especially King Louis XIV of France, the exemplars of the era called the **age of absolutism.** The theory of absolute monarchy held that rulers received sovereignty directly from God. They governed by **divine right,** representing within their realm the sovereignty of God over all things. This idea rested on the exegesis of such biblical statements as "No authority exists unless it comes from God." Churches taught obedience to the monarch as a religious duty: God had given sovereignty, and "No one but God can judge the king." Resisting a monarch was to attack God's order. An anonymous poem of the eighteenth century entitled "The Vicar of Bray" summarized the alliance of throne and altar in a succinct rhyme:

> Unto my flock I daily preached
> Kings were by God appointed,
> And damned was he that durst resist
> Or touch the Lord's anointed.

Those who dared to attack a monarch paid a horrific price, as the man who tried to kill King Louis XV of France suffered in 1757 (see Document 19.1). True autocratic monarchy—most often called **despotism**—was rare, but parts of central and eastern Europe still lived under despotic rulers who were unrestrained by laws. A despot might strangle an opponent with his bare hands, have another torn apart by dogs, or have his own son and heir flogged to death, as Tsar Peter the Great of Russia did.

Limited Monarchies. Most monarchs could not exercise such unrestrained powers. Their governments were limited monarchies, limited by privileges that earlier rulers had granted, a legal system enforced by independent courts, the nobility, the powers of an established state religion, the rights delegated to an assembly, or financial dependency on others. The Braganza kings of Portugal were limited by the power of the Catholic Church; the Bourbon kings of the Two Sicilies, by having to ask an assembly for the money to rule. The Bourbon kings of France faced a resurgent

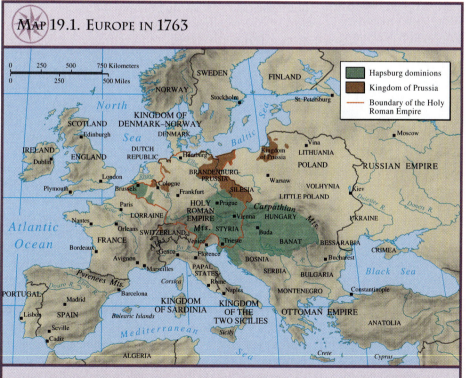

MAP 19.1. EUROPE IN 1763

Eighteenth-century Europe still did not include the modern states of Germany and Italy. Central Europe was loosely united in the Holy Roman Empire, dominated by the Hapsburg Empire. The state that would later lead German unification, Prussia, was just emerging as a great power, supplanting Swedish leadership on the Baltic and annexing new lands. France had reached its approximate modern borders through the wars of Louis XIV.

DOCUMENT 19.1

THE COURT SENTENCE ON ROBERT-FRANÇOIS DAMIENS, 1757

Robert-François Damiens was an unemployed army veteran of ill-temper and deeply held, but muddled, religious convictions. After the Jesuits fired him from a menial job in Paris, Damiens formed the opinion that only the death of King Louis XV could resolve the complex religious battles of the age. In January 1757, as Louis XV entered his carriage at Versailles, Damiens rushed forward to stab and assassinate the king, but he failed. Convicted of regicide in the royal courts, Damiens was sentenced to a barbarous and gruesome execution intended to underscore the inviolability of kings. This short excerpt from the transcript of his trial describes his punishment. After it ended, Damiens's house was burnt down; his father, wife, and daughter were banished; and his surviving relatives were forced to change their name. Several eyewitness accounts of the execution circulated in the late eighteenth century, making the case a frequently cited indictment of monarchy.

[Damiens shall be] taken and conveyed in a cart, wearing nothing but a shirt, holding a torch of burning wax . . . to the Place de Grève, where, on a scaffold that will be erected there, the flesh will be torn from his breasts, arms, thighs and calves with red-hot pincers, his right hand, holding the knife with which he committed the said parricide, burnt with sulphur, and, on those places where the flesh will be torn away, poured molten lead, boiling oil, burning resin, wax and sulphur melted together and then his body drawn and quartered by four horses and his limbs and body consumed by fire, reduced to ashes and his ashes thrown to the winds.

Source: Pièces originales et procédures du procès fait à Robert-François Damiens (Paris, 1757).

Question: How could eighteenth-century laws justify such grotesque capital punishment?

---

aristocracy that used the law courts (*parlements*) to thwart the royal will.

Constitutions. The most formal restrictions on royal sovereignty were constitutional laws. Few states possessed a constitution in the modern sense of a single written document. Sweden adopted the strictest constitution of the era in 1720. The Swedish nobility accepted the rule of a queen on the condition that she accept a document limiting her power. Most constitutions were less formal, usually a set of customary privileges claimed by the aristocracy as their national traditions. In Hungary, the Magyar aristocracy held virtual **auton-**

omy. When the Hapsburgs incorporated Hungary into the Austrian Empire, the Hungarians insisted on their ancient constitution and rebelled when they believed it was violated. The English constitution is the most studied model of limiting monarchical power, but it, too, did not exist in a single document stating these limits. It was a body of constitutional law dating back to the Magna Carta of 1215 in which King John had acknowledged limits to his power.

An unusual form of limited monarchy existed in Poland, where succession to the throne occurred by election. A representative body (the *Sejm*) of the Polish landowning gentry (the *szlachta*) chose each new king and claimed traditional rights, called "the five eternal principles," including the right to renounce allegiance to the king.

Republics. Republican governments held that sovereignty belonged to the citizens, usually to some privileged portion of them. **Republicanism** slowly evolved into the modern sense of republic—in which sovereignty is held by citizens who elect a government and delegate limited powers to it—but this form did not apply during the Old Regime. Most of the republics of 1715 were **oligarchies**—the rule of the few instead of the rule of one—typically small city-states in Italy. The only great power to attempt republican government during the eighteenth century was revolutionary France during the 1790s.

The Evolution of Government: Parliaments, Ministers, and Cabinets

Most countries of the Old Regime, except autocratic states such as Russia, possessed a representative assembly, typically called a **parliament** today but more often called a **diet** (from the Latin *diaeta*, meaning "a place of assembly"). Diets had existed in Europe for centuries. The oldest was the Icelandic Althing, founded in 930 CE. In some strong monarchies, such as France and Spain, assemblies existed in theory but not in practice. The French **Estates-General** had once been a powerful body, elected by all classes of the population and able to limit taxation. However, it met only when convoked by the king, and between 1614 and 1789, French kings never called a meeting. In Württemberg, Duke Eberhard Ludwig ruled for 40 years, from 1693 to 1733, and permitted only one meeting of the Diet during his entire reign. That meeting opposed a standing army and the levying of taxes, but the duke proceeded to raise an army, collect taxes, and prevent further meetings of the Diet. Only the British Parliament and the Swedish Rikstag had genuine legislative power.

Royal Advisers and Cabinets. The most powerful political figures of the eighteenth century were usually the advisers chosen by the monarch to manage the government. Another important trend in political history was the slow evolution of these royal advisers into a modern government. Advisers gradually became ministers of state, charged with the direction of a **bureaucracy,** such as the Ministry of Finance or the Ministry of War. In efficient governments, the advisers worked together as a cabinet of ministers, pursuing a common policy. During the eighteenth century, this evolved into the cabinet system of government in Britain, culminating in the recognition of one minister as the head of the government—the **prime minister.** Only the most energetic and able of monarchs, such as Frederick the Great of Prussia, served as their own prime minister, directing the bureaucracy. Instead, such strong leaders as Sir Robert Walpole in Britain (served 1721–1742) or Cardinal Fleury in France (served 1726–1743), laid the bases of modern ministerial government.

Ministerial Responsibility.

The final stage of this evolution is known as **ministerial responsibility,** when the prime minister and the cabinet no longer served at the king's pleasure but were responsible to Parliament and held office only as long as a majority supported them. Signs of ministerial responsibility were evident in eighteenth-century Britain, but the idea developed in the nineteenth century and was not widely accepted until the twentieth century. Many ministers were selected by royal whim. The most powerful adviser might be the king's private secretary, as was Alexandrea de Gusmao, the strongest statesman in midcentury Portugal. Or power might be hidden behind a minor office. For example, the title of Adam Moltke, who dominated the government of Denmark for a generation, was master of the royal household. The two most influential advisers to King Louis XV of France were the man who had been his childhood tutor and one of the king's mistresses.

THE RISE OF PARLIAMENTARY GOVERNMENT IN HANOVERIAN ENGLAND

The strength of parliamentary government in England was the result of seventeenth-century revolutions that limited the royal power of the Stuart kings. When it became clear that the royal line was dying out, Parliament asserted its supremacy and selected a German princess from the House of Hanover (a relative of the Stuarts) as the heir to the throne. Thus, in 1714, the throne of England passed to a German, the elector of Hanover. He took the title of King George I, beginning the House of Hanover. His heirs took the names George II and

George III, so eighteenth-century England is known as *Georgian England* as well as *Hanoverian England.*

George I and the Rise of Parliament.

King George I did not speak English, and he never bothered to learn the language of his new kingdom, although he had already learned Latin, French, and Italian. He preferred life in Germany and made long trips to Hanover, where he kept a series of plump mistresses whom the English press loved to satirize. The king married his own cousin, then accused her of adultery, divorced her, and imprisoned her for 30 years. This monarch did not win the affection of the English people, who generally considered him indolent and ignorant. One of the sharpest tongued Englishmen, Samuel Johnson, summarized him simply: "George I knew nothing and desired to know nothing; did nothing and desired to do nothing." The character of King George I contributed to the supremacy of Parliament. He showed little interest in government, and because of the language barrier, even his addresses to Parliament had to be read by someone else. Parliament asserted itself with a coronation oath, requiring each monarch to swear to obey parliamentary statutes. It established a mandatory term of office for itself and gained tighter control over the budget and the army. But the most important effect of George I's disinterest in governing was that it allowed the development of the cabinet system of government.

Sir Robert Walpole and the Rise of the Cabinet System.

George I's adviser Sir Robert Walpole became the first prime minister in British history and the architect of the cabinet system. Walpole did not come from the titled nobility but was the son of large landowners with nearly a dozen manors. His marriage to a merchant's daughter brought him a dowry of £20,000 and the independence for a parliamentary career. He championed the Hanoverian succession and won the confidence of the royal family, who allowed him independence to shape the government. Walpole also had to win the confidence of Parliament, and he did so through remarkable managerial skills. He won the backing of the landowning **gentry** by cutting the land tax from 20 percent to 5 percent. He gained the faith of others by restoring order to British finances after a crisis that was caused by stock speculation known as the South Seas Bubble. He got the support of manufacturing interests with a policy favorable to foreign trade. The key to Walpole's success, however, was probably his **patronage system,** in which he tried to find a job or an income for everyone who would support him. "There is enough pasture for all the sheep," Walpole said. His opponents thought this scandalous. Jonathan Swift put it bluntly: "The whole system of his ministry was corruption; and he never gave bribe or pension without frankly telling the receivers what he expected

FIGURE 19.1 *Walpole and Cabinet Government.* Sir Robert Walpole (1676–1745) is considered the first prime minister of England, an office he held from 1721 to 1742. (As his lace, silk, and jewels testify, he prospered in office.) He is therefore one of the most important founders of modern representative government in Europe and one of the foremost architects of the cabinet system of government. In the painting by Joseph Coopy, Walpole is shown speaking to the other cabinet ministers seated around the table. They are all middle-aged, expensively dressed men of the propertied elite that dominated eighteenth-century politics, men who might be expected to own (and gamble on) a sleek race horse and hang its picture in their meeting room. Note that eleven people comprise this cabinet. Modern European cabinets contain two to three times as many members.

from them." Yet in this way, Sir Robert Walpole held power for 21 years and laid the foundations of modern parliamentary government.

Parliament. The British Parliament of the eighteenth century was far from a modern, democratic legislature. The upper house, the House of Lords, remained a bastion of the aristocracy where membership was inherited by the eldest son along with the family title. The lower house, the House of Commons, was elective, but voting was limited to adult males who paid 40 shillings a year in property taxes, on the theory that men of property had a vested interest in orderly government. This meant that fewer than 250,000 voted—approximately 3 percent of the nation. In addition to the poor, women, criminals, Catholics, Jews, some Protestants (notably Quakers), and nonbelievers were barred from voting. A Qualification Act required that to become a member of Parliament **(M.P.)** a candidate must own land worth £300, leaving a tiny fraction of the nation eligible for office. Walpole, however, encouraged the dominance of the House of Commons and accepted that his cabinet stood collectively responsible to that body.

Deference. British voters typically deferred to the leadership of a small elite of great landowners. According to a study of British politics at the accession of King George III, this pattern of **deference** meant that a few prominent families controlled the House of Commons. The constituency of Wenlock in western England, for example, had a few hundred electors. Throughout the eighteenth century, they deferred to the leadership of the Forester family, choosing eight members of that family to represent them in the House of Commons. Some constituencies, called **pocket boroughs,** were owned by a single family, which had the seat in its pocket and chose the M.P.; others, called **rotten boroughs,** had so few votes that the seat could be bought. In 1761, the borough of Sudbury openly advertised that its seat in the House of Commons was for sale. The vast lands owned by the Duke of Newcastle included seven boroughs for which he personally selected the M.P. In such ways, 111 wealthy landowners controlled more than 200 seats in Parliament.

The Party System. Eighteenth-century England also witnessed the origins of a political **party system.** Members of Parliament generally split into two large factions, not yet political parties in the modern sense, called the **Tory** and **Whig** parties. The Tories were somewhat more conservative (in the sense of supporting royal authority) than the Whigs (who were monarchists and defenders of the Hanoverian settlement but who spoke for parliamentary supremacy). The leaders of both factions typically came from the aristocracy. Political parties did not yet dominate elections. A famous study of politics in the Georgian age concluded that party did not determine the outcome of a single election in the voting of 1761. Nonetheless, the Whigs—including Walpole—won a majority in the first elections under King George I and generally dominated British politics for the next two generations.

William Pitt. The strongest of Walpole's successors, William Pitt the Elder, strengthened the position of prime minister and the cabinet system of government. Like Walpole, Pitt was not born to the aristocracy, but he managed to die holding both the nickname "the great commoner" and the noble title the Earl of

FIGURE 19.2 Hogarth's Canvassing for Votes. Parliamentary elections in the eighteenth century were notoriously corrupt. Some seats (called *pocket boroughs*) were owned outright by a great landowner who possessed the entire constituency. Other seats (called *rotten boroughs*) had so few voters that the election could be bought. This print by William Hogarth (1697–1764), sarcastically titled *Canvassing for Votes,* is filled with a satire of contemporary politics. The centrality of political corruption is shown by the central figure of a farmer who vote is being sought by the hosts of two competing taverns (representing the two political parties) who are clearly paying for his vote. The banner overhead depicts more money flowing out from the government.

rotten boroughs and to give seventy-two more seats to London and other populous areas. Pitt's bill failed in 1785, however, and fairer electoral laws had to wait for half a century.

King George III. George III was the most complex and important of the Hanoverian kings. He was the first Hanoverian to be born and educated in England. Although some British historians have described him as "an unbalanced man of low intelligence," George began his long reign (1760–1820) as a popular, hard-working king, considered a decent man of domestic virtues (in contrast to his predecessors and many of his ministers) and high patriotism. George III was also the first Hanoverian to intervene deeply in politics, the first to try to rule. He was stubborn and arbitrary, and he fought with his ministers, dismissing them from office. He tried to abolish the emerging system of political parties, and for about a dozen years, he effectively ran the government through the choice of weak ministers and lavish application of Walpole's patronage system. George III is often best remembered for the mental imbalance that began to afflict him in 1765—now thought to have been caused by the metabolic disease porphyria—and led to his being stripped of royal powers in 1811. But for many years, he was a formidable political figure, strong enough to order the arrest of Wilkes, who was expelled from Parliament.

Chatham. He was the grandson of a merchant who had made a fortune trading in India in illegal competition with the East India Company. That wealth had bought Pitt's marriage into high society and his seat in Parliament representing a famous rotten borough, Old Sarum. Pitt was polished and Oxford educated; his rise in Parliament was largely the result of exceptional oratorical skills. As prime minister during the Seven Years' War of 1756–1763, Pitt's vigorous leadership helped to secure global victories over France and demonstrated the strength of cabinet government in times of crisis.

Wilkes, Pitt the Younger, and the Reform of Parliament.

The evolution of parliamentary government in England was an important stage in the growth of European civilization, but it remained open to criticism. The most radical voice came from the son of a distiller, John Wilkes. Wilkes had an Oxford education and a helpful marriage to a wealthy older woman, whose dowry financed his campaign to abolish rotten boroughs and redistribute seats in a fairer representation of the population. Such reform won an important ally in 1783, when William Pitt the Younger (the son of Pitt the Elder) introduced a bill to disenfranchise thirty-six

Protest in the Streets. The political process did not stop with kings, parliaments, and radical reformers: the eighteenth century was an age of turbulent protest. One study has identified 275 urban disturbances in Britain between 1735 and 1800. The most common problem that drew crowds into the streets was hunger. Scarce or expensive bread caused food riots because many people lived on the margins of survival. Labor riots were also common during periods of high unemployment. Such protests in England frequently became anti-Irish demonstrations, such as the 1736 riots of London construction workers fearful that Irish immigrants were taking their jobs and driving down the price of labor.

Anti-Catholicism. Religious hatred was a common cause of riots in the eighteenth century, and English crowds regularly expressed their anti-Catholicism with

PARLIAMENT IN THE EIGHTEENTH CENTURY

Parliamentary government was the institution that most distinguished the English monarchy from the other great powers. The lower house of Parliament, the elective House of Commons, effectively limited the power of the Hanoverian kings in contrast to the absolute monarchies of continental Europe. Note how the physical arrangement divides Parliament into two sides (the government and the opposition), encouraging a two-party system. Note also the dress of the men present: they are clearly drawn from the comfortable classes. But not all members of the educated classes found the cozy government by the elite acceptable. The Oxford-educated John Wilkes entered Parliament on the strength of his wife's dowry but earned notoriety on his wits. He published a barbed weekly journal named the *North Briton*, where he offended many people by discussing rumors of M.P.s sleeping with the king's mother. He used his notoriety to call for the radical reform of Parliament, such as the abolition of rotten boroughs, as this document shows.

The House of Commons. Parliamentary government was the institution that most distinguished the English monarchy from the other great powers. The lower house of Parliament, the elective House of Commons, effectively limited the power of the Hanoverian kings in contrast to the absolute monarchies of continental Europe. The House of Commons, shown here listening to a speech by William Pitt, was far from modern democracy, however, and was still dominated by the landowning aristocracy. Note how the physical arrangement divides Parliament into two sides (the government and the opposition), encouraging a two-party system.

John Wilkes on Reform of Parliament, 1776

All wise governments, and well-regulated states, have been careful to mark and correct the various abuses, which a considerable length of time almost necessarily creates. Among these, one of the most striking and important in our country is the present unfair and inadequate representation of the people of England in Parliament. . . .

[N]o less than 22 towns sent members to the Parliament of Edward I [in the thirteenth century], which have long ceased to be represented. The names of some of them are scarcely known to us. . . . What a happy fate has attended the boroughs of Gatton and Old Sarum, of which, although [they are now deserted ruins] the names are familiar to us: the clerk regularly calls them over, and four respectable gentlemen represent their departed greatness. . . . Great abuses, it must be owned, contrary to the primary ideas of the English constitution, were committed by our former princes, in giving the right of representation to several paltry boroughs. . . . The

marked partiality for Cornwall, which single county still sends, within one, as many members as the whole kingdom of Scotland, is striking. . . .

[I]t has been demonstrated that this number of 254 members [of Parliament] are elected by no more than 5,723 persons. . . . [T]he mean, and insignificant [constituencies], so emphatically stiled the rotten part of our constitution, should be lopped off, and the electors of them thrown into the counties; and the rich, populous, trading towns, Birmingham, Manchester, Sheffield, Leeds, and others, be permitted to send deputies to the great council of the nation.

From Wilkes, John, *Wilke's Speeches in Parliament* (London, 1777).

Question: How does the British Parliament compare to representative institutions in the other great powers?

"pope-burnings." When the House of Commons in 1778 voted to abolish legal restrictions on the 78,000 Catholics living in England, the public uproar grew into one of the largest riots of the century. A vehement defender of Protestant dominance, an M.P. named Lord George Gordon, in June 1780 led 60,000 militant Protestants in a march on Parliament that precipitated 3 days of anti-Catholicism riots, known as the Gordon Riots or the "No Popery Riots." Mobs assaulted Catholic chapels, major prisons, and the Bank of England.

CONTRASTING VIEWS OF EIGHTEENTH-CENTURY LONDON

The Gordon Riots.

Urban riots were a recurring feature of life in eighteenth-century Europe, even in the prosperous states of the west. London suffered severe riots, of which the worst were the Gordon Riots of 1780, when crowds attacked Catholic

The Bank of England.

churches and church property under the banner of "No Popery." The first illustration here shows rioters setting fire to Newgate Prison in London. In addition to such crowd violence, the eighteenth century had appalling crime rates and a rudimentary police force of watchmen, constables, and thief-takers. A modern police force was not established until 1825.

The second illustration shows a very different London. This is the Bank of England, founded in 1694, an icon of order, stability, tranquility, and prosperity. The artist has gone to great lengths to illustrate a peaceful London, a clean and serene great city where people of property stroll securely, women are safe on the streets, and child and dog can safely play. Both illustrations express an element of truth about the eighteenth century, and the historian's job often involves assimilating such contradictory images into a coherent pattern.

Question: What factors best explain this contrast and the selection of one image of the past instead of the other?

George III used the army to quell the riots, killing 285 members of the crowd. Gordon was tried for treason and acquitted; his campaign delayed Catholic emancipation for 50 years.

Britain and the Struggles of Empire

The eighteenth century was an age of nearly constant warfare for Britain; wars were fought in Europe, in North America, in India, and on the high seas. The British contested both French and Spanish power in Europe—fearing the hegemony of either Catholic power—and battled the French for global empire. And

British military policy was successful in both objectives. The War of the Spanish Succession (1701–1714) checked the French pursuit of continental hegemony, and a simultaneous war in North America (Queen Anne's War) resulted in a significant growth in English power. The War of the Quadruple Alliance (1718–1720) seriously curtailed Spanish power.

War and Debt. War was one of the few political questions that deeply interested the Hanoverian kings. George I and George II gladly left English domestic politics in the hands of Walpole, but they resisted his policy of peace and international commerce. Both kings

Britain's Wars in the Eighteenth Century

Britain fought almost constant wars, both in Europe and around the world, during the eighteenth century. The wars led to great indebtedness because they cost more than Britain's total government income, so they led to both a continuing national debt and to the invention of the modern income tax. The century began with 14 years of war (1701–1714), longer than World War I and World War II combined, fought in Europe as the War of the Spanish Succession and in America as Queen Anne's War. Britain was back at war in 1718–1720 (the War of the Quadruple Alliance), 1739–1748 (the War of Austrian Succession, King George's War, and the War of Jenkins Ear), 1756–1763 (the Seven Years' War, the French and Indian War, the Bengal Wars), and 1773–1783 (the American Revolution). For Europe, the Seven Years' War was the most expensive war, but the American Revolution cost Britain more. The British war debt is shown in Table 19.1 and the global range of fighting is shown in Map 19.2.

Table 19.1 British War Finances, 1702–1783

War	War Expenditure (in millions)	Government Income (in millions)	Deficit in Loans (in millions)	Percentage Borrowed
War of the Spanish Succession, 1701–1713	£93.6	£64.2	£29.4	31.4
War of the Austrian Succession, 1740–1748	£95.6	£65.9	£29.7	31.1
Seven Years' War, 1756–1763	£160.6	£100.6	£60.0	37.4
American Revolution, 1776–1783	£236.5	£141.9	£94.6	39.9
Total	£586.3	£372.6	£213.7	36.4

Source: Adapted from data in Kennedy, Paul, *The Rise and Fall of the Great Powers* (New York: Random House, 1987, p. 81).

believed that the English army and navy represented the best defense of their Hanoverian homeland, and they accepted costly warfare to defend it. George II was the last king of England to take personal command of an army in the field, fighting in the War of the Austrian Succession in 1743. George III thus inherited a huge **national debt** (£138 million) along with the throne, the result of military profligacy. He, too, fought constant wars, however, and quintupled the English national debt to £800 million, 73 percent of which was directly due to war (see Table 19.1). This uncontrolled military expenditure and national debt necessitated the adoption of the first **income tax** in 1798.

The Seven Years' War. The immense war debt that King George III inherited was the cost of participation in the first true world war—the Seven Years' War in Europe (1756–1763), and its simultaneous theaters known as the French and Indian Wars in North America and the Bengal Wars in India. This global war produced a mixed blessing: the British Empire won but wound up deeper in debt; Britain became the dominant colonial power in the world, but she thereby acquired even greater administrative costs.

The American Revolution. The British nation—like many others during the Old Regime—was loathe to pay the taxes needed to repay war debts, support military expansion, and meet the expenses of empire. In 1764, the Tory government chose a compromise it thought safe: new taxes would be imposed in the colonies, which were the source of many imperial costs, but not in the British Isles. The issue of this policy was the Stamp Act of 1765, a tax on the American colonies, requiring that a tax stamp be attached to official documents such as a will, a liquor license, or a college degree. The furious reaction in many colonies held that such taxes could not be imposed under British law without the consent of those being taxed. Representatives of nine American colonies (Britain possessed more than thirty colonies in the Americas) assembled in a Stamp Tax Congress and adopted an an-

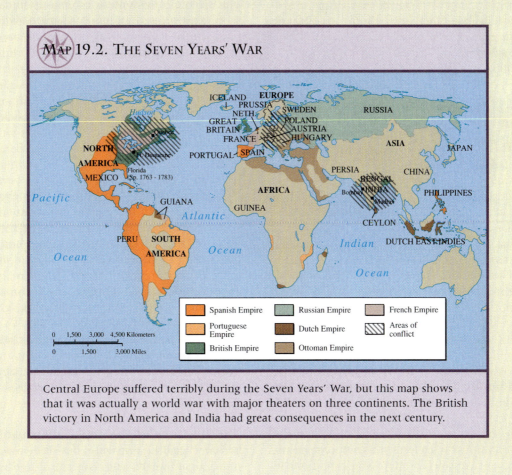

MAP 19.2. THE SEVEN YEARS' WAR

Spanish Empire
Portuguese Empire
British Empire
Russian Empire
Dutch Empire
Ottoman Empire
French Empire
Areas of conflict

Central Europe suffered terribly during the Seven Years' War, but this map shows that it was actually a world war with major theaters on three continents. The British victory in North America and India had great consequences in the next century.

gry resolution challenging the decision of Parliament as subverting "the rights and liberties of the colonists." The confrontation over taxation simmered for a decade and led to the American Revolution of 1776–1783. Parliament initially backed down in the face of American protests and rescinded the Stamp Tax in 1766, but renewed protests led Parliament to adopt the punitive Coercive Acts of 1774 and to quarter troops in Boston. A few months later, in April 1775, the battles of Lexington and Concord began the military phase of the revolution.

Although the British had won a global war in 1763, they were in a weaker position in 1775. They were deprived of the help that Americans had given them during the Seven Years' War. There was now no continental war to preoccupy and divide the European powers. One by one, the European powers exploited Britain's vulnerable position and declared war upon her. France entered the war in 1778, Spain in 1779, and Holland in 1780.

France and the American Revolution. The financial and military assistance of these states—especially the French—plus the division of British opinion over the war, helped decide the war. France sent increasingly larger armies, such as the force of 6,000 men that arrived with Count Jean de Rochambeau in 1780. By the later phases of the war, French forces were decisive. In the battle fought at Yorktown, Virginia, in 1781, the largest army was neither British nor American but French. Facing such growing forces, the British accepted the independence of thirteen of her American colonies in 1783.

Ireland. The American Revolution obliged the British to reconsider the situation in other territories. Both nearby (in Ireland) and around the world (in India), Britain faced problems. The Anglo-Protestant domination of Ireland had grown steadily during English battles with Catholicism at home and abroad in the seventeenth and eighteenth centuries, especially after the Protestant victory in the battle of the Boyne in 1690.

FIGURE 19.3 *The Colonies Reduced.* A decade before the American Revolution, Benjamin Franklin created this gruesome, revolutionary image and used it on his cards. It depicts the beaten figure of Britannia who has lost a battle and all four of her limbs. Those severed limbs are identified as American colonies (New England, New York, Pennsylvania, and Virginia), and the caption describes the amputations as "Great Britain: Her Colonies Reduced." In the background, the Royal Navy sails away in the aftermath of defeat.

One striking consequence of these struggles could be seen in **land tenure.** In 1603, Catholics had owned 90 percent of the land in Ireland; in 1778, they owned 5 percent (see Table 19.2). Catholics protested their eviction from the soil, which had left them at the mercy of absentee landlords who collected extortionate rents. When Parliament considered improving conditions in Ireland, such as the Relief Act of 1778, the result was a Protestant backlash. Protestants in the northern counties of Ulster founded the Protestant Volunteers, a **paramilitary** force of 40,000 armed men to defend their privileged position. The House of Commons ca-

pitulated to the Protestants by creating a Protestant-dominated parliament in Ireland known as Grattan's Parliament, which survived until Ireland was merged into the United Kingdom in 1801.

THE VULNERABLE MONARCHY OF BOURBON FRANCE

In contrast to the situation in England, the French monarchy carried the powers of absolutism into the eighteenth century: Louis XIV, *le Roi Soleil* (the Sun King), the most powerful of the seventeenth-century monarchs, died in 1715 after the longest reign in the history of European monarchy, nearly 73 years. Advocates of limiting absolutism had placed their hopes in the heirs of Louis XIV, but within a single year (1711–1712), Louis's son, grandson, and eldest great-grandson all died. The death of Louis XIV consequently brought to the throne his 5-year-old great-grandson, Louis XV, who would reign for most of the eighteenth century (from 1715 to 1774).

The Regency of the Duke d'Orléans. Louis XIV had practiced the distrustful but shrewd administrative principle of fragmenting power near to the throne, and he extended this policy after death by a will dividing the powers of the **regency** to rule France until Louis XV came of age. The regent of France during the childhood of Louis XV was his cousin, Philippe II, the Duke d'Orléans, a liberal and tolerant man, although profli-

---

TABLE 19.2 LAND OWNERSHIP IN IRELAND, 1603–1778

The English conquered the eastern coast of Ireland in the twelfth century and retained control of part of Ireland for 500 years. When the Irish rebelled against the English occupation in the seventeenth century, England (under Oliver Cromwell) conquered the entire island and began a policy colonizing it with Scots, Welsh, and English Protestants. This led to the seizure of land—ownership was taken from Irish Catholics and given to Protestant colonists. Among the long-term consequences of this was a significant amount of absentee ownership that shipped agricultural produce to market in England, a policy that became extremely controversial if Ireland faced famine. The following table shows the complete reversal of land ownership in just 75 years.

YEAR	% CATHOLIC OWNERSHIP	% PROTESTANT OWNERSHIP
1603	90	10
1641	59	41
1688	21	79
1703	15	85
1778	5	95

Source: Edwards, Ruth D., *An Atlas of Irish History*, 2nd ed. (London: Methuen, 1973, p. 178).

Question: To what extent does this seizure of land help explain subsequent Irish rebellions against British rule?

gate enough to be considered dissipated even in the context of royal families. The duke skillfully obtained full power by making a deal with the chief judicial body in France, the **Parlement** of Paris: the parlement invalidated the will of Louis XIV, and in return, Philippe d'Orléans allowed the fifteen parlements of France greater powers to review (and block) royal decrees. Thus, when Louis XV reached age 13 and began to rule without a regent in 1723, he inherited a streamlined government, but he faced well-entrenched opposition from the aristocratic parlements.

Louis XV. Louis XV was an intelligent and capable young man, amiable enough to be called Louis "the Well-Beloved." He was not interested in controlling the government as his great-grandfather had; he liked the idea of absolutism but lacked enthusiasm for the daily chores of governing. Consequently, at age 16, Louis XV entrusted the government of France to his tutor, Cardinal Fleury, who served as the virtual prime minister of France (without the title) between 1726 and 1743. Louis, who had been married at age 15 for reasons of state, amused himself with a variety of women while Fleury used his long tenure, as Walpole did in Britain, to stabilize and organize the government. When Fleury died, Louis XV tried to restore the system of Louis XIV—ruling personally instead of trusting a minister to govern. Like George II of England, he took command of his army and led it into battle in 1744. Ministers who wanted too much power were reduced to the shadows, as was a finance minister of 1759 who left behind his name for that condition: Étienne de Silhouette. Instead of trusting a prime minister and a cabinet, Louis chiefly took advice from his official mistress, the Marquise de Pompadour. She exerted a generally liberal and enlightened influence on French policy, but she was not able to master the king's greatest problem: like George III of England, he found that he had inherited a government deep in debt, with disordered finances and no ready solutions. Louis XIV's deathbed words to his great-grandson had been prophetic: "My child, you are about to become a great king. Do not imitate . . . my liking for war." Even more than England, France would pay a terrible price for the indebtedness caused by war.

The French Financial Crisis and the Resurgent Aristocracy

The foremost problem facing Louis XV was the disastrous state of French finances created by high military expenses and low taxation. The wars of Louis XIV left France in debt and near bankruptcy. The debt amounted to 36 percent of the government's budget in 1739. Royal opulence compounded the problem: the

FIGURE 19.4 *Marquise de Pompadour.* The Marquise de Pompadour (1721–1764) was the mistress of King Louis XV of France and exercised enormous influence over French politics for nearly 20 years, from 1745 to 1764. In this portrait, the French court painter Francois Boucher (1703–1770) has tried to depict Pompadour as both the beautiful woman and the intelligent woman that she was. Note that she is shown with folio volumes, scrolls, and a globe scattered at her feet while she stands at piano, suggesting her musical talent.

cost of maintaining the royal family, splendid palaces such as Versailles, and the life of the royal court exceeded 10 percent of the national budget, whereas all expenditures on social welfare, including royal pensions, received only 8 percent of the budget. The extravagant spending on luxuries could reach absurd levels. A single piece of furniture for a royal palace, gilded and bejeweled, cost more than the servant who dusted it could earn in 2,000 years (see *French Finances in the Eighteenth Century*).

Taxes. Cardinal Fleury established financial order in France, but he could not resolve the underlying problems of inadequate taxation and therefore could not eliminate the debt. The principal direct tax, the *taille,* was collected on land and property, but it was inadequate because the aristocracy, the church, and some towns had exemptions from it. Attempts to create an

French Finances in the Eighteenth Century

The following bill was presented by a Parisian jeweller in 1760 for a single piece of furniture, a jeweled, lacquered writing desk called an *escritoire*, with flower vase, powder box, and sponge case. To understand this level of royal spending, consider that a wealthy nobleman, such as the Count of Tavannes, might have an annual gross revenue from his land of less than 100,000 livres (the Count received 86,000 in 1788). The annual wages for the count's chef were 945 livres; a maid received 70 livres.

TABLE 19.3 THE COST OF ROYAL EXTRAVAGANCE— A WRITING DESK

COMPONENT	COST IN FRENCH LIVRES
Jewels	66,000
Gold	3,464
Miniature portrait of the empress	600
Lacquer	528
Labor (sub-contract for jewelry work)	6,148
Labor (cabinet maker, joiner, and lock maker)	360
Packaging box with copper mounts	30
Labor (packaging)	28
Total	77,158

Source: Condensed from data in Mitford, Nancy, *Madame de Pompadour* (New York: E. P. Dutton, 1968, p. 276).

TABLE 19.4 THE FRENCH NATIONAL BUDGET

Note that this simplified version of the budget shows some success in lowering the cost of the national debt, because service on the debt has fallen to 30 percent. The figure remains frighteningly high, however, and to meet these expenses, the government had to borrow 5 percent of the total, thereby sending the debts back upward.

EXPENSES	PERCENTAGE OF BUDGET
Army	33
Service on Debt	30
Royal Court	10
Royal Pensions (awarded for past services)	6
All other	21

Question: Do these data suggest a crisis in eighteenth-century France?

income tax without exemptions, such as the ***dixième*** (10 percent) of 1710, had been blocked by the aristocracy, the church, and the parlements. The right to collect indirect taxes, such as tax stamps on documents, had been sold to **"tax farmers"** for a fixed sum, while they collected whatever excess they could. Many traditional taxes, such as the salt tax *(gabelle)*, had been cut for some regions and could not be increased.

Financial Crisis. The Seven Years' War converted an intractable financial problem into a national crisis. France was populous, rich, and powerful, but the government was facing bankruptcy. The war cost France most of its colonial empire and 50 percent of its world trade. The national debt rose to 62 percent of the national budget in 1763, and it was growing because of huge interest obligations and a rigid tax structure; new loans to restructure the debt could reduce the percentage of the budget consumed but perpetuate the problem. So finances became the dominant issue in France during the twilight years of the Old Regime. Ultimately, neither side won. The financial crisis led France to one of the greatest revolutions of modern history.

Ineffectiveness of Louis XV. King Louis XV, once beloved, was unable to handle these problems. His indebted and ineffective government plus his life of luxury and debauchery produced unpopularity and stately torpor. The death of Madame de Pompadour in 1764 left the king in despair. He slowly became an eighteenth-century stereotype, the aging voluptuary. After a few years of entertaining himself with a royal brothel at Versailles known as Deer Park, Louis selected another official mistress in 1769. Unfortunately, Madame du Barry lacked the insights and education of Madame de Pompadour. The dominant figure in the French gov-

FIGURE 19.5 *Portrait of King Louis XV.* King Louis XV (1710–1774) came to the throne at age 5 after both his grandfather and his father had died. After a regency governed France during Louis's childhood, he came to throne and the initial nickname of "Louis the Well-Beloved"; but his weak leadership left France with badly disordered finances and severe losses in war.

ernment after the Seven Years' War was Duke Étienne de Choiseul, a capable soldier-statesman who had been sponsored by Madame de Pompadour. Choiseul effectively rebuilt French military strength after 1763 but not French finances.

To his credit, Louis XV attempted a solution. He ordered that a wartime tax, the ***vingtième***—"the twentieth," a 5 percent income tax that fell on all classes—remain in force.

Aristocratic Resistance.
This provoked a virtual rebellion of aristocrats who believed themselves exempt from such taxes. The aristocratic lawyers and magistrates of the ***noblesse de robe,*** who controlled the parlements of the higher court system, formed the center of the resistance. The Parlement of Paris ruled that the king's decree was illegal. In the south of France, the Parlement of Toulouse even arrested the royal governor who tried to enforce the tax law. Louis XV capitulated to the parlements in 1764, rescinding the vingtième and changing his government. This did not end his battles with the parlements. When he tried to introduce a road building program in Brittany, relying on a royal **corvée** to provide labor, Breton nobles and the Parlement of Rennes protested.

The frustrated king ordered the arrest of the president of the Parlement of Rennes, but this provoked a united protest from all fifteen parlements, claiming

that they represented the nation whenever the Estates-General (which had last met in 1614) was not in session. As the Parlement of Rouen stated, they considered themselves "the custodian and the depository" of the French constitution, and the king must bend before the law. This time the king stood firm. In 1766, he sent royal troops to occupy the seat of the Parlement of Paris, then personally appeared before the parlement to express his anger. "I will not allow," Louis told the magistrates, "this usurpation of power. The magistrates are my officers, charged with the truly royal duty of rendering justice to my subjects." Louis insisted that the duties of the parlements did not restrict his sovereignty: "In my person only does the sovereign power rest. (To me alone belongs legislative power, unconditionally and indivisibly."

René de Maupeou.
To underscore his claim to absolute power, Louis XV named a new government, headed by René de Maupeou, to fight the parlements. In 1771, Maupeou abolished the parlements and created a simpler court system in which the magistrates were salaried state employees instead of owners of their office. He hoped to create a new tax system, both fairer and sufficient for the fiscal crisis, without facing an aristocratic veto. The aristocracy, backed by many philosophes who detested royal absolutism, naturally raised vociferous opposition. But much opinion also supported the king. Voltaire stood with Maupeou's dismissal of the parlements, saying that he would rather be governed by a fine lion than by 200 rats.

Louis XVI.
The aristocracy won the day in 1774, when Louis XV died. His 19-year-old grandson, Louis XVI, possessed generally good intentions, but he was too timid and inexperienced to stand up to the nobility. His first acts were to dismiss Maupeou and to restore the parlements. Consequently, he faced a strengthened aristocracy throughout his reign. In 1777, when Joseph II of Austria visited his sister, Queen Marie Antoinette, in Paris, he concluded that the government of France was "an aristocratic despotism."

Louis XVI also inherited the desperate financial situation. In the year of his coronation, the state's revenues were 5 percent below its expenditures, increasing a debt that consumed a third of the budget just in interest payments. Those problems soon worsened. Beginning in 1778, France was again at war, supporting—and financing—the American Revolution. Other problems were beginning. The foremost source of French wealth was agriculture, and in 1774 an agricultural recession began. Farm profits, which translated into tax revenue, plummeted in 1775, and they never again during the Old Regime reached the levels of 1772–1774. The decade between 1777 and 1786 saw five harvests in which the average farmer lost money, plus two other poor harvests.

THE PARLEMENT OF PARIS PROTESTS A ROYAL EDICT, 1776

The desire to relieve the burdens of the people is too worthy of praise in a sovereign and conforms too much to the wishes of your parlement for the latter ever to conceive the thought of dissuading Your Majesty from such a noble and legitimate goal.

But when projects that hold out this pleasing prospect lead to real and aggravated injustices, and even imperil the constitution and tranquility of the state, it is our faithful duty, without seeking to place obstacles in the way of your beneficence, to set the barrier of the law against the imprudent efforts being made to pledge Your Majesty to a course of action the dangers and stumbling-blocks of which have been concealed from you. . . .

This is not, Sire, a struggle between rich and poor, as some have tried to convince you. It is a question of Estate, and a most important one, since it is a matter of knowing whether all your subjects can and must be treated indiscriminately, whether differences in conditions, ranks, titles and preeminence must cease to be acknowledged among them. To subject nobles to a tax to redeem the corvée *. . . is to declare nobles subject to the* corvée *like commoners. . . . [N]oblemen, the descendants of those ancient knights who placed or preserved the crown on the head of Your Majesty's forefathers . . . could be exposed to the humiliation of seeing themselves dragged off to the* corvée!

Question: What is the foremost concern of the parlement?

Turgot and Reform. The reign of Louis XVI did show signs of hope, as a result of a reforming ministry led by the minister of finance, Robert Turgot, and the interior, Chrétien Malesherbes. Malesherbes was a liberal who had defended the publication of the *Encyclopédie.* Turgot was a minor aristocrat who had reached high office in a typical way for a venal society: he bought his position for 100,000 livres. He was also a freethinker and a leader of the enlightened economic school of the **Physiocrats,** whose doctrines (which had much in common with early capitalism) he explained in the *Encyclopédie.* In a series of decrees known as the Six Edicts (1776), Turgot and Malesherbes laid the basis for economic recovery. The edicts abolished the monopoly of the guilds to stimulate **economic competition.** They abolished the burden of the corvée on peasants and replaced it with a tax on all landowners. And they eliminated most **internal tariffs** on the grain trade to bring down the price of bread. At the same time, Turgot cut government spending, especially in the portion of the budget devoted to royal pensions and the royal court.

Necker and Continuing Efforts at Reform. The reforms of 1774–1776 made many enemies. The opposition of the parlements, pressure from powerful guilds, and intrigues at court brought down Turgot in 1776, and Malesherbes followed him. The Parlement of Paris, for example, claimed that the Six Edicts "imperil the constitution" (see Document 19.2). The magistrates carried the day: guild monopolies, the corvée, and internal tariffs were all restored. Another capable minister of finance, a Swiss-born, Protestant financier named Jacques Necker, succeeded Turgot. Necker had made a fortune as a banker during the Seven Years' War. His home was one of the most influential centers of the Enlightenment, where his wife, Suzanne (a prominent writer and the daughter of a Swiss pastor), and their daughter, Germaine (later famous as the Baroness de Staël, also a distinguished writer), directed a brilliant **salon.** Necker lived at the center of a network of financial, political, and intellectual leaders, and they shaped a series of enlightened reforms during his ministry from 1778 to 1781. He drafted a royal decree abolishing the limited form of **serfdom** that survived in France, although it applied only to royal lands. It condemned serfdom in principle and urged aristocrats to follow the king's lead; it did not force abolition in respect for the principle of private property. Few aristocrats followed the king, so serfdom lingered in France, especially in eastern France, where the parlement—most of whose members owned serfs— refused to register the royal decree.

The Assembly of Notables. The successors of Turgot and Necker as ministers of finance during the 1780s were utterly unable to break the logjam by which the aristocracy blocked meaningful tax reform. Charles de Calonne, a courtier and less able financier, skirted the edges of bankruptcy by continually increasing the debt. He, too, concluded that a new tax was essential and proposed a land tax, to be paid by aristocrats and the church as well as commoners. To win aristocratic support, an Assembly of Notables (a body of uncertain constitutional basis) was called in 1787; the assembly failed to agree on anything except opposition to Calonne's tax. This led to Calonne's ouster and yet another minister of finance, who sought even bigger loans, asked the parlements to approve new taxes, and met yet another rejection.

The Estates-General. The consequence of the aristocratic rejection of new taxes was that the French national debt reached 100 percent of the budget in 1789. A second consequence was that the aristocracy forced Louis XVI to call elections for the Estates-General. The Parlement of Besançon had proposed that solution in 1783, and others had adopted the idea. Louis resisted, trying instead his grandfather's idea of abolishing the parlements in 1788. He finally conceded defeat, however, and agreed to a meeting of the Estates-General in May 1789—which led directly to the French Revolution.

THE HAPSBURG EMPIRE IN THE AGE OF MARIA THERESA AND JOSEPH II

In contrast to Britain, where Parliament had broken the power of the king, or to France, where the resurgent aristocracy was restricting the power of the king, in Austria the Hapsburg family still held nearly absolute power during the eighteenth century. The political evolution in Austria—known as **enlightened despotism**—showed how monarchy could respond to new problems.

The Hapsburg Empire. The Hapsburg Empire dominated Germanic central Europe at the start of the eighteenth century, dwarfing its rivals in size, population, and military might. Prussia numbered only 1.6 million persons and Bavaria, 2.0 million; the Hapsburg lands held 11.0 million. In the first decades of the century, Hapsburg armies under the skillful command of Prince Eugene of Savoy had fought well in the War of the Spanish Succession, the peace treaties of 1714 gave the Hapsburgs the Austrian Netherlands (Belgium), and Lombardy. Wars with the Ottoman Empire at the end of the seventeenth century had acquired the Kingdom of Hungary, including vast territories in eastern Europe. Thus, in 1714, Vienna controlled lands from Brussels in the west to Milan in the south, Belgrade in the east, and Prague in the north—plus the crown of the **Holy Roman Empire** (the nearly powerless, 700-year-old political structure that loosely linked the German states together).

Charles VI. The Hapsburg emperor, Charles VI, who reigned from 1711 to 1740, faced daunting political problems. His heterogeneous, polyglot realm was united only by the person of the Hapsburg monarch. Hungary gave Charles the most difficulty. The **magnate class** (the Hungarian nobility) had been largely autonomous under the Turkish sultan, and their diet expected no less from the Hapsburgs. Some Hungarian nobles even claimed a remarkable right, the *jus resistandi,* which legalized resistance to central authority. Charles VI realized that "[I]t is very important that quiet should prevail in this country," and he made numerous concessions to the Hungarians, such as promises to continue their Diet, to tolerate religious minorities (many nobles were Protestants), and not to tax the magnates. Such concessions to regional rights, however, meant that Austria lagged behind rivals such as Prussia in the development of a centralized authority and bureaucracy.

The Salic Law and Women Monarchs. The second formidable political problem confronting Charles VI was the issue of his heir. His only son died in infancy, and all Hapsburg lands thus probably would pass to his daughter, Maria Theresa, who could not become Holy Roman Empress (because the **Salic law** excluded women) but who could, under Austrian law, inherit the family dominions. Charles knew that powerful men might challenge his succession if the throne passed to a woman; he therefore devoted much of his reign to guaranteeing Maria Theresa's succession and preventing a war of Austrian succession. For Charles, the issue was not protecting his daughter or defending the rights of women, it was the perpetuation of the dynasty and the territorial integrity of the far-flung Hapsburg lands. For his subject peoples, however, his death would open the prospect of independence or enhanced autonomy. For the European powers, it suggested the dismemberment of the Hapsburg Empire.

The Pragmatic Sanction. The solution Charles VI proposed was a document called the Pragmatic Sanction. It proclaimed that the Hapsburg lands were indivisible, and it outlined the Austrian succession through Maria Theresa. Charles obtained the agreement of his family and published the Pragmatic Sanction in 1719. For the next 20 years he bargained within the empire and abroad, buying acceptance of the Pragmatic Sanction. Negotiations with the Hungarian Diet produced its acceptance in 1723, at the price of further weakening Viennese central authority over Hungary. A lifetime of diplomatic bribery bought the consent (sometimes recanted and bought again) of the European powers. Britain, for example, accepted the Pragmatic Sanction by a treaty of 1731; Charles paid Britain by closing the Austrian trading company (the Ostend Company) that competed with the British in global commerce. The king of Spain signed in return for the duchy of Parma.

Maria Theresa and the War of the Austrian Succession. Maria Theresa inherited the Hapsburg dominions in 1740 at the age of 23, and she stayed on the throne until her death in 1780. She possessed energy and determination but an empty treasury and a weakened army. She began to reorganize the government, but the Pragmatic Sanction failed almost immediately. Her realm accepted her, and the Hungarians were chivalrous in her defense, but the Duke of Bavaria, the king of Spain, and the elector of Saxony each claimed the Hapsburg crown for himself. The Holy Roman Empire sided with Bavaria, choosing the duke to be emperor. The king of Prussia demanded the province of Silesia as his price for honoring the Pragmatic Sanction. When Maria Theresa refused to surrender Silesia, the Prussians invaded it, beginning a series of wars known collectively as the War of the Austrian Succession (1740–1748).

The war went poorly for Maria Theresa at first. The Prussians occupied Silesia. France, Spain, and Bavaria joined an alliance against her. The support of Britain

FIGURE 19.6 *Queen Maria Theresa (1717–1780).* Maria Theresa sat for dozens of portraits that stressed her domesticity, showing her as a good mother surrounded by her children. But she was also a very strong monarch who overcame much opposition. This illustration suggests that side of her character: here she plays cards with her generals, and most of the chips are in front of her.

and Holland, however, prevented the partitioning of the Hapsburg Empire. When the Duke of Bavaria died in 1745, the electors of the Holy Roman Empire acknowledged the stability of Maria Theresa's position by choosing her husband, the Duke of Lorraine, as Emperor Francis I. The belligerents reached the same conclusion about Maria Theresa in 1748, ending the War of the Austrian Succession in a treaty that sustained the Pragmatic Sanction except for permitting Prussia to retain Silesia.

The Seven Years' War. The Hapsburg Empire had survived the coronation of a woman, but Maria Theresa's empire remained internally divided and less efficient than those of her rivals. Conditions improved when she entrusted the government to a strong **chancellor** (chief minister), Count Kaunitz, but he could not block the rise of Austria's hungry rival for leadership in central Europe, Prussia. Within a few years, Austrian armies again found themselves engaged with the Prussians. The Seven Years' War (1756–1763) devastated both countries, leaving no true victors. When peace came again in 1763, the Austrian Empire remained firmly in the grip of Maria Theresa, but even larger financial and administrative problems plagued her. She faced the problems of recovery and reorganization, even establishing a national budget for the first time in her reign. The death of her husband in 1765, however, plunged her into grief: in a world of arranged

loveless marriages Maria Theresa had been deeply attached to Francis. The young, exuberant empress who had loved theatricals and dances became a solemn, withdrawn, and increasingly religious figure who gave more and more of the government to trusted nobles such as Count Kaunitz.

The Hapsburg Monarchy and the Enlightened Despotism of Joseph II

Emperor Joseph II. Solving the postwar financial problems of the 1760s led Maria Theresa into conflict with the aristocracy. In 1764, she tried to force the Hungarians to carry a fairer share of imperial taxes, but the Hungarian Diet blocked her plans. Resistance to tax reform led Maria Theresa in a surprising direction— toward the **emancipation** of the peasantry from the bondage of serfdom. Maria Theresa's most influential adviser in the emancipation of the serfs was her son, Joseph, whose reign in Austria would later provide the best illustration of enlightened despotism in eighteenth-century European monarchism. Joseph was Maria Theresa's first son, born most inconveniently in 1741, when his mother was confronted with the War of the Austrian Succession. His mother ordered that he not be given a rigorous, military education, and Joseph consequently acquired many of his ideas from reading the philosophes, not from strict tutors.

Joseph came to see himself as the embodiment of the Enlightenment, the person who could link reason with absolute powers. When his father died in 1765, Joseph became the Holy Roman Emperor and coregent with his mother in Austria. Maria Theresa shared some of her son's reformist ideas but tried to keep tight control of him and his friends, whom she called the **Aufklärungs** (Enlightenment) Party. After her death in 1780, Joseph could enthusiastically write, "I have made philosophy the legislator of my empire," but the same was not true of Maria Theresa. She had learned to rule in tough circumstances, and her policies often showed this. She believed in the use of torture, she was a brutal anti-Semite who launched a pogrom to drive all Jews out of Bohemia, and she often betrayed a startling insensitivity to the life of a peasant nation. But her stern, and sometimes cruel, policies created the stable, centralized government with a well-regulated army and well-balanced treasury that would make the enlightened policies of her son possible.

Enlightened Despotism in Austria. The mixed personalities of mother and son launched enlightened despotism in Austria with a compromise version of emancipation of the serfs. Years of famine and periodic peasant rebellion had shown that the serfs needed relief. Joseph urged his mother to act, and Maria Theresa accepted his arguments, writing, "The lords fleece the

JOSEPH II'S ENLIGHTENED DESPOTISM IN AUSTRIA

Joseph II, the eldest son of Maria Theresa, was the Holy Roman Emperor for 25 years and shared power with his mother (women could not be emperor) in Austria from 1765 to 1780 before ruling in his own right until 1790. Joseph was a stubborn and impatient young man who repeatedly argued with his mother about adopting more far-reaching reforms. His typical self-image was significantly different from hers. In the illustration, one of many versions of this theme, Joseph (in full dress uniform) teaches modern agricultural methods to a peasant. As the document shows, however, Joseph was sincere in his desire to improve the conditions of his people. This decree, abolishing serfdom in the province of Bohemia in 1781, was one of a series of such decrees for the provinces of the realm. It is one of the most dramatic accomplishments of enlightened despotism. In 1781, serfdom still existed in parts of France. It survived in Prussia until 1806 and in Russia until 1861.

Joseph at Plow.

Joseph II Abolishes Serfdom in Bohemia

Henceforth serfdom in Bohemia is abolished in its entirety. In its place a moderate form of subjection is introduced and the following arrangement has the force of law:

1. Every subject is entitled to marry if he announces his intention beforehand and if he fills in an official form, for which there is no charge.

2. If he observes the commercial regulations prevailing in his district, every subject is free to leave his lord's estate to seek employment or to settle elsewhere in the province. But those subjects who leave their lords to settle in an estate elsewhere must obtain a free release certificate, to prove to their new lord that their old lord has released them from all obligations.

3. The subjects can learn the trades and professions of their choice and can pursue their livelihood where they find it without needing special papers, which moreover are abolished altogether.

4. In the future, no subject will be obliged to perform domestic services for his lord; except that (5) orphans are obliged to serve lords who have acted as guardians without remuneration, but the period of service must not exceed three years. . . .

Finally, 6. All other dues incumbent on the subject, whether in the form of services, money or in kind, which derive from his tenure of the lord's land and which remain binding even after the abolition of serfdom, are fixed by the urbarial patents (royal decrees). Apart from these, nothing more can be demanded of the subject. However, after the abolition of serfdom, the subjects still owe their lords obedience, in accordance with the laws. . . .

Source: Frass, Otto, *Quellenbuch zur österreichischen Geschichte* (Vienna, 1959), II: 4.

Question: Does the emancipation of the serfs make Joseph II an enlightened leader?

---

peasants dreadfully. . . . We know, and we have proof of the tyrannical oppression under which the poor people suffer." Maria Theresa hesitated to act against the interests of the great landowners, but the tax-resistance of the Hungarian nobles angered her enough to proceed. The emancipation of the peasantry in the Hapsburg Empire began with an imperial decree of 1767 named the Urbarium. This gave Hungarian peasants a leasehold on the soil that they worked and the legal freedom to leave the land without the permission of the local lord. It did not, however, abolish the **robot**, the compulsory labor tax that peasants owed to lords. During the 1770s, mother and son slowly extended this emancipation. Peasant obligations were separately reduced in Austrian Silesia (1771), then in lower Austria (1772), Bohemia and Moravia (1775), and Styria (1778). After a rebellion by Bohemian peasants in 1775, another imperial decree converted the detested robot into a money tax.

Serfdom Abolished in Austria. Joseph II carried this work to its logical conclusion—the complete emancipation of the serfs—after the death of his mother in 1780.

JOSEPHINISM—JOSEPH II AND THE CATHOLIC CHURCH IN AUSTRIA

Letter on Taxation, 1785

The present system of taxation in my dominions, and the inequality of the taxes which are imposed on the nation, form a subject too important to escape my attention. I have discovered that the principles on which it is founded are unsound, and have become injurious to the industry of the peasant; that there is neither equality, nor equity . . . it can no longer continue. . . .

I give you the necessary orders to introduce a new system of taxation, by which the contribution, requisite for the wants of the state, may be effected without augmenting the present taxes, and the industry of the peasant, at the same time, be freed from impediments. Make these arrangements the principal object of your care, and let them be made conformably to the plan which I have proposed.

Letter on Religious Toleration, 1787

Till now the Protestant religion has been opposed in my states; its adherents have been treated like foreigners; civil rights, possession of estates, titles, and appointments, all were refused them.

I determined from the very commencement of my reign to adorn my diadem with the love of my people, to act in the administration of affairs according to just, impartial, and liberal principles; consequently, I granted toleration, and removed the yoke which had oppressed the Protestants for centuries.

Fanaticism shall in the future be known in my states only by the contempt I have for it; nobody shall any longer be exposed to hardships on account of his creed; no man shall be compelled in the future to profess the religion of the state. . . . [M]y Empire shall not be the scene of abominable intolerance.

Joseph II's Argument for the Abolition of the Monasteries

Many eighteenth-century governments struggled with established churches over traditional privileges and powers. One increasingly important theme in this struggle was the assertion of the primacy of the state. Catholic monarchs had often contested the papacy's authority, and the principle that the king of France had special rights over the Roman Catholic Church in France had been repeatedly asserted as the doctrine of Gallicanism. Joseph II launched an Austrian version of this struggle to establish state authority over the church in the late eighteenth century, a doctrine known as Josephinism. One of the major stages in this struggle came over the monastic orders in Austria. The following excerpt is from a report by Kaunitz stating the government's antimonastic argument.

All opinions previously expressed seem to assume that it is doubtful whether or not there are more monks than necessary. I, on the other hand, consider that their present number is as exag-

His decree of 1781 (the *Untertanspatent*) gave peasants in Austria, Bohemia, and Galicia the right to appeal to the state in any disputes with their lords. That same year he abolished serfdom in Austria. Peasants obtained the right to marry, to move to the city, and to learn a trade without permission. Then, between 1781 and 1785, Joseph extended this emancipation to his other domains. Joseph II had practical reasons for his policy, such as asserting royal power against the aristocracy and creating a more efficient economy, but the ideas of the Enlightenment were an important factor. As the Patent to Abolish Serfdom of 1781 stated in its preface, "reason and humanity alike require this change." That did not mean, however, that Joseph was simply a gentle philosopher: he was both despot and enlightened. He had autocratic instincts, and those around him often commented on his domineering, uncompromising, irritable character.

Church-State Relations and Josephinism.

Maria Theresa's financial needs and Joseph II's reforming zeal led to similar policies regarding the Catholic Church. The financial crisis of 1763 convinced the devout empress that she should challenge some of the tax exemptions and privileges of the church. She began by asking the church to make a greater "voluntary contribution" to the treasury and to limit future property donations to the church (which became tax-exempt land), but the Vatican refused. This led to imperial decrees restricting the church's acquisition of land, beginning with a patent that applied to the duchy of Milan in 1767. Thus, the financial crisis brought the monarchy into conflict with the church just as it had with the nobility, and this led to a variety of reforms. In 1768, the first tax on the clergy was created. In 1771, a decree established the maximum amount of property that an individual could bring to the church when joining a monastic order.

In this struggle, Joseph pressed his mother even harder than he did against the aristocracy, and after her death, he acted vigorously. Between 1781 and 1789, Joseph and Kaunitz closed more than 700 monasteries with 36,000 members. "It is clear," Kaunitz wrote, "that

gerated as it is unnecessary and is so disadvantageous to the state and religion that failure to correct this undetected but cancerous abuse will lead inevitably to the Catholic states of Europe falling more and more into decay, and the non-Catholic states increasing more and more in power and wealth.

It seems to me that the following principles can serve as an irrefutable proof of this assertion:

(1) As is well known, the clerical estate is dedicated to celibacy and is therefore very disadvantageous to the propagation of the human race. Those who are admitted to this estate are for most part the pick of the citizens in physical and intellectual gifts.

(2) They are withdrawn for all time from agriculture, from military service, from the arts and professions, from manufacturing, and the factories, from commerce, etc. . . . in a word from almost all other useful civil occupations in society. . . .

(3) In most countries, their estates and possessions are far greater than all the laity's put together and yet there is no Catholic state in which the laity, considering their numbers and the important, onerous, and multifarious services they perform for society, do not bear a vastly greater fiscal burden than the clergy.

(4) Indeed, in many countries, the clerical estate is freed entirely from the obligation to contribute to this burden, although it enjoys all the advantages of the state's constitution. The load is borne solely by the other citizens.

(5) In addition, because the ownership never changes, the possessions of the clergy are withdrawn from circulation, as a result of which the sovereign loses the benefits which normally accrue to him from the various transfers of property. . . .

(6) This is not to mention the enormous part of their fortune which derives from the payments of the brotherhoods . . . for the reading of masses, from secret donations, and from other sources. Because this information cannot be checked reliably, it cannot be taxed.

It is clear that the clerical estate in general, and the monastic order in particular, because their members are of both sexes, are exceedingly harmful to both the state and civil society, that they can be justified only on the grounds of necessity. . . . Therefore the only question seems to be whether the present number of regular clergy of both sexes can be restricted and reduced without harming the essential interests of the Catholic religion.

It is universally known that the Church existed for more than three centuries before anyone knew anything about monks. Consequently their introduction was quite arbitrary and had nothing to do with the essence of Christianity. . . . Consequently, it is incontrovertible that there are far too many monks, for the church can do without them altogether.

Source: Maass, Ferdinand, Der Josephinismus. Quellen zu seiner Geschichte in Osterreich, 1760–1790 (Vienna, 1953, 2:139–140).

Question: Does Josephinism seem like an enlightened policy, or does it seem like an attack on the Catholic Church?

the clerical state in general and the monastic orders in particular are exceedingly harmful to both the state and civil society" (see *Josephinism—Joseph II and the Catholic Church in Austria*). Joseph II seized the lands of the dispersed orders, thereby raising revenues for the state and converting church properties into schools. In all matters, he tried to break the power of Rome over the Catholic Church in Austria, a national religious policy known as **Josephinism.**

Enlightened Reforms. Historians have also praised Joseph II for enlightenment in responding to many of the great concerns of the philosophes: his censorship ordinance of 1781 relaxed the restrictions on the press, his toleration of religious minorities, and the Beccarian modernization of law codes. His Edict of Toleration reversed the harsh policies of his mother and extended the rights of full citizenship to Protestants and Jews. Such minorities were allowed to enter businesses and professions or to hold previously closed offices. Joseph's edict on the Jews, for example, bluntly stated that "the leaders of local communities must instruct the subjects in a rational manner that the Jews are to be regarded like any other fellow human beings and that there must be an end to the prejudice and contempt which some subjects, particularly the unintelligent, have shown towards the Jewish nation." Minorities obtained the right to hold religious services, although regulations still restricted such details as the right to have churches with steeples or bells. Joseph's policy was again a mixture of enlightened ideals and practical politics. Emancipating the minorities brought people of talent into state service and promoted economic growth. Joseph admitted this in the Edict of Toleration, saying that he granted it because he was "convinced on the one hand of the perniciousness of all restraints on conscience and, on the other, of the great benefits to religion and the state from a true Christian tolerance."

Joseph II's legal reforms came in a series of decrees in the 1780s, chiefly 1787–1788. He introduced both a new Civil Code and a new Penal Code. Together they abolished torture and the death penalty (except in military courts martial), introduced civil marriage and burial, ended class distinctions in the law, permitted religious intermarriage, eliminated several categories of crime (such as witchcraft and religious apostasy), and even forbade the ancient aristocratic tradition of primogeniture, which concentrated inheritance in the hands of the eldest son. These reforms did not make Joseph universally popular, nor did they make the centralized powers of the state (such as strong police) welcome. He had infuriated the aristocracy and the Catholic Church by attacking their traditional privileges. He was hated in many provinces, where he enforced the rule of Vienna over local customs, including the mandatory use of the German language in business and government.

THE ARMY, THE BUREAUCRACY, AND THE RISE OF HOHENZOLLERN PRUSSIA

One of the most important political facts of the eighteenth century was the rise of Prussia as an important European power. The elector of Brandenburg (a small region around Berlin) had acquired the province of Prussia in the seventeenth century, making the com-

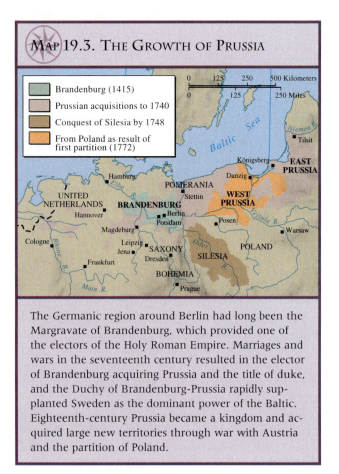

MAP 19.3. THE GROWTH OF PRUSSIA

Brandenburg (1415)
Prussian acquisitions to 1740
Conquest of Silesia by 1748
From Poland as result of first partition (1772)

The Germanic region around Berlin had long been the Margravate of Brandenburg, which provided one of the electors of the Holy Roman Empire. Marriages and wars in the seventeenth century resulted in the elector of Brandenburg acquiring Prussia and the title of duke, and the Duchy of Brandenburg-Prussia rapidly supplanted Sweden as the dominant power of the Baltic. Eighteenth-century Prussia became a kingdom and acquired large new territories through war with Austria and the partition of Poland.

bined state of Brandenburg-Prussia an important, but still secondary, German state. The Holy Roman Empire recognized this state as the Kingdom of Prussia in 1701. It was an absolute monarchy with an impotent Diet and obedient aristocracy, known as the **Junker** class, whose obedience had been rewarded with land in the newly acquired regions. It was one of the most autocratic states in Europe, but strict, able administration by the House of Hohenzollern provided a solid basis for development.

The Hohenzollern Kings. The ruler at the beginning of the century, Frederick I, did little to advance Prussia into the ranks of the great powers. He admired the sophisticated life of the French royal court at Versailles and devoted his reign to making Berlin glitter with the same elegance. The generation gap between Frederick and his son, King Frederick William I, who reigned from 1713 to 1740, could not have been larger. Frederick William was a cruel, semiliterate man who detested his father's world as effeminate; he favored drunken nights with his advisers and soldiers. In the words of their successor Frederick II, Frederick I sought to turn Berlin into the Athens of Germany, then Frederick William I tried to make it Sparta. Although contemporary observers found King Frederick William personally loathsome, they acknowledged that he was the person who converted Prussia into a European power. His son, Frederick II—whose love of books, music, French, and men so horrified his father that he beat him violently, imprisoned him, and considered executing him—became Frederick "the Great" partly because he inherited the strong state that his father built.

The Rise of Prussia. The rise of the Prussian state under Frederick William derived from several factors: the unchallenged authority of the monarchy, the subservience of the aristocracy to a duty called state service, an emphasis upon building a strong bureaucracy and the army officer corps, and the hoarding of resources through parsimony and the avoidance of war. Frederick William I, in short, neither admired nor copied western models of government. He took the concept of compulsory **state service** by the aristocracy from despotic Russia. Prussian nobles were expected to serve as army officers or as civil servants; in return they obtained a monopoly of many posts and great control over the peasants on their estates. Frederick William's administration of Prussia rested on more than the domestication of the aristocracy and the conscription of bureaucrats. He made Prussia a center of the study of **cameralism** (state administration) and founded university positions in cameral studies. This set standards of professionalism for civil servants and bred a **bureaucracy** admired for its efficiency. What began as a duty for conscripted aristocrats grew into an honor that brought distinction. The best indication of Prussian administrative efficiency came in state finances. Monarchs in France, Spain, and Austria faced bankruptcy; Frederick William had inherited nearly empty coffers himself. But his Ministry of Finance, created in 1713, and its tax-collecting bureaucracy soon became the envy of Europe. A study of Frederick William's finances has shown that he doubled his revenue while reducing expenditures—chiefly by cutting the extravagant royal court that his father had maintained.

The Prussian Army. King Frederick William I became known as a miser, but he did not economize on military expenditures. European armies were changing in the early eighteenth century; larger armies, maintained in peacetime, were becoming common. Württemberg had a standing army of 6,000 men in 1700; Poland, an army of 12,000. Saxony and Spain kept peacetime armies of approximately 30,000 men. Frederick William inherited a standing army set at 27,000 men and more than tripled its size to 83,000, launching a tradition of Prussian **militarism.** To do this, he divided Prussia into military districts, assigning a quota of new soldiers to each; when recruitment fell short, he added **conscription.** This meant that Prussia kept 4 percent of its population in uniform, a number previously unthinkable—but Prussia had an army superior to most of its neighbors. An important element of this policy, however, was that soldiers be taken from the lowest levels of society so that the large army not disrupt the productive classes of peasants and workers. Criminals and debtors were released from prison to serve in the army. As Frederick II later explained this policy, "useful, hardworking people should be guarded as the apple of one's eye" because they paid the taxes that supported the army. The doctrine of state service gave sons of the aristocracy a monopoly of the ranks in the officer corps, and this meant that nearly 15 percent of the aristocracy was serving as army officers. Prussia, as Voltaire wryly commented, was not so much a country with an army to defend it, as it was an army with a country to support it.

Frederick William built the Prussian army upon such rigid discipline that he became known as "the sergeant-king." The Prussian ideal, known as *Kadavergehorsam,* was an army that gave cadaver obedience—even the dead would still obey orders for fear of punishment. Creating this obedience went far beyond the famous **goose-step** drilling of Prussian soldiers: flogging and even mutilation were common punishments. The penalty for desertion was to have one's nose and an ear cut off, followed by a life sentence to slave labor. Nonetheless, desertion remained so common that Prussian army regulations required the cavalry to surround the infantry during any march through a wooded area. Capital punishment could be administered for merely raising a hand against an officer. This did not mean that Frederick William I frequently risked the lives of his soldiers. Prussia remained neutral in three major wars during his reign. When he did choose to fight, against troubled Sweden, he continued the expansion of Prussia with the acquisition of Pomerania on the Baltic coast.

THE PRUSSIAN MONARCHY OF FREDERICK THE GREAT

Frederick William I's kingdom was inherited by his third son, the 28-year-old Frederick II, in 1740. The new king got absolute power, an enlarged kingdom, an efficient administration, a full treasury, and a feared army—the material opportunity to become Frederick the Great. His life did not begin that way. As a third son, he had not been expected to reach the throne. As a son of Frederick William, he had been expected to accept a rigid education and rigorous military training. Instead, Frederick had rebelled against his father at age 18; formed an intimate relationship with his tutor, Lt. Katte; and tried to run off with him. Frederick William sentenced both men to death for desertion, forced Frederick to witness the beheading of his lover, and then imprisoned him with a suspended death sentence. Frederick accepted military training and learned his lessons well but infuriated his father by deciding that French literature and music were more interesting (see Document 19.3). Frederick became an excellent flute player and wrote flute compositions throughout his life. When he came to power and built Sans Souci ("Carefree")—an ornate palace with French gardens— in Potsdam, outside Berlin, he delighted in the visits of Johann Sebastian Bach, with whom he played duets, and Voltaire, with whom he debated philosophy. Frederick became such a voluminous writer that his collected works run for thirty volumes.

Frederick the Great. Frederick II did not become known as Frederick the Great for writing poetry and incidental pieces for the flute. He turned to the task of government with enthusiasm and extended his father's accomplishments. To the bureaucracy he added a system of competitive examinations for promotions and his own tireless labor as "the first servant of the state." He insisted on daily written reports from his ministries and poured over them in a bureaucratic toil that would have been unthinkable for most monarchs. And when Frederick II decided on ways to improve his kingdom, he did not hesitate to act. He believed that "Agriculture is the first of all arts. Without it there would exist neither merchants nor poets nor philosophers." Consequently, when he learned of the benefits of the potato, he set an example by eating potatoes in public.

ENLIGHTENED DESPOTISM IN PRUSSIA

Frederick the Great of Prussia is among the most complex figures of the eighteenth century. On one hand, he was a military man. The rise of the Prussian state rested on an unusually large army for a small state, a thoroughly trained army that was maintained with brutal discipline. Frederick the Great, who spent more time in warfare than music, approved of the flogging of his soldiers because he expected cadaver obedience from them—the will to follow his orders even after death. Nonetheless, Frederick presented a cultivated and intellectual side to his monarchy. He was a fine musician and spent many hours composing his own music. He certainly wished to be seen as an enlightened monarch, as he shows in his letter (one of a long series of letters) to the French philosopher Voltaire.

Frederick II Portrays His Enlightenment

Frederick II to Voltaire, October 24, 1773

I have been returned from my journeys more than a month. I have travelled into Prussia to abolish servitude, reform barbarous laws, promulgate others more rational, open a canal . . . and to establish a police in a country where the name had before been unknown. . . . I have ordered sixty villages to be built in Upper Silesia where there was land still uncultivated, each village to consist of twenty families. I have caused high roads to be made among the mountains . . . I shall not speak to you of the troops; that is a subject too severely prohibited at Ferney [Voltaire's home] for me to touch upon them. . . .

This system is neither that Richelieu nor of Mazarin [meaning, not absolutism]; but is that of the good of the people who ought to form the principal object of the magistrate's care . . .

Frederick II to Voltaire, September 8, 1775

Taste will not extend itself through Germany till the classic authors—Greek, Roman, and French—shall have been maturely studied. Two or three men of genius . . . will naturalize those masterpieces of literature which other nations have produced. . . .

From *Letters of Frederick II and Voltaire* (London, 1789).

Question: Does Frederick II seem enlightened?

When this did not persuade the nation to adopt the new food, Frederick distributed free seed potatoes to the peasants in 1744, then issued an edict demanding that they grow potatoes or have their ears and noses cut off. The Prussian army checked on crops being grown, and Prussia became a nation of potato eaters. Modern scholarship has argued that this nutritional change (growing more potatoes and less grain, thereby producing more calories per acre) was the single most important factor in the rapid growth of German population.

Frederick the Great's Enlightened Despotism.

Another part of Frederick II's reputation rests on his claim to enlightened despotism alongside Joseph II of Austria. At the beginning of his reign, Frederick showed promise of becoming one of the most enlightened statesmen of the century. Within a few months, he abolished torture in criminal procedures, established freedom of religion, granted limited freedom of the press, and founded the Berlin Academy of Science. That early promise was poorly fulfilled, however. Frederick remained attached to the ideals of the Enlightenment,

in theory, but his later years saw few reforms and they were chiefly to improve Prussian finances, curing the problems he had created himself with long wars.

Frederick the Great and Prussian Militarism.

The rebellious and artistic Frederick became Frederick the Great as a soldier. Unlike his father, he was not reluctant to use the Prussian army. He came to the throne of Prussia at age 28 in May 1740, 5 months before Maria Theresa inherited the Austrian throne; in December 1740, Frederick invaded Silesia without warning. Of his first 23 years on the throne of Prussia, Frederick was at war with Austria for 15 years. He began by ignoring the Prussian promise of 1726 to honor the Pragmatic Sanction, and invading Silesia in the first of three wars, he would fight with Maria Theresa, sometimes called the Silesian Wars. Frederick II had gone into combat for the first time at age 22, and he knew the battlefield better than any other European monarch. He was neither a brilliant innovator nor a great battlefield strategist, but he was a superb tactician who found ways to defeat larger, or better placed,

FIGURE 19.7 *Frederick the Great.* "Old Fritz" Frederick the Great of Prussia (1712–1786) was one of the most complex personalities of modern history. He remained a military man all his life, presiding over an army built on cruel discipline and used constantly, sometimes in wars of aggression. He proudly retained the military great coat that he wears here because it was pierced by several bullets during his campaigns. He is seen here late in life, when he was fondly known as "Old Fritz" but worn out by his campaigns. It would be equally easy, however, to depict a different side of Frederick: he was one of the most sophisticated, sensitive, and intelligent of modern rulers, a man who made flute concerts and discussions with philosophers central features of life at his country residence, Sans Souci ("Carefree").

armies by concentrating his forces against a portion of his enemies. His success as a general was linked to a strategy of exhaustion in which he fought in indirect ways (such as occupying territory and destroying crops or commerce) rather than engaging in grand battles until one side or the other was annihilated. This won Silesia, Frederick's reputation as a genius, and international recognition of Prussia as a great power.

Frederick II continued to build the Prussian army. Frederick William's army of 83,000 approached 200,000 near the end of Frederick II's reign. He did this by subordinating all government activity to the military. During a peacetime buildup in 1752, Frederick gave the army 90 percent of the Prussian budget. His arms factory at Potsdam manufactured 15,000 muskets per year, and the military warehouses at Berlin and Breslau stored enough grain to feed 60,000 soldiers for 2 years. Frederick also expanded the army by implementing the plan of a Prussian civil servant, Justus Moser, for army reserves. Moser conceived the idea of universal military training with most citizens remaining active in a militia in case they were needed.

Prussia and the Seven Years' War. Frederick's militarism nearly destroyed Prussia. During the 1750s, Count Kaunitz engineered a diplomatic revolution that allied the Hapsburgs with Russia and England and included promises of the return of Silesia to Austria. Frederick chose war and kept Silesia, but following the Seven Years' War, Prussia was, in the words of one historian, "a bleeding stump, drained of vitality." The war killed more than 10 percent of the population (500,000 of 4.5 million), and by 1763 boys of age 14 were being conscripted to fight. More than 100 towns and villages had been burnt to the ground, and 13,000 families had lost their homes. The devastated towns of Prussia included Berlin, which the Russian army put to the torch in 1760. The overflowing treasury that Frederick II had inherited had been squandered on war, forcing Frederick to face the critical question of eighteenth-century government: taxation. "No government can exist without taxation," he wrote. "This money must necessarily be levied on the people; the grand art consists of levying so as not to oppress." He, like his peers, failed at the "grand art." Taxes were levied in inverse proportion to the ability to pay them: the rich and powerful had exemptions from taxation, so the poor and the middling were expected to carry the burden. That system worked in comfortable times, but the Seven Years' War broke it. Far from paying taxes, much of the population was near starvation in 1763. The monarch himself, although only 51 years old, seemed broken by age: his back was stooped, his face gaunt, his teeth missing, and he was plagued with both diarrhea and hemorrhoids. He returned to Berlin in military triumph known as "der alte Fritz" (Old Fritz)—partly an affectionate compliment, partly a sad comment. "It is a poor man who is coming home," the king acknowledged in 1763.

Little room existed for enlightenment in the despotism of Frederick the Great's later years. He was still remembered as the king who had insisted that "[A]ll religions must be tolerated," but he extended few freedoms. When the German dramatist Gotthold Lessing followed Voltaire's footsteps to Berlin with high hopes, he left protesting against a stifling environment:

> Don't talk to me about your Berlinese freedom
> of thought and writing. It only consists of the
> freedom to make as much fun as you like of
> religion. . . . Let someone in Berlin stand up for

the rights of the peasants, or protest against despotism and exploitation as they do now even in France and Denmark, and you will soon know by experience which country is to this day the most slavish in Europe.

Some modern scholars, however, have concluded that Frederick was the greatest of the enlightened despots. One French historian, impressed by a king of intellect and culture, concluded that he possessed "the most complete character of the eighteenth century, being the only one to unite idea with power."

CATHERINE THE GREAT AND DESPOTISM IN ROMANOV RUSSIA

The eighteenth century began in Russia, as it did in France, with one of the most powerful autocrats of the seventeenth century still holding the throne. When Peter the Great of Russia died in 1725, he left behind a royal succession even more troubled than Louis XIV's legacy to France. The French got a 5-year-old king and a resurgent aristocracy; the Russians got a generation of chaotic government in which one heir to the throne was tortured to death, one former serf was crowned, and a council of nobles exercised central power in Russia until 1762, when a strong monarch, Catherine II, arrived on the throne.

Catherine II. Catherine was the daughter of an impoverished German duke who had married her off at age 16 to a feeble-minded grandson of Peter the Great, the grand-duke Peter. After childhood worries that a spinal deformity would make Catherine an ugly, unmarriageable drain on her family, she grew into an attractive woman with deep black hair contrasting with a pale complexion. Before she had matured into such physical attractiveness, however, the future empress had built her identity around her education and her strong, probing mind. Her intelligence won the attention of the Russian royal family when hunting for a wife for the uneducated heir to the throne, Grand-Duke Peter. When Peter was unable to consummate the marriage, members of the royal family who were desperate to perpetuate the dynasty advised Catherine to find a lover who could produce children. She cheerfully complied and began a series of affairs that were among the most notorious features of her reign—although they hardly distinguished her from the behavior of male monarchs such as George I of England or Louis XV of France.

Catherine's lovers have historical importance because one of them, Grigori Orlov, an officer in the royal guards, helped her usurp the throne. When her husband was crowned Tsar Peter III in 1762, the army began to con-

spire against him because he favored an alliance with a recent Russian enemy, Frederick the Great of Prussia. Orlov became a leader of this conspiracy. When Peter threatened the arrest of his estranged wife, a **military coup** overthrew him and named Catherine empress. Her husband soon died in prison, apparently killed by one of Orlov's brothers and possibly with the connivance of Catherine, who ascended the throne at age 32.

Catherine II of Russia reigned from 1762 until 1796. She initially faced significant opposition because she was a foreigner, Lutheran-born in an Orthodox land, and sexually scandalous. She obtained (and used) great power largely because she was able to strike a bargain with the aristocracy—the *dvorianstvo* class. Like Frederick II of Prussia, the basis of her reign became this compromise: she would enhance the position of the aristocracy and make no reforms at their expense. Catherine settled the deal by seducing the foremost leader of the old nobility, Nikita Panin, who then endorsed her claim. Thereafter, she exercised autocratic powers with a skill that rivaled Peter the Great, earning a reputation for enlightened despotism, although the evidence is greater for her despotism than for her enlightenment.

She initially accepted—but then later opposed—an imperial *ukase* (decree) drafted by Panin that would have delegated legislative power to a council of nobles. She did restore to the nobility freedoms it had lost under Peter the Great. She abolished compulsory state service by all aristocrats but kept nobles in high diplomatic and military posts, winning the gratitude of many. She granted a monopoly on vodka production to nobles, winning others.

Catherine and the Aristocracy. Catherine II best placated the aristocracy by her policy on serfdom. She had read enough of the philosophes to be an enlightened enemy of serfdom in principle, and one of her first decrees upon coming to the throne had been to alleviate the conditions of serfs on the royal estates. Given that European Russia contained 50 million peasants—55 percent of them serfs on the royal estates—this was no small matter. And Catherine talked of abolishing serfdom. Her actions, however, were different: she consistently extended the power of aristocrats over their serfs. A decree of 1765, for example, gave them the right to send troublesome peasants to Siberia.

Catherine's shrewd politics solidified her despotic authority by raising the Russian aristocracy to a level of power that they had not previously known. The culmination of this trend occurred in 1785 when Catherine issued the Charter of the Nobility, which codified the collective rights of the dvorianstvo, such as freedom from state service. It gave aristocrats the sole right to acquire serfs, which town dwellers and even free peasants had sought. It excluded the aristocracy from taxation and from corporal punishment.

CATHERINE THE GREAT'S INSTRUCTIONS FOR A NEW LAW CODE, 1767

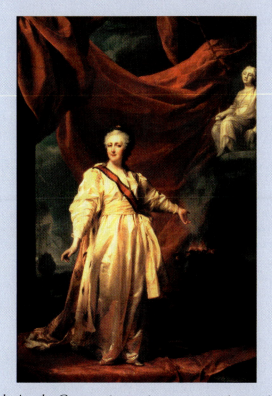

Catherine the Great. Catherine the Great seriously considered reforming the Russian legal system, but she never succeeded in doing it. In 1767, she summoned a commission to review the study. She allowed many of its members to be elected and free subjects (including many peasants) to petition the commission. Catherine gave the commission a set of guiding principles from which this extract is taken.

Of the situation of the people in general

33. The laws ought to be so framed as to secure the safety of every citizen as much as possible.

34. The equality of the citizens consists in this: that they should all be subject to the same laws.

35. This equality requires institutions so well adapted as to prevent the rich from oppressing those who are not so wealthy as themselves. . . .

36. General or political liberty does not consist in that licentious notion, that man may do whatever he pleases.

37. In a state or assemblage of people that live together in a community where there are laws, liberty can only consist in doing that which every one ought to do, and not to be constrained to do that which one ought not to do.

38. A man ought to form in his own mind an exact and clear idea of what liberty is. Liberty is the right of doing whatsoever the laws allow: And if any one citizen could do what the laws forbid, there would be no more liberty, because others would have an equal power of doing the same.

39. The political liberty of a citizen is the peace of mind arising from the consciousness that every individual enjoys his peculiar safety; and in order that the people might attain this liberty, the laws ought to be so framed that no one citizen should stand in fear of another; but that all of them should stand in fear of the same laws.

Question: How does Catherine's enlightened despotism compare to that of Frederick II and Joseph II?

Catherine and Enlightened Despotism. Partly for consolidating imperial power for 30 years and partly for her enlightened reforms, Catherine II became known as Catherine the Great. The enlightened side of her record, however, is ambiguous. She read many of the philosophes before ascending to the throne, and she was apparently much influenced by Blackstone, Beccaria, and Montesquieu. She corresponded with Voltaire and hosted Diderot on a visit to Russia. Her devotion to the ideals of the Enlightenment, however, remained stronger in theory than in action. She found it difficult to enact the ideas she liked. Diderot was dazzled to find "the soul of Brutus in the body of Cleopatra," but Catherine thought the philosopher's schemes were "sheer prattle." She wrote to him in 1770, rejecting many reforms for Russia, "All your work is done on paper, which does not mind how you treat it. . . . But I, poor empress, must work upon human skin, which is much more ticklish and irritable."

Catherine's Grand Instructions on Reform. Catherine's greatest effort at enlightened government produced almost no result. In 1767, she summoned a Legislative Commission of 564 delegates, representing all classes except the serfs. Only twenty-eight members were named to the commission, and the rest were elected. Catherine charged the commission with the task of considering the complete reform of the laws of Russia. To guide the commission, Catherine prepared one of the most famous documents of her reign, the Grand Instructions (*Nakaz*) of 1767 (see Document 19.4). These instructions contained both halves of

EMILIAN PUGACHEV PROCLAIMS THE EMANCIPATION OF THE SERFS, 1774

Emilian Pugachev. Pugachev was a Cossack who deserted from the Russian army a year after the Imperial Government ended the autonomy of his homeland. He led other Cossacks, runaway serfs, and dissident minorities in a 2-year rebellion against Catherine the Great, during which time he announced that he was the true tsar of Russia and issued edicts as tsar. In the following decree, Pugachev emancipates the serfs of Russia.

We, Peter III, by the Grace of God Emperor and Autocrat of All Russia, etc.

This is given for nationwide information.

By this personal decree, with our monarchical and fatherly love, we grant [freedom] to everyone who formerly was in serfdom or in any other obligation to the nobility; . . . while to the Cossacks [we restore] for eternity their freedoms and liberties; we terminate the [military] recruiting system, cancel personal and other monetary taxes, abolish without compensation the ownership of land, forest, pastures, fisheries, and salt deposits; and we free everyone from all taxes and obligations which the thievish nobles and extortionist city judges have imposed on the peasantry and the rest of the population. We pray for the salvation of your souls and wish you a happy and peaceful life here [on earth] where we have suffered and experienced much from the above-mentioned thievish nobles. Now since our name, thanks to the hand of providence, flourishes throughout Russia, we make hereby known by this personal decree the following: all nobles who have owned [estates granted by the state] or [inherited estates], who have opposed our rule, who have rebelled against the empire, and who have ruined the peasantry should be seized, arrested, and hanged; that is, treated in the same manner as these unchristians have treated you, the peasantry. After the extermination of these opponents and thievish nobles everyone will live in a peace and happiness that shall continue to eternity.

Question: Does Pugachev seem like an enlightened despot?

enlightened despotism. They opened by asserting that "[T]he sovereign is absolute, for there is no other authority but that which centers in his single person." That statement of despotic power was followed by many enlightened principles: Catherine opposed torture and capital punishment, called for a government based on the division of powers, and indicated her hostility to serfdom. The potential for change was enormous. As Panin reacted to the Nakaz, "[T]hese principles are strong enough to shatter walls!" But despite the great promise of its beginning, the Legislative Commission of 1767–1768 did not reform Russia. It received more than 1,400 petitions (more than 1,000 of them from free peasants), held more than 200 meetings, and quibbled over details. The commission agreed to vote Catherine a new title ("the Great and All-Wise Mother of the Fatherland"), but it could not agree upon a legal code. At best, it gave Catherine ideas for later years.

Pugachev's Rebellion. The need for reform in Russia was dramatized by a rebellion of serfs and the Cossacks of southern Russia in 1773–1775, known as Pugachev's Rebellion. Emilian Pugachev was a Cossack—a people who had lost their autonomy in 1772—and a deserter from the Russian army. He organized discontented serfs, Cossacks, and religious minorities into a rebel army in 1773. Pugachev announced that he was Czar Peter III, claiming he had been dethroned by Catherine and the great nobles. He formed a "royal court" among the rebels and proclaimed the emancipation of the serfs, giving them the incentive to fight for his victory (see Document 19.5). Pugachev's rebels withstood the Imperial army for nearly 2 years, capturing the town of Kazan and stimulating serf rebellions throughout the region. The government took Pugachev so seriously that new defenses were built around Moscow to prepare for his attack. The rebellion collapsed in 1775, when Pugachev's own forces betrayed him. He was taken to St. Petersburg, exhibited in an iron cage, and then beheaded. Catherine ordered that Pugachev not be tortured but agreed that his questioning could include the artful extraction of his teeth. Her principles against torture did not protect Pugachev's followers. Special troops scoured the countryside, tracking down rebellious serfs. Most were executed "according to Christian canon"—cutting off their hands and feet before beheading them, then leaving the bodies to rot at roadside while heads were displayed on pikes in town.

Catherine II achieved her most important reforms in the aftermath of Pugachev's rebellion, but they did little to improve the conditions of serfdom. First, she reorganized the government of Russian provinces in 1775 by dividing Russia into fifty administrative provinces, each subdivided into districts. Local nobles were named to head district governments. Councils, elected by town dwellers as well as nobles, shared in the government. Separate courts were established for nobles, burghers, and free peasants. Catherine carried this administrative reform further in 1785, when she issued the Charter of Towns. Following the strict hierarchy of corporative society, the charter divided the urban population into six legal categories, ranging from the great merchants and leaders of the wealthiest guilds down to manual laborers. It allowed all six categories of town dwellers, including the unskilled working class, to participate in elections for the town council. Catherine the Great thus gave signs of enlightened aspiration, and she achieved a few noteworthy changes. But the foremost characteristic of her reign was still despotism, and the condition of the serfs worsened significantly under her rule.

CONCLUSION

As the eighteenth century drew toward a close, Europe remained a civilization dominated by the institutions of monarchy and aristocracy. This was true in all five of the great powers, although the nature of monarchy and aristocracy varied sharply from state to state. In western Europe, the absolute powers of the throne had been broken in England and were being severely tested in France; in central and eastern Europe, the monarchs of Austria, Prussia, and Russia retained more despotic powers, although this typically rested upon some compromise with the nobility. The debate continues as to whether these monarchs are better understood as despots or as enlightened rulers. This question could also be extended down the social scale, to examine the rule of aristocrats over the peasantry. Were the British Parliament, the French parlements, the Prussian Junkers, the *dvoriano* wiser rulers locally than the enlightened despots were nationally?

All governments of the Old Regime faced a similar set of problems. Warfare was near the top of the list; the eighteenth century was among the more bellicose in European history. The century began with two wars in progress involving great powers, and between 1701 and the beginning of the French Revolution in 1789, only 22 years passed when none of the great powers was at war. One of the foremost problems created by these wars was economic: the monarchies of Europe became debtor states, and governments searched for new taxes to pay for war debts. This cycle of problems became intertwined with the struggle over monarchial powers. Although the outcome still remained unclear in the late eighteenth century, these problems threatened the end of the age of royal power.

Review Questions

- How were forms of European government changing in the eighteenth century?
- What were the principle stages of the growth of parliamentary government in eighteenth-century England, and what were the principle areas in which monarchs remained active?
- What were the foremost problems confronting the French monarchs in the eighteenth century, and how did they address them?
- Why is the Hapsburg monarchy of the late eighteenth century considered an example of enlightened despotism?
- How was enlightened despotism in Prussia different from that in Austria?

For Further Study

Readings

Black, Jeremy, and Porter, Roy, eds., *Dictionary of Eighteenth-Century History* (London: Penguin, 1996). Provides biographic sketches of most of the important figures of the century.

Doyle, William, *The Old Order, 1660–1800* (Oxford: Oxford University Press, 1978).

Hufton, Olwen, *Europe: Privilege and Protest, 1730–1789*, 2nd ed. (Oxford: Blackwell, 2000).

Rudé, George, *Europe in the Eighteenth Century: Aristrocracy and the Bourgeois Challenge* (New York: Praeger, 1973). These last three surveys of the century, presented from different perspectives, offer a more detailed introduction to the era.

InfoTrac College Edition

For additional reading, go to your online research library at *http://infotrac.thomsonlearning.com*.

Using Key Terms, enter the search terms:
William Pitt   *Frederick the Great*
Seven Years' War

Using the Subject Guide, enter the search term:
Catherine II

THE POLITICAL EVOLUTION OF THE EIGHTEENTH CENTURY

1690	1700	1710	1720	1730	1740	1750	1760	1770	1780	1790	1800

PARLIAMENTARY GOVERNMENT IN BRITAIN

Kings: 1714–1727: George I

1727–1760: George II

1760–1820: George III

Prime Ministers: 1721–1745: Robert Walpole

1783–1801: William Pitt the Younger

1776–1783: American Revolution

1707: Union of England and Scotland Creates "Great Britain"
1720: South Seas "Bubble" Ruins Investors
1720s: Walpole Establishes "Cabinet System" of Government as First "Prime Minister"
1757: John Wilkes Elected to Parliament Demanding Reform
1778: Commons Vote to Eliminate Catholic Restrictions
1780: Gordon (anti-Catholic) Riots
1780: Yorkshire Petition for Parliamentary Reform
1783: Pitt's Reform Bill to Redistribute Seats
1785: Reform of Parliament Bill Fails
1787: Parliament Votes to Keep Test Acts

ENLIGHTENED DESPOTISM IN CENTRAL AND EASTERN EUROPE

1762–1796: Catherine II (the Great) of Russia
1740–1780: Maria Theresa of Austria
1765–1790: Joseph II of Austria
1764: Maria Theresa Reforms Tax Code
1765: Joseph II Coregent with His Mother
1767: *Urbarium:* Decree Begins Emancipation of Peasantry
1767–1768: Taxation of Church Begun
1771–1778: Taxes on Peasantry Lowered
1771: Restrictions Imposed on Gifts of Land to Church
1781: Josephinism: Edict of Toleration: Full Rights for Protestants and Jews
1781: Joseph Begins Reform of Legal System
1781: Decree Increases Rights of Peasantry
1781–1789: Joseph Closes 700 Monasteries
1785: Joseph Introduces Physiocratic Tax Law
1787–1788: Joseph's Civil Code and Penal Code

THE POLITICAL EVOLUTION OF THE EIGHTEENTH CENTURY—CONT'D

1690	1700	1710	1720	1730	1740	1750	1760	1770	1780	1790	1800

ENLIGHTENED DESPOTISM IN CENTRAL AND EASTERN EUROPE—Cont'd

1740–1748: War of the Austrian Succession

1756–1763: Seven Years' War

1748: Prussia Obtains Silesia from Austria

1760: Russians Burn Berlin

1740–1786: Frederick II (the Great) of Prussia

1740: Frederick Introduces Competitive Exams for Bureaucracy

1740: Frederick Abolishes Torture in Criminal Procedures

1740: Frederick Establishes Freedom of Religion

1740: Frederick Founds the Berlin Academy of Science

1744: Frederick Forces Introduction of Potato in Prussia

1772: Frederick Launches First Partition of Poland

1782: Codification of Prussian Law

Web Sites

http://www.chateauversailles.fr   The official site of the French royal palace, with an English tour and history available.

http://www.fordham.edu/halsall/mod/modsbook11.html   The "enlightened despots" section of the Internet Modern History Sourcebook maintained at Fordham University. It offers documents from Russia, Austria, and Prussia.

http://www.spartacus.schoolnet.co.uk   The "Encyclopedia of British History" option offers very helpful large sections on Members of Parliament, Britain 1600–1750, and parliamentary reform, 1750–1832.

Visit the Western Civilization Companion Web Site for resources specific to this textbook:
http://history.wadsworth.com/hause02/

 The CD in the back of this book and the Western Civilization Resource Center at *http://history.wadsworth.com/western/* offer a variety of tools to help you succeed in this course, including access to quizzes; images; documents; interactive simulations, maps, and timelines; movie explorations; and a wealth of other sources.

FOCUS QUESTIONS

🔹 What made the eighteenth-century clash of cultures so severe that people accepted punishments such as those administered to the Chevalier de la Barre?

🔹 What were the ways in which European culture was transmitted and questioned?

🔹 What were the foremost elements of Enlightenment thought, and what conclusions did they lead to?

Chapter 20

THE CULTURE OF OLD REGIME EUROPE

*I*n the spring of 1766, the judges of Abbeville, a small town of Picardy in northern France, considered the case of an impetuous young man named the Chevalier de la Barre. The chevalier (a knight) came from an important family (his grandfather had been a lieutenant general of France), but he faced serious charges. He was an enthusiastic critic of church and monarchy, stimulated by a controversial book that had been published in 1764, Voltaire's *Philosophical Dictionary.* The chevalier had demonstrated his opposition to intolerance and persecution by singing impious songs, and he had been brought to court after refusing to remove his hat when a procession of Capuchin monks passed. His judges decided that these crimes merited a careful investigation, so the young man was tortured (fully legal under eighteenth-century law) to determine how many **sacrileges** he had committed. The justices then ordered that the tongue that sang impiously be torn out and that the disrespectful hand be cut off. The Chevalier de la Barre was then burnt to death over a slow fire, along with a copy of the *Philosophical Dictionary.*

This chapter looks at the cultural ferment of eighteenth-century Europe. It begins by looking at traditional **"high culture"**—the art and architecture, the music and drama of the educated classes. A transition occurred from the **baroque** style to a revival of **classicism,** which became the dominant style in the arts of the eighteenth century. The discussion then focuses on **"popular culture"** in the lives of ordinary people. It compares a basic institution of high culture, the **salon,** with the equivalent institution of popular culture, the **coffeehouse.** Although other themes seemed to dominate the culture of the eighteenth century, Christianity remained central to European civilization. Chapter 20 explains the religious division of Europe into Protestant, Catholic, and Orthodox regions and examines the position of Jewish, Islamic, and dissenting Christian minorities. Most of the chapter is devoted to the dominant intellectual phenomenon of the eighteenth century, **the Enlightenment,** whose advocates—like the Chevalier de la Barre—often found themselves in the midst of a great clash of cultures. Later sections explore the basic concepts that connected enlightened thought—**natural law, reason, and progress**—and the conflict with church and state.

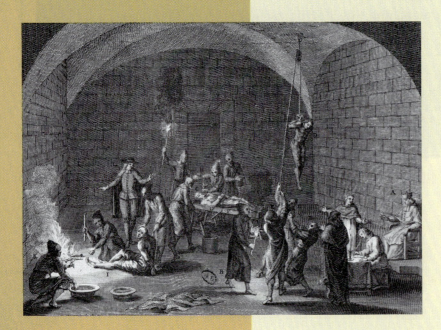

HIGH CULTURE: FROM THE BAROQUE TO THE CLASSICAL

Baroque and Rococo. The predominant cultural style of the seventeenth century, known as the **baroque,** still dominated many of the arts in the early eighteenth century. The baroque appealed to the emotions and spirituality through the ornately decorated, the extravagantly expressed. Whether looking at the energetic statues of Bernini, paintings of suffering martyrs by Caravaggio, or the voluptuous pastel nudes of Rubens, the viewer was overwhelmed by the lavish baroque style. Architects brought baroque emotions to palaces and churches, composers brought them to oratorios and fugues, artisans even sought the baroque style in gilded chairs and writing tables. This style culminated in an extravagant artistic style, characterized by fanciful curved forms and elaborate ornamentation, known as **rococo.** Frederick the Great's Sans Souci Palace was rococo—there a warrior king could write French poetry, compose flute music, and dispute philosophers in a home he helped to design, with the gaudy yellow walls and the plump cherubs a soldier wanted.

FIGURE 20.1 *Secular Rococo Architecture.* As the monarchs of Europe emulated the French Bourbons in building lavish new palaces, they did not make precise copies of Versailles. Instead they built luxurious homes in the newest architectural style. The Wittelsbach family, who ruled the south German state of Bavaria, were among the most active builders, and their palaces included Schloss Nymphenburg at Munich, whose gilded rococo "Hall of Mirrors" is shown here. An Italian architect began construction of this Baroque palace, which was a gift for the king's Italian wife, in the late seventeenth century; the central portion of the palace was completed under German architects between 1715 and 1728, and parts of the rococo decoration were being added as late as 1757.

Neoclassicism. Historians chiefly remember the high culture of the eighteenth century for the reaction against the baroque style. A revival of the styles and aesthetics of the classical Greco-Roman world rapidly supplanted the baroque during the middle decades of the century. The elegant simplicity of classical architecture—characterized by symmetry, mathematical proportions, the harmony of forms, and severe rules—became a vogue in the 1740s after archaeologists began to excavate the Roman cities of Pompeii and Herculaneum, which had been buried (and preserved) by volcanic ash in 79 CE. A classical revival swept European architecture, producing such masterpieces as the Romanov Winter Palace in St. Petersburg (now the Hermitage Museum), La Scala opera house in Milan, and the Royal Crescent in Bath, England. In some cases, neoclassical buildings closely resembled classical structures built 1,800 years earlier.

This "neoclassicism," or simply classicism, soon came to dominate the arts of the eighteenth century. Histories of the ancient world, such as Edward Gibbon's *The Decline and Fall of the Roman Empire,* became popular reading together with the ancients themselves. Universities required Latin and Greek of their students, and in some countries, an honors degree in classics became the best route to a high-paying job or a government post. Painters, sculptors, dramatists, poets, and composers all mined classical literature for inspiration. The French painter Jacques-Louis David, for example, inspired a generation of politicians with his dramatic canvases depicting stirring moments in Roman history. Music was perhaps most shaped by eighteenth-century classicism. The strict attention to form, the mathematical precision, and the symmetry learned from architecture became the basis of a new music: the development of the sonata, the symphony, the string quartet, and the concerto so changed musical composition that the name classical music remained long after the classical era.

Popular Culture in the Eighteenth Century

In recent decades, cultural historians have paid closer attention to the culture of the lower classes, as distinct from the high culture of the elite. The distinction is not absolute, because high culture and popular culture are often remarkably similar. In the eighteenth century, the plays of Shakespeare were popular with the agricultural classes of rural England, who welcomed the touring troops of actors who brought drama to the countryside. In

FIGURE 20.2 *The Classical and the Neoclassical.* One of the finest surviving works of Roman architecture is the Maison Carré, a Corinthian temple constructed in 16 BCE in Nîmes, France, where large numbers of Roman army veterans were given land in their retirement. (Southern France holds many others examples of classical Roman architecture—theaters, baths, aqueducts, and coliseums.) The Parisian church of St. Mary Magdalen, known as La Madeleine, was begun in 1764 and redesigned several times. The final version, a neoclassical temple with imposing Corinthian columns, bears a striking resemblance to the Maison Carré, built 1800 years earlier.

London, David Garrick's famous theater on Drury Lane was as popular with the artisans and laborers who flocked to the cheap seats as it was with the wealthy who bought the boxes. In the capitals of opera such as Milan and Vienna, few shopkeepers could afford to attend the lavish productions. But Mozart had a popular following, too, and versions of his operas were produced in lower-class music halls.

Popular culture and high culture also intersected for the converse reason: the well-bred, well-educated, and well-off also frequented the robust entertainment of ordinary folk. The world of popular culture—a world of rope-walkers, jugglers, and acrobats; of village bands and workers' music halls; of folktales and folk song; of races, fights, animal sports, and gambling; of marionettes, pantomimes, and magic lantern shows projected on smoke; of inns, taverns, public houses ("pubs"), cafes, and coffeehouses; of broadsheets and limericks; of carnivals and fairs; of entertainment in public parks and on the village commons—was not the exclusive province of the laboring classes who gave these their meanings and values. High culture honored this intersection by regularly borrowing from popular culture, from the folk theme that reappeared as a leitmotif in a symphony or the tales of oral culture that reappeared in learned anthologies.

Salons. A good illustration of the parallels in high culture and popular culture can be seen in two of their centers: the salon (high culture) and the coffeehouse (popular culture). The salon, a social gathering held in a private home where notable literary, artistic, and political figures discussed the issues of the day, characterized the educated world of high culture in the eighteenth century. Salons were typically organized and directed by women of grace and style, often aristocrats, who shaped European culture by sponsoring rising young talents, protecting unpopular opinions, finding financial support for impoverished writers, and sometimes fostering political intrigues. The salons glorified conversation—about the republic of letters, the arts, politics and policies, scandal and gossip, and wit and flirtation. Salon hostesses were sometimes the wives, daughters, or mistresses of powerful men, such as the duchess de Maine, the mistress of Philippe d'Orléans, and the regent of France; some were prominent intellectuals in their own right. Their ranks included women such as Madame de Lambert, the author of *Advice of a Mother to Her Daughter* (1734), which advocated university education for women. Another salon hostess, Louise d'Epinay, won the French academy's prize for 1774 for her *Conversations with Emile.*

The Spread of the Salon. The habit of organizing salons originated in the French aristocracy, but it was adopted by other elements of the educated classes and spread across Europe. By the middle of the century, salons were flourishing in London, Berlin, Vienna, Rome, and Copenhagen, usually assuming a national character somewhat different from Parisian salons. In England, they ranged from the formal salon of Elizabeth Montagu, the granddaughter of Lady Mary Wortley Montagu, who forbade such frivolity as playing cards, to the less formal salon of Mary Monckton, the Countess of Cork, which included such prominent figures as Samuel Johnson. Montagu's salon included some poorer intellectuals who could not afford the fine evening clothing of the wealthy; one member wore humble blue worsted stockings, giving rise to the term **bluestockings,** which evolved into a term for women intellectuals. Salons in the German states provided an opportunity for Jewish families to win social acceptance previously denied them. Moses Mendelssohn began the habit of holding open houses for intellectuals, and his daughter, Dorothea von Schlegel, built on this habit to emulate the French salons. Most German salons, however, insisted on a stricter sexual respectability than characterized Parisian salons.

Coffeehouses. The coffeehouse served a similar cultural role for other social strata. Coffeehouses—and sometimes taverns, which were less expensive and less formal—served as meeting houses, reading rooms, and debating halls. The daily newspaper was at the center of this phenomenon. Dailies were born and began to flourish in the eighteenth century, starting with *The Daily Courant* in London in 1702. Moscow had a newspaper later that same year, Berlin a daily paper from 1704, and Rome from 1716. Paris even had a women's newspaper, advocating the equality of the sexes—*Les Journal des Dames,* founded in 1759—before it had a daily newspaper. Larger Sunday newspapers appeared in London in 1780. Until the technological innovations of the midnineteenth century, however, these newspapers remained expensive and their circulation low. Subscription libraries and "reading societies" appeared in the German states as early as 1704. But the coffeehouse provided the most popular solution by subscribing to multiple newspapers, holding public readings of newspaper stories for the benefit of the illiterate majority, and providing the sociable setting.

The towns and cities of eighteenth-century Europe were filled with coffeehouses. Coffee was a new beverage to Europeans. The first coffeehouse in central Europe opened in Vienna in 1683, after a few sacks of coffee were taken from a retreating Turkish army. After the eighteenth-century boom, the Viennese all but lived in 15,000 coffeehouses. The first coffeehouse opened in Paris in 1672 and soon failed; in 1754, however, 56 were flourishing. There were none in London in 1650, but more than 2,000 had opened by 1725. Coffeehouses became so popular in Berlin that Frederick the Great blocked the importation of coffee as a drain on the national wealth—a hint at how expensive coffee was initially. Other governments feared that coffeehouses were centers of subversion where the lower orders met to discuss dangerous ideas. The king of Sweden considered coffee a dangerous poison and outlawed it in 1756. The popular mood was better captured by Bach, however, who produced a "Coffee Cantata" after visiting a coffeehouse.

RELIGION AND EIGHTEENTH-CENTURY CULTURE

Christianity stood at the center of European culture in the eighteenth century, as it had for more than 1,000 years. Although European civilization was almost exclusively a Christian civilization, it was split into many conflicting **sects.** The religious map of the Old Regime followed lines drawn by the Peace of Westphalia in 1648, which had ended a period of ferocious religious warfare. At the simplest level, most of northern Europe was **Protestant,** most of southern Europe was **Roman Catholic,** and much of eastern Europe was **Orthodox.** Protestant Europe included Great Britain, the Dutch republic, the northern German states (notably Hanover, Saxony, and Prussia), all of Scandinavia, part of divided Switzerland, and pockets in eastern Europe (notably in Hungary). Catholic Europe included Portugal, Spain, France, all of the Italian states, the southern German states (notably Bavaria), and the Austrian Empire, plus most of the population in religiously divided Ireland and Poland. Orthodox Europe included Russia plus large portions of Poland and the Ottoman Empire (such as Greece and Serbia).

FIGURE 20.3 *Mme. de Châtelet and Voltaire at Cirey.* One of the most extraordinary women of the Enlightenment was the Marquise Emilie du Châtelet (1706–1749), shown here hosting a gathering at her home, the Château de Cirey in northeastern France. She learned Latin and Italian with her father, but at age 19 married into a noble family and moved into Cirey. Her husband preferred a military life, however, and chose to live with the army. Emilie du Châtelet then moved to Paris, where she entered salon society but chose to become a scientist herself, as well as a hostess. At 27, now well-trained in mathematics in the sciences, she met Voltaire and the two became longtime lovers. They returned to Cirey, where they hosted literary gatherings typical of the age, but more often Emilie turned to her studies. She published several scientific works in the 1740s and encouraged a scientific focus for salon gatherings. One of her most influential accomplishments was the translation of Newton's *Principia Mathematica* into French. She died in childbirth at 43.

Religious Minorities. This religious division of Europe left many minority populations inside hostile countries. Important Catholic minorities existed in Britain (only 2 percent of the population, but including many powerful families), Holland (35 percent), Switzerland (40 percent),

FIGURE 20.4 *A French Coffeehouse.* In the 1700s, coffeehouses offered social settings for people to meet; debate current ideas; and read the new, expensive, daily newspapers. Coffeehouses subscribed to the multiple copies of newspapers and held public readings. Although governments feared that coffeehouses were centers for subversion, where discontents met to discuss ideas dangerous to authoritarian regimes, by the late 1700s, coffeehouses were flourishing all across Europe, especially in London, Paris, and Vienna.

and Prussia (especially after the annexation of Silesia). Similar Protestant minorities were found in Ireland (30 percent), France (2 percent, but disproportionately important, like Catholics in Britain), Piedmont (2 percent), Poland (4 percent), and Hungary (23 percent). In addition to Christian minorities, Europe contained small Jewish and Muslim populations. Jews were forbidden to live in some countries (notably Spain) but were a noteworthy minority (less than 1 percent) in many states, especially Britain, France, Holland, and Prussia; they constituted larger minorities in eastern Europe, chiefly in Poland (7 percent), Hungary (2 percent), Russia, and the Ottoman territories. Muslims were almost entirely confined to the Ottoman Empire, concentrated in the provinces of modern Bosnia and Albania.

Protestantism. Protestant Europe included three predominant faiths: **Anglicanism, Calvinism,** and **Lutheranism.** Virtually all of the membership of the Anglican Church (the Church of England) was found in England, Wales, Scotland, and Ireland. Lutheranism was the dominant form of Protestantism in the German states and Scandinavia, and Lutheran minorities were scattered in many east European states. A variety of Calvinist churches—usually called the **Reformed Church**—existed in western Europe. Their traditional center was Geneva, where Calvin had established his church. Calvinist churches were predominant in Switzerland, Holland (the Dutch Reformed Church), and Scotland (the Presbyterian Church); Calvinist minorities existed in many states, notably France—where the Reformed Church was illegal, although 500,000, known as **Huguenots,** followed it in secret—Prussia (where Huguenot refugees were invited to settle), and Hungary.

In addition to these primary Protestant churches, many smaller sects existed in 1700, and more were founded during the eighteenth century. Small populations of diverse Protestants—such as **Quakers** (the Society of Friends) in England and the **Baptists** in central Europe—lived even within Protestant states. In England, approximately 8 percent of the population, collectively called **Dissenters** or **Nonconformists,** belonged to Protestant sects outside of the Church of England.

Catholicism. The Roman Catholic Church was more unified and centralized than Protestantism, but it, too, encompassed diversity. Catholicism remained united by the authority of the pope and by the hierarchical administrative structure directed by the **Vatican.** However, the eighteenth-century papacy was too weak to resist the absolute monarchs of Catholic lands. Louis XIV of France had created a virtually autonomous French Catholic Church, often called the Gallican Church. (**Gallicanism** meant that the king named French cardinals and bishops himself and decided whether papal decrees would apply in France.) Other Catholic monarchs copied the French administrative independence from Rome, as the kings of Piedmont did in the early eighteenth century and Joseph II of Austria did later (a policy known as **Josephinism**). Variations of Catholicism also depended on the local strength of individual orders (such as the **Jesuits**) or doctrines (such as **Jansenism**). The Jesuits began the eighteenth century as the most important of all Catholic orders. They were rigorously trained men who had acquired global influence through their educational and missionary efforts, and they had increasingly turned their attention to politics. Their role in statecraft made the Jesuits controversial, however, and they were expelled from Portugal in 1759, from France in 1762, from Spain and many Italian states in 1767, and finally dissolved by Pope Clement XIV in 1773. Jansenism, named for a Dutch theologian, was equally controversial for teaching an austere, puritanical—almost Calvinistic—form of Catholicism, particularly in Belgium and France, and the doctrine was condemned by a papal bull.

Contrasts of Catholicism and Protestantism.
Important differences existed between Catholicism and

MAP 20.1. RELIGIOUS POPULATIONS IN EIGHTEENTH-CENTURY EUROPE

Catholic majority
Orthodox majority
Orthodox minority

Muslim majority
Protestant majority
Protestant minority

(1865) Date of Jewish Emancipation

Note the range of dates for Jewish Emancipation (the date at which Jews were given equal civil rights). France and Holland became centers of opportunity for Jews, but many states, from Portugal to Russia, continued to deny equal rights into the twentieth century. Is there a correlation between the Enlightenment debate on toleration and the acceptance of equal rights?

Protestantism, shaping cultural differences in Europe. These extended far beyond matters of faith—beyond the fine points of theological doctrines, such as the nature of Christian sacraments or the route to salvation. Protestant pastors, unlike Catholic priests, married and raised families, often producing dynasties of preachers when their sons also entered the church and their wives and daughters took leading roles in Protestant organizations. Protestant states abolished the monastic orders that existed in Catholic countries and seized church lands; thus, the church had a greater physical presence in Catholic countries through land ownership and especially the far greater size of the clerical population. The Catholic Church owned 10 percent of the land in France (30 percent in some regions), 15 percent of Castile and central Spain, and 40 percent of Naples and southern Italy. The ecclesiastical population of Portugal has been estimated at 80,000 to 300,000—at least 4 percent of the population, and perhaps as much as 15 percent. A study of the island

of Corsica has found that a population of 220,000 people sustained sixty-five monasteries. The situation was dramatically different in England, where a population of 5.8 million, 90 percent of whom were nominally Anglican, sustained 11,000 clergymen in the Church of England—less than 0.2 percent of the population.

Christian Culture. Within these variations, all of Europe lived in a deeply Christian culture. Churches provided most of the social services that existed for the poor, crippled, aged, orphaned, released prisoners, and reformed prostitutes. Hospitals and schools were run by the church, not by the state. Schools provide perhaps the best illustration of the Christian character of European civilization.

Literacy. Few people received a formal education in the eighteenth century—most of the population in all countries remained illiterate—but most of the schools that existed were run by churches. The Presbyterian Church ran most of the schools in Scotland, the Anglican Church ran the majority of the schools in England, the Lutheran Church dominated Scandinavian education, and the Orthodox Church conducted most of the schools in Russia. In many Catholic countries—including Spain, Portugal, Poland, and most of the Italian states—the church totally controlled teaching. Religion formed a large part of the educational curriculum. The need to be literate to read the Bible was frequently the decisive reason in creating new schools, especially in Protestant faiths that stressed Bible reading.

Christianity and High Culture. Religion remained central to both high culture and popular culture, but Christian themes no longer dominated painting and sculpture, and literature had entered a thoroughly secular age; European culture reflected an "age of reason" more than an "age of faith." Still, the arts of the eighteenth century relied heavily on religion. Goethe's

The Culture of Old Regime Europe 483

FIGURE 20.5 *Ecclesiastical Rococo Architecture.* Much of the finest rococo architecture is found in the eighteenth-century churches of Germanic central Europe. The Abbey Church at Ottobeuren, shown here, uses colored stucco, marble, frescoes, and gilded frames to achieve a spectacular image of celestial grandeur.

Faust (1773), one of the masterpieces of German literature, is a Christian tragedy of lost faith and damnation. The dominant buildings of the age were royal palaces and stately homes, yet many of the structures that characterized baroque and rococo architecture were churches, such as the lavish Karlskirche in Vienna or the rococo churches of Bavaria. Composers may have favored secular subjects for the flourishing opera of the eighteenth century, but many of the masterpieces of baroque music originated in Christianity, such as Marc-Antoine Charpentier's powerful *Te Deum*. Johann Sebastian Bach long earned his living as cantor and organist at the Thomaskirche in Leipzig, where he composed a huge array of music on Christian themes, such as his Mass in B minor. And perhaps no music composed in the eighteenth century is more famous than Handel's *Messiah*.

Christianity and Popular Culture. Christianity similarly remained central to popular culture and the rhythms of daily life. The sound of church bells marked the time of day for most Europeans, and a church clock was often the only timekeeping that the poor knew until late in the eighteenth century. Sunday remained the day of rest—often the only day of rest—for shopkeepers, laborers, and peasants alike. The only vacation most people knew came from religious holidays and festivals, and the calendar of the Old Regime was filled with such days. In addition to the universal holidays of the Christian calendar, such as Christmas and Easter, every region, village, and occupation added the celebration of patron saints. Few events of the year were more popular in village life than the annual religious festival.

Established Churches. Most governments maintained an official state religion (called the **established church**), rewarding its members and limiting the rights of nonmembers. In Denmark and Sweden, non-Lutherans could not teach, hold public office, or conduct religious services. Prussia excluded non-Lutherans from many occupations, a barrier that persuaded the father of Karl Marx to convert from Judaism to Lutheranism in order to practice law. In Britain, a series of laws called the **Test Acts** excluded non-Anglicans from military command, sitting in parliament, or attending Oxford or Cambridge universities. Catholics could not live in London, nor Protestants in Paris, in 1750. Restrictions were stricter in regions where the **Inquisition** (a judicial arm of the papacy, established in the thirteenth century to suppress heresy) retained power. More than 700 Spaniards condemned by the Inquisition were burnt at the stake between 1700 and 1746; the last burning for heresy in Spain came in 1781. The Inquisition exerted a greater force on European culture by regulating behavior. A trial before the Inquisition in 1777 listed some of the behavior that true Christians must cease: (1) eating meat on Friday; (2) crossing one's legs during a church service; (3) believing that the Earth revolved around the sun; (4) not believing in acts of the faith, such as ringing church bells during a storm to beg God to stop it; (5) owning prohibited books, listed on the church's Index of Forbidden Books; (6) corresponding with non-Catholics; and (7) disputing the idea that only Catholics could go to Heaven. No Protestant equivalent of the Inquisition existed, but that did not make Protestant lands models of toleration. Denmark forbade Catholic priests from entering the country under threat of the death penalty.

THE ENLIGHTENMENT AND ITS ORIGINS

The eighteenth century is one of the most famous periods in the history of European thought. Historians often call that century the **Age of Enlightenment** (or the Age of Reason) because eighteenth-century writers considered their epoch more enlightened than earlier eras. It was an age that cherished universities, learned academies, scientific laboratories and observatories, libraries, philosophic journals, books (especially great reference works), and talking about all of them. Although the term *the Enlightenment* was not used during the eighteenth century, synonymous terms—particularly the German term, *Aufklärung*—were used.

The Philosophes. The history of the Enlightenment focuses on the influential thinkers and writers of the age. They are usually identified by a French name, the *philosophes,* which is a broader term than *philosophers* in English. The importance of the Enlightenment rests in the circulation of the ideas of the philosophes among a small literate population and the influence of these ideas in changing the Old Regime. The central ideas of the Enlightenment are frequently simplified to a few basic concepts. The philosophes often differed, but a few concepts were nearly universal: (1) **skepticism**—questioning the validity of assumptions about society and the physical world without regard for traditional authority; (2) belief in the existence of **natural laws**—such as the law of gravity—that govern both the social and physical worlds; (3) confidence that human **reason,** rigorously applied, can discover these natural laws and establish them as the basis of human activity; and (4) optimism that the application of reason and obedience to natural laws will produce **progress,** leading to the perfection of human institutions.

One of the most eminent German philosophes, Immanuel Kant, summarized many of these attitudes in an essay of 1784 titled "What Is Enlightenment?" His definition of Enlightenment was the liberation of individuals from direction by others (see Document 20.1). Kant held that people achieved this liberation when they resolved to use their reason and to follow its dictates. Thus, he suggested a Latin motto for the Enlightenment: *Sapere aude!* (literally, "Dare to know!"), which he translated as "Have the courage to use your own reason!"

Origins of the Enlightenment. The Enlightenment developed from several trends in European thought. Skepticism had been one of the dominant themes of seventeenth-century philosophy, chiefly associated with the French philosopher René Descartes. In works such as the *Discourse on Method* (1637), he had advocated universal doubt; that is, the doubting of everything until it can be proved. Pierre Bayle had even taken the dramatic step of applying skeptical philosophy to the Bible. Bayle, a Frenchman whose advanced ideas forced him to live in the greater freedom of Holland, proposed "a detailed refutation of the unreasonable deference given to tradition," and he included Christianity within that tradition. All religious questions, including the reading of the Bible, "require the use of reason."

The Scientific Revolution. A second fundamental source of the Enlightenment thought was the scientific revolution of the seventeenth century, especially Sir Isaac Newton's synthesis of

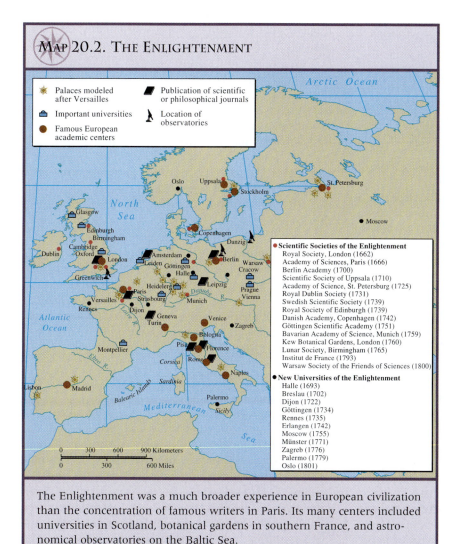

MAP 20.2. THE ENLIGHTENMENT

Palaces modeled after Versailles
Important universities
Famous European academic centers
Publication of scientific or philosophical journals
Location of observatories

Scientific Societies of the Enlightenment
Royal Society, London (1662)
Academy of Sciences, Paris (1666)
Berlin Academy (1700)
Scientific Society of Uppsala (1710)
Academy of Science, St. Petersburg (1725)
Royal Dublin Society (1731)
Swedish Scientific Society (1739)
Royal Society of Edinburgh (1739)
Danish Academy, Copenhagen (1742)
Göttingen Scientific Academy (1751)
Bavarian Academy of Science, Munich (1759)
Kew Botanical Gardens, London (1760)
Lunar Society, Birmingham (1765)
Institut de France (1793)
Warsaw Society of the Friends of Sciences (1800)

New Universities of the Enlightenment
Halle (1693)
Breslau (1702)
Dijon (1722)
Göttingen (1734)
Rennes (1735)
Erlangen (1742)
Moscow (1755)
Münster (1771)
Zagreb (1776)
Palermo (1779)
Oslo (1801)

The Enlightenment was a much broader experience in European civilization than the concentration of famous writers in Paris. Its many centers included universities in Scotland, botanical gardens in southern France, and astronomical observatories on the Baltic Sea.

IMMANUEL KANT ON ENLIGHTENMENT

Immanuel Kant (1724–1804) was a distinguished German philosopher and a professor of logic and metaphysics at the University of Königsberg in eastern Prussia. He was already famous for his greatest work—*The Critique of Pure Reason* (1781)—when he published the essay "What Is Enlightenment?" (1784), from which the following excerpt is taken.

Enlightenment is man's leaving his self-caused immaturity. Immaturity is the incapacity to use one's intelligence without the guidance of another. Such immaturity is self-caused if it is not caused by lack of intelligence, but by lack of determination and courage to use one's intelligence without being guided by another. Sapere Aude! Have the courage to use your own reason! is therefore the motto of the enlightenment.

Through laziness and cowardice, a large part of mankind, even after nature has freed them from alien guidance, gladly remain immature. It is because of laziness and cowardice that it is so easy to usurp the role of guardians. It is so comfortable to be a minor! If I have a book which provides meaning for me, a pastor who has conscience for me, a doctor who will judge my diet for me, and so on, then I do not need to exert myself. I do not have any need to think; if I can pay, others will take over the tedious job for me . . .

But it is more nearly possible for a public to enlighten itself: this is even inescapable if only the public is given its freedom. . . . All that is required for this enlightenment is freedom; and particularly the least harmful of all that may be called freedom, namely the freedom for man to make public use of his reason in all matters.

From Kant, Immanuel, "What Is Enlightenment?" in *The Philosophy of Kant*, Carl J. Friedrich, ed. (New York: Modern Library, 1949).

Question: What implications does Kant's argument have for the role of religion?

the accomplishments of many scientists. Newton had built upon a **scientific revolution** that had destroyed the **geocentric theory** of the universe, instead placing the sun at the center in a **heliocentric theory.** This required sweeping, counterintuitive adjustments in European thought. For the heliocentric theory to be true, the Earth must move, at tremendously high speeds, around the sun and the sun did not rise or set, it merely appeared to do so because the rotation of the Earth turned a viewer toward or away from the Sun. Christian theologians fought such conclusions. The Catholic Church placed the writings of astronomers on the **Index of Prohibited Books,** arguing that Christians should worry about how to go to heaven, not how the heavens go. The Enlightenment canonized Newton because he convinced the intelligentsia that the new astronomy was correct and the churches were wrong. His greatest fame resulted from stating the Principle of Universal Gravitation (the law of gravity) in his masterwork, *Principia Mathematica* (1687). The "universal" element of the law of gravity fascinated the philosophes of the eighteenth century. Newton proved to them that human reason could discover "the universal qualities of all bodies whatsoever." Voltaire, who popularized Newton's work in *Elements of the Philosophy of Newton* (1738), proclaimed him "the greatest and rarest genius that ever rose for the ornamentation and instruction of the species." The English poet Alexander Pope was equally lavish in praising the Newtonian synthesis in his *Essay on Man* (1734): "Nature and nature's law lay hid in night/God said, 'Let Newton be,' and all was light." And around the Western world, philosophes placed a bust of Newton in their study—as Thomas Jefferson did at Monticello—as a reminder that human reason could find universal natural laws.

Classicism. A third source of Enlightenment thought, alongside philosophic skepticism and scientific rationalism, was the revival of classicism. Like the humanists of the Renaissance, the philosophes revered the Greco-Roman past, but with a different emphasis. To them, antiquity represented the historical model of a society that had revered scientific observation and reasoned objectively from these observations. This admiration of antiquity implied the rejection of knowledge supported only by authority, dogma, or superstition—the traits that the philosophes often associated with the history of Europe after the fall of Rome.

Natural Law, Reason, and Progress

When the Scientific Revolution convinced the European intelligentsia that natural laws existed, the philosophes concluded that laws governing human activity—the organization of governments, economic relations, the efficient operation of prisons, and the writing of history—similarly "lay hid in night." Such laws merely awaited the Newton of economics or penology. The belief in natural law was not new; ancient authors had asserted its existence, too. The

Scientific Revolution merely allowed thinkers to embrace this old idea with a new self-confidence.

Natural Law and Political Theory.

One of the leading figures of the French Enlightenment, the Baron Charles-Louis de Montesquieu illustrates this interest in natural law in his writings on political theory. Montesquieu was a wealthy provincial noble, educated in law, who inherited a position in the Parlement of Bordeaux. Although he was elected the chief justice of the parlement, he was more interested in theories of government than in the day-to-day drudgery of his highly political job. He sold his office—such positions were often the property of nobles in the eighteenth century—and turned to writing. His *The Spirit of the Laws* (1748) became one of the most widely influential books of the century, joining the seventeenth-century works of John Locke, who had attacked the divine right of royalty and asserted the divine royalty of right, in laying the foundations of modern political theory.

Positive Law and Natural Law.

Montesquieu began *The Spirit of the Laws* by asserting that people, like the physical world, are "governed by invariable laws." This did not mean laws promulgated by the government and enforced by the courts; Montesquieu called that type of law **"positive laws."** Instead, Montesquieu meant laws in a scientific sense—laws that exist in nature, laws that state "fixed and invariable relationships" just as much as the law of gravity did. For example, Montesquieu believed that natural law proclaimed the need for food and the attraction of the sexes. Other natural laws governing human relations were less certain. Montesquieu, for example, asserted that people were, by nature, peaceful rather than warlike. One consequence of asserting the existence of natural laws and trying to define them was that they might be different from the positive laws enforced by the government or the moral laws of the established church.

The Spread of Natural Law Theory.

Philosophes such as Montesquieu insisted that positive law must therefore be changed to agree with natural law. "The intelligent world," he wrote, "is far from being so well governed as the physical." References to "nature" and "nature's law" are found in a great variety of eighteenth-century works in addition to Newton's physics, Pope's poetry, and Montesquieu's political theory. The most typical work of the Enlightenment, the *French Encyclopedia of the Arts and Sciences* (the *Encyclopédie*), devoted three full articles to natural law. Jean-Jacques Rousseau wrote one of the famous books in the history of education, *Emile,* or "Concerning Education" (1762), stressing natural education. "Nature," he wrote, "never

deceives us; it is always we who deceive ourselves." The first draft of the American Declaration of Independence proclaimed that people were entitled to independence and self-government by "the Laws of Nature." Not all philosophes used the theory of natural law, however. But even those who rejected it—as did the Scottish philosopher David Hume, who called it a "fallacious and sophistical" theory—discussed the idea at length.

Skepticism and Rationalism.

To discover natural laws, the philosophes relied on skepticism and **rationalism** (the application of reason to all things). Skepticism meant questioning and criticizing everything. "A thing is not proved when no one has ever questioned it," wrote one of the editors of the *Encyclopédie.* "Skepticism is the first step toward the truth." Kant insisted on the skeptical evaluation of everything, including church and state, in *The Critique of Pure Reason* (1781):

> Our age is the age of criticism, to which everything must be subjected. The sacredness of religion, and the authority of legislation, are by many regarded as grounds for exemption from the examination by this tribunal. But, if they are exempted, they become the subjects of just suspicion, and cannot lay claim to sincere respect, which reason accords only to that which has stood the test of a free and public examination.

Reason.

Most philosophes shared this glorification of reason. Montesquieu stressed that reason must be the basis of law. An American philosophe, Thomas Jefferson, advised: "Fix reason firmly in her seat, and call on her tribunal for every fact, every opinion." Denis Diderot, the coeditor of the *Encyclopédie,* wrote that the philosophe must be "actuated in everything by reason."

The insistence on rationalism caused collisions between the philosophes and the established authorities. This was especially true of the Christian churches, which insisted on the primacy of faith as a standard of knowledge rather than, or in addition to, reason. One of the first popes directly rejected reason as the standard of the church, arguing that "[i]f the word of God could be comprehended by reason, it would no longer be wonderful." The conflict between reason and faith had interested many thinkers across the centuries, but faith had remained the Christian standard even after the Protestant Reformation, when Martin Luther had condemned reason as "the Devil's Harlot." Despite such conflicts, the philosophes were generally confident that the use of human reason to discover natural laws would produce a better world. Thus, the glorification of reason led to an optimistic cult of progress. The French

TABLE 20.1 LANDMARK WORKS OF THE ENLIGHTENMENT

1702 Daniel Defoe's *The Shortest Way with Dissenters* satirizes intolerance.

1710 Gottfried Leibnitz's *Théodicée* proclaims this "the best of all possible worlds."

1721 Baron Montesquieu's *Persian Letters* derides French institutions.

1725 Madame de Sévigné's posthumous *Letters* reveal life of the aristocracy.

1725 Giambatista Vico's *Principles of a New Science* proposes a science of society.

1729 Sir Isaac Newton's *Principia Mathematica* is translated into English from Latin.

1733 Voltaire's *Letters Concerning the English* popularizes Newtonian science and representative government.

1734 Madame de Lambert's *Advice of a Mother* advocates university education for women.

1736 Bishop Joseph Butler's *Analogy of Religion* defends Christianity against Deism.

1737 Lady Mary Wortley Montagu's *The Nonsense of Common Sense* questions accepted ideas.

1739 David Hume's *A Treatise of Human Nature* states utilitarian principles.

1739 Sophia's *Woman Not Inferior to Man* asserts the equality of women.

1741 Johann Süssmilch's *The Divine Order* pioneers the field of statistics.

1748 David Hume's *Essays Concerning Human Understanding* states case for complete skepticism.

1748 Baron de Montesquieu's *The Spirit of the Laws* establishes study of comparative government.

1751 Denis Diderot and Jean d'Alembert publish the first volume of the *Encyclopédie.*

1755 Jean-Jacques Rousseau's *Discourse on the Origin of Inequality* attacks the social order of Europe.

1755 Samuel Johnson publishes first comprehensive dictionary of the English language.

1758 Claude Helvétius's *De l'esprit* asserts the principle of enlightened self-interest.

1759 Voltaire's *Candide* satirizes ideas and institutions of the eighteenth century.

1762 Jean-Jacques Rousseau's *The Social Contract* propounds radical ideas about rights and liberties.

1762 Jean-Jacques Rousseau's *Emile* urges "natural" education.

1763 Voltaire's *Treatise on Tolerance* denounces religious intolerance.

1764 Cesare Beccaria's "Treatise on Crimes and Punishments" urges penal reforms.

1764 Voltaire's *Philosophical Dictionary* criticizes both church and state.

1768 Joseph Priestley's *Essay on the First Principles of Government* stresses the happiness of citizens.

1770 Baron d'Holbach's *The System of Nature* attacks organized religion.

1771 First edition of the *Encyclopedia Britannica* appears.

1776 Edward Gibbon's *The Decline and Fall of the Roman Empire* is published.

1776 Adam Smith's *The Wealth of Nations* outlines principles of capitalist economics.

1777 John Howard's *The State of the Prisons* exposes horrible prison conditions.

1779 Gotthold Lessing's *Nathan the Wise,* a dramatic poem on toleration, is published.

1781 Immanuel Kant's *Critique of Pure Reason* is published.

1781 Moses Mendelssohn's *On the Civil Amelioration of the Condition of the Jews* is published.

1781 Johann Pestalozzi's *Leonard and Gertrude* advocates the reform of education.

1782 Joseph Priestley's *History of the Corruptions of Christianity* criticizes the church.

1784 Immanuel Kant's "What Is Enlightenment?" urges people to dare to use their reason.

1788 Immanuel Kant's *Critique of Practical Reason* states "the categorical imperative" for behavior.

1789 Jeremy Bentham's *Introduction to the Principles of Morals and Legislation* is published.

1792 Mary Wollstonecraft's *A Vindication of the Rights of Woman* calls for equal education.

1795 Marquis de Condorcet's *Progress of the Human Spirit* proclaims the doctrine of progress.

1798 Thomas Malthus's *Essay on the Principle of Population* foresees world overpopulation.

Question: Does this list of works and ideas merit the term the Age of Reason?

---

mathematician Jean d'Alembert, Diderot's coeditor of the *Encyclopédie,* thought "it is impossible to deny that philosophy has shown progress among us. Day by day natural science accumulates new riches." The greatest champion of the doctrine of progress was another French mathematician, Marquis Antoine de Condorcet, whose *Progress of the Human Spirit* (1795) foresaw nothing less than "the indefinite perfectibility of the human race"—a passage written shortly before Condorcet died in a prison of the French Revolution.

The French Enlightenment and the Encyclopédie

France as the Center of the Enlightenment.

Although skepticism and rationalism attracted the educated classes of many regions, the home of the Enlightenment was in France, where the authority of church and throne were already weakened and the political duel between the aristocracy and the monarchy created an environment more favorable to radical thought than existed in most of Europe. The most famous and internationally read philosophes were French, as the universal use of a French word for them suggests. Voltaire's famous satiric novel *Candide* (1759), filled with witty criticism of the Old Regime, went through eight editions in the year of its publication alone. Rousseau's radical political tract *The Social Contract* (1762) had thirteen French editions in 1762–1763. Montesquieu's *The Spirit of the Laws* (1748) saw twenty-two French editions by 1751 and ten editions in its English translation by 1773; it had appeared in Dutch, Polish, Italian, and German editions by the 1780s and was so widely read that it was translated into Latin for the benefit of well-educated people in regions with less common languages, such as Hungary.

The *Encyclopédie*.

Nothing characterizes the French leadership of the Enlightenment better than the publication of the twenty-eight volumes of the *Encyclopédie* by Diderot and d'Alembert between 1751 and 1772. Many of the most famous writers of the eighteenth century contributed to what was perhaps the greatest intellectual accomplishment of the Enlightenment. The idea of compiling an encyclopedia was not new. The word itself came from the classical Greek *encyclios*—meaning instruction in the whole circle of learning—in both the arts and the sciences. Many famous efforts had been made to encompass the entire circle of learning, from Pliny's *Natural History* in the first century CE through a number of encyclopedic works in the seventeenth century.

Diderot.

Denis Diderot was an unlikely figure to produce the *Encyclopédie*. He was the son of a lower-middle-class family—his father was a cutlery maker—in provincial France. Diderot received his formal education from the Jesuits, then prepared for a career in the church so devoutly that he fasted, slept on straw, and wore a hair shirt. Further study in Paris, however, changed Diderot into a Bohemian writer who broke with church and family alike, angering the former with his writing and the latter with his behavior. Like many philosophes, Diderot's writings earned him poverty and time in a royal prison. Thus, he eagerly accepted the opportunity to edit an encyclopedia, which was originally intended to be merely a translation of an English work.

The resultant *Encyclopédie* was a work of uneven quality and numerous inaccuracies, but it nonetheless became *the* encyclopedia. It owed its fame and influence to two characteristics. First, it was a collaborative enterprise, not simply the work of its editors. The contributors included many of the most influential writers of the Enlightenment; Condorcet, Montesquieu, Rousseau, and Voltaire all wrote for the *Encyclopédie*, with Voltaire alone contributing more than forty articles. Baron Paul d'Holbach wrote on the history of religion, including daring essays on priests and theocracy that made him one of the most controversial philosophes. Two leading Physiocrats, François Quesnay and Jacques Turgot, summarized the economic ideas that dominated contemporary thought and would be adopted by many governments. Such contributors guaranteed the *Encyclopédie* a large readership and extended the influence of the French Enlightenment across Europe.

Notoriety of the *Encyclopédie*.

The second reason for the importance of the *Encyclopédie* was that the ideas and opinions that it contained made it notorious. The *Encyclopédie* did not merely record information, it became a forum for the philosophes. They began in the first volumes by criticizing despotic government and the established church; subsequent volumes contained direct attacks. As early as 1752, with only two volumes in print, King Louis XV of France ordered the *Encyclopédie* "to be and to remain suppressed." The support of friends in high places—especially the king's mistress, Madame de Pompadour—allowed publication to proceed, but it did so amidst controversy. In 1759, French courts turned the work over to a panel of churchmen and scholars to censor. The government again denounced it, this time for causing "irreparable damage to morality and religion." Pope Clement XIII condemned it for "false, pernicious, and scandalous doctrines and propositions, inducing unbelief and scorn for religion." None of these threats, including excommunication for mere possession of it, stopped the publication.

The Enlightenment beyond France

The German Enlightenment.

French leadership may have been unquestioned, but the Enlightenment was a widespread experience. The German Enlightenment (the Aufklärung) drew on the excellence of German education, from compulsory education laws to superior universities. Rulers even encouraged the process in some regions. Frederick the Great of Prussia considered himself a philosophe and corresponded with Voltaire. He wrote dozens of books and composed more than 100 symphonies, sonatas, and concertos. And he typically bought five copies of each book by the philosophes, to have one at each of his palaces. Frederick kept Prussian intellectuals on a short leash, however, and once said that the way to punish a region was to have it governed by philosophers. But he allowed

THE *ENCYCLOPÉDIE*

Few books have had more impact than the *Encyclopédie* had on eighteenth-century Europe. The first volume appeared in 1751, and volume twenty-eight was published in 1772. Many of the most important writers of the Enlightenment, including Condorcet, Montesquieu, Rousseau, and Voltaire, contributed to this collective work—Voltaire contributing more than forty articles. King Louis XV attempted to suppress the publication in 1752, and the French courts tried to censor it in 1759; but none of these blocked its circulation around Europe. The subtitle of the *Encyclopédie* was the "Universal Dictionary of the Arts and Sciences," and exceptionally detailed illustrations accompanied most of the articles. The accompanying illustration depicts the stages of making a mirror.

Excerpts from the Encyclopedia

Each of the subjects in bold type is an entry in the *Encyclopédie* from which a brief excerpt is taken.

Censors of Books. Name given to men of learning who are in charge of the examination of books to be printed. . . . These censors have been created in various states in order to examine literary works and pass judgment on books which are to be printed, so that nothing would become public that could seduce minds with false doctrines or corrupt morals with dangerous maxims.

Intolerance. The word intolerance is generally understood to designate the savage passion that prompts us to hate and persecute those who are in error. . . . Ecclesiastic intolerance consists in considering as false all religions other than one's own. Teaching, persuasion, and prayer—these are the only legitimate means of spreading the faith. Whatever means provoke hate, indignation, and scorn are blasphemous. . . . Whatever means would tend to incite men to rebellion, bring the nations under arms, and drench the earth with blood are blasphemous.

Natural Law. The term is taken to designate certain principles which nature alone inspires and which all animals as well as men have in common. On this law are based the union of male and female, the begetting of children as well as their education, love of liberty, self-preservation, concern for self-defense. We understand by natural law certain laws of justice and equity which

only natural reason has established among men, or better, God has engraved in our hearts. The fundamental principles of law and all justice are: to live honestly, not to give offense to anyone, and to render unto each whatever is his. . . . Since this natural law is based on such fundamental principles, it is perpetual and unchangeable: no agreement can debase it, no law can alter it or exempt anyone from the obligation it imposes.

Negroes. For the last few centuries the Europeans have carried on a trade in Negroes whom they obtain from Guinea and other coasts of Africa and whom they use to maintain the colonies established in various parts of America and in the West Indies. To justify this loathsome commerce, which is contrary to natural law, it is argued that ordinarily these slaves find the salvation of their souls in the loss of their liberty, and that the Christian teaching they receive, together with their indispensable role in the cultivation of sugar cane, tobacco, indigo, etc., softens the apparent inhumanity of a commerce where men buy and sell their fellow men as they would animals used in the cultivation of the land.

From Diderot, Denis, D'Alembert, Jean le Rond, et al., *The Encyclopédie; Selections*, trans. Nelly S. Hoyt and Thomas Cassirer (Indianapolis: Bobbs-Merrill, 1965).

Question: Do any of these excerpts suggest a reason for censoring the *Encyclopédie?*

---

sufficient tolerance that letters flourished, as they had begun to do under his grandfather (Frederick I), whose Berlin had boasted the first subscription library (1702), one of the first newspapers (the *Vossische Zeitung,* 1704), and an Academy of Sciences (1711). Hapsburg Austria, in contrast, was largely closed to the Enlightenment by strict censorship, intolerance of minorities, and the hostility to science of the Austrian Catholic Church.

Alchemists outnumbered chemists in Vienna in the early eighteenth century.

Leibnitz. The German Enlightenment produced a number of notable figures. The century began with Gottfried von Leibnitz, Newton's equal as a mathematician and superior as a philosopher, presiding over the Berlin Academy. Leibnitz's reputation suffered somewhat when Voltaire's *Candide* ridiculed a sentence taken out of context from his *Théodicée* (1710): "God created the best of all possible worlds." His philosophy, however, did much to establish the scientific concept of natural law in eighteenth-century thought. And Leibnitz came closer than Voltaire to being the intellectual who mastered all fields of thought, from the scientific to the philosophic.

Leaders of the German Enlightenment. At the end of the century, the Aufklärung produced Germany's greatest poet, Wolfgang von Goethe. Goethe was at the center of a remarkable intellectual circle in Weimar that marks the beginnings of modern German literature; it included the poet and dramatist Friedrich von Schiller and the philosopher Gottfried von Herder. The dramatist Gotthold Lessing in Leipzig and Berlin, the philosopher Moses Mendelssohn in Dessau and Berlin, Immanuel Kant in Königsberg, Johann Süssmilch (one of the founders of the science of statistics) at Berlin, and the Bavarian Academy of Sciences in Munich show that the German Enlightenment spread widely across central Europe.

Other European Centers of the Enlightenment. A Swedish Enlightenment, evident in northern Europe, was known as the Gustavian Enlightenment because it was encouraged by King Gustavus III of Sweden. It centered on the Swedish Royal Academy of Sciences (1741), Linnaeus's Botanical Gardens at Uppsala (1741), and the Swedish Academy at Stockholm (1786). There was also a noteworthy Neapolitan Enlightenment and a Scottish Enlightenment, which included Adam Smith (one of the founders of **capitalist economics**), David Hume (one of the greatest skeptics of the age), and James Hutton (one of the founders of modern geology). The prestige of the Enlightenment was so great that historians in every country have labored to show their national role in it, but for some regions—such as Spain, Portugal, and eastern Europe—the local Enlightenment was limited. In Spain, the hostility of the church limited the movement to a minority of the governing class. The largest periodical in Spain had a circulation of 630 copies, and a daring aristocrat who spoke publicly of the importance of reason was brought before the Inquisition on charges of heresy.

THE ENLIGHTENMENT AND CHRISTIANITY

Wherever the Enlightenment stirred the educated classes, it had important implications for European civilization. This becomes especially clear when one views the relationship between the Enlightenment and Christianity. Many of the philosophes bluntly attacked Christian beliefs and institutions, challenging the

churches in ways that might have led them to the stake in other eras. Hume, for example, applied skepticism to Christianity: "[T]he Christian religion not only was at first attended by miracles, but even at this day cannot be believed by any reasonable person without one." Diderot called Christianity "the most prejudicial of all the superstitions of the earth" (see Document 20.2). Privately, he denounced the Judeo-Christian deity as "a partial God who chooses or rejects, who loves or hates, according to his caprice; in short, a tyrant who plays with his creatures." Such ideas were not limited to one or two radical, de-Christianized writers. Tom Paine attacked the concept of the Trinity—"The notion of a Trinity of Gods has enfeebled the belief in one God"—and the Bible:

> Whenever we read the obscene stories, the voluptuous debaucheries, the cruel and tortuous executions, the unrelenting vindictiveness with which more than half the Bible is filled, it would be more consistent that we call it the word of a demon than the word of God. It is a history of wickedness that has served to corrupt and brutalize mankind.

Voltaire's *Candide* ridiculed churchmen by depicting a friar who seduces women, monks who consort with prostitutes, and priests who spread venereal disease; other churchmen committed robbery, torture, and murder. Edward Gibbon ended his monumental, six-volume *The Decline and Fall of the Roman Empire* with the conclusion that Christianity was one of the primary causes of the fall of Rome. He portrayed a church filled with "the inevitable mixture of error and corruption" contained in all human institutions.

Voltaire. The most famous critic of Christianity during the Enlightenment was Voltaire, the pen name of a Frenchman named François-Marie Arouet. Voltaire, the frail child of a Parisian legal official, received the finest classical education from the church,  at the Jesuit collège Louis-le-Grand. A priest who admired Voltaire's intelligence led him into a freethinking group whose members did not hesitate to criticize or deride any institution (see *Voltaire and the Enlightenment*). Voltaire threw himself into this sport and wrote a poem satirizing the regent, the Duke of Orléans. Under the arbitrary legal system of the Old Regime, this poem was sufficient grounds for Voltaire's imprisonment without a trial. Thus, at age 23, Voltaire was thrown into the Bastille (a large fortress-prison in Paris) for 11 months. Shortly after his release, Voltaire

DIDEROT ON THE CHURCH

Portrait of Denis Diderot

Denis Diderot studied to become a priest but instead became one of the church's sharpest critics. The following excerpt is taken from a short work that he published in 1775, "Discourse of a Philosopher to a King."

Sire, if you want priests you do not need philosophers, and if you want philosophers you do not need priests; for the ones being by their calling the friends of reason and the promoters of science, the others the enemies of reason and the favorers of ignorance, if the first do good, the others do evil.

You have both philosophers and priests; philosophers who are poor and not very formidable, priests who are rich and very dangerous. You should not much concern yourself with enriching your philosophers, because riches are harmful to philosophy, but your design should be to keep them; and you should strongly desire to impoverish your priests and to rid yourself of them. . . .

But, you will say to me, I shall no longer have any religion.

You are deceived, Sire, you will always have one; for religion is a climbing and lively plant which never perishes; it only changes form. That religion which will result from the poverty and degradation of its members will be the least troublesome. . . .

And if you deign to listen to me, I shall be the most dangerous of all philosophers for the priests. For the most dangerous is he who brings to the monarch's attention the immense sums which these arrogant and useless loafers cost his state; he who tells him, as I tell you, that you have a hundred and fifty thousand men to whom you and your subjects pay about a hundred and fifty thousand crowns a day to bawl in a building and deafen us with their bells. . . .

Since you have the secret of making a philosopher hold his tongue, why not employ it to silence the priest?

From Diderot, Denis, "Disclosure of a Philosopher to a King," in *Denis Diderot, Interpreter of Nature*, trans. Jean Stewart and Jonathan Kemp (New York: International Publishers, 1943).

Question: Is Diderot convincing in his assertion that there is a dichotomy between reason and faith and therefore a king must choose between them?

Deism. Few ideas that Voltaire championed caused more controversy than a religious doctrine known as **Deism.** Deists believed in a single God who created the universe but does not intervene in it. They rejected formal religion and religious institutions as unnecessary, and they criticized religions based on miracles, revelations, and the supernatural. Deists were often called **freethinkers** because they questioned everything and expected reasoned proof of it. Deism had originated in late seventeenth-century England, and it won many converts among the educated classes (including Benjamin Franklin and Thomas Jefferson in America) before the French philosophes popularized it as a logical consequence of rationalism. Montesquieu and Voltaire (who favored the term **theism**) spread the doctrine wider. Voltaire's *Sermon of the Fifty*, begun in the 1730s but not published until the 1760s, stated deist arguments bluntly, deriding the "absurd fables" of Christianity (see *Voltaire and the Enlightenment*).

Toleration. Voltaire's principal criticism of Christianity was the intolerance that he found among Christians. He devoted much of his life to championing the principle of **toleration,** and he returned to the theme so often that he made it one of the most important legacies of the Enlightenment (see *Voltaire and The Enlightenment*). Voltaire was not the first philosophe to adopt this theme. Daniel Defoe had already written a stinging satire in 1702 titled *The Shortest Way with Dissenters*, a book that persuaded too few people because Defoe was pilloried in public stocks and sent to prison. Voltaire's *Treatise on Tolerance* (1763) denounced the Catholic Church for the mentality that led to the cruel murder of Jean Calas, a Protestant merchant who was tortured to death in 1761 on the fallacious charge that he had murdered his son to prevent him from converting to Catholicism. Voltaire demanded that Christians learn complete tolerance: "It does not require any great art of studied elocution to prove that Christians ought to tolerate one another. I will go even further and say that we ought to look upon all men as our brothers. What! call a Turk, a Jew, a Siamese, my brother? Yes, of course; for are we not all children of the same father, and the creatures of the same God?" Voltaire returned to this theme in his *Philosophical Dictionary* (1764): "Of all religions, Christians ought doubtless to inspire the most tolerance, although hitherto the Christians have been the most intolerant of men." For the next edition of this dictionary, Voltaire added the story of the Chevalier de la Barre to illustrate the horrors of religious intolerance.

Moses Mendelssohn and Toleration. By the end of the eighteenth century, many other philosophes adopted Voltaire's theme. Moses Mendelssohn, the great Jewish philosopher of the Enlightenment, published a powerful plea for the freedom of conscience,

insulted another powerful noble who arranged to have the young poet beaten by a gang of thugs and imprisoned in the Bastille a second time. Voltaire wisely chose exile in England after his second release.

the toleration of minorities, and the separation of church and state—*Jerusalem* (1783). Mendelssohn also served as the model for the title character in Lessing's passionate call for toleration, *Nathan the Wise* (1779).

Chrisitianity and the Enlightenment. The criticism that the philosophes leveled on Christianity became so widespread that some historians have called the eighteenth century an age of modern paganism. However, the Enlightenment was not simply an atheist campaign. Some of the most distinguished philosophes were churchmen, such as the Anglo-Irish philosopher George Berkeley, an Anglican bishop. The institutional hostility of the Catholic Church to the Enlightenment did not stop many individual Catholic churchmen from being enthusiastic participants. One study of the *Encyclopédie* has shown that in some regions of France, priests bought the majority of copies. Indeed, reformers and priests were often members of the same family; Roland de la Platière, who would become one of the leaders of the French Revolution, had four brothers, and they were all priests. Pope Benedict XV was an intellectual himself, a friend of Montesquieu and Voltaire. In 1744, he permitted the publication of Galileo's condemned works; in 1757, he stopped enforcing the decrees against books teaching the heliocentric theory of the universe. Many philosophes sought to reconcile Christianity and science, theology and reason, as Leibnitz did in *Théodicée*.

THE ENLIGHTENMENT AND GOVERNMENT

The Enlightenment had equally grave implications for the monarchical governments of the Old Regime. The same application of skepticism and rationalism, the same search for natural laws, meant criticism of monarchy and aristocratic privilege. Rousseau, for example, bluntly styled himself "Jean-Jacques Rousseau, enemy of kings" and did not hesitate to sign letters to Frederick the Great that way. Diderot was more dramatic with his hostility: "Let us strangle the last king with the guts of the last priest!" Voltaire, who had good reasons to despise the powerful, treated them to the same acidic ridicule in *Candide* as churchmen received. When Candide and a companion arrived in a new kingdom, for example, they "asked one of the lords-in-waiting how he should behave in saluting His Majesty; should he fall on his knees or should he grovel, should he put his hands on his head or his behind, or should he just lick the dust off the floor . . . ?"

Censorship. The criticism of a monarch who could imprison authors without a trial was a risky business. Voltaire's stay in the Bastille and Diderot's in the dungeon at Vincennes are only two of the most famous ex-

amples of the attempts to control troublesome writers. A study of French records has shown that the police kept thorough files on French authors; fully 10 percent of all writers in 1750 had spent some time in prison, usually the Bastille. The police used royal *lettres de cachet* (an arrest warrant signed by the king) to pursue such critics of the government, especially pamphleteers. Arrest by lettre de cachet need not specify any crime; the king's words "because it pleases us" were sufficient grounds. Authors risked public whippings or even life sentences to the galleys for publishing their ideas. And many authorities regularly censored the works of even the most famous writers. Rousseau's *Emile,* for example, was not only condemned by the Catholic Church and placed on the Index of Prohibited Books but was also condemned by the Sorbonne (University of Paris), the General Assembly of the Clergy, and the Parlement of Paris. Fortunately for Rousseau, only his book was burnt in a public ceremony.

Circumventing Censorship. Consequently, early eighteenth-century writers sought indirect ways, such as Voltaire's satires, to make their point. When Archbishop François Fénelon wanted to criticize the king, he hid his satire in the form of an ancient epic. Fénelon's *Télémaque* reports the travels of the son of the Homeric hero, Ulysses; by describing Telemachus's visits to strange lands, Fénelon could comment on many forms of government and hide his comments on France. The book was banned and consigned to public fires anyway. Montesquieu similarly disguised his first critical comments in an epistolary novel (a novel in the form of letters), *The Persian Letters* (1721). These fictional letters were purportedly written by Persian visitors to Europe, whose naive comments hid barbs. One letter, for example, explains that the king of Spain owns many gold mines, but the king of France (who owns none) is richer because he has found a way to make unlimited money from the vanity of his subjects: he sells them offices, titles, and honors (such **venal offices** were common in the eighteenth century).

Attacking Censorship. One strong criticism of government occurred naturally to writers—attacking **censorship.** Claude Helvétius, a rich government official under Louis XV, made one of the most vigorous attacks in 1758. His *De l'esprit* ("Essays on the Mind") was blunt: "To limit the press is to insult the nation; to prohibit the reading of certain books is to declare the people to be either fools or slaves." His book was condemned by the parlement and burnt by the public executioner in 1759. In England, where the tolerance of ideas was slightly greater—but censorship was practiced nonetheless—even jurists gave the philosophes some support. William Blackstone, a judge, a member of parliament, and one of the founders of modern university training in law, published four volumes of the extremely influential

VOLTAIRE AND THE ENLIGHTENMENT

Voltaire has been called "the greatest of the philosophes" and esteemed as one the greatest champions of humanity; portraits, busts, and statues of him abound, far beyond France. Voltaire was also one of the most despised men of the eighteenth century, twice imprisoned in the Bastille (and only released on the condition that he leave the country). He lived in England for several years in the 1720s, in Prussia in the 1750s, and then spent the last 20 years of his life in Switzerland. Two hundred years later, some writers still argue that the upheaval of the late eighteenth century was "the fault of Voltaire" or that subsequent social critics were "Voltaire's Bastards."

Deism—*Voltaire's* Sermon of the Fifty *(1760)*

Despite his Jesuit education, Voltaire's early works show many aspects of his Deism (such as the demand for tolerance or the denunciation of superstition), but he fully developed his ideas during a period of Bible study in the 1740s. His writings of the 1750s and 1760s (including *The Sermon of the Fifty* from which this excerpt is taken) began to state his Deism more vigorously. For the remainder of his life, his Deism and his humanitarianism were closely intertwined and his assault on Christianity more vigorous.

For a year, fifty well-educated, pious, and reasonable persons have been gathering every Sunday in a populous and mercantile town. They say prayers, and afterwards a member of the society delivers a talk. Then they have dinner, and after the meal they take up a collection for the poor. Each presides in his turn; it is up to the

A nineteenth-century print depicting one of the arrests of Voltaire (the figure in black in the center, with walking-stick raised). Note that Voltaire and the other gentlemen in this print all wear silk hose and culottes rather than full-length trousers—a class distinction that would soon become important to revolutionaries.

president to say the prayer and give the sermon. Here is one of those prayers and one of those sermons.

Prayer
God of all worlds and all beings. . . . let us preserve your pure religion; and keep us free from all superstition. If one can insult you by unworthy sacrifices, then abolish those sordid mysteries; if one can dishonor the Divinity with absurd fables, may these fables perish forever. . . . Preserve the purity of our morals, the friendship our brethren have for one another, the benevolence they feel to all men, their obedience to the laws, and their wisdom in private conduct; may they live and die worshiping one God alone. . . .

Commentaries on the Laws of England (1765–1769). He cautiously concluded: "The **liberty of the press** [bold added] is indeed essential to the nature of a free state, but this consists in laying no previous restraints upon publication, not in the freedom from censure for criminal matter when published."

Defending Censorship. As with the parallel battle against religious intolerance, not everyone agreed with the attack on censorship. Conservatives rallied to the

defense of the government, just as they stood by the church. Samuel Johnson, a journalist and lexicographer, is a good example. Johnson was a deeply conservative man who despised writers such as Voltaire and Rousseau and thought it a splendid idea that writers of their sort should be sent to penal colonies. And he stoutly defended censorship: "No member of society has a right to teach any doctrine contrary to what society holds to be true." As the Enlightenment progressed, political writers became bolder in their criticism.

Sermon

My brethren, religion is the secret voice of God which speaks to all men; it should unite, and not divide them all; hence any religion that belongs to only one people is false. . . . May this great God who listens to me; this God who surely cannot have been born of a girl, nor died on the gibbet, nor be eaten in a piece of dough, nor have these books [of the Bible] filled with contradictions, madness and horror; may this God, creator of all the worlds, have pity on that sect of Christians that blasphemes him! May he lead them back to the holy and natural religion. . . . Amen

From Peter Gay, ed., *Deism: An Anthology* (Princeton: Van Nostrand, 1968, pp. 145–158).

Voltaire on Toleration and Persecution from his Philosophical Dictionary *(1769)*

Perhaps Voltaire's most passionate campaign was fought on behalf of the principal of toleration. He denounced the religious prejudice that led to persecution and even torture, as it did for the young freethinker, the Chevalier de la Barre. Voltaire produced a second edition of the *Philosophical Dictionary* in 1769 so that he could include an angry passage about this episode.

Persecution. Who is a persecutor? It is he whose wounded pride and furious fanaticism irritate the prince or the magistrate against innocent men guilty only of the crime of holding different opinions. . . . When the persecution of the Protestants began in France . . . who spied on these unfortunates, who took arms against them with deliberate fury, and who consigned them to the flames to wreak their vengeance on them? . . . Who started these persecutions? Jealous priests, who armed the prejudices of the magistrates. . . . O god of mercy! if any man can resemble the malignant being who is depicted as ceaselessly busy in destroying your works, is it not the persecutor?

Prejudice. A prejudice is an irrational opinion. Thus throughout the world all sorts of opinions are instilled into children before they are able to use judgement. . . . It is out of prejudice that you respect a man dressed in a certain way, who behaves solemnly and talks in the same way. Your parents told you that you should bow to this man. You respect him before you know whether he deserves your respect. You grow in age and knowledge. You perceive that this man is a charlatan eaten up with pride, selfishness, and guile. You despise what you once revered, and prejudice yields to judgement. . . . If your nurse told you that Ceres presides over corn, or that Vishnu and Zaca have several times taken human form, or that Summonocodom came to cut down a forrest, or that Odin is waiting for you in his hall somewhere in Jutland, or that Mohammed or somebody else made a journey into heaven; if then your tutor drove into your brain what your nurse engraved there, you will keep hold of it for life. Should your judgement seek to rise above these prejudices, your neighbors, above all the women, scream impiety and frighten you.

Toleration. What is toleration? It is the prerogative of humanity. We are all steeped in weakness and errors: let us forgive one another's follies, it is the first law of nature. . . . It is clear that every individual who persecutes a man, his brother, because he does not agree with him, is a monster. This is obvious enough. But the government, the magistrates, the princes, how should they behave to those who have a different form of worship? . . . Of all religions, the Christian is undoubtedly that which should instil the greatest toleration, although so far the Christians have been the most intolerant of all men.

From Voltaire, *Philosophical Dictionary,* ed. and trans. Theodore Besterman (New York: Penguin, 1972, pp. 333–334, 343, 387–389).

Question: How do the behavior and treatment of Voltaire and the Chevalier de la Barre differ?

The Critique of Monarchy. The opposition of Louis XV, the French courts, and the Catholic Church did not stop the publication of the *Encyclopédie.* Its essay on "Government" shows how radical the criticism had become. It stated that society exists under a civil constitution that invests rulers with their power, but those rulers are "bound therein by the laws of nature and by the law of reason." Nature and reason both dictated that the "purpose in any form of government [is] the welfare" of civil society. Thus, the bold argument continued: society should expect "to abrogate laws that are flaws in a state" and even to revoke "the allegiance and the jurisdiction in which they are born" by changing the government.

English Political Theory. Such ideas were not new to the Enlightenment. The English political theorist John Locke had made eloquent statements of them in the late seventeenth century, especially in his *Two Treatises of Government* (1690). Voltaire returned to France from his

MONTESQUIEU ON LAW, LIBERTY, AND GOVERNMENT

Baron Charles-Louis de Montesquieu (1689–1755)

The Spirit of the Laws

Law in general is human reason inasmuch as it governs all the inhabitants of the earth: the political and civil laws of each nation ought to be only the particular cases in which human reason is applied. . . .

There are three species of government: republican, monarchical, and despotic. . . . A republican government is that in which the body, or only a part of the people, is possessed of the supreme power; monarchy, that in which a single person governs by fixed and established laws; a despotic government, that in which a single person directs everything by his own will and caprice. . . .

There is no word that admits of more various significations, and has made more varied impressions on the human mind, than that of Liberty. . . . Political liberty does not consist in an unlimited freedom. . . . Liberty is a right of doing whatever the laws permit. . . .

It is necessary from the very nature of things that power should be a check to power. A government may be so constituted, as no man shall be compelled to do things which the law does not oblige him, nor forced to abstain from things which the law permits. . . .

In every government there are three sorts of power: the legislative, the executive in respect to things dependent on the law of nations; and the executive in regard to matters that depend on the civil law. . . . When the legislative and executive powers are united in the same person, or in the same body of magistrates, there can be no liberty.

From Montesquieu, Baron de, *The Spirit of the Laws*, trans. Thomas Nugent (Cincinnati: Clarke, 1873).

Question: It is often asserted that Montesquieu shaped the thinking of the "founding fathers" of the American republic. Does this excerpt suggest that might be true?

the only one of earth that has successfully regulated the power of its kings by resisting them; and which, after repeated efforts, has established that beneficial government under which the Prince . . . is restrained from doing ill."

Montesquieu's *The Spirit of the Laws*. Baron Montesquieu, however, produced the most widely studied political analysis of the era (see Document 20.3). His *Spirit of the Laws* stands as the founding work of modern comparative government. Montesquieu adopted the ancient political observation—used by both Aristotle and Cicero—that three basic forms of government exist: a republic, in which the people or their representatives govern; a mixed monarchy, in which a king reigns with constitutional limits and aristocratic checks upon his power; and a despotism, in which the monarch holds unchecked, absolute power. Montesquieu contended that none of these was a perfect, universal form of government because governments should be appropriate to local conditions. He proposed features of the ideal government, however, such as "liberty," which he carefully defined: "Liberty does not consist in an unlimited freedom. . . . Liberty is a right of doing whatever the laws permit."

This line of reasoning led Montesquieu to state two of the most famous political theories of the eighteenth century: (1) the **theory of the separation of powers** and (2) the **theory of checks and balances.** Montesquieu first argued that the centers of power within the state—the executive, the legislative, and the judicial powers—should not be held by the same person or institution. "When the legislative and executive powers are united in the same person . . . there can be no liberty." He then added that these separated centers of power should check and balance each other: "Power should be a check to power." Such ideas had many dramatic implications for the eighteenth century. They meant, for example, that powerful institutions controlled by the aristocracy, such as the French parlements, must check the potential despotism of a king.

Paine. By the late eighteenth century, the Enlightenment produced even more radical political arguments. Tom Paine, the son of a quiet English Quaker family who became an active participant in both the American and the French revolutions, wrote passionate pamphlets and carefully reasoned multivolume works of political theory. One of his pamphlets, *Common Sense* (1776), attacked monarchical government and advocated a republic—arguments aimed at the British colonies in America. His *Rights of Man* (1791–1792) defended the legislation of the French Revolution, attacked monarchical government, and called on the English to overthrow George III. The government of Britain indicted him for treason.

exile in England (1726–1729) filled with similar willingness to write of his opposition to absolutism. His *Philosophical Letters* (1734) praised the English for their form of government and suggested it as a model for the rest of Europe. "The English nation," he wrote, "is

◄ FIGURE 20.6 *Thomas Paine.* Tom Paine (1737–1809) was one of the most radical political writers of the eighteenth century. He was born in a Quaker family in England, but after a bankruptcy, he emigrated to the American colonies, where he supported himself through his writing. *Common Sense*, a forty-seven-page pamphlet that he published in 1776, called for a revolution against British rule, and Paine supported the American Revolution in several ways, including military service. In 1787, he returned to Europe, in time to observe the French Revolution, which inspired him to write *The Rights of Man* (1791–1792), supporting the revolution and calling on the English to follow the same course and overthrow their monarchy.

Bentham. Jeremy Bentham took Enlightenment political and social thought in yet another direction. Bentham was a lawyer with a comfortable inherited income that allowed him to pursue his writing, which he deeply imbued with Enlightenment attitudes. He saw his writings as "an attempt to extend the experimental method of reasoning from the physical branch (sciences) to the moral." His *Principles of Morals and Legislation* (1789) called for rationalist legislation, favoring the least possible legislation and the least possible government. "Every law," Bentham believed, "is an evil, for every law is an infraction of liberty." This reasoning contained the germ of one of the dominant political gospels of the nineteenth century, **classical liberalism,** although the term most often associated with Bentham's thought is **utilitarianism**—the theory that laws and institutions should be measured by an ethical standard, following the standard of "the greatest happiness for the greatest number."

Rousseau. Perhaps the most radical political theorist of the Enlightenment was Jean-Jacques Rousseau (1712–1778), a Franco-Swiss philosophe who never experienced the comfortable life that Montesquieu, Voltaire, and Bentham knew. Rousseau was the son of a watchmaker and a pastor's daughter. He was born in austere Calvinist Geneva, where stern laws regulated behavior. His mother died in the week of his birth, and his father deserted him as a child, fleeing imprisonment for dueling. Rousseau was raised by his mother's strict religious family and apprenticed to an engraver, but he ran away from Geneva at age 16. During the remainder of his youth, Rousseau wandered as a vagabond. He survived as a beggar, domestic servant, tutor, music teacher, and the kept lover of an older woman. When he settled in Paris in 1744, he had a hatred of the rich but gave no signs of converting this into literary fame. Some of Rousseau's revolutionary anger showed in an early essay, the *Discourse on the Origin of Inequality* (1755) (see *Jean-Jacques Rousseau [1712–1778]*). His concern was not "natural" inequality among individuals, but "moral or political inequality, because it depends on . . . the consent of mankind." The discourse went on to demand nothing less than the complete reorganization of society to eliminate inequalities based on factors such as rank or race. Before the discourse was finished, Rousseau attacked the concept of private property, which he considered "the worst of our institutions" (see *Jean-Jacques Rousseau [1712–1778]*).

The Social Contract. The same passion characterized Rousseau's more complex masterpiece, *The Social Contract* (1762), one of the founding works of modern political thought (see *Jean-Jacques Rousseau [1712–1778]*). It opened with one of the most famous sentences of the Enlightenment: "Man is born free, but is everywhere in chains." The great human emancipation that Rousseau desired led him to propose a right of revolution—a right to "shake off the yoke" of oppressive government—and to suggest an ideal government that mixed democracy and authoritarianism. Rousseau, the enemy of kings, admired democracy and stimulated its growth in Europe with sentences such as: "No man has a natural authority over his fellow men." This reasoning led Rousseau to the right to resist forced obedience to authority: "As soon as [a people] can throw off its yoke, and does throw it off, it does better; for a people may certainly use, for the recovery of their liberty, the same right that was employed to deprive them of it." Rousseau also believed, however, that democracy would only work with "a people who were Gods." He criticized democracy because "it is contrary to the natural order" that a minority should always be governed by a majority. Thus, he introduced the concept of an abstract force, called **"the general will,"** which would compel all members of society to desire the common good. Paradoxically, Rousseau's ideas thus encouraged both a democratic egalitarian attack on the Old Regime and a form of absolutism, the very concept of which had led to the initial Enlightened critiques of government.

The Spread of Rationalism

The Enlightenment had a tremendous impact on Western civilization because it spread skepticism and rationalism to many fields of human activity. Even the study of history felt the influence of these doctrines. Gibbon's *The Decline and Fall of the Roman Empire*, for example, showed the advantages of a reasoned study of the sources. The Neapolitan Enlightenment offered

The Culture of Old Regime Europe **497**

JEAN-JACQUES ROUSSEAU (1712–1778)

Jean-Jacques Rousseau, 1712–1778 (after Ramsay)

Rousseau's radicalism, and his impact on revolutionary history, can be seen in these two brief excerpts from his writing—the first excerpt attacks the concept of private property and the second states a right of revolution. His deist writings got Rousseau into more trouble than his political radicalism did; the Parlement of Paris ordered his arrest for his attack on religion, not for the right of revolution. (He fled to avoid arrest, only to see Geneva censor his works too. For the last decade of his life, Rousseau moved frequently to avoid legal harassment.)

Jean-Jacques Rousseau's Discourse on the Origin of Inequality

The first man who, after fencing in a piece of ground, took it into his head to say: This is mine, and found people simple enough to believe him, was the true founder of civil society. How many crimes, wars, murders, how many miseries and horrors would not have been spared the human race by him who, pulling up the stakes or filling in the ditch, had cried out to his fellow men: Take care not to listen to this impostor; you are lost if you forget that the fruits belong to all and the earth to none.

Jean-Jacques Rousseau's The Social Contract

Book One
I wish to inquire whether, taking men as they are and laws as they can be, it is possible to establish some legitimate and certain rule of administration in civil affairs. . . .

Subject of this First Book
Man is born free but everywhere he is in chains. One believes himself the master of others, and yet he is a greater slave than they. How has this change come about? What can render it legitimate? I believe that I can settle this question.

If I considered only force and the results that proceed from, I should say that so long as a People is compelled to obey and does obey, it does well; but that, so soon as it can shake off the yoke and does shake it off, it does better; for, recovering their freedom by virtue of the same right by which it was taken away, either they are justified in resuming it, or there was no justification for depriving them of it . . .

From Rousseau, Jean-Jacques. *The Social Contract, or Principles of Political Right* (London, J.M. Dent, 1913).

Question: What factors might explain the fact that Rousseau was not imprisoned for his political ideas, but faced arrest for less provocative religious ideas?

---

similar lessons in history. Giambattista Vico's *Principles of a New Science* (1725) urged scientific standards: scholars should seek "the universal and eternal principles (such as every science must have)." Another Neapolitan historian, Pietro Giannone, suggested that this meant historians must write "histories of the kingdom" that contained more than the "lives of the kings." So Giannone began his masterwork with the words, "The history of the Kingdom of Naples which I am undertaking will not deafen readers' ears with the clash of arms and the din of battle. . . . This is to be a civic history."

Beccaria. Another leader of the Enlightenment in Italy, Cesare Beccaria, applied the scientific standards of careful observation and reasoning to another human activity, the punishment of crimes. Beccaria, a wealthy Milanese noble, studied prison conditions in Milan, and he was horrified by the conditions he discovered: criminal charges were brought in secret, the accused had few opportunities to offer a defense and produce evidence, trials held before a jury were rare, **torture** was used both to determine guilt and to punish it, barbarous physical punishments such as branding and mutilation were commonplace, and people were executed for minor crimes. Beccaria's *Treatise on Crimes and Punishment* (1764) marked the beginning of modern criminology, and it led to more humane standards in European civilization. His argument was simple: "It is better to prevent crimes than to punish them" (see Document 20.4). Therefore, he said, "Every punishment that does not arise from absolute necessity is tyrannical." Beccaria accepted preventive punishments—to stop a criminal from committing the same act again or to inhibit someone else from committing that crime—but he argued forcefully against any form of torture. However, he found it "a cruelty consecrated by custom in most nations."

The Enlightenment and the Status of Women.

The Enlightenment occupies a complex place in the history of women. On one hand, women remained in an utterly unequal position before the law, lacking many of the most basic of human rights, and few esteemed philosophes challenged this injustice. Indeed, some of the most noted (and even most radical) philosophes helped perpetuate the inequality. Yet simultaneously, one of the most far-reaching Enlightenment criticisms of the human condition focused on the inequality of women. The word **feminism** did not yet exist—it was a late-nineteenth-century coinage—and no organized campaigns for women's rights had been established. But several philosophes shaped later developments by challenging accepted attitudes about the inferiority of women and thus laid the basis of modern equality.

A few prominent philosophes, such as Condorcet and Holbach, championed the equality of women. In 1787, Condorcet published an essay which stated the case for the natural equality of women: "The facts prove that men have or believe they have interests that are very different from those women, because everywhere they have made oppressive laws against them, or at the least have established a great inequality between the two sexes." Condorcet even called for the right of women to vote and hold office—more than 150 years before France granted those rights. Others writers, such as Montesquieu and Diderot, discussed the problems of women's status with sympathy yet concluded that women were destined for what has been called "enlightened domesticity"—a life of improved conditions but in the home.

Rousseau and Antifeminism.

The Enlightenment also produced important arguments against the equal rights of women, arguments which contributed to the unequal treatment of women for more than a century. Rousseau published two influential books on education: *The New Héloise* (1761) and *Emile* (1762). He asserted that women lacked the intellectual ability for higher education, so he argued that the education of women should teach the skills needed to serve men: "The search for abstract and speculative truths, principles, axioms in the sciences, and everything that tends to generalize ideas is not within the compass of women: all their studies must deal with the practical. Their job is to apply the principles that men discover." Clearly, the humanitarianism of the Enlightenment, so vigorously stated in the combat for religious tolerance and against censorship, did not extend to the full equality of women.

Sophia.

A few educated women, despite lacking the advantages of their famous colleagues, began to publish reasoned arguments about the condition of the sexes. It is indicative of the status of women that one of the most forceful works, an English pamphlet titled *Woman Not*

DOCUMENT 20.4

BECCARIA ON PENAL REFORM

Cesare Beccaria (1738–1794) was a Milanese nobleman and a leader of the Italian Enlightenment. His *Tratto dei Delitti e delle Pene* (*Treatise on Crime and Punishment,* 1764), from which the following excerpt is taken, advocated many fundamental reforms such as the abolition of both torture and capital punishment.

Of the Right to Punish. *Every act of authority of one man over another, for which there is not an absolute necessity, is tyrannical. It is upon this that the sovereign's right to punish crimes is founded; that is, upon the necessity of defending the public liberty, entrusted to his care, from the usurpation of individuals. . . .*

Of the Intent of Punishments*. . . . [I]t is evident that the intent of punishments is not to torment a sensible being, nor to undo a crime already committed. Is it possible that torments and useless cruelty, the instrument of furious fanaticism or the impotency of tyrants, can be authorized by a political body? Can the groans of a tortured wretch recall the time past or reverse the crime he has committed?*

The end of punishment, therefore, is no other than to prevent the criminal from doing further injury to society and to prevent others from committing the same offense. . . .

Of Torture. *The torture of a criminal during his trial is a cruelty consecrated by custom in most nations.*

It is used with the intent of either making him confess his crime, or explaining some contradictions, or discovering his accomplices, or for some kind of metaphysical and incomprehensive purgation of infamy. . . . The very means employed to distinguish the innocent from the guilty will most effectually destroy all difference between them.

From Beccaria, Cesare, *An Essay on Crimes and Punishments* (London: J. Almon, 1785).

Question: Is Beccaria a convincing opponent of torture?

Inferior to Man, was published anonymously in 1739 by an author known only as "Sophia, A Person of Quality" (see Document 20.5). "Everyone who has but a degree of understanding above the idiot," Sophia wrote, can "observe the universal prevalence of prejudice and custom in the minds of Men." Sophia did not mince words: men exercised a "tyrannical usurpation of authority" over women.

Mary Wollstonecraft.

The most influential advocate of the equality of the sexes, and one of the most important founders of feminist thought, was another Englishwoman—Mary Wollstonecraft. Wollstonecraft, the daughter of an alcoholic and abusive father, learned to

"SOPHIA" ON WOMEN'S EQUALITY WITH MEN

"Sophia, A Person of Quality" was the pseudonym of an unknown author who anonymously published a forceful pamphlet on the equality of women in 1739. This work, *Woman Not Inferior to Man*, or "A Short and Modest Vindication of the Natural Right of the Fair Sex to a Perfect Equality of Power, Dignity, and Esteem with Men," employed many of the basic concepts of the Enlightenment, as the following excerpt shows.

If a celebrated Author had not already told, that there is nothing in nature so much to be wonder'd at as THAT WE WONDER AT ALL; it must appear to every one, who has but a degree of understanding above the idiot, a matter of the greatest surprize, [sic] to observe the universal prevalence of prejudice and custom in the minds of the Men. One might naturally expect to see those lordly creatures, as they modestly stile themselves, everywhere jealous of superiority, and watchful to maintain it. Instead of which, if we except the tyrannical usurpation of authority they exert over us Women, we shall find them industrious in nothing but courting the meanest servitude. Was their ambition laudable and just, it would be consistent in itself, and this consistency would render them alike imperious in every circumstance, where authority is requisite and justifiable: And if their brutal strength of body entitled them to lord it over our nicer frame, the superiority of reason to passion, might suffice to make them blush to submit that reason to passion, prejudice, and groundless custom. If this haughty sex would have us believe they have a natural right of superiority over us, why do not they prove their charter from nature, by making use of reason. . . .

What I have hitherto said, has not been with an intention to stir up any of my own sex to revolt against the Men, or to invert the present order of things, with regard to government and authority. No, let them stand as they are: I only mean to show my sex, that they are not so despicable as the Men would have them believe themselves.

Question: Is Sophia's argument built on similar principles to those used by other writers of the Enlightenment?

support herself despite having only a limited education. She and her sister directed a school near London, and this led Wollstonecraft to begin writing texts and tracts on education. Success introduced her to literary circles in London, where she met radical writers who encouraged her to continue her writing. She practiced some of her radical ideas in her own life, living with a man and having a child outside marriage. Wollstonecraft found only limited happiness, however, and once attempted to drown herself in the Thames River.

From these poignant experiences, Mary Wollstonecraft found the materials for her masterwork, *A Vindication of the Rights of Woman* (1792). (See Chapter 24, Document 24.5.) She, too, constructed her argument for women in the language of the Enlightenment. "In what," she asked, does human "pre-eminence over the brute creation consist? The answer is clear . . . in Reason." Because women possessed reason as well as men, they were equally pre-eminent and should be treated that way: "[I]f they be really capable of acting like rational creatures, let them not be treated like slaves." And she proclaimed her own, unequivocal stand, unwilling to submit to domination by men: "I love man as my fellow; but his scepter, real or usurped, extends not to me, unless the reason of an individual demands my homage; and even then the submission is to reason, and to not to man."

CONCLUSION

The culture of the eighteenth century has been one of the most widely admired and praised ornaments of European civilization. Traditionalists have been drawn to the last great age of the European aristocracy, the last period of universal monarchy, and the last epoch in which established churches directed most of the population. They have been fascinated by the glittering opulence of baroque culture and dazzled by spectacular palaces, stately homes, and opulent rococo churches. This was the last flowering of the hierarchical world of the old elites, and its richness will long be admired.

But the eighteenth century is more often remembered as the age of a new elite, of the educated and articulate philosophes. The members of this elite often came from the old centers of privilege (Montesquieu was a baron and Condorcet, a marquis), but many influential voices had modest origins (Rousseau was a runaway apprentice and Wollstonecraft, a self-supporting teacher). Historians have argued about the influence of this new elite. How much influence did their skepticism and rationalism actually have? Their progressive ideas challenged the Old Regime in the most fundamental ways, but did this challenge produce change? The century would end with the vast upheaval of the French Revolution, in which aristocracy, clergy, and royalty all lost their historic roles in European society. But historians have never agreed whether the old elites had failed so badly that they precipitated the revolution, or whether the new elites had stimulated revolution with their criticisms. Does revolution originate in the ideas of cultural and intellectual history? In the problems and failures of political and military history? Or in the troubles seen in social history and economic crises?

Review Questions

• What was the difference between high culture and popular culture?

- What were the strengths and weaknesses of Christianity in eighteenth-century Europe?
- How would you explain the basic concepts of the Enlightenment: skepticism, natural law, reason, and progress?
- What was the Enlightenment critique of Christianity?
- What was the Enlightenment critique of monarchy?

For Further Study

Readings

Burke, Peter, *Popular Culture in Early Modern Europe* (New York: Harper, 1978). Covers a broader period than just the eighteenth century and the Enlightenment (c. 1500–1800). Looks at the nature, forms, and transmission of popular culture.

Cragg, Gerald, *The Church and the Age of Reason, 1648–1789,* revised edition (London: Penguin, 1970). A good, brief study of Christianity in Europe during the age of skepticism and the critique of the Enlightenment.

Darnton, Robert, *The Great Cat Massacre* (New York: Basic Books, 1984). A provocative look at cultural history across the social classes. Considers the peasantry through Mother Goose and folktales and workers through the title story of the cat massacre before turning to topics such as the *Encyclopédie* and Rousseau.

Gay, Peter, *The Enlightenment: An Interpretation,* 2 vols. (New York: Norton, 1977). The best-known history of the Enlightenment. It discusses the links between the philosophes and general culture and the role of the Enlightenment in creating the modern world.

Reill, Peter H., and Wilson, Ellen J., eds., *Encyclopedia of the Enlightenment* (New York: Facts on File, 1996). An excellent reference and source of detailed information on individuals, institutions, and ideas of the Enlightenment prepared by two scholars at UCLA.

InfoTrac College Edition

For additional reading, go to your online research library at *http://infotrac.thomsonlearning.com.*
Using Key Terms, enter the search term:
Enlightenment

Using the Subject Guide, enter the search terms:
Voltaire   *Rousseau, Jean-Jacques*
Wollstonecraft, Mary

Web Sites

http://www.wsu.edu/dee/ENLIGHT/ENLIGHT.HTM
A valuable site created by the World Civilizations program at Washington State University. It includes a good glossary, sections on topics such as *philosophes* and Rousseau, and links to other sites.

http://www.newadvent.org/cathen This site offers the entire 1908 edition of the Catholic Encyclopedia, which provides the perspective of the church (which differs from many histories) on some of the issues of the Enlightenment, such as entries on Deism, the Inquisition, Reason, Toleration, and Rousseau's *Social Contract.*

Visit the Western Civilization Companion Web Site for resources specific to this textbook:
http://history.wadsworth.com/hause02/

The CD in the back of this book and the Western Civilization Resource Center at *http://history. wadsworth.com/western/* offer a variety of tools to help you succeed in this course, including access to quizzes; images; documents; interactive simulations, maps, and timelines; movie explorations; and a wealth of other sources.

EUROPEAN CULTURE IN THE EIGHTEENTH CENTURY

1700	1710	1720	1730	1740	1750	1760	1770	1780	1790	1800	1810

THE ENLIGHTENMENT IN FRANCE

L'Encyclopédie Published in France

1721: Montesquieu's *Persian Letters* Satirizes French Institutions
1725: Mme de Sévigné's Posthumous *Letters* Depict the Life of the Aristocracy
1733: Voltaire's *Letters Concerning the English* Popularizes Newton
1734: Mme de Lambert's *Advice of Mother* Calls for Education of Women
1738: Voltaire's *Elements of the Philosophy of Newton*
1748: Montesquieu's *Spirit of the Laws* on Governments
1751: Diderot and d'Alembert Publish vol. 1 of *L'Encyclopédie*
1755: Rousseau's *Discourse on the Origin of Inequality*
1758: Helvétius's *De l'esprit* Defends "Self-Interest"
1759: Voltaire's *Candide* Satirizes Ideas and Institutions
1762: Rousseau's *Social Contract* on Government
1763: Voltaire's *Treatise on Tolerance* Criticizes Religions
1763: Rousseau's *Emile* Urges "Natural" Education
1770: d'Holbach's *System of Nature* Attacks Religion
1795: Condorcet's *Progress of the Human Spirit*

THE ENLIGHTENMENT AROUND EUROPE

1729: Newton's *Principia* Translated from Latin into English
1734: Alexander Pope's *Essay on Man*
1736: Bishop Butler's *Analogy of Religion* Attacks Deism
1737: Lady Montagu's *The Nonsense of Common Sense*
1739: Hume's *Treatise of Human Nature* States "Utilitarian" Principles
1739: Sophia's *Woman Not Inferior to Man*
1748: Hume's *Concerning Human Understanding* Calls for Skepticism
1755: Dr. Johnson Publishes First Comprehensive English Dictionary
1771: First Edition of *Encyclopedia Britannica*
1776: Gibbon's *Decline and Fall of the Roman Empire*
1776: Adam Smith's *Wealth of Nations*
1777: Howard's *State of Prisons* Shows Bad Conditions
1792: Wollstonecraft's *Vindication of the Rights of Woman*
1798: Malthus's *Essay on the Principle of Population*

1710: Leibnitz's *Théodicée* Proclaims This "The Best of All Possible Worlds"
1741: Süssmilch's *The Divine Order* Pioneers Field of Statistics
1779: Lessing's *Nathan the Wise* on Toleration
1781: Kant's *Critique of Pure Reason*
1781: Mendelssohn's *Amelioration of the Condition of the Jews*
1784: Kant's "What Is Enlightenment?"
1725: Vico's *Principles of a New Science* Proposes a "Science of Society"

1764: Beccaria's *Treatise on Crimes and Punishments* Urges Legal and Penal Reforms
1781: Pestalozzi's *Leonard and Gertrude* Advocates Reform of Education

Chapter 21

THE FRENCH REVOLUTION AND NAPOLEON, 1789–1815

FOCUS QUESTIONS

- What were the primary causes of the French Revolution?
- What were the primary results of the French Revolution?
- Why did France go to war with the rest of Europe?
- Why did France experience the Reign of Terror?
- How did Napoleon Bonaparte acquire power?
- What effects did Napoleon's domestic policies have on France and Europe?

On Monday morning, January 21, 1793, citizen Louis Capet, formerly known as King Louis XVI of France, was taken for a final coach ride from imprisonment in the Temple and past thousands of soldiers controlling crowds in the snow-packed streets of Paris. In the Place de la Révolution, just outside the gardens of his former Tuileries Palace, Louis, stiff and overweight at age 38, climbed the steep steps of a scaffold with his hands tied behind his back. His neck was too fat to fit properly into the wooden groove at the base of the guillotine, so the descending blade made a mess of his neck and jaw and created a large amount of blood. At 10:22 AM, an assistant executioner held up the dripping head for the crowd to see, and people rushed forward to dip handkerchiefs into the blood. The French had abolished monarchy.

Chapter 21 surveys the French Revolution (1789–1799) and the Napoleonic regime that followed (1799–1815). In an extraordinary upheaval that many people remembered for its Reign of Terror (1793–1794), Louis XVI was only one of millions of victims. The French Revolution is a story of great violence and great achievements. It begins with the Old Regime's economic and social problems that led to a series of revolutionary governments that abolished the monarchy, the aristocracy, and the established church. A revolutionary bill of rights and an idealistic constitution promised an age of liberty and equality—and the revolutionary government fulfilled much of this promise by abolishing slavery and emancipating religious minorities. But the revolution also produced public executions and dictatorial governments. Ultimately, before the new French republic had reached its tenth anniversary, many of its people cheered a soldier, Napoleon Bonaparte, who destroyed it, created an authoritarian regime, and led France into a decade and a half of war. One of the best known passages in English literature, the opening of Charles Dickens's *A Tale of Two Cities* (1859), summarizes the duality of the revolutionary age: "It was the best of times, it was the worst of times . . . it was the spring of hope, it was the winter of despair."

THE ORIGINS OF THE FRENCH REVOLUTION

Economic Crisis. The French Revolution arose out of an intractable economic crisis and the inability of the government to resolve it. King Louis XVI could neither raise taxes nor pay his bills. A recession and falling prices hurt farmers and workers. Manufacturing suffered in competition with the English, especially in the textile industry. Unemployment reached dangerous levels, exceeding 80,000 in Paris in December 1788 (approximately one-third of the adult workforce), while poor harvests in 1787–1788 produced shortages of wheat, which rose in price to record levels by mid-1789. The price of bread in Paris, normally eight or nine *sous* for a 4-pound loaf, hit 14.5 sous. Such circumstances often caused rioting in preindustrial Europe.

Riots and the Crowd. Ominous signs were evident in 1788–1789 that France was a volatile society. Bread riots occurred in many districts. Some villages refused to ship their grain. In towns, crowds, often led by women, attacked granaries, mills, and bakeries. The crowds typically forced sales at **"the just price"** (an old Christian idea); in Rouen, for example, they cut the price of bread in half. Another example of urban unrest, the Réveillon riots, occurred at Paris in April 1789. Workers at the Réveillon wallpaper factory protested a pay cut by burning the owner in effigy and pillaging his home and factory; more than 200 rioters were killed by royal troops. Historians still debate how the crisis of the late 1780s became a revolution, arguing about the relative importance of political, economic, and cultural factors. (For example, to what extent did the ideas of the Enlightenment precipitate a revolution, and to what extent did revolution just make eighteenth-century critics famous?)

Four Overlapping Revolutions. Historians generally agree that such troubles became a revolution when four overlapping movements converged: (1) An aristocratic revolution had been building for many years, as aristocrats used institutions such as the parlements to thwart the king, especially on tax reform. This revolution forced Louis XVI to hold elections for the Estates-General in 1789. (2) A bourgeois revolution challenged the aristocratic leadership of the reform movement and sought to limit aristocratic control of high government offices. (3) A peasant revolution went beyond disturbances over grain and became an armed uprising against the remnants of feudalism. This rebellion connected the common people to the reformers and made it extremely difficult for Louis XVI to act against them.

FIGURE 21.1 *Poor Harvests and the Monarchy.* Many problems confronted Louis XVI in the late 1780s. One of the most urgent was a succession of poor harvests in a country where many people lived by a meager subsistence diet in normal times and where food riots had become a common occurrence in times of scarcity. In this sympathetic image, the king is shown dispensing charity to the grateful poor in the winter of 1788–1789.

FIGURE 21.2 *The Three Estates.* The late eighteenth century was a great age of political cartooning, and the cartoons were often very pointed. In this French cartoon from 1789, titled "The Awakening of the Third Estate," representatives of the first estate (the clergy) and the second estate (the aristocracy) recoil in shock as the representative of the third estate (the other 97 percent of the population) stirs to activity. The third estate has removed the iron shackles placed upon it and prepares to stand up but first reaches for a weapon. Note the ominous activity in the background: the crowd tears down the Bastille and parades two heads at the top of pikes.

(4) An urban working-class revolution turned the fury of the crowd to large political targets. The revolution of the crowd pressed reformers to extend the revolution.

THE ESTATES-GENERAL AND THE BEGINNING OF THE REVOLUTION (1789)

Elections for the Estates-General. Faced with bankruptcy, Louis XVI promised his critics in November 1787 that he would hold elections for the Estates-General (the first since 1614) within 5 years. Under continuing pressure, Louis finally agreed that representatives from each of the three **estates** (the clergy, the aristocracy, and all others) that comprised the population of France (see Chapter 17) could assemble in May 1789. His decision launched the first modern political debate in French history. Should the third estate (97 percent of the population) have more deputies than the others? Should the three estates meet together or separately? What issues should the Estates-General discuss? Such questions produced a flood of political pamphlets. The most famous of these was written by a provincial priest, the Abbé Emmanuel Sieyès, who defended the third estate in a work entitled *What Is the Third Estate?* (see Document 21.1). Sieyès's answer was "Everything!" The aristocracy, he added, was like "some horrible disease eating the living flesh of some unfortunate man."

The Cahiers. Louis XVI agreed to double the representation of the third estate, but he insisted on preserving traditions—the estates would meet separately. He permitted freedom of the press for the elections and asked that each district submit statements of their grievances (*cahiers des doléances;* see Table 21.1). Most **cahiers** condemned absolutism and praised constitutional monarchy; many pledged loyalty to Louis XVI, but none acknowledged his "divine right." They called for a French parliament to control taxation and legislation. The cahiers attacked hated aspects of the Old Regime (such as the arbitrary royal power of arrest by *lettres de cachet*) and demanded new freedoms (such as freedom of the press). Each cahier also expressed the interests of the estate that produced it. The first estate, for example, wanted clerical control of education, denounced immorality in the press, and objected to the toleration of Protestantism.

The National Assembly. The Estates-General met in Versailles, a short walk from the royal palace. It opened with a royal speech asking for new taxes. The deputies of the third estate, chiefly lawyers, rejected holding such discussions in separate meetings, and they asked other deputies to join them in legislating reforms. Nine priests agreed, and the combined group pro-

DOCUMENT 21.1

THE ABBÉ SIEYÈS'S *WHAT IS THE THIRD ESTATE?* (1789)

Emmanuel Joseph Sieyès (1748–1836), remembered as the Abbé Sieyès, was a Catholic priest who became a prominent leader of the French Revolution. On the eve of the revolution, he was a vicar in the cathedral town of Chartres, where he sympathized with the reform movement. He was a little known figure in 1789, when he published *What Is the Third Estate?* The pamphlet was so impressive that he was soon offered the post of archbishop of Paris. He served several regimes during the revolutionary era, including Napoleon's, where he was made a count.

The plan of this essay is fairly simple. We have three questions to ask:

1. *What is the Third Estate? Everything.*
2. *What has it been thus far in the political order? Nothing.*
3. *What does it demand? To become something. . . .*

It is enough at this point to have made it plain that the pretended usefulness of a privileged order for public service is only vain imagination; that without it, all that is tiresome in such service is done by the Third; that without it, the higher positions would be infinitely better filled; that they should naturally be the prize and reward for talent and recognizable services; and that if the privileged have succeeded in usurping all the lucrative and honorific posts, it is both an injustice shocking to the majority of citizens and a betrayal of the public interest.

Who, then, would dare to say that the Third Estate does not contain everything needed to form a complete nation? It is like a strong, robust man, one of whose arms is still enchained. If the privileged order were removed, the nation would not be something less, but something more. What would it be without the privileged order? Everything, but an everything free and flourishing. Nothing can function without it; everything would function infinitely better without the others. . . .

What is a nation? A body of associates living under a common law and represented by the same legislature. . . . Is it not certain that the noble order has privileges, exemptions, even rights distinct from the rights of the great body of citizens? Thereby it is apart from the common order. . . . The Third therefore includes everything that belongs to the nation; and everything not of the Third cannot be regarded as being of the nation. What is the Third? Everything.

Question: This document is often considered one of the founding writings of the doctrine of nationalism. Why?

claimed itself the French National Assembly. A political revolution had begun. The deputies were locked out of their meeting hall, so they assembled at a nearby indoor tennis court and swore not to adjourn without preparing a constitution. Within a few days, 612 of 621

TABLE 21.1 ISSUES DISCUSSED IN THE CAHIERS

If one judges by the *cahiers des doléances* (kye'-yay deh doh-lay-ahnss'), the issues that most concerned the French on the eve of the revolution were, first, taxation and, second, representative government. One scholarly study has analyzed the cahiers and found that the most widely discussed subjects were those presented in this table. Note the comparative degree of concern with taxation and electoral estates. Note also that each estate had self-interests, but one seems more concerned with human rights.

Following are the issues discussed in the cahiers in the order of their importance to each estate.

Question: On what concerns do the estates most agree?

CAHIERS FROM CHURCH PARISHES	CAHIERS FROM THE NOBILITY	CAHIERS FROM THE THIRD ESTATE
1. Taxation in general	1. Regular meeting of Estates-General	1. Taxation in general
2. Salt tax *(gabelle)*	2. Taxation in general	2. Provincial Estates
3. Tax on alcohol	3. Veto on taxation for Estates-General	3. Regular meeting of Estates
4. Salt monopoly	4. Provincial Estates	4. Vote by head at Estates
5. Tax on legal acts	5. Censorship	5. Veto on taxation for Estates
6. Compulsory road work	6. Personal liberties	6. Customs duties
7. Provincial Estates	7. Allocation of taxes	7. Tax on legal acts
8. Direct tax *(taille)*	8. Government pensions	8. (tie) Government pensions
9. Praise of Louis XVI	9. *Lettres de cachet*	8. (tie) Censorship
10. Tax advantages of clergy	10. Customs duties	10. Careers in military
16. Regional and local roads	12. Private property	14. Weights and measures
26. The tithe	18. Government debt	15. Personal liberties
38. The poor	23. Constitution	36. Private property
39. Weights and measures	29. Tax advantages of nobility	42. Criminal penalties
44. Payments to clergy	35. Ennoblement through office	46. Taxes on manufacture

Adapted from Markoff, John, *The Abolition of Feudalism: Peasants, Lords, and Legislators in the French Revolution* (University Park, PA: Pennsylvania State University Press, 1996, pp. 30–32).

---

deputies of the third estate had signed the Tennis Court Oath; 149 priests and a few nobles joined them.

The king naturally resisted these events. He did not panic because he had learned from dealing with the parlements that he could suspend their business, transfer the meeting to a distant province, or even arrest troublesome leaders. Thus, he simply declared the decisions of the third estate illegal. He offered the hope of a constitution, with important reservations. "The King wills," he said, "that the traditional distinctions between the three orders of the state should be preserved in its entirety." Deputies of the defiant third estate chose to continue the National Assembly. As one liberal deputy, the Count de Mirabeau, said, "We shall not leave our places except by the power of bayonet." Louis considered using the army, but his ability to use French troops against the National Assembly was uncertain. Few were stationed in Versailles, and their loyalty was dubious. One regiment had refused to fire on demonstrators, and another had vowed not to act against the third estate. So Louis called in German and Swiss reinforcements from the provinces (foreigners constituted

25 percent of his army). He still felt confident enough to do nothing when the National Assembly discussed a constitution. The revolution, however, quickly passed beyond his ability to control it.

The Revolutionary Crowd: The Bastille and the Great Fear

The political revolution begun by the aristocracy and expanded by the deputies of the third estate changed in July 1789, driven by crowds of commoners in both town and country. **The revolutionary crowd** ("the mob" to hostile observers) has been the subject of historical controversy. Some authors depict the crowds as purely destructive and conclude that they were comprised of criminals, vagabonds, and the unemployed. Edmund Burke, the most eloquent enemy of the revolution, called the crowd "a band of cruel ruffians and assassins." Recent study, however, has shown that the revolutionary crowds were composed of wage earners, journeymen, artisans, and shopkeepers (see Table

FIGURE 21.3 *Tennis Court Oath.* One of the decisive moments at the beginning of the French revolution came on June 20, 1789, when the representatives of the third estate, who had proclaimed that they were a "national assembly," arrived for their meeting and found themselves locked out of their meeting hall by orders of the king. The representatives are seen here learning of the royal order. Instead of giving up, as the rainy day might have encouraged, they found a nearby indoor tennis court and there took the famous "tennis court oath" not to disband until they had drafted a constitution.

21.2). Of the people arrested during the Réveillon riots, for example, 19 percent came from the building trades (chiefly masons), 13 percent from transportation workers (chiefly dock workers), and 12 percent from the clothing trades (chiefly cobblers).

The Crowd in July 1789. The Parisian crowd changed the revolution in July 1789. The price of bread, fear of foreign troops, concern that the National Assembly would be closed, and the agitation of revolutionary orators (notably Camille Desmoulins, a 29-year-old radical lawyer) created a volatile situation. On July 11, the king dismissed his most popular advisor, Jacques Necker, alarming moderates. Parisians burned the customs gates to the city as a protest against the tariffs that they blamed for the high price of bread and wine. The next day, German soldiers fired on a crowd, and a riot followed. On the morning of July 14, 8,000 people attacked a royal barracks and took 32,000 muskets and 12 artillery pieces. They used those arms later that day in the most famous act of the revolutionary crowd—the attack on the **Bastille.**

The Crowd Storms the Bastille. The Bastille was a formidable fortress, towering more than 100 feet (38 meters) over eastern Paris. It was less important for the seven prisoners it held than as a symbol of despotism, in which such famous prisoners as Voltaire had been confined. (Studies have found that 10 percent of all French writers of the eighteenth century were locked up in the Bastille at least once.) Perhaps more important, it held 5 tons of gunpowder, defended by only eighty-two French soldiers and thirty-two Swiss. During a 4-hour battle on July 14 (which became a French national holiday), one soldier and ninety-eight civilians were killed. The victorious crowd, which included many cabinetmakers and cobblers but no lawyers (see Table 21.2), finished the day with an act that led to their image as a blood-thirsty mob: the brutal murder of the governor of the Bastille. Louis XVI spent the day hunting; his diary entry for July 14 read: "Nothing." The next day, stunned by the news from Paris, he went to the National Assembly and promised to withdraw the provincial troops.

The Great Fear. Neither the king nor the National Assembly had adjusted to the insurrection in Paris when similar events occurred in rural France. The rural disturbances of July and August 1789, known as the **Great Fear,** were a response to rumors. Some rumors held that the king wished to liberate the peasantry but expected them to take the lead. Worse rumors held that aristocrats, frustrated by events in Versailles, were preparing some terrible revenge or that armies of vagrants (whose numbers were high) were to be set loose on the peasantry. Peasants armed themselves in self-defense. When brigands did not appear, the frightened population turned their anxiety on the chateaux of their seigneurs. Some aristocrats were forced to renounce their feudal rights. In other places, peasants burned the records of the feudal dues that they owed, and sometimes the chateau as well.

THE LEGISLATIVE REVOLUTION OF THE NATIONAL ASSEMBLY (1789–1791)

The actions of the Parisian crowd and the peasantry had two important effects on the National Assembly (also called the Constituent Assembly because it was writing a constitution). First, they strengthened the assembly because the king could not suppress it without fear of violence. Second, the rebellions encouraged the deputies to extend the revolution.

The Night of August 4. A legislative revolution began on "the night of August 4." Debates on the Great Fear led to a remarkable scene: some aristocrats proposed ending their own privileges. Without preparation or committee studies, the deputies voted a series

TABLES 21.2 SOCIAL COMPOSITION OF REVOLUTIONARY GROUPS*†

Percentage of Workers in Each Trade Who Were Arrested at the Bastille (1789)

TRADE	PERCENTAGE
Furniture	17.1
Building	14.2
Clothing	10.1
Metal	10.1
Transport	6.8
Food	5.3
Other	36.4

Percentage of Emigrés by Social Groups (1789–1799)

SOCIAL GROUP	PERCENTAGE
Third estate	58.0
Peasantry	19.4
Workers	14.3
Clergy	25.2
Nobility	16.8

*Note: Total percentage may exceed 100 because of rounding.

†Source: Jones, Colin, ed., *The Longman Companion to the French Revolution* (London: Longman, 1988, pp. 120, 168, 186, 199); and Rudé, George, *The Crowd in the French Revolution* (Oxford: Oxford University Press, 1959, pp. 246–248).

Percentage of Deputies in the Convention by Profession (1792–1795)

PROFESSION	PERCENTAGE
Lawyers	47.7
Businessmen	8.9
Clergy	7.3
Civil servants	6.8
Medicine	6.1
Farmers	5.1
Other	18.1

Percentage of the Membership in the Jacobin Clubs by Profession (1793–1795)

PROFESSION	PERCENTAGE
Shopkeepers	45.0
Farmers	9.6
Businessmen	8.2
Lawyers	6.8
Other professions	6.9
Civil servants	6.7
Other	16.8

Question: What conclusions can be drawn from the variations in social groups represented in these data?

---

of decrees that began with: "The National Assembly completely abolishes the feudal regime." The night of August 4 marked the end of feudal servitude and taxes, the feudal rights of the aristocracy (such as hunting on peasant farmland), the manorial courts of aristocratic justice, "tithes of every description" owed to the Catholic Church, and the sale of public offices, which were opened to all citizens.

The Rights of Man. Three weeks later, the National Assembly adopted another historic document, a French bill of rights named the Declaration of the Rights of Man (see Document 21.2). It promised freedom of religion, freedom of speech, freedom of the press, due process of law, and the prohibition of cruel and unusual punishment. It did not grant equal rights to religious minorities (Protestants received this in December 1789; Jews had to wait until September 1791), freedom for the black slaves in French colonies (adopted in February 1794), or equal rights for women (which the revolution never accepted, see *Inequality for Women*)—

but in 1789 it was the greatest statement of human rights in Europe.

The Revolutionary Journée of October 5. Louis XVI rejected the August reforms. This action defended tradition, but it angered the National Assembly and the people of Paris. The people forced the issue. Their fears of a royal counterrevolution were exacerbated by the food crisis. The harvest of 1789 was good, but a late season drought had slowed the work of the water-powered mills that ground grain into flour. Thus, August and September 1789 again witnessed bread riots led by the women of Paris. Historians call those days on which the action of the crowd changed the course of events *revolutionary journées* (revolutionary days). The angry housewives and working women of Paris led such a **journée** on October 5, 1789. Their target was the king. When Louis blocked the August reforms, talk circulated in Paris about a march to Versailles to bring him to Paris. On the rainy Monday morning of October 5, the women of Paris did just that. A procession of several

FIGURE 21.4 *Storming the Bastille.* On July 14, 1789, a popular uprising succeeded in capturing a 100-foot-tall fortress-prison in Paris, known as the Bastille. This event, celebrated each year as a French national holiday, had many emotional overtones about attacking tyranny and liberating prisoners, but the chief aim of the crowd was to seize the supply of gunpowder stored in the Bastille. Royal troops killed ninety-eight civilians in their attack on the fortress, but afterward the crowd took their revenge: the governor of the prison who had refused to surrender to them was brutally murdered and his head paraded around on a pike.

thousand set out for Versailles, chanting "Let's fetch the baker!" A few hours later, a reluctant Lafayette led the National Guard to support them. After a small clash on the grounds of the royal palace, Louis XVI agreed to accept the August decrees and to move into his Tuileries Palace (today the Louvre Museum) in Paris.

Political Clubs. The National Assembly moved to Paris, too, confident that it now controlled France. The deputies deprived the king of the right to dismiss them or to veto the constitution they were writing. Their effort to shackle royal power included one mistake: they excluded royal ministers from the assembly. This

Georges Danton

blocked the evolution of a cabinet system of government and the principle of ministerial responsibility to parliament. The move to Paris stimulated the growth of political clubs (the precursors of political parties), which became one of the distinguishing features of the revolution. These clubs had roots in the salons of the Old Regime, organi-

zations such as Masonic lodges, and the excited political meetings of 1788–1789. They became the voice of Parisian radicalism and then the center of revolutionary power. One of the most influential clubs was the Cordeliers, named for a Catholic order whose monastery it rented. The Cordeliers included three of the most prominent radicals of the city: Camille Desmoulins (the orator who helped to precipitate the attack on the Bastille), Jean-Paul Marat (a physician whose radical newspaper, *The Friend of the People,* had shaped the journée of October 5), and Georges Danton (a radical lawyer who had married into middle-class wealth and purchased a venal office in the royal courts). The most important club, the Jacobins, drew their name from a rented Jacobin convent and their membership from Parisian small businessmen (see Table 21.2). The Jacobins were especially influential because their membership included more than 200 deputies. Jacobins ranged from moderates such as Lafayette to radicals such as Robespierre, but the latter soon predominated. In the first year, the club grew to more than 1,200 members and 150 affiliated provincial clubs. The term **Jacobinism** soon entered political discourse to identify their militant ideas and actions.

The Revolution and the Church. Pushed by these radical clubs, the National Assembly continued its revolutionary legislation. Its attention soon fell on the Catholic Church, which seemed to hold an answer to the economic crisis. In November 1789, the revolutionary, and nonreligious, Bishop of Autun, Charles Talleyrand, convinced the assembly to "put at the disposal of the nation" all lands belonging to the church. This confiscated a huge amount of land—typically 20 percent of the farm land in a region, although it reached 40 percent in some areas. The assembly then sold interest-bearing bonds, called *assignats,* secured by this land. The **assignats** gradually circulated as revolutionary paper money. The notes could be redeemed for land and the value of the land was sufficient to cover them, but the public had little confidence in paper money, so assignats depreciated in value. By late 1792, inflation had taken 40 percent of their value. Other legislation on the church followed. The loss of its lands and the abolition of the mandatory tithe left the church with limited income. This led the assembly to create a new relationship between the church and the state, known as the Civil Constitution of the Clergy of July 1790. The Civil

PERSPECTIVES ON THE FRENCH REVOLUTION

The early stages of the French Revolution witnessed a torrent of legislation, fundamentally changing France. The revolutionary legislature, shown here debating the end of feudalism, made a good start to creating liberty and equality in France, as the idealistic view of equality suggests.

The Legislative Revolution.

All Mortals are Equal.

The Reunion of the Estates-General, Forming the New Constitution, May 1789.

Constitution converted priests into state employees and doubled their salaries, but it cut the number, income, and powers of the aristocratic bishops by changing their posts into elective state offices. Clerics had to swear loyalty to the constitution or be removed from office. By mid-1791, 60 percent of French priests (the **"juring,"** or constitutional, **clergy**) had accepted this arrangement; more than 95 percent of the bishops refused. The revolution—which had begun with many churchmen such as the Abbé Sieyès at the forefront—was soon de-

nounced by Pope Pius VI, and a schism between the church the government lasted for the rest of the decade.

The Legislative Revolution. The legislative revolution proceeded rapidly. The assembly addressed the economic crisis in 1790 by abolishing internal tariffs, nationalizing royal land, and creating a land tax. None of these reforms was as far-reaching as the election of a committee to prepare a simple, uniform system of weights and measures (1791), which gave the world the **metric system.** The assembly sought governmental efficiency by reorganizing local government (1789) and by abolishing the parlements (1790). Following the idealistic urging of Maximilien Robespierre, the deputies led Europe to recognize the rights of minorities (see Document 21.3): it decreed the civil equality of Protestants (1789) and ex-slaves (1791), and it decriminalized homosexuality by abolishing antisodomy laws (1791). The assembly also continued to attack the elite of the Old Regime: in 1790, it abolished monasteries, most religious orders, and the nobility. One of its most far-reaching reforms, however, restricted the rights of workers. The Chapelier Law of 1791 abolished the guilds and outlawed trade unions, shaping French labor history for nearly a century.

Women and the Revolution. One omission in this torrent of reform was women's rights, despite the active role of women in the revolution. The pamphlet campaign of early 1789 had included women's grievances; one petition to the king, for example, had called for educational and economic opportunities. A few women in religious orders had voted for representatives of the first estate. More than a dozen women had been among the conquerors of the Bastille. Women had led demonstrations over bread and the march on Versailles. They had formed political clubs, such as Théroigne de Méricourt's Friends of the Law, which was denied affiliation by the Cordeliers. And when the Declaration of the Rights of Man failed to mention women, Olympe de Gouges responded with a brilliant manifesto entitled Declaration of the Rights of Women (1791). "Man, are you capable of being just?" she asked. Although a few men, such as Condorcet, responded supportively, the answer remained no. Traditional attitudes about the role of women in society persisted, fears about the subservience of women to the church abounded, and a multitude of arguments (such as the lesser education of women) were advanced to perpetuate male dominance. Soon, the revolutionaries even closed women's clubs.

The Constitution of 1791. In September 1791, the National Assembly produced the first written constitution in French history. This document incorporated many of the decrees of the previous months. The Declaration of the Rights of Man formed the preamble. Louis XVI retained power as a constitutional monarch, but most power was vested in a unicameral parliament called the Legislative Assembly, which he could not dissolve. Elections were complicated and based on limited suffrage. Adult male citizens were divided into **"active" citizens** (who got to vote, based on how much tax they paid) and **"passive" citizens** (who had full civil rights, but no vote). Elections were indirect: active citizens chose representatives who met to elect deputies. This allowed 4.3 million people to vote, fewer people than had voted for the Estates-General but higher percent-

age than the electorate for the House of Commons in Britain.

The Flight to Varennes. Before the Constitution of 1791 took effect, another dramatic event changed the course of the French Revolution. On June 20,

DOCUMENT 21.2

THE DECLARATION OF THE RIGHTS OF MAN (1789)

1. *Men are born and remain free and equal in rights. Social distinctions can be based only upon public utility.*
2. *The aim of every political association is the preservation of the natural and imprescriptible rights of man. These rights are liberty, property, security, and resistance to oppression.*
3. *The source of all sovereignty is essentially in the nation; no body, no individual can exercise authority that does not proceed from it in plain terms.*
4. *Liberty consists in the power to do anything that does not injure others. . . .*
5. *The law has the right to forbid only such actions as are injurious to society. . . .*
6. *Law is the expression of the general will. All citizens have the right to take part personally, or by their representatives, in its formation. It must be the same for all, whether it protects or punishes. . . .*
7. *No man can be accused, arrested, or detained except in the cases determined by the law. . . .*
8. *The law ought to establish only penalties that are strictly and obviously necessary. . . .*
9. *Every man being presumed innocent until he has been pronounced guilty. . . .*
10. *No one should be disturbed on account of his opinions, even religious. . . .*
11. *The free communication of ideas and opinions is one of the most precious rights of man; every citizen then can freely speak, write, and print, subject to responsibility for the abuse of this freedom. . . .*
14. *All the citizens have the right to ascertain, by themselves or by their representatives, the necessity of the public tax, to consent to it freely. . . .*
17. *Property being a sacred and inviolable right, no one can be deprived of it, unless a legally established public necessity evidently demands it, under the condition of a just and prior indemnity.*

From Anderson, Frank M., ed., *The Constitutions and Other Select Documents Illustrative of the History of France, 1789–1907* (Minneapolis: 1908).

Question: Why is this document considered one of the most important in modern European history?

ROBESPIERRE ON EQUALITY FOR MINORITIES (1791)

The Rights of Jews (1791)

How could one . . . accuse the Jews of persecutions of which they themselves have been the victims in different countries? On the contrary, those are national crimes which we should expiate by restoring to them the imprescriptible rights of man of which no human power could deprive them. . . . Restore them to happiness, to the Patrie [homeland], to virtue by giving back to them the dignity of men and of citizens. Let us remember that it can never be politic, whatever one may say, to condemn a large group of men living in our midst to degradation and oppression. How could the interests of society be grounded upon the violation of the eternal principles of justice and reason which are the very basis of all human society?

The Rights of African Blacks in the Colonies (1791)

But what then, especially in the colonies, are the civil rights left to [African blacks] without political rights? What is a man deprived of the rights of an active citizen in colonies under the domination of whites? He is a man who cannot take part in any way in political deliberations, who cannot influence, either directly or indirectly, the most moving, the most sacred interests of the society of which he is a member. He is a man who is governed by magistrates whose selection he cannot determine in any way....He is a degraded being whose fate is left to caprice, to passions, to the interests of a higher caste.

Question: Was Robespierre a defender of human rights?

FIGURE 21.5 *Arrest of Louis XVI and Marie Antoinette at Varennes.* On June 20, 1791, Louis XVI and the royal family fled Paris for the eastern frontier in a plan to join the émigrés and the foreign powers allied against the revolution. A postmaster recognized the king, and at the village of Varennes, the National Guard arrested him. In this romanticized, royalist illustration from the nineteenth century, the king is seen explaining himself to a menacing crowd while Marie Antoinette shelters their children. Louis XVI returned to Paris as a prisoner. "There is no longer a king in France," he said, and a republic was indeed proclaimed a year later.

EUROPE AND THE FRENCH REVOLUTION (1789–1792)

The French Emigrés. The arrest of Louis XVI accelerated the growth of counterrevolutionary opinion. The most dramatic expression of this in France had been emigration from the country. The **émigrés** (those who fled) had been led by the king's younger brother and future successor, the Count of Artois, who left in July 1789. Each major event of the revolution increased the number of émigrés. The total ultimately reached 104,000. Adding 25,000 people who were deported (chiefly nonjuring priests), 2 to 3 percent of the population left France. Most émigrés came from the third estate, but priests and aristocrats fled at higher rates (see Table 21.2). In contrast, counterrevolutionary emigration to Canada during the American Revolution took 3 to 5 percent of the population. The émigrés concentrated in Koblenz and other towns near the border where they sought assistance from the crowned heads

1791, Louis XVI fled for the eastern frontier. A postmaster recognized the king, and at the village of Varennes, the National Guard arrested him. Louis XVI returned to Paris as a prisoner. "There is no longer a king in France," he said. His flight to Varennes led to talk of abolishing the monarchy and creating a republic. For more than a year after the king's arrest, however, the revolutionary government allowed an aristocrat to continue publishing a royalist newspaper on his behalf.

INEQUALITY FOR WOMEN

Olympe de Gouges (1748–1793) was the illegitimate daughter of a provincial butcher. She ran away with a soldier at age 16 and wound up as a writer in Paris. She supported the revolution and founded a club for women that Robespierre closed. Her opposition to Robespierre and her opposition to the execution of Louis XVI sent her to the guillotine in 1793, by which date revolutionary committees had bluntly rejected her appeal. Compare the words of her articles with the similar provisions in the *Declaration of the Rights of Man*.

Olympe De Gouges's Declaration of the Rights of Woman (1791)

Man, are you capable of being just? It is a woman who poses the question; you will not deprive her of that right at least. Tell me, what gives you sovereign empire to oppress my sex?

1. *Woman is born free and lives equal to man in her rights. . . .*
4. *Liberty and justice consist of restoring all that belongs to others; thus, the only limits on the exercise of the natural rights of woman are perpetual male tyranny; these limits are to be reformed by the laws of nature and reason. . . .*
10. *No one is to be disquieted for his very basic opinions; woman has the right to mount the scaffold; she must equally have the right to mount the rostrum.*

The Committee of General Security Rejects Women's Rights (1793)

Should women exercise political rights and meddle in affairs of government? To govern is to rule the commonwealth by laws, the preparation of which demands extensive knowledge, unlimited attention and devotion, a strict immovability, and self-abnegation . . . Are women capable of these cares and of the quality they call for? In General, we can answer no. . . .

[W]omen's associations seem dangerous. If we consider that the political education of men is at its beginning, that all its principles are not developed, and that we are still stammering the word liberty, then how much more reasonable is it for women, whose moral education is almost nil, to be less enlightened concerning principles?

From Gouges, Olympe de, *Declaration of the Rights of Woman*. 1791. In Levy, Darline G., Applewhite, Harriet B., and Johnson, Mary D., eds., *Women in Revolutionary Paris, 1789–1795* (Urbana: University of Illinois Press, 1979).

Question: Does the committee report of 1793 give an adequate answer to the declaration of 1791?

---

of Europe, aided rebellions in southern France, and built ties to nonjuring priests, especially in western France where a bitter civil war would soon be fought.

Sympathy for the Revolution. The émigrés got little help at first. Educated opinion was divided but generally favored the idealism of revolutionary goals over the émigré nobles. The English poet William Wordsworth summarized the enthusiasm of the educated classes in a few lines of poetry: "Bliss was it in that dawn to be alive, But to be young was very heaven!" Such opinions were not limited to intellectuals. Charles James Fox, a leader of the Whig Party in Britain, called the revolution "much the greatest event that ever happened, and much the best."

Edmund Burke's Criticism. The most thoughtful critic of the revolution was Fox's rival in the House of Commons, Edmund Burke. Burke became one of the founders of modern conservatism with his attack on the revolution, *Reflections on the Revolution in France* (1790). "France," he wrote, "by the perfidy of her leaders, has utterly disgraced the tone of lenient council." The revolution was an "undignified calamity."

Pope Pius VI's Response. The most influential early enemy of the revolution was Pope Pius VI, who chiefly directed his anger at the Civil Constitution because it removed the church from papal control. In April 1791, he sent the **encyclical letter** *Caritas* to French bishops, forbidding the oath to the constitution. That oath, Pius insisted, was "the poisoned fountainhead and source of all errors." The French assembly answered by annexing the papal territory of Avignon (once the seat of the medieval papacy). Soon the French ambassador at Rome had been murdered, Parisian crowds had burnt the pope in effigy, and Pius VI had become a leader of the European counterrevolution.

Austria's Brunswick Manifesto. The arrest of the French royal family at Varennes persuaded Leopold II to help his sister and her family. In July 1791, he sent a circular letter to the monarchs of England, Spain, Prussia, Naples, Sardinia, and Russia, urging them to join him in a protest to the French. He wanted "to vindicate the liberty and honor of the most Christian King and his family and to limit the dangerous extremes of the French revolution." Most rulers were unwilling to act. King George III of Britain abstained because the revolution weakened France, and he believed it was divine retribution for the French intervention in the American Revolution. The only ruler who joined Leopold II was King Frederick William II of Prussia. Together they issued the Brunswick Manifesto (1792), which denounced "the anarchy in the interior of France." Soon they would invade France.

European Polarization—Republicanism versus Monarchism.
European opinion gradually became polarized. As a Dutch conservative wrote in 1791, two parties were forming in all nations. One, a party of popular sovereignty and democratization, attacked all governments "except those arising from the free consent of those who submit to it." The other party held traditional values and, therefore, counterrevolutionary sentiments. It accepted government "by one or several persons over the mass of the people, a government of divine origin and supported by the church." The French Revolution was only the largest part of a democratic revolution that included liberal Polish nobles struggling against Russian influence; English dissenters campaigning for parliamentary reform; Rhineland Jews seeking emancipation; Irish peasants dreaming of French aid against the English; and Dutch, Belgian, and Swiss "patriots" who revived earlier rebellions.

Ireland and the French Revolution.
In Ireland, for example, the French Revolution stimulated rebellion against English rule. Lord Edward Fitzgerald and Wolfe Tone led the United Irishmen in seeking independence. Fitzgerald, a veteran of the American Revolution, a member of the Irish parliament, and a twenty-first generation member of the Catholic nobility and Tone, a Protestant radical pamphleteer, visited France to observe the revolution and to seek aid. Fitzgerald was so moved by the revolution that he renounced his ancient title. The ironic result of this reveals the complexity of debate over the revolution: devout Irish Catholic peasants ignored the attitude of the papacy and lit candles in prayer for the success of the French, who had attacked the church but who might also attack the English.

THE LEGISLATIVE ASSEMBLY AND THE WARS OF THE REVOLUTION (1792)

The Political Left, Right, and Center.
Elections for the Legislative Assembly took place in the aftermath of the flight to Varennes and the promulgation of *Caritas* and the Brunswick Manifesto. The new assembly of 745 deputies left a permanent mark on political discourse as a coincidence of its seating arrangement in a semicircular amphitheater. As a speaker faced the assembled deputies, conservative members who defended the king sat on the right side. This group, led by members of the Feuillant Club, became the Right. On the left wing sat the radical members from the Jacobin and Cordeliers clubs. Less militant revolutionaries, who later became known as the Girondins (because many came from the region of the Gironde), sat in the middle. Thus was born the political vocabulary of **"left," "right,"** and **"center."**

The Coming of the War of 1792.
International tension distracted the Legislative Assembly from further reform. Instead, the assembly adopted legislation against the émigrés, branding those who did not return as conspirators. In February 1792, the state seized their property. Similar decrees against **nonjuring priests** followed in November 1792. Such legislation worsened French relations with the Austro-Prussian alliance. In March 1792, a belligerent, counterrevolutionary Francis II had succeeded to the Hapsburg throne. By this time, the Girondins, whose foreign policy was more radical than their revolutionary aims, dominated the French assembly. They argued that war with the counterrevolutionaries would rally the French to defend the revolution, test the sympathies of Louis XVI, and export the revolution to other peoples. The leading Girondist, Jacques Brissot, said simply: "War is a blessing to the nation." Francis II and Brissot had led their countries to war by April 1792.

The War of 1792 and the First Coalition

A Prussian army invaded eastern France in August 1792 and won several victories, but the course of the war shifted in September, when a French army under General Charles Dumouriez defeated the Prussians in an artillery duel near the town of Valmy, bolstering republican enthusiasm. In the words of the German poet Wolfgang von Goethe, the battle of Valmy meant that "here and today begins a new age in the history of the world." This was poetic exaggeration, but it made a point: the allies would not quickly crush the French Revolution. A few weeks later, Dumouriez and an army of 45,000 underscored that point by marching into Hapsburg lands on France's northern border (today's Belgium) and winning a decisive victory at the town of Jemappes.

The First Coalition.
The War of 1792 grew into the War of the **First Coalition** (1793–1795) when Britain, Spain, and Russia joined the alliance against the revolution, which had become passionately antimonarchical. Although this seemed like one of the most unevenly matched wars in history, the French not only

survived it but also occupied the lowlands, the German Rhineland, and Northern Italy. They were able to do so because the revolution, among its other accomplishments, transformed the nature of modern warfare.

Modern Infantry. France had a larger population than most of her rivals, and in the early years of the revolution, high unemployment made recruitment easy. The army grew from 180,000 men in 1789 to 650,000 in 1793. Then in August 1793, the assembly decreed **universal military conscription** (the *levée en masse*), placing the entire nation "in permanent requisition for army service." France soon had an unprecedented 1 million men in uniform. A conscript army of this size could not function according to the time-honored rules of European warfare. Although armed with the proceeds of revolutionary confiscations, it could feed itself only by living off the lands it conquered. Moreover, tactics had to be revised because intensive training had become impossible. Under reforms adopted by "the organizer of victory," Lazare Carnot, the French infantry advanced in deep columns instead of the traditional line, taking advantage of its superior numbers and revolutionary enthusiasm to overwhelm more disciplined enemies.

THE FIRST REPUBLIC (1792)

The Convention. The War of 1792 changed the revolution and led to the abolition of the monarchy and the creation of a republic. Once again, the Parisian crowd took the initiative. Austro-Prussian threats on Louis XVI's behalf inspired demonstrations against the king, including an attack on the Tuileries Palace. The Legislative Assembly then suspended Louis's remaining powers and reenacted all legislation he had vetoed. Then, in "the revolution of August 10" the assembly decided to create a new legislature. It would be called the Convention in honor of the Constitutional Convention recently held in America. Representatives to the Convention would be elected by **universal suffrage** (defined as adult males), and they would write a more democratic constitution. Among its final acts, the Legislative Assembly moved Louis XVI to a royal prison and urged the Convention to abolish the monarchy.

Revolutionary Authoritarianism. The late summer of 1792 also saw ominous signs of revolutionary authoritarianism. The assembly sent commissioners into provincial France hoping to rally support, but their powers often created opposition. Then the assembly required a loyalty oath of all government employees, and it gave those who refused two weeks to leave the country. Other laws permitted searches of homes for arms and counterrevolutionary suspects. The attack on the Catholic Church also continued. All surviving Catholic associations (such as teaching orders) were abolished, religious processions and public ceremonies were prohibited, and divorce was legalized.

The September Massacres. This same period witnessed one of the worst atrocities of mob violence, known as the September Massacres. The allied invasion, the implications of the Brunswick Manifesto, and the defection of people such as Lafayette (seen as proof of widespread treason) created fears of a conspiracy linking the internal and external enemies of the revolution. The resultant panic was like the Great Fear of 1789, but this time the target was suspected enemies rather than châteaux. There were sixty-five lynchings around France. In Paris, the result was a massacre. During the first week, the government did nothing for 5 days while the mobs slaughtered 1,100 inmates, three-fourths of whom were nonpolitical prisoners such as common criminals and prostitutes.

The Elections of 1792. Elections for the Convention thus took place in volatile circumstances. The 749 new deputies were chiefly lawyers (47.7 percent); fifty-five were priests and several others were former aristocrats, including Louis's revolutionary cousin, the former Duke of Orléans, now called Philippe Egalité (see Table 21.2). The deputies were young—two-thirds were younger than age 44. No faction held a majority, but universal suffrage and the war produced a radical body. Jacobins and their allies, called **Montagnards** (mountain dwellers) because they sat in the upper levels, accounted for 40 percent of the seats; their ranks included a Parisian delegation led by such radicals as Danton, Marat, and Robespierre. The Girondins and their allies, led by Brissot and Roland, fell to less than 25 percent. The first year of the Convention was a struggle for predominance between these two factions, and the Jacobins won.

Abolition of Monarchy. The Convention proclaimed a new order during its first week. Deputies voted unanimously to abolish the monarchy and create a republic. A committee began work on a new constitution, to be submitted to the people for ratification. When the Convention later invented a new calendar, this week in September would begin the new year, and September 1792 started Year I of the republican era.

The Trial of Louis XVI. The success of republican armies in 1792–1793 meant that the greatest issue before the Convention became the fate of Louis XVI. A committee recommended that he be tried for treason, based on his secret contacts with the governments that had invaded France. The trial of the king before the Convention began in December. Few doubted his guilt, revealed by his secret correspondence, and the deputies convicted him by a vote of 683–0. The debate over his sentence, however, caused bitter divisions. Jacobins advocated the customary death penalty for

REGICIDE, REVOLUTION, AND EIGHTEENTH-CENTURY CULTURE

The Execution of Louis XVI. Citizen Capet, the former King Louis XVI of France (in the white shirt), is shown as he begins to mount the steps of the guillotine on January 21, 1793. Louis is accompanied by his Irish confessor, the Abbe Edgeworth, who would later escape to England and become chaplain to Louis's brother who became King Louis XVIII in 1814. Note the large number of troops used to guarantee order on the day of the execution. The trees in the background are the edge of Louis's former gardens, the Tuileries. Before them are seen some of the grim details of the execution: the board to which Louis will be strapped and the basket that will catch his head.

this crime. Passionate speakers insisted that "[k]ings are in the moral order what monsters are in the natural." Many leaders of the revolution, such as the Abbé Sieyès, favored execution; even the king's cousin voted with the regicides. Louis XVI was condemned by a vote of 387–334 and beheaded on the guillotine in January 1793. The virtues of republican government and the acceptance of **tyrannicide** had become interwoven with European culture in the eighteenth century (see *Regicide, Revolution, and Eighteenth-Century Culture*). The republic and regicide had now moved to the center of French political life.

Constitution of the Year 1. War consequently dominated the life of the Convention (1792–1795), but deputies still aspired to reform society. Noteworthy laws envisioned schools open to all citizens. Robespierre, who had long championed the rights of minorities, scored his greatest triumph with the abolition of slavery in French colonies (February 1794), pushing the republic far ahead of Britain or the United States. The Convention's constitution, adopted in June 1793 and known as the Constitution of the Year I, summarized much of this egalitarian idealism. It began with an expanded version of the Declaration of the Rights of Man; stating, "The aim of society is the common welfare." That led to a constitutional assertion (Article Twenty-One) of the welfare state: "Every French citizen has a right to existence. . . . Public assistance is a sacred debt. . . . Society owes subsistence to its unfortunate citizens, either in providing work for them, or in assuring the means of existence for those who are unable to work."

TABLE 21.3 CONNECTIONS: REGICIDE, REVOLUTION, AND EIGHTEENTH-CENTURY CULTURE

510 BCE	44 BCE	1610 CE
Junius Brutus overthrows last of Rome and founds Republic	Brutus and Senators kill Caesar to save the Roman Republic	Henry IV of France assassinated after wars of religion

1649	1661	1730–1731
Charles I of England tried and beheaded in republican revolution	Body of Cromwell exhumed and publicly hanged for crime of regicide	Voltaire's tragedies *Brutus* and *The Death of Caesar* depict Roman revolution and regicide favorably

1757	1762	1770s
Louis XV of France survives assassination attempt by Damiens	Tsar of Russia killed by aristocrats bringing Catherine II to the throne	French philosophes criticize the royal torture of Damiens (who tried to kill King Louis XV)

1780	1784	1787
Houdon sculpts American revolutionary hero George Washington as Roman hero Cincinnatus	Neoclassical paintings of Jacques-Louis David praise stern republican virtues of Rome	*Comédie-Française* stages dramas of Roman revolution in modern dress

JULY 1789	JUNE 1791	SEPTEMBER 1791
Louis XVI obliged to return from Versailles and live in Tuileries Palace	Louis XVI flees Paris but is detained at town of Varennes and returned	Assembly suspends royal powers of Louis XVI

AUGUST 1792	SEPTEMBER 1792	NOVEMBER 1792
Crowd attacks Tuileries Palace and Louis is jailed	Saint-Just tells the Convention, "Every citizen has the same right over a king that Brutus had."	Louis XVI documents found incriminating him

DECEMBER 1792	JANUARY 1793	JANUARY 21, 1793
Convention votes to try Louis XVI under its own jurisdiction	Trial of Louis XVI: Convention convicts Louis VI of "conspiracy against the nation" and votes to execute him	Louis XVI executed on the guillotine

CIVIL WAR AND THE REIGN OF TERROR (1793–1794)

Whatever the intentions and accomplishments of the Convention, it is chiefly remembered for one of the most horrifying periods of modern history, the **Reign of Terror** (1793–1794), when thousands of people were publicly executed. At the same time, a bloody civil war took tens of thousands of lives. The central issue in both tragedies was whether the revolution or the counterrevolution would prevail.

Victories of the Coalition. The crisis began with the war against the European coalition. In early 1793, the Austrians defeated the armies of General Dumouriez and moved toward the French frontier. While the French braced themselves for an invasion, Dumouriez stunned them by defecting to the allies, making military catastrophe seem imminent. In addition to the Austrians on the northern frontier, Prussians were besieging French forts in the east, Italian troops were invading from the southeast, the Spanish army had crossed the southern border, and the English navy was threatening several ports. In Paris, many people agreed that the war effort required desperate measures.

The Vendée and Civil War. The Convention's efforts to defend France, however, enlarged the problem. Plans to draft 300,000 men produced antidraft riots across France, chiefly in the west. This, plus continuing food shortages, the execution of the king, and the **de-Christianization** of France, created opposition to the republic. By March 1793, peasant rebels in the Atlantic region of the Vendée had won several battles against the government. The Convention soon had to take units of the regular army from the frontier to combat the Vendéens, who now called themselves the Royal Catholic Army. Resistance to the Convention spread quickly, particularly to cities that resented the centralized control of Paris. In May 1793, moderates in Lyons overthrew the Jacobin municipal government. Their **federalist** revolt against centralization soon reached Marseilles and Toulon, and by the summer of 1793, the federalists were as great a problem as the Royal Catholic Army. When the new government of Lyons executed the deposed Jacobin mayor, the Convention sent an army to besiege the city.

Toussaint L'Ouverture and Slave Rebellion in St. Domingue.
Ironically, the republic also faced an uprising from people who felt that the revolution had not yet gone far enough. The French colony of St.

FIGURE 21.6 *Slave Revolt.* One of the most historic events that the French Revolution stimulated was a slave rebellion in the French colony of St. Domingue (today Haiti), where a revolutionary assembly of French colonists met in April 1790. Mutinies began in august 1790, and an uprising of slaves began in November 1790. In 1791, the slave insurrection shown in this illustration produced one of the first great heroes of black resistance to slavery, Pierre Toussaint L'Ouverture (1743–1803), the son of slaves and the man whose leadership would create the first black republic. Toussaint was so respected that when the French Revolution abolished slavery in 1794, the convention offered him the rank of general to join them. Toussaint accepted because his former supporters (the British and the Spanish) still kept slavery. Napoleon later turned on Toussaint, imprisoned him, and restored slavery, but his armies could not suppress the slave rebellion.

Domingue (today Haiti) faced a slave rebellion supported by the English and the Spanish. This uprising produced one of the greatest black heroes of the resistance to slavery, François Toussaint, known as Pierre Toussaint L'Ouverture. Toussaint was an educated ex-slave who had risen to the powerful position of steward on a large plantation before joining the rebellion. His abilities were so highly regarded that when the Convention abolished slavery (February 1794), the deputies offered Toussaint the rank of general to join them; he accepted because the British and the Spanish kept slavery.

The Reign of Terror.
The context of the **Reign of Terror,** therefore, was a desperate fight to save the republic and the revolution. The men of the Convention, who had executed Louis XVI, were also fighting for their lives, and they chose harsh measures. The revolution had already turned toward authoritarianism under the Legislative Assembly. The Convention went much further, reducing newly won liberties to a Jacobin **dictatorship.** Enactment of the constitution was postponed and severe laws adopted (see Document 21.4). Advocacy of a monarchical restoration and economic crimes such as hoarding were made capital crimes, to be tried before a special Revolutionary Tribunal. The freedom of the press to criticize the revolution was curtailed. A Law of Suspects expanded police powers, allowing the arrest of anyone "who by their conduct, their connections, their remarks, or their writings show themselves the partisans of tyranny or . . . the enemies of liberty." And a twelve-person executive committee with ill-defined powers, called the Committee of Public Safety, was created.

Robespierre and the Committee of Public Safety.
Under the leadership of Maximilien Robespierre, the Committee of Public Safety defended the revolution ferociously. In June 1793, the Convention was purged of moderate deputies, chiefly Girondins. A Reign of Terror, directed against spies, traitors, counterrevolutionaries, profiteers, hoarders, and corrupt officials, had begun. Leaders of the Convention spoke with extraordinary candor. Danton called for them to "drink the blood of the enemies of humanity." Louis Saint-Just, an uncompromising 26-year-old terrorist, was even more chilling: "Punish not only traitors, but even the indifferent." Robespierre dominated the Committee of Public Safety and explained the meaning of the terror (see Document 21.5). The puritanical provincial lawyer who had built his career as an opponent of capital punishment and a defender of human rights led a terror that he defined as "nothing but prompt, severe, inflexible justice."

The Guillotine.
The instrument of this severe justice was the **guillotine,** a machine for human decap-

LEGISLATING A REIGN OF TERROR

Press Law (March 1793)

1. *Whoever shall be convicted of having composed or printed works or writings which incite to the dissolution of the national representation, the reestablishment of monarchy, or any other power which constitutes an attack upon the sovereignty of the people shall be . . . punished with death.*
2. *The vendors, distributors, and hawkers of these works or writings shall be condemned to an imprisonment which shall not exceed three months, if they declare the authors, printers, or other persons from whom they have obtained them; if they refuse[,] . . . two years in prison.*

The Law of Suspects (September 1793)

1. *Immediately after the publication of the present decree, all the suspect persons who are in the territory of the republic and who are still at liberty shall be placed under arrest.*
2. *These are accounted suspect persons: (i) those who by their conduct, their connections, their remarks, or their writings show themselves the partisans of tyranny or federalism and the enemies of liberty; (ii) those who cannot . . . justify their means of existence. . . . (iv) Public functionaries suspended or removed from their functions by the National Convention. . . .*

(v) Those of the former nobles . . . who have not constantly manifested their attachment to the revolution; (vi) those who have emigrated from France.

Law on Dangerous Priests (October 1793)

1. *Priests subject to deportation and taken with arms in their hands[,] . . . [t]hose discovered in possession of permits or passports delivered by French émigré leaders[,] . . . [a]nd those provided with any counter-revolutionary symbols, shall be delivered within twenty-four hours to the executioner of condemned criminals and put to death. . . .*
12. *Ecclesiastics who have taken the oath [of the Civil Constitution], as well as that of liberty and equality, . . . and shall be denounced [for violating the oath] shall be embarked without delay and transferred to the east coast of Africa. . . .*
18. *Every citizen is required to denounce the ecclesiastic whom he shall know to be subject to deportation.*

From Anderson, Frank M., ed., *The Constitution and Other Select Documents Illustrative of the History of France, 1789–1907* (Minneapolis: 1908).

Question: Can any conditions of war and civil war justify such violations of liberty?

---

itation. The guillotine became a gruesome symbol of the terror, crudely called "the republican razor" or "the widow" (because it made so many). It had been introduced, however, by a physician, Dr. Joseph Guillotin, as a humanitarian form of swift execution, in contrast to the horrible tortures employed by the Old Regime such as being broken on the wheel or drawn and quartered.

The Executions. The Reign of Terror lasted for 13 months, from June 1793 until July 1794. During those months, tribunals around France ordered an estimated 14,000 to 17,000 executions; the most famous, the Revolutionary Tribunal of Paris, accounted for more than 2,700 (see Table 21.4). The overwhelming majority of the executions (71 percent) were in regions of civil war, especially the Vendée; of those, 75 percent were rebels caught with weapons in their hands. Despite stereotypes in popular literature, most of the people executed were workers (31 percent) and peasants (28 percent), not aristocrats (8 percent) or priests (7 percent). The revolutionary tribunals acquitted many people. The tribunal at Marseilles, for example, acquitted more than 50 percent of the accused and sentenced 31 percent to death. The Parisian tribunal sent many famous figures to the guillotine: members of the royal family (such as the Duke of Orléans), leaders of the Old Regime (Malesherbes), noted scholars (the distinguished chemist Antoine Lavoisier), leading Girondins (Brissot), and feminists (Olympe de Gouges) all died there. Some, such as Condorcet, escaped that fate only by committing suicide.

The Vendée. The civil war was especially bloody. Lyons was conquered, with ruthless reprisals, in October 1793; more than 1,600 people were executed. The Vendéen counterrevolution dragged on for years, with enormous casualties and mass executions of rebels. One ferocious representative of the revolution in the Vendée—Jean-Baptiste Carrier—drowned prisoners in the Loire River by the hundreds, proclaiming, "We shall turn France into a cemetery rather than fail in her regeneration." A minimum of 80,000 Vendéens died; some estimates for the civil war put the dead at more than 200,000. (By contrast, total war-related deaths during the American Revolution were fewer

ROBESPIERRE ON THE REVOLUTION AND ITS IDEALS

It is time to define clearly the goal of the Revolution and the end which we wish to reach. . . .What is the goal toward which we strive? The peaceful enjoyment of liberty and equality . . .

We wish an order of things where all the base and cruel passions are chained, all generous and beneficent passions aroused by the laws . . . where distinctions are born only of equality itself; where the citizen is obedient to the magistrate, the magistrate to the people, and the people to justice; where the country assures the well-being of each individual . . .

What kind of government can realize these wonders? Only a democratic or republican government: these two words are synonymous, in spite of the abuses of popular usage. . . .

[W]hat is the fundamental principle of democratic or popular government. . . ? It is virtue; I speak of the public virtue which produced so many marvels in Greece and Rome, and which ought to produce even more astonishing ones in republican France; of that virtue which is nothing else but love of the country and its laws. . . .

If the force of popular government in peace is virtue, that of popular government in revolution is both virtue and terror; virtue, without which terror is deadly; terror, without which virtue is powerless. Terror is nothing but prompt, severe, inflexible justice; it is then an emanation of virtue.

From Robespierre, Maximilien, "Discours et rapports a la convention" (Paris: 1965). In Adams, Wallace, ed. *The Western World,* vol. 2 (New York: Dodd, Mead, 1970).

Question: Was Robespierre a defender of liberty?

than 10,000; in the American Civil War, more than 600,000.)

THE THERMIDORIAN REACTION AND THE DIRECTORY (1794–1799)

Thermidor. The Reign of Terror reached its peak in December 1793–January 1794, when 49 percent of the executions (mostly in the west) occurred. In Paris, however, the Jacobin dictatorship accelerated the terror in June and July 1794, accounting for 57 percent of the executions there. Like the god Saturn in classical mythology, the revolution consumed its own children; even Danton was executed. Revulsion and fear then produced a conspiracy against Robespierre. The Convention ended the terror by arresting him in what is called the **Thermidorian reaction** (named for the month in the republican calendar). Robespierre attempted suicide, but he, Saint-Just, and other leading Jacobins went to the guillotine.

The End of the Jacobian Revolution. During 1794–1795, the Convention labored to remove the more extreme aspects of the Jacobin dictatorship, starting with the abolition of the Jacobin clubs. The tribunals were closed, and prisoners were released. The Law of Suspects was repealed and new judicial guarantees instituted. The Convention recalled deputies who had been purged. To placate federalists, the powers of the central government were reduced. An amnesty was offered to all rebels who laid down their arms. Freedom of religion was gradually restored, with churches separated from state control. Following these efforts to restore order, the Convention wrote a new constitution to keep it. The Constitution of the Year III (1795) was the third in the short history of the revolution. It, too, began with a declaration of rights, significantly renamed the Declaration of the Rights and Duties. Article One stated a right of security alongside liberty and equality.

The Directory. France remained a republic with a broad suffrage including most (male) citizens, but it was constituted with safeguards, such as the separation of powers. A bicameral legislature, for example, included a lower house that introduced all legislation and an upper house with the power to block it. As a further safeguard, the upper house was a Council of Ancients, whose 250 members had to be at least 40 years old—a reaction to the fact that in 1793, Robespierre had been 35 years old, Danton 34, and Saint-Just 26. The new government was called the Directory because the constitution also created an executive branch with that name. The Directory had five members, chosen by the legislature from among its own members and prohibited from succeeding themselves. The Convention bequeathed great difficulties to the Directory. Economic problems were so severe that government ministers were given salaries measured in wheat because the currency was so unstable. Royalism was resurgent, and in some regions this had produced a **"white terror"** (white being the symbol of royalism) against former Jacobins. Simultaneously, however, new militants demanded further revolution. Gracchus Babeuf, a radical journalist, founded the Conspiracy of Equals in 1795, to restore the Constitution of the Year I and to create greater egalitarianism. Babeuf's manifesto bluntly proclaimed, "In a true society, there should be neither rich nor poor."

The Directory preserved the moderate republic by using the army against royalists, executing extremists such as Babeuf, and repudiating much of the national

TABLE 21.4 THE REIGN OF TERROR, 1793–1794

Number and Percentage of Each Class Executed by the Paris Revolutionary Tribunal		
CLASS	**NUMBER**	**PERCENTAGE**
Nobles	533	19.4
Clergy	240	8.7
Middle class	1,443	52.6
(Upper	903	32.9)
(Lower	540	19.7)
Workers	478	17.4
Unknown	53	1.9
Total	2,747	

Number and Percentage of Each Class Executed Throughout France		
CLASS	**NUMBER**	**PERCENTAGE**
Nobles	1,156	8.2
(Old	878	6.2)
(Robe	278	2.0)
Clergy	920	6.5
Middle class	3,452	24.6
(Upper	1,964	14.0)
(Lower	1,488	10.6)
Workers	4,389	31.2
Peasants	3,961	28.1
Unknown	200	1.4
Total	14,078	

Originally titled "Executing the Executioner," this period engraving shows guillotines reaching to the horizon and representing the different groups executed.

From Greer, Donald, *The Incidence of the Terror during the French Revolution: A Statistical Interpretation* (Cambridge, MA: Harvard University Press, 1935, p. 164); and Jones, Colin, ed., *The Longman Companion to the French Revolution* (London: Longman, 1988, p. 120).

Question: A traditional stereotype holds that the French Revolution especially attacked priests and aristocrats. Do these numbers support that view?

debt. It won a final victory in the Vendée in 1796 but became increasingly conservative when elections in 1797 returned only 13 of the surviving 216 members of the Convention. The Directory was soon characterized by the return of individuals who had gone into hiding or fled the country. Talleyrand became foreign minister in July 1797; Sieyès became a director in 1799. The Directory thus attempted to stand in the political center, dreading both Jacobinism and royalism. It was a republic that distrusted republicanism, reflecting French exhaustion and apathy. This made it vulnerable to conspiracies, as Talleyrand realized when he attended a meeting of the directors, and guards confiscated his cane as a potential weapon. "It appears to me," he said, "that your government is terribly afraid of being poked with a stick." He was not surprised when the Directory fell in a military coup d'état in 1799.

THE REVOLUTIONARY WARS AND THE RISE OF NAPOLEON (1785–1799)

Napoleon's Background. Napoleon Bonaparte (1769–1821) was born the second son of a minor Italian noble on the island of Corsica. The family became French when Louis XV bought Corsica from the republic of Genoa, whose government had become exasperated with Corsican rebellion. Napoleon's father had accepted the French occupation, a French patent of nobility, and a position in the government of Corsica. In 1778, he sent 9-year-old Napoleon to the Royal Military Academy for sons of the aristocracy, where the skinny, provincial Bonaparte was unpopular, but a good student. His mathematical skills determined his

NAPOLEON AND THE GRAND ARMY OF FRANCE

MAP 21.1. SPREADING THE FRENCH REVOLUTION: THE SISTER REPUBLICS

French political thought and revolutionary action excited much enthusiasm in Europe, and the arrival of French revolutionary armies was even welcomed in some places by those who sought the abolition of monarchy. This map shows the "sister republics" that French armies created, as Napoleon's armies did in Italy.

Napoleon's rise to fame as a commander coincided with the exportation of the revolution into neighboring states, where some people welcomed republican government but the local governments naturally resisted. Revolutionary armies and popular uprisings created "sister republics" in many areas, but these quickly became French satellites. Napoleon's early victories led to the creation of several sister republics in Italy, where some hailed him as a champion of Italian nationalism. In winning these early victories, Napoleon demonstrated his skill at leading soldiers, as his Proclamation of 1796 shows. But just as the republics changed, so did the life of Napoleon's soldiers, as the diary of one soldier from 1812 shows.

Napoleon's Proclamations to His Soldiers (1796)

March 1796

Soldiers, you are naked, ill fed! The government owes you much; it can give you nothing. Your patience, and the courage you show in the midst of these rocky mountains, are admirable; but they win you no glory. You bask in no fame. I seek to lead you into the most fertile plains in the world. Rich provinces, great cities will be in your power. There you will find honor, glory, and riches. Soldiers of Italy, are you lacking in courage. . . ?

April 1796

Soldiers! In the last two weeks you have won six victories, you have captured the banners of twenty-one enemy armies, fifty pieces of artillery, several fortifications, you have conquered the richest part of Piedmont, and you have taken 15,000 prisoners while killing or wounding more than 10,000 men. Until now you have fought for sterile rocks, made famous by your efforts but worth little to your Patrie [homeland]. . . . Lacking everything, you have supplied everything. You won battles without cannon, you crossed rivers without bridges, you made forced marches without shoes, you made camp without brandy and sometimes without bread.

future: the artillery needed officers who could calculate trajectories. He graduated 2 years early, in 1785, and became a lieutenant in the royal artillery.

Napoleon's Personality. Napoleon harnessed his high intelligence to hard work. "Work is my element," he later wrote in a diary. He proved this as a young officer by working 18 hours per day, typically eating only one meal and sleeping 4 or 5 hours. He kept these habits as emperor; on the 2 nights before his victory at Austerlitz (1805), Bonaparte slept a total of 3 hours. This trait enabled him to issue more than 80,000 writ-

ten orders in his 15-year reign, an average of fifteen documents per day. Even "the love of a woman," he noted at age 22, "is incompatible with one's life work."

Napoleon's Political Thought. Lieutenant Bonaparte was a political radical. He had read the philosophes and admired Rousseau. He had contempt for the church and hatred for kings: "There are few of them who have not merited dethronement," he wrote. When the revolution began, he joined the Jacobin club. His revolutionary politics and the emigration of royalist officers led to Napoleon's rapid promotion. Then, in

Soldiers of liberty! Only republican phalanxes could have endured what you have endured. Soldiers, we owe you our thanks! The Patrie will owe its prosperity to your efforts. . . .

The two armies which recently boldly attacked you are now fleeing from you in terror: wicked men who laughed at your misery . . . are now confounded and trembling.

But, soldiers you have done nothing compared to what remains to be done. . . . You still have great battles to fight, cities to capture, rivers to cross. Is there anyone among you whose courage is flagging? . . . No? All of you wish to return to your villages, filled with pride, able to say, "I was with the victorious Army of Italy."

. . . [M]y friends, I promise you victory. But there is one condition which you must swear to honor: to respect the people whom you liberate. . . . Otherwise you would not be the liberators of the people; you would be their scourge. . . .

People of Italy! The French army comes to break your chains. The French people is the friend of all peoples. . . . [Y]our property, your religion, your customs will be respected. We are fighting as generous enemies, and we only want to crush the tyrants who enslave you.

The Hardships of Napoleon's Soldiers (1812)

An 18-year-old stonemason from Westphalia named Jakob Walter was among the thousands of Germans who were conscripted to fight in Napoleon's Grande Armée. After serving in the campaigns of 1806–1807, Walter was called to serve in the invasion of Russia. His autobiographical account of that campaign provides a startling record of the hardships endured by solders. The Russian campaign is famous for the suffering of the French retreat; note that this description is from the start of the invasion, and the worst was yet to come.

Daily the hardships increased, and there was no hope of bread. My colonel spoke to us once and said that we could hope for no more bread until we crossed the enemy border. The most anyone might get was a little lean beef, and hunger made it necessary to dig up the fields for the potatoes already sprouting, which were, however, very sweet and almost inedible. One also heard everywhere that several men had already shot themselves because of hardships . . . Finally we came to the Memel River, where the Russian border was. . . . We now believed that, once in Russia, we need do nothing but forage—which, however, proved to be an illusion. The town on Poniemon was already stripped before we could enter, and so were all the villages. Here and there a hog ran around and then was beaten with clubs, chopped with sabers, and stabbed with bayonets; and, often still living, it would be cut and torn to pieces. Several times I succeed in cutting off something; but I had to chew and eat it uncooked, since my hunger could not wait for a chance to boil the meat. . . .

Meanwhile it rained ceaselessly for several days, and the rain was cold. It was all the more disagreeable because nothing could be dried. Bodily warmth was our only salvation from freezing to death. I had on only one pair of blue linen trousers, which I had bought at Thorn, since I had thrown away my underwear because of the former heat. Thus I was constantly wet for two days and two nights, so that not a spot on my body was dry. . . . I could not see the way at night and slid in every direction on account of the clay. Indeed, the soldiers fell about me so incessantly that most of them were completely covered with mud and some were left lying behind. . . .

From Walter, Jakob, *The Diary of a Napoleonic Foot Soldier*, Marc Raeff, ed. (New York: Doubleday, 1991, pp. 40–42).

1793, Napoleon found himself in the right place at the right time. Returning from Corsica to the south of France shortly after the people of Toulon had turned their port over to the British, Napoleon was placed in command of the artillery. In 3 months, Napoleon had forced the British to withdraw. Toulon capitulated to the army of the republic, and Napoleon became a general at age 25. The fall of Robespierre resulted in Napoleon's imprisonment for Jacobinism, but the republic needed successful generals and soon restored his rank. When royalist demonstrations in Paris threatened the Directory, General Bonaparte used his artillery, loaded with small balls (the size of grapes), on the crowd. By killing demonstrators with **"a whiff of grapeshot,"** he preserved the government, won powerful friends, and received his choice of commands.

The Wars of the Revolution. French armies were in a strong position in 1795. The lowland provinces of modern Belgium had been taken from the Austrians and annexed to France. The coalition had collapsed over the division of Poland. A peace treaty with Prussia had given France the left bank of the Rhine River and recognized a French claim to Holland. The Dutch had been given their own republic, the first of several **"sister republics"** in western Europe created by French armies. Spain had left the war against France, and Britain had no troops on the continent. Victory in the Vendée freed French armies.

The Italian Campaign of 1796 and the Sister Republics. Napoleon chose to attack the Austrians on the French border, drive them from northern Italy, and force them to accept peace. His victory at the battle of Arcola (near Venice) in November 1796 cost the Austrians more than 40 percent of their army (see Table 21.5). Within a few months, Napoleon had created two more sister republics in Italy: the Ligurian republic (formerly Genoa) and the Cisalpine republic (Lombardy, Modena, and part of Venetia). Italian nationalists began to dream that Bonaparte was the hero who would liberate Italy and unify the small Italian states into a strong modern state. In October 1797, Francis I of Austria signed the Treaty of Campo Formio, accepting French expansion and the sister republics. Other sister republics soon followed in Switzerland (the Helvetian republic), central Italy (the Roman republic), and southern Italy (the Neapolitan, or Parthenopean republic). Although the sister republics were nominally independent states allied to the French republic, they were actually client states of limited republicanism. After Napoleon proclaimed himself emperor in 1804, they became sister monarchies. (The Batavian Republic, for example, became the Kingdom of Holland, with Napoleon's brother Louis as its king.)

The Egyptian Campaign of 1798. Britain remained the most persistent opponent of the French republic. Lacking the naval power to invade Britain and seeking a strategy to use against it, Napoleon chose to challenge British control of the Mediterranean by invading Egypt. He arrived in Egypt in 1798 with an army of 38,000 and a corps of archeologists who helped found Egyptology. A sweeping victory against Egyptian forces in the battle of the Pyramids (the battle was fought a few miles from the great pyramid of Giza) gave him Cairo, but a British fleet commanded by Horatio Nelson destroyed the French fleet (only two frigates escaped) at the battle of Aboukir Bay—the first of three great victories by a young hero (Nelson was a captain at age 20) that saved Britain from the devastation Napoleon would bring to the continent.

Lord Admiral Horatio Nelson

The Coup d'état of Brumaire, 1799. When Napoleon Bonaparte returned to France in 1799, he was a national hero and he was dangerous. He combined aristocratic birth with a Jacobin youth. He had won great battles against foreign enemies and had saved the Directory from its royalist enemies. Now he delivered learned lectures on ancient Egypt and met with prominent scholars. Politicians soon had visions of the "man on horseback" saving France from the Directory, and Napoleon seized that opportunity. He overthrew the Directory in a military **coup d'état** in the month of **Brumaire** (November) 1799, making *Brumaire* a synonym for "coup." The coup had the support of several leaders of the Directory, notably Sieyès (the dominant director); Napoleon's brother Lucien (president of the legislature); and the unscrupulous minister of police, Joseph Fouché (a mathematics teacher who had been a Jacobin during the Reign of Terror, then a leader of the Thermidorian reaction). Napoleon blithely announced that "the Revolution is at an end," and within one month he had produced the Constitution of the Year VIII (1799), dissolving the republic.

NAPOLEON'S DOMESTIC POLICIES IN FRANCE (1799–1814)

The Consulate. The Constitution of 1799 created the Consulate, an authoritarian regime with some democratic elements. It put executive power in the hands of three consuls but added that "the decision of the First Consul [Napoleon] shall suffice." Legislative power was fragmented among many bodies: one to draft bills, a separate body to debate them, another to vote on them, and a fourth to rule on the constitutionality of these acts. All were elected by universal manhood suffrage, but it was diluted by three stages of indirect voting: voters chose representatives, who chose representatives, who chose a list of representatives from which the first consul named the legislators. Even with such restrictions, Napoleon permitted only "a single party and a single will."

Plebiscites. The nearest approach to popular sovereignty in Napoleonic government was the **plebiscite.** Some legislation, such as the constitution itself, was submitted to a direct vote of adult men. A plebiscite of February 1800 ratified the Constitution of 1799 by a reported vote of 3 million to 1,500. Electoral fraud, directed by Lucien Bonaparte as minister of the interior, doubled the favorable vote. The actual vote fell far below the turnout in 1793; in Paris, only 23 percent voted. It is also noteworthy that Napoleon enforced the constitution before holding the plebiscite. For the next century, Bonapartists would advocate the plebiscite as the basic instrument of universal suffrage.

The Emperor Napoleon. Napoleon's reign, from 1799 to 1814, mixed such techniques with a refined Old Regime despotism and revolutionary reformism. The trend of his regime, however, was unmistakably toward dictatorship. "Liberty," he said, "is a need felt by a small class of people. . . . [T]herefore, it may be repressed with impunity." He produced his second constitution in 1802, awarding himself the consulate for life. Two years later, his third constitution (France's sixth of the revolutionary era) created a hereditary empire and reduced the legislative bodies to mere ornaments. He celebrated with an elaborate coronation, crowning himself at Notre Dame Cathedral in December 1804.

Napoleon and the French Revolution. Napoleon was not a simple counterrevolutionary, but he used his autocratic powers to undo some of the works of the French Revolution. To preserve the traditional family, he restricted divorce and allowed police harassment of homosexuals. Hoping to boost the economy of Caribbean colonies, he legalized slavery again. Denouncing the "pretensions of gilded Africans," he imprisoned Toussaint L'Ouverture, who died in a French jail in 1803. And Bonaparte reestablished nobility as an honor for his generals and civil servants. Whereas Louis XVI had named approximately ten nobles per year, Napoleon averaged one a day.

Censorship and the Police. In January 1800, Napoleon closed sixty of the seventy-three newspapers in France, and he soon shut others. "Three hostile newspapers," Napoleon told his staff, "are more to be feared than a thousand bayonets." Next he extended censorship to the theaters. Then he took control of all printing, requiring the submission of all manuscripts to the government for prior censorship. His thought control even reached into the mails when he instructed postmasters to open letters and take notes for him. Fouché's police enforced such regulations.

The Opposition. Napoleon generally dealt harshly with his opponents. He ended Vendéen resistance by ordering an army "to burn down two or three large villages as a salutary example." He jailed political prisoners, including many former Jacobin colleagues, without a trial. A plot against him in 1804 led to the execution of a dozen people, including a member of the royal family, the Duke d'Enghien, whom Napoleon seized by invading neutral Baden. But Napoleon never succeeded in silencing, or chose not to silence, all of his critics. In a remarkable example of defiance, Germaine de Staël, Necker's brilliant daughter, called Napoleon "Robespierre on horseback." She organized a Parisian salon, with participants ranging from royalists to Jacobins, as a center of criticism. Napoleon was a misogynist who referred to women as "machines for making babies," but Madame de Staël fascinated him and he merely banished her from Paris. She continued to insist that defending freedom in France was more important than winning foreign wars.

Napoleon's Enlightened Despotism and the Concordat of 1801. A balanced portrait of Napoleon must also see an enlightened side to his despotism. He tried to reunite France by welcoming home émigrés willing to accept his regime, and many aristocrats accepted the amnesty of 1802 to serve Napoleon. A similar compromise reestablished the Catholic Church. Napoleon had no religious faith himself, and his motive was purely pragmatic. He deposed one pope in 1798 and imprisoned another in 1809. He believed, however, that "[r]eligion is excellent stuff for keeping the common people quiet." This led him to negotiate the **Concordat** (a treaty with the Vatican) of 1801 with Pope Pius VII, recognizing Catholicism as "the religion of the vast majority of French citizens" and permitting it to be "freely practised." This treaty cost the Vatican many concessions. Pius VII accepted the confiscation of church lands, agreed that priests would be salaried employees of the state, permitted Napoleon to name French bishops, and even allowed a clerical "oath of fidelity" to the government. The result of this compromise was an integration of church and state, managed by a Ministry of Religion, which employed all priests and paid them a state salary.

Protestants and Jews. In reestablishing Catholicism, Napoleon preserved the revolutionary protection of religious minorities. Protestants (chiefly **Calvinists** in the Reformed Church plus the Lutherans of Eastern France) received their own state charter (which salaried pastors) in 1802. Napoleon did not share the monarchial hostility toward Protestants and comfortably relied on Protestant generals and bankers. Jews obtained new guarantees of their emancipation, although this did not prevent outbreaks of anti-Semitism in eastern France. Napoleon's attitudes toward Jews were sometimes suspect, but his defense of Jewish emancipation made France a center of nineteenth-century toleration. The Jewish population of Paris, which had been fewer than 500 in 1789, reached 3,000 in 1806, a tribute to his comparative toleration. And Napoleon carried Jewish emancipation into regions that his armies conquered, especially in western Germany.

The Napoleonic Code. Napoleon even enhanced some ideas of the revolutionary era. He completed a Jacobin project for the codification of French laws, producing the **Civil Code** (known as the Napoleonic Code) of 1804, then codes of commercial law (1807) and penal law (1810). The codes eliminated scores of antiquated laws, perpetuated much revolutionary

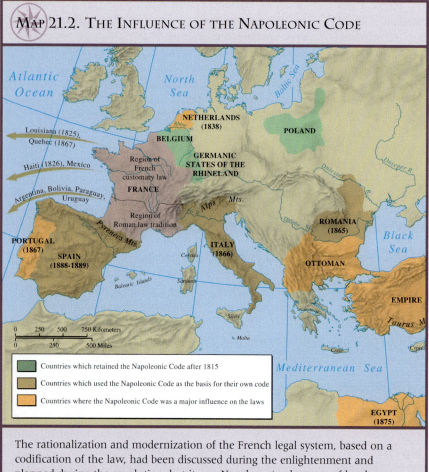

MAP 21.2. THE INFLUENCE OF THE NAPOLEONIC CODE

Countries which retained the Napoleonic Code after 1815

Countries which used the Napoleonic Code as the basis for their own code

Countries where the Napoleonic Code was a major influence on the laws

The rationalization and modernization of the French legal system, based on a codification of the law, had been discussed during the enlightenment and planned during the revolution, but it was Napoleon (and a team of legal experts) who achieved this dream, beginning with a Civil Code (subsequently called the Napoleonic Code) in 1804. As this map shows, it was one of the most influential legal codes in European history.

legislation, and standardized the laws. Among the most far-reaching elements of the codes were detailed laws of private property, which protected people who had acquired property during the revolution. The Napoleonic Code was also bluntly paternalistic, explicitly treating women as subordinates of men and blocking their emancipation throughout the nineteenth century. French armies carried the Napoleonic Code abroad, making it the most influential modern legal system. Poland, Belgium, and some of the west German states kept it after Napoleon's fall. Romania, Italy, and Spain later adopted substantial parts of it; in the Netherlands and Portugal, reformers were greatly influenced by it.

Education and Meritocracy. Napoleon also revived the revolutionary effort to expand education. A national school system existed, but only on paper. Napoleon considered the schools, like the churches and the law, to be instruments of social stability. "My principle aim," he said, "is to secure the means for directing political and moral opinion." Thus he provided the widest educational opportunity in the world, but his schools operated with "military discipline." Napoleon's greatest accomplishment as the heir of the French Revolution was to sustain and expand a democratic **meritocracy,** often called **"the career open to talent."** In a world still characterized by corporate society, the Napoleonic Empire offered great opportunities for the able, whatever their social origin or religion. No institution provided greater opportunities than his army, where soldiers could rise rapidly through the ranks despite humble origins. In a Napoleonic cliché, every soldier had a field marshal's baton in his knapsack, and it was up to him to find it. His closest marshal, Joachim Murat, was the son of an innkeeper. In an act that would have been unthinkable under the monarchy, Murat married Napoleon's sister Caroline and became king of Naples.

THE NAPOLEONIC WARS (1804–1815)

The Draft and the Birth of Mass Armies. Napoleon devoted most of his time to war; he stayed in France for only one-third of the days in his reign. When he became First Consul in 1799, France was at war with the remnants of the Second Coalition. France still relied on the numerical strength provided by the levée en masse, but battles were comparatively small. Napoleon's victory at Arcola, for example, had matched 20,000

French soldiers against 17,000 Austrians. During the next 15 years, Napoleon fought nearly permanent war against Europe. His armies occupied Madrid, Rome, Vienna, Berlin, and Moscow. This required the standing conscription of young Frenchmen, usually for 5 years. By 1814, he had drafted 2.6 million men and led more than 1 million of them to their death.

These huge numbers help to explain Napoleon's victories (see Table 21.5). The revolutionary army at Valmy had numbered only 59,000. By the time of the Third Coalition (1805–1807), Napoleon often sent 100,000 men into a battle, and that number soon seemed small. Much of his success came from having the largest army or from maneuvering until he obtained numerical superiority. When he had the advantage, Napoleon was ruthless. The Prussians learned this at the battle of Jena (1806): a French army of 96,000 crushed a Prussian force of 53,000, then pursued them relentlessly. Napoleon lost 5.2 percent of his army, whereas the Prussians lost 47.2 percent. When Napoleon lost such advantages, he began to lose battles. Numbers alone do not account for Napoleon's military reputation, however. His skillful use of artillery, especially concentrated artillery firing rapidly (versus the accepted wisdom of conserving ammunition), won some battles. His use of elite cavalry units as shock troops to attack infantry won others. But his military greatness was less a matter of brilliant strategies than inspired opportunism.

Changes in Warfare.
As warfare changed from small professional armies fighting small formal engagements to the ruthlessness of mass armies, other changes followed. In 1793, the Austrian army in the Netherlands had paid rent to Dutch farmers for permission to camp in their fields. When the retreating Austrians found themselves pushed against the Rhine River without sufficient money to pay for ferry service across the river, instead of seizing the ferries, the Austrians awaited the French and surrendered. Napoleon encountered a different psychology of war when he invaded Russia in 1812. The Russians used a **"scorched earth"** strategy: they burnt the farms and fields of the Russian peasantry instead of leaving food supplies for the French.

The War of the Third Coalition, 1805–1807.
By 1805, Napoleon faced a Third Coalition of Britain, Austria, and Russia. He prepared for an invasion of England until October 1805, when Admiral Horatio Nelson's fleet destroyed the French fleet near the Spanish coast off Cape Trafalgar, depriving Napoleon of the naval power needed for an invasion. Napoleon thereupon marched his army into central Europe and won major victories over the Austrians at Ulm (October 1805) and combined Austro-Russian forces at Austerlitz (December 2, 1805). Napoleon was so proud of his great victory at Austerlitz that he adopted all children of the French sol-

diers killed in that battle, promising that the government would support them, educate them, and find husbands for the daughters and jobs for the sons. (This also made December 2 the greatest patriotic day for Bonapartists.) He then pressed his troops on, and they defeated the Prussians, who had belatedly joined the coalition, at Jena (October 1806) and the retreating Russians at Friedland (June 1807). The defeat of Prussia allowed Napoleon to occupy Berlin, where he underscored his victory by dismantling and taking back to Paris one of the symbols of the city—the classic chariot atop the Brandenburg gate, known as the Quadriga. The price of such humiliation would be the awakening of a fearsome German nationalism. But in 1807, in less than 2 years of fighting, Napoleon had gained control of central Europe.

Napoleonic Europe.
Napoleon exploited his victories to redraw the map of Europe. He abolished the Holy Roman Empire, reducing Francis I to emperor of Austria. In 1806 he amalgamated western Germany into a puppet state called the Confederation of the Rhine. Holland was made a kingdom and given to his brother, Louis Bonaparte. The territory that Prussia had seized partitioning Poland was taken from her to form another client state, the Grand Duchy of Warsaw. Italy was divided into three regions: Northern Italy became the Kingdom of Italy, with Napoleon as the nominal king; central Italy was directly annexed to France; and southern Italy became the Kingdom of Naples, with Napoleon's brother-in-law, Murat, named king. Territory along the Adriatic Coast (previously governed by Venice) and the northern coast of Germany were also directly annexed to France. Spain was given to another brother, Joseph Bonaparte.

By 1810, most of Europe was under Napoleon's control, with Portugal, Britain, Scandinavia, Russia, and most of the Balkans remaining free. Prussia and Austria retained their independence, but they faced numerous controls. Prussia, for example, was limited to an army of 42,000 men and was made to host a French garrison. Austria, after attempting a Fourth Coalition and suffering another defeat at Wagram in 1809, was bound to France by a marriage in 1810 between Napoleon and Francis's teenaged daughter, Maria Louisa. As an angry Russian aristocrat said in the opening sentence of Leo Tolstoy's War and Peace, the great cities of Europe "are now just family estates of the Buonapartes."

The Continental System and the Peninsular Campaign.
Napoleon tried to fight Britain with **economic warfare**. His Berlin Decree of 1806 ordered the cessation of all commerce and communication with Britain. This plan, known as the Continental System, failed because it required more cooperation than Napoleon could compel. The loss of easy access to inexpensive English manufactures caused some Europeans to

TABLE 21.5 THE MILITARY CAMPAIGNS OF NAPOLEON

CAMPAIGN AND DECISIVE BATTLE	STATES AT WAR	SIZE OF ARMY	RATIO OF FORCES	NUMBERS LOST	PERCENTAGE OF ARMY LOST	PEACE TREATY
Italian Campaign						
Battle of Arcola (1796)	France	20,000	1.2:1	4,500	22.5	Treaty of Campo
	Austria	17,000		7,000	41.2	Formio (1797)
Egyptian Campaign						
Battle of the Pyramids (1798)	France	25,000	1.2:1	300	1.2	
	Turks	21,000		5,000	23.8	
Italian Campaign						
Battle of Marengo (1800)	France	28,000	1.1:1	7,000	25.0	Treaty of Lunéville
	Austria	31,000		14,000	45.2	(1801)
War of Third Coalition						
Battle of Austerlitz (1805)	France	73,200	1.2:1	9,000	12.3	Treaty of Pressburg
	Austria	85,400		27,000	31.6	(1805)
Battle of Jena (1806)	France	96,000	1.8:1	5,000	5.2	
	Prussia	53,000		25,000	47.2	
Battle of Friedland (1807)	France	80,000	1.3:1	8,000	10.0	Treaty of Tilsit
	Russia	60,000		20,000	33.3	(1807)
Austrian Campaign						
Battle of Wagram (1809)	France	170,000	1.2:1	32,000	18.8	Treaty of
	Austria	146,000		40,000	27.4	Schönbrunn (1809)
Russian Campaign						
Battle of Borodino (1812)	France	133,000	1.1:1	30,000	22.6	
	Russia	120,000		44,000	36.7	
Battle of the Nations						
Battle of Leipzig (1814)	France	195,000	1:1.9	73,000	37.4	Treaty of Paris (1813)
	Allies	365,000		54,000	14.8	
The 100 Days						
Battle of Waterloo (1815)	France	72,000	1:1.7	32,000	44.4	Second Treaty of Paris
	Allies	120,000		22,000	18.3	(1815)

Question: What important trends can be observed in these data?

Arthur Wellesley, Duke of Wellington

defy the Continental System. When Tsar Alexander I of Russia refused to cooperate, Napoleon decided to invade Russia. He did so despite unresolved difficulties in western Europe, where the Spanish resistance to Joseph Bonaparte had already created an independent Cortes (the Cortes of Cádiz, 1810–1813), which produced the liberal constitution of 1812, modelled on the French constitution of 1791. The Spanish had received the support of a British army commanded by Sir Arthur Wellesley. Spanish and British armies were already pushing back the French in Wellesley's brilliant Peninsular Campaign, which would earn him the title of the Duke of Wellington.

The Russian Campaign (1812). Napoleon's Grande Armée of 600,000 men nonetheless invaded Russia in June 1812 and initially won several battles. This included Borodino, the bloodiest battle of the nineteenth century where 44,000 Russians were killed in a single day. (In contrast, 55,000 Americans were killed in the decade of the Vietnam War.) Russian armies, however, typically retreated without permitting decisive engagements, following the scorched earth strategy of Marshal Mikhail Kutuzov. Even when Moscow fell to Napoleon,

MAP 21.3. THE NAPOLEONIC EMPIRE

Legend:
- French empire
- Under French control
- Allied to France
- Napoleon's route, 1812
- Battle site
- SPAIN Members of the Grand Coalition against Napoleon (1809-1814)

At its peak, the Napoleonic Empire (and its client states) stretched from Madrid to Moscow. France had annexed vast territories in the lowlands, western Germany, Italy, and even on the Adriatic. Spain and much of Germany, Italy, and Poland were under French control.

the Russians refused peace negotiations and set fire to their own city. Napoleon, the author of the maxim that "an army marches on its stomach," found himself with an impossibly long supply line and few prospects for survival by plunder, as the winter neared. His only choice was to retreat, which exposed his army to attacks from the rear, the tactic with which he had devastated opponents. He retreated, leaving nearly 300,000 French soldiers dead in Russia, with another 200,000 taken prisoner. Viewed from the other side of the field, this was an epic triumph, celebrated by Tolstoy in *War and Peace* (1866) and by Peter Tchaikovsky in *The 1812 Overture.*

Napoleon's Defeat and Abdication. Napoleon's defeat in Russia led directly to the collapse of his empire. Just as 1812 became a year celebrated in Russian patriotism, 1813 became a triumphal year of German nationalism. Frederick William III of Prussia immediately joined the Russians and urged Germans to unite against

Napoleon. The leading statesman of the new allied coalition was the Austrian foreign minister, Prince Klemens von Metternich, who brought Austria into the war against France after Napoleon had rejected the generous offer of peace based on the "natural frontiers" of France (shrinking the country back to the Rhine River).

The war in central Europe involved immense armies, especially in a decisive battle near the city of Leipzig (Saxony) in October 1813. This engagement, known as the *Völkerschlact* (the Battle of the Nations) to German patriots, saw the allies produce combined forces of 365,000 men, nearly double Napoleon's army and ten times the size of typical armies in the 1790s. Napoleon was thoroughly beaten. Shortly thereafter, allied armies poured into France from several directions. They occupied Paris in March 1814, and Napoleon abdicated a few days later. The victorious allies granted France a lenient peace treaty, the Peace of Paris (1814), restoring the frontiers of 1792. Napoleon was exiled to the Italian island of Elba in comfortable conditions, and the Bourbon family was restored to the throne of France. The new king, Louis XVIII, was the brother of Louis XVI; he had survived the revolution by joining the émigrés in 1791. (He skipped the title of Louis XVII in deference to the son of Louis XVI, who had died in prison.)

Waterloo (1815). In the following year, Napoleon escaped from Elba and with the support of his veterans seized control of France for a brief reign known as "the 100 days." The alarmed allies refused negotiations, and Napoleon marched an army into Belgium, where the British were garrisoned. British forces under the Duke of Wellington (joined by a Prussian army at a critical moment) defeated him at Waterloo, just south of Brussels, on June 18, 1815. The Napoleonic era was over, although the emperor lived on until 1821, exiled

FIGURE 21.7 *"The Napoleonic Wars."* The great neoclassical painter Jacques-Louis David became court painter to Napoleon and created several immense canvases glorifying his regime. None was greater propaganda than (left) his "Napoleon Crossing the Alps" en route to his victory in Italy and following the path of earlier conquerors whose names are immortalized in Alpine stone. The heroic rider astride a fiery charger is far from the truth, however. Napoleon chose a cautious crossing of the Alps on the back of a sure-footed burro. The white stallion remains, but little of the romantic heroism of Napoleon seen in Jacques-Louis David's painting survives in (right) Ernest Meissonier's "The French Campaign, 1814." Here, a somber emperor leads an exhausted army that had been beaten repeatedly for 2 years.

to house arrest on the remote British island of St. Helena in the south Atlantic.

CONCLUSION

The revolutionary era of 1789–1815 challenged, but did not destroy, the Old Regime. What began as a profound economic and governmental crisis in France grew into an attack on monarchical government, aristocratic privilege, and established religion. The French Revolution presented Europe with a breathtaking array of alternative ideas (many of which had been discussed and tried earlier) that would shape the political evolution of Europe until the present—constitutional monarchy, the abolition of monarchy, republican government, universal suffrage, the abolition of feudalism, the abolition of the aristocracy, constitutional government, bills of rights, the abolition of slavery, the abolition of state religions and the emancipation of religious minorities, the welfare state, the abolition of torture, universal military liability and the mass army, rationalized legal codes, standards of private property, and so forth.

But the clash between the Old Regime and such revolutionary ideas also produced some of the most horrifying violence in modern political history—the state executions of the Reign of Terror, the days of crowd violence, the ferocity of civil war, and the devastation of mass armies and total warfare. Consequently, across Europe (and across historical literature), many people loved, and many others hated, the idea of the French Revolution. A great conservative, Edmund Burke, thought the revolution (an irrational, proscribing, plundering, ferocious, bloody, and tyrannical democracy." But a great liberal, Thomas Jefferson, believed that "[e]very man who loves freedom has two homes, his own and France."

Review Questions

- What were the principal origins of the French Revolution?
- How and why did the Estates-General become the National Assembly?
- What was the importance of the revolutionary crowd in 1789?
- How did the rest of Europe react to the French Revolution?
- Why did France go to war with the rest of Europe? What was the outcome of this war?
- What were the major problems facing the Convention? What were the most important actions taken by the Convention?
- Why did the French Revolution turn to the Reign of Terror? What were the policies of the government during the Reign of Terror? What was the scope of the Reign of Terror? Who were its victims?

- What was the Thermidorian reaction? How did the Directory change the French republic?
- How did Napoleon Bonaparte come to power in France?
- Which of Napoleon's domestic policies suggest that Napoleon was a despot? Which of his domestic policies suggest that he was an heir of the revolution?

For Further Study

Readings

Chandler, David G., ed., *Dictionary of the Napoleonic Wars* (New York: Simon and Schuster, 1993). Excellent reference for the military history of the regime; written by the leading expert in the field.

Doyle, William, *The Oxford History of the French Revolution* (Oxford: Oxford University Press, 1988). The best current, detailed history of the revolution.

Holtman, Robert, *The Napoleonic Revolution* (Baton Rouge: Louisiana State University Press, 1981). A concise and sympathetic examination of Napoleon's accomplishments.

Jones, Colin, ed., *The Longman Companion to the French Revolution* (London: Longman, 1988). An excellent reference for chronologies and data.

Palmer, R. R., *The Age of the Democratic Revolution: A Political History of Europe and America, 1760–1800,* 2 vols. (Princeton: Princeton University Press, 1959–1964). A classic study of the French Revolution as but one part of an "age of revolution," seen in the context of the American Revolution, as well as many other revolutions.

Scott, Samuel F., and Rothaus, Barry, eds., *Historical Dictionary of the French Revolution, 1789–1799,* 2 vols. (Westport, CT: Greenwood Press, 1985). Valuable for short sketches of important individuals, institutions, and events.

THE FRENCH REVOLUTION

1789	1790	1791	1792	1793	1794

The French Monarch 987–1792   The (First) Republic 1792–(1799)

1789: *Cashiers* Express Grievance
May 1789: Meeting of Estates-General
June 1789: Tennis Court Oath
    June 1789: Deputies of Third Estate Proclaim "National Assembly"
    July 1789: Parisian Crowd Storms the Bastille
    July–August 1789: Peasant Uprising: the Great Fear
    July 1789: Beginning of Emigration of Nobles
    August 1789: Night of August 4 Abolishes Feudalism
    August 1789: Declaration of the Rights of Man
    October 1789: Women's March on Versailles
        July 1790: Louis XVI Accepts Constitution
        July 1790: Constitution Abolishes Parlements
        July 1790: Civil Constitution of the Clergy
            June 1791: Varennes Flight and Arrest of Louis XVI
            August 1791: Pillnitz Declaration: Austro-Prussian Intervention
            October 1791: Legislative Assembly Elected
                1792: Invasion of France by First Coalition
                August 1792: Mob Storms Tuileries Palace
                September 1792: September Massacres in Paris
                September 1792: French Defeat Prussian Army at Valmy
                September 1792: Election of the National Convention
                September 1792: Convention Abolishes the Monarchy
                November 1792: Revolutionary Armies Defeat Austria at Jemappes
                December 1792: Trial of Louis XVI Begins
                    January 1793: Execution of Louis XVI
                    March 1793: Royalist Revolt in Vendée
                    April 1793: Dictatorship of Committee of Public Safety
                    July 1793: British Siege of Toulon Makes Bonaparte a Hero
                    August 1793: Levy en masse for Army
                    October 1793: Revolution Crushes Federalist Resistance in Lyons
                    October 1793: Reign of Terror Executes Moderates (Girondins)
                    November 1793: Abolition of Christian Worship for a Cult of Reason
                        July 1794: Fall of Robespierre and End of the Terror

InfoTrac College Edition

For additional reading, go to your online research library at *http://infotrac.thomsonlearning.com.*

Using Key Terms, enter the search term
Reign of Terror

Using the Subject Guide, enter the search terms
Louis XVI   Napoleon
Madame de Stael

Web Sites

http://chnm.gmu.edu/revolution   "Liberty, Equality, Fraternity: Exploring the French Revolution," an outstanding site with hundreds of images and documents, maintained at George Mason University.

http://www.fsu.edu/~napoleon/   "The Institute on Napoleon and the French Revolution," a valuable site, maintained at Florida State University.

Visit the Western Civilization Companion Web Site for resources specific to this textbook:
http://history.wadsworth.com/hause02/

The CD in the back of this book and the Western Civilization Resource Center at *http://history.wadsworth.com/western/* offer a variety of tools to help you succeed in this course, including access to quizzes; images; documents; interactive simulations, maps, and timelines; movie explorations; and a wealth of other sources.

The West in the World

EUROPE AND THE WORLD IN 1800

Much of the world remained *terra incognita* to Europeans in 1800. Although explorers like French commander Louis-Antoine de Bougainville and English captain James Cook had undertaken dramatic missions of discovery in the South Pacific in the 1760s and 1770s, European knowledge of the region barely extended past coast lines. The interior of Australia (where the first European settlement was established in 1788) remained a mystery. Similarly, the interior of Africa was so little known that the continent was truly a "dark continent." Europeans did not know, for example, where the headwaters of the Nile River rose. Similarly, much of south Asia and east Asia had not yet been seen by European eyes.

Important regions of the world had fallen to European imperial conquest—notably the Americas and the East Indies in the age of exploration and much of India in the colonial wars of the eighteenth century—but far more remained self-governing, such as China, Japan, and Southeast Asia; virtually all of Africa and the Middle East; and the vast majority of the 25,000 islands of Pacific Oceania.

Europeans had long had contact with Africa, especially the North African territories under the suzerainty of the Ottoman Empire, and held a few coastal bases and numerous connections due to the importance of the Trans-Atlantic slave trade. But the states of Europe were not yet able to impose their will on Africa. A disease barrier, such as the deadly effects of malaria, largely kept Europeans out of Africa, but European military technology was not yet sufficiently advanced (until the arrival of automatic weapons in the late nineteenth century) to overcome African advantages in defense of their homeland. In many regions of Africa, a

A view of the harbor in Canton, China, around 1800. The white buildings atthe center fronting the water are part of the Western trading compound.

warrior culture such as the Kano aristocracy of Hausaland, the Salum Kingdom of Senegal, the centralized Yoruba states of Nigeria, or the Muslim theocracies of the Sudan provided formidable resistance (and frequent African wars and jihads).

Asia in 1800 had little interest of closer connections with Europe. Europeans had long been in contact with China, but they had achieved relatively little. A Jesuit presence was tolerated in return for a continuing introduction to Western science. A strictly limited trade was endured, but Europe offered almost nothing that the Chinese sought, except silver. The Manchu Dynasty had been in decline, however, and Europeans stood on the brink of a period of forcing their will on China, initially because Europeans craved numerous products of China such as tea, silk, and porcelain.

Japan under the Tokugawa shoguns (1603–1867) remained largely closed to Westerners. Until 1720, even the importation of European books or the study of European subjects remained banned. Despite European efforts, such as a diplomatic mission sent by Catherine the Great of Russia in 1793, the shogunate spurned friendly relations and rejected treaties with the West. Some coastal commerce continued, but it was strictly limited.

Similar rejections of the West and its ways characterized the rest of Asia. In Korea, for example, Catholicism was banned in 1785. Much of Southeast Asia remained a tributary of China and followed the Chinese example of limited relations with the West, although French interest in Vietnam had already begun by the late eighteenth century, when they helped rebels to capture Saigon. The only exceptions to this pattern came in territories long occupied as colonies, such as the Philippines, where the Spanish had established an occupying presence, centered in Manila, in the sixteenth century, and a Spanish governor general ruled the archipelago and reported back to the Council of the Indies in Spain. The governor possessed a commercial monopoly after a Spanish decree of 1751 and a chartered monopoly, the Royal Philippine Company, after 1785. In contrast to other regions of Asia, the Philippines consequently had a large presence of Catholic missions—Jesuits, Franciscans, Dominicans, and Augustinians—and frequent cultural clashes with the Muslim population.

The Spanish imperial presence also dominated central and south America in 1800. Spanish viceroys and intendants, serving under the administrative direction of the Council of the Indies in Spain, governed a region far larger than Spain itself. In Spanish America, as in the Philippines, however, European rule was met with repeated insurrections, such as the Maya Rebellion in Chiapas in 1712 or the Rebellion of Túpac Amaru in the Viceroyalty of Peru in 1780–1782. European rule in the Americas, like European efforts toward a greater penetration in Africa and Asia, was simply not welcome.

Chapter 22

INDUSTRIALIZATION AND THE SOCIAL AND ECONOMIC STRUCTURE OF EUROPE

FOCUS QUESTIONS

- How did the industrial system of factory manufacture develop in England?
- What changes in agriculture and manufacturing preceded the factory system?
- How was the new industrial economy related to changes in cities and the social class structure?
- How do historians analyze the conditions of daily life for workers?
- How did the countries of continental Europe compete with Britain during the industrialization of the nineteenth century?

*I*n early June 1832, a tired and nervous 23-year-old woman named Elizabeth Bentley who lived in Leeds met with a group of important men from London who asked her to describe her experiences working in one of the textile mills that characterized the new industrial system that had developed in England. Elizabeth explained that she had begun full-time work at age 6 to help support her widowed mother, and she had found the work very hard. During the 6-month busy season, she explained, her workday began at 5 AM and lasted until 9 PM, with only a 40-minute break to eat at noon. During the merciful slow season, she worked only from 6 AM to 7 PM. But it was hard work even then, she stressed to the gentlemen—she was on her feet for her entire 13-hour (or 16-hour) workday, and she had to lift a lot of heavy things. The worst part, she said, was when she worked in the carding room where the fibers were prepared—it was so dusty that she couldn't breath. Then her respiratory problems got so bad that Elizabeth Bentley couldn't keep her job and now lived in the poorhouse.

Chapter 22 looks at the process of industrialization in Europe that began in the late eighteenth century and by 1900 had dramatically transformed the economy and social structure. It begins by explaining two **demographic changes** associated with industrialization: a population explosion and urbanization. It explains a "vital revolution" produced by agricultural changes that fed a larger population, then focuses on the industrialization of Great Britain, often called the **Industrial Revolution.** After examining the positive and negative sides of life in the new urban world, the chapter focuses on the changing class structure of Europe, with special attention to the new middle class and the urban working class. It then discusses the impact of industrialization on women, children, and the family. This leads to what has been called the standard of living debate: Did the conditions of daily life improve or deteriorate during industrialization? The chapter ends by tracing the spread of industrialization across Europe, stressing the "take-off" phase of industrial growth during the mid-nineteenth century, followed by the **"second industrial revolution"** in which German industrial output began to match and even outstrip that of Great Britain.

The Population Explosion (1750–1914)

One of the most important developments in modern European history was a dramatic increase in population during the eighteenth and nineteenth centuries. The population of Europe had been slowly rising for centuries, but severe checks, caused by poor diet and nutrition, epidemic disease, primitive medical care, warfare, and repressive government, had limited that growth. Great Britain offers a vivid illustration. After William the Conqueror won control of England in 1066, he ordered a survey of his new realm; the resultant Domesday Survey (1086) determined that England had a population of 3.5 million. A good estimate of England in 1750 is a population of 6.5 million, which meant an increase of 3 million people in 700 years, an average growth rate of less than 1 percent per decade.

Population Growth (1700–1900). In contrast to that history of slow population growth, what happened during the late eighteenth century and the nineteenth century must be called a **population explosion.** A continent inhabited by perhaps 110 million people in 1700 became a continent of 423 million people in 1900 (see Table 22.1). This near quadrupling in Europe meant a growth rate of nearly 10 percent per decade, compared with the historic pattern of less than 1 percent. Britain, where the European population explosion began, provides the best illustration of this growth. Beginning in 1750, the British Isles experienced three consecutive decades of 6 percent population growth, followed by stunning decennial increases of 9 percent, 11 percent, 14 percent, and 18 percent. The astonishing population boom meant that a country that had grown by 3 million people over 700 years then grew by 11 million people in 100 years.

Population Growth Rates. The British population explosion continued into the nineteenth century and became a widespread (although not universal) European phenomenon. During the eighteenth century, population growth in most of the major states of Europe was approximately 35 to 40 percent—36 percent in the Austrian Empire, 37 percent across the Germanic states of central Europe, 39 percent in the Italian states, and 40 percent in Spain. France, the most populous and most powerful state of western Europe, experienced a slightly faster rate of growth (55 percent) but did not approach the remarkable 82 percent growth in Britain. In the nineteenth century, the rate of growth in Austria, Italy, and Spain increased to 70 to 85 percent, but the British rate of growth had soared to more than 150 percent, causing the **population density** (the ratio of inhabitants to territory) to surpass 100 inhabitants per square mile in large portions of Europe. Only Germany and Russia—where population growth was more than 200 percent—kept up with Britain. France, which pioneered modern **birth control** practices, did not experience such a dramatic population explosion, and the nineteenth-century growth rate there (45 percent) was lower than that of the eighteenth century (55 percent).

TABLE 22.1 The European Population Explosion, 1700–1900

The data in this table reflect historical boundaries at the date shown and therefore are not perfectly comparable. For example, the population of Alsace-Lorraine is included in France in 1800 and in Germany in 1900.

State	1700 Population (in millions)	1800 Population (in millions)	% Growth, 1700–1800	1900 Population (in millions)	% Growth, 1800–1900
Austria-Hungary	11.0	15.0	36.4	25.9	72.7
European Russia	17.0	29.0	70.6	106.2	266.2
France	17.3	26.9	55.5	39.0	45.0
Germany	13.5	18.5	37.0	56.4	204.9
Italy	13.0	18.1	39.2	33.4	84.5
United Kingdom	8.9	16.2	82.0	41.5	156.2
Spain	7.5	10.5	40.0	18.1	72.4

Calculated from data in Barbuscio, Jack, and Dunn, Richard M., *European Political Facts, 1648–1789* (London: Macmillan, 1984, pp. 335–353); Cook, Chris, and Paxton, John, *European Political Facts, 1848–1918* (London: Macmillan, 1978, pp. 213–232); Goodwin, A., ed., *The New Cambridge Modern History,* vol. 8 (Cambridge: Cambridge University Press, 1965, pp. 714–715); and Mitchell, B. R., *European Historical Statistics, 1750–1970* (London: Macmillan, 1975, pp. 19–24).

Question: What factors could explain the great differences in growth rates shown in the last column?

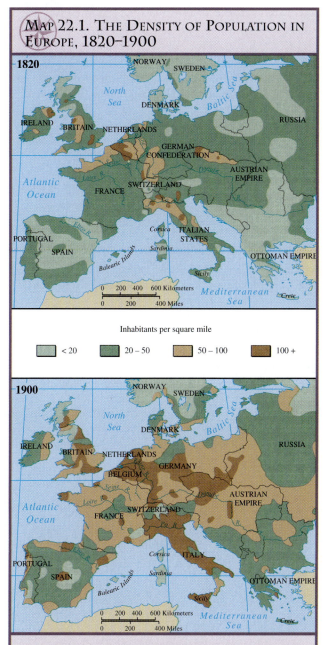

MAP 22.1. THE DENSITY OF POPULATION IN EUROPE, 1820–1900

1820

Inhabitants per square mile

< 20	20 – 50	50 – 100	100 +

1900

The density of population, measured by the number of inhabitants per square mile, increased dramatically during the population explosion of the nineteenth century, as the changing shading of these two maps shows. In 1700, the most densely populated regions of Europe were the lowlands (today's Netherlands and Belgium) and the old urban regions of Italy, which had more than 100 inhabitants per square mile. The map of 1820 shows that this trend extended to northern Ireland, parts of England, part of Northern France, and several regions of Germany. By 1900, vast regions of Europe held more than 100 inhabitants per square mile.

Reverend Malthus and the Malthusian Principle. The beginning of this population explosion so shocked one English economist, the Reverend Thomas Malthus, that he wrote the most famous book about population ever published, *An Essay on the Principle of Population* (1798), in which he warned about the dangers of this trend. Malthus argued that unchecked population growth tended to increase at a geometric rate (one, two, four, eight, sixteen, thirty-two), while the means of subsistence to support those people increased only at an arithmetic rate (one, two, three, four, five, six). The contrast between these two rates, known as **the Malthusian principle,** prompted the pessimistic conclusion that without some preventive restraints on population increase, the future of humankind would be a story of catastrophic checks on population.

The Vital Revolution. The conquest of the **biological Old Regime,** through the improvement of diet and the conquering of disease, amounts to a great **vital revolution.** The vital revolution that began in the late eighteenth century and extended through the twentieth century is arguably the most important revolution in modern history, even when compared with famous political and economic revolutions.

The Birthrate. Demographers measure the vital revolution with a variety of statistics, but the most important are straightforward: the **birthrate** and the **death rate.** The population of Europe had grown very slowly for centuries for the simple reason that the birthrate and the death rate remained similar. If one studies the birth and death data for early eighteenth-century Britain, the balance of the biological Old Regime becomes clear. In 1720, the birthrate per 10,000 people (314) and the death rate (311) were almost identical. Then in 1730, the death rate (349) exceeded the birthrate (339), and that pattern continued in 1740. Thus, for the first generation of the century, the biological Old Regime kept a virtually even balance between births and deaths. Beginning in 1750, however, British birthrates remained steady at a high level (between 366 and 377 per 10,000) for decades, while the death rate plummeted, hitting 300 in 1770, then falling to 211 by 1820. The huge gap between 366 births and 211 deaths per 10,000 population is the demographer's measure of the vital revolution, the source of the population explosion, and the pattern that frightened Malthus.

The Death Rate. The European death rate, especially the **infant mortality rate,** had remained frightfully high during the eighteenth century, and in many years, the death rate surpassed the birthrate. Studies of regions of Europe that had higher birthrates than Britain did—such as Lombardy in northern Italy—have shown

THOMAS MALTHUS ON THE PRINCIPLE OF POPULATION (1798)

Malthus (1766–1834) was both an Anglican clergyman and a prominent political economist. When he examined the figures for British population growth, he concluded that the widely accepted opinion linking a large, expanding population to prosperity was not necessarily true. He was not the first to question this wisdom (Adam Smith and David Hume had both suggested the same thing), but he was the first to develop a full argument about the dangers of this demography. The dangers that Malthus pointed out were one of the important elements in the widespread perception of economics as "the dismal science." His answer to the problem, especially expounded in the second edition, was to urge "moral restraint" (meaning sexual restraint). Later in the nineteenth century, reformers known as neo-Malthusians would use his theories in their campaign for the legalization of birth control.

I think that I may fairly make two postulata. First, That food is necessary to the existence of man. Secondly, That the passion between the sexes is necessary and will remain. . . .

Assuming then, my postulata as granted, I say that the power of population is indefinitely greater than the power of the earth to produce subsistence for man. Population, when unchecked, increases in a geometrical ratio. Subsistence increases only in an arithmetical ratio. A slight acquaintance with numbers will shew the immensity of the first power in comparison of the second. . . .

[In eighteenth-century Britain and America], the population has been found to double itself in twenty-five years. This ratio of increase, though short of the utmost power of population, we will take as our rule, and say that population, when unchecked, goes on doubling itself every twenty-five years, or increases in a geometrical ratio. . . .

If I allow that by the best possible policy, by breaking up more land and by great encouragements to agriculture, the produce of this island [Britain] may be doubled in the first twenty-five years, I think it will be allowing as much as any person can well demand. In the next twenty-five years, it is impossible to suppose that the produce could be quadrupled. It would be contrary to all our knowledge of the qualities of land. The very utmost that we can conceive is, that the increase in the second twenty-five years might equal the present produce. Let us then take this for our rule . . . and allow that by great exertion, the whole produce of the Island might be increased every twenty-five years, by a quantity of subsistence equal to what it at present produces. The most enthusiastic speculator cannot suppose a greater increase than this. . . . It may be fairly said, therefore, that the means of subsistence increase in an arithmetic ratio. . . .

Taking the population of the world at any number...the human species would increase in the ratio of: 1, 2, 4, 8, 16, 32, 64, 128, 256, 512, etc. and subsistence as: 1, 2, 3, 4, 5, 6, 7, 8, 9, 10, etc. In two centuries and a quarter, the population would be to the means of subsistence as 512 to 10. . . . No limits whatever are placed to the productions of the earth; they may increase for ever and be greater than any assignable quantity; yet still the power of population being a power of a superior order, the increase of the human species can only be kept commensurate to the increase of the means of subsistence . . .

From Malthus, Thomas, *An Essay on the Principles of Population* (London, 1798).

Question: Why might Malthus's contemporaries have considered this essay to be part of a "dismal science"?

---

that great increases in the number of births did not necessarily produce a significant population increase. If the twin guardians of the biological Old Regime, diet and disease, were not beaten, the death rate simply consumed the higher birthrate. The vital revolution of the late eighteenth century owed more to the improvement of diet than to the conquest of disease: the benefits of the **Columbian exchange,** such as the potato, and an **agricultural revolution** meant that Europe could feed a larger population. The great medical advances of the vital revolution mostly came in the nineteenth and twentieth centuries, although the slow conquest of smallpox had begun with Mary Wortley Montagu (Mahn'-ta-gew) and Edward Jenner in the eighteenth century.

The Urbanization of Europe

The vital revolution led to the urbanization of European civilization. For more than 2,000 years, the greatest centers of European civilization—from ancient Athens and Rome through the Italian city-states of the Renaissance to London and Paris in the Old Regime—had been its cities. By 1750, European cities had been growing in size and numbers for centuries. But the eighteenth century was not yet an urban society; in every country, the majority of the population lived on farms and in small villages.

British Urbanization. The British census of 1850 found that more than 50 percent of the population lived in towns and cities, making Britain the first predomi-

THE VITAL REVOLUTION

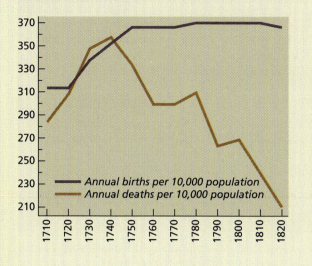

Source: Plotted from data in Voilliard, Odette, et al., eds, *Statisques d'histoire économique* (Strasbourg: Université de Strasbourg, 1964, p. 12).

Question: According to this graph, why did the population of Britain increase?

lived in metropolitan areas of 100,000 or more, whereas only 4.6 percent of France and 2.3 percent of Spain lived in such urban regions. The great Swiss cities of Geneva (31,000) and Zürich (17,000) were suddenly smaller than British towns such as Bradford (104,000). In 1800, two of the ten largest cities in Europe (London and Dublin) were in the United Kingdom; by 1850, four of the ten largest (London, Liverpool, Glasgow, and Manchester) were in the United Kingdom; and in 1900, the population of London was greater than the twenty largest cities of 1800 combined.

Continental Urbanization. When the effects of the population explosion reached continental Europe, so did urbanization. Just as Manchester, Birmingham, Leeds, and Sheffield had exploded from regional towns into major urban centers, new cities grew in Europe. Essen, in the Ruhr valley of western Germany, changed from a small town of 4,000 people in 1800 to a sprawling city of 295,000 at the start of the twentieth century. The transformation of Łodz (Poland) was even more dramatic: a village of 200 people in 1800 became a city of 315,000 in 1900. By 1900, only three of the largest cities in Europe were in Britain.

THE AGRICULTURAL REVOLUTION (1700–1914)

The first explanation of the vital revolution was an improved food supply. Although the nineteenth century still experienced famines in some regions (especially Russia) and occasional disasters such as the potato famine of the 1840s (chiefly Irish, but important in the German states, too), the pattern of regular subsistence crises that characterized early modern history ended by the middle of the nineteenth century. The average European diet was poor by twenty-first-century standards, but it had significantly improved since the eighteenth century, producing better general health, greater resistance to disease, and higher rates of healthy reproduction.

Food Supply, Prices, and Preservation. The improved food supply is best seen in late eighteenth-century Britain, where the population explosion began. Despite restrictive **tariffs** on grain imports, known as the **Corn Laws,** Britain imported an increasing amount of food after 1780, and this provided partial support for a larger population. British grain imports stood at 200,000 tons in 1780, rising to 3.7 million tons in 1800, and then 7.5 million tons in 1840. At the same time, the improvements in internal transportation—canals, toll roads, and railroads—reduced food prices in urban areas. Food shipment also improved as new technology

nantly urban society in history. The early nineteenth century was consequently a period of remarkable urban growth. Between 1750 and 1800, nineteen towns in Europe doubled in size, and fifteen of them were located in Britain. No town in France, none in the Italian states, nor any in Russia grew so rapidly, but in northern England—from Lancashire in the west, across the midlands to Yorkshire in the east—seven towns doubled in size. And the impact of the population explosion was just beginning. During the next half-century, 1800–1850, seven British cities (five of them in northern England) tripled in size, some nearly quintupling.

British cities were not huge by twenty-first-century standards, but they were astonishing by contemporary standards because the population explosion had not yet transformed the continent. The port of Liverpool, a town that had become prosperous during the slave trade, grew so fast in the early nineteenth century that it surpassed such capital cities as Moscow and Madrid in size (see Table 22.2). In 1850, the British Isles contained seven cities larger than Rome, the historic center of Europe. Nearly one-fourth of the British population

TABLE 22.2 POPULATIONS FOR THE MAJOR CITIES OF EUROPE, 1800–1900

This table shows the populations of the largest cities in Europe from 1800 to 1900. Changes in city size during this period illustrate the relationship between industrialization and urbanization: the period of rapid industrialization witnessed even more rapid urban growth. British cities are highlighted in bold-faced type. Note the importance of British cities in the data for 1850, a date often chosen as the point at which Britain had become a predominantly industrial society.

Europe in 1800		Europe in 1850		Europe in 1900	
CITY	POPULATION	CITY	POPULATION	CITY	POPULATION
London	**1,117,000**	**London**	**2,685,000**	**London**	**6,586,000**
Paris	547,000	Paris	1,053,000	Paris	2,714,000
Naples	427,000	St. Petersburg	489,000	Berlin	1,889,000
Moscow	250,000	Naples	449,000	Vienna	1,675,000
Vienna	247,000	Vienna	444,000	St. Petersburg	1,267,000
St. Petersburg	220,000	Berlin	419,000	Moscow	989,000
Amsterdam	201,000	**Liverpool**	**376,000**	Hamburg	931,000
Lisbon	180,000	Moscow	365,000	Budapest	732,000
Berlin	172,000	**Glasgow**	**357,000**	**Liverpool**	**704,000**
Dublin	**165,000**	**Manchester**	**303,000**	**Manchester**	**645,000**

Source: Mitchell, B. R., *European Historical Statistics, 1750–1970* (London: Macmillan, 1975, pp. 76–78); and Cook, Chris, and Paxton, John, *European Political Facts, 1848–1918* (London: Macmillan, 1978, pp. 213–232).

Question: If the urban data for 1850 suggest a period of British leadership, do the data for 1900 suggest the rise of a competing power?

allowed the preservation of food for transportation, beginning with the adoption of a sterile canning process that a Parisian chef, François Appert (A-pair'), had invented for Napoleon's armies in 1804.

Improved Harvests. The greatest source of an improved food supply in Britain, however, was an increase in British harvests so significant that historians have called it an agricultural revolution. The agricultural revolution involved both extensive use of land (more acres planted) and intensive use of the land (higher yields per acre). The stimulus to both developments was simple: grain prices rose with the population, previous bad harvests had left few grain reserves, and a generation of war with France sometimes interrupted the importation of grain (which fell from 4.6 million tons to 2.9 million tons in the years following 1810).

Extensive Use of the Land. Extensive use of the soil provided obvious possibilities. Land could be reclaimed by draining marshes and wetlands, such as the fens of eastern England or the marshes of central Italy. In other regions of Europe, especially Scandinavia and eastern Europe, sparsely populated woodlands and wildernesses could be cleared and planted. Wherever the science of **agronomy** established modern **crop ro-**

tation, the tradition of leaving fields lie fallow every third year could be abandoned. This alone produced a 10 percent increase in arable land in some regions.

Intensive Use of the Land. The most impressive side of the agricultural revolution—more intensive use of the land—achieved an unprecedented rise in European productivity. Scientific farming, such as improved understanding of fertilizers, significantly improved the harvest per acre. The beginnings of modern farm mechanization—from Jethro Tull's 1701 development of **seed drills** (a machine that planted seeds in orderly rows) to replace the manual broadcasting of seeds, to Andrew Meikle's (Mike'-ul) invention of the **threshing machine** (which separated edible grain from straw without the manual flailing of the harvested wheat) in 1784—produced more efficient harvests. Such developments increased the ratio of grain harvested to grain sown. In Britain, the wheat harvest went from a yield of 7:1 to a ratio of 10.6:1; at that rate, the British harvest was nearly twice as productive per acre as the rest of Europe and three times as successful as farming in eastern Europe.

New Crops. New crops were also an important part of the agricultural revolution. The introduction of winter

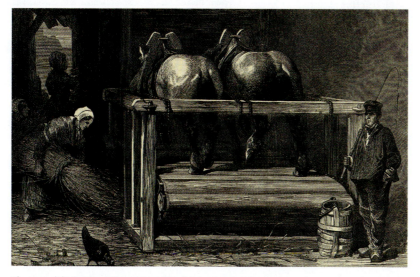

FIGURE 22.1 *The Threshing Machine.* One of the most basic improvements in the food supply has come from steadily improved methods of threshing—that is, methods of separating the edible grain or seed from the plant or husk holding it. Civilization advanced from shelling by hand, through beating on hard ground, to use of a tool known as the flail to beat the grain. At each stage of this evolution, it became possible to feed a larger population with less work. One of the most important stages came in 1786, when Andrew Meikle invented the first successful threshing machine. This image shows an early nineteenth-century Belgian version of Meikle's thresher. The woman is feeding stalks of grain between two rotating drums, which are driven by the pace of the horses.

mons for the use of all residents. No one could plant crops on the commons, but anyone could graze animals, forage for food (such as berries or acorns), and gather firewood there. Enclosure of the commons within fences meant that the land could be plowed to increase the national grain production, but the traditional rights of citizens ended, forcing many of them off the land. Enclosure in a larger sense ended the **open-field system** of agriculture, in which the land was divided into numerous small strips. In 1700, 50 percent of English farmland, and most continental farmland, was in open-field strips. By 1850, virtually all of rural Britain was enclosed.

Enclosure and Agricultural Efficiency.

Each enclosure required an act of Parliament, and 4,000 such acts of enclosure were voted between 1750 and 1850, although a General Enclosure Act of 1801 served as a model for most others. By these acts, the commons lands were sold in some villages and distributed among the landowners in others. This led to the consolidation of individual strips into single farms and the failure of small farms where the owners had depended on the commons. The resulting farms were larger than the sum of the strips because they incorporated the paths that had separated the strips, and they became larger yet as uncompetitive small farms were absorbed. By the early nineteenth century, two-thirds of British farmland was in large estates. Enclosure raised agricultural production as well as controversy. The benefits were larger than simply that more land was put under the plow and therefore more food was produced. Enclosure of the commons meant the segregation of herds of livestock, reducing disease transmission and permitting selective breeding. The breeding experiments conducted with sheep by Robert Bakewell, for example, saw the average weight of sheep brought to market rise from 28 pounds in 1710 to 80 pounds in 1795. Larger farms encouraged crop rotation because the entire acreage did not have to be planted in the same subsistence grain for the farm family. Consolidation of the open-field strips meant that farm equipment did not have to be moved great distances.

The Human Effects of Enclosure.

Enclosure provoked opposition because of the human effects on the rural population. Marginal farmers suffered worst. Without strips of common farmland, many families

crops in some regions, the continuing arrival of new American crops from the Columbian exchange, and the steady acceptance of root crops (such as the potato and the sugar beet) greatly changed European diets. The potato grew in more northerly climates and poorer soils than most grains; it had a 3- to 4-month cycle to harvest, compared with 10 months for many grains; and a single crop yielded twice as much nutrition per acre as grains did. Consequently, by the early 1840s, one-third of the population of England and one-half of Scotland lived on the potato. Even higher rates of potato consumption were found in Ireland and parts of Germany.

The Controversy over Enclosure

Clearing forests or swamps and harvesting more crops per acre were not the only changes by which the agricultural revolution fed the growing population of the British Isles. The greatest source of new acreage being farmed resulted from a controversial political decision known as **enclosure.** This term simply means the enclosing of farmland within fences. The laws of enclosure, however, had more profound results than that description suggests (see Document 22.2), leading some historians to argue that it was a necessary condition for industrialization. By ancient tradition, most villages in Britain reserved a portion of local land called **the com-**

TWO VIEWS OF THE ENCLOSURE OF THE COMMONS

Oliver Goldsmith supported the antienclosure view in his poem "The Deserted Village" (1770).

> Sweet smiling village, loveliest of the lawn,
> Thy sports are fled, and all thy charms withdrawn;
> Amidst thy bowers the tyrant's hand is seen,
> And desolation saddens all thy green:
> One only master grasps the whole domain. . . .
> Far, far away, thy children leave the land.
> Ill fares the land, to hastening ills a prey,
> Where wealth accumulates, and men decay;
> Princes and lords may flourish, or may fade . . .
> But a bold peasantry, their country's pride,
> When once destroy'd, can never be supplied.

Frederic Eden argued in favor of enclosure in *The State of the Poor* (1797).

> [T]he allegation has been so often repeated, that the laboring classes of the nation have been injured by the consolidation . . . [that] the author trusts it will not be deemed foreign to his purpose to remark that, if large farms do, in fact . . . lessen labor, and thence enable the cultivators of the earth to bring its various produce to market at a cheaper rate, it seems decidedly to prove that they are of great national utility. . . .
>
> If the consolidation of several small farms into one should be found . . . to bear hard on the owners of small farms, and perhaps on cottagers and laborers, this is an evil to be lamented indeed, but not of such a magnitude as that it should be suffered to counteract the greater good which may be expected to result from the improvement. At any rate, the inconveniences and the distresses thus provided can be but temporary; whilst the advantages to be expected from a contrary system are such as promise to be permanent.

From Eden, Frederic, *The State of the Poor* (London: 1797); and Baker, Kenneth, ed., *The Faber Book of English History in Verse* (London: Faber, 1988).

Question: How can historians reconcile the view that enclosure meant "Ill fares the land" with the view that enclosures "are of great national utility"?

could not survive by agriculture. Others faced failure because they had depended on the commons to graze a pig or a few geese. As one angry poet put it, "The law locks up the man or woman who steals the goose from off the Common; / But leaves the greater villain loose who steals the common from the goose." Historians have debated the amount of suffering caused by enclosure, and they have generally agreed that it is a question of long-term gains for most of society versus short-term suffering for much of society.

HANDCRAFT, COTTAGE INDUSTRY, AND THE STEAM ENGINE (1700–1850)

Industrialization. The agricultural revolution, the vital revolution, and the population explosion of late eighteenth-century and nineteenth-century Europe were all important factors in making possible a dramatic transformation of the European economy known as **industrialization,** in which manufactured goods began to replace agriculture as the dominant sector of the economy. Large-scale factory production began to replace handcraft manufacture; machinery and inanimate power sources began to replace human labor. Such large-scale industrialization did not happen suddenly or universally—factories, traditional production, and agriculture coexisted within a country, and usually within a region. Nonetheless, industrialization was such a dramatic change that contemporaries and historians (especially in Britain) have sometimes called it the Industrial Revolution.

Textile Production. The pressure of growing population demanded (and rewarded) great increases in the production of essential goods, such as the woolen and cotton textiles needed for clothing. Such goods had long been made by traditional handwork methods of spinning thread and weaving cloth. This handwork production of textiles had spawned a form of manufacturing known as **cottage industry,** in which entrepreneurial middlemen engaged people to produce textiles in their homes, provided them with raw materials, paid them for finished work, then transported the goods to town for sale. This form of employment in home spinning and weaving lasted throughout the nineteenth century in some regions, but beginning in the mideighteenth century, technological innovations replaced human skills and power with machines. Industrialization was the broad process by which machines, operated by hundreds of people in urban factories, replaced the production of handcraft workers in small shops and cottages.

The Steam Engine. The age of industrialization was opened by a new technology—the steam engine, which provided the power source for many other innovations that followed. The idea of exploiting steam power was not new. It had been known in the ancient world and had long been the subject of study and experimentation—one needed fire; a container of water; and an idea for containing, channeling, and applying the force of steam. No single person invented the **steam engine,** although popular culture in English-speaking countries credits James Watt and the French credit Denis Papin (Pa-pan′), who first conceived of using steam to force a piston up a cylinder. In reality, the steam engine was the culmination of the work of many people. Several engineers, notably Thomas Newcomen (New-kuh′-mun) in 1712, developed practical steam engines applying Papin's idea. The Newcomen engine generated five horse power and worked to drive a pump removing water from a mine. By the 1720s, working steam engines were being tested from Königsberg (Kur′-nigs-

burg; today, Kaliningrad) in East Prussia to Liege in Belgium. Paris used a steam engine to pump a water supply from the Seine in 1726.

James Watt. James Watt developed the first effective machines in the 1770s. Watt was a maker of precision instruments for scientists at the University of Glasgow and had patented improvements to the Newcomen engine in 1769. Watt devised an efficient means of condensing steam, which meant that the steam engine required less fuel. The initial use for Watt's steam

James Watt

engine continued to be in mining: steam-powered pumps could remove water from mine shafts that passed below the water table. This permitted much deeper mining, which facilitated vastly greater coal extraction; in turn, the coal could then be burned to operate more steam engines.

Use of the Steam Engine. As coal became more plentiful and less expensive and as steam engine technology proved successful, the engine found other applications. Steam-powered bellows at forges changed metallurgy, producing more and finer steel, which, in turn, made better steam engines. Steam-powered mills for grinding grains or sugar freed millers from dependence on rivers and water mills. Experiments applied steam power to heating city buildings and to transportation, including the first steam automobile (1769), steamboat (1783), and railroad locomotive (1804). The locomotive was the perfect symbol of the steam revolution because it was merely a giant steam engine with wheels attached.

The Age of Iron and Coal

Industrialization quickly came to depend on plentiful resources of iron, from which the machinery of steam technology was made, and coal, with which it was powered. Both iron and coal had been mined in Europe for centuries, but the scale of this mining was small. The total European output of pig iron in 1788 was approximately 200,000 metric tons, of which the British mined 69,000 tons. Most countries produced so little iron that they kept no national records of it. Coal mining was a similarly small-scale industry.

FIGURE 22.2 *The First Railway Locomotive.* Perhaps the most important evolution of the steam engine was to put a large steam engine on wheels and use steam power to move the wheels. The steam locomotive is essentially a large water tank with a firebox to boil the water and produce steam. The first successful steam engine was built by George Stephenson (1781–1848) in 1830 and named the "Rocket." It served as the first railway, the Stockton–Darlington line in England.

THE INDUSTRIAL REVOLUTION IN BRITAIN

The process of industrialization in Great Britain in the late eighteenth and early nineteenth centuries demanded great supplies of both coal (which was required to power steam engines by boiling water and to fire the forges in which the machinery of industrialization was made) and iron (from which the machinery was made). Mines and factories became sources of jobs, wealth, and power, which gave Britain world leadership in many ways. But it also came at a horrifying social cost.

Question: What standards should historians use to analyze the historical experience of industrialization—an experience that created terrible labor conditions and devastated the environment yet produced employment for many and vast wealth and power for a nation?

◄ *A Coal Mine during Early Industrialization.* Coal was a primary power source of industrialization. Pumps driven by steam engines (which were powered by burning coal), such as the Newcomen engine, made it possible to tunnel below the water table and extract large amounts of previously unavailable coal. Note the details in this contemporary illustration of a coal mine, which depicted child labor: boys and girls were used to cart the coal in narrow areas because they were cheaper than pit ponies. A lamp is located where a miner works (lower left), but an open flame risked an explosion if the miner encountered underground gases. Consider together this image and the data in Table 22.3.

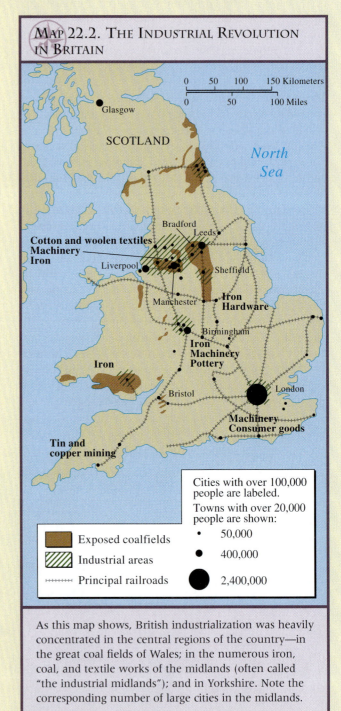

MAP 22.2. THE INDUSTRIAL REVOLUTION IN BRITAIN

Glasgow

SCOTLAND

North Sea

Bradford
Leeds

Cotton and woolen textiles
Machinery
Iron

Liverpool

Sheffield

Manchester

Iron Hardware

Birmingham

Iron Machinery Pottery

Iron

Bristol

London

Machinery Consumer goods

Tin and copper mining

0   50   100   150 Kilometers
0   50   100 Miles

Cities with over 100,000 people are labeled.
Towns with over 20,000 people are shown:
• 50,000
● 400,000
⬤ 2,400,000

▨ Exposed coalfields
▨ Industrial areas
╫╫╫╫ Principal railroads

As this map shows, British industrialization was heavily concentrated in the central regions of the country—in the great coal fields of Wales; in the numerous iron, coal, and textile works of the midlands (often called "the industrial midlands"); and in Yorkshire. Note the corresponding number of large cities in the midlands.

British Mineral Resources. The age of steam power clearly favored those countries with abundant (and easily available) iron and coal resources. Great Britain had the good fortune to possess exceptionally rich deposits of both natural resources. When the steam engine permitted—then demanded—greater coal mining, Britain exploited those resources (see *The Industrial Revolution in Britain*) to become the world's first industrial power and

TABLE 22.3 DEATH OF CHILD MINEWORKERS IN BRITAIN IN 1838

Nineteenth-century mines were extremely dangerous places to work, even for experienced adults. There was little government safety regulation due to the laissez-faire mentality of early capitalism, and there were numerous dangers. Mines extended far below the water table, and even with elaborate pumping systems, a child could drown far from the sea. As children were used to replace pit ponies in pulling coal carts down tram lines, many were crushed by a runaway tram full of coal. If they became tangled with the ropes used to raise great weights, they could even be crushed by having their body pulled into (or through) a pulley.

CAUSE OF DEATH	YOUNGER THAN AGE 13	AGE 13–18	AGE 18–21	TOTAL
Mine collapses and rock slides	15	14	72	101
Gas explosions	13	18	49	80
Falling down shaft	14	16	36	66
Drowning in mines	3	4	15	22
Crushed by tram	4	5	12	21
Gas suffocation	0	2	6	8
Drawn over pulley	3	0	3	6
Other	6	5	36	47
Total	**58**	**64**	**229**	**351**

Source: Compiled from data in Longmate, Elizabeth, *Children at Work, 1830–1885* (London: Longman, 1981, p. 35).

TABLE 22.4 EUROPEAN COAL PRODUCTION, 1820–1840

The data in this table are national outputs of coal in millions of tons.

COUNTRY	1820	1830	1840
Austria	0.1	0.2	0.5
Belgium	*	2.3	3.9
Britain	17.7	22.8	34.2
France	1.1	1.8	3.0
German states	1.3	1.8	3.9

*Belgium was part of the Netherlands in 1820.

Mitchell, B. R., *European Historical Statistics, 1750–1970* (London: Macmillan, 1975, pp. 360–361).

to establish an enormous lead in industrial might. During the French Revolution and the Napoleonic Wars (1789–1815), the British output of pig iron more than tripled; with peace, the output had tripled again by the early 1830s. (Output went from 69 metric tones in 1788 to 248 metric tons in 1806, then to 1,016 metric tons in 1835.) In 1850, Britain smelted 2.3 million metric tons of iron, more than half of the total supply of iron in the world. British coal mining similarly overwhelmed the rest of the world. In 1820, the Austrian Empire mined 100,000 tons of coal and the German states slightly more than 1 million tons; Britain mined 17.7 million tons. Twenty years later, Austria and the German states had tripled their output, but that was barely one-tenth of Britain's 34.2 million tons of coal. By midcentury, Britain mined more than two-thirds of the world's coal. Consequently, the British also generated more steam power than all of continental Europe combined. The British dominance in coal, iron, and steam production built an industrial leadership so great that Britons naturally spoke of their "industrial revolution."

THE MACHINE AGE (1770–1850)

The availability of inexpensive steam power and iron for machinery led to an age of remarkable inventiveness. In the century between 1660 and 1760, the British government had registered an average of six new patents per year; applications of steam technology drove that average to more than 200 patents per year in the 1770s, more than 500 per year in the 1790s, and nearly 5,000 per year by the 1840s. The British inventions of the early industrial age were not the result of excellent technical schools; continental schools such as the Schemnitz (Shem'-nits) Academy in Hungary or the École des Ponts et Chaussées (the first engineering school) in France were far superior. Most British inventions were the inspiration of tinkerers and artisans. One of the most important inventors of the early industrial age, Richard Arkwright, was a semiliterate barber with an exceptional mechanical aptitude.

Cotton and the Textile Industry. The earliest beneficiary of the new technology was the textile industry. Woolen goods had been a basic British export for centuries; in the early eighteenth century, woolens accounted for 25 to 33 percent of export revenue. Cotton goods were a newer export, produced from raw cotton imported from Britain's American colonies. In 1700, textile manufacturing had not changed much from medieval industry. Fibers were spun into thread by hand, perhaps with a spinning wheel, perhaps with simpler tools such as the distaff. The threads were then woven into cloth on handlooms. Spinning was usually done by women (hence the terms *spinster* or *distaff side* to refer to women); weaving, by men in a **sexual division of labor.** The entire handcraft process fit comfortably into a rural cottage.

New Inventions in the Textile Industry. The new technology of the steam age soon threatened cottage industry. Machines first changed the spinning of thread: James Hargreaves's **spinning jenny** (see *Women and Spinning in the Industrial Revolution*) allowed

one person to spin thread onto multiple spindles, producing 10 times as much thread—soon 100 times as much thread—as a good manual spinner. Arkwright's **water frame** mechanized the spinning of threads to produce stronger thread with less labor. The **spinning mule** of 1779 combined the spinning jenny, the water frame, and the steam engine to produce forty-eight spindles of high-quality thread simultaneously. Looms were also mechanized: the mechanical improvement of John Kay's **flying shuttle loom** allowed one person to do the work of two, and Edmund Cartwright patented the first steam-powered loom in 1785.

The Factory System. The consequence of this new technology was the textile factory. There, the steam engine could be linked to the spinning mule, to the power loom, or to banks of dozens of each. All goods, from raw cotton to coal, could be delivered to a single, convenient site, chosen for inexpensive transportation costs such as proximity to mines, location on a river, or nearness to a great harbor. Instead of having the looms of cottage industry scattered around the countryside, they were now grouped together in a single building or factory complex, where an overseer could control the pace and quality of work. Steam-powered textile machinery produced high-quality cloth in vast quantities.

English Textile Leadership. The first steam loom factory opened at Manchester, in northern England, in 1806. By 1813, there were 2,400 power looms operating in Britain, concentrated in Lancashire, the Midlands, and Yorkshire. A decade later, there were more than 10,000 textile factories using power looms in Britain; at midcentury, 250,000. The resultant change in the scale of textile manufacturing was even greater than those numbers suggest. Whereas a master weaver with thirty years of experience could produce two bolts of cotton cloth a week on a handloom, a 15-year-old boy at a power loom could produce seven bolts. Britain dominated global commerce in textiles, especially in the British Empire and Latin America, and British merchants began to dream of the day they could sell a shirt to everyone in China.

The Woolen Industry. The woolen industry, which had older traditions, resisted the innovations that transformed the cotton industry and mechanized more slowly. Most wool remained hand-loomed in 1840. Cotton, however, was a new industry without such resistance to change. It even attracted innovation, such as patents to make cotton velvet, to create ribbed cloth for stockings, or to print patterns on cotton cloth. Consequently, cottons surpassed woolens as Britain's foremost export in 1803; by 1830, cotton—a plant not native to the British Isles—accounted for more than 50 percent of Britain's foreign trade income, and more than half of the world's cotton cloth came from Britain.

WOMEN AND SPINNING IN THE INDUSTRIAL REVOLUTION

Women have traditionally been so closely associated with the job of spinning fibers to make thread that the vocabulary of spinning has come to identify women. Those who have not married might be called "spinsters," and all women might be identified as being the "distaff" side. The following images show how women's work dominated the spinning of thread from rural cottages to huge cotton mills.

Traditional Spinning. In this nineteenth-century print, women in a farm cottage work at a large, manual spinning wheels to produce thread.

Spinning in a Cotton Mill. In this English print depicting a cotton mill in 1851, women still work at spinning thread, but they now tend to enormous banks of power machinery that spins hundred of spools of thread at once. In this idealized image, the women work at a comfortable pace and the overseer (the man at far right) does not mind that two of them have stopped working and are talking with each other.

The Railroad Age

The new economy required improved transportation. Food had to be transported to factory towns in far greater quantities. Iron, coal, machinery, raw wool, and cotton had to be brought together. Manufactured goods had to be distributed. People had to be moved in large numbers. The railroad solved these problems, but the first steam locomotive was not built until 1804, and the first public railway—the Stockton-to-Darlington Railway—did not open until 1825. Railroads were the culmination of industrialization in Britain, not the cause of it.

Transportation before the Railroad. Transportation in Britain had improved significantly in the century before 1825. The trip between London and Edinburgh that took 12 days in 1734 required 4 days in 1762 and 40 hours on the eve of the railroad age. The chief developments in eighteenth-century transportation involved canal, road, turnpike, and bridge build-

ing. Britain had 2,000 kilometers of canals in 1700 and 6,500 kilometers in 1830. Transportation on rivers and these canals was the most efficient means of moving great weights, such as shipments of iron and coal. The development of canals serving Manchester cut the cost of coal to factory owners by 50 percent in the late eighteenth century, so the textile boom there owed more to waterways than to railways. Canals and rivers, however, had one major drawback: they sometimes froze in the winter, ending the distribution of goods.

Roads. Road building and maintenance improved tremendously during the eighteenth century. In 1700, Britain relied on a system of compulsory labor, similar to the French *corvée* (kor-vay'), under local supervision to do roadwork. Consequently, many roads in England were in worse condition than when the Romans evacuated in the fourth century. Then, in 1706, Parliament legalized **turnpike trusts**—associations allowed to

THE FACTORY SYSTEM

The A. Bajac Factory, Liancourt, Oise, in the Late Nineteenth Century. The development of steam-powered machines led to vast factories where many machines could be linked to a single power source. In this interior view of a factory making agricultural machines, note the seemingly endless vista of workers, the large number of windows letting in natural light—key to manufacturing before electricity—and the compartmentalization of labor. The overseers enforced strict work rules, such as no talking, singing, or sitting down.

Work Rules in a Prussian Factory, 1844

Good order and harmony must be looked upon as the fundamentals of success, and therefore the following rules shall be strictly observed. . . .

(1) The normal working day begins at all seasons at 6 AM precisely and ends, after the usual break of half an hour for breakfast, an hour for dinner and half an hour for tea, at 7 PM. . . . Workers arriving two minutes late shall lose half an hour's wages; whoever is more than two minutes late may not start work until after the next break. . . .

(2) When the bell is rung to denote the end of the working day, every workman . . . shall leave his workshop and the yard,

but is not allowed to make preparations for his departure before the bell rings. Every breach of this rule shall lead to a fine of five silver groschen. . . .

(3) No workman . . . may leave before the end of the working day without having first received permission from the overseer. . . .

(4) Repeated irregular arrival at work shall lead to dismissal. . . .

(6) No worker may leave his place of work otherwise than for reasons connected with his work.

(7) All conversation with fellow-workers is prohibited. . . .

(9) Every worker is responsible for cleaning up his space in the workshop. . . .

(12) It goes without saying that all overseers and officials of the firm shall be obeyed without question and shall be treated with due deference. Disobedience will be punished by dismissal. . . .

(15) Every workman is obliged to report to his superiors any acts of dishonesty or embezzlement on the part of his fellow workmen. If he omits to do so, and it is shown after the subsequent discovery of a misdemeanor that he knew about it at the time, he shall be liable to be taken to court as an accessory after the fact.

NOTE: A *groschen* was a small silver coin worth approximately one penny; 5 groschen in 1844 was a significant part of one day's wages.

From: Pollard, Sidney, and Holmes, Colin, eds., *Documents of European Economic History,* 3 vols. (New York: St. Martin's, 1968).

Question: Contemporary critics of the factory system called such factories "dark satanic mills." Do this illustration and document support that description?

---

build and operate **toll roads.** By 1750, there were 143 of these trusts in Britain, and they had opened 5,500 kilometers to toll roads. People and goods could move faster and more comfortably, if one could afford the tolls. As industrial development demanded better transportation, the turnpike trusts grew rapidly; in 1790, 519 trusts operated 24,100 kilometers of roads.

Technical Advances and Transportation. Many technical advances made the British transportation sys-

tem the best in Europe. An ironmaster named Abraham Darby III, whose family had built the world's largest **blast furnaces** (a furnace for smelting ore in which a "blast" of air speeds the extraction of minerals from the ore) and foundry, constructed the world's first iron bridge—a 295-foot-long "wonder of the age" that amazed gawking tourists and changed transportation. Similarly, a Scottish engineer named John McAdam (Muh-kad'-em) improved roads—subsequently called **macadamized roads**—by cambering them for

FIGURE 22.3 *The Industrialization of Travel.* The disappearance of coach services and the expansion of railroad service can be only partly explained in the contrast of these two images, which were created to show progress. The railroads did drive most competing coaching lines out of business, but the contrast was not quite this severe.

drainage and paving them with crushed stones. (The blacktopped road treatment known as macadam was named in his honor, but it was not yet in use.) The improvement in highway transportation was so dramatic that the coach companies began to remove the qualification "God Willing" from their time schedules.

Development of the Railroad. The railroad was the culmination of these trends and was so successful that it ended the age of canals and coaching. Railroads began with an old idea borrowed from the coal mines. Since the seventeenth century, collieries had used wooden rails to guide horse-drawn coal wagons; by the 1760s, many mines were switching to cast iron rails. Richard Trevithick (Trev'-uh-thik), an English mining engineer, won the race to develop the first practical vehicle to carry passengers and goods by designing a high-pressure steam engine in 1800. In early 1804, Trevithick's locomotive, riding on colliery iron rails, pulled five wagons containing seventy passengers and 10 tons of iron ore, for a distance of 9.5 miles at a speed of nearly 5 miles per hour.

The First Railroads. George Stephenson, an inventor who had devised the miner's safety lamp, built on Trevithick's work to start the age of railroad service. Stephenson built the 43-kilometer Stockton-to-Darlington line in the early 1820s to serve the heavy industries of the midlands—so the first train became known as **Stephenson's Rocket.** He then turned to a more important line, a railroad linking the mills of Manchester with the port of Liverpool. Many people opposed this development, and dire predictions were made of the impact of railroads: the smoke and sparks from coal-burning locomotives would kill flora and fauna, start wildfires, and destroy foxhunting. When the Liverpool–Manchester line opened in 1830, however, it carried 445,000 passengers and 98,000 tons of goods in its first full year. Stephenson's railroad was

so successful that of the twenty-nine stage coach services between Manchester and Liverpool in 1830, only one remained in business in 1832.

Continental European Railroads. On the continent, where rapid industrialization did not begin until after the end of the Napoleonic Wars in 1815, a railroad-building boom that started in the late 1830s supported industrialization. For much of the midnineteenth century, Britain kept a huge lead in railroad lines, as it did in iron, coal, steam, and textiles. Ten years after the Stockton–Darlington line opened, no railroads had been built in Austria, the Italian states, Russia, or Spain; all of the German states combined contained only 6 kilometers of railroad track. Fifteen years after the railroad age began, 63 percent of all European track was in Britain (see Table 22.5). Railroads were already changing the continental economy, however. A railway linking the Belgian seaport of Antwerp with the Rhine River port of Cologne was inaugurated in 1843; the **Iron Rhine** became one of the world's industrial arteries and made the third largest port in the world (after London and New York). In the second half of the nineteenth century, gigantic railroad stations became a dominant feature of the urban landscape and a central nexus of the economy.

THE URBAN WORLD (1770–1914)

The impact of industrialization on European society was most vivid in the rapidly growing cities. The population explosion, the decline in agricultural employment, the rise of the factory system, and the improvements in transportation combined to uproot thousands of people and draw them to the cities—a process known as **urbanization.**

The Variety of Towns and Cities. Unprecedented growth changed the nature of cities and urban life, but there was a range of types of towns and cities. Older towns often still stood within their medieval defensive walls. In many towns, the urban and the rural were still intertwined, sometimes with farmland within the walls and usually with important farming surrounding the town. Town dwellers often had gardens or even orchards. Livestock still lived inside towns, and it was not

TABLE 22.5 THE RAILROAD AGE IN EUROPE

COUNTRY	Railroad Track Open (in kilometers)			
	1825	1835	1845	1850
Great Britain	43	544	3,931	9,797
Ireland	n.a.	n.a.	150	865
Austrian Empire	n.a.	n.a.	728	1,357
Belgium	n.a.	20	577	854
Denmark	n.a.	n.a.	n.a.	30
France	n.a.	141	875	2,915
German states	n.a.	6	2,143	5,856
Italian states	n.a.	n.a.	152	620
Netherlands	n.a.	n.a.	153	176
Russia	n.a.	n.a.	144	501
Spain	n.a.	n.a.	n.a.	28
Switzerland	n.a.	n.a.	n.a.	25
Total on the Continent	n.a.	167	4,772	12,362
Total in Europe	43	711	8,853	23,024
% of European Lines in the United Kingdom	100%	77%	46%	46%

n.a. = Not available.

Source: Mitchell, B. R., *European Historical Statistics 1750–1970* (London: Macmillan, 1975, pp. 581–582).

Question: How does the extent of railroad development, shown here, compare to population, shown in Table 22.1?

unusual to see a pig or rooster wandering the streets. A 1786 census of Hanover—an important German capital and the home of the English royal family—found 365 head of cattle living within the walls, but no sidewalks, paved streets, or sewer system. The new industrial towns had similar conditions: transplanted animals lived alongside uprooted workers in the shadow of the factory.

London and the Emergence of the Modern City.
The modern city emerged painfully during the late eighteenth century and nineteenth century. London began the habit of numbering street addresses and invented sidewalks in the 1760s. Watt developed steam heating for his office, and his steam pipes were the first **central heating.** Experiments with the newly plentiful supply of coal led William Murdock to the invention of indoor lighting—the burning of coal gas provided more illumination than candles did. By 1807, the city of London was installing Murdock's **gaslights** on the streets; by 1820, gaslights were common in the homes of the well-to-do. The 1820s also saw London and Paris invent new public transportation systems: the horse-drawn **omnibus** (a bus available to the public) soon supplemented by urban railroads. The French Revolution stimulated another big change in city life— the invention of the **restaurant,** a result of the emigration of aristocrats who left behind many unemployed chefs. In 1789, Paris had only one restaurant (as distinct from cafés, inns, or taverns); in 1804, there were more than 500 and the institution was spreading. By the middle of the nineteenth century, the manufacturing economy had created vast **department stores** (such as the Bon Marché in Paris) and even arcade shopping centers (such as the Galleria in Milan).

Manchester and Industrial Cities.
Urban life during industrialization was not always as rosy as the image of restaurants and department stores suggests. The industrial and manufacturing towns such as Manchester, Essen (A'-sen), and **Łodz** (Woodg') initially grew too fast for basic amenities to keep pace with the population (see *The Nineteenth-Century Urban World*). Housing, fresh water, sewers, and sanitation were dangerously inadequate. An attractive environment (such as trees or clean air) or convenient services (such as shops or schools) were even rarer. Many contemporaries recorded their horror at the sight of factory towns. Charles Dickens depicted Manchester as a dreadful place, blackened by the soot of ubiquitous coal burning. Elisabeth Gaskell, who rivaled Dickens for vivid details, described the nightmare of life in such conditions. In *Mary Barton* (1848), Gaskell described the squalid conditions of life in a slum cellar, where starvation and typhus competed for the lives of a family sleeping on beds of damp straw.

Pollution and the Urban Environment.
Even the old cities could not keep up with their growth. In the Westminster district of London, residents living within one block of Parliament complained to the government in 1799 about the stinking odor of their street, which had not been cleaned of horse and human waste in 6 months. In that same district of the richest city on Earth, **air pollution** (chiefly from coal burning) was so terrible during hot weather that Parliament usually voted for an early summer recess. But those who went north for the summer, as the poet laureate Robert Southey did, might not escape deplorable conditions. The air in Edinburgh was so bad, Southey claimed, that "you might smoke bacon by hanging it out the window."

Haussmann and Urban Renewal in Paris.
Much of nineteenth-century urban history became the story of **urban renewal.** Paris became a much

THE NINETEENTH-CENTURY URBAN WORLD

The rapid urbanization of Europe during the nineteenth century was one of the most dramatic transformations in European history. These images depict two different stages in that transformation. In the first, the town is seen still surrounded by the rural world and closely related to it, although the beginning of its industrialization can be seen. In the second, the city has grown so large that urban renewal is needed to handle the new roles of the city.

Question: What other images of nineteenth-century urban change might be depicted here?

Factories at Le Creusot, France, in the Midnineteenth Century. Manufacturing soon changed the appearance of cities. Not only did they grow larger and the skyline grow taller, the factory system led to the chimneys and smoke seen here.

Urban Renewal in Paris in the 1850s and 1860s. Many European cities retained characteristics of the medieval and early modern town in the nineteenth century. During the reign of Napoleon III in France, Paris introduced the world to massive projects of urban renewal, directed by Baron Haussmann. In this scene, narrow medieval streets are being replaced by a long, wide, and straight boulevards by tearing down many of the surrounding buildings.

more pleasant city with the construction of the comprehensive **sewer system** that Victor Hugo described as a setting of *Les Misérables.* In 1800, Paris had a total of 20 kilometers of sewers; by the late nineteenth century, it had more than 2,000 kilometers. Paris became a model of urban renewal in the 1850s, when a comprehensive plan for the city, developed under Baron Georges Haussmann (Owes'-mann), tore down many of the dark buildings and narrow streets surviving from medieval Paris and replaced them with the broad boulevards and graceful residences of a "city of light." With modern sewers, street lighting, public transportation, and a central food distribution market (*"Les Halles"*), **Haussmanization** became the model of urban renewal. The Austrian government similarly modernized Vienna by tearing down the fortifications that screened the city and replacing them with a broad, circular boulevard known as the *Ringstrasse,* along which the city built its public buildings—an opera house, a new city hall (*Rathaus*), a university, the stock exchange, a National Theater, Parliament, and Palace of Justice.

CHARLES DICKENS DESCRIBES CONDITIONS IN MANCHESTER (*HARD TIMES*, 1854)

Observers were often startled by living conditions in the early Industrial Revolution, and many of them wrote vivid descriptions of what they had seen. The most famous include an unattractive portrait of Manchester in Charles Dickens's novel *Hard Times* (1854) and a blunt denunciation of conditions there in Friedrich Engels's *The Condition of the English Working Class* (1845). Many others can be compared with these. Alexis de Tocqueville, chiefly remembered for his description of America in *Democracy in America* (1835), also visited Britain and wrote about life in Manchester. Elizabeth Gaskell, a novelist whose pictures of industrial conditions rivals Dickens's, was especially vivid in *Mary Barton* (1848). Other startling descriptions can be found in the report of a parliamentary investigation known as the *Ashley Report* (1851). The following excerpt from Dickens, gives a hint of contemporary shock.

Coketown [Manchester] . . . was a town of red brick, or of brick that would have been red if the smoke and ashes had allowed it; but as matters stood it was a town of unnatural red and black, *like the painted face of a savage. It was a town of machinery and tall chimneys, out of which interminable serpents of smoke trailed themselves forever and ever, and never got uncoiled. It had a black canal in it, and a river that ran purple with ill-smelling dye, and vast piles of buildings full of windows where there was a rattling and a trembling all day long, and where the piston of the steam engine worked monotonously up and down like the head of an elephant in a state of melancholy madness. It contained several large streets all very like one another, and many small streets still more like one another, inhabited by people equally like one another, who all went in and out at the same hours, with the same sound upon the same pavements, to do the same work, and to whom every day was the same as yesterday and tomorrow, and every year the counterpart of the last and the next.*

Question: Where does Dickens's description fit in the urban development seen in the box *Continental European Industrialization?*

CHANGING CLASS STRUCTURES IN THE NINETEENTH CENTURY

The beginning of the industrial age changed the **social structure** of the city (the division of the population into multiple socioeconomic groups) as much as it changed the physical appearance. Industrialization created a new elite of middle-class wealth, based on **capital,** not land—a wealth of merchants, manufacturers, industrialists, and financiers. The British social critic Thomas Carlyle called them "Captains of Industry"; others referred to "Lords of the Loom" or "Railroad Kings" or dozens of similar titles. Heavily industrialized regions, such as Alsace, created a wealthy aristocracy of the new rich. The Koechlin family of Mulhouse (Alsace) went from the comfortable life provided by a successful weaver in a cottage industry to the immense wealth of factory owners within a single generation. The leading families of this **industrial bourgeoisie** formed an elite with different interests than the landed aristocracy. During the nineteenth century, this small social group joined with other parts of the **urban middle class** (or **bourgeoisie**), such as the older elite of middle-class wealth (such as mercantile, shipping, or banking wealth) and the educated middle-class professions (such as doctors, lawyers, or professors) to challenge the political dominance of the Old Regime alliance of monarchy, aristocracy, and established churches. For members of these diverse sectors of the middle class, the nineteenth century was an era of increasing prosperity, an exciting and comfortable epoch.

The Urban Working Class. The new bourgeoisie may have been the most influential class in the changing society of the industrial age, but it was relatively small. A larger change in the social structure was the rapid growth of an urban **working class,** whose members operated the steam engines, power forges, spinning mules, power looms, and trains. The working class—or **proletariat** as this social class was frequently called—often formed a majority of a town's population, particularly if domestic servants (the largest source of work for women in the nineteenth century) are included. A study of the social structure in Belgian textile towns found that approximately half of the population was employed as spinners or weavers in the new factories. The social structure was not simply a world of bosses and workers, however. Towns might still include farmers and farm laborers, and they certainly included the traditional artisanal trades and crafts (25 percent of the population in many towns). In most towns, the professions, the middle-class elite, and the upper classes of wealth remained a small percentage of the population, typically less than 5 percent.

Age, Gender, and the Family

Women in the Labor Force. The new industries initially favored the employment of men in most jobs, but the textile adopted a **sexual division of labor** that had typified cottage industry: women did most of the spinning, and men did most of the weaving. Many employment traditions broke down, however. Machines often required few skills and little strength to make superior textiles; factory owners therefore favored women and children for much wage labor because they worked for lower wages than men did. Women soon held a majority of the jobs in the textile industry (see Table 22.6), and other occupations soon underwent a change in which women held most or all of the jobs (otherwise known as **feminization**). Factory owners spoke of a woman's dexterity, or reliability, and many thought (often erroneously) of women as a less truculent labor force. Low wages, however, were the explanation for the growing employment of women. A study of women workers in London in 1848, for example, found that women earned 34 percent of men's wages. When Parliament investigated working conditions, factory owners candidly admitted that they preferred women because they could pay them less and because women would work hard to provide for their children. As one mill owner testified, women "are attentive, docile . . . and are compelled to use their utmost exertions to procure the necessities of life." This low-paid existence was so precarious that thousands of women were forced into prostitution (which was legal) to survive, a fact visible on the streets of most European cities.

The Family Wage Economy. Whether the factory hired men, women, or children, industrialization changed the nature of a working family's economy. Instead of the tradition where a husband, wife, and children might often work together, sharing work in a **family economy**—at different tasks on a farm, in domestic production, or in a small shop—the new urban employment often split the family apart in individual employment for individual wages. As factory wages remained low, such employment often led all family members to take full-time employment, and it encouraged large families in which children went to work at an early age. Economic historians label this new arrangement a **family wage economy,** because the family survived by all members pooling their earnings from different jobs.

Domestic Service and Traditional Jobs. Many older towns that did not become centers of textile manufacturing or heavy industry, such as York (England), continued to prosper on traditional handicraft manufacturing and as commercial and marketing centers. The social structure in those towns was different, especially when considering gender. Woman constituted nearly one-third of the labor force in York in 1851 (a typical figure for the nineteenth-century economy), but barely 1 percent of working women held jobs in factory manufacturing (see Table 22.6). Far more women—30 percent of working women—worked in traditional handcraft manufacturing and small shops. But most of the working women of York labored in the century's chief occupation for women, **domestic service.** The middle-class prosperity of industrialization and the low wages paid to women of the working class created a market in which all members of the middle class were expected to keep household servants, and even members of the lower middle class, such as shopkeepers, could afford a cook or a maid. Across Europe, the unmarried daughters of the lower classes filled these posts; they often did so eagerly, because a servant's post meant a more comfortable life than factory work did.

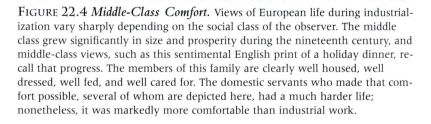

FIGURE 22.4 *Middle-Class Comfort.* Views of European life during industrialization vary sharply depending on the social class of the observer. The middle class grew significantly in size and prosperity during the nineteenth century, and middle-class views, such as this sentimental English print of a holiday dinner, recall that progress. The members of this family are clearly well housed, well dressed, well fed, and well cared for. The domestic servants who made that comfort possible, several of whom are depicted here, had a much harder life; nonetheless, it was markedly more comfortable than industrial work.

TABLE 22.6 EMPLOYMENT IN BRITISH COTTON FACTORIES BY GENDER, 1835

The data presented in this table clearly demonstrate the importance of women's labor during the Industrial Revolution; in every region of the United Kingdom, women represented the majority of the workforce in the cotton mills. Long before the twentieth-century discussion of women working outside the home, they were essential to the economy.

REGION	NUMBER OF MEN	% OF MEN	NUMBER OF WOMEN	% OF WOMEN
England	88,266	48.2	94,861	51.8
Ireland	1,639	38.0	2,672	62.0
Scotland	10,529	32.3	22,051	67.7
Wales	452	39.3	699	60.7
Total United Kingdom	100,886	45.6	120,283	54.4

Aspinall, A., and Smith, Anthony E., eds., *English Historical Documents*, vol. 11 (London: Eyre and Spottiswoode, 1959, p. 512).

Question: What conclusions about working women can be drawn from these data?

TABLE 22.7 CHILD LABOR IN THE FRENCH TEXTILE INDUSTRY, 1845

INDUSTRY	NUMBER OF CHILDREN EMPLOYED	CHILDREN AS A % OF THE INDUSTRY'S LABOR FORCE	CHILDREN IN THE INDUSTRY AS A % OF ALL CHILD LABOR
Cotton	44,828	18.3	31.2
Woolen	26,800	18.6	18.7
Cotton blend	11,038	23.9	7.7
Silk	9,326	5.6	6.5
Hemp and flax	7,232	12.8	5.0
Wool and silk	4,765	12.5	3.3
Textile total	103,989	—	72.4

Source: Weissbach, Lee S., *Child Labor Reform in Nineteenth Century France* (Baton Rouge: Louisiana State University Press, 1989, p. 19). Reprinted by permission of the publisher.

Question: What conclusions about the life of children can be drawn from these data?

died in mine collapses, thirteen died in gas explosions, three drowned, and four were crushed by trams.

Child Labor. Although working women faced terrible exploitation during industrialization, the treatment of working children was even worse. In the agricultural society of the Old Regime, children had worked as part of the family economy, and they had begun farm work at an early age. Urban children whose families possessed the resources to obtain an apprenticeship for them had to leave home by their early teens, and some trades took apprentices at a much earlier age. But none these experiences prepared observers for the exploitation of children in the early industrial era.

Child Labor in Mining. Children were employed in mining (see *The Industrial Revolution in Britain*) as early as age 5 to 7 years. Mine owners argued that children were needed because their size enabled them to fit into tight places. Often, however, they were used for tasks such as sorting coal or even to replace the ponies that pulled ore carts. Small wages were as important as small size. Studies of child labor during industrialization have found that these practices accounted for 15 to 20 percent of all mining labor. It was unhealthy, dangerous work, and hundreds of children died in the mines each year. In 1838, for example, 122 British workers younger than age 18 died in the mines; fourteen were preteenage children who died by falling down mineshafts, fifteen

Child Labor in Factories. The factory age expanded the use of child labor. Factories such as Josiah Wedgwood's famous pottery typically employed as much as 30 percent of their labor force in workers younger than age 18. The textile mills pushed that policy to new extremes. Studies have found that, on average, 40 to 50 percent of those employed in the early British cotton mills were younger than age 18; the worst offenders relied on children for 70 to 80 percent of their labor and employed strict discipline to keep the children docile. A study of child labor in France in the 1840s (see Table 22.7) found that textile mills employed more than 72 percent of all child labor in France, and both the cotton and woolen industries still relied on children for nearly 20 percent of their labor force. European society initially permitted this treatment of children because the prevalent political philosophy (**classical liberalism,** see Chapter 24) and economic theory (**laissez-faire capitalism,** see Chapter 24) both insisted that governments not intervene in the economic process or regulate industries. Parliament reluctantly concluded that it must nonetheless intervene and regulate child labor, which it did in a series of **Factory Acts;** the Factory Act of 1833 limited children aged 13 to 18 to 69 hours of work per week and children aged 9 to 13 to 48 hours of work.

The Standard of Living Debate

The subject of the exploitation of women and children in the industrial economy raises one of the most heated debates in modern historical scholarship, a controversy known as the **standard of living debate.** On one side of this debate, social historians depict the ghastly living and working conditions of workers in the early industrial age; on the other side, economic historians show a steady improvement across the nineteenth century in the cost of living and the standards of living for the working class. The optimists look back at the new industrial towns and see affordable workers' cafés in the bright illumination of Murdock's gaslights. When the pessimists look back, they smell the stench of uncollected refuse in the streets and the foul dampness in typhus-infested cellar bedrooms. Both viewpoints contain an important historical truth, and the debate is not resolved.

Critics of Industrialism. The early critics of industrialization were numerous. They ranged from England's greatest romantic poet, William Wordsworth, who wrote in 1814, "I grieve when on the darker side of this change I look," to the co-founder of **Marxist socialism** (see Chapter 24), Friedrich Engels. Engels, the son of a rich German industrialist, lived in Manchester and studied manufacturing there in 1844. His conclusion was brutal: "I charge the English middle class with mass murder." The contemporary British historian who coined the name Industrial Revolution also reached a shocking conclusion; he called industrialization "a period as terrible as any through which a nation every passed."

Life in a Factory Town. The anger of such critics has derived chiefly from the conditions in the new factories and life in the factory towns. Life in that world had an undeniably grim side (see Chapter 23). Conditions in the textile factories were so bad that another poet, William Blake, named them "dark Satanic mills." These unregulated workplaces had terrible safety standards; with no guards on the new machinery, mutilating accidents were common. Factories were typically unbearably hot, so men, women, and children worked stripped to the waist. But the environment was hardly erotic: machines overwhelmed the ears with a deafening roar, the nose with overheating grease, and the eyes and lungs with cotton or coal dust. This combination gave Manchester the world's highest rate of bronchial ailments, a life expectancy sharply below the national average, and a horrifying infant mortality rate of 50 percent.

Factory Work. Jobs in these dreadful conditions also required workers to adapt to a new discipline (see *The Factory System*). Most workers came from the countryside, where they had been accustomed to agricultural work defined by the rhythms of nature—the seasons, daylight, weather—or to such self-disciplined labor as spinning or weaving at home. Factory work was a regime of rules, enforced by an overseer with the threat of fines or dismissal; regimentation came not from nature, but from the clock and the pace of a machine. Typical industrial work rules forbade singing or even talking. Fines for talking would be deducted from wages. The first large spinning factory in England fired an average of twenty workers per week and averaged a 100 percent turnover within 1 year. One of the most famous novels of the century, Gustave Flaubert's *Madame Bovary,* ends with the thought that life in the dark satanic mills was appropriate punishment for sin. The protagonist of the novel, Emma Bovary, commits adultery and then suicide. Her relatives refuse to accept the care of Emma's orphaned daughter; the child is punished for the shame of Emma's behavior by being sent to earn her living in a cotton mill.

The Defense of Industrialization. Other contemporaries defended the conditions of industrialization. Frederic Eden began the optimistic tradition with his defense of agricultural enclosures in *The State of the Poor* (1797). Eden acknowledged that the consolidation of farms might hurt small farmers and farm laborers, but he argued that the difficult straits that they faced were "but temporary" and they must be balanced against "the greater good which may be expected from the improvement." Early champions of industry went further in their defense of the factory system. Andrew Ure, a Scottish scientist angered at the criticism of industrialization, wrote a thoroughly optimistic book in 1835 titled *The Philosophy of Manufactures* (see Document 22.4). To Ure, the factory system was nothing less than "the great minister of civilization." He found workers to be "willing menials" who were "earning abundant food, raiment, and domestic accommodation without perspiration at a single pore."

Improvements in the Standard of Living. Economic historians have shown much data to support the optimistic view that industrialization improved life for most people. The most obvious argument is that of the conquest of the biological Old Regime and the significantly increased life expectancy (see Chapter 23). Newborn infants in 1700 had an average life expectancy of less than 40 years; by 1824, it had reached 50 years. Witnesses might describe terrible living conditions during industrialization, but increased life expectancy must prove that conditions had improved in some substantial ways.

Wages and Expenses. Wages of workers did not improve greatly, and in some preindustrial occupations (such as a handloom weaver) they declined severely.

ANDRE URE ON THE FACTORY SYSTEM, 1835

Andrew Ure (1778–1857) was a Scottish chemist and the author of several reference books about chemistry, mining, and manufacturing. He wrote *The Philosophy of Manufactures* (1835) to respond to the criticism of factory conditions.

In my recent tour, continued during several months, through the manufacturing districts, I have seen tens of thousands of old, young, and middle-aged of both sexes—many of them too feeble to get their daily bread by any of the former modes of industry—earning abundant food, raiment, and domestic accommodation without perspiring at a single pore, screened meanwhile from the summer's sun and the winter's frost, in an apartment more airy and salubrious than those of the metropolis, in which our legislative and fashionable aristocracies assemble. In those spacious halls, the benign power of steam summons around him his myriads of willing menials, and assigns to each the regulated task, substituting for painful muscular effort on their part the energies of his own gigantic arm and demanding in return only attention and dexterity to correct such little aberrations as casually occur in his workmanship. The gentle docility of this moving force qualifies it for impelling the tiny bobbins of the lace machine with a precision and speed inimitable by the most dexterous hands, directed by the sharpest eyes. Hence, under its auspices . . . magnificent edifices, surpassing far in number, value, usefulness, and ingenuity of construction the boasted monuments of Asiatic, Egyptian, and Roman despotism, have within the short period of fifty years risen up in this kingdom to show to what extent capital, industry, and science may augment the resources of the state while they meliorate the condition of its citizens. Such is the factory system, replete with prodigies in mechanics and political economy, which promises in its future growth to become the great minister of civilization.

From Ure, Andrew, *The Philosophy of Manufacturers* (London: C. Knight, 1835).

Question: Compare this reading to the previous excerpt from Charles Dickens. Is it possible to reconcile these two views?

But the data show a general pattern of improvement. Whereas a carpenter working in the London region had to work 13 or 14 days in 1800 to earn enough money to buy a suit, the same carpenter's wages in 1830 bought a suit in 7 or 8 days. Industrialization also provided enough wages for luxuries that workers previously could not afford, from sugar and tea to fish and chips. By the 1840s, railway expansion led to inexpensive excursion tickets. Railroads reinforced the rigid social structure of nineteenth-century Europe by segre-

gating passengers according to the class of tickets they bought, but the existence of cheap second- or third-class tickets led to the birth of the working-class holiday. For the first time, most of the population of London could afford a day trip to the seashore. Workers had little leisure time to enjoy this benefit, but inexpensive rail travel allowed more than one-third of the total population of Great Britain to visit the world exposition in London in 1851.

FROM THE BRITISH INDUSTRIAL REVOLUTION TO CONTINENTAL EUROPEAN INDUSTRIALIZATION (1770–1850)

Early Industrialization in Europe. British industrialization dwarfed the manufacturing of any other country in the late eighteenth and early nineteenth centuries, but Britain was not unique in experiencing industrial development. In the textile industry, for example, Belgium had been an important manufacturer of cloth for centuries and rapidly industrialized following the British example. Textile towns such as Manchester developed across Europe from Ghent (Belgium), to Mulhouse (Alsace), to Łodz (Poland). Many regions experienced their own industrial revolutions. Industrialization in the Rhône valley of southeastern France, for example, ensured predominance in the manufacture of silk. Mechanical and chain-driven looms came into use there in the 1770s (although they had been known in China for centuries). By the 1780s, more than 23 percent of the population of Lyons worked in the silk industry. The delicacy of silk work delayed the development of a power silk loom, but when one was developed in the midnineteenth century, Lyons remained the center of silk manufacturing, partly because of its location near the rich coalfields of St. Etienne. French textile industrialization also produced an extraordinary new technology. In 1808, a silk weaver named Joseph Jacquard (Jac-kar') invented a loom to weave elaborate patterns in silk; Jacquard devised cards with holes punched in them to control the weaving, anticipating computer technology by 150 years.

Delays in Continental Industrialization. The industrialization of continental Europe was slowed by the French Revolution and the Napoleonic Wars. Postwar economic problems were severe, and Europe remained in a **depression** until 1820. Governments hurried to demobilize their expensive armies, which left hundreds of thousands of veterans unemployed. Jobs were scarce because governments also canceled wartime contracts for food, uniforms, and equipment, leading to the dismissal of agricultural, textile, and metallurgical workers. Most governments were deep in war debt; Prussia, for example, could barely pay the interest on war loans. Governments promised to cancel the war taxes needed for big armies, but that created the combination of high debt and reduced revenue when governments needed huge sums of money to rebuild the regions devastated by war. Roads and bridges required immediate attention to support the recovery of commerce. Consequently, Britain enjoyed a long lead in industrialization.

Textile Industrialization on the Continent.
Nevertheless, Europe experienced steady industrialization in the first half of the nineteenth century. Traditional textile regions, such as Alsace and Normandy in France or Catalonia in Spain, rapidly adapted to the age of the spinning mule and the power loom. A study of the Alsatian textile industry has shown its expansion from a total of 48,000 spindles in 1812 to 466,000 spindles in 1828. There were only 426 power looms in Alsace in 1827, but more than 18,000 in 1856. The strength of continental textiles in the nineteenth century is imbedded in the English language. In addition to the elegant jacquard patterns, the world was soon wearing a sturdy type of cotton denim, which came from Nîmes (de Nîmes in French).

The Railroad Age on the Continent.
Another sign of continental industrialization was the beginning of the railroad age in the 1830s and 1840s. The French opened a small line in 1828 to connect the coalfields of St. Etienne with the national canal and river system, but they were slow to build a large railroad network. No passenger service was established between Paris and Lyons until the 1850s. In most countries, the first tracks were laid in the 1830s or 1840s. Progressive statesmen such as Count Camilio Cavour (Ka-voor') of Piedmont-Sardinia made their reputations as early champions of the railroad. Cavour was convinced that "their economic importance will be from the outset magnificent," and by 1850, the Italian states had more miles of track than Russia and Spain combined.

Prussian Industrialization.
The country that most profited from the beginning of continental industrialization was Prussia. This was partly the result of Prussian military success, which led to the annexation of rich mineral deposits. The wars of Frederick the Great had acquired the coalfields of Silesia, and the defeat of Napoleon brought Prussia the iron and coal deposits of the Rhineland. The Prussian government also encouraged industrialization. Karl Freiherr vom Stein reorganized the government after the catastrophic loss to Napoleon at Jena in 1806. Stein secured the abolition of serfdom in 1807, and the emancipation edict had far-reaching economic provisions that opened landownership and granted the aristocracy the freedom to choose any occupation. Friedrich von Motz, the Prussian minister of finance in the 1820s, presided over a similar modernization that included the abolition of **internal tariffs; free-trade treaties** with neighboring German states; and finally the formation of the *Zollverein* (Tsoll'-fa-rine), a **customs union** of trading partners that propelled Prussia toward the economic leadership of central Europe. As Friedrich List, the champion of the Zollverein as a way to have free trade among German states but to protect German manufacturers against foreign competitors, argued in *The National System of Political Economy*, Prussian industry must be developed and protected because "Industry is the mother and father of science, literature, the arts, enlightenment, freedom, useful institutions, and the national power of independence." King Frederick William IV of Prussia encouraged industrialization by his love of trains, whereas his rival, the emperor of Austria, detested railroads and impeded their construction.

THE EUROPEAN INDUSTRIAL "TAKE-OFF" (1850–1914)

Economic historians use the term **take-off phase** to describe the period when a nascent industrial economy begins to expand rapidly. For much of western and central Europe, the take-off of industrialization occurred in the middle of the nineteenth century. The word **capitalism** was coined during this midcentury generation (1851), and Karl Marx published his famous critique of industrial capitalism, *Das Kapital* (1867). The British celebrated their new society in a spectacular world's fair in London, known as the Crystal Palace Exhibition (1851), which showed the world the latest technical and mechanical wonders. Not surprisingly, some historians call this period the **"age of capital."**

Contrasting Patterns of Industrialization.
Industrialization did not spread evenly across Europe, and the great powers did not industrialize in the same ways. A few regions (especially in Germany) industrialized rapidly enough to constitute an industrial revolution. Some important states (notably France) industrialized at a steady, but less dramatic, pace which suggests an industrial evolution. Other areas (such as Russia) remained overwhelmingly agricultural, and major industrialization did not accelerate until the late nineteenth century. Nor did the take-off phase mean that continental production caught up to Britain in a single generation. Between 1851 and 1869, British heavy industry

CONTINENTAL EUROPEAN INDUSTRIALIZATION

TABLE 22.8 THE TAKE-OFF OF HEAVY INDUSTRY IN EUROPE, 1851–1869

The data in this table show that Britain was already heavily industrialized in 1851, but none of the other great powers was. The data summarize output in millions of metric tons and show growth in percentages. Note that the huge growth in iron and coal output in France and the Germanic states of central Europe—their industrial take-off—still left them far behind British production. Note also the comparison between French industrialization and German industrialization, which is much more rapid; this contrast had great implications for the balance of power on the continent.

| COUNTRY | Output in 1851 | | Output in 1860 | | Output in 1869 | | Growth 1851–1869 | |
	IRON	COAL	IRON	COAL	IRON	COAL	IRON	COAL
Austria	0.5	1.0	n.a.	3.2	0.7	6.6	40.0	560.0
Britain	9.7	50.2	8.2	81.3	11.7	109.2	20.6	118.9
France	1.8	4.4	3.0	8.3	3.1	13.5	72.2	202.3
Zollverein	0.8	7.8	1.3	16.7	3.1	34.3	287.5	339.7

Source: Compiled from data in Mitchell, B. R., *European Historical Statistics, 1750–1970* (London: Macmillan, 1975, pp. 360–361, 387).

A Late Nineteenth-Century Steel-Making Factory. The arrival of the blast furnace, such as the one shown in this image, greatly increased the output of steel, but it also created a harsh environment of intense heat where workers typically had shortened life expectancies.

TABLE 22.9 EUROPEAN RAILROAD EXPANSION, 1850–1870

Data reflect kilometers of railroad track in use.

COUNTRY	1850	1860	1870
Austria	1,357	2,927	6,112
Belgium	854	1,729	2,897
Britain	9,798	14,603	19,987
France	2,915	9,167	16,465
Germany/ Zollverein	5,856	11,089	17,211
Italy	620	2,404	6,429
Russia	501	1,626	10,731
Spain	28	1,649	5,295

Compiled from data in Mitchell, B. R., *European Historical Statistics, 1750–1970* (London: Macmillan, 1975, pp. 581–584).

continued to grow at a steady rate; iron production increased by 20 percent and coal production by 119 percent. The French growth rate in iron production tripled British growth and nearly doubled it in coal. However, in 1869, French iron production remained barely one-fourth of the British total and coal production stood at one-eighth. German rates did not yet threaten British leadership either, but the Zollverein had passed France and the rate of growth portended a future Anglo-German rivalry.

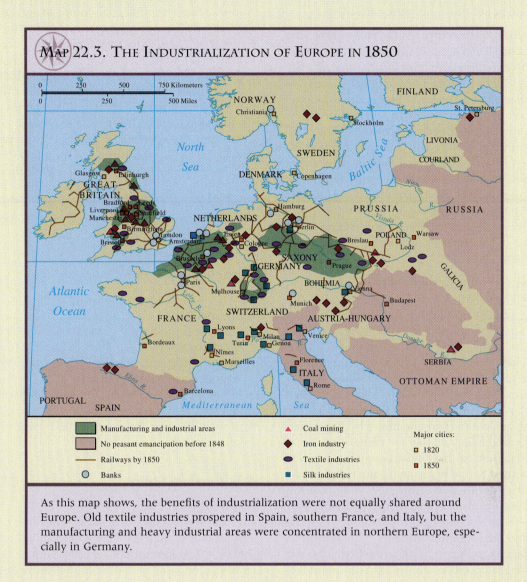

MAP 22.3. THE INDUSTRIALIZATION OF EUROPE IN 1850

Legend:
- Manufacturing and industrial areas
- No peasant emancipation before 1848
- Railways by 1850
- Banks
- Coal mining
- Iron industry
- Textile industries
- Silk industries
- Major cities: 1820, 1850

As this map shows, the benefits of industrialization were not equally shared around Europe. Old textile industries prospered in Spain, southern France, and Italy, but the manufacturing and heavy industrial areas were concentrated in northern Europe, especially in Germany.

Questions: What conclusions do these sources suggest about the balance of power on the continent? Compare the data in Table 22.9 on European railroads in 1850 with the image of industrialization shown in Map 22.3. What correlations do you see? Note the data on iron and coal output in 1851 shown in Table 22.8. Compare the data for individual countries to their representation in Map 22.3. Do the two sources give the same impression of industrial might?

European Railroad Building. The continental industrial take-off can also be seen in the expansion of railroad networks. The midcentury was an age of railway construction across the continent. Austria, Belgium, Italy, and Spain all built large national systems. Russia remained backward; in 1850, tiny Belgium had a larger railroad network. By 1870, a Russian building program had added more than 10,000 kilometers of track, but that meant that a country of more than 22 million square kilometers was served by half as much railroad track as Great Britain, a country of 300,000 square kilometers. The railway systems of France and Germany both neared the size of the British network in 1870, but they, too, were much larger.

French Industrialization. Such data show that France industrialized at a significant pace but never experienced the exponential rate of change that characterized the British or German industrial revolutions. No population explosion occurred in France, and the government never completely abandoned the mercantilist tradition of a centrally **directed economy.** The mid-century government of Napoleon III encouraged the industrial take-off with institutions such as the Crédit Foncier, which provided low-interest business loans. A French Railroad Law of 1857 guaranteed the interest payments of private railroad bonds, so investors could not lose. This law so stimulated railroad building that a system with 2,915 kilometers of track in 1850 grew to 16,465 kilometers before 1870.

Krupp and German Industrialization. German industrial development varied regionally, with the greatest strength concentrated in Prussia and the Rhineland. The German take-off was rapid. Between 1851 and 1857, the number of Prussian joint-stock companies, and their total capitalization, tripled. Prussian legislation encouraged British-style laissez-faire capitalism. New mining laws, for example, ended state control of coal mines, broke the powers of the miners' guild, and cut the taxes on mines by 50 percent. Prussian coal production sharply increased. The Krupp Works of Essen showed the similar growth of the metallurgical industry. Krupp was a small, and nearly bankrupt, iron foundry with seven employees when it began to manufacture ordnance in 1837. Alfred Krupp pioneered new techniques of steel production, produced an exceptional steel cannon in 1847, won the firm's first government contract in 1859, and within a decade had made the Krupp Works the largest arms manufacturer in central Europe. Krupp's iron and steel mills made it one of the largest industrial combines in the world, and Krupp artillery would help to win a similar military leadership for Germany.

CONCLUSION

Historians and social scientists use the term *revolution* with abandon, in contexts far different from such famous political revolutions as the American Revolution and the French Revolution, including the economic history examined in this chapter. But the Industrial Revolution and the spread of urban industrial society truly merit the term—for producing some of the most profound changes that humanity has experienced. If one focuses on economic structures and the society associated with them, industrialization was the biggest change in the human condition since the shift from hunting-and-gathering civilizations to agricultural societies. If one focuses on modern history, the Industrial Revolution (and the vital revolution examined in Chapter 23) must stand alongside the French Revolution as the strongest forces shaping modernity.

The population explosion that began in the late eighteenth century, the subsequent urbanization of Europe, the development of the new technology of manufacturing and the new employment of the factory system, the age of mass production, rapid railroad transportation, transformed family relations and alterations in the status of women and children, the mixture of dreadful conditions and rising expectations, and so forth, combined to change the world more than the monarchs and marshals of political revolutions did.

Review Questions

- What was the population explosion, and what were its causes?
- What was the nature of manufacturing before the steam engine?
- How did the steam engine help transform the European economy and society?
- What are the two sides of the "standard of living debate"?
- How did British and continental European industrialization differ?

For Further Study

Readings

Bunch, Bryan, and Hellemans, Alexander, eds., *The Timetables of Technology* (New York: Simon and Schuster, 1993). A detailed chronology of inventions (such as the spinning jenny or the water frame) organized by fields such as energy, communication, medical, and tools.

Deane, Phyllis, *The First Industrial Revolution*, 2nd ed. (Cambridge: Cambridge University Press, 1979). Excellent shorter survey of the century 1750–1850.

Landes, David, *The Unbound Prometheus: Technological Change and Industrial Development in Western Europe from 1750 to the Present Day* (Cambridge: Cambridge University Press, 1969). A detailed volume in the Cambridge Economic History that provides a comparative study of industrialization with a focus on technology.

Mantoux, Paul, *The Industrial Revolution in the Eighteenth Century: An Outline of the Beginning of the Modern Factory System in England* (Chicago: University of Chicago Press, 1961). The classic statement of the origins and phases of the Industrial Revolution that has been much revised but remains the basic starting point.

THE INDUSTRIAL AGE TO 1914

1800	1810	1820	1830	1840	1850	1860	1870	1880	1890	1900	1910

TEXTILE FACTORIES

1769: Richard Arkwright Patents Water Frame, a Hydraulic Spinning Machine
1770: James Hargreaves Patents the Spinning Jenny, a Machine to Spin Eight Threads at Once
1771: Richard Arkwright Founds First Cotton Spinning Factory in Derbyshire
1779: Samuel Cromption Invents the Spinning Mule, Combines Water Frame and Spinning Jenny
    John Kay Invents Flying Shuttle Loom
1783: Cylindrical Printing of Fabrics Introduced
1785: Bleaching of Fabric with Chlorine Introduced
1785: Edmund Cartwright Patents First Steam-Powered Loom
1787: Steam Engine Introduced in a Cotton Mill in Orléans, France
1789: First Cotton Factory Entirely Operated by Steam Opens in Manchester, England
1793: American Eli Whitney Invents Cotton Gin to Extract Raw Cotton in Large Quantities
    1801: Joseph Jacquard Invents Mechanical Loom to Weave Patterns in Silk
    1805: Jacquard Introduces Punch-Card System of Controlling Machines
    1806: First Steam-Powered Loom Factory Opens in Manchester
    1810: First Strike of Textile Workers in Manchester
    1813: 2,400 Power Looms in Britain
    1812: Alsatian Textile Industry Grows from 427 Power Looms to 6,000 (1837) to 18,000 (1856)
    1816: Marc Isambard Brunel Patents Knitting Machine to Knit Tubular Fabric (for Stockings)
    1830: Barthelemy Thimonnier Invents the First Sewing Machine
    1833: British Factory Act Begins Age of Government Regulation of Factories
    1841: French Factory Act Limits Child Labor (but Widely Ignored)
    1845: Power Loom for Machine-Made Carpets Invented
    1884: Rayon Invented, the First
    Synthetic Thread

RAILROADS

1769: Joseph Cugnot of France Builds a Steam Automobile Carrying Four People at 2.25 mph
    1804: Richard Trevithick Invents First Steam-Powered Locomotive and Hauls 10 Tons of Iron 10 Miles
    1814: George Stephenson Steam Locomotive *Blucher* Hauls Cargo Faster Than Horse-Drawn
    1825: George Stephenson Creates First Public Railway (Stockton-to-Darlington, UK)
    1828: French Railroad Links Coalfields of St. Etienne with French Canal System
    1830: Manchester-to-Liverpool Railway Opens and Railway Boom Begins
    1830: British Government Begins to Use Rail Lines to Deliver Mail
    1831: Lyons-to-St. Etienne Railway Opens
    1832: Franz Anton von Gerstner Designs Closed Railroad Passenger Car
    1837: First Railroads Serving Paris Open: Paris–St. Germain, Paris–Versailles
    1840: First Railroad Dining Cars in Use; Train Speeds Reach 50 mph
    1842: Prussian Railway Fund Gives Government Aid for Railroad Building
    1842: French Railway Law Gives Government Aid
    1843: First Railroads Over the Alps Begun (Completed in 1854)
    1843: Iron Rhine Railway Connects Port of Antwerp with Rhine River
    1846: Great Western Railroad Reaches 67 mph
    1847: Union of German Railways Standardizes Rail System in Germany
    1850s: First Rail Passenger Service between Paris and Lyon Opens
    1857: French Railroad Law Aids Private Railroad Construction
    1861: First Rail Tourist Guide to France Published
    1871: Mt. Cenis Tunnel Opens, Cut 8.7 Miles
    through Alps
    1879: Werner von Siemens Demonstrates
    Electric Railway at Berlin Exposition
    1881: First Electric Train Line (Berlin)
    1889: First Steel Railway Bridge Crosses
    Firth of Forth (Scotland)
    1891: Trans-Siberian Railway
    Begun (Finished 1904)

Continued

1800	1810	1820	1830	1840	1850	1860	1870	1880	1890	1900	1910

URBANIZATION

1760s: London Begins Numbering Buildings with Street Addresses and Installing Sidewalks

1784: Aimé Argand of Switzerland Invents First Effective Oil Lamp

1784: James Watt Demonstrates Use of Steam Pipes to Heat Buildings

1799: Wilhelm Lampadius Demonstrates Coal-Gas Lighting in Dresden, Saxony

1801: Philippe Lebon Demonstrates Effective Gas Lighting in Paris

1804: Paris Invents the Restaurant, Increasing from 1 (1789) to 500 (1804)

1807: London Begins to Install William Murdock's Gaslights on Streets

1811: Freiberg, Saxony, Becomes First City Illuminated by Gas Light

1820s: Horse-Drawn and Steam-Powered Omnibus Lines Open in London and Paris

1827: Invention of Glass Pressing Machine Makes Mass Production of Windows Possible

1829: Gas Lighting Introduced on Streets of Paris

1829: Enlarged Specialty Stores Open in Paris

1830s: First Department Stores Open in Newcastle and Manchester, England

1837: First Paved Sidewalk in Paris

1844: Experimental Electric Lights Used in Place de la Concorde, Paris

1850: Joseph Paxton Builds Glass Walled Crystal Palace, Glass Buildings Follow in Dublin (1852) and Munich (1854)

1850: Paris Begins Construction of Major Sewer System

1851: First Parisian Department Store Opens

1852: American Elisha Otis Invents Safety Elevator, Making High-Rise Buildings Possible

1856: Paris Annexes Eleven Surrounding Suburbs

1857: Gas Lighting Installed on Grands Boulevards of Paris

1857: London Begins Excavation for Underground Trains

1860: Baron Haussmann Begins Urban Renewal of Paris

1863: London Opens First Underground Railway

1863: Food Distribution Center (Les Halles) Opens in Central Paris

1867: Joseph Monier Invents Reinforced Concrete

1868: Paris Installs Pneumatic Mail System for High-Speed Delivery across Town

1869: Bon Marché Department Store built in Paris: World's Largest Store before 1914

1879: Edison (USA) and Swan (GB) Develop Electric Lamps

1879: London Installs First Telephone System

1884: Paris Requires Trash Collection

1885: First 10-Story Skyscraper Built in Chicago

1887: Siemens Introduces Electric Elevator in Mannheim, Germany

1889: Eiffel Tower Built, Tallest Structure in World until 1930

1896: Budapest Subway

1898: Paris and Vienna Subways

1910: Neon Lights

Milward, Alan S., and Saul, S. B., *The Economic Development of Continental Europe, 1780–1870* (London: Allen & Unwin, 1979). First of two volumes of continental economic history, offering a good synthesis of much scholarship.

InfoTrac College Edition

For additional reading, go to your online research library at *http://infotrac.thomsonlearning.com.*

Using Key Terms, enter the search term *Industrial Revolution*

Using the Subject Guide, enter the search term *industrial development*

Web Sites

http://www.spartacus.schoolnet.co.uk/Textiles.htm   This is a British educational site that covers many topics of modern history. Some materials are at an introductory level, but it provides well-chosen excerpts from primary sources on subjects such as child labor and life in the factories.

http://www.bbc.co.uk/history/   Enter "industrialisation" in the search engine. This is a corner of a BBC Web site, which contains a variety of historical materials. The section on industrialization offers seven sections, on topics such as the railroad.

Visit the Western Civilization Companion Web Site for resources specific to this textbook:
http://history.wadsworth.com/hause02/

The CD in the back of this book and the Western Civilization Resource Center at *http://history.wadsworth.com/western/* offer a variety of tools to help you succeed in this course, including access to quizzes; images; documents; interactive simulations, maps, and timelines; movie explorations; and a wealth of other sources.

FOCUS QUESTIONS

- What were the principal patterns in nineteenth-century European demography, and what were the explanations for them?
- What was the principal pattern in the history of contagious disease in nineteenth-century Europe? How did it happen?
- What is meant by the term *vital revolution?* How does one explain it?
- What was the principal pattern of the birthrate in nineteenth-century Europe? How can it be explained?
- Were there new patterns to marriage in nineteenth-century Europe?
- What were the principal debates about human sexuality in nineteenth-century Europe?

Chapter 23

DAILY LIFE DURING THE VITAL REVOLUTION OF THE NINETEENTH CENTURY

*I*n the summer of 1810, a noted English writer named Fanny Burney, who had married a Frenchman and found herself caught in France when war resumed between Britain and France, began to be disturbed by a "small pain" in her breast which grew increasingly severe. Although she did not recognize the gravity of her situation, her observant husband did, and he pleaded with her to visit a surgeon. Fanny Burney resisted this idea for several months until her best friend joined her husband in insisting. When the diagnosis of advancing breast cancer could no longer be denied, Fanny's husband obtained the services of one of the most eminent surgeons in Europe, the Baron Larrey, who had become famous in the service of Napoleon and had previously performed a successful mastectomy, saving a woman's life. Thus, in late September 1811, Fanny Burney received a visit at her home from a team of seven men, headed by Dr. Larrey. After she had sipped a wine cordial, she lied down on a simple bed, and a light handkerchief was draped over her face, she was held down while Dr. Larrey thrust a surgical knife into her until it scraped her breast bone, allowing him to remove her entire breast while she remained wholly conscious. The first successful use of medical anesthesia remained 35 years in the future.

Fanny Burney's horrifying ordeal vividly suggests how different from today daily life remained in 1810. This chapter examines dramatic changes in the everyday existence of Europeans during industrialization. The biggest changes were so dramatic that they constitute a **vital revolution.** In 1800, the average European had a life expectancy at birth of about 35 years. A boy born in 1900 could expect 50 years and his sister 52 years. Historians attribute 15 percent of all European deaths during the 1700s to smallpox; in a typical year, smallpox, typhus, and typhoid accounted for 35 percent of all deaths. By the early 1900s, these diseases caused less than 1 percent of deaths in the most advanced regions of Europe. Chapter 23 discusses this great change. The history of this vital revolution often receives less attention than the actions of princes, popes, and presidents, but no leader affected daily life as much as the conquest of disease and the improvement of diet.

THE DEMOGRAPHY OF THE VITAL REVOLUTION (1750–1914)

The Increase in Life Expectancy

Nineteenth-century **demography** is a good illustration of historical perspective; that is, the subject looks very different if viewed from the perspective of the early eighteenth century or the early twenty-first century. The **life expectancy** of a European male born today is 72 to 74 years; females average 78 to 81 years. (The figures for the United States are 72 and 79 years, respectively. See Table 23.1.) Typical rates for 1750 ranged between 28 and 33 years. Thus, a mean life expectancy of 50 years seems short or long, depending on one's perspective. The benefits arrived unequally, and many regions did not experience them until the twentieth century. Scandinavians already expected 55 to 60 years of life for a child born in 1900, whereas Russians still lived in a **biological Old Regime** with life expectancies of 30 to 35 years (see Table 23.1).

Death and Social Class. Life expectancy also varied by social class; the wealthy usually lived longer than laborers did. A study conducted for the British Parliament in 1842 found that in Manchester, the average age at death was 38 for professionals, 20 for shopkeepers, and 17 for the working class.

Death Rates. A study of improving life expectancy starts with the decreasing **death rate**. The annual mortality rate in the eighteenth century usually exceeded 30 deaths per 1,000 population; it reached 35 to 36 deaths per 1,000 in England in the 1740s. That rate plummeted during the nineteenth century. The lowest mortality rate in Europe on the eve of World War I was a Danish rate of 13.2 per 1,000. (Rates today are near 12 per 1,000.) The worst rates were in southern and eastern Europe: Spain had a death rate of 22.8 per 1,000 and Russia, 29.0, and both represented significant improvements over eighteenth-century rates. The unhealthy environment of cities meant that rates there resembled rural eighteenth-century rates; mortality in Moscow and St. Petersburg was 30 to 35 per 1,000 in the 1880s. Paris (24.4), Berlin (26.5), and Vienna (28.2) also had high death rates.

Death and Childhood. The falling mortality rate resulted chiefly from declining infant and childhood mortality. A study of Dutch demography has found more than 23 percent of all deaths in Holland in 1811 were infants younger than 1 year of age; 41 percent of the dead were younger than 10. Such figures fell sharply. French rates fell from 16.2 percent of all infants dying in the year of their birth (1840) to 11.1 percent (1910); British rates fell from 15.4 percent (1840) to 10.5 per-

COUNTRY	PERIOD	MALE LIFE EXPECTANCY AT BIRTH (IN YEARS)	FEMALE LIFE EXPECTANCY AT BIRTH (IN YEARS)
England and Wales	1838–1854	39.9	41.8
	1901–1910	48.5	52.3
	2002	75.3	78.0
France	1817–1831	38.3	40.8
	1908–1913	48.4	52.4
	2002	75.2	83.1
Germany	1871–1881	35.5	38.4
	1910–1911	37.4	50.6
	2002	74.6	81.1
Italy	1876–1887	35.1	35.4
	1901–1911	44.2	44.8
	2002	76.1	82.6
Russia	1896–1897	31.4	33.3
	2002	62.3	73.0
Spain	1900	33.8	35.7
	1910	40.9	42.5
	2002	77.2	82.6
Sweden	1816–1840	39.5	43.5
	1901–1910	54.5	56.9
	2002	77.2	82.6
United States	2002	74.5	80.2

TABLE 23.1 LIFE EXPECTANCY IN THE NINETEENTH CENTURY AND 2002

Source: Armengaud, André, "Population in Europe, 1700–1914," in Cipolla, C., ed., *The Industrial Revolution* (London: Collins, 1973, p. 36); and *The CIA Fact Book 2002*, *www.cia.gov/cia/publications/factbook/index.html*.

Question: Which European countries appear to have been the healthiest and the least healthy at the start of the twentieth century?

cent (1910). These rates, too, were worse in southern and eastern Europe. Russian **infant mortality** was horrifying—51.9 percent between 1864 and 1879 and 30.5 percent on the eve of World War I. (The U.S. rate is poor today, but it barely surpasses 1 percent for the total population; in France and Germany, the rate in 2002 was less than 0.5 percent.) Infant mortality rates remained high in cities. Madrid and Bucharest both had rates of 21 percent in 1909; Moscow, nearly 32 percent. In the prosperous west, rates were high in manufacturing towns. Roubaix, a French textile center, had an infant mortality rate nearly twice the national average. Death rates remained terrible throughout the years of childhood. In 1897, nearly 50 percent of the children born in rural Russia died before age 5, and 68.7 percent did not reach 10. As terrible as such numbers seem, they nevertheless represented significant improvement in comparison to those of the eighteenth century. In 1750, the death rate in London for children younger than age 5 had been more than 75 percent; in 1914, only 15 percent of English children died before their fifth birthday. The important facts, therefore, are the decline of infant mortality (discussed later in this chapter) and the consequent increase in life expectancy.

DISEASE AND MEDICINE IN NINETEENTH-CENTURY EUROPE (1796–1912)

Contagious Disease. The foremost explanation of falling death rates lies in the history of **contagious disease.** One study has suggested that diseases explain 94 percent of all European deaths in the year 1850. The dominion of disease included wars; typhus killed more of Napoleon's soldiers than Wellington's army or the Russian army did. That pattern remained true across the century: typhus, typhoid, cholera, and smallpox killed more soldiers than enemy fire did. As late as the Boer War (1899–1902), the British army lost 6,425 soldiers in combat and 11,327 soldiers to disease. Contagious diseases killed more people than heart attacks or cancer did, because fewer people lived long enough to experience degenerative problems. At midcentury, even measles killed more people than cancer did. In 1848, the British deaths from diseases carried by **microorganisms** stood at 1,296 per 100,000 population (see Table 23.2); today's death rate for deaths attributable to acquired immunodeficiency syndrome (AIDS; 8.6), cancer (199.2), and heart disease (311.9) combined do not reach half of that 1848 rate for contagious diseases.

Smallpox. In the late eighteenth century, European civilization had begun the conquest of contagious diseases, but the lesson of smallpox **vaccination** was learned very slowly. In Edward Jenner's homeland (England), less than 1 percent of the population was vaccinated in 1801 (5 years after his historic discovery of the procedure). Bavaria adopted compulsory vaccination in 1807 and the British government required it in 1835, but many states were slower. Vaccination of all Germans became mandatory in 1874, during the smallpox epidemic of 1870–1875, which killed more than 500,000 people in Europe. The Vatican outlawed vaccination, and Catholic states suffered higher death rates. Spain did not require vaccination until 1902, but the new policy did not come in time to prevent 37,000 Spanish smallpox deaths between 1901 and 1910. Even these numbers seem small compared with the horrors of public health in Russia. Four hundred thousand Russians died of smallpox in 1901–1910, while one

Orthodox sect still fought against vaccination, calling the resultant smallpox scar "the mark of the Anti-Christ." In contrast, Denmark recorded only thirteen smallpox deaths during that decade, and Sweden became the first country ever to go through an entire year (1895) with no smallpox deaths.

Childhood Disease and Immunity. Tragedies such as the smallpox epidemic of 1870–1875, or the Spanish and Russian crises of 1901–1910, are noteworthy facts, but the virtual disappearance of smallpox in Denmark and Sweden is more important in understanding the nineteenth century as an age both of disease and the conquest of it. **Childhood diseases**—such as measles, whooping cough, and scarlet fever—account for less than 0.1 percent of deaths in the Western world today, but they remained virulent killers during the nineteenth century. An outbreak of scarlet fever killed nearly 20,000 children in Britain in 1840. The inhabitants of Denmark's Faeroe Islands suffered badly in 1846 because they had experienced 65 years without a case of the measles. No one had acquired immunity to the disease in childhood, and when a worker brought measles to the islands, 78 percent of the population (6,100 people) caught the disease and 106 adults died.

Cholera. The most persistent **epidemic disease** of nineteenth-century Europe was cholera, an acute diarrheal disease usually transmitted through contaminated drinking water. Major epidemics swept Europe repeatedly—in 1817–1823, 1826–1837, 1846–1863, 1865–1875, and 1881–1896. They typically arrived from India, where cholera was **endemic** along the Ganges River. That path of infection, combined with poor public health standards, meant that Russia suffered terribly from cholera. One study has found that Russia endured 58 years of cholera epidemic between 1823 and 1926. In that century, 5.5 million Russians contracted cholera and 2.1 million of them died. A cholera epidemic of 1831–1833 was especially severe. It initially moved from India to Persia to Russia. The Russian army sent to suppress the Polish revolution of 1830–1831 carried cholera into central Europe. This biological tax on military action took 1,835 lives in Berlin (nearly 1 percent of the population) before moving westward. The epidemic reached Glasgow (population 202,000) in February 1832, and before it left, 1.6 percent of the city had died. When the epidemic struck Paris, it killed 2.5 percent of the population, 19,000 people (see *Cholera in Nineteenth-Century Europe*). A catastrophe such as this in present-day New York City would kill 183,000 people in 10 months. Such numbers were basic facts of life in the nineteenth century. London had 20,000 cholera deaths in 1849–1853, chiefly because the city dumped untreated sewage into the Thames River and collected drinking water nearby. Between 1853 and 1856, cholera killed 52,000 people in Britain and 140,000 in France,

Typhus. Dreadful military hygiene meant that eighteenth- and nineteenth-century armies regularly lost more soldiers to typhus than they did on the battlefield. Typhus, characterized by high fevers, is spread by the bite of a body louse that thrives in poor sanitary conditions. It was commonly found in armies, jails, and slums. This illustration, originally titled "Hunger Typhus," shows the interior of a fever hospital at Moscow in 1892.

DISEASE	1848 DEATHS PER MILLION	Population 1901 DEATHS PER MILLION	PERCENT CHANGE
Airborne Diseases	7,259	5,122	−29.4
Tuberculosis (respiratory)	2,901	1,268	−56.3
Bronchitis, pneumonia, influenza	2,239	2,747	+22.7
Scarlet fever and diphtheria	1,016	407	−59.9
Whooping cough	423	312	−26.2
Measles	342	278	−18.7
Smallpox	263	10	−96.2
Ear, pharynx, larynx infections	75	100	+33.3
Water- and Food-Borne Diseases	3,562	1,931	−45.8
Cholera, diarrhea, dysentery	1,819	1,232	−32.3
Typhoid and typhus	990	155	−84.3
Tuberculosis (nonrespiratory)	753	544	−27.8
Venereal Diseases	50	164	+228.0
Syphilis	50	164	+228.0
Other Diseases Attributable to Microorganisms			
Convulsions and teething	1,322	643	−52.4
Appendicitis and peritonitis	75	86	+14.7
Puerperal fever	62	64	+3.2
All others	635	458	−27.9
Total	12,965	8,468	−34.7
Other Death Rates	8,891	8,490	−4.5
Heart diseases	698	1,673	+139.7
Cancer	307	844	+174.9
Violence	761	640	−15.9

NOTE: Data for 1848 are an average for the period 1848–1854.
Calculated from data in McKeown, Thomas, *The Modern Rise of Population* (London: Academic Press, 1976, pp. 54–55, 58, 60, 62).

Question: Against which diseases did society make the greatest progress during the nineteenth century?

not counting 18,000 Anglo-French soldiers who died of cholera during the Crimean War.

Cholera and Sewage. John Snow, an English doctor, proved that cholera was spread by contaminated water in one of the most memorable studies in medical history. During a cholera epidemic in the Soho district of London in 1854, Snow mapped the houses in which cholera deaths occurred and compared this with the location of public stand-pumps for water. Finding that the

CHOLERA IN NINETEENTH-CENTURY EUROPE

Sewer Systems. Between 1854, when John Snow demonstrated a connection between sewage-contaminated drinking water and cholera, and 1884, when Robert Koch identified the organism that transmitted cholera, progressive city governments launched sewer building and clean water programs. British and French programs contributed to a significant reduction in cholera by the 1890s, while other societies, such as Germany and Russia, suffered terribly. Here, construction progresses under Fleet Street on London's new common sewer.

The nineteenth century witnessed the slow conquest of smallpox, following Jenner's remarkable discovery of a vaccine in 1796, and the plague was no longer a serious problem. Instead, the worst disease of the century was cholera, which struck Europe in repeated epidemics. Cholera is an acute diarrheal disease, typically spread by a bacillus in contaminated water (although that was not known until 1854), which then lodges in the intestine. The cholera epidemic of 1832 killed more than 2 percent of the population of Paris, a rate at which hundreds of thousands would die in today's great metropolitan areas.

Heinrich Heine Describes the Cholera Epidemic of 1832 in Paris

Heine (1797–1856) was already a noted poet when he took up residence in Paris in 1831.

I speak of the cholera, which for a time has reigned here unrestrictedly, felling its victims by the thousands without regard for rank or opinion.

One had not been apprehensive about that pestilence because the word from London was that it caused comparatively few deaths. In fact, the initial idea seemed to be to deride it. . . . Its arrival was officially announced on the 29th of March; and as this was the middle of Lent, the Parisians swarmed more gaily than ever on the boulevards, where masks were even seen, mocking the fear of the cholera. . . . That night, the balls were more crowded than ever; hilarious laughter drowned the loudest music. . . .

It was soon discovered that this was no joke; the laughter died, and several wagon-loads of people were driven directly from the ball to the Hôtel Dieu, the main hospital, where they arrived in their gaudy fancy dress and promptly died. As in the first shock

deaths were concentrated near a single pump, Snow simply disabled the pump by removing its handle, and the epidemic ended. After this experiment, sewer systems and water filtration plants spared Britain and France the worst ravages of later epidemics.

Disease and Social Class. This lesson, like smallpox vaccination, was accepted only slowly, however. Snow's message might have prevented the epidemic of 1884–1885, which killed more than 120,000 people in Spain, or the epidemic of 1892–1893, which ravaged the German port of Hamburg, killing 8,600 people in a few months (see Table 23.3). A study of

the Hamburg epidemic has highlighted the correlation between social class and disease: the higher a person's annual income, the lower the chance of catching cholera or of dying from it. The poor died at a rate twelve to thirteen times higher than the rich did. Both Hamburg and its more affluent suburb of Altona took their water from the same source, but Altona had a filtration system. Hamburg had a death rate of 13.4 per 1,000; Altona, 2.1. The rich and famous did die—the composer Peter Tchaikovsky died later in that same epidemic—but the public health standards for their neighborhoods spared them much of the suffering found in cities.

TABLE 23.3 THE HAMBURG CHOLERA EPIDEMIC OF 1892

ANNUAL INCOME IN MARKS (1 MARK = 25¢)	NUMBER OF PEOPLE	% WHO CAUGHT CHOLERA	% WHO DIED
800–1,000	28,647	11.4	6.2
1,000–2,000	32,848	10.0	5.5
2,000–3,500	14,544	4.7	2.7
3,500–5,000	6,125	4.0	2.2
5,000–10,000	5,649	3.1	1.6
10,000–25,000	3,328	1.8	1.0
25,000–50,000	1,182	1.7	1.1
50,0001	834	0.6	0.5

From Evans, Richard J., *Death in Hamburg* (Oxford: Oxford University Press, 1987, p. 408). Used by permission of the publisher.

MAP 23.1. CHOLERA EPIDEMICS THROUGHOUT EUROPE IN THE 1800s

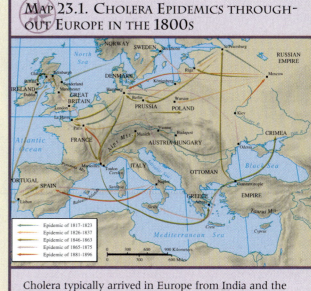

Cholera typically arrived in Europe from India and the Middle East, traveling via Russia and the Ottoman Empire. Although epidemics often spread over land, they usually broke out in port cities first. Thus, Marseilles, Hamburg, and Naples were often at the center the epidemics of the nineteenth century. As this map shows, cholera soon reached the great cities of Europe, giving Paris, Berlin, and St. Petersburg terrible epidemics.

the cholera was thought to be contagious, the older guests of the Hôtel Dieu raised cruel screams of fear; those dead were said to have been buried so fast that not even their checkered fool's costumes were taken off them; and merrily as they lived they now lie in their graves.

There is nothing like the confusion with which security measures were now suddenly taken. A Sanitation Commission was created, first aid stations were established everywhere, and ordinances concerning public hygiene were put into effect at once . . . It was as if the end of the world had come. Especially at streetcorners, where the red-painted wine shops are, groups gathered and consulted. . . . The people grumbled bitterly, seeing how the rich fled and, loaded with doctors and drugs, escaped to healthier climes. Resentfully, the poor man saw that money had become a prophylactic even against death. . . .

My barber told me that an old woman on Faubourg Montmartre sat by her window all night counting the corpses which were carried past; she counted three hundred, and when dawn broke she herself was seized by the chills and cramps of cholera and shortly died. Wherever one looked in the streets there were funerals . . .

Medicine, Public Health, and the Conquest of Disease

Medical Limits in 1800. In 1800, the medical profession was virtually powerless to prevent diseases, the foremost exception being Jenner's smallpox vaccine, discovered in 1796 and announced in 1798. Physicians had no power over infectious diseases because they did not know what caused them. They also had limited ability to control pain or to perform surgery because they lacked **anesthetic drugs.** During the vital revolution of the nineteenth century, those facts changed: scientists proved the **germ theory of disease transmission** (which led to antiseptic surgery and to the conquest of many infectious diseases), and they discovered effective anesthetics. Nothing in all of modern history is more important than these facts for the improved quality of daily life.

Germs and Disease. The germ theory of disease transmission held that organisms invisible to the naked eye caused contagious diseases. These *microorganisms* (a term coined in 1880) might be spread by air (as was smallpox), by water or food (as was cholera), or by sexual intercourse (as was syphilis). The germ theory had been proposed by a Roman physician in the first century

BCE, but physicians repeatedly rejected it in favor of other theories, such as the **humoral theory** (humors in the body were unbalanced) of the ancient world. The microscope revealed the existence of microorganisms in the seventeenth century, but scientists still favored the **miasmal theory** of diseases, which stressed vapors arising from the ground. The medical establishment remained so reluctant to accept the germ theory that in 1892 a German physician drank a beaker full of cholera bacteria to prove that microorganisms did not cause the disease. He did not die, but his theories did.

The Germ Theory. The germ theory was important for several reasons. First, it led to greater cleanliness, thereby reducing disease transmission. Without the knowledge that invisible organisms transmitted disease, no need existed for antiseptic conditions. Without **antisepsis,** doctors' offices, hospitals, and surgeries were deadly places. Hospitals packed fifty or sixty people into shared wards, where they also shared diseases. Operating rooms had walls and floors impregnated with the waste of recent operations, the floors typically sprinkled with sawdust to soak up the mess. Surgeons wore frock coats, spattered with the blood of their patients; they tied whipcord, used to sew incisions shut, to their buttonholes, where it dangled in the blood of other patients. Doctors treated one patient after another often without washing their hands, and surgeons operated without washing their implements. Not surprisingly, survival rates were low. Even maternity wards were deadly, often having a 25 to 30 percent death rate for new mothers from **puerperal fever,** spread by physicians who performed examinations with unwashed fingers. General infections were so common that they were simply called **"hospital disease."** As Florence Nightingale later lamented, "The very first requirement in a hospital is that it should do the sick no harm."

Pasteur, Koch, and the Germ Theory. The research of French chemist Louis Pasteur and German physician Robert Koch convinced the medical world to accept the germ theory of disease transmission. Pasteur's early work proved that microorganisms in the environment caused fermentation in beverages and the decay of organic matter. This knowledge led Pasteur, Koch, and others to the identification of the bacilli causing various diseases and then to the creation of vaccines against them. Pasteur's research showed how to keep dairy products and beer fresh by eliminating microorganisms (through **pasteurization**) and led to a vaccination against rabies. Koch conducted similar work on tuberculosis, and in 1882, he isolated the bacillus of the disease that had killed an encyclopedia full of the creative artists of the nineteenth century, including the English romantic poet John Keats (at 25),

FIGURE 23.1 *Pasteur in His Laboratory.* Few individuals in modern history have made a greater contribution to the improvement of life for all of humanity than the French chemist Louis Pasteur (1822–1895), shown here in his lab at Pasteur Institute. Pasteur's studies of microorganisms—in subjects as diverse as the fermentation of beverages, the diseases of silkworms, the cause of anthrax, and rabies—made him the father of the "germ theory" of disease transmission. His work, along with that of other noted scientists such as Robert Koch, began an age of the conquest of infectious diseases and saved uncounted lives.

the Polish pianist Frederic Chopin, the French painter Paul Gauguin, the Russian dramatist Anton Chekhov, and the Italian violinist Nicolo Paganini.

Semmelweis and Female Mortality in Childbirth. Even before Pasteur's proof of the germ theory, a few physicians had called for **antiseptic medicine** without being able to prove their case. The greatest early champion of antisepsis was Dr. Ignaz Semmelweis, whose ideas earned him the nickname "the savior of mothers" as well as the scorn of his colleagues. Semmelweis was an assistant in Vienna's maternity clinic in the 1840s. He observed high rates of puerperal fever among women whose doctors treated patients in other parts of the hospital, and this convinced him that simple cleanliness could reduce the death rate. Semmelweis asked that doctors wash their hands in a chloride of lime solution before delivering a baby. He required such antisepsis in the Viennese delivery ward in 1847, and within a few weeks, the death rate from puerperal fever fell from 18 to 2 percent. Semmelweis could not demonstrate why antisepsis succeeded, however, and the medical profession rejected his conclusion; the savior of mothers was branded a charlatan and driven from his job after he also supported the revolution of 1848. The Medical Association

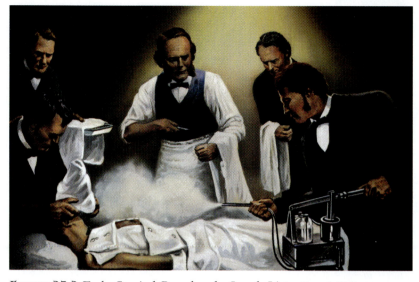

FIGURE 23.2 *Early Surgical Procedure by Joseph Lister.* Joseph Lister (1827–1912) became the father of antiseptic surgery by devising the spray shown in this illustration. Lister, shown at the center, had been studying the infection of wounds when he read Louis Pasteur's work on microorganisms. This led Lister to the conclusion that a cleansing agent that would kill germs could greatly improve the survival rate in surgery. The result was the carbolic acid spray depicted here, a procedure that reduced the death rate in Lister's surgery over the next year by two-thirds. Note, however, that Lister and the other physicians shown here still operate in their street clothes without gloves, face masks, or hair-covering.

a pump to spray a carbolic acid mist across the surgery soon won acceptance, although simpler forms of antisepsis took a surprisingly long time to arrive. An American surgeon introduced rubber gloves (originally intended to protect his hands from the carbolic acid) in 1889, a Polish doctor began to use gauze face masks, and a German doctor suggested the steam sterilization of instruments in 1896.

Anesthesia. Pasteur, Koch, Semmelweis, Lister, and others greatly improved the human condition, but none of their work was more welcomed than were the discoveries of anesthetics. Untreatable pain was a fact of life in 1800. The agony of being fully conscious in a dentist's chair, in a delivery room, or on a surgical table was one of the nightmares of existence before 1846 (see Document 23.1). Before the discovery of anesthetics, patients might have been drugged with alcohol or opium, but they were more often expected to bite down on a bullet. The greatest skill of a surgeon was speed in cutting the body: Dr. James Syme of Edinburgh became famous for his ability to amputate at the hip in ninety seconds; Baron Larrey reported performing "about 200" amputations during the first day of the battle of Borodino in 1812, a rate of one major surgery every 7.2 minutes for 24 hours.

of Vienna proclaimed it "time to stop all this nonsense about chlorine handwash" and abandoned his innovation. Semmelweis died in a straitjacket during the same year that a British surgeon became famous for demonstrating the success of antisepsis.

Lister and Antiseptic Medicine. Joseph Lister became the father of antisepsis instead of Semmelweis. Lister had been studying wounds when he read Pasteur's work and concluded that microorganisms caused the infections he saw. He tested carbolic acid as a cleansing agent to kill such organisms in a successful experiment in 1865. His essay "On the Antiseptic System of Treatment in Surgery" (1867) quickly led to a decline in operating room deaths from 45 to 15 percent. In places where Lister's ideas were not adopted, the contrast was startling. At the start of the Franco-Prussian War of 1870–1871, Lister published a paper on the application of his method to war wounds, and the British even sent appropriate supplies to both France and Germany. Yet German records for the battle of Metz show a mortality rate of 41 percent for upper extremity wounds, 50 percent for lower extremity wounds, and 77 percent mortality for penetrating injuries of the knee. On the French side, army surgeons performed 13,000 battlefield amputations without antisepsis during the war; they had a 76% death rate. Clean rooms, the storage of surgical threads in antiseptics, and

The Slow Adoption of Anesthetics. Sir Humphrey Davy, a British chemistry professor, discovered the anesthetic property of nitrous oxide (laughing gas) in 1800. His laboratory assistant, the distinguished chemist and physicist Michael Faraday, discovered the similar properties of ether in 1815. No medical application was made of these discoveries until dentists began experimenting with ether and chloroform in the 1840s. Dental success led in 1846 to the first major surgery (a leg amputation) performed on a patient under anesthesia. Syme and other British physicians began to campaign for the adoption of anesthesia in 1847. Professor James Young Simpson, a Scottish obstetrician, introduced the use of anesthesia in childbirth and campaigned in the British

Sir Humphrey Davy

Fanny Burney, whose ordeal was introduced in the opening paragraph of this chapter, described it herself in a lengthy journal-letter (composed over several weeks) to her sister Esther. What she could not add was a note about the long-term success of her surgery: she lived for nearly 30 years after it.

My dearest Esther,—and all my dears to whom she communicates this doleful ditty, will rejoice to hear that this resolution [to have surgery] once taken, was firmly adhered to, in defiance of a terror that surpasses all description, and the most torturing pain. Yet— when the dreadful steel was plunged into the breast—cutting through veins—arteries—flesh—nerves—I needed no injunctions not to restrain my cries. I began a scream that lasted unintermittingly during the whole time of the incision—and I almost marvel that it rings not in my ears still! so excruciating was the agony.

When the wound was made, and the instrument was withdrawn, the pain seemed undiminished, for the air that suddenly rushed into those delicate parts felt like a mass of minute but sharp and forked poniards, [daggers] that were tearing the edges of the wound—but when I again felt the instrument, describing a curve, cutting against the grain if I may so say, while the flesh resisted . . . I thought I must have expired. . . . The instrument this second time withdrawn, I concluded the operation over—Oh, no! presently the terrible cutting was renewed—and worse than ever. . . .

To conclude, the evil was so profound, the case so delicate, and the precautions necessary for preventing a return so numerous, that the operation, including the treatment and the dressing, lasted 20 minutes! a time, for sufferings so acute, that was hardly supportable—however, I bore it with all the courage I could exert, and never moved, nor stopt them, nor resisted.

From Burney, Fanny, *Selected Letters and Journals*, Hemlow, Joyce, ed. (Oxford: Oxford University Press, 1986.)

Questions: Is this account sufficient evidence that the discovery of anesthesia was one of the most important facts of nineteenth-century history? Or are the famous battles or books of the century more important?

medical journal *Lancet* for the adoption of his procedure. The medical profession accepted anesthetics in surgery at once but resisted them in the delivery ward. Many still held that the agony of childbirth was God's will in telling Eve "in sorrow thou shalt bring forth children."

Carrel and Anastomosis Even with antisepsis and anesthesia, the death rate remained high when an artery was cut from such causes as compound fractures, knife wounds, or caesarian sections. Surgeons could not perform satisfactory **anastomosis** (the rejoining of the two ends of a severed artery). The president of the Royal College of Surgeons in Britain warned young physicians, "the abdomen, chest, and brain will forever be closed to operations by a wise and humane surgeon." When the president of France was stabbed in the abdomen in 1894 (in the company of several famous physicians) and the blade nicked a vein, it was a death sentence. This episode prompted a French medical student, Alexis Carrel, to study the problem, and in 1902, he performed the first successful anastomosis, which earned him the Nobel Prize in 1912 and opened the doors to the dramatic development of surgery in the twentieth century.

FOOD, DRINK, DRUGS, AND THE VITAL REVOLUTION (1800–1914)

The vital revolution of the nineteenth century was not simply a history of medical science. The increased availability of food and the improvement of diet also played a significant role. Well-fed people resist illness better and live longer. The average European diet of 1850 or 1890 was neither as diverse nor as nutritious as the diet most Europeans enjoy today, and it appears dreadful to most modern readers. However, historical perspective again demands that one compare it with the diet of earlier centuries; seen in that context, the nineteenth-century diet represented a significant improvement.

Increase in Average Height. The simplest proof that the European diet improved during the nineteenth century is that Europeans grew taller. At the beginning of the century, the average soldier—selected for good health and strength—stood between 5′1″ and 5′2″ tall. Napoleon conquered Europe with warriors of that stature. To be sure, there were variations in height. The aristocracy had a better diet and already stood closer to 5′6″. The average height of west European soldiers did not reach 5′6″ until 1900, when Scandinavian countries produced averages of 5′7″. This growth can be explained only by dietary changes. No institution kept similar records of the height of women across the century, but the average height was clearly below 5′ in 1800 and across that line by 1900. A study of skeletons conducted by the Museum of London found that the average male in Victorian London stood 5′5″ and the average female stood 5′1″. Queen Victoria herself stood 5′. That study also found that average heights in England had declined from the middle ages to the mid-nineteenth century, as the quality of the average diet declined (see Table 23.4).

Carbohydrates as the Basic Diet. Dietary improvements arrived slowly, with significant variations by social class and region. A study of the Belgian city of Antwerp in 1850 found that the population of 88,000 people still received two-thirds of its calories from carbohydrates, mostly from bread (see Table 23.5). Workers and the poor received 75 percent or more of their calories from bread. August Bebel's study of the German diet in the 1880s found a similar situation, although more calories came from potatoes. In Spain, the daily per capita consumption of bread remained above two pounds through the first half of the twentieth century. The grains that Europeans ate were beginning to change, as heavy, dark grains such as rye were replaced by wheat (a traditional distinction of the well-to-do) as people could afford the change. In 1700, 40 percent of English bread was rye bread, but a century later the portion of rye had fallen to 5 percent. Scandinavia followed a similar pattern, but rye remained the staple grain in Germany.

Meat and Variation in Diet. The study of Antwerp found that 10 percent of people's calories came from meat and nearly a quarter from animal products in 1850—a big change from eighteenth-century averages. Similar studies of the German diet in the midnineteenth century found an average of 1.3 ounces of meat per day—little if compared with today, but an amount that would have indicated prosperity in the eighteenth century. An increased consumption of fruits and vegetables came more slowly; they typically remained expensive or seasonal food for most people.

Gradual Improvements in the Diet. Most studies of food consumption show steady improvement across the nineteenth century. A study of workhouse diets in Britain, for example, found that men received 2,350 calories in the 1880s and 1890s, an improvement of nearly 20 percent from the 1830s. Thus, the poorest level of British society, whom the government treated with intentional stringency, ate better, too. Similarly, a study of German diets found that by 1910 per capita meat consumption had reached 4.5 ounces per day. Even if much of this came in tin cans, or much of it was horse meat (a habit promoted in European armies), this average would have seemed utopian in the eighteenth century.

Food Prices and Diet. The chief explanation for this improvement is that food prices declined significantly. The age of free trade ended tariffs on food and permitted the importation of cheaper food from around the world. In London, for example, the Napoleonic Wars had kept the price of a loaf of bread—then a 4-pound loaf—artificially high at 11 to 17 pence, and it had fallen to a range of 8 to 12 pence in peacetime under the **Corn Laws** (tariffs on grain). The repeal of the Corn Laws in 1846 produced a price of 7 to 8 pence per loaf, dropping to an average of five to six pence for the years 1895–1914. Thus, even if workers' wages remained unchanged during the entire century, in 1900, they bought nearly three times as much bread as they had in lean years at the start of the century and nearly twice as much bread as they had under the Corn Laws.

The Science of Agriculture and Diet. Agronomy and technology also drove down food prices. The foremost advances in agricultural science came from the chemistry labs, like Justus von Liebig's institute at the Universities of Giessen and Munich. Liebig, one of the founders of modern chemical analysis, demonstrated in 1840 that there were four key inorganic elements in rich soil (nitrogen, potassium, lime, and phosphoric acid) and that farmland required each to be productive. He and his students launched the age of soil analysis and replenishment through **chemical fertilizers,** which they began to produce. Together, Liebig's chemical analysis and fertilizer factories led to the end of the traditional agriculture of the **fallow field.**

FIGURE 23.3 *Liebig's Chemistry Laboratory, Circa 1842.* Baron Justus von Liebig (1803–1873) became the founder of organic chemical analysis and agricultural chemistry working in this laboratory at Giessen (Hesse) in the 1840s and 1850s. Among the accomplishments of this lab were the discovery of chloroform and the first nitrogen-rich fertilizers for plants, a discovery that significantly increased agricultural productivity in the nineteenth century.

DIET AND INCREASED HEIGHT

The height of the average European male is nearly 5'10'' in northern countries today, a dramatic increase when compared with the historic record shown here. An improved diet is the basic explanation.

TABLE 23.4 AVERAGE HEIGHTS IN EUROPE

	Average Heights of European Military Recruits		Average Heights in London, Based on Skeleton Studies	
			Medieval London	
COUNTRY	**SOLDIER IN THE 1800s**	**SOLDIER IN 1900**	**MALE**	**FEMALE**
Italy	5'1''–5'2'' (1800)	5'4''	5'7½''	5'3''
			Tudor-Stuart	
			MALE	**FEMALE**
Britain (18-year-olds)	5'3'' (1866)	5'4''	5'7½"	5'2"
France	n.a.	5'5''		
Britain (21- to 23-year-olds)	5'5'' (1858)	5'6''		
			Georgian Working-Class	
			MALE	**FEMALE**
Denmark	5'5'' (1835)	5'6''	5'7¼''	5'1¼''
			Victorian London	
			MALE	**FEMALE**
Netherlands	5'4'' (1864)	5'6''		
Norway	n.a.	5'7''		
Sweden	5'6'' (1890)	5'7''	5'5½''	5'1¼''

n.a. = Not available.

From Floud, Roderick, et al., *Height, Health, and History: Nutritional Status in the United Kingdom, 1750—1980* (Cambridge: Cambridge University Press, 1990, pp. 14, 25—26, 136–137); and Werner, Alex, *London Bodies: The Changing Shape of Londoners from Prehistoric Times to the Present Day* (London: Museum of London, 1998, p. 108).

Question: Why were average heights in midnineteenth-century England actually lower than those for the eighteenth century?

Shipping, Prices, and Diet. Vacuum canning, refrigeration, and steam ships enabled Europeans to exploit the agricultural wealth of Argentina, Australia, Canada, and the United States. The cost of shipping goods fell sharply. A study of French costs has shown that shipping goods by sea in 1825 added 6 centimes to the price for every kilometer that a ton of food was shipped, and once these goods reached France, highway transportation added 35 centimes for every kilometer a ton was carted. In 1905, when steamships had

TABLE 23.5 THE AVERAGE DAILY DIET AT ANTWERP IN THE 1850s

	CONSUMPTION PER CAPITA, PER DAY	NUMBER OF CALORIES	CALORIES AS A PERCENTAGE OF TOTAL CONSUMED
Animal Products			
Butter	32.0 grams	240	10.6
Eggs	0.348 grams	26	1.1
Meat	104.0 grams	234	10.3
Salt fish	12.0 grams	32	1.4
Subtotal		532	23.4
Beverages			
Beer	0.367 liters	163	7.2
Coffee	12.0 grams	12	0.5
Gin	0.015 liters	40	1.8
Wine	0.015 liters	12	0.5
Subtotal		237	10.0
Carbohydrates			
Potatoes	700.0 grams	490	21.6
Rye flour	45.0 grams	140	6.2
Wheat flour	284.0 grams	880	38.8
Subtotal		1,510	66.6
Total		2,279	100

Adapted from data in Lis, Catharina, *Social Change and the Labouring Poor: Antwerp, 1770–1860* (New Haven, CT: Yale University Press, 1986, p. 182).

Question: What are the most surprising features of this average diet from the 1850s?

replaced sails, sea transportation had fallen to 2.4 centimes (a decrease of 58 percent); railroads had similarly replaced horse-drawn carts, and land transportation had fallen to 5.4 centimes (a decrease of 84 percent). Thus, foreign-food prices fell simply because bringing it to market cost less. This competition drove down the price of locally produced food.

Canning and Refrigeration. In the late nineteenth century, canning and refrigeration greatly improved

FIGURE 23.4 *Canned Food.* In the kitchen of Ritchie and McCall's preserved meat factory in Houndsditch, London, 1852, workers are canning meat. Methods of preserving food in sealed metals cans—by boiling them (as seen on the left)—were developed for the military in the first years of the nineteenth century, without knowing why this "canning" worked. The cost of canned food remained high when it first reached the stores in the 1830s because the first cans were all handcrafted. A worker produced approximately one can per hour, so a single can of meat or fish cost nearly as much as a working-class family paid for a week's rent. By the 1870s, factory methods had increased production, prices had fallen, and the average family's diet improved.

the European diet, which had relied on the traditional preservation techniques of smoking, salting, or drying. The preservation of foods by heating them (thereby killing bacteria) and storing them in airless tin cans (an idea for which Nicholas Appert won a prize offered by Napoleon, for feeding his army) began to yield widespread improvements in diet in the 1850s and 1860s, but canning did not initially offer great availability of canned fruit or vegetables, because demand was highest for canned meats, and canning was expensive (cans were hand-made). Machine-made cans began an age of cheaper canned food in 1868. The first effective refrigeration of foods (an ammonia-based refrigeration) was developed in the 1870s. This led to a dramatic moment in food history in 1878, when a French ship docked at Le Havre with a cargo of more than 5,000 full carcasses of cattle, all well-preserved. By the 1880s, inexpensive meat from Australia, New Zealand, Argentina, Canada, and the United States was transforming the European diet.

Diet and Social Class. Data showing total consumption in a nation, or data divided to state average consumption, can be misleading. Individual consumption still varied greatly by social class. A study of the English diet in 1900 has suggested that a typical working-class family of four had a weekly food budget of 15 shillings (about $3.75), whereas a middle-class family spent 15 shillings per person. Well-to-do families, who took pride in lavish entertaining, spent 30 shillings per person. Working-class meals still consisted chiefly of starches, with few fruits or vegetables; meat chiefly came at a special Sunday meal, with occasional supplements such as bacon, sausage, or rabbit.

The Middle-Class Diet. In contrast, food was a status symbol for the middle classes, the material proof of their success in reaching a standard of living previously limited to the wealthy. Overeating became a conspicuous social process; obesity, a mark of distinction. Standards of both manly and womanly appearance favored robust figures, showing that a person did not live on a modest budget. One of the best-selling books of the 1890s was an advice manual for women titled *How to Become Pleasingly Plump.* Many public figures at the turn of the twentieth century cast such large shadows. The prime minister of Britain on the eve of World War I, Sir Henry Campbell-Bannerman, weighed nearly 280 pounds, and his wife was almost as obese. They ate four meals every day, such as the prime minister's regular favorite: a bowl of mutton-broth soup, a fish course of either herring or salmon, then a roast lamb, followed by a grouse, and culminating in multiple desserts (usually an apple tart with fresh strawberries), then gingerbread and butter. His predecessor at the start of the century, the marquess of Salisbury, was only slightly smaller.

The Working-Class Diet. The health risks of a working-class diet were different from those of middle-class overeating. The foremost problem (beyond obtaining sufficient food) was the adulteration of food. As Europe changed from an agricultural society, in which people produced the food that they ate, to an urban society, in which people purchased their food in markets, unscrupulous merchants exploited the unregulated economy to sell **adulterated food.** A parliamentary commission found that bread often contained chalk, plaster of Paris, sand, or lime. Powdered clay was mixed with cocoa, ground nut shells with pepper. Sulfuric acid was added to gin, producing a drink with a memorable bite. Sugar was debased with a dried residue from soap boilers. Parliament concluded that 62 percent of all food sold in London was corrupted, but the government hesitated to act due to the principle of laissez-faire capitalism that the state should not intervene in the economic process. The problem was not limited to British cities, and many countries debated pure food laws versus pure capitalism before accepting the government regulation of food, drink, and drugs. The Dutch pioneered such legislation in 1829, and regulations against adulterated food soon followed in France, Belgium, Prussia, and Spain. British merchants continued to insist upon an unregulated market until scandals forced pure food legislation in 1860 and 1872.

Chemically Engineered Food Substitutes. The adulteration of food made people initially skeptical of altered or synthetic foods, which began to appear in the nineteenth century. Only after large advertising campaigns did people begin to accept pasteurized milk in which microbes had been killed by sterilization. Two American chemists synthesized a compound in 1879 and accidentally discovered that it was extremely sweet tasting; their saccharin was an effective sugar substitute, but people who knew about the corruption of sugar with soap wastes were reluctant to accept a sugar containing no sugar. One of the first successful substitute foods—often called by the German term *Ersatzessen*—was a flour made from potatoes instead of grains. Margarine, the most widely used **ersatz food,** was invented in a French laboratory in 1869, in response to a contest sponsored by Napoleon III to discover an affordable substitute for butter. The prizewinning recipe was a mixture of beef fat and ground cow's udders. This may seem a scant improvement on the outlawed adulteration, but it was just a short step to the use of vegetable oil instead of rendered beef fat to create the commercially successful margarine sold to the urban working class.

Alcoholic Drink in the Nineteenth Century

Alcohol and Taxes. The nineteenth century was an age of high consumption of alcohol compared with the early twenty-first century, but not compared with the eighteenth century. The ravages caused to the human body by excessive alcohol or drugs were poorly understood, and physicians regularly prescribed narcotics as painkillers; some even recommended heavy alcohol consumption. Governments did little to control alcohol or opium sales in 1800. As with food capitalism, opposed government restrictions on the market and perpetuated an open market. Furthermore, alcohol taxes kept most governments in business. In 1870, Britain had virtually no income tax but raised 35 percent of its total revenue on alcohol taxes. In Ireland, 54 percent of all government revenue was raised by taxes on alcohol. End-of-the-century Russia raised even more income through a government monopoly on vodka.

Alcohol and Society. Heavy drinking was socially acceptable. William Pitt the Younger frequently addressed Parliament while drunk; on important occasions, he

stepped behind the speaker's chair and induced vomiting before making a critical speech. Even the more puritanical Gladstone drank a sherry mixture in Parliament to ease his way through 3-hour speeches. Another prime minister made himself light-headed with ether before speaking, and a fourth took a jolt of opium dissolved in alcohol. If the rich and powerful behaved that way, it is hardly surprising that people who lived in a world of epidemic disease, short life expectancy, 70- to 80-hour workweeks, no welfare legislation or retirement, and minimal diets found solace and sociability in cafés, pubs, and beer halls. Nor was heavy drinking limited to the cities. In regions where **viticulture** dominated the economy, peasant wine drinking was often prodigious. In more northern regions, beer making was often part of the household economy and a staple of the diet.

Alcohol Consumption. A variety of records reveal the extent of nineteenth-century drinking. The Antwerp study found that beer consumption in the 1820s averaged two bottles per day (23 ounces) for every man, woman, and child in the population, plus approximately one bottle of wine and one bottle of gin each per month; by the 1850s, nearly 10 percent of all calories consumed in the city came from alcohol. A similar survey of France in 1900 found a per capita annual consumption rate of 180 liters of wine (240 standard bottles), 27 liters of beer (more than three cases of 12-ounce bottles), and 4.7 liters of distilled spirits (more than 5 bottles of alcohol). Those averages include the entire population. If one excludes children younger than age 14 (more than 30 percent of the population in 1900), every adult in France had to consume 325 bottles of wine per year; clearly, a significant portion of the population drank more than a bottle per day, all year long, much of it distilled to make a rough brandy. A study of Russia found that spending on vodka exceeded total spending for education, books, oil, gifts, priests, the poor, weddings, and funerals, which may explain why the government chose to tax vodka instead of books. The home secretary (Minister of the Interior) in Britain offered a slightly different perspective in 1871: there was one pub for every 182 people in the kingdom, without counting refreshment rooms in railway stations, private clubs, and liquor stores. The founder of the Salvation Army pointed to this fact when he pronounced the British to be "a population sodden with drink."

Opposition to Alcohol Consumption. Such drinking led to efforts to control sales of alcoholic beverages. The first European **temperance society** was organized in Ireland in 1818, and such groups spread across the British Isles during industrialization. Many motives could be discerned behind the temperance campaign. Some reformers were motivated by religious morality and saw drinking as sinful; others acted from the perspective of social class—sometimes to help families in

FIGURE 23.5 *The Dangers of Alcohol.* The rate of alcohol consumption in Europe had been enormous in the eighteenth century and was still remarkably high in the nineteenth century. The first organizations seeking the regulation of alcohol sales and the moderation of consumption began to appear in the first half of the nineteenth century. This French poster from 1850 satirizes those who worship "The Very Holy Bottle"—patron of the noisy, marriage breakers, swindlers, bad payers, drunkards, and bad husbands.

poverty, sometimes in fear of the poor and crime, sometimes angry about alcohol and absenteeism from work. Although the upper classes were notoriously heavy drinkers, most reformers agreed with employers that drink was "the curse of [the] working class." British law regulated the opening hours of alehouses in 1828 and began the licensing of pubs in 1830. Scottish clergymen won the first prohibition of alcohol—no sales on Sundays—in 1853.

Opium Use in the 1800s

Laudanum. By the time that temperance leagues became active in European cities, advocates of social control were also becoming concerned about opium and cocaine, both of which were legally available. Opium, derived from an easily cultivated flower, has been used medicinally since ancient Mediterranean civilizations; one of the oldest known Egyptian papyri praises its painkilling powers. A Swiss physician popularized medical opium in the sixteenth century in a compound he named **laudanum** ("highly praised"). Laudanum, a tincture of opium dissolved in alcohol, became a basic medication, and by 1800 it was widely consumed by all who could afford it.

Opium Export. Britain imported tons of opium every year. Most of this stock was reexported to the Far East, where the British were the world's pushers—they had used opium addiction as a means of opening Oriental markets, and they fought two Opium Wars (1839–1842 and 1856–1858) to keep their drug markets open. Even

subtracting the reexportation of opium, the British home market was enormous. Domestic consumption grew from 8.5 tons of opium in 1827 to 30.5 tons in 1859, spawning a network of respectable importers, auctioneers, brokers, and merchants (see *Opium*). British governments shared in this lucrative trade through an opium tariff until 1860. The abolition of the tariff cut the price of opium to approximately one shilling (25 cents) per ounce, roughly an agricultural laborer's weekly wages in 1860.

Opium and Social Class. Opium was initially a drug of the educated and upper classes because of its cost and its circulation by physicians. In the early nineteenth century, addiction was far more common among famous writers than criminals or the poor. Virtually the entire literary community of romanticism used opium. Thomas De Quincey became famous for his book titled *Confessions of an English Opium Eater* (1856), which bluntly said, "Thou hast the keys of paradise, O just, subtle, and mighty opium!" Coleridge became renowned for a poem ("Kubla Kahn") that he composed after an opium-induced fantasy. Byron took a brand of laudanum called the Black Drop, and satisfied references to it appear in his writing. Shelley used opium to relieve stress. Keats consumed such large quantities that he even considered using it for suicide. Elizabeth Barrett Browning's spinal problems made her dependent on a daily dose of opium, and her husband concluded that "sleep only came to her in a red hood of poppies." Sir Walter Scott began taking huge quantities during an illness and wrote at least one of his novels under its influence. Similar lists could be drawn of political figures (the friends of George IV often found him stupefied by opium) or even famous preachers (William Wilberforce was an addict because of his ulcer medication). This situation lasted until the Pharmacy Act of 1868 introduced the first restrictions, because the government feared that workers were starting to use opium for its pleasure-giving properties. Further restrictions appeared in the 1890s, when the government began to fear that immigrants, especially the Chinese, congregated in "opium dens" and plotted crimes.

CHANGING ATTITUDES AND BEHAVIOR ACROSS THE LIFE CYCLE

Birth and Birth Control

The subject of human reproduction led to much controversy during the nineteenth century. The century witnessed a significant decline in the birthrate, which is explained by a variety of birth control practices.

OPIUM

The Opium Room. Throughout the nineteenth century, the opium trade remained a legal business, and the drug was imported into Europe in huge quantities, where it was legally sold in drug stores. In 1859, the British market consumed more than 30 tons of opium. In this illustration, respectable opium merchants examine their stock.

TABLE 23.6 OPIUM USE IN ENGLAND, 1827–1877

YEAR	OPIUM IMPORTS (IN TONS)	TOTAL HOME CONSUMPTION (IN TONS)	HOME CONSUMPTION (IN POUNDS PER 1,000 PEOPLE)
1827	56.6	8.5	1.31
1837	40.3	18.5	2.48
1847	n.a.	23.0	2.67
1857	68.2	28.0	2.92
1867	136.8	n.a.	n.a.
1877	303.7	n.a.	n.a.

n.a. = Not available.

Condensed from data in Berridge, Virginia, and Edwards, Griffith, *Opium and the People: Opiate Use in Nineteenth Century England* (New Haven, CT: Yale University Press, 1987, tables 1–2, pp. 272–274).

Question: Do these data show that England had a drug problem in the nineteenth century?

Physicians, churches, and governments generally opposed the circulation of birth control information and the use of contraceptives, however. In fact, they considered them immoral and made them illegal in most places.

Contraception. The search for a reliable means of **birth control** is as old as human records, and discussions of it are found in pre-Christian records. The early church opposed contraception and medieval canon law forbade it, but ideas about avoiding pregnancy nonetheless circulated in popular culture. The population explosion that began in the late eighteenth century persuaded nineteenth-century reformers to circulate birth control information. These **neo-Malthusians** proposed a variety of (semireliable) means of contraception: the insertion of a barrier (such as a sponge), as a rudimentary form of the diaphragm; the use of simple chemical douches (such as vinegar), as a rudimentary spermicide; and the practice of male withdrawal before ejaculation, modestly described by the Latin term *coitus interruptus.* Condoms made from animal membranes had been tried for centuries, and a reusable condom of vulcanized rubber (hence its nickname) was clandestinely marketed in the 1870s, although the modern, thinner condom made of latex was not invented until after World War I.

Contraceptives and the Birthrate. Such methods of contraception—plus abortion, infanticide, and abandonment—were first used on a scale large enough to check population growth in France. The French birthrate in 1810 was 317 births per 10,000 population, 15 percent lower than the rate in Britain (375 per

BIRTH CONTROL IN VICTORIAN ENGLAND

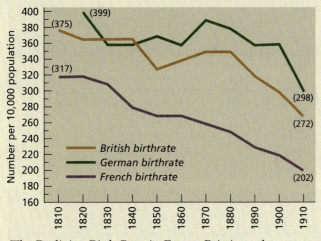

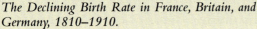

The Declining Birth Rate in France, Britain, and Germany, 1810–1910.

Annie Besant Surveys Birth Control Options (1877)

All thinkers have seen that since population increases more rapidly than the means of subsistence, the human brain should be called in to devise a restriction of the population, and so relieve man from the pressure of the struggle for existence. . . . Malthus proposed . . . the delay of marriage. . . . [But] the more marriage is delayed, the more prostitution spreads. . . . Later, thinkers, recognizing at once the evils of over-population and the evils of late marriage . . . have advocated early marriages and small families. . . . [Yet] how is this duty to be performed?

The check we will take first is 'natural laws'. . . . Women are far less likely to conceive midway between the menstrual periods than either immediately before or after them.

The preventive check so generally practiced in France . . . consists simply in the withdrawal of the husband previous to the emission of the semen, and is, of course absolutely certain as a preventive. . . . The preventive check advocated by Dr. Knowlton is, on the other hand, entirely in the hands of the wife. It consists in the use of the ordinary syringe immediately after intercourse, a solution of sulphate of zinc, or of alum, being used instead of water. There is but little doubt that this check is an effective one . . . [but] there are many obvious disadvantages connected with it as a matter of taste and feeling. The same remark applies to the employment of the baudruche, a covering used by men of loose character as a guard against syphilitic diseases, and occasionally recommended as a preventive check.

The check which appears to us to be preferable, as at once certain, and in no sense grating on any feeling of affection or of delicacy, is that recommended by Carlile many years ago in his Every Woman's Book. *. . . To prevent impregnation, pass to the end of the vagina a piece of fine sponge. . . .*

There is a preventive check attempted by many poor women which is most detrimental to health, and should therefore never be employed, namely, the too long persistence in nursing one baby in the hope of thereby preventing the conception of another. Nursing does not prevent conception. . . .

Another class of checks is distinctly criminal, i.e., the procuring of abortion. Various drugs are taken by women with this intent, and too often their use results in death, or in dangerous sickness.

From Besant, Annie, *The Law of Population* (London: Freethought Publishing Company, 1877).

10,000); the rate in the German states was even higher (395 per 10,000). The difference between the French and the Anglo-German birthrates widened during the nineteenth century, even when the British birthrate started falling. By 1910, the French birthrate (202 per 10,000) was 26 percent below the British rate (272 per 10,000) and 32 percent below the German rate (298 per 10,000). By the early twentieth century, the French had reached **zero population growth** (a balance between births and deaths), despite the opposition of leaders who foresaw the depopulation of France. This trend, combined with other demographic data, leaves no doubt that the French were practicing birth control on a significant scale.

The Battle over Contraception. British radicals tried to spread such information. Richard Carlile, a tinsmith and printer, published a manual in 1838 titled *Every Woman's Book* advocating the use of a sponge barrier. It and an American manual, *Fruits of Philosophy* (1832), which advocated a vinegar douche, were censored, and some booksellers were imprisoned, but their ideas circulated. In 1877, Annie Besant, a preacher's wife and campaigner for unpopular causes, and Charles Bradlaugh, a social reformer, defied the courts and sold 125,000 copies of these reprinted works. Besant summarized the various methods of birth control in *The Law of Population* (1877), which conservatives branded as "a dirty, filthy book . . . that no human would allow on his table . . . and no decently educated English husband would allow even his wife to have" (see *Birth Control in Victorian England*). Besant was sentenced to 6 months in prison, but the verdict was overturned on a technicality.

Women's Clinics. Similar controversies developed in many countries. Dr. Alleta Jacobs, the first woman physician in the Netherlands, opened the world's first **birth control clinic** in Amsterdam in 1882, despite great opposition from the medical profession. In other countries, radical feminists, such as Dr. Madeleine Pelletier in France, made the control of reproduction an essential element of women's rights. Pelletier even published one of the first works claiming the right to abortion. By the end of the century, information about both birth control and abortion circulated widely. A study of Spain has found significant use of contraception in the cities, especially in Catalonia. A study of a Berlin working-class clinic in 1913 found that 64 percent of the women used birth control.

Abortion in the 1800s. Historical data on abortions are among the least reliable evidence confronting historians, but provocative records survive on this controversial subject. A study of **abortion** in France in the late nineteenth century concluded that approximately 250,000 abortions per year were performed there. It was illegal to perform or to obtain an abortion throughout those years, but only 100 to 200 French women were convicted of the crime each year. Physicians' records from small villages show varying local rates, from 3 to 18 percent of all pregnancies ending in abortion. In contrast, fully 40 percent of the working-class women interviewed in Berlin in 1913 admitted that they had at least one abortion; the entire group had terminated almost one-third of their pregnancies by abortions. The means of abortion that they reported were startling: one simply "jumped off chairs and stools." Another "sent for a [chemical] remedy that was advertised in the newspaper." And a third "poked around with a quill a little bit until blood came." Descriptions of similar means of aborting unwanted pregnancies occur in late nineteenth-century novels, such as Zola's grim portrayal of peasant life in France, *The Land* (1887). Such sources suggest that midwives performed many of the abortions. Despite the medical, legal, social, and religious obstacles, European women practiced birth control and abortion on a large enough scale during the nineteenth century to sharply lower birthrates.

Illegitimacy in Nineteenth-Century Europe. The increasing use of birth control did not mean that social problems associated with childbirth, such as **illegitimacy,** abandonment, and infanticide, disappeared. Illegitimacy began to increase in the late eighteenth century and grew during the nineteenth century, until 8 percent of all European births in the 1880s were illegitimate. This pattern varied regionally, with the highest national averages being found in Germanic central Europe. Austria, Germany, Denmark, and Scandinavia had a combined illegitimate birthrate above 10 percent, with the highest figure being in Austria (14.9 percent in 1889). Much lower rates were found in regions with early marriages (such as Serbia, which reported 1.1 percent illegitimacy) or the strictest sexual mores (such as Ireland, which reported 2.7 percent). Conversely, where late marriages were the norm, illegitimacy rose. A demographic study of rural Portugal found that, in villages where landless peasants could not marry until late in life, illegitimacy reached as high as 73 percent of all births. As the data for Ireland and Austria show, national religions were not the determining factor in illegitimate births.

Infanticide and Child Abandonment. **Infanticide** and the **abandonment** of newborn infants (often the same thing) remained serious social problems, as they had been in the Old Regime. In Britain, the law stated that infanticide must be treated as murder, but it also said "it must be proved that the entire body of the child has actually been born into the world in a living state" before the child was legally alive and the act was legally murder. Killing an infant as it emerged from the womb thus received some legal protection, and it was a horrifying, but not uncommon, urban experience of mid-Victorian England to find dead babies in the streets, in trash heaps, or in rivers. Abandonment was sufficiently common in Victorian England that George Eliot (the pseudonym of Mary Ann Evans) could make it a central element of *Adam Bede* (1859) and make the mother who left her child to die in the woods (Hetty Sorrel) a sympathetic character.

Frequency of Infanticide and Abortion. In France, infanticide was so common that at least 1,000 women were indicted for it every year from the 1840s to the 1880s; annual arrests did not fall below 500 until 1901. One study estimates that the crime reached its nineteenth-century peak at 12 percent of all births in 1862–1863. In the years 1817–1820, the abandonment of babies at Paris hospitals equaled one-third of the births recorded in the city, although many of these infants were undoubtedly brought to Paris from the countryside. The abandonment of babies at public institutions in France reached a recorded peak of 164,319 in 1833. Thus, abandonment or infanticide may have claimed 40 percent of all babies in some years. Abandonment was most common in regions where effective contraception was not well known, especially in eastern Europe. Catherine the Great had established **foundling homes** in Moscow and St. Petersburg, but abandoned babies soon overflowed these institutions, which then became processing centers

TABLE 23.7 ABANDONED CHILDREN IN ST. PETERSBURG, 1830–1845

The range of percentages is due to the possibility that none of the abandoned babies was a registered birth and the possibility that all of the abandoned babies were registered births. These percentages do not reflect the possibility that some babies were born outside of St. Petersburg but abandoned there.

Year	New Entries to St. Petersburg Foundling Home	Percentage of Births in St. Petersburg	Newborns Abandoned
1830	4,091	9,661	29.7–42.3
1835	5,226	10,313	33.6–50.7
1840	4,604	13,339	25.7–34.5
1845	5,808	19,276	23.2–30.1

Calculated from data in Ransel, David L., "Abandonment and Fosterage of Unwanted Children: The Women of the Foundling System," in Ransel, David L., ed., *The Family in Imperial Russia: New Lines of Historical Research* (Urbana, IL: University of Illinois Press, 1978, p. 193).

Question: Why would mothers abandon so many babies?

for shipping unwanted babies to the countryside. In the 1830s, the foundling home of St. Petersburg had 25,000 children on its rolls, with 5,000 being added each year; by the 1880s, the home in St. Petersburg was receiving 9,000 abandoned newborns per year, and the home in Moscow, 17,000 (see Table 23.7). A study of the province around Moscow has found that more than 10 percent of the babies born there in the late nineteenth century were abandoned by their mothers. The problem was most urgent for the large numbers of women who were domestic servants in the cities—25 percent of women in Moscow, 37 percent in St. Petersburg. Marriage was difficult for these women and economic survival virtually impossible if they lost their posts, as they would if they had a child. Children who reached the foundling homes suffered terribly: Between 75 and 90 percent of them died each year. Similar patterns existed in western Europe, and critics were not totally wrong when they called foundling homes a system of "legalized infanticide."

Childhood and Youth

The Changing Experience of Childhood. No stage of the life cycle experienced a more dramatic change in daily life than the young did. The history of childhood and adolescence in nineteenth-century Europe saw the conquest of childhood diseases—a con- quest that changed childhood from an experience in which 50 percent of the population died to one in which less than 10 percent did; it also saw the emergence of the idea that youth was a distinct phase of life, leading to new attitudes and laws about different treatment of the young. And the Industrial Revolution utterly transformed the primary activities of the young, first shifting their economic roles with employment in mines and factories and later requiring years of mandatory schooling instead of work.

The Legal Definition of Childhood. The British led Europe toward a new legal treatment of the young by defining new borders between youth and adulthood. Nineteenth-century laws limited the maximum number of hours that children could work and the minimum number of years that they must attend school; laws defined the age at which the young could consent to sex or to marriage and the age at which they could be sentenced to death. For most of the nineteenth century, the age of sexual consent for girls was twelve; a reform of British criminal law in 1875 raised this to thirteen (the French standard), and another reform in 1885 set the age of consent at sixteen. A study of French criminal justice has shown that, despite such early ages of consent, the single most common felony against persons in the late nineteenth century was the molestation of young girls. The young similarly received at least nominal protection in penal law. For most of the century, British prison populations were segregated by gender, social class, and types of crimes committed, but they were not segregated by age; a 10-year-old thief would be imprisoned with adult criminals. British penal reforms of 1854 created reformatories for youthful offenders, with 15 being considered the age of adulthood. A Children's Act of 1908 created separate prisons (borstals) for the young and set the age of adulthood (for hanging, for example) at 16, to match the sexual statutes.

Limitations on Child Labor. Industrialization and urbanization transformed the economic life of the young. For many, life shifted from being farm workers in a household economy, or urban apprentices already separated from their families, to working in mines and factories and contributing to a family wage economy. By the 1840s, child labor had become so common that governments began to regulate it. In France, for example, 18 to 24 percent of all workers in textile factories were children, and the law limited children below the age of 12 to 8 hours of work per day.

Education and Literacy. The Old Regime legacy of children working at an early age in agriculture, factories, mines, or apprenticeships left little room for universal education. The great majority of the population of Europe was illiterate in 1800. A study of French schooling in the early nineteenth century found that more than 15,000 towns (40 percent of the communities in France) had no schools whatsoever. A study of Russia on the eve of emancipation (1861) found that 0.8 percent of the population was attending school. The German states had long been the leaders of European education because they had a tradition of compulsory education. In the 1850s, nearly 95 percent of Prussian adults had received at least 8 years of primary education; by the 1890s, virtually 100 percent of German children received a primary education (see *Education and Literacy in the 1800s*).

The Rise of Compulsory Education.

Most of Europe did not copy the German principle of compulsory education until the late nineteenth century. In 1850, the combined elementary school enrollments in Hungary, Portugal, and the Ottoman Empire amounted to fewer than 100,000 pupils—fewer than 5,000 in all of the Turkish provinces, only 18,000 in Portugal. Jules Ferry, an earnest lawyer and five-term Minister of Education in France, gave Europe another model in the late 1870s and early 1880s: mandatory, free, secular, universal education in state-run schools. British education, shaped by the Forster elementary education reforms of Gladstone's "great ministry" (1868–1874), provided a competing model that encouraged private, fee-paying schools. By 1914, schooling had replaced disease as the basic fact of childhood. British primary school enrollments increased twentyfold, from 278,000 in 1850 to 6.3 million in 1910.

The Conquest of Illiteracy.

The foremost consequence of compulsory education laws was the birth of nearly universal literacy. Although the vast majority of Europeans had been illiterate in 1800, this varied somewhat from one region to another, differed for men and for women, and followed the standards of social class or occupation; but the result was usually the same: most people could neither read nor write. Studies of marriage records—by checking the signatures on wedding certificates—reveal the scope of illiteracy. In 1800, 53 percent of the women married in England signed with an "X." As late as 1870, 58 percent of Italian men and 77 percent of Italian women still signed marriage certificates with an "X." The Russian census of 1897 found 71 percent of men and 87 percent of women to be illiterate. Other studies have shown how illiteracy varied by a family's social position or occupation. A study of French army recruits in the 1830s found that illiteracy was rare among the sons of professionals (less than 1 percent) or civil servants (2.4 percent) but high among the sons of factory workers (58.9 percent), peasants (83.5 percent), or domestic servants (96.0 percent). Similar variations occurred within the regions of a country. A study of Italian illiteracy in 1911 found it low in the more prosperous north (Piedmont, 11 percent; Lombardy, 13 percent) but high in the poorer south (Sicily, 58 percent; Calabria, 70 percent).

The School Day.

The life of schoolchildren in the nineteenth century consisted chiefly of the memorization of facts. As Mr. Gradgrind, a teacher in Charles Dickens's *Hard Times* (1854), explained, "Now what I want is Facts. . . . Facts alone are wanted in life." There remained some variation about which facts pupils must memorize, but little doubt existed about this form of education. Girls and boys received different schooling, with some boys being groomed for higher education and girls usually denied such preparation. Private schools (where tuition was charged) often stressed religious studies, whereas state schools in both the French and German models insisted on strictly secular education. The master of a famous British school for the elite, Rugby School, stated his mission this way: "It is not necessary that this should be a school of 300 or 100, or of 50 boys, but it is necessary that it should be a school of Christian gentlemen." The French Ministry of Education, in contrast, removed Christianity from the classroom and the curriculum, teaching instead a secular moral philosophy. Most schools taught a little mathematics, more history (especially the national history), some geography (particularly as colonial empires grew), little literature, less science (sometimes omitted entirely), and a great deal of Latin and Greek, which were requirements for higher education. Classics remained the key to a university education throughout the century; although Oxford and Cambridge relaxed their Greek requirement at the turn of the twentieth century, proficiency in Latin remained *sine qua non* (indispensable) at universities well into the 1900s.

Conservative Reaction to Compulsory Education.

Compulsory education, like other social changes, often conflicted with traditional values and behavior. Just as conservatives opposed some of the new medical practices, such as vaccination and anesthesia, and they fought against birth control and abortion, many conservatives opposed compulsory education (see Document 23.3). They argued that state-run schools gave the government too much power or that the family would be weakened. Religious leaders inveighed against the "godless school." Such arguments slowed, or blocked, universal education in some countries. The Spanish accepted only a minimum of universal education: the Moyano Education Law of 1857, which remained the basis of Spanish education until the 1960s, made schooling obligatory only until age nine and provided free schooling only for the poor. The tsarist government in Russia rejected compulsory

EDUCATION AND LITERACY IN THE 1800S

The creation of free, secular, compulsory public schools was one of the greatest accomplishments of nineteenth-century Europe, contributing significantly to the rise of democracy, a modern economy, women's rights, and the breakdown of rigid class systems. These developments began with the conquest of illiteracy.

TABLE 23.8 THE RISE OF UNIVERSAL EDUCATION IN EUROPE, 1849–1914

	Primary Pupils		University Students	
COUNTRY	NUMBER (YEAR)	NUMBER (YEAR)	NUMBER (YEAR)	NUMBER (YEAR)
Austria	1,450,000 (1850)	4,691,000 (1910)	11,439 (1850)	39,416 (1910)
Britain	278,000 (1850)	6,295,000 (1910)	n.a.	n.a.
France	3,322,000 (1850)	5,049,000 (1910)	n.a.	41,190 (1910)
Germany	n.a.	n.a.	21,432 (1880)	70,183 (1910)
Hungary	18,000 (1850)	2,549,000 (1910)	838 (1850)	12,951 (1910)
Italy	1,025,000 (1861)	3,473,000 (1910)	6,504 (1861)	26,850 (1910)
Ottoman Empire	5,000 (1858)	2,000,000 (1895)	n.a.	n.a.
Russia	n.a.	1,835,000 (1891)	n.a.	13,033 (1891)
Spain	1,005,000 (1855)	1,526,000 (1908)	7,528 (1857)	20,497 (1914)

n.a. = Not available.

Data drawn from Mitchell, B. R., *European Historical Statistics, 1750–1970* (London: Macmillan, 1975, pp. 750–773); Cook, Chris, and Paxton, John, *European Political Facts, 1848–1918* (London: Macmillan, 1978, pp. 307–315); and Keltie, J. Scott, ed., *Statesman's Yearbook* (London: Macmillan, 1891, pp. 855–856).

Question: What countries seem to have changed the most with universal schooling?

education there and prevented provinces such as Finland from establishing it.

Marriage and the Family in the 1800s

Age at Marriage. European law in the nineteenth century still permitted marriages at an early age. British law allowed girls to marry at 12 and boys at 14 for most of the century. Orthodox canon law accepted marriage at 13 for girls and 15 for boys. Literature from the era reminds readers that early marriages did occur, such as the nurse in Pushkin's *Eugene Onegin* (1833), who married at 13. The history of European marriage during the nineteenth century, however, is different from what the law permitted (see *Marriage and Family*). Marriage generally occurred much later—at, or after, age 25—and the average age at marriage increased, reaching into the thirties in some regions. Women typically married at a younger age than men did.

Marriage in Western Europe. The average age at marriage in Britain in the early nineteenth century was approximately 25 for women and 26 for men. A study of Belgium in 1800 found a range of marital ages for men of roughly 25 to 32, depending upon their occupation; the same data found women marrying at 24 to 30. The latest averages were in Ireland, where marriage was traditionally linked to sufficient landholding to support a family. The potato famine of the 1840s taught the tragedy of having a family but no ability to feed it. One-fourth of the population of Ireland during the late nineteenth century never married, and those who did married at an age of economic security: 38 for men and 30 for women. A study of Württemberg during industrialization found that most men in agricultural and working-class occupations could not afford to marry until their early thirties.

Marriage in Eastern Europe. A dramatic contrast to these marital patterns existed in eastern Europe. A

TABLE 23.9 THE DECLINE OF ILLITERACY IN EUROPE, 1800–1910

The figures in this table show the percentage of newlyweds signing wedding certificates with an "X."

YEAR	England MEN	England WOMEN	France MEN	France WOMEN	Italy MEN	Italy WOMEN	Prussia MEN	Prussia WOMEN	Germany MEN	Germany WOMEN
1800	n.a.	53	72	n.a.	n.a.	n.a.	n.a.	n.a.		
1820	n.a.	n.a.	46	65	n.a.	n.a.	n.a.	n.a.		
1830	n.a.	n.a.	n.a.	n.a.	n.a.	n.a.	12	32		
1840	33	49	n.a.	n.a.	n.a.	n.a.	6	19		
1850	31	36	n.a.	n.a.	n.a.	n.a.	3	8		
1860	26	36	30	45	n.a.	n.a.	3	4		
1870	20	27	27	40	58	77				
1880	14	19	16	25	48	70				
1890	7	8	8	14	42	62			2	3
1900	3	3	5	6	n.a.	n.a.			0	1
1910	3	4	n.a.	n.a.					0	0

n.a. = Not available.

Source: Keltie, J. Scott, ed., *Statesman's Yearbook* (London: Macmillan, 1891); Kaelble, Hartmut, *Industrialization* (New York: St. Martin's, 1986, pp. 90–91).

Question: Which of the great powers had compulsory education laws in 1860?

study comparing Sweden and Serbia in 1900 found huge differences for people in their twenties. Only 8 percent of Swedish men and 20 percent of Swedish women were married at age 20 to 24, but the Serbian figures were 50 percent for men and 84 percent for women. The Serbian pattern also characterized nineteenth-century Russia, where the average age at marriage in the 1830s was 18 for both sexes. Serfs could not postpone marriage until they possessed land of their own unless they planned never to marry. Even after emancipation, most Russian peasants in 1868 were married by age 20. These marital patterns, like those in Ireland or Württemberg, appear to have been a direct result of the economic condition of the population.

Changes in the Institution of Marriage. The institution of marriage changed during the nineteenth century. One aspect of this change was the transition from an agricultural economy to an industrial economy, which broke down the historic pattern of a **household economy** in which a husband and wife shared the labor of farm or shop, creating instead a **family wage economy** in which a husband and wife typically worked at separate jobs and pooled their wages to maintain the home. Other important changes in marriage were appearing by the end of the nineteenth century, largely the result of the successes of the women's movement. The historic pattern of **patriarchal marriage**—of a husband's authority and a wife's obedience—a pattern sanctified by law, religion, and custom, was breaking down. Married women were winning fundamental economic rights, such as the control of their own property or wages, beginning with the British Married Women's Property Acts of 1857–1882. The breakdown of the patriarchal marriage, which has continued during the twentieth century, soon touched all aspects of family life, such as control of the children.

COMPULSORY EDUCATION

Conservative Arguments against Compulsory Public Education

The French Ministry of Education, under the direction of a historian named Victor Duruy, did much to modernize education during the 1860s. Duruy gave libraries to primary schools, improved the salaries of teachers, sharply increased the number of schools for girls, expanded adult education, and reformed teacher training. Duruy supported the ideas of free and compulsory education, but he was a generation ahead of his time; conservative opposition to compulsory schooling was too strong, and such laws were not adopted until the 1880s. The following document was prepared in Duruy's Ministry of Education to summarize the conservative arguments.

The arguments against obligatory education can be listed under seven different headings:

1. It is a limitation upon paternal authority. The State has no right to intervene in the family to diminish the power of its head.

2. The obligation of a father to send his son to a public school cannot be reconciled with freedom of conscience, because the child is vulnerable to a religious education contrary to the faith which his father wishes to give him.

3. It is a diminution of the resources of the family: the child of the poor person performs a host of small jobs which attenuate misery for them both. Thus the government intervenes in the workplace . . . and reduces productivity.

4. Making education obligatory gives the government the sort of power which it should not have.

5. Given the present state of the schools, it is economically impossible to open them to all children.

6. The forced presence in the schools of children who refuse to learn and disrupt other students will destroy discipline.

Compulsory Schooling. Few laws in modern history have changed the world as much as the universal education laws adopted in Europe in the late nineteenth and early twentieth centuries. The most immediate impact was on the lives of children, like these children in France, 1889. But the consequences—such as the training of an educated class of women to be teachers, or the creation of literate consumers who could read advertising, or the education of the public in preparation for electoral politics—were far-reaching. (The painting is *The Children's Class,* 1889 [oil on canvas] by Henri Jules Jean Geoffroy.)

7. Finally, compulsory education, if it is not also free education, will create a heavy new tax on peasants and workers.

From "French Ministry of Education Yearbook" (1863), trans. Steven C. Hause, ed. M. Chaulanges et al., *Textes historiques, 1848–1871: le milieu du XIXe siècle* (Paris: Delagrave, 1975).

Question: Do these arguments adequately justify a failure to create, or a policy of weakening, a public school system

---

Divorce. A third fundamental change in the nature of marriage, the legal right to end the marriage, developed during the nineteenth century. The French Revolution instituted **divorce,** but that law was repealed by the restored monarchy. The Prussian legal code of 1794 made divorce comparatively easy there, and Bismarck imposed divorce on Catholic Germany during the *Kulturkampf* of the 1870s. Legislation of 1857 in Britain and 1884 in France permitted divorce, and Scandinavian countries adopted similar statutes. Men and women (but significantly more women) increasingly exercised this right during the late nineteenth century. British divorces climbed from 178 per year in the late 1850s to surpass 1,000 for the first time in 1906. Divorce rates rose more rapidly in France. The first full year of divorce (1885) saw 4,000 marriages dissolved; that number doubled by 1895, tripled by 1905. By the early twentieth century, both France and Germany were seeing 15,000 divorces

MARRIAGE AND FAMILY

Despite persistent stereotypes about the past, marriage often occurred at later ages than in the twentieth century. These data suggest that the explanation may have been economic.

TABLE 23.10 MARRIAGE PATTERNS IN NINETEENTH-CENTURY EUROPE

Mean Age at Marriage in Belgium, 1800

OCCUPATION	MEN	WOMEN
Artisans	26.8	26.6
Farmers	30.6	27.8
Servants	26.3	27.3
Shopkeepers	26.0	24.1
Spinners	29.9	29.8
Weavers	25.6	23.9
Others	32.1	27.5

Mean Age at Marriage in Württemberg, 1880–1914

OCCUPATION	MEN	WOMEN
Agriculture	32.8	29.4
Metalworker	32.2	27.4
Textile worker	32.8	30.1

Belgian data from Gutman, Myron P., *Toward the Modern Economy: Early Industry in Europe, 1500–1800* (New York: Knopf, 1988, p. 169); German data from Schomerus, Heilwig, "The Family Life-Cycle: A Study of Factory Workers in Nineteenth Century Württemberg," in Evans, Richard J., and Lee, W. R., eds., *The German Family: Essays on the Social History of the Family in Nineteenth and Twentieth Century Germany* (Totowa, NJ: Barnes and Noble, 1981, p. 183).

TABLE 23.11 FAMILY SIZE IN WÜRTTEMBERG, GERMANY, IN THE 1850S AND 1860S

OCCUPATION OF FATHER	Percentage of Families Having				
	0 CHILDREN	1–3 CHILDREN	4–6 CHILDREN	7–9 CHILDREN	10 OR MORE CHILDREN
Agricultural	31.3	33.6	22.8	7.2	4.8
Metal industry	17.1	59.9	17.1	2.9	2.9
Textile industry	21.4	32.2	25.0	14.2	7.2

From Schomerus, Heilwig, "The Family-Life-Cycle: A Study of Factory Workers in Nineteenth Century Württemberg," in Evans, Richard J., and Lee, W. R., eds., *The German Family: Essays on the Social History of the Family in Nineteenth and Twentieth Century Germany* (Totowa, NJ: Barnes and Noble, 1981, p. 185).

Question: What might account for the differing ages at marriage?

per year. Such figures do not compare with the **"divorce revolution"** of the late twentieth century, but the social trend was clear, as the Catholic Church argued in blocking divorce in Italy and Spain.

Decline in Size of Families. The combination of later marriage, the increased use of birth control, and the legalization of divorce meant that the average size of European families declined. The economic system no longer rewarded large families when children were obliged to attend school. The vital revolution that conquered many childhood diseases meant that parents could be confident of children surviving into adulthood without having ten or twelve of them. Whereas ten or more children had been a common **family size** during the Old Regime, less than 10 percent of the population now had such large families. By the 1850s, German peasants averaged four or fewer children; even textile workers had smaller families (see *Marriage and Family*). Families continued to shrink during the nineteenth century. Completed family size for all British marriages of the 1860s included four children; for marriages in the early twentieth century, the average had fallen to two children.

Size of Households. A typical household of nineteenth-century Europe still retained some characteristics of the Old Regime, however. A household still meant all of the people who lived together under a common roof, and that included servants, apprentices, or boarders. A study of Nottingham in midcentury found that more than 20 percent of households contained a lodger, and well-to-do families had an average of two servants. Most of these domestic servants were unmarried women, and such service was the largest source of employment for women during the century. More than 700,000 women worked as servants in mid-Victorian Britain, nearly twice as many as labored in textile industries, or twenty times as many as were engaged in all forms of education. Even middle-class families could afford at least one servant because the wages paid were shockingly low. A study of Austrian household structure illustrates how nineteenth-century families became smaller, but household size remained large. Viennese census data reveal that a typical master baker and his wife had five children. But their household contained eighteen residents: six journeymen bakers, two shopgirls, and the family's three domestic servants. In another illustration, a widowed textile manufacturer in his sixties lived in a household of nine people: his two sons who had become his partners in their thirties and still lived at home, his five household servants, and his coachman.

SEXUAL ATTITUDES AND BEHAVIOR IN THE NINETEENTH CENTURY

Victorianism. The nineteenth century lingers in popular memory as an age of prudery and puritanical restrictions. To describe a person or an idea as "Victorian" (derived from the name of the Queen of England, who reigned for most of the century) is to connote repressive attitudes about human sexuality commonly associated with the era. This stereotype of **Victorianism** contains much truth. Respectable women who consulted a physician normally went with a chaperone; they would point out their ailments on a doll rather than touch themselves. Gynecological examinations were per-

formed only in extreme cases, and genteel opinion held that women should endure much pain before submitting to the indignity of a pelvic exam. Prudishness governed polite conversations. The words for bodily functions (sexual or not) were unacceptable, and this ban forbade such outrages to delicate ears as sweating, which was deemed much too animalistic. Decent people did not refer to *legs*—a word thought to inflame sexual passions—but rather referred to *limbs.* This taboo included the legs on furniture, and truly respectable families placed a cloth skirt around a piano, lest the sight of its limbs provoke prurient thoughts. This **puritanism** culminated in *Lady Gough's Book of Etiquette,* which stated the moral principle that books in a family library must be organized so that those written by men not lay next to those written by women—unless the authors were married.

Contrasting Permissiveness. This image of the nineteenth century contains much truth, but it hides truth as well. The early nineteenth century, when fashionable dress at continental balls permitted the exposure of a woman's breasts, did not correspond to the prudery of later years. Many people believed that foreign countries teemed with a sexuality unknown at home (as the British viewed France), although that may reveal more about their own behavior away from home. The upper classes, including Queen Victoria's family, did not behave by the standards of middle-class Victorianism. Victoria's predecessor on the throne, William IV, lived with a mistress for 20 years and had ten illegitimate children with her; Victoria's husband, Prince Albert, was the child of a broken marriage; and Victoria's heir, the future Edward VII, had a legion of lovers, from a famous actress to a duchess who always curtsied before climbing into the royal bed. Such exceptions to the Victorian stereotype were widespread: nude bathing at the seashore was commonplace for much of the nineteenth century, and the mid-Victorian House of Commons declined to outlaw it in 1857. Somehow bourgeois prudery coexisted with startling exceptions, such as permitting Lewis Carroll to enjoy the hobby of photographing naked young girls, including the Alice for whom *Alice in Wonderland* was written.

The Double Standard. Historians have studied many aspects of human sexuality hidden by the stereotype of Victorianism. Subjects such as **the double standard,** prostitution, venereal disease (VD), and homosexuality have all drawn the attention of social historians. The double standard—different standards for men and women, or for different social classes, or between the public and the private—behind Victorianism is clear. Sometimes it was a matter of hypocrisy: the governing and opinion-making classes said one thing in public and behaved differently in private. During

Napoleon III's Second Empire, for example, the government of France stoutly defended public morality. When Gustave Flaubert published *Madame Bovary* (1857), which dared to suggest that a respectable married woman might choose to commit adultery, the government immediately indicted Flaubert for outraging public morals. The public agreed so heartily that when Edouard Manet first exhibited *Olympia*, destined to become one of the most noted paintings of the century but depicting a nude woman reclining in bed, guards had to be hired to protect it from vigilante moralists. The private morality of the Bonaparte family was somewhat different from their public standard, and they welcomed the friendship of Flaubert. The emperor was as lusty as Edward VII, and his biography is filled with episodes such as the costume ball at which he found one of his mistresses, a teenaged countess who wore a transparent costume.

The Double Standard for Men and Women.
Another variant of the sexual double standard expected different behavior from men and women. Unmarried women were expected to remain virginal until marriage; unmarried men were assumed to be sexually active. Adultery was a serious crime for married women but less so for men. (In French law, a husband only committed adultery by bringing a concubine into the marital home, but the murder of an adulterous wife was not always a crime.) Flaubert probably would not have been arrested had his novel been about Doctor Bovary, describing the adultery of a prominent man. The respectable double standard even taught that women did not have sexual urges. As late as 1905, an Oxford physician could seriously testify that nine out of ten women disliked sex, and the tenth was invariably a harlot.

Prostitution.
Given the double standard of sexual behavior, the late age of marriages, and the desperate economic situation of women from the lower classes, it is not surprising that prostitution thrived during the nineteenth century. Legal and open prostitution was a striking feature of European cities, and some authors have claimed that in periods of economic distress, prostitution became the largest single form of women's employment. Women (often servants) who had been seduced and left with a child had little legal support (they could not even sue to prove paternity in most countries) and usually no economic support. The situation was even worse for rape victims, who found many respectable jobs closed to them. Even widows could be driven to consider prostitution by their economic plight. Single factory workers, trying to live on a fraction of a man's wages, faced few alternatives besides supplementing their wages through prostitution (see Document 23.2).

DOCUMENT 23.2

A BRITISH PROSTITUTE DESCRIBES HER LIFE (1849)

Henry Mayhew was a journalist in London, well known to his contemporaries as a comic writer; he was one of the founding editors of *Punch*. Mayhew is better remembered by scholars today for his serious side, shown in a series of sensitive articles about the daily life of the poor. These articles were collected in several volumes under the title *London Labour and the London Poor* (1851–1862). The following excerpt is one of Mayhew's most moving. He originally published it in *The Morning Chronicle* in 1849, under the title "Prostitution among Needlewomen."

She told her tale with her face hidden in her hands, and sobbing so loud that it was difficult to catch her words. . . .

I used to work at "slop work"—at the shirt [hand-sewing] trade—the fine full-fronted white shirts; I got 2-1/2 pence each for them [approximately 5¢]. . . . By working from five o'clock in the morning to midnight each night I might be able to do seven in the week. That would bring me in 17 1/2 pence for my whole week's labor. Out of this the cotton must be taken, and that came to 2 pence every week, and so left me 15 1/2 pence to pay rent and living and buy candles with. I was single and received some little help from my friends; still it was impossible for me to live. I was forced to go out of a night to make my living. I had a child and it used to cry for food. So, as I could not get a living for him and myself by my needs, I went into the streets and made a living that way. . . .

My father was an independent preacher, and I pledge my word that it was the low price paid for my labor that drove me to prostitution. I often struggled against it, and many times I have taken my child into the streets to beg rather than I would bring shame on myself and it any longer. I have made pin cushions and fancy articles—such as I could manage to scrape together—and taken them into the streets to sell, so that I might get an honest living, but I couldn't. Sometime I should be out all night in the rain, and sell nothing at all, me and my child together. . . . I was so poor I couldn't have even a night's lodging on credit. One night in the depth of winter his legs froze to his side. . . .

[A]t last I left the "house" [workhouse] to work at umbrella covering. . . . I then made from 3 shillings to 4 shillings a week [36–48 pence, 75¢–$1], and from that time I gave up prostitution. . . . Had I remained at shirt making, I must have been a prostitute to this day.

From Mayhew, Henry, *London Labour and London Poor* (London: Morning Chronicle, 1862).

Question: Why did this woman choose prostitution?

The Scope of Prostitution.
The London police estimated that 6,000 full-time prostitutes worked in the city in the 1860s and 25,000 in Britain; reformers claimed that the true number was ten times higher. The number of prostitutes was much higher if one includes

the thousands of working women driven to supplement their wages by part-time prostitution. The data behind such assertions are notoriously variable. The number of women who registered with the Parisian police as legal prostitutes increased from 1,293 in 1812 to 6,827 in 1914, and police records show that 10,000 to 30,000 Parisian women were arrested each year for unregistered prostitution. The police estimated 34,000 prostitutes in Paris in the 1850s, 35,000 to 40,000 at the turn of the twentieth century. Similar estimates for Germany range from 100,000 to 330,000 women in 1914. All such numbers must be treated with caution: some Victorian moralists counted any unmarried woman living with a man as a prostitute.

Regulated Prostitution and Abolitionism.
Britain, France, and Italy all enacted state-regulated prostitution. Most German states permitted municipal brothels, although after 1871 Berlin tried to eliminate them. Governments accepted regulated prostitution because it helped control VD in naval bases and army garrisons. Prostitutes were required to have regular medical examinations and receive treatment for VD. Laws such as the British Contagious Diseases Acts of 1864 and 1866 gave the police exceptional powers to arrest

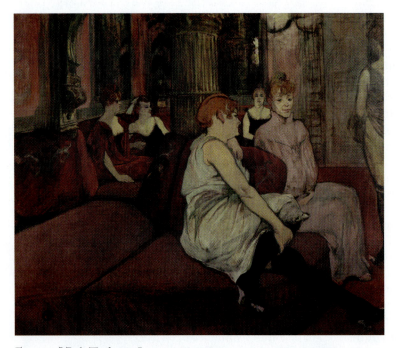

FIGURE 23.6 *Toulouse-Lautrec.* Prostitution was legal and regulated by the government in nineteenth-century Europe, and it was one of the principle occupations of women in urban Europe, rivaled only by domestic service and work in textile factories in the number of working women. The police of Paris estimated that there were 35,000 to 45,000 prostitutes working there in 1900, although only 6,000 to 7,000 were legally registered with the government. Many of the paintings of Henri de Toulouse-Lautrec (1864–1901) depict the world of Parisian prostitution, such as this vivid scene of a brothel, *In the Salon at the Rue des Moulins* (1894).

any woman who was unescorted in public and to order her to have a medical examination. This abuse of women, combined with the moral opposition to prostitution and the desire to help prostitutes, led to **abolitionist** campaigns, such as Josephine Butler's, which won the suspension of the Contagious Diseases Acts in 1883 and their repeal in 1886. Women, typically Protestant reformers who linked moral reforms with feminism, launched abolitionist campaigns in many countries, as Avril de Sainte Croix did in France and Emilie de Morsier did in Switzerland.

Venereal Disease. Governments were right to worry about VD rates. The rate of infection and the death rate for syphilis in the 1890s were both higher than the rates for AIDS a century later. One French study found that the leading cause of death in Europe was tuberculosis (which killed 150,000 per year), but syphilis was a close second (140,000), killing three times as many people as cancer did (40,000). In Britain, where Lord Randolph Churchill demonstrated the universality of VD by slowly dying from syphilis in public, nearly 7,000 people died of VD in 1901—a death rate of 16.4 per 100,000 population (a total of 450 people died of HIV/AIDS in Britain in 1999). A German medical study of 1900 estimated even higher rates of infection there and asserted that 50 percent of German men had a VD, usually gonorrhea, and 20 percent had syphilis.

Homosexuality. European laws to regulate prostitution or to control VD were mild compared with the draconian laws against homosexuality. Although eighteenth-century toleration had extended to the decriminalization of homosexuality in revolutionary France, the nineteenth-century double standard had criminalized it again. All sexual acts between men were illegal in most countries, and sexual intercourse between men (usually called *buggery* or *sodomy* in the nineteenth century) was often a capital crime. Dutch law allowed the execution of convicted homosexuals in 1800, and twenty-two trials had taken place for the crime in 1798; however, imprisonment or banishment was the usual punishment. There were seventeen convictions for homosexuality at Amsterdam in the decade 1801–1810, and none resulted in an execution. Sexual intercourse between men remained a capital crime in Britain until 1861, and one or two men were hanged for it annually in the early nineteenth century. Gay men thus faced extreme dangers from blackmailers, as happened to Lord Castlereagh; the pressure led to his suicide in 1822. Others, such as the notoriously bisexual Lord Byron, fled the country.

Slow Reform of Laws against Homosexuality.
The nineteenth-century reforms of sexual statutes typically perpetuated the criminalization of homosexuality but reduced the penalties. The penal code of the German Empire forbade "unnatural vice" between men, but sentences ranged from 1 day to 5 years. British law remained more severe. The Criminal Law Amendment Act of 1885 allowed life imprisonment for homosexuality, but it also created the lesser crime of "gross indecency," for which men could be sentenced to 2 years of hard labor. When that statute was reformed in 1912, it permitted the flogging of homosexuals without a jury trial. These statutes remained in force until 1967. Such statutes did not even mention lesbianism, an unthinkable subject to most Victorian legislators.

The Oscar Wilde Scandal.
The criminalization of homosexuality led to dramatic scandals and trials at the turn of the twentieth century. The most famous trial involved a celebrated Irish writer, Oscar Wilde. Wilde was arrested following an acrimonious and public battle with the marquess of Queensbury (a bully chiefly remembered for formulating the rules of boxing), the father of his lover. Wilde was convicted in 1895 and imprisoned until 1897, an experience that he related in *Ballad of Reading Gaol* (pronounced Redding Jail) (1898). The government could have indicted many other prominent homosexuals—such as the members of the Bloomsbury set (named for a district of London), which included the economist John Maynard Keynes, the biographer Lytton Strachey, and the novelist E. M. Forster—but the government would have been obliged to arrest several of its own members.

Scandals in the German Army.
A larger scandal over homosexuality occurred in Germany, where the central figures were not intellectuals but the commanders of the German army, members of the imperial government, and close associates of Kaiser Wilhelm II. The policy of the German army was to court martial homosexuals if they had been publicly identified. That policy led to two dramatic trials in 1903–1906, at which several officers were named, including the commander of the royal guard who was a member of the royal family. This led to the public admission that Prince Friedrich Heinrich of Prussia was gay. The German public soon received admissions of homosexuality from a long list of public figures, ranging from the director of the state theater to the royal equerry. As the number of homosexuals in royal and military circles became clear, one segment of the German press turned to homophobic attacks; Kaiser Wilhelm II blamed the entire experience neither on the criminalization of homosexuality nor on the men who had broken his laws, but on the machinations of "international Jewry." He reached this bizarre and ominous conclusion because the journalist who had named high-ranking gays was Jewish. Thus, a scandal that might have led to discussion of decriminalization led instead to increased anti-Semitism.

CONCLUSION

Historians have traditionally stressed the political history of the past. From this perspective, the great revolution that shaped the nineteenth century was the French Revolution (see Chapter 21). As economic change assumed greater importance in the study of the past, historians also placed great emphasis on the great changes wrought by the Industrial Revolution (see Chapter 22). Many historians today place the French and Industrial Revolutions together as the "twin revolutions" that created modern Europe. Social historians have not yet won similar recognition for the importance of the vital revolution, which also changed life in modern Europe, even though in some ways, it is more important in understanding life in the past. The sharp decline in infant mortality, the widespread fall of the death rate from infectious diseases, and the corresponding increase in life expectancy have touched everyone. So the medical and dietary improvements that made these new conditions of everyday life possible must also be central to our understanding the past.

Review Questions

- How did life expectancy change in the nineteenth century? Why?
- What was the relative importance of contagious disease among the causes of death in nineteenth-century Europe?
- What were the principal steps in the conquest of disease and in medical treatment in the nineteenth century?
- How was the European diet changing during the nineteenth century? What developments explain such changes?
- What were European attitudes towards alcohol and drugs in the nineteenth century?
- To what extent was birth control used in nineteenth-century Europe? Did this have an impact on European demography?
- How significant were the levels of abortion, infanticide, and child abandonment?
- What was the legal status of birth control and abortion?
- How common was illegitimacy?

- How did the nature of childhood change in the nineteenth century?
- What were the important nineteenth-century patterns in schooling and literacy?
- What was the typical age at marriage in the nineteenth century? What explains this pattern?
- How did the institution of marriage change during the nineteenth century?
- What was the typical family size and structure?

For Further Study

Readings

Evans, Richard, *Death in Hamburg: Society and Politics in the Cholera Years, 1830–1910* (London: Penguin, 1987). An excellent, detailed study of the impact of the cholera epidemics of the nineteenth century in northern Germany.

Flandrin, Jean-Louis, and Montanari, Massimo, eds., *Food: A Culinary History from Antiquity to the Present* (New York: Penguin, 2000). A detailed introduction to the history of food, with specialized chapters by many experts.

McNeill, William H., *Plagues and Peoples* (New York: Doubleday, 1977). A pioneering study of the importance of disease across many centuries of human history.

References

Kiple, Kenneth F., ed., *The Cambridge World History of Food*, 2 vols. (Cambridge, UK: Cambridge University Press, 2000). An authoritative, 2,000-page encyclopedia of food history.

Kohn, George C., ed., *Encyclopedia of Plague and Pestilence* (New York: Facts on File, 1995). A worldwide reference source for the history of major epidemics.

Trager, James, ed., *The Food Chronology* (New York: Henry Holt, 1995). A year-by-year reference source for food history.

InfoTrac College Edition

For additional reading, go to your online research library at *http://infotrac.thomsonlearning.com.*

Using the Subject Guide, enter the search terms: *demographic transition   Louis Pasteur puerperal fever*

Web Sites

http://www.cwru.edu/artsci/dittrick/home.htm   A medical history site maintained at Case Western Reserve University. It includes sections on their Museum of Medical History and Image Collection.

http://medhist.ac.uk   A site maintained by the Wellcome Library of Medical History in London. It includes extensive sections such as medical history from different eras.

http://www.gti.net.mocolib1/kid/food.html   A site established by a public library in Morris County, New Jersey, known as "The Food Timeline." It includes many valuable links.

Visit the Western Civilization Companion Web Site for resources specific to this textbook:
http://history.wadsworth.com/hause02/

 The CD in the back of this book and the Western Civilization Resource Center at *http://history. wadsworth.com/western/* offer a variety of tools to help you succeed in this course, including access to quizzes; images; documents; interactive simulations, maps, and timelines; movie explorations; and a wealth of other sources.

DAILY LIFE DURING THE VITAL REVOLUTION OF THE NINETEENTH CENTURY

1800	1810	1820	1830	1840	1850	1860	1870	1880	1890	1900	1910

1804: Napoleon Becomes Emperor of France

1815: Congress of Vienna Ends Napoleonic Era

1832: Reform Bill Sets Britain on Course of Liberal Evolution

Revolution of 1848 Across Europe

1859–1860: War of Italian Unification

1861: Emancipation of Serfs in Russia

1870–1871: Franco-Prussian War

1882: Triple Alliance Formed

DEMOGRAPHY

1801: First Census in Britain

1820: Life Expectancy in France Hits 38 for Men, 41 for Women

1870: Life Expectancy in Germany Hits 36 for Men, 38 for Women

1890: Life Expectancy in Russia 31 for Men, 33 for Women

DISEASE AND MEDICINE

1796: Jenner Demonstrates Smallpox Vaccination

1808: Typhus Kills More French Soldiers Than Spanish Armies Do

1826–1837: Great Cholera Epidemic Crosses Europe

1840: Scarlet Fever Epidemic Kills 20,000 Children in Britain

1850: 94 Percent of All Deaths Are Due to Contagious Disease

1853–1856: 140,000 Cholera Deaths in France

1865: Lister Demonstrates Antiseptic Surgery

1874: Smallpox Vaccination Made Mandatory in Germany

1881: Pasteur Proves Germ Theory

1882: Koch Isolates Tuberculosis Bacillus

1884–1885: 120,000 Cholera Death in Spain

BIRTH AND BIRTH CONTROL

1800: Population Explosion in Britain Hits 16 Million: 82 Percent Increase in a Century

1820s: Average Age at Marriage in Britain is 25 for Women, 26 for Men

1833: 164,319 French Babies Abandoned at Public Institutions

1838: *Every Woman's Book* Advocates Sponge Barrier Contraception

1840s: 1,000 French Women Indicted for Infanticide Annually

1870s: Condoms of Vulcanized Rubber

1877: Annie Besant Campaigns for Birth Control

1880s: 8 Percent of Births Illegitimate

1880s: 10 Percent of Babies in Moscow Abandoned by Their Mothers

1900: Population Explosion in Germany Passes 200 Percent in Nineteenth Century

1900s: French Birthrate Hits Zero Growth Level

1913: Pelletier Publishes *The Right of Abortion*

FOCUS QUESTIONS

- What were the stated objectives of the victors at the Congress of Vienna? Did their accomplishments correspond to their objectives?
- How did the conservative governments of the age of Metternich try to maintain domestic order? How successful were they?
- What were the causes of social unrest and revolution in the age of Metternich?
- How did the emerging doctrines known as the "-isms" agree or differ in response to the issues of this era?

Chapter 24

THE DEFENSE OF THE OLD REGIME, 1815–1848

On the afternoon of August 16, 1819, more than 60,000 people (mostly workers) staged an orderly assembly in open fields, known as St. Peter's Fields, at Manchester, England. They had many economic grievances to protest, but they had assembled to hear a radical speaker demand political reforms in Parliament, which was still controlled by a small elite. The conservative government, still fearful of French revolutionary thought, tried to use an old law, known as the Riot Act, to arrest the speaker and disperse the crowd. When mounted troops of the yeomanry rode into the crowd, panic ensued and the authorities sent in the Fifteenth Hussars, royal cavalry who had fought at the battle of Waterloo, with sabers drawn. Eleven members of the protesting crowd were killed, and more than 400 were wounded in what sympathizers soon derisively named the Peterloo massacre. The conservative government blamed the mobbites, sentenced the speaker to prison, and adopted a series of laws to restrict the freedom to protest.

The story of the Peterloo massacre summarizes the central political tension of early nineteenth-century Europe. The coalition that defeated Napoleon in 1812–1815 supported monarchy and the institutions of the Old Regime. During the next generation (1815–1848), victorious conservatives tried to restore their world. Chapter 24 examines this era, often called the age of Metternich in honor of its leading conservative statesman. It starts with monarchists reasserting the Old Regime at the Congress of Vienna and at the postwar conservative alliance and the chapter looks at the congress system designed to preserve that order. But the restoration of the Old Regime was widely resisted, and a variety of political movements—collectively known as **the "-isms"**—challenged the old order, as did a wave of revolutions in 1830–1832.

THE CONGRESS OF VIENNA AND THE DEFENSE OF THE OLD ORDER (1814–1848)

The Quadruple Alliance against Napoleon. A quadruple alliance of Russia, Prussia, Austria, and Britain was needed to defeat Napoleon. Armies of these allies reached Paris in 1814. Napoleon received a generous settlement in return for his unconditional abdication. He kept the title of emperor (with a promised income of 2 million French francs) and received the Italian island of Elba to govern. Similar leniency characterized the treaty given to France, the Treaty of Paris, which restored the Bourbon monarchy. The eldest brother of Louis XVI thus returned to Paris "in the baggage of the allies." He took the title of Louis XVIII, in respect for Louis XVI's son who had died in prison. The allies considered Louis XVIII a member of the counterrevolutionary coalition, so France lost recently annexed territory (such as Belgium) but kept the borders of 1792 without losing older provinces (such as Alsace).

The Congress of Vienna, 1814–1815. These treaties were secondary issues to the allies, who wanted to reconsider the entire map of Europe and restore the prerevolutionary order. Representatives from hundreds of states assembled in Vienna in 1814 for this peace congress and to celebrate the end of the revolutionary era. The decisions of the Congress of Vienna were made by the four strongest allies. The most influential statesman was the foreign minister of Austria, Prince Klemens von Metternich. He was a native of the Rhineland, and he had been raised in the French language, which he spoke at home; Metternich entered Austrian service only after a French army drove him from his Rhenish estates in 1794. His ideas, however, won the confidence of the emperor of Austria, Francis I; they agreed that revolutionary ideas were "moral gangrene." Francis trusted Metternich to maintain a world with "no innovations" (see Document 24.1). Enlightenment was so unwelcome, wrote the poet Heinrich Heine, that he should be remembered as "Prince Mitternacht" (midnight).

The Principle of Legitimacy. The allies shared variants of Metternichian **conservatism.** Britain was represented by the foreign secretary of a conservative government, Viscount Castlereagh. He was such a forceful spokesman for the aristocratic cause that the poor of London lined the streets to cheer his funeral procession. Prussia was represented by Prince Karl von Hardenberg who earned a reputation for **liberalism** for Prussian domestic reforms but who defended Prussian interests and international order with tenacity. The tsar of Russia, Alexander I, the most complex and intelligent monarch of the age, often chose to represent Russia in negotiations himself. These counts, viscounts, dukes, and princes stated a guiding philosophy for the Congress of Vienna: the principle of **legitimacy.** Every province in Europe should be returned to its legitimate ruler, and the people of each province should be restored to their place in the legitimate (Old Regime) social order. In theory, the doctrine of legitimacy meant the re-creation of pre-1789 frontiers, monarchies, and social systems—the divinely ordained order. In reality, the decisions made at Vienna stemmed from self-interest. Compensation was a truer name for the philosophy of the congress, and the four allies each annexed territory without a pretense of legitimacy. Whole regions of Europe—such as Belgium, Genoa, Lombardy, Norway, Poland, and Saxony—became the pawns of the great powers. Russia kept Finland (which it had annexed during the war) and gained most of Poland. The Russian concession to legitimacy was to give Congress Poland its own constitution. Prussia annexed half of neighboring Saxony and several small

FIGURE 24.1 *Delegates at the Congress of Vienna.* The peace congress following the defeat of Napoleon was one of the most glittering assemblies in the history of the European nobility. The statesmen portrayed here redrew the map of Europe in between dancing at congress balls, while other aristocrats celebrated in a party that lasted for months. Prince Metternich, who dominated European affairs for the next generation, is the dandy in tight white breeches standing to the left of center. Lord Castlereagh, whose party life eventually led to his suicide, is seated at the center with legs crossed. Prince Talleyrand sits at the right, with his arm on the table and his crippled foot hidden.

MAP 24.1. EUROPE AFTER THE CONGRESS OF VIENNA, 1815

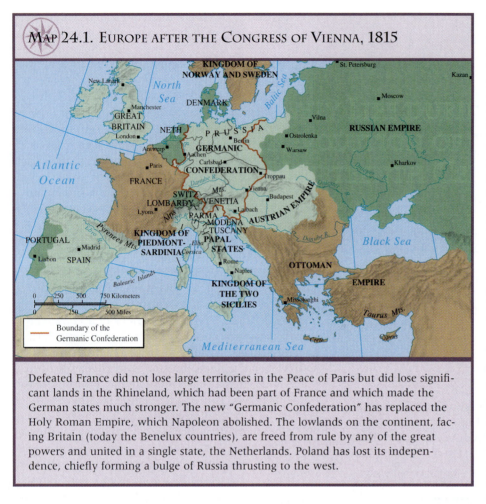

Defeated France did not lose large territories in the Peace of Paris but did lose significant lands in the Rhineland, which had been part of France and which made the German states much stronger. The new "Germanic Confederation" has replaced the Holy Roman Empire, which Napoleon abolished. The lowlands on the continent, facing Britain (today the Benelux countries), are freed from rule by any of the great powers and united in a single state, the Netherlands. Poland has lost its independence, chiefly forming a bulge of Russia thrusting to the west.

states in the Rhineland. This changed the course of European history because an enlarged Prussia acquired great industrial potential and a presence in western Europe.

Talleyrand and Territorial Compensation at Vienna.

Britain and Austria demanded compensation to balance the gains of the Prussians and Russians. This led to a two-against-two stalemate until the four powers asked a fifth diplomat to join them—Louis XVIII's foreign minister, Prince Charles-Maurice de Talleyrand.

Talleyrand

Talleyrand had served the Old Regime as a bishop, the French Revolution as a legislator, and Napoleon as a diplomat, so he was comfortable when self-interest was more important than principle. He shifted the **balance of power** by supporting Britain and Austria, so they, too, received compensation. The British

took new colonies in Africa, Asia, and the Americas, plus strategic islands, such as Malta; they also insisted that a friendly state (but not a great power) control the lowlands from which an invasion of England might be launched. Consequently, the predominantly Protestant, Dutch-speaking Netherlands annexed the Catholic, predominantly French-speaking region of Belgium. The Hapsburgs had previously ruled this region (then known as the Austrian Netherlands), so Austria took compensation in northern Italy: Lombardy and the Republic of Venice.

The German and Italian Questions.

Even after their mutual aggrandizement, the great powers did not follow the principle of legitimacy in addressing the small states of Germany and Italy. They did not resurrect the Holy Roman Empire, which had confederated 200 German states in central Europe until Napoleon abolished it in 1806. Instead, the allies restored only thirty-nine German states, linked in a loose German Confederation with a weak Diet at Frankfurt. The dispossessed rulers kept their titles, their personal estates, and good reasons to doubt the meaning of legitimacy. Italians had their own reasons to question the validity of that principle. Lombards and Venetians discovered that they were legitimate Austrians; the Genoese learned that their historic government was not legitimate because it had been a republic; and others, such as the Tuscans, found that their legitimate rulers were members of the Hapsburg family.

Napoleon and "the 100 days."

Napoleon Bonaparte escaped from his lenient exile on Elba in March 1815 and returned to France during these negotiations—an episode known for its duration, the Hundred Days. Louis XVIII fled and his army defected to Napoleon, but the allies rejected Napoleon's claim to the throne and assembled armies in Belgium under the Duke of Wellington, who had defeated Napoleon's armies in Spain. A combination of British and Prussian armies defeated Napoleon outside Brussels at Waterloo, and his reign ended with harsher settlements. Napoleon became a British prisoner of war,

FIGURE 24.2 *Napoleon on Board the* **Bellerophon.** In this scene, Napoleon Bonaparte stands on the deck of a British warship, the *H.M.S. Bellerophon,* and watches the coastline of France recede from his sight for the last time, in July 1815. The event occurred 1 month after Napoleon's defeat at Waterloo, and he was still hoping that he would be given asylum in England. However, the British government rejected this idea, and another warship soon carried him to his final exile, on the remote island of St. Helena, a small volcanic island in the south Atlantic more than 1,000 miles west of southern Africa. The Duke of Wellington knew of St. Helena because the ship that had returned him from service in India had stopped at this remote outpost. Napoleon endured a form of house arrest on the island, suffering equally from the irksome policies of the British governor and from stomach cancer. He died in 1821 at age 52, and his remains were returned to France in 1840.

and they held him under house arrest on the island of St. Helena until his death in 1821. A Second Peace of Paris made the French pay for accepting Napoleon's return. France lost more Rhineland territory to Prussia and more of Savoy to the kingdom of Piedmont-Sardinia, had to pay an indemnity of 700 million francs, and endured the military occupation of northeastern France until it was paid.

The Conservative Alliance and the Congress System

The Holy Alliance. After the difficult negotiations at Vienna and the shock of the Hundred Days, the allies resolved to protect their newly restored order. Alexander I, who was attracted to religious mysticism, proposed a **Holy Alliance** in which they would pledge to act according to the teachings of the Bible. Most statesmen agreed with Castlereagh that this was "sublime nonsense" (one called it a "holy kiss"), but they promised to act "conformably to the words of the Holy Scriptures." In case that did not work, they also re-

newed the Quadruple Alliance against French armies and French ideas. Austria, Britain, Prussia, and Russia pledged "to employ all their means to prevent the general tranquility from again being disturbed."

The Congress System. The allies also protected the conservative order by planning regular meetings to discuss international problems. This led to a series of small congresses (known collectively as the **congress system**), also shaped by Metternich, during the next decade. In 1818, a congress met at Aachen to recognize that the French had paid the indemnity and to welcome the government of Louis XVIII into a Quintuple Alliance to maintain the status quo. A more important congress met in 1820 at Troppau, where the three eastern powers (Austria, Prussia, and Russia) adopted the **Troppau Protocol,** asserting the right of the allies to intervene in smaller countries if the conservative order were threatened. A congress of 1821 used this principle to justify an Austrian invasion of the Italian states to suppress radical rebels. The congress system faced a difficult decision in 1822, when a liberal revolution occurred in Spain. The Troppau Protocol called for armed intervention to crush the revolution, but that meant a French invasion of Spain. The allies decided that they were less afraid of a French army than of a French constitution and accepted the ironic position of cheering French military victories.

Protecting the Old Order: Religion

Religious Revival. The conservatism of the post-1815 world is especially clear in the religious revival of that era. After an age in which philosophes satirized churches and the educated classes became skeptics, after a revolution in which churches were closed and their property seized, after an economic revolution that de-Christianized many workers, and after a cynical conqueror imprisoned the pope and used religion as an instrument of political policy, many Christians were eager for their own restoration of old values and institutions.

The Vatican and Conservative Order. The Vatican was a leader of the new conservatism. Pope Pius VII had slept in French jails during the revolutionary era and now retaliated against French ideas. He restored the Jesuit order, reestablished the Inquisition,

METTERNICH ON *THE CONSERVATIVE'S FAITH* (1820)

Prince Klemens von Metternich (1773–1859), Austria's foreign minister, was the dominant figure in European politics in the era between the defeat of Napoleon in 1815 and the widespread revolutions in 1848. He hosted the Congress of Vienna in 1814–1815; stated the conservative, counterrevolutionary political philosophy of the age; and organized the "congress system" of frequent meetings of the great powers to suppress all signs of revolution. Metternich was instrumental in adopting the Carlsbad Decrees in Germany, which tightened censorship and strictly regulated universities, and for the doctrine known as the Troppau Protocol, which allowed the armies of the larger states to intervene in the affairs of smaller neighbors to stop revolutions. The following document, which he sent to the emperors of Austria and Russia in 1820, explains his conservative values and his reasons for his policies.

Kings have to calculate the chances of their very existence in the immediate future; passions are let loose and league together to overthrow everything which society respects as the basis of its existence: religion, public morality, laws, customs, rights, duties are all attacked, confounded, overthrown, or called in question. The great mass of people are tranquil spectators of these attacks and revolutions. . . . It is principally the middle class of society which this moral gangrene has affected, and it is only among them that the real heads of the party [of revolution] are found . . .

We are convinced that society can no longer be saved without strong and vigorous resolutions on the part of the Governments . . . in establishing the principle of stability, [which] will in no wise exclude the development of what is good, for stability is not immobility. . . . Union between the monarchs is the basis for the policy which must now be followed to save society from total ruin. . . . Respect for all that is; liberty for every Government to watch over the well-being of its own people; a league of all Governments against all factions in all states; contempt for the meaningless words which have become the rallying cry of the factious; . . . refusal on the part of every monarch to aid or succour partisans under any mask whatever. . . . We are certainly not alone in questioning if society can exist with the liberty of the press. . . . Let the monarchs in these troublous times be more than usually cautious. . . .

From Metternich, Klemens von, *Memoirs of Prince Metternich*, 5 vols., trans. Mrs. Alexander Napier (New York: Scribner's, 1880–1882).

Question: Why does Metternich consider the middle class to be the problem for monarchy?

---

and reconstituted the Index of Prohibited Books. Catholics were forbidden to believe that the Earth rotated around the sun or to read Gibbon's *History of the Decline and Fall of the Roman Empire.* In the papal states, Pius annulled Napoleonic laws of religious toleration and reintroduced persecution of the Jews, who were returned to the ghetto and compelled to attend mass once a week. Pius ended freedom of speech and the press, outlawing statements of heresy, **radicalism,** or immorality. His criminal code permitted torture but outlawed vaccinations and street lighting as radical innovations.

The Battle against Secularism and Rationalism.
Pope Pius VIII continued this effort to return to the Old Regime. As he explained in the encyclical *Traditi humilitati nostrae* (1829), the church must combat **secularism** in all its forms, including public schools, civil marriage, and divorce. Pius believed Catholics should return to a religion based on faith and Christian mysteries. A leading Catholic intellectual, the viscount René de Chateaubriand, had championed this in *The Genius of Christianity* (1802). Christians, Chateaubriand argued, must reject **rationalism** because it rejected religious mysteries: "It is a pitiful mode of reasoning to reject whatever we cannot comprehend" (see Document 24.2).

Conservatism in Spain.
Even political liberals embraced religious conservatism in some countries. In Spain, liberals fought an obsessively religious monarch, King Ferdinand VII, who was so devout that he personally embroidered robes for statues of the Virgin Mary in Spanish shrines. Yet Spanish liberals shared his religious beliefs. When they imposed a constitution in 1820, they rejected religious freedom. Article 12 said simply, "The religion of the Spanish nation is, and shall be perpetually, Apostolic Roman Catholic, the only true religion. The nation protects it by wise and just laws and prohibits the exercise of any other religion whatsoever."

The Evangelical Protestant Awakening. A somewhat different conservatism characterized Protestantism. **Evangelical churches** (especially Pietists in Lutheran countries and Methodists elsewhere) denounced the evils of the modern world and taught obedience to established authority, as did the Vatican. Methodist governing statutes stated: "None of us shall, either in writing or in conversation, speak lightly or irreverently of the government." Prince Metternich could not have said it better. Even hymns could be counterrevolutionary: "The rich man in his castle, The poor man at the gate, God created both of them, And ordered their estate." An evangelical **"awakening"** swept Britain, the north German states, and Scandinavia and even won converts in Belgium, Switzerland, and France. This development was so important that some historians have argued that the spread of Methodism in the British working class was a reason why Britain never experienced a major revolution during industrialization.

Puritanism. Protestants stressed another element in conservatism: **Puritanism** and its restrictions on behavior. Evangelicals insisted on strict sexual morality, campaigned for the prohibition of alcoholic beverages, and fought blasphemous language. The most famous illustration of the Protestant effort to supervise morals is the work of Dr. Thomas Bowdler and his sister Harriet. The Bowdlers worked so avidly to censor immoral literature that they left their name behind for expurgated **(bowdlerized)** works. They abridged Shakespeare to produce *The Family Shakespeare* in 1818. The bowdlerized Shakespeare eliminated all passages that might "raise a blush on the cheek of modesty," such as Hamlet's famous remarks to Ophelia about sex.

Protecting the Old Order: The Law

Censorship. Historians often characterize Metternichian government as an effort to curb dissent. Every state in Europe adopted such legislation as a bulwark against revolution. Freedom of the press and freedom of speech were the first targets. Russian restrictions were so severe that writers spoke of a "censorship terror." Two of the greatest figures of Russian literature, Alexander Pushkin and Fyodor Dostoevsky, were exiled—Pushkin for writing "Ode to Liberty" and Dostoevsky for belonging to a radical organization. In Scandinavia, the tales of Hans Christian Andersen were banned for corrupting the youth; Dante's *The Divine Comedy* was forbidden in Prussia because the title seemed blasphemous to a censor.

The Family. Such counterrevolutionary legal restrictions did not stop with obvious political targets; they also had profound effects on individual families. In

---

VISCOUNT FRANÇOIS-RENÉ DE CHATEAUBRIAND ON *THE GENIUS OF CHRISTIANITY* (1813)

Chateaubriand (1768–1848) was one of the leading authors of the Christian revival that followed the revolutionary age. He was a noble who had served in the royal army and fought the revolution, then joined the émigrés. Although he served under Napoleon, he supported the Bourbon Restoration and became Minister of Foreign Affairs. His works (especially *Atala* and *René*) are often cited as the beginning of Romanticism in French literature. *The Genius of Christianity* (originally published in English as *The Beauties of Christianity*) was very popular in the early nineteenth century. This passage, which describes Chateaubriand's thoughts during a sea voyage to America, contain many of the elements of Romanticism. Note the strength of religious faith in contrast to "disputing men of science," the deeply emotional tone, the importance of the senses, and the emphasis upon nature.

We often arose at midnight and sat down on the deck, where we found only the officer of the watch and a few sailors in profound silence. . . . God of Christians! It is on the waters of the abyss, and on the expanded sky, that thou has particularly engraven the characters of thy omnipotence! Millions of stars sparkling in the azure dome of heaven . . . a sea unbounded by any shores; infinity in the skies and on the waves! Never didst thou affect me more powerfully with thy greatness than in those nights . . . !

I am nothing; I am only a simple, solitary wanderer: oft have I heard men of science disputing on the subject of a Supreme Being, and I have not understood them; but I have invariably remarked that it is in the prospect of the sublime scenes of nature that this unknown being manifests himself to the human heart. . . .

He who had not recognized in this prospect the beauty of the Deity had been greatly to be pitied. Religious tears involuntarily flowed from my eyes. . . . this is a scene which defies the art of the painter and the eloquence of the writer, and which the whole heart of man is scarcely sufficient to embrace!

From Chateaubriand, François-René de, *The Beauties of Christianity*, vol. 1 (London, 1813, pp. 186–189).

Question: What important elements of Romanticism are seen in this excerpt?

France, for example, the government sought to rebuild the traditional family. The chief legal expression of this effort was the repeal of the divorce law adopted during the French Revolution. As Louis de Bonald, a philosopher of monarchism, explained: "Just as political democracy allows the people, the weak part of political

THE KARLSBAD DECREES, 1819

Supervision of Universities

1. The sovereign [of each German state] shall choose for each university an extraordinary commissioner. . . . The duty of this commissioner shall be . . . to observe carefully the spirit with which the professors and tutors are guided in their public and private lectures; . . . to give the instruction a salutary direction, suited to the future destiny of the students. . . .

2. The governments of the states . . . reciprocally engage to remove from their universities and other establishments of instruction, professors and other public teachers against whom it may be proved, that . . . in abusing their legitimate influence over the minds of youth . . . they shall have shown themselves incapable of executing the important functions entrusted to them. . . .

3. . . . [L]aws . . . against secret or unauthorized associations at the universities shall be maintained in all their force and vigor.

Press Censorship

1. . . . [N]o writing appearing in the form of a daily paper or periodical pamphlet . . . shall be issued from the press without the previous consent of the public authority.

From "Karlsbad Decrees," in *The Annual Register* (1819). (London: J. Dodsky, 1820).

Question: Would these laws produce a significant change for university students?

control of a government commissioner, fired liberal professors, and closed student clubs. (Among the dangerous professors fired were the brothers Grimm, dismissed by the University of Göttingen.) Francis I liked this policy; as he told a group of teachers in 1821: "I do not need scholars but obedient citizens." The arbitrary arrest and trial of teachers followed. In Prussia, the harassment of liberal professors became a police recreation. This regulation of the schools reached its nadir when Friedrich Froebel opened the first kindergarten in 1837. Froebel believed that preschool children could learn through games and activities. The Prussian government, however, deemed this a revolutionary principle that undermined the authoritarian model of education. Kindergartens were outlawed.

German education laws provided a model for other countries. Shortly after the promulgation of the Karlsbad Decrees, Alexander I adopted a similar program. His instructions for the University of Kazan (1820) eliminated free speech and freedom of inquiry: "No harmful or seductive literature or speeches in any form shall be permitted to spread through the university." Alexander, like Francis I, thought that "[t]he soul of education, and the prime virtue of the citizen, is obedience." His restrictions did not surpass the zeal of the French. In 1816, the government expelled the entire student body of their elite engineering school, the École Polytechnique (including Auguste Comte, a founder of sociology), for radicalism. Such attitudes also reached England, where one member of Parliament (M.P.) denounced plans for more schools by arguing that education only taught the masses "to despise their lot in life instead of making them good servants; instead of teaching them subordination, it would render them fractious[,] . . . insolent to their superiors."

society, to rise against the established power, so divorce, veritable domestic democracy, allows the wife, the weak part, to rebel against marital authority. In order to keep the state out of the hands of the people, it is necessary to keep the family out of the hands of wives and children." Metternich adopted similarly motivated family legislation in Austria. A Marriage Law of 1820, for example, forbade marriage by beggars, people receiving relief, the unemployed, and migrants; it also required a "marriage permit," without which servants, journeymen, and day laborers could not marry.

Schools and the Karlsbad Decrees. The policy of social control made schools a favorite target of conservative governments. An assembly of German student groups (known as *Burschenschaften*) at the Wartburg Festival of 1817 showed an enthusiasm for nationalism that disturbed the government. Metternich's regulations for schools, announced at Karlsbad in 1819 (see Document 24.3), put German universities under the

The Police. The most severe Metternichian restrictions were the political use of the police and judiciary. Modern police forces did not exist in 1815, but the revolutionary era had taught many lessons about policing. Metternich had observed the methods of the French police, such as keeping files on suspects, organizations, or periodicals. He and Count Joseph Sedlnitzky founded one of the first effective police systems, using these bureaucratic techniques. Sedlnitzky merged the police and postal service, so letters could be read before delivery, and he used internal passports to limit the movement of people and ideas within the empire.

Repressive Legislation in Britain. In Britain, the counterrevolutionary policies of Lord Liverpool's government (1812–1827) rivaled those in more despotic states. A **Habeas Corpus** Suspension Act denounced "a traitorous conspiracy" of radicals and authorized the arrest of "such persons as his majesty shall suspect are conspiring." A **Seditious Meetings** Act restricted the right of assembly by requiring prior approval for meetings of fifty or more people. A set of repressive laws, collectively called the Six Acts, forbade the publication of anything the government considered seditious, authorized arbitrary searches and seizures, banned many public meetings, and taxed newspapers to make them too expensive for most of the public. The Liverpool government did not hesitate to use the British army against workers, as it did during the Spa Fields (London) Riot of 1816. This policy led to tragedy at Manchester in 1819, when the Hussars ended a protest meeting with their sabers in the Peterloo massacre.

Severity of Judicial System.

British conservatives used the judiciary as effectively as the Austrians used the police. More than 200 crimes were punishable by death, and these laws were often used for political effects, such as controlling workers. In 1833, the courts taught a lesson to workers by executing a 9-year-old apprentice for stealing 2 pence (about 4 cents) worth of ink from his master's shop. British judges more often solved political problems by ordering the **transportation** of troublesome people to penal colonies in Australia. Irish nationalists and labor militants were especially liable to receive such sentences. One of the first efforts to organize a labor union in Britain resulted in the transportation of six farm workers (the Tolpuddle martyrs) in 1834 for taking a secret oath. The conditions of penal servitude were harsh and included **corporal punishment;** one Irish nationalist received 100 lashes for singing a rebel song.

Continental Justice.

Politicized justice also typified the continent. Many governments, especially the Prussian, used the crime of *lèse majesté* (anything offensive to the dignity of the ruler) to control dissent. King Frederick William III showed the usefulness of this law in 1819. He had promised his Rhenish provinces a constitution when he annexed them in 1815, but he reneged. When a group of Rhinelanders reminded him with a petition, he ordered their arrest for lèse majesté. French justice illustrates another method for controlling the troublesome. *Les Misérables,* Victor Hugo's novel with a criminal protagonist (Jean Valjean), describes criminals being chained to a stake in a public square and branded with a hot iron so that honest folk could identify them and avoid them. Lesser criminals merely had to carry a passport with the distinctive mark of a criminal to warn employers and the police.

CHALLENGES TO THE OLD ORDER: THE "-ISMS" OF THE NINETEENTH CENTURY

The changes that had shaken Europe in the generation before 1815—the intellectual ferment of the Enlightenment, the political upheaval of the French Revolution, the social transformation of industrialization—had all produced pressures to reform the Old Regime. After 1815, these ideas of change began to crystallize into political doctrines (or ideologies). These new doctrines are known as the "-isms" because they took names ending in *ism,* a linguistic vogue that began with the word *liberalism* (coined in 1820), continued with the terms **nationalism** and **socialism** in the 1830s, and soon included such doctrines as radicalism, capitalism, Marxism, and **feminism.** These doctrines were sometimes compatible with each other and sometimes in conflict with each other, but they all called for changes in the Metternichian order.

FIGURE 24.3 *Peterloo Massacre.* Under the provisions of the Six Acts, the British government had the right to close political meetings, by force if necessary. Depicted here, in the most outrageous application of the law, the British cavalry use sabers to break up a meeting at Manchester in 1819. Note the crowd being attacked: both men and women are present, and all are dressed very well.

Liberalism.

The first of these doctrines—liberalism— was derived from the Latin word *liber* (free) to denote a doctrine about individual freedom. Early nineteenth-century liberalism (sometimes called **classical liberalism** to distinguish it from later liberalism) sought individual freedoms (such as freedom of speech), laws extending such liberty to more individuals (such as minorities), and the removal of

TABLE 24.1 THE EVOLUTION OF THE "-ISMS" IN NINETEENTH-CENTURY EUROPE

Complex doctrines, such as the "-isms," often have multiple shades of meaning for different individuals and groups, making careful definition important. Such doctrines also shift their meaning (and their relationships with each other) over time. "Conservatism" once suggested defending and conserving monarchism while trying to repress "republicanism"; yet later conservatives became staunch defenders of republican government. "Nationalism" was once a radical doctrine that threatened the established order, so conservatives fought to suppress it; within a century, however, nationalism and conservatism had become closely allied in many countries. Capitalism was originally the economic doctrine associated with liberalism, not conservatism. Use of such terms should therefore carefully note the specific feature of the "-ism" being discussed and be conscious of changes over time.

DOCTRINE	FEATURES	EVOLUTION OF THE IDEAS
Monarchism (coined in 1838)		
Divine Right monarchism	• Alliance of church and state • Structured corporative society • State management of economy	Gradual disappearance from European political discourse
Constitutional monarchism	• Constitutional laws limiting monarchy • Elective legislatures with restricted suffrage	Gradual compromise with new elite

Burke, *Reflections on the French Revolution* (1790): defense of tradition and order

Conservatism (coined in 1835)	• Defense of monarchy against republicanism • Defense of established religion • Defense of traditional social stratification • Defense of land-based economy • Opposition to democratic revolution	Gradual acceptance of liberal political reforms Gradual acceptance of economic liberalism

Chateaubriand, *Genius of Christianity* (1802): intellectual and cultural inspiration of nationalism, conservatism, and liberalism
Hegel, *Phenomenology of Spirit* (1807): stirs German nationalism

Romanticism (coined in 1803)	• Independence of nationalities from foreign rule, by revolution as needed	Gradually replaced by realism as dominant cultural theme

Hugo, *Les Misérables* (1862): sympathy for the poor and revolution
Mazzini, *Instructions for Young Italy* (1831): manual for nationalist unification

Nationalism (coined in 1836)	• Unification of states and territories of the same nationality • Initial alliance with liberalism and radicalism • Economic policies to help the nation, including tariffs	Gradual shift from alliance with liberalism to conservatism

List, *National System of Political Economy* (1841): rejects liberal economics for developing nations
Smith, *Wealth of Nations* (1776): defines economic freedom — Gradually known as capitalism

Capitalism (coined in 1851)	• Economic liberalism • Free trade among nations: no tariffs • Weak, noninterventionist state • Minimal state welfare or regulation • Freedom of individuals to act (laissez faire)	Gradual adoption as conservative economics

impediments to liberty (such as laws favoring members of an established national church). To achieve such aims, liberals commonly demanded two fundamental documents: (1) a constitution establishing a representative government and specifying its powers and (2) a bill of rights guaranteeing individual liberties. Few countries possessed such constitutions or bills of rights, and most monarchs opposed them. Liberals, therefore, were among the primary opponents of the Metternichian restoration.

TABLE 24.1 THE EVOLUTION OF THE "-ISMS" IN NINETEENTH-CENTURY EUROPE—CONT'D

DOCTRINE	FEATURES	EVOLUTION OF THE IDEAS
Liberalism (coined in 1820)	• Political liberalism • Constitutional restriction of state • Legislative power in representative government • Bill of rights guarantee of individual rights	Gradual adoption of agenda of radicalism and some socialism, leaving name **"classical liberalism"** for original ideas
Mill, *On Liberty* (1859): champions individual rights		
Radicalism (coined in 1820)	• Support of political freedoms of liberalism • Universal suffrage democracy • Republican government • Equality in politics and society • Separation of church and state: secularism	Gradual absorption into liberalism and evolutionary socialism
Wollstonecraft, *Vindication of the Rights of Women* (1792)		
Mill, *Subjection of Women* (1869): champions women's rights		
Feminism (coined c. 1890)	• Inclusion of women in liberal and radical agenda • Expansion of social agenda of "-isms" such as education • Alliance with differing groups supporting women	
Fourier, *Theory of Four Movements* (1808): proposes cooperative organization of society		
Utopian socialism	• Early criticism of industrial society • Emphasis on greater economic equality	Early disappearance from discourse
Bernstein, *Evolutionary Socialism* (1899): argues democracy will produce socialism		
Socialism (coined in 1832)		
Evolutionary socialism	• Acceptance of liberal-democratic political institutions • Support of strong state to aid and protect the weak • Program of social and economic equality • Early support of feminism	
Marx and Engels, *The Communist Manifesto* (1848)		
Marx, *Capital* (1867)		
Revolutionary socialism	• Revolution to seize power • Strong government of the working class • Abolition of private property • State ownership of production and distribution	Gradually known as Marxism and Communism
Marxism (coined in 1897)		
Proudhon, *What Is Property?* (1840)		
Anarchism (coined in 1642)	• Abolition of the state and private property	

Question: Which of the "-isms" has changed the most since the early nineteenth century?

Nationalism. A second ideology—nationalism—created additional problems for conservatives, although a century later it would be a central doctrine of twentieth-century conservatism. This doctrine shifted discussion toward the collective rights of a nation. Nationalists asserted that it was possible to identify distinct nations, based on shared characteristics such as language. This nationalism is illustrated by a German song, Ernst Arndt's *Where Is the German's Fatherland?*: "Where is the German's Fatherland? Name me at length that mighty

The Defense of the Old Regime, 1815–1848   603

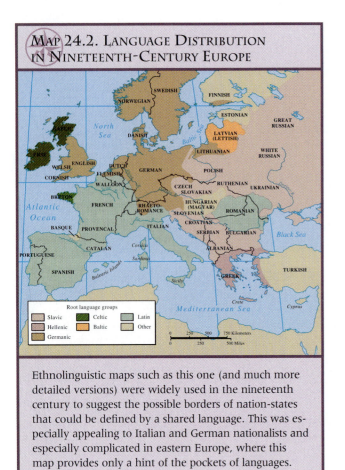

MAP 24.2. LANGUAGE DISTRIBUTION IN NINETEENTH-CENTURY EUROPE

Ethnolinguistic maps such as this one (and much more detailed versions) were widely used in the nineteenth century to suggest the possible borders of nation-states that could be defined by a shared language. This was especially appealing to Italian and German nationalists and especially complicated in eastern Europe, where this map provides only a hint of the pockets of languages.

land! 'Where'er resounds the German tongue, Where'er its hymns to God are sung.' " Other nationalists defined their nation by a shared culture, history, or religion. All advocated the creation of nation-states independent from foreign rule, uniting members of the nation in a single, self-governing state.

Nationalism and Liberalism. Nationalists considered these objectives more important than the political rights that liberals sought. As a Rumanian nationalist said in the 1840s, "The question of nationality is more important than liberty. Until a people can exist as a nation, it cannot make use of liberty." One could be both a liberal and nationalist, seeking a nation-state that granted liberty, as Giuseppe Mazzini did in his movement called Young Italy (see Document 24.4), but the two objectives often conflicted with each other. Most often, nationalists and liberals were allies because they both fought against the political structures of the Old Regime, but that alliance rarely endured.

Radicalism. Governments especially dreaded *radicalism,* the term they usually applied to democratic movements. Radicals endorsed liberalism but demanded

more; whereas liberals were willing to accept a limited franchise, radicals called for a democratic franchise and sometimes for the abolition of monarchy (making their doctrine **republicanism**). In the words of Mazzini, radicals "no longer believed in the sanctity of royal races, no longer believed in aristocracy, no longer believed in privilege." Radical movements, such as the Decembrists in Russia and the Chartists in Britain, however, made conservatives think of Robespierre and the guillotine.

Socialism. The term *socialism* was also coined in the 1830s to identify doctrines stressing social and economic equality. **Marxist socialism** did not become a significant political philosophy until after midcentury, but many forms of pre-Marxist socialism existed. The earliest, known as **utopian socialism,** grew from critiques of industrial society. Robert Owen, the son of a poor Welsh artisan, made a fortune as a textile manufacturer and devoted his wealth to improving industrial conditions. He branded the factory system "outright slavery" and called for a new social order based on cooperation instead of competition.

Utopian Socialism. Owen applied his ideas to his own factories at New Lanark, Scotland, where he limited his profits and invested in building a comfortable life for his workers. This won Owen an international reputation, but neither industrialists nor governments copied his ideas. Utopian socialism took different forms in France. The founder of French socialism, Count Henri de Saint-Simon, reversed the pattern of Owen's life: he was born to the nobility, squandered his fortune, and died in poverty. He was a hero of the American Revolution, a prisoner of the French Revolution, and a critic of the Industrial Revolution. He denounced all economies in which "man has exploited man" and called for a new order based on the principle "from each according to his capacity, to each according to his productivity." Charles Fourier proposed utopian communities, which he called *phalansteries.* Fourier envisioned an idealistic, but highly structured, society whose members shared labor and freedom.

Varieties of Socialism. Other pioneers called for a **cooperative socialism** of workers, a **Christian socialism** based upon Jesus's devotion to the poor, or a **democratic socialism,** on the theory that the poor would have a majority in a true democracy and create a socialist society. The champion of democratic socialism was a French journalist, Louis Blanc, who developed the idea of a strong socialist state that regulated the economy and provided work for the unemployed in national workshops.

Feminism. A final doctrine of social change—feminism—had not yet acquired that name, a late

MAZZINI'S INSTRUCTIONS FOR YOUNG ITALY, 1831

Giuseppe Mazzini (1805–1872) in 1830.

Guiseppe Mazzini (1805–1872) was one of the founders of Italian nationalism and the modern state of Italy. He greatly influenced nationalist thinking in many countries. Mazzini created a secret society, Young Italy, dedicated to the unification of all Italian states under a self-governing republic. His manifesto for Young Italy, from which the following excerpt is taken, was widely emulated.

Young Italy is a brotherhood of Italians who believe in a law of Progress and Duty, and are convinced that Italy is destined to become one nation. . . . By Italy we understand —(1) Continental and peninsular Italy, bounded on the north by the Alps . . . and on the east by Trieste; (2) The islands proved Italian by the language of the inhabitants, and destined . . . to form a part of the Italian political unity.

Young Italy is Republican and Unitarian.

Republican because theoretically every nation is destined, by the Law of God and humanity, to form a free and equal community as brothers; and the republic is the only form of government that ensures this future. . . . Because our Italian tradition is essentially republican; our great memories are republican; the whole history of our national progress is republican; whereas the introduction of monarchy amongst us was coeval with our decay and consummated our ruin. . . .

Young Italy is Unitarian because without unity there is no true nation.

The means by which Young Italy proposes to reach its aim are education and insurrection, to be adopted simultaneously, and made to harmonize with each other.

From Mazzini, Giuseppe, *Life and Writings* (London: Smith, Elder, 1880).

Question: Does Mazzini's version of nationalism seem more closely associated with liberal or conservative political doctrines?

---

nineteenth-century coinage, but already called for reconsideration of the role of women in European society. Pioneers such as Mary Wollstonecraft (see Document 24.5) and Olympe de Gouges had opened discussion of the woman question so effectively that the Metternichian reaction could not contain this debate. European legal systems, especially the Napoleonic Code, but also the British common law tradition and the Germanic Frederician Code, explicitly held women in an inferior position. The rights of women were exercised for them by men (first their fathers, then their husbands). Women were expected to remain confined to limited **spheres of activity**—*Kinder, Kirche, Küche* (children, church, cooking) in a famous German cliché. Formal education (especially higher education) and educated occupations were closed to them. The legal condition of women within marriage and the family began with an obligation to obey their husbands, who legally

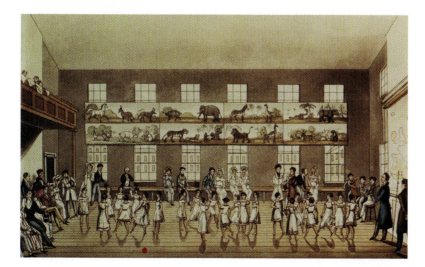

FIGURE 24.4 *Utopian Socialism at New Lanark.* The most successful of the utopian idealists was Robert Owen (1771–1858), an exceptionally able man who went to work in a cotton mill at age 10, was the manager of a mill by age 19, and was wealthy enough to buy the mills at New Lanark, Scotland, at 29. Owen devoted his wealth to creating a model community for the workers at New Lanark, providing them with unmatched working conditions and housing, a nursery and a school for the children of workers, evening education classes for workers, and a cooperative. Thus, this scene of daughters of cotton mill workers dancing the quadrille at the New Lanark free school provides a remarkable illustration of the forms of socialism.

MARY WOLLSTONECRAFT, *A VINDICATION OF THE RIGHTS OF WOMAN* (1792)

Mary Wollstonecraft (1759–1797) was born to a poor Irish family born in England. Her youth was marked by an abusive, alcoholic father and the early death of her mother, but Mary managed to educate herself. During the 1780s, she published a book on the education of girls and ran a short-lived school, but chiefly supported herself as a governess. In 1790, she took a post with a London publisher through whom she entered radical political circles. She lived in Paris during the early days of the French Revolution and defied public morality by giving birth to an illegitimate daughter, although she attempted suicide due to her lover's infidelities. In 1796, she began an affair with the noted radical William Godwin, and when she became pregnant again (with the daughter Mary who would become famous as Mary Shelley), she married Godwin despite their mutual principles against marriage. She died of puerperal fever a few days after giving birth. *A Vindication of the Rights of Woman* shows the impact of her debates in radical circles, her attention to the French Revolution, and her deep concern with the education of women.

If marriage be the cement of society, mankind should all be educated after the same model, or the intercourse of the sexes will never deserve the name of fellowship, nor will women ever fulfill the peculiar duties of their sex, till they become enlightened citi-

zens, till they become free by being enabled to earn their own subsistence, independent of men; I mean, to prevent misconstruction, as one man is independent of another. Nay, marriage will never be held sacred till women, by being brought up with men, are prepared to be their companions rather than their mistresses. . . . So convinced am I of this truth, that I will venture to predict that virtue will never prevail in society till the virtues of both sexes are founded on reason . . .

I have already inveighed against the custom of confining girls to their needle, and shutting them out of all political and civil employments; for by thus narrowing their minds they are rendered unfit to fulfil the peculiar duties which nature has assigned them. . . . [I]t is not the enchantment of literary pursuits, or the steady investigation of scientific subjects, that leads women astray from duty. No, it is indolence and vanity—the love of pleasure and the love of sway, that will reign paramount in an empty mind. I say empty emphatically, because the education which women now receive scarcely deserves the name. . . .

From Wollstonecraft, Mary, *A Vindication of the Rights of Woman* (London, 1891, pp. 247, 252–253).

Question: Why should women be educated in the same way as men?

---

controlled their wives' wages, children, and bodies. Divorce was illegal in many countries and rare everywhere (it required an act of Parliament in Britain).

Romanticism: European Culture in the Age of Metternich

Classicism. The standards of neoclassical culture that had characterized the Old Regime did not survive into the postrevolutionary era. Even before the French Revolution, **classicism** had come under attack for its strict rules, formal styles, and stress upon reason. When the Congress of Vienna assembled in 1815, European high culture had become quite different. The new style, known as **Romanticism,** reached its apogee in the age of Metternich and continued to be a force in European culture past midcentury.

Romanticism. Romanticism is difficult to define because it was a reaction against precise definitions and rules, and that reaction took many forms. The foremost

characteristic of Romanticism was the exaltation of personal feelings, emotions, or the spirit, in contrast to cold reason. The emphasis on feelings led in many directions, from the passions of romantic love to the spirituality of religious revival. Other attitudes also characterized Romanticism: a return to nature for themes and inspiration, the admiration of the Middle Ages instead of classical Greece and Rome, a fascination with the exotic and the supernatural, and the canonization of the hero or genius.

Romanticism in Literature. The emphasis on feelings had begun in the late eighteenth century. Rousseau, one of the central figures of Enlightenment rationalism, was a transitional figure, a precursor of Romanticism who had also argued, "To exist is to feel!" Rousseau stimulated a reaction against unqualified rationalism by his emphasis upon nature: in his view (especially in his treatise on education, *Emile*), humans were by nature good but corrupted by society. This view provided a simultaneous critique of both rationalism (because supposedly rational society is the source of corruption) and

HEGEL'S *THE PHILOSOPHY OF HISTORY*

Georg Wilhelm Friedrich Hegel (1770–1831) was one of the most influential thinkers of the age of Romanticism. He was a philosopher who held posts at several German universities, beginning at Jena (where he taught at the time of Napoleon's devastating victory over the Prussian army at Jena in 1806) and culminating in the philosophy professorship at Berlin (1818–1831). Hegelianism, a philosophy of the Absolute, shaped the thinking of two generations of German university students (including Karl Marx, his student at Berlin) and the nature of European Romanticism, especially the political doctrines that evolved in the era. Hegel's ideas appealed to thinkers of differing beliefs— monarchists, conservatives, liberals, radicals, nationalists, and, of course, Marxists all drew on Hegel. The following excerpt comes from *The Philosophy of History,* originally delivered as lectures in 1822. Note the implications of Hegel's thoughts for German nationalism and the important turn that Hegel gives to German liberalism.

Germany was traversed by the victorious French [Napoleonic] hosts, but German nationality delivered it from this yoke. One of the leading features in the political condition of Germany is that code of Rights which was certainly occasioned by French oppression, since this was the especial means of bringing to light the deficiencies of the old system. The fiction of an Empire [the Holy Roman Empire] has utterly vanished. It is broken up into sovereign states. Feudal obligations are abolished, for freedom of property and of person have been recognized as fundamental principles. Offices of State are open to every citizen, talent and adaptation being of course the necessary conditions. The government rests with the official world, and the personal decision of the monarch constitutes its apex; for a final decision is, as was remarked above, absolutely necessary. Yet with firmly established laws, and a settled organization of the State, what is left to the sole arbitration of the monarch is, in point of substance, no great matter. It is certainly a very fortunate circumstance for a nation, when a sovereign of noble character falls to its lot; yet in a great state even this is of small moment, since its strength lies in the Reason incorporated in it. . . .

The History of the World is nothing but the development of the Idea of Freedom. But Objective Freedom—the laws of real Freedom—demand the subjugation of mere contingent Will . . . what has happened, and is happening every day, is not only not "without God," but is essentially His Work.

From Hegel, G. W. F., *The Philosophy of History* (New York: Colonial Press, 1899, pp. 455–457).

Question: Is Hegel's argument compatible with the monarchical conservatism of the age of Metternich?

Christianity (because it rejects the doctrine of original sin). Johann von Goethe, arguably the greatest German poet, similarly bridged the change from the classical to the romantic. His short novel, *The Sorrows of Young Werther,* depicted feelings so strong that the protagonist's suicide began a vogue for melancholy young men killing themselves as Werther had, with moonlight falling across the last page of Goethe's book. The name of the school of German literature that evolved around Goethe, the *Sturm und Drang* ("storm and stress") movement, suggests the intensity of this emphasis on feelings. Romanticism was the triumph of that emphasis. Another great figure of German culture, the philosopher G. W. F. Hegel, stimulated a rejection of Enlightenment rationalism by his critique of the leading intellect of the German Enlightenment, Immanuel Kant. Hegel did not argue for the rejection of rationalism but rather for an understanding its errors. Hegel's writing often seems opaque to modern readers, but it shaped many of the doctrines of the nineteenth century (see Document 24.6).

Romanticism in the Arts. At the peak of Romanticism, the British poet William Wordsworth simply defined poetry as "the spontaneous overflow of powerful feelings," and the landscape painter John Constable similarly insisted that "[p]ainting is another word for feeling." The return to nature inspired much romantic poetry, especially Wordsworth's. It produced two generations of landscape painters, such as Constable and J. M. W. Turner, who found inspiration in natural scenery. This mood even extended to symphonic music, inspiring Beethoven's *Sixth Symphony,* known as the Pastoral Symphony. The romantic fascination with medieval Europe likewise had far-reaching influence. The most visible expression of it was a Gothic revival in architecture. This produced both new construction in the flamboyant Gothic style of the late Middle Ages (such as the new Palace of Westminster, home of the British Houses of Parliament, built in 1836) and campaigns to preserve surviving Gothic masterpieces (such as Viollet-le-Duc's restoration of the Notre Dame Cathedral in Paris). The same inspiration stimulated historical literature such as Hugo's *The Hunchback of Notre Dame,* Sir Walter Scott's *Ivanhoe,* and Alexandre Dumas's *The Three Musketeers;* its most lasting effect on Western literature, however, was probably the invention of the Gothic horror story, a style made famous by Mary Shelley's *Frankenstein.*

Romanticism and Politics. Many of these themes made Romanticism compatible with the political conservatism of the era. The focus on nature turned high culture toward the rural world, home of aristocratic power and the bastion of conservative sentiments. The focus on the Middle Ages restored cultural emphasis on a world of unchallenged monarchy and universal Christianity, instead of the republicanism, constitutionalism, and liberalism. The dethronement of rationalism and the recovery of emotion encouraged the revival of religions of faith, mystery, and miracle. But another side of Romanticism found a powerful voice in the liberal and national revolutions of the early nineteenth century. The revolutionary sympathies of some romantics can be seen in Eugène Delacroix's painting *Liberty at the Barricades;* the radical poems of Percy Bysshe Shelley; the angry novels of Victor Hugo, such as *Les Misérables;* and even Giuseppe Verdi's powerful opera *Rigoletto* (which depicts the scandalous behavior of a monarch). Beethoven's opera *Fidelio,* a hymn to liberty, inspired a century of reformers and revolutionaries with a moving scene in which the victims of tyranny are released from prison singing, "Oh happiness to see the light. . . . Oh Freedom, Freedom come to us again."

Romanticism and Nationalism. The link between Romanticism and nationalism was especially strong because many nationalists built their philosophy on the nation's shared culture. Many peoples found identity in folk tales, and their compilation (such as the work of the brothers Grimm in Germany) became a form of romantic nationalism. So did the recovery of the history of national minorities (as distinct from the history of their foreign government), as Frantisek Palacky did for the Czechs in his multivolume *History of Bohemia.* Nationalist themes were equally powerful for romantic artists, as Francisco Goya showed in a powerful work titled "3 May 1808," depicting the firing squad execution of Spanish freedom fighters. The strongest expression of romantic nationalism, however, was in music. All across Europe, nationalist composers drew inspiration from patriotic themes and folk music: Frédéric Chopin's polonaises (Polish pieces), Bedrich Smetana's tone poems about Czech scenes (*Ma Vlast* [My Country]), or Franz Liszt's *Hungarian Rhapsodies.*

Challenging the Old Order: Revolutions (1815–1825)

Despite their precautions, the conservative forces in power after 1815 could not prevent revolutions. More than a dozen revolutions, from Portugal to Russia, took place in the decade following the Congress of Vienna, plus historic rebellions in the British and Spanish empires. Historians normally describe these upheavals as liberal-national revolutions because most rebellions sought national independence (in Serbia, Ireland, Greece, and Spanish America) or constitutional government (in Spain) or both (several Italian states).

The Carbonari and Revolutionary Societies. Conservatives believed that these revolutions were nurtured and led by radical secret societies and used this to justify restricting civil rights. Such societies did exist, the most famous being an Italian society known as the *Carbonari* ("the charcoal burners"). **Carbonari** swore an oath to fight despotism and seek governments based on popular sovereignty, to oppose clericalism and seek

FIGURE 24.5 *Liberty Leading the People.* Eugène Delacroix (1798–1863), who was widely thought to be the illegitimate son of Talleyrand, was one of the most important leaders of the Romantic style of painting. Perhaps following the interests of his father, Delacroix painted several works devoted to political images, including this scene of the revolution of 1830 in France, one of the most famous paintings of the nineteenth century. Note the barricade at the base of the painting and the pile of paving stones (often dug up for barricades), and the images of poverty but the collaboration of workers and bourgeois.

FIGURE 24.6 *Third of May 1808.* Franciso Goya created one of the most moving political pictures of the century in this work, simply titled *Third of May 1808.* It depicts the public execution of civilians—one of them defiant to the end—before the eyes of a weeping crowd. Spain, which had been fighting on the French side in the Napoleonic Wars, was in the process of having its king dismissed and Napoleon's brother Joseph placed on the throne instead.

secular institutions, and to challenge the foreign domination of the Italian states; in 1820, the Neapolitan chapter claimed 100,000 members. Similar societies existed in most countries—in the circles of Greek businessmen (the Hetairos), in Polish universities (Adam Mickiewicz founded his nationalist society at the University of Vilna in 1817), in the officer corps of the Russian army (the Society of the South in Ukraine and the Society of the North at St. Petersburg), in Masonic lodges in Spain, and among Napoleonic war veterans attending German universities who founded the Burschenschaften (the student organizations which worried Metternich so much that he insisted on the strict supervision of German universities).

Rebellions and Revolutions, 1816–1823.

With or without the encouragement of such societies, political uprisings were frequent occurrences in the age of Metternich. While the Congress of Vienna met, a Serbian uprising against Ottoman Turkish rule began, the first in a series of Balkan revolts against the government in Constantinople. In 1816, Britain faced a slave rebellion in the Caribbean. A year later, a Carbonari-led liberal revolution was suppressed in the papal states. These uprisings provoked the conservative powers to adopt the Troppau Protocol in 1818, but barely 2 years later came the successful Spanish revolution (stimulated by King Ferdinand VII's abolition of the constitution of 1812 and by the impact of wars of independence in Spanish America), which was a nagging problem for the congress system in 1820–1823. In

FIGURE 24.7 *Meeting of the Carbonari, c. 1815–1830.* The *carbonari* (the charcoal burners) were the most famous of the revolutionary secret societies of the early nineteenth century. They originated in southern Italy during the resistance to the Napoleonic government, and after the defeat of Napoleon, versions of the carbonari grew in several Italian cities, dedicating themselves to liberal and national revolution in Italy. A version of the society, with a parallel name, also developed in France during the Bourbon Restoration. The existence of such societies was the rationale for many of the repressive laws of the age of Metternich. In this image, members of the society hold a clandestine meeting, ironically illuminated by an oil-burning lamp.

1820, revolutions also broke out in Portugal and Naples (both seeking constitutions), then at Palermo, in Sicily. Congresses of 1821 and 1822 sent Austrian armies to fight liberals in Italy, and French troops into Spain. By 1823, the conservative alliance had defeated the Spanish and Italians, treating the defeated rebels with savage cruelty; in Italy, captured rebels had their right hands cut off before being sent to Austrian dungeons. The British opposed the application of the Troppau Protocol elsewhere. The British navy supported the Monroe Doctrine (proclaimed by the United States to block allied intervention in America), so most of Latin America won its independence from Spain. As the

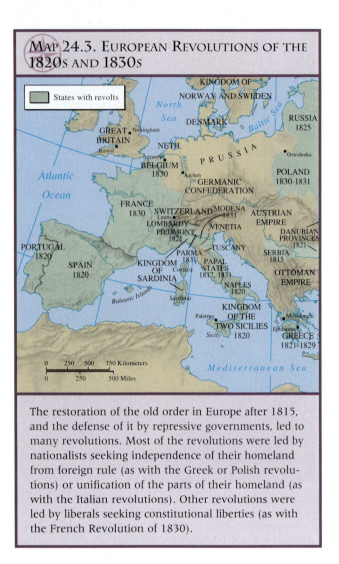

MAP 24.3. EUROPEAN REVOLUTIONS OF THE 1820s AND 1830s

States with revolts

KINGDOM OF NORWAY AND SWEDEN

North Sea

DENMARK

Baltic Sea

RUSSIA 1825

GREAT BRITAIN
Nottingham
Bristol

NETH.

Antwerp
BELGIUM 1830
Aachen

P R U S S I A

Ostrolenka

Atlantic Ocean

GERMANIC CONFEDERATION

POLAND 1830-1831

FRANCE 1830
Lyons
SWITZERLAND
MODENA 1831
LOMBARDY
PIEDMONT 1821
VENETIA

AUSTRIAN EMPIRE

Danube R.

DANUBIAN PROVINCES 1821

PORTUGAL 1820

SPAIN 1820

PARMA 1831
KINGDOM OF SARDINIA
Corsica
PAPAL STATES 1817, 1831
TUSCANY
SERBIA 1815

NAPLES 1820

OTTOMAN EMPIRE

Balearic Islands

Sardinia

KINGDOM OF THE TWO SICILIES 1820
Palermo
Sicily

Missolonghi
Epidaurus
GREECE 1821-1829

Mediterranean Sea

0   250   500   750 Kilometers
0   250   500 Miles

The restoration of the old order in Europe after 1815, and the defense of it by repressive governments, led to many revolutions. Most of the revolutions were led by nationalists seeking independence of their homeland from foreign rule (as with the Greek or Polish revolutions) or unification of the parts of their homeland (as with the Italian revolutions). Other revolutions were led by liberals seeking constitutional liberties (as with the French Revolution of 1830).

British foreign secretary bragged to Parliament, "I have called the New World into existence to redress the balance of the old."

Revolution in the Ottoman Empire. The conservative alliance broke apart over the revolutions in the Balkans, where the Ottoman Empire was slowly disintegrating. Revolutions broke out in Serbia, Greece, and the Rumanian provinces of Moldavia and Wallachia (on the border of Russia), but it was the Greek revolution of 1821–1827 that broke the Metternichian alliance. After the Serbs won autonomy in their revolution, a Greek congress at Epidaurus declared independence in 1822. According to the principles of the Troppau Protocol, the great powers should have supported the legitimate Turkish government. Metternich was almost alone in favoring that policy. Romantic **philhellenism** stimulated a pro-Greek policy in Britain and France, and for once governments agreed with the radical Shelley who wrote: "We are all Greeks. Our laws, our literature, our

religion, our arts, have their roots in Greece." Russian policy was less sophisticated but more adamant: the Ottoman Empire deserved no help from the Holy Alliance because it was not a Christian state.

The Greek Revolution. The Greeks won their independence in a long, brutal war that still echoes in Greco-Turkish enmity. Greek Orthodox clergymen proclaimed a "war of extermination" against Islamic infidels, leading to the killing of 25,000 civilians within 6 weeks; the sultan proclaimed an Islamic Holy War that produced 40,000 civilian corpses. Along the way, the patriarch of the Orthodox Church was hanged and his body thrown into the Bosporus. This killing did not end until Britain, France, and Russia broke with Metternich and intervened in 1827. The counterrevolutionary alliance collapsed (there were no full congresses after 1822) because self-interest had prevailed over doctrine; ironically, the most conservative state in Europe had caused this.

AUTOCRACY IN ROMANOV RUSSIA (1801–1855)

Alexander I. The tsar of Russia held enormous power in Metternichian Europe. No monarch had contributed more to the defeat of Napoleon Bonaparte: Napoleon's *Grande Armée* had perished in Russia in 1812, and Russian troops had occupied Paris in 1814. The tsar's support had sustained the congress system, and his defection during the Greek revolution had destroyed it. Russian internal affairs were less simple. The enigmatic Alexander I had come to the throne in 1801 at the age of 24, after the assassination of his father, in which Alexander may have been involved. He was a tall and handsome youth who favored skintight uniforms; he had become overweight by 1815, but his vanity and his robust sexuality (which ranged from his sister to religious mystics) put him in corsets instead of loose-fitting clothes. This same Alexander was considered the most intelligent monarch of the age by both Thomas Jefferson and Napoleon Bonaparte (excepting himself). Alexander held more absolute power than anyone else in Europe, and with it came the opportunity to propel Russia into the modern age by timely reforms (such as the abolition of serfdom) or to become the champion of the Old Regime. Alexander considered both.

Speransky and Russian Liberalism. Many historians describe Alexander I as the hope of Russian liberalism. He received a liberal education from his tutor, and he began his reign closely associated with a liberal adviser, Michael Speransky. Speransky was the son of a priest; his brilliance at school earned him a

Figure 24.8 *Alexander I, Russia's Emperor.* Tsar Alexander I of Russia (1777–1825) came to the throne following a conspiracy that deposed his father, Tsar Paul I. His regime awakened many liberal hopes for reform, but it became increasingly autocratic with the passage of time. Alexander expanded the Russian Empire through war with the Ottoman Empire and through negotiation at the Congress of Vienna, where, in recognition of his important role in defeating Napoleon, he won the annexation of most of Poland. He took an active role in leading Russian diplomacy at Vienna, in creating the conservative Holy Alliance of 1815, and in sustaining the congress system of counterrevolutionary diplomacy.

government job and caught the interest of the tsar. He was a good administrator, well organized and able to write clear prose, who mixed liberal sentiments with bureaucratic caution. Speransky swayed Alexander to consider reforms. He founded four new universities (doubling the total in the empire), at Kazan, Kharkov, Warsaw, and St. Petersburg. He gave the Poles a constitution and allowed them to reopen their parliament (the *Sejm*). This led to a constitution for Finland and to discussions with Speransky about a Russian constitution. Alexander also restrained the persecution of minority religions and proclaimed religious toleration. Most important, he abolished serfdom in his Baltic provinces between 1816 and 1819 while hinting that this was a pilot project for the emancipation of all Russian serfs.

Alexander's Depotism. Alexander I remained, however, an autocrat unchecked by a constitution, an independent judiciary, or a parliament. He was a monarch closer to eighteenth-century enlightened despotism than to nineteenth-century liberalism, presiding over the most feudal economy in the world. He held conquered peoples against their will, no matter how generously he treated them. In his later years, Alexander preferred reactionary advisers. He yielded to their contempt for Speransky and banished his friend to Siberia (although he later made him governor-general of that province). In his place, Alexander entrusted Russian domestic policy to a leading reactionary, Alexis Arakcheyev. Arakcheyev was a cruel and arrogant man unlikely to abolish serfdom; he once ordered a young serf flogged to death because she did a poor job at her sweeping. Alexander also capitulated to religious conservatives and abandoned the policy of toleration, which they considered "a sin against the Holy Ghost." Religious repression resumed in 1821.

The Decembrist Rebellion. Alexander's death in 1825 precipitated a crisis in Russia. He had no children who could inherit the throne, so it should have passed to his eldest brother, Constantine, the governor-general of Poland; but Constantine had renounced his right to the throne in 1822. This brought to the throne Alexander's youngest brother, Nicholas, whose training (by a sadistic military tutor) had been for military command, not for government. The accession of Nicholas I in December 1825 precipitated a rebellion led by liberal army officers. These **Decembrists** wanted to abolish the monarchy, write a constitution, and free the serfs, but their poorly organized revolt was quickly crushed. Nicholas found that many of the Decembrists were nobles who had been his friends (including two princes and a major general), but he responded harshly nonetheless. Of the Decembrists, 5 were hanged and 121 others were sentenced to hard labor in Siberia. The episode left the tsar bitter and even less tolerant of liberalism.

The Autocracy of Nicholas I. Restrictive legislation was severely tightened under Nicholas I. He created a new branch of the government, the Third Section, to centralize the police. The head of the Third Section, General Alexander Benckendorff, vigorously enforced a Censorship Law forbidding all publications not "useful or at least harmless." The law even banned works considered "full of grammatical errors." Nicholas I relied on the Ministry of Education to control minorities; the educational system became an instrument for the **Russification** of minorities and the submission of everyone to the authority of the church and the state. This policy was summarized in a famous slogan: "Autocracy! Orthodoxy! Nationality!" Historians sometimes contrast the repressive regime of Nicholas I with

The Defense of the Old Regime, 1815–1848

FIGURE 24.9 *Nicholas I, Emperor of Russia.* Tsar Nicholas I of Russia (1796–1855) ascended to the throne unexpectedly in 1825. He was the third son of Tsar Paul I, but his eldest brother (Alexander I) died childless and next elder brother, Constantine, abdicated his claim to the throne. Nicholas was a 31-year-old military man, and he ruled Russia with the firm grip of a military autocrat. He suppressed a Russian rebellion at his accession (the Decembrist Revolt), a Polish revolution in 1830, the Hungarian revolution of 1848–1849, and more than 700 serf rebellions in Russia, earning him the nickname of the "gendarme of Europe."

the liberal flirtations of Alexander I. More than 700 peasant uprisings occurred during his reign, and Nicholas repressed them with the same anger that he had shown the Decembrists. His eagerness to use the Russian army earned him the nickname "the gendarme of Europe." But contrasts are never as simple as they seem. Just as Alexander had shown an attachment to autocracy by entrusting the government to Arakcheyev, Nicholas I showed at least a mild interest in reform by recalling Speransky from Siberia and allowing him to finish his codification of Russian law.

THE LIBERAL-MONARCHICAL COMPROMISE IN FRANCE (1814–1848)

The Bourbon Restoration. The allies's restoration of the Bourbon royal family in 1814–1815 required a delicate compromise between Metternichian conservatism and deeply rooted French liberalism. Allied armies could put Louis XVIII on the throne, but the Bourbons could lose it again if Napoleon were correct when he jibed that they "had learned nothing and forgotten nothing" during the revolutionary era. The Bourbon compromise rested upon Louis's acceptance of a constitution and parliament. Louis insisted that his "constitutional charter" was a royal gift to the nation (not their natural right) and that the Bourbons still had a divine right to the throne; in return, the charter also included the liberal principles of equality before the law, freedom of religion, and freedom of the press (see Document 24.7). This constitution created a Chamber of Deputies, elected by 88,000 well-to-do men (0.3 percent of the population), of whom 15,000 (0.06 percent) were eligible to be candidates. This contrasted with the French republic of 1792 with its universal manhood suffrage and Britain, where 2.5 percent of adult men voted in 1815. The most democratic states in Europe were Norway and Sweden, where 10 percent voted, yet France remained decidedly more liberal than Austria, Prussia, Russia, or Spain, where there were no parliaments.

The Aristocratic Reaction in France. Reactionary nobles hated this compromise and favored a Metternichian, or even Russian government. These ultraroyalists (or **"ultras"**) were led by Louis XVIII's younger brother, the Count of Artois. The ultras had returned to France from 20 years in exile, determined to revive the Old Regime. They relied on Louis's having no surviving sons, so Artois would inherit the throne. This prompted Louis to remark presciently that the fate of the Bourbon Restoration depended on his outliving his brother. The French compromise seemed vulnerable during the first year of the Bourbon Restoration. Revenge against the supporters of previous regimes saw prominent supporters of Napoleon executed, peerages revoked, officers court martialed, and government employees fired. The worst outrage was a vigilante bloodbath, known as the **White Terror,** directed against republicans and Protestants. More than 200 people were killed in the White Terror in the south of France. Louis XVIII, however, prevented the ultras from gaining control of the government and from returning to former owners the lands taken during the French Revolution. The successful peasant and middle-class proprietors who had purchased this "national property" received constitutional guarantees that their land was inviolable.

Victory of the Ultras. Louis preserved his moderate compromise until 1820, when the son of Artois (and the heir to the throne) was assassinated. The king—tired, obese, 65, and suffering from a bad case of the gout— then capitulated to many of the ultras' demands. French censorship became so strict that authors could be imprisoned if their books "cast disfavor" on the government, the police received the power to make arrests based solely on suspicion, and the Sorbonne was placed under

THE FRENCH CHARTER OF 1814: A COMPROMISE CONSTITUTION

The French had adopted a constitution in 1791, then four new constitutions in the revolutionary and Napoleonic era, but formal constitutions remained rare in Europe. The monarchical victors would have preferred a world without constitutions, but they also recognized the dangers of denying a constitution in France. The result was a compromise, by which King Louis XVIII granted the following constitution, so delicately constructed that it was called a "constitutional charter" rather than a constitution.

Louis, by the grace of God, King of France. . . .

Divine Providence, in recalling us to our estates after a long absence, has laid upon us great obligations. . . . A constitutional charter was called for by the actual conditions of the kingdom; we promised it . . . although all authority in France resides in the person of the king. . . .

Public Law of the French

1. *Frenchmen are equal before the law, whatever may be their titles. . . .*
2. *They contribute without distinction, in proportion to their fortunes, towards the expenses of the state.*
3. *They are all equally admissible to civil and military employments.*
4. *Their personal liberty is likewise guaranteed. . . .*
5. *Every one may profess his religion with equal freedom, and shall obtain for his worship the same protection.*
6. *Nevertheless, the Catholic, Apostolic, and Roman religion is the religion of the state. . . .*
8. *Frenchmen have the right to publish and to have printed their opinions, while conforming with the laws which are necessary to restrain abuses of that liberty.*
9. *All property is inviolable. . . .*

Form of the Government of the King

13. *The person of the King is inviolable and sacred. His ministers are responsible [to him]. To the King alone belongs the executive power.*
14. *The King is the supreme head of the state, commands the land and sea forces, declares war, makes treaties.*

From Anderson, Frank M., ed., *The Constitutions and Other Select Documents Illustrative of the History of France, 1789–1907* (Minneapolis, 1908).

Question: In what ways is this constitution a compromise?

the control of a bishop and liberal professors were fired. The electorate for the Chamber of Deputies was sharply reduced while the rich were given a second vote.

Charles X. The breakdown of Louis XVIII's compromise worsened in 1824, when Artois came to the throne as King Charles X. Historians have characterized Charles as a blind reactionary, an image that contemporary cartoonists fostered by drawing the king with his crown covering his eyes. Charles earned this image when he named the leading ultra, Count Jean-Baptiste Villèle, premier. Villèle's government adopted a Law of Indemnity (1825) to repay aristocrats who had lost land during the revolution and a Law of Sacrilege, making irreligion a capital crime.

The Revolution of 1830. Such extreme conservatism ended middle-class, liberal acceptance of the compromise and precipitated a revolution in 1830 that drove Charles X from the throne. When Charles tried to keep ultras as his ministers without the support of the Chamber of Deputies, elections in May 1830 showed

that even rich voters opposed him. Then Charles responded in July 1830 with strict decrees known as the July Ordinances, tightening censorship further, dissolving the chamber again, and reducing electoral eligibility once more. The July Ordinances provoked a vehement reaction in the Parisian press. Adolphe Thiers, the editor of a liberal newspaper and a future president of France, drafted a protest stating, "The government has violated legality and we are absolved from obedience." The Chamber agreed that the king had violated the constitution, but newspapermen and politicians did not overthrow the king. Their anger became a revolution when radical insurgents took to the streets of Paris. After a few incidents of rioting (such as breaking windows in government buildings), crowds built barricades across the streets in working-class districts. Charles X, who had learned a lesson from the execution of his eldest brother, fled into exile.

Louis Philippe. The revolution of 1830 ended the rule of the Bourbon dynasty and removed the ultras from power, but France remained a monarchy. The

FIGURE 24.10 *The Charter or Death, July 1830.* In this anonymous painting, French Republicans, in opposition to King Charles X's oppressive reign, revolt and demand a return to the Charter issued under Louis XVIII. Once again the populace battled Royalist troops and toppled a regime. The reign of Louis Philippe followed in France and revolts echoed across Europe.

The Bourgeois Monarchy. The July Monarchy became so renowned for supporting banking, business, and industrial interests that it was also called **the Bourgeois Monarchy.** One of France's keenest political observers during the 1840s, Alexis de Tocqueville (Tawk'-veel), saw this at once: "Posterity will perhaps never know to what degree the government of this time is a capitalist enterprise in which all action is taken for the purpose of profit." A major novelist of the era, Honoré de Balzac, was more acidic in *Cousin Bette* (1847), writing that the heart of French civilization was "the holy, venerable, solid, adored, gracious, beautiful, noble, ever young, almighty Franc." Karl Marx was blunt: the regime was "a joint-stock company for the exploitation of French national wealth."

liberal opponents of Charles X agreed on his cousin, Louis Philippe, the Duke of Orléans, as a new king (see Table 24.2). Louis Philippe possessed moderate liberal credentials. He had initially supported the French Revolution and served in its armies; he then fled France during the Reign of Terror. His father had even served in the Convention and voted for the execution of Louis XVI. Louis Philippe had courted the liberal opposition during the restoration and convinced many of them that he represented "the republic in a single individual."

The July Monarchy. The Orleanist Monarchy, also called the July Monarchy (1830–1848), began with a liberalized constitution but few dramatic changes. Louis Philippe expanded voting rights from 90,000 to 170,000 (0.5 percent of the nation). He relaxed censorship but still tried to control the press. He brought new social strata into the government, but that chiefly meant that an elite of wealth was joined to that of the aristocracy. Louis Philippe did select many of his chief ministers, such as Thiers and the historian François Guizot from middle-class liberals, but they were cautious men who feared democracy. Guizot became the chief architect of the Orleanist version of the French compromise, and he achieved greater success than Louis XVIII in creating a liberal constitutional monarchy comparable to the government in Britain.

Industrialization and Unrest. Orleanist sympathies for business and industry had two important consequences. France experienced an important era of banking growth, railroad building, and industrial expansion after 1830, and the new regime deserves credit for its role in French industrialization and modernization. Simultaneously, however, the workers, shopkeepers, and students who had formed the crowds that drove Charles X into exile realized that the revolution of 1830 had made little difference in their existence. So France experienced further upheavals. In 1834, Louis Philippe needed a tenth of his army to control a silk weavers' strike in Lyon. In 1835, an embittered radical built an "infernal machine" of twenty-five rifles in an iron rack and fired them with a single trigger. He killed eighteen people in a royal procession but only bruised the king. While France remained prosperous, such assaults remained isolated events; in the mid-1840s, however, a severe depression led to yet another French revolution.

THE REVOLUTIONS OF 1830

The Belgian Revolution. Metternich once observed that when Paris caught a cold, Europe sneezed. In 1830, that meant revolutions across Europe (see Table 24.3). The sneezing began in August 1830 with unrest in the Belgian provinces of the Kingdom of the Netherlands. The French-speaking, Catholic population of Belgium was larger than the Dutch-speaking, predominantly Calvinist population of Holland. The king was Dutch, the capital was Amsterdam, officeholders were chiefly Dutch, and national institutions predominantly Dutch. As a Belgian nationalist asked in the summer of 1830,

TABLE 24.2 FRENCH ROYAL FAMILIES OF THE NINETEENTH CENTURY

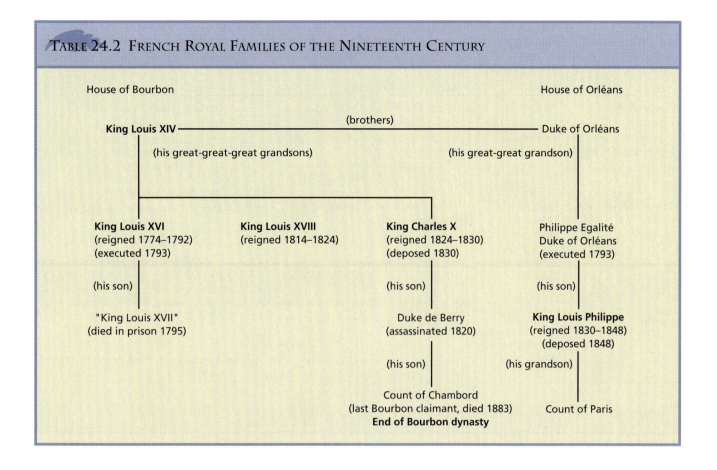

House of Bourbon   House of Orléans

King Louis XIV ————————————— (brothers) —————————————— Duke of Orléans

(his great-great-great grandsons)   (his great-great grandson)

King Louis XVI	King Louis XVIII	King Charles X	Philippe Egalité
(reigned 1774–1792)	(reigned 1814–1824)	(reigned 1824–1830)	Duke of Orléans
(executed 1793)		(deposed 1830)	(executed 1793)

(his son)   (his son)   (his son)

"King Louis XVII"		Duke de Berry	King Louis Philippe
(died in prison 1795)		(assassinated 1820)	(reigned 1830–1848)
			(deposed 1848)

(his son)   (his grandson)

Count of Chambord   Count of Paris
(last Bourbon claimant, died 1883)
End of Bourbon dynasty

"By what right do two million Dutchmen command four million Belgians?" The Belgian revolution of 1830 followed the French pattern: an insurrection of workers forced the issue, but the educated elite seized control of the situation. A national congress proclaimed Belgian independence in October 1830, but reluctant, middle-class Belgians supported the revolution only after the Dutch army bombarded Antwerp.

Belgian Independence. Although Louis Philippe gave the Belgians military assistance, they won their independence at the negotiating table. The British sympathized with Belgian nationalism but feared French influence. When the Belgians accepted a German prince (an uncle of Queen Victoria) as their ruler instead of a French king, British support assured Belgian independence. Belgium adopted a liberal constitution, more advanced than either the British or French constitutions, in 1831. It guaranteed freedom of the press and freedom of religion, then promised many other "inviolable" individual liberties (such as the right of association in unions), and it promoted secularization by establishing civil marriage. All of the great powers signed a treaty guaranteeing the independence and neutrality of Belgium.

Revolutions in Germany. Insurrection spread across Europe from France and Belgium. German anti-tax and food riots in 1830 revealed dissatisfaction with Metternichian Germany, but they produced no major revolution. A few smaller states, notably Saxony (1831), Brunswick (1832), and Hanover (1833), granted constitutions. Metternich considered granting a constitution in Austria, but Emperor Francis I insisted that he would tolerate "no innovation," so Metternich used the Germanic Confederation to stop the revolutions and impose a new series of repressive laws, known as the Six Articles.

Revolution in Poland. The revolution of 1830 reached Poland a few weeks after crossing the Rhine. The Polish November Rising did not seek a constitution (which already existed) but an end to Russian rule. It began with a Polish army mutiny provoked when the tsar prepared to send units to crush the French and Belgian revolutions. The Sejm declared Polish independence in January 1831. Nicholas decided that "the Poles must be made happy in spite of themselves" and sent a Russian army of 115,000 to teach them happiness. After the defeat of the Polish army at Ostrolenka and the fall of Warsaw, Poland was reunited with Russia.

TABLE 24.3 CHRONOLOGY OF THE REVOLUTIONS OF 1830

DATES	COUNTRY	REVOLUTIONARY EVENTS	OUTCOME
July 1830– August 1830	France	• Paris rebels over "July Ordinances" • King Charles X abdicates	• Revised constitution, 1830 • King Louis Philippe, 1830
August 1830– December 1832	Belgium	• Brussels and Belgium rebel against Dutch rule, 1830 • Belgium declares independence, 1830, and passes constitution, 1831	• Dutch army shells Antwerp, and French army expels Dutch army from Belgium, 1832 • London Conferences recognize Belgium, 1830–1832
September 1830– June 1832	German states Saxony, Hesse, Brunswick, and Hanover	• Rulers dethroned, 1830 • Constitutions granted, 1831	• Metternichian "Six Articles" restore old order, 1832
November 1830– February 1832	Poland	• Polish people rebel against Russian rule, 1830 • Sejm declares Polish independence, 1831	• Russian army suppresses revolt, 1831 • Polish constitution abolished, 1832
February 1831– January 1832	Italian states Modena, Parma, and Papal States	• Pope grants administrative concessions	
1831	Switzerland	• Demonstrations in Swiss cities, 1831 • Ten cantons adopt liberal constitutions, 1831–1833	• Austrian army suppresses revolt, 1831–1833

Question: Where did the revolutionaries of 1830–1831 have the most success?

Nicholas I then exacerbated Polish nationalism with his retribution: military tribunals convicted 80,000 Poles of rebellion, and the army marched them to Siberia in chains; a program of **Russification** ended all official use of the Polish language and closed the universities at Warsaw and Vilna; and the Polish army, the Polish constitution, and the Polish Diet were all abolished.

Revolutionary Violence in Britain. Historians do not typically list Britain among the revolutions of 1830. Nonetheless, Britain experienced revolutionary activity in 1830–1832. Rural violence, known as the Captain Swing Riots, began in Kent and covered southeastern Britain. Farm workers protested their poverty by burning hayricks and smashing the new threshing machines (the name Captain Swing came from the swinging flail used in hand threshing). More riots followed at Bristol, Nottingham, and Derby in 1831. The British may have avoided a revolution when Parliament conceded reforms that the liberal middle classes wanted, thus preventing the alliance of propertied classes with revolutionary workers that had toppled Charles X in France. Thomas Macaulay, an eloquent leader of British liberalism, warned Parliament that "great and terrible calamities" were imminent. The House of Commons, Macaulay insisted, must "reform that you may sur-

vive." Parliament did adopt a series of historic reforms, which perpetuated its image as a model of representative government—notably the Reform Bill of 1832 (for parliamentary reform), the Factory Act of 1833 (regulating hours and conditions), and the Abolition of Slavery Act of 1833.

Workers and Women Revolutionaries. The revolutions of 1830 are important for additional reasons beyond the struggles for national independence or liberal constitutions. They showed the beginnings of important new social movements that would shape the nineteenth century. The best known of these is the rise of working class radicalism; the events of 1830 (especially in Paris) provided a preview of subsequent risings. Other movements, such as the early campaign for women's rights, also received a stimulus from the revolutions of 1830 (see Document 24.8). In France, for example, the revolution led to the foundation of a feminist newspaper titled *La Femme Libre* (the Free Woman), which asked, "Shall we women remain passive spectators of this great moment for social emancipation that is taking place before our eyes?" The combination of the revolution of 1830 and the utopian socialism of men such as Charles Fourier (who promised women an equal role) encouraged French feminism in the 1830s and 1840s. This group included Jeanne Deroin, a self-educated teacher and journalist who later became the first French woman to run for office; Eugénie Niboyet, whose Protestant zeal for moral reform led her to socialism and then to feminism; and Flora Tristan, whose Fourierism made her an advocate of equal rights for women.

THE ADVANCE OF LIBERALISM IN BRITAIN (1801–1846)

Strength of Aristocracy. Historians usually cite Britain as the homeland of nineteenth-century liberalism and contrast it to the Metternichian reaction in central Europe. Truth exists in this contrast, but it should not obscure the strength of conservatism in post-1815 Britain. The landed aristocracy still dominated politics and society (see Table 24.4). They composed less than 0.002 percent of the population but received more than 29 percent of the national income. Dukes, earls, and viscounts filled the cabinet. The House of Commons was elected by less than 3 percent of the population. If liberal reforms succeeded in that house, the House of Lords still held an aristocratic veto. The **patronage system** allowed this elite to perpetuate aristocratic domination of army and navy commands, the diplomatic corps, high government posts, and the leadership of the Church of England.

Ireland. The English record on minority nationalism resembled that of Metternich and Nicholas I. An Act of Union of 1801 had absorbed Ireland into the United Kingdom, and the Protestant ascendancy of the eighteenth century had transferred land ownership and political power in Ireland to the Protestant minority. The

---

DOCUMENT 24.8

AN APPEAL TO WOMEN—FEMINISTS PROCLAIM A WOMEN'S REVOLUTION OF 1830

At the moment when all peoples are aroused in the name of Liberty and the proletariat calls for its own emancipation, shall we women remain passive spectators of this great moment for social emancipation that is taking place before our eyes?

Is our condition so happy that we ourselves have no demands to make? Until now woman has been exploited and tyrannized. This tyranny, this exploitation must cease. We are born free, like man, and half the human race cannot, without injustice, be in servitude to the other half. . . .

We demand equality in marriage. We prefer celibacy to slavery! . . .

Liberty, equality—that is to say, a free and equal chance to develop our faculties: this is the victory we must win, and we can succeed only if we unite in a single group. Let us no longer form two camps—that of the women of the people and that of privileged women. Let our common interests unite us.

From Bell, Susan G., and Offen, Karen M., eds., *Women, the Family, and Freedom: The Debate in Documents,* vol. 1 (Stanford, CA: Stanford University Press, 1983).

Question: Why should women participate in the revolution of 1830?

Catholic peasantry faced poverty and famine; suffering was so severe that some Irish nationalists have accused the British of genocide. Even British visitors to the Irish countryside were horrified by the suffering. Sir Walter Scott wrote of his 1825 visit: "Their poverty has not

FIGURE 24.11 *The British House of Commons.* Westminster Palace, the seat of the British Parliament, was a royal palace until the sixteenth century. A portion of it contained the House of Commons, shown here in the early 1800s. Note the distinctive physical arrangement of the seating, which divides Parliament into two parties who sit facing each other. Members of the cabinet are seated in the front row on the left, with their supporters behind them. The opposition sits on the right. Although this building was destroyed by fire, and the next structure by a German fire bomb in 1941, the distinctive seating survives.

TABLE 24.4 THE BRITISH ARISTOCRACY IN THE EARLY NINETEENTH CENTURY	
The Nobility	326 families, with 8,000 members, ranked in descending order of title
	4 princes and princesses of royal blood
	19 dukes and duchesses
	18 marquesses and marchionesses
	103 earls and ladies
	22 viscounts and viscountesses
	160 barons and baronesses
The Clergy (spiritual nobility)	26 archbishops and bishops
The Lesser Nobility	540 families—baronets—with hereditary titles "Sir" and "Lady"
	350 families—knights—with non-hereditary titles "Sir" and "Lady"
The Gentry	6,000 families of landowning "squires"
Gentlemen	20,000 families with inherited income and coats of arms

Question: Does the aristocracy seem an important portion of a country with a population of nearly 21 million in 1820?

been exaggerated: it is on the extreme verge of human misery." Twenty years later, conditions were even worse, and during the potato famine of 1845–1848, Ireland lost more than 25 percent of its population—experiencing more than 1 million deaths and losing 1.5 million refugees in a population of 8 million. Starving peasants ate their domestic pets.

Daniel O'Connell. Ireland needed a great defender, but the first parliamentary champion of Ireland could not take his seat in the House of Commons because British law excluded Catholics from office. Daniel O'Connell was a Jesuit-educated member of the Catholic gentry. He demanded the repeal of the Act of Union and the treatment of Ireland "not as a subordinate province, but . . . as a separate and distinct country." Lawful repeal was hardly likely. O'Connell could attract 100,000 people to a rally, but the House of Commons stood against him by 529–534. His experiences in the French Revolution, however, had convinced O'Connell of the horror and futility of revolution, and he continued to work for a parliamentary victory and reject violence (see Document 24.9).

The Reform Bill of 1832. Early nineteenth-century Britain was not yet a model of liberal democracy. However, Parliament accepted some important reforms between 1832 and 1846. Members did not democratize Britain, displace the governing elite, or encompass the radical agenda, but they made Britain the liberal leader of Europe. The reform of Parliament in 1832 illustrates the nature of British liberal reform. It had been discussed since the 1780s, but little had been achieved except outlawing the sale of seats in the House of Commons (1809). The Reform Bill of 1832, won by the moderate liberals in a Whig government, enfranchised the new business and industrial elite, expanding the electorate from 2.1 percent of the population to 3.5 percent. The bill abolished **"rotten boroughs"** such as Old Sarum, the ruins of a medieval town that had no residents but still sent two members to Parliament. This eliminated fifty-six constituencies whose 111 seats were transferred to manufacturing towns such as Birmingham and Manchester, neither of which had representation in Parliament before 1832.

Regulatory Legislation. Liberal industrial reforms were modest in their range, but they pioneered European regulatory legislation. A Factory Act of 1833 established a maximum working day in textile mills for young children (9 hours) and for teenagers (12 hours, or 72 hours per week) and planned for inspectors to enforce these terms. The Factory Act of 1844 extended the regulatory principle to women working in the textile mills, limiting their daily work to 12 hours and their Saturday work to 9 hours (a 69-hour week) and added the requirement of protective screening around machinery. Further regulatory legislation followed: a Mines Act (1842) prohibited underground work for boys younger than age 10 and for all women; the Ten Hours Act (1847) lowered the workday for women and teenaged boys to 10 hours (a 59-hour week) without provisions for enforcement. These laws have been controversial. Laissez-faire liberals opposed them, arguing that the state had no right to interfere with private business, and feminists have questioned the different treatment of men and women as paternalistic.

Emancipation of Religious Minorities. Another controversial form of liberal legislation involved the emancipation of the religious minorities—everyone who was not a member of the established Church of England. In 1815, only Anglicans could be elected to Parliament, command in the army, or enroll at Oxford; this intentional discrimination was created by a series of laws called the **Test Acts.** Unlike the French, who had promised religious freedom in the Constitutional Charter of 1814, or the Belgians, who provided a model of toleration in their Constitution of 1831, the British relaxed religious discrimination so slowly that it sur-

BRITISH CAMPAIGNS FOR THE RIGHTS OF MINORITIES

Daniel O'Connell Demands Catholic Emancipation, 1824

In the experimental despotism which England fastened on Ireland, her mighty appetite for slavery was not gorged; and because our unfortunate country was proximate, and polite in the endurance of the burden so mercilessly imposed, it was inferred that slavery could be safely extended far and wide, and an attempt was therefore made on the American colonies. . . . [T]he Americans—the God of heaven bless them for it!—shook off the thralldom. . . . The independence of America was the first blush of dawn to the Catholic, after a long and dreary night of degradation. . . .

In Ireland, we have been blamed for being agitators. I thank God for being one. Whatever little we have gained, we have gained by agitation, while we have uniformly lost by moderation. That last word is repeated so often that I am completely sick of it. I wonder some gentlemen do not teach a parrot to repeat it.

Baron Macaulay Pleads for Jewish Emancipation, 1833

When the question was about Catholic emancipation, the cry was "See how restless, how . . . encroaching, how insinuating is the spirit of the Church of Rome. See how her priests compass earth and sea to make one proselyte, how indefatigably they toil. . . . [W]ill you give power to the members of a church so busy, so aggressive, so insatiable?"

Well, now the question is about people who never try to seduce any stranger to join them, and who do not wish anybody to be of their faith who is not also of their blood. And now you exclaim, "Will you give power to the members of a sect which remains sullenly apart from other sects. . . . "

The honourable member [of parliament] for Oldham tells us that the Jews are naturally a mean race, a sordid race, a money-getting race; that they are averse to all honourable callings; that they neither sow nor reap; that . . . usury is the only pursuit for which they are fit; that they are destitute of all elevated and amiable sentiments. Such, Sir, has in every age been the reasoning of bigots. They never fail to plead in justification of persecution the vices which persecution has engendered. . . . We treat them as slaves. . . . We drive them to mean occupations. . . . We long forbade them to possess land. . . . We shut them out from all paths of ambition. . . . During long ages we have, in all our dealings with them, abused our immense superiority of force.

From Great Britain, Parliament, *Hansard's Parliamentary Debates*, April 17, 1833 (London: T. C. Hansard, 1833); and Peterson, Houston, ed., *The World's Greatest Speeches* (New York: Schuster and Son, 1953).

Question: Does O'Connell make an effective argument for agitation?

---

vived into the late nineteenth century. Parliament granted nonconforming Protestants (**"dissenters,"** such as Methodists and Presbyterians) equal opportunity in 1828. In the same year, County Clare (Ireland) forced a larger reconsideration by electing O'Connell to Parliament, although Catholics were still excluded. Many conservatives considered Catholic emancipation to be a "suicidal measure" and fought bitterly against it, but after a conservative hero, the Duke of Wellington, accepted the idea, the Tories made it law in 1829. The Catholic Emancipation Act did not end religious discrimination in British laws. The new oath of office still required M.P.s to swear "on the true faith of a Christian." This excluded Quakers (who would not swear), plus Jews and nonbelievers (who were not Christians). Parliament debated Jewish emancipation, but four separate bills failed between 1830 and 1836. Even when a London constituency elected a Jewish M.P. in 1847 (Lionel Rothschild, of the famous banking family), Parliament refused to seat him. The debate on Jewish rights showed how far Britain remained from the liberal ideal: a majority still believed in such anti-Semitic clichés as collective Jewish responsibility for the crucifixion.

Women's Rights. Another reform debate introduced Parliament to an issue that would demand attention for more than a century—women's rights. Although Queen Victoria sat on the throne, the women of her nation had no legal identity apart from their husbands or fathers. The law treated them as minor children and in some cases lumped them together with criminals and the insane. Husbands owned and controlled their wives' property. Husbands exercised legal control of children. A father sentenced to prison could specify that his children be raised by his mistress instead of the

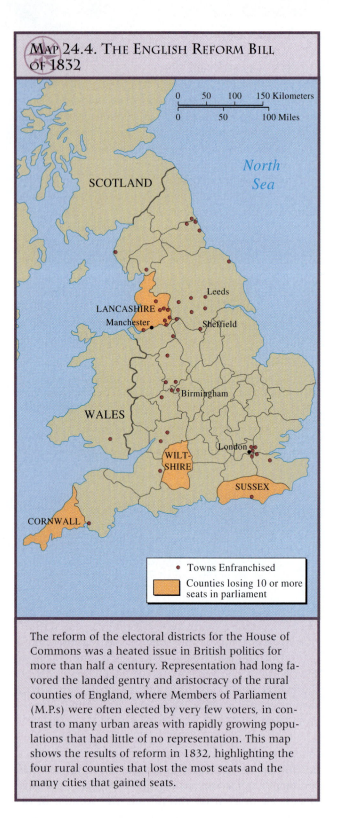

MAP 24.4. THE ENGLISH REFORM BILL OF 1832

North Sea

SCOTLAND

Leeds

LANCASHIRE

Manchester   Sheffield

Birmingham

WALES

London

WILT-SHIRE

SUSSEX

CORNWALL

• Towns Enfranchised

▮ Counties losing 10 or more seats in parliament

The reform of the electoral districts for the House of Commons was a heated issue in British politics for more than half a century. Representation had long favored the landed gentry and aristocracy of the rural counties of England, where Members of Parliament (M.P.s) were often elected by very few voters, in contrast to many urban areas with rapidly growing populations that had little of no representation. This map shows the results of reform in 1832, highlighting the four rural counties that lost the most seats and the many cities that gained seats.

children's legal mother. Cultural attitudes sustained this treatment, and most women accepted it. In a best-selling book of 1842, for example, a woman tried to teach young women "to be content to be inferior to men" (see Document 24.10). Queen Victoria gave

scant help to the campaigns to change such attitudes and laws. She once wrote: "The Queen is most anxious to enlist everyone who can speak or write to join in checking this mad, wicked folly of 'Women's Rights' . . . with all its attendant horrors. . . . [I]t is a subject which makes the Queen so furious that she cannot contain herself." Ironically, the force of her example as a strong woman simultaneously served to advance the cause of emancipation, which she opposed.

Caroline Norton, Infant Custody, and Married Women's Property. The first changes in the legal restrictions on women resulted from the work of an outraged individual instead of a women's movement. Caroline Norton, the wife of an M.P., had an intimate friendship with a Whig prime minister, Lord Melbourne. This so enraged her husband (a confessed adulterer) that he sued the prime minister for alienation of his wife's affections. Caroline Norton then discovered she would not be allowed any role or representation in the trial because the law considered her interests to be represented by her husband. The suit failed, and the Nortons separated (she could not even divorce her husband), with the law awarding custody of their children to the father. Caroline Norton thereupon launched a pamphlet campaign that led to the Infant Custody Act of 1839, giving mothers limited rights over their infant children to age seven. Her role in the evolution of women's rights did not stop with that victory. She came from a talented family (her grandfather was the dramatist Richard Sheridan), and she supported herself comfortably by writing. In the 1850s, her husband, now badly debt ridden, legally seized all of her royalties as his property, and Caroline Norton became a central figure in the campaign to obtain a **Married Women's Property Act.**

Repeal of the Corn Laws and Chartism. Other issues received more attention than women's rights, both from contemporaries and subsequent historians. The chief interest of middle-class liberals was the repeal of the Corn Laws, the high tariffs on imported grain that kept the price of bread high, the landowning class prosperous, and workers hungry. Repeal, however, would produce cheaper bread, healthier workers (who still relied on starches for 50 percent of their total calories), and business profits (because workers need not be paid so much if bread were not dear). To win repeal, British liberals (led by Manchester business interests) founded the Anti–Corn Law League, which became the international model of a political lobbying group. At the same time, a parallel campaign of working-class radicals known as the **Chartist movement** (named for the National Charter of 1838) outlined a democratic program: universal manhood suffrage, the secret ballot, the abolition of property qualifications to serve in Parliament, the payment of

FIGURE 24.12 *Poet Caroline Norton.* Caroline Norton was the granddaughter of the noted Anglo-Irish dramatist Richard Brinsley Sheridan, the author of such witty plays as *The School for Scandal.* Caroline demonstrated literary skill herself and helped support her husband, a barrister and M.P. named George Norton. When Caroline had a love affair with Prime Minister Melbourne, Norton sued him for alienation of affection, beginning a long series of legal proceedings in which Caroline Norton discovered how severely limited the rights of women were. She then used her considerable literary talents to champion two important feminist reforms, an Infant Custody Act (giving mothers some rights over their children) and a Married Women's Property Act (giving married women the right to own property, such as their own earnings).

salaries to M.P.s (so the poor could serve), the creation of equal-sized constituencies, and annual elections. Chartism produced huge public rallies on behalf of democracy and sent large petitions to Parliament, but it lacked the support of powerful insiders.

The fate of these two campaigns shows the cautious approach of European liberals. The leaders of the repeal campaign, John Bright (the M.P. son of a cotton mill owner) and Richard Cobden (a wealthy Manchester textile factory owner), succeeded by courting conservatives. They convinced moderate Tories, led by Sir Robert Peel (now dubbed Re-Peel), to adopt free trade as economic orthodoxy. The same coalition, however, would not accept Chartism. The Chartists included radicals such as Feargus O'Connor, a newspaper editor whose willingness to consider violence frightened both the conservative government and the liberals who claimed to be his allies. Although Chartism summarized most elements of modern democracy, it did not come close to adoption.

INTERNATIONAL LIBERALISM AND SLAVERY (1815–1848)

Servitude in Europe. Nothing better illustrates the strength of conservative regimes and the weakness of liberal reformers in Metternichian Europe than the persistence of serfdom in eastern Europe and slavery in European colonies. In 1700, virtually every state in Europe had practiced one of these forms of enslavement

FIGURE 24.13 *Trading in Slaves.* In this abolitionist broad-side showing English traders and their cargo, the text reads:
Fleecy locks and black complexion
Cannot forfeit Nature's claim
Skins may differ but affection
Dwells in Black and White the same

in some part of its territory. Britain had no serfs at home but had built slave economies in America. France had both serfdom at home and slavery in its colonies. Most of Russia, Prussia, and Austria lived in serfdom. During the Enlightenment, three important states abolished serfdom: Savoy, Baden, and Denmark. The abolition of serfdom during the French Revolution led to the spread of this idea to Switzerland, Poland, Prussia, and Bavaria. The French abolition of colonial slavery did not, how-ever, persuade other slave states to follow, although Denmark and Britain both ended their slave trades and the United States stopped the importation of new African slaves.

Abolitionism. **Abolitionists** thus faced a great task in 1815. They won a few victories between 1815 and 1848, but millions of people in Western civilization remained in slavery or serfdom throughout the age of Metternich. Alexander I abolished serfdom in his Baltic provinces, and the revolutions of 1830 ended serfdom in several German states. At the beginning of 1848, however, feu-dal obligations still restricted peasants in the Austrian and the Hungarian portions of the Hapsburg Empire, in

a dozen German states (including Saxe-Coburg-Gotha, the homeland of Queen Victoria's consort), in the Danubian provinces, and in Russia. The campaign against colonial slavery also made some progress yet left millions of people in bondage. The Congress of Vienna adopted a proclamation ending the slave trade in princi-ple, but the same treaties accepted the existence of colo-nial slavery and returned lost colonies to Denmark, France, the Netherlands, and Spain knowing that these were to be slave economies. Europe then ignored the agreement ending the slave trade.

Sugar and Slavery. The growing love of sweet foods demanded great quantities of cane sugar from Caribbean plantations, where sugar often accounted for 90 percent of the exports. Few people paused with the poet William Cowper, who wrote, "Think how many backs have smarted/For the sweets your cane affords." Thus, Bourbon France shipped more than 125,000 new slaves to the Caribbean between 1814 and 1831, and other slave states behaved similarly. In 1828 alone, 100,000 more African slaves were shipped to the Americas, despite the closing of the market in British colonies and the United States. Historians have calculated that one slave died for every ton of sugar shipped.

Emancipation in Latin America. The Spanish revolution of 1820 led to a victory for abolitionism when the Spanish colonies won independence. The revolutionaries did not plan to end slavery at first, but Simon Bolivar realized that liberating slaves would in-crease his chances of victory. Bolivar adopted military manumission (freeing the slaves in areas conquered) in his campaigns after 1815, and his speech to the rev-olutionary congress of 1821 led to a Manumission Law. Bolivar thus doubly earned the nickname *El Libertador* (the liberator) by freeing a region from Spain and a class from slavery, but slavery persisted in those Spanish territories that did not win indepen-dence. Coffee and sugar plantations in Cuba required more than 200,000 slaves and those in Puerto Rico, 17,500.

Abolition in British Colonies. Abolitionists won another important victory in British colonies. The British antislavery movement, led by Quakers and other Dissenters, had been gaining strength since the late eighteenth century. They found an effective leader in William Wilberforce, an M.P. and the head of an Anglican evangelical sect. Wilberforce founded the Antislavery Society with the aim of abolishing all slav-ery, and his movement flooded Parliament with peti-tions. In its first year, the Antislavery Society opened 220 local chapters and submitted 825 petitions, with hundreds of thousands of signatures. Abolitionism gained strength during the turbulent years of 1830–1832, when many members of Parliament feared a revolution in Britain. At that moment, the British Caribbean experienced another slave rebellion (the third since 1815). On Christmas Day 1831, more than 20,000 Jamaican slaves revolted. The British army quelled the revolt, but 14 whites and 200 slaves were killed and 312 more slaves were later executed. The message from Jamaica, alongside the news from Paris, Brussels, and the Kentish countryside, persuaded the Whig government to abolish slavery in the British colonies in 1833.

Conclusion

The history of the post-Napoleonic era in Europe (1815–1848) can be told from two contrasting perspectives: (1) by focusing on Prince Metternich and the conservative governments of the era, who sought to preserve and protect the Old Regime society of monarchy, aristocracy, and established religion, or (2) by focusing on the reformers and revolutionaries who challenged that order and sought to change or overthrow it. Thus, it can be described as age of general European peace (a generation without war among the great powers) and increasing economic prosperity (see Chapter 22), to the credit of the conservative governments, or it can be described as an age of widespread domestic conflict (expressed in oppression of minorities, repressive laws, and frequent rebellions), to their shame. The dominant character of the era was actually in the continuing clash of those who defended the old order and those who challenged it. The outcome of that contest is clear today, and the old order is largely gone, but it remained a dramatic contest in 1848.

Review Questions

- What were the objectives and accomplishments of the victors at the Congress of Vienna?
- How did the conservative governments of the age of Metternich try to maintain domestic order?
- What were the causes of social unrest and revolution in the age of Metternich?

- What were the causes and outcomes of the revolutions of 1830?
- To what extent was Britain genuinely different from the continent?

For Further Study

Readings

Cook, Chris, and Paxton, John, eds., *European Political Facts, 1789–1848* (London: MacMillan, 1981). Valuable lists of ministers and chronologies of major events.

Cook, Chris, and Stevenson, John, eds., *Modern European History, 1763–1991* (London: Longman, 1992). Includes short biographies of many figures.

Ford, Franklin, *Europe, 1780–1830,* 2nd ed. (New York: Addison-Wesley, 1989). A good statement of traditional views of the restoration era.

Gildea, Robert, *Barricades and Borders: 1800–1914,* 3rd ed. (Oxford: Oxford University Press, 2003). A volume in the *Short Oxford History of the Modern World*, providing the newest survey of political history of the nineteenth century.

Howsbawn, E. J., *The Age of Revolution, 1789–1848* (New York: Vintage, 1999). A readable and provocative survey of the era by a prominent Marxist historian.

InfoTrac College Edition

For additional reading, go to your online research library at *http://infotrac.thomsonlearning.com.*

Using Key Terms, enter the search terms
Liberalism   *Nationalism*

Using Subject Guide, enter the search terms
Congress of Vienna   *Metternich*

Web Sites

http://www.victorianweb.org/ A large and valuable collection of materials on Victorian Britain, founded by the National University of Singapore and maintained today at Brown University.

http://www.spartacus.schoolnet.co.uk/ The Spartacus educational site contains sections on slavery, the emancipation of women, and parliamentary reform.

http://www.departments.bucknell.edu/russian/chrono2.html A detailed chronology of Imperial Russian History, with some links to related sites, maintained at Bucknell University.

THE DEFENSE OF THE OLD REGIME, 1815–1848

	1815	1820	1825	1830	1835	1840	1845	1850

THE CONGRESS SYSTEM

1815: Peace of Paris
1814–1815: Congress of Vienna
1815–1830: The Congress System
Principle of Legitimacy Stated
Kingdom of Netherlands Created
Germanic Confederation Created
"Congress Poland" Awarded to Russia
Prussian Expansion in Rhineland
Holy Alliance
Quadruple Alliance against France
1818: Quintuple Alliance against Revolution
1820: Troppau Protocol to Suppress Revolution
1822: Congress of Verona against Spanish Revolution
1823: French Invasion of Spain

DOMESTIC UNREST AND LIBERAL-NATIONAL REVOLUTIONS

Britain:
1817: Coercion Acts Suspend Habeas Corpus
1819: Peterloo Massacre of Reform Agitators
Six Acts to Control Press and Meetings
Chartist Agitation
1836: Workingmen Association's "Charter"
1839: Chartist Riots
1842: Second Charter Calls
for Democracy

France:
1820: Assassination of Heir to Throne
Revolution of 1830   Labor Unrest in Cities
July Ordinances to Control Press
Barricades in Paris
Overthrow of Bourbon Dynasty
Foundation of Orleanist Monarchy
1831: Lyons Silk-Weavers Revolt
1834: Urban Riots in Paris and Lyons

German States:
Student Movement   Revolutions of 1830
1815–1819: *Burschenschaften* Flourish
1817: Wartburg Festival Celebrates Nationalism
1819: Karlsbad Decrees Regulate Universities
1830: Revolutions in Smaller States
1833: Revolution in Hanover

Chapter 25

EUROPE IN AN AGE OF NATIONALISM, 1848–1870

FOCUS QUESTIONS

- What were the aspirations of the revolutionaries of 1848, and which were achieved?
- How were similar aspirations for change expressed and achieved in Great Britain?
- How were great reforms accomplished in Imperial Russia?
- How did Italy achieve unity after the defeat of nationalism in 1848?
- How did Germany achieve unity after the defeat of nationalism in 1848?

On a chilly February morning in 1848, a 19-year-old university student in the German Rhineland town of Bonn sat in his attic room, hard at work. He was not working on his studies, of course, but was engaged in a typical act of the romantic age, writing an epic tragedy. A friend burst into the room and exclaimed that a revolution in Paris had driven King Louis Philippe from the throne, and the crowds had proclaimed a French republic. The student, Carl Schurz, a radical who dreamt of proclaiming a German republic, stopped writing and dashed to the street to join a demonstration of his friends. Schurz later became a respected leader of a republic, but that republic was the United States, where he fled into exile when the revolution of 1848 was crushed in Germany.

Chapter 25 looks at the turbulent epoch following the stability enforced by the Metternichian system. It begins with the revolutions of 1848, revolutions that swept up many youthful rebels like Carl Schurz and convulsed two dozen countries. The Old Regime—and conservatism—survived: Europe in 1870 was still governed by monarchs. Gradual liberalization was under way from Britain to Russia, but greater change came on the battlefield. Europe experienced five wars between 1854 and 1870: the Crimean War, the War of Italian Unification, and three wars for the unification of Germany that ended in a decisive struggle between France and Prussia. The modern states of Germany and Italy emerged from these conflicts.

625

THE REVOLUTIONS OF 1848

Overview of the Revolutions. The event that conservatives had feared for a generation (and which Marxists predicted for the next century)—widespread revolutions—swept Europe in 1848 (see Table 25.1). Governments fell in France, the Italian states, the German states, and the Austrian Empire; revolutionary turmoil lasted for 2 years. Liberals and nationalists initially won great victories. Constitutions, bills of rights, and even republics sprang up. Enthusiasm for national autonomy, independence, or unification was so universal that the revolutionary period became known as "the springtime of peoples." The alliance of nationalism and liberalism drove monarchs to abdicate and sent their ministers into exile. The king of France and, his chief minister, François Guizot (Ghee'-zoh) and the emperor of Austria and Metternich were all driven from the stage of international politics. By 1850, however, the revolutions of 1848 had collapsed in the face of military repression. Some constitutions survived, as did a few revolutionary accomplishments, but counterrevolutionary governments dominated the 1850s.

Origins of the Revolutions. Historians have explained the revolutions of 1848 in many ways. Liberals have stressed the repressive nature of government in the Metternichian era. More conservative historians have blamed the discontent of the **intelligentsia,** calling 1848 a "revolt of the intellectuals." Others have noted the willingness of the increasingly influential middle classes (such as bankers, manufacturers, merchants, and professionals) to accept revolutionary change because they had few attachments to the aristocratic regime. Marxists have pointed to the importance of the growing urban laboring class living in poverty, whereas social historians have examined **urbanization** (many cities doubled in size between 1800 and 1848) and found an array of problems in housing, public health, and crime.

Economic Origins of Revolution. One of the more convincing explanations of the origins of the revolutions has come from economic historians. In the late 1840s, Europe simultaneously experienced the last great **subsistence crisis** (in which people faced the danger of starvation) as a result of agricultural failure and the first severe **depression** of the industrial age. Crop failures meant expensive bread (which had also preceded the French Revolution); the downturn in the business cycle meant high unemployment.

The Agricultural Crisis of the 1840s. The agricultural crisis began with the **potato famine** of 1845, caused by a blight that destroyed much of the crop in 4

TABLE 25.1 THE REVOLUTIONS OF 1848

DATES	COUNTRY	REVOLUTIONARY EVENTS	OUTCOME
January 1848–May 1848	Naples	• Revolt in Sicily • Short-lived constitution and independence	• Revolt crushed
February 1848–June 1849	France	• Revolt in Paris • Abdication of the king • Formation of republic	• President Louis-Napoleon overthrows Second Republic
March 1848–August 1849	Piedmont-Sardinia	• Constitution granted • War declared on Austria	• Austrian victories force king to abdicate • Constitution endures
March 1848–August 1849	Austria	• Emperor abdicates • Metternich flees • Constitutions in Austria and Hungary • Nationalist uprisings	• Austrian and Russian armies suppress all revolutions
March 1848–July 1849	Vatican States	• Pope Pius IX grants constitution • Mazzini proclaims republic and pope flees	• French troops crush the republic and restore the pope
March 1848–August 1849	Venice	• Demonstrations drive out Austrian army • Proclaims republic	• Republic capitulates to Austrian army
March 1848–December 1848	Prussia	• Revolution in Berlin • King grants constitution	• King dismisses assembly, keeps constitution
March 1848	Lombardy	• Revolution in Milan forces Austrian evacuation	• Austria reconquers
March 1848–June 1849	Germany	• National assembly in Frankfurt abolishes confederation and debates German unity	• Assembly fails to create unity; dismissed by army

THE AGRICULTURAL CRISIS OF THE 1840s

Bread Riots in Berlin. Europe suffered one of the worst depressions of the industrial age during the middle and late 1840s. Unemployment reached frightening levels in many occupations, and crops failed in several regions. When crop failure was added to unemployment, Europe experienced widespread food riots. This German illustration depicts bread riots in Berlin in the spring of 1847 in which families sack a local bakery. Note the prominent role of women.

TABLE 25.2 THE POTATO FAMINE AND THE COLLAPSE OF IRISH POPULATION

YEAR	POPULATION OF IRELAND	POTATO CROP FAILURES	YEAR	POPULATION OF IRELAND	POTATO CROP FAILURES
1821	6.8 million	Partial crop failure	1848		Potato blight: famine
1822		Partial crop failure	1849		Potato blight: famine
1830		Partial crop failure	1850		Partial crop failure
1831	7.8 million	Partial crop failure	1851	6.6 million	Partial crop failure
1832		Partial crop failure	1860		Potato blight: famine
1833		Partial crop failure	1861	5.8 million	Potato blight: famine
1834		Partial crop failure	1862		Potato blight: famine
1835		Partial crop failure			
1836		Partial crop failure			
1837		Partial crop failure			
1839		Partial crop failure			
1841	8.2 million	Partial crop failure			
1844		Partial crop failure			
1845		Potato blight: famine			
1846		Potato blight: famine			
1847		Crop healthy but famine continues			

Courtesy of Dr. Kathryn A. Walterscheid, based on data from Keating, John, *Irish Famine Facts* (Dublin: Teasgasc, 1996); O Grada, Cormac, *The Great Irish Famine* (London: Macmillan, 1989); Woodham-Smith, Cecil, *The Great Hunger* (London: Penguin, 1962); and Clarkson, L. A., and Crawford, E. Margaret, *Feast and Famine: A History of Food and Nutrition in Ireland, 1500–1920* (Oxford: Oxford University Press, 2001).

Questions: Was there a correlation between famine and revolution in Ireland? Between unemployment, hunger, and revolution in Berlin? Were both Germany and Ireland centers of the revolutions of 1848?

years. Ireland suffered horribly from this catastrophe (see *The Agricultural Crisis of the 1840s*), and all regions that depended on the potato as a staple of the diet (such as the German states) had problems. Grain famines followed in 1846 and 1847, causing hardship for many people and mortal danger for some. In the Alsatian industrial center of Mulhouse, for example, the price of bread increased 67 percent during this crisis; in some German states, the price of staple foods rose between 250 and 450 percent. **Food riots,** such as the riot that ravaged Berlin in 1847, returned to the European political scene.

The Depression of the 1840s.

The depression of the 1840s multiplied the suffering and political agitation that grows when food does not. The member states of the Zollverein experienced a mild depression in textiles, but a collapse in business and banking. Between August 1847 and January 1848, 245 firms and 12 banks failed in Prussia alone. France experienced a fearful collapse of the textile industry; consumption of cotton fell by 30 percent, reducing output to the lowest level in the industrial era. The human meaning of such numbers was reduced income or unemployment while the price of food was skyrocketing. In Silesia, one of the hardest hit regions in Prussia, an estimated 75 percent of the population sought **poor relief.** In Paris, unemployment exceeded 40 percent in most trades and ranged between 50 and 75 percent in the worst cases. An angry Parisian radical summarized the situation: "While half of the population of Paris dies of starvation, the other half eats for two."

The Revolution of February 1848 in France.

The revolutions of 1848 began in the homeland of revolution—France. The constitutional monarchy of Louis Philippe had evolved into an alliance of moderate conservatives and moderate liberals that the premier, François Guizot, considered "the golden mean." Guizot's perfect balance allowed 0.7 percent of the population to vote in 1845 while preserving the status quo for the propertied classes of landlords and capitalists. During the winter of 1847–1848, his opponents tried a truly French form of protest: the banquet. Respectable middle-class critics of the regime organized large dinners and added inflammatory political oration to the menu. The **banquet campaign** culminated in a great banquet scheduled for Paris in late February 1848, but the Guizot government prohibited that assembly. Critics of the regime met nonetheless, to march to their locked banquet hall. Workers and students swelled the parade, and by nightfall **barricades**—the physical sign of rebellion in Paris—were again appearing in the streets. Louis Philippe dismissed Guizot, and when that did not placate the demonstrators, he fled the country. As Alexis de Tocqueville observed, it was an open question whether a revolution had overthrown the monarchy or the monarchy had collapsed. **Republicans,** led by a radical deputy named Alexandre Ledru-Rollin (Lay'-drew Row-lan'), seized the Hôtel de Ville (the town hall), proclaimed the Second Republic, and named a provisional government.

The Democratic Revolution in France.

The French Revolution of 1848 did not immediately fall into the hands of moderates as had the revolution of 1830. Republicans kept control but were soon divided between those who favored Ledru-Rollin's democratic program (a republican constitution, universal manhood suffrage, parliamentary government, a cabinet responsible to a majority) and social radicals who demanded help for workers and the poor. Ledru-Rollin had more support, so the provisional government concentrated on political change: it abolished "all forms of monarchy," all titles of nobility, and laws restricting political activity. Its most enduring accomplishment was to abolish slavery in the French colonies (for the second time); reforms soon overturned included the abolition of the death penalty and the abolition of censorship. In contrast, it attempted only one idea for what radicals called **the social republic,** Louis Blanc's **National Workshops.** The workshops were a relief plan for the unemployed. (The government's first assignment for relief workers was to remove the barricades.) Democratic elections

FIGURE 25.1 *Barricades in Paris.* One of the characteristic features of revolutions in modern France was the construction of barricades closing streets—mounds were constructed from nearby vehicles, trees, furniture from surrounding buildings, and paving stones from the streets. Barricades, such as the one shown here, gave revolutionaries a strong position to confront government troops, and the neighboring buildings could hide snipers or provide objects to drop on soldiers.

in April 1848 gave moderate republicans a large majority; shortly thereafter, it curtailed support for workers.

The June Days. The immediate consequence was a second insurrection in June 1848. Unemployed workers, fearful that the **counterrevolution** had begun and remembering how monarchists had stolen the revolution of 1830, called for popular action. Blanc summarized their position succinctly: "The bread or the bomb!" The republican government answered the demonstrations of "the June days" by giving General Louis Cavaignac dictatorial powers. Cavaignac unleashed the army on Paris and reduced unemployment with killings, arrests, and deportations. Others saw his accomplishment as ending a workers' uprising and preserving the republic, threatened by the workers' uprising. The assembly adopted a radical constitution in November 1848, but it had permanently alienated one of its strongest constituencies, the working class. The Second Republic managed to elect one president, but it never elected another.

The Spread of Revolution in 1848—"The Springtime of Peoples"

The March Revolutions in Germanic Europe.
The February revolution in Paris encouraged March revolutions in many places. It first stimulated demonstrations across the Rhine in Offenburg (Baden), where radicals demanded freedom of the press, freedom of assembly, and other basic liberties. This reform movement quickly spread through the towns of the Rhineland, such as Heidelberg and Bonn (see Document 25.1 later in this chapter). German radicals raised posters announcing that "[o]ur brothers in France have bravely led the way" and calling on Germans to follow. In many of the smaller German states, rulers quickly capitulated. Monarchs named liberal governments in Baden, Württemberg, and Saxony. The king of Bavaria abdicated. Revolution spread throughout the German Confederation in March 1848, changing central Europe so much that Germans thereafter described the pre-March (**Vormärz**) era as an antediluvian past.

The Revolution in Berlin.
The German revolutions of 1848 centered on three cities: Berlin, Vienna, and Frankfurt. In Berlin, liberal demonstrations led to the building of barricades. King Frederick William IV sent the army into the streets, and their brutality made the liberal cause more popular. The dead included several women, the "amazons of the German revolution" and harbingers of a women's rights movement. Frederick William considered all-out war on the revolution but capitulated to it instead of leading to a bloodbath. Within a few days, he abolished censorship, called elec-

tions for a new Diet (the United **Landtag;** Lahnt'-tag), and promised a liberal constitution. His "beloved Berliners," however, did not quit the barricades until he had withdrawn the army and joined them in saluting the bodies of the rebels.

The Nationalist Revolutions in Austria.
In Vienna, Prince Metternich also resisted demands for liberalization and soon had more problems than he could handle. The most ominous was the awakening of **nationalism** throughout the empire, especially Hungarian nationalism, led by Lajos Kossuth. Kossuth was a reforming journalist who had spent 4 years in prison for political crimes and had been elected to the Hungarian Diet in 1847. When the news from Paris reached Buda (still a separate town, across the Danube from Pest), Kossuth inflamed opinion with a patriotic speech demanding Hungarian **autonomy.** Revolutionary expectations grew rapidly, and by 1849, Kossuth was the leader of an insurrection that declared Hungarian independence. The Hungarian rebellion encouraged the other peoples of the Hapsburg Empire to seek freedom. In April 1848, Czech patriots led by the historian František Palacky won a separate Parliament for Bohemia. Similar claims quickly arose in Moravia (another Czech province), in Galicia (a predominantly Polish province in the north), in Dalmatia (a mixed Slavic province on the Adriatic coast), in Croatia (a southern province), and in Transylvania (a predominantly Rumanian province in the east). In the eastern half of the empire, these nationalist expectations were complicated by the claim of the Hungarians to exercise the full sovereignty previously held by the Austrians.

The Liberal Revolution in Vienna.
A liberal revolution also occurred in Vienna in March 1848. After 1 day of fighting between the army and demonstrators, Metternich fled to exile, leaving the Austrian government in the hands of a feeble-minded emperor, Ferdinand I, and an intimidated group of advisers. After 2 more days of demonstrations, Ferdinand promised press freedom, a constitution, and an Austrian Parliament; he and the royal court then abandoned Vienna to the liberals. The liberal revolutionaries achieved two lasting successes in Austria—the abolition of serfdom and the granting of civil rights to Jews, who were allowed for the first time to live in the cities, enter the professions, and to marry freely.

The German National Revolution.
The liberal victories in Prussia and Austria encouraged German nationalists to dream of a parallel triumph to unify the German states. They faced many problems, however, starting with disagreements among themselves. Many nationalists favored a comprehensive German nation-state—their "Germany" stretched "Wher'er is heard the

THE REVOLUTIONS OF 1848

A University Student in the Revolution of 1848

Carl Schurz (1829–1906) was a 19-year-old German university student in Bonn when the revolution of 1848 began. His radical politics during the revolution forced him to flee into exile, and he settled in the United States, where he became a lawyer and a political ally of Abraham Lincoln. His American career included serving as a Union general during the Civil War, senator from Missouri, a cabinet member, and editor of a New York newspaper. Had he not been born in Germany, he would probably have become a serious presidential candidate. His memoirs cover his youth in Germany, and the following excerpt describes the role of students in the revolution.

One morning toward the end of February 1848, I sat quietly in my attic chamber, working hard on my tragedy of Ulrich von Hutten, *when suddenly a friend rushed breathlessly into the room, exclaiming: "What, you sitting here! Do you not know what has happened?"*

"No; what?"

"The French have driven away Louis Philippe and proclaimed the republic."

I threw down my pen—and that was the end of Ulrich von Hutten. *I never touched the manuscript again. We tore down the stairs, into the street, to the market square, the accustomed meeting place for all the student societies after their midday dinner. Although it was still forenoon, the market was already crowded with young men talking excitely. There was no shouting, no noise, only agitated conversation. What did we want there? This probably no one knew. But since the French had driven away Louis Philippe and proclaimed the republic, something of course must happen here too. . . . We were dominated by a vague feeling as if a great outbreak of elemental forces had begun. . . .*

The next morning there were the usual lectures to be attended. But how profitless! The voice of the professor sounded like a monotonous drone coming from far away. What he had to say did not seem to concern us. The pen that should have taken notes remained idle. At last we closed our notebooks with a sigh and went away, impelled by a feeling that now we had something more important to do—to devote ourselves to the affairs of the fatherland. And this we did by seeking again as quickly as possible the company of our friends, in order to discuss what had happened and what was to come. . . . First in line, the convocation of a national parliament. Then the demands for civil rights and liberties, free speech, free press, the right of free assembly, equality before the law. . . .

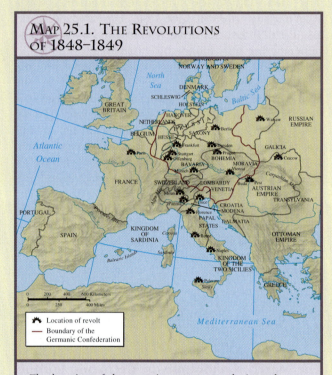

MAP 25.1. THE REVOLUTIONS OF 1848–1849

The location of the most important revolutions shown on this map suggests how important nationalism was in driving the revolutions. Although the revolution at Paris was a liberal-democratic revolution, and liberal principles contributed to many others, the great majority of the revolutions involved the national aspirations of Italians, Germans, or the minority peoples of the Hapsburg Empire.

Great news came from Vienna. There the students of the university were the first to assail the Emperor of Austria with the cry for liberty and citizens' rights. Blood flowed in the streets, and the downfall of Prince Metternich was the result. The students armed themselves as the armed guard of liberty. In the great cities of Prussia, there was a mighty commotion. . . . [W]e in the little university town of Bonn were also busy preparing addresses to the sovereign, to circulate them for signature, and to send them to Berlin. . . . [W]e too had our mass demonstration. A great multitude gathered for a solemn procession through the streets of the town. The most respectable citizens, not a few professors, and a great number of students and people of all grades marched.

German tongue!" This ***grossdeutsch*** (grohs-doyt'-sch; large Germany) nationalism was important to Austrians, who thought that Germany included the Hapsburg Empire. Grossdeutsch nationalism, however, threatened the non-German peoples of that empire, who feared their treatment as minorities in a larger and stronger German state. Pragmatic nationalists favored a ***kleindeutsch*** (kline-doyt'-sch; little Germany) solution that excluded Hapsburg lands or included only the German-speaking portion of them. Prussians, the rivals of

Austrians for leadership of Germany, generally favored *kleindeutsch* nationalism, because it meant either the exclusion or the dismemberment of Austria.

The Frankfurt Parliament.

The home of German nationalism during the revolutions of 1848 was the free city of Frankfurt, the seat of the German Confederation. Revolutionaries in many states called for a national Parliament to replace the confederation's Diet, and elections for the Frankfurt Parliament took place across Germany in April 1848. More than 800 members of this "parliament of professors" (although bureaucrats and lawyers were more numerous) met at the Paulskirche in Frankfurt. Under the leadership of a liberal lawyer from Hesse, Heinrich von Gagern (fon Gah'-gern), the Frankfurt Parliament produced fervent rhetoric, but not a treasury, an army, or effective leadership of German nationalism. Liberals wrote an idealistic **constitution** for unified Germany. It stripped the nobility of privileges, opening the bureaucracy and the officer corps to commoners; it abolished the pillory, branding, and other forms of corporal punishment; it proclaimed "The Fundamental Rights of the German People," including civil liberties; and it promised free state education. The pressure of nonvoting women "observer-delegates," championing the program of a German feminist newspaper, the *Frauenzeitung* (the *Women's Newspaper*), did not persuade the men of 1848 to add **women's rights.**

The Italian Revolutions.

Another dramatic chapter in the springtime of peoples began in the Italian states. Sicily rose against its Neapolitan monarch for its fifth insurrection in 18 years. When news of Metternich's fall reached northern Italy, revolutions broke out in Venice and Milan in the same week. In Venice, Daniele Manin (Mah-neen') proclaimed a republic. In Milan, barricades and street fighting known as "the five glorious days," expelled the Austrian garrison from Milan. This news inflamed northern and central Italy, and revolt spread to Parma and Florence, where rebels drove out pro-Austrian rulers and adopted constitutions. King Charles Albert of Piedmont-Sardinia supported the Italian revolution rather than face upheaval at Turin. When the Austrian army retreated from Milan, Piedmont declared war on Austria.

The Revolution in Rome.

The refusal of Pope Pius IX to join the Italian war led to a democratic insurrection at Rome in November 1848 in which the pope's prime minister and personal confessor were both killed. Pius fled Rome, and revolutionaries abolished his temporal powers. The Roman Republic attracted two of the heroes of Italian nationalism: Giuseppe Mazzini (Maht-zeen'-ee; the theorist who had created Young Italy) and Giuseppe Garibaldi (Gair-uh-ball'-dee; a Genoese radical who became the most famous general of the Italian

wars). Despite papal threats to excommunicate all voters, they organized the Roman Republic as a "pure democracy." One of Garibaldi's first acts was to abolish the **Jewish ghetto** and emancipate Roman Jews. Like the emancipation of the serfs in Germany, the emancipation of the Jews became one of the lasting accomplishments of the Italian revolution of 1848.

Victory of Counterrevolution.

In mid-1848, the age of Metternich seemed over at Turin, Milan, Venice, and Rome, as it did in Berlin, Vienna, and Frankfurt. Austrian revolutionaries planned to grant Lombardy its independence. There were some contrary trends, however. The suppression of the "June Days" in Paris showed the determination of the propertied classes to preserve order. Greater counterrevolutionary determination came from Russia, where Tsar Nicholas I earned the nickname of being "the gendarme (policeman) of Europe" for sending the Russian army to crush Polish and Hungarian revolutions. While constitutional governments were still being formed in Italy, an Austrian general dramatically changed events. Count Joseph Radetzky (Ra-debt'-ski), the Austrian chief-of-staff during the Napoleonic Wars, commanded the garrison driven from Milan. Radetzky regrouped his forces and crushed a combined Italian army in the battle of Custozza (Cous-toe'-zuh; July 1848). The outcome at Custozza (a village in Venetia) left few doubts: revolutionaries could not defeat determined professional armies, and they could not drive the Austrians from Italy.

1848 in Smaller States.

The French, German, and Italian revolutions were the most significant upheavals of 1848, but important changes occurred in many countries, often when alert monarchs voluntarily introduced liberal innovations. In Denmark, a new king (Frederick VII) came to the throne in 1848 and launched a reform program culminating in the Danish constitution of 1849. Frederick accepted constitutional limits on his powers, a strengthened Parliament, widespread manhood suffrage (15 percent of the population voted in 1850 versus 4 percent in Britain), guarantees of civil liberties, and the emancipation of religious minorities. In the Netherlands, King William II agreed to liberal constitutional revision. The Dutch liberals, led by a noted constitutional jurist, Johan Thorbecke, won new parliamentary authority at the expense of the throne, including the principle of ministerial responsibility to a majority in Parliament.

The Conservative Counterrevolution (1849–1852)

Most of the changes made during the revolutions of 1848 did not survive for long. Conservatives, typically led by army commanders like Radetzky, went on the counteroffensive in 1849 and reasserted principles of the Old Regime. Constitutions and reforms were nullified; royal authority reasserted. Pius IX summarized conservative sentiment in December 1848: "We . . . declare null and of no effect, and altogether illegal, every act" of the governments of 1848. The end of slavery in French colonies, the abolition of serfdom in Germany, and the emancipation of Jews in Austria and Italy remained a legacy of the revolutionary moment, but few of the governments and none of the republics of 1848 endured. The Italian republics at Venice and at Rome fell in 1849; the French Second Republic became so conservative that it helped to suppress the Roman Republic and was itself overturned in 1851. The nationalist fires of 1848 turned to ashes everywhere. By 1850, a Neapolitan radical concluded, "The concept of nationality sufficed to bring about the insurrection, but it was not enough to bring victory." Alexis de Tocqueville had foreseen such problems in early 1848. "In a rebellion, as in a novel," he said, "the most difficult part to invent is the end."

The Military Defeat of the Revolutions.
Armies ended most of the revolutions. A cheery German prince summarized the situation in late 1848: "It takes soldiers to put democrats in their place." Europe had briefly been led by revolutionaries: Ledru-Rollin in Paris, Mazzini and Garibaldi in Rome, Manin in Milan, and Kossuth in Buda. At the end of the day, the true victors were generals such as Cavaignac in France and Radetzky in Austria. By 1850, Kossuth would be in prison and his radical colleagues in exile. Manin spent the rest of his life in Paris, Ledru-Rollin and Mazzini found exile in London, and Garibaldi became a citizen of the United States and spent the early 1850s as a candle maker on Staten Island. Radetzky, meanwhile, ended his days as the governor-general of Lombardy and Venetia.

The Counterrevolution in Austria.
The military conquest of the revolution began in Prague in June 1848. The enraged army commander of Bohemia, Prince Alfred zu Windischgrätz (Vint'-ish-grahts), whose wife had been killed in riots there, ignored his orders and bombarded the city. Windischgrätz subdued Prague, then turned his armies on the Hungarians and took Buda and Pest a few weeks later. One month after the shelling of Prague, Radetzky (also resisting imperial instructions) defeated the Piedmontese at Custozza. Windischgrätz led a polyglot imperial army against Vienna in late October 1848 and shelled his third capital into submission. The army then peremptorily executed the leaders of the government, including Robert Blum, the leader of the Saxon revolution who was visiting Vienna as the vice president of the Frankfurt Parliament. The generals entrusted the Austrian Empire to a reactionary aristocrat, Prince Felix Schwarzenberg (Sh-varts'-en-berg), the brother-in-law

of Windischgrätz and a member of Radetzky's staff. Schwarzenberg and the generals arranged for the mentally deficient emperor Ferdinand to abdicate and for his son to renounce the throne. This brought the emperor's 18-year-old grandson, Franz Joseph, to the throne. The new emperor reigned for an exceptionally long time (from 1848 to 1916) and became the sentimental symbol of the twilight of an empire. In 1848, he was simply the pawn of counterrevolutionaries who asserted that he was not bound by concessions that he had not personally made.

The Counterrevolution in Prussia.
The military counterrevolution in Austria stiffened the will of King Frederick William IV of Prussia. A few days after the bombardment of Vienna, he again sent the army into Berlin. Under the shrewd leadership of a conservative minister of the interior, Baron Otto von Manteuffel (Mahn-toy'-full), the Prussian counterrevolution took a more moderate form than the Austrian reaction. The revolutionary Parliament was dismissed, but Manteuffel appeased liberals by persuading the king to grant his promised constitution with a bicameral legislature. Manteuffel understood that constitutions could be conservative weapons, too. Thus, the Prussian Constitution of 1850 restated the principle of divine right and protected the Hohenzollern family by reserving crown domains that produced a huge income. The Prussian army remained an unrestricted state within the state. The government depended on the support of the king, not the Parliament. The lower house of that Parliament (the Landtag) was elected by a broad manhood suffrage, but the electorate was subdivided (by taxes paid) into three classes, each of which elected one-third of the deputies.

The Counterrevolution in Frankfurt.
The defeat of the revolution in Vienna and Berlin doomed the national revolution at Frankfurt. In March 1849, the desperate delegates offered the crown of a unified Germany to Frederick William. Under pressure from conservatives, he rejected "a crown from the gutter," which would make him "the serf of the revolution." Austria and Prussia recalled their delegates, and the city of Frankfurt refused to host the assembly any longer. A rump Parliament briefly met in Stuttgart, but the Württemberg army disbanded it. Prince Schwarzenberg seized the opportunity to block all manifestations of nationalism. He particularly tried to kill the kleindeutsch vision of Germany, which elevated Prussia at the expense of Austria. His greatest victory came at the expense of the Prussians, who were obliged in 1850 to disavow a kleindeutsch union and to accept the re-creation of the Austrian-dominated German Confederation, in an agreement known to Austrians as the Olmütz (Owe'-l-muhts) Convention and to Prussians as the "humiliation of Olmütz."

The Counterrevolution in France. None of these counterrevolutionary victories was as startling as the events in France. General Cavaignac had demonstrated the limits of the French Revolution in June 1848 by using the army against protesting workers. In December 1848, he sought the presidency of the republic against Ledru-Rollin. French voters, however, spurned both men in favor of an aspirant monarch. Prince Louis-Napoleon Bonaparte, the nephew of Napoleon Bonaparte, won more than 70 percent of the votes; he had far greater name recognition in provincial France (where most voters were still illiterate), and his name stood for order after revolutionary chaos and it evoked the glorious triumphs of his uncle.

Louis-Napoleon Bonaparte. Louis-Napoleon proceeded to create an authoritarian regime. In short order, Louis-Napoleon reintroduced censorship, restricted universal suffrage, outlawed political clubs, gave the Catholic Church control of French education, and arrested radicals. One of the founders of French feminism, Jeanne Deroin (De-row-ann'), had dared to run for office in 1849, after the assembly had laughed at her petitions; Louis-Napoleon restored order by throwing her in prison. He also demonstrated how far the republic had changed from its radical origins by sending the French army to Rome to fight on the side of counterrevolution and restore Pope Pius IX to temporal authority.

The French Second Empire. By December 1851, the Second Republic cast only a pale shadow of the liberal-democratic program of 1848, and President Bonaparte ended the pretense by overthrowing the republic in a military **coup d'état** (coo day-tah'), an echo of his uncle's destruction of the first republic in 1799. The echo continued when President Bonaparte created a Second Empire with himself as Emperor Napoleon III (honoring Napoleon and his son, who never reigned, as predecessors). The French Second Empire (1852–1870) began as a counterrevolutionary regime well suited to the Europe of Nicholas I, Schwarzenberg, and Pius IX. Yet Napoleon III differed from them in significant ways. He shaped France into a unique blend of Caesarism and modern democracy. The French Second Empire was an authoritarian regime—at its best a modern form of enlightened despotism, at its worst a hint of the modern police state. On one hand, Napoleon III gave a significant boost to the modernization of the French economy

FIGURE 25.2 *Soldiers Clearing the Streets during the Coup of 1851.* Louis-Napoleon Bonaparte had twice attempted a coup d'état against the regime of King Louis Philippe, but his efforts had resembled a comic opera more than the military campaigns of his uncle. In 1851, however, Louis-Napoleon (then President of France) executed a coup so successful that it long served as a textbook illustration of how to seize power. This scene depicts soldiers patrolling the streets on the night of the coup, making certain that no crowds gather to demonstrate or attempt to build barricades.

and a great assist to the industrialization of France, while remaining sensitive to the condition of workers, whose rights he expanded. On the other hand, a Law of Suspects (1858) allowed the government to banish or imprison anyone previously convicted of a political offense, including virtually all of the leaders of 1848; under this act, more than 500 republicans were transported to Algeria. Although Napoleon III tried to reshape his regime into a "liberal empire" in the 1860s and allowed an opposition party, republicans never forgot that he was the "despicable assassin of the republic." No one branded him more effectively than Victor Hugo (Hew'-go) who sat in the legislature of 1848. From exile, Hugo published a political diatribe entitled *Napoleon the Little,* taunting him as "this mummer, this dwarf, this stunted Tiberius." A fairer judgment would remember both sides of this complex man; but few understood him and many agreed with Bismarck's remark that Napoleon III was "the sphinx without a riddle."

THE LABOR MOVEMENT AND THE RISE OF SOCIALISM (1791–1869)

Even while victorious counterrevolutionaries dreamt of restoring the old order, the social and economic transformation of industrialization created great pressures for the social changes that they resisted. One of the foremost consequences of industrialization was the rise of a labor movement expressing the needs of the **industrial working class** (often known as the **proletariat**). The dreadful working and living conditions associated with industrialization were well known by midcentury, but neither conservative governments (typically dominated by great landowners) nor their liberal opposition (typically dominated by industrialists and manufacturers) did much to address the problem. Consequently, labor unrest and labor movements grew. These took two different forms: (1) associations of workers in the **trade unions,** seeking to persuade employers to grant better wages and working conditions, and (2) political movements, usually socialist, seeking to create governments that would govern in the interest of the laboring class.

Trade Unionism. Trade union movements grew slowly because they were illegal. In some countries, the legislation abolishing the monopolies of medieval guilds (such as the Chapelier [Shah-pell-ee'-a] Law of 1791 in France) also blocked unions. The traditional privileges of guilds survived in parts of Europe, however. German governments were still trying to legislate the principle of *Gewerbefreiheit* (guh-vair'-buh-fry-height; the freedom to practice an occupation) in the 1850s; Denmark, Sweden, and Russia adopted such laws in the 1860s. In other countries, legislation explicitly banned trade unions, as a series of **Laws of Association** did in France and Italy or **Combination Acts** (regulating the right of people to join in any form of association) did in

Britain. Changes in the Combination Acts in 1824–1825 permitted the first legal unions, although they could neither strike nor restrain business. Other laws also restricted workers, as the Tolpuddle martyrs discovered in 1834, when they were convicted of the crime of taking a secret union oath. Nonetheless, British trade unionism grew during the 1840s, and the prosperity of the 1850s accelerated this growth. The Amalgamated Society of Engineers, a union of mechanics founded in 1850, created a model of successful organization, based on collecting dues and offering services. Such unions of skilled labor (sometimes called **the labor aristocracy**) flourished during the 1850s and 1860s, culminating in a potentially powerful alliance of unions—the **Trades Union Congress**—founded in 1868. Without the right to organize freely and to strike against their employers, the labor movement remained moderate (see Document 25.1) and worker's aspirations (such as the 40-hour workweek—an idea that originated in the Australian labor movement—or paid annual vacations) remained a distant dream.

Trade Unions on the Continent. Continental Europe trailed Britain in labor organization. The revolutions of 1848 stimulated a German labor movement, but few organizations survived the political repression of the 1850s. It was the late 1860s before stronger unions appeared in Germany, and these were created by the workers' political movement. A variety of workers' societies, such as traditional journeymen's societies *(compagnonnages),* competed in France despite the Chapelier Law. Napoleon III felt paternalistic sympathy for French workers and approved liberal laws of 1864–1868 legalizing their associations. When he died in exile years later, representatives of labor unions were the only French delegation at Napoleon III's funeral.

Varieties of Socialism. A second workers' movement, focusing on political activity, developed alongside trade unionism. The early socialist movement encompassed a wide range of political doctrines, from the **radical democracy** of Chartism to the **anarchism** (the abolition of all government) of Pierre-Joseph Proudhon (Pru-don') and Mikhail Bakunin (Bah-kew'-nin). Socialism began to emerge as the dominant political philosophy of the workers' movement in the 1860s, and **revolutionary socialism,** especially **Marxism,** became the most discussed form of socialism, although it was always in competition

FIGURE 25.3 *Anti-Unionism.* This British cartoon from the 1830s is an attempt to discredit the labor movement. The scene shown here is an upper-class version of how workers behave when given time off. Given Sundays off, they go to gin palaces rather than church (all three buildings are labeled "gin") and spend their money getting fall-down drunk, fighting, and ignoring their ill-clad children. Respectable society looks on in amazement and disgust.

with varieties of nonrevolutionary socialism, best known as **evolutionary socialism.**

Marxism. Karl Marx was born to a comfortable middle-class Jewish family that had converted to Lutheranism because of the legal requirements for Marx's father to practice law in Trier. At the University of Berlin, Marx became an enthusiastic student of G. W. F. Hegel (Hay'-gl), the German idealist philosopher who deemphasized the individualism of liberal philosophy and taught the preeminence of the state. Marx was deeply impressed with Hegelianism and adopted many of Hegel's concepts of the state and power, as well as the **dialectic method** of argument (in which an idea, or a **thesis,** is always in conflict with its **antithesis** until they merge into a **synthesis**). Marx planned to become a philosophy professor, but his membership in a radical student organization during the age of Metternich closed that career to him. A brief stint as a journalist, which introduced Marx to industrial conditions, ended when censors closed his newspaper. Marx, already radicalized, began a life in exile. In France, he learned revolutionary politics; in London, he studied capitalist economics. By the 1850s, Marx had already published several socialist works, and he had collaborated with Friedrich Engels (a factory owner's son) on *The Communist Manifesto* (1848), a concise statement of the **theory of class struggle** (see *Revolutionary Socialism and Evolutionary Socialism*). They wrote: "The history of all hitherto existing society is the history of class struggles." Only by overthrowing bourgeois society could peasants and industrial workers achieve social justice—hence their slogan, "Workers of the world, unite!" By the 1860s, Marx—still in exile—was seeking to unite and direct European socialism through the International Workingmen's Association, founded in London in 1864. This association (later called the First International) assembled leaders of the workers' movement in annual congresses and kept them informed of events in other countries.

Evolutionary Socialism. Marxist socialism was only one variant in the emerging working-class political movement of the 1860s. Although it was the strongest version of revolutionary socialism (which accepted the violent overthrow of the government as the means to power), it faced much competition from advocates of **evolutionary socialism** (who believed that democratic elections would lead to socialism and therefore opposed violent revolution). Marx had little influence in Britain and was virtually unknown in France. He was not even dominant in his native Germany, where Ferdinand Lassalle (Leh-sal'), and later August Bebel (Bay'-bul), had more influence. Lassalle, a successful lawyer and spellbinding orator, had organized workers at Leipzig in 1862 and created the Universal German

Workingmen's Association in 1863. His theory of **state socialism,** in which governments would adopt socialist programs without being overthrown by a Marxist revolution, initially appealed to German workers, but Lassalle died in a duel in 1864. A more radical workers' party appeared in 1868, organized by Bebel and Wilhelm Liebknecht (Leeb'-keh-nekt). Their first party congress, held at Eisenach (Eye'-suh-nahk) in 1869, showed that socialism remained close to radical republicanism; the Eisenach program sought democratic reforms, not revolution.

DOCUMENT 25.1

PROGRAM OF AN EARLY TRADE UNION

A *draper* is a dealer in cloth, such as the cloth that might be used for curtains (or "drapes"). Sometimes the term also included dealers in clothing and other dry goods. As a consequence of the industrialization of textile manufacturing, there was a great expansion of the drapers' business and rapidly changing conditions of work. Drapers consequently made one of the first efforts to found a union during the industrial age. The following is the program of the drapers' union of 1845 in Britain.

The object of this association shall be to obtain an abridgment of the hours of business in the linen and woolen drapery, silk mercing, hosiery, haberdashery, lace and other trades, with a view to the physical and moral and intellectual improvement of those engaged therein:

1. by appealing to the public to abstain from shopping in the evening, by means of public meetings, sermons, lectures, tracts, and the press.

2. by representing to employers the evils arising from late hours of business and the advantage which would accrue from closing their shops at an early hour.

3. by impressing upon the minds of assistants the importance of using the time at their disposal in the improvement of their mental faculties, by the aid of literary institutions, lectures, and libraries, and by urging upon them the desirableness and advantages of industry in business, correctness of behavior, and intellectual acquirements.

4. by employing only such means as are of a peaceful and conciliatory nature, and by refusing to sanction or adopt any measure having a tendency to coerce or injure the interests of employers....

From "Rules of the Metropolitan Drapers' Association," in Schaefer, Ludwig, et al., eds., *Problems in Western Civilization* (New York: Scribner's, 1965).

Question: Does the drapers' union seem like a revolutionary organization or to be making radical demands?

REVOLUTIONARY SOCIALISM AND EVOLUTIONARY SOCIALISM

Marx. Karl Marx initially sought an academic career and studied philosophy under Hegel at the University of Berlin. When his radical politics blocked that career, Marx turned to journalism, and in 1842, he became the editor of the *Rheinische Zeitung,* published at Cologne. In this image, the 24-year-old editor (the bearded man holding a newspaper) is shown in the pressroom of his newspaper. When he published an attack on censorship in 1843, the government closed the newspaper.

Marx and Engels' Communist Manifesto

An international association of workers, meeting at London in November 1847, voted to draft a statement of its program and entrusted this task to Karl Marx and Friedrich Engels. Their Manifesto was originally written in German, translated into French and published in 1848 (without much impact on the revolutions of 1848), and was subsequently printed in many languages: an English edition appeared in 1850, and a Russian edition appeared in 1869.

The history of all hitherto existing society is the history of class struggles. . . . The bourgeoisie, historically, has played a most revolutionary part. The bourgeoisie . . . has pitilessly torn asunder the motley feudal ties that bound man to his "natural superiors" . . . [but] the modern bourgeois society, that has sprouted from the ruins of feudal society, has not done away with class antagonisms. It has but established new classes, new conditions of oppression, new forms of struggle in place of the old ones. . . . The epoch of the bourgeoisie possesses, however, this distinctive feature: it has simplified class antagonisms. Society as a whole is more and more splitting up into two great hostile camps, into two great classes directly facing each other: Bourgeoisie and Proletariat. . . .

All property relations in the past have continually been subject to historical change. . . . The French Revolution, for example, abolished feudal property. . . . In this sense, the theory of the Communists may be summed up in the single sentence: Abolition of private property. . . .

Do you mean the property of the petty artisan and of the small peasant, a form of property that preceded the bourgeois form? There is no need to abolish that. . . . Communism deprives no man of the power to appropriate the products of society; all that it does is to deprive him of the power to subjugate the labor of others by means of such appropriation. . . .

MID-VICTORIAN BRITAIN (1846–1869)

If industrial conditions were heading toward revolution, the revolution would logically be expected to come in Great Britain, the birthplace of industrial society. The British census of 1851 showed the changes associated with the industrial revolution: more than 50 percent of the population lived in towns and cities, making Britain the first urban society in history. Comparative data show how unusual Britain was: the French census of 1851 found only 25.5 percent of the population in towns, the Spanish figure (1857) was 16.2 percent, and the Austrian figure (1857) was 8.5 percent.

Britain in 1848. Despite the pressures of urbanization and industrialization, Britain had avoided revolution in 1848. Historians have explained this in many ways.

[I]n the most advanced countries the following [program] will be pretty generally applicable:

1. Abolition of property in land and application of all rents of land to public purposes.

2. A heavy progressive or graduated income tax.

3. Abolition of all right of inheritance. . . .

5. Centralization of credit in the hands of the State, by means of a national bank with State capital and an exclusive monopoly.

6. Centralization of the means of communication and transport in the hands of the State.

7. . . . [F]actories and instruments of production owned by the State. . . .

8. Equal liability of all to labor. . . .

10. Free education for all children in public schools.

The Communists everywhere support every revolutionary movement against the existing social and political order of things. . . . The Communists disdain to conceal their views and aims. They openly declare that their ends can be attained only by the forcible overthrow of all existing social conditions. Let the ruling classes tremble at a Communistic revolution. The proletarians have nothing to lose but their chains. They have a world to win.

From Marx, Karl, and Engels, Friedrich, *The Communist Manifesto* (New York: Rand, 1927).

The Eisenach Program of German Socialism, 1869

The leading voice of German socialism for most of the late nineteenth century was August Bebel, the co-founder of the socialist party at Eisenach in 1869 and the party's parliamentary leader for nearly a half-century. The founding program, known as the Eisenach Program, stands in dramatic contrast to the revolutionary socialism of Karl Marx, through its fundamental commitment to democracy and reform by democratic means.

1. Granting universal, equal, direct, and secret vote to all males over 20 years of age for the (national) parliament, the legislatures of the individual states . . . etc. The elected representatives should receive adequate compensation.

2. Introduction of direct legislation [that is, initiative and veto right] by the people.

3. Elimination of all privileges based upon social rank, property ownership, birth, and religious belief.

4. Establishment of a popular militia in the place of a standing army.

5. Separation of church and state and separation of education from the church.

6. Compulsory education at the level of primary schools and free instruction in all public educational institutions.

7. Independence of the judiciary, introduction of the jury system and courts of trade disputes, introduction of public and oral court proceedings, and free legal aid.

8. Elimination of all indirect taxes and introduction of a single direct progressive income and inheritance tax.

9. Elimination of all laws regarding the press and the right to free association; introduction of a standard working day; limits on women's work and prohibition of child labor.

10. State support for cooperatives and state credits for independent producers' cooperatives with democratic guarantees.

From *The Eisenach Program*, reprinted in Steenson, Gary P., "Not One Man! Not One Penny!" German Social Democracy, 1863–1914 (Pittsburgh: University of Pittsburgh Press, 1981).

Question: What is the greatest difference in these two programs?

Some have stressed the role of working-class religions (especially **Methodism**) that inculcated values such as the acceptance of one's social position and obedience to one's superiors. Charles Dickens put this into a prayer: "O let us love our occupations . . . and always know our proper stations." Others have extended this view to stress the importance of **deference** to the leadership of the upper class. As the constitutional scholar Walter Bagehot (Badg'-ut) put it, "The English constitution in its palpable form is this: the mass of the people yield obedience to a select few." Economic historians have insisted that the answer is simpler: the working-class standard of living was steadily improving. A more traditional view stresses the importance of timely, but gradual, liberal reforms.

Irish Nationalism. Yet mid-Victorian Britain faced problems. The kind of nationalist rebellion that struck

BARBARA BODICHON ON THE STATUS OF MARRIED WOMEN, 1854

In an effort to awaken support for women's rights, Barbara Bodichon tried to educate the public about the treatment of women in English law. She stated the situation bluntly.

A man and wife are one person in law; the wife loses all her rights as a single woman, and her existence is, as it were, absorbed in that of her husband. He is civilly responsible for her wrongful acts, and in some cases for her contracts; she lives under his protection or cover, and her condition is called coverture.

In theory, a married woman's body belongs to her husband; she is in his custody, and he can enforce his rights by a writ of habeas corpus; but in practice this is greatly modified. . . .

A man may not lend, let out, or sell his wife; such transactions are considered as being against public decency, and they are misdemeanors.

A wife's personal property before marriage [such as stock, shares, money in hand, money at bank, jewels, household goods, clothes, etc.] becomes absolutely her husband's, unless when settled in trust for her, and he may assign or dispose of it at his pleasure, whether he and his wife live together or not. . . .

Neither the Courts of Common Law nor of Equity have any direct power to oblige a man to support his wife. . . .

Money earned by a married woman belongs absolutely to her husband. . . .

The legal custody of children belongs to the father. During the lifetime of a sane father, the mother has no rights over her children, except limited power over young infants, and the father may take them from her and dispose of them as he sees fit. . . .

From Bodichon, Barbara, "A Brief Summary in Plain Language of the Most Important Laws of England Concerning Married Women," in Hollis, Patricia, ed., *Women in Public, 1850–1900. Documents of the Victorian Women's Movement* (London: Unwin Hyman, 1979).

Question: What are Bodichon's strongest points in showing the need for women's rights?

central Europe might have occurred in Ireland, for the Irish problem was as severe as the plight of Czechs or Hungarians. The potato blight of the 1840s led to such a terrible famine that more than 1 million people died and another 1 million fled the country. The British responded by passing repressive laws. When the moderate Daniel O'Connell died in 1847, the leadership of Irish nationalism passed briefly to the Young Ireland movement, founded on the Mazzinian model by William Smith O'Brien. O'Brien tried to raise an insurrection at Tipperary in July 1848, but he failed and was sentenced to penal **transportation** to Tasmania (being

transported to a penal colony in Australia). In the 1850s, one of O'Brien's associates, James Stephens, founded the Irish Republican Brotherhood as a secret society dedicated to armed rebellion. Stephens's republican rebels became better known as the **Fenians** (Fee'-nee-uns; honoring ancient Gaelic warriors, the *Fianna*). The Fenians planned an uprising in 1867 (for which they pioneered fundraising among Irish immigrants in America) but were thwarted by informers.

Emancipation of Minorities. In domestic affairs, Parliament advanced cautiously toward liberal-democratic government. This evolution extended civil rights to British Jews through the Jewish Disabilities Act of 1858, a generation after Catholic emancipation. The House of Lords had blocked Jewish (and Atheist) emancipation on the argument that Britain was a Christian state and must therefore have a Christian Parliament. In typical British gradualism, Jewish emancipation provided only equal political rights; Oxford and Cambridge remained closed to them until a further reform in 1871.

Barbara Bodichon and Women's Rights. The women's rights campaign also made historic progress during the 1850s. Parliament had briefly addressed this subject after Caroline Norton's struggle to win the Infant Custody Act of 1839, but no government adopted the principle of women's rights. In the 1850s, another energetic woman with high political connections, Barbara Bodichon (Bow'-dee-shon), resumed the campaign for the rights of married women. Bodichon had been one of the first women to attend Bedford College at the University of London. She managed her own school for women, and there encountered the burden that the law placed on a married woman. Bodichon published a pamphlet to educate the public: *A Brief Summary in Plain Language of the Most Important Laws of England Concerning Married Women* (1854). "A man and wife are one person in law," she explained. "The wife loses all her rights as a single woman, and her existence is . . . absorbed in that of her husband" (see Document 25.2). That loss of legal identity was so complete that if a woman had her purse stolen, the thief could be arrested only for stealing the property of her husband. Bodichon undertook a **petition campaign** and gathered tens of thousands of signatures that encouraged Parliament to take a first (and naturally, partial) step toward equal rights, the **Married Women's Property** Act of 1857. Encouraged by this progress and by the Matrimonial Causes Act of 1857 (which created Britain's first **divorce** courts), Bodichon devoted her resources to financing *The Englishwoman's Journal* (1858), which became the leading voice of British feminism.

Electoral Reform. The most debated mid-Victorian reform was electoral. Radicals had been disappointed in 1832, and in the 1850s, they mounted another campaign to expand the electorate. John Bright produced a list of seventy-one constituencies with a population equal to metropolitan Manchester, noting that those boroughs held 117 seats in Parliament to Manchester's 3. Several bills to expand the franchise or to redistrict seats failed during the next decade, until reform won a surprising champion—Benjamin Disraeli (Diz-ray'-lee), a leader of the Tory Party. Disraeli concluded that "change is inevitable" and decided that it would be best if a conservative government arranged this "leap in the dark."

The Reform Bill of 1867.

Disraeli's Reform Bill of 1867 doubled the electorate from approximately 1 million (4.2 percent of the population) to 2 million. It enfranchised urban males who paid £10 per year in rent. It also adjusted the overrepresentation of England (which held 72 percent of the seats in the kingdom) compared with Scotland, Wales, and Ireland, and it partly corrected the underrepresentation of cities. Disraeli's reform bill still stopped far short of full democracy: it denied rural workingmen the vote and explicitly excluded women by giving the vote to "every man." The parliamentary debate included the first introduction of women's suffrage, however, championed by the liberal philosopher John Stuart Mill. Mill advocated women's suffrage in a speech insisting that the denial of women's rights was "repugnant to the . . . principles of the British constitution." His motion received seventy-three votes in a house of 658 members, but that defeat led to the formation of suffrage societies in Birmingham, Manchester, and Edinburgh within the year. Two years later, Parliament accepted a partial form of **women's suffrage** when the Municipal Corporations Act (1869) allowed single women to vote in municipal elections.

THE CRIMEAN WAR (1853–1856)

Between 1815 and 1853, the Metternichian balance of power had given Europe a degree of stability in international affairs and a general peace among **the great powers** Britain, France, Prussia, Austria, and Russia. They had often fought smaller states and revolutionary governments but not each other since the defeat of Napoleon.

Power Politics in 1850.

The Crimean War was fought around the Black Sea (chiefly on the Russian peninsula of the Crimea). It demonstrated two important changes in the post-Metternichian world. First, the public discussion of international politics had changed. **Ideology** (such as monarchism versus republicanism) no longer defined relations—the politics of self-interest did. The Metternichian system had (in theory) united the great powers to defend the **status quo;** during the Crimean War, the great powers were candidly motivated by national interests, and they were willing to fight for them. As the nationalist foreign secretary of Britain, Lord Palmerston (Pahl-mer-stun'), told Parliament, "We have no eternal allies and we have no perpetual enemies. Our interests are eternal and perpetual, and these interests it is our duty to follow."

Armies and Warfare in the Industrial Age.

The second change in post-Metternichian power politics had more frightening implications: the Crimean War gave the world its first glimpse of war in the industrial age, teaching lessons that were amplified during the 1860s by the American Civil War and the wars of German unification. Metallurgical advances, the factory system using interchangeable parts, and steam-powered transportation industrialized war. At the start of the 1850s, British soldiers were still fighting with the "Brown Bess," a **smooth-bore musket** quite similar to British equipment in 1700. By 1853, they began using weapons with **rifled barrels,** accurate over much greater distances. The large-scale use of rifles whose barrels were machined to close tolerances marks the beginning of industrialized warfare. It was made possible by the French invention of the Minié (Mee-nee'-ay) ball (1849), a conical bullet for rifled barrels that could be mass-produced. The next step in the industrialization of warfare came when an American, Samuel Colt, used automatic milling machines to produce interchangeable parts for the firearms themselves. His display at the Crystal Palace Exhibition of 1851 convinced the British to build an arms plant using mass-production techniques at Enfield in suburban London. The Enfield rifle and the Minié ball revolutionized warfare.

The Eastern Question.

The Crimean War originated in the **eastern question,** the complex issue of the survival (or the partition) of the Ottoman Empire. In the late seventeenth century, the Ottoman Empire had encompassed all of southeastern Europe, almost to the gates of Vienna. By the end of the Napoleonic Wars, the Ottomans had lost vast territories to the Hapsburg Empire (including both Hungary and Transylvania) and to the Russian Empire (which annexed the Crimea in 1783 and Bessarabia in 1812). In the 1850s, Sultan Abdul Mejid ruled the eastern Mediterranean, the Balkans, the Middle East, and most of northern Africa. His authority was weak in many regions: Egypt had won autonomy in 1811; Serbia, in 1817; and the provinces of Moldavia and Wallachia (Wall-a'-key-uh; the Danubian provinces), in 1829. Greece won independence in 1830. The European powers disagreed on the fate of the Ottoman Empire. Russia, coveting further expansion, favored the dismemberment of the empire; the British, fearing Russian ambitions, were determined to protect their naval superiority in the Mediterranean and the land routes to India by keeping

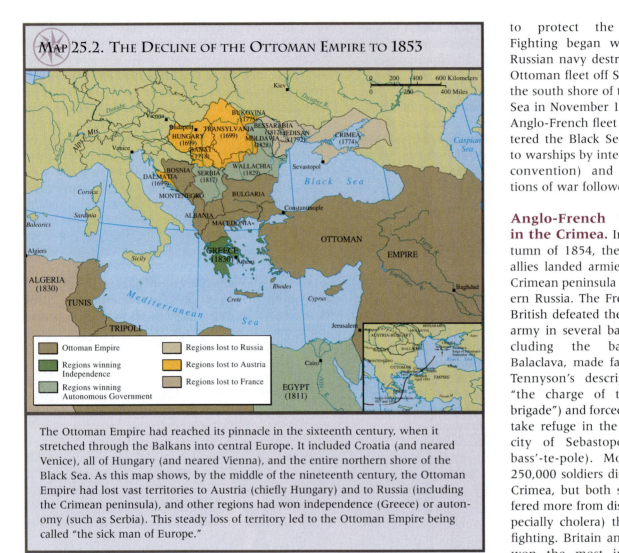

MAP 25.2. THE DECLINE OF THE OTTOMAN EMPIRE TO 1853

Ottoman Empire

Regions winning Independence

Regions winning Autonomous Government

Regions lost to Russia

Regions lost to Austria

Regions lost to France

The Ottoman Empire had reached its pinnacle in the sixteenth century, when it stretched through the Balkans into central Europe. It included Croatia (and neared Venice), all of Hungary (and neared Vienna), and the entire northern shore of the Black Sea. As this map shows, by the middle of the nineteenth century, the Ottoman Empire had lost vast territories to Austria (chiefly Hungary) and to Russia (including the Crimean peninsula), and other regions had won independence (Greece) or autonomy (such as Serbia). This steady loss of territory led to the Ottoman Empire being called "the sick man of Europe."

to protect the sultan. Fighting began when the Russian navy destroyed the Ottoman fleet off Sinope on the south shore of the Black Sea in November 1853. The Anglo-French fleet then entered the Black Sea (closed to warships by international convention) and declarations of war followed.

Anglo-French Victory in the Crimea. In the autumn of 1854, the western allies landed armies on the Crimean peninsula of southern Russia. The French and British defeated the Russian army in several battles (including the battle of Balaclava, made famous by Tennyson's description of "the charge of the light brigade") and forced them to take refuge in the besieged city of Sebastopol (Seh-bass'-te-pole). More than 250,000 soldiers died in the Crimea, but both sides suffered more from disease (especially cholera) than from fighting. Britain and France won the most important battles of the Crimean War in part because their soldiers carried rifles with a range of 1,000 yards, whereas the Russian army still used smooth-bore muskets with a range of 200 yards. The Crimean War showed the need for modern transport as well. Russian logistics depended on 125,000 wooden carts pulled by draft animals, and it soon became obvious that they could not provide enough fodder for their support. The lesson was not lost on the more efficient armies of the 1860s, which learned to use railroads to transport both men and material.

The Peace of Paris, 1856. The Crimean War was not fought to a decisive conclusion. Several events brought it to a victorious end for the allies: Piedmont-Sardinia (whose government wanted the friendship of Britain and France) joined the war against Russia, Austria (whose government feared Russian advances in the Balkans) threatened to do the same, and Nicholas I died. A peace conference at Paris in early 1856 quickly settled matters: Russia conceded some Danubian territory,

"the sick man of Europe" alive. These interests defined the alliances of the Crimean War: Britain and the Ottoman Empire (joined by France and later Piedmont-Sardinia) fought Russia.

The Origins of the Crimean War. The immediate origins of the war were in the politics of 1848. A Russo-Ottoman dispute began when the sultan accepted revolutionary refugees fleeing the Russian army. A Franco-Russian dispute followed when Napoleon III tried to build his reputation as a defender of the Catholic Church by obtaining from Abdul Mejid the right to protect Catholic interests in Jerusalem. Nicholas I wanted similar rights to protect Orthodox interests, but the British and French blocked him. Such minor conflicts came to a head in May 1853, when an angry Nicholas instructed the Russian army to occupy the Ottoman provinces of Moldavia and Wallachia. This provoked Britain and France to send a joint fleet

FIGURE 25.4 *Interior of the Redan.* None of the participants (chiefly Britain, France, and Russia) in the Crimean War (1853–1856) covered themselves in glory. It was perhaps the most foolish, unnecessary war of the century, a monument to poor statesmanship. More than 150,000 soldiers died of disease, and another 60,000 perished as a result of such ill–conceived combat as the "charge of the light brigade." In this scene, intended to convey a heroic image, British troops stand guard at a fortified position during the siege of Sevastapol.

promised to respect the integrity of the Ottoman Empire, and acquiesced in the neutralization of the Black Sea.

RUSSIA IN THE ALEXANDRINE AGE (1855–1881)

Tsar Alexander II. The 37-year-old Tsar Alexander II who came to the throne of Russia in 1855 differed greatly from his father. He had spent a happier childhood, raised by humane tutors without the military discipline imposed on Nicholas. Alexander's personality was complex. He was an ascetic who sometimes slept on straw on stone floors. He had high moral aspirations and once spent a night locked in solitary confinement in one of his prisons to understand the conditions there. As crown prince, he joined the government commission studying the "flogging gentry." He seemed well suited to be the man who freed more than 20 million people from serfdom and earned the nickname "the tsar liberator." Yet his morals permitted him to take young girls as mistresses, and his reforms were insufficient to prevent six assassination attempts in 4 years.

Emancipation of the Serfs. Alexander II assumed the throne in 1855, determined to emancipate the serfs. One of his first acts was a manifesto giving the aristoc-

racy a pragmatic explanation: "I am convinced that . . . it is better to begin to destroy serfdom from above than to wait for that time when it begins to destroy itself from below." The 30-year reign of Nicholas I had seen 556 **serf rebellions,** an average of more than one uprising per month; in the first years of Alexander's reign, the rate increased to 80 peasant rebellions per year. In 1857, the new tsar named a secret committee, headed by his liberal adviser Nikolai Milyutin (Mill-yew'-tin), to prepare for **emancipation.** Alexander II followed the advice of the Milyutin Commission and issued an edict *(ukase)* of emancipation in March 1861 on the same day that Abraham Lincoln took the oath of office as president of the United States. The details of emancipation were so complex that they required nearly 500 pages. The basic provision ended serfdom, freeing 22,192,000 people, the majority of the Russian peasantry. Another obliged the serf-owners (most of whom opposed emancipation) to give the serfs land as a part of the emancipation. Serfs obtained "the full rights of free rural inhabitants," their homes, and arable land. Landowners, however, kept title to the land until the former serfs gradually paid for it. In the interim, the imperial government compensated landowners with bonds, and former serfs were obliged, through collective village obligations, to make the **redemption payments** on these bonds. Until the completion of redemption payments, peasants owed some labor to their landlords and shared their village's obligation. Emancipation began with enlightened principles but perpetuated involuntary servitude (see *The Emancipation of the Serfs in Russia*).

Alexander's Liberal Reforms. Alexandrine liberalism went beyond the emancipation edict of 1861. Alexander II did not grant a constitution or a parliament, but his reforms made them logical expectations. In 1864, he created elective district assemblies *(zemstva)* with powers of local government. The **zemstva** were chosen by a three-class franchise similar to the voting for the Prussian Landtag. Legislation had to win the approval of the provincial governor, but this still left the assemblies a role in public health, education, and transportation. Educational reforms flowed from local self-government. Between the creation of the zemstva in 1864 and the end of Alexander's reign in 1881, 14,500 new schools opened in Russia. The tsar encouraged this

THE EMANCIPATION OF THE SERFS IN RUSSIA

A Radical Prince Describes the World of Serf-Owning Aristocrats

Prince Peter Kropotkin (1842–1921) was born to the Russian nobility and spent his childhood in luxury. He became a geographer of distinction, known for his exploration of Siberia. Kropotkin slowly turned to social criticism, however, attacking the world into which he had been born. He entered radical politics in western Europe and spent several years in French prisons for his anarchism.

Wealth was measured in those times by the number of "souls" that a landed proprietor owned. So many "souls" meant so many male serfs: women did not count. My father, who owned nearly twelve hundred souls, in three different provinces, and who had, in addition to his peasants' holding, large tracts of land which were cultivated by these peasants, was accounted a rich man. He lived up to his reputation, which meant that his house was open to any number of visitors, and that he kept a very large household. We were a family of eight, occasionally ten or twelve; but fifty servants at Moscow, and half as many more in the country, were considered not one too many. Four coachmen to attend a dozen horses, three cooks for the masters and two more for the servants, a dozen men to wait upon us at dinner-time (one man, plate in hand, standing behind each person seated at the table), and girls innumerable in the maidservants' room—how could any one do with less than this?

From Kropotkin, Peter, *Memoirs of a Revolutionist* (Boston: Houghton Mifflin, 1899).

TABLE 25.3 SERFS AND PEASANTS IN IMPERIAL RUSSIA

PEASANT POPULATION	1858 CENSUS
Serfs on privately owned estates	20,173,000
Serfs on imperial lands	2,019,000
Total serfs	22,192,000
Peasants on state lands	18,308,000
Peasants from state lands working in factories and mines	616,000
Peasants from state lands allowed to work in private factories	518,000
Peasants freed by military service	1,093,000
Total peasants	**20,535,000**

Source: Lyashchenko, P. I., *History of the National Economy of Russia* (New York: Macmillan, 1949); and Conte, Francis, ed., *Les Grands dates de la Russie et de l'URSS* (Paris: Larousse, 1990, p. 131).

Question: Are any other of the great social reforms of the nineteenth century as important as the emancipation of 22 million serfs?

---

trend by extending freedom to the universities. In 1864, the imperial government also reformed the judiciary and the criminal code. The new edicts, based on the principle of equality before the law, created an independent judiciary with a professional bar, abolished corporal punishment, and introduced the jury system in criminal cases.

The Limits of Alexander's Westernization. The reforms of 1861–1865 whetted the Russian appetite for further liberalization. During the remaining 16 years of his reign, Alexander disappointed those who wanted more. He granted self-government to the cities in 1870 and reformed the army, reducing the term of service from 25 years to 9 in 1874. But his liberalism stopped short of full **Westernization** (emulating Western systems of government, institutions, and policies as opposed to a **Slavophile** program of following Russian traditions). He brought Russian institutions near to the level of the Austrian Empire, but not to Anglo-French standards. He began the economic modernization of his empire but did not bring it into the industrial age. A tragedy of historical development is that those who begin to modernize a backward country often awaken expectations that they cannot fulfill. The tsar liberator became caught in this trap of rising expectations. He ameliorated the strict rule of Poland and amnestied thousands of his father's political prisoners, yet confronted a major Polish revolution in 1863. He reopened universities and granted them greater freedom, yet they became centers of intellectual discontent pressing for more reforms. Alexander liberalized the press laws and harvested radical criticism. He emancipated the serfs but still faced peasant rebellions (one occurred in Kazan as early as April 1861). Revolutionaries repeatedly tried to kill him. They ultimately succeeded, and the reign that had begun with such promise ended with his blood on the pavement.

THE UNIFICATION OF ITALY: THE RISORGIMENTO (1847–1870)

Count Cavour. No event of the Crimean War was more surprising than the declaration of war on Russia by Piedmont-Sardinia, a distant state with no direct interests at stake. That decision was the carefully calculated work of the Piedmontese premier, Count Camillo di Cavour (Cah-vour'), the foremost architect of Italian unification. Cavour was a wealthy landowner with an advanced education in engineering and an admiration for England, which he knew much better than Sicily or Calabria. He was a short, plump, florid-faced man, a constantly cheerful hard worker who began the day at 5 AM. His skills combined the pragmatism of the engineer and business executive with the cynical dexterity of the diplomat. Cavour had long advocated the liberalization of Italy. He meant the term broadly: scientific agriculture, modern banking, railroad building, and free trade capitalism were as important as secularized institutions, a free press, and representative government. He became prominent in 1847, when he founded a newspaper, *Il Risorgimento* (Ree-sore-gee'-men-toe; The Revival), to champion Italian independence and progressive reforms. The newspaper became the leading voice of liberal-nationalism, making its title a synonym for the process of unification.

Piedmont-Sardinia. The revolutions of 1848 convinced most observers that rebellion in the streets would not drive the Austrians out of Italy. The leadership of a strong state, plus foreign assistance, would be needed. Both seemed distant during the reaction of 1849. In the south, Ferdinand of Naples was arresting, imprisoning, and torturing more than 20,000 of his citizens. In Lombardy and Venetia, Marshal Radetzky dispensed the justice of the military tribunal—a few executions, many floggings, more imprisonments, and thousands of exiles. Pope Pius IX proscribed 7,000 people and executed priests with republican sympathies. Only in Piedmont, where King Charles Albert had abdicated in favor of his son, King Victor Emmanuel II, did the liberalism of 1848 survive. Victor Emmanuel kept the constitution (the *Statuto*) that his father had granted, despite an Austrian offer to cancel Piedmont's war indemnity if he abrogated the document. In 1850, Victor Emmanuel promulgated the Siccardi Laws, written by Cavour, limiting the powers of the Catholic Church by abolishing church courts, permitting civil marriage, and restricting the number of church holidays. This version of separation of church and state, which Cavour called "a free church in a free state," persuaded nationalists such as Garibaldi and Manin to recognize the leadership of Piedmont. Cavour became premier in 1852 and kept that post for the rest of the decade, culminating in his leadership of Piedmont during a war of unification in 1859.

Napoleon III and French Intervention. Cavour prepared for the war of 1859 by courting Britain and France. After sending the Piedmontese contingent to the Crimea in 1855, he raised the Italian question at the Paris Peace Conference of 1856. Cavour next sought an alliance with Napoleon III. He sent his teenaged cousin (and lover), the Countess Virginie di Castiglione (Ka-stee-yee-owe'-nay), to become Napoleon's mistress and an Italian secret agent. He even profited from the attempt of a disgruntled nationalist, Felice Orsini (Or-see'-nee), to kill Napoleon. The emperor seemed chastened by Orsini's conspiracy, as if embarrassed that he had slighted the Italian cause; he allowed Orsini to make a series of patriotic pronouncements ("So long as Italy is enslaved, death is a blessing") before sending him to the guillotine. Cavour won his French alliance in 1858. He and Napoleon III met covertly at the mineral springs resort of Plombières (Plom-bee'-air) in eastern France and reached a secret agreement. Napoleon pledged a French army of 200,000 men (larger than the entire Piedmontese army) "to drive the Austrians out of Italy once and for all and to leave them without an inch of territory south of the Alps." Cavour promised to return to France the province of Savoy (lost in 1815) and the coastal region of Nice, although his own mother was a Savoyard and Garibaldi had been born in Nice. In addition, Piedmont-Sardinia pledged 10 percent of its annual budget to pay the French war costs.

The War of 1859. The Italian War of 1859 (known to Italians as the "War of Independence") needed little provocation. Cavour mobilized the Piedmontese army, and the Austrians demanded that he demobilize it. When Cavour refused, the Austrians invaded Piedmont (April 1859) to teach him a lesson. This gave Napoleon III an excuse to send the French army to protect Piedmont. Bloodless revolutions soon drove pro-Austrian rulers from the central Italian states of Parma, Modena, and Tuscany. Allied armies entered Lombardy in June 1859 and forced the Austrians to retreat after the battle of Magenta (a village near Milan), which gave its name to the purplish-red color as a result of the quantity of blood spilled there. After another bloody but inconclusive battle, at Solferino (Sol-fair'-ee-no) in eastern Lombardy, the Austrian army retreated into a defensive complex of fortresses known as the Quadrilateral, and Napoleon III (who had seen battle for the first time) withdrew in nausea. More than 75,000 soldiers were killed in less than 2 months of fighting, 40,000 of them in a single day at Solferino. (In contrast, the United States lost 50,000 in a decade of fighting in Vietnam a century later.)

The Geneva Convention and the Red Cross. Napoleon III was not the only person horrified at the spectacle of industrialized armies slaughtering each

ITALIAN UNIFICATION

Portrait of Camillo Benso. Count Camillo di Cavour (1810–1861).

Napoleon III. Emperor Napoleon III of France (1808–1873).

◄ *Meeting of Victor Emmanuel and Garibaldi.* King Victor Emmanuel II of Piedmont-Sardinia (1820–1878) meets Giuseppe Garibaldi (1807–1882) in southern Italy, after Garibaldi and the "red-shirts" have defeated the forces of the Kingdom of the Two Sicilies.

other. J. Henri Dunant, a wealthy Swiss banker traveling in northern Italy, witnessed the battle of Solferino. The sight of the wounded, left to die in piles on the battlefield, so shocked Dunant that he devoted himself to creating an international organization to care for wounded soldiers. His efforts led to an international conference at Geneva and the (first) **Geneva Convention** (1864) in which twelve European states accepted Dunant's proposed relief society, the International Red Cross. In one of the final tragedies of Solferino, Dunant spent his en-

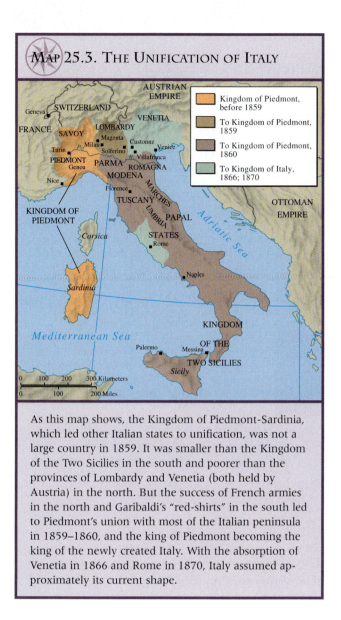

MAP 25.3. THE UNIFICATION OF ITALY

Kingdom of Piedmont, before 1859

To Kingdom of Piedmont, 1859

To Kingdom of Piedmont, 1860

To Kingdom of Italy, 1866; 1870

As this map shows, the Kingdom of Piedmont-Sardinia, which led other Italian states to unification, was not a large country in 1859. It was smaller than the Kingdom of the Two Sicilies in the south and poorer than the provinces of Lombardy and Venetia (both held by Austria) in the north. But the success of French armies in the north and Garibaldi's "red-shirts" in the south led to Piedmont's union with most of the Italian peninsula in 1859–1860, and the king of Piedmont becoming the king of the newly created Italy. With the absorption of Venetia in 1866 and Rome in 1870, Italy assumed approximately its current shape.

tire fortune on this effort and lived thereafter in poverty, although he shared the first Nobel Peace Prize in 1901.

The Peace Treaty of Villafranca. After the battle of Solferino, Napoleon III sought peace with the Austrians without consulting Victor Emmanuel II. Napoleon and Franz Joseph met privately at Villafranca (a village in Venetia) in July 1859 and agreed on terms: Austria would keep Venetia but cede Lombardy to France, which could, in turn, give it to Piedmont. Victor Emmanuel accepted this agreement, despite the fury of Cavour, and yielded Nice and Savoy to France after plebiscites in the central states (Parma, Modena, Romagna, and Tuscany) made it clear that they would join Lombardy in merging with Piedmont.

Garibaldi and the War in the South. Before this new Italian state could be organized, another uprising began in Sicily. Garibaldi, as impetuous and idealistic as he had been in 1848, seized the initiative. With the connivance of Cavour, he raised a volunteer army of 1,067 men, dressed them in red woolen shirts, and launched an invasion of Sicily (see *Giuseppe Garibaldi and Italian Unification*). Garibaldi's red-shirts (also known as "the 1,000") evaded the Neapolitan navy, trekked overland across Sicily, and were received as liberators in Palermo after defeating the Neapolitan army and setting up a provisional government. Garibaldi next crossed to the mainland, where the Neapolitan army dissolved, allowing the red-shirts to enter Naples. Garibaldi planned to continue his march northward to take Rome, believing that "[t]he Vatican is a dagger in the heart of Italy," and an uprising to support him began in the papal states in September 1860.

The Kingdom of Italy. Cavour seized the opportunity provided by Garibaldi's victories to unite northern and southern Italy. Using the Roman rebellion as an excuse to intervene, Cavour sent Piedmontese armies into the Papal States where they won rapid victories. After plebiscites in Sicily, southern Italy, and central Italy favored union with the north, the Kingdom of Italy was proclaimed in March 1861. Victor Emmanuel became the first king of Italy, and the Statuto provided the basis of an Italian constitution, including a parliamentary government elected by limited suffrage (2 percent of the population). The new kingdom did not include Venetia (which was still Austrian) or Rome (where the French army remained, still defending the pope). Garibaldi attempted another uprising in 1862 to annex Rome as the natural capital of Italy, but he was beaten in a small skirmish and retired to his farm, where he plowed fields behind a team of jackasses he named Napoleon III, Pius IX, and Immaculate Conception. Venetia joined Italy in 1866, when Austria lost the Seven Weeks' War with Prussia, and Rome became the capital of Italy after French troops withdrew in 1870 (see following discussion). A plebiscite of October 1870 completed the unification of Italy, but in one sense, the new Italy included few Italians; barely 2 percent of the population spoke a standard Italian language, and most of the nation spoke local dialects. As one wit observed, because Italy now existed it would be necessary to invent the Italians.

BISMARCK AND THE UNIFICATION OF GERMANY (1848–1871)

Prussian Leadership in Germany. Following the revolutions of 1848, Germany remained a loose confederation of thirty-nine independent states: one empire (Austria); five kingdoms (Prussia, Bavaria, Württemberg, Saxony, and Hanover); one princedom

GIUSEPPE GARIBALDI AND ITALIAN UNIFICATION

◀ *Garibaldi and the 1,000.* Giuseppe Garibaldi was the greatest military hero of Italian unification. He had fought for Italy since his youthful association with Mazzini in the 1830s had led him into exile in South America (where he also became a revolutionary hero). He had returned to Italy to fight for the Roman Republic of 1848, and the victory of the counterrevolution and the restoration of Pope Pius IX had led to a second exile, this time in the United States. He returned to Piedmont in the 1850s and commanded an army corps in 1859. When Napoleon III withdrew the French army, Garibaldi organized a volunteer army (known as "the 1,000") to continue the war in Sicily and the south. After the unification, he lived on an island estate off the shore of Sardinia, where he berated his team of jackasses, named Napoleon III and Pius IX. In this romanticized image, the greatly outnumbered red-shirts and their Sicilian volunteers defeat the army of the Kingdom of Two Sicilies in the battle of Calatafimi (Sicily) in May 1860.

Garibaldi Calls Italians to Arms, 1860

Italians! The Sicilians are fighting against the enemies of Italy, and for Italy. It is the duty of every Italian to succour them with words, money, arms, and, above all, in person.

The misfortunes of Italy arise from the indifference of one province to the fate of others.

The redemption of Italy began from the moment that men of the same land ran to help their distressed brothers.

Left to themselves, the brave Sicilians will have to fight, not only the mercenaries of the Bourbon [of the government of Naples], but also those of Austria and the Priest of Rome.

Let the inhabitants of the free provinces lift their voices in behalf of their struggling brethren, and impel their brave youth to the conflict.

To arms! Let me put an end, once and for all, to the miseries of so many centuries. Prove to the world that it is no lie that Roman generations inhabited this land.

From *The Annual Register: 1860* (London: J. G. and F. Rivington, 1861).

(Hesse); and an assortment of grand duchies, duchies, principalities, and free cities. Although the Hapsburgs had long dominated central European affairs, the leadership of the German states was shifting to Prussia for many reasons. The expansion of Prussia at Vienna in 1815 had affirmed Prussian dominance of northern Germany. The German states north of the Main River were also oriented toward Prussia by the **confessional division** of Germany into a Protestant north and Catholic south. States such as Hanover (95.7 percent Protestant), Hesse (83.1 percent), Mecklenburg (99.3 percent), and Saxony (98.1 percent) were more comfortable with Lutheran Prussia than with Catholic Austria; many of their leaders had been educated at the Protestant universities of Jena, Halle, and Berlin. Industrial leadership and command of the Zollverein also made Prussia the economic leader of central Europe. German liberals preferred Prussian to Austrian leadership. Neither could be mistaken for a radical republic, but the Prussian record of reforms, from Stein and Hardenburg in 1807 to the constitution of 1850 (with an elective Landtag), was more appealing than the oppression of Metternich or Schwarzenberg.

The Prussian Army. The Prussian domination of Germany ultimately depended on the army, the same institution that had accounted for the rise of Prussia in the eighteenth century. Prussia, alone among the great

MAP 25.4. THE UNIFICATION OF GERMANY, 1866–1871

Prussia, 1862

United with Prussia in 1866–1867 as North German Confederation

United with North German Confederation in 1871 as German Empire

Annexed in 1871 after Franco-Prussian War

Boundary of German Confederation, 1815

Boundary of German Empire, 1871

Prussia had grown significantly since becoming a kingdom in 1701, acquiring eastern territories from Poland and Sweden in the eighteenth century, then large portions of Saxony and the Rhineland in 1815. As this map of German unification shows, in 1862 Prussia already held the largest portion of the territory that became Germany. War with Denmark in 1864 brought Schleswig, and war with Austria in 1866 resulted in the Prussian-dominated North German Confederation. War with France brought the south German states into union with the confederation as the German Empire, which acquired Alsace-Lorraine from defeated France.

powers, had not gone to war since the defeat of Napoleon, so statesmen did not appreciate the importance of Prussian army reforms undertaken by Gerhard von Scharnhorst and Count von Gneisenau after 1806. They had made all Prussian men liable for military service between ages 20 and 39, including a well-organized system of reserve duty that made the army potentially much larger than its apparent size. The reforms also included (1) the revolutionary principle of commissioning and promoting officers on the basis of ability, thus abolishing the aristocratic monopoly of rank (yet perpetuating some exclusions, such as Jews); (2) the creation of schools in which to train officers; and (3) the development of a **General Staff** to provide the army with organization and planning. The Prussian General Staff had been quick to learn the lessons of war in the industrial age; they had, in the words of the nationalist historian Heinrich von Treitschke, "faith in the God who made iron."

The Prussian Constitutional Crisis. The international tensions of the 1850s convinced the new king of Prussia, William I, that further reforms of the army were in order. In 1859, William named a new minister of war, General Albrecht von Roon, to supervise those reforms; Roon, in turn, selected a friend, General Helmuth von Moltke (Molt'-kuh), to serve as chief of the general staff. Roon and Moltke needed a great deal of money for this undertaking, but their attempt to get financing precipitated a constitutional battle with the Landtag, where a liberal majority claimed the constitutional **power of the purse**—the right to approve such expenditures. Roon fulminated that "in the sewer of doctrinaire liberalism, Prussia will rot without redemption," but the liberals held out.

Otto von Bismarck. The constitutional battle over the Prussian budget lasted for nearly 3 years before a desperate king selected another of Roon's friends, Otto von Bismarck, to head the government. Bismarck was a hotheaded and mistrustful Junker, who had followed a diplomatic career to ambassadorial posts in Frankfurt, St. Petersburg, and Paris. He was also a brilliantly pragmatic conservative who favored **Realpolitik** (Ray'-ahl-poh-lih-teek; a policy of realism) to defend the old order. As Bismarck put it, he "listened for the footsteps of God through history, and tried to grab hold of His coattails." Bismarck's Realpolitik made him at times a virtual dictator, led Prussia into three wars during the 1860s, and shoved German liberals into outer darkness; but he emerged as the greatest German politician of the century, and at the end of his term as chancellor, a Prussian-dominated Germany had become the strongest state in Europe.

Bismarck and the Constitutional Crisis. Bismarck defeated the Landtag liberals by ignoring them and the constitution. He decided that "necessity

GERMAN LEADERS

The unification of Germany in 1871 was the accomplishment of military men—in Bismarck's words, Germany was created by "iron and blood," not by "speeches and the decisions of a parliamentary majority." All of the leaders of unification (including Bismarck) had a military background.

King William I of Prussia. King William I of Prussia (1797–1888), the first emperor of Germany (1871–1888). William was the second son of a monarch and thus had a military career as a young man, fighting in the campaign against Napoleon of 1814–1815.

Albrecht von Roon. Count and Field Marshal Albrecht von Roon (1803–1879), Prussian Minister of War (1859–1873), who expanded and reorganized the Prussian army.

alone is authoritative" and acted without legislative approval. Bismarck levied taxes, collected revenue, and spent money—all without legislation, without a budget, and without accounting. Roon and Moltke acquired breech-loading rifles (Johann von Dreyse's "needle gun") and Krupp cannons; these weapons soon acquired substantial real estate. "Better pointed bullets than pointed speeches," Bismarck believed. He explained his audacity in one of the most famous speeches of the century. He told a Landtag committee that it was the army that made Prussia great, not liberal ideals. "The great issues to the day," he said defiantly, "will not be decided by speeches and the decisions of a parliamentary majority—that was the mistake of 1848 and 1849—but by iron and blood" (see *Otto von Bismarck*). These words stuck. Bismarck became

"the Iron Chancellor" and Germany became a land of **iron and blood** militarism instead of liberalism.

The Danish War of 1864. Bismarckian diplomacy and the Prussian army created a kleindeutsch Germany between 1864 and 1871. Bismarck first won the friendship of Tsar Alexander II of Russia by helping him during the Polish revolution of 1863. He next positioned Prussia as the defender of German nationalism by supporting the confederation in a dispute with Denmark over two duchies, Schleswig and Holstein, located at their common border. In a dispute over the inheritance of these provinces, the German Confederation endorsed the claim of a German prince and in July 1863 called for the use of force against Denmark. Within a year, Bismarck had produced an anti-Danish alliance with Austria and a war

Otto von Bismarck. Count (later Prince) Otto von Bismarck (1815–1898), posing in uniform near Paris during the Franco-Prussian War.

Moltke at Versailles, 1870. Count and Field Marshal Helmuth von Moltke (1800–1891), chief of the Prussian General Staff (1857–1882), relaxing at the French royal palace of Versailles during the Prussian victory of 1870–1871.

with Denmark. The Danes held out for 5 months before surrendering Schleswig and Holstein. Bismarck did not free the duchies; instead, he negotiated the Convention of Gastein (August 1865) by which Holstein became Austrian and Schleswig, cut off by Austrian territory, became Prussian. This difficult situation soon provided the dispute that led to a war between Austria and Prussia.

The Biarritz Agreement. Bismarck prepared Prussia for a war with Austria by the skillful diplomacy that made him the most renowned statesman of the late nineteenth century. Two months after his treaty with Austria, Bismarck held anti-Austrian negotiations with Napoleon III at Biarritz on the southwestern coast of France. Using vague assurances of fair compensation to France (perhaps in Belgium, perhaps in Luxembourg, perhaps on the Rhineland frontier), Bismarck won a promise of French neutrality in the event of an Austro-Prussian War as well as French help in making a similar deal with Italy. The Biarritz agreement of October 1865 was followed by a Prusso-Italian alliance (April 1866); Italy would help Prussia in a war with Austria in return for Venetia. Confident that he had secured the sympathies of Russia, France, and Italy, Bismarck provoked the Austrians into war, much as Napoleon III and Cavour had done in 1859.

The Austro-Prussian War of 1866. By June 1866, Austria and Prussia were fighting an unexpectedly lopsided Seven Weeks' War. Moltke directed a Prussian army whose needle-guns enabled them to fire five to seven times per minute from crouching or lying positions; the Austrians used muzzle-loading guns that

OTTO VON BISMARCK

Bismarck's "Iron and Blood" Speech

Our blood is too hot; we prefer armor too heavy for our slight body, but we should put it to use nevertheless. The eyes of Germany are not fixed on Prussia's liberalism, but upon her power.

Bavaria, Württemberg, and Baden may choose the liberal path. No one for that reason will allot Prussia's role to them. Prussia must gather up her strength and hold it in readiness for the favorable

moment—a moment which has already been let pass on several occasions. Prussia's borders under the Treaty of Vienna are not suitable for a healthy national life. The great questions of the day will not be decided by speeches and the decisions of a parliamentary majority— that was the mistake of 1848 and 1849—but by iron and blood.

From Kohl, H., ed., "Die politischen Reden des Fürsten Bismarck," in Schaefer, Ludwig, et al., eds., *Problems in Western Civilization* (New York: Scribner's, 1965).

TABLE 25.4 HUMAN LOSSES IN THE WARS OF GERMAN UNIFICATION, 1864–1871

Danish War (1864)		Seven Weeks' War (1866)		Franco-Prussian War (1870–1871)	
COUNTRY	**LOSSES**	**COUNTRY**	**LOSSES**	**COUNTRY**	**LOSSES**
Austria	1,100	Italy	11,197	France	580,000
Prussia	2,423	Prussia	22,376		
Allied Total	**3,523**	**Allied Total**	**33,573**	Prussia	130,000
Denmark	11,000	Austria	87,844		
		German allies	24,628		
		Allied Total	**112,472**		

Note: Losses include the category of prisoners-of-war.

Calculated from data in Cook, Chris, and Paxton, John, *European Political Facts, 1848–1918* (London: Macmillan, 1978, p. 177).

Question: What evidence does this table give of Prussian military superiority?

required soldiers to remain standing while firing two or three rounds per minute. Moltke had also learned the lessons of the American Civil War on the use of railroads to mobilize large armies. The first advantage meant that Austria suffered four times as many casualties as Prussia; the second enabled Moltke to move a fresh army into a decisive battle at the Bohemian town of Königgrätz. The Austrians, whose introduction to industrialized warfare cost them more than 12,000 men per week, surrendered shortly after the battle of Königgrätz (also known as the battle of Sadowa, for a neighboring village). Europe had entered a new age of warfare. As one military observer of the wars of German unification put it, "The armies taking the field today differ from those commanded by the Duke of Wellington [in 1815] as much as the latter differed from the Roman legions."

The North German Confederation. The stunning Prussian victory over Austria changed the balance of power in Europe and confirmed the Prussian hegemony in central Europe. By the Treaty of Prague (August

1866), the Hapsburg Empire surrendered Venetia to Italy and acquiesced in a Prussian reshaping of Germany. Franz Joseph had to swallow his own Olmütz. The German Confederation of 1815, the last remnant of centuries of Austrian hegemony in central Europe, was abolished. Several of the north German states (including Hanover) were absorbed into an enlarged Prussia. All other German states north of the Main (Mine) River (including Hesse and Saxony) were brought into a new confederation under Prussian domination, the North German Confederation. A few southern states (chiefly Baden, Württemberg, and Bavaria) retained their independence, although Bismarck brought them into the economic orbit of the Zollverein and into military alliances with Prussia. Bismarck resisted the desires of army leaders and the king to annex Austrian territories because he wanted Austrian support in the future.

The Ausgleich of 1867. Even with Bismarck's generous terms of peace, the Austrian Empire had urgent problems. Fearing that the minority peoples of the empire who had arisen in 1848–1849 might begin a civil war following the humiliation of Königgrätz, the Austrian government reached a compromise (*Ausgleich*; Ows'-gl-eyek) with the Hungarians. The Ausgleich was negotiated by Francis Deák (Day'-ahk), a moderate liberal who had resisted Kossuth's radicalism in 1848–1849; he sought only the restitution of the ancient Hungarian constitution granting self-government in domestic affairs. In accepting this degree of Hungarian **autonomy,** the Austrians converted the empire into a dual monarchy known as the Austro-Hungarian Empire. Vienna continued to control the western half of the empire (containing Czech, Slovene, and Italian minorities), but the Magyars now controlled the east, cheerfully accepting the task of keeping the Slavic peoples (Croatians, Bosnians, Poles, Romanians, Slovaks, Ruthenians, White Russians, and Serbs) of the empire subordinated.

Origins of the Franco-Prussian War.

Prussia's unanticipated victory in the Austro-Prussian War created a crisis in Franco-Prussian relations. One month after the battle of Königgrätz, Napoleon III reminded Bismarck of their Biarritz agreement. He requested, for the promised compensation, that France receive her eastern frontiers of 1814 (which included the Rhineland) plus additional territory such as Luxembourg. Bismarck categorically refused such compensation as offensive to German nationalism, intentionally angering the French as he had recently provoked the Austrians. Poor relations deteriorated into a Franco-Prussian War due to a dispute over Spain. In September 1868, the Spanish army overthrew the corrupt regime of Queen Isabella and created a liberal regime based on a newly elected Córtes. The Córtes created a constitutional monarchy but had difficulty finding a member of the European royalty to accept the throne. Finally, in the summer of 1869, Prince Leopold of Hohenzollern-Sigmaringen, a Catholic relative of King William I of Prussia, accepted the Spanish throne. The candidacy of a Hohenzollern prince alarmed the French, who envisioned allied armies on their southern and eastern borders, and they demanded that Leopold withdraw. The French applied diplomatic pressure and blocked the Hohenzollern candidacy in June 1870, but this episode nonetheless led to a Franco-Prussian War in July. At a meeting between William I and the French ambassador at the resort town of Bad Ems (Hesse), the ambassador pressed the king to disavow the candidacy and to promise that it would never be revived. William reported the incident to Bismarck in a telegram that became known as the Ems Dispatch. Bismarck edited the telegram to make it seem like an arrogant French insult, then released the text to the nationalist press, hoping to goad the French into war. He succeeded; France declared war 2 days later.

The Franco-Prussian War.

The Franco-Prussian War of 1870–1871 again demonstrated the superiority of the Prussian army and the advantages of the industrial age. General von Moltke used railroads and the telegraph to mobilize his armies with remarkable efficiency. The German invasion first drove the French army out of their frontier province (Alsace). Then, after less than a month of war, Prussian armies won a crushing victory at Sedan (September 1870) and took the emperor prisoner. Despite these defeats, France did not capitulate quickly because a revolutionary republican government in Paris was determined to continue the fight. Forcing a French surrender required a 4-month siege of Paris, which held out despite Krupp artillery shelling residential districts; Parisians lived on zoo animals, domestic pets, rats, and shoe leather before accepting an armistice in January 1871.

Proclamation of the German Empire.

The surprising defeat of the French army (which Europeans had still considered the successor to Napoleon I's armies) had tremendous consequences for Europe. France lost Alsace and part of adjacent Lorraine, accepted a proclamation of German unification (made at the French royal palace of Versailles), and endured a German triumphal march down the Champs Elysée. Bismarck's Frankfurt Peace Treaty also cost France a huge indemnity (5 billion francs) and the military occupation of northeastern France until it was paid. The result, however, was German unification: Bismarck's merger of the North German Confederation and the south German states into the German Empire (known as the Second Reich, in recognition of the Holy Roman Empire, which Napoleon had abolished).

European Consequences of the War.

For France, *l'année terrible* (the terrible year) included another violent revolution and virtual civil war before the creation of a lasting republic (the Third Republic) during the 1870s. For Italy, the war meant the completion of Italian unification because the recall of the French garrison from Rome permitted the Kingdom of Italy to annex most of the remaining territory of the Papal States. For all of Europe, the greatest consequence of the war was a shift in the **balance of power:** the scales now tipped towards Berlin, not Paris.

CONCLUSION

The early nineteenth century witnessed a conservative victory in the revival of the Old Regime. That victory was constantly challenged by a revolutionary age that culminated in the widespread revolutions of 1848. Those revolutions failed in their nationalist ambitions and most of their liberal ambitions, leaving counterrevolutionary governments in full control, but they nonetheless opened an area of dramatic changes. The dramatic changes of the midnineteenth century, however, came on the battlefield rather than the barricade. Nearly 20 years of war transformed the map of Europe and the balance of power: the era underscored the dangerous weakness of the Ottoman Empire; destroyed the German Confederation; created the modern states of Italy and Germany; revealed the weakness of the Austrian Empire, which was transformed into the Austro-Hungarian Empire; and marked a historic transition from a century of French hegemony in Europe to a century of German hegemony. There were very important liberal triumphs during the era (such as the emancipation of the serfs in Austria and Russia; the emancipation of the Jews in Britain, Italy, and Austria; the end of slavery in the French colonial empire; and the continuing progress of constitutional, parliamentary government), but they paled in importance compared to the wars of the era.

Review Questions

- What were the results of the revolutions of 1848?
- What varieties of working-class movements were developing?
- How did the emancipation of the serfs in Russia happen?
- How was the unified state of Italy created?
- How was the unified state of Germany created?

For Further Study

Readings

Bottimore, Tom, ed., *A Dictionary of Marxist Thought* (Cambridge: Harvard University Press, 1983). A very valuable aid in understanding the complexities of Marxism.

Cook, Chris, and Paxton, John, eds., *European Political Facts, 1848—1918* (London: Macmillan, 1978). A valuable reference book for chronologies, officeholders, and economic data.

Hobsbawm, E. J., *The Age of Capital, 1848–1875* (New York: New American Library, 1979). A readable and provocative survey of the era.

Mitchell, Sally, ed., *Victorian Britain: An Encyclopedia* (New York: Garland, 1988). A comprehensive reference work, especially strong in topical entries.

Pflanze, Otto, *Bismarck and the Development of Germany,* 2nd ed. (Princeton: Princeton University Press, 1990). The first volume of this comprehensive study covers the period of unification.

Smith, D. M., *Victor Emanuel, Cabour, and the Risorgimento* (Oxford: Oxford University Press, 1971). The standard work on Italian unification.

Sperber, Jonathan, *The European Revolutions, 1848–1851* (Cambridge: Cambridge University Press, 1994). The up-to-date, comprehensive survey of the revolutions.

InfoTrac College Edition

For additional reading, go to your online research library at *http://infotrac.thomsonlearning.com.*

Using the Subject Guide, enter the search terms

revolutions of 1848	*Italian unification*
Bismarck, Otto von	*Communist Manifesto*
Crimean War	

Web Sites

http://www.ohiou.edu/~chastain/ An exceptional Web site that provides a comprehensive and detailed encyclopedia of the revolutions of 1848, created by a professor at Ohio University.

http://www.spartacus.schoolnet.co.uk/TU.htm One of the parts of a British educational site, devoted to the Trade Union movement. Provides biographies of trade unionists, summaries of trade union legislation, and summations of important issues.

Visit the Western Civilization Companion Web Site for resources specific to this textbook:
http://history.wadsworth.com/hause02/

 The CD in the back of this book and the Western Civilization Resource Center at *http://history.wadsworth.com/western/* offer a variety of tools to help you succeed in this course, including access to quizzes; images; documents; interactive simulations, maps, and timelines; movie explorations; and a wealth of other sources.

Chapter 25

EUROPE IN AN AGE OF NATIONALISM, 1848–1870

1845	1850	1855	1860	1865	1870

THE REVOLUTIONS OF 1848

February: Revolution in Paris and Abdication of King Louis Philippe
March: Revolution Spreads to German and Italian States
Constitution Granted in Piedmont
Emperor of Austria Abdicates and Metternich Flees
Italians Drive Austrian Army from Venice and Milan
Revolution in Berlin: King Grants a Constitution
May: French Constituent Assembly Elected to Plan a Second Republic
May: German Parliament Assembles at Frankfurt to Prepare for Unification
June: Workers' Uprising in Paris Suppressed
October: Constitution of Second Republic Adopted
December: Louis-Napoleon Elected President
 1849: Republic of Rome Proclaimed and Temporal Power of Pope Ended
 Hungarian Republic Proclaimed but Russia Helps Austria
 Austrian Army Suppresses Revolution in Empire
 King of Prussia Refuses Frankfurt Offer of Crown
 Frankfurt Parliament Dissolved without Constitution or Unity
 French Army Crushes Roman Revolution and Restores Pope
  1851: Coup d'état Overthrows Republic in France
  1852: Second Empire Proclaimed in France

ITALIAN UNIFICATION

January 1859: Napoleon III and Cavour Meet to Plan Cooperation
April 1859: Austria Provoked into War and Invades Piedmont
May 1859: Napoleon III Sends French Army to Aid Piedmont
June 1859: Austrians Routed at Battle of Solferino
July 1859: Armistice gives Lombardy to Piedmont
August 1859: Central Italian States Unite with Piedmont and Lombardy
 March 1860: Piedmont Gives Nice and Savoy to France
 May 1860: Garibaldi and "the 1,000" Land in Sicily and Win It for Italy
 August 1860: Garibaldi's Forces Invade Southern Italy and Take Naples
 September 1860: Piedmontese Armies Invade Papal States
 March 1861: Kingdom of Italy Proclaimed
  1866: Italy Acquires Venice due to Austro-Prussian War
  1870: Italy Acquires Rome Due to Franco-Prussian War

GERMAN UNIFICATION

1859: General von Roon Begins Reform of Prussian Army
 1861: Prussian Parliament Refuses to Pay for Army Reforms
 1862: William I Names Bismarck Chancellor of Prussia to Solve Constitutional Crisis
 1863: Bismarck Gains Russian Friendship by Providing Support against the Polish Revolution
 1864: Prussian and Austria Defeat Denmark and Take Schleswig-Holstein
 1865: Bismarck Gains French Neutrality in Biarritz Meeting
 1866: Prussia Defeats Austria in Seven Weeks' War
  1867: Austria Accepts Dual Monarchy of Austria-Hungary
  1867: Prussia Achieves Partial Unity in North German Confederation
   1870: Franco-Prussian Crises over Hohenzollern Candidacy
   1870: Franco-Prussian War and Prussian Victory at Sedan
   1870: Prussian Besieges Paris
    1871: Paris Capitulates and France Makes Peace
    1871: Southern States Agree to Join German Empire

FOCUS QUESTIONS

- To what extent was the newly unified Germany a part of the liberal-democratic pattern of western Europe, and to what extent was it still more like the eastern autocracies?
- In what ways did Britain and France illustrate a pattern of the steady victory of liberal-democratic institutions and laws, and in what ways did they not?
- What were the demands of the labor movement and the women's movement for a more democratic society, and to what extent did the movements succeed?
- How should historians characterize European culture at the turn of the twentieth century?

Chapter 26

EUROPE IN THE BELLE ÉPOQUE, 1871–1914

On the afternoon of May 3, 1908, a 60-year-old widow dressed in mourning black marched past the doorman at a Paris polling place into the precincts reserved by law for men alone. Hubertine Auclert (Oh-clair'), who had founded the women's suffrage movement in France nearly 30 years earlier, expressed the frustration of those decades of trying to persuade men to accept equality by grabbing a wooden ballot box and smashing it to the ground. While a poll worker gasped "Sacrilege!", Auclert stomped on the male ballots and denounced "unisexual suffrage." She was arrested a few moments later.

The story of Hubertine Auclert's demonstration, like the protests of minority nationalities or striking workers or other feminists, illustrates the paradox of the period at the end of the nineteenth century, known as the *Belle Époque* (Bell Ay-pock'; the beautiful era). The turn of the twentieth century seemed beautiful because it was a period of unusual peace and prosperity compared with the preceding century or the following half-century: between the Paris Commune of 1871 and the beginning of World War I in 1914, no European wars broke out among the great powers and no wave of revolutions arose. A long recession troubled people during the 1870s and 1880s, but the Belle Époque experienced nothing so severe as the great depressions of the 1840s or 1930s.

Chapter 26 examines Europe during this era of relative tranquility. It surveys the four greatest powers (the German Empire, the French Third Republic, Great Britain, and the Russian Empire) and shows how each

made progress toward democratic societies, yet attitudes and institutions of the Old Regime persisted. Historians must analyze the paradox of a progressive world—seen in the creation of universal education in France by Jules Ferry, and the foundation of social security in Germany by Otto von Bismarck, or the broadening of the English franchise by William Gladstone—in balance with such undemocratic experiences as the Bismarckian attack on the Catholic Church during the *Kulturkampf* (Kul-tour'-camph; the clash of cultures), the anti-Semitism of the Dreyfus affair in France, and the British refusal of home rule to the Irish.

THE GERMAN EMPIRE (1871–1914)

The Second Empire. The Prussian victory in the Franco-Prussian War enabled Bismarck to bring the south German states (Baden, Bavaria, and Württemberg [Vur'-tem-berg]) into a union with the Prussian-dominated North German Confederation. The result was the German Empire (called the Second Empire, or Second Reich). Unquestionably the most powerful state on the continent, it stretched from the newly annexed French provinces of Alsace and Lorraine in the west to the Lithuanian frontier on the Baltic Sea (900 miles away); its population roughly equaled that of France and Spain combined. The German army had proved its mastery of the battlefield; German industry was beginning to demonstrate a comparable superiority. Just as the French had been forced to swallow German military leadership, the British increasingly lost ground to German industrial might. Germany surpassed Britain in iron consumption by the late 1890s, then in coal consumption in the early twentieth century (see *German Leadership in Europe*).

The Federal Structure of Germany. Although the German army and economy were the most modern in Europe, the government and its institutions remained rooted in the eighteenth century. Prussia had created Germany, and the German constitution (1871) showed the dominance of Prussia. The empire was a federal government of twenty-five unequal states. Many historic states survived with their monarchies intact but subordinated to the Prussian king, who was crowned emperor *(Kaiser)* of Germany. The empire thus contained four kingdoms (Prussia, Bavaria, Saxony, and Württemberg), six grand duchies, five duchies, seven principalities, and three free cities. All states retained some sovereignty, with separate constitutions, taxes, and laws. The Bavarians even obtained "special rights" and kept their own postal service and diplomatic corps. An enlarged Prussia, however, encompassed 65 percent of all German territory, 62 percent of the population, and the richest economic areas (the Saar, the Ruhr, and Upper Silesia). The Prussian-dominated imperial government controlled the army, decisions of war or peace, and such central economic institutions as banking and the railroads.

Government of Germany. The emperor of Germany (the king of Prussia, William I) held genuine power under the new constitution, which was significantly less democratic than that of the regimes in Britain and France. The emperor named a **chancellor**—the architect of unification, Prince Bismarck—to direct the government. The chancellor was appointed and never faced a general election; he remained responsible to the emperor (who could dismiss him at any time) and could govern without the support of a legislative majority. Bismarck held office without leading any political party and without a parliamentary majority. He frankly admitted that his primary job was to preserve the monarchy: "The Prussian crown must not allow itself to be thrust into the powerless position of the English crown." The German legislature contained a lower house (the *Reichstag* [Rikes'-tahg]), elected by universal manhood suffrage (at age 25), and an upper house representing the states. The Reichstag's approval was needed for new legislation or a new budget, but the chancellor could perpetuate an old budget indefinitely and ignore the Reichstag. This constitution was a compromise between eighteenth-century absolutism and nineteenth-century popular sovereignty, a fact underscored by the absence of any German bill of rights. The constitution did include some human rights, such as a guarantee of equal rights for Jews.

Bismarck and Defense of the Empire. During the "founding years" of the 1870s and 1880s, Bismarck built an alliance of conservative interests to support his government and battle its enemies. By 1879, he had gained the backing of the landowning aristocracy, the growing class of wealthy industrialists, and the supporters of militarism and nationalism—an alliance that set the direction of German history. The support of this coalition enabled Bismarck to fight the *Reichsfeinde* (Rikes'-fine-duh; enemies of the empire), whom he thought threatened the new empire, whether internal or external enemies.

Pius IX and Ultramontanism. Bismarck's target during the 1870s was the Catholic Church, which had become vigorously assertive during the pontificate of Pope Pius IX (1846–1878). He had been elected pope as a Liberal, sympathetic to Italian nationalism and had been an important reformer in his first years, granting a constitution for the Papal States. However, he became extremely reactionary after the Roman revolution of 1848 (when he was driven from the throne by a Roman Republic). He proclaimed doctrines sought by conservatives (such as the dogma of the Immaculate Conception), and in a document known as the Syllabus of Errors, he denounced the ideas of liberalism (such as civil marriage or education in public schools). During the final stage of the unification of Germany, Pius convened in Rome an assembly known as the Vatican Council. The council promulgated new Catholic dogma in a document known as *Pastor aeternus,* including the belief in **papal infallibility** (when speaking on matters of faith and morals). The result of Pius's conservative actions had been to strengthen **ultramontanism** (ultra-mahn'-tan-ism), the belief that all Catholic authority came from Rome (the other side of the mountains for most Europeans) and that Catholics must follow the

GERMAN LEADERSHIP IN EUROPE

MAP 26.1. EUROPE IN 1871

Legend:
- German Empire
- Austria-Hungary
- Italy
- France
- Ottoman Empire

The great changes in the map of Europe between 1815 and 1871 were largely in central Europe: the creation of the vast German Empire, the unification of Italy, and the formation of a "dual monarchy" in Austria-Hungary.

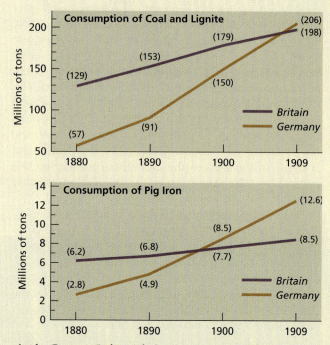

Anglo-German Industrial Competition, 1880–1909. Coal was an essential measure of industrial might because it was burned to power steam engines, including railroad locomotives. Iron was essential for industry machinery, including the rails. (Source: Baker, J. Ellis, *Modern Germany* [New York: 1919], reproduced in Snyder, Louis L., ed., *Documents of German History* [New Brunswick, NJ: Rutgers University Press, 1958, pp. 306–307].)

Question: Does this set of graphs show that Britain was falling behind in the industrial competition with Germany?

---

directions of the pope, especially in combat with modern world.

The Kulturkampf. Bismarck saw ultramontanism as a threat to the German Empire's authority because he expected all Germans to accept the primacy of the state, not of the pope. This led him to a battle with the Catholic Church known as the **Kulturkampf** (the struggle of cultures). The new empire held a Protestant (mostly Lutheran) majority, dominated by a Protestant state and monarch, but it included a large Catholic minority. The Syllabus of Errors explicitly opposed cooperation with Protestantism and resisted the power of the state. Bismarck disagreed. Between 1872 and 1875, Prussia adopted a series of **"May laws"** increasing state control in matters previously left to churches and ex-

pelling clerics who lacked state certification. By 1876, no Catholic bishops were left in Prussia (outside of prison) and 1,400 parishes were vacant.

Antisocialism. Bismarck ended the Kulturkampf in the late 1870s, when the more conciliatory Pope Leo XIII succeeded Pius IX, and Bismarck began to worry about a new enemy that threatened the empire. German elections gave the Social Democratic Party (SPD [for Sozialdemokratische Partei Deutschlands]) nearly 10 percent of the vote. Bismarck responded with an Anti-Socialist Law of 1878, which prohibited socialist meetings, closed socialist newspapers, restricted socialist fundraising, and permitted the harassment of the leaders of the SPD. Because the Second Reich had no bill of rights, this was all legal under German law.

TABLE 26.1 POPULATION OF THE GREAT POWERS AT THE END OF THE NINETEENTH CENTURY		
	POPULATION IN 1871	POPULATION IN 1901
Imperial Germany	41.1 million	56.4 million (1900)
France	36.1 million (1872)	39.0 million
United Kingdom	31.5 million	41.5 million
Italy	27.6 million	33.4 million
Austria-Hungary	20.2 million (1869)	25.9 million (1900)

Dates for data differ owing to differing census years in respective countries.

Source: Cook, Chris, and Paxton, John, eds., *European Political Facts, 1848–1918* (London: Macmillan, 1978, pp. 213–232).

TABLE 26.2 ARMY BUDGETS OF THE GREAT POWERS AT THE END OF THE NINETEENTH CENTURY		
	ARMY ESTIMATES FOR 1870	ARMY ESTIMATES FOR 1900
Germany	$46.7 million	$163.5 million
France	$73.0 million	$135.3 million
Great Britain	$65.2 million	$104.1 million
Austria-Hungary	$36.0 million	$58.4 million
Italy	$31.1 million	$52.6 million

Army estimates for 1870 represent amount budgeted before the war of 1870.

Data in pounds sterling converted at £1 = $4.866 (1890 rate).

Adapted from Taylor, A. J. P., *The Struggle for Mastery in Europe, 1848–1918* (Oxford: Oxford University Press, 1954, p. xxvii).

Question: What factors might explain the tremendous increase in army expenditures?

Bismarck's Welfare State. Bismarck's battle with socialism did not stop the growth of German trade union membership or reduce the number of socialist voters, so he changed his tactics. Concluding that "[s]omething positive should be done to remove the causes for socialism," he borrowed some of the legislative ideas that made socialism appealing. The deeply conservative Bismarck became one of the founders of the **welfare state,** telling the Reichstag that the state had "the duty of caring for its helpless fellow-citizens," adding that "[i]f someone objects that this is socialism, I do not shrink from it in the least." German **health insurance** began in 1883, **workers' accident compensation insurance** in 1884, and **old age and disability pensions** in 1889. These programs were kept small by granting pensions at age 65 when the average life expectancy at birth was 41 years. (Life expectancy did not reach 65 years until the 1940s.)

Kaiser William II. The death of Kaiser William I in 1888 nearly led to the liberalization of Germany, a course favored by his son, Frederick III. Frederick reigned for only a few weeks, however, before dying of throat cancer at age 57, and his son, Kaiser William II, led Germany in a different direction. William II (often known by the German form of his name, Wilhelm) came to the throne at age 29. He had no links to the dreams of 1848, the constitutional crisis of the 1850s, or the wars of the 1860s. Born with a deformed arm as the consequence of a forceps delivery, he was aggressive and arrogant to hide his insecurity. Bismarck tried to restrain the impulsive young emperor: "The Kaiser is like

FIGURE 26.1 *Pius IX.* Pope Pius IX ("pio nono") reigned in one of the longest papacies (1846–1878) in history, and he had a tremendous impact on both Catholic doctrine and European politics. His pontificate produced the dogma of the Immaculate Conception, the Syllabus of Errors (of modernity), and the doctrine of papal infallibility. In politics, he clashed with Italian Nationalists and Republicans in 1848 and with Bismarckian Conservatives and Nationalists in Kulturkampf.

a balloon. If you don't hold fast to the string, you never know where he'll be off to." However, William II decided in 1890 to retire the aging old chancellor. This episode, known as **"the dropping of the pilot,"** clearly reflected the young emperor's intention to rule personally. In William's words, "If Frederick the Great had had such a chancellor, he would not have been Frederick the Great."

Wilhelmine Germany. The leaders of Wilhelmine Germany were consequently men of less ability than Bismarck. They attempted to set a "new course" in the 1890s but accomplished little change in domestic affairs. Their greatest task was often to restrain the undemocratic instincts of the kaiser. William summarized his political sentiments when he attended a colonial exposition and observed a crude display of an African king's hut with the skulls of his rivals posted outside: "If only I could see the Reichstag stuck up like that!" The strongest chancellor of Wilhelmine Germany, Count (Prince after 1905) Bernhard von Bülow (Byou'-low), maintained the Bismarckian conservative coalition by giving higher agricultural tariffs to the Junkers and larger military contracts to industrialists. Bülow directed German energies to "world policy" *(Weltpolitik)*. With the enthusiasm of the em-

peror and the energy of a strong minister of the navy, Admiral Alfred von Tirpitz, the Bülow government (1900–1909) undertook a major arms race (especially in naval construction), the extension and consolidation of a German colonial empire (reluctantly begun by Bismarck), and the assertion of German leadership in global issues.

THE FRENCH THIRD REPUBLIC (1870–1914)

The war of 1870–1871 destroyed the French Second Empire as it created the German Second Empire. Napoleon III was taken prisoner at Sedan in September 1870. When the news reached Paris, a bloodless revolution announced the creation of a Third Republic (the name honoring the republics of 1792 and 1848). The Third Republic became the first republic in European history to last long enough to offer a viable alternative to monarchy. Despite a rocky start and a history filled with crises, the French Third Republic also survived a generation longer than the German Reich did.

The National Assembly. The capitulation of Paris in January 1871 led to an armistice in which the French elected a National Assembly that would negotiate a peace treaty and write the constitution of postwar France. Although Republicans and Parisians talked, fighting to the bitter end, monarchists and the provinces favored peace. A majority of the nation would have voted against monarchy if that were the issue, but they accepted monarchist representatives as the price of peace. A French National Assembly chose Adolphe Thiers (Tee-air'), a leader of the Orleanist monarchy and a critic of Napoleon III, as its executive. His government negotiated the Frankfurt Peace Treaty of May 1871, which cost France Alsace, much of Lorraine, and a 5-billion-franc (1-billion-dollar) war **indemnity.** (An *indemnity* is a punitive bill presented by the victors, as distinct from **reparations,** which are charged after some wars to rebuild devastated territory.)

Adolphe Theirs (1797–1877)

The Paris Commune. While the monarchist government of Thiers deliberated in suburban Versailles, Paris elected a municipal government, known as the Paris Commune of 1871, which denied the authority of the Versailles government. The **Commune** was a mixture of Republicans, Socialists, and anarchists. It did not last long enough to prepare a full program, but the Communards favored **decentralized government, the separation of church and state,** and a variety of social programs. Although it became a famous symbol in socialist literature, the Commune never even threatened the Bank of France or the Stock Exchange. It (and smaller communes in other cities) survived only for a few weeks from March to May 1871 before falling in a bloody civil war. Thiers used the French army to attack Paris (while the German army watched), and Versailles troops fought Communards street by street, executing anyone who was armed. The Communards responded with a similar ferocity, executing hostages (including the archbishop of Paris) and destroying monarchist monuments. Under the direction of a candidly cruel general, the Marquis de Gallifet (Gal-ih-fay'), the army punished the city. Gallifet felt justified in executing wounded prisoners (wounds were evidence of being involved in the fighting) or white-haired prisoners (who were thought old enough to have fought in the revolution of 1848, too). The monarchical revenge on Paris killed ten times as many Parisians (an estimated 25,000) as the Reign of Terror had guillotined there (2,600). An additional 40,000 military trials produced 10,000 sentences of imprisonment or deportation to a penal colony.

The Constitution of the Third Republic.
Following this civil war, the French had great difficulty in agreeing on a government during the 1870s. The National Assembly held a monarchist majority, but they were split among supporters of three royal families: the Bourbon **legitimists,** who wanted to crown the grandson of Charles X; the Orleanists, who favored the grandson of Louis Philippe; and the Bonapartists, who supported Napoleon III or his son. While these factions squabbled, by-elections filled vacant seats with Republicans, until even Thiers admitted that France must become a republic. The constitutional laws of the Third Republic were finally adopted in 1875. Monarchist deputies tried to make the new regime conservative—to guard against democracy and to provide for a future monarchical restoration. The constitution created a strong lower house of Parliament (the Chamber of Deputies), which was elected by universal manhood suffrage, and balanced it with an upper house (the Senate) elected indirectly. The head of the government (the premier) needed the support of a majority in the Chamber of Deputies.

The Ferry Reforms and Secularization.
In the late 1870s and the 1880s, Republicans created many of the basic laws and institutions of modern France. Moderates led by a quiet lawyer named Jules Ferry (Fair-ree'), who was twice premier and five times minister of education, and radical Republicans led by the more flamboyant Georges Clemenceau compromised on an initial program. The Ferry laws of the early 1880s created one of the basic institutions of democracy—a public school system that was free, secular, and compulsory. This legislation opened secondary schools to women and to children of the poorer classes. Although the population of France increased by less than 8 percent between 1883 and 1913, secondary school enrollment grew by 106 percent. The number of girls in secondary education grew from 11,100 to 55,700. The creation of secular schools was just one step in the republican **secularization** of France. Secular society (often called *laic* in French) included secular hospitals, civil marriage and burial, and divorce.

Anticlericalism.
Republicans sought a secular state, which they considered one of the foremost legacies of the French Revolution, because they realized that the church remained allied with the monarchy against republicanism and democracy (see Document 26.1) As Gambetta (Gam-bet'-uh) once put it, "Clericalism, there is the enemy!" Throughout the Third Republic, French Republicans supported a program of **anticlericalism**—opposition to the influence of the church in politics, not opposition to freedom of religion. The schools showed their success: whereas 44 percent of all French children (60 percent of all girls) were educated by the church in 1876, less than 1 percent (0.05 percent of all boys) were in 1912. Some radicals, like Clemenceau (Clem-en-so') urged Republicans to continue to the program of secularization with the complete separation of church and state—to abolish the Ministry of Religion (established by Napoleon) and to eliminate national budget expenditures for churches and the salary of priests, pastors, and rabbis.

Radicalism.
The political program of French radicals went beyond anticlericalism, secularism, and the separation of church and state. They debated innovations such as an income tax, welfare legislation on the German model, and even **proportional representation** (a democratic idea designed to give representation to minorities), but they did not include such basic democratic issues as the full political and civil rights of women. Most Republicans still hesitated to adopt such reforms (see Document 26.2).

Boulangism.
A conservative reaction against this republicanism swept France in the late nineteenth century. A popular minister of war, General Georges Boulanger, became the symbolic leader of this reaction, and monarchists, nationalists, and Catholics rallied to **"Boulangism,"** hoping that he would overthrow the republic. Boulangists won many seats in Parliament in

WILHELMINE GERMANY

William II. Kaiser William II of Germany (1859–1941) in imperial regalia and a heroic pose that disguised his withered arm. William was the grandson of William I, and he came to the throne at age 29 because his grandfather and father both died in 1888. William's determination to take an active role in the direction of Germany's destiny has led to the period after 1888 being known as "Wilhelmine Germany."

1245

Dropping the Pilot. Otto von Bismarck was the dominant statesman in Europe for nearly 30 years. In 1890, the 31-year-old Kaiser William II ended that era by dismissing the 75-year-old Bismarck—the chancellor of Germany served at the pleasure of the monarch, not the Parliament. The cartoon shown here, from the British magazine *Punch,* summarized that event with a nautical metaphor, "the dropping of the pilot," which became a widely used term for Bismarck's retirement. During the next generation, the German ship of state lacked such a skilled hand at the helm.

the late 1880s and taught the world a lesson in electoral demagoguery, but the general, fearing conspiracy charges against him, fled the country and committed suicide. Right-wing enemies of the republic resumed the attack in the 1890s, when several republican politicians were involved in a corruption scandal surrounding a failed French attempt to build a canal across the Isthmus of Panama.

Anti-Semitism. The Panama Canal scandal of 1892–1893 awakened one of the ugliest elements in European antidemocratic politics—**anti-Semitism.**

Anti-Semitism remained widespread in late nineteenth-century Europe; newspapers and political parties blatantly called themselves anti-Semitic, and the Catholic Church still held Jews morally responsible for the crucifixion of Jesus. Vienna elected Karl Lueger, an anti-Semite, as its mayor, and he fired Jewish officials and segregated the schools. In Germany, the Anti-Semite Party elected deputies to the Reichstag in every election from 1887 to 1912 and held eleven to sixteen seats after 1893. In Russia, the **pogroms** (direct attacks on Jewish communities) killed thousands and led millions to flee the country.

General von Schlieffen. Count and General Alfred von Schlieffen (1833–1913) served as Chief of German General Staff for 15 years under William II (1891–1906), and his role was one of the most important in German military history. He devoted himself to the problem of fighting a two-front war against both France and Russia. The result was the Schlieffen Plan, which would lead Germany to invade neutral Belgium at the start of World War I.

Admiral von Tirpitz. Admiral Alfred von Tirpitz (1849–1930) served as chief of the naval staff in the early 1890s before becoming William II's Secretary of State for the Navy in 1897. Tirpitz became the father of the German battle fleet by sponsoring a series of naval construction laws beginning in 1898. He gave Germany the second strongest battle fleet in the world but thereby contributed greatly to the deterioration of Anglo-German relations.

The Dreyfus Affair. French anti-Semitism produced the most dramatic human rights battle of the nineteenth century—the Dreyfus (Dry'-fus) affair. The French army was one of the few European armies of the 1890s to open its officer corps to Jews, and Captain Alfred Dreyfus was 1 of 300 French Jewish officers in the 1890s. Dreyfus was serving as an artillery expert on the French General Staff in 1894 when counterintelligence found evidence that artillery secrets from the General Staff were reaching the Germans. Bigoted officers convicted Dreyfus of treason and sentenced him to solitary imprisonment on Devil's Island (off the northern coast of South America), although they never possessed a shred of evidence against him. When evidence of Dreyfus's innocence began to accumulate in the late 1890s, **Dreyfusards** organized to free him, founding one of the world's first **human rights** organizations, the League of the Rights of Man. An anti-Dreyfusard coalition of monarchists, conservative Catholics, nationalists, militarists, and anti-Semites defended the army and its verdict. French anti-Semitism remained a nasty element throughout the Dreyfus affair, but the battle came to focus on the issues of justice and

JULES FERRY ON THE SECULAR STATE, 1876

The late 1870s and the 1880s witnessed the triumph of republicanism in France and the adoption of numerous reforms. One of the central themes of these reforms was secularism. Laws were adopted, such as the legalization of divorce, which responded to the concerns of secular society, not to the wishes of the church. Basic institutions, such as schools, were made public, secular institutions rather than church-run. One of the central figures in the effort to create the secular (or *laic*) state was Jules Ferry who was twice premier and five times minister of education. He defended the secular state in a speech to the Chamber of Deputies in 1876.

I pronounce the words secular state without any trepidation, even though, for some of our honorable colleagues they would seem to have a certain radical, anarchist, or revolutionary flavor. Yet I am not saying anything new, revolutionary, or anarchist when I maintain that the state must be secular, that the totality of society is necessarily represented by secular organizations.

What, exactly, is this principle? It is a doctrine that [the church] prides itself on having introduced to the world: the doctrine of the separation of temporal and spiritual power. Yes, Christianity introduced the doctrine of the separation of these two domains. . . . However, there is one reproach we could make against the church in this matter. After taking four or five centuries to introduce this doctrine, the church has then spent seven or eight centuries attacking it. (Applause on the left.)

Gentlemen, what was the key accomplishment, the major concern, the great passion and service of the French Revolution? To have built this secular state, to have succeeded in making the social organisms of society exclusively secular, to have taken away from the clergy its political organization and role as a cadre within the state—that, precisely, is the French Revolution in its full reality. Well, now, we do not presume to convert the honorable members seated on this side of the Chamber [the monarchists, seated on the right] to the doctrines of the revolution. We only wish it to be understood that we do not deviate from these doctrines. Convinced that the first concern, the first duty of a democratic government is to maintain incessant, powerful, vigilant, and efficient control over public education, we insist that this control belong to no other authority than the state. We cannot admit, we will never admit, and this country of France will never admit that the State can be anything but a secular one. ("Very Good!" shouts from left and center)

From *Journal officiel de la République française,* June 3, 1876, as translated in Goldstein, Jan, and Boyer, John W., eds., *Nineteenth-Century Europe: Liberalism and Its Critics* (Chicago: University of Chicago Press, 1988, p. 358).

Question: What is secularism for Jules Ferry?

---

individual rights balanced against the interests of the state. The fight continued until a second court martial reconvicted Dreyfus in 1899, and an outraged president of the republic pardoned him.

The Birth of Zionism. It was shocking to the educated world, and especially to European Jews, that liberal and tolerant France could be the home of such anti-Semitism. One of the shocked was an Austrian journalist named Theodor Herzl (Hairtz'-zul) who published *The Jewish State* in 1896. Herzl posed a painful question: "Are we [Jews] to 'get out' now and to where? Or, may we remain? And how long?" He concluded that Jews must prepare to found a Jewish State outside of Europe, in a region such as Palestine, and he founded a movement called Zionism to achieve that homeland and security.

Separation of Church and State. The immediate importance of the Dreyfus affair was that it led to elec-

toral victories for the Republicans, Radicals, and Socialists who defended Dreyfus. This made the left-wing majority feel strong enough to return to its reform agenda. In 1901, they dissolved many associations of the Catholic Church, and in 1905, they separated church and state, ending both state financial support for and state regulation of the churches. In 1906, Clemenceau became premier for the first time (at age 65) and created the first Ministry of Labor, which he entrusted to a Socialist. In 1907, feminists won one of their foremost goals, a **Married Women's Property Act** known as the Schmahl Law (for the woman who had campaigned for it); until this reform, property in a marriage was owned by the husband alone, even including a wife's wages at work. The radicals also laid the basis of the French welfare system. Earlier governments had established state aid for neglected children (1889) and a medical assistance program (1893). Republicans now provided state support for hygienic housing (1902), needy children (1904), the aged and the infirm

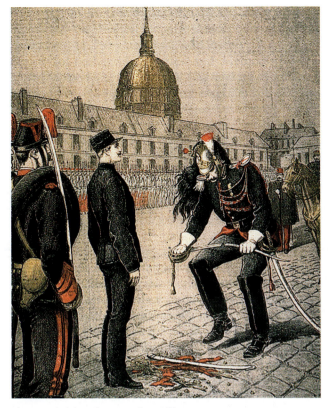

FIGURE 26.2 *The Dreyfus Affair.* The 1894 court martial (on a charge of spying for Germany) of Captain Alfred Dreyfus, a Jewish officer on the French General Staff, led in 1898–1899 to the most passionate human rights debate of the nineteenth century, when the innocence of Dreyfus was discovered but the army refused to reconsider its verdict. The debate between Dreyfusards, who demanded a revision of the verdict, and defenders of the army awakened some of the most vehement anti-Semitism of the century. In this image, Dreyfus has been stripped of his rank and watches as his sword is broken in a ceremony before he was sent to solitary confinement on Devil's Island.

CLEMENCEAU'S RADICAL-DEMOCRATIC PROGRAM, 1881

Article 1. Revision of the constitution. Abolition of the Senate and the Presidency. . . .

Article 2. Individual freedom. Liberty of the press, of meetings, of association, guaranteed by the constitution. . . .

Article 3. Separation of church and state. Suppression of state aid for churches. . . .

Article 4. The right of children to a full education. Secular, free, obligatory education.

Article 5. Reduction of the term of military service. Obligatory military service for all citizens. . . .

Article 6. Judicial system free and equal for all. Judges elected for short terms. . . . Abolition of the death penalty.

Article 7. Sovereignty of universal suffrage. . . . [S]horter terms of office for elected officials. . . .

Article 9. Autonomy for local governments. Town governments to control their own administration, finances, police. . . .

Article 11. Tax reform. . . . Suppression of indirect consumption taxes. Progressive taxes on capital or income.

Article 13. Legalization of divorce.

Article 14. Reduction in the length of the working day. Suppression of work by children younger than fourteen. . . . Creation of retirement savings for the aged and the injured.

Article 15. Revision of labor laws. . . . Responsibility of employers for work-related accidents, guaranteed by insurance.

From Clemenceau, Georges, "Cahier des électeurs," trans. Steven C. Hause, *La Justice,* November 19, 1881.

Question: What was radical about this program?

(1905–1906), retirement pensions (1910), and large families (1913).

The Democratic Agenda. Such reforms still left a large democratic agenda on the eve of World War I. Despite vehement feminist protests by Hubertine Auclert and Madeleine Pelletier in 1908 and the peaceful demonstrations of hundreds of thousands of suffragists, women's suffrage remained far from acceptance. Even amid increased labor violence and equally large demonstrations, the 40-hour workweek remained a utopian dream. And despite their electoral successes, the Radicals were unable to win a majority for proportional representation, the right of government employees to strike, a graduated income tax, maternity leaves for new mothers, or the abolition of the death penalty.

Simply debating such issues, however, made France a leader of European democratic thought.

LATE VICTORIAN AND EDWARDIAN BRITAIN (1868–1914)

Great Britain also remained a leader in the evolution of liberal-democratic institutions. Smaller states were often pioneers in adopting radical reforms—as the Scandinavian states were with women's rights—but Britain and France defined the model of parliamentary democracy for the great powers. The British model remained one of gradual evolution, but the years before 1914 witnessed two important periods of rapid change.

FIGURE 26.3 *Hubertine Auclert.* Auclert founded the women's suffrage movement in France in the 1880s, and by the early twentieth century, she had become frustrated enough at the obstinate refusal of men to accept equal rights for women that she briefly used violent tactics. Her most famous demonstration—depicted here on the front cover of *Le Petit Journal* May 17, 1908—was to invade a Parisian polling place on election day in 1908, smash a ballot box to the ground, and trample on the exclusively masculine ballots. The woman with her arm upraised is Auclert—who knocked over the box alone and was arrested, tried, and fined.

William E. Gladstone.

The first period of intensive reform came during a Liberal government of 1868–1874, elected after the expansion of the franchise in 1867. The leader of this government was one the greatest figures of nineteenth-century liberalism, William E. Gladstone. Gladstone had been elected to Parliament at age 22, following a brilliant career at Oxford, where he had won first-class honors in two separate fields. He began his career as a cabinet minister at age 34 and served as a member of Parliament (M.P.) for more than 60 years. Gladstone served four terms as prime minister of Britain, beginning with his "great ministry" (1868–1874) and ending with a cabinet in his eighties (1892–1894). He brought to govern-

FIGURE 26.4 *Gladstone's First Home Rule Bill.* William E. Gladstone (1809–1898) served four terms as prime minister of England and achieved many of the basic liberal reforms of the era, including the introduction of the secret ballot, the opening of primary schooling to all children, and the ending of some forms of legal discrimination against religious minorities. Gladstone declined to address some issues (such as women's suffrage) and suffered repeated defeats in his attempts to grant home rule to Ireland. In this image, Gladstone (the standing figure in black at left-center) addresses Parliament on his Home Rule Bill of 1886.

ment a religious scholar's moralistic temperament that made him resemble an Old Testament patriarch. Gladstone supported his moralism with an intellect that dominated Parliament. He could speak for 3 hours without a break or summarize an arduous debate with a long quotation in Latin without translation, leaving few M.P.s who could match him.

Gladstone's Great Ministry.

Gladstone's great ministry adopted nearly a dozen major reforms. He did not attempt another expansion of the franchise (although that was on his agenda) or to give women the vote (which was not in his plans). He did, however, enhance British democracy with a **Secret Ballot Act** of 1872. The Elementary Education Act of 1870 (known as the Forster Act for its author, William Forster) made primary schooling available to all children in England and Wales, from age 5 to 13. In contrast to the Ferry laws in France, the Forster Act subsidized private, tuition-paying schools and created state schools only, as Forster put it, "to complete the present voluntary system, to fill up the gaps." In Britain as in France, adult illiteracy quickly fell, from 20 percent of adult males (1870) to 2 percent (1900). Gladstone similarly opened higher education. A **University Tests Act** (1871) abolished religious barriers to enrollment at Oxford and Cambridge, permitting Catholics, Jews, and nonbelievers to matriculate. At the same time, two colleges at Cambridge were opened to women, although women remained ineligible for degrees until after World War I.

Gladstone's government also tackled army reform, judicial reform, trade union rights, the civil service, and the Irish question. The sale of commissions as officers in the army was abolished, and the term of military enlistment was reduced from 12 years to 6. Judicial reforms ended imprisonment for debt and created appellate courts. Workers won the complete legalization of **trade unions** and the recognition of their **right to strike,** but not the right to picket their employers. Civil service reforms created a modern bureaucracy by abolishing the **patronage system** of giving jobs to friends and supporters in favor of competitive examinations for all posts except those in the Foreign Office. Gladstone's great ministry also began to address the Irish question. An Irish Land Act gave some protection to Irish farmers who rented lands and could be evicted after poor harvests. Gladstone also disestablished the Church of Ireland (the Anglican Church in Ireland), meaning that the people of Ireland (90 percent Catholic) were no longer required to provide tax support for a Protestant state church. Such reforms built cooperation between the Liberal Party and Irish M.P.s, who pressed Gladstone to take the next logical step—grant the Irish **home rule** (autonomy) in domestic matters.

Benjamin Disraeli. The end of Gladstone's great ministry returned to office his long-time rival, the conservative prime minister Benjamin Disraeli. In contrast to Gladstone's sober strengths, Disraeli sparkled with wit and style. He derided Gladstone's much-praised oratory as "harebrained chatter." Disraeli had flirted with reforms in his earlier career, but in his second term as prime minister (1874–1880), he steered a more traditional course, satisfying conservatives opposed to liberal reformism. As one conservative essayist, Thomas Carlyle, had summarized the attack on Gladstonian liberalism: Britain was a nation of "mostly fools," and it was dangerous to "believe in the collective wisdom of individual ignorance." Disraeli shrewdly turned the government's attention away from domestic issues and aimed for British success in foreign and colonial affairs. In 1875, he adroitly purchased control of the French-built Suez Canal, giving Britain control of the route to India and great influence in Egypt. In 1876, his government adopted the Royal Titles Bill, which named Queen Victoria "Empress of India" and put her title on a par with those of the emperors of Austria-Hungary, Germany, and Russia. (Four months later, a grateful queen named Disraeli the Earl of Beaconsfield.) In 1878, he personally represented Britain at the Congress of Berlin, where he successfully defended the British interest in preserving the Ottoman Empire (rather than seeing Russia pose a potential threat to India).

Gladstonian Democracy. Gladstone returned to his reform agenda in a second ministry (1880–1885) after shocking conservatives by introducing campaigning to British politics: he toured the nation and appealed directly to the voters. This time Gladstone sought democratization and Irish **home rule** (Irish self-government in domestic issues, while remaining part of Britain). His Representation of the People Bill (1884) extended the vote in rural Britain and brought the kingdom closer to the universal manhood suffrage that existed in France and Germany (see *The Democratization of Britain*). This was the third great reform bill of the nineteenth century, following those in 1832 and 1867; collectively, they increased the size of the electorate eleven-fold. Domestic servants were still denied the vote, however, as were all women.

Parnell and Home Rule. The Irish question presented greater difficulties. Home rule had become the objective of Irish politicians in the 1870s, when Isaac Butt, a lawyer and the son of a Protestant clergyman, had formed a coalition of Catholics and Protestants to seek it. When Butt's movement won the support of most Irish M.P.s in 1874, it became the Irish Home Rule League. A few years later, the league found a popular successor to Butt in Charles Stewart Parnell, a Protestant landowner who had entered Parliament in 1875 at age 29. Parnell managed to unite Irish nationalists, including the more militant and republican Fenians (Fee'-nee-uns); the British increased his popularity by imprisoning him and watching while he organized a farmers' **rent strike** from his cell. Parnell denounced revolutionary violence in 1882, after the assassination in Dublin of the two leading cabinet members for the government of Ireland, an act known as the Phoenix Park murders. Parnell and his followers developed nonviolent tactics such as the **boycott** of uncooperative landlords; the name of that tactic came from a campaign in which no servants, no farm workers, no shopkeepers, and not even the postman would acknowledge the existence of a landlord in County Mayo named Charles Boycott.

The First and Second Home Rule Bills. Gladstone adopted the cause of home rule in 1886 and at the age of 77 introduced the first Home Rule Bill with a 3-hour, 30-minute speech. This issue shattered the Liberal Party. Ninety-two Liberal M.P.s, led by the prominent Liberal spokesman of the 1840s, John Bright, and Bright's protégé, a wealthy manufacturer from Birmingham, Joseph Chamberlain, left the party and formed their own faction, the **Unionists** (who insisted on preserving the union with Ireland). Gladstone strove to build a majority in favor of home rule but suffered another setback when Irish M.P.s were divided by a scandal over Parnell's love affair with the wife of another M.P. Gladstone defended Parnell, observing that "I have known eleven prime ministers, ten of whom

THE DEMOCRATIZATION OF BRITAIN

TABLE 26.3 THE DEMOCRATIZATION OF THE BRITISH ELECTORATE

	England and Wales		Scotland		Ireland		United Kingdom	
YEAR	ELIGIBLE VOTERS	% OF TOTAL POPULATION	ELIGIBLE VOTERS	% OF TOTAL POPULATION	ELIGIBLE VOTERS	% OF TOTAL POPULATION	ELIGIBLE VOTERS	% OF TOTAL POPULATION
1831	435,000	3.1	5,000	0.2	76,000	0.9	516,000	2.1
1833	656,000	3.5	64,000	2.7	92,000	1.2	812,000	3.4
1866	1,054,000	5.3	105,000	3.4	205,000	3.5	1,364,000	4.7
1868	1,960,000	9.8	236,000	7.7	222,000	3.8	2,418,000	8.4
1883	2,618,000	10.1	310,000	8.3	224,000	4.3	3,152,000	9.0
1885	4,380,000	16.9	551,000	14.7	738,000	14.3	5,669,000	16.3

Source: Compiled from data in Cook, Chris, and Keith, Brendan, *British Historical Facts, 1830–1900* (London: MacMillan, 1975, pp. 115, 232–233).

The People's Budget

The provision for the aged and deserving poor—was it not time something was done? It is rather a shame that a rich country like ours—probably the richest in the world, if not the richest the world has ever seen—should allow those who toiled all their days to end in penury and possibly starvation. It is rather hard that an old workman should have to find his way to the gates of the tomb, bleeding and footsore, through the brambles and thorns of poverty. We cut a new path for him. . . . There are many in the country blessed by Providence with great wealth, and if there are amongst them men who grudge out of their riches a fair contribution towards the less fortunate of their fellow countrymen they are very shabby rich men.

We propose to do more by means of the Budget. We are raising money to provide against the evils and sufferings that follow from unemployment. We are raising money for the purpose of assisting . . . to provide for the sick and the widows and orphans. . . .

Some of our critics say, "The taxes themselves are unjust, unfair, unequal, oppressive—notably so the land taxes. . . ." They are now protesting against paying their fair share of the taxation of the land, and they are doing so by saying, ". . . You are putting burdens upon the people which they cannot bear." Ah! they are not thinking of themselves. Noble souls! . . . [W]e were so impressed by this tearful appeal that at last we said, "We will leave [small landowners] out."

From George, Lloyd, *The Times*, July 31, 1909.

Question: How effective does Lloyd George's argument seem?

---

were adulterers," but Parnell's career, and the chances for home rule, were ruined. Gladstone obtained the prime ministry for the fourth time in 1892. He introduced a second Home Rule Bill a few months later (1893), and his Liberal majority carried it through the House of Commons. A decade of debate, however, had entrenched conservative opposition to home rule. Lord Randolph Churchill, an aggressive Tory M.P. who had once led the progressive wing of the party, fought Gladstone under the slogan "Home Rule Means Rome Rule." This campaign encouraged resistance in the Protestant population of Northern Ireland, where mili-

tants warned that "Ulster will fight." Such passions led the conservative majority in the House of Lords to crush the second Home Rule Bill (419–441).

The Labour Party and Taff Vale. The early twentieth century witnessed a second period of radical reform in Britain, comparable to Gladstone's great ministry. The Liberal Party built a new majority in 1905, sometimes supported by the twenty-nine M.P.s of the new Labour Party, which had been organized in 1906 by a Scottish miner, Keir (Kear) Hardie, and a Scottish journalist, Ramsay MacDonald. One of the first legislative actions of the new government, the Trades Disputes Act of 1906, responded to the labor movement's greatest grievance. Gladstone's Trades Disputes Act of 1871 had given legal recognition to unions, and they had gradually gained such rights as picketing. In 1901, however, the House of Lords had rendered a dramatically antilabor ruling in a legal case known as the *Taff Vale Railway Company v. Amalgamated Society of Railway Servants.* The Taff Vale ruling held that a union could be sued for the actions of its members and that a union could be held liable for a company's losses during a strike. The Liberal government of 1906 repaid labor support by overturning the Taff Vale decision and restoring the **right to strike and picket,** through the Trade Disputes Act.

David Lloyd George and the Welfare State.

The Liberal coalition found its radical voice in David Lloyd George, who typified the changing nature of liberalism from a **laissez-faire** doctrine of noninterventionist government to an activist doctrine of **governmental intervention** to protect the vulnerable. Lloyd George, a Welsh lawyer possessed with a charming yet ferocious mastery of debate, drafted the government's economic policies as **chancellor of the exchequer** (minister of finance) and led Britain into the age of welfare legislation. A Workmen's Compensation Act (1906) greatly expanded benefits, the Old Age Pensions Act (1909) replaced the workhouse system, and the National Insurance Act (1912) introduced health and unemployment insurance. The cornerstone of the Liberal welfare state was the budget that Lloyd George introduced in 1909. The "People's Budget" attacked the conservative tradition that the state could spend large sums for military preparations (such as large new battleships) but not for social welfare (see Document 26.3). Lloyd George further angered conservatives by proposing to pay for these expenditures by taxing the rich.

The Parliament Act.

The Lloyd George budget led to the democratization of Parliament (by ending the power of the House of Lords to block legislation) and thereby led to hopes for a third Home Rule Bill. The House of Lords, which remained an unelected body defending the interests of the landed aristocracy, held the power to veto any legislation except a budget. Lloyd George, however, had presented them with an irresistible target. Lords vetoed the People's Budget of 1909, creating a constitutional crisis and exposing itself to a Liberal assault. The Liberal government turned to the new king, George V (reigned 1910–1936), and asked him to support them in defending the prerogatives of the House of Commons. George V reluctantly promised to ennoble 400 commoners (enough new peers to create a Liberal Party majority in the House of Lords) if the Conservative nobles would not back down.

Forced to choose between surrendering their obstructionist power and the prospect of Lloyd George selling hundreds of titles to the highest radical bidder, the Tories capitulated. The result was the Parliament Act of 1911. The House of Lords surrendered its claim to power over the budget and lost its absolute veto over all legislation. The Lords retained a **suspensive veto:** they could delay a law by vetoing it for 2 consecutive years, but they could not block a bill on its third passage of the Commons.

The Third Home Rule Bill.

This democratization of Parliament raised Irish hopes for home rule because they still had the support of a Liberal majority in the House of Commons. When the third Home Rule Bill sailed through the House of Commons in 1912 and was vetoed again in the House of Lords, it seemed certain that Ireland would receive self-government in 1914. Protestants in Northern Ireland warned of civil war. Ironically, a war of another kind blocked home rule: World War I began in 1914, shortly before home rule would have become law, and Liberals suspended the issue until the war's end. The Irish felt betrayed by the British political system and would rise up during the war in the Easter Rebellion of 1916.

Women's Suffrage.

Although the Irish did not win self-government until 1920, the Liberals had tried harder on their behalf than they had for women's rights. The first women's suffrage debate in Parliament (1867) and the right of women to vote in local elections (1869) had arrived before the first Home Rule Bill (1886), but neither of the major parties was willing to adopt the cause of votes (or candidacy) for women. Gladstone consciously chose to exclude women's suffrage from his electoral reform bill (1884). Thus, as suffrage became a widespread issue across Europe, Britain seemed scarcely closer to change in 1906 than 30 years earlier.

IMPERIAL RUSSIA ON THE EVE OF REVOLUTION (1881–1914)

Russian Backwardness.

The Russian Empire remained markedly different from Britain, France, and Germany in the late nineteenth century. Despite the abolition of serfdom in 1861, Russian society was more typical of the Old Regime than of the industrialized liberal democracies of western Europe. Ninety percent of the population still lived in a rural world. Urbanization was so slight in 1870 that capitals such as Helsinki (26,000) or Kiev (71,000) remained mere towns. Despite the reforms of the Alexandrine age, Russia remained a peasant society ruled by aristocratic landowners unrestrained by a parliament, a constitution, or a

A CONSERVATIVE CRITIQUE OF DEMOCRACY

Konstantin Pobedonostsev (poe'-beh-don-awst-seff) expressed his opposition to the liberalization of Russia in his memoirs, published after Count Sergei Witte had begun to lead Russia toward Westernization.

Among the falsest of political principles is the principle of the sovereignty of the people, the principle that all power issues from the people, and is based upon the national will—a principle which has unhappily become more firmly established since the time of the French revolution. From it proceeds the principle of parliamentarianism, which, today has deluded much of the so-called "intelligentsia," and has unfortunately infatuated certain foolish Russians. It continues to maintain its hold on many minds with the obstinacy of a narrow fanaticism, although every day its falsehood is exposed more clearly to the world. . . .

What is this freedom by which so many minds are agitated, which inspires so many insensate actions, so many wild speeches, which leads the people so often to misfortune? In the democratic sense of the word, freedom is the right to political power, or, to express it otherwise, the right to participate in the government of the state. This universal aspiration for a share in government has no constant limitations, and seeks no definite issue, but incessantly extends. . . . Forever extending its base, the new democracy now aspires to universal suffrage—a fatal error, and one of the most remarkable in the history of mankind. . . . In a Democracy, the real rulers are the dexterous manipulators of votes. . . . [T]hey rule the people as any despot or military dictator might rule it.

From Pobedonostsev, Konstantin, *Reflections of a Russian Statesman* (London: Robert Long, 1898).

Question: How valid does this critique of democracy seem?

---

bill of rights. The distribution of land at **emancipation** had not created a class of peasant landowners with small farms. More than 80 percent of the peasant land in Russia was owned communally (although some regions, such as Lithuania, had significant private ownership). These **communal farms** of the late nineteenth century fell short of western standards; a study of 1900 found that 83 percent of all peasants still used wooden plows.

The Assassination of Alexander II. Russian backwardness produced many tragedies, such as the killing of Alexander II in 1881. An old witticism of European statecraft said that Russia was "an absolute monarchy tempered by **regicide** [bold added]." That remark became somewhat less amusing after 1879, when a group of radicals founded a revolutionary society named the

People's Will *(Narodnaia Volia)*. Their program resembled democratic socialism in the west (a Russian parliament, universal suffrage, freedom of speech and the press, peasant ownership of the land, and worker control of the factories), but their chief activity was assassination. The People's Will made five unsuccessful attempts to kill Alexander II, including burrowing under railroad tracks to blow up his train, before succeeding on their sixth attempt.

The Reactionary Reign of Tsar Alexander III. The murdered tsar's son, Alexander III (reigned 1881–1894), had the Romanov family's extraordinary height (6'6'' in a world where the average height was less than 5'6'') and exceptional strength (he once intimidated a statesman at the dinner table by tying a piece of silverware into a knot), but he had none of the liberal sentiments that had made his father the most significant Russian reformer of the century. Alexander III's mind had been shaped by his chief adviser, Konstantin Pobedonostsev, a deeply conservative, antidemocratic man who opposed the **Westernization** of Russia as destructive to national traditions. His official position as procurator of the holy synod (minister of religion) enabled him to state the regime's philosophy. He taught that popular sovereignty was "among the falsest of political principles" and that universal suffrage was "a fatal error, and one of the most remarkable in the history of mankind" (see Document 26.3). Pobedonostsev and the head of the secret police, Vyacheslav Plehve, presided over a police state that cracked down on dissident groups. They tightened censorship, established firmer control over schools, and reduced the independence of the judiciary. **Russification** was again imposed on minorities. Jews suffered especially severe restrictions, but Catholics in Poland and small sects, such as the "Old Believers," also endured harassment. Nearly 8,000 trials of political opponents were held in the 1880s. Alexander II's reforms were diluted, and two-thirds of the eligible voters for the *zemstva* were disenfranchised; turn-of-the-century St. Petersburg thus had an electorate of 7,000 men in a population of 1,267,000 (0.6 percent).

Russian Revolutionary Movements. The repressive regime of Alexander III, Pobedonostsev, and Plehve provoked a revolutionary opposition. **Populist movements,** collectively known as the *Narodniki,* continued the Russian tradition of peasant socialism and assassinations, although the government broke up the most militant terrorist groups. Early industrialization in Moscow and St. Petersburg led some dissidents to Marxism. George Plekhanov (Pleh-kahn'-off) began to introduce Marxism into Russia in the 1880s, and imperial censors assisted him by permitting the publication of *Das Kapital,* reasoning that it was too boring to be a threat.

Tsar Nicholas II. Alexander III died of natural causes in 1894, bringing to the throne his son, the last tsar of Russia, Nicholas II. Nicholas was a more sensitive and intelligent man than his father, but he was less forceful and resolute. He was fortunate to inherit a capable statesman, Count Sergei Witte (Vit'-teh), whom Alexander had named minister of finance in 1892. Witte's tenure in that post and subsequent leadership as prime minister marked the first sustained effort to bring Russia into the industrial age. He pressed the cause of economic Westernization with a vigor unseen since Peter the Great, arguing that an unindustrialized Russia would be unable to compete in the European state system. During the 1890s, Witte's view of Russia's future supplanted Pobedonostsev's **Slavophile** insistence on guarding Russia's separate historic evolution.

The Russian Economy. The Russia of the 1890s had far to go before it could compete with western Europe. The empire had a large labor supply, but restraints on its mobility remained because former serfs had an obligation to help their commune repay the **redemption bonds** given to the landowners at the time of emancipation. Nearly 10 percent of the imperial budget depended on these redemption payments, and rural communities kept a maximum working population in the fields. Factories consequently remained few in number and small in size before the expansion of the 1890s. A study of Ukraine has shown that factories tripled their average workforce (to 4,600 workers) during that decade. Russian agriculture had the potential to feed this urban population and to raise capital by exporting surpluses, but it remained too backward to fulfill the promise. At the turn of the twentieth century (1898–1902), Russian farmers produced an average yield of 8.8 bushels of grain per acre, whereas British farmers supported an urban population by producing 35.4 bushels per acre. As late as 1912, the entire Russian Empire contained a total of 166 tractors.

Sergei Witte and Russian Industrialization. Sergei Witte addressed Russian backwardness in several ways. Taxes on the sale of alcohol provided the largest source of revenue, so Witte built a state monopoly on such sales. He put the Russian currency (the ruble) on the gold standard to enhance credit with foreign lenders. Russia already carried a large national debt, which amounted to 5.5 billion rubles in 1891—nearly six times the annual budget of the empire. Such debt had become so integral to European economics that Russia was still repaying Dutch loans of 1778 and 1815 and devoted nearly 27 percent of its budget to loan repayments. Witte believed that "[n]o country has ever developed without foreign capital" and sought new loans. He used this investment to found a national bank, provide state aid in building factories, and construct the Russian railroad system. Witte created a system of state-controlled (60 percent ownership) railways. He doubled the total of working track in Russia during the 1890s, including the construction of the Trans-Siberian Railroad, a 5,000-mile link between Moscow and the Pacific port of Vladivostok. The cost of this program, however, was a national debt so severe that state-supported progress in other areas was impossible.

The Revolutionary Opposition. Industrialization increased political discontent. The living and working conditions that characterized early industrialization everywhere increased the revolutionary violence that Russia had experienced for a generation. Attempted assassinations became a regular feature of Russian politics. During the 1890s, two prime ministers, an education minister, a provincial governor, and an uncle of the tsar were among those killed. With no parliament, underground radical parties flourished. Plekhanov organized the Russian Social Democratic Party in 1898, and agrarian radicals from the populist tradition created a competing organization, the Socialist Revolutionary Party, in 1901. This underground—largely led by people from educated, middle-class backgrounds—became more complex in 1903, when the Social Democrats held a party congress in London and split in two.

Lenin. The London congress marked the emergence of Lenin in Russian politics. Lenin (the adopted name of a lawyer born Vladimir Ulyanov) was radicalized by the execution of his older brother for plotting against the tsar. Arrested in 1895 and sent to Siberia for spreading propaganda in St. Petersburg, Lenin reached Switzerland in 1900 and there published a revolutionary newspaper, *Iskra* (the Spark), to be smuggled into Russia. He joined Plekhanov (also an intellectual living in exile) in building the Social Democratic Party, but he soon rejected Plekhanov's idealistic socialism in favor of a more revolutionary doctrine. Lenin called for a small party of revolutionary leaders instead of a mass movement. In a clever propaganda stroke, Lenin named his small faction of the party the **Bolsheviks** (the majority), branding the more numerous supporters of Plekhanov the **Mensheviks** (the minority).

Liberal-Democrats. In addition to the underground activities of the Social Democrats and the Social Revolutionaries, open opposition to tsarist autocracy existed and included a liberal-democratic movement among Westernizers who wished to emulate the development of Britain and France. This movement drew its strength from the intelligentsia, the liberal professions, educated urban circles, and *zemstvo* workers who combined to organize the Union of Liberation in 1903. This group was a nascent liberal political party, critical of autocracy and calling for a constitution, a parliament, and a bill of rights.

The Revolution of 1905.

Russia experienced a major revolution in 1905. Crushing defeat in the Russo-Japanese War of 1904–1905 (see Chapter 27), led to this revolt. In mid-1904, Plehve was killed in a terrorist bombing. A few weeks later, zemstvo delegates assembled for a congress in St. Petersburg and asked Nicholas II to call a Russian Parliament. During the winter of 1904–1905, as the Russian army suffered reverses in the Orient, strikes and demonstrations began. By early January, 10,625 factories were closed and 125,000 strikers were out. A turning point came on Sunday, January 9, 1905, when an Orthodox missionary to the working-class slums of St. Petersburg, George Gapon, led a protest march to deliver a petition to Nicholas II. Gapon (known as Father Gapon, although he had not completed his study for the priesthood) had been organizing illegal trade unions since 1903 and had recently led his followers out on strike. Their petition to the tsar called for Russian democracy and help for workers and peasants. Before marchers could reach the royal palace, however, the army fired on them. This "Bloody Sunday" massacre left 70 marchers dead and 240 wounded. In Gapon's words, this "killed our faith in the tsar." He escaped to London but was assassinated there. Strikes, demonstrations, and a naval mutiny (aboard the battleship Potemkin in the Black Sea) followed.

The Constitution of 1906.

Nicholas II vacillated in response to the revolution of 1905. Count Witte was not a great champion of liberalism, and when workers orga-

FIGURE 26.5 *The Revolution of 1905.* A decisive moment in the coming of revolution to Russia in 1905 came on Sunday, January 22. After 3 weeks of strikes and 5 days of a general strike, a procession of workers marched to the Winter Palace in St. Petersburg to present a petition to the tsar. As the marchers neared the palace, troops opened fire on them, killing 70 and wounding 240 in what became known as "Bloody Sunday." This massacre made a quick end to labor unrest unlikely.

nized councils **(soviets),** he responded by ordering the arrest of the entire St. Petersburg soviet; fifty-two representatives were tried and fifteen leaders, including the young Leon Trotsky, were sent to Siberia. Witte was a pragmatist, however. He encouraged the tsar to concede to many of the revolutionary demands, and he drafted the documents (the August Manifesto and the October Manifesto) in which Nicholas did so. The August Manifesto promised a limited parliament (the **Duma**) to be elected by limited suffrage. When unrest continued and a general strike was called, Nicholas II granted further concessions in the October Manifesto: a Russian constitution, a Duma with significant legislative powers, and virtually universal suffrage. The Russian Constitution of 1906 did not mark the complete surrender of autocracy. It opened with a section titled "On the Nature of the Supreme Autocratic Power." Article Four of that section stated: "Supreme autocratic power belongs to the Emperor of All the Russias. To obey his power, not only through fear but also by conscience, is commanded by God Himself." Subsequent articles gave the tsar the sole right to introduce legislation, an absolute veto over any work of the Duma, and the power to name or dismiss the government. Nicholas II nonetheless detested the constitution and soon fired Witte for leading him to it.

The Dumas.

Four turbulent Dumas met under this constitution. The first two lasted for a few months in 1906 and 1907, before the tsar prorogued them.

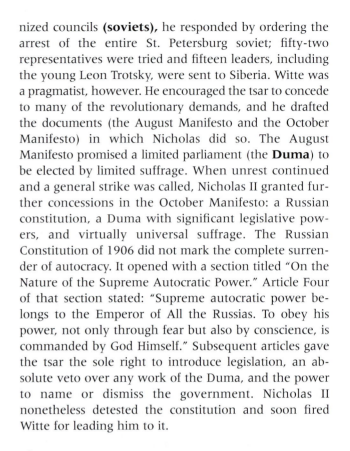

Nicholas II decreed a new electoral law in 1907, giving greater representation to the wealthy, so the Third Duma (1907–1912) obtained a conservative majority. Even middle-class Liberals, organized as the Constitutional Democratic Party (known by a Russian abbreviation, the *Kadets*) under the leadership of Professor Pavel Milyukov (Mill'-you-koff), opposed this government, angry that meaningful reform moved at a maddeningly slow pace. Nicholas II had promised in 1904 a program of accident and illness insurance for workers. That idea, the first piece of Russian welfare legislation, led to a draft policy in 1905, a proposal to the Duma in 1908, study by a special committee in 1910–1911, and debate by the Duma in 1912.

Peter Stolypin and Terrorism.

The dominant political figure of the Duma was the new prime minister (1906–1911), Peter Stolypin (Stoh-lee'-pin), a conservative noble who had won favor for his role in suppressing the revolution in the provinces. Stolypin was not a simple antiparliamentary reactionary. He accepted the Duma and the principle of liberal modernization, but within the context of strictly enforced law and order. He met radical extremism with state extremism, and Russia saw both in large quantities. Historians have estimated that 17,000 terrorist assassinations (in 23,000 attempts) took place between 1905 and 1914. Any official was a target. In a single day, attempts were made on every policeman walking the streets of Warsaw and Lodz; on another, one-fourth of the police force of Riga was killed. Terrorists still favored bombs and even used small children to deliver them; the youngest arrested was an 11-year-old girl who had been paid 50 kopecks (approximately 25 cents) for the delivering a bomb.

The Assassination of Stolypin. Stolypin responded with both state violence and noteworthy reforms. He allowed instant trials in the field and the execution of sentences on the spot. Suspected terrorists were hanged in such numbers that the noose became known as a "Stolypin necktie." At the same time, however, he liberalized censorship, expanded education, and defended freedom of religion. Perhaps the most important idea of Stolypin's government was support for peasant landownership. This program created a class of 9 million landowning peasants in Russia by 1914. No legislation could save Stolypin, however. He was the most hated man in Russia, and he was shot to death (by an assassin who could have killed the tsar instead) at the Kiev Opera House in 1911. This level of hatred and violence did not augur well for the solution of Russia's manifold problems, and time was running out. Stolypin's successors were increasingly consumed by foreign problems in the Balkans, problems that would soon lead to another war, another disastrous defeat, and another violent revolution.

CONTINUING INDUSTRIALIZATION AND WORKING-CLASS MOVEMENTS

The Second Industrial Revolution. As the problems confronting Imperial Russia show, the Belle Époque faced difficult adjustments to the consequences of continuing industrialization. A **second industrial revolution** during the late nineteenth century shared many characteristics of early industrialization. It saw rapid population growth, steady urbanization, and an agricultural revolution sufficient to feed the cities. But many changes also were evident in the new industrialization.

The European economy overcame the dominance of Britain. Germany (and the United States) matched

TABLE 26.4 EUROPEAN STEEL PRODUCTION, 1871-1911			
	Output of Steel in Tons		
COUNTRY	**1871**	**1891**	**1911**
Austria-Hungary	36,000	495,000	2,174,000
Belgium	n.a.	222,000	2,028,000
Britian	334,000	3,208,000	6,566,000
France	80,000	744,000	3,837,000
Germany	143,000	2,452,000	14,303,000
Italy	n.a.	76,000	736,000
Luxembourg	n.a.	111,000	716,000
Russia	7,000	434,000	3,949,000
Spain	n.a.	90,000	323,000
Sweden	9,000	172,000	471,000

n.a. = Not available.

British industrialization, and many countries were sufficiently industrialized to compete effectively. The foci of industrialization also changed: steel replaced iron at the center of heavy industry, electricity began to replace steam as the source of industrial power, and new industries such as the chemical industry challenged the preeminence of textiles.

Population and Urbanization. The continuing **population explosion** that made Germany the dominant state of Europe were especially vivid in **urbanization.** In 1880, Britain remained the only country in the world where a majority of the population lived in towns and cities. Belgium, which had led early industrialization on the continent, was drawing close at 43 percent urban, but both France and Germany remained merely 33 percent urban. By the early years of the twentieth century, Germany had changed into an urban society. In 1800, Berlin's 172,000 people had made it the largest city in the German states; in 1910, unified Germany contained seventeen cities larger than Berlin had been, including the industrial cities of Essen and Duisberg in the Rhineland that had grown from sleepy villages of 4,000 people into capitals of heavy industry with populations exceeding 200,000.

The Food Supply. The continuing population explosion and urbanization in Europe were made possible by dramatic improvements in the food supply. For most of the continent, the historic epoch of **subsistence** and periodic famine had ended. A significant part of the increased food supply was the result of the success of industrialization. The development of **inorganic fertilizers** greatly increased food production in countries—such as

Germany—that possessed a strong chemical industry. The revolution in farm machinery also expanded European production. French farmers, for example, were conservative and slow to accept new machinery. Yet between 1888 and 1908, French agriculture changed from a national total of 200 reaping machines and 50 harvesters to 15,000 reaping machines and 25,000 harvesters.

Imported Food. The European food supply also profited greatly from importation. Vast tracts of rich virgin soil were being plowed in Argentina, Australia, Canada, Russia, and the United States. The acceptance of food in tin cans, the invention of ammonia-based refrigeration, and the availability of quick and inexpensive steam shipping brought the harvest of the world to the tables of Europe. Grain from the American Middle West cost 53 cents per bushel to ship from Chicago to London in 1870; by 1919, that price had fallen to 16 cents per bushel. The price of wheat in Europe consequently tumbled from $1.50 per bushel in 1870 to 85 cents per bushel in 1900.

The Age of Steel. The greatest stimulus to the second industrial revolution came from new materials, new energy, and new industries. Steel became the symbol of the new industrialization. The making of steel—distinguished from iron by a higher carbon content—has been known since ancient times. It was preferred for its hardness, its strength in relation to weight, and its plasticity, but the process required to adjust the carbon content in steel had been too expensive for widespread use. In the 1850s, a British metallurgist named Henry Bessemer invented a simpler process for making steel. By sending a blast of air through molten iron, Bessemer was able to heat iron to the point where it obtained the desired carbon content. By the 1870s, Bessemer's **"blast furnaces"** were being widely adopted in industrial countries because governments craved steel for heavy artillery, railroads, and warships. In 1871, the total European output was less than 1 million tons of steel; in 1913, tiny Luxembourg alone produced 1.3 million tons of steel. Britain had entered the steel age with the continuing advantage of plentiful iron and coal plus the pioneering role in blast furnace development. But Britain did not start with an insurmountable lead. Germany, which also possessed abundant iron and coal, closed the production gap in the 1880s and passed Britain in steel production in the 1890s. By the start of the twentieth century, Germany produced 20 percent more steel than Britain. In 1911, Germany produced as much steel as Britain, France, and Russia combined, and on the eve of World War I, German steel production stood at eighteen times the European total of 1870. The second industrial revolution had broken the industrial dominance of Britain.

Chemical Industries. The German leadership of the second industrial revolution was even more notable in chemical industries. Chemical engineering shaped late nineteenth-century industrialization just as mechanical engineering had shaped early industrialization. The initial importance of chemistry came in the textile industry: the manufacture of cotton cloth required large quantities of alkalis, sulfuric acid, and dyes, and the expansion of textile manufactures necessitated expansion of chemical industries. Many noted chemical industries, such as Friedrich Bayer's company in Germany, originated in support of the textile industry. Bayer developed synthetic dyes from coal tar to replace the natural dyes used to color cloth; his **aniline dyes** permitted a vast range of new, durable colors in clothing and became a tremendous commercial success. Bayer and Company soon diversified and developed other products, such as the first aspirin, patented in 1899.

The Working Class. One of the consequences of industrialization and urbanization was that the largest social issue confronting governments was the question of the working class. Most workers lived arduous lives and had many valid grievances. Rapid urbanization had produced dreadful living conditions in working-class **slums.** The importation of cheap food improved the diet of most workers, but it also led to the **depression** of 1873–1894 with periodic high **unemployment.** A study of the London working class in 1887 found that 52.3 percent of the population experienced short-term unemployment and 30.1 percent of the population was unemployed for 12 weeks or more. Governments slowly emulated the Bismarckian welfare laws of the 1880s and offered workers some measure of unemployment insurance, accident compensation, health care, or retirement benefits, but the welfare state was still in a rudimentary form and provided limited security. Working conditions were deplorable in many occupations. The coal miners and steelworkers whose labor sustained heavy industry had life expectancies 10 years less than that of other men; those who operated a Bessemer blast furnace often died in their thirties. Most jobs required a minimum of 5.5 ten-hour days per week, and many expected 6 twelve-hour days (see *The Working-Class Movement of the Late Nineteenth Century*). Minimum wage legislation, overtime pay, and paid vacations did not exist.

Trade Unionism. Trade unions grew quickly under these conditions, as a new wave of unionization (called **syndicalism** in some countries) spread from the skilled crafts to less skilled occupations. By the early twentieth century, the leading industrial states (Britain, Germany, and the United States) each counted more than 1 million union members. In Britain, more than 20 percent of the adult population belonged to unions in 1913.

Elsewhere, lesser industrialization and restrictive legislation kept union membership smaller. Spanish unions included only 0.02 percent of the population in 1889 and 0.2 percent in 1910. Two patterns were clear: only a minority of workers belonged to unions, and their numbers were growing significantly.

As their memberships grew, trade unions called strikes to win improved conditions. At the turn of the twentieth century, France experienced an average of nearly 1,000 industrial strikes per year, reaching a peak of 1,319 strikes involving 509,274 strikers in 1906. A study of these strikes has found that 56 percent sought higher wages, 15 percent sought shorter working hours, 13 percent sought the rehiring of fired workers, and 4 percent sought the abolition of certain work rules. By the eve of World War I, Britain, France, and Germany were each losing nearly 5 million working days to strikes every year; Europe was entering an age of mass participation more direct than the trend toward democratization.

Antiunionism. Governments responded to trade union militancy with restrictive legislation and the use of force. In Britain, the Masters and Servants Act (1867) made any breach of contract a criminal offense instead of a civil offense; the Criminal Law of 1871 created a new category of crime—conspiracy—for acts committed by more than one person and included collective acts that were not crimes for individuals; and the Protection of Property Act (1875) set stiff criminal penalties for compelling a person to commit (or not commit) an act such as joining a strike. Armed with such legislation, and the pro-management sentiments that produced it, governments did not hesitate to use military force against disruptive workers in Britain or France like government in Russia had.

State Violence against Strikers. Unemployed workers demonstrated in central London in the fall of 1887. The government responded by banning labor marches. When workers persisted, they were met by armed police in the "Bloody Sunday" clash of November 1887. Three of the unemployed were killed, and several hundred were injured. Similarly, strikes by coal miners in the Ruhr valley in 1889 led to violent clashes (known as the Herne riots) when the German government called out two battalions of infantry and a squadron of cavalry to oppose the strikers. French troops fired on strikers at the northern industrial town of Fourmies in 1891, killing nine and wounding thirty-five; the conservative government responded to the massacre by arresting Karl Marx's son-in-law, who had spoken there 2 days earlier, for inciting a riot. At Łodz (in Russian Poland), forty-six workers were killed in a clash in 1892; ninety-two died in a confrontation in Sicily in 1893. And Georges Clemenceau, who had risen to political prominence as a democratic radical and friend of workers, did not hesitate to call out the troops against French strikers in 1906; he even seemed to relish being called "the number one cop in France."

The Growth of Democratic Socialism. Workers responded with another form of mass politics—supporting political parties that promised to create governments sympathetic to them. This converted **socialism** from a theory into a mass movement. Intellectuals who typically led socialist parties combined a program of political democracy with social benefits. The Austrian Socialist Party was led by a physician, the Belgian Socialist Party by a lawyer, and the French and German parties by professors. The foremost French Socialist, Jean Jaurès, began his career by writing a Latin dissertation to earn a professorship at the University of Toulouse. The clearest example of middle-class intellectuals shaping socialism was the Fabian Society founded in Britain in 1883. Its leaders were a novelist (H. G. Wells), a dramatist (George Bernard Shaw), and a brilliant couple (Sidney and Beatrice Webb) who founded both a university (the London School of Economics) and several periodicals. Such leaders espoused **democratic socialism** and believed they would ultimately win an electoral majority. In programs such as the Erfurt Program of the German socialist party, they called for radical democracy similar to the Chartist program of the 1830s or the advanced constitutions of 1848; "universal suffrage" (often including women's suffrage), secret ballots, salaried representatives, and proportional representation were typical political objectives. The 8-hour working day, government regulation of working conditions, and free medical care were typical social goals of democratic socialism (see *The Growth of Socialist Parties*).

Revolutionary Socialism. All over Europe, however, democratic Socialists contended with Marxists for control of working-class political movements. Philosophical disputes, such as the **abolition of private property** (meaning the property of production and distribution in the economy) and the theory of **class conflict** (which eliminated the possibility of cooperation with bourgeois governments), separated these two wings of the socialist movement. The greatest of these disagreements involved the seizure of power. Marxists expected the working-class victory to come through **violent revolution.** "Force," Marx and Engels wrote, "is the midwife of every old society pregnant with a new one." Democratic Socialists were divided on subjects such as private property or class conflict, but they rejected violent revolution and believed that they could achieve their objectives through elections. The greatest philosophic rejection of Marxism was advanced by a German Socialist, Edouard Bernstein, who developed the theory of **evolutionary**

The Working-Class Movement of the Late Nineteenth Century

Workers during 1886 Dock-Workers' Strike, London. By the late nineteenth century, workers had won the right to organize and to strike in many Western countries, producing an era of great labor unrest. By the end of the century, strikes to improve the living conditions of workers were taking millions of working days per year. This image depicts strikers during one of the most successful strikes, the London Dock-Workers' strike of 1889. More than 10,000 dockers stayed on strike for 4 weeks, causing so much dislocation to the British economy that they won a significant raise, the principle of extra pay for overtime, and the end of piecework payment. Their success stimulated the rapid growth of trade unions for unskilled workers, more than 200,000 of whom joined unions in the next year.

TABLE 26.5 THE AVERAGE WORKWEEK

OCCUPATION	HOURS IN BRITAIN	HOURS IN FRANCE
Baker	70	78–96
Brickmaker	54–69	96–108
Chemical worker	53–70	64.5–72
Construction	50–55	72–48
Foundry	48–72	72–84
Metalworker	54	63–66
Miners	42.5–55	51–60
Paper worker	66–78	63
Printer	53–54	60
Railway ticket agent	56–62	90–96
Railway guard	64–70	96–108
Restaurant waiter	96	101
Textile worker	56	66–72
Tailor	54–96	66–96

Source: Cross, Gary, *A Quest for Time: The Reduction of Work in Britain and France, 1840–1940* (Berkeley, CA: University of California Press, 1989, p. 235). Used by permission of the publisher.

socialism. He was driven into exile by Bismarck's harassment of Socialists in the 1880s and edited a newspaper in Zürich, where he developed his socialism in contact with British democratic Socialists. During the 1890s, he lived in London and wrote *Evolutionary Socialism* (1899) to demonstrate the errors of *The Communist Manifesto* and to advocate gradual, democratic socialism. Marx's theory of revolution, Bernstein wrote, was "a mistake in every respect."

Socialist Parties. Divisions within the socialist movement initially produced competing socialist parties in many countries, but political realism soon obliged Socialists to contain their disagreements within a unified party. Thus, French evolutionary Socialists (led by Jaurès) and French Marxists (led by Jules Guesde) created a unified party, known by the French initials *SFIO*, in 1905. British Socialists, from the Fabians to the Marxist Social Democratic Federation, combined to create the Labour Party in 1906. Followers of Marx and Bernstein learned to live together within the SPD. Collaboration allowed ideological debates at the congresses of the international movement known as the Second International (1889–1914), but it also led to

TABLE 26.6 THE GROWTH OF UNION MEMBERSHIP

COUNTRY	Union Membership				
	1890	1900	1905	1910	1913
Britain	1,576,000	2,022,000	1,997,000	2,565,000	4,135,000
Germany	344,000	851,000	1,650,000	2,435,000	3,024,000
United States		869,000	1,959,000	2,184,000	2,753,000
France			203,000	358,000	400,000
Russia			123,000		
Austria-Hungary	47,000	135,000	482,000		
Sweden		180,000		136,000	
Belgium	13,000	43,000		116,000	
Spain	3,000		41,000		

Compiled from data in Seligman, Edwin R. A., ed., *Encyclopedia of the Social Sciences,* vol. 8 (New York: Macmillan, 1937, pp. 9–41).

TABLE 26.7 STRIKES IN EUROPE

PERIOD	Belgium		Britain		France		Germany	
	AVERAGE ANNUAL STRIKES	DAYS LOST	AVERAGE ANNUAL STRIKES	DAYS LOST	AVERAGE ANNUAL STRIKES	DAYS LOST	AVERAGE ANNUAL STRIKES	DAYS LOST
1896–1900	122	801,000	758	6,948,000	568	1,991,000	774	
1901–1905	94	2,451,000	427	2,744,000	691	3,132,000	1,363	2,853,000
1906–1910	155	1,606,000	479	5,701,000	1,236	4,629,000	2,712	4,954,000

Compiled from data in Cook, Chris, and Paxton, John, *European Political Facts, 1848–1918* (London: Macmillan, 1978, p. 323).

Question: Do these tables help to explain each other?

electoral success. Bismarck's fears notwithstanding, few Socialists could be found in European parliaments in the 1880s, but they were among the largest parties in 1914. The German SPD held more than 25 percent of the seats in the Reichstag, making it the second largest party; French Socialists were the second largest block in the fragmented Chamber of Deputies with 22 percent of the seats. And in the 1914 elections, the Swedish Socialist Party showed that evolutionary Socialists might be right: it became the largest party in Parliament with eighty-seven seats against eighty-six conservatives (see *The Growth of Socialist Parties*).

THE GROWTH OF WOMEN'S RIGHTS MOVEMENTS (1870–1914)

The Family Wage Economy. Industrialization stimulated other movements. None had more far-reaching importance than the women's rights movement. Industrialization contributed to the rise of feminism by transforming the roles of women in Western societies. It broke down the traditional **household economy** in which women labored at home, sharing in agricultural duties or the work of a family-run shop, plus

THE GROWTH OF SOCIALIST PARTIES

The Erfurt Program of the German Social Democratic Party (1891)

[T]he Social Democratic Party of Germany demands, to begin with:

1. Universal, equal, and direct suffrage, with secret ballot, for all elections, of all citizens of the realm over twenty years of age, without distinction of sex. Proportional representation, and until this is introduced, legal redistribution of electoral districts after every census. Biennial legislative periods. Holding of the elections on a legal holiday. Compensation for the elected representative. Abolition of every limitation of political rights, except in the case of legal incapacity.
2. Direct legislation through the people, by means of the right of proposal and rejection. . . .
3. Education of all to bear arms. Militia in the place of the standing army. . . .
4. Abolition of all laws which limit or suppress the right of meeting and coalition.
5. Abolition of all laws which place women . . . at a disadvantage as compared with men.
6. Declaration that religion is a private affair. Abolition of all expenditure of public funds upon . . . religious objects. . . .

7. Secularization of schools. Compulsory attendance at the public national schools. Free education. . . .
8. Free administration of justice, and free legal assistance. . . . [J]udges elected by the people. Appeal in criminal cases.
9. Free medical attendance, including midwifery, and free supply of medicines. Free burial.
10. Graduated income and property tax for defraying all public expenses. . . . Abolition of all indirect taxes. . . .

For the protection of the working classes, the Social Democratic Party of Germany demands, to begin with:

1. An effective national and international legislation for the protection of labor, on the following principles:
   a. Fixing of a normal working day, which shall not exceed eight hours.
   b. Prohibition of the employment of children under fourteen.
   c. Prohibition of night work except . . . [in necessary cases].
   d. An unbroken rest of at least thirty-six hours in every week. . . .
2. Supervision of all industrial establishments, investigation and regulation of the conditions of labor.

---

non–wage-paying work such as spinning yarn or making candles. That economic model yielded to a **family wage economy** in which women (and children) provided less home labor and more wage-earning labor. Families increasingly bought their yarn or ready-made clothing, candles, or vegetables; women increasingly worked outside the home to pay for them.

Women in the Economy. A study of women in the French labor force reveals these momentous changes in the lives of women. In 1872, less than 25 percent of the total female population of France worked for wages. In 1906, nearly 40 percent of the total female population (54 percent of women age 20 to 60 and 60 percent of women in their early twenties) worked for wages. Furthermore, the work women did was changing. The largest employers remained agriculture, the textile industry, domestic service, and prostitution, but governments were opening white-collar positions (typically in postal and telephone services), the age of the department store was creating sales positions, the needs of businesses were opening secretarial and clerical jobs, and compulsory education laws were providing teaching jobs.

Attitudes to Working Women. Women's employment varied across Europe—Russian law closed the civil service to women, whereas a Swedish law of 1864 opened all employment to women—but the impact was similar. Educated and energetic women in increasing numbers (although still a minority of women) demanded equality with men. Conservatives, and some men who thought themselves radicals, resisted equality as staunchly as they resisted the demands of workers. Pope Leo XIII's encyclical letter **Rerum Novarum** was clear on the subject of working women: "Women are not suited for certain occupations; a woman is by nature fitted for home-work, and it is that which is best adopted at once to preserve her modesty and promote the good bringing up of children and the well-being of the family."

The Women's Rights Movement in France. The women's rights movement was relatively small in the 1870s, but militants articulated comprehensive programs. Hubertine Auclert, the leading French militant of the 1870s, summarized such a program for her organization, *Droit des Femmes* (Dwah day Fem'; Women's Rights): "The ultimate objective of *Droits des femmes* is: The perfect

TABLE 26.8 SOCIALIST DEPUTIES IN EUROPEAN PARLIAMENTS

| COUNTRY | Number of Socialist Deputies | | | | | | | | PERCENTAGE OF SEATS IN 1914 PARLIAMENT |
	1880	1885	1890	1895	1900	1905	1910	1914	
Austria (Social Democrats)	0	0	0	0	0	0	28	33	20.4
Belgium (Workers Party)	0	0	0	28	32	32	32	39	21.0
Britain (Labour Party)	0	0	0	0	2	2	29	42	6.3
France (Socialist Party)	0	0	0	31	57	46	78	130	22.0
Germany (Social Democrats)	9	24	35	44	56	81	43	110	27.7
Italy (Socialist Party)	0	0	0	15	33	29	41	52	10.2
Sweden (Social Democrats)	0	0	0	0	0	13	34	87	37.8

Compiled from data in Cook, Chris, and Paxton, John, *European Political Facts, 1848–1918* (London: Macmillan, 1978, pp. 115–143).

equality of the two sexes before the law and in morality" (see Document 26.4). **Feminists** (a term that Auclert pioneered in the 1880s) debated priorities, but comprehensive programs soon resembled Auclert's: full political rights, open education and careers, equal civil rights, and equal pay. The suffrage campaigns of Auclert during the 1880s attracted only a handful of followers. The women's rights majority, led by Léon Richer and Maria Deraismes, the founders of the French League for the Rights of Women, favored programs concentrating on civil and legal rights. A similar situation existed in Italy, where Maria Mozzoni fought for women's civil and economic rights but avoided a doctrine on suffrage.

The Women's Rights Movement in Germany.
Pioneering feminists in most of western and northern Europe favored a strategy of starting with limited programs and postponing the issue of women's suffrage. Louise Otto-Peters, the founder of the German women's rights movement, focused on civil rights. The generation of German feminists that followed her, such as Anita Augsburg and the General Federation of German Women's Associations, also began with limited

demands. Not until the early twentieth century did women's rights advocates in most countries begin to seek political rights. Augsburg reached this position in 1898 but did not create her suffrage league (the German Union for Women's Suffrage) until 1902.

The Women's Rights Movement in Britain.
The strongest movement developed in Britain. Women in England and Wales won the vote and eligibility for office at the local level in 1869, and they pressed, with growing militancy, for full political rights for the next 50 years. Between 1870 and 1914, approximately 3,000 women were elected to local boards and councils in Britain, but these offices were chiefly on school boards and social agencies dealing with infant mortality or unsanitary housing—positions considered a natural part of the "women's sphere." Such entry-level posts would ultimately change politics, however, as women like Eleanor Rathbone used them as a starting point for the development of the welfare state.

Suffragists and Suffragettes.
British women, led by Lydia Becker and Millicient Garrett Fawcett, organized

HUBERTINE AUCLERT'S PROGRAM FOR WOMEN'S RIGHTS

Hubertine Auclert (1848–1914) was a daughter of prosperous farmers and inherited enough money to devote her life to a political cause. She founded the women's suffrage campaign in France and organized demonstrations on behalf of women's rights. During the 1880s, she edited the leading newspaper of militant feminism in France, *La Citoyenne* (The [Female] Citizen). Frustrated by the rate of progress, she considered violent protest in the early twentieth century but kept faith in democratic programs as the following illustrates.

The ultimate objective of Droit des femmes is: The perfect equality of the two sexes before the law and in morality.

PROGRAM: Droit des femmes will seek, from the beginning and by all means in its power:

1. *The accession of women, married or not, to full civil and political rights, on the same legal conditions as apply to men.*
2. *The reestablishment of divorce.*
3. *A single morality for men and for women; whatever is condemned for one cannot be excusable for the other.*
4. *The right for women to develop their intelligence through education, with no other limitation than their ability and their desire.*
5. *The right to knowledge being acquired, the free accession of women to all professions and careers for which they are qualified at the same level as applies to men (and after the same examination).*
6. *The rigorous application, without distinction by sex, of the economic formula: Equal Pay for Equal Work.*

From Hause, Steven C., *Hubertine Auclert: The French Suffragette* (New Haven: Yale University Press, 1987).

Question: Why might men have opposed this program?

the first large suffrage movement and won support in the House of Commons. **Suffragists** (advocates of women's suffrage) obtained majorities—but not the support of either major party—in the House of Commons, and the conservative majority in the House of Lords blocked the reform. The women's suffrage movement in Britain became one of the most radical movements in Europe in the early twentieth century. Fawcett, the widow of a radical M.P. who shared many of his parliamentary duties because of his blindness, presided over the unification of several suffrage leagues into a National Union of Women's Suffrage Societies in 1897. It grew from 16 founding societies to more than 400 in 1913. Even during this period of rapid growth, some suffragists formed new organizations to attempt more radical tactics than Fawcett used. They were dubbed **"suffragettes"** by a newspaper hoping to ridicule the movement, but

militants accepted the label and made it famous. The most famous suffragettes, Emmeline Pankhurst and her daughters, Christabel and Sylvia, founded the Women's Social and Political Union (WSPU) in 1903 and led it to violent tactics (against property, not people) such as smashing store windows. Emmeline Pankhurst decided that they "had to do as much of this guerilla warfare as the people of England would tolerate." That decision had dreadful results: when arrested, she (and several other strong women) infuriated the government by going on a hunger strike. When hunger strikers suffered declining health, the government chose to force-feed them. This sequence of events culminated in the notorious Cat-and-Mouse Act of 1913—suffragist prisoners would be released until they recovered.

Continental Suffragism. Despite the remarkable example of the WSPU, moderation characterized the struggle for women's suffrage in most of Europe. Large suffrage movements had developed by 1914, but WSPU tactics were rare. Irish women staged several violent protests, and in France, Auclert and Pelletier briefly attempted violent demonstrations but found no support. Instead, the movements in France, Germany, Italy, and Russia chose campaigns of respectable moderation. Their organizations grew large by 1914 (the French Union for Women's Suffrage had 12,000 members in 75 regional chapters), but none won the right to vote.

Civil Rights of Women. Feminists also concentrated on other targets. Many favored modernization of legal codes, such as the Napoleonic Code in France or the Pisanelli Code in Italy, which made wives subordinate to husbands. The most basic reform sought was a **Married Women's Property Act,** such as the British had adopted in stages between 1856 and 1882, and several countries (chiefly in Scandinavia) followed. French women obtained this right with the Schmahl Law of 1907; German women did not win it before World War I. Most women's rights advocates also sought the legalization of divorce. This was permissible in the German Lutheran tradition and had been established in British law in 1857. The campaign was more difficult in Catholic countries because Pope Leo XIII strongly opposed divorce and issued an encyclical in 1880 stating that "[d]ivorce is born of perverted morals." French women won a limited form of divorce in 1884; Spanish and Italian women did not.

Women's Educational Rights. Women's rights advocates generally had more success in seeking educational opportunities. The University of Zürich became the first to open to women (1865), and other Swiss universities followed in the 1870s. Russian women briefly won a series of university rights, but these were rescinded in 1881 because of the involvement of some women in radical political groups. Germany, home of the most highly praised and emulated universities of the late nineteenth century, resisted higher education for women. The state of Baden was the most progressive, offering women a secondary school curriculum to prepare for universities in 1893 and then opening higher education to them in 1900. The Prussian Ministry of Education was more conservative and perpetuated a secondary school curriculum stressing "Household Arts" to teach "feminine precision, neatness, and patience" while denying young women the prerequisites for entering universities. The distinguished University of Berlin thus remained closed to women until 1908. In 1914, German universities enrolled a combined total of slightly more than 4,000 women, who formed 6.2 percent of the student population. The situation was only slightly better for women in France, where 4,254 women students (10.1 percent of enrollment) studied in 1913.

EUROPEAN CULTURE DURING THE BELLE ÉPOQUE (1870–1914)

Cultural Styles of the Belle Époque. The Belle Époque was a period of great cultural creativity, but no single style dominated the arts and typified the era. Unlike the baroque and classical styles of the eighteenth century, or the Romanticism of the early nineteenth century, no style summarizes the cultural trends of the era. Instead, the Belle Époque was an age of vitality expressed in conflicting styles. In painting, the realism of 1870 gave way to a succession of new styles, such as impressionism, fauvism, cubism, and expressionism. **Realism** lingered in novels and drama of social comment, spawning a style known as naturalism—such as Emile Zola's novels of ordinary life in France or Henrik Ibsen's plays of angry social criticism—but poetry evolved into an introverted and sometimes mystical style called symbolism. Music, architecture, philosophy, sculpture, and the decorative arts produced no style that dominated the era.

Impressionism. The best remembered cultural style of the Belle Époque was **impressionism,** a style of painting that originated in France from the 1860s to 1880s. Impressionism produced several of the greatest artists of the century, such as Claude Monet, whose painting *Impression: Sunrise* (1874) led to the name. And impressionism influenced the other arts, from music (Claude Debussy is sometimes called an impressionist) to poetry (the symbolist poets are also called impressionists). But the Belle Époque was an era of so much change that it cannot be called the "age of impressionism."

Styles in Architecture. Belle Époque architecture illustrates both the jumble of cultural styles and the emergence of the dramatically new. Late nineteenth-century architecture primarily suggests an age of revivalism, because almost all past styles were exploited; the Bavarians built another great castle in neo-rococo style, the most noted new building in central Vienna (a theater) was in neo-baroque style, the Hungarian parliament on the banks of the Danube in Budapest was neo-Gothic, the most-discussed new church of the age in Paris was neo-Romanesque, the Dutch National Museum built in Amsterdam was neo-Renaissance, and the vast Gum Department Store in Moscow was neoclassical. Despite this cacophony of styles of the past, an exciting architecture of the twentieth century began to emerge in the closing years of the nineteenth. The French built the tallest structure on earth for their world's fair of 1889 (the centennial of the revolution), and they built the Eiffel Tower in structural steel. By the 1890s, this use of steel and the American-born style of building skyscrapers, by attaching a masonry exterior to a metal frame, had begun a profound change in the appearance of cities. Walter Gropius, a German architect who had tremendous influence on the visual arts of the new century, built the first steel frame building with glass walls in 1911.

Innovation in the Arts. Developments in architecture at the birth of the twentieth century had parallels throughout the arts. Startling innovators broke with tradition. In music, the rejection of the nineteenth-century symphonic heritage led to efforts to compose atonal music after 1900, culminating in 1914 with Arnold Schoenberg's system of composing to destroy the feeling of tonality. Other composers, such as Igor Stravinsky, boldly created dissonant harmonies.

Such music so offended traditional tastes that performances were sometimes met with howls of protest from the audience; the first performance of Stravinsky's ballet *The Rite of Spring* provoked a riot in Paris in 1913. Horrified traditionalists even saw the rules of dancing begin to break down as free dance abolished the following of steps or prescribed positioning.

Modern Art. The breakdown of traditional styles was especially controversial in the visual arts, where the popularity of photography and the cinema pressed painters to find artistic expression that these new arts could not rival. **Realism** lasted into the late nineteenth century, championed by artists like Edouard Manet, who argued that "[w]e must accept our times and paint what we see." But nonrepresentational styles of painting steadily emerged, and they still evoke hostility from traditionalists a century later. As an avant-garde French poet, Guillaume Apollinaire observed about this **modernism:** "Painters, while they still look at nature, no longer imitate it, and carefully avoid any representation of natural scenes. . . . Real resemblance no longer has any importance." The most inventive artist of the twentieth century, Pablo

Picasso, began his career producing works of emotional realism, but after 1904, he pioneered a style known as **cubism** in which shapes and structures (such as the human face) were simplified into geometric outlines. Picasso pushed the breakdown of realism so far that a face might have two eyes on the same side of the nose. Denounced for his nonrepresentational styles, Picasso responded that his art was "a lie that tells the truth." Painting was no longer simply a depiction of the physical world; it revealed hidden truths about a two-faced world.

European Thought. European thought during the Belle Époque followed a similar course. The most influential works of the era drew on the new discipline of psychology. Novelists from Fyodor Dostoevsky (whose *The Brothers Karamazov* appeared in 1879–1880), through Joseph Conrad (whose *Lord Jim* appeared in 1900), to Marcel Proust (whose first volume of *Remembrance of Things Past* appeared in 1913) relied on psychological detail and insight. The inner life of characters and their subconscious motivation gained emphasis as central features of the novel. Psychology also reshaped European philosophy. Friedrich Nietzsche, a pastor's son who reacted against the piety of his home, was such a brilliant student that he became a professor at the University of Basel at age 24. Nietzsche wrote with psychological insight about the sublimation of passions and instincts, the relativity of morals, and what he called "the will to power." He had contempt for contemporary cultural and moral values and, in works such as *Thus Spoke Zarathustra* (1883), argued that "God is dead" and Christianity is based on the mentality of slaves. Such arguments did not have much immediate impact, but they grew increasingly influential in European thought.

Freud and Darwin. Perhaps the most influential thinkers of the Belle Époque were two scientists: Sigmund Freud, the Austrian neurologist who founded the science of **psychoanalysis**, and Charles Darwin, the English naturalist who developed the **theory of evolution** by natural selection. Freud's study of psychoneuroses in the 1890s led him to an analytic technique of the "free association" of thoughts, a process that he named "psychoanalysis." Throughout Freud's thought ran the concept of the **unconscious**, present in everyone's mind and emerging in dreams, jokes, and slips of the tongue. This led him to the analysis of dreams. The *Interpretation of Dreams* (1900) stated his first model of the workings of the mind, a model that evolved into a description of three competing subconscious elements of the mind: the ego, the superego, and the libido (or id). Freud's attention to the libido as the seat of emotional (and especially sexual) urges led to his famous stress on sexual explanations (especially those with origins in infantile sexuality) in *Three Contributions to the Sexual Theory* (1905). Many of Freud's theories have been controversial, and some are simply wrong, but Freud's impact on European thought

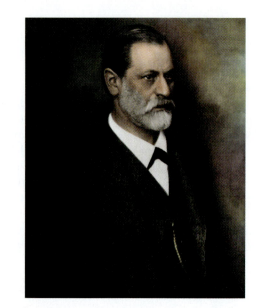

FIGURE 26.6 *Sigmund Freud.* Sigmund Freud (1856–1939), an Austrian medical doctor and professor of neuropathology at the University of Vienna, was the founder of psychoanalysis. The most widely influential thinker of the Belle Époque, Freud taught the world the importance of the subconscious mind beyond the orderly patterns of rational thought. His ideas about a broad range of subjects, including children, women, dreams, and sexuality, remain controversial a century later but have had an enormous impact on Western thought.

has been so enormous that he remains the most influential author of his era.

Darwin. Darwin had presented his theories in two controversial works: *On the Origin of Species* (1859), which demonstrated how **natural selection** worked, and *The Descent of Man* (1871), which applied evolution to humanity. The theory of evolution—that plants and animals naturally experience a process of gradual change into a more complicated or advanced state—had been advanced by many scientists. Darwin's greatest contribution was to demonstrate natural selection as the means of evolution. He first did this by studying the evolution of the beaks of birds in the Galapagos Islands, showing how the environment favored certain shapes of beaks, thus birds with such an advantage were naturally selected for survival and reproduction. Darwin's application of evolution to human history was enormously controversial because it conflicted with the biblical account of human origins, but scientists steadily accepted his theory. Social theorists in many fields soon appropri-

*Charles Darwin
(1809–1882)*

ated (and misappropriated) Darwin's ideas. The most widespread derivation during the Belle Époque was known as **"social Darwinism."** This doctrine applied a crude version of natural selection to human society and then asserted that certain people were suited for dominance and they would triumph, following what Herbert Spencer called "the survival of the fittest." Such social Darwinism was used to justify the class system, unregulated capitalist competition, racism, and imperialism.

CONCLUSION

The name *Belle Époque* was not created during the generation before 1914; it was a nostalgic label created after the suffering of World War I made the prewar era seem immensely appealing. As with most nostalgia, the perception of a "beautiful era" is debatable. It is surely appropriate when the perspective is war and peace in Europe: between 1871 and 1914, the great powers experienced

1871–1914

1865	1870	1875	1880	1885	1890	1895	1900	1905	1910

1871: Constitution of German Empire
1871–1890: Otto von Bismarck Chancellor of Germany
1870s: Bismarck's Battle with German Catholics: The *Kulturkampf*
1873: First of Prussian "May Laws" to Regulate Catholicism
1878: German Antisocialist Law
1880s: Bismarck's Battle with Socialists and Trade Unions
1880s: Bismarck's Health Insurance, Pension, and Welfare Legislation
1888: Death of Emperor William I
1890: Emperor William II Forces Bismarck to Retire
1890s: Rapid Growth of Trade Union Movement
1891: Erfurt Program of German Socialists
1890s: Germany Begins *Weltpolitik* and Colonial Empire
1902: Women's Suffrage Union Founded

1870: Third Republic Proclaimed in Paris
1870s: Struggle between Monarchists and Republicans to Write New Constitution
1870s: Léon Richer and Maria Deraismes Advance Program of Women's Rights
1871: Revolutionary Government in Paris, the Commune, Crushed by French Army
1875: Constitution of Third Republic Adopted
1880s: French Secular Laws, Trade Unions, Free Press, Divorce
1880s: Ferry Laws Establish Universal, Compulsory, Free, Secular Education
1881: Hubertine Auclert Launches Women's Suffrage Movement
1885–1889: Boulangism Threatens Overthrow of French Republic
1892–1893: Panama Scandal Awakens Anti-Semitism
1894–1906: Dreyfus Affair Divides France
1900s: Labor Unrest and Strikes
1905: Separation of Church and State
1907: Married Women's Property Act

1868–1874: William Gladstone's "Great Ministry" Adopts Reform Legislation
1870s: Growth of "Home Rule" Movement in Ireland
1870s: Growth of Women's Rights Movement and Suffragism
1874–1880: Government of Benjamin Disraeli Shifts Attention to British Empire
1882: Married Women's Property Act
1884: Third Reform Bill brings Britain Nearer to Democracy
1886: Gladstone's Home Rule Bill Splits Liberal Party
1893: Second Home Rule Bill blocked by House of Lords
1893: Labour Party (ILP) Founded
1901: Death of Queen Victoria
1903: Pankhursts Begin Militant Suffragism
1906: Lloyd George Budget for Welfare
1911: Parliament Act Limits Lords
1912: Third Home Rule Bill

nearly half a century without war among themselves. Thus, the fortunate generations of the Belle Époque lived in a much more tranquil world than those of 1848–1871 or 1914–1945. The Belle Époque was also fortunate in making significant progress toward a democratic society. Each of the great powers was more democratic in 1914 than it had been in 1870.

Despite such positive signs, it would be wrong to exaggerate the Belle Époque as a golden age. Minority populations suffered in all the great states—as the Irish did in Britain, Jews did in most countries but especially Russia and France, and Catholics did in Germany. Nor did the working-class movement or the women's rights movement believe that Europe had yet reached a golden age. And European culture, characterized by a jumble of styles rejecting traditional culture, reflected this dissatisfaction.

Review Questions

- What were the strengths and weaknesses of the German Second Reich?
- How successful was the French Third Republic, as Europe's first enduring republic, in establishing democracy?
- To what extent was Britain a democracy by 1914?
- What were the aspirations of the workers' movement and the women's movement?

For Further Study

Readings

Cook, Chris, and Paxton, John, eds., *European Political Facts, 1848–1918* (London: Macmillan, 1978). Excellent source for checking basic facts on governments, ministers, elections, political parties, treaties, and so forth.

Cook, Chris, and Stevenson, John, eds., *The Longman Handbook of Modern European History, 1763–1991*, 2nd ed. (London: Longman, 1992). Excellent for checking dates and chronologies; provides good economic data.

Hobsbawm, E. J., *The Age of Empire, 1875–1914* (New York: Vintage, 1989). A provocative volume in a multi-volume history by a noted historian, offering a stimulating left-wing perspective.

Stone, Norman, *Europe Transformed, 1878–1919*, 2nd ed. (Oxford: Blackwell, 1999). A more conservative counterpoint to Hobsbawm as a survey of the era.

Tuchman, Barbara, *The Proud Tower* (New York: Ballantine, 1996). A highly accessible introduction to the era by one of the most popular historians of the past generation.

InfoTrac College Edition

For additional reading, go to your online research library at *http://infotrac.thomsonlearning.com*.

Using the Subject Guide, enter the search terms:

Otto von Bismarck William Gladstone
anticlericalism suffragists

Web Sites

http://www.victorianweb.org This is a huge site with many links, maintained by the National University of Singapore.

http://www.spartacus.schoolnet.co.uk/ A British school site with a variety of files helpful for the Belle Époque, such as the women's rights movement and Imperial Russia.

http://www.marxists.org/ Includes an encyclopedia of Marxism and a Marxist history section. The Marxist history section leads to a large section of the Paris Commune among many other topics.

Visit the Western Civilization Companion Web Site for resources specific to this textbook:
http://history.wadsworth.com/hause02/

 The CD in the back of this book and the Western Civilization Resource Center at *http://history.wadsworth.com/western/* offer a variety of tools to help you succeed in this course, including access to quizzes; images; documents; interactive simulations, maps, and timelines; movie explorations; and a wealth of other sources.

The West in the World

EUROPE AND THE WORLD IN 1900

The relationship between Europe and the world had changed dramatically by 1900, when an era of European global hegemony was nearing its apogee. Western science had made possible the conquest and occupation of most of the world: medical science and the booming chemical industry mass-produced quinine tablets, which overcame the disease barrier of malaria. Other tropical diseases, such as yellow fever, were similarly conquered by 1900.

Simultaneously, the European arms race produced weaponry, which overcame all but the most determined resistance: all-steel, steam-powered ships created global navies of new speed and power. In 1884, an Anglo-American inventor, Hiram Maxim, demon-

strated a remarkable automatic weapon. Machine guns had been employed before, such as the Gatling gun of the American Civil War and the *mitrailleuse* of the Franco-Prussian War, but the Maxim gun could efficiently slaughter hundreds of people per minute. As the *Encyclopedia Britannica* put it in 1902, "It was used with great effect in the Zulu War and in the Sudan." Great effect indeed: at the battle of Omdurman (Sudan) in September 1898, General Horatio Herbert Kitchener led a British army of 26,000, equipped with the Maxim gun, against 45,000 Mahdists (militant Muslims), who had driven out the British in the 1880s. In the single day of the battle, Kitchener lost 500 men; the Maxim gun enabled the British to kill more than 15,000 Sudanese.

A complex combination of factors—such as nationalism, militarism, economic expansionism, and missionary zeal (see Chapter 27)—led European governments to pursue the conquest of much of the world in the late nineteenth and early twentieth centuries. This age of conquest, usually called "the new imperialism," was often justified in terms of humanitarianism and widespread benefits for human kind (plus, of course, the special benefits to the imperial power). But at the bottom, it rested on attitudes such as racism and social Darwinism.

The age of the new imperialism began in the years after the Franco-Prussian War of 1870–1871, but Europeans had been gradually expanding their claims to governing distant lands throughout the century. The British navy steadily acquired, and the British government claimed, new islands around the globe—from Malta in the Mediterranean (1800), to Pitcairn Island in the Pacific (1809), Ceylon (Sri Lanka) in the Indian Ocean (1815), the Falkland Islands in the South Atlantic (1820), and Trinidad (1802) and Tobago (1815) in the Caribbean—and it was still claiming new islands, such as Samoa in 1899 and Tonga in 1900.

The French similarly expanded their claims around the world. A French expedition to Algiers in 1830, intended to be a punitive mission to redress insults to French honor, resulted in the conquest and occupation of Algeria until 1962. The French also expanded their

The cover a French magazine illustrates the battle of Omdurman in the Sudan, September 1898. With the benefit of the cannon and the Maxim gun, General Kitchener defeated Muslim forces twice the size of the British troops.

outposts on the west coast of Africa and gradually occupied Senegal.

Throughout the nineteenth century, European governments sent "exploratory missions" into Africa, making great cultural heroes of the individuals who survived. Mungo Park explored the region of the Gambia and the Niger in West Africa in 1805–1806, laying a British claim to the area but dying in the process. In 1827–1828, René Caillié led a French expedition from the shores of west Africa northward across the Sahara, beginning a series of French expeditions that would result in future French claims to the entire Saharan region. A British missionary, David Livingstone, became one of the most famous people in the Victorian era by crossing the Kalahari Desert in 1849, then returning to Africa for a second expedition (1853–1856) that brought European the news of the Victoria Falls. This was followed by second and third expeditions, until he was so famous that a competition arose to go to Africa and find Dr. Livingstone. Other European missions went up the Congo River (to "the heart of darkness") and down the Nile River (in search of its source).

Despite all of this European activity, Africa remained a complex quilt of self-governing peoples in 1878. But the new European advantages soon led to a "scramble for Africa" so overwhelming that by 1914, virtually the entire continent had fallen to European conquest. (Liberia, in the west, remained independent under American protection; Ethiopia, in the east, remained independent although claimed by Italy, thanks to the defeat of the Italians in the battle of Adua in 1896.)

A similar pattern of exploration followed by conquest brought the British control of the Australian continent in the nineteenth century. The first colonial population, which consisted of convicts transported from Britain, arrived in the colony of New South Wales in 1788, in a convoy of 11 ships and 717 prisoners. By the first decades of the century, free colonists were joining the transported population and British governors (including the infamous William [1806–1809]) were named. Control of the entire continent proceeded steadily: western Australia (1820), Tasmania (originally Van Dieman's Land, 1825), South Australia (1836), and Queensland (1850), until the Commonwealth of Australia united the colonies in 1901. The British conquest of Australia caused terrible problems for the Aborigines already living there, but worse confrontations occurred in neighboring New Zealand, where the native Maori peoples fought the British in a series of fierce wars beginning in 1845.

Chapter 27

IMPERIALISM, WAR, AND REVOLUTION, 1881–1920

FOCUS QUESTIONS

- Does the Bismarckian system of alliances seem a guarantee of peace or a cause of war?
- What motivated the European new imperialism of the late nineteenth century?
- What issues in international relations explain the European arms race at the beginning of the twentieth century?
- What diplomatic mistakes led to the catastrophe of World War I?
- Why was World War I so devastating?
- Did the Russian revolution grow out of internal problems in Russia or Russian defeat in the war?

On a cool night in late April 1914, a group of Serbian students sat together beneath flickering gas lamps at the *Zlatna Moruna,* a modest café in Belgrade that they favored for the meetings of *Narodna Odbrana* (Defense of the People), a group dedicated to achieving Serbian nationalism through terrorism. They discussed the day's mail, which included a newspaper clipping sent anonymously from Bosnia; the clipping reported that the heir to the throne of Austria would visit the Bosnian capital of Sarajevo in late June. That newspaper clipping changed Europe forever because the seven young men who read it were later armed and waiting when the Archduke's four-car parade passed through Sarajevo on June 28. As the motorcade passed through Sarajevo, one member of the group, Nedjelko Cabrinovic, stepped forward and threw a bomb. The archduke deflected the device, but its subsequent explosion drew blood on the archduchess (who had joined her husband because it was their fourteenth wedding anniversary) and wounded three people in the next car, plus thirteen onlookers. After angrily completing his state visit, Archduke Franz Ferdinand insisted on visiting the wounded at the hospital, a decision that led his open car past another member of the café group, a 19-year-old student named Gavrilo Princip, who managed to kill both the archduke and archduchess by shooting Franz Ferdinand in the neck and his wife, Sophie, in the stomach. Princip, who already had severe tuberculosis and would die in prison, sparked the beginning of World War I, which would kill 15 million people and destroy four of the empires of Europe.

Chapter 27 looks at three great experiences that shaped European (and global) history in the twentieth century: (1) the **new imperialism** (1881–1914) in which the great European powers seized control of most of Africa and much of Asia; (2) World War I (1914–1918), which destroyed the last monarchical empires of the Old Regime; and (3) the Russian Revolution (1917–1920), which posed a new and powerful form of mass politics to compete with democracy. The chapter begins with the background of these great events during two generations of peace. It examines the Bismarckian alliance system, which divided Europe into two opposing sides, and the militarism and arms race, which made this division so dangerous. The discussion of World War I shows how the "great war" (as contemporaries called it) introduced Europe to a century of **total war**—in both its destructive battles and life on the home front. The final section focuses on the Russian Revolution of 1917, which established Lenin's Communist government in Russia, a regime that introduced Europe to twentieth-century totalitarianism.

THE BISMARCKIAN SYSTEM OF ALLIANCES (1871–1890)

Bismarck and German Diplomacy after 1871. The German victory in the Franco-Prussian War led to the creation of a unified German Empire so strong both militarily and economically that it dominated Europe, yet Chancellor Otto von Bismarck still feared French revenge. After 1871, he aimed to protect Germany by negotiating treaties that would guarantee the support of other powers and deny France potential allies. He achieved both goals through a web of alliances collectively known as the **Bismarckian system,** with which he dominated European diplomacy for 20 years (1871–1890). Bismarck's accomplishment radically altered European statecraft. Whereas the Metternichian system had kept the peace by a delicate **balance of power** in which none of the great powers became too dominant and none felt too threatened, the Bismarckian system kept peace through the lopsided superiority of the German alliances and the comparative weakness of France.

French Policy after 1871. French nationalists nonetheless dreamt of the day of revenge—*la revanche* (ruh-vahnsh')—on Germany, the day when the republic would reclaim the lost provinces of Alsace and Lorraine, whose borders were marked on the maps of French schools in a deep black. Realistic nationalists such as the hero of 1870, Léon Gambetta (Gam-bet'-uh), understood that Germany had become too powerful to fight alone and the French must wait for *revanche;* they should "[t]hink of it always, speak of it never." Despite a war scare in 1875 and a tense period during the Boulangist (Boo'-lahn-jist) nationalism of the late 1880s, no French government planned a war of revenge.

The Three Emperor's League. The first treaty in Bismarck's alliance system was the Three Emperors' League *(Dreikaiserbund)* of 1873, an outgrowth of state visits exchanged by William I of Germany, Franz Joseph of Austria-Hungary, and Alexander II of Russia. The Dreikaiserbund (Dry-ky'-zer-bunt) represented an amicable understanding (an *entente* [ahn-tant']) among recent rivals who shared a belief in monarchical solidarity. (France remained the only republic in monarchical Europe.) The king of Italy soon embraced this counterrevolutionary league, siding with Germany despite the debt Italians owed to the French from their wars of unification. The British remained outside this league, favoring a policy of continental nonalignment that came to be called **splendid isolation.**

The Balkan Wars and the Eastern Question. The development of the Bismarckian system accelerated as a result of warfare in the Balkans in 1875–1878,

which convinced Bismarck to seek more formal treaties. The provinces of Bosnia and Herzegovina (see *The Eastern Question*) rebelled against Ottoman rule in 1875, and Serbia intervened to support them. The Serbs had won autonomous government in their rebellion of 1817 and had become the center of **Pan-Slavism,** an ardent nationalism dedicated to the unity of the southern Slavic peoples of the Balkan subcontinent. The insurrection against the Ottoman Empire spread to Bulgaria in 1876, and the Turks responded with a violent repression known in the European press as "the Bulgarian horrors." The enlarged Balkan War forced the European powers to address the problem of southeastern Europe that had come to be called **the eastern question.**

The Sick Man of Europe. The eastern question concerned the survival of the Ottoman Empire—still known as **"the sick man of Europe"**—and the fate of territories under the control of Constantinople. The eastern question posed the danger of Austro-Russian conflict because both governments coveted Ottoman territory in the Balkans. To avoid such a confrontation, Bismarck adopted the role of **"the honest broker"** of the eastern question and presided over the Congress of Berlin (1878) to end the fighting. The British endorsed the congress because it served their policy of preserving the Ottoman Empire rather than dismantling it. The Berlin settlement placated Turkish honor by returning some territory lost in the fighting, and it awarded Balkan territory to both the Russians (Bessarabia) and the Austrians (Bosnia-Herzegovina). Bismarck bought French backing with support for colonial expansion. The Slavic nationalist movements of the Balkans—both Serbian and Bulgarian—were not satisfied: Serbs won their independence, but Pan-Slavs saw Bosnia lost to Austria; the Bulgarians won independence, but lost much territory promised to them in a preliminary treaty, the Treaty of San Stefano.

The Triple Alliance. The Balkan crisis of 1875–1878 drove Bismarck to negotiate a close military alliance with Austria-Hungary known as the Dual Alliance (1879), which became the new cornerstone of his alliance system. The Hapsburg prime minister and foreign minister was a Hungarian, Count Julius Andrássy (Ahn-drahsh'-ee), who held no grudge against Germany for the war of 1866. Secret terms of the Dual Alliance promised military assistance if either country were attacked by Russia and guaranteed neutrality if attacked by any other country. Bismarck labored simultaneously to retain Russian friendship by preserving and strengthening the Three Emperors' League; he understood that "[i]n a world of five powers, one should strive to be *à trois*" (on the side with three). Italy, motivated by a growing colonial rivalry with France in North Africa, joined the Dual Alliance in 1882, con-

THE EASTERN QUESTION

The eastern question was perhaps the most persistent diplomatic problem of the nineteenth century. At the simplest level, the question was this: who shall control the territories of the vast, but weak, Ottoman Empire. Nationalist movements sought independence in many regions, some of the great powers (especially Austria and Russia) sought to annex some regions, and some of the great powers (especially Britain) were determined to preserve the Ottoman Empire.

MAP 27.1. THE BALKANS AFTER THE CONGRESS OF BERLIN

The Ottoman Empire had once extended almost to the gates of Vienna, but it had been receding for two centuries. The Balkan Wars of 1875–1878 and the resolution of these wars at the Congress of Berlin (1878) marked a major start in the Ottoman retreat. Serbia and Bulgaria won independence and Austria absorbed Bosnia.

Delegates at the Congress of Berlin (1878). When the Balkan Wars of 1875–1878 threatened the survival of the Ottoman Empire and the disruption of the Balkans and the Middle East, Chancellor Bismarck of Germany organized a European peace conference at which the great powers imposed a settlement on the belligerents, preserving the Ottoman Empire and preventing a wider conflict. This illustration depicts the statesmen assembled at Berlin. Bismarck is the large man with a mustache, second from the right. Benjamin Disraeli of England is the man with a goatee, standing at left center and leaning on a cane. Note how many diplomats wear military insignia.

verting the pact into the Triple Alliance. Germany thus acquired explicit security against France, although Bismarck publicly presented the treaty as merely a bulwark of the monarchical order.

The Reinsurance Treaty. To underscore his desire for Russian friendship, Bismarck later negotiated another Russo-German treaty known as the Reinsurance Treaty (1887). This document gave a German pledge not to support Austrian aggression against Russia, and it was accompanied by significant German investment in Russian industrial development. Both governments reiterated their devotion to the **status quo** (to keeping things unchanged). Finally, Bismarck orchestrated a series of secondary treaties, such as the Mediterranean Agreements (1887), which involved other governments (including Britain and Spain) in the defense of the status quo. The network of his treaties became so complex that Bismarck enjoyed the self-bestowed image of being a juggler who could keep five balls in the air at once.

THE NEW IMPERIALISM (1881–1914)

An Age of Global Conquest. The great powers exploited the European peace to annex large empires around the world, an expansion known as the **new imperialism.** In 1871, only 10 percent of Africa had fallen under European control. Britain held the Cape Colony in South Africa and a few strips of West Africa. France had seized Algeria in 1830 and had long controlled part of West Africa, including Senegal; Portugal retained southern colonies dating back to the fifteenth and sixteenth centuries, but most of the continent remained self-governing. By 1914, Europeans claimed virtually the entire continent, leaving independent only Liberia (under American influence) and Ethiopia (claimed by Italy but unconquered). This new imperialism had also ended self-government in the Pacific by

1914. There, the Japanese—who took the Ryuku Islands in 1874 and Formosa (Taiwan today) in 1895—and the Americans—who took Hawaii, the Philippines, and part of Samoa in the 1890s—joined Europeans in building oceanic empires. Simultaneously, Britain and Russia expanded in southern Asia, Britain and France occupied most of Southeast Asia, and all of the industrial powers (including Japan and the United States) menaced China. Empires were growing so fast that a leader of British imperialism, Colonial Secretary Joseph Chamberlain, gloated, "The day of small nations has long passed away. The day of empires has come."

Empires before 1870. Europeans had been claiming empires around the world for centuries. Britain, France, Spain, Portugal, Denmark, and the Netherlands all held colonies taken before the nineteenth century. According to an estimate made in 1900, the frontiers of Russia had been advancing into Asia (much as the United States pushed westward) at the rate of 55 square miles per year since the sixteenth century. In the century between the 1770s and the 1870s, Russia fought six wars against the Ottoman Empire and four wars against Persia, in the course of which its tsars annexed the Crimea, Georgia, and Armenia, then advanced into southern Asia and prepared to take Afghanistan. Newly unified Italy and Germany were eager—against Bismarck's better judgment—to join this club. As Kaiser Wilhelm II said in a speech of 1901, echoing Count Bernhard von Bülow's *Weltpolitik,* Germans also expected "our place in the sun."

Traditional Colonialism and the New Imperialism. Europeans had previously built **colonial empires,** in which they sent colonists to live in distant colonies. The new imperialism of 1881–1914 included little of this style of colonialism. Europeans sent soldiers to explore and conquer, officials to organize and administer, missionaries to teach and convert, and merchants to develop and trade, but few families of colonists. When Germany annexed African colonies in the 1880s, more Germans chose to emigrate to Paris (the capital of their national enemy) than to colonize Africa.

Economics and Empire. Earlier empires had also been based on the commerce of **mercantilism.** Colonies provided such diverse goods as pepper, tulip bulbs, opium, slaves, but they were expected to strengthen or to enrich the imperial state. Economic interests still drove the new imperialism, but the motor had changed. Imperialists now spoke of markets for **exports,** especially textiles. They dreamt, in the imagery of one British prime minister, of the fortunes to be made if every Oriental bought a woolen nightcap. The rise of trade unions inspired industrialists to covet cheaper, more manageable, **colonial labor.** Financiers

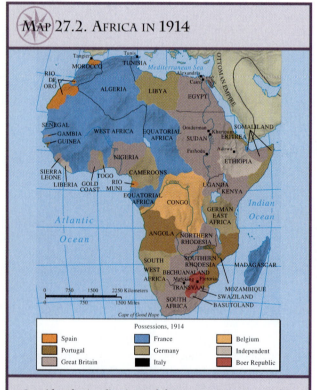

MAP 27.2. AFRICA IN 1914

Possessions, 1914

- Spain
- Portugal
- Great Britain
- France
- Germany
- Italy
- Belgium
- Independent
- Boer Republic

Consider the implications of the comparative size and location of European empires. When British imperialists looked at this map of Africa, for example, they dreamt of a Cape-to-Cairo railroad; when French imperialists looked at it, they saw a concentration of Francophone civilization. What rivalries do the maps suggest?

needed to find markets for investing the **capital** that was accumulating from industrial profits. As a leading French imperialist, Jules Ferry, said, "Colonial policy is the daughter of industrial policy" (see Document 27.1).

The Cost of Empire. The new imperialism, however, cannot be explained entirely by economics. Colonies cost imperial governments great sums of money for military, administrative, and developmental expenses that far exceeded the tax revenues they produced. Many private enterprises also lost money on imperialism. In the early twentieth century, the five largest banks in Berlin appealed to the government to stop acquiring colonies because they were losing ventures. Individual investors usually lost money in colonial stocks, which frequently paid neither dividends nor interest and were sold as patriotic investments. Some businesses, and the elite who controlled them, did make great profits from captive markets; textile towns and port-cities prospered in this way and championed imperialism. It was not a coincidence that Joseph Chamberlain, one of the greatest champions of British imperialism, represented the manufacturing town of Birmingham (where he had been mayor) in Parliament.

Cecil Rhodes. A few individuals made staggering fortunes overseas, as Cecil Rhodes did in the African diamond fields. Rhodes was a struggling cotton farmer who bought a diamond claim and hired Africans to work it. When he died, he was considered the richest man on Earth. His power was so enormous that a colony was named for him (Rhodesia, today Zimbabwe), and his fortune was so immense that it endowed (a bequest of £6 million) the Rhodes scholarships to Oxford for students from Britain, Germany, and the United States. Not surprisingly, Rhodes was an ardent imperialist who supported wars of imperial expansion (such as the Boer War of 1899–1902) and lamented that he could not annex the stars. Even the fantasy of striking it as rich as Rhodes, however, cannot fully explain why governments ran deficits to pay for empire.

Nationalism. The new imperialism must also be understood in terms of nationalism, militarism, and racism. Imperialist politicians insisted that empire was the measure of a nation's greatness. Nationalist organizations, such as the Pan-German League, pressed their government to take more territory. It would "awaken and foster the sense of racial and cultural kinship" of Germans to know that their country occupied a city on the coast of China. Journalists, teachers, and scholars promoted similar attitudes about the greatness of empire. As a Cambridge historian wrote in 1883, "[T]here is something intrinsically glorious in an empire 'upon which the sun never sets'." Even Cecil Rhodes insisted that his motives began with his **nationalism.** "I con-

tend," he wrote, "that we [the British] are the first race in the world, and the more of the world we inhabit, the better it is for the human race. I believe it to be my duty to God, my Queen, and my Country to paint the whole map of Africa red [the color typically used to depict British colonies], red from the Cape to Cairo."

DOCUMENT 27.1

JULES FERRY ON FRENCH IMPERIALISM (1885)

Jules Ferry (1832–1893) was a wealthy middle-class lawyer who served as premier of France in the 1880s. He was a moderate Republican and one of the founders of the Third Republic. His greatest accomplishments came in the creation of the French educational system, but he also became a leading champion of imperialism. The following document is excerpted from one of his parliamentary speeches.

Our colonial policy . . . rests upon our economic principles and interests, on our humanitarian visions of order, and on political considerations. . . .

[Interruptions by hecklers: "Yes, 20,000 corpses!" and "Ten thousand families in mourning!"]

Why have colonies from an economic standpoint? . . . [C]olonies are, for wealthy countries, an advantageous investment. France, which has exported a great amount of capital abroad, must consider this aspect of the colonial question. There is, however, another point, even more important: . . . For countries like France, devoted to exports by the nature of their industry, the colonial question is a question of markets. . . .

Gentlemen, there is a second point, a second set of ideas, that I must also raise: the humanitarian and civilizing side of imperialism. The honorable Camille Pelletan [another deputy] scoffs at this point. . . . He asks, "What is this civilization that one imposes with cannon shells?" . . . One must answer that superior races have rights with regard to the inferior races. They have rights because they have duties. They have the duty to civilize the inferior races. . . . Can anyone deny that it was good fortune for the people of equatorial Africa to fall under the protection of France and Britain?

. . . I add that French colonial policy . . . is inspired by another truth which you must reflect upon: a navy such as ours cannot survive with the shelters, defenses, supply bases. Just look at the map of the world. . . . No warship, no matter how perfectly organized, can carry more than a fourteen day supply of coal, and a warship short of coal is only a derelict on the high seas.

From *Journal officiel de la république française*. Debates of July 28, 1885, trans. Steven C. Hause (Paris: Imprimerie des journaux officiels).

Question: How well does Ferry's speech explain French imperialism?

Militarism. **Militarism** was also a significant factor in imperialism. The conquest of distant lands required larger armies and bigger budgets. Decoration, promotion, and territory were more easily won against preindustrial armies. Lord Kitchener became famous for commanding the outnumbered army that conquered the Sudan in 1896–1898. Kitchener's army of 25,000 defeated an army of 50,000 because they were equipped with Maxim guns (early machine guns), weapons that the explorer Henry Morton Stanley had proclaimed to be "of great service in helping civilization to overcome barbarism." The Maxim gun enabled Kitchener's forces to kill large numbers of Sudanese with relative ease; at the decisive battle of Omdurman, the British suffered 500 casualties and killed more than 15,000 Sudanese—"giving them a good dusting" in Kitchener's words. Thus, although the nineteenth century appears to be an age of peace for Britain when viewed in a European context, it was an epoch of constant warfare when viewed in a global context (see Table 27.1). In a tragic irony, Europeans saw the effect of the Maxim gun in Africa but could not envision its impact on a future war in Europe.

Missionaries and Humanitarianism in Imperialism. In addition to economic and political explanations of imperialism, Western cultural attitudes are also important in understanding the new imperialism. These range from religion and humanitarianism to social Darwinism and racism. Christian missionaries formed the vanguard of imperialist intervention in Africa and Asia, and it was not uncommon for missionaries to provide information to their governments or to advocate further imperial annexation. Missionaries won converts in some regions: Nigeria and Madagascar, for example, are both more than 40 percent Christian today; the most famous missionary in Africa, David Livingstone, however, converted only one person (whom he later threw out of the church for backsliding into paganism). In other regions, people resisted Christianity as an imperialist intervention; as one Indian put it, "Buddha came into our world on an elephant; Christ came into our world on a cannonball." Missionaries also taught Western attitudes and behavior, such as denouncing the depravity of seminudity in tropical climates. Textile manufacturers were not alone in concluding that "[b]usiness follows the Bible." Europeans also justified imperialism by speaking of humanitarianism. Some used crude stereotypes about abolishing cannibalism or moralistic arguments about ending polygamy; others took pride in the campaign to end the slave trade, which Europeans had done so much to develop. More educated arguments cited the abolition of practices such as Suttee in India (the tradition by which a widow threw herself on her husband's funeral pyre) or the benefits of Western medicine.

Social Darwinism and Racism. Humanitarian justifications for imperialism were often cloaked in terms such as the French doctrine of *la mission civilatrice* (the **civilizing mission**) or the title of Rudyard Kipling's poem "The White Man's Burden" (1899). Such terms suggested the argument of **social Darwinism**—that Western civilization was demonstrably superior to others, the most fit to survive. This led to the simple corollaries that (1) in Jules Ferry's words, "superior races have rights with regard to inferior races" and (2) they had a duty to help "backwards" peoples. Kipling, for example, urged advanced states: "Fill full the mouth of Famine/And bid the sickness cease." One British army officer praised the conquest of Africa in an 1883 book because "the less advanced and the more primitive tribes" would benefit from it. Even humanitarianism contained an element of the **racism** common in imperialism. Europeans had often viewed colonial peoples as heathens or savages. Late nineteenth-century social Darwinism worsened such stereotypes by promoting the pseudoscientific notion that all races were locked in a struggle for survival, a struggle to be won by the fittest. Imperialists cheerfully concluded that their own nation would win this struggle. In some of the worst cases, such as the administration of Heinrich Goering (the father of Hermann Goering) in German Southwest Africa (today Namibia), war was waged so relentlessly on the African population (the Hereros peoples in southwest Africa) as to seem a war of extermination. Racial attitudes were sometimes bluntly expressed. A president of the United States spoke of his desire to help his "little brown brothers" (the people of the Philippines). A tsar of Russia joked about going to war with "little yellow monkeys" (the Japanese, who promptly defeated the Russians). By the early twentieth century, Western racism was so unchallenged that a major zoo exhibited an African in a cage alongside apes.

The Scramble for Africa

North African Origins of the New Imperialism. Historians often cite the French occupation of Tunis in 1881 as the beginning of the new imperialism. French pride had been hurt by the events of 1870–1871, and it had received another blow in 1875, when the British purchased control of the Suez Canal (built by the French in the 1860s) from the khedive of Egypt. Bismarck used the distrust generated by the Suez issue to reawaken Anglo-French rivalry. At the Congress of Berlin in 1878, he encouraged the French to claim Tunis, and the congress approved. Jules Ferry, who became premier of France in 1880, used the excuse of raids by Tunisian tribes into Algeria to proclaim a French **protectorate** (one of many euphemisms for conquered territory) over Tunis—an act that promptly benefited Bismarck by driving the Italians (who had

TABLE 27.1 A CHRONOLOGY OF THE BRITISH IMPERIAL WARS, 1815–1900

DATE	WAR	LOCATION	RESULT
1815	Ceylonese War	Indian Ocean	Ceylon made crown colony
1816	Barbados Rebellion	Caribbean	Slave revolt suppressed
1817–1819	Assam Intervention	Southeast Asia	Assam ceded to Britain
1823	Guiana Rebellion	South America	Slave revolt suppressed
1824–1826	First Burmese War	Southeast Asia	Further annexations from Burma
1831	Jamaica Rebellion	Caribbean	Slave revolt suppressed
1832	Falklands Campaign	South America	Falklands taken from Argentina
1834–1835	Sixth Kaffir War	South Africa	Xhosa lands opened to settlement
1838–1842	First Afghan War	South Asia	Successful British invasion
1839	Aden Campaign	Arabia	Port-town of Aden seized
1839–1842	Opium War	China	Hong Kong seized
1843	Sind War	India	Baluchi lands annexed
1844–1847	First Maori War	New Zealand	Maori uprising defeated
1845–1846	First Sikh War	India	Sikh rebellion beaten
1846–1847	Seventh Kaffir War	South Africa	Xhosa lands annexed
1848–1849	Second Sikh War	India	Punjab annexed to India
1850–1853	Eighth Kaffir War	South Africa	Xhosa defeated
1852–1853	Second Burmese War	Southeast Asia	British merchants protected
1856–1857	Persian War	South Asia	Shah forced to concede land
1856–1857	Second China War	China	Trade policies defended
1857–1858	Sepoy Mutiny	India	Mutineers defeated
1860–1861	Second Maori War	New Zealand	Taranaki resistance beaten
1863–1866	Third Maori War	New Zealand	Taranaki uprising defeated
1867–1868	Abyssinian War	East Africa	Abyssinian threats ended
1868–1872	Fourth Maori War	New Zealand	Maori resistance broken
1873–1874	First Ashanti War	West Africa	Ashanti capital taken
1877–1878	Ninth Kaffir War	South Africa	Annexation of all Kaffir lands
1878–1879	Zulu War	South Africa	Natal saved from Zulus
1878–1880	Second Afghan War	South Asia	Pro-British government installed
1880–1881	South African War	South Africa	British withdraw from Boer lands
1882	Egyptian War	Egypt	Nationalist uprising defeated
1884–1885	First Sudanese War	North Africa	Mahdist rebellion defeats English
1885–1892	Third Burmese War	Southeast Asia	Burma made British colony
1896	Second Ashanti War	West Africa	Ashanti beaten
1896–1899	Second Sudanese War	North Africa	Sudan reconquered
1899–1902	Boer War	South Africa	Boers defeated
1900	Third Ashanti War	West Africa	Ashanti lands annexed
1900	Boxer Rebellion	China	Nationalist uprising beaten

competing claims in North Africa) into the Triple Alliance. The British responded by using nationalist riots as an excuse to extend their control of Egypt in 1882. They bombarded Alexandria, occupied Cairo, and placed Egypt under the thumb of a British consul. Nationalist rebellion moved south to the Sudan in 1883. It acquired a religious fervor from an Islamic leader known as the Mahdi (messiah); the Mahdists defeated several British garrisons, notably the forces of General Gordon at Khartoum (1885), and sustained an autonomous government until Kitchener's victory at Omdurman a decade later.

The Scramble for Empire. Anglo-French imperialism in North Africa provoked a race among European governments, known as the **"scramble for Africa,"** to claim colonies in sub-Saharan Africa. In the 5 years between 1882 and 1887, Europeans claimed more than

FIGURE 27.1 *The Conquest of Africa.* The European conquest of Africa in the late nineteenth century was popularized at home in many ways: in churches, where it was depicted favorably for helping missionary efforts; in schools, where the new popularity of geography depicted empire as a conquest of knowledge; in business, where empire meant new markets; and in this illustration for a children's game. This board game, bluntly named "The Conquest of Africa," was based on the travels of the missionary David Livingstone (1813–1873) and the explorer Henry Morton Stanley (1841–1904).

2 million square miles of Africa. (The United States today totals less than 3.7 million square miles.) In 1884 alone, Germany took more than 500,000 square miles as German Southwest Africa, Cameroon, and Togo; 2 years later, they added nearly 400,000 square miles as German East Africa (today Tanzania). King Leopold II of Belgium took the largest single claim—nearly 1 million square miles of central Africa known as the Congo—following the approval of a meeting of the imperial powers in Berlin in 1885. Leopold then founded a company that brutally exploited the Congo as a gigantic rubber plantation, under the ironic name of the Congo Free State. (Leopold's regime was so brutal that some historians speak of a **holocaust** in Africa.) Even land grabs that huge could not compete with the British and French empires; by 1914, Great Britain and France each controlled approximately 5 million square miles of Africa.

The Fashoda Crisis of 1898. The scramble for Africa had many repercussions in European diplomacy, chiefly the reopening of the colonial rivalry between Britain and France. After General Kitchener's victory at Omdurman, his troops confronted a small French exploratory mission, the Marchand mission, which had crossed Africa from west to east in a heroic march and was camped on the upper Nile at the Sudanese town of

Fashoda. Kitchener and Marchand both planted their flags at Fashoda, but the size of Kitchener's forces obliged the French to leave. The Fashoda crisis showed that France remained vulnerable in 1898, but the French withdrawal later facilitated improved relations.

The Boer War, 1899–1902. In the months that followed, the vulnerability of British diplomatic isolation (from any alliance) was exposed by Britain's involvement in the Boer War (1899–1902). The Boers, white settlers of mixed Dutch and Huguenot descent, had created a republic, the Transvaal, in Bantu territory north of the Britain's Cape Colony in South Africa. The British annexed the Transvaal in 1877, but a revolt in 1880–1881 and a convincing victory at Majuba Hill in 1881 earned the Boers autonomy under the strong leadership of President Paul Kruger. Tensions remained high, however, especially after the discovery of vast deposits of gold in the Transvaal. An Anglo-Boer war broke out in 1899. The Boers won initial victories, besieged the British at Mafeking and Ladysmith, and earned international sympathy, especially after the British placed 120,000 Boer women and children in **concentration camps** (the first use of this term) to limit support for Boer guerrillas and 20,000 died, chiefly from disease. Massive British reinforcements under General Kitchener reversed the course of the war in 1900, lifting the siege of Mafeking, capturing the Boer capital of Pretoria, and again annexing the Transvaal. The Boer leaders continued resistance by 2 years of guerrilla fighting before accepting the British victory in the Treaty of Vereeniging in 1902.

African Resistance to Imperialism. The Boer War was the largest imperial war in Africa, but it should not distract attention from the wars of African resistance to imperialism. The British annexation of the Transvaal, for example, led them into the Zulu War of 1879, where the battle of Isandhlwana showed that a poorly equipped African army could defeat Europeans. The Ashanti tribes of West Africa, in what is now Ghana, resisted the British in four wars during the nineteenth century, three of them fought between 1873 and 1896. The Ashanti, too, won battles against the British. The French likewise experienced defeats in fighting two Dahomeyan wars (in present-day Benin); the Mandingo tribes (in present-day Ivory Coast) resisted French occupation of the interior for 13 years

FIGURE 27.2 *Pioneers of Civilization.* In this anti-British cartoon from a French newspaper, sarcastically titled "Pioneers of Civilization," British imperialism in Africa is shown as the killing of everyone in Britain's path. The British soldier, literally armed to the teeth, stands on the corpse of black Africa and grins, oblivious to the pleas of the dying.

(1885–1898), making a great hero of their chief, Samory. The Hereros (Bantu tribes of southwest Africa) and the Hottentots withstood the German army for nearly 6 years (1903–1908). They did not capitulate until the Germans had reduced the Herero population from 80,000 to 15,000. The Ethiopians threw out European invaders; Emperor Menelik II resisted an Italian occupation in 1896, and his forces annihilated an Italian army in the massive battle of Adowa, which involved more than 100,000 combatants.

The Victory of European Numbers and Science. Europeans eventually won most imperial wars. The advantage of modern armament is a sufficient explanation, as Kitchener demonstrated in the bloody engagement on the plains of Omdurman. In the blunt words of one poet, "Whatever happens we have got/The Maxim Gun, and they have not." Europeans also held a numerical advantage whenever they chose to use it; defeats usually summoned reinforcements that Africans could not match, as the Bantus, the Zulus,

and the Boers learned. The Italian army was outnumbered by 80,000 to 20,000 at Adowa. If Italy had wanted Ethiopia badly enough to obtain a four-to-one advantage (the Italian army and militia of the 1890s numbered nearly 3 million men), they, too, might have won. Europeans also succeeded in imperial conquests because of biological and medical advantages. Westerners had an advantage in nutrition that translated into larger, healthier armies, and invaders carrying smallpox, whooping cough, or the measles sometimes carried a biological weapon better than gunpowder. Conversely, African diseases (especially malaria) had long blocked European penetration of the continent. When the French occupied Tunis in 1881, malaria killed twenty-five times as many soldiers as combat did. Europeans knew that quinine, derived from the bark of the cinchona tree, prevented malaria, and scientists isolated the chemical in 1820, but not until the late nineteenth century did they synthesize quinine in adequate quantities to provide an inexpensive daily dose for large armies. Such scientific conquests made possible the military conquest of Africa.

Imperialism in Asia and the "Opening of China"

European Empires in Asia. Europeans began their conquests in Asia in the early sixteenth century. By the late nineteenth century, Britain dominated most of south Asia (present-day India, Pakistan, Sri Lanka, and Bangladesh) and Australasia (present-day Australia and New Zealand). They had begun to expand into Southeast Asia, annexing much of Burma (now Myanmar) in 1853. This led them into competition with the French who landed troops in Annam (present-day Vietnam) in 1858. Most of the East Indies had been claimed by the Dutch (present-day Indonesia was the Dutch East Indies) or the Spanish (the Philippines) for centuries. China and Japan had largely resisted Western penetration, except for toeholds such as Hong Kong, which the British leased in 1841.

The New Imperialism in Asia. The new imperialism refreshed the European appetite for Asia. Between 1882 and 1884, the French subjugated the region of modern Vietnam, and their expedition continued until Cambodia (1887) and Laos (1893) were connected with Annam to form French Indo-China, after years of fighting (see Document 27.2) This prompted the British to complete their annexation of Burma (1886) and to reach south for the Malay States (present-day Malaysia), which became a British-run federation in 1896. By the turn of the twentieth century, Siam (Thailand) was the only independent state in the entire subcontinent, and Siamese freedom depended on

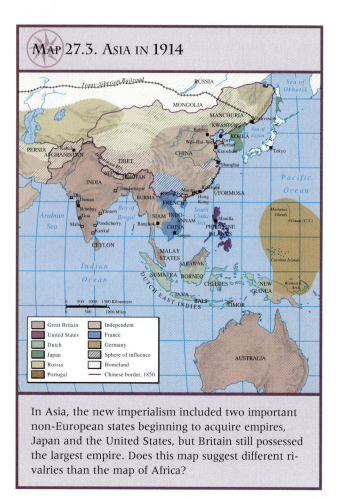

MAP 27.3. ASIA IN 1914

Great Britain
United States
Dutch
Japan
Russia
Portugal
Independent
France
Germany
Sphere of influence
Homeland
Chinese border, 1850

In Asia, the new imperialism included two important non-European states beginning to acquire empires, Japan and the United States, but Britain still possessed the largest empire. Does this map suggest different rivalries than the map of Africa?

German missionaries had been killed in that region. These events launched another imperialist scramble, this time known as the **"opening of China."** Unlike their outright annexation of land in Africa, European governments used the genteel device of pressing the Manchu government to sign 99-year leases for **treaty ports** along the coast of China. During 1898, the Germans extracted a lease to Kiaochow, the Russians to the Liaodong peninsula and Port Arthur, the French to Kwangchow in the south (near to Indo-China), and the British to both Wei-Hai-Wei in the north and Kowloon (near Hong Kong) in the south.

The Race for Pacific Islands. While Europeans were extracting leases to Chinese territory, another war shifted imperialist attention further east, to the islands of the Pacific Ocean. The Spanish-American War of 1898—chiefly fought in the Caribbean, following a Cuban insurrection against Spanish rule in 1895—completed the collapse of the Spanish colonial empire. The victorious United States, which had won an important naval victory against the Spanish at Manila, claimed the Philippine archipelago (the largest Spanish colony) and fought a 3-year war (1899–1901) to subdue Filipino nationalists. The United States chose to follow European imperialism and established an American government for the islands. This stimulated a race to claim the remaining islands of the Pacific. Germany and the United States, both eager for bases to support global fleets, led this rush. Between 1899 and 1914, Germany claimed dozens of north Pacific islands (such as the Mariana Islands, the Caroline Islands, and the Marshall Islands, which would become famous battlegrounds of World War II). The United States took Hawaii (1898), Guam (1898), and Wake Island (1900), while joining Germany and Britain in dividing the Samoan Islands (1899). By 1914, no self-governing atoll survived in the Pacific.

Asian Resistance. The Asian resistance to Western imperialism, like the African resistance, was repeatedly expressed with arms. The opening of China in 1898 precipitated a turbulent period in Chinese history that included a major uprising against foreigners, the Boxer Rebellion (1900–1901). The Boxers, the European name for a paramilitary organization of Chinese nationalists who hoped to expel all foreigners from China, began the uprising by attacking Christian missionaries and their converts. Violence spread to Beijing, culminating in the murder of the German ambassador and a siege of Western legations. A multinational expedition put down the Boxer Rebellion and conducted punitive missions in provincial China.

Japan and the West. Japan provided the most successful opposition to European imperialism in Asia. European intervention against the Japanese in 1895,

Anglo-French inability to compromise. Most of Southeast Asia had been under the loose suzerainty of the Manchu Dynasty of China, and the European conquests of 1882–1896 exposed the vulnerability of that regime. Japan's easy military victory in the Sino-Japanese War of 1894–1895—the result of a decade of rivalry over Korea, which Japan seized in 1894—underscored that lesson. The Treaty of Shimonoseki ended that war, with China granting independence to Korea and ceding the province of Kwantung (west of Korea) and the island of Formosa (Taiwan) to Japan.

The Opening of China. Europeans could not resist exploiting the infirmity of the Chinese Empire. Initial European intervention, however, was against the Japanese, who were obliged to return Kwantung to China. Then, in 1896, the Russians extracted a treaty allowing them to build the Trans-Siberian Railway across the Chinese province of Manchuria to the Russian port of Vladivostok. Shortly thereafter, the Russians simply occupied Manchuria. In early 1897, the Germans followed the Japanese and Russians into China by occupying the northern port-city of Kiaochow after two

A CHINESE GOVERNOR DENOUNCES FRENCH IMPERIALISM (1883)

The Opening of China. In this political cartoon from a French newspaper in 1898, the imperialist powers carve up China. Seated around the dish, labeled China, are Queen Victoria of England, Emperor William II of Germany, Tsar Nicholas II of Russia, and Emperor Mutsuhito of Japan, while the allegorical representative of France, Marianne, looks on. Note that the European powers seem much more concerned with each other than with the Chinese.

I, Vice-commandant . . . Liu Yung-fu publish this proclamation so that it be read in the four cardinal points [of the compass].

The country of Annam [modern Vietnam] . . . was a tributary of the Chinese Empire. The entire world, and even children five years old, knows that Annam is tributary of China; why does France seem to be ignorant of this fact? . . . The greed of the French is equaled only by the voracity of the shark. They wish to absorb the Empire of Annam. . . .

I have had to have brave soldiers come. They are at Hanoi. On May 13 and 14, they attacked the Catholic Mission. On the nineteenth, they fought with the French troops. The gunfire resounded like thunder. The flesh of the men has shivered from it. . . . [O]ur soldiers are courageous and are not afraid to march forward even if they have to fight one against ten. In this fight, we killed some French chiefs: a commandant with five bands [on his uniform], a captain, and two lieutenants. The number of soldiers killed is incalculable. . . . [W]e pursued them [the French] as far as the West Gate. Then the gate was closed and they have not dared to show themselves. Their conduct is condemned by the gods and by men. They merit that punishment, which is the vengeance of Heaven alone.

If France is aware of her faults and regrets them, she will withdraw her troops.

From Yung-fu, Liu, *Revue indo-chinoise*, 40 (1932):166, as reproduced in Ludwig Schaefer, et al., eds., *Problems in Western Civilization* (New York: Scribner's, 1965).

Question: How does this document of 1883 compare with Jules Ferry's justification of French imperialism in 1885?

---

followed by provocations such as the Russian occupation of Manchuria, lease to Port Arthur, and penetration of Korea led to the Russo-Japanese War of 1904–1905. The Japanese attacked Port Arthur in February 1904, trapping the entire Russian Pacific fleet except for the ships icebound at Vladivostok. A few weeks later, the Japanese army landed in Korea, advanced into Manchuria, and defeated the Russian army. In the spring of 1905, a Russian European fleet reached the Orient only to be destroyed (thirty-three of forty-five ships were sunk) in the battle of Tsushima Strait between Japan and Korea. The crushing defeat of Russia led to a peace treaty of 1905 ceding territory to

Japan, contributed to revolution in Russia, and would soon led to a new European diplomatic alignment.

Asian Nationalism. Resistance to European imperialism went beyond the Indo-Chinese wars of the 1880s, the Boxer uprising of 1900, and the Japanese victory of 1904–1905. Well-organized nationalist movements appeared in the early twentieth century. In 1908, for example, a group of moderate nationalists wrote a constitution for the Indian National Congress (later, the Congress Party), calmly stating their objective of winning self-government by constitutional means. The African National Congress (ANC) of South Africa originated at a similar meeting in 1912. Many of the nationalists who would later lead the twentieth-century resistance to Western imperialism emigrated to Europe, where they received formal and informal education in dealing with European governments. Ho Chi Minh, the leader of Vietnamese armed resistance to French, Japanese, and American imperialism, lived in France as a young man; there he joined in the foundation of the French Communist Party.

Gandhi and Nonviolent Resistance. Perhaps the most impressive resistance to imperialism was begun by an Indian lawyer, Mohandas Gandhi. Gandhi began his career as a lawyer defending Indian laborers in South Africa in 1889. There he developed a policy of **nonviolent resistance** known by the Sanskrit word *Satyagraha.* Despite harassment, beatings, and imprisonment, Gandhi stood with the moral force of Satyagraha and gained a global reputation. When the frustrated British deported him to India, Gandhi brought passive resistance to Indian nationalism. His ability to lead hundreds of thousands of people in peaceful **civil disobedience** and **noncooperation** would ultimately be a major factor in the British loss of India.

THE DIPLOMATIC REVOLUTION (1890–1914)

The Decline of the Bismarckian System. Imperial rivalries strained the Bismarckian system in Europe, but Bismarck's network of alliances survived until Kaiser Wilhelm II sent him into retirement in 1890. The young emperor followed the advice of one of Bismarck's rivals, Baron Fritz von Holstein, to revise the Bismarckian system because Bismarck's promises to Russia risked losing the close alliance with Austria. Therefore, despite repeated Russian requests, the kaiser decided not to renew the Reinsurance Treaty of 1887, and it lapsed 3 months after the dismissal of Bismarck. Instead, Wilhelm expanded the Triple Alliance in 1891, giving larger promises of support to Austria-Hungary and Italy.

The Franco-Russian Alliance, 1891–1894. The consequence of the lapsing of Reinsurance Treaty was Franco-Russian friendship. One year after Bismarck's departure, a French fleet paid a symbolic visit to the Russian port of Kronstadt (near St. Petersburg) and Franco-Russian negotiations began; French pledges of loans to help industrialize Russia quickly led to the August Convention of 1891, an informal guarantee of cooperation. Avid French diplomacy expanded this into a military treaty, the Franco-Russian Alliance of 1894. Through this pact, the tsar pledged to use the full

Russian army against Germany if Germany invaded France; the reciprocal French promise gave Russia security against Austria and Germany. France and Russia agreed that they would "take counsel together on all questions which are calculated to jeopardize the peace of the world." To be ready for war, they also pledged to mobilize their armies (to put them on a status of war readiness) as soon as any member of the Triple Alliance began **mobilization.** The Franco-Russian Alliance was the first major step in a **diplomatic revolution** in which the dominance of the Bismarckian alliance would be challenged.

Anglo-German Rivalry. The 1890s witnessed a further weakening of the German position as a result of deteriorating Anglo-German relations. The rise of Germany as an industrial power caused a rivalry for markets and aroused hostile public opinion in both countries. The **jingoistic press** contributed significantly to the worsening relations. The **trade rivalry** made the British question their tradition of free trade, and newspapers were soon denouncing goods "Made in Germany." German imperialism and German sympathy for the Boers (the kaiser sent a notorious telegram of encouragement to President Kruger in 1896) worsened relations further. German colonies contributed to the emergence of a larger problem: the German decision to build a great navy. Through the efforts of Admiral von Tirpitz, Germany adopted an ambitious Naval Law in 1898 and expanded this construction program with a second Naval Law in 1900. The British, who had long counted on "ruling the waves" as their insurance against invasion, had adopted a vigorous naval building

FIGURE 27.3 *Kaiser Wilhelm II, King of Prussia; von Tirpitz; and von Moltke.* In this early twentieth-century photograph, the emperor of Germany, Wilhelm II, stands at left listening intently to his navy Minister, Admiral Alfred von Tirpitz (1849–1930) and his army Chief of Staff, General Helmuth von Moltke (1848–1916).

policy in 1889 known as **the two-power standard;** that is, they would build a navy equal to the combined forces of any two rivals. This policy, in combination with the German naval laws, led Europe into a dangerous **arms race.**

Théophile Delcassé and the Entente Cordiale. When the Fashoda crisis rekindled Anglo-French colonial disputes in 1898, some British statesmen, led by Joseph Chamberlain, argued that the government must abandon **splendid isolation** and enter the European alliance system. Chamberlain suggested resolving Anglo-German differences and negotiating an Anglo-German alliance, but his unofficial talks with minor diplomats in 1898–1901 failed to persuade either the Prime Minister, the Marquis of Salisbury, or Chancellor von Bülow, and they were flatly rejected by the kaiser. The French foreign minister who yielded to Britain in the Fashoda crisis, Théophile Delcassé, responded by seizing the opportunity to open Anglo-French negotiations over their generations of colonial differences. By skillfully expanding colonial negotiations, Delcassé became the architect of an entente with Britain, creating a diplomatic revolution that ended British isolation and the hegemony of the Triple Alliance. His central accomplishment was an Anglo-French agreement of 1904 known as the Entente Cordiale (cordial understanding). The entente was not a military treaty comparable to the Triple Alliance or the Franco-Russian Alliance. It simply resolved colonial disputes: France recognized British preeminence in Egypt, and Britain accepted the French position in Morocco. Starting with this *quid pro quo* (something in return for something), the two governments were able to end squabbles around the globe.

The Moroccan Crisis of 1905. The German reaction to the Entente Cordiale was to provoke an international crisis over Morocco in 1905. Germany, which had a growing commercial interest in Morocco, had been excluded from talks on the subject, although Delcassé had conducted negotiations on Morocco to acquire the support of Spain (by giving up the Moroccan coast opposite Spain) and of Italy (by backing an Italian claim to Tripoli). The Moroccan Crisis (later called the first Moroccan Crisis) resulted from a state visit by Kaiser Wilhelm II to Tangier, Morocco, where he made a strong speech in defense of Moroccan independence. When Delcassé proposed that some territorial concession be made to Germany to recognize the French position in Morocco, the kaiser refused. This confrontation led, at the invitation of the sultan of Morocco, to an international conference at Algeciras (Spain) in 1906. At this conference, Delcassé's diplomacy succeeded again, although he was driven from office in France by fears that he was dangerously provoking Germany. The crisis strengthened the Entente Cordiale and prompted closer Anglo-French military conversations, and when a vote was taken at Algeciras, only Austria supported Germany.

The Anglo-Russian Entente. The survival of the Entente Cordiale convinced the Reichstag to adopt Germany's third Naval Law in 1906, but that in turn frightened the British enough to negotiate their territorial disputes with Russia in south Asia (Persia and Afghanistan). The Russians recognized the need for this negotiation after their defeat by Japan in 1905. The resultant Anglo-Russian Entente of 1907 divided Persia into spheres of influence and exchanged a Russian agreement to stay out of Afghanistan in return for British support for Russian naval access to the Mediterranean.

The Triple Entente. This Anglo-Russian understanding, in combination with the Anglo-French Entente Cordiale and the Franco-Russian Alliance, created the Triple Entente. The Triple Entente did not include the explicit military provisions of the Triple Alliance, but Britain, France, and Russia soon entered into talks to plan military cooperation. Whereas French diplomats once worried about their isolation by Bismarck, the diplomatic revolution made Germans speak angrily of their *Einkreisung* **(encirclement)** by hostile competitors. The diplomatic revolution had replacement German diplomatic hegemony with a new balance of power between competing alliances.

FIGURE 27.4 *The Entente Cordiale.* In a diplomatic revolution of enormous historical importance, Britain dropped its traditional "splendid isolation" and France won potential support against Germany when the two countries signed the Entente Cordiale (the cordial understanding) of 1904, resolving old colonial disputes between the two countries. The architect of this agreement, Théophile Delcassé, thus completed a revolution by which the French counteracted the dominance of the German Triple Alliance. In this contemporary postcard, the president of France and the king of England are seen dancing together while Delcassé hangs onto the English coattails.

THE EASTERN QUESTION AND THE ROAD TO WAR (1878–1914)

This division of Europe into two competing alliances meant that a local crisis could precipitate a general war. Europe held several grave local problems, but the worst remained the eastern question. Bismarck's Congress of Berlin in 1878 had not settled this issue. It had merely temporized by placating the great powers; it did nothing to resolve Balkan nationalist claims or to settle the internal problems of the Ottoman Empire.

Balkan Crises and Wars. Fighting resumed in the Balkans in the 1880s and had become severe by 1885, when Bulgarian nationalists in the region of East Rumelia sought unity with Bulgaria and Serbia went to war to prevent the creation of a large Bulgaria on its frontier. Fighting broke out twice in the 1890s, then two more times in the early twentieth century before the next major crisis, known as the Balkan crisis of 1908. The crisis began with a long-simmering rebellion of **Westernizers** (modernizers who advocated a west European model) inside the Ottoman Empire, known as the Young Turk rebellion. The victorious **Young**

Turks won numerous concessions from the Sultan and exposed the inability of the government in Constantinople to resist changes, encouraging nationalists in the Balkans.

Pan-Slav Nationalism. Almost constant crises wracked the Balkans from 1908 to 1914. Austria-Hungary, which had established a claim to Bosnia and Herzegovina in 1878, took advantage of the Ottoman crisis to annex the two provinces in 1908. This act outraged Pan-Slav nationalists in Serbia who had long seen Serbia as the "Piedmont of the Balkans" and anticipated a merger with Bosnia in a union of the southern Slavs (called Yugo Slavs in the Serbian language). After the annexation, Slavic nationalists turned increasingly to revolutionary societies, such as the Black Hand and the Narodna Odbrana, to achieve unity. The 1911 statutes of the Black Hand stated the danger bluntly: "This organization prefers terrorist action to intellectual propaganda." The Hapsburg monarchy was soon to discover that this was not an idle threat. None of the European powers was pleased by the annexation of Bosnia, but none intervened to prevent it. The continuing weakness of the Ottoman Empire, militancy of Balkan nationalism, and reluctance of the great powers to intervene led to a sequence of crises.

The Balkan Wars, 1912–1913. In 1911, a second Moroccan crisis occurred, in which Germany sent the gunboat *Panther* to Morocco to protect German interests, and the French conceded territory in central Africa to resolve the dispute. In 1912, a war broke out in North Africa, in which Italy invaded Tripoli to acquire their compensation for French gains in Morocco. Later that year, open warfare spread to the Balkans when Serbia, Montenegro, Bulgaria, and Greece joined to attack the Ottoman Empire and detach some of the few remaining Turkish provinces in Europe. The Italians soon joined this First Balkan War (1912–1913) by invading the Dodecanese Islands off the coast of Turkey. After the Turks had conceded territory to them, the belligerents quarreled among themselves; several states fought Bulgaria in the Second Balkan War (1913) to redivide the spoils, but nationalist ambitions remained unsatisfied.

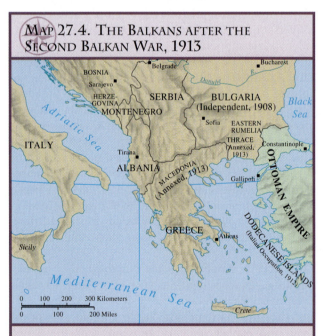

MAP 27.4. THE BALKANS AFTER THE SECOND BALKAN WAR, 1913

Compare this map with Map 27.1. Note the trend of the shrinking Ottoman Empire. In 1878, all of the green shaded areas (Albania, Macedonia, East Rumelia, and Thessaly) remained part of the empire; by 1913, the empire held only a small foothold in Europe. Nonetheless, this pattern of independence from Constantinople worsened nationalist violence rather than ending it.

MILITARISM AND THE EUROPEAN ARMS RACE (1871–1914)

Imperial competition, alliance system rivalries, and the Balkan crises were all happening in an age of militarism. Europe in 1900 was the scene of a heated arms race, sustained by a mentality that glorified military action. When Bismarck negotiated the Triple Alliance in 1879, the typical great power army was smaller than

500,000 men; by 1913, the average exceeded 1 million men, with mobilization plans for armies of 3 million to 4 million men (see *Militarism and the Arms Race*).

The Naval Construction Race. The naval construction race between Britain and Germany was the most costly part of the arms race. The industrial age had made it possible to build enormous, steam-powered, steel battleships, equipped with long-range artillery. These battleships, known as **dreadnoughts** (from the expression "Fear God and Dread Nought"), were staggeringly expensive, and the construction of submarine fleets added significantly to the total (see *Militarism and the Arms Race*). Before the shipbuilding mania of the 1890s, Britain had an annual naval budget of £13.8 million. This consumed more than 15 percent of government revenues, or more than twice the amount spent on education, science, and the arts combined (£6.1 million). Then, between 1890 and 1914, annual British naval expenditures more than tripled to £47.4 million. (The total revenue raised by the British income tax in 1913 was £44 million.) The German naval budget, meanwhile, almost quintupled from £4.6 million (1871) to £22.4 million (1914).

Militarism and Industrialization. Few people yet understood the implications of this marriage between militarism and industrialization. Cavalry troops wearing brightly colored eighteenth-century uniforms and sabers remained the image of a heroic army, although a more accurate image of an army in 1900 portrayed its machines: rapid-firing heavy artillery (such as the Krupp guns that had shelled Paris) and machine guns (such as the Maxims that had slaughtered the Sudanese). And no army could be stronger than the chemical industry that stood behind it; mass armies, and the total war that they implied, became possible only when chemists devised ways to manufacture millions of tons of explosives and the small arms munitions required by millions of soldiers. The wartime role of the chemical industry would take an even more macabre turn when poison gas became an option.

Militarism and the Glorification of War. The arms race was accompanied by a popular **militarism** glorifying war. "Eternal peace is a dream, and not even a beautiful one," held one famous general. An outspoken German commander, General Friedrich von Bernhardi, published a remarkable book titled *Germany and the Next War* (1911), in which he insisted that "war is a biological necessity." Bernhardi devoted a chapter to demonstrating "the right to make war" and then another to "the duty to make war." His conclusion came down to a simple choice: "world power or downfall." Writers everywhere popularized such attitudes. In the words of an Italian journalist, "We wish to glorify war—the only health-giver of the world." Or, in those of an American philosopher, "War is a school of strenuous life and heroism."

The Schlieffen Plan. Militaristic governments produced elaborate plans (in peacetime) for possible wars. German planners, for example, were ready for an invasion of the British Isles or of Texas (supporting a Mexican invasion of the southwestern United States), although they naturally lavished their most meticulous attention, such as the creation of precise railroad timetables, on plans to invade France. The most famous peacetime **war plan** was the Schlieffen Plan, named for the German general who devised it in 1892 in response to the Franco-Russian rapprochement and the fear that Germany might have to fight a **war on two fronts** at once. Schlieffen reasoned that the Russians would be slow to mobilize, but the French, able to employ modern communications and transportation, would be an immediate threat. The Schlieffen Plan therefore directed the German army to begin any war by concentrating all possible forces against the French; a rapid victory there would permit defeating the Russians afterward. To win that rapid victory over the French, the plan proposed to start any war (without regard to where it originated) by invading neutral Belgium. As the German strategist Karl von Clausewitz had explained a century earlier, "The heart of France lies between Brussels and Paris." The German plan for marching to Brussels and then pivoting southward was so precise that it included a timetable for each day's progress, culminating in a triumphal parade through Paris on day thirty-nine.

Plan XVII. French war planners also believed that the next war would be decided by a rapid offensive. Their 1913 regulations were straightforward: "The French army, returning to its tradition, henceforth admits no law but the offensive." It was expounded through a document known as Plan XVII, drafted by French generals for the reconquest of Alsace and Lorraine. Most of the French army was to be concentrated on the eastern frontier and then march into Alsace, but French planners so poorly understood what an industrial war would be like that they rejected camouflage uniforms for their great offensive and dressed soldiers in bright red trousers.

THE BALKAN CRISIS OF JULY 1914

Europeans little recognized the gravity of their situation in the early twentieth century; their rivalries for markets and empire, their nationalist ambitions and hatreds, their alliances and battle plans, their militarism, and their crude social Darwinian belief in "the survival of the fittest" all threatened the devastation of their civilization. Putting the matter most succinctly, Winston Churchill noted, "Europe in 1914 was a powder keg

MILITARISM AND THE ARMS RACE

TABLE 27.2 THE EUROPEAN ARMY BUILDUP, 1879–1913

COUNTRY	1879		1913	
	STANDING ARMY IN PEACETIME	FULLY MOBILIZED ARMY FOR WAR	STANDING ARMY IN PEACETIME	FULLY MOBILIZED ARMY FOR WAR
Austria-Hungary	267,000	772,000	800,000	3,000,000
Britain	136,000	600,000	160,000	700,000
India	200,000		249,000	
France	503,000	1,000,000	1,200,000	3,500,000
Germany	419,000	1,300,000	2,200,000	3,800,000
Russia	766,000	1,213,000	1,400,000	4,400,000

From Taylor, A. J. P., *The Struggle for Mastery in Europe* (Oxford: Clarendon Press, 1954); and Kennedy, Paul, *The Rise and Fall of the Great Powers* (New York: Random House, 1987).

Question: What justified this enormous expansion of armies in peacetime?

Although the late nineteenth century was a long period of peace among the European great powers, it was also a period of widely accepted militarism and preparation for war. Soldiers were being drafted for longer periods of service, and standing armies were being expanded into the millions of soldiers and reserves. An arms race was placing huge burdens on government budgets. Yet Europe culture embraced concepts of struggle, conflict, and heroic war.

Heinrich von Treitschke on The Glorification of War

Heinrich von Treitschke (1834–1896) was a distinguished German historian at the University of Berlin beginning in 1874. Although Treitschke was a Saxon, his passionate nationalism made him a champion of Prussian and then German nationalism. His chief work was a five-volume history of Germany in the nineteenth century, but he expressed many of his outspoken theories (including the excerpt given

where everybody smoked." When yet another Balkan crisis occurred in the summer of 1914, European governments precipitated a monstrously destructive war, known to contemporaries as "the Great War" and to later generations as World War I. Some historians have called it "the suicide of the old Europe."

The Assassination of Archduke Franz Ferdinand. The Balkan crisis of 1914 began in the Bosnian city of Sarajevo. A 19-year-old Serbian nationalist and member of the Narodna Odbrana, Gavrilo Princip, assassinated the heir to the Hapsburg throne, the Archduke Franz-Ferdinand, during a state visit to Sarajevo in late June. The Austrian government blamed the murder on the Serbian government, which knew of the planned assassination and did not stop it. After se-

curing a promise that their German allies would support them in a confrontation with Serbia—a pledge known as **the blank check**—the Austrians sent a 48-hour **ultimatum** to Serbia: the government must dissolve nationalist societies, close nationalist periodicals, end anti-Austrian propaganda, fire anti-Austrian members of the government, allow Austrian investigation of the crime inside Serbia, and arrest officials implicated . . . or expect war. The Russian government meanwhile warned that it would not tolerate an Austrian invasion of Serbia. The Russians, too, received assurances that their allies, the French, would support them—President Poincaré of France was visiting Russia during the crisis and stood by France's staunchest ally. When Serbia accepted most, but not all, of the ultimatum, the Austrians declared war on July 28, 1914, exactly 1 month after the assassination in

here) in his lectures, which were later published under the title *Politics.*

Brave peoples alone have an existence, an evolution or a future; the weak and the cowardly perish, and perish justly. The grandeur of history lies in the perpetual conflict of nations, and it is simply foolish to desire the suppression of their rivalry. . . .

Without war, no state could be. All those we know of arose through war, and the protection of their members by armed force remains their primary and essential task. War, therefore, will endure to the end of history, as long as there is a multiplicity of states. . . .

It is then the normal and reasonable thing for a great nation to embody and develop the essence of the state, which is power, by organizing its physical strength in the constitution of the army. We live in a warlike age; the over-sentimental philanthropic fashion of judging things has passed into the background, so that we can once more join hands . . . in calling war the forceful continuation of politics. . . . We have learned to perceive the moral majesty of war. . . . The greatness of war is just what at first sight seems to be its horror—that for the sake of their country men will overcome the natural feeling of humanity, that they will slaughter their fellow men who have done them no injury.

First Battle Squadron of Dreadnoughts Steaming down the Channel in 1911. The most expensive item in the arms race of 1900 was the new all-steel, all big-gun battleships known as "dreadnoughts" (from the expression "Fear God but dread naught.") In this illustration, the British First Squadron of Dreadnoughts steams down the English Channel in 1911 in a show of power.

From von Treitschke, Heinrich, *Politics,* 2 vols., trans. Blanch Duqdale and Torbenck Bille (New York: Macmillian, 1916).

Question: Do Treitschke's ideas seem more like the product of the German wars of unification or the popularity of social Darwinism?

Sarajevo; they bombarded the Serbian capital, Belgrade (on the border), the next day.

The August Crisis and the Expansion of the War. The Third Balkan War quickly became a general European war. The Russians responded to the bombardment of Belgrade by ordering the mobilization of their army. The Germans, whose Schlieffen Plan was predicated upon the Russians being slow to mobilize (allowing the Germans to fight France first, then Russia), demanded that the Russian army stand down. When the Russians did not, the German army invaded Belgium. This violation of the international treaty on Belgian neutrality ("a scrap of paper" in the words of German Chancellor Bethmann-Hollweg) persuaded the British to recognize that their interests were on the side

of the French. For centuries, British policy had opposed the dominance of the lowlands (from where an invasion of England might be launched) by any strong power—by Spain, later by France, or now by Germany. European declarations of war rained down in the first days of August 1914, until the members of the Triple Alliance (except Italy) and the Triple Entente were at war with each other over a crisis of Balkan nationalism.

Enthusiasm for War. As the British foreign secretary commented—after a long cabinet meeting had decided on war and the streetlights of London outside his window were being extinguished for daybreak—"The lights are going out all over Europe." That somber statement was a good metaphor for the 4 years of darkness that followed; at the time, however, public opinion greeted

FIGURE 27.5 *The Balkan Crisis of 1908.* The eastern question produced a Balkan crisis in 1908, two Balkan Wars in 1912 and 1912–1913, and the 1914 crisis that precipitated World War I. In this cartoon from the Balkan Crisis of 1908, Emperor Franz Joseph of Austria-Hungary tears the provinces of Bosnia and Herzegovina from the Ottoman Empire while Tsar Nicholas II of Russia takes Bulgaria.

the war with great enthusiasm and brisk sales were made of French (and German) dictionaries for the "stroll to Paris" (or Berlin). No great pacifist movement arose to resist the war. Kaiser Wilhelm II confidently spoke of a quick victory: "Paris for lunch, St. Petersburg for dinner." Only limited expressions of antiwar sentiment were heard after Jean Jaurès, the leading advocate of the socialist doctrine of organizing workers against war, was assassinated by an ultrapatriotic war enthusiast on July 31. (This assassination occurred 3 days after the shelling of Belgrade and the day before the mobilization of the French and German armies.) In Germany, socialist deputies to the Reichstag arose to lead their colleagues in singing the national anthem, *"Deutschland, Deutschland, über alles"* ("Germany, Germany, above everything else").

The Expansion of the War.

Other belligerents entered the war slowly. The Ottoman Empire, whose continuing collapse in the Balkans had been such a factor in sparking the war, followed its close ties with Germany and its historic rivalry with Russia to join the central powers in October 1914. Italy remained neutral, declaring

that the Triple Alliance was binding only if Germany or Austria were invaded, not when they invaded small neighbors. The Italians then negotiated with both sides and eventually joined the entente powers in 1915, when a secret Treaty of London promised them significant territorial compensation at the expense of the Hapsburg Empire. The United States likewise remained neutral despite significant pro-British sentiment. Although a dispute over submarine warfare clouded German–American relations, President Woodrow Wilson kept the country out of war and contributed to efforts for a negotiated peace until entering the war on the side of the entente powers in 1917. Before the fighting ended in November 1918, twenty-seven countries joined the battle.

THE GREAT WAR: WORLD WAR I (1914–1918)

A World War. The decisive **theater of the war** (sector of fighting) was the **western front** in France and Belgium, although the largest armies met on the **eastern front,** and fighting reached into the Middle East, Africa, and the Pacific Islands. More than 60 million men were mobilized to fight, including millions of Africans, Indians, Canadians, Australians, and Americans. The French, for example, conscripted 519,000 Africans to fight in Europe; British and French colonial troops combined suffered more than 250,000 casualties. By 1917, the belligerents included Japan and China (both on the side of the western Allies), Turkey (on the side of Germany and the Central Powers), and many smaller states supporting the western Allies. Somehow the governments of Siam, Liberia, and Peru all found reasons to declare war on Germany.

The Western Front. Initial fighting in the west nearly resulted in a German victory in 1914. The Schlieffen Plan led to the German occupation of Brussels on the sixteenth day of the war, and a German army of 1.5 million men pushed far into France by the thirty-fifth day. Simultaneously, the French invasion of Alsace and Lorraine (known as the battle of the frontiers) failed, and the French were driven back with heavy losses—27,000 men were killed on a single day, the bloodiest day in French history. In early September, the German army stood within a few miles of Paris. Victory seemed imminent, and the chief of staff, General Helmuth von Moltke (nephew of the Moltke of the 1860s), violated the plan and sent part of the army to the eastern front to protect Prussia. In a week of desperate fighting along the Marne River, during which the military governor of Paris (General Joseph Gallieni) gambled the city's garrison by shuttling them to the front in Parisian taxicabs, the French stopped the German advance and forced the invaders to retreat to more defensible positions.

MAP 27.5. THE WESTERN FRONT IN WORLD WAR I

Legend:
- Farthest German advance, September 1914
- German offensive, March – July 1918
- German advances
- Winter, 1914 – 1915
- Armistice line
- Allied advances

Note the position of the lines separating the two sides, established when an offensive advance was stopped. Note how close the initial German invasion came to Paris in September 1914 and how much of Belgium and France were still held by Germany at the time of the armistice in 1918. Between those two lines, the line of dashes shows how far back from Paris the Germans were pushed by early 1915. The arrows show the extent to which massive offensives achieved advances of the front line. Note that Verdun remains the hinge for these shifts of the line.

Stalemate in the West. Victory at the Marne saved France at a horrifying price. Of 1.3 million French field troops at the start of the war, more than 600,000 were killed, wounded, or taken prisoner in 1 month of fighting. The casualty rate among infantry officers reached two-thirds. The aftermath of the battle of the Marne was a different war. After a "race to the sea" stretched the opposing armies from the English Channel to Switzerland, they fought a defensive war in which massive battles hardly budged the opposing army—a **war of attrition** in which both sides slowly wore the other down by small increments. By Christmas of 1914, with more than 1 million men killed on the western front, both armies had dug into fixed positions and faced each other from a system of earthen **trenches.** Trenches were typically 7 to 8 feet deep and 6 to 7 feet wide, dug in parallel lines with connecting lateral trenches and

open latrines. They were often filled with mud, bones, standing water, vermin, or the unburied dead, and despite timbering, tended to collapse. (Nonetheless, it was somehow possible for Ludwig Wittgenstein to write one of the densest works of twentieth-century philosophy, the *Tractatus Logico-Philosophicus,* in Austrian trenches.) Despite staggering casualty rates, the front line did not move more than 10 miles in the next 3 years.

The Eastern Front. In the east, Russian armies engaged the Austrian army in Galicia and invaded East Prussia, while most of the German army participated in the Schlieffen Plan in the west. The Russians won some initial victories in Galicia, but the German and Austrian armies soon defeated the poorly equipped and commanded Russians. An outnumbered German army, led by a Prussian aristocrat and veteran of the wars of unification (General Paul von Hindenburg) and a young staff officer who had distinguished himself in the west (General Erich von Ludendorff), stopped the Russian invasion at the battle of Tannenberg in August 1914, taking more than 100,000 prisoners. Two weeks later, Hindenburg's army defeated the Russians again at the battle of the Masurian Lakes, taking another 125,000 captives and driving a demoralized enemy from Prussia. The Russian defeat was so complete that the commander shot himself, whereas Hindenburg became a national hero who was later elected president of Germany in 1925.

Russian Collapse and the Treaty of Brest-Litovsk. Large armies and vast territory still protected the tsarist government, but the first year of fighting cost nearly 1 million soldiers plus all of Poland and Lithuania. The Russians recovered sufficiently to stage a great offensive against the Austrians in 1916 (the Brusilov Offensive), but that campaign cost 1 million men and worsened demoralization. Subsequent losses were so enormous (more than 9 million Russian military casualties, including 1.7 million deaths and 2.2 million civilian deaths) that in early 1918 a revolutionary government negotiated a separate peace in the Treaty of Brest-Litovsk, surrendering 1 million square miles of territory (and 62 million inhabitants) to Germany to abandon the war, and leaving Germans with the feeling that they had won half of the war.

World War I on Secondary Fronts. By 1915, secondary fronts had expanded the European conflagration into a world war. In the first weeks of the war, British and French colonial armies conquered most of the German colonies in Africa. In southern Europe, Italy joined the western Allies in 1915, and an Italo-Austrian front witnessed two years of indecisive fighting. In late 1917, the Italians were badly defeated by forces under General Ludendorff at the battle of Caporetto, but that action came too late to change the outcome of the war.

WORLD WAR I ON THE WESTERN FRONT

Although hundreds of thousands of men died fighting in the eastern (or Russian) front, the Italian front, the Balkans front, the middle eastern front, the colonial front, or at sea, the resolution of World War I came on the western front, where Germany had invaded Belgium and France. Britain, the British Empire, and the United States all joined in fighting Germany on the western front, where the death toll mounted into the millions before Germany accepted unconditional surrender.

Robert Graves on Life in the Trenches

Robert Graves was a British poet and author who was nineteen when World War I began. He first won fame for his autobiography, published in the 1920s, that covered the war years. This excerpt is from that autobiography, titled *Goodbye to All That*.

After a meal of bread, bacon, rum, and bitter stewed tea sickly with sugar, we went . . . up a long trench to battalion headquarters. The trench was cut through red clay. I had a torch [flashlight] with me which I kept flashed on the ground. Hundreds of field mice and frogs were in the trench. They had fallen in and had no way out. The light dazzled them and we could not help treading on them. . . .

The trench was wet and slippery. The guide was giving hoarse directions all the time. "Hole right." "Wire high." "Wire low." "Deep place here, sir." "Wire low." I had never been told about the field telephone wires. They were fastened by staples to the side of the trench, and when it rained the staples were always falling out and the wire falling down and tripping people. . . . The holes were the sump-pits used for draining the trenches. We were now under rifle fire. . . . The rifle bullet gave no warning. . . . [W]e learned not to duck to a rifle bullet, because once it was heard it must have missed. . . . In a trench the bullets, going over the hollow, made a tremendous crack. Bullets often struck the barbed wire in front of the trenches, which turned them and sent them spinning in a head-over-heels motion. . . .*

Our guide took us up to the front line. We passed a group of men huddled over a brazier. They were wearing waterproof capes, for it had now started to rain, and capcomforters, because the weather was cold. They were little men, daubed with mud. . . . We overtook a fatigue-party struggling up the trench, loaded with timber lengths and sandbags, cursing plaintively as they slipped into sumpholes and entangled their burdens in the telephone wire. Fatigue parties were always encumbered by their rifles and equipment, which it was a crime ever to have out of reach. . . . [W]e had to stand aside to let a stretcher-case past.

From Graves, Robert, *Goodbye to All That* (London: Cape, 1923).

Questions: To what extent did commanders, governments, and people at home understand what the front was like? Would it have made any difference if they could have read accounts such as this?

In the Balkans, the Serbians initially held out against the Austrians, but the Balkan War quickly expanded; Turkey joined the Central Powers in 1914, and Bulgaria followed in 1915. Romania joined the western Allies in 1916. Turkish participation led to bloody fighting in the Middle East. A Russo-Turkish War nearly annihilated the Armenians, who were caught between the warring parties; in 1915, the Turks accused the Armenians of pro-Russian sympathies and began their eviction, a death march known as the Armenian Massacre. The British intervened in the Middle Eastern front (following Churchill's advice) and, in 1915, landed an army at Gallipoli, a peninsula in the Aegean Sea near the narrow passage of the Dardanelles. This ill-conceived attempt to open the straits and supply the Russians ended in 1916 with heavy British losses and a Turkish victory that established the reputation of Mustapha Kemal (later known as Atatürk), who became the first president of the postwar Turkish republic. Britain countered by aiding an Arab revolt whose success (such as the campaign led by Colonel T. E. Lawrence in Arabia) hastened the Ottoman collapse.

The War at Sea. An important part of World War I took place at sea, but it was not the anticipated duel of dreadnoughts. Both sides were extremely cautious with their expensive super-battleships and rarely sent them to fight. Of fifty-one British, French, and German dreadnoughts afloat in 1914, only two were sunk during the entire war. The British failed to win a decisive victory against the German fleet at Jutland in May 1916, but they effectively blockaded Germany, allowing only 10 percent of prewar imports to reach shore. The **blockade** caused severe food shortages in Germany late in the war, a period remembered for one of the few crops available as the "turnip winter." The German navy scored its own dramatic successes with submarines. Between late 1916 and late 1917, German submarines sank more than 8 million tons

WORLD WAR I ON THE EASTERN FRONT

The term *eastern front* refers to a vast theater of war stretching from the Baltic Sea to the Black Sea. Three great empires fought there for nearly 4 years—Germany and Austria-Hungary joining to battle Imperial Russia. (Fighting on the Italian and Balkan fronts is usually not considered part of the eastern front.) Conflict began with Russian invasions of East Prussia and then Austrian Galicia. Following the Schlieffen Plan, most of the German army had been concentrated on the western front, but the smaller German forces in the east defeated larger Russian armies at the battles of Tannenberg and the Masurian Lakes. This brought to prominence the two victorious German commanders, General von Hindenburg and General von Ludendorff, who directed fighting on the eastern front for the next few years. The Russians had initial success against the Austro-Hungarian army in Galicia and won further victories in the Brusilov Offensive of 1916, but staggering levels of Russian casualties plus great hardships on the home front led to a revolution in Russia and a separate peace treaty on the eastern front. The Treaty of Brest-Litovsk of March 1918 gave Germany control of enormous territory in eastern Europe, containing nearly 30 percent of the population of pre-war Russia and stretching from Finland, through the Baltic States and Poland, to Belarus and Ukraine.

MAP 27.6. THE EASTERN FRONT IN WORLD WAR I

- — Russian advances: 1914 – 1916
- · · · Deepest German penetration
- —— Brest–Litovsk boundary: 1918
- ⚔ Battle site, 1914
- (CRIMEA) Regions

Note the extent of German annexations following their victory on the eastern front. Germany acquired the Baltic states (Estonia, Latvia, and Lithuania), Poland, and part of White Russia (Belarus). Russia also ceded the Ukraine (which was placed under a German governor and expected to feed the German armies) and Finland (which was only partially occupied by the Germans).

of Atlantic shipping, threatening the British food supply but contributing to the American entry into the war on Britain's side. In 1915, German submarines sank passenger liners with Americans aboard and American ships carrying goods to Britain. Sentiment boiled over when the *Lusitania*, a passenger liner en route from New York to England with a cargo that included arms, went down with 139 Americans aboard. Germany placated American opinion with a promise not to sink passenger liners but withdrew that promise to resume **unrestricted submarine warfare** in 1917; only 4 days after the latter an-

nouncement, the United States broke relations with Germany and, 2 months later, entered the war.

Trench Warfare and the Machine Gun in the West

World War I was ultimately decided on the western front. There, Belgium, Britain, France, Germany, large numbers of colonial troops, and, ultimately, the United States continued the war of attrition in which hundreds

FIGURE 27.6 *World War I at Sea.* Although the great powers had spent enormous amounts of money in building great fleet of battleships, these dreadnoughts rarely fought in significant battles during the war. Instead, the most important combat at sea was submarine warfare that came to dominate merchant shipping to and from Europe. In this German illustration of 1915, a submariner scans the horizon searching for British shipping.

of thousands of men died in offensives that failed to break the stalemate. Heavy artillery bombardment could not produce a breakthrough: Krupp guns virtually leveled the fortifications at Verdun without producing a breakthrough. The German introduction of poison gas (such as phosgene and mustard gas) at the battle of Ypres (Belgium) in 1915 and the British use of the first tanks in 1916 did not break the defensive lines.

Verdun and the Somme. Two of the most murderous battles of human history were fought on this front in 1916—the German offensive at Verdun and an Anglo-French counterattack along the Somme River—but neither battle broke the existing defensive positions. The fighting around Verdun cost France 542,000 casualties and Germany 434,000 but shifted the lines only slightly. The French commander at Verdun, General Henri Pétain, became famous for claiming that the Germans "shall not pass" and a national hero when they did not. (Pétain's reputation, like Hindenburg's, suffered greatly when he became a postwar head of state.) Even while the carnage at Verdun continued, the British and French began their own offensive on the Somme River. After 7 days and

nights of artillery bombardment on the German trenches (see *World War I on the Western Front*), Allied soldiers went "over the top," walking toward the German lines, with 66 pounds of equipment strapped to their backs. They marched into a storm of machine gun fire, and by nightfall, 40 percent of the British frontline troops and 60 percent of British officers were dead. In 1 day of fighting, the bloodiest day in the history of the British army, they suffered 20,000 deaths—devastating when compared with an American death toll of 58,000 in the entire Vietnam War. One British soldier who survived by narrow margin was J. R. R. Tolkien, who had contracted a severe case of trench fever and was invalided home shortly before the battle of the Somme began; most of his friends died in the assault. When the Allies finally stopped their attack, they had pushed the German lines back a maximum of seven miles, at the combined cost of 1.2 million casualties.

The Home Front

Civilian populations also suffered terribly during the war. Seven million civilians were killed, and in several countries (notably in the Balkans and eastern Europe), more civilians were killed than soldiers. Civilian populations spared direct contact with the fighting typically endured lesser hardships. The war brought about martial law in many countries (starting with Germany), press censorship and the jailing of journalists (including one who was a cabinet minister in France), harassment of foreigners and pacifists, suspension of many peacetime activities (British schools even canceled cricket), and dreadful propaganda (such as reports that the Germans were bayoneting babies in Belgium).

Rationing and the Cost of Living. Transportation, food, clothing, and fuel were requisitioned, regulated, or rationed by governments. The scarcity and inflated prices of daily necessities frequently left the home front as hungry as the army. The war doubled the price of consumer goods in Britain, tripled prices in France, and quadrupled those in Germany (see *Life on the Home Front in World War I*). The Allied blockade made the situation so bad in Germany that even the invention of *ersatz* foods (substitute foods, often adulterated) left the people with less than half of the nutrition in their prewar diet. During the "turnip winter" of 1916–1917, much of the population survived on that humble tuber. In Russia, the scarcity of food and fuel was so severe that it was a major factor in the outbreak of revolution in 1917.

Women in the Labor Force. The war also led to dramatic changes on the home front. The most important change resulted from the mobilization of so many men to fight. In France, 43 percent of all adult men were conscripted, a total of 8.4 million men over 5 years. All of the powers, except Britain, drafted their armies before the war; Britain was forced to end the volunteer army in 1916 when the death rate became too high to replace with volunteers. To replace conscripted soldiers in their peacetime jobs, the French government welcomed 184,000 colonial workers into France, creating immigrant communities that would later become controversial. The principal solution for the labor shortage, however, was the recruitment of women. The war sharply increased the percentage of women in the labor force (especially in Britain and France), and it put women into jobs from which they had previously been excluded. In France, for example, women had constituted more than 35 percent of the prewar workforce. Then the French state railroads increased women workers from 6,000 to 57,000. The Ministry of Education added 30,000 women in secondary education. Banks, businesses, and the government all hired women to replace men on clerical and secretarial staffs.

Women in Munitions Factories.
The largest opening for women, however, was in munitions factories, which required a huge new labor force. An estimated 1.5 *billion* artillery shells were fired during the war; in Flanders, a preposterous sum of 3,000 artillery shells per square meter were fired. (Unfortunately, one-third of these shells never exploded; recovery teams are still working on this problem at the start of the twenty-first century, and they have an estimated fifty years of work remaining.) This colossal demand for explosives employed 15,000 Frenchwomen in 1915 and 684,000 in 1917, with similar numbers laboring in Britain (see *Life on the Home Front in World War I*). Without these masses of women workers, armies could not have continued to fight. The women received much less pay than the men they replaced, labored in poisonous conditions, were denied most rights to protest, and typically lost their jobs at the war's end, but they contributed significantly to the long-term evolution of women's rights.

Exhaustion and Armistice (1917–1918)

Rebellion, Mutiny, and Revolution.
By 1917, Europe was exhausted. Combat deaths were approaching 8 million; total war deaths, 15 million. Britain experienced a rebellion, France witnessed a mutiny, Germany faced starvation, and Russia faced a revolution. Even the arrival of the American Expeditionary Force did not create a breakthrough, although the American army fired more artillery shells in the first three hours of its first major battle (at the Meuse and Argonne) than it had fired in the entire Civil War.

Ireland's Easter Rebellion of 1916.
In April 1916, Patrick Pearse and the Sinn Fein (Gaelic for "ourselves alone") led an unsuccessful Irish nationalist uprising known as the Easter Rising. A German submarine landed Sir Roger Casement on the Irish coast to begin the rebellion, but Germany subsequently failed to provide promised aid. After a week of fighting, Pearse, Casement, and others were executed and many Irish nationalists were imprisoned. This setback only temporarily halted the Irish Revolution that produced a larger Anglo-Irish War in 1919–1921.

The French Mutiny of 1917 and Widespread Demoralization.
Fully half of the units of the French army mutinied in 1917. Twenty thousand men deserted, more refused to attack (not to defend), and the **mutiny** did not end until commanders took the most draconian action: 3,000 French soldiers (often chosen by lot) were executed—more than the total executed on the guillotine in Paris during the French Revolution. Similar demoralization (but not mutiny) took root in the British army after the commander, Sir Douglas Haig, ordered another offensive in Flanders; known as the battle of Ypres, this campaign claimed 400,000 British lives. In Germany, where the civilian government was directed by the army high command and the virtual dictatorship of General Ludendorff, the Allied blockade was bringing the nation to the brink of starvation, and German discontent was so severe that defiant strikes and sabotage became widespread in early 1918. In Berlin alone, more than 250,000 workers refused to continue, and although their short strike ended, revolutionary conditions did not. Antiwar sentiment developed in many places.

The Spanish Influenza.
The last months of the war brought one more epic tragedy to the world. A virulent form of influenza struck in the trenches of the western front and flourished when soldiers carried it home. Before the **pandemic** ended in 1919, it had become the greatest public health disaster of modern history. More than 2 billion people worldwide contracted the disease, and somewhere between 22 million and 30 million people died from it—twice as many as died in the fighting. The disease spread from France to Spain, where it killed an estimated 8 million Spaniards, who constituted more than 40 percent of the 1910 population. Thus, it was dubbed the Spanish influenza. Returning British colonial troops spread the disease in India, where an estimated twelve million people perished from it. In the United States, this flu caused 500,000 deaths, making it the worst plague in American history. By comparison, AIDS killed 125,000 people in its first decade.

The Armistice.
Among the states fighting on the western front in 1918, Germany felt the exhaustion of war the most acutely. The Allied naval blockade and the American entry into the war left little doubt that Germany would be defeated, although the fighting had not been pushed onto German soil. As the army neared

LIFE ON THE HOME FRONT IN WORLD WAR I

World War I transformed life on the home front dramatically. Some towns were devastated by the fighting, and others received thousands of refugees from the war zone. Further behind the lines, life was changed by serious shortages of necessities, such as food and fuel, and the disappearance of many small luxuries. Scarcity led to severe inflation.

One of the most basic changes resulted from the departure of millions of men for the front: women now held many jobs previously closed to them. Indeed, none of the armies could have continued fighting for long without the support of women war workers, especially in the munitions industry.

TABLE 27.3 WARTIME INFLATION IN THE PRICES OF CONSUMER GOODS

	Prices as a Percentage of 1913 Prices					
COUNTRY	1914	1915	1916	1917	1918	1919
France	102	140	189	262	340	357
Germany	106	142	153	179	217	415
Great Britain	100	127	160	206	227	242
Italy	96	133	201	299	409	364

Source: *History of the World Economy in the Twentieth Century*, vol. 2: Gerd Hardach, *The First World War, 1914–1918* (Berkeley, CA: University of California Press, 1977, p. 119).

TABLE 27.4 WARTIME RATIONS IN GERMANY

	Rations as a Percentage of the 1913 Diet	
FOOD	JULY 1916 TO JUNE 1917	JULY 1918 TO DECEMBER 1918
Butter	22	28
Cheese	3	15
Eggs	18	13
Fish	51	5
Flour	53	48
Meat	31	12
Potatoes	71	94
Rice	4	0
Sugar	49	80

Source: *History of the World Economy in the Twentieth Century*, vol. 2: Gerd Hardach, *The First World War, 1914–1918* (Berkeley, CA: University of California Press, 1977, p. 172).

Question: What sectors of civilian population would suffer the worst from these conditions?

collapse, the German generals called for an **armistice** in mid-1918. In early November, the German navy at Kiel mutinied rather than continuing to fight, and revolution spread to Munich—where a short-lived socialist republic of Bavaria was proclaimed—and other cities. Two days later, Kaiser Wilhelm II abdicated and fled to Holland. Militant Socialists (known as the Spartacists, after an ancient Roman slave rebellion), led by Karl Liebknecht and Rosa Luxemburg, sought to establish a communist regime in Berlin. A hastily formed republican government led by Matthias Erzberger met the Allied commander in chief, French Marshal Ferdinand Foch, in a railroad boxcar outside Compiègne, France, and accepted strict Allied terms for an armistice that made further fighting impossible. Thus, the fighting stopped at a symbolic moment—the eleventh hour of November 11.

War Losses. The human cost of the war was staggering, and grim numbers only sketch its outlines (see Table 27.5). More than 60 million soldiers were mobilized to fight, and nearly 15 million people were killed (8 million combatants and 7 million civilians), not counting the tens of millions who fell to the Spanish influenza and other war-related diseases. Most of the great powers saw between 33 percent and 75 percent of all military personnel suffer war wounds, and 10 percent to 17 percent

Women Munition Workers in Paris.

Sylvia Pankhurst on the Situation of Women War Workers

With the largest armies in history mobilized to fight the war, the European powers found themselves critically short of labor at home. Millions of women made the war effort possible by bringing in the harvest, by serving as replacement workers in dozens of occupations, and by staffing the munitions factories that supplied armies in the field. Here Sylvia Pankhurst discusses the situation of women munitions workers.

Propaganda was insistent to get women into the munition factories, and every sort of work ordinarily performed by men. The sections clamouring for the military conscription of men saw in the industrial service of women a means to their end. Feminists who were advocates of Conscription for men believed themselves adding to the importance of women by demanding that women also should be conscripts. . .
.

From all over the country we cited authentic wage scales: Waring and Gillow paying 3½ d. an hour to women, 9d. to men for military tent making; the Hendon aeroplane works paying women 3d. per hour, at work for which men got 10d. per hour; women booking clerks at Victoria Station getting 15s. a week, though the men they replaced got 35s.; and so on, in district after district, trade after trade. . . .

Firms like Bryant and May's, the match makers, were now making munitions. Accustomed to employ large numbers of women and girls at illpaid work, they knew by long experience that piece rates would secure them a higher production than could be induced by a bonus. Without a care for pre-war standards, in a trade new to their factory, they had fixed for munition work, often perilous and heavy, similar sweated piece rates to those paid for matches. . . .

The Munitions Act was being used to prevent workers from changing their employment in order to secure higher wages, or positions of greater responsibility, or to obtain work nearer home . . . Leaving certificates were refused when the work was proving prejudicial to the health of the worker. . . . As the War progressed, trade after trade was put under the Munitions Act. Employers were eager to seize the powers it gave them.

From Pankhurst, Sylvia, "The Home Front" (London, 1932), in Brian Tierney and Joan Scott, *A Documentary History of Western Societies*, vol. 2 (New York: McGraw-Hill, 1984).

Question: Were women war workers treated fairly under the circumstances?

---

killed; the death rate for infantrymen averaged 22 percent. A generation of young European men was lost.

THE RUSSIAN REVOLUTION AND CIVIL WAR (1917–1920)

The most important home front crisis of the war took place in Russia from 1917 to 1920. A revolution in 1917, known as the February Revolution, ended the Romanov monarchy, and a second revolution a few months later (the Bolshevik, or October, revolution)

brought Lenin and the Bolsheviks to power. A subsequent civil war (from 1918 to 1920) led to the creation of a communist state.

The Vulnerability of Imperial Russia. The government of Nicholas II already faced extreme difficulties on the eve of World War I. The peasant majority of the nation had never achieved the economic freedom or landownership implicit in their emancipation of 1861. A growing working class, created by the beginnings of Russian industrialization, was enduring conditions as bleak as those in England in the 1840s. Minority populations such as the Poles felt the nationalist ambitions for

TABLE 27.5 LOSSES IN WORLD WAR I, 1914–1918

Country	Total Men Mobilized	Combat Deaths	Percentage of Forces Killed	Military Casualties	Percentage of Forces Wounded	Civilian Deaths	Total War Dead	Percentage Population Killed
Austria-Hungary	7,800,000	1,200,000	15.4	7,000,000	90.0	300,000	1,500,000	5.2
Belgium	267,000	14,000	5.2	93,000	34.8	30,000	44,000	0.6
British Empire	8,900,000	947,000	10.6	3,200,000	35.2	30,000	977,000	2.4
Bulgaria	560,000	87,000	15.5	267,000	47.7	275,000	362,000	8.3
France	8,400,000	1,400,000	16.2	6,200,000	73.2	40,000	1,440,000	3.6
Germany	11,000,000	1,800,000	16.1	7,100,000	64.9	760,000	2,500,000	3.8
Greece	230,000	5,000	2.2	27,000	11.7	132,000	137,000	2.8
Italy	5,600,000	460,000	8.2	2,200,000	39.1	n.a.	n.a.	
Montenegro	50,000	3,000	6.0	20,000	40.0	n.a.	n.a.	
Portugal	100,000	7,000	7.2	33,000	33.3	n.a.	n.a.	
Rumania	750,000	336,000	44.8	536,000	71.4	275,000	611,000	8.1
Russia	12,000,000	1,700,000	14.2	9,200,000	76.3	2,000,000	3,700,000	2.4
Serbia	707,000	125,000	17.7	331,000	46.8	650,000	775,000	17.6
Ottoman Empire	2,900,000	325,000	11.4	975,000	34.2	2,200,000	2,500,000	10.1
United States	4,740,000	115,000	2.4	204,000	6.7		115,000	0.1

Source: Calculated from data in Cook, Chris, and Paxton, John, *European Political Facts, 1848–1918* (London: Macmillan, 1978, pp. 188–189, 213–232); Langer, William L., ed., *An Encyclopedia of World History* (Boston: Houghton-Mifflin, 1968, p. 976); and *The World Almanac and Book of Facts, 1997* (Mahwah, NJ: World Almanac Book, 1996, p. 184).

Question: Do these numbers explain why the years 1916–1918 witnessed revolutions and army mutinies in many countries?

self-rule that had swept Europe, and religious minorities, especially the Jews, detested the regime that persecuted them. Much of the intelligentsia aspired to have the individual rights and representative government they saw in western Europe.

Wartime Suffering in Russia. In addition to these problems, World War I was a catastrophe for Russia. The Russian army's inferior preparation and equipment led to shocking defeats. In 1915, the army suffered shortages of rifles, ammunition, and clothing; conscripts were even sent into battle without equipment. Army morale collapsed. On the home front, ill-planned mobilization caused a shortage in skilled labor and ultimately led to shortages of critical supplies and to chaos in supply transportation and distribution. The cost of basic consumer goods rose dramatically as the government printed worthless money to pay for the war; a pound of meat and a sack of potatoes each increased by 700 percent (see Table 27.6 in *The Russian Revolution*). Food shortages became severe because peasants refused to sell grain for paper money. The government seemed mired in scandals and corruption; notable criticism arose sur-

rounding Grigori Rasputin (a religious mystic who was close to the royal family), who was dramatically assassinated by a group of prominent aristocrats. Russia had no stable government: four prime ministers were dismissed in slightly more than 2 years, and the tsar remained at the front with his army. Even moderates in the Duma expressed outrage at the incompetence and repressiveness of the government. Pavel Milyukov, a historian who had been a leader of the liberal-democratic faction in 1905, a founder of the Constitutional Democratic Party (Kadets) in the Duma, and the leading liberal critic of the war government, put it bluntly: "How did Russia get here? Stupidity or treason?"

Strikes and Unrest. In 1916, real wages fell by approximately 20 percent, prompting more than 1,400 strikes in Russian cities. Sporadic mutinies began in the demoralized army. An imperial decree ordered conscription of 400,000 people for civilian labor, and violent resistance broke out, particularly in southern portions of the empire. By winter, bread was becoming scarce in major cities, and the price of the limited supplies was climbing daily.

The February Revolution. The February Revolution of 1917 began, like many rebellions of the Old Regime, when food shortages made life intolerable for urban workers. The year began with 50,000 workers striking in Petrograd (formerly St. Petersburg), and the number grew to 80,000 in the following month. Demonstrations and bread riots, led by women as they had been in the French Revolution, occurred in early March 1917 (February in the old Russian calendar). By March 10, Petrograd was in the grip of nearly general strikes, and Nicholas II ordered the army to "end them tomorrow." After officers ordered soldiers to fire on the crowd on March 11, killing 150 civilians, discontented soldiers of the Petrograd garrison mutinied on March 12 and joined the demonstrators. The tsar tried to suspend the Duma, but parliamentary leaders refused to disband. The revolutionary tide in Petrograd was rapidly passing by the Duma, however, and the mutineers elected a competing body. They created a council (a *soviet*) of soldiers, which joined with a soviet of labor deputies, led by Alexander Kerensky (a socialist lawyer), to set up an alternative government. On March 13, the Petrograd soviets began publishing their own newspaper, *Izvestia,* to encourage the election of workers' soviets elsewhere; on March 14, the Petrograd Soviet issued Order #1 (*Prikaz* #1), calling on soldiers throughout the army to elect their own soviets to take control from imperial officers—the fate of the regime was settled.

The Provisional Government. On March 15, 1917, 6 days after the first Russian protest marches and 4 days after the army fired on the crowd, Tsar Nicholas II abdicated for himself and for his son, passing the throne to his brother, the grand duke Michael, who also refused the crown. Leaders of the Duma, the Petrograd Soviet, and many of the *zemstva* assumed power and announced a Provisional Government headed by Prince Georgi Lvov, a liberal aristocrat and Kadet who presided over the national union of all of the zemstva. This government included democratic centrists such as Lvov and Milyukov and democratic Socialists such as Kerensky, but none of the leading Bolsheviks, who were returning from exile and attacking the government in their newspaper, *Pravda,* which circulated openly in Russia. The Provisional Government, under Lvov and shortly thereafter under Kerensky, won international praise for its democratic program—an amnesty for political crimes, a constitutional assembly elected by universal suffrage, equal rights for minorities, and full civil liberties—but it remained a severely divided coalition. Lenin, who was in exile in Zürich, urged the soviets to withdraw their support for the government, and conservatives (many of whom rallied behind the Cossack commander of the Petrograd garrison, General Lavr Kornilov) considered a coup d'état to forcibly suppress the Bolsheviks.

Problems of the Provisional Government. During its brief existence, the Provisional Government faced numerous problems. It remained at war with Germany, and the governments of Britain, France, and the United States (whose help Russia desperately needed) all wanted it to remain part of the wartime coalition that could now be described as a democratic alliance against autocracy. The Provisional Government may have sealed its own fate in April 1917, when Foreign Minister Milyukov reaffirmed the Russian promise to the Allies to remain in the war by a document known as the Milyukov Note. Furthermore, the government did not have an easy solution for the shortages of food and other critical supplies. In the spirit of a democratic revolution, the Provisional Government recognized the independence of Poland and Finland, established the 8-hour workday and granted freedom of religion; yet the war's unpopularity never allowed the government to consolidate a hold on Russian public popularity. The Petrograd Soviet of Workers' and Soldiers' Deputies, meanwhile, still held the backing of those critically important groups, while the continuation of the war caused support for the Provisional Government to dwindle rapidly.

The October Revolution of 1917

Lenin and the April Theses. The most tenacious opposition to the Provisional Government came from Lenin and his supporters in the **Bolshevik** (literally, "majority" although they were a minority) faction of revolutionary socialism. Lenin had spent the war in exile in Switzerland until his clandestine return (aided by the Germans, who expected his politics to weaken Russia) in April 1917. He expounded a simple, yet highly effective program (see *The Russian Revolution*) known as the April Theses: (1) immediate peace, even at the cost of a harsh German treaty; (2) immediate redistribution of land to the peasants; (3) transfer of political power from the Provisional Government to the soviets; and (4) transfer of the control of factories to committees of workers. The promises of the April Theses (particularly peace) contrasted vividly with the policies of the Provisional Government (especially the Milyukov Note, see *The Russian Revolution*). Lenin's program of land and peace first won the Bolsheviks a majority on the Moscow Soviet and then made Lenin's foremost lieutenant, Leon Trotsky (whose real name was Lev Bronstein), the head of the Petrograd Soviet by the early autumn of 1917. Trotsky, a Ukrainian Jewish peasant who had entered radical politics as a teenager, was a leader of the revolution of 1905 and one of the most effective leaders of the Bolshevik revolution.

The Bolshevik Seizure of Power. Even with the appeal of the April Theses, the Bolsheviks had the support

THE RUSSIAN REVOLUTION

Nowhere were conditions on the home front worse than in Russia, where shortages were so severe that many cities experienced significant unrest. The result was series of revolutions known as the Russian Revolution: a democratic revolution in early 1917, the Bolshevik revolution in late 1917, and an ensuing civil war.

The Bolshevik Decree on Peace, November 1917

The workers' and peasants' government, created by the Revolution of October 24–25, and basing itself on the Soviets of Workers', Soldiers', and Peasants' Deputies, calls upon all the belligerent peoples and their governments to start immediate negotiations for a just, democratic peace.

By a just or democratic peace, which the overwhelming majority of the working class and other working people of all the belligerent countries, exhausted, tormented, and racked by the war, are craving—a peace that has been most definitely and insistently demanded by the Russian workers and peasants ever since the overthrow of the tsarist monarchy—by such a peace, the government means an immediate peace without annexations (i.e., without the seizure of foreign lands, without the forcible incorporation of foreign nations) and without indemnities.

The Government of Russia proposes that this kind of peace be immediately concluded by all the belligerent nations, and expresses its readiness to take all the resolute measures now, without the least delay. . . .

The government considers it the greatest of crimes against humanity to continue this war over the issue of how to divide among the strong and rich nations the weak nationalities they have conquered.

. . . At the same time, the government declares that it does not regard the above-mentioned peace terms as an ultimatum; in other words, it is prepared to consider any other peace terms, and insists only that they be advanced by any of the belligerent countries as speedily as possible.

From Golder, Frank, *Documents of Russian History, 1914–1917* (New York: Century, 1927).

Question: Does this proposal seem a persuasive reason to abandon the monarchy?

of only a small minority of Russians. When the Petrograd Soviet of Workers' and Soldiers' Deputies held a Pan-Russian Congress in June and July 1917, only 105 of 822 delegates were Bolsheviks, who were far outnumbered by both Mensheviks and rural radicals just among the revolutionary parties. Lenin and Trotsky responded by forming a Military Revolutionary Committee to prepare for a second Russian revolution of 1917 and created their own military force—the Red Guards—composed of soldiers from the Petrograd garrison and armed workers, forces that were essential in open battles against Kornilov's troops. A Bolshevik party congress held in August 1917 resolved upon the conquest of power by an armed insurrection, although most of the party was unprepared for action. Lenin and Trotsky won the backing of the party's leadership (the Central Committee) after the Russian army suffered more reverses, and they orchestrated a minutely planned coup to seize power in Petrograd in early November (October in the old Russian calendar). Two days of violent fighting gave the Bolsheviks control of the Winter Palace and then of Petrograd. The Bolshevik revolution spread to Moscow on the third day, and within a week, soviets of workers and soldiers held Moscow, Smolensk, and Kazan.

Lenin and the Bolshevik Government. An All-Russian Congress of Soviets immediately endorsed the Bolshevik revolution and approved a new government, which Lenin organized with himself at its head. This Council of Commissars (later called the *Politburo*) included Trotsky as *commissar* (minister) of foreign affairs and his bitter rival, Joseph Dzhugashvili, known as Stalin ("the man of steel"), as commissar for the nationalities. Stalin, the son of a Georgian shoemaker, was one of the few Bolshevik leaders who could honestly claim to be a member of the working class. He had entered an Orthodox seminary at age 20 but had been expelled for his Marxism, and before the war, he had been arrested six times and twice sent to Siberia for revolutionary politics. The Council of Commissars acted quickly to consolidate the Bolshevik position by issuing Lenin's decrees on peace and land. Although the decree on peace secured much support, elections for a constituent assembly gave the Bolsheviks only 25 percent

Lenin Exhorting the Crowd. Among the strongest weapons that Lenin and the Bolsheviks had against Kerensky and the Provisional Government was the simple call for peace, a weapon that could be used in repeated speeches in the street. This photograph of Lenin addressing the revolutionary crowd in Moscow later became famous because of a secondary detail—the figure standing on the steps and facing the camera is Trotsky, who was edited out of most subsequent versions of this picture to hide his prominence in the revolution.

TABLE 27.6 THE COST OF BASIC RUSSIAN CONSUMER GOODS		
Commodity	**April 1914**	**April 1917**
Sack of potatoes	1 ruble	7 rubles
Sack of wheat flour (36 lb.)	2.5 rubles	16 rubles
Sack of rye flour	6.5 rubles	40 rubles
Pound of meat	10 kopecks	70 kopecks
Lard	12 kopecks	90 kopecks
A pair of shoes	5–8 rubles	40 rubles
One cubic meter of firewood	3 rubles	20 rubles

The 1914 ruble equaled 100 kopecks or 50 cents.

Source: Ferro, Marc, *La Révolution de 1917*, vol. 1 (Paris: Flammarion, 1967); and Conte, Francis, *Les Grands dates de la Russie et de l'URSS* (Paris, Larousse: 1990, p. 175).

Question: Does this increase in prices help explain the Revolution of 1917?

of the vote. The council responded by creating a new **secret police,** known as the *Cheka,* to fight opponents of the revolution. The Cheka, which was not greatly different from the tsarist secret police, laid the basis for the new regime to become a police state. And it showed that Lenin meant his words of 1902: "We have never rejected, and cannot reject, terror." Not surprisingly, Lenin and Trotsky closed the constituent assembly in January 1918, on the second day of its meetings.

The Peace of Brest-Litovsk. Lenin and Trotsky fulfilled their promise to bring peace. The high command of the German army agreed to talks at Brest-Litovsk (in modern-day Belarus) in December 1917. They presented Russia with severe terms (far more severe than the treaty later given to defeated Germany), and the Treaty of Brest-Litovsk in March 1918 showed that Lenin and Trotsky were determined to have peace. They gave up Finland, the Baltic States, Poland, White Russia (Belarus), Ukraine, and Bessarabia. When the Germans capitulated to the Western Allies in November, however, Russia repudiated the treaty.

Civil War (1918–1920)

The Bolshevik seizure of power in late 1917 did not give them control of the entire Russian Empire. They had begun as a small faction in Russian politics, and they won control in Petrograd because they were well organized, had the will to act (and to act ruthlessly), and understood that land and peace were more popular than parliamentary democracy. "No amount of political freedom," Lenin noted, "will satisfy the hungry." The Bolshevik government, however, faced opposition in many regions of the empire, often from larger and more popular forces. The result was a Russian civil war that continued long after the end of the world war.

Renewed War in Russia. When the civil war began, the Bolsheviks (renamed the Communist Party in 1918) had sufficient forces for a coup d'état but not for a war. However, they faced civil war on several fronts. They shifted the capital from Petrograd to Moscow, a city less vulnerable to foreign-supported armies, because they faced early defeats. White (anti-Bolshevik) forces soon

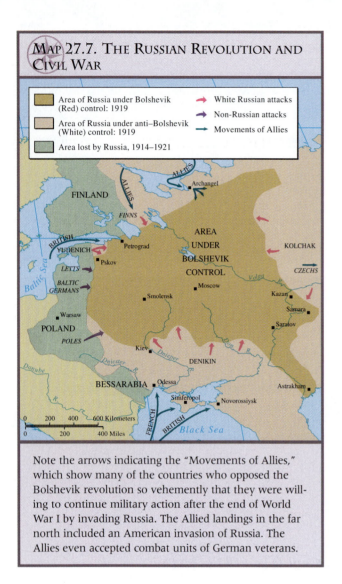

Note the arrows indicating the "Movements of Allies," which show many of the countries who opposed the Bolshevik revolution so vehemently that they were willing to continue military action after the end of World War I by invading Russia. The Allied landings in the far north included an American invasion of Russia. The Allies even accepted combat units of German veterans.

controlled Siberia (where they installed Admiral Alexander Kolchak as their ruler), the southern regions around Kazan, and Ukraine, where the Cossacks joined the anti-Bolshevik coalition. Trotsky, named commissar for war, organized a volunteer (later conscript) army known as the Red Army to fight the counterrevolutionary **Whites,** and brutal civil war soon stretched across the Russian Empire. It included a war with the Cossacks in southern Russia, wars of independence in Ukraine and the Baltic states, intervention by several of the western Allies, campaigns in the Caucasus that led to the secession of south Asian provinces, and even war in the Far East, where the Japanese invaded Russia. The intervention of the western Allies scored some brief success in Ukraine, where the Allies supported early victories by General Anton Deniken. The Americans staged a landing at Archangel, and the British and French briefly

supported a puppet government in Northern Russia at Archangel, but neither the British nor the Americans were willing to accept significant involvement in the war. For a while, this produced a bizarre situation in which German anti-Bolsheviks fought together with western Allies until western forces withdrew from Russia in September 1919.

Communist Victory. A Communist victory in the civil war was complete in most regions by 1920. The Whites were poorly coordinated among the many fronts, badly divided in their plans for Russia, and heavily dependent on the Western world. The western Allies, however, were simply too exhausted by years of fighting Germany to be interested in another prolonged battle. Shortly after the Allies stopped supplying the Whites, the Red Army won the civil war. Ukraine (1919) and the Caucasian states (1920) were annexed again, although the Baltic states (Estonia, Latvia, and Lithuania) kept their independence. The most famous episode of the civil war did not occur on a battlefield. In the summer of 1918, the Communist government ordered the execution of Nicholas II and his family (who had been held prisoner at Ekaterinburg, on the Asian side of the Ural Mountains) when it appeared possible that the White armies of Kolchak might liberate them.

Communist Government. During the civil war, Lenin began to consolidate Communist power. In 1918, a Congress of Soviets adopted a new constitution for Russia. (the country did not become the Union of Soviet Socialist Republics [USSR], or Soviet Union, until 1922). The constitution attempted to create a **"dictatorship of the proletariat,"** including one-party government and restrictions on freedoms of speech, press, and assembly. The government, now led by a five-man Politburo, demonstrated the police powers of this dictatorship after a socialist woman attempted to assassinate Lenin in 1918. They did so by killing thousands of critics of the regime in a policy called **"the red terror,"** a grim introduction to the authoritarian violence that Europe would face during most of the twentieth century. The most far-reaching policy of the new Communist state had global implications. In the spring of 1919, Lenin created the Third International (the Comintern, 1919–1943) to link Communist parties in all countries and to support revolutions around the world. Revolutionary situations existed in many war-weary countries, exemplified by the Spartacist revolt in Berlin in early 1919. Béla Kun, a protégé of Lenin, established a short-lived Bolshevik government in Hungary in late 1919. These events alarmed anticommunist capitals around the world and led to a postwar **"red scare"** in many countries.

CONCLUSION

The vast human tragedies examined in Chapter 27 provide an essential context for historians who look back at the Belle Époque at the end of the nineteenth century or for those who look ahead to the larger tragedies of the first half of the twentieth century. The Belle Époque, attractive as it may be, must be understood as sowing the seeds of the total war and revolution that ravaged Europe between 1914 and 1920 and as the same epoch as the imperial conquest of millions of square miles around the globe. The glorification of war

IMPERIALISM, WAR, AND REVOLUTION

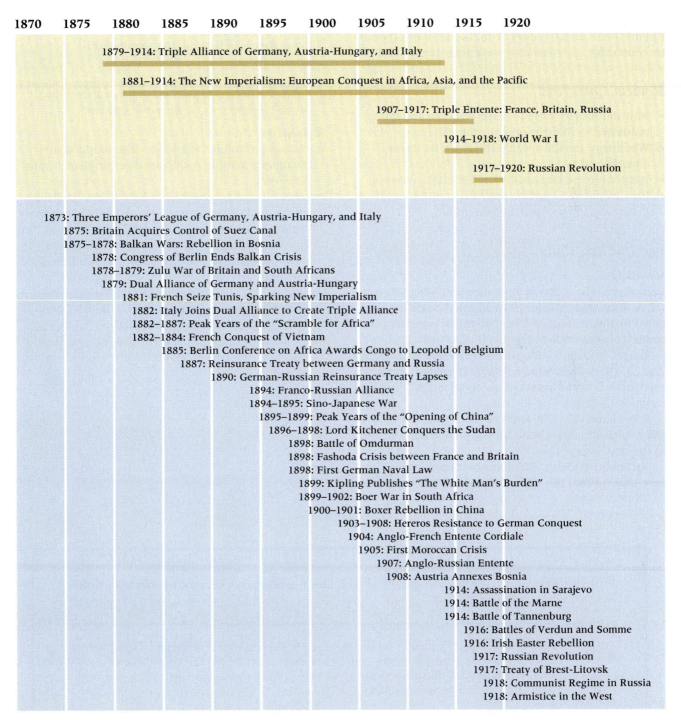

1870	1875	1880	1885	1890	1895	1900	1905	1910	1915	1920

1879–1914: Triple Alliance of Germany, Austria-Hungary, and Italy

1881–1914: The New Imperialism: European Conquest in Africa, Asia, and the Pacific

1907–1917: Triple Entente: France, Britain, Russia

1914–1918: World War I

1917–1920: Russian Revolution

1873: Three Emperors' League of Germany, Austria-Hungary, and Italy
1875: Britain Acquires Control of Suez Canal
1875–1878: Balkan Wars: Rebellion in Bosnia
1878: Congress of Berlin Ends Balkan Crisis
1878–1879: Zulu War of Britain and South Africans
1879: Dual Alliance of Germany and Austria-Hungary
1881: French Seize Tunis, Sparking New Imperialism
1882: Italy Joins Dual Alliance to Create Triple Alliance
1882–1887: Peak Years of the "Scramble for Africa"
1882–1884: French Conquest of Vietnam
1885: Berlin Conference on Africa Awards Congo to Leopold of Belgium
1887: Reinsurance Treaty between Germany and Russia
1890: German-Russian Reinsurance Treaty Lapses
1894: Franco-Russian Alliance
1894–1895: Sino-Japanese War
1895–1899: Peak Years of the "Opening of China"
1896–1898: Lord Kitchener Conquers the Sudan
1898: Battle of Omdurman
1898: Fashoda Crisis between France and Britain
1898: First German Naval Law
1899: Kipling Publishes "The White Man's Burden"
1899–1902: Boer War in South Africa
1900–1901: Boxer Rebellion in China
1903–1908: Hereros Resistance to German Conquest
1904: Anglo-French Entente Cordiale
1905: First Moroccan Crisis
1907: Anglo-Russian Entente
1908: Austria Annexes Bosnia
1914: Assassination in Sarajevo
1914: Battle of the Marne
1914: Battle of Tannenburg
1916: Battles of Verdun and Somme
1916: Irish Easter Rebellion
1917: Russian Revolution
1917: Treaty of Brest-Litovsk
1918: Communist Regime in Russia
1918: Armistice in the West

and the arms race might have been seen as signposts on the road toward the precipice. Yet Europeans embraced war with naïve enthusiasm in 1914, scarcely understanding the nightmare they welcomed. How belle could the époque be that had this denouement?

Conversely, the devastation of 1914–1920 also pointed Europe toward the future. World War I was only the opening chapter in an age of total war, and the horrifying story of 15 million war dead was only the prelude to a larger war that would claim more than 50 million lives. Similarly, the Soviet dictatorship of 1917–1920 offered only a hint of the terrors of dictatorship to come. But the international history of 1871–1920 forms the basic context for understanding those tragedies to come.

Review Questions

- How did Bismarck try to preserve peace and the status quo in international relations?
- What were the European motives for the "new imperialism"?
- What were the origins of World War I?
- How would you describe the success of the Bolsheviks in the Russian Revolution?

For Further Study

Readings

Carr, E. H., *The Bolshevik Revolution, 1917–1923*, 3 vols. (New York: Macmillan, 1950–1953). Somewhat outdated by the opening of Soviet archives, but provides a classic detailed study of the revolution.

Langer, William L., *European Alliances and Alignments*, 2nd ed. (New York: Knopf, 1960). The classic study of the Bismarckian alliance system; long and detailed but superb scholarship.

Pakenham, T., *The Scramble for Africa, 1876–1912* (New York: Random House, 1991). A good introduction to the new imperialism.

Tuchman, Barbara, *The Guns of August* (New York: Macmillan, 1962). An immensely readable introduction to World War I.

References

Olson, James S., ed., *Historical Dictionary of European Imperialism* (New York: Greenwood, 1991).

Pope, Stephen, and Wheal, Elizabeth-Anne, eds., *The Macmillan Dictionary of the First World War* (London: Macmillan, 1997).

Shukman, Harold, ed., *The Blackwell Encyclopedia of the Russian Revolution* (London: Blackwell, 1988).

InfoTrac College Edition

For additional reading, go to your online research library at *http://infotrac.thomsonlearning.com*.

Using Key Words, enter the search terms:
new imperialism   *World War I*

Using the Subject Guide, enter the search terms:
Lenin, Vladimir I   *Bismarck, Otto von*

Web Sites

http://www.lib.byu.edu/~rdh/wwi/   The World War I Document Archive, a site posted at Brigham Young University.

http://www.spartacus.schoolnet.co.uk/FWW.htm   A British educational site that covers many topics of modern history, including this section on the first world war. Some materials are at an introductory level, but it provides well-chosen excerpts from primary sources.

http://www.bbc.co.uk/history/war/easterrising/index.shtml A valuable, detailed site, posted by the BBC and containing many primary materials.

http://www.barnsdle.demon.co.uk/russ/rusrev.html   A collection of links (of mixed value) to sites helpful for the revolution.

Visit the Western Civilization Companion Web Site for resources specific to this textbook:
http://history.wadsworth.com/hause02/

The CD in the back of this book and the Western Civilization Resource Center at *http://history. wadsworth.com/western/* offer a variety of tools to help you succeed in this course, including access to quizzes; images; documents; interactive simulations, maps, and timelines; movie explorations; and a wealth of other sources.

Chapter 28

EUROPE IN AN AGE OF DICTATORSHIP, 1919–1939

Berlin family taking an evening stroll on January 3, 1923, could stop in a neighborhood *Bäckerei* (bakery) and purchase a standard one kilo loaf of rye bread (2.2 pounds), the staple of the German diet, for 163 marks. This was a shocking price to everyone because 1 year earlier, in January 1922, bread had cost less than 4 marks. It had crept up to nearly 9 marks in July, hit 22 marks in October, and skyrocketed when winter came. But no one yet knew how bad rocketing prices could be. By early July 1923, the family's loaf of rye bread had hit the absurd price of 1,895 marks. Four weeks later, a loaf cost more than 8,000 marks. In early September, bread hit 273,684 marks, although that seemed modest because butchers asked 4 million marks for a kilo of beef. On October 1, bread prices stood at nearly 9.5 million marks for a loaf, and 3 weeks later that seemed cheap: during the week of October 22, bread prices hit 1 billion 389 million marks for a loaf! The skyrocket reached its apogee on November 19, 1923, when bread sold for 233 billion marks a loaf, reasonably cheap compared with the price of kilo of beef at 4 trillion 800 billion marks.

An old Europe lay in ruins in 1919. Five years of world war had swept away four empires: the Russian, German, Hapsburg, and Ottoman Empires. Chapter 28 looks at Europe in the generation after World War I. It begins with the peace settlement reached at Paris in 1919 and postwar problems (such as the reconstruction of devastated areas) and attitudes (such as conservative desires to preserve the old Europe) that derived from the war. Subsequent sections discuss the problems of postwar democracies, such as the Great Depression of the 1930s, and the controversial governments (such as the Popular Fronts in France and Spain) that tried to address them. The chapter then examines the rise of dictatorships as the typical form of European government, discussing Fascist Italy, Nazi Germany, and Communist Russia.

THE PEACE OF PARIS AND POSTWAR RECONSTRUCTION (1919–1929)

The Paris Peace Conference. The fighting in World War I ended with the Compiègne armistice of November 1918, which disarmed Germany to make further combat impossible. The Paris Peace Conference that assembled in January 1919 similarly disarmed German diplomacy; a German delegation was allowed to come to Versailles but not to negotiate. (The Allies held separate conferences for each of the defeated powers at palaces around Paris; peace with Germany was planned at the royal palace in suburban Versailles.) The German republic, founded after the abdication of Kaiser Wilhelm II, could only hope that the treaty would be based on the idealistic Fourteen Points stated in early 1918, in a speech by U.S. president Woodrow Wilson (who had endorsed "peace without victory" as late as 1916).

The Big Four. Although dozens of states sent diplomats to Paris, the basic elements of the treaties were negotiated among representatives of the "Big Four" wartime allies— chiefly by Wilson, Premier Georges Clemenceau (Kleh-mahn'-sew) of France, and Prime Minister David Lloyd George of Britain, and sometimes including Premier Vittorio Orlando of Italy. This was similar to the situation at Vienna in 1815 (where France had initially been excluded from negotiations among the four victorious great powers) but differed in one important aspect: one of the great powers that had fought long for the allied cause, Russia, was an excluded pariah state in 1919, governed by Communist revolutionaries who had negotiated a separate peace.

Clemenceau and Lloyd George. The most important authors of the postwar world were Clemenceau and Lloyd George, neither of whom felt bound by Wilson's program. Lloyd George (who started a program similar to the Fourteen Points before Wilson) had run for reelection in the Khaki Election of December 1918 promising to punish German **war criminals** and saying, "I'll hang the

Kaiser!" Clemenceau, whose political career spanned two German invasions of France, scoffed at Wilsonian idealism with snide reminders that even God presented only ten Commandments. Europe, Clemenceau once remarked, might consider Wilsonian moral leadership when the president ended racial segregation in the United States. Unlike the situation at Vienna in 1815, the Allies were never so idealistically divided that they invited Germany to participate in negotiations. German diplomats had their first formal meeting with Allied diplomats in May 1919, and a draft treaty was presented to them; Clemenceau introduced the treaty by saying, "The time has come to settle accounts." The Germans, who were not given a chance to negotiate compromises, bitterly called the treaty a ***diktat*** (a dictated peace), but nonetheless they signed it in June 1919. The German response to the peace treaty—in contrast to the French response to the Frankfurt Treaty of 1871—became one of

MAP 28.1. EUROPE IN 1919

Lost immediately after World War I
- By Russia
- By Germany
- The Rhineland—Demilitarized Zone of Germany
- By Bulgaria
- By Austria–Hungary

The peace settlements of 1918–1923 created, or ratified, dramatic changes in the map of Europe and the Middle East. The colored key shows the territory lost by the Central Powers and the territory required to be demilitarized. Note that Germany lost significant lands, chiefly to Poland in the east, but the Austrians lost virtually their entire empire. Note also that Russia, which had fought on the victorious side, lost more territory than either Germany or Austria.

the most severe problems of the following generation and a major factor in the resumption of war in 1939.

The Versailles Treaty. The Versailles Treaty returned Alsace and Lorraine to France, awarded frontier territory to Belgium and Lithuania, restored to Denmark land lost in the war of 1864, and made major concessions to Poland. The most controversial decision gave part of West Prussia to the reborn state of Poland, which Prussia had played a leading role in destroying in the eighteenth century. Such an arrangement created a **Polish Corridor** to the Baltic Sea, but it isolated East Prussia as an exclave surrounded by Poland and thus fostered German hatred for the treaty (similar to the French reaction to the loss of Alsace in 1871). Germany was also stripped of all its colonies and Russian territory annexed by the Treaty of Brest-Litovsk in 1918. The Saar (Sar) River basin, a coal-rich region in the Rhineland, was detached from Germany, and France gained control of the Saar mines for 15 years, after which a **plebiscite** would determine the status of the region. The Saar had been part of France in the revolutionary and Napoleonic era and was detached in the Second Peace of Paris in 1815. The German army was limited to 100,000 men, a number chosen intentionally because it was smaller than that of the Polish army. Germany was denied heavy artillery, submarines, and an air force, and the entire Rhineland was **demilitarized.**

The War Guilt Clause. The most controversial section of the Versailles Treaty was Article 231, known as the war guilt clause. This article made Germany accept responsibility for causing the war. On this basis, the German nation was to pay **reparations** (the repair bill) for all civilian damage caused by the war (in contrast to the **indemnity** (punishment) payments that France had been made to pay in 1815 and 1871), a subject destined to become another of postwar Europe's greatest controversies. When critics asked Clemenceau if he thought that future historians would conclude that Germany had caused the war, he answered that they certainly would not conclude that Belgium had invaded Germany in 1914. As a concession to Wilson and to ensure the enforcement of the treaty, the Allies also created a permanent international assembly known as the League of Nations—whose founding covenant spoke of reducing armaments and ending war but established few instruments of enforcement. The Versailles Treaty was thus an awkward compromise among the victors, and it remained controversial among them (especially in Britain), so they never did a good job of enforcing it when Germany refused to cooperate.

Peace with the Hapsburg Empire. Secondary treaties signed at Paris registered the collapse of two great empires, recognized more than a dozen new coun-

tries, and addressed territorial problems that would remain unresolved throughout the twentieth century. The Hapsburg monarchy had broken apart in mid-1918, creating separate states of Austria and Hungary. Minority populations of the empire joined Poland (Upper Silesia) and Romania (Transylvania) or the newly created states of Czechoslovakia and Yugoslavia. The Treaty of St. Germain with Austria recognized these changes as a *fait accompli* (fay' tuh-comb-plee'; an already accomplished fact) and obliged the Austrians to cede the frontier territory of the south Tyrol and the Istrian Peninsula to Italy as promised in the Treaty of London of 1915. Even so, Orlando walked out of the conference to protest other "unredeemed promises" of territory, such as the town of Fiume (Fee'-oo-may) on the Adriatic. The once-mighty Hapsburg Empire, which had dominated central Europe for centuries, was reduced to an Austria only 12 percent of its size in 1914, with a population of 6 million and a treaty forbidding union with Germany. The Hungarians were made to accept the Treaty of Trianon, by which they lost 75 percent of their prewar territory. Serbia, whose **Pan-Slavic nationalism** had done so much to provoke the war (and had suffered so much during the war), was rewarded with the creation of Yugoslavia, which included Montenegro, part of Macedonia, Bosnia and Herzegovina, Croatia, and Slovenia. Both Czechoslovakia and Yugoslavia would disintegrate before the end of the century.

Peace with the Ottoman Empire. Europe paid less attention to the breakup of the Ottoman Empire—an empire that had lasted for more than six centuries—despite the fact that its fate had led to so many wars in the previous century. The empire had begun to crumble during the war. The Treaty of Sèvres, signed by the sultan in 1920, bequeathed the twentieth century some of its most difficult problems. Turkish Nationalists, led by Atatürk (At'-uh-turk), the military hero who had stopped the British at Gallipoli, fought both the sultan and the treaty. The sultanate was abolished in 1922 in favor of a secular state, and Atatürk won a new treaty in 1923; however, Turkey nonetheless received much harsher treatment than Germany had in the Versailles Treaty. The powerless sultan surrendered all non-Turkish portions of the former Ottoman Empire, although these territories did not become independent. The Middle Eastern states of Syria and Lebanon were carved out and assigned to French control (by a League of Nations **mandate**), and Palestine, Trans-Jordan, and Iraq were assigned to British control. Two of the peoples of the empire, the Armenians and the Kurds, were largely ignored by Allied mapmakers. Greece claimed most of European Turkey and part of the Turkish coast, launching another century of Greco-Turkish enmity. Italy took Rhodes and several other Mediterranean islands. Atatürk initiated the modernization of Turkey,

POSTWAR RECOVERY

TABLE 28.1 INDUSTRIAL RECOVERY AFTER WORLD WAR I

COUNTRY	1913	1919	1920	1921	1922	1923	1924	1925	1926	1927	1928
Output of Crude Steel (in thousands of metric tons)											
Belgium	2,467	334	1,253	789	1,565	2,297	2,875	2,549	3,339	3,680	3,905
France	4,687	1,293	2,706	3,099	4,538	5,222	6,670	7,464	8,617	8,349	9,479
Germany	17,609	8,710	9,278	9,997	11,714	6,305	9,835	12,195	12,342	16,311	14,517
Output of Coal (in thousands of metric tons)											
Belgium	24,371	18,483	22,143	21,807	21,209	22,922	23,362	23,097	25,230	27,551	27,587
France	40,844	22,441	25,261	28,960	31,913	38,556	44,982	48,091	52,453	52,875	52,440
Germany	277,342	210,355	219,416	236,962	256,353	180,474	243,189	272,533	285,240	304,447	317,136

Source: Mitchell, B. R., *European Historical Statistics, 1750–1970* (London: Macmillan, 1975, pp. 362–365, 400, 430).

Question: These data are presented to show the time it took Western Europe to return to the peacetime production levels of 1913. What other observations can one make from them?

---

addressing issues from the adoption of the Roman alphabet to the rights of women, but he governed a much smaller state, with only a small toehold in Europe.

Peace with the Soviet Union. Russia had been part of the Triple Entente and had entered the war as an ally of Britain and France, but the October Revolution of 1917 had led to a new government that concluded a separate peace treaty with the central powers (the Treaty of Brest-Litovsk of 1918) and left the war. The harsh German peace treaty stripped the Soviet Union of vast territory on its western border. The Allies meeting in Paris had no inclination to restore this territory to their former ally—partially because they felt betrayed by the separate Russian peace and largely because they strongly opposed the ideology of the Communist government. Indeed, Britain, France, and the United States all intervened directly in the Russian civil war, opposing the Soviets, and briefly held Russian territory at Archangel and Murmansk in 1918–1919. In total, the Paris Peace Conference accepted the existence of independent states in eastern Europe, forming a barrier known as the *cordon sanitaire* (cor-dawn' sah-nee'-tair; a term borrowed from medical quarantines) to block the spread of Communism.

The Reconstruction of Europe in the 1920s

War Losses. The cost of World War I cannot be measured precisely. More than 8 million soldiers and 7 million civilians died in the fighting; including war-related epidemics, roughly 20 million Europeans perished. France and Germany lost approximately 10 percent of their labor force, and Britain lost one-third of all men aged 15 to 24 according to the 1911 census. The casualty rate in some armies surpassed 50 percent of all personnel. The German and the Austro-Hungarian armies each reported more than 5 million wounded in the war. The French wounded included 740,000 crippled men, *mutilés de guerre* (mew-tee-lay' deh gair) who would be living reminders of the war for 50 years. The British needed forty-eight new mental hospitals just to house the 65,000 cases of acute shell shock. Little wonder that a British novelist, D. H. Lawrence, wrote, "We have all lost the war. All Europe." The living and the dead alike were a "lost generation." The poet Ezra Pound expressed a deeper bitterness:

> There died a myriad,
> And of the best, among them,
> For an old bitch gone in the teeth,
> For a botched civilization. . . .

TABLE 28.2 DEFICIT FINANCING OF WORLD WAR I

The figures are in billions of 1913 dollars.

COUNTRY	EXPENDITURE	INCOME	DEFICIT
France	32.9	5.1	27.8
Germany	37.9	5.2	32.7
Great Britain	46.7	13.3	33.4
Russia	18.3	5.0	13.3
United States	16.6	6.0	10.6

Source: Calculated from data in *History of the World Economy in the Twentieth Century*, vol. 2: Gerd Hardach, *The First World War, 1914–1918* (Berkeley: University of California Press, 1977, pp. 155, 293).

Question: In what other circumstances might a government borrow more than six times its income (as France did) or seven times its income (as Germany did)?

Postwar Reconstruction. One of the first tasks of the 1920s was the rebuilding of devastated war zones, such as this town in northern France. In that war zone, more than 6,000 square miles had been laid to waste and 1,039 villages were completely destroyed.

Economic Recovery

Economic Devastation in Europe. Economic data show similar devastation. The cost of World War I still cannot be counted (veterans and widows still receive benefits), and even the direct costs, such as government spending and destroyed property, can only be estimated. Postwar calculations translate into nearly 100 trillion late twentieth-century dollars. Economic historians have shown what this meant in local cases: 6 percent of all Belgians lost their homes, the nation lost 75 percent of its railroad cars, and farmers lost 66 percent of all pigs in prewar totals. The devastation in France was worse. The fighting had laid waste to more 6,000 square miles of northeastern and eastern France; 9,000 small factories and 5,000 large factories were destroyed, as were 15,000 miles of railroad and 33,000 miles of highway. Europe needed nearly a decade of peace merely to approach 1913 levels of production (see *Postwar Recovery*).

The Global Economy. The slow recovery of Europe permitted the United States to achieve dominance in the global economy. Whereas France mined 7 million tons of coal in 1924, the United States mined 485 million tons; whereas Germany produced 9 million tons of steel that year, the United States produced 45 million tons. By 1929, the United States accounted for 34.4 percent of global industrial production, whereas Britain, France, and Germany combined accounted for 25.7 percent. Belgium suffered a typical slow recovery: Belgians matched their prewar coal output by 1926, but textiles never reached their prewar levels. **Debt** slowed the recovery. Governments had financed the war by borrowing rather than taxing. The French government, for example, had a total wartime income of $5.1 billion, but they spent $32.9 billion. British and German debts were even worse. Germany had contracted loans totaling 98 billion gold marks (approximately $25 billion), and that indebtedness still left a deficit of nearly $8 billion (see *Postwar Recovery*). The combined effect of such staggering debts plus the immensity of the reparations payments led many economists to conclude, as John Maynard Keynes (Canes) did in *The Economic Consequences of the Peace*, that Allied economic expectations were unrealistic.

Postwar Inflation and Unemployment. Postwar conditions worsened these problems. Fighting the war on credit had led to runaway inflation. Prices increased by 264 percent in Italy and by 302 percent in Germany

POSTWAR INFLATION

TABLE 28.3 THE PRICE OF ONE KILO (2.2 POUNDS) OF RYE BREAD IN BERLIN, 1922–1923	

Note: The mark was worth approximately 25 cents before the war.

DATE	COST
January 1922	3.91 marks
February	4.62
March	6.74
April	7.39
May	7.68
June	7.93
July	8.60
August	12.70
September	18.42
October	22.37
November	55.83
December	153.69
January 3, 1923	163.00
July 4	1,895.00
August 6	8,421.00
September 3	273,684.00
October 1	9.474 million marks
October 22	1.389 billion marks
November 5	78 billion marks
November 10	233 billion marks

Combined data from Feldman, Gerald D., *The Great Disorder: Politics, Economics, and Society in the German Inflation, 1914–1924* (Oxford: Oxford University Press, 1993, p. 622); and Widdig, Bernd, *Culture and Inflation in Weimar Germany* (Berkeley: University of California Press, 2001, p. 46).

German Inflation of 1923. Despite repeated revisions of the allied demand for reparations, Germany repeatedly defaulted on scheduled payments, even payments in kind (such as coal). Germany defaulted in late December 1922 and in early January 1923, leading Belgium and France to exercise their treaty rights and occupy the rich Ruhr valley and extract coal themselves. The German government paid workers not to work with the Allies and simply printed paper money (with no backing) to pay them. The result was hyperinflation in which paper money became virtually worthless.

Question: What changes should be expected in daily life when prices are rising this dramatically?

during the war, and they did not stabilize when the fighting ended. Germany endured another 162 percent increase in prices from 1920 to 1921, and the worst was yet to come; from 1922 to 1923, **inflation** made the German mark (valued at 25 cents in 1913) virtually worthless (see *Postwar Inflation*). The price of bread in Berlin went from 0.63 marks per loaf in 1918 to 163 marks in January 1923, then to 1,895 marks in July, 9.5 million marks in October, and 233 billion marks in November. This inflation devastated German society almost as badly as German arms had devastated Belgium—

people living on a fixed income were ruined. **Unemployment** posed other problems. Although unemployment had stood at 3 percent before the war, the **demobilization** of armies left millions of veterans jobless. Unemployment hit 15 percent in 1921 and stayed above 10 percent for years. Having seen the role of disgruntled soldiers in the Bolshevik revolution, governments were eager to remedy this situation. Many nations adopted their first unemployment compensation laws because conservatives wanted to help veterans; Italy did so in 1919, and Austria and Britain followed in 1920.

The Conservative Reaction of the 1920s

Conservative Political Victories. One widely shared postwar sentiment was a desire to recover the remembered tranquility of antediluvian Europe. In an awkward American coinage, people wanted a "return to normalcy." This led to conservative electoral victories in many countries. British voters dismissed their wartime leader, Lloyd George, and gave the Tories a huge victory in 1924. The French sent Clemenceau into retirement and elected a Chamber of Deputies so full of **veterans** that it was called the "horizon blue" assembly (because of their uniform color). Conservative Catholic parties won landmark victories in the Belgian elections of 1919 and 1921 and in the Austrian elections of 1920 and 1923.

Conservative Morality: Controlling Drink and Drugs. The conservative reaction typically encompassed efforts to guard morality. This led to the prohibition of alcoholic beverages in the United States and Bolshevik Russia and to lesser restrictions on drink (commonly the perpetuation of wartime regulations) around Europe. The French continued a ban on certain alcoholic beverages (such as absinthe), and a British law of 1921 strictly regulated the hours when pubs could sell drinks (ending early, interrupting sales during the day, and cutting hours in half). Many countries imposed higher taxes on alcohol, on the theory that people would accept these **"sin taxes."** And most of Europe, which had allowed the consumption of **narcotic drugs** during the prewar Belle Époque, joined in an international convention against such drugs in 1925.

Conservative Morality: Controlling Sexuality and Reproduction. Many countries rewrote laws on sexuality and reproduction, marriage, and divorce. Many democracies adopted stricter censorship based on sexual content. The new film industry was widely censored by organizations such as the British Board of Film Censors (created in 1920). Many publications were censored because conservatives considered them to be **pornography.** D. H. Lawrence's novel, *Lady Chatterley's Lover,* which one conservative reviewer called "the most evil outpouring that ever besmirched the literature of our country," was widely censored. Regulation of **prostitution** was introduced in Germany, Spain, and Russia; stricter regulations were adopted in Holland, Scandinavia, Switzerland, and Italy. The leading voice for a conservative morality was Pope Pius XI, who stated strict standards for Catholics in 1930, in the encyclical *Casti connubi* (see Document 28.1). He opposed **birth control, abortion,** and **divorce;** birth control, for example, was branded "criminal abuse" and "intrinsically vicious." Many governments, motivated by population losses as much as by morality, outlawed birth control or abortion. In 1920, the French banned not only birth control and abortion but also information about them. Madeleine Pelletier, the prewar feminist who had championed women's right to have abortions, was jailed in an asylum under these laws and died there. Ireland made it a felony to sell, import, or advertise any birth control

---

POPE PIUS XI ON MARRIAGE, BIRTH CONTROL, ABORTION, AND DIVORCE

Pius XI (served 1922–1939) was a conservative pope. His encyclical *Casti connubi* (1930), from which the following excerpts are taken, gave the first comprehensive statement of the church's position of many issues concerning the family.

Domestic . . . order includes both the primacy of the husband with regard to the wife and children, the ready subjection of the wife and her willing obedience, which the Apostle commends in these words: "Let women be subject to their husbands as to the Lord, because the husband is the head of the wife, as Christ is the head of the Church." This subjection, however, does not deny or take away the liberty which fully belongs to the woman. . . .

First consideration is due to the offspring, which many have the boldness to (avoid) . . . by frustrating the marriage act. . . . But no reason, however grave, may be put forward by which anything intrinsically against nature may become conformable to nature and morally good. Since, therefore, the conjugal act is destined primarily by nature for the begetting of children, those who in exercising it deliberately frustrate its natural power and purpose sin against nature and commit a deed which is shameful and intrinsically vicious. . . .

Another very grave crime is to be noted, Venerable Brethren, which regards the taking of the life of the offspring hidden in the mother's womb. Some wish it to be allowed and left to the will of the father or the mother; others . . . ask that the public authorities provide aid for these death-dealing operations. . . . Venerable Brethren, however much we may pity the mother whose health or even life is gravely imperiled in the performance of a duty allotted to her by nature, nevertheless what could ever be a sufficient reason for excusing in any way the direct murder of the innocent?

The advocates of the neo-paganism of today . . . continue by legislation to attack the indissolubility of the marriage bond, proclaiming the lawfulness of divorce. . . .

Opposed to all these reckless opinions, Venerable Brethren, stands the unalterable law of God, fully confirmed by Christ, a law that can never be deprived of its force by the decrees of men, the ideas of a people, or the will of any legislator: "What God hath joined together, let no man put asunder."

From Pius XI, "Casi Connubi," in Anne Fremantle, *The Papal Encyclicals* (New York: Putnam, 1956).

Question: What consequences can be expected from the church issuing this document?

VERA BRITTAIN ON THE DEMOBILIZATION OF WORKING WOMEN

Vera Brittain (1893–1970), the daughter of a well-to-do manufacturing family, enrolled in Oxford University over her parents' objections but withdrew to serve as a nurse during World War I. The war politicized her, and Brittain became a vigorous champion of both feminism and pacifism after the war. She recorded her experiences and reactions from this period in *Testament of Youth* (1933) and *Testament of Friendship* (1940). The following excerpt is taken from one of her political works published after the war.

During the war, women passed rapidly into trades hitherto considered unsuitable for them, such as transport, munitions, motor manufacture and shipbuilding, and were found to be specially well-adapted to organization, supervision, and process work of all kinds. Work hitherto thought too heavy or too highly skilled was made quite feasible by means of lifting tackle (now generally considered desirable for men also) and special training, as well as by the more adequate nourishment of the worker. Numbers of women were brought back into manual labor, often the most strenuous. . . .

In industry the temporary relaxation of Trade Union regulations led to women being universally employed to replace or supplement men. . . . Statistics given by the War Cabinet Committee on Women in Industry in Great Britain and Ireland show that the 5,966,000 women who were employed in July 1914 had increased by July 1918 to 7,311,000. . . . Because of this increase in numbers, as well as owing to the efficiency shown by women in every type of occupation, the Women's Employment Committee foresaw

an extension of openings for women . . . and believed that employers would gladly continue to use them after the war. . . .

These sanguine hopes were doomed to disappointment. The war had certainly given the world an object lesson in woman's achievement, but men in general showed a disturbing tendency to be appalled rather than encouraged by this demonstration of unexpected ability. . . . With the end of the necessity which had provoked war-time agreements, both sides [labor and management] were anxious to return to the old advantageous positions. . . .

The immediate result of demobilization was to add a sentimental argument to the already familiar economic and social arguments against the work of women. The Restoration of the Pre-War Practises Act, which became law in July 1918 effactually dispelled any lingering optimism as to the improvement of women's position in industry owing to the war. Women were discharged wholesale; they were not only turned out of old industries, but out of many new ones. . . . By the autumn of 1919 three quarters of a million of the women employed at the time of armistice had been dismissed. . . . By 1923, the number of [union] women was reduced to 480,000. . . little more than half that of 1913.

From Brittain, Vera, *Women's Work in Modern England* (London: Douglas, 1928).

Question: In what ways are Vera Brittain's concerns about the role of women compatible, or incompatible, with those of Pope Pius XI?

---

device. Mussolini criminalized abortion in 1930, although Italian women still obtained 500,000 illegal abortions annually. Britain was an unusual exception where an abortion law of 1929 allowed the operation until the twenty-eighth week of pregnancy, and a birth control clinic, founded by Marie Stopes, opened in 1921. Few European governments followed Pius's urging to outlaw divorce, which was still a relatively uncommon phenomenon. British courts, for example, granted a total of 3,747 divorces in 1920. However the details varied, the postwar mood of moral reform was larger than a Christian religious revival. At the Islamic southeastern edge of Europe, Atatürk reformed Turkish marital law and outlawed polygamy.

Conservative Morality: Controlling Marriage and the Position of Women.

Casti connubi also restated traditional views of the position of women. It instructed Catholics to accept "the primacy of the husband" and "the ready subjection of the wife" who must

obey him. Many governments saw an economic benefit in this traditional view. War work by millions of women had encouraged feminists to believe that women would soon win equality in jobs and wages. They did not. Fewer Frenchwomen were working in 1921 than had been in 1906, despite the loss of 1.4 million male workers in the war. In Britain, 750,000 women lost their jobs in the first year of peace; by 1923, women were a smaller portion of labor unions than they had been in 1913, even though nearly 1 million British workers had been lost (see Document 28.2) This pattern was repeated across the continent. Although most of the major powers granted women's suffrage during or after the war, old attitudes about women remained strong.

The Changing Conditions of Life in Europe

Although Europe endured tragic difficulties following World War I, seeing the era solely in terms of its problems would be misleading. Historians must keep many perspectives on the past. Cultural historians, for example, explore the mixture of vitality and decadence known in America as "the roaring twenties." The Weimar Republic is a tragic failure in the history of democracy, but its vigorous cultural history fascinates historians who look at expressionist painting, Bauhaus architecture, or the novels of Thomas Mann instead of dictatorship and depression. Historians of popular culture find an exciting interwar world by considering the impact of the automobile, aircraft, or telephone. For example, private autos in use in Britain rose from 79,000 in 1919 to 2,034,000 in 1939; British Imperial Airways began overseas passenger service in 1924 and the German Lufthansa airline started service in 1926; and the telephone, which was introduced in London in 1879 but still limited to an elite of 10,000 homes in Britain on the eve of the war, became widely available (the two-millionth phone was installed in Buckingham Palace in 1931). Historians of science treat epochal developments in physics, where scientists such as Albert Einstein, Max Planck, Enrico Fermi, and Ernest Rutherford transformed understanding of the physical world; the atom, long considered the indivisible basis of all matter, was first split in 1932.

A Revolution in Health. Among the many differences from the past that are examined by social historians of the early twentieth century, the most notable may be the dramatic decline in infant mortality rates (see Table 28.4). Under the **biological Old Regime,** between 20 and 30 percent of all babies never reached their first birthday. By 1940, most of Europe had a infant mortality rate below 10 percent as a result of the accelerated conquest of epidemic diseases. The death rate from diphtheria for British children fell by 49 percent; measles, by 76 percent; and scarlet fever, by 83 percent. Hundreds of thousands of Europeans who would have died of conta-gious diseases in the nineteenth century now reached adulthood. In 1921, two French scientists developed a vaccine against tuberculosis, the greatest scourge of Belle Époque Europe. The most remarkable lifesaving discoveries of the interwar era—the **antibiotic** treatment of wounds and diseases—did not have a great impact until the generation of World War II. Two of the twentieth century's most important Nobel Prizes in Physiology or Medicine were awarded to men whose work contributed greatly to the conquest of disease: Scottish bacteriologist Alexander Fleming in 1945 and German chemist Gerhard Domagk in 1939. (The Nazi government made Domagk decline the prize, however.) Domagk's work led to the development of sulfa drugs, a treatment nontoxic to humans yet powerful in combating infectious diseases. Fleming discovered penicillin in 1928, although its development was left to others (Ernst Chain and Sir Howard Florey shared the 1945 Nobel Prize in Physiology or Medicine) and the drug was not synthesized until the war. Such **"miracle drugs"** were first used experimentally in 1932; penicillin saved thousands of soldiers' lives in World War II and became widely available after the war.

European Culture after the Deluge

The Great War caused deep cultural despair in Europe. It spawned pessimism in some people, cynical frivolity in others, bitterness in many, and spiritual barrenness in most. In the imagery of the Irish poet William Butler Yeats in "The Second Coming":

Things fall apart; the centre cannot hold;
Mere anarchy is loosed upon the world.
The blood-dimmed tide is loosed, and everywhere
The ceremony of innocence is drowned;
The best lack all conviction, while the worst
Are full of passionate intensity.

TABLE 28.4 THE DECLINE OF INFANT MORTALITY IN EUROPE, 1900–1940

	Deaths of Infants Younger Than 1 Year of Age, as a Percentage of Live Births					
YEAR	AUSTRIA	BRITAIN	FRANCE	GERMANY	RUSSIA	SWEDEN
1900	23.1	15.4	16.0	22.9	25.2	9.9
1910	18.9	10.5	11.1	16.2	27.1	7.5
1920	n.a.	8.0	12.3	13.1	n.a.	6.3
1930	10.4	6.0	8.4	8.5	n.a.	5.5
1940	7.4	5.7	9.1	6.4	n.a.	3.9

n.a. = Not available.

Source: Mitchell, B. R., *European Historical Statistics, 1750–1970* (London: Macmillan, 1975, pp. 130–131); data for 1991 from *The World Almanac and Book of Facts 1993* (Mahwah, NJ: World Almanac Books, 1992), passim.

Question: What conclusions about differing conditions in these countries can be proposed, based on these data?

Dadaism and Surrealism. This postwar mood produced the absurdities of **dadaism** (dah-dah'-iz-um) and **surrealism,** the alienated literature of modernism, and ubiquitous antiwar sentiments. Dada was the response of iconoclastic intellectuals—an intentionally meaningless art, an anarchistic "antiart." According to the Dadaist Manifesto of the Romanian poet Tristan Tzara, European culture should abandon everything from logic to good manners and teach spontaneous living. The German painter George Grosz found that dadaism suited his mood of nihilism and painted under the slogan *"Kunst ist tot!"* (Art is dead!). The more sophisticated doctrine of surrealism also purged reason from art, replacing it with images from the subconscious or the absurd, as painters such as René Magritte and Marcel Duchamp demonstrated. Duchamp shocked the art world by exhibiting a sculpture entitled "Fountain." It was a urinal, turned upside down and signed "R. Mutt."

Modernism. The masterpieces of literary **modernism** showed similar responses to the war. The poetry of T. S. Eliot, such as *The Waste Land* (1922), stated a disillusioned lament for European civilization and asked "what branches grow/Out of this stony rubbish?" Another of the great works of modernism, James Joyce's *Ulysses* (1922), broke down the logical structure of the novel and fashioned a story about the commonplace events of a single day, verbalized in an inventive but sometimes incoherent form called **stream of consciousness.** *Ulysses* focused on the postwar mood of Leopold Bloom who, like Europe, had become bitter and dispirited.

Kafka. The creative artist who best typified the postwar despair of European culture was Franz Kafka (Kaff'-kuh), an Austrian-Czech writer so powerful that his name became an adjective. The **kafkaesque** world is incomprehensible yet menacing, complex, bizarre, absurd, and ominous. Kafka wrote of people so alienated that one of them awakens to find himself transformed into a large insect; others are held in a prison where preposterous commands are tattooed onto their bodies; another is brought to a bizarre trial in which the charges are never specified; and yet another is hired for a frustrating job that seems to have neither instructions nor anyone to explain it.

Anti-War Sentiment. One of the central themes of this postwar mood was anger at war and the society that produced it or profited from it. Erich Maria Remarque (Ruh-mark'), a German writer who later joined a flood of intellectual **émigrés** to America, penned one of the most famous antiwar novels ever written, *All Quiet on the Western Front* (1929), describing the experiences of a group of schoolboys in the dehumanizing life of the trenches. Jaroslav Hasek's *Good Soldier Schweik* (1923) made fun of armies and officers (Hasek used some of his own commanders' names) by showing how easily everyone is fooled by a soldier acting stupid. Wilfred Owen's posthumously published poetry (he was killed in France 1 week before the armistice) described the suffering of the common soldier and burned with loathing for the war. Vera Brittain, a British volunteer nurse during the war, used her experiences to write of pacifism with such conviction that she became an officer of the Women's International League of Peace and Freedom. George Grosz, the German graphic artist so embittered by the war that he had turned to dadaism, used savage caricature to attack the government, the military, and the classes that prospered while others suffered.

The Cultural Revolution of Film. Ironically, the most important development in European culture in the early twentieth century was not linked to World War I and the postwar despair. A cultural revolution had begun in the early years of the century, and it triumphed dramatically in the 1920s and 1930s. The new technologies of radio and motion pictures led to the democratization of culture, the creation of mass culture. Two French chemists, Louis and Auguste Lumière (Loo-me'-air), presented the first public showing of a motion picture in 1895, a 1-minute film of workers leaving their factory. The first narrative film, the American-made *The Great Train Robbery,* appeared in 1903, and the silent film industry was born in the following decade. Charles Pathé, the first movie mogul, achieved the commercial exploitation of the Lumière brothers' cinematograph and made Paris the world center of the motion picture industry in the years before 1914. Although the center of the industry had shifted to Hollywood by the 1920s, booming film industries developed in interwar Europe. The British, French, and German industries each were producing more than 100 feature films per year by the early 1930s.

Radio. An Italian inventor, Guglielmo Marconi (Marr-cone'-ee), launched the world into the age of broadcasting in 1895, shortly before the Lumières showed the first film. Marconi's "wireless telegraphy" did not develop as rapidly as the cinema did, but individual radio transmissions in Europe and America began in the decade before the war. The first broadcast of a program of music occurred at Graz (Austria) in 1908, and the world's first station broadcasting regularly scheduled radio programs began its transmissions in Pittsburgh in 1920. That same year, the British government created a broadcasting monopoly, the BBC (British Broadcasting

Company, later Corporation), and it produced the first European daily programming in 1922. Radio, like the movies, became widespread in interwar Europe. By 1930–1931, radio reached most households in western and central Europe; there was a radio set for every twelve people in Britain, one per every fifteen people in Germany.

EUROPEAN DEMOCRACY AFTER WORLD WAR I

Most of Europe lived under parliamentary democracy in 1920 but under authoritarianism in 1939. The era began with popularly elected parliaments in the new states of Eastern Europe, from the Finnish and Estonian assemblies of 1919 to the Turkish republic of 1922 and the Greek republic of 1924.

Women's Suffrage. The enthusiasm for democracy included an expansion of its definition. Between 1915 and 1922, eighteen European countries gave women the right to vote in national elections. The trend began in Scandinavia, where Norway had led the way before the war. Denmark enfranchised women in 1915, with Finland (1917) and Sweden (1918) following. The idea then took root in the new regimes of Eastern Europe and in the Austrian and German republics. Ironically, **women's suffrage** found less acceptance in western Europe. Britain allowed women to vote only at the age 30 until an equal franchise law was passed in 1928. In France, a conservative Senate blocked women's suffrage in 1922 and prevented women from voting until 1944. Belgium, Italy, Portugal, and Switzerland (the last state in Europe to accept women's suffrage) also rejected enfranchisement.

Proportional Representation. A second expansion of democracy was proportional voting to give representation to minorities. Under traditional procedures, a group receiving 10 percent of the vote seldom won an election; advocates of **proportional representation** said that group deserved 10 percent of the seats in a legislature. Belgium had employed proportional representation since 1899, and varieties of that system were adopted in France, Germany, and Italy at the end of the war.

The Overthrow of Democracy in Eastern Europe. Despite such trends, democracy did not flourish during the interwar years. By 1939, dictatorships had replaced more than a dozen parliamentary democracies. The newly independent states were especially vulnerable. General Józef Pilsudski used the Polish

FIGURE 28.1 *Women's Suffrage.* Women won the right to vote in many European states during or immediately after World War I—including the Soviet Union (1917), Britain (1918), and Germany (1918), but not France or Italy. Most of the states granting equal political rights to women were those writing the constitution of a new regime, not old governments that had been persuaded to admit women. Here British women protest that they do not receive the right to vote until age 30.

army to hold dictatorial power for nearly 15 years after his coup d'état of 1926. Monarchies abolished political freedoms in Yugoslavia and Albania. In Hungary, Admiral Miklós Horthy governed (from 1920 to 1944) as the regent for a vacant monarchy; he retained a Parliament, but curtailed the electoral process, held a veto over legislation, and created an anachronistic upper house of Parliament controlled by nobles.

The Age of Dictatorship. As the failed democracies of Eastern Europe suggest, the era between 1919 and 1945 became an age of **dictatorship**—the rule of one leader, one party, and many police. Characteristic regimes or the era include the Communist dictatorship of Joseph Stalin in the Soviet Union (ruled 1924–1953); the Nazi dictatorship of Adolf Hitler in Germany (ruled 1933–1945); the Fascist dictatorship of Benito Mussolini in Italy (ruled 1922–1945); the military dictatorships of General Primo de Rivera (ruled 1922–1930) and General Francisco Franco in Spain (ruled 1936–1975); Antonio Salazar in Portugal (ruled 1926–1968); and the wartime dictatorship of Marshal Henri Philippe Pétain (Pay'-tan) in France (ruled 1940–1945). World War II accelerated this trend, and by 1941, only five parliamentary democracies survived in Europe: Britain, Ireland, Iceland, Sweden, and Switzerland.

German Democracy in the 1920s: The Weimar Republic

After the abdication of Kaiser Wilhelm II in 1918, a provisional government held elections for a constituent assembly to meet in the Saxon city of Weimar (Veye'-marr) and create a German republic. The 59-year-old emperor would live longer than the republic that replaced him. The provisional government put down the Sparticist revolt of German Communists at Berlin in January 1919 and accepted the responsibility for signing the Versailles Treaty in June 1919. Consequently, the Weimar Republic began governing in the summer of 1919, detested by both the Communist left and the nationalist right. The Weimar constitution contained universal suffrage, proportional representation, popular referenda, the abolition of aristocratic privilege, and basic individual freedoms. It entrusted the government to a chancellor, who needed the support of a majority in the Reichstag, but it also created a 7-year presidency with special powers to suspend the constitution during emergencies.

Right-Wing Anti-Republicanism. Right-wing opposition to the Weimar Republic flourished immediately and dominated the early 1920s. Paramilitary leagues of war veterans, known as the *Freikorps* (Free Corps), remained a violent factor in German politics. Extremists assassinated the socialist premier of Bavaria in 1919, then Matthias Erzberger (who had bravely accepted the job of signing the Versailles Treaty) in 1921 and Walter Rathenau (the foreign minister) in 1922. Freikorps troops supported monarchists in seizing control of Berlin in the *Kapp Putsch* (coup) of 1920, and the German army refused to fire on them; the Putsch was only blocked by a general strike of Berlin workers. Nationalists blamed Republicans for a supposed civilian betrayal of the German army in 1918—the **"stab-in-the-back"** (*Dolchstoss*) **myth** of the German defeat—even though their military hero, General Erich Friedrich Ludendorff (Loo'-den-dorf), had been the person who admitted that military victory was impossible and called for peace. Ludendorff participated in what became the most famous right-wing conspiracy of the 1920s—the Munich Beer Hall Putsch of November 1923. This attempted coup introduced the world to Adolf Hitler and his small National Socialist German Workers' Party ("Nazi" for short). The Beer Hall Putsch was easily stopped, and Hitler was convicted of high treason and sentenced to prison for 5 years, where he dictated *Mein Kampf* (My Struggle) before his early release (see Document 28.3). Hitler's book offered a muddle of hatreds (of Communism, Jews, the Versailles Treaty,

democracy, and the Weimar Republic), stating the right-wing agenda at the time. Initially it found few readers.

German Economic Weakness. The success of parliamentary democracy in Germany depended on winning the support of the middle classes and the peasantry away from the alternatives proposed by Nationalists or Communists. Many Germans were alienated, however, by the economic catastrophes of the early 1920s. The imperial government had destroyed the value of the mark by its vast borrowing and the reckless printing of money. Territorial losses and reparations payments compounded the problem. The inflation of 1922–1923 destroyed the savings, pensions, and income of millions of Germans. Consequently, the German middle class, especially the lower middle class, never developed fond ties to the Weimar government.

Gustav Stresemann and the Spirit of Locarno. The German republic did recover and prosper after 1924. A coalition of moderate Socialists, Democrats, and the Catholic Party (the *Zentrum*) brought stability to the government. An international agreement, the Dawes Plan (1924), readjusted reparations and created a stable currency. Industrial production rose. A strong and capable foreign minister, Gustav Stresemann (Stray'-seh-mahn), risked the ire of Nationalists by pursuing conciliatory policies. Stresemann, the brilliant son of an innkeeper, had risen in politics as Ludendorff's protégé and had been an ardent Nationalist and imperialist, but he reconsidered his beliefs during the right-wing violence of the early 1920s,

FIGURE 28.2 *The Spirit of Locarno.* For a short period in the middle and late 1920s, it seemed possible that France and Germany had overcome the generations of war between the two countries and reached an amicable understanding. The promising agreement was a treaty signed at Locarno in 1925, a work of conciliation by the foreign ministers of France (Aristide Briand, 1862–1932, on the right) and Germany (Gustav Stresemann, 1878–1929, on the left), who shared the Nobel Peace Prize in 1926.

DOCUMENT 28.3

HITLER'S ANTI-SEMITISM IN *MEIN KAMPF* (1925)

The first part of *Mein Kampf*, from which the following excerpt is taken, was written during Hitler's imprisonment and published in 1925. It provided unmistakable indications of his racist thoughts and intentions. Hitler asserted that the Jews were lowest of all the races and that they destroyed the civilization of other races; they were responsible for World War I and for the Bolshevik revolution.

It is difficult today, if not impossible, for me to say when the word "Jew" first gave me cause for particular thought. In the paternal household during the lifetime of my father I cannot remember ever having heard the word. I believe the old gentleman would have considered the particular emphasis on this term to be cultural backwardness. . . . Nor did I find any inducement in school which could have led me to change this adopted point of view. . . . Not until my fourteenth or fifteenth year did I come across the word "Jew" in connection with political discussions. I reacted with mild aversion. . . .

There were few Jews in Linz. In the course of the centuries their outward appearance had become Europeanized and had taken on a human look; in fact, I even took them for Germans. . . .

Then I came to Vienna. . . . Once, as I was strolling through the Inner City, I suddenly encountered an apparition in a black caftan and black hair locks. Is this a Jew? was my first thought. . . . The longer I stared . . . the more my question assumed a new form: Is this a German? . . . I bought for a few pennies the first anti-Semitic pamphlets of my life. . . .

The cleanliness of this people, moral and otherwise, I must say, is a point in itself. By their very exterior you could tell that these were no lovers of water, and, to your distress, you often knew it with your eyes closed. . . .

I became acquainted with their activity in the press, art, literature, and the theater. . . . As soon as one cut ever so carefully into such a tumor, one found, like the maggot in a rotting corpse, . . . a little Jew. Nine-tenths of all literary filth, artistic trash, and theatrical idiocy can be set to their account. . . .

Then a flame flared up within me. . . . I went from weak cosmopolitan to fanatical anti-Semite. Hence, today I believe that I am acting with the will of the Almighty Creator: by defending myself against the Jew, I am fighting for the work of the Lord.

From Hitler, Adolph, *Mein Kampf* (Boston: Houghton Mifflin, 1943).

Question: How can this excerpt be compared with other racist arguments?

---

especially after the murders of Erzberger and Rathenau. His cooperation with the French foreign minister Aristide Briand (Bree'-ahnd) restored normal peacetime conditions. Briand had risen in French politics as a socialist ally of Jean Jaurès, but Socialists expelled him from the party for accepting a cabinet post in a bourgeois government and he began a long career as a centrist. Between 1906 and 1932, he held twenty-six cabinet appointments. As the leading voice of postwar French foreign policy, Briand twice (in 1924 and 1929) agreed to ease reparations payments. Briand and Stresemann negotiated the Locarno (Low-car'-no) Treaty (1925), reaffirming the Franco-German frontier drawn in the Versailles Treaty. Stresemann led Germany into the League of Nations (1926) as the equal of Britain and France. In short, peace and prosperity seemed possible when Stresemann and Briand shared the 1926 Nobel Peace Prize for creating the "spirit of Locarno."

Postwar Democracy in Britain and France

The older democracies also experienced difficult times in recovering stability. Britain and France struggled with economic problems, faced social unrest, and turned to conservative governments for most of the 1920s.

Women's Rights in Britain. At the end of the war, the British government had addressed two of its greatest prewar problems: women's rights and the government of Ireland. Lloyd George's Representation of the People Act (1918) gave women the vote at age 30, and the Equal Franchise Act (1928) finally granted women suffrage on the same basis as men. In 1919, American-born Lady Nancy Astor became the first woman to sit in the House of Commons; by 1929, there were 69 women candidates and 14 women members of Parliament (M.P.s) (of 615 seats). British women won other important rights in the Sex Disqualification Act of 1919, which abolished gender barriers to universities, the professions, and public positions, and the Matrimonial Causes Act of 1923, which gave women equality in divorce law. The Law of Property of 1926 gave all women the right to hold and dispose of property on the same terms as men. Important as all of this legislation was, it fell short of full equality for women, as dismissed war workers learned. Even those women who kept their jobs in the 1920s and 1930s still worked for less than half of a man's wages, and such pay disparity was not improving. Working women's percentage of men's earnings was 48.2 percent in 1924 and 48.1 percent in 1935.

Europe in an Age of Dictatorship, 1919–1939 **729**

Irish Independence. The British addressed the Irish question with mixed success. Three years after the Easter Rebellion of 1916, Irish Nationalists again rebelled against British rule. In a treaty of 1921, twenty-six (largely Catholic) counties of Ireland gained independence as the Irish Free State; however, six other counties (with a large Protestant population) in the northern region of Ulster remained a part of the United Kingdom. This ended the unity of the "British Isles," which lasted for barely a century and a half (having begun with the eighteenth-century absorption of Scotland and Ireland). The Irish Treaty also precipitated an Irish civil war between pro-treaty moderates and antitreaty Nationalists; pro-treaty forces that accepted the border dividing Ireland won. The continued widespread acceptance of this treaty and this northern border led to the reopening of the Irish question in 1969, when a militant minority of the Irish Republican Army (IRA), known as the Provos, began a terrorist campaign intended to end the union of Britain and Northern Ireland and to reunite the north with the south. The Irish Free State was officially proclaimed, and the Irish Constitution adopted, in 1922, and independent Ireland joined the League of Nations in 1923; in 1937, a new constitution replaced the Irish Free State with the Republic of Ireland (Eire).

British Economic Problems. The most severe problem that interwar Britain faced was neither the women's rights question nor the Irish question. It was an economical problem. Prewar unemployment had been 3.3 percent, and it remained low until the demobilization of soldiers and women workers. Unemployment hit 14.8 percent in 1921 (nearly 1 million people jobless) and stayed above 10 percent for the remainder of the decade. Productivity stood at a fraction of prewar levels, and many of these (such as coal production) were never reached again. The cost of living in 1921 had risen to four times the level of 1914. By 1922, marches of the unemployed and hungry had become a common feature of British daily life, such as the **hunger march** of unemployed workers from Glasgow to London. And the home of capitalist free trade orthodoxy watched as its imports doubled its exports.

Ramsay MacDonald and Labour Party Socialism. Britain was one of the most heavily unionized states in the world, with 30 percent of workers belonging to trade unions in 1921. The miners' unions were especially militant, and they led major strikes in 1919 and 1921. (Miners attempted to organize a **general strike** including railway and transport workers, but on "Black Friday," these other workers abandoned the strike.) Although elections in early 1924 created a short-lived Labour Party government in which Ramsay MacDonald became Britain's first socialist prime minis-

ter, angry workers obtained little welfare legislation except the Housing Act of 1924 and the Pension Act of 1925. MacDonald, the illegitimate son of a farm laborer and a servant, had risen through self-education to become the leading theorist of British socialism. He rejected Marxist doctrines of **class warfare** and violent revolution and believed in an evolutionary, **democratic socialism** as "the hereditary heir of liberalism." After MacDonald granted diplomatic recognition to the USSR, however, the evolutionary process restored conservatives to power, and Stanley Baldwin (the son of a rich industrialist) formed his second government. (MacDonald would ultimately serve three terms as prime minister—in the Labour governments of 1924 and 1929–1931 and then in the national coalition government of 1931–1935.)

Stanley Baldwin and the Trade Disputes Act. Social unrest worsened under both governments. Mine owners lowered wages and lengthened the working day, leading to another wave of strikes, which culminated in the 11-day general strike (when all workers were expected to leave their jobs) of 1926. More than 2.5 million workers in a labor force of 6 million walked out. The Baldwin government, fearful of the revolutionary potential of the general strike, made enough concessions to bring back moderate workers. With the general strike beaten, conservatives quickly passed the Trade Disputes Act of 1927 limiting the right to strike. General strikes, sympathy strikes, and strikes in many occupations (such as the police) became illegal.

Raymond Poincaré and Conservatism in France. The postwar government in France was a similar conservative coalition, led by Raymond Poincaré (Pwan'-car-ay). Poincaré, educated as both an engineer and a lawyer, had held elective office since the 1880s, culminating in the wartime presidency. As premier in the early 1920s, Poincaré concentrated on the rebuilding of France and a nationalist agenda. He expected the strict enforcement of the Versailles Treaty and ordered a military occupation of the Ruhr (permitted by the reparations agreement) when Germany defaulted on payments in 1923. French conservatives supported Poincaré in treason trials of wartime pacifists, the dissolution of the militant confederation of trade unions (the CGT), aid to big business and the peasantry, and concessions to the Catholic Church. During the middle and late 1920s, Briand persuaded the conservative coalition to relax its anti-German nationalism, and Poincaré acquiesced in this policy to concentrate upon economic recovery. French problems were so bad that Poincaré asked and received the right to solve them by decrees without a vote of the Chamber of Deputies. He stabilized the French franc in 1926–1928 by devaluing it to 20 percent of its prewar value. This meant that the government repudiated 80 percent of its foreign debt written in francs, chiefly war bonds.

The Recovery of France. When Poincaré retired in 1929, his accomplishments included a stable currency, a growing economy, record industrial production, and the reconstruction of most war-damaged regions. Briand had simultaneously won guarantees of peace. French conservatives had accepted a measure of proportional representation in 1919 but rejected women's suffrage in 1922. They had taken a significant step in the evolution of the European welfare state by adopting a **social insurance** law in 1928, based on workers contributing 3 percent of their income to an insurance fund and employers matching that 3 percent. This was refined in the National Workmen's Insurance Law of 1930 to provide government benefits for sickness, old age, and death. Many resentments simmered below the surface, but France appeared to have made a strong recovery.

THE GREAT DEPRESSION OF THE 1930S

By 1928, Europe had largely recovered from the ravages of World War I. Total productivity stood 13 percent above the 1913 level, slightly stronger in western Europe (16 percent). The year 1929, however, marked the beginning of the worst economic **depression** of the twentieth century. This crisis began in the United States with the collapse of stock market values known as the Wall Street Crash, and it spread to a global collapse from 1929 to 1932. Most of Europe felt the depression begin in 1930, and it soon became the deepest of the industrial age, comparable only to the depression of the 1840s, which contributed to the outbreak of the revolutions of 1848. The collapse of the American stock values, the loss of American credit, the recall of American loans, the rise of American tariffs, and the withering of exports to America caused deep declines in European production and frightening levels of unemployment. European finances were locked into a precarious **gold standard,** in which governments were required to hold sufficient gold to back their paper money; limited supplies of gold and unrealistic exchange rates meant that governments could not support expansion. As unemployment rose, small shops went bankrupt; as world trade collapsed, big industries such as shipbuilding closed down. In 1931, when banks could not obtain repayment of outstanding loans, a wave of **bank failures** swept Europe. After a great Austrian bank, the Kredit-Anstalt, failed, much of the banking system of Eastern and Central Europe collapsed, and the wave of bank closings flowed back to the United States. Most of Europe was still struggling to recover from this cycle when World War II began in 1939.

Unemployment in the Depression. The most dramatic measure of the crisis of the 1930s is in unemployment data (see *Unemployment in the Great Depression of the 1930s*). Despite the recovery of the late 1920s, Europe had not returned to the low levels of joblessness seen in 1913–1914 (3 to 4 percent), but no one was prepared for the catastrophic unemployment of the 1930s. Most of Europe had double-digit unemployment in 1930, then rates above 20 percent in 1931–1932. Many countries experienced 30 percent jobless rates; the Dutch lived with unemployment averaging 31.7 percent for 7 years (1932–1938).

The Depression and Democracy. The Great Depression tested the Western world's belief in liberal-democratic government and capitalist economics. Many countries abandoned democracy in favor of authoritarian leadership; many surviving democracies (such as France and the United States) found that they had to provide their citizens with significantly higher levels of welfare benefits. All countries (including Britain, France, and the United States) abandoned some classic precepts of market capitalism, such as **free trade;** many adopted the eighteenth-century economics of autarchy (self-sufficiency). And most states abandoned the gold standard—as England did in 1932 and the Netherlands did in 1936.

Britain in the Depression. Britain illustrates the severity of the crisis. The National Insurance Act of 1911 gave Britain the largest unemployment insurance program in Europe, but it covered less than two-thirds of British workers and provided only 15 weeks of benefits. (German unemployment legislation, by comparison, covered less than half of the labor force.) When unemployment in old industrial centers reached horrendous proportions, as it did in the Welsh coal-mining town of Merthyr Tydfil (62 percent in 1934) and the English shipbuilding town of Jarrow (68 percent in 1934), such insurance was insufficient. A National Coalition government of all major parties (1931–1935) adopted drastic measures: the end of the gold standard, the **devaluation** of the pound sterling (£) by nearly 30 percent (from a value of $4.86 to $3.49), and the adoption of **protective tariffs** (including a new Corn Law in 1932). Effectively, the greatest theory of nineteenth-century British capitalism had been reversed. The coalition also cut the wages of government employees (such as teachers and soldiers) and reduced unemployment benefits.

The Depression and Fascism in Britain. The depression produced a volatile situation in Britain. Riots in London, Liverpool, and Glasgow greeted the announced economies in 1931. Part of the royal navy mutinied. The **crime rate** soared. (The burglary rate for stores and

UNEMPLOYMENT IN THE GREAT DEPRESSION OF THE 1930s

Unemployment in Britain. Although the table shows staggering national rates of unemployment during the great depression, some industries and communities faced even worse rates. This photograph shows marchers in 1936 from Jarrow (an industrial town in northern England), where two-thirds of the male population was unemployed.

FIGURE 28.3 *Sir Oswald Mosley.* Fascist movements—or similar authoritarian movements that were both antidemocratic and anticommunist—existed in many countries in the 1930s. In this photograph, British fascists, dressed in the blackshirt uniforms made infamous on the continent, give the Nazi salute to Sir Oswald Mosley, a former member of parliament who was the leader of the British Union of Fascists.

shops in 1938 was 556 percent of the rate in 1900.) The unemployed marched on Parliament—one protest was known as the Jarrow Marches because much of that town marched to London in 1936 when unemployment there hit 96 percent, closing virtually every store in the town. British democracy survived, but not without enduring the birth of Fascist and racist movements such as Sir Oswald Mosley's British Union of Fascists, founded in 1932. British Fascism initially obtained the support of some prominent figures and the endorsement of one major newspaper (the *Daily Mail*). But Mosley increasingly adopted German **anti-Semitism** (blaming the international crisis on "Jewish masters of usury"), and his Blackshirts ("thugs" in the style of the Italian Fascist Party) became increasingly involved in **street violence.** The government responded to a street battle in east London in 1936 with **anti-Fascist legislation** (the Public Order Act of 1937), and the movement went into decline. Mosley was jailed at the start of World War II.

The Depression and the Stavisky Scandal in France.
The French Third Republic came even closer to collapsing. French unemployment quintupled in

TABLE 28.5 UNEMPLOYMENT DURING THE GREAT DEPRESSION, 1930–1939

The data in this table are from the League of Nations.

			Percentage of Labor Force Unemployed			
YEAR	UNITED STATES	BRITAIN	GERMANY	NETHERLANDS	NORWAY	POLAND
1930	7.8	14.6	15.3	9.7	16.6	8.8
1931	16.3	21.5	23.3	18.1	22.3	12.6
1932	24.9	22.5	30.1	29.5	30.8	11.8
1933	25.1	21.3	26.3	31.0	33.4	11.9
1934	20.2	17.7	14.9	32.1	30.7	16.3
1935	18.4	16.4	11.6	36.3	25.3	16.7
1936	14.5	14.3	8.3	36.3	18.8	15.6
1937	12.0	11.3	4.6	29.2	20.0	14.6
1938	18.8	13.3	2.1	27.2	22.0	12.7
1939	16.7	11.7	n.a.	21.8	18.3	14.1

Source: *Annuaire statistique de la Société des Nations, 1939–1940* (Geneva: League of Nations, 1940, pp. 70–71).

n.a. = not available

Questions: Note the different patterns of unemployment data in these countries and try to explain national variations. Why would Poland have lower unemployment in the early 1930s? Why did German unemployment drop off so sharply?

1932 and passed the 1.3 million mark in early 1933. The government, long considered unstable, became a series of short-lived cabinets: four different cabinets in 1930, three in 1931, five in 1932, four in 1933, and four in 1934. As one wit observed, tourists went to London to see the changing of the guard and to Paris to see the changing of the government. The Stavisky (Stuh-vis'-key) affair of 1933–1934 showed that the French government was as corrupt as it was ineffectual. This scandal began when Alexandre Stavisky, a Ukrainian-born swindler, confessed to selling fraudulent bonds with the assistance of prominent politicians. Stavisky's death in a reported suicide and the dubious nature of investigations created a volatile antiparliamentary mood in France.

The Leagues and French Fascism. Several far-right-wing organizations, known as *ligues* (leagues) flourished in France during these troubled years. Colonel de la Rocque's *Croix de feu* (The Fiery Cross) and Pierre Taittinger's *Jeunesses Patriotes* (Young Patriots) had grown during the economic hard times, and they promoted the doctrine that it was "time to put rotten parliamentarianism on vacation." Members of the French Fascist leagues seized on the Stavisky scandal as the excuse for antiparliamentary riots in central Paris in February 1934. Thousands of right-wing demonstrators battled with police in an attempt to attack the Chamber of Deputies. The republic survived the Stavisky riots, but 15 people were killed and more than 1,000 injured. As in Britain, the government responded with legislation to control right-wing extremism, but Fascist plots (such as the *Cagoulard*—the "hooded men" conspiracy of 1938) were still being discovered on the eve of World War II.

Léon Blum and the Popular Front in France

The Popular Front. The depression, the Stavisky affair, and the February 1934 riots led, paradoxically, to a strengthening of the Third Republic, because they frightened political leaders into creating a powerful coalition of left-wing groups, known as a **popular front.** The French Popular Front of 1936–1938 united parties that had long fought each other, because fears of a Fascist Putsch brought them together. Moderate

Democrats of Édouard Daladier's (Dah-lah'-dee-ay) Radical Party, democratic Socialists, trade unionists, and even Communists (frightened by the spread of Fascism, which was strongly anti-Communist) supported the Popular Front under the leadership of Léon Blum (Bloom), the head of the Socialist Party. Blum, a Jewish intellectual and a distinguished jurist, had entered politics at the time of the Dreyfus affair. He opposed both Poincaré's conservatism and French Communism while rebuilding the democratic socialist party (SFIO) during the 1920s. After riots in 1934, France became alarmed about the strength of Fascism, and Blum took the lead in creating the Popular Front. He brought it to victory in the 1936 parliamentary elections, becoming the first Jewish prime minister in French history.

Léon Blum. Léon Blum held office for only 1 year before the Popular Front began to crumble, but he achieved Europe's most profound response to the depression: a 40-hour workweek, paid annual vacations of 4 weeks, a 12 percent raise for workers and civil servants, and the acceptance of collective bargaining. Under Blum's direction, France also abandoned some aspects of capitalist economics: he nationalized the Bank of France and parts of the armaments industry and undertook government regulation of basic food prices. The Blum government also restored a degree of order in France and calmed the worst fears of industrialists by ending the wave of sit-down strikes and factory occupations that had swept the country and by abandoning socialist plans to nationalize more industries. When Blum proposed further financial reforms in 1937, however, the Radical Party deserted him and he was obliged to resign, to the cheers of many conservatives who felt "better Hitler than Blum."

THE SPANISH SECOND REPUBLIC AND THE SPANISH CIVIL WAR (1931–1939)

Spain entered the twentieth century in an age of governmental instability under a constitutional monarchy (1874–1923) that lasted until General Primo de Rivera created a military dictatorship (1923–1930). The Spanish Second Republic was created in 1931 after Primo de Rivera allowed local elections, which produced an outpouring of support for a republic.

The Spanish Republic. The Spanish republic of 1931 was among the frailest of Europe's parliamentary democracies, and it faced many threats. A regional revolt broke out in 1934, when Catalonia pro-

claimed itself independent. The republic was also internally divided between groups of moderate Catholic Republicans led by Prime Minister Alcalá Zamora and groups of more radical, **anticlerical** Republicans led by Manuel Azaña. Its radical constitution alarmed landowners, who feared **nationalization** of property; the leaders of the church, who resisted its program of **secularization;** and the army, whose officer corps was greatly reduced by forced retirements at half pensions. These groups formed the nucleus of a resurgent right-wing in Spanish politics. Primo de Rivera's son launched a Spanish Fascist movement known as the *Falange* in 1933; it later stopped using the word *Fascist,* but it remained emphatically antidemocratic. The program of the Falange was clear: "Our State will be a totalitarian instrument. . . . We shall immediately abolish the system of political parties."

The Spanish Civil War. The crisis of Spanish democracy culminated in the Spanish Civil War of 1936–1939. War began when General Francisco Franco led a revolt of army units stationed in Spanish Morocco, and it spread to become an army revolt in the garrison towns in Spain. The Falange joined General Franco in forming a coalition of Nationalists seeking to abolish the Second Republic and restore traditional order to Spain. A similar coalition of Loyalists (loyal to the republic), including Catalan rebels, defended the republic. The Loyalists held most of the great cities of Spain, such as Madrid and Barcelona, but the Nationalists held most of the military strength. Franco was the son of a naval paymaster, educated in a military academy, and made his reputation in colonial wars in the 1920s. His reckless bravery in combat (perhaps a compensation for his insecurity at standing only 5'3'') made him the youngest general in Europe (at age 33) in 1926. His mixture of nationalism, military dictatorship, Falangist Fascism, monarchism, and clericalism did not precisely fit the mold of Fascist movements elsewhere, but it won the military support of both Mussolini, who sent Franco 75,000 soldiers, and Hitler during the civil war. The Soviet Union similarly aided the republic. General Franco, proclaimed chief of the Spanish state by the insurgents in late 1936, led the Nationalist armies in the steady destruction of the republic and the Basque and Catalan separatist regimes. The civil war ended in 1939 after Barcelona fell to an assault by allied Nationalist and Italian troops, then Madrid surrendered. Over 3 years of fighting, more than 700,000 people died in combat and at least 100,000 civilians died. More than 100,000 Spaniards disappeared into Franco's **concentration camps** or were simply executed. General Franco replaced the republic with a dictatorship that lasted until his death in 1975.

THE GLOBAL STRUGGLE FOR FREEDOM FROM EUROPE

The most ironic problem confronting the European democracies was that they opposed self-government outside of Europe. Native leaders, nationalist organizations, and armed uprisings already characterized the global resistance to imperialism before 1914. The success of Japanese arms in 1905 and Chinese revolutions in 1900 and 1911 inspired Asian Nationalists, just as the Young Turk Revolution of 1908 and the Arab Revolt of 1916 stirred the Islamic world. By 1919, most regions of the world heard voices such as that of the Bengali poet Rabindranath Tagore, who won the Nobel Prize for Literature for the simple force of lines such as his prayer, "My father, let my country awake."

Empires and the World War. World War I exposed the vulnerability of European armies and eroded the moral position of Western propaganda. The Allies had proclaimed that they were fighting to make the world "safe for democracy." They had promised peace based on principles such as **"national self-determination"** (in the words of Wilson's Fourteen Points), and they recruited millions of Africans and Asians to serve Europe under these banners. India sent 1.3 million soldiers and replacement laborers to aid Britain; Algeria, Indochina, and West Africa sent 650,000 to France. A few colonial voices had questioned the war, as John Chilembwe did in East Africa (see Document 28.4). He simply asked why Africans were "invited to shed our innocent blood in this world's war." (Chilembwe wound up being shot by the police.) Most Nationalists, including Ghandi, stood by their wartime governments until 1918, hoping that their loyalty would be rewarded.

Resistance to Postwar Neo-Imperialism. But World War I did not bring democracy or national self-determination to Africa and Asia. Instead, it created new colonies (particularly in the Middle East) through the League of Nations **mandate system** of assigning territory, like former Ottoman or German lands, to the great powers to govern. Before the ink had dried on the peace settlements, Nationalists again challenged European imperialism. An Egyptian nationalist party, the Wafd, led an insurrection in 1919 and thereafter combined passive resistance and terrorism until the British granted them independence in 1922. A Syrian national congress proclaimed independence from France in 1920, and a similar congress at Nablus in 1922 called for the independence of Trans-Jordan and Palestine from Britain. The French rejected Syrian independence and took Damascus by force; thereafter they faced a decade of Druse rebellion and an all-out war in 1925–1927.

DOCUMENT 28.4

JOHN CHILEMBWE ON THE EUROPEAN EMPIRES IN AFRICA (1914)

We understand that we have been invited to shed our innocent blood in this world's war. . . .

On the commencement of the war we understood that Africa had nothing to do with the civilized war. But now we find that the poor African has already been plunged into the great war. A number of our people have already shed their blood, while others are crippled for life. And an open declaration has been issued. A number of police are marching in various villages persuading well built natives to join in the war. The masses of our people are ready to put on uniforms ignorant of what they have to face or why they have to face it.

We ask the Honorable Government of our country which is known as Nyasaland, Will there be any good prospects for the natives after the end of the war? Shall we be recognized as anybody in the best interests of civilization and Christianity after the great struggle is ended? . . .

Let the rich men, bankers, titled men, storekeepers, farmers and landlords go to war and get shot. Instead the poor Africans who have nothing to own in this present world, who in death leave only a long line of widows and orphans in utter want and dire distress are invited to die for a cause which is not theirs. . . . We hope in the Mercy of Almighty God that some day things will turn out well and that Government will recognize our indispensability, and that justice will prevail.

From Chilembwe, John, *The Nyasaland Times,* November 26, 1914. In R.C. Bridges, et al., eds., *Nations and Empires* (London: St. Martin's, 1969).

Question: Are Chilembwe's arguments primarily shaped by the experience of colonialism or by universal values that might have shaped European opinion too?

Zionism and Palestine. The British granted Trans-Jordan autonomy in 1923 and independence in 1928, but they kept control of Palestine, where the question of a Jewish state was already an explosive issue. The European-based **Zionist movement** (dedicated to the creation of a Jewish state) had grown significantly, and the British had promised "a national home for the Jewish people" in the Balfour Declaration of 1917. But Jewish immigration into Palestine led to anti-Jewish riots in 1921 and 1929, so the British backed down and curbed immigration in 1930. A Pan-Arab Congress of 1937 called for Palestinian independence and condemned the projected Jewish state, but neither Palestinians nor Zionists would accept British compromises.

Gandhi and Civil Disobedience. Anti-imperialism took a different form in India. Ghandi began his nonviolent **civil disobedience** movement, the *satyagraha,* in April 1919 and the noncooperation movement in 1920. He was jailed in 1922 but still insisted on nonviolence: "I discovered in the earliest stages that pursuit of the truth did not admit of violence being inflicted upon one's opponent, but that he must be weaned from error by sympathy and patience." The Indian nationalist movement, known as the Congress, grew increasingly radical yet accepted Ghandi's doctrines. By the 1930s, Ghandi had become such a revered leader that when he announced a "fast unto death," the British capitulated to his demands in 6 days.

Anti-Imperialism in Asia. Other patterns of anti-imperialism flourished in the Far East. A scholarly Buddhist monk, U Ottama, led Burmese resistance to Britain by blending religious revival and nationalism. Islam similarly strengthened nationalism in the East Indies; on the island of Java (modern-day Indonesia), the Sarekat Islam had 2.5 million members opposing the Dutch in 1919. When Asian nationalist movements did not ally with such religious revivals, they often found secular support in newly formed Communist parties. The Indonesian Communist Party, organized in 1920, was typical; it drew more members by linking poverty with opposition to the Dutch than by linking poverty to Marxist-Leninist analysis. In French Indochina, Ho Chi Minh (a pseudonym meaning "He Who Enlightens") likewise found supporters for his Vietnamese Young League of Revolutionaries by uniting nationalism and communism.

MUSSOLINI AND FASCIST ITALY (1919–1939)

The Italian constitutional monarchy survived World War I, although the king held little power. Victor Emmanuel III (reigned 1900–1947), the grandson of the monarch of the Risorgimento, remained a figurehead monarch throughout the Fascist era. Italians had been slowly creating a parliamentary democracy, although they were accustomed to fewer civil liberties than existed in Britain or France. An electoral law of 1912 introduced "universal manhood suffrage" and another gave proportional representation (but not yet women's suffrage) in 1919.

Italy and World War I. Italy had candidly fought World War I for territorial compensation. It had quit the Triple Alliance and joined the entente powers for the deal they offered in the Treaty of London (1915): Italy would annex the frontier province of the Tyrol,

the Istrian Peninsula at the head of the Adriatic Sea, the Dalmatian coast opposite Italy, and an African colony. When Premier Vittorio Orlando asked for this territory at the peace conference, however, President Wilson, who had not participated in the London Treaty, insisted that those regions be distributed on the basis of nationality. Consequently, Italy received only the southern Tyrol and Istria; the town of Fiume and the Adriatic coast became part of Yugoslavia. Angry Italian Nationalists, the **irredentists,** continued to demand the unredeemed territories. Italy paid heavily for its new territory: 5 million men had been called to military service, and 500,000 were killed in combat and an additional 2.2 million were **casualties** (all forms of war injuries). Italy suffered the devastation of Venetia, a huge national debt, 400 percent inflation (see Table 28.6), massive unemployment, and violent social unrest.

Mussolini and the Rise of Fascism. The combination of embittered nationalism and economic hardship produced many authoritarian movements in Europe; in Italy, it led to Fascist dictatorship. Benito Mussolini founded the Italian Fascist movement at Milan in 1919. Mussolini, the son of a radical blacksmith who had named him in honor of Benito Juárez (the Mexican anticlerical), had been an elementary

---

TABLE 28.6 INFLATION AND THE COST OF LIVING IN ITALY

In this table, the base 1914 cost of living = 100. Total inflation during World War I (1914–1918) was 264.1 percent; during demobilization (1919–1921), 55.5 percent; and during the war and demobilization (1914–1921), 416.8 percent.

YEAR	COST OF LIVING INDEX	ANNUAL INFLATION RATE (%)
1914	100.0	—
1915	107.0	7.0
1916	133.9	25.1
1917	189.4	41.4
1918	264.1	39.4
1919	268.1	1.5
1920	352.3	31.4
1921	416.8	18.3

Source: Instituto centrale di statistica, *Sommario di statistiche storiche italiane, 1861–1955* (Rome: 1955, p. 172).

Question: When prices rise so steeply and so constantly, which social groups suffer the most and which ones might benefit?

school teacher, a trade union organizer, and a socialist journalist before the war. At the start of the fighting, he converted to vehement nationalism; he served as a private until being wounded and discharged. At the end of the war, he organized angry unemployed veterans at Milan into the *Fascio di Combattimento* (Combat Group). These black-uniformed street fighters (Blackshirts) embraced his program of strict discipline and authority. They accepted an ancient Roman symbol of such authority, the *Fasces* (a bundle of rods bound around an axe), which led to their name *Fascisti,* or Fascists. They accepted funding from large landowners and industrialists to use violence to break up trade union meetings, beat up striking workers, and terrorize peasants. During the Italian "red scare" of the *biennio rosso* (1918–1920) when Socialists and Communists led constant strikes, Mussolini built Fascist popularity by a mixture of extreme nationalism and violent anti-Bolshevism. Between 1919 and 1921, the Blackshirts progressed from bullies into killers. They believed, as Mussolini put it, that "a certain kind of violence is moral."

Italian Fascism. In 1921, Mussolini organized **Fascism** as a political party, and his doctrine (see Document 28.5) provides the model for understanding the varieties of European Fascism in the interwar years. The essential element of Fascism was a political program vehemently opposed to all other forms of government. It was a counterrevolutionary revolution, opposed to the revolutionary tradition of 1789, which encouraged liberal-democratic forms of parliamentary government across Europe, and equally opposed to the new revolutionary tradition of 1917, which stimulated socialist or Communist forms of government. Yet, it was not a reactionary demand to return to monarchical authority. The Fascist alternative offered a strong authoritarian government (which became totalitarian government) buttressed with nationalism and militarism. Fascist **totalitarianism,** soon established with local variations in many European countries, was similar to Communist totalitarianism in creating a one-party state that was headed by a single leader with dictatorial powers; maintained in power by a secret police and the use of violence; and unrestrained by constitutional laws, liberties, and thoughts of human rights. Such totalitarianism differed from Communist totalitarianism by stressing nationalism instead of internationalism, by re-

jecting class conflict (old aristocrats and wealthy bourgeois could both flourish), and by preserving capitalist concepts such as private property. Mussolini's variety of Fascism produced a less totalitarian dictatorship than subsequent varieties (especially Nazi Germany). He packaged his antiparliamentary, anti-Communist nationalism in a rhetoric about heroism, courage, and sacrifice. He created a **cult of leadership** around himself in the role of Il Duce (the leader) and promised leadership that would change the peace treaty and the economic crisis.

The Fascist Seizure of Power. Mussolini's appeal attracted enough votes under proportional representation to elect him and thirty-four supporters to the Chamber of Deputies in 1921. Mussolini won less than 10 percent of the vote, yet he successfully exploited Italian troubles and government weakness to gain dictatorial powers in 1922. This began with the "march on Rome" in October 1922, when Mussolini led thousands of Fascists in a demonstration seeking his appointment as premier. "Either they will give us the government or we shall seize it," Mussolini said. When armed Fascists seized arsenals, railroad stations, and telephone and telegraph offices, the king relented and appointed Mussolini to office. Within 1 month, he persuaded Parliament to give him dictatorial powers for 1 year to restore economic order without the delays of the democratic process. Mussolini used his power to pack the courts, the administration, and local government with his supporters; simultaneously he browbeat the king into naming a Fascist majority in the Italian Senate. As

FIGURE 28.4 *The Fascist March on Rome.* The culmination of Mussolini's seizure of power in postwar Italy came on October 28, 1922, when he personally led a demonstration—a march of thousands of fascists—demanding that the king name him prime minister. In this photograph of the leaders of the march, Mussolini is in the center, wearing white diagonal sash.

THE LEADERS OF EUROPEAN FASCISM

European totalitarian movements of the 1930s typically used simple new titles, such as "leader," for the dictator. Adolph Hitler became the *der Führer* (the leader), Benito Mussolini became *Il Duce* (the leader), and Francisco Franco became *el caudillo* (the head). As these photographs show, fascist dictators also preferred the image of being military men rather than political leaders.

Hitler. Adolph Hitler (1889–1945) was one of the angry World War I veterans who joined the reactionary movement against democratic government after the war. He founded an extremist group and attempted to seize power in Munich in 1923 in the "Beer Hall Putsch." This act of treason led to a 5-year prison sentence, during which he dictated the text of his hate-filled book, *Mein Kampf,* outlining his opposition to democracy, the peace treaty, and Jews. After his parole, Hitler built his extreme nationalist party, the Nazi Party, and used a mixture of legal and violent means to reach the chancellorship of Germany in 1933. Within months he had taken dictatorial powers and soon prepared to lead Germany into a war that would devastate Europe and lead to millions of deaths. He committed suicide in the last days of the war.

his dictatorial powers neared their expiration, Mussolini issued a new electoral law, the Acerbo Law of 1923, which abolished proportional representation and awarded 67 percent of the Chamber of Deputies to the party with the most votes, even if it obtained only one-fourth of the votes.

Mussolini and the Fascist Party built their dictatorship on the parliamentary elections of 1924. They exploited their control of the courts and local government, used direct intimidation and violence as needed, and relied on outright fraud in counting the votes. This combination earned the Fascists a two-thirds majority in Parliament and a Fascist government. When a leader of the Socialist Party, Giacomo Matteotti (Maht-tay-oat'-tee) (whose book *The Fascisti Exposed* details Fascist political violence), denounced this undemocratic seizure of power, Fascist thugs kidnapped him and stabbed him to death. When socialist, liberal, and Catholic deputies walked out of Parliament in a protest known as the Aventine Secession, the Fascist majority permanently expelled them. Journalists critical of Fascism were jailed.

Mussolini. Benito Mussolini (1883–1945) began his political career as a socialist journalist and edited the Socialist Party's newspaper *(Avanti)* at the start of World War I, but the war converted him into an ardent nationalist. After the war (in which he served as a private and was wounded), Mussolini joined the right-wing combat against his old friends on the left, and in 1919 he organized the first Fascist group in Italy, the *Fascio di Combattimento.* By 1921, these street thugs were organized as a political party and, by 1922, Mussolini had seized control of the government. As dictator of Italy for more than 20 years, he led his country into a disastrous war, at the end of which Italian partisans executed him.

Franco. Francisco Franco (1892–1975) built his career as a military leader in the Spanish empire, leading the fight against the Riffs in Morocco, where Spanish armies won a major victory in 1926. Franco and other military leaders were not sympathetic to the Spanish Republic, founded in 1931, and when the civil war began in 1936, Franco was chief of the Spanish General Staff and immediately organized the army to fight against the republic. By the fall of 1936, Franco was commander-in-chief of the insurgents and claiming the title of Chief of the Spanish State. With the military assistance of Fascist Italy and Nazi Germany, Franco forces defeated the republican loyalists and regional separationists in 1939, when he assumed dictatorial powers. Although sympathetic to the Nazis (he sent troops to help fight Russia), Franco kept Spain out the Second World War and thus his dictatorship survived into the late twentieth century.

Fascist Dictatorship. The Fascist dictatorship in Italy quickly uprooted democratic society. All opposition parties—monarchical, democratic, Catholic, and socialist—were abolished, creating a one-party state. Universal suffrage was abolished, and voting was defined by the amount of taxes paid. In Mussolini's words, "We have buried the putrid corpse of liberty." A Fascist Grand Council named members of Parliament and voters ratified their selections, yet Mussolini kept the power to govern by decree. Strict press censorship was installed. All local officials were made appointive. A **secret police** (the OVRA), using a law that permitted capital punishment for political offenses, cracked down on opponents of the regime. Despite such powers, Mussolini never created a total dictatorship because he never broke the independent power of the army, the Catholic Church, or the wealthy upper classes.

Fascist Economics. The Fascist regime focused its attention on economic recovery, and it had noteworthy successes although problems remained. Mussolini

MUSSOLINI ON FASCISM (1932)

Although this essay appeared under Mussolini's name, as the summary of his thought, it was actually written by Giovanni Gentile (1875–1944), a philosophy professor at the University of Rome who had served as Mussolini's Minister of Education.

Fascism . . . was born of the need for action, and it was itself from the beginning practical rather than theoretical; it was not merely another political party but, even in the first two years, in opposition to all political parties. . . . The necessity for action did not permit research or any complete elaboration of doctrine. The battle had to be fought . . . against Liberalism, Democracy, Socialism, and the Masons. . . .

Fascism . . . believes neither in the possibility nor the utility of perpetual peace. It thus repudiates the doctrine of Pacifism—born of a renunciation of the struggle and an act of cowardice in the face of sacrifice. War alone brings up to its highest tension all human energy and puts the stamp of nobility upon the peoples who have the courage to meet it. . . .

Fascism (is) the complete opposite of . . . so-called scientific and Marxian socialism . . . Fascism, now and always, believes in holiness and heroism; that is to say, in actions influenced by no economic motive, direct or indirect. . . . Above all, Fascism denies that class war can be the preponderant force in the transformation of society.

. . . After Socialism, Fascism combats the whole complex system of democratic ideology, and repudiates it. . . . Fascism denies that the majority, by the simple fact that it is a majority, can direct society . . . [and] it affirms the inequality of mankind, which can never be permanently leveled. . . . Fascism denies, in democracy, the absurd conventional untruth of political equality. . . . Fascism has taken up an attitude of complete opposition to the doctrines of Liberalism, both in the political field and the field of economics (Capitalism). . . .

The Fascist negation of Socialism, Democracy, and Liberalism must not be taken to mean that Fascism desires to lead the world back to the state of affairs before 1789. . . . Absolute monarchy has been, and it can never return. . . .

The foundation of Fascism is the conception of the State, its duty and its aim. Fascism conceives of the State as an absolute, in comparison with which individuals or groups are relative. . . . The State (is) custodian and transmitter of the spirit of the people, as it has grown up through the centuries in language, in customs, and in faith. . . . Whoever says Fascism implies the State.

From Mussolini, Benito, *The Political and Social Doctrine of Fascism* (London: Hogarth Press, 1933).

Question: What are the central concepts of Fascism seen in this document?

---

abandoned capitalism in favor of **state planning** and state intervention, but he kept private property and profit. These steps never achieved the self-sufficient economy he sought. The "battle for wheat" increased farm acreage and production, but Italy remained dependent on imports. Unemployment was cut sharply by extending education, expanding the army, and hiring thousands for public works projects (such as draining swamps to become farmland). Labor unrest was controlled by abolishing trade unions and outlawing strikes; management was regulated and made to accept state arbitration. To keep a tranquil economy and state direction of it, Mussolini created what he called the **corporate state.** All occupations were organized into **"syndicates"** (a syndicate even existed for intellectuals); groups of syndicates were linked as **"corporations."** Representatives of occupations met in a quasi-legislative body called the National Council of Corporations. The council and a Ministry of Corporations theoretically directed the economy, but the corporate state never had clearly defined powers. It generally supported propertied interests and management, and its biggest creation was a bloated bureaucracy.

HITLER AND NAZI GERMANY (1928–1939)

Adolph Hitler and the Nazi Party similarly exploited the legacies of World War I—angry nationalism and economic crisis—in Germany. Like Mussolini and the Fascists, they mixed the legitimate political process with violence to seize power, destroy democracy, and build a dictatorship.

Rise of the Nazi Party. The Nazis remained a small and ineffective party during the Weimar recovery of the mid-1920s. In the parliamentary elections of 1928, the Nazi Party had a membership of 100,000 and received a meager 2.6 percent of the votes cast. The party attracted some support for its strident nationalism and denunciation of the Versailles Treaty, but its growth chiefly came during economic crisis. Although the full name of the party, the German National Socialist Workers' Party, suggests that it was a working-class party, most urban workers voted against the Nazis. The Nazis drew their electoral strength from small farmers and the lower-middle-class occupations known as the *Mittelstand*—chiefly small shopkeepers, artisans, and retail merchants). Such groups had suffered greatly in the nation's ordeal since 1914 and were strongly nationalistic, vulnerable to economic crises, and without strong voices in the political process. When the depression hit Germany in 1930 and produced high unemployment (30.1 percent in 1932) many people saw a solution in strong leadership.

The Nazi Party in the Depression.

Adolph Hitler seized power through the political crisis of the German depression. Reichstag elections in 1930 showed frightened voters seeking new solutions: both the Communist Party and the Nazi Party registered large gains, and at the time Hitler led a delegation of 107 deputies. Part of this electoral success stemmed from the effectiveness of Nazi propaganda, managed by Joseph Goebbels and presented in spell-casting oratory by Hitler. Goebbels, the chief author of fulsome Nazi propaganda images of a tall, blond, Aryan race of supermen, was himself a short and dark-haired man with a withered foot from childhood polio. In addition to artful propaganda, Nazi success resulted from using the intimidation and violence that Mussolini had taught. Nazi **storm troops**—originally the brown-shirted SA (short for *Sturmabteilungen*, literally "storm troopers") and later Heinrich Himmler's black-shirted SS (short for *Schutzstaffel*, or "defense echelon")—fought street battles, especially against leftists. The growth in Nazi popularity persuaded Hitler to run for the presidency of Germany in 1932, but he was overwhelmingly beaten (20 million to 13 million votes) by the 85-year-old incumbent Field Marshal von Hindenburg. In two separate Reichstag elections that year, the Nazis polled 37 percent and 33 percent of the popular vote but became the largest party in a fragmented Reichstag. Party membership stood at a mere 849,000 of a population of 66 million.

Hitler Named Chancellor.

Hitler became chancellor of Germany by gaining the support of Reichstag conservatives led by Franz von Papen, a Catholic aristocrat and former General Staff officer who had married into one of the wealthy industrial families of the Saar. Von Papen had dedicated his political career to preserving the leadership of the **Junker** and industrial elite, and he believed that Hitler would do this. When Hitler became chancellor in early 1933, his lieutenant, Hermann Goering (a World War I fighter pilot and hero who had won the Iron Cross), became minister of the interior, with control of the police. Hitler immediately

called Reichstag elections. The Nazis increased their electoral violence, harassing opponents, intimidating voters, and even burning the Reichstag building. The Reichstag fire was blamed on Communists and used to justify the suspension of civil liberties, including both freedom of speech and the press.

The Nazi Dictatorship.

Nazi violence achieved 44 percent of the votes and a parliamentary majority through the alliance with von Papen. The Reichstag then voted Hitler dictatorial powers for 5 years in the Enabling Act of March 1933, which allowed him to change the constitution and to promulgate laws. (Similar Enabling Laws had been used to deal with the economic crisis and Ruhr invasion of 1923.) Hitler used these powers to begin a policy that he called *Gleichschaltung* (Glike'-shalt-tung; coordination); this policy simply meant the consolidation of a lasting Nazi dictatorship (see Table 28.7). In the first few months of the Gleichschaltung, the Nazis created a secret police force (the Gestapo), a law permitting the arrest of dissenters, secret trials in People's Courts, and the first concentration camps (Dachau, near Munich, and Buchenwald, near Weimar) for the detention of political opponents. In the first 9 months of the Nazi dictatorship, more than 100,000 people (chiefly political opponents at first) were arrested and sent to the concentration camps. Elective local governments, labor unions, other political parties, the upper house of Parliament, the presidency, and civil liberties were all abolished. The regime did not merely establish censorship, it made censorship a public celebration. In May 1933, Nazis began the practice of public book burnings with a great bonfire in central Berlin. Books whose authors or content were considered decadent or "un-German" (including those by Einstein, Freud, Marx, and Brecht) were committed to the flames by teams of students and professors in their black university gowns. Nazi violence also increased. On the "Night of the Long Knives" in June 1934, Himmler (a frail and sickly man with an enormous drive for power) directed the SS to murder approximately 1,000 people—opponents of the Nazis and unreliable party members, including the leaders of the SA.

Persecution of the Jews.

The Nazi persecution of the Jews (approximately 1 percent of the German population) began almost immediately. Two months after Hitler became chancellor, the state ordered the boycott of all businesses owned by Jews and the seizure of their bank accounts. This government-backed boycott closed many Jewish businesses. The purge of the bureaucracy ousted Jewish civil servants, professors, and public school teachers. The Nuremberg Laws of 1935 (and 250 supplemental decrees) defined Jews as anyone who had one Jewish grandparent (increasing the number of Jews

TABLE 28.7 CONSOLIDATION OF NAZI POWER, A CHRONOLOGY OF THE GLEICHSCHALTUNG

The German Reichstag voted Adolph Hitler dictatorial powers for 5 years in the Enabling Act. Hitler used these powers to consolidate the Nazi dictatorship as a totalitarian state, in a process known as the *Gleichschaltung*.

January 1933	Adolf Hitler and Franz von Papen negotiate alliance of nationalist parties
January 1933	Hitler named chancellor with Hermann Goering as minister of interior
February 1933	The Reichstag Fire: Parliament burned and blamed on Communists
February 1933	Goering reorganizes the police and creates the Gestapo (secret police)
February 1933	Basic civil liberties (freedom of speech, press, assembly) suspended
February 1933	Law allowing for *Schutzhaft* (protective custody) for dissenters
February 1933	Political opponents sent to Dachau, the first concentration camp
March 1933	The Enabling Act gives Hitler dictatorial powers for 5 years
March 1933	People's Court created to try "treason" cases in secret
March 1933	Roundup arrest of German Communists, interred at Oranienburg
April 1933	Elective local governments abolished and Nazi governors appointed
April 1933	The civil service, schools, universities purged
April 1933	Government launches boycott of Jewish businesses
April 1933	Roundup arrest of leading German Socialists
May 1933	Labor unions and strikes outlawed
May 1933	Great Berlin book-burning: 25,000-volume fire
July 1933	All other political parties dissolved
July 1933	Sterilization Law for the disabled, gypsies, blacks
January 1934	Upper House of German Parliament abolished
May 1934	Judicial system overhauled and civil liberties curtailed
June 1934	Night of the Long Knives: purge of the Nazi Party
August 1934	Office of president eliminated and its powers given to the *Führer*, Hitler

Question: At what point in the Gleichschaltung might champions of democracy and liberty have resisted it?

---

to 2.5 million, or 4 percent of the population). These decrees stripped Jews of their citizenship, forbade intermarriage, barred them from many occupations, and restricted where they could live. Discrimination and harassment turned to violence in the late 1930s, and 72 percent of German Jews fled the country before emigration became impossible. On the *Kristallnacht,* the "Night of the Broken Glass" (named for thousands of broken windows), in November 1938, the SS launched a **pogrom.** Rioters killed approximately 100 Jews, trashed more than 7,000 businesses (completely destroying 815 shops), and burned 191 synagogues. More than 20,000 Jews were arrested in the following weeks, and many of them were sent to concentration camps such as Dachau.

Nazi Persecution of Others. Nazi persecution was not limited to the Jews. Political opponents were the first to suffer under the new police state. Communists were rounded up and interred in March 1933, barely 1 month after Hitler became chancellor, and the arrest of leading Socialists followed in April 1933; high office

was no protection, as the prime minister of Oldenburg discovered when he was arrested in early March. Between July 1933 and April 1935, Nazi campaigns were launched against homosexuals, gypsies, the disabled, and members of several religious sects, especially Jehovah's Witnesses. A law of 1933, for example, permitted the government to order the sterilization of the disabled (and several other groups), and tens of thousands of people were forcibly sterilized. This started a campaign that culminated in Operation T4, which began in 1939 to "grant mercy death" to the disabled—which meant the murder of thousands of disabled people. The Nazi attempt to exterminate members of such groups, especially Jews, in the concentration camps (for which the word **genocide** was coined) did not begin until after World War II had started.

Nazi Social Policies. Nazi social policy also affected women, children, schools, and churches. Nazi policy toward women, for example, sought their return to the supposed traditional "women's place": *Kinder, Kirche,*

Küche (children, church, kitchen). This led to efforts to drive women out of the workplace and higher education. The first Nazi economic plan, for example, sought to cut the employment of women by 200,000 per year, and educational policy cut the enrollment of women in German universities from 18,315 in 1932 to 5,447 in 1939. The regime strongly encouraged motherhood, which had long been a central theme of the Nazi program. This led to **pro-natalist** policies ranging from grants for large families and strict laws against abortions to punishments for remaining unmarried. World War II later changed many of these policies, bringing women back into the workplace and the universities, but Nazi ideology remained antifeminist.

Nazi Economics. Hitler, like Mussolini, kept a capitalist economy in the narrow sense that he accepted private property and individual profit; however, he quickly converted Germany to a government-planned and government-directed economy. The Nazi Four Year Plan of 1936 outlined German **autarchy**—a self-sufficient economy. Some industries, such as the Krupp Works and IG Farben, willingly collaborated with the Nazi plan and profited from government backing (and slave labor). Self-sufficiency made striking progress in some fields, such as gasoline production, which was 44 percent synthetic by 1938. Some industries, such as Ruhr coal, profited from Nazi help, such as forced labor, but kept independent policies. Nazi economic policies ended German unemployment. The unemployment rate of 30.1 percent in 1932 hit 4.6 percent in 1937, whereas the rest of the industrialized world remained in double digits. This was achieved through compulsory programs: conscription for military service, employment in state-funded armaments industries, drafted labor in public works projects (such as building the highway system known as the autobahn), and labor camps for young men and women. The regime financed these programs with other extreme measures, including renouncing reparations payments, forcing involuntary loans to the government, and confiscating Jewish wealth (initially a 20 percent tax on Jewish property in 1938). Dictatorship thus achieved a form of recovery. Coal production, which stood at 110 million tons in 1933, reached 188 million tons in 1939 (a 71 percent increase); steel production rose from 7.6 million tons to 23.7 million tons (a 212 percent increase).

STALIN AND SOVIET COMMUNISM (1924–1939)

Among the dictatorships that characterized Europe in the 1930s, none was more harshly totalitarian than the dictatorship that Joseph Stalin built in the Soviet Union. Historians cannot say with certainty how many people died as a consequence of Stalin's horrifying policies of the 1920s and 1930s, but numbers between 10 million and 20 million are usually suggested. The total count of Russian suffering resulting from World I, the civil war, Stalin's dictatorship, and World War II might have added a mind-boggling 50 million deaths to the normal death rate.

The Russian Economy and the NEP. After a decade of world war, revolution, and civil war, the Russian economy lay in ruins in 1921. The output of mining and heavy industries stood at 21 percent of the prewar level, compared with figures closer to 50 percent in Belgium, France, or Germany—Russian pig iron production in 1921, for example, amounted to 100,000 tons, compared with 4.2 million tons in 1913. Exports (and the capital that they raised) had virtually ceased, standing at 1.3 percent of the 1913 total. To address this crisis, Lenin and the Politburo leadership adopted a New Economic Policy (NEP) that mixed Communist theories **of state ownership** and planning with capitalist theories of private ownership and the free market. The NEP, Lenin

FIGURE 28.5 *Nazi Anti-Semitism.* Anti-Semitism was a central element of Nazi doctrine long before the party came to power, and this led to anti-Semitic policies from the earliest days of the regime. One of the most ominous moments came on November 9, 1938, known as the *Kristallnacht* (night of the broken glass). Nazi hooligans attacked Jews (killing more than 100), burnt synagogues, and trashed more than 7,000 Jewish businesses—whose broken windows, shown here, gave Kristallnacht its name.

explained, was a matter of taking one step backward to take two steps forward. Under the NEP, 98 percent of heavy industry, factory manufacturing, mining, and public services were state-owned; simultaneously, however, 90 percent of handicraft manufacturing, small shops, and agriculture remained privately owned. At the time of Lenin's death, 54 percent of all Soviet income still came from the private sector.

The Rise of Stalin. Lenin died in 1924 following his third stroke and a period of speechless incapacitation. He had favored Trotsky to succeed him and urged the removal of Stalin, but Stalin used his leadership post in the Communist Party and maneuvered in the Politburo to isolate Trotsky. During a period of **collective leadership** in the mid-1920s, Trotsky was edged out of the Politburo (1925), out of the party (1927), and out of the country (1929); a Stalinist agent assassinated him in Mexico in 1940. After defeating Trotsky, Stalin then used an ideological battle to divide the Politburo and purge other leaders. The issues were the NEP and Stalin's doctrine known as "socialism in one country." Stalin asserted that the Soviet Union could create a Communist society alone and that the NEP should be retained as the first step. His rivals on the left wing of the Politburo (whom he branded **left deviationists**) backed Trotsky's idea of **permanent revolution**— work for revolution everywhere and continuing revolution in Russia. Stalin won this argument, and the left deviationists were ousted. In 1927, however, Stalin turned against his supporters in that fight; he purged them as **right deviationists** because they still supported the NEP. By 1928, Stalin's dictatorial power was unchallenged. He then announced his "new socialist offensive," borrowing ideas from the left deviationists and abolishing the NEP.

Stalin's Police State and the Gulags. One of the foremost attributes of Stalin's dictatorship was the **police state.** The tsarist secret police and the Bolshevik Cheka (reorganized as the OGPU in 1922) formed the basis of Stalin's secret police, known by a series of Russian acronyms, beginning as the NKVD (in 1926) and ending up as the KGB (from 1954). Under Feliks Dzerzhinsky and Nikolai Yezhov, the Soviet secret police became one of the most feared institutions in the world. The Bolsheviks had already established Holmogor concentration camp in Siberia for political prisoners in 1921 and had begun to use such camps **(gulags)** for forced labor in 1923. Stalin expanded this into an immense network of prison camps—named the Gulag Archipelago by Nobel Prize–winning novelist Aleksandr Solzhenitsyn (see *Daily Life in the Stalinist Police State*). Many details about the gulags remain unclear, but at least 10 million people (18 million by some estimates—some as young as 9 years old) were sent to

such notorious camps as Kolyma or Magadan in eastern Siberia. By 1938, 5 percent of the population was jailed. Prisoners in the gulag labored at preposterous tasks such as building a railroad across the Arctic. At Pelvozh camp on the Arctic Circle, prisoners slept four to a straw pallet, with 3 feet of space each; worked 14-hour shifts through the Siberian winter, except when the temperature fell below minus 50° Fahrenheit; dressed in light clothing and felt boots; and were fed a diet of approximately one thousand calories per day.

Collectivization and the Communist State. Stalin used these instruments of terror to build the Communist state. He ended the NEP and its privately owned shops and farms. The **nationalization** of this property (a process called **collectivization**) led to bitter fights, especially among the successful class of landowning peasants known as the **kulaks.** There were approximately 25 million peasant farms in the Soviet Union in 1928, with a livestock population of 28 million pigs and 66 million cattle. By 1932, collectivization had created nearly 250,000 large state farms *(sovkhoz)*, where the government employed peasant workers to farm state land, and collective farms *(kolkhoz)*, where state land was leased to a peasant community that farmed it as a collective enterprise. In this process, 39 million private farms disappeared. The kulaks resisted collectivization by burning crops, smashing farm implements, and slaughtering livestock. Thus, by 1934, the Soviet livestock population had plummeted to 11 million pigs and 33 million cattle. Stalin answered with a brutal repression aimed at nothing less than "the liquidation of the kulak class." Between 5 million and 6 million peasants were executed in their villages or died in the gulags; another 4 million died in the famine of 1933, a direct consequence of collectivization. Ilya Ehrenburg, the poet of Stalinism, explained: "Not one of them was guilty of anything; but they belonged to a class that was guilty of everything."

Soviet Industrialization and the Five-Year Plan. Stalin used the grains and profits of collectivized agriculture to feed and finance the forced industrialization of the Soviet Union. He placed the economy under a central planning office *(Gosplan)* that drafted a series of **Five-Year Plans** directing the creation of an industrial economy. The first Five-Year Plan (1928–1932) encompassed the collectivization of agriculture and rapid industrialization (see Table 28.8). The cost of these plans in human suffering was horrifying, but they accomplished the goal of industrialization (although they did not meet their production targets in heavy industry).

Russia had lagged far behind Western Europe throughout the nineteenth century; by 1940, however, the Soviet Union had the third largest industrial economy in the world (behind the United States and Germany), and at Stalin's death in 1953 it stood second. The same

DAILY LIFE IN THE STALINIST POLICE STATE

Aleksandr Solzhenitsyn Describes Being Arrested

Aleksandr Solzhenitsyn is a Russian writer who won the Nobel Prize for Literature in 1970. He served 8 years in a concentration camp for the crime of criticizing Stalin in a letter to a friend.

For several decades political arrests were distinguished in our country precisely by the fact that people were arrested who were guilty of nothing and were therefore unprepared to put up any resistance whatsoever. There was a general feeling of being destined for destruction, a sense of having nowhere to escape from the OGPU-NKVD (which, incidentally, given our internal passport system, was quite accurate). . . . People leaving for work said farewell to their families every day, because they could not be certain they would return at night. . . .

By and large, the [police] had no profound reasons for their choice of whom to arrest and whom not to arrest. They merely had over-all assignments, quotas for a specific number of arrests. These quotas might be filled on an orderly basis or wholly arbitrarily. . . .

The majority [of those arrested] sit quietly and dare to hope. Since you aren't guilty, then how can they arrest you? . . . Others are being arrested en masse, and that's a bothersome fact, but in those cases there is always some dark area: "Maybe he was guilty." . . . Why, then, should you run away? After all, you'll only make your situation worse; you'll make it more difficult for them to sort out the mistake. . . . You even walk down the stairs on tiptoe, as you are ordered to do, so your neighbors won't hear. . . .

Sometimes the principal emotion of the person arrested is relief. . . . When all around they were hauling in people like yourself and still had not come for you; for some reason they were taking their time. After all, that kind of exhaustion, that kind of suffering, is worse than any kind of arrest. . . . Once a person was arrested, he was never released; and [there was] the inevitability of a tenner, a ten-year sentence.

From Solzhenitsyn, Alexandr, *The Gulag Archipelago*, trans. Thomas Whitney (New York: Harper & Row, 1973).

Nadezhda Mandelstam Describes Life in Lubianka Prison

Nadezhda Mandelstam (1899–1980) was a Russian writer and the wife of the poet Osip Mandelstam, who died in a Stalinist camp after writing a poem critical of Stalin. Nadezhda's memoirs describe her husband's experience.

At the very first interrogation, M. [her husband] had admitted to being the author of the poem on Stalin, so the stool pigeon's task could not have been to find out something that M. was hiding. Part of the function of these people was to unnerve and wear down prisoners under interrogation, to make their life a misery. Until 1937 our secret police made much of their psychological methods, but afterwards these gave way to physical torture, with beatings of the most primitive kind. . . .

M. was put through the physical ordeal which had always been applied. It consisted mainly of not being allowed to sleep. He was called out every night and kept for hours on end. Most of the time was spent not on actual questioning, but in waiting under guard outside the interrogator's door. . . . The ordeal by deprivation of sleep and a bright light shining right in the eyes are known to everybody.

The principles and aims of mass terror have nothing in common with ordinary police work or with security. The only purpose of terror is intimidation. To plunge the whole country into a state of chronic fear . . . on every floor of every building there must always be several apartments from which the tenants have been taken away. The remaining inhabitants will be model citizens.

From Mandelstam, Nadezhad, *Hope against Hope*, trans. Max Hayward (London: Collins & Harvill, 1971).

Question: What is the most chilling aspect of the police state seen in these memories?

Five-Year Plans that starved the kulaks increased Soviet coal production from 36 million tons (1928) to 166 million tons (1940), steel production from 4 million tons to 18 million tons. Production often fell short of Gosplan's targets (leading to the purge of so-called **plan wreckers**), and both efficiency and quality suffered, but Stalin made the Soviet Union into an industrial power.

The Great Terror. During this time, Stalin relied on police terror to maintain his dictatorship. He began a new series of purges directed by Yezhov in 1936 that later grew into the Great Terror (1936–1939). This **purge** struck millions of members of the Communist Party, including virtually all surviving leaders of the Bolshevik revolution of 1917. Many of Stalin's old comrades, such as Nikolay Bukharin, the intellectual leader of the right deviationists, were convicted in public **"show trials"** after confessing to absurd charges such as being Nazi agents. In 1937, the purge decimated the officer corps of the Red Army, including the chief of staff and seven leading generals. By the end of the Great Terror, approximately 1 million people had been

TABLE 28.8 SOVIET INDUSTRIALIZATION UNDER THE FIVE-YEAR PLAN, 1928–1932

OUTPUT	1928 TOTAL	TARGET IN THE PLAN	1932 TOTAL
Gross industrial production (in billions of 1927 rubles)	18.3	43.2	43.3
Consumer goods production (in billions of 1927 rubles)	12.3	25.1	20.2
Gross agricultural production (in billions of 1927 rubles)	13.1	25.8	16.6
Hard coal production (in millions of tons)	35.4	75.0	64.3
Iron ore production (in millions of tons)	5.7	19.0	12.1
Steel production (in millions of tons)	4.0	10.4	5.9
Electricity generated (in billions of kilowatt hours)	5.1	22.0	13.4

Source: Nove, Alec, *An Economic History of the USSR* (London: Penguin, 1969, 1982, p. 192).

Question: Was the Five-Year Plan of 1928–1932 a success?

killed (including both Bukharin and Yezhov) and 8 million to 10 million people sent to the gulags.

CONCLUSION

During the first half of the twentieth century, Europe experienced as much suffering as it had in any epoch. War, revolution, and epidemic disease had killed more than 25 million people and consumed billions of dollars in 1914–1921, but the following decades experienced only limited respite. Europe needed the entire decade of the 1920s to rebuild its devastated regions and to recover prewar levels of population and production. Even during the recovery of the 1920s, nationalism and economic crisis threatened new catastrophes. By the 1930s, democracy was collapsing in Europe and dictatorship was becoming the typical form of government. These dictatorships, especially the totalitarian regimes in Nazi Germany and Soviet Russia, soon created a degree of suffering that would overshadow even the 25 million dead. Thus, the generation after World War I never recovered the fondly recalled tranquility of the Belle Époque, never truly rebuilt a peacetime society. World War II, which would begin in Europe in 1939, was in fact the continuation and resolution of the first.

Review Questions

- In what ways was the Peace of Paris a harsh treaty and in what ways was it a fair treaty?
- How well did the democracies in Britain and France recover from World War I?
- How were dictatorships established in Italy and Germany?
- What were the characteristics of the totalitarian governments?

For Further Study

Readings

Conquest, Robert, *The Great Terror: A Reassessment* (Oxford: Oxford University Press, 1990). A thorough introduction to the nightmares of Stalinism.

Kershaw, Ian, *Hitler*, 2nd ed. (London: Longman, 2001). A short and accessible condensation of the highly regarded two-volume Kershaw study of Hitler.

Mayer, Charles, *Recasting Bourgeois Europe: Stabilization in France, Germany, and Italy in the Decade after World War I* (Princeton: Princeton University Press, 1975). Excellent introduction to the problems of establishing democracy after the war.

References

Cannistraro, Philip V., ed., *Historical Dictionary of Fascist Italy* (Westport, CT: Greenwood, 1982).

Cortada, James W., ed., *Historical Dictionary of the Spanish Civil War, 1936–1939* (Westport, CT: Greenwood, 1982).

Kirk, Tim, ed., *The Longman Companion to Nazi Germany* (London: Longman, 1999).

McCauley, Martin, ed., *The Longman Companion to Russia since 1914* (London: Longman, 1998).

InfoTrac College Edition

For additional reading, go to your online research library at *http://infotrac.thomsonlearning.com*.

Using the Subject Guide, enter the search terms:

Stalin	*Hitler*
Mussolini	*Great Depression*

Web Sites

http://www.spartacus.schoolnet.co.uk   A British educational site with sections on Weimar Germany, Nazi Germany, and French interwar politics.

http://www.fordham.edu/halsall/mod/modsbook42.html
This is the "Fascism in Europe" section of the Modern History Sourcebook maintained at Fordham University.

http://www.uncp.edu/home/rwb/hst430_w.htm   A site maintained at the University of North Carolina, Pembrooke, that provides links to numerous sites for Nazi Germany.

EUROPE IN THE AGE OF DICTATORSHIP, 1919–1939

1915	1920	1925	1930	1935	1940

1930–1939: Great Depression in Europe

1936–1937: Popular Front in France

1919–1933: Weimar Republic in Germany

1933–1945: Nazi Regime in Germany

1922–1944: Fascist Regime in Italy

1936–1939: Spanish Civil War

1926–1953: Stalin's Regime in Soviet Union

1919–1923: Peace of Paris Treaties with Germany, Austria, and Turkey
1919: Weimar constitution Creates Republic in Germany
1921: Anglo-Irish Treaty Creates the Irish Free State without Northern Ireland
1922: French Senate Blocks Women's Suffrage
1922: Mussolini's "March on Rome" to Seize Power in Italy
1923: Runaway Inflation in Germany
1923: Hitler's "Beer Hall Putsch" Attempt to Seize Power in Germany
1923: Acerbo Law Gives Mussolini Basis to Establish Dictatorship
1924: Ramsay MacDonald Becomes Britain's First Socialist (Labour) Prime Minister
1924: Death of Lenin
1925: Locarno Treaty Creates Era of Franco-German Cooperation
1926: Stalin Establishes Dictatorship in USSR
1930: Depression Begins in Europe (1929 in U.S.A.)
1930: *Casti connubi* Sets Strict Standards for Catholics
1930: Britain Grants Women Equal Suffrage
1932: Hitler Beaten for Presidency of Germany
1933: Hitler Named Chancellor of Germany
1933: Enabling Act Makes Hitler Dictator
1935: Nuremberg Laws Strip Jews of Citizenship
1936: Léon Blum premier of French Popular Front
1936–1939: Spanish Civil War
1936–1939: Great Terror in USSR

Visit the Western Civilization Companion Web Site for resources specific to this textbook:
http://history.wadsworth.com/hause02/

 The CD in the back of this book and the Western Civilization Resource Center at *http://history.wadsworth.com/western/* offer a variety of tools to help you succeed in this course, including access to quizzes; images; documents; interactive simulations, maps, and timelines; movie explorations; and a wealth of other sources.

FOCUS QUESTIONS

- What problems were so severe that Europeans would enter a general war less than 20 years after ending a general war that had killed 15 million people?
- How were the Axis powers able to conquer most of Europe by 1942?
- How were the Allied powers able to defeat the Fascist alliance that dominated Europe from the Atlantic to Moscow?
- How can the Holocaust be described in understandable terms?
- What were the chief objectives and accomplishments of the victorious Allies?

Chapter 29

EUROPE IN AN AGE OF TOTAL WAR: WORLD WAR II, 1939–1945

*I*n the late summer of 1939, with war already raging in Asia and only days away from beginning in Europe, a famous 60-year-old scientist from Princeton University sat down at a typewriter and wrote a two-page letter that would lead, 6 years later, to the sudden end of World War II and, even later, to the most terrifying aspect of the cold war of the late twentieth century. Albert Einstein, who had won the Nobel Prize in 1921 and had been a professor of physics in Berlin until 1933, was writing to the president of the United States about "recent work" in his field that suggested the need for "quick action on the part of the Administration" because "it may become possible to set up a nuclear chain reaction in a large mass of uranium." This meant the possible development of "extremely powerful bombs," Einstein wrote, and the government might want to note that the United States possessed "only very poor ores of uranium in moderate quantities" and that Germany now controlled the uranium mines of Czechoslovakia and was currently funding studies of uranium at the Kaiser-Wilhelm-Institut in Berlin.

Europe had lived through a generation of great suffering between 1914 and 1939, but the worst was yet to come when the age of total war culminated in the largest war in history. Between 1939 and 1945, World War II killed an estimated 40 million Europeans, most of them noncombatants; the global total neared 60 million. The Soviet Union, which had suffered millions of deaths in World War I, the Russian Revolution and civil war, and Stalin's terror of the 1930s, now endured an estimated 25 million deaths. Simultaneously, in one of the most horrifying chapters in human history, Nazi Germany attempted the complete extermination of the Jews of Europe. Nearly 11 million people, including 6 million Jews, died in German death camps. World War II ended with enormous civilian casualties as a result of the aerial bombardment of major cities. The most ominous bombing came in the events that ended the war in Asia—the detonation of atomic bombs over the Japanese cities of Hiroshima and Nagasaki.

Chapter 29 covers the events of World War II from its origins in the Peace of Paris of 1919 to the diplomatic conferences at the end of the war (no formal peace conference was held), the world's discovery of the Holocaust in Europe, and the war crimes trials (the Nuremberg Trials) of 1945–1946.

THE LONG ARMISTICE AND THE ORIGINS OF WORLD WAR II

The two world wars of the twentieth century were closely related to each other, with the second originating from the disputed outcome of the first. Winston Churchill, whose history of World War II won him the Nobel Prize for Literature, saw the wars as a new Thirty Years' War, interrupted by a long armistice in which weary and devastated countries rebuilt their capacity to fight. The Peace of Paris that ended World War I, and the bitter nationalism that it produced, linked the two wars. Opposition to the peace treaties was especially strong in the dictatorships that emerged during the 1920s and the 1930s, and in some cases, the treaties were a significant factor in the rise of such dictatorships.

The Paris Treaties of 1919. Defeat gave German territory to France, Belgium, Denmark, and Poland; moreover, German Nationalists were outraged by the war guilt clause, reparations payments, military restrictions, and the demilitarization of the Rhineland. Similarly, defeat cost Russia Finland, the Baltic states, Poland, and Bessarabia; the loss of these buffers on Russia's western frontier produced anxiety in the Kremlin because neighboring states were vehemently anti-Communist. Victory failed to satisfy Italian Nationalists because the treaties had denied Italy some of the territory that the Allies had promised as compensation for Italian participation in the war. Even in victorious Britain and France, many asked if World War I had been worth its cost. Many British and American critics of the treaties opposed French efforts to enforce the treaty, making the campaign of German and Italian critics easier.

Revisionism. Battles over revising the peace treaties began while the ink on them dried. In 1919 alone, six armed disputes broke out over territorial settlements in Europe. The new state of Czechoslovakia and the reborn state of Poland fought over a frontier district, as did Austria and Hungary (both now small remnants of the once vast Hapsburg Empire). Italian Nationalists occupied the town of Fiume (Fee-oo'-may) on the Yugoslavian border, which had been denied to Italy in the peace treaty. Germans protested the loss of much of Prussia. Thus, when the League of Nations was formally organized in January 1920, it inherited a host of problems of **revisionism** spawned by the Peace of Paris.

German Reparations. The gravest issue of the early 1920s was the Versailles Treaty's provision for **reparations** payments by Germany to fund the reconstruction of war-torn Belgium and France. A series of Allied conferences labored to refine this question, but German failures to make payments produced the first severe postwar crisis in 1923, when the Weimar government did not deliver in-kind payments of timber. The frustrated Poincaré (Pwan'-car-ay) government in France, supported by the Belgians (but not by the British or the Americans), insisted on enforcing the treaty and occupied part of western Germany to extract in-kind payments (especially coal) directly. This led to a Franco-Belgian occupation of the Ruhr valley in January 1923, to a rupture of cooperation among the former western allies, and to a German campaign of noncooperation. To encourage noncooperation, the Weimar government paid striking workers by simply printing new money, therefore fueling the devastating **inflation** of 1923. The occupation of the Ruhr failed to provide France with reparations and cost the French hostile international opinion; Britain and America organized to save the German economy through the Dawes Plan and the French retreated.

The Spirit of Locarno. A more optimistic mood characterized Franco-German relations during the later 1920s, the result of good relations between two statesmen, Aristide Briand (Bree'-ahnd) and Gustav Stresemann (Stray'-seh-mahn). This short-lived period of hope produced its most noteworthy success in the Locarno (Low-car'-no) Treaty of 1925 in which France, Belgium, Germany, Britain, and Italy guaranteed the western borders of Germany (thereby gaining German acceptance of the retrocession of Alsace and Lorraine to France) and established arbitration treaties to resolve future disputes. In the same spirit, Briand and Stresemann collaborated to secure German admission to the League of Nations in 1926. At its most idealistic moment, the "spirit of Locarno" stretched to create the idealistic Kellogg–Briand Pact (or the Pact of Paris) of 1928, in which the powers accepted a proposal by U.S. Secretary of State Frank B. Kellogg for the renunciation of aggressive war. Although it was ratified by many states and embraced by the League of Nations, this toothless treaty contained no means of enforcement, not even trade sanctions. Dawes received the Nobel Peace Prize in 1925, Briand and Stresemann shared the prize for 1926, and Kellogg received it in 1929, but these awards were more a measure of the world's hopes for peace in Europe than a measure of success at creating and maintaining it.

Italian Irredentism. The most insistent challenge to the peace treaties of 1919 initially came from Italy. Mussolini was in power for less than a year when he attempted to annex the island of Corfu (Core'-foo) (off the coast of Albania and Greece) in mid-1923, only to be forced to back down under British pressure. He had better fortune in advancing Italian **irredentist nationalism** (seeking to incorporate "unredeemed" territory of the nation) by resolving the Fiume question in a 1924 treaty with Yugoslavia, which recognized the

Italian annexation of the town. An Italo-Albanian agreement of 1926 made the small Balkan state a virtual protectorate of Fascist Italy, a preliminary step in the annexation of Albania in early 1939. In 1928, Mussolini negotiated treaties of friendship with two countries with whom he envisioned future wars—Ethiopia and Greece.

The Ethiopian Crisis.

Ethiopia was especially important to Italian Nationalists because it had been the site of the humiliating colonial defeat of 1896 (the battle of Adowa) and had been an important Italian claim denied at Paris in 1919. In 1934, Mussolini used the excuse of border clashes between Ethiopia and the Italian colony of Somaliland to resume the attempted conquest. An Italian invasion of Ethiopia in 1935 led the League of Nations to declare Italy an aggressor state and to apply **economic sanctions** such as an embargo on selling military goods or giving financial assistance to Italy. The League, however, could not agree on severe sanctions (such as shutting off Mussolini's oil supplies) and thus gave little effective support to Ethiopia, which was formally annexed by Italy in 1936. The weakness in dealing with the Ethiopian question was a sign that the Western powers lacked the resolve to stop aggression in Europe.

German Rearmament.

Nazi Germany exploited Western irresolution. Hitler was a product of World War I, and his efforts to abrogate the Versailles Treaty led to World War II. For most of the 1930s, World War I victors did nothing to stop him. Hitler had made his intentions clear in *Mein Kampf* and in German political debate; within weeks of coming to power in 1933, he showed his determination to change the 1919 settlement by walking out of disarmament negotiations and the League of Nations. The most fateful Western inaction came in early 1935, when Hitler bluntly renounced the disarmament provisions of the treaty and reintroduced military conscription. The disarmament clauses had permitted Germany only a small army (seven divisions in 1933) and no air force or submarines. France, and perhaps Poland, could have withstood that Germany. Nazi conscription and construction, however, built an army of 52 divisions by 1939, backed by a *Luftwaffe* (air force) of more than 4,000 planes and a navy with 54 submarines. Hitler found battlefield training for this army by sending units to fight in the Spanish Civil War. The Luftwaffe, for example, polished the dive-bombing tactics that it would use in World War II by bombing the Basque town of Guernica. Fascist cooperation in Spain led to an Italo-German alliance of 1936, which Mussolini dubbed the **Axis.** The Anti-Comintern Pact (1936) expanded this alliance to include Japan, and the Pact of Steel (1939) tightened the Axis.

The Remilitarization of the Rhineland.

Hitler's second great challenge to the Versailles Treaty came in early 1936, when he renounced the Locarno Treaty and ordered the **remilitarization** of the Rhineland (sending the German army into the region bordering France). The French army could have stopped this, but the French and the British governments were indecisive and still bickering over the Ethiopian question. France had a caretaker government on the eve of the most important election of the interwar era—the depression election of Léon Blum's Popular Front government; Britain had a newly elected Conservative government unwilling to send British soldiers to the continent again or to support sanctions in the League of Nations. Consequently, the World War I allies did nothing to stop the remilitarization of the Rhineland, and Hitler (whose rearmament had only just begun) won a risky gamble.

German War Plans.

Hitler's victories in 1935–1936 encouraged him to overthrow the rest of the Versailles restrictions and to plan the expansion of Germany. Hitler outlined his war plans to German military leaders in 1937. The record of that meeting, known as the Hossbach Memorandum, reveals Hitler's thinking: "The German racial community," he said, must have *Lebensraum* (Lay'-bens-rowm; "living space"), and he projected a new European war before 1943 (see Document 29.1).

The Anschluss.

Hitler achieved most of his territorial goals without war. A plebiscite in the Saar (Sar) in 1935 restored that region to Germany by an overwhelming vote, lending some credence to Hitler's demands for revision of the Versailles Treaty. He did not seek further territory, however, until March 1938, when he annexed Austria, an act he preferred to call the *Anschluss* (Ahn'-shloos; union), which had been forbidden by the treaty. After promising to respect Austrian independence and then browbeating the chancellor of Austria, Kurt von Schuschnigg, into disbanding Austrian militias and granting an amnesty to Austrian Nazis, Hitler used the excuse of Austrian unrest (largely provoked by Austrian Nazis) to invade that country. The Austrians did not offer military resistance, and the Western powers again did nothing. (France was again in the midst of a ministerial crisis, and the British were disposed to accept the Anschluss.) In a sham plebiscite, 99.75 percent of Austrians were reported to support the annexation, not counting the votes of, among others, concentration camp internees.

The Sudetenland and the Munich Crisis.

Shortly after the annexation of Austria, Hitler returned to his oratorical theme of "protecting the 10 million Germans living outside the Reich" and reopened the question of Czechoslovakia. He demanded that the Czechs cede to Germany the Sudetenland (Soo-dayt'-n-lahnd), a border region of western Bohemia that contained a German

MAP 29.1. THE ROAD TO WAR, 1936–1939

Germany

German advances:

Reoccupied Rhineland, March 1936

Annexed Austria, March 1938

Annexed Sudetenland, October 1938

Occupied Bohemia and Moravia, March 1939

Annexed Memel, March 1939

Italy

Annexed Albania, April 1939

Poland and Hungary

Annexed Czech territory, 1938 and 1939

( ) Former independent nations: Albania, Austria, and Czechoslovakia

This map shows the important stages in the German and Italian efforts to revise the peace settlement of 1919, beginning with the German remilitarization of the Rhineland in 1936. Note the geopolitics of German revisionism in central and eastern Europe, suggesting that Poland would certainly be a target soon.

population (2.8 million Germans compared with 700,000 Czechs) plus Czechoslovakia's natural defenses (the Sudeten mountains and frontier fortresses) and one-third of its industry. When Hitler stated this claim as giving the Sudetenland "the right of **self-determination,**" the prime minister of Britain, Neville Chamberlain, agreed to meet with him to discuss the Czech question. Although Hitler made clear his intention to annex the Sudetenland, British and French (but not the Czech) diplomats prepared for the Munich Conference of October 1938 with Hitler. There, Chamberlain and the French premier, Édouard Daladier (Da-lah'-dee-ay), agreed to the annexation of the Sudetenland and pressured the Czech government of President Edvard Beneš (Ben'-esh) (who thereafter resigned) into accepting it. The effect was to reduce Czechoslovakia to a Nazi client state. In early 1939, Czechoslovakia was abolished, most of it (Bohemia and Moravia) becoming a German protectorate.

DOCUMENT 29.1

THE HOSSBACH MEMORANDUM ON THE GERMAN NEED FOR WAR, 1937

After World War II, the Allies searched German archives for documents to be used in the Nuremberg war crimes trials. The chief document used by prosecutors to prove that Hitler intended war is known as the Hossbach Memorandum, named for the colonel who took minutes at the meeting. The memorandum records a discussion at a conference between Hitler and German military leaders in November 1937.

The Führer initially said that the subject matter of today's conference was of such high importance that further detailed discussion would probably take place in Cabinet sessions. However, he, the Führer, had decided not to discuss this matter in the larger circle of the Reich Cabinet because of its importance. . . .

The Führer then stated: The aim of German policy is the security and the preservation of the nation, and its propagation. This is, consequently, a problem of space. The German nation is composed of 85 million people, which . . . form a homogeneous European racial body which cannot be found in any other country. On the other hand, it justifies the demand for larger living space (Lebensraum) more than for any other nation. . . . The German future is therefore dependent exclusively on the solution of the need for Lebensraum. . . .

The German question can be solved only by way of force, and this is never without risk. The battles of Frederick the Great for Silesia, and Bismarck's wars against Austria and France had been a tremendous risk. . . . If we place the decision to apply force with risk at the head of the following exposition, we are only left to reply to the questions "when" and "how."

The rearming of the German Army, the Navy, and the Air Force, as well as the formation of the Officers' Corps, are practically concluded. Our material equipment and armaments are modern, with further delay the danger of their becoming out-of-date will increase. . . . In comparison with the rearmament of other nations, which will have been carried out by that time, we shall begin to decrease in relative power. . . . It is certain, however, that we can wait no longer.

From *Nürnberg War Crimes Trials Documents. Nazi Conspiracy and Aggression,* vol. 3 (Washington, DC: U.S. Government Printing Office, 1946–1948).

Question: Does this document prove that Germany's leaders planned a war?

Appeasement. The Western capitulation to Hitler's demands at Munich became known as a policy of **appeasement**—appeasing dictators by surrendering to their demands. A 1938 newsreel records the return of Prime Minister Chamberlain from Munich and clarifies

APPEASEMENT AND THE MUNICH CRISIS, 1938

Neville Chamberlain

Neville Chamberlain was the son of Joseph Chamberlain, the Unionist leader who had broken with Gladstone over Irish Home Rule. He had risen through the Conservative Party in the 1920s and 1930s, becoming prime minister in May 1937 with a foreign policy of urgent rearmament but avoidance of war through appeasement of the legitimate grievances of the Axis powers. He accepted the Anschluss of Germany and Austria, then the German claims to the Sudetenland, on the grounds of preserving the peace. He quarreled with his own foreign secretary (who resigned before the Munich Conference) and drew the ire of hard-liners in his own party, led by Winston Churchill. Churchill was also the son of a prominent Victorian politician, Lord Randolph Churchill, who had fought Gladstone. He strongly opposed Chamberlain's diplomacy and said so loudly. When war came, Churchill succeeded Chamberlain as prime minister in May 1940. The following excerpts are from their statements in Parliament on the Munich crisis.

Neville Chamberlain Defends His Policy

When the House met last Wednesday, we were all under the shadow of a great and imminent menace. War, in a form more stark and terrible than every before, seemed to be staring us in the face. Before I sat down, a message had come which gave us hope that peace might yet be saved, and today, only a few days after, we all meet in joy and thankfulness that the prayers of millions have been answered, and a cloud of anxiety has been lifted from our hearts. . . .

I would like to remind the House of two things it is very essential not to forget . . . The first is this: We did not go there [to the Munich Conference] to decide whether the predominantly German areas in the Sudetenland should be passed over to the German Reich. That had been decided already. . . . What we had to consider was the method. The second point to remember is that time was one of the essential factors. All the elements were present on the spot for the outbreak of a conflict which might have precipitated the catastrophe. We had populations inflamed to a high degree; we had extremists on both sides ready to work up and provoke incidents; we had considerable quantities of arms. . . .

---

his policy: a pleased Chamberlain waves the Munich agreement and proclaims that he has won "peace in our time." Public opinion in both Britain and France shared in the sense of relief that a war, fought over "far-off countries of which we know little" (such as Serbia in 1914), had been avoided. To Chamberlain's opponents, led by Winston Churchill, Chamberlain and Daladier had made craven concessions to avoid fighting (see *Appeasement and the Munich Crisis, 1938*).

The Invasion of Poland. World War II began when Hitler sought to revise the eastern border of Germany, where the Polish Corridor and the free city of Danzig (Dan'-sig) separated East Prussia from the rest of Germany. This, Hitler told the world, was his last territorial demand in Europe. Stalin neither believed this nor waited for further Anglo-French concessions. He answered Western appeasement with the Nazi–Soviet Nonaggression Treaty, also known as the Molotov–Ribbentrop (Moll'-eh-toff–Rib'-ben-trop) Pact for the foreign ministers who signed it. Germany and the Soviet Union promised not to attack each other and to remain neutral in a war with a third party. They sealed the bargain with secret provisions of the treaty reprising the eighteenth-century partition of Poland. Germany would take the western two-thirds while the Soviet Union absorbed eastern Poland and the Baltic republics. This treaty stunned opinion worldwide—Joachim von Ribbentrop, after all, was also the author of the largest anti-Communist alliance in the world, the Anti-Comintern Pact linking Germany, Italy, and Japan. The stunned silence did not last. A few days after concluding this treaty, Hitler used a dispute over Danzig as his excuse to send an army of 1.25 million men into Poland. Two days after the invasion began in September 1939, Britain and France declared war on Germany.

THE YEARS OF AXIS CONQUEST (1939–1942)

Blitzkrieg in Poland. The war in Poland showed that technology had again changed warfare. The use of tanks and airplanes to support an invading army created a powerful offensive force, in contrast to the de-

In my view the strongest force of all, one which grew and took fresh shapes and forms every day, was the force not of any one individual, but was that unmistakable sense of unanimity among the peoples of the world that war somehow must be averted. . . . Ever since I assumed my present office, my main purpose has been to work for the pacification of Europe, for the removal of those suspicions and those animosities which have so long poisoned the air. . . . The question of Czechoslovakia is the latest and perhaps the most dangerous. Now that we have got past it, I feel it may be possible to make further progress along the road to sanity.

Winston Churchill Attacks Appeasement

I will . . . begin by saying the most unpopular and unwelcome thing. I will begin by saying what everybody would like to ignore or forget but which must nevertheless be stated, namely, that we have sustained a total and unmitigated defeat, and that France has suffered even more than we have. . . .

The utmost my right honorable friend, the Prime Minister, has been able to secure by all his immense exertions . . . has been that the German dictator, instead of snatching his victuals from the table, has been content to have them served to him course by course . . . If the House will permit me to vary the metaphor: £1

Winston Churchill

was demanded at the pistol's point. When it was given, £2 were demanded at the pistol's point. Finally, the dictator consented to take £1 17s. 6d. and the rest in promises of good will for the future. . . .

I have always held the view that the maintenance of peace depends upon the accumulation of deterrents against the aggressor, coupled with a sincere effort to redress grievances. . . . Do not suppose that this is the end. This is only the beginning of the reckoning. This is only the first sip, the first foretaste of a bitter cup which be proffered to us year by year unless by a supreme recovery of moral health and martial vigor, we arise again and take our stand for freedom in the olden time.

From Great Britain, *Parliamentary Debates*, House of Commons, 1938. vol. 339, pp. 41–50, 544–552, passim.

---

fensive war of barbed wire and machine guns fought in 1914–1918. Even the infantry had changed, with mechanized units able to move rapidly. The German army (the *Wehrmacht* [Vair'-mockt]) possessed another major advantage: it was more than twice as large as the Polish army, and twenty-two divisions could not stop fifty-four. The Luftwaffe destroyed most of the Polish air force on the ground in the first hours of the war, and the Wehrmacht swept across Poland so fast that the campaign was called a ***blitzkrieg*** (blitz'-kreeg; lightning war). The Germans reached Warsaw in barely 1 week, after a time-warp spectacle of Polish cavalry on horseback, with sword and lance, fighting in the same campaign that introduced German Panzer tanks.

Total War in Poland. The opening days of the campaign presented one of the most hellish aspects of **total war**—the attack on civilian populations. Hermann Goering ordered the "saturation bombing" of Warsaw, and the Polish capital was pounded into submission by Luftwaffe "dive-bombers" *(Stukas)*, which dove toward the city with nerve-shattering whistles mounted in the wings. During a 4-week battle, the Luftwaffe leveled 15

percent of all buildings and killed 40,000 civilians. After 2 weeks of the German devastation of Warsaw, Stalin sent the Red Army into eastern Poland, as foreseen in the Nazi–Soviet Pact and as a precaution against a German seizure of the rich oil resources of Galicia and Romania. German and Russian armies met in central Poland during the third week of the war; a few days later, independent Poland had disappeared. With 60,000 Polish dead and 200,000 Polish wounded, Polish suffering was just beginning. Approximately 6 million Poles would die before the war's end, including more than 3 million Polish Jews. Fleeing to the Russian sector gave no safety; when a Polish army tried this, the Red Army executed 4,200 Polish officers in the Katyn Forest massacre outside Smolensk.

The Phony War of 1940. World War II seemed to have ended before it could spread. Italy and the United States declared neutrality. Britain (sitting behind the traditional security of the English Channel) and France (sitting behind the supposed security of the Maginot [Maj'-eh-no] Line fortifications built across eastern France in the 1920s and 1930s) found themselves in a

MAP 29.2. WORLD WAR II IN EUROPE AND NORTH AFRICA

World War II: Europe and Africa

- German-Italian Axis: 1939
- Axis satellites and allies: 1941
- Axis conquests: 1939–1942
- Allied powers and areas under Allied control
- Neutral nations
- Axis offensives: 1939–1942
- Farthest Axis advance: 1941–1942
- Allied offensives: 1942–1945
- Soviet annexations: 1939–1940

Note the arrows depicting the early victorious campaigns of the Axis powers and the shading to show the furthest extent of Axis conquest, which stretched from the Pyrenees Mountains between Spain and France almost to the Caspian Sea in south Asia. Then note the arrows showing the Allied counteroffensives that met in central Germany 1945.

"phony war," sarcastically called the *sitzkrieg* (sitting war). Stalin took advantage of this moment to annex the Baltic states and then, in November 1939, to attack Finland. The Finns held out for weeks behind exceptional fortifications devised by their commander, General Carl von Mannerheim, who refused to concede territory to the Russians, even after Stalin bombed Helsinki: "We shall fight to the last old man and the last small child. We shall burn our forests and houses . . . and what we yield will be cursed by the scourge of God." The Finns hoped for Western aid that never arrived. The League of Nations expelled the USSR, and many countries sent limited supplies and sympathy, but the Finns were forced to surrender in March 1940 (after the Russian manpower advantage reached fifty-to-one) and to yield frontier territory.

The Atlantic War. The war continued in the west in 1939–1940, but it was hidden from sight, on the high seas. Britain's lifeline remained, as it had been in World War I, on the Atlantic. German submarines (*Unterseeboots*, or **U-boats**) had nearly beat the British in the first war, and an experienced U-boat commander, Admiral Karl Doenitz, now headed the German navy. However, Hitler (like Napoleon before him) had paid far less attention to naval preparation for war than he lavished on his army, leaving Doenitz a total submarine fleet of only fifty-six vessels in 1939. Doenitz launched total war on the seas (including ordering attacks on passenger ships in convoy for Britain), and the battle of the Atlantic began shortly after the invasion of Poland. A British liner was sunk by a German U-boat on the first day of the war, and **"wolf-pack"** U-boat tactics sank nineteen ships in 2 weeks and forty before the fall of Poland. In two shocking episodes for British morale, a U-boat sank a major British aircraft carrier (with the loss of 514 men) in September, and another snuck into the British base at Scapa Flow and sank the battleship *Royal Oak*. By spring, Doenitz's men had sunk 688,000 tons of merchant shipping. As the German U-boat fleet increased, so did the toll in the battle of the Atlantic. By 1942, it had reached 14 million tons.

The Invasion of Denmark and Norway. The sitzkrieg ended in April 1940, when Germany attacked Denmark (with whom it had a nonaggression treaty) on the flimsy pretext that the Danes would not be able to defend themselves against an Allied attack. In reality, this attack was Germany's first step in controlling Scandinavian iron and steel. The surprised Danes could offer no resistance, and units of the Nazi army reached Copenhagen in only a few hours, forcing the king to capitulate within 24 hours of the start of the war. On the same day as the Danish campaign, units of the Luftwaffe occupied the airports at Oslo and other major towns, and the German navy entered every major fjord on the Norwegian coast. The Norwegians—who had housed and fed thousands of German children during the starvation in the closing phase of World War I—were as astonished as the Danes had been. The king of Norway and the government fled to the north, and Britain and France landed a few troops there, but the Allies (and a Norwegian government in exile) were soon forced to evacuate. German conquest had reached the Arctic Circle. A Nazi sympathizer agreed to lead a **collaborationist government** that cooperated with the invaders, and Major Vidkun Quisling thereby made his last name a synonym for traitor.

The Invasion of Belgium and the Netherlands.

The blitzkrieg came to Western Europe in May 1940 with a German assault on the Low Countries (a 4 AM sneak attack positioned to flank the fortifications of the French Maginot Line) and then on northern France. The great cities of Amsterdam, Antwerp, and Brussels all suffered bombardment; the great port city of Rotterdam (despite being declared an open city) was virtually flattened in withering Stuka attacks, which reduced 2 square miles of the city center (including 25,000 private residences) to rubble. The destruction of Rotterdam convinced the British Royal Air Force (RAF) to bring the same sense of total war to German cities, and this strategy would devastate Germany later in the war. The Dutch army suffered 100,000 casualties (25 percent of the army) in just 5 days of fighting, enough to force a surrender. The queen, and a government in exile, managed to escape to Britain, leaving the Dutch under the brutal rule of a Nazi governor, Artur Seyss-Inquart, a meek little man who plundered the country for nearly 5 years and sent more than 5 million Dutch citizens to forced labor camps in Germany. (Seyss-Inquart would be executed as a war criminal in 1946.) A simultaneous Panzer tank attack on Belgium sliced between France and Belgium, and Brussels fell. The Belgians, who had endured more than 4 years of bloodletting without yielding in 1914–1918, surrendered to the Nazis in 1 week.

The BEF Evacuation from Dunkirk.

The British had sent a large **expeditionary force** (the BEF) to the continent, but this army was cut off and trapped near the coast of the English Channel at Dunkirk (the northernmost port in France), with its entire left flank exposed by the fall of Belgium and the Luftwaffe pounding it at will. Facing almost certain catastrophe, the British chose to evacuate the BEF. In one of the most important retreats in military history, the British used every available boat (mostly civilian) from the English coast to ferry their army back across the channel. Nearly 340,000 men (including 140,000 French and Belgian soldiers) abandoned their equipment and the continental war, but thanks to the armada of 900 small craft (and Hitler's strange decision to halt the Panzer assault at Dunkirk), they survived to fight Germany on more favorable terms.

The Fall of France.

A vulnerable and demoralized France faced the Nazi blitzkrieg without the allies of 1914. Although the French army of 800,000 regular forces and 5.5 million trained reserves was considered the strongest army in Europe, it took no significant action against Germany during the sitzkrieg; instead it sat in the Maginot fortications and awaited a German attack. Many of the strongest units of the French army were lost in the debacle in Belgium, however, and much of the French air force had been destroyed on the ground in a preemptive Nazi attack. Then, 2 days after the Dunkirk evacuation, 120 divisions of the Wehrmacht poured into northern France, outflanking the Maginot Line instead of challenging it. The blitzkrieg shattered quickly assembled French lines, as the Nazis drove past Sedan, the site of the German victory of 1870, and Verdun, the symbol of French resistance in 1916. By mid-June (after less than 2 weeks of fighting), the French army was in chaos, with more than 100,000 casualties. The government evacuated Paris, which lacked significant defenses, to spare it the fate of Warsaw and Rotterdam. With the fall of France seeming imminent, Mussolini declared war on Britain and France, invading the Riviera with an army of 400,000 men. France had been routed. When the government turned to Marshal Henri Philippe Pétain (Pay'-tan), the hero of Verdun, he immediately surrendered. A gleeful Hitler accepted the French surrender in Compiègne, signed in the very railroad boxcar where Imperial Germany had capitulated in 1918 (Hitler ordered the boxcar to be taken back to Berlin as a tourist attraction). The Wehrmacht staged a victory parade down the Champs Elysées and hung a giant Nazi banner from the Eiffel Tower.

Vichy France.

The fall of France led to a German peace much harsher than the Versailles Treaty. Germany reannexed Alsace and Lorraine, then occupied the northern half of France (including Paris) plus the entire Atlantic coast; all the territory was placed under a German military government. This partition of France ended the Third Republic, which had often been a troubled regime but had been Europe's greatest pioneer of republican government in a monarchical world. A **rump state** of southern France, known as Vichy (Vee'-she) France because its capital was the spa of Vichy, was led by the 84-year-old Marshal Pétain and a former conservative premier, Pierre Laval (Luh-vahl'), who served as Pétain's most important deputy. They replaced French constitutional democracy with an authoritarian government that had no constitution,

THE TWO FRANCES IN 1940

Two generals, one a great national hero and the other virtually unknown to most of the nation, claimed to speak for France in 1940. Henri Philippe Pétain the hero of World War I, accepted the crushing defeat of France by the Germans, accepted a small rump state of France (while Germans occupied Paris), accepted a policy of collaboration with the victors, presided over the destruction of the Third Republic (and the arrest of many of its leaders), and proposed the creation of a new France through a "National Revolution." Charles de Gaulle, a little known general who had been a junior officer in the war of 1914–1918, and who would emerge as the greatest political leader of twentieth-century France, insisted that, despite the shocking fall of France, the French were not defeated and they must continue their resistance of German rule. Here are excerpts from their views of two different states of France.

◄ *Henri Philippe Pétain (c. 1940).* Marshal Pétain (1856–1951) had one of the most contradictory careers of the twentieth century—hailed for much of his life as a national hero who had saved France in war, he died in the disgrace being convicted of treason for his collaboration with Nazi Germany in war. In World War I, Pétain had been the French commander at Verdun, where the greatest German offensive of the war was stopped at a terrible price. In World War II, he presided over the armistice of 1940 and the collaborationist Vichy Government that helped the German war effort.

Pétain on the New Order in France, October, 1940

In October 1940 Marshal Pétain broadcast a radio message to the French people. It was his manifesto for a new, antirepublican France.

Frenchmen!

Four months ago, France received one of the biggest defeats in her history. . . . [T]he disaster is but the reflection of the weaknesses and blemishes of the old political regime. Yet many of you were attached to that regime. As you voted every four years, you had the impression that you were free citizens in a free State. . . .

On this mound of ruins we must now reconstruct France. The New Order must not in any sense imply a return. . . .

The new regime will be a social hierarchy. It will not rest on the false idea of the material equality of men but on the necessary idea of the equality of opportunity given to all Frenchmen to prove their ability to serve. . . . So will arise the true elites, which the former regime spent years destroying. . . .

Some may fear that the new hierarchy will destroy the liberty to which they cling and for which their fathers fought at the price of their blood. They need have no fear. Authority is necessary to safeguard the liberty of the State. . . .

---

collaborated with the Third Reich, and launched a Fascist "National Revolution" (see *The Two Frances in 1940*). The Vichy regime symbolized the revolution by changing the French national motto from "Liberty, Equality, Fraternity" to "Work, Family, Fatherland." It underscored the end of liberty by arresting leaders of the Third Republic, such as Léon Blum, who was sentenced to life imprisonment and later sent to the German concentration camp at Buchenwald. Pétain and Laval restricted freedoms, regulated basic institutions, institutionalized anti-Semitism (including rounding up Jews for the Germans), and collaborated significantly in the German war effort (such as conscripting French labor for German war industries).

Charles de Gaulle and Free France.
The highest-ranking leader of France to escape was General Charles de Gaulle (de-Gall'), who had been an obscure brigade

commander in 1939 and whose government post in June 1940 was undersecretary for war. De Gaulle had favored fighting to the bitter end, but when Pétain chose to surrender, de Gaulle fled to London, where he organized a government in exile known as Free France. On his first day in London, he addressed a famous radio appeal to the French people: "Has the last word been said? Has all hope disappeared? Is this defeat definitive? No! Believe me." This powerful broadcast (reproduced on clandestine posters around France) sealed de Gaulle's wartime leadership. By 1941, some 45,000 French troops from the Dunkirk evacuation and French colonies had rallied to him, although the British and Americans tried to replace him.

The Battle of Britain.
The first German defeat came when Hitler turned his attention to Britain in the summer of 1940. To prepare for an invasion of Britain, the

What does freedom, abstract freedom, mean in 1940 to the unemployed worker or the ruined small employer—except freedom to suffer helplessly in a vanquished nation? We are really only losing some deceptive illusions of freedom, in order to make sure of saving the substance. . . . In economic policy . . . two essential principles will be our guides: the economy must be organized and controlled. Coordination of private activities by the State.

De Gaulle's Call-to-Arms, June 18, 1940

The Government, alleging the defeat of our armies, has begun relations with the enemy in order to end the combat.

Yes, we have been overwhelmed by the armored land and air forces of the enemy.

. . . But has the last word been spoken? The last hope disappeared? Is the defeat definitive? No!

Believe me, I who speak to you know the situation and I tell you that nothing is lost for France. . . . Because France is not alone! She is not alone! She is not alone! She has a vast empire behind her. She can ally herself with the British Empire which controls the seas and which continues the struggle. She can, like England, use without limit the immense industry of the United States. . . .

I, General de Gaulle, now in London, summon French officers and soldiers who are now on British territory or who will be, with their weapons or without their weapons, . . . to contact me. Whatever may happen, the flame of French resistance must not be extinguished and will not be extinguished.

Tomorrow, as today, I will speak to France by radio from London.

◀ **Charles de Gaulle (c. 1940).** General Charles de Gaulle (1890–1870) was an obscure military and political figure in 1940. He had served in the infantry and been captured at the battle of Verdun in 1916. After the war, he lectured at the army staff college, where he advocated a new military strategy based on the mobility of tanks. He had just been promoted to brigadier general and named undersecretary of war in 1940 when Germany invaded France. De Gaulle's refusal to accept surrender made him the leader of France's government in exile during the war and France's greatest national hero after the war. It would lead him to a two-term presidency of France (1958–1969) and the leading role in drafting the constitution of France's current government, the Fifth Republic.

From "l'Appel du 18 juin," Olivier Wieviorka and Christophe Prochasson, eds., *La France du XXe siècle: documents d'histoire* (Paris: Seuil, 1994). Trans. Steven C. Hause.

Question: What are the convincing elements of these appeals?

Luftwaffe contested the RAF for control of the skies over the English Channel. The future of Britain, and perhaps of Europe, rested with approximately 5,000 pilots during this battle of Britain and with an untested British invention—**radar**—which enabled them to spot planes 75 miles away from the coast of England. The Luftwaffe sent as more than 2,100 planes over England, greatly outnumbering RAF defenses. During July 1940, the British lost nearly half of the RAF, but they shot down German planes at a higher rate and denied them control of the skies. Hitler dared not risk sending an invasion armada to sea. As the new prime minister of Britain, Winston Churchill, put it, "Never . . . was so much owed by so many to so few."

The Blitz. The battle of Britain entered a horrifying second phase in September 1940, a phase that vividly showed how total war could choose civilian targets.

Hitler decided to break British morale by obliterating London in terrorizing bomber raids called the **blitz.** Twenty-three consecutive days of bombing rained nearly 20,000 tons of bombs down on the city, destroying more than 450,000 private homes and killing 30,000 civilians—but failing to break the British will. Nothing symbolized British resistance better than the leadership of Winston Churchill, one of the greatest wartime leaders in European history. Churchill was the descendant of an eighteenth-century military hero and the son of a prominent Conservative member of Parliament (M.P.) and a wealthy American mother. He worked exceptionally hard, but he had an infuriating personality, few friends, and a record of political failure. But Winston Churchill possessed a rare eloquence that summoned up resistance to the Nazis. In his maiden speech as prime minister, he had told the nation he had nothing to offer "but blood, toil, tears, and sweat." But,

FIGURE 29.1 *The Battle of Britain.* The first defeat that Nazi Germany suffered, and the first turning point in the course of the war in Europe, came in an air war fought over Britain in the summer of 1940. The German Luftwaffe, with 2,800 aircraft, was asked to win control of the skies in preparation for an invasion of England, but the Royal Air Force (RAF), with 700 fighters, prevented them from doing so. In this photo, RAF pilots have just received a radar warning of approaching bombers and run to their Hurricane fighters to intercept the German planes.

The War in North Africa.

Despite victory in the battle of Britain, 1941–1942 was a dark time for opponents of the Axis. An Italian invasion of Egypt (from their colony in Libya) threatened the Suez Canal and Middle Eastern oil supplies; both targets were so important that when British defenders drove the Italians from Egypt, Hitler reinforced the Axis effort with an elite German Panzer army known as the *Afrika Korps,* commanded by an exceptional tank commander, General Erwin Rommel, who forced the British to retreat. By June 1942, the Afrika Korps was threatening to take the Suez Canal.

The War in the Balkans.

Simultaneously, Italian armies invaded Greece (October 1942) and opened war in the Balkans. The Wehrmacht also entered this theater, supporting the Italians in Greece and then invading Yugoslavia. Belgrade (severely bombed by the Luftwaffe in punishment for continued resistance) and Athens both fell to German occupation. The war in the Balkans continued as a guerrilla war, however, and Yugoslav partisans led by Josip Broz (known as "Tito") never surrendered. The Yugoslav **resistance** was probably the most vigorous in Europe, surpassing even the efforts of the more famous French resistance: fighting was so ferocious in the Balkan theater that Yugoslavia (a nation of 14 million people in the 1930s) would lose 1.5 million to 2 million people.

he soon added, if the nation paid that price, "should the British Empire last for a thousand years, people would say 'This was their finest hour'."

Lend-Lease and the Atlantic Charter.

The battle of Britain drew the United States closer to the war. President Roosevelt was sympathetic, and he inched America toward intervening against the steady opposition of **isolationists.** In the aftermath of the Dunkirk evacuation, Roosevelt sent $43 million worth of surplus arms (such as 600,000 rifles) to Britain. In August, he struck a "destroyers for bases deal" to protect Atlantic shipping by sending fifty-one aging American destroyers to Britain. The conservative U.S. Congress limited arms sales by a strict "cash-and-carry" policy, but Roosevelt fought this short-sighted policy and called on Congress to aid threatened democracies. The fruit of Roosevelt's efforts was the Lend-Lease Act of March 1941, which empowered the president to send arms to any nation deemed "vital to the defense of the United States." Congress initially authorized an appropriation of $7 billion for Lend-Lease arms (which grew to $50 billion during the war), and supplies began to flow from "the arsenal of democracy" to the enemies of Hitler. In August 1941, FDR and Churchill met on a warship off Newfoundland and agreed on the Atlantic Charter, a statement of war aims and postwar plans comparable to the Fourteen Points of World War I (see Document 29.2) They renounced territorial gain, called for "the destruction of Nazi tyranny," and spoke of human rights.

The German Invasion of Russia.

The most important theater of World War II in Europe was the eastern front. Hitler, like Napoleon before him, turned from his failure to invade England and attacked Russia. This was the logical culmination of Hitler's determination to gain *Lebensraum* in the east, a calculation eased by his racist conviction of Slavic inferiority.

In June 1941, he launched Operation Barbarosa, hitting the Soviet Union along a 2,000-mile front in three massive offensives—toward Leningrad, Moscow, and Kiev. Finland resumed its war with the Soviet Union in the north while Hungary and Romania supported Germany in the south. The Nazi blitzkrieg again won quick victories. Soviet armies were in disarray, partly because of Stalin's purge of army commanders in the 1930s and partly because of Stalin's belief that Hitler would not attack him. (The USSR was still shipping food and military aid to Germany in the spring of 1941.) By autumn, the Wehrmacht had penetrated hundreds of miles into the Soviet Union. In the north, they laid siege to Leningrad and subjected it to the treatment that had obliterated Warsaw, Rotterdam, and Belgrade. In the center, German bombers hit Moscow in the first weeks of the war, and German armies drew within sight of the city by late fall. In the south, the Wehrmacht overran the Ukraine, taking Minsk, Kiev, and Odessa and finally planting the swastika on the banks of the Black Sea, as they had hung it from the Eiffel Tower and the Parthenon. Hitler seemed near to dominion over continental Europe. His empire stretched from the Arctic Circle in Norway to the desert of western Egypt, from the French Pyrenees to the Crimea. But he had opened Pandora's box; for the next 3 years, 90 percent of German deaths would happen on the eastern front.

WORLD WAR II ON THE HOME FRONT

The Home Front in Britain. Life on European **home fronts** during World War II was naturally austere. Total war made the home front part of the theater of war, as London discovered during the blitz. The British, who imported much of their food, faced strict rations of basic foods (such as meat, butter, sugar, eggs, and tea), the total loss of many foreign foods (such as oranges, bananas, and chocolate), and reliance on foods not previously eaten (such as shark and whale). **Rationing** identity cards were issued in September 1939 (during the Polish campaign), and the first rationing began in January 1940. Britons would live with rationing for the next 14 years—a period extending long past the end of the war but necessary in order to rebuild the economy. Many families dug up their lawn or flowers to plant vegetables, and towns in Britain (as in many other countries) matched that effort by plowing public parks or athletic playing fields; the moat around the Tower of London, for example, was converted to such a garden. Families in the south of England also learned to live without their children; 1.5 million children were moved outside German bombing range, many to refuge in Canada and the United States. The government curtailed free-market capitalism in favor of a **regulated economy.** Strikes were outlawed, the workweek increased to 54 hours, and the Ministry of Labor received the power to reassign workers to different jobs. The war effort also demanded much higher taxes. With one-third of all men between the ages of 16 and 64 serving in uniform, women again entered the workforce at much higher levels, not only in factory jobs but also in a wide range of replacement positions (such as the police force, which lost many personnel to the military).

THE ATLANTIC CHARTER, AUGUST 1941

As they had in World War I, Western leaders were determined to state that they were fighting to preserve democracy.

A Joint Declaration by the President and the Prime Minister . . . to make known certain common principles. . . .

FIRST, Their countries seek no aggrandizement, territorial or other;

SECOND, They desire to see no territorial changes that do not accord with the freely expressed wishes of the people concerned;

THIRD, They respect the right of all peoples to choose the form of government under which they will live; and they wish to see sovereign rights and self-government restored to those who have been forcibly deprived of them;

FOURTH, They will endeavor with due respect for their existing obligations, to further the enjoyment by all states, great or small, victor or vanquished, of access, on equal terms, to the trade and to the raw materials of the world which are needed for their economic prosperity.

FIFTH, They desire to bring about the fullest collaboration between all nations in the economic field with the object of securing, for all, improved labor standards, economic adjustment, and social security.

SIXTH, After the final destruction of the Nazi tyranny, they hope to see established a peace which will afford to all nations the means of dwelling in safety within their own boundaries, and which will afford assurance that all the men in all the lands may live out their lives in freedom from fear and want;

SEVENTH, Such a peace should enable all men to traverse the high seas and oceans without hindrance;

EIGHTH, They believe that all of the nations of the world, for realistic as well as spiritual reasons, must come to the abandonment of the use of force. . . . They will aid and encourage all other practicable measures which will lighten for peace-loving peoples the crushing burden of armaments.

Question: Which elements of the charter most seem produced by wartime attitudes?

Civilians on the Eastern Front. Domestic conditions were worse in the theaters of war because civilian populations were considered legitimate targets of total war. Russians suffered enormously. Civilians living in areas overrun by the German army endured severe privation and frequent atrocities; these people had scarcely recovered from the suffering of forced collectivization and a subsequent famine in the 1930s. For those caught directly in the fighting, the meaning of total war was abundantly clear: the 3 million people of

FIGURE 29.2 *The Home Front.* In total war, there was scant respect for the distinction between a "battle front" and a "home front"—and civilian populations suffered terrible attacks in many countries. At the very start of the war, Germany conducted a saturation bombing of cities such as Warsaw and Rotterdam, and the allies did the same thing to German cities later in the war. One of the most famous, and important, of the attacks on civilian centers was the German bombing of London, known as "the blitz." This illustration shows one consequence of these German air raids: many families fled their homes and slept on the platforms of the London subway system.

Leningrad endured a German siege lasting 890 days, and 600,000 of them died of starvation.

Collaboration and Resistance in France.

Wartime deprivation was especially severe in France (and other Nazi-occupied regions) because the conquerors requisitioned a large share of food and clothing. Shoes became scarce commodities, and many people wore newspaper lining in their clothing for winter warmth. Life was further complicated by the collaboration of defeated countries such as Vichy France. The Nazi puppet government of Pétain and Laval sent more than 1 million Frenchmen to do forced labor in Germany just as they arranged the Nazi requisition of 3 million tons of wheat and 1 million tons of meat.

Conditions in France deteriorated so far that even wine was rationed. An underground resistance movement, composed of many separate groups (chiefly Communist, but with a large Catholic element), was collectively known as the Maquis or the French Forces of the Interior (FFI). Approximately 2 percent of the population took the risks of espionage, sabotage, or simple defiance, but the Maquis made a significant contribution to later stages of the war. Similar resistance movements existed in all occupied countries, with especially active movements in the mountain regions of Greece and Yugoslavia.

The German Home Front.

Hitler initially strove to cushion most of the German civilian population from the impact of the war because he feared the collapse of the home front, which had been a significant factor in the German defeat in 1918. Thus, military deferments remained common until 1942. Rationing was introduced in August 1939, but the level was kept unusually high (a weekly supply of 1 pound of meat, 5 pounds of bread, 12 ounces of cooking fat, 12 ounces of sugar, and 1 pound of *ersatz* [er'-zahts] coffee [artificial substitute coffee] per person), largely through food supplies plundered abroad. Behind such comforts, however, hid a nightmarish expression of Nazi total war at home: a **euthanasia** program to eliminate "useless mouths," launched at the start of the war. Between 100,000 and 200,000 of the elderly, the severely ill, the disabled, the mentally ill, and even the severely injured World War I veterans were put to death by the government through the willing cooperation of doctors, nurses, and hospital administrators. Only when Clemens von Galen, the bishop of Munster, courageously protested in 1941 did the government suspend the program (planning to resume it after victory), fearing a propaganda catastrophe if army units learned of the program of euthanasia for crippled veterans.

THE GLOBAL WAR

The Greater East Asia Co-Prosperity Sphere.

The European war had been preceded by an Asian war, which began when Japan invaded China in 1937. The Japanese had been building an Asian empire for half a century. While acquiring Formosa (won in the Sino-Japanese War of 1895), Korea (won in the Russo-Japanese War of 1904–1905), and Manchuria (occupied in 1931), Japanese Nationalists developed the dream of a Greater East Asia Co-Prosperity Sphere—a slogan to cover Japanese conquest and dominance of East Asia. A second Sino-Japanese War began in 1937, and by the end of that year, the Japanese Empire stretched across China as far south as Shanghai. In the

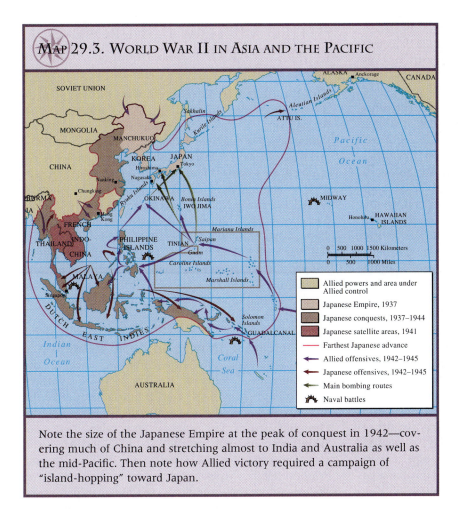

MAP 29.3. WORLD WAR II IN ASIA AND THE PACIFIC

SOVIET UNION

MONGOLIA

MANCHUKUO

CHINA

KOREA

JAPAN
Tokyo
Hiroshima
Nagasaki

BURMA

Chungking

Nanking

Hong Kong

FRENCH
INDO-
CHINA

THAILAND

MALAYA

Singapore

DUTCH EAST INDIES

Indian
Ocean

AUSTRALIA

Sakhalin

Kurile Islands

OKINAWA
Ryukyu Islands

Bonin Islands
IWO JIMA

PHILIPPINE
ISLANDS

Mariana Islands
Saipan
TINIAN
Guam

Caroline Islands

Marshall Islands

Solomon
Islands

GUADALCANAL

Coral
Sea

ALASKA
Anchorage
CANADA

Aleutian Islands

ATTU IS.

Pacific
Ocean

MIDWAY

Honolulu
HAWAIIAN
ISLANDS

0 500 1000 1500 Kilometers
0 500 1000 Miles

Legend:
- Allied powers and area under Allied control
- Japanese Empire, 1937
- Japanese conquests, 1937–1944
- Japanese satellite areas, 1941
- Farthest Japanese advance
- Allied offensives, 1942–1945
- Japanese offensives, 1942–1945
- Main bombing routes
- Naval battles

Note the size of the Japanese Empire at the peak of conquest in 1942—covering much of China and stretching almost to India and Australia as well as the mid-Pacific. Then note how Allied victory required a campaign of "island-hopping" toward Japan.

teriorated during the war in China. American sympathies for the Chinese government of Generalissimo Chiang Kai-Shek (Chang Kye'-shek) led to the prohibition of exporting war materials to Japan. Protests, warnings, and recriminations crossed the Pacific Ocean in 1940–1941. In July 1941, the military dictatorship of Japan resolved to establish the Greater East Asia Co-Prosperity Sphere "no matter what international developments take place." A few weeks later, all armed forces in the Philippine Islands were placed under the command of General Douglas MacArthur to ready them for war, and President Roosevelt froze Japanese assets in the United States. Trade between the two countries ceased. In August 1941, Roosevelt warned Japan against any further expansion in Asia, stating that the United States would "take immediately any and all steps necessary" to protect its interests. Japan responded with a surprise attack on the home base of the U.S. navy at Pearl Harbor (near Honolulu, Hawaii) on December 7, 1941. The attack crippled the U.S. Pacific Fleet, destroying 19 warships and 150 naval aircraft and resulting in 3,000 American casualties. Denouncing "a date which will live in infamy," the United States declared war on Japan. The Japanese had made simultaneous attacks on British forces in Asia (notably in Hong Kong and Malaya), so the British also declared war. Germany and Italy then declared war on the United States, linking the Asian and European wars into World War II.

course of this conquest, the Japanese army committed some of the most ruthless atrocities of the age of total war. The "rape of Nanking," which followed the conquest of that city, included the massacre of approximately 300,000 Chinese civilians, often in extremely cruel ways such as using live people for bayonet practice. (The name of this brutality was not misplaced: the Japanese army made rape an organized aspect of total warfare, victimizing perhaps 80,000 women in Nanking.) After the fall of France in June 1940, the Japanese army landed forces in French Indochina and began the expansion of the co-prosperity sphere into Southeast Asia, where they hoped to obtain war materials. The further expansion meant a collision with the British Empire, which stretched across Asia from India to Singapore to Australia. Japanese expansion similarly menaced American territories in the Pacific, stretching from Hawaii to the Philippine Islands.

Pearl Harbor. Britain and the United States were both drawn into the Asian war by Japanese attacks in December 1941. Japanese–American relations had de-

Japanese Victories in Asia. In the 6 months following the attack on Pearl Harbor, the Japanese won important victories across Southeast Asia. They invaded the Philippines in late December 1941, drove General MacArthur to retreat, and won control of the islands in March 1942, taking a large army captive on the peninsula of Bataan. Another Japanese army drove the British out of Hong Kong in December 1941, and a third successfully invaded Burma in January 1942, cutting off British forces, which retreated to the stronghold of Singapore, but the Japanese took that city after a 2-week siege in February 1942. Sixty thousand British prisoners of war fell to the Japanese. Allied armies were beaten in Indonesia in March 1942, and by spring, the Japanese Empire stretched from the gates of India almost to the international dateline, from Korea nearly to Australia.

Defeat of Japan in the Pacific Theater. The turning point of the war in Asia came in a series of air–sea battles in the Pacific in 1942. In the battle of the Coral Sea (May 1942), the first naval battle ever fought between ships so distant that they could not see each other, the United States stopped the Japanese advance and probably saved Australia and New Zealand. In the battle of Midway (May–June 1942)—named for the U.S.-held Midway Islands, northwest of Hawaii and at the approximate midpoint of the Pacific—a U.S. fleet under Admiral Chester Nimitz fought one of the largest naval engagements in history, inflicting heavy losses on the Japanese and forcing Admiral Yamamoto to retreat. By the summer of 1942, the war in the Pacific had become a succession of island-hopping—amphibious invasions slowly driving toward Japan. After victories by British armies in Burma and Australian armies in New Guinea, Allied forces under Admiral Lord Louis Mountbatten slowly defeated the Japanese armies of Southeast Asia. The United States dislodged the Japanese from Guadalcanal (in the Solomon Islands) in early 1943 and began the reconquest of the Philippines. Bloody fighting followed on many islands, especially in the Marshall Islands and Guam in 1944 and on Okinawa in 1945, but an invasion of Japan also awaited.

FIGURE 29.3 *Pearl Harbor.* World War II had begun in Asia in 1937 and in Europe in 1939, so fighting was already global before the United States entered the war at the end of 1941. The American entry was the result of a Japanese surprise attack on the American naval base at Pearl Harbor, outside Honolulu, Hawaii. On Sunday morning, December 7, 1941, most the United States' Pacific Fleet was at anchor at Pearl Harbor. The 8 battleships and 43 smaller vessels (but not 3 aircraft carriers, which were on duty elsewhere) were comparatively easy targets for 360 Japanese aircraft. The attack sank five battleships and killed more than 2,000 men. In this photo, the USS *West Virginia* and the USS *Tennessee* are in their death throes.

ALLIED VICTORY IN EUROPE (1942–1945)

Victory in North Africa. Another turning point of the war in Europe came in 1942. British armies in North Africa under the command of Field Marshal Montgomery stopped the advance of the Afrika Korps in the battle of El Alamein. While the German army regrouped, an Anglo-American army of 100,000 men, under the command of General Dwight D. Eisenhower, landed in French North Africa in November 1942—less than 1 year after Hitler had declared war on the United States. This amphibious operation required 850 ships and was at that time the largest such landing in history. Caught between the armies of Eisenhower and Montgomery, the Axis armies in North Africa suffered a series of defeats, and the last Axis troops in North Africa surrendered in May 1943.

The Defeat of Italy. Even before the victory in Africa, Roosevelt and Churchill had met at the Casablanca Conference of January 1943 and decided that the next stage of the war in Europe would be the invasion of Italy, "the soft under-belly of Europe" in Churchill's words. The Allies began bombing raids over Sicily and combined British, Canadian, and American armies, commanded by Eisenhower, invaded in July. Palermo fell in 2 weeks, and the Allies began bombing Naples. Before they could cross to the Italian peninsula, however, Mussolini was deposed in a sudden coup, ending 21 years of Fascist rule in Italy and dissolving the Fascist Party. As the British and American armies made their first landings near Naples, Italy unconditionally surrendered in September 1943. German armies still occupied Milan, Rome, and Naples, and the Italian campaign therefore became a slow battle up the peninsula in 1943–1945, expedited by a landing behind German lines at Anzio in early 1944. Rome did not fall until June 1944. As the German army began to pull out of Italy, Mussolini was captured by Italian anti-Fascists while attempting to escape to Switzerland and was shot without a trial.

The Eastern Front. While the victories in North Africa and Italy were important steps in the defeat of the Axis, the decisive theater of the war was the eastern front. The

German invasion of Russia had been stopped by the winter of 1941–1942 and the determined defense of Moscow led by General Georgy Zhukov (Zhoo'-koff). Zhukov was the son of illiterate peasants and had a gruff and unsophisticated style, but he was one of the first commanders to master tank warfare. He so distinguished himself by saving Moscow that Stalin sent him to Leningrad, where Zhukov ordered that the city be defended street by street and that officers who retreated be shot. German assaults (which cost them 200,000 soldiers) and bombardment failed to break Leningrad. When the siege ended in early 1943, half of the population of Leningrad had died.

Stalingrad. The turning point of World War II in Europe came in southern Russia. The Wehrmacht had already lost nearly 2 million men on the eastern front before the Red Army began to counterattack in the winter of 1942–1943. A campaign on the Volga River at Stalingrad was the beginning of the end of Nazi Germany, an epic battle comparable to Verdun in World War I. The Red Army encircled a German army of 300,000 men at Stalingrad and relentlessly attacked in horrifying conditions where temperatures dropped to −49° Fahrenheit. When the Germans gave up in February 1943, a veteran army that had sped across Belgium and Holland was reduced to 91,000 starving, frostbitten prisoners of war, only 6,000 of whom eventually survived Russian imprisonment. After the battle of Stalingrad, the Wehrmacht attempted another offensive, the largest tank battle in history—the battle of Kursk, a rail center south of Moscow. This 9-day battle involved more than 2 million combatants, 5,000 planes, and 6,000 tanks. The Wehrmacht lost badly, as the Red Army threw seemingly endless numbers of men and equipment into the battle. Then began a long German retreat. The Russian army recaptured Smolensk in September 1943, liberated Kiev in November, and crossed the frontier into Poland in January 1944.

The Western Front. The Allies had long planned to open a western front against Germany. Stalin pressed this policy to reduce the burden of the eastern front, where Russian deaths had passed the 10 million mark. The western Allies responded with Operation Overlord, a plan to invade northern France with a combined army of five divisions (two British, two American, and one Canadian), commanded by General Eisenhower. They prepared elaborately, staging men and materiel in southern England and conducting bombing raids over Germany. The RAF struck Berlin with 900 tons of bombs in March 1943, then concentrated on the industrial Rhineland. The bombing of Essen cut the output of the Krupp armaments complex by 65 percent.

FIGURE 29.4 *D-Day.* The turning point of World War II on the western front of Europe came on June 6, 1944, when the Allies staged the greatest amphibious landing in history, in Normandy on the northern shore of France. Newly devised landing craft such as the one shown in this photograph put an army of more than 150,000 men ashore in the first day, losing slightly more than 2,000 killed. In less than 2 weeks, the success of the D-Day invasion had put nearly 500,000 soldiers into the western front.

D-Day. The result was the largest amphibious invasion in history, landing on the shores of Normandy on D-Day, June 6, 1944. An armada of 5,000 ships carrying 150,000 soldiers (plus thousands of vehicles and tons of supplies) landed on the French coast. A total of 2,000 men were killed upon landing, but in less than 2 weeks, the numbers reached nearly 500,000 soldiers and 90,000 vehicles, opening the western front. Such numbers underscore the remarkable war productivity of American industry: by June 1944, American factories were producing enough war materiel to replace everything lost in the invasion within 6 months. The Normandy landings led to a rapid breakthrough by Allied tank forces, and by midsummer, Germany clearly had lost the second battle of France, permitting armies of the British Empire, the Free French, and the United States to press into western Germany while the Russians invaded eastern Germany. This setback precipitated an attempt to assassinate Hitler by a conspiracy within the Wehrmacht. The plot involved several senior officers, but the central figure was Colonial Claus von Stauffenberg, who carried a bomb into a conference among Hitler and his military advisers. Hitler survived and the conspirators were brutally executed (Hitler filmed their deaths for evening entertainment).

V-1 and V-2 Rockets. Hitler responded to the reverses of June–July 1944 with one last surprise: a wave of rocket attacks whose technology presaged the cold war and the space race. A German research program (which included many scientists who would later work in the United States and contribute to the space race of the 1950s and 1960s, such as Dr. Wernher von Braun) at Peenemünde, on the Baltic coast, achieved significant advances in rocketry. The results were the V-1 rockets—flying bombs with a ton of explosives traveling 370 miles per hour—which hit London in the summer of 1944, and more sophisticated V-2 rockets, which struck London and Antwerp that autumn. V-1 and V-2 attacks (the "V" stood for "revenge") delivered more than 70,000 tons of explosives to Britain, approximately four times the amount that the Luftwaffe dropped in 1940; the rockets killed nearly 80,000 people but had little effect on the course of the war.

The Defeat of Germany. Allied armies reached Paris in August 1944 and speeded the liberation of France by making further landings in the south of France. Lyons, Brussels, and Antwerp were all liberated in September 1944, and western armies crossed into western Germany in that same month. The Allies officially recognized Charles de Gaulle's government of liberated France in October. Although the Wehrmacht staged a strong counteroffensive through the Ardennes Forest in December 1944, the Nazi regime was crushed between western and Soviet armies. The Red Army had reached Warsaw in July 1944, and a Polish uprising joined in throwing off the Nazi occupation. The Russian army, however, waited for the Nazis to crush the Polish resistance (245,000 Poles were killed) before advancing on Warsaw, because Stalin reasoned that Polish resistance to a German occupation could easily become Polish resistance to a Russian occupation. As France was being freed in the west,

TABLE 29.1 THE ESTIMATED CASUALTIES OF WORLD WAR II

COUNTRY	KILLED IN COMBAT	WOUNDED	CIVILIANS KILLED	TOTAL KILLED
Allied Casualties				
Australia	23,000–26,000	39,000–180,000		23,000–26,000
Belgium	8,000–10,000	56,000	60,000–76,000	68,000–86,000
Britain	244,000–264,000	370,000	60,000–93,000	304,000–357,000
Canada	32,000–37,000	53,000		32,000–37,000
China	1.3–2.2 million	1.8 million		1.3–2.2 million+
Denmark	3,000–4,000		2,000–3,000	5,000–7,000
France	200,000–400,000	400,000	200,000–350,000	400,000–750,000
Greece	17,000–74,000	47,000	325,000–391,000	342,000–465,000
India	24,000–32,000	64,000		24,000–32,000
Netherlands	7,000	3,000	200,000	207,000
New Zealand	11,000	17,000		11,000
Norway	1,000–2,000		7,000–8,000	8,000–10,000
Poland	123,000–600,000	530,000	5 million+	c. 6 million
United States	292,000	670,000	6,000	298,000
USSR	6.0–7.5 million		2–9 million+	8–20 million
Yugoslavia	305,000–410,000	425,000	1.2 million	1.5–1.6 million
Axis Casualties				
Bulgaria	7,000–10,000		10,000	17,000–20,000
Finland	79,000–82,000		2,000–11,000	81,000–93,000
Germany	3.3–4.4 million		780,000+	4.1–5.2 million
Hungary	140,000–180,000		280,000–290,000	420,000–470,000
Italy	78,000–162,000		146,000	224,000–308,000
Japan	1.2–2.0 million		280,000+	1.5–2.3 million
Romania	300,000–350,000		200,000	500,000–550,000

Adapted from data in Louis L. Snyder, ed., *Louis L. Snyder's Historical Guide to World War II* (Westport, CT: Greenwood, 1982, p. 126).

Note: Figures show range from lowest to highest estimates. German data include Austria. Holocaust victims are counted in homeland civilians.

Question: What conclusions can be drawn from these data?

Russian troops were crossing into East Prussia. The Red Army approached Berlin in early 1945, just as the U.S. army was crossing the Rhine River. The Allied bombing of Germany had been ferocious, and Churchill was determined "to make the rubble bounce." With the war nearly over, Allied bombers delivered a horrifying final blow, a last testament to the nature of total war: the historic Saxon city of Dresden, known as "the Florence of Germany," was subjected to 2 days of nightmarish bombing, killing more than 130,000 civilians.

V-E Day. Mussolini and Hitler died 1 day apart in April 1945. Whereas Il Duce was killed by Italian partisans, der Führer committed suicide in the ruins of Berlin a day later. Hitler's war had cost Germany more than 3 million combat deaths; more than twice that number of Russian soldiers had died, as compared with a combined total of approximately 1 million British, French, and American troops (see Table 29.1). Roosevelt also died in April, a few days before the unconditional surrender of Germany on V-E Day (Victory in Europe Day). Finishing the war in Asia thus fell to Roosevelt's vice president, Harry S. Truman.

The Atomic Bomb and V-J Day. President Truman made the painful decision to use the atomic bomb on Japan to avoid the frightful costs of invading Japan. In the late 1930s, experiments with splitting the atom had begun to convince physicists around the world of the potential of a weapon based on **nuclear fission.** In 1939, a group of distinguished European émigré scientists (notably Enrico Fermi, Leo Szilard, and Albert Einstein) at American universities began to worry that Nazi Germany might be working on such an atomic bomb. This resulted in a historic letter from Albert Einstein to President Roosevelt explaining these possibilities. Roosevelt responded with top-secret (even from Congress) funding for the Manhattan Project to construct a nuclear fission bomb. An international team of scientists (many of them Jewish refugees driven from Europe by Nazi racial policies), fearful that Werner Heisenberg and other German scientists were ahead of them, succeeded in the summer of 1945. The first atomic bomb exploded at a desert site near Alamogordo, New Mexico. It generated the explosive power of 20,000 tons of TNT, vaporized all surrounding equipment, and startled even its inventors. J. Robert Oppenheimer, the director of the Manhattan Project laboratory, was moved to recall a line of Hindu scripture, "I am become Death, the destroyer of worlds." The European war had already ended, and the awesome new weapon quickly ended the Asian war. The United States bombed the Japanese city of Hiroshima on August 6, 1945, killing 68,000 people instantly and nearly 100,000 in the next few weeks; the city of Hiroshima today counts more than 231,000 civilian casualties. A second A-bomb,

FIGURE 29.5 *The A-Bomb.* The first atomic bomb was exploded by an international team of scientists working in the desert of the American southwest, near Alamogordo air base in New Mexico, on July 16, 1945. Three weeks after that successful test, on August 6, 1945, an American B-29 bomber dropped the first atomic bomb used in combat on the Japanese city of Hiroshima. In this image, the bomb dropped on Hiroshima, known as "Little Boy," creates its signature mushroom cloud, which would become one of the frightful images of the cold war. This awesome weapon killed 68,000 civilians immediately and more than 100,000 over time. Three days later, a second atomic bomb was dropped on the city of Nagasaki.

dropped on Nagasaki 3 days later, killed another 35,000 and convinced the Japanese to surrender.

THE HOLOCAUST (1941–1945)

German Concentration Camps. In 1945, the world learned the details of a crime as incredible as the destructive force of the atomic bomb: during the war, the Nazis had used their **concentration camps,** which had initially housed political prisoners and forced laborers, for the systematic murder of millions of people. Rumors of Nazi horrors had circulated earlier, but they had not been widely known and they did not provoke Allied governments to act. The original network of

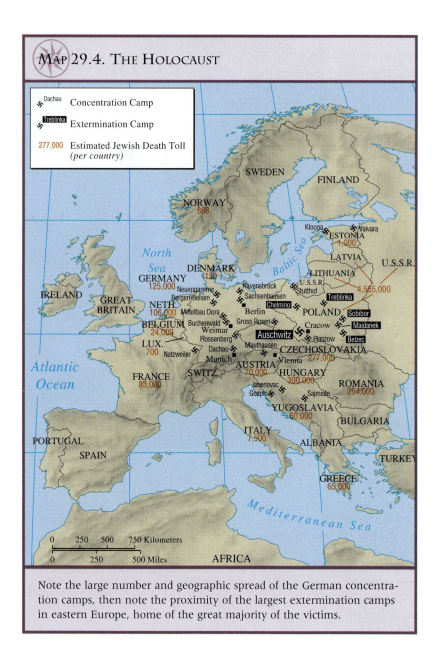

MAP 29.4. THE HOLOCAUST

ᛋ Dachau	Concentration Camp
ᛋ Treblinka	Extermination Camp
277,000	Estimated Jewish Death Toll *(per country)*

Note the large number and geographic spread of the German concentration camps, then note the proximity of the largest extermination camps in eastern Europe, home of the great majority of the victims.

the disabled, the mentally ill, and members of sects such as the Jehovah's Witnesses were all marked for extermination, and they died in large numbers—from 5,000 German and Austrian homosexuals to 200,000 gypsies. Millions of Poles and Soviet prisoners of war (both nations were *Untermenschen*, or subhumans, in the Nazi racial cosmology) also perished in the German concentration camps. But the Final Solution was aimed first at the Jews, nearly 6 million of whom were killed (two-thirds of all European Jews), including 1.5 million children.

The Wannsee Protocol and Genocide. Under the direction of Himmler, Reinhard Heydrich, and Adolf Eichmann, the concentration camps became a universe of slave labor and starvation, then of brutality so savage that it included medical experimentation on live people and ultimately factories for the efficient killing of people. Nazi officials had begun to discuss "a complete solution of the Jewish question" in 1941, and the concentration camps started to become death camps that year. Then in January 1942, fifteen leading Nazi officials met at Wannsee, in suburban Berlin, to plan **genocide;** in the Wannsee Protocol, they pledged to achieve the Final Solution. This led to grisly experimentation to find an efficient means of committing genocide: the Sobibor camp killed 200,000 to 250,000 people by carbon monoxide poisoning, before the managers of the Auschwitz–Birkenau complex discovered the efficacy of Zyclon-B (a form of prussic acid) for gassing inmates. Poison gas was typically administered to groups of people locked into large rooms made to resemble showers; great furnaces were built to burn the bodies. More than 1.1 million people were killed in this way at Auschwitz, and meticulous Nazi bureaucrats kept detailed records of their murders. At his postwar trial, the Nazi commandant of Auschwitz, Rudolf Hoess, calmly described the entire procedure (see Document 29.3).

Resistance to the Holocaust. The Holocaust witnessed heroism amid the horror. Fascist Italy joined in anti-Semitic legislation (such as a 1938 law forbidding intermarriage with Jews) and had interned foreign-

camps, including Dachau (near Munich), Buchenwald (near Weimar), and Sachsenhausen (near Berlin), expanded during the war, especially in Poland, the site of such notorious camps as Auschwitz (near Cracow) and Treblinka (near Warsaw). Adolph Hitler had described himself in *Mein Kampf* as a "fanatical anti-Semite," and he gave the world many signs of his murderous intent. In a speech to the Reichstag in January 1939, Hitler had warned that the Jewish race in Europe would be exterminated in the next world war. This psychotic anti-Semitism culminated in a grotesque plan to "purify Aryan blood," known as the Final Solution (*Endlösung*).

The Final Solution. The **Final Solution** was mass murder; approximately 11 million people were killed in the Nazi camps. Gypsies, homosexuals, Communists,

THE COMMANDANT OF AUSCHWITZ CONFESSES

Rudolf Hoess (1900–1947) was a decorated World War I veteran who spent much of the 1920s in prison for killing a teacher who had insulted the memory of a Nazi hero. He joined the SS and spent his career working in the concentration camps, rising from a corporal at Dachau to be the commandant of Auschwitz (1940–1943). Under his supervision, 2.5 million inmates were murdered, and Hoess earned an SS commendation for efficiency. At his trial he gave a remarkably calm and detailed confession of his life as a mass murderer.

In the summer of 1941—I can no longer remember the exact date—I was suddenly summoned to the Reichsführer SS (Himmler) in Berlin directly by his adjutant's office. Contrary to his normal practice, he received me without his adjutant being present and told me, in effect:

"The Führer has ordered the final solution of the Jewish question and we—the SS—have to carry out this order. The existing extermination centers in the east are not in a position to carry out the major operations which are envisaged. I have, therefore, earmarked Auschwitz for this task, both because of its favorable communications and because the area envisaged can be easily sealed off and camouflaged. . . .

"You will maintain the strictest silence concerning this order, even vis-à-vis your superiors. After your meeting with Eichmann (Himmler's SS assistant) send me the plans for the proposed installations at once. The Jews are the eternal enemies of the German people and must be exterminated. Every Jew we can lay our hands on must be exterminated. . . ."

Shortly afterwards, Eichmann came to see me in Auschwitz. . . . We discussed how the extermination was to be carried out. Gas

was the only feasible method, since it would be impossible to liquidate by shooting the large numbers envisaged, and shooting would place too heavy a burden on the SS men who had to carry it out, particularly in view of the women and children involved.

Eichmann informed me of the method of killing by exhaust fumes from vans, which had been implemented in the east hitherto. However, it was out of the question to use it in Auschwitz on the mass transports that were envisaged. . . . My deputy . . . (had) used gas to exterminate the Russian prisoners of war. He crammed individual cells with Russians and, protected by gas masks, hurled Zyclon-B into the cells which caused death immediately. . . . During Eichmann's next visit, I reported to him about this use of Zyclon-B and we decided to employ this gas for the future mass extermination program. . . .

Auschwitz reached its high point in the spring of 1944. . . . A triple track railway line leading to the new crematoria enabled a train to be unloaded while the next one was arriving. . . . All four crematoria operated at full blast. . . . The last body had hardly been pulled from the gas chambers and dragged across the yard behind the crematorium, which was covered in corpses, to the burning pit, when the next lot were already undressing in the hall for gassing.

From Hoess, Rudolph, "Nuremberg testimony," in J. Noakes and G. Pridham, eds., *Nazism, 1919–1945. A History in Documents and Eyewitness Accounts*, vol. 2. (New York: Schocken, 1988).

Questions: Is this drilling confession proof that Hoess was criminally insane? Or does it show the incredible crimes that ordinary people are capable of committing?

---

born Jews, but Mussolini resisted genocide and refused to deport 44,000 Jews to the death camps, enabling 85 percent of Italian Jews to survive the war. Although Vichy France collaborated by deporting foreign-born Jews, a heroic Protestant village in southern France, Le Chambon, led by Pastor André Trocmé, saved 5,000 Jews by hiding them, and a Capuchin monk at Marseille, Marie Benoît, saved 4,000 by providing papers allowing them to escape. Danes ferried Jews to safety in Sweden so effectively that 7,000 Danish Jews escaped and only 51 died in the camps. A single Swedish diplomat, Raoul Wallenberg, organized a system that saved 10,000 Budapest Jews. (In a tragic irony, Wallenberg himself died in Soviet captivity.) A German businessman, Oskar Schindler, saved Jews from Auschwitz by taking them to work in his factory. Jewish self-defense also had notable moments: in April 1942, the Jewish ghetto of Warsaw fought back and

killed 5,000 German soldiers. Such heroic resistance highlights the less heroic responses of most governments and churches; the governments of neutral Switzerland and powerful America, and even the Vatican of Pope Pius XII, were all informed in 1942 (by a Polish hero named Jan Karski) of the nightmare yet declined the opportunity to behave heroically (or even to bomb the railroad tracks leading into Auschwitz).

CONFERENCE DIPLOMACY AND PEACE IN EUROPE IN 1945

No peace or treaty ended World War II in Europe. Churchill, Stalin, and Roosevelt had prepared for Germany's unconditional surrender at a series of summit conferences during the war. The Tehran Conference

THE NUREMBERG TRIBUNAL (1945)

The Nuremberg Trials. An international military tribunal sat at Nuremberg, Germany, between November 1945 and October 1946, to try twenty-two of the highest-ranking Nazi officials. Hitler, Himmler, and Goebbels all chose death and were not tried. In this trial photograph, the primary defendants sit in the wooden dock in the center: the figure leaning far forward is Hermann Goering (who would also commit suicide), followed (left to right) by Rudolph Hess (who would be sentenced to life in prison); Nazi Foreign Minister Joachim von Ribbentrop (who would be hanged in 1946 as a war criminal); General Wilhelm Keitel, head of the supreme command of the German army (later hanged); Alfred Rosenberg, Nazi political writer (later hanged); and Hans Frank, Nazi jurist and administrator of Poland (later hanged).

The Charter of the Nuremberg Tribunal (1945)

The following acts, or any of them, are crimes coming within the jurisdiction of the Tribunal for which there shall be individual responsibility:

*(a) **Crimes against peace**. Namely, planning, preparation, initiation, or waging of a war of aggression or a war in violation of international treaties, agreements, or assurances, or participation in a common plan or conspiracy for the accomplishment of any of the foregoing.*

*(b) **War crimes**. Namely, violations of the laws or customs of war. Such violations shall include, but not be limited to, murder, ill treatment, or deportation to slave labor or for any other purpose of civilian population of or in occupied territory, murder or ill treatment of prisoners of war or persons on the seas, killing of hostages, plunder of public or private property, wanton destruction of cities, towns, or villages, or devastation not justified by military necessity.*

*(c) **Crimes against humanity**. Namely, murder, extermination, enslavement, deportation, and other inhumane acts committed against any civilian population before or during the war or persecutions on political, racial, or religious grounds in execution of or in connection with any crime within the jurisdiction of the Tribunal, whether or not in violation of the domestic law of the country where perpetrated . . .*

The fact that the defendant acted pursuant to an order of his government or of a superior shall not free him from responsibility but may be considered in mitigation of punishment if the Tribunal determines that justice so requires.

From Potsdam Protocol, Article 6. In U.S. Department of State, Bulletin, 13:320 (August 12, 1945): 224.

Question: Do these concepts of crime still work in international law?

---

of 1943, for example, projected new frontiers for Poland and discussed the dismemberment of Germany. The Dumbarton Oaks Conference (in Washington, D.C.) planned an international organization—the United Nations (UN)—to keep the peace. Churchill and Stalin met in Moscow in 1944 and agreed to divide Eastern Europe into **"spheres of influence"**; the USSR would be preeminent in Romania and Bulgaria and have influence in Hungary and Yugoslavia.

Yalta and Potsdam. The most important wartime conference took place in early 1945 in the Russian re-

sort town of Yalta on the Crimean peninsula. Churchill, Roosevelt, and Stalin agreed to divide Germany into four zones of military occupation, with France administering the fourth. (Stalin accepted only three zones, but Britain and America divided their zones to give the French a role.) They pledged the "complete disarmament, demilitarization, and dismemberment" of Germany, including the right of occupying powers to remove German wealth, such as dismantling factories. The Potsdam Conference (in suburban Berlin in the summer of 1945) finalized the **partition** of Germany. The Allies agreed that Germans must "atone for the terrible crimes committed under the leadership of those whom, in the hour of their success, they openly approved and blindly obeyed." The boundary between a reduced Germany and a recreated Poland would be defined by two rivers, the Oder–Neisse Line. Much of historic Prussia thus became part of Poland.

Nuremberg Trials. The Potsdam Protocol also stated the right of the victors to hold trials of **war criminals.** Similar trials had been planned after World War I, when the Allies had drawn up a list of 890 people to be tried, beginning with Kaiser Wilhelm II. But the trials begun at Leipzig in 1921 collapsed when the German high court accepted the exculpatory plea of individuals who were "just following orders." The Potsdam Protocol avoided this problem by chartering an Allied tribunal to sit at Nuremberg and by defining the crimes that would come before it (see *The Nuremberg Tribunal [1945]*). This included **"crimes against humanity"** for acts committed against civilian populations. Twenty-two Nazi leaders were accordingly tried at the Nuremberg Trials of 1945–1946, and twelve were sentenced to death. Hitler, Joseph Goebbels, and Heinrich Himmler were all dead, but Goering and Ribbentrop were among the prominent Nazis at Nuremberg. Others were tried in the east, and war crimes trials continued throughout the postwar era: Israel convicted and executed one of the architects of the Holocaust, Adolf Eichmann, in 1962; a French court convicted the Gestapo chief in Lyons (Klaus Barbie) as late as 1987, then tried a Vichy police official, Maurice Papon, in 1997. Similar trials (and informal revenge) covered the war zone. In France, 800 Vichy collaborationists were executed during the Liberation. The hero of World War I, Marshal Pétain, was convicted of treason for his collaboration with the Nazis; although de Gaulle spared Pétain's life in respect for his age and his historic role in World War I, Pierre Laval was executed. No court applied the Nuremberg precedent to other conflicts until 1996 when the United Nations began war crimes trials for atrocities committed in the Bosnian War.

The United Nations. An international conference at San Francisco in 1945 adopted the Dumbarton Oaks plan and founded the United Nations to replace the League of Nations (which had been so ineffectual in preventing World War II) and "to save succeeding generations from the scourge of war." Fifty-one countries (excluding the Axis powers) committed themselves to the idea of **"collective security."** (The UN reached 191 members in 2003 when Switzerland joined.) The UN Charter created a General Assembly to represent all countries and to debate international issues. Primary responsibility for keeping the peace, however, was given to a Security Council, which had five permanent members (the United States, the USSR, Britain, France, and China) and six elected members. The Security Council chose a secretary-general, the chief administrative officer of the UN, who could bring issues to the council but had little power to act. Many UN bodies were subsequently created, beginning with an International Court of Justice. The charter of the UN had tried to launch the postwar era on a positive note, and this led to the adoption in 1948 of the Universal Declaration of Human Rights, the first effort in history to state minimal human rights for the world (see Document 29.4).

DOCUMENT 29.4

THE UNIVERSAL DECLARATION OF HUMAN RIGHTS, 1948
PREAMBLE

This declaration, adopted by the United Nations, was the world's first international statement of human rights.

Whereas recognition of the inherent dignity and of the equal and inalienable rights of all members of the human family in the foundation of freedom, justice, and peace in the world,

Whereas disregard and contempt for human rights have resulted in barbarous acts which have outraged the conscience of mankind. . . .

Now, therefore, the General Assembly proclaims this universal declaration of human rights as a common standard of achievement for all peoples and all nations. . . .

Article 1. All human beings are born free and equal in dignity and rights. They are endowed with reason and conscience and should act towards one another in a spirit of brotherhood.

Article 2. Everyone is entitled to all the rights and freedoms set forth in this Declaration, without distinction of any kind, such as race, color, sex, language, religion, political or other opinion, national or social origin, property, birth, or other status. . . .

Article 3. Everyone has the right to life, liberty and security of person.

Article 4. No one shall be held in slavery or servitude. . . .

Article 5. No one shall be subjected to torture or cruel, inhuman or degrading treatment or punishment.

Article 6. Everyone has the right to recognition everywhere as a person before the law.

Article 7. All are equal before the law and are entitled without discrimination to equal protection.

From Brownlie, Ian, ed., *Basic Documents of Human Rights* (Oxford: Clarendon, 1992).

Question: What other human rights might be listed in the first seven paragraphs today?

Conclusion

The statistics on people killed during World War II, like those during World War I, are mind-numbing. Perhaps 50 million people (the numbers will always remain estimates at best) met a violent death in World War II, more than half of them noncombatant civilians. Perhaps 75 million people (far more than the total population of Britain or France today) perished as a result of the two parts of the combined Thirty Years' War of the twentieth century. The history of this epic dance of death is no less mind-numbing if it is portrayed as individual suffering—of women raped and then disembow-eled at Nanking, of London homeowners blown to bits at their dinner table, of children choking to death on poison gas at Auschwitz, or of teenaged conscripts freezing to death at Stalingrad. Whatever the amount of this suffering that the historian can assimilate, it should be sufficient to suggest that the twentieth century was one of the most violent and destructive centuries in all of human history. And it should suffice to raise doubts about the Enlightenment vision of the progress of the human race. At the most generous, agreement can be reached with the historian who labeled the first half of the twentieth century "the age of catastrophe." The epoch ended with high hopes for the future—seen in

Europe in the Age of Total War, 1939–1945

1936	1937	1938	1939	1940	1941	1942	1943	1944	1945

Germany Renounces Locarno Treaty and Remilitarizes Rhineland
Italy and Germany Sign Axis Pact and Anti-Comintern Treaty with Japan
Hossbach Memorandum Outlines German War Plans
Germany Annexes Austria and Demands Sudetenland from Czechoslovakia
Britain and France Appease Germany at Munich Conference
Germany Annexes Remainder of Czechoslovakia
Nazi–Soviet Non-Aggression Pact
Germany Invades Poland in Blitzkrieg Campaign
Britain and France Declare War but Stay out of Poland
USSR Invades Eastern Poland, Baltics, and Finland
Fall of Poland and Katyn Forest Massacre
Battle of Atlantic Begins at Sea with German U-Boat Success
Germany Conquers Denmark and Norway
Germany Conquers Netherlands and Belgium
British Evacuate Continent from Dunkirk
Italy Declares War on France and Joins German Invasion
Fall of France to Germany and Reduction to Vichy France
De Gaulle Organizes French Government in Exile
Battle of Britain in Air and Germans bombing of London in "Blitz"
US Aids Britain in "Destroyers For Bases" Deal
U.S. Lend–Lease Aid to Britain and Atlantic Charter
Germany Invades USSR
Japan Attacks U.S. and Germany Declares War
Italo-German Victory in Balkans
Warsaw Ghetto Uprising
Wannsee Protocol on "Final Solution"
Allied Landings in North Africa
Turning Point in the Pacific: Battle of Coral Sea
Germany Beaten in North Africa
Allies Invade Italy
Battle of Stalingrad
Tehran Conference of Allies
Allied Bombing of Germany
D-Day Landing in France
V-1 and V-2 Rockets Hit England
Liberation of France
Fall of Berlin to Russians
Yalta Conference
First Atomic Bomb Used
United Nations Founded
Potsdam Conference

the principles of war crimes trials, the ambitions of the United Nations, and the ideals of the Universal Declaration of Human Rights—but mixed confidence that the world would actually adhere to them.

Review Questions

- What were the origins of World War II?
- What were the stages of Axis conquest in World War II?
- What were the chief characteristics of "total war"?
- What were the stages of the Allied victory in World War II?

For Further Study

Readings

Churchill, Winston, *The Second World War,* 6 vols. (Boston: Houghton Mifflin, 1948–1953). A notable history by a war leader; admired for its exceptional prose, it is one of the few histories ever to win the Nobel Prize for Literature.

Hilberg, Raoul, *The Destruction of the European Jews,* 3 vols., 3rd ed. (New Haven, CT: Yale University Press, 2003). The newest update of the standard history of the Holocaust.

Hogan, David J., ed., *The Holocaust Chronicle* (Lincolnwood, IL: Publications International, 2000). A thorough chronology of the final solution accompanied by comprehensive illustrations.

Snyder, Louis L., *Louis L. Snyder's Historical Guide to World War II* (Westport, CT: Greenwood Press, 1982). A lengthy dictionary of the war.

Taylor, A. J. P., *The Origins of the Second World War* (New York: Antheneum, 1983). An older, highly readable account of the origins of the war that caused great controversy when it appeared.

Weinberg, Gerhard L., *A World at Arms: A Global History of World War II* (Cambridge: Cambridge University Press, 1994). The newest comprehensive history (1,200 pages) by a noted scholar.

InfoTrac College Edition

For additional reading, go to your online research library at *http://infotrac.thomsonlearning.com.*

Using Key Word search, enter the search terms:

Auschwitz   *Stalingrad*
D-Day   *Hiroshima*

Web Sites

http://www.ushmm.org/   The Web site of the United States Holocaust Memorial Museum in Washington, D.C., presents a wide range of information, often following the special exhibitions at the museum. Provides extensive Web links for the Holocaust.

http://www.yale.edu/lawweb/avalon/imt/imt.htm   The Web site of the Avalon Project of the Yale University Law School; it provides an extensive collection of electronic documents, especially useful for the Nuremberg war crimes trials and for documents on World War II.

http://www.bbc.co.uk/history/war/wwtwo/index.shtml   A Web site developed by the BBC, providing multimedia sources and especially strong on individual recollections of the war.

Visit the Western Civilization Companion Web Site for resources specific to this textbook:
http://history.wadsworth.com/hause02/

The CD in the back of this book and the Western Civilization Resource Center at *http://history. wadsworth.com/western/* offer a variety of tools to help you succeed in this course, including access to quizzes; images; documents; interactive simulations, maps, and timelines; movie explorations; and a wealth of other sources.

Chapter 30

THE SOCIAL AND ECONOMIC STRUCTURE OF CONTEMPORARY EUROPE

*I*n early May 1924, a 27-year-old woman, pregnant with her fourth child, sat down at a table in rural England to write a letter to a famous person, in search of advice. The writer was the wife of a farm laborer who earned 1 pound and 7 shillings a week ($6.60 in 1924), and her family's financial situation had deteriorated to the point that to be able to feed her children, she could eat only a few meals herself. Her son could not go to school because they couldn't afford to buy shoes for him to wear. When she had asked her mother (an almost equally desperate woman with several children) for advice, her mother replied that she "must stop having children." The only way that the woman could see to stop having children, she wrote at the time, was "to leave my husband and go into the workhouse. . . . If you can advise me I would be very grateful." The recipient of this letter, a 44-year-old physician named Marie Stopes, did indeed know a better way to stop having children—a way that didn't rely on avoiding sexual relations. Marie had become famous 6 years earlier for publishing a book titled *Married Love,* which had, to the dismay and denunciation of the clergy, vigorously defended a woman's right to sexual pleasure within marriage. Her advice, however, came from another of her writings, *Wise Parenthood,* which had presented a clear guide to contraception, and from her experience of operating a birth control clinic in North London since 1921, Britain's first family planning clinic. There is no record of how well the farmwife fared with Marie Stopes's birth control advice, but it was advice that dramatically changed the social and economic patterns of twentieth-century Europe.

The twentieth century opened with both the economic structures and the social structures of Europe in the middle of a continuing historic change. Chapter 30 surveys these changes, beginning with a study of the population of Europe—one of the most important indicators of socioeconomic change since the middle of the eighteenth century. The chapter shows how population growth continued, then slowed greatly, then shifted to a pattern of population loss by the end of the twentieth century. The century began with a mixed economy of agriculture and industry, in which industrialization was the dominant trend. Agriculture steadily shrank as a segment of the European economy until it employed less than 10 percent of the population of western Europe at the end of the century. The triumph of the industrial economy did not last long, however, as a third sector of the economy—the service sector—became dominant. Chapter 30 concludes with a look at social changes. It explains how the vital revolution of modern history accelerated, reducing the mortality rate so much that the average life expectancy of Europeans grew from 45 years in 1900 to 75 years in 1990.

POPULATION TRENDS IN EUROPE SINCE 1900

Trends across the Modern Centuries. At the beginning of the modern era in the early eighteenth century, Europe had an estimated population of slightly more than 100 million persons. By the end of the twentieth century, Europe numbered more than 500 million inhabitants—approximately doubling the population of the United States. Most of that population growth came during the population explosion that began in the mideighteenth century and continued during the nineteenth century. In 1900, the population of Europe stood at 423 million, meaning that three-fourths of Europe's modern growth had occurred before the twentieth century (see Table 30.1). By the end of the twentieth century, the rate of growth had fallen sharply, and some European countries had actually begun to lose population. The full impact of that trend will not be known until the middle of twenty-first century because demographic totals are often seen a generation after the start of a trend; however, demographers now foresee the prospect that many European countries will shrink in total population between 2000 and 2050. Studies done by the United Nations (UN) find the biggest downward trend in Russia, which is already losing population and is projected to fall from 145 million in 2000 to 101 million in 2050 if current trends continue. Germany and Italy would also lose millions in total population.

Population and Power. The population history of the major states of Europe underscores modern political history. In 1700, France possessed a great **demographic advantage** (a larger army in the simplest terms) over all of its rivals in western and central Europe; France was nearly 50 percent more populous

than all German states added together and three times as populous as Great Britain. By the beginning of the twentieth century, France had less than three-fourths of the population of unified Germany and approximately the same population as Britain. A **population explosion** had quadrupled Germany and quintupled Britain (fueling an era of tremendous economic growth) but had only nearly doubled the population of France. Reunified Germany remains the largest state in the European Union (EU), with a population that exceeded 82 million in 2003; Britain, France, and Italy each numbered nearly 60 million, more than 70 percent of the populace of Germany. Russia, whose size supported a dominant position in Europe after 1945, reached a population of 283 million in 1988 (just before the breakup of the Soviet Union). At that time, the USSR was approximately 15 percent larger than the United States during the cold war (or 15 percent larger than Britain, France, Germany, and Italy combined).

The Baby Bust. The primary cause of the striking change in current European population trends is a precipitous decline in European birthrates since the 1980s (see Table 30.2). Demographers are calling this development the **baby bust** (a term used in contrast to a **baby boom** in periods of population growth, such as the era after World War II). A stable population requires a **fertility rate** of 2.1 children per woman, assuming that immigration and emigration are not a factor. As the birthrate falls below 2.1, the prospect of long-term population decline increases. UN demographers expect that Germany, with a fertility rate of 1.35 in 2002, will lose up to 10 percent of its population by 2050; Italy, with a rate of 1.23 births per woman, could lose 20 percent or more. The impact of these trends is so large that demographers estimate that if Europe quickly returned to a fertility rate of 2.1, it would still lose 24 percent its to-

TABLE 30.1 THE GROWTH OF EUROPEAN POPULATION, 1700–2000

COUNTRY	ESTIMATED POPULATION IN 1700	CENSUS POPULATION C. 1900	CENSUS POPULATION C. 2000	GROWTH RATE 1700–2000	GROWTH RATE 1900–2000
	(in millions)			(in percent)	
France	19.3	38.5	59.8	210	55
Germany	13.5	56.4	83.3	517	48
Italy	13.0	32.5	57.7	344	78
Spain	7.5	18.6	40.1	435	156
Britain	6.4	37.0	59.8	834	62
Russia	16.0	126.4	145.0	806	15

Question: Compare the pattern of growth for the modern era (1700–2000) with the pattern of growth for the twentieth century (1900–2000). What are the major changes that happened during the twentieth century?

TABLE 30.2 THE BABY BUST: FALLING BIRTHRATES IN EUROPE

TOTAL FERTILITY RATES IN 2002

COUNTRY (RANKED BY GROWTH RATE)	FERTILITY RATE (2002)	UN ESTIMATES OF POPULATION LOSS BY 2050
Turkey	2.43	Population growth
United States	2.06	Probable gain
Ireland	1.90	Probable gain
France	1.89	Probable gain
Norway	1.80	Probable gain
Netherlands	1.72	Probable gain
United Kingdom	1.60	Probable gain
Sweden	1.64	0 to −10%
Germany	1.35	0 to −10%
Greece	1.27	0 to −10%
Spain	1.15	0 to −10%
Switzerland	1.41	−10% to −20%
Poland	1.26	−10% to −20%
Italy	1.23	−20% or more
Russia	1.14	−20% or more

Fertility rate = lifetime live births per woman.

Fertility rate need to sustain population = 2.1.

United Nations data posted at *http://www.undp.org*.

Questions: What factors might explain the contrast between a fertility rate higher in Switzerland than in Spain yet a greater loss of population in Switzerland than in Spain? Or the probable gain of population by France and the United Kingdom, although their fertility rates are below 2.1?

tal population by 2060. Thus, the baby bust raises complex questions about the balance of power within Europe and the continued preeminence of Europe as a center of world power. (Will smaller populations be an advantage or a disadvantage?) And they require careful historical examinations of developments such as birth control and immigration (which allows some regions to grow despite low birthrates).

Urbanization. One of the most important consequences of the European population explosion of the eighteenth and nineteenth centuries was the **urbanization** of European civilization. During the eighteenth century, Europe had been a rural society, with the vast majority of the population living on farms and in small villages. By 1850, Britain had become the first country in history to have the majority of its population living in cities. Although much of Europe still remained rural in 1900, nineteenth-century Europe had become an urban civilization. Population migration from agricultural communities had made London and Paris the largest cities in the world, and it had changed dozens of small towns into large cities.

Twentieth-Century Urbanization. The trend toward urbanization continued in the twentieth century. By 1950, the majority of the population of western and central Europe lived in cities. Metropolitan Paris, the region containing the city and its suburbs, quadrupled in size during the twentieth century, growing from 2.3 million people in 1900 to 8.7 million in 1991. Yet Paris is far from the most dramatic example. Milan grew more than eight-fold, from 493,000 in 1900 to 4.3 million in 1991; Moscow, the center of the post–World War II communist empire, went from less than 1 million to more than 8 million; and the Essen agglomeration, the center of German industrial might in the Rhine–Ruhr valleys, grew from 119,000 to 6.5 million (see Table 30.2).

Global Urbanization. Despite the dramatic urbanization seen in these figures, the rate of European urban growth, like total population growth, actually slowed in the twentieth century and was moderate compared with the global trend. At the start of the twenty-first century, London and Paris were no longer the largest cities in the world. By 1950, New York City had surpassed them and London ranked second and Paris fourth. In 1975, Paris stood ninth and London eleventh in the world; in 2000, Paris ranked nineteenth and London twenty-fifth. Tokyo, at 26.4 million, is approximately three times their size. Several cities, such as Mexico City and São Paulo to Mumbai and Calcutta are nearly twice the size of London or Paris. Only those two European cities rank in the world's thirty largest cities. In many ways, the European city representative of global trends is Athens, which has exploded from a national capital of 111,000 in 1900 to a rambling metropolitan region of 3.1 million in 2000, nearly 50 percent of the Greek population. (By comparison, Berlin contains less than 5 percent of the population of Germany, and less than 7 percent of Italians live in Rome.)

Variation of Urbanization within Europe. Twentieth-century European urbanization, like so many historic patterns, has not been the same in western and eastern Europe. On the eve of World War II, the population of Romania was still 82 percent rural, a figure more typical of the western or central Europe before the French Revolution. Whereas Britain had become more than 50 percent urban in 1850, as late as 1975, eight countries remained predominantly rural, led by Bosnia (31.3 percent urban) and Albania (32.7 percent). Even in 2000, the majority of the population of Albania, Bosnia, Moldova, and Slovenia lived in small rural communities, compared with 17 percent of western Europe (see *Urbanization Since 1900*).

European Emigration in 1900. Urbanization has not been the only important trend in European **population migration.** At the turn of the twentieth century, Europe was losing millions of people through **emigration** to other parts of the world. Between 1871 and 1914, Sweden lost 1.5 million emigrants—chiefly to the United States—who accounted for more than one-third of the population of Sweden in 1870. Over that same time period, more than 3.2 million people (chiefly Irish) left Great Britain; thus, Britain, the richest state in the world, lost nearly 8 percent of its 1901 population to emigration. More than 2 million people (chiefly Jews) fled Russia during the revolution of 1905 and its aftermath. Italian population loss was perhaps the most striking. In the early 1880s, Italy lost 1 million people every 5 years; by the early 1890s, Italy was losing 1 million people every 3 years; and in the first decade of the twentieth century, 1 million people left Italy every 18 months. By 1913, the rate of Italian exiles had reached nearly 900,000 per year. This meant that Italy was losing 2.5 percent of its total population every year, roughly the equivalent to losing the entire population of Rome (542,000), Venice (161,000), and Florence (135,000) annually.

The twentieth century thus began with Europe losing 1.3 million people per year. Some fled to avoid religious persecution and others fled to avoid conscription into monarchical armies, but most emigrants left for greater economic opportunities. Millions of Europeans lived in such poverty in 1900 that flight to the Americas, Australia, or the scattered corners of European empires was preferable to hunger at home. World War I nearly stopped European emigration, and in the 1920s, many states (led by the United States) adopted much stricter policies on accepting immigrants. Nonetheless, the wars and revolutions of twentieth-century Europe shifted millions of people across national frontiers, such as the repatriation of 1.2 million Greeks from Turkey after World War I, the migration of 200,000 Magyars from Transylvania to Hungary in the 1920s, the escape of thousands of Germans from totalitarian terror during the 1930s, or the flight and expulsion of nearly 7.5 million Germans from eastern Europe after World War II.

Immigration into Europe. None of these migrations changed Europe as profoundly as the arrival of millions of non-Europeans as a result of decoloniza-

tion. By the end of the twentieth century, Europe's migration pattern had completely reversed the pattern of 1900. Millions of non-Europeans sought to immigrate to Europe because economic opportunity was much greater there. Much of the late twentieth-century **immigration** into Europe had its origins in the history of European colonial empires and in the age of decolonization that followed World War II. The end of empire forced imperialist governments to reintegrate European-born colonists and their descendants; the Franco-Algerian War of 1954–1962, for example, led more than 1 million *pieds noirs* (peed nwar; French colonists in Algeria) to return to France in the 1960s. In many cases, the indigenous population of European colonies had the legal right to migrate to the imperial state or had legal preference in normal immigration. For example, after the Dutch East Indies won their independence as Indonesia in 1949, the Netherlands absorbed 300,000 immigrants from their former colony. The independence of the *Maghreb* (Mah'-greb; the Arabic term for north Africa—Morocco, Algeria, and Tunisia) from France resulted in an influx of millions of North Africans starting in the late 1960s and peaking in the 1980s. Until Britain adopted strict—and often racially motivated—immigration controls in mid-1962, hundreds of thousands of south Asians (chiefly from India and Pakistan) and blacks from the West Indies migrated to Britain (see *Immigration to Europe*). These migrations of non-Europeans into Europe reversed long-standing patterns of population movement; in the case of Britain, for example, the largest group of immigrants had remained Irish through the 1960s.

North African Immigration to France. France provides a dramatic illustration of this transformation of European population. By 1982, immigrants formed nearly 7 percent of the population of France; counting the families of immigrant workers, France was more than 8 percent immigrant. At the beginning of the twentieth century, less than 3 percent of the populace was foreign-born, and nearly 90 percent of the immigrants came from other parts of Europe—immigrants were chiefly Belgians and Italians who found work across the border. By the end of the century, immigration had quadrupled and most French immigrants were Algerians (22 percent) and Moroccans (12 percent). Nearly half of all French immigrants came from Africa; meanwhile, Italian and Belgian immigration into France fell to less than one-sixth of its previous rate. And the religious minorities in France, which had been approximately 2 percent Protestant and 1 percent Jewish in 1900, approached 10 percent Islamic in 2000.

The Immigration of Guest Workers. Another important form of migration accompanied European

URBANIZATION SINCE 1900

TABLE 30.3 THE GROWTH OF EUROPEAN CITIES SINCE 1900

CITY	POPULATION IN 1900	POPULATION IN 2000	PERCENTAGE OF NATIONAL POPULATION IN THIS CITY (2000)
Paris	2,300,000	9,630,000	16.3
Constantinople/Istanbul	874,000	8,953,000	13.4
Moscow	989,000	8,367,000	5.8
London	6,600,000	7,640,000	12.9
Essen (Rhine–Ruhr)	119,000	6,531,000	8.0
St. Petersburg	1,300,000	4,635,000	3.2
Milan	493,000	4,251,000	7.4
Madrid	540,000	3,976,000	10.0
Lisbon	356,000	3,861,000	38.5
Berlin	1,889,000	3,319,000	4.0
Athens	111,000	3,116,000	29.4

Note: Data are totals for urban *agglomerations*.

Data for 1900 from Mitchell, B. R., *European Historical Statistics, 1750–1970* (London: Macmillan, 1975, pp. 76–78); 1900 data for Constantinople from *Statesman Yearbook, 1901*. Data for 2000 from United Nations Population Information Network, posted at *http://www.un.org/popin/data.html*.

Question: What interpretations do the data on the percentage of population living in a single city suggest?

prosperity in the late twentieth century. The UN estimated in 1973 that the Common Market states plus Austria, Norway, Sweden, and Switzerland included 7.5 million foreign workers. West Germany, for example, held 2.6 million **guest workers** (*Gastarbeiter*) who constituted 12 percent of the German labor force. Nearly 20 percent of those workers came from Turkey, a figure that surpassed 33 percent by the late 1980s. The Turkish population of Germany passed 2 million in the 1990s. Although their guest-worker status (and an extremely strict German citizenship law of 1913) denied them the rights of immigrants, a study in 1977 found that 25 percent of all German guest workers had resided there for at least a decade.

Migration from Eastern Europe. Migration patterns shifted again in the 1990s, following the breakup of the Soviet empire, as thousands of eastern Europeans sought a better life in the west. The foreign-born population of Germany, for example, again increased dramatically after 1989. Tens of thousands of ethnic Germans returned (claiming citizenship under a 1913 law), hundreds of thousands of refugees arrived (for example, 320,000 Bosnians fled the Yugoslav War), and tens of thousands of Soviet Jews were granted residence. These trends, along with the strict laws and a plummeting birthrate, combined in the late 1990s to create a situation in which more than 20 percent of the babies born in Germany were born to non-Germans. Such immigration trends of the

Urbanization. The concentration of population in large metropolitan regions, which had begun in late eighteenth-century Britain and had characterized many regions in the nineteenth century, continued throughout the twentieth century. At the start of the century, when traffic snarls involved horse-drawn vehicles, Europe already contained half a dozen congested cities of populations of more than 1 million. By 1938, when this photograph was taken on a London shopping street, urbanization had spread to many more regions, but congestion had only changed the style of vehicle.

TABLE 30.4 THE SLOW URBANIZATION OF EASTERN EUROPE, 1950–2000			
	Urban Population as Percentage of National Population		
COUNTRY	1950	1975	2000
Western Europe	67.9	78.4	82.6
Eastern Europe	39.3	60.1	68.2
Albania	20.3	32.7	42.3
Belarus	22.6	50.3	68.2
Bosnia	13.7	31.3	43.0
Bulgaria	25.6	57.5	67.5
Croatia	22.3	45.1	57.7
Czech Republic	40.9	63.7	74.5
Hungary	39.3	52.8	64.5
Macedonia	23.4	50.6	59.4
Moldova	16.6	35.8	41.6
Poland	38.7	55.4	62.3
Romania	25.5	46.1	55.1
Russia	44.7	66.4	72.9
Slovakia	30.0	46.3	57.4
Slovenia	19.9	42.4	49.2
Ukraine	39.2	58.3	67.9
Yugoslavia	19.0	43.0	51.6

United Nations Population Information Network, posted at *http://www.un.org/popin/data.html.*

Question: What are the economic implications of these data?

late twentieth century led to tense political situations in many European countries. Most states had defined their identity in images shaped by nineteenth-century nationalism: a shared language, religion, culture, and history created a nation-state. Many states now confronted the reality of cultural diversity. At the start of the twenty-first century, immigration remained one of the hottest political issues in European politics, with numerous restrictions placed on migrants from outside the EU. Nonetheless, in 2002, Britain still accepted 1.1 immigrants for every 1,000 population; Italy, 1.7 per 1,000; and Germany, 4.0 per 1,000. (The rate in the United States is 3.5 per 1,000.) One of the strongest reasons for the continued acceptance of immigration is economic: in 2003, the EU reported that more than three-fourths of all European population growth (and, therefore, a growing labor pool) came from immigration.

THE ECONOMIC STRUCTURES OF EUROPE SINCE 1900

The Persistence of Agricultural Civilization.
Agriculture dominated the economy of Europe through the eighteenth century but began to lose preeminence during industrialization. Nineteenth-century industrialization, however, should not obscure the persistence of agricultural society. Just as the European political history

IMMIGRATION TO EUROPE

Immigration into Europe. In the 1950s and 1960s, several of the major states of Europe experienced waves of immigration from outside Europe, typically from their colonies or former colonies. In this photograph, a passenger ship from the Caribbean has landed at the British port of Southampton, and hundreds of immigrants from the West Indies are disembarking for residence in the United Kingdom, which was profoundly changed by the new population and the reaction to it.

TABLE 30.5 COMMONWEALTH IMMIGRATION INTO BRITAIN

Annual Net Commonwealth Immigration

YEAR	WEST INDIES	PAKISTAN AND INDIA	BANGLADESH
1960	49,700	5,900	2,500
1961	66,300	23,750	25,100
1962	35,041	22,100	24,943
January–June	31,800	19,050	25,080
July–December	3,241	3,050	2137
1972	1,176	3,634	23,515

Source: Adapted from data in Butler, David, and Sloman, Anne, eds., *British Political Facts, 1900–1975,* 4th ed. (London: Macmillan, 1975, p. 268).

Question: What explains the sharp decrease in immigration?

---

of 1900 depicts the progress of democracy and the persistence of monarchical government and aristocratic privilege, the European economic history of 1900 must show the progress of industry alongside a surviving agricultural society. In eastern Europe, where industrialization had not yet advanced greatly, the huge majority of the population was still engaged in agriculture. In France, a major industrial power, less than one-third of the labor force worked in industrial occupations. Even Germany, the greatest industrial powerhouse of the continent, had less than half of its population engaged in the industrial workforce in 1900 (see *The Changing Role of Agriculture in Twentieth-Century Europe*).

The Gradual Decline of Agriculture. Despite the strength of agricultural society at the beginning of the twentieth century, a trend was clear: agriculture was steadily employing fewer people and producing a smaller share of the **gross national product** (GNP). By 2001, agriculture accounted for only 2.6 percent of the French GNP, 1.1 percent of the German GNP, and 0.8 percent of the British GNP. On the eve of the World War I in 1914, many states, including Austria and Italy, still found the majority of their population on the farm. By 1930, comparatively few regions—such as Ireland, eastern Europe, and the Balkans—still had such rural economies. Some of those areas remained strongly agricultural long after World War II. In Ireland, nearly 50 percent of the population was engaged in agriculture as late as 1960, but the European trend was clear: in Russia, where 75 percent of the population had been employed in agriculture at the beginning of the century, less than 25 percent were employed there by 1960; in Britain, a scant 3.6 percent of the population lived by agriculture in 1960. By 2001, agricultural employment had fallen to just 1.4 percent of the population in Britain.

Although agriculture was no longer at the center of the European economy and employed comparatively few people, late twentieth-century European agriculture was neither weak nor unimportant. In France, where the agricultural economy was especially persistent, peasant farmers still formed 35 percent of the labor force at the end of World War II. Three million people left French farming between 1945 and 1980, but French agricultural production increased during that period because of modern machinery and improved farming methods. When 35 percent of the French labor force was engaged in farming, fewer than 30,000 tractors were in use; by 1967, there were more than 1.1 million. With less than 10 percent of the population engaged in agriculture in the 1980s, France was nonetheless the second largest food exporter in the world.

Continuing Industrialization

The decline of an agriculture-dominated economy in twentieth-century Europe corresponded to continuing industrialization. Most of Europe was highly industrialized by the late twentieth century, even compared with the most advanced economies of 1900. In 1980, for example, industrial output in Czechoslovakia, Poland, or Spain far exceeded the British standard of 1900; Italian output more than tripled that standard.

Anglo-German Industrial Leadership. The data on industrialization also reveal the strength of the European great powers. The British, who had the dominant economy in 1900, continued to expand their industrial output during the twentieth century despite the century's multiple catastrophes. British industrialization increased by 27 percent from 1900 to the eve of World War I; by more than 33 percent from 1900 to 1928, despite the consequences of World War I; by more than 75 percent from 1900 to 1938, despite the Great Depression of the 1930s; by more than 100 percent between 1900 and 1953, despite World War II; and by more than 200 percent by the late twentieth century. The German economy, which had been challenging British economic preeminence in 1900, surpassed British output before World War I and remained the dominant industrial economy in Europe until World War II. Although the divided and devastated Germany fell behind in the years following World War II, by 1963, West German industrial output matched that of the British and within a decade far exceeded it. The combined output of West and East Germany in the 1980s doubled British production. French industrial output, which had never approached British levels during the nineteenth century, did not reach the Anglo-German levels of 1900 until the mid-1950s. A French industrial resurgence after 1960, however, brought France close to British levels: French industrial output had stood at 41 percent of British output at the beginning of World War II, but it reached 82 percent of British output in 1980. Italy achieved a comparable industrial boom, expanding from 18 percent of Britain's production in 1913 to 72 percent in 1980. Simply put, at the beginning of the nineteenth century, Britain had a dominant lead in European industrial production, and then, at the beginning of the twentieth century, Britain shared dominance with Germany, and by the end of the twentieth century, many European states had industrialized to competitive levels with Britain and Germany (see *European Industrialization in the Twentieth Century*).

The Rise and Fall of Russian Industry. The industrial output data underscore a change in European political and military power during the twentieth century. Russian industrialization had been meager before World War I; in the late 1920s, the USSR still managed only 53 percent of British output, or 46 percent of German output. Before the death of Stalin in 1953, however, the Soviet Union had significantly surpassed the industrial production of both Britain and West Germany. By 1963, Soviet output exceeded that of British and German combined, and by 1980, it nearly equaled the output of Britain, Germany, France, and Italy combined. The collapse of the Russian economy during the last years of the USSR and its breakup in the 1990s left the new Russia of the twenty-first century far behind western Europe again. In 2001, the Russian GNP stood at one-third the Italian GNP, one-fourth the French GNP, and one-sixth the German GNP.

Gross National Product and Standard of Living. Similar economic data provide a different perspective if historians seek to illustrate the standard of living instead of political and military power. Whereas GNP combines agricultural and industrial output, as well as other economic sectors, **GNP per capita** considers this figure in terms of population—thus, it indicates the standard of living. From this perspective, neither the Soviet Union nor western European powers match Sweden's accomplishment. Although the Swedes had only 52 percent of the per capita GNP in Britain at the start of the twentieth century, they had surpassed the British by 1950 (partly by avoiding participation in the world wars) and had become 20 percent more prosperous than Britain and 17 percent more prosperous than West Germany in 1980.

Global Context. The economic evolution of the twentieth century also requires a global perspective on European industrial might. On the eve of World War I, nearly 58 percent of the world's total industrial produc-

The Changing Role of Agriculture in Twentieth-Century Europe

Agriculture remained the dominant sector of the economy in many parts of Europe in 1900, and surprisingly old traditions persisted. Human and animal labor plowed more fields than tractors did. This changed dramatically during the twentieth century. Although agriculture remained central to health and prosperity, it steadily declined as a source of employment. Whereas 75 percent of the population of eighteenth-century Europe had labored in the agricultural world, by the late twentieth century, a modern economy employed less than 10 percent of the labor force in agriculture. Tractors replaced field hands in harnesses.

The Persistence of Agricultural Society in 1900.

tion came from Europe, with Britain holding a global share of 14 percent and Germany holding 15 percent. Europe still produced more than 50 percent of the world's industrial output on the eve of World War II. By 1980, European production had fallen to 44 percent and Japanese production (9.1 percent) nearly equaled British (4.0 percent) and German production (5.3 percent) combined. The United States, which represented 32 percent of global production in 1913, still accounted for 31.5 percent in 1980, although that stable share is distorted by the post–World War II rise to nearly 45 percent of global production (1953), whereas Europe had still not recovered from wartime devastation.

The Postindustrial Economy. The relative decline in European industrial output in the late twentieth cen-

tury raises several related issues. The European economy came to be dominated by a new sector, neither industrial nor agricultural. In the course of this transition to a **postindustrial economy,** Europe (and the United States) deindustrialized their economies to a significant degree, allowing uncompetitive industries to close and many forms of traditional industrial production to go overseas (especially to Asian countries), where production costs (particularly labor) are much lower. By the 1990s, **deindustrialization** had changed many sectors of the industrial and manufacturing economy (including such traditional sectors as steel and textiles) because Western countries could import goods cheaper than manufacturing them. No image of the European economy of 2000 would have been more startling to Europeans of 1900 than the contrast between the powerful smoke-

TABLE 30.6 AGRICULTURAL SOCIETY IN 1900

COUNTRY	YEAR	PERCENT OF POPULATION EMPLOYED IN AGRICULTURE	PERCENT OF POPULATION EMPLOYED IN INDUSTRY
Austria	1910	53.1	22.6
Britain	1901	9.1	51.2
France	1906	42.7	30.2
Germany	1907	37.8	43.0
Italy	1901	58.7	24.2
European Russia	1897	74.9	9.7
Spain	1900	61.8	12.3

Calculated from tables in Mitchell, B. R., *European Historical Statistics, 1750–1970* (London: Macmillan, 1975, pp. 153–163).

Question: Which state had the most advanced economy in 1900 and which had the most backward?

TABLE 30.7 THE DECLINE OF AGRICULTURAL EMPLOYMENT, 1910–2001

COUNTRY	Percentage of Labor Force Engaged in Agriculture				
	c. 1910–1911	c. 1930–1931	c. 1960–1961	1981	2001
Austria	53.1	31.7	18.4	10.3	5.8
Britain	8.6	6.0	3.6	3.2	1.4
France	41.0	35.6	20.0	8.4	4.1
Germany	37.8	29.0	13.4 (west)	5.2	2.6
			17.4 (east)		
Ireland	42.9	25.3 (north)	13.0% (north)	17.3	7.0
		52.1 (republic)	48.6 (republic)		
Italy	55.4	35.5	29.0	13.4	5.2

Data for 1910, 1930, and 1960 calculated from tables in Mitchell, B. R., *European Historical Statistics, 1750–1970* (London: Macmillan, 1975, pp. 153–163); data for 1981 and 2001 from the European Union's *Eurostat Yearbook 2002: The Statistical Guide to Europe*, p. 67.

Question: Do these data provide a reasonable index of comparative modernization or must other factors be considered?

---

stacks of 1900 and the shuttered factories at the end of the century.

The Service Economy

By the end of the nineteenth century, the focus on industrial production no longer presented a complete picture of European economies and social structures. A third sector of the economy had been growing for several generations, and by the second half of the twentieth century, it had become as important as industrial employment. By 1980, this third sector, called **the service sector,** dominated the economy of western Europe (see Table 30.10). In 1910, industry employed 41 percent of the population, compared with 30 percent for agriculture. In 1980, the service economy employed 55 percent of the labor force of western Europe, while industry had declined to 39 percent and agriculture took only 6 percent. In 1910, Europeans had expected a continually expanding industrialization; in 1980, Europe had a postindustrial economy. The service sector did not dominate any East European economy at the time of the revolutions of 1989, although East Germany (41 percent service to 49 percent industry) and Czechoslovakia (41 percent service to 48 percent industry) were drawing close.

Defining the Service Economy. The service sector, also called the tertiary sector, had always existed; it had originally been a relatively small, but necessary, companion to the industrial economy. The simplest distinction between industrial employment and service employment

EUROPEAN INDUSTRIALIZATION IN THE TWENTIETH CENTURY

By the end of the nineteenth century, many European states were well-advanced in the development of industrial economies. The accompanying map shows that in 1914, the industrialization that had once been concentrated in the British Midlands and the German Rhineland stretched across the continent. Britain had become the first industrial economy by 1850, and British industrialization remained a standard for comparison well into the twentieth century. Table 30.8 uses the standard of British output in 1900 to show industrial growth during the twentieth century and to show how other states (such as Germany and Russia) surpassed the British.

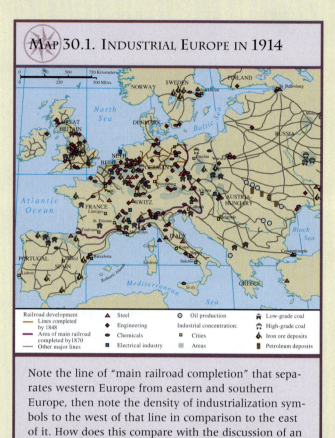

MAP 30.1. INDUSTRIAL EUROPE IN 1914

Railroad development			
Lines completed by 1848	▲ Steel	⦿ Oil production	Low-grade coal
Area of main railroad completed by 1870	◆ Engineering	Industrial concentration:	High-grade coal
Other major lines	● Chemicals	Cities	Iron ore deposits
	■ Electrical industry	Areas	Petroleum deposits

Note the line of "main railroad completion" that separates western Europe from eastern and southern Europe, then note the density of industrialization symbols to the west of that line in comparison to the east of it. How does this compare with the discussion of an "Elbe–Trieste Line" in Chapter 17?

is that the former produces material goods and the latter produces customer services. Industrial employment includes most jobs in fields such as manufacturing, heavy industry, mining, construction, and energy. It is typically manual labor—blue-collar work—paid by hourly or daily wages. The service sector has long included such smaller categories as banking and insurance, commerce and trade, journalism and communications, and a growing list of public employees. Employment in the service sector often requires more education and less physical labor and includes the white-collar work performed in offices. The late twentieth century, however, saw a boom in lower-paid and less-skilled service jobs, such as food serving in fast-food restaurants. White-collar service employees often (but not universally) receive an annual or monthly salary, however many hours they work, frequently

adding up to better total compensation. The greatest growth in the service economy by the start of the twenty-first century, however, was in hourly wage work.

Bureaucracy and Public Service. One of the areas of most rapid growth in the service economy of the twentieth century has been government employment. This category is much larger than the image of anonymous bureaucrats filling the offices of a national capital. Millions of public school teachers or postal workers are also employees of the tertiary sector. The French Ministry of Education employed 121,000 people in 1896 and more than 1 million people in 1984; in the same years, the French Ministry of Posts grew from 70,000 workers to 513,000. Thus, in a century during which the population of France increased by less than

TABLE 30.8 THE GROWTH OF EUROPEAN INDUSTRIAL OUTPUT

	Percentage of British Industrial Output in 1900					
COUNTRY	1913	1928	1938	1953	1963	1980
Britain	127	135	181	258	330	441
France	57	82	74	98	194	362
Germany	138	158	214	224	416	747
West Germany				180	330	590
East Germany				44	86	157
Italy	23	37	46	71	150	319
Poland	*	16	19	31	66	169
Spain	11	16	14	22	43	156
Sweden	9	12	21	28	48	83
Soviet Union	n.a.	72	152	328	760	1,630

*Did not exist as an independent country.

n.a. = Not available.

Sources: Adapted from data in Bairoch, Paul, "International Industrialization Levels from 1750 to 1980," *Journal of European Economic History,* 11 (1982), pp. 299, 331; and Ambrosius, Gerold, and Hubbard, William H., *A Social and Economic History of Twentieth Century Europe* (Cambridge: Harvard University Press, 1989, p. 187).

Question: Based on these data, what is the most dramatic story of twentieth-century industrialization in Europe?

44 percent, employees in one ministry increased by 768 percent and by 639 percent in another. The police, the judicial system, and—as a natural consequence of taxing to finance all of the others—the Ministry of Finance also grew much faster than the population did.

The Service Economy of the Early Twentieth Century.
The service sector was already an important part of the European economy at the start of the twentieth century, but it was clearly tertiary. In 1910, for example, 41 percent of German labor was employed in industry, 37 percent in agriculture, and 22 percent in service. The service sector accounted for 26 percent of employment in France and only 18 percent of employment in Italy that year. European employment data for 1930 show that different economies co-existed in Europe. Poland remained a traditional, rural economy, with 66 percent of the population employed in agriculture. Germany remained a strongly industrial economy, with 40 percent of employment in industry, 29 percent agricultural, and 31 percent in service. Britain demonstrated the emerging pattern of the twentieth-century economy with only 6 percent of labor in agriculture and slightly more workers in the service sector (48 percent) than the industrial (46 percent).

Post-1945 Boom of the Service Economy.
The growth of the tertiary economy chiefly occurred after World War II. By 1980, 61 percent of all workers in Sweden were in the service sector. More than 50 percent of employment in Britain, France, and Germany were in service. Meanwhile agricultural employment

TABLE 30.9 GNP PER CAPITA AND GNP DISTRIBUTION, 2001			
		Percentage of Income Going to Population in the . . .	
COUNTRY	PER CAPITA GNP (2001)	RICHEST 10%	POOREST 10%
United States	$34,320	30.5%	1.8%
Norway	$29,620	21.8%	4.1%
Germany	$25,350	28.0%	2.0%
Italy	$24,160	27.4%	1.9%
Sweden	$24,180	20.1%	3.4%
United Kingdom	$24,160	27.5%	2.1%
France	$23,990	25.1%	2.8%
Spain	$20,150	25.2%	2.8%
Poland	$ 9,450	24.7%	3.2%
Russia	$ 7,100	36.0%	1.8%

United Nations data posted at *www.undp.org.*

Question: Can you draw any conclusions by comparing the data on the income share of the top 10 percent and the bottom 10 percent? If so, what?

had fallen to less than 10 percent of the labor force in Britain (3 percent), Germany (4 percent), Sweden (5 percent), France (8 percent), and Austria (9 percent). Thus, industrial employment still remained important in all European economies, but nowhere did it account for a majority of the labor force, as it had in Britain in 1910 (52 percent). In some economies, industrial employment was declining. In Britain, it fell from 49 percent in 1950 to 42 percent in 1980; in Sweden, from 45 percent in 1960 to 34 percent in 1980.

Age, Gender, and the Labor Force

Economists who study the economic vitality of a society use an index called the **participation rate** to measure the volume and distribution of labor in an economy. Changes in the components of the participation rate tell historians much about a changing society. The total participation rate merely counts all employed persons plus all part-time workers, expressed as a percentage of the population. As a healthy economy grows, so does the participation rate. This simple index provides economic historians with a long perspective on the twentieth century. In 1900, Europe had experienced a generation of internal peace and had a generally solid economy; thus, the participation rate was high. Between 1910 and 1950, Europe was devastated by multiple catastrophes—World War I, the Russian Revolution, the Great

FIGURE 30.1 *The Industrial Economy.* At the beginning of the twentieth century, heavy industry was considered the source of a nation's power and wealth. This view of the Krupp Works at Essen in 1912 was a fair representation of the great strength of the German economy and the dream of the future for less developed economies.

TABLE 30.10 THE SOCIOECONOMIC STRUCTURE OF TWENTIETH-CENTURY EUROPE

	Percentage of Working Population														
	1910			1930			1950			1960			1980		
COUNTRY	AG.	IND.	SER.	AG.	IND.	SER.	AG.	IND.	SER.	AG.	IND.	SER.	AG.	IND.	SER.
Austria	32	33	35	32	33	35	33	37	30	24	46	30	9	37	54
Britain	9	52	40	6	46	48	5	49	46	4	48	48	3	42	56
France	41	33	26	36	33	31	27	36	37	22	39	39	8	39	53
Germany	37	41	22	29	40	31	23	43	38	14	48	38	4	46	50
Greece	50	16	34	54	16	30	51	21	28	56	20	24	37	28	35
Ireland	51	15	34	48	16	36	40	24	35	36	25	40	18	37	45
Italy	55	27	18	47	31	22	42	32	26	31	40	29	11	45	44
Poland	77	9	14	66	17	17	54	26	20	48	29	23	31	39	30
Spain	56	14	30	n.a.	n.a.	n.a.	50	26	25	42	31	27	14	40	46
Sweden	49	32	19	39	36	25	21	41	38	14	45	41	5	34	61
Yugoslavia	82	11	7	78	11	11	71	16	13	63	18	19	29	35	36

Note: Data for Austria, Greece, Ireland, Poland, and Yugoslavia for 1910 are post–World War I data, c. 1920. Data for Germany for 1950, 1960, and 1980 are for West Germany only.

Ag. = Agriculture; Ind. = industry; n.a. = not available; Ser. = service.

Questions: Which of the data suggests the leading economics of 1910? Which for 1980?

Depression, the Spanish Civil War, World War II, the Holocaust—and European economies suffered terribly. The internal peace of the cold war and the economic miracle between 1950 and the revolutions of 1989, however, overcame the catastrophes of the first half of the century to build a stronger economy. Economists assert that the prosperity of turn-of-the-century rests on a stronger economy than the prosperity of 1910 by showing that the participation rate had grown, despite the collapse of 1910–1950, and by correlating participation with productivity.

Age and the Participation Rate. This arcane tool of economic analysis is more interesting to historians who ask, "Who is participating in the economy? Who is working and who is not?" Between 1870 and 1940, for example, age became a significant factor in the changing participation rate. Compulsory education laws subtracted millions of teenagers from the labor force, thereby reducing the participation rate. The economic role of older ages has also affected the participation rate. In 1900, few programs guaranteed a paid retirement, so many people remained in the labor force beyond age 65, thereby keeping the participation rate higher. At the beginning of the twenty-first century, European governments have widespread retirement

programs that enable people to reduce or stop productive labor by age 65 (and often earlier). Yet Europe also has a steadily growing population of citizens past the age 65. In most European countries, 15 to 20 percent of the population have reached age 65, and that percentage is increasing every year. In 2001, the figure stood at 16 percent in Britain and France, 17 percent in Germany, and 18 percent in Italy (compared with 12 percent in the United States). Demographers expect the rate to pass 20 percent in many states within a decade, led by Italy with an anticipated rate of more than 22 percent. Thus, a steadily increasing portion of the population is dropping out of the participation rate. Put differently, the answer to the question "Who works?" sharply changed in the twentieth century as a result of compulsory education laws and widespread higher education, welfare programs, and increased longevity.

The Workweek. At the same time that the economic participation rate was being reduced by new social attitudes toward age, the labor movement succeeded in its long battle to reduce the workweek. Full-time employment in 1900 typically meant a 6-day, 55-hour workweek; many occupations still expected 60 to 72 hours per week. When European countries began to regulate the workweek, standards set in the 1920s were usually

Figure 30.2 *The Service Economy.* The biggest change in Western economies during the twentieth century was the growth of a third sector of the economy, neither agricultural nor industrial, which became the dominant sector of European economies after World War II. This service economy depicted itself—as in this photograph from the early days of the computer revolution in the 1960s—as the modern and efficient sector of the economy, as compared with the smokestack economy of heavy industry and large factories. (Note that men work with the office computer at this date.)

close to a 48-hour week; only during the massive unemployment of the Great Depression of the 1930s did countries start to adopt the century-old labor dream of a 40-hour workweek. During the European prosperity of the late twentieth century, workers in many countries of the EU (led by Belgium, Sweden, and France) obtained workweeks of 35 to 40 hours.

Paid Vacations. The twentieth-century labor movement also won paid vacations. Norway introduced the first paid vacations, guaranteeing all workers 2 weeks in a 1919 law. Several other western countries—including Britain and France—adopted this concept in the 1930s. It became the universal standard in postwar Europe as well as the minimum standard, because France and the Scandinavian countries increased paid vacations to 3 weeks. After 1970, the same prosperity that allowed workweeks of less than 40 hours provided minimum paid vacations of 4 weeks in EU countries, and the most progressive granted 5 or 6 weeks. Numerous traditional holidays (which varied greatly by country) meant that many European workers actually worked a 10-month year, often of workweeks below 40 hours, before retiring at often strikingly young ages. These trends had important implications for the European economy.

Growth of the Participation Rate. The consequence of this century of transforming traditional labor was to cut both its participation rate and its productivity rate. Economic historians estimate that the annual total number of hours worked by each individual worker has been cut in half. Despite all the changes that achieved this reduction—advocated by the young, the elderly, and the labor movement—other factors were so dramatic that the total participation rate and total productivity increased. One final economic trend explains this apparent paradox: the growing and changing employment of women.

Women in the Economy. Throughout modern history, working women have been a large and essential part of the European economy, although not always in ways that were noted in economic statistics. In the household economy of the eighteenth century, women worked alongside men in farms or shops. In the family wage economy of the industrial era, women entered the wage-earning labor force and their numbers in economic statistics grew significantly.

At the beginning of the twentieth century, women formed 30 to 35 percent of the salary- and wage-earning labor force in western Europe. Those percentages did not shift dramatically for most of the twentieth century, although historical circumstances sometimes caused noteworthy trends. For example, much greater employment of women was evident during both world wars and for brief postwar periods when large numbers of men were lost. (In the USSR, the death rate in World War II so reduced the postwar male labor pool that women remained employed at a high rate for the entire next generation.) The employment of women sometimes fell sharply as a consequence of conservative social policy based on the theory that women belonged in more traditional roles; Mussolini, for example, managed to reduce women's share of jobs from 32 percent in 1910 to 23 percent in 1930. Despite such secondary trends, the foremost trend was that the employment of women did not significantly change between 1910 and 1970 (see *Women in the Twentieth-Century Economy*). In the first two-thirds of the century, the rate rose just 3 percent in Britain and 2 percent in Sweden, and fell 3 percent in France and 6 percent in Italy.

The Changing Work Role of Women. In the last third of the twentieth century, the employment of women in western Europe changed significantly. Between 1970 and 1990, women went from 32 percent of the British labor force to 44 percent; that is, the number of women employed grew by more than one-third. The growth in the employment of women was equally dramatic in France and Italy, and it was very marked in Sweden, where women went from 30 percent of the labor force to 48 percent—meaning that the number of working women grew by more than 60 percent in one

WOMEN IN THE TWENTIETH-CENTURY ECONOMY

Women Office Workers. Women had played central roles in the domestic economy of the eighteenth-century agricultural world and in the family wage economy of nineteenth-century industrialization. The largest employers of women changed steadily, however. Farming, domestic service, textile factories, and prostitution had once the dominant employers of women. But in the late nineteenth century, large numbers of women began to be employed in department stores and other sales jobs; in teaching, postal, and telephone service; and in increasingly large numbers as office workers, although chiefly performing secretarial and clerical work. This British photograph of an open-plan business office in 1936 shows how dominant women had become in some sectors of the economy.

TABLE 30.11 WOMEN IN THE EUROPEAN LABOR FORCE, 1910–1990

	Women as a Percentage of Total Labor Force				
COUNTRY	c. 1910	c. 1930	c.1950	c. 1970	c. 1990
Britain	29.5	29.8	30.8	32.4	43.5
France	36.7	36.6	33.9	33.2	42.3
Germany	30.7	35.6	36.3	37.4	40.8
Italy	31.6	22.6	25.1	25.1	34.5
Sweden	27.8	31.0	26.4	29.8	47.8

Compiled from data in Mitchell, B. R., *European Historical Statistics, 1750–1970* (London: Macmillan, 1975, pp. 153–163); and *The Information Please Almanac, Atlas, and Yearbook 1994* (Boston: Houghton Mifflin, 1994, p. 136).

Question: Do any of the national differences in the data shown in this table indicate the importance of a government's social policy?

generation. This transformation of the labor market was most dramatic in regions where women previously had limited access to jobs. Women accounted for only 18 percent of the Greek labor force in 1961 and nearly doubled that share to 32 percent in a single decade. In Hungary, the employment of women nearly doubled between 1945 and 1980. As late as 1960, women provided 52 percent of all labor on Soviet collective farms and constituted 76 percent of all physicians in the USSR. A generation later, in 1987, these numbers had declined to 43 percent of agricultural labor and 69 percent of physicians.

The high levels of the employment of women in the twentieth century are especially noteworthy because the two greatest job markets for women in the nineteenth century—domestic service and the textile industry—both collapsed. The role of textiles in west European industry shrank by 75 percent between 1901 and 1975. Nonetheless, the participation of women in the labor force increased, and the explanation involves several fac-

tors. The nineteenth-century and early twentieth-century economy had a limited variety of jobs available to women—typically jobs deemed similar to a woman's role in housework, as both domestic service and textile work illustrate. Much of the explanation, therefore, is found in a new range of employment available to women. War work—demonstrating that women could effectively perform many jobs previously denied to them—was important in this trend but is insufficient as a sole explanation, as the postwar demobilization of women suggests. The rise of the service economy was probably more important. Millions of new jobs were created, without a tradition of being held by only one gender. The resulting demand for workers virtually required the participation of women in the economy, especially in government and business offices. At the same time, demographic changes facilitated the participation of women. As the birthrate fell sharply, women spent far less of their lives providing child care, thereby making themselves available for employment. At the same time that the service economy was booming and families were shrinking, a reinvigorated women's rights movement in the late twentieth century effectively advocated for the equal treatment of women. This meant that women were not only entering new types of jobs but obtaining more jobs requiring skill or education. It did not mean, however, that women acquired wage equality in the late twentieth century; women were still typically concentrated in lower-level positions, earning lower wages than men.

DAILY LIFE IN EUROPE: THE VITAL REVOLUTION AFTER 1900

The twentieth century witnessed dramatic demographic changes, which continued the **vital revolution** that began in the eighteenth century and flourished during the nineteenth century. None of these changes was more important for understanding life in the modern world than the falling **death rate** (deaths per 1,000 population) and the increase in **life expectancy** (average life span in years from birth). In 1900, many regions of Europe—from Spain in the west to Poland in the east—had an annual death rate of 25 to 30 deaths per 1,000 population (some regions and subcultures had even higher rates). In the worst areas, including much of Russia, the rate was normally greater than 30 per 1,000. In the healthiest areas of western and northern Europe, mortality generally ranged between 15 and 20 per 1,000. By the 1930s, however, the death rate had fallen below 20 per 1,000 in all corners of the continent; by the 1960s, many countries were reporting mortality figures below 10 per 1,000 (see *Mortality and Life Expectancy in the Twentieth Century*).

The Decline of Infant Mortality. The vital revolution of modern European history chiefly rested upon a decline in **infant mortality** (death before age 1), and this trend accelerated dramatically in the twentieth century (see *Mortality and Life Expectancy in the Twentieth Century*). In 1900, Europeans expected at least 15 percent of newborn children to die within their first year of life. In prosperous Germany, the rate for infant mortality was 23 percent, and in Russia, more than 25 percent. As late as the 1920s, advanced countries such as France (12 percent) and Germany (13 percent) still had high rates. Between 1920 and 1950, the infant death rate was cut in half, then halved again between 1950 and 1970, and finally halved once more between 1970 and 1990. Thus, the century witnessed the infant mortality rate in England fall from 15.4 percent to 0.7 percent, and in Germany from 22.9 percent to 0.7 percent.

The Improvement of Life Expectancy. The sharp decline in infant mortality explains much, but not all, of the decline in death rates. The vital revolution of the twentieth century also saw the population cohort aged 65 years or older grow steadily. The combination of better diet and nutrition, better sanitation and public health standards, and greatly improved medical knowledge and health care delivery systems improved prospects for all. The consequence was a remarkable increase in life expectancy. A boy born in Germany in 1910 had a life expectancy of 37.4 years, and the average boy born in Germany in 2002 can expect 74.6 years of life (see *Mortality and Life Expectancy in the Twentieth Century*). A Russia girl born in 1896 had a life expectancy of 33.3 years; Russian girls born in 2002 can expect to live 73.0 years. For many Europeans, life expectancy doubled in the span of a century. The twenty-first century is highly unlikely to produce a vital revolution of this magnitude, because another revolution would make 150-year-old people common. Even without such developments, increasing life expectancy is creating a significantly older society. In 1910, only 6 to 7 percent of the population of Europe was age 65 or older; in the 1980s, western and northern Europe had 12 to 17 percent of the population in that age cohort.

PATTERNS IN THE LIFE CYCLE IN EUROPE SINCE 1900

Marriage and Divorce

Although many of the demographic trends of modern history find their explanation in subjects such as diet or disease, some important explanations must come from human behavior rooted in institutions such as marriage and the family. Both institutions changed significantly during the twentieth century.

Age at Marriage. During the eighteenth and nineteenth centuries, economic restraints created a trend toward marriage at a later age. Couples did not marry without a steady job or a plot of land; many waited until they had accumulated savings or property. By the start of the twentieth century, the average age at which British men married had exceeded 26 years. For Irish men, the age was past age 30. Women in both societies married at slightly younger ages. The trend toward later marriage continued into the twentieth century, and on the eve of World War I, British men were typically marrying at age 27 or 28. In the 1920s, however, that trend began to change and the age at marriage began to fall. By the 1960s, British men were marrying a full 3 years younger, at age 24 or 25; British women, at age 22 or 23. In eastern Europe, where earlier marriages had been common, that trend remained a dramatic contrast to western Europe. Although western European marriage laws permit a girl to marry at an early age—at 15 in both Denmark and France and at 12 in Ireland—only 2 or 3 percent of marriages involved teenaged women. In Belarus, however, 26 percent of all marriages involved teenaged girls and 3 percent involved girls age 15 or younger. Poland reported 22 percent and Bulgaria 38 percent of all marriages involved teenaged girls.

Limitations on Childbearing. If the trend toward younger ages at marriage in western Europe and very young marriages in eastern Europe had appeared in an earlier century, it would have had a significant impact on European population because the number of childbearing years within marriage would have increased. At the start of the twentieth century, the average woman had 14 to 15 childbearing years within marriage. By the 1980s, however, that number had fallen to less than 5 years, despite younger marriages. Much of the explanation for this phenomenon has come from the restriction of childbearing years through the use of **artificial birth control**. Another part of the explanation is that the earlier marriages of the twentieth century were not necessarily longer marriages because divorce often truncated marriages during childbearing years.

Divorce. In 1900, divorce remained illegal in several countries (such as Italy and Spain), difficult to obtain in some (such as Britain), and only recently adopted in others (such as France). As twentieth-century society accepted divorce, it witnessed both the spreading legalization of divorce and a **divorce revolution**—the exponential growth of the rate at which marriages were dissolved (see Table 30.15). Even the most devoutly Catholic states of Europe allowed divorce by the end of the century. Public support in a referendum of 1970 led to the legalization of divorce in Italy, although the law there remains cautious and requires a 3-year separation before a divorce is granted. The Spanish republic introduced divorce in 1932, but it remained legal in Spain only until Franco revoked it in 1938. Divorce was not reinstituted there until 1981, but Spain then adopted a liberal divorce law. The last Western nation to prohibit divorce was Ireland, whose constitution expressly banned it; a referendum in 1995—the closest vote in Ireland's history—amended the constitution to permit divorce, and courts upheld the first divorce in 1997. In other countries, the divorce rate grew rapidly. By 1990, 30 percent of marriages in France and Germany ended in divorce, and more than 40 percent of marriages in Britain, Denmark, Russia, and Sweden were dissolved. The trend was vivid in post–World War II Britain. In 1950, there were 11.5 marriages and 0.4 divorces per 1,000 population, translating to a marriage to divorce ratio of 29-to-1; that ratio steadily fell to 9-to-1 in 1960 and to less than 3-to-1 in 1980. Approximately one-fourth of British divorces ended marriages before they had lasted 5 years, and the majority of divorces ended marriages shorter than 10 years. Divorce thus significantly reduced childbearing to less than 15 years within marriage.

Childbirth, Birth Control, and Abortion

The Falling Birthrate. Despite the pattern of earlier marriages, the birthrate fell sharply during the twentieth century, producing the **baby bust** discussed previously (see Table 30.2). The falling birthrate of the twentieth century is dramatic in numbers, but it is also complicated. The German birthrate of 28.2 births per 1,000 population in 1910 dropped to 9.0 per 1,000 in 2002, a remarkable decline of 68 percent. In Britain, the rate fell from 28.6 per 1,000 in 1900 to 11.3 per 1,000 in 2002, a fall of 60 percent. The Russian birthrate fell by an astonishing 78 percent in the same period (see Table 30.16). The demographic history of the twentieth century, however, is not a simple story of consistently falling birthrates. Indeed, observers at midcentury did not discuss the implications of a baby bust but rather a baby boom (a period in which the birthrate goes up sharply), which followed World War II. In France, the birthrate had declined to 14.8 live births per 1,000 population on the eve of the war; a decade later, in 1945–1949, the rate had risen to 20.1 per 1,000. In most of Europe, birthrates increased during the baby boom of the 1950s, peaking in the early 1960s. Thus, Britain, France, and Germany all had higher birthrates in 1960 than they had in 1930.

Family Size. One natural consequence of the low birthrate was that family size became much smaller during the twentieth century. During the eighteenth and nineteenth centuries, the average family size in western and central Europe had been close to five persons. This remained true in Victorian Britain during the Industrial Revolution, when family size had averaged 4.75 members. Significant regional variation was evident in family size, with larger families being typical of rural communities and smaller families found in towns. The falling birthrates of the twentieth century rapidly reduced average family size. In Vienna, family size fell from 4.7 in 1890 to 4.1 in 1910, then to 3.2 in 1934, and down to 2.3 in 1961. Berlin and Hamburg both had averages of 1.9 in 1993, whereas communities of fewer than 5,000 people held average families of 2.6 members. In Italy, average family size remained at 4.3 members as late as 1951, when one-third of all Italian families contained five or more members. By

Mortality and Life Expectancy in the Twentieth Century

One of the clearest measures of the vital revolution has been the steady decline in the death rate. Table 30.12 shows that some regions, such as England and Sweden, had already experienced the most dramatic decline in death rates during the nineteenth century, but other countries, such as France, Italy, and Spain, saw their death rates cut in half. The foremost explanation for the declining death rate was the dramatic reduction in infant mortality, show in Table 30.13. The conquest of childhood diseases enabled many countries to eliminate more than 90 percent of infant deaths. One of the most striking results of the falling death rate is seen in Table 30.14: the twentieth century witnessed a remarkable increase in life expectancy.

TABLE 30.12 THE TWENTIETH-CENTURY DECLINE IN DEATH RATES

COUNTRY	Death Rates per 1,000 Population			
	1910	1930	1960	1990
England	13.8	12.0	11.8	11.2
France	18.2	15.7	11.2	9.3
Germany	16.6	11.0	11.4	11.2
Greece	n.a.	16.8	7.8	9.3
Italy	19.2	14.1	11.7	9.4
Poland	*	14.9	7.6	10.2
Russia	28.2	17.8	7.2	n.a.
Spain	22.5	16.6	8.7	8.5
Sweden	13.9	11.6	10.0	11.0
United States	14.7	11.3	9.3	8.6

*Did not exist as an independent country.

n.a. = Not available.

Sources: Mitchell, B. R., *European Historical Statistics, 1750–1970* (London: Macmillan, 1975, pp. 127–132); Mitchell, B. R., *The Fontana Economic History of Europe: Statistical Appendix, 1920–1970* (London: Collins, 1974, pp. 28–34); *The World Almanac and Book of Facts 1995* (Mahwah, NJ: World Almanac Books, 1994, pp. 740–839, 959); *Information Please Almanac, Atlas, and Yearbook 1994* (Boston: Houghton Mifflin, 1994, p. 135); and U.S. Bureau of the Census, *Historical Statistics of the United States* (Washington, D.C.: U.S. Government Printing Office, 1960, p. 28).

1980, the average Italian family had 2.8 members in the prosperous north and 3.3 members in the more rural south, and less than 15 percent of Italian families had five or more members. By the 1990s, Italy had become the state most likely to experience a population decline in the twenty-first century.

Illegitimacy. The decline in twentieth-century birthrates and family size happened despite changing sexual attitudes to greater toleration of illegitimate births. In 1990, more than 25 percent of all births in Great Britain were illegitimate and 44.7 percent of births in Denmark were outside of marriage. A century earlier, Victorian Britain had low social tolerance of illegitimacy and the rate had been 5 percent. Even in Catholic countries, the stigma previously attached to having children outside of marriage had diminished. In conservative Ireland, 12 percent of 1990 births were illegitimate. In France, the number reached 26.3 percent in 1990 and passed 33 percent in 1995. The French showed the new

TABLE 30.13 THE TWENTIETH-CENTURY DECLINE IN INFANT MORTALITY

COUNTRY	1850	1900	1920	1950	1970	1990	2001
England	162	154	80	30	18	7	6
France	146	160	123	52	20	7	4
Germany	297	229	131	55 (West)	23 (West)	7	4
				72 (East)	20 (East)		
Italy	*	174	127	64	30	8	4
Poland	*	*	187	108	34	13	8
Russia	n.a.	252	n.a.	81	26	27	18
Sweden	146	99	63	21	12	6	3
Brazil						60	
India						78	
Nigeria						75	
United States	131	141	79	23	20	9	7
White						8	
Black						18	

*Did not exist as an independent country.

n.a. = Not available.

Sources: Mitchell, B. R., *European Historical Statistics, 1750–1970* (London: Macmillan, 1975, pp. 127–132); Mitchell, B. R., *The Fontana Economic History of Europe: Statistical Appendix, 1920–1970* (London: Collins, 1974, pp. 28–34); *The World Almanac and Book of Facts 1995* (Mahwah, NJ: World Almanac Books, 1994, pp. 740–839, 959); *The World Almanac and Book of Facts 1997* (Mahwah, NJ: World Almanac Books, 1996, p. 964); *Information Please Almanac, Atlas, and Yearbook 1994* (Boston: Houghton Mifflin, 1994, p. 135); and U.S. Bureau of the Census, *Historical Statistics of the United States* (Washington, D.C.: U.S. Government Printing Office, 1960, p. 26).

TABLE 30.14 INCREASED LIFE EXPECTANCY IN TWENTIETH-CENTURY EUROPE

COUNTRY	PERIOD	MALE LIFE EXPECTANCY AT BIRTH (IN YEARS)	FEMALE LIFE EXPECTANCY AT BIRTH (IN YEARS)
France	1908–1913	48.4	52.4
	2002	75.2	83.1
Germany	1910–1911	37.4	50.6
	2002	74.6	81.1
Italy	1901–1911	44.2	44.8
	2002	76.1	82.6
Russia	1896–1997	31.4	33.3
	2002	62.3	73.0
United Kingdom	1901–1910	48.5	52.3
	2002	75.3	80.8
United States	1900	46.3	48.3
	2002	74.5	80.2

Sources: Mitchell, B. R., *European Historical Statistics, 1750–1970* (London: Macmillan, 1975, pp. 127–132); Mitchell, B. R., *The Fontana Economic History of Europe: Statistical Appendix, 1920–1970* (London: Collins, 1974, pp. 28–34); *The World Almanac and Book of Facts 1995* (Mahwah, NJ: World Almanac Books, 1994, pp. 740–839, 959); *Information Please Almanac, Atlas, and Yearbook 1994* (Boston: Houghton Mifflin, 1994, p. 135); U.S. Bureau of the Census, *Historical Statistics of the United States* (Washington, D.C.: Government Printing Office, 1960, p. 28); and *CIA Fact Book—2002* at *http://www.cia.gov/cia/publications/factbook/*.

Questions: Do the data in these three tables offer convincing evidence that a "vital revolution" took place in the twentieth century? Which data are the most persuasive?

social acceptability of unmarried childbirth in 1996, when the nation celebrated the illegitimate birth of President Jacques Chirac's first grandchild. Although some parts of Europe maintained strict attitudes toward illegitimacy in the 1990s—such as Greece, where the rate was 2.1 percent—it was not traditional sexual morality that kept the birthrate low in Europe.

Birth Control. The most important explanation of falling birthrates has been the widespread practice of birth control. Information about contraception, and contraceptive devices, remained illegal in most of Europe well into the twentieth century. In the 1920s, some countries (led by France) adopted stiff new prohibitions to recover population losses during World War I, but champions of women's rights in some Western countries challenged this trend. Aletta Jacobs still maintained the world's first birth control clinic, which she had opened in Amsterdam in 1878. In 1921, a paleobotanist at the University of London, Marie Stopes, opened the first

TABLE 30.15 DIVORCE IN EUROPE, 1910–1990

COUNTRY	NUMBER OF DIVORCES IN 1910	NUMBER OF DIVORCES IN 1990	DIVORCES AS A PERCENTAGE OF MARRIAGES (1990)
Britain	701	165,700	41
France	15,125	106,096	31
Germany	13,008	128,729	30
Italy	0	30,778	8
Russia	n.a.	n.a.	42
Sweden	n.a.	n.a.	44

n.a. = Not available.

Sources: Robertson, Priscilla, *An Experience of Women* (Philadelphia: Temple University Press, 1982, p. 250); Phillips, Roderick, *Untying the Knot: A Short History of Divorce* (Cambridge: Cambridge University Press, 1991, pp. 185–186); *The Economist,* December 25, 1993; Cronin, Martha, and Nasser, Julia, "Number of Marriages and Divorces in E.C. Countries," *Europe* (June 1992), p. 4; and *Information Please Almanac, Atlas, and Yearbook 1994* (Boston: Houghton Mifflin, 1994, p. 839).

Question: Do these numbers justify the use of the term *divorce revolution?*

TABLE 30.16 THE DECLINE IN EUROPEAN BIRTHRATES, 1910–2002

COUNTRY	Birthrates per 1,000 Population				
	1910	1930	1960	1990	2002
Britain	24.2	15.3	17.9	13.9	11.3
France	18.8	17.0	18.0	13.5	11.9
Germany	28.2	16.3	18.0	11.4	9.0
Italy	32.0	24.5	18.6	9.8	8.9
Russia	44.2	43.4	22.4	12.7	9.7
Spain	31.3	27.6	21.4	10.2	9.3
Sweden	23.7	14.4	14.5	14.5	9.8
United States					14.1

Source: Mitchell, B. R., *European Historical Statistics, 1750–1970* (London: Macmillan, 1975, pp. 127–132); Mitchell, B. R., *The Fontana Economic History of Europe: Statistical Appendix, 1920–1970* (London: Collins, 1974, pp. 28–34); *The World Almanac and Book of Facts 1995* (Mahwah, NJ: World Almanac Books, 1994, pp. 740–839, 959); *Information Please Almanac 1994* (Boston: Houghton Mifflin, 1994, p. 135); and *U.S. Bureau of the Census, Historical Statistics of the United States* (Washington, D.C.: U.S. Government Printing Office, 1960, p. 23).

Question: Although the trend line from 1910 to 2002 is clear, a different pattern existed between the 1930 and 1960 data. What explains this pattern?

British birth control clinic—the Mothers' Clinic for Constructive Birth Control. Stopes's *Contraception: Its Theory, History, and Practice* was published in 1923, and she continued to fight for easy public access to contraceptives as president of the Society for Constructive Birth Control.

Opposition to Birth Control. Strong opposition to birth control clinics and contraceptives existed in the interwar years. Many governments favored a policy of **pro-natalism,** the encouragement of higher birthrates. The conservative coalition led by Raymond Poincaré in France, the Fascist government of Benito Mussolini in Italy, and the Nazi regime in Germany, all strove to encourage motherhood and to increase the population. In 1932, French conservatives enshrined in law a Family Code that provided a cash award after the first baby was born to a married couple, then provided a monthly payment of 10 percent of wages for the second child and 20 percent of wages for the third. The Vatican strongly supported pro-natalism, as evidenced in 1930, when Pope Pius XI issued the first encyclical opposed to birth control, *Casti connubi.* Pius XI left no doubt about the "correct" moral position for Catholics: "Any use what-

soever of matrimony exercised in such a way that the [sex] act is deliberately frustrated in its natural power to generate life is an offense against the law of God and of nature, and those who indulge in such are branded with the guilt of a grave sin." Some Catholic states responded to *Casti connubi.* The Irish not only outlawed birth control but also deemed it a felony to import, sell, or advertise any birth control device or any birth control instructions (such as Marie Stopes's book).

Contraceptives. European birthrates, however, show that millions of people, including Catholics, ignored both the church and the state, choosing to practice birth control. Birth control advocates, often led by champions of women's rights—who argued that women (rather than the state) should have control of their own bodies—won changes in restrictive laws after World War II. Postwar scientists also changed the nature of contraception. The first latex condoms were introduced in the 1880s, although they did not become widely available until the 1930s; these inexpensive and relatively reliable condoms made widespread birth control successful, and an estimated 8.5 billion were sold in 1993. The principle behind **oral contraceptives—**

FIGURE 30.3 *A Feminist Demonstration.* Demonstrations for women's suffrage had focused public attention on women's rights, but the vote was far from the only goal of feminist groups, which sought equality in a broad range of civil, economic, educational, legal, professional, social, and reproductive rights. In this early twentieth-century demonstration in London, the leader is Marie Stopes, the president of the Society for Constructive Birth Control.

changing a woman's balance of hormones—was well understood in the 1940s, and supplementary hormone pills were developed and tested in the 1950s. The first oral contraceptive, Enovid, was marketed in the United States in 1960, and "the pill" was introduced in Britain as Conovid in 1961. France legalized contraceptives in 1967, and although conservative French governments restricted this law in many indirect ways, the French people voted with their bodies. An International Conference on Population held in 1994 estimated that France had the highest rate of contraception in the world. Eighty percent of all married Frenchwomen used contraceptives, compared with a rate of 70 to 80 percent reported in many other countries (including the United States). Spain legalized contraceptives after the death of General Franco, and 500,000 Spanish women began using the pill in the first 3 years that it was legal. After a long and passionate debate, Ireland legalized contraceptives in 1985 for women older than age 18. And the government of Ireland even began to provide free contraceptives (although not condoms) to recipients of government-supported health care.

Conservative Opposition. Conservatives, led by the Vatican, did not abandon the battle against birth control information and devices. When the birth control pill became popular in many Western countries in the late 1960s, Pope Paul VI reiterated the church's total opposi-

tion to birth control in his 1968 encyclical *Humanae vitae* (Of Human Life). Despite the clear evidence that Catholics accepted and used birth control, Pope John Paul II maintained the strenuous rejection of all contraceptives in policy statements of 1987, 1995, and 1998. John Paul II's 1995 encyclical *Evangelium vitae* (The Gospel of Life) forcefully asserted that birth control was one of modern society's "crimes against life" and "a significant cause of grave moral decline."

Abortion before 1945. The most controversial check on population growth, however, was not birth control but abortion. Abortion had long been illegal, but had nonetheless been widely practiced in most of Europe. Pope Pius IX denounced abortion and made it an excommunicatory sin, warranting exclusion from the Catholic Church, in 1870. British laws of 1803 and 1861 expressly outlawed abortion, providing penalties up to life imprisonment. The same statutes also criminalized many forms of assisting an abortion, such as sharing an abortifacient medication. The criminal code of newly unified Germany in 1871 made abortion a serious crime, carrying a 5-year prison sentence. The French legislation of 1920 that targeted birth control also tightened laws against abortion, establishing large new fines and longer prison sentences for performing an abortion, having an abortion, or providing information about abortion. Under those statutes, a prominent French feminist who had long championed a woman's right to control her own body, Dr. Madeleine Pelletier, was imprisoned (and died) in a mental asylum in 1939. Mussolini promulgated strict antiabortion legislation in 1930, branding abortion a crime against "the health of the race." The foremost exception to the strict laws against abortion came in the Soviet Union, where Lenin's government legalized abortion in 1920. The decree required all physicians to perform an abortion if a pregnant woman requested it during the first 10 weeks of pregnancy. Stalin, however, revoked this decree and recriminalized abortion in 1936.

The Legalization of Abortion. The changing attitudes in post–World War II Europe led to the reversal of the legislation outlawing abortion (see Table 30.17). Shortly after Stalin's death, in 1955, the Soviet Union again legalized abortion. Abortion became legal in

Britain in 1968, and nearly 24,000 legal abortions were performed that year. In the next 20 years, the number of legal abortions performed in Britain grew nearly eight-fold, reaching 184,000 in 1990. At that rate, nearly 20 percent of all pregnancies in Britain ended in an abortion. By the 1970s, the legalization of abortion had become a trend in Europe. Simone Veil, the minister of health, persuaded Jacques Chirac's conservative government to legalize abortion in France in 1974. A French endocrinologist, Dr. Etienne Baulieu, developed an abortifacient drug known as RU 486, and in 1980, it became widely available there. Italian voters went to the polls in the spring 1981 referendum and approved abortion by a 2-to-1 margin, despite papal opposition declaring abortion murder. Belgium legalized abortion in 1990. Although Ireland did not legalize abortion, a controversial case in 1995 allowed Irish clinics to assist Irish women to obtain abortions abroad. In 2003, abortion was available on demand in most of Europe, including France, Germany, Italy, and Russia.

Abortion in Eastern Europe. The highest rates of abortion were typically found in eastern Europe. In 1999, Russia had an abortion rate of 1,695 per 1,000 live births (63 percent of all pregnancies ended in an abortion), a rate more than four times as high as that in the United States. More pregnancies ended in a legal abortion than resulted in a live birth in Belarus, Estonia, Romania, and Bulgaria—partly because contraceptives remained largely unavailable. A contrary pattern existed in Poland, where the Catholic Church played an important role in both the revolution of 1989 and the election of Lech Walesa to the presidency, and abortion was again outlawed in 1997.

TABLE 30.17 LEGAL ABORTIONS PERFORMED PER 1,000 LIVE BIRTHS IN EUROPE, 1999	
COUNTRY	ABORTIONS
Russia	1,695
United States	387
France	254
Britain	233
European Union	193

Source: World Health Organization data, *International Herald Tribune*, February 16, 2001.

Question: What factors might account for the differing rates of abortion?

THE CONTINUING VITAL REVOLUTION

The vital revolution of modern European history is chiefly explained in terms of diet and disease (see Chapters 18 and 22). Twentieth-century European history—with its larger population, lower death rates, longer life expectancy, smaller families, and reduced agricultural sector of the economy—must return to these factors for explanations.

The Vital Revolution and Agriculture. To understand the role of food in the vital revolution of the twentieth century, one must resolve a puzzle of trends. Between 1900 and 1990, the population of Europe increased from 423 million to 501 million, agricultural employment declined dramatically (from 32 percent of the population in Austria to 9 percent and from 41 percent of the population in France to 8 percent), and the amount of land devoted to agriculture decreased (by 15 percent in western Europe). Whereas the vital revolution of the eighteenth century had led to extensive use of the land—such as clearing forests, draining swamps, and enclosing common lands—to feed a growing population, the vital revolution of the twentieth century fed a growing (albeit more slowly) population with less land and fewer workers.

Grain Production. Grain has long been the key to understanding agriculture and the diet, and studies of grain production show the success of European agriculture during the twentieth century. Total European production (excluding Russia) of all grains—wheat, rye, barley, oats, and corn (maize)—stood at slightly less than 100 million tons in 1900. Good harvests preceded World War I, and production had grown by nearly 25 percent in 1913, before plummeting during the war. The European grain harvest reached prewar levels by 1929–1930 but had only slightly exceeded them when World War II devastated agriculture and reduced production far below 1900 levels.

In 1945, war-torn Europe produced less than 70 million tons. Between World War II and 1980, however, European agriculture experienced a miracle comparable to that of European industry. Total grain production nearly quadrupled, surpassing 250 million tons in the late 1970s. The average diet of twentieth-century Europeans became much healthier, and food costs were a much smaller percentage of the average person's income at the end of the twentieth-century than they were at the beginning.

Agronomy and Mechanized Agriculture. The agricultural miracle and its contribution to the vital revolution are the result of a tremendous investment in agronomy. The mechanization of agriculture—the widespread use of machinery such as tractors, harvesters, and threshers—has transformed farming and required fewer people to produce more food. On the eve of World War II, fewer than 300,000 tractors were being used in all of European farming; in 1980, the total was exceeded 8 million. Although many environmental problems have been attributed to the use of agricultural chemicals—both for fertilizing the soil and as pesticides—such use has contributed in large part to increasing the yield per acre. The success of biologists in developing new strains of crops or new breeds of animals has also greatly improved food production. A UN study of agriculture in Czechoslovakia between 1948 and 1978 shows how much these things have transformed agriculture. In the traditional Czech agriculture that persisted in 1948, the UN calculated that the chief production factors were natural soil fertility, climatic conditions, and ground preparation; these variables explained 80 percent of the harvest size. In the modernized Czech agriculture of 1978, the UN concluded that the most important variables were fertilization, seed quality, and the use of pesticides—which accounted for 65 percent of harvest size.

Infectious Disease. Although the success of European agriculture is important, the foremost factor in understanding the vital revolution of the twentieth century is the conquest of disease. In 1901, the largest cause of death was respiratory diseases, including influenza and pneumonia, which appeared on 16.8 percent of all death certificates. Tuberculosis (7.5 percent) and cholera (7.3 percent) each killed almost as many people as heart disease (9.9 percent). Childhood diseases such as whooping cough, measles, scarlet fever, and smallpox were still more significant causes of death (5.9 percent) than cancer (5.0 percent). By 1990, British deaths from infectious disease had fallen from 49.9 percent to 0.4 percent. Smallpox had ceased to exist as an epidemic disease, and zero deaths were reported attributable to cholera, typhoid, diphtheria, or scarlet fever. Whooping cough and measles killed a total of 8 children, compared with more than 20,000 in 1901.

The Persistence of Contagious Disease. The conquest of epidemic disease had begun at the end of the eighteenth century with Edward Jenner's smallpox vaccination. It made significant progress during the second half of the nineteenth century when Louis Pasteur established the germ theory of disease transmission and biochemists such as Pasteur and Robert Koch began the slow process of finding vaccines that could protect people from other infectious diseases. Nonetheless, the twentieth century dawned on a world still in the grip of epidemic disease. The nineteenth century ended with yellow fever and malaria still preventing the construc-

tion of the Panama Canal, and the bubonic plague remained a rare but virulent killer that ravaged both Honolulu and San Francisco. The twentieth century began with a typhoid epidemic in New York City (1903), a polio epidemic in Sweden (1905), 1.3 million deaths from bubonic plague in British India (1907), virtually annual cholera epidemics in Russia (until 1926), and a British report that the Anglo-Boer War in South Africa (1899–1902) had a British death rate from disease five times higher than the death rate from enemy fire. The association between war and disease would persist in World War I. Tetanus spread through the trenches of the western front in 1915, a typhus epidemic took 150,000 lives in Serbia in 1915, and another typhus outbreak killed 3 million people in Russia beginning in 1917. The Spanish influenza pandemic of 1919 became the most horrifying disease since the Black Death. Although it originated elsewhere, the disease took its name from the fact that nearly 80 percent of the Spanish population became infected. In 2 years, according to conservative estimates, it killed 22 million people worldwide, more than twice the number of combat deaths that occurred in World War I. In short, infectious disease was still a catastrophic feature of life in the early twentieth century. Some diseases, such as malaria in Italy and cholera in Russia, remained endemic. Some, such as polio, came in frightening epidemics (such as the one that crippled Franklin Roosevelt). And some, such as influenza and venereal diseases, were universal pandemics. The sexually transmitted human immunodeficiency virus (HIV), which leads to acquired immunodeficiency syndrome (AIDS), especially frightened the Western world at the end of the twentieth century, although Western infection rates were very low (0.1 percent of the adult population in Britain and Germany, 0.3 percent in France, 0.4 percent in Italy, 0.6 percent in the United States, and 0.9 percent in Russia) compared with the horrifying infection rates in Africa and Asia (20.1 percent of the adult population in South Africa, 33.4 percent in Swaziland, and 38.8 percent in Lesotho).

Medical Progress. Although infectious disease remained a critical issue at the beginning of the twenty-first century, the twentieth century made dramatic medical progress that shaped the vital revolution. The first Nobel Prizes were awarded in 1901; the prize in physics went to Wilhelm Roentgen for the discovery of X-rays and the first prize in physiology or medicine went to a bacteriologist in Koch's Berlin laboratory for the discovery of the diphtheria antitoxin, which became a universal childhood inoculation in the twentieth century. In 1909, another German scientist, Paul Ehrlich, opened research into a new family of antibacterial therapeutic drugs with his development of an arsenic-based treatment for syphilis named Salvarsan. Syphilis had been one the greatest scourges of the Belle Époque, killing more Europeans per year than AIDS did at the end of the century. Salvarsan cut the syphilis infection rate in western Europe by more than 50 percent before the World War I, although its application was restricted by moralists who denounced the drug, claiming it encouraged sin.

The Conquest of Contagious Diseases. Many of the most deadly diseases of European history gradually fell to the laboratory work of microbiologists, biochemists, and pathologists. After diphtheria and syphilis, yellow fever, typhus, tetanus, scarlet fever, bubonic plague, malaria, measles, and polio were all conquered or contained in Europe. Perhaps the most historic moment in this conquest of disease came in 1979, when the World Health Organization (WHO) announced that smallpox, the dreaded disease that had formerly killed tens of thousands of Europeans every year, had been totally eradicated. The last case of smallpox, WHO reported, had passed without transmission in 1977. Smallpox can, however, be revived because the governments of the United States and Russia have both stored samples of the smallpox virus, and fears remain of the use of smallpox in biological warfare.

Miracle Drugs. The identification of the bacteria and viruses responsible for contagious diseases and the development of vaccines and drug therapies stand at the center of the vital revolution of the twentieth century. No element of this story is more dramatic than the discovery of the powerful drugs that became available after 1945, popularly known as the **miracle drugs.** Their discovery began in the late 1920s, when Scottish physician and bacteriologist Alexander Fleming discovered penicillin, and was accelerated in 1935, when German pathologist Gerhard Domagk reported the discovery of the first antibacterial drug in a group called sulfa drugs. Many scientists contributed to the understanding and development of these miracle drugs. A French-American bacteriologist, René Dubos, developed the technique for isolating antibacterial agents in 1939. An Australian-born British pathologist, Sir Howard Florey, developed Fleming's penicillin into a powerful drug in 1940. Shortly thereafter, Selman Waksman, an American microbiologist, introduced one of the strongest miracle drugs—streptomycin—in 1944. During the late 1940s, a dozen new drugs followed from this collective effort. Thus, for much of the late twentieth century, miracle

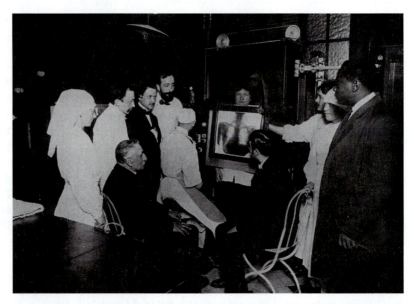

FIGURE 30.4 *Medical Technology.* In the late autumn of 1895, a German physics professor, Wilhelm Roentgen (1845–1923), was studying materials that fluoresced when exposed to cathode rays when he discovered a short-wave radiation that passed through metals and paper alike. Within months, doctors were using Roentgen's "x-rays" to see inside the human body. Roentgen, who in 1901 won the first Nobel Prize in Physics, had launched a revolution in medical technology that contributed significantly to the continuing vital revolution. In this illustration, a group of people examine a woman's rib cage as stands behind a simple x-ray machine.

drugs such as penicillin seemed to hint at the complete conquest of disease. That optimism had faded by the 1990s, however, as viruses evolved that were resistant to many antibiotics. The fight against contagious diseases was not the only great medical contribution to the vital revolution of the twentieth century—a century that saw such remarkable procedures as open-heart surgery, a range of organ transplantation, and even successes with artificial organs.

CONCLUSION

A danger confronts historians who depict life in the past too realistically—such a life can seem to have been characterized by unrelieved suffering. The grim struggle of eighteenth-century peasants, living chiefly on bread and dying at early ages, or the shocking daily life of workers during the early days of industrialization, often laboring 80 hours per week, do not make life in the past seem attractive. Students of the twentieth century must witness immense, perhaps immeasurable amounts of suffering—such as during World War I, the Russian Revolution, the Great Depression, Fascist dictatorships, Stalin's terror, and the many horrors of World War II, notably the Holocaust. Among the many corrections to this portrait of the past are the socioeconomic developments of the vital revolution of the twentieth century discussed in this chapter. Despite the nightmares of the 1914–1945 era, the twentieth century witnessed remarkable progress. The stabilization of population, the expansion of the postagricultural economy, the transition of the role of women in society, the falling death rate and the rising life expectancy all contributed to relieving any sense of ubiquitous suffering.

1900–2000

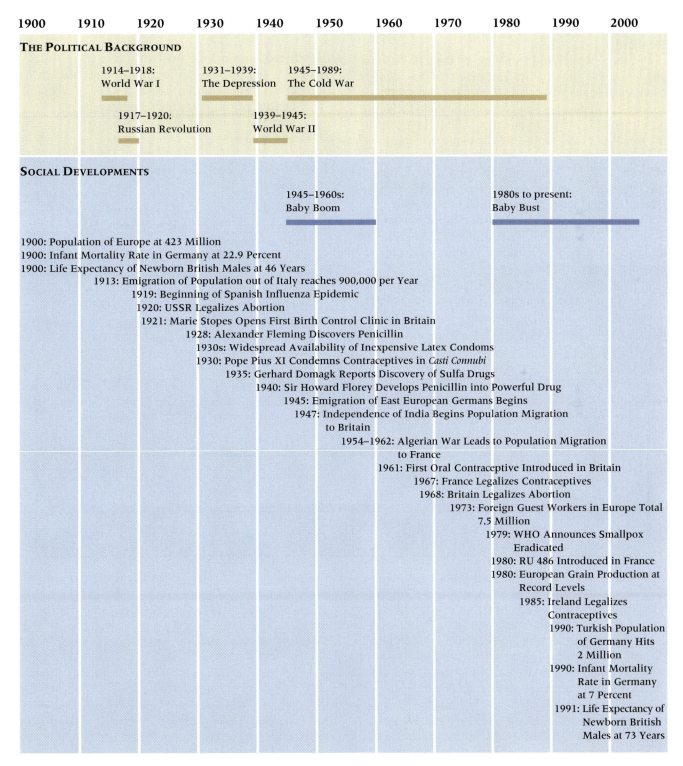

| 1900 | 1910 | 1920 | 1930 | 1940 | 1950 | 1960 | 1970 | 1980 | 1990 | 2000 |

THE POLITICAL BACKGROUND

1914–1918:
World War I

1931–1939:
The Depression

1945–1989:
The Cold War

1917–1920:
Russian Revolution

1939–1945:
World War II

SOCIAL DEVELOPMENTS

1945–1960s:
Baby Boom

1980s to present:
Baby Bust

1900: Population of Europe at 423 Million
1900: Infant Mortality Rate in Germany at 22.9 Percent
1900: Life Expectancy of Newborn British Males at 46 Years
1913: Emigration of Population out of Italy reaches 900,000 per Year
1919: Beginning of Spanish Influenza Epidemic
1920: USSR Legalizes Abortion
1921: Marie Stopes Opens First Birth Control Clinic in Britain
1928: Alexander Fleming Discovers Penicillin
1930s: Widespread Availability of Inexpensive Latex Condoms
1930: Pope Pius XI Condemns Contraceptives in *Casti Connubi*
1935: Gerhard Domagk Reports Discovery of Sulfa Drugs
1940: Sir Howard Florey Develops Penicillin into Powerful Drug
1945: Emigration of East European Germans Begins
1947: Independence of India Begins Population Migration
to Britain
1954–1962: Algerian War Leads to Population Migration
to France
1961: First Oral Contraceptive Introduced in Britain
1967: France Legalizes Contraceptives
1968: Britain Legalizes Abortion
1973: Foreign Guest Workers in Europe Total
7.5 Million
1979: WHO Announces Smallpox
Eradicated
1980: RU 486 Introduced in France
1980: European Grain Production at
Record Levels
1985: Ireland Legalizes
Contraceptives
1990: Turkish Population
of Germany Hits
2 Million
1990: Infant Mortality
Rate in Germany
at 7 Percent
1991: Life Expectancy of
Newborn British
Males at 73 Years

Review Questions

- What were the chief patterns of population change during the twentieth century?
- What were the chief changes in the European economy during the twentieth century?
- What were the chief twentieth-century contributions to the vital revolution?

For Further Study

Readings

Ambrosius, Gerold, and Hubbard, William H., *A Social and Economic History of Twentieth Century Europe* (Cambridge, MA: Harvard University Press, 1989). Somewhat outdated by not covering the period after the breakup of the Soviet Union, but a solid introduction to the trends of demography and economic structure.

Coleman, David, ed., *Europe's Population in the 1990s* (Oxford: Oxford University Press, 1996). An excellent survey of developments in marriage patterns, fertility levels, family size, migration, mortality, and aging.

McLaren, Angus, *A History of Contraception* (Oxford: Blackwell, 1996). A well-written survey of Western attitudes and behavior by a leading historian of sexual behavior and reproduction.

Phillips, Roderick, *Untying the Knot: A Short History of Divorce* (Cambridge: Cambridge University Press, 1991). A concise introduction to changing attitudes and behavior, condensing a larger scholarly work.

References

Mitchell, B. R., ed., *European Historical Statistics, 1750–1970* (London: Macmillan, 1975). In need of an update to the twenty-first century, but an invaluable resource for social and economic data.

Stearns, Peter N., ed., *Encyclopedia of European Social History*, 5 vols. (New York: Scribner's, 2001). Excellent support for many of the themes of this chapter, from demography to religion, written by dozens of prominent scholars.

InfoTrac College Edition

For additional reading, go to your online research library at *http://infotrac.thomsonlearning.com.*

Using Key Words, enter the search terms
birthrate   immigration
Alexander Fleming

Using the Subject Guide, enter the search term:
baby bust

Web Sites

http://www.un.org   The home page of the United Nations, which leads to dozens of collections of socioeconomic data, such as the long-range population projections at *http://www.un.org/esa/population/ publications/longrange/.*

http://www.cia.gov/cia/publications/factbook/   The CIA Factbook provides global data on dozens of subjects, from birthrates to HIV rates.

Visit the Western Civilization Companion Web Site for resources specific to this textbook:
http://history.wadsworth.com/hause02/

The CD in the back of this book and the Western Civilization Resource Center at *http://history. wadsworth.com/western/* offer a variety of tools to help you succeed in this course, including access to quizzes; images; documents; interactive simulations, maps, and timelines; movie explorations; and a wealth of other sources.

Chapter 31

EUROPE IN THE AGE OF THE COLD WAR, 1945–1975

*I*n the first week of September 1962, General Charles de Gaulle, the president of France and a graduate of the prestigious French military academy at St. Cyr, a man who had served as a junior officer throughout the 1914–1918 war with Germany and symbolized the French determination to resist German conquest during the second war in 1939–1945, made a state visit to the Federal Republic of Germany. De Gaulle concluded speeches at Bad Godesberg, Hamburg, and Munich by raising his large body to its fullest height, then thrusting both long arms into the air and shouting "Long live Germany! Long live German–French friendship!" At a roar of approval from his German audience, de Gaulle added the shout, *"Sie sind ein grosses Volk!"* ("You are a great people!"). One of the dominant features of modern European history was changing. More than a century and a half of warfare was becoming friendship, a stunning diplomatic revolution that would be ratified in the Franco-German Elysée Treaty of 1963 and shape European history into the twenty-first century.

Europe was again a devastated continent in 1945, with homes, industries, transportation systems, and entire cities in ruins. Chapter 31 begins by describing the territorial changes that resulted from World War II and the years of austere living that Europeans faced to rebuild. The steady economic recovery of western Europe, with aid from the U.S. Marshall Plan, produced growing prosperity in the late 1950s and the 1960s. The West German economy recovered so fast rate that it became known as the "economic miracle." Whereas Soviet satellite states were created in eastern Europe, Western democracies evolved in different ways. The British, under Prime Minister Clement Attlee, developed the welfare state; the French, following the ideas of Jean Monnet, developed a new form of capitalism within a planned economy; and the Germans, under the leadership of Konrad Adenauer, created a successful democracy in contrast to the failed Weimar democracy of the 1920s. As Europe recovered, it faced a global rivalry between the two strongest victors of World War II—the Soviet Union and the United States. This struggle never led to open warfare between the rivals, but confrontations between powers with atomic weapons were so menacing that the rivalry was called the cold war. The chapter ends by examining two of postwar Europe's greatest accomplishments: decolonization—the dismantling of ancient colonial empires—and the beginning of European economic unity with the creation of the European Economic Community (EEC).

FOCUS QUESTIONS

- Why did some of the Allies of World War II become the bitter rivals of the cold war in the 1940s?
- What new features did Britain and France introduce to western government after 1945?
- How did the age of European colonial empires end?
- What were the major events in the evolution of the economic unity of western Europe?
- How did the cold war change in the 1960s and 1970s?

POSTWAR EUROPE (1945–1949)

German Losses of Territory. No peace conference was held at the end of World War II, and no treaty was drawn up with the Axis powers. The map of postwar Europe was the consequence of Allied wartime conferences at Tehran, Yalta, and Potsdam and the political realities of the military situation in 1945. Germany was reduced in size and partitioned into four **zones of military occupation.** East Prussia, the isolated exclave of prewar Germany that had been cut off by the Polish Corridor, was taken from Germany and divided by Poland and the USSR; the Soviet annexation converted the Prussian city of Königsberg into the Soviet city of Kaliningrad, and the Polish annexation included the former free city of Danzig, now the Polish city of Gdansk. The eastern frontier of Germany was moved westward to a line defined by the Oder and Neisse Rivers, giving Poland thousands of square miles of Prussia (roughly historic Silesia and Pomerania). This shift converted the German cities of Stettin and Breslau into the Polish cities of Szczecin and Wroclaw. In the west, France reacquired Alsace and Lorraine; in the north, Denmark recovered Schleswig. The initial division of Germany was into three zones of military occupation, under the British, American, and Russian armies. In the west, Britain and the United States shared their zones with France (which Stalin had refused to do), creating a four-power occupation. The city of Berlin, although located deep in the Soviet zone of occupation, was likewise divided into sectors administered by the great powers.

The Map of Eastern Europe. The territorial changes were less dramatic in the remainder of Europe. Austria was again detached from Germany; like Germany, it was divided into zones of occupation. Austria, Czechoslovakia, Hungary, Yugoslavia, and Romania were all restored to their approximate frontiers of 1919. The most important changes in eastern Europe involved the march of the Soviet Union westward. The Baltic states of Estonia, Latvia, and Lithuania (annexed in 1939) remained part of the USSR, as did slices of eastern Poland (much of White Russia, or Belarus), Czechoslovakia (much of Ruthenia), and Romania (the province of Bessarabia). This reversed the perspective of the Peace of Paris: the 1919 treaties had created a *cordon sanitaire* of small east European states as a barrier to the spread of Bolshevism, but eastern Europe now stood as a buffer zone protecting an expanded Soviet Union from Western militarism and anti-Communism.

Postwar Population Migration. The territorial changes of 1945 led to a period of great migration, especially of the German population scattered in many states and now expelled. More than 8 million Germans left Poland and the Baltic states for Germany. They were joined by nearly 3 million Germans who had been driven out of Czechoslovakia (chiefly the Sudeten Germans); more than 1 million Germans fleeing the Soviet zone of occupied Germany;

MAP 31.1. THE EUROPEAN TERRITORIAL SETTLEMENT AFTER WORLD WAR II

- ········ National boundaries in 1949
- Allied occupation of Germany and Austria 1945–1955
- Territory lost by Germany
- Territory gained by Soviet Union
- —— "Iron Curtain" after 1955
- 1945 Year communist control of government was gained

Note the position of the "Iron Curtain" separating western Europe from the Soviet bloc in the east. An earlier version of this map would have included Yugoslavia in the Soviet bloc. How does this division of Europe compare to earlier lines, such as the Elbe–Trieste Line shown in Chapter 17?

and nearly 1 million Germans from Hungary, Yugoslavia, and Romania. Approximately 13 million Germans were uprooted from 1945 to 1947. Similarly, some 3.5 million Poles moved into the territory newly acquired from Germany, and 1.5 million Poles fled the territory acquired by the USSR. Hundreds of thousands of Italians (leaving the Istrian Peninsula, which was now Yugoslavian), Turks (driven from Bulgaria), and Ukrainians (leaving Poland for Ukraine) shared this experience.

The Austerity of the 1940s and the Economic Recovery

Devastation. Much of Europe lay in ruins in 1945. Great cities from London and Antwerp to Dresden and Leningrad were devastated. Of all German housing, 40 percent was damaged or destroyed, and 95 percent of Berlin was in rubble. More than half of the surviving productive capacity of German industry was dismantled and shipped to Russia. European transportation had collapsed amidst bombed out ports, rails, roads, and bridges. In Holland, 60 percent of the transportation network was destroyed, industrial output amounted to only 25 percent of the 1939 level, and thousands of acres of farmland lay flooded. As millions of war refugees spread across the continent, tuberculosis and malnutrition stalked displaced persons everywhere.

Austerity of Daily Life. The primary characteristic of postwar Europe was the austere existence of the survivors. The European production of bread grains in 1945 stood at 50 percent of the prewar level. Food was rationed in most of Europe; bread was rationed in Britain, although it had not been rationed during the war. The wheat crop in France for 1945 totaled 4.2 million tons, compared with 9.8 million tons in 1938, the last year of peace (see Table 31.1). The United Nations (UN) estimated that 100 million people were receiving 1,500 calories or fewer per day. Governments tried to control prices, but scarcity caused inflation. Between 1945 and 1949, prices tripled in Belgium and quintupled in France. Hungary suffered perhaps the worst inflation in world history, and the national currency was printed in 100 trillion pengö notes. Black markets selling food, fuel, and clothing flourished. Simultaneously, military demobilization created widespread unemployment.

The Marshall Plan. The recovery of Europe in the late 1940s and early 1950s relied on **planned economies,** which were managed by governments, and foreign aid. Jean Monnet, a distinguished French economist and civil servant, became the father of European **mixed economies** (based on a mixture of capitalist and socialist principles) that relied on **state planning,** such as his Monnet Plan of 1947. UN agen-

cies such as the World Bank and the United Nations' International Children's Emergency Fund (UNICEF) channeled assistance to Europe, but the United States played the greatest role. In June 1947, Secretary of State George C. Marshall proposed a program of American aid to Europe. Between 1948 and 1952, the Marshall Plan sent $13 billion to Europe; the greatest recipients were Britain ($3.2 billion), France ($2.7 billion), and Germany and Italy ($1.4 billion each). The USSR rejected aid. During 1948, West European industrial production reached 80 percent of its 1938 level in most countries (60 percent in Holland and West Germany). European economies showed signs of recovery but shortages, unemployment, and austerity continued throughout the early 1950s. By 1957, however, Prime Minister Harold MacMillan of Britain was able to say that "most of our people have never had it so good."

EASTERN EUROPE AND THE ORIGINS OF THE COLD WAR (1945–1949)

A Cold War. From the fall of Berlin in 1945 to the fall of the Berlin Wall in 1989, the west European democracies and the United States confronted the Soviet Union and its satellite states in eastern Europe in a tense conflict; this conflict is known as the **cold war,** because the two sides did not enter direct armed conflict with each other. During the most intense phase of the cold war, which stretched between two dramatic crises (the Berlin blockade of 1948 and the Cuban missile crisis of 1962), the world lived in constant dread of the possibility of nuclear war.

Russian War Losses. The origins of the cold war lay in eastern Europe, where the Red Army occupied vast regions in 1945. Russia had survived its third invasion from the west in modern times, outlasting Hitler just as it had survived Napoleon and the kaiser. The Soviet war effort had taken two or three times as many lives (as many as 20 million to 25 million people by the largest estimates) as British, French, German, and American deaths combined. Stalin, who ruled the USSR until his death in 1953, concluded that he must exploit the power vacuum in Europe to guarantee Russian security.

The USSR and Eastern Europe. The summit conferences at Moscow, Yalta, and Potsdam gave the Soviet Union a strong position in Eastern Europe. Churchill had recognized Romania and Bulgaria as falling in the Soviet **"sphere of influence,"** and the USSR had been conceded the occupation of the eastern one-third of Germany. In Yugoslavia, the managed elections of 1945 (in which all opposition parties abstained) gave 90 per-

AUSTERITY IN POSTWAR EUROPE

The late 1940s were austere times in both western and eastern Europe. Employment recovered slowly, reconstruction of devastated zones took years, and replacement of lost infrastructure delayed everything. Production of everything, from food to basic consumer goods recovered slowly, and rationing lasted into the 1950s.

▶ *Postwar Austerity.* The body language and facial expressions of these men speak volumes about European austerity in the late 1940s. The bicycle had again become a scarce and expensive commodity, coveted by most of the population as the dream of mobility to everything from more distant jobs to courtship.

TABLE 31.1 FOOD PRODUCTION IN POSTWAR EUROPE

| COUNTRY | Commodity (millions of metric tons) | | | | |
	WHEAT	POTATOES	SUGAR BEETS	MILK	CATTLE (MILLIONS)
Belgium					
1938	0.5	3.3	1.2	3.1	1.7
1945	0.3	1.2	0.9	1.1	1.5
Czechoslovakia					
1938	1.8	7.4	3.9	4.2	4.8
1945	1.1	6.8	3.2	2.0	4.1
France					
1938	9.8	17.3	8.0	13.8	15.6
1945	4.2	6.1	4.5	7.9	14.3
Italy					
1938	8.2	2.9	3.3	n.a.	7.7
1945	4.2	1.5	0.4	n.a.	5.9
Poland					
1938	2.2	34.6	3.2	10.3	10.6
1945	0.8	21.9	3.5	2.8	3.3
Russia					
1938	40.8	42.0	16.7	29.0	50.9
1945	13.4	58.3	5.5	26.4	44.1

n.a. = Not available.

Source: Mitchell, B. R., *European Historical Statistics, 1750–1970* (London: Macmillan, 1975).

Question: Which of the columns of data contain the most important information for understanding the austerity of the 1940s?

cent of the vote and the presidency to the hero of the resistance (and prewar secretary general of the Communist Party), Marshal Tito, who held that office until his death in 1980. Multiparty democracies were announced in Poland, Hungary, and Czechoslovakia,

and Communist parties formed a strong minority in each state. These democracies bore the burdens of postwar austerity from 1945 to 1947, and each democracy was so fragile that the Communist Party—backed by the Red Army—was able to seize control of the government. Poland, Czechoslovakia, and Hungary all fell to such Stalinist coups between 1947 and 1949.

Communist Coup in Czechoslovakia.
A dramatic example of the Communist takeover in eastern Europe occurred in Czechoslovakia in 1948. Edvard Beneš, the prewar president of Czechoslovakia and head of the government in exile during the war, returned to Prague to lead a provisional government, and he was reelected president of the republic. Free parliamentary elections in 1946 gave Czech Communists 38 percent of the vote and 114 seats; their four strongest rivals (Catholic, democratic, and socialist parties) won 178 seats. This produced a coalition government with a Communist prime minister, Klement Gottwald, and Communist management of key ministries such as the Ministry of the Interior. The Gottwald government attempted to nationalize several Czech industries, just as Socialists were doing in Britain and France; Gottwald followed Soviet orders and refused to accept Western aid, such as the Marshall Plan, for the rebuilding of Czechoslovakia. These policies led to bitter disputes with more conservative coalition partners, conflicts that Gottwald resolved in early 1948 by staging a coup d'état, naming a Communist government, and blocking elections. This coup included the mysterious death of Czechoslovakia's most prominent statesman, Foreign Minister Jan Masaryk, whose fall from a high window was labeled a suicide by the government; many other non-Communists were purged from high office. Managed elections then named Gottwald president, from which position he solidified a Communist dictatorship. A new Czech Constitution of 1948 proclaimed a People's Democratic Republic on Soviet lines.

Hungary.
Similar coups created Communist states in Hungary and Poland, where Communist-led provisional governments and the presence of the Red Army facilitated the takeovers. In Hungary, free elections using secret ballots in September 1945 gave the Communist Party only 22 percent of the vote, the third highest share, and provided 70 seats in parliament. This share was far less than that of the Smallholders Party, an anti-Communist party that garnered 57 percent of the vote and 245 parliamentary seats. Charges of a conspiracy and "plotting against the occupying forces" (the Red Army) were brought against leaders of the new republic, who were rapidly purged. This led Hungary to new elections in 1947 and a reported 95.6 percent vote for a Communist coalition. A Soviet-inspired constitution of 1949 proclaimed Hungary a People's Republic.

Poland.
The Communist position in Poland was strong in 1945 because many non-Communist leaders had been killed in the Warsaw uprising of 1944. Two competing governments in exile claimed to represent Poland—one that spent the war in Moscow and another that spent it in London. When the Red Army liberated Poland, Stalin installed the pro-Soviet government in the Polish town of Lublin, and it formed the basis of the postwar compromise government. The Communist-led provisional government did not hold elections until 1947, when its coalition received 80.1 percent of the vote and Western protests arose, declaring the elections unfair. In a pattern similar to the events in Hungary and Czechoslovakia, the government nationalized land and industries, fought with the Catholic Church, punished collaborators (more than 1 million people were disenfranchised), adopted a new constitution, and purged the party. Although other parties continued to exist, the Communist government won a reported 99.8 percent of the vote in the elections of 1952.

The Iron Curtain.
The creation of Communist dictatorships allied to the Soviet Union provoked a strong reaction in the West. Winston Churchill, a lifelong anti-Communist, sounded the alarm against Soviet expansionism in a speech delivered at a small college in Missouri in March 1946. Churchill said that "an iron curtain has descended across the Continent," and the term **Iron Curtain** became the Western world's cold war symbol for the division between the democratic West and the Communist East.

The Truman Doctrine.
The West first confronted Communist expansionism in the Balkans. Greece had been a scene of intense partisan fighting throughout the war. The Greek resistance was predominantly composed of Communists—a situation similar to that in Yugoslavia and, to a slightly lesser degree, France—whereas the Greek government was a monarchy. The conflict between the resistance and the government produced sporadic fighting in 1944–1945 and degenerated into a Greek Civil War (1946–1949), which is widely seen as an attempted coup d'état by Greek Communists. This civil war focused Western attention on the Balkans, specifically on the vulnerability of Turkey and the strait linking the Black Sea and the Mediterranean. The geopolitical importance of this region combined with growing Western anxieties about Communist expansionism led President Harry S. Truman to announce aid to Greece and Turkey in 1947. This policy became the Truman Doctrine: the United States would "support free peoples who are resisting attempted subjugation by armed minorities or by outside pressures." The Truman Doctrine of aid to threatened countries blended with the Marshall Plan for aid in economic recovery; humanitarian assistance and military assistance were intertwined instruments of the cold war. American aid contributed significantly

WINSTON CHURCHILL ON AN "IRON CURTAIN" IN EUROPE (1946)

A shadow has fallen upon the scenes so lately lightened, lighted by the Allied victory. Nobody knows what Soviet Russia and its communist international organization intends to do in the immediate future, or what are the limits, if any, to their expansive and proselytizing tendencies.

I have a strong admiration and regard for the valiant Russian people and for my war-time comrade, Marshal Stalin. There is deep sympathy and good-will in Britain—and I doubt not here also—toward the peoples of all the Russias. . . . We understand the Russian need to be secure on her western frontiers by the removal of all possibility of German aggression. We welcome Russia to her rightful place among the leading nations of the world. . . .

It is my duty, however . . . to place before you certain facts about the present position in Europe.

From Stettin in the Baltic to Trieste in the Adriatic, an iron curtain has descended across the Continent. Behind that line lie all the capitals of the ancient states of central and eastern Europe. Warsaw, Berlin, Prague, Vienna, Budapest, Belgrade, Bucharest, and Sofia, all these famous cities and the populations around them lie in what I might call the Soviet sphere, and all are subject, in one form or another, not only to Soviet influence but to a very high and in some cases increasing measure of control from Moscow.

Police governments are pervading from Moscow. . . . The communist parties, which were very small in all these eastern states of Europe, have been raised to preeminence and power far beyond their numbers and are seeking everywhere to obtain totalitarian control.

From Churchill, Winston, Speech at Fulton, Missouri, March 5, 1946. *Current History*, April 1946, pp. 358–361.

Question: To what extent does the Iron Curtain explain the cold war?

---

to the victory of the Greek monarchy over Communist guerrilla forces in 1949.

The Berlin Airlift. The most dramatic American intervention in the early days of the cold war came in the Berlin Airlift of 1948. To protest the increasing merger of the British and American zones in West Germany (dubbed "Bizonia" in 1946), the Soviet Union began to interfere with western access to Berlin and in July 1948 sealed off the city by closing all land access through the Soviet zone of eastern Germany. The United States considered opening the route to Berlin by force but instead chose to launch Operation Vittles—daily flights of humanitarian aid to sustain a city of 2 million. The Berlin Airlift delivered more than 8,000 tons of food and supplies daily, with British and American flights landing every 5 minutes around the clock until the Soviet Union lifted its blockade in the spring of 1949.

NATO and the Warsaw Pact: Containment and Confrontation

NATO. The Truman Doctrine and the U.S. policy of **containment** of Communism within countries where it had been established soon prompted military alliances. Britain, France (where the government was doubly nervous because French Communists won more than 25 percent of the votes, making it the largest party in Parliament), and the Benelux states had signed a defensive treaty in March 1948. The blockade of Berlin and the Czech coup of 1948 led to the 1949 expansion of this alliance into the North Atlantic Treaty Organization (NATO). Italy, Portugal, Norway, Denmark, Iceland, Canada, and the United States joined the original Allies in a twelve-member alliance—a defensive alliance of Western democracies—that stationed American forces throughout Europe. Greece and Turkey were added to NATO in 1949. According to one British wit, the purpose of NATO was to keep the Russians out, keep the Americans in, and keep the Germans down. The alliance possessed no forces of its own, but relied on the forces of the members states; it never entered combat during the entire history of the cold war, but it kept the Russians out of, and the Americans in, western Europe.

The Warsaw Pact. When a reunited West Germany joined NATO in 1955, the Soviet Union countered by forming the Warsaw Pact, an alliance linking the USSR, East Germany, Poland, Czechoslovakia, Hungary, Romania, Bulgaria, and Albania. Members of the Warsaw Pact pledged to respond to aggression against any member state; although such preparations never led to war between NATO and Warsaw Pact nations, this proviso was used by the USSR to send troops into member states where Communist government was being challenged. Throughout the cold war, NATO and the Warsaw Pact kept large armed forces facing each other, with thousands of American and Soviet troops stationed in allied countries—with nuclear weapons.

The Cold War in Asia. The cold war was much larger than a European struggle. Dozens of global crises threatened to bring the two sides to combat. The most dangerous of these crises occurred in Asia. In 1949, Mao Zedong's Chinese Communists won the war for control of China that they had begun in the 1930s. Mao took

TABLE 31.2 CHRONOLOGY OF COLD WAR EVENTS IN EUROPE FROM 1945 TO 1975

1945	Yalta meeting on postwar settlement
1945	Potsdam conference on the division of Germany
1946	Churchill's "Iron Curtain" speech on the division of Europe
1946	Civil war in Greece; Communist guerrillas against monarchist government
1947	Truman Doctrine of aid against Communist takeovers
1948	Communist coup in Czechoslovakia
1948	The Marshall Plan of American aid for European recovery
1948	Soviet blockade of Berlin circumvented by Berlin Airlift
1949	North Atlantic Treaty Organization (NATO) alliance linking United States, Canada, and western Europe
1949	Communists seize power in Hungary
1949	Three western zones of occupation united to form Federal Republic of Germany
1951	USSR explodes its first atomic bomb
1951	British Foreign Office officials Guy Burgess and Donald Maclean defect to the USSR after long careers as Soviet spies
1952	United States explodes the first hydrogen bomb at Eniwetok Atoll in the Pacific
1952	Great Britain explodes its first atomic bomb
1953	Death of Stalin and rise of Khrushchev
1953	Uprising in East Germany suppressed
1955	West Germany joins NATO
1955	Soviet Union organizes Warsaw Pact of East European states
1956	Anglo-French invasion of Egypt over Suez Canal
1956	Soviet Army suppresses Hungarian revolution
1957	Soviet launching of *Sputnik* begins space race
1960	USSR shoots down American U-2 spy plane over Russia
1960	France explodes its first nuclear bomb
1961	USSR achieves first manned space flight
1961	Berlin Crisis and construction of the Berlin Wall to block emigration
1962	United States forces USSR to withdraw missiles in Cuban missile crisis
1962	Solzhenitsyn reveals details of the Soviet gulag
1963	Partial Test Ban Treaty signed, beginning relaxation of cold war tensions
1963	France rejects Test Ban Treaty and plans its own nuclear force de frappe
1966	France withdraws from NATO command
1967	Six-Day War in Middle East revives grave cold war tensions
1968	Nuclear Nonproliferation Treaty Signed
1968	USSR and Warsaw Pact nations suppress Czech liberalization
1969	United States puts astronauts on moon
1970	Rioting in Poland over austerity program
1970	Heads of West Germany and East Germany hold first official meeting
1972	President Nixon visits Moscow and signs Strategic Arms Limitation Talks (SALT) Treaty
1973	West Germany and East Germany both join the UN
1975	Helsinki Accords on human rights mark age of détente

Beijing and drove his nationalist opponents, led by Chiang Kai-Shek, off the mainland to the island of Formosa (now called Taiwan). In early 1950, the U.S. Pacific Fleet patrolled the waters around Taiwan to prevent a Communist invasion. A few weeks later, Mao and Stalin agreed on a Sino-Soviet alliance. And a few weeks after that, the armies of Communist North Korea invaded the south of that partitioned country and captured the capital city of Seoul. The UN adopted a resolution to send troops to Korea to block aggression—a resolution made possible because the Soviet delegate was boycotting the UN Security Council meeting and therefore was not present to cast a veto. President Truman sent the U.S. army, commanded by the hero of the Pacific theater of World War II, General Douglas MacArthur, to join UN contingents from several countries in the small portion of the South Korean peninsula around Pusan still held by the South Koreans. After a UN counteroffensive, including an amphibious landing at Inchon, the North Korean army was driven back across the border (the thirty-eighth parallel) and MacArthur drove deep into North Korea, reaching the border of Manchuria. Then, in November 1951, Mao responded with Chinese "volunteers" (from the Red Army) to help the North. The Korean War (1950–1953), which had begun with a near victory by North Korea and led to the great danger of another world war, resulted in a stalemate and a cease-fire, perpetuating both the division of Korea and cold war anxieties.

Nuclear Terror. The most frightening aspect of such cold war confrontations was the constant threat of nuclear war. The United States was the sole possessor of the **atomic bomb** for just 4 years (1945–1949), until,

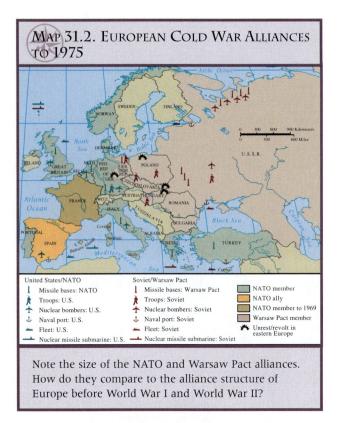

MAP 31.2. EUROPEAN COLD WAR ALLIANCES TO 1975

United States/NATO
- | Missile bases: NATO
- Troops: U.S.
- Nuclear bombers: U.S.
- Naval port: U.S.
- Fleet: U.S.
- Nuclear missile submarine: U.S.

Soviet/Warsaw Pact
- | Missile bases: Warsaw Pact
- Troops: Soviet
- Nuclear bombers: Soviet
- Naval port: Soviet
- Fleet: Soviet
- Nuclear missile submarine: Soviet

- NATO member
- NATO ally
- NATO member to 1969
- Warsaw Pact member
- Unrest/revolt in eastern Europe

Note the size of the NATO and Warsaw Pact alliances. How do they compare to the alliance structure of Europe before World War I and World War II?

in 1949, the Soviet Union, with significant assistance from atomic spies, detonated its first nuclear bomb. For the next quarter-century, the United States and the USSR engaged in a nuclear **arms race** that constantly increased the destructive power of both sides. The United States exploded the world's first **hydrogen bomb**—a bomb many times more destructive than the atomic bombs used on Hiroshima and Nagasaki—in 1952 but held this lead for only a few months. The arms race then shifted to the technology of delivering nuclear bombs. In 1953, the United States tested the first **intermediate-range ballistic missile** (IRBM), capable of carrying bombs long distances, and both sides developed **intercontinental ballistic missiles** (ICBMs) that could reach each other's cities.

The Space Race. The nuclear arms race shared much of its technology with a concurrent **space race** between the USSR and the United States. The space age—and an era of Soviet superiority in space—began in 1957, when a Russian rocket carried the first artificial **satellite,** Sputnik, into orbit. A month later, the Soviets launched a second satellite, sending a dog into space and safely retrieving it. When President Dwight D. Eisenhower rushed an American rocket to show the world that U.S. space technology did not lag far behind, it exploded a few feet off the ground and became known as the American "Dudnik." The Soviet lead in the space race continued into the 1960s, when the USSR sent the first

person into outer space, the cosmonaut Yuri Gagarin. The U.S. space program of the 1960s showed that the **"missile gap"** was narrowing; launches of American astronauts and Soviet cosmonauts into space soon became commonplace. President John F. Kennedy committed the United States to winning the space race by being the first country to put people on the moon, and in 1969, the United States succeeded when the Apollo astronauts landed on the moon.

The Arms Race. While the space race glamorized one aspect of the cold war arms race, the United States quietly took the lead in another technology with the capacity to rain atomic bombs on the Soviet Union; the United States built a fleet of nuclear submarines with atomic missiles aboard. By the early 1970s, technology had produced the MIRV. The MIRV was a hydra-headed missile that could deliver separate bombs (multiple independent reentry vehicles in the cold war lexicon) to several cities from one missile. Both sides continued to stockpile nuclear weapons and their delivery systems long after they had attained the capacity to obliterate civilization, a situation called **mutually assured destruction.**

Concurrently, both sides developed the philosophy of using nuclear weapons. The United States, for example, threatened the use of nuclear weapons to force negotiations that ended the Korean War and, again in 1962, to force the USSR to withdraw its missiles from Cuba. Both sides seriously discussed strategies such as **massive retaliation,** using nuclear bombs in conflicts instead of fighting traditional ground wars. One of the keenest metaphors of the cold war appeared on the cover of a scientific journal: a clock showing that the human race had reached 1 minute before midnight.

Peaceful Coexistence. The nuclear arms race and the space race were enormously expensive, and this cost ultimately had much to do with the end of the cold war. An early sign that this was an extremely expensive burden for the USSR came in 1959, when Stalin's successor, Nikita Khrushchev, proposed the concept of **peaceful coexistence**—that the capitalist world and the Communist world should accept each other's existence with a "live-and-let-live" attitude (see Document 31.2). Many in the West doubted Khrushchev's sincerity (he had recently made another speech, taunting the West with the message, "We will bury you!"), and few were yet willing to gamble on a relaxation of cold war preparedness. Many Europeans came to favor peaceful coexistence by the late 1960s, when it came to be called a policy of relaxed tensions (*détente* in the French vocabulary of diplomacy).

Nonintervention. As the nuclear balance of power became an ominous balance of terror, the cold war became a delicate stalemate based on the self-restraint of both sides. The NATO allies restrained themselves from direct interventions in Communist countries, although discontent with Communist rule provided opportunities. A workers' revolt in East Berlin was put down by force in 1953, beginning an era of uprisings behind the Iron Curtain. A Hungarian rebellion in 1956 led to fighting in the streets of Budapest and the creation of a reformist government under Imre Nagy. Nagy pledged to withdraw Hungary from the Warsaw Pact and to become neutral. A few weeks later, the Red Army invaded Hungary. The Soviet intervention led to the flight of 200,000 Hungarians to the west, 25,000 casualties in combat, and 2,000 executions (including Nagy) in reprisal. The NATO powers still chose not to go to war over Hungary. Similarly, the Soviet Union restrained itself from direct intervention in Western wars, such as the Anglo-French invasion of Egypt in 1956 known as the Suez War (the invasion was an attempt to keep control of the Suez Canal). Later, when the United States fought the Vietnam War (1965–1975), the second Asian war based on the containment of Communism, the USSR and China gave assistance to North Vietnam and to the Communist guerrilla armies of the Viet Cong, but both countries refrained from directly entering the war.

THE USSR UNDER STALIN AND KHRUSHCHEV (1945–1964)

The Soviet Demand for Security. No country suffered more severely from World War II than the Soviet Union. In the western quarter of the country, more than 70,000 villages were classified as destroyed. In a war zone of 800,000 square miles (Germany and Poland combined occupy only 210,000 square miles), 50 percent of all residences and 80,000 schools were lost. Twenty-five million Soviet deaths during the war overshadow every other tragedy in a century of megadeath, and such a loss of life explains why Stalin demanded postwar security for the USSR.

Soviet Economic Recovery. Stalin began the reconstruction of the Soviet Union by plundering defeated Germany. The Yalta and Potsdam agreements recognized a Soviet right to reparations from Germany and permitted Stalin to collect them "in kind." This meant the confiscation and shipment of billions of dollars worth of surviving German industry to the USSR. Recovery was entrusted to the state planning agency, Gosplan, which drafted a Five-Year Plan for 1946 to 1950. With severe enforcement, the Soviet Union exceeded the production quotas set in this plan and gave the world a name for workers who exceed their quotas, **Stakhanovites** (taken from the name of a miner who

---

DOCUMENT 31.2

NIKITA KHRUSHCHEV ON PEACEFUL COEXISTENCE (1959)

Nikita Khrushchev often used the annual Party Congress of the Communist Party to make dramatic speeches. At the congress of 1956, he opened the age of de-Stalinization in Russia in a speech attacking "the crimes of the Stalin era." In 1959, at the Twentieth Party Congress, he declared that the basis of foreign policy should be the "peaceful coexistence" of states with differing social systems, inviting a détente in cold war tensions. Western nations did not start to trust this concept for another decade.

We all of us well know that tremendous changes have taken place in the world. Gone, indeed, are the days when it took weeks to cross the ocean from one continent to the other or when a trip from Europe to America, or from Asia to Africa, seemed a very complicated undertaking. The progress of modern technology has reduced our planet to a rather small place; it has even become, in this sense, quite congested. And if in our daily life it is a matter of considerable importance to establish normal relations with our neighbors in a densely inhabited settlement, this is so much more necessary in the relations between states, in particular states belonging to different social systems. . . . What then remains to be done? There may be two ways out: either war—and war in the rocket H-bomb age is fraught with the most dire consequences for all nations—or peaceful coexistence. . . .

The problem of peaceful coexistence between states with different social systems has become particularly pressing. . . . The Soviet people have stated and declare again that they do not want war. If the Soviet Union and the countries friendly to it are not attacked, we shall never use any weapons either against the United States or against any other countries. . . . Precisely because we want to rid mankind of war, we urge the Western powers to peaceful and lofty competition.

From Krushchev, Nikita, "On Peaceful Coexistence," in Ludwig Schaefer et al., eds., *Problems in Western Civilization* (New York: Scribner's, 1965).

Question: Why would Western governments reject these words?

---

far exceeded his quota). Stalin promised that Soviet output would triple prewar levels, and by 1960, that standard had been met, although agricultural recovery was slower. Ironically, the speed of the Russian recovery increased cold war tensions because it underscored the enormous potential of the Soviet Union. And when the USSR launched Sputnik into orbit, no one could doubt the Soviets' technical potential.

Stalin's Dictatorship. Soviet security and recovery both rested on Stalin's dictatorship. His brutality had not diminished with age, and in 1948, he ordered yet another purge. The new repression was conducted by his senior lieutenant, Georgy Malenkov (a survivor of the Politburo of the 1930s), and the head of his secret police, Lavrenty Beria. This purge did not match the Great Terror of the 1930s, but it took a terrifying toll, especially on Soviet cultural life (writers and filmmakers were prominent victims). The purges then moved through the military, the bureaucracy, and the Communist Party, with anti-Semitism being a common feature. This culminated in the so-called Doctors' Plot of 1952, when Stalin accused Jewish physicians in the Kremlin of poisoning Soviet leaders.

The Death of Stalin. When Stalin died of a cerebral hemorrhage in early 1953, Malenkov and Beria claimed power. Despite the idealistic constitution of 1936, the USSR had no formal system for the transfer of power. Senior leaders feared that the rule of Malenkov or Beria meant continued terror. The army arrested and shot Beria on a charge of "plotting to restore Capitalism"; Beria's secret police was reorganized as the KGB. Malenkov was dismissed from office, but to show that Stalinism had ended, he was merely sentenced to end his career as the manager of a hydroelectric plant in provincial Kazakhstan.

Nikita Khrushchev. After a period of **"collective leadership"** (when power was shared), Nikita Khrushchev emerged as Stalin's successor. Khrushchev, the son of a Ukrainian miner, had joined the Communist Party as an illiterate worker in 1918. He rose rapidly under Stalin's regime and participated in some of its crimes during the 1930s, but his dictatorship differed from Stalinist bloodletting. At the Communist Party Congress of 1956, Khrushchev announced a program of change and openly attacked Stalin. He denounced "the crimes of the Stalin era," admitting to a startled world Stalin's "grave abuse of power . . . which caused untold harm to our Party" through "the most cruel repression." Details awaited another generation, but Soviet intellectuals were encouraged to begin a gradual dissent, circulated in self-published journals (often typed at home) called *samizdat* publications. As symbols of his **de-Stalinization,** Khrushchev removed Stalin's body from public display and renamed Stalingrad as Volgograd. Three years later, at another party congress, he made his famous call for relaxed economic controls and peaceful coexistence with the West. Westerners were shocked by Khrushchev's crude and blustering style. For many, the enduring image of Nikita Khrushchev was a fat man in a rumpled suit, banging his shoe on a podium and shouting. Soviet dissidents still faced harassment and the *gulag* (the Siberian network of prison camps) under Khrushchev, and when he fell from power in 1964, the Soviet Union remained a dictatorship. However, Khrushchev had taken the first steps toward the age of détente.

GREAT BRITAIN: CLEMENT ATTLEE AND THE BIRTH OF THE WELFARE STATE

The Recovery of Democracy. In contrast to eastern Europe and the Soviet Union, postwar western Europe experienced the recovery of parliamentary democracy. Britain, France, the Benelux countries, Italy, the Scandinavian states, and even the reunited zones of Western Germany were stable democracies by the 1950s. Spain and Portugal kept their prewar autocratic governments, but these fell after the death of Franco (1975) and Salazar (1970). The postwar Western democracies were more than mere restorations, however, and several governments expanded the European definition of democracy.

Clement Attlee and the Welfare State. Postwar Britain led the evolution of European democracy by founding the modern **welfare state.** The British electorate rejected Winston Churchill's conservative government in 1945—much as the French had rejected Clemenceau after World War I or the Russians would reject Gorbachev after the revolutions of 1989—giving the Tories only 39.9 percent of the vote in parliamentary elections. The new Prime Minister, Clement Attlee, received an overwhelming majority in Parliament (393–213) with which to enact socialist plans for a welfare state. Attlee had been born to an upper-class family and sensitized to the needs of the poor through social work in the East End of London. After World War I, he became a lecturer at the London School of Economics, a nondogmatic socialist, and a leading Labour member of Parliament (M.P.). His government planned a new British democracy based on two broad policies: (1) the adoption of welfare legislation by which the state provided all citizens with basic services "from the cradle to the grave" and (2) the **"nationalization** of leading elements" of the British economy (state ownership)following the theory that state profits would pay for welfare services.

The Beveridge Report. Attlee's welfare program derived from an idealistic wartime plan, the Beveridge Report of 1942, which called for government insurance to protect the nation. The Beveridge Report laid the basis for the National Health Act (1946) and the National

THE BRITISH WELFARE STATE

The postwar government of Prime Minister Clement Attlee (1945–1951) created the modern welfare state in Britain. Attlee based the government's welfare program on the Beveridge Report of 1942, which proposed a system of social insurance. Aneurin Bevan (1897–1960), Attlee's Minister of Health, presided over the creation of Britain's National Health Service in 1948.

The House of Commons Debates the National Health Act (1946)

Mr. Bevan (Labour): The first reason why a health scheme of this sort is necessary at all is because it has been the firm conclusion of all parties that money ought not to be permitted to stand in the way of obtaining an efficient health service. Although it is true that the [current] national health insurance system provides a general practitioner service and caters for something like 21 million of the population, the rest of the population [24 million] have to pay whenever they desire the services of a doctor. It is cardinal to a proper health organization that a person ought not to be financially deterred from seeking medical assistance at the earliest possible stage. . . .

In the second place, the [current] national health insurance scheme does not provide for the self-employed, nor, of course, for the families of dependents. . . .

Furthermore . . . in an overwhelming number of cases, the services of a specialist are not available to poor people. . . . In the older industrial districts of Great Britain hospital facilities are inadequate. Many of the hospitals are too small—very much too small. Furthermore—I want to be quite frank with the House—I believe it is repugnant to a civilized community for hospitals to have to rely upon private charity. . . .

Mr. Law (Conservative): . . . We accept the principle [of a national health system], and we accept the consequences that flow from it. . . . We are gladly committed to the principle of a 100% service. . . . We understand, once we accept the principle, that we

Clement Attlee (1883–1967), Father of the Welfare State.

are committed to a far greater degree of coordination, or planning as it is usually called, than we have ever known before . . .

[However, Conservatives] believe that [Bevan] could have established a health service equally comprehensive, better coordinated and far more efficient, if he had not been determined to sweep away the voluntary hospitals; if he had not been determined to weaken the whole structure of English local government . . . , and if he had not sought to impose upon the medical profession a form of discipline which, in our view and theirs, is totally unsuited to the practice of medicine, an art, a vocation . . . which depends above all else upon individual responsibility, individual devotion, and individual sympathy.

Question: What explains the Conservative reaction to the National Health plan?

Insurance Act (1946), laws that promised "a national minimum standard of subsistence" to everyone.

In return for a regular payroll deduction, all citizens received sick leave benefits, retirement pensions, maternity benefits, unemployment compensation, widow's and orphan's allowances, and medical care. One of the first reforms of the welfare state was a program to provide British schoolchildren (many of whom had poor nutrition from years of privation) with free milk at school, and this image did much to popularize the wel-

fare state. Beveridge, Attlee, and the minister for health and housing, Aneurin Bevan, gave western Europe the model for a democratic welfare state.

Nationalization. The Labour government also carried out the second half of its program, the nationalization of key industries. State ownership had been a central objective of European socialists since the late nineteenth century and a cornerstone of Labour Party programs since 1918. The idea had gained respectability in the 1920s, when a conservative government had created the British Broadcasting Corporation as a state corporation. Nationalization gained further appeal during the depression of the 1930s, when big business was widely blamed for the terrible unemployment. The Attlee government compensated the owners of private firms that were nationalized into **public corporations,** and the Tory Party made only limited protests when Attlee nationalized the Bank of England in 1945 and civil aviation in 1947 (creating the parent corporation of British Air). Conservatives more vigorously contested the nationalization of the coal mines (1946) and the iron and steel industries (1950); when Churchill returned to power in 1951, his government allowed most of Labour's nationalizations to stand, denationalizing (which would later be termed **privatizing**) only iron and steel and road haulage. A broad conservative attack on the policies of the Attlee years did not come until the Margaret Thatcher era, which began in 1979. Both denationalization and the dismantling of the welfare state defined her government, making Attlee and Thatcher the two defining prime ministers of British twentieth-century social policy.

Harold Wilson. Subsequent Labour governments under Harold Wilson (1964–1970 and 1974–1976) expanded the new sense of British democracy by legislating equal rights. The Race Relations Act (1965) outlawed racial discrimination, and the Sexual Offenses Act (1967) legalized homosexual acts by consenting adults. An Abortion Act (1967), one of the first legalizations of abortion in Europe; an Equal Pay Act (1970); and the Equal Opportunities Act (1975) legislated the three chief aims of the women's rights movement. These Labour reforms of the Wilson era survived Thatcher's conservatism better than Attlee's reforms.

Northern Ireland. Postwar Britain experienced a significant variety of social discontent: numerous strikes by powerful trades unions, populist (and racist) anger at the large numbers of African and Asian immigrants arriving in Britain, protests against nuclear weapons, and a growing nationalism in Wales and Scotland. But the most severe social crisis began in Northern Ireland, the six counties of Ulster which had remained with Great Britain when Ireland became independent, in 1968. A Catholic **civil rights movement,** seeking to end discrimination in employment and housing by the Protestant-controlled government, prompted vehement opposition (such as attacking civil rights marchers) by militant Protestants, who were led by the Reverend Ian Paisley (Paisley was sentenced to 3 years in prison in 1969). When riots broke out in Belfast and Londonderry in 1969, Britain responded by calling out the army, which led to a catastrophe in 1972, when British troops shot thirteen unarmed

Catholic demonstrators. By 1974, Britain had assumed direct rule in Northern Ireland, as religious strife led to frequent violence.

THE FRENCH FOURTH REPUBLIC: JEAN MONNET AND THE PLANNED ECONOMY

Postwar Nationalization. The reestablishment of a French republic also involved the rejection of a famous wartime leader, resulting in General de Gaulle's retirement in 1946. His provisional government, which returned in the aftermath of D-Day, began preparations for the constitution of a Fourth Republic and made momentous decisions that changed French society. De Gaulle feared a Communist coup in France because many of the leaders of the wartime Resistance had been Communists. To block the Communists (by stealing some of their appeal), the conservative de Gaulle chose a dramatic step: he adopted the socialist program of nationalization that Léon Blum had begun in the 1930s. The state took control of energy and the utilities (gas, oil, and coal); most insurance companies and banking; and some prominent industrial companies, such as Renault and Air France. Twenty percent of the French economy had been nationalized by the late 1940s—a program of conservative nationalization even larger than the Labour Party's efforts in Britain.

Women's Rights. De Gaulle and the wartime government in exile also agreed to grant women the vote in postwar elections. For some, this decision was based on the simple justice of equal rights, but others considered this another anti-Communist decision because they believed a common stereotype holding that women would vote conservatively, as their priests directed. Suffrage and candidacy were important steps in equal rights for women, but they did not lead to a large role for women in French politics; until the socialist parliamentary victory in the spring of 1997, France remained nearly last among European states in electing women. (The French did, however, accept a woman as prime minister—Edith Cresson in the 1990s—whereas Germany and the United States entered the twenty-first century without ever accepting a woman as the head of government.) Thus, de Gaulle's concession of the vote did not convince all French women that they had yet won equality. One prominent intellectual, Simone de Beauvoir, responded with a landmark manifesto of women's rights, *The Second Sex* (1949), arguing that women were "still bound in a state of vassalage." The late twentieth-century reinvigoration of **feminism** throughout the Western world owed much to de Beauvoir's book, and the next generation of feminists hailed her as "the mother of us all."

SIMONE DE BEAUVOIR ON THE EMANCIPATION OF THE "SECOND SEX"

Simone de Beauvoir. Simone de Beauvoir's (1908–1986) book *The Second Sex* (1948) was the founding work of the second wave of European feminism, which grew after World War II.

Simone de Beauvoir (1908–1986), the daughter of a respectable bourgeois family, was a rebel against the standards of her world. She became a leader of Parisian intellectual society, a novelist, and a philosopher closely associated with Jean-Paul Sartre and the school of existentialist philosophy, which held that people create their identity through acts of will throughout their existence.

French Law no longer lists obedience among the duties of a wife, and every Frenchwoman now has the right to vote; but these civil liberties remain only theoretical while they are not accompanied by economic freedom. A woman supported by a man—a wife or a mistress—is not emancipated from him because she has a ballot in her hand; if customs now constrain her less than before, this has not profoundly changed her situation; she is still bound in a state of vassalage. It is through paid employment that women have covered most of the distance separating them from men; nothing else can guarantee her freedom. Once woman ceases to be a parasite, the system based on her dependence falls apart; there is no longer any need for men to mediate between women and the universe.

From Beauvoir, Simon de, *Le Deuxieme Sexe*, vol. 2, *L'Expérience vecue*. Excerpt trans. Steven C. Hause (Paris: Gallimard, 1950).

Question: What is the most important element in de Beauvoir's view of emancipation?

The Fourth Republic. The French postwar elections divided power among three parties, each with 25 percent of the seats: a Catholic party (the MRP), the socialist party of Léon Blum (who had survived Nazi imprisonment), and the Communist Party (which remained popular because of its role in the wartime resistance). The new version of French parliamentary democracy, the Fourth Republic (1946–1958), greatly resembled the Third Republic (1871–1940), including its **ministerial instability** (frequent changes of government) because no party held a majority. Wars of decolonization—especially the Algerian War (1954–1962)—destroyed the Fourth Republic in 1958, resulting in the return of Charles de Gaulle to politics and the creation of the strong presidential government (as he had sought in 1945–1946) in the constitution of the Fifth Republic.

Jean Monnet and the Planned Economy. One of the greatest French contributions to European postwar democracy was a democratic version of **economic planning.** Jean Monnet, an economist whose ideas reshaped both France and Europe, never led the government of France, but his Plan for Modernization and Equipment (1946), embodied in the government's First Plan (1947–1953) and its Second Plan (1954–1957), shaped the postwar recovery. Monnet created an **"in-dicative plan"** that set goals in important sectors of the economy (such as mining or transportation) and then provided government assistance to private businesses for reaching those goals—thus maintaining most elements of a capitalist economy. Unlike rigorous state planning in the Soviet Union, Monnet's plan was not compulsory, and it did not create government control over private firms. Monnet thus pioneered the **"mixed economy,"** combining elements of capitalist and non-capitalist economics. French steel output doubled between 1950 and 1960, wheat output doubled between 1950 and 1962, and other governments soon followed Monnet's lead.

Gaullism and the Conservative Republic. As the French economy recovered, France became more conservative. The popularity of the Communist Party declined sharply, from 25 percent of the seats in Parliament in 1945 to 5 percent in 1988. The governments of the 1950s were so conservative that they even changed the traditional French insistence on **secular education;** the Barange Law (1951) gave state aid to Catholic schools. When Charles de Gaulle founded the Fifth Republic in 1958, the conservative coalition in France—known as Gaullism—won a solid majority of electoral support and retained power throughout the 1960s and

1970s. Gaullist conservatives, however, did not try to privatize the nationalized sectors of the economy, to abandon the state direction of a mixed economy, or to dismantle the growing welfare state. Indeed, Gaullists extended French welfare benefits several times, especially in the 1970s, when they expanded a state-run system of old-age pensions for the entire nation.

THE FEDERAL REPUBLIC OF GERMANY: KONRAD ADENAUER AND THE ECONOMIC MIRACLE

Communist East Germany. The rebirth of German democracy followed a more difficult course. The four-power occupation of Germany created conflicting administrations. In the Soviet zone, the revived German Communist Party, led by survivors from the Weimar Republic such as Walter Ulbricht, failed to win a majority in the elections of 1946 but took control of the government with Soviet approval. By 1948, the Soviet zone was a one-party state at the center of the cold war, and millions of East Germans were emigrating to the West. The flood of refugees going west became so embarrassing that in 1961 Ulbricht closed the border. He erected a dramatic barrier in Berlin: the Berlin Wall—a brick, concrete, barbed wire, and machine gun impediment to travel—which became the most vivid symbol of the Iron Curtain.

The Federal Republic of Germany. The Western powers slowly united their zones in Germany. Britain and the United States began the economic merger of their zones in 1946; when the French accepted German unity, the allies created the German Federal Republic (widely known as West Germany) in May 1949. The allies required that the Federal Republic's constitution (known as the *Grundgesetz,* or basic law) protect regional rights (a **federal system** of government), create authority without authoritarianism, and include a liberal bill of rights.

The leading founder of the Federal Republic of Germany was Konrad Adenauer, a lawyer who had served as mayor of Cologne and a deputy during the Weimar Republic. Adenauer had survived the Nazi era in an early retirement, and he had twice been arrested by the Gestapo. He founded a conservative party, the Christian Democratic Union (CDU), which was heavily Catholic but nevertheless tried to avoid the confessional identity of the prewar Center Party. The CDU stood for **anti-Communism, free-enterprise economics,** and social conservatism, but Adenauer, like many British and French conservatives, defended the welfare state and drew on Bismarck's example in the 1880s to advocate **"socially responsible" capitalism.**

Konrad Adenauer's Germany. The CDU mixture of conservatism and socialism won a narrow plurality of the votes for the German parliament (the *Bundestag*) in the 1949 elections; the party expanded that margin to win every national election of the 1950s and 1960s. Adenauer won the chancellorship of West Germany by a single vote by allying with a moderate third party, the Free Democrats, against a strong Social Democratic Party. Adenauer's personality was more authoritarian than democratic, but his 14-year chancellorship (1949–1963) firmly established Germany as a Western democracy. Because of his influence, the capital of the new republic was situated in the small (100,000 population in 1939) Rhineland manufacturing town of Bonn, where he had been a student, and the Federal Republic was sometimes called the Bonn Republic.

The Economic Miracle. The greatest accomplishment of the Bonn Republic was an economic recovery called the *Wirtschaftswunder* (Virt'-shafts-vun-der; **economic miracle**). The Wirtschaftswunder owed much to American policy: defeated Germany was included in the Marshall Plan of 1948 and was given $3.5 billion by 1961 in an effort to prevent the spread of Communism. Much of the credit for the recovery also belongs to the finance minister in Adenauer's cabinet, Ludwig Erhard. Erhard was a professor of economics at the University of Munich and the principal author of the CDU program linking free-enterprise economics with social welfare—a German version of the **progressive conservatism** that de Gaulle had introduced in France in 1945–1946. He presided over a monetary policy that penalized savings and favored the purchase of commodities. His demand-driven economy created a huge increase in production (see Table 31.3). German steel production had been 13.7 million tons in 1910, and East and West Germany together produced only 13.1 million tons in 1950. By 1960, West Germany alone produced 34.1 million tons. Translated into a consumer economy, this meant that West Germany manufactured only 301,000 automobiles in 1950 but more than 3 million in 1960. This rapid growth of production virtually eliminated unemployment, which fell below 1 percent.

The German Model. Credit for the hard-won German prosperity also belongs to several other groups whose spirit of consensus and compromise produced a **German model** of labor peace and political stability, which contrasted dramatically with the labor unrest in other west European countries. A generation of workers lived with long workweeks (typically 48 hours) and low wages (25 cents per hour in the 1950s or less than half of the American standard) in return for social benefits, such as 4 to 6 weeks of paid vacation per year. During the first decade of the twentieth century,

TABLE 31.3 THE GERMAN ECONOMIC MIRACLE, 1945–1969

PRODUCT	1949	1954	1959	1964	1969
Coal (1,000 tons)	177.0	217.6	237.3	255.0	229.8
Pig iron (1,000 tons)	7,140.0	12,512.0	21,602.0	27,182.0	33,764.0
Steel (1,000 tons)	9,156.0	17,434.0	29,435.0	37,339.0	45,316.0
Petroleum (1,000 tons)	842.0	2,666.0	5,103.0	7,673.0	7,876.0
Natural gas (million cubic meters)	534.0	87.0	388.0	1,975.0	8,799.0
Private cars (thousands)	104.0	561.0	1,503.0	2,650.0	3,380.0
Electricity (million kilowatt-hours)	40.7	70.5	106.2	164.8	226.1

Source: Mitchell, B. R., *European Historical Statistics, 1750–1990* (London: Macmillan, 1975, pp. 366, 372, 395, 402, 467, 481).

Question: Do these data justify the term *economic miracle?*

Germany had lost an annual average of 6.5 million working days to strikes; during the 1960s, West Germany lost an average of 0.3 million working days. At the same time, leaders of German business and industry guaranteed this labor peace by accepting the principle of the welfare state and the generous benefits for workers. A similar peace existed in German politics because the CDU's chief opposition, the Socialist Party, adopted a program at Bad Godesberg in 1959 that stated a clearly democratic form of socialism, accepted most aspects of capitalist society, and renounced Marxism and concepts such as class war (see Document 31.4).

The Elysée Treaty of 1963. Perhaps the most significant accomplishment of Konrad Adenauer or de Gaulle was the reversal of a more than 150 years of Franco-German hostility. In December 1961, Chancellor Adenauer proposed to President de Gaulle that the two statesmen hold regular consultations. That led, in the summer of 1962, to Adenauer's state visit to France, during which the two leaders attended mass together at Reims Cathedral, one of the greatest symbols of the German devastation of northern France in two world wars. In September, General de Gaulle, made his historic visit to Germany and his dramatic shout of "Long live Germany! Long live German–French friendship!" The result was a visit by Adenauer to the Elysée Palace (the presidential residence) in Paris in January 1963, where he and de Gaulle signed a treaty of Franco-German cooperation, known as the Elysée Treaty, which renounced their "age-old rivalries"; planned close economic cooperation; and facilitated student exchanges (a total of 4 million between 1963 and 2003) to build future understanding. "It is good for our children," said Adenauer in signing the treaty.

EUROPE AND THE WORLD: THE AGE OF DECOLONIZATION (1945–1975)

The End of Empire. When World War II ended, European states still held vast global empires. Most of Africa, the Middle East, South and Southeast Asia, the East Indies and Pacific Oceania, and the Caribbean remained under imperial rule. Movements for national independence had begun in many of these areas before the war. After the war, the imperial powers learned that they could not keep their empires even by fighting major wars. The resulting breakup of European colonial empires, called **decolonization,** is one of the most important themes of twentieth-century world history. As one non-Western nationalist put it, decolonization changed "the international structure more profoundly than did the two terrible world wars." That change happened rapidly. Most of South Asia and the East Indies (more than 500 million people) won self-government between 1946 and 1950. Most of Africa (more than thirty countries) won independence between 1956 and 1966.

Patterns of Decolonization. Three major patterns of decolonization emerged in the 1940s: (1) the pattern set by the British in India (granted independence in 1947) showed that Europeans could end imperialism when convinced that they must do so or pay a terrible price, (2) the pattern set by the French at the Brazzaville Conference of 1944 showed that some governments would struggle to retain empires, and (3) the pattern set by the people of the Dutch East Indies (who fought 1945–1949) showed that colonial peoples could win their independence by force.

THE BAD GODESBERG PROGRAM OF THE GERMAN SOCIAL DEMOCRATIC PARTY, 1959

The experiences of World War II and the cold war forced European socialist parties to reevaluate their programs and to develop a democratic socialism suited to the late twentieth century. They were so successful in stating new socialist programs that Britain, France, and Germany all elected important socialist governments in the late twentieth century. One of the most important restatements of the socialist program occurred in West Germany, where the Socialist Party (the SPD) had not revised its program since the Weimar Republic. The Bad Godesberg program of 1959 represented a major turning point in the history of democratic socialism: the program no longer mentioned Marx or concepts of class warfare and it accepted many aspects of capitalist society, but it effectively stressed the importance of human rights and social security.

Fundamental Values of Socialism

Socialists aim to establish a society in which every individual can develop his personality and as a responsible member of the community, take part in the political, economic and cultural life of mankind. . . .

Democratic socialism, which in Europe is rooted in Christian ethics, humanism, and classical philosophy, does not proclaim ultimate truths—not because of any lack of understanding for or indifference to philosophical or religious truths, but out of respect for the individual's choice in these matters of conscience in which neither the state nor any political party should be allowed to interfere.

The Social Democratic Party is the party of freedom of thought. It is a community of men holding different beliefs and ideas. Their agreement is based on moral principles. . . .

Basic Demands for a Society Worthy of Man

. . . All peoples must submit to the rule of international law backed by adequate executive policy. War must be ruled out as a means of policy.

All peoples must have equal opportunities to share in the world's wealth. Developing countries have a claim to the help of other peoples.

We are fighting for democracy. Democracy must become the universal form of state organization and way of life. . . .

We resist every dictatorship, every form of totalitarian or authoritarian rule because they violate human dignity, destroy man's freedom and the rule of law. . . .

In the democratic state, every form of power must be subject to public control. The interest of the individual must be subordinated to the interest of the community. . . .

The Economy

The goal of Social Democratic economic policy is the constant growth of prosperity and a just share for all in the national product, a life in freedom without undignified dependence and without exploitation. . . .

Effective public control must prevent the abuse of economic power. . . .

Public ownership is a legitimate form of public control which no modern state can do without. It serves to protect freedom against domination by large economic concerns. . . .

The competition economy does not guarantee by itself just distribution of income and wealth. This can only be achieved through measures of economic policy. . . .

The Social Democratic Party aims to create conditions in which everybody is able to save part of his rising income and acquire property . . .

Social Responsibility

Every citizen has the right to a minimum state pension in case of old age or inability to earn a living. . . .

The Social Democratic Party demands comprehensive health protection. . . .

Working hours should be progressively shortened without prejudice to income levels and in step with the development of the economy. . . .

Everyone has a right to a decent place in which to live. It is the home of the family. . . .

Equality of rights for women should be realized in the legal, economic, and social spheres. Women must be given equal opportunities in education and occupational training, in the choice and practice of professions and in earnings. . . .

State and society must protect, support, and strengthen the family. . . .

From *Basic Programme of the Social Democratic Party of Germany* (Bonn: Social Democratic Party, 1959, pp. 5–17, 20–22); reprinted in John W. Boyer and Jan Goldstein, eds., *Twentieth-Century Europe* (Chicago: University of Chicago Press, 1987, pp. 528–539).

Question: Do socialism and democracy seem compatible?

British Decolonization: India. The British acceptance of decolonization began with the election of the Attlee government in 1945. Labour Party doctrine had included colonial independence since a 1926 program denounced the empire as "based on the absolute subjection of the native population." British economic weakness and war weariness also made resistance unlikely. Gandhi's continued campaign of nonviolent resistance *(Satyagraha)*, massive demonstrations, and the astute political leadership of Jawaharlal Nehru won Indian independence in 1947. The most difficult issue facing the British was not granting independence (they realized that they had little choice), but the conditions of such independence: conflicts between the Muslim and Hindu populations of India led to its partition into a largely Hindu India (with Nehru as its first prime minister) and a largely Muslim Pakistan, a bitter parting that led to violence from 1946 to 1948 and India–Pakistan Wars in 1965, 1971, and 1984.

British Decolonization: The Middle East. British withdrawal (again with little choice) from the Middle East created another explosive situation. The collapse of the Ottoman Empire and the British role in an Arab revolt of 1916 had left Britain in control of much of the Middle East after World War I as part of a colonial mandate. The British administration of Palestine, Trans-Jordan, and the Arabian peninsula (today, Israel, Jordan, Saudi Arabia, and the Arabian gulf states) found itself at the center of the Zionist effort to create an independent Jewish homeland. The British accepted the basic principle of **Zionism** in the Balfour Declaration during World War I, and this assumed great importance when the British occupied Jerusalem and the Peace of Paris put Palestine under British control. A migration of European Jews to Palestine began during the interwar years, as did the first Arab–Jewish strife in Palestine, but British steps toward the creation of Israel were slow and Jewish settlers formed a **terrorist organization,** the Irgun, to fight for independence. World War II and the Holocaust greatly accelerated both the pace of Jewish settlement and the Arab–Jewish conflict in Palestine. When the British attempted to block massive immigration after 1945, the Irgun turned on the British and in 1946 blew up the King David Hotel (British headquarters), killing ninety-one people. The UN took up the Palestine question in 1947 and adopted a resolution calling for the **partition** of Palestine, but Jewish settlers proclaimed the state of Israel in 1948. This proclamation led to an Arab–Israeli war, the first of a series of wars in the Middle East, fought in 1956, 1967, and 1973. Britain withdrew, the UN failed to mediate the crisis, and the region remained a war zone.

French Decolonization. The French began the postwar era struggling to retain their colonial empire instead of withdrawing, as the British were obliged to do in India and Palestine. A French effort to block decolonization started with the doctrine of **assimilation.** Advocates of assimilation believed that colonial peoples could be integrated, or assimilated, into a French-speaking and French-cultured civilization in which both the metropolitan and the overseas territories were principal parts. That philosophy shaped both the

DOCUMENT 31.5

THE ELYSÉE TREATY OF 1963

France and Germany fought repeated wars with each other in the modern era—notably during the French Revolution, the Napoleonic Wars, the Franco-Prussian War, and World Wars I and II. This treaty, "bringing an end to age-old rivalries," was no small historical development, although the context of the cold war obscured its importance to many observers in 1963. The following text forms the preamble to the treaty's specific sections on diplomatic and military cooperation, educational and economic collaboration.

General Charles de Gaulle, President of the French Republic, and Dr. Konrad Adenauer, Chancellor of the Federal Republic of Germany,

Convinced that the reconciliation of the German people and the French people, bringing an end to the age-old rivalries, constitutes a historic event which profoundly transform the relations of the two peoples,

Conscious of the solidarity which unites the two peoples both with respect to their security and with respect to their economic and cultural development,

Observing particularly that young people have become aware of this solidarity and find themselves called upon to play the determinant role in the consolidation of French-German friendship,

Recognizing that a strengthening of the cooperation between the two countries constitutes a vital stage along the road to a untied Europe, which is the goal of the two peoples,

Have agreed to the organization and to the principles of the cooperation between the two States as they are stated in the Treaty signed this day . . .

Embassy of France in the United States.

From France, Embassy of the French Republic, *The ElyséeTreaty* (Washington, D.C., 1963).

Question: What other treaties of modern history can be compared with the Elysée Treaty for preserving the peace of Europe?

Brazzaville Conference, where the French promised "the material and moral development of the natives" but not independence, and the colonial provisions in the constitution of the Fourth Republic (1946): France and her colonies formed an indissoluble French Union. So the French fought independence, which was a costly policy. While the British were granting independence to Burma (1947), the French army was in the early stages of a long war in Southeast Asia (1947–1954), where they suffered a stunning military defeat at Dien Bien Phu (a valley in northern Vietnam) in 1954

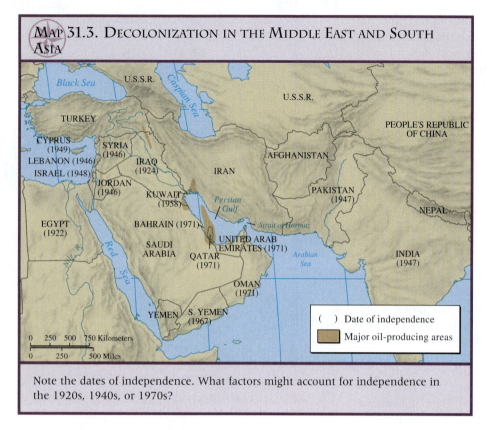

MAP 31.3. DECOLONIZATION IN THE MIDDLE EAST AND SOUTH ASIA

Note the dates of independence. What factors might account for independence in the 1920s, 1940s, or 1970s?

until accepting independence 4 years later. Variations of this pattern were repeated in all European empires. The French faced guerilla warfare from Ho Chi Minh's Vietminh forces in Vietnam until withdrawing in 1954. The British fought against the Mau Mau movement of Jomo Kenyatta in Kenya from 1948 to 1957, and Kenyatta's secret society was so successful that the term Mau Mau entered the English language as a verb, meaning to terrorize or to threaten. The last European country to accept decolonization, Portugal, had to battle guerrilla warfare in Mozambique until 1975.

Decolonization and the Cold War. Decolonization became intertwined with the cold war. The Soviet Union realized that the peoples of Africa and Asia were fighting their mutual enemies, so Moscow supported movements of national liberation. Some of the nationalist leaders seeking independence were also Communists, such as Ho Chi Minh, one of the founders of the French Communist Party. Some national liberation movements hid an uncomfortable alliance between Communist elements and nationalists; this happened in the Dutch East Indies, where the leadership was anti-Communist and later conducted a bloody purge of Communists. The United States and the European imperial powers often reacted to decolonization as if it were simply a theater of the cold war where the policy of containment applied. This led to further Western hostility to many independence movements and was a major factor for American involvement in Vietnam.

before finally accepting the independence of Indochina. While independent Burma produced a secretary-general of the UN, U Thant, the victory of Vietnamese nationalism required a total of 19 years of war, which continued against the United States (1965–1975). Before the French war in Southeast Asia had ended, the Fourth Republic became involved in yet another war of decolonization, the Algerian War, which would result in both the independence of Algeria and the collapse of the Fourth Republic itself.

Guerilla Warfare and Terrorism. Guerilla warfare (irregular combat by small groups acting independently, especially by surprise) and **terrorist attacks** (the use of violence, often extreme violence, and intimidation to coerce a government or a population) became common features of decolonization. Guerrilla warfare (and its name) had originated in Europe during the Spanish resistance to Napoleon's invasion in 1808–1814, and its techniques had been widely used by the European resistance to Nazi and Italian occupation during World War II. Two days after the surrender of Japan in 1945, Indonesian leaders proclaimed a republic of Indonesia in the East Indies, under the presidency of Achmed Sukarno, who had led resistance since 1927. When the Dutch refused independence, they had to struggle against an Indonesian People's Army, fighting by guerilla attacks rather than traditional open battles,

The Victory of Decolonization. The turning point in decolonization came between 1957 and 1962. During those years, both Britain and France acknowledged the end of their empires and more than two dozen countries gained their independence. France had lost the disastrous war in Indochina in 1954. Britain and France had suffered further embarrassment in the Middle East during the Suez War of 1956. In 1957, the British West African colony of Gold Coast had become the independent state of Ghana under the leadership of Kwame Nkrumah. Nkrumah, sometimes called "the Ghandi of Africa" for his leadership of sub-Saharan independence, became the voice of the new Africa and a revered father figure to many **anticolonialists.** In 1958, he led the first conference of independent African states by condemning Western colonialism and racism. Two years later, the UN adopted a Declaration against Colonialism stating that the ideals of the World War II Allies, embodied in the UN Charter and the UN Declaration of Human Rights, must apply to the peoples of Africa and Asia, too. The remaining European empires of Belgium, Britain, France, Portugal, and Spain, plus the United States, did not support this resolution, but they could not overcome global support for it.

The End of Empire. Conservative governments in Britain and France, long the staunchest imperialists, recognized that the age of empire—or "the great western party," as one black leader termed it—was over. Prime Minister Harold MacMillan acknowledged this in a 1960 speech discussing the "wind of change" blowing across the African continent. His Tory government of 1957–1964 granted Ghana, Kenya, Nigeria, and four other territories independence. President de Gaulle, who had courageously granted Algerian independence at the risk of French civil war, presided over the inde-

pendence of thirteen more French African colonies between 1958 and 1962.

THE EUROPEAN ECONOMIC COMMUNITY (1945–1975)

The most historic trend in postwar Europe may not have been reconstruction and prosperity, the revival of democratic government, the cold war between the West and the Soviet bloc, or even the age of decolonization, but the progress toward European unity.

Paul-Henri Spaak and the Origins of European Unity. Postwar cooperation began with the negotiation of free trade agreements. A 1948 treaty linked Belgium, Luxembourg, and the Netherlands in the Benelux Customs Union. The Organization for European Economic Cooperation (OEEC) united sixteen non-Communist states, from Iceland and Scandinavia in the north to Turkey and Iberia in the south, for the distribution of American aid from the Marshall Plan. The OEEC sparked debates about European unity, especially after the selection of Paul-Henri Spaak of Belgium as the first president of its council. Spaak called for political institutions to accompany economic unity, and a 1949 treaty founded the Council of Europe to begin such cooperation.

Robert Schuman and Jean Monnet. Meaningful economic integration began in 1950. The foreign minister of France from 1948 to 1953, Robert Schuman, a liberal Catholic born in Luxembourg who saw himself as a "European," successfully championed a new plan devised by Jean Monnet. The plan dictated that the democracies of western Europe should pool their coal and steel resources under an international authority to speed recovery. Britain—in a fateful decision that long separated the British from the evolution of European unity—

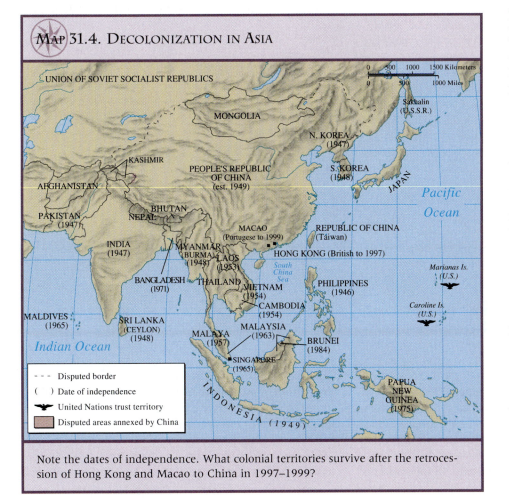

MAP 31.4. DECOLONIZATION IN ASIA

UNION OF SOVIET SOCIALIST REPUBLICS

MONGOLIA

Sakhalin (U.S.S.R.)

N. KOREA (1947)

KASHMIR

PEOPLE'S REPUBLIC OF CHINA (est. 1949)

S. KOREA (1948)

JAPAN

AFGHANISTAN

PAKISTAN (1947)

BHUTAN

NEPAL

INDIA (1947)

MYANMAR (BURMA) (1948)

MACAO (Portugese to 1999)

REPUBLIC OF CHINA (Táiwan)

Pacific Ocean

LAOS (1953)

HONG KONG (British to 1997)

South China Sea

Marianas Is. (U.S.)

BANGLADESH (1971)

THAILAND

VIETNAM (1954)

PHILIPPINES (1946)

Caroline Is. (U.S.)

CAMBODIA (1954)

MALDIVES (1965)

SRI LANKA (CEYLON) (1948)

MALAYA (1957)

MALAYSIA (1963)

BRUNEI (1984)

Indian Ocean

SINGAPORE (1965)

INDONESIA (1949)

PAPUA NEW GUINEA (1975)

- - - Disputed border
( ) Date of independence
United Nations trust territory
Disputed areas annexed by China

0   500   1000   1500 Kilometers
0   500   1000 Miles

Note the dates of independence. What colonial territories survive after the retrocession of Hong Kong and Macao to China in 1997–1999?

THE END OF EMPIRE

European colonial empires, vast territories around the globe that had been steadily taken since the fifteenth century, broke up in the generation following World War II. The age of decolonization, shown on the maps of Africa and Asia, was largely over by 1975, but it encompassed widespread violent resistance and guerilla war to convince Europeans to capitulate. Many of the leaders of the colonial peoples who won independence from European empires were the leaders of this anti-imperialist resistance or rebellion.

Kwame Nkrumah on an Independent Africa (1961)

For centuries, Europeans dominated the African continent. The white man arrogated to himself the right to rule and to be obeyed by the non-white; his mission, he claimed, was to "civilize" Africa. Under this cloak, the Europeans robbed the continent of vast riches and inflicted unimaginable suffering on the African people.

All this makes a sad story, but now we must be prepared to bury the past with its unpleasant memories and look to the future. All we ask of the former colonial powers is their goodwill and co-operation to remedy past mistakes and injustices and to grant independence to the colonies in Africa. . . .

It is clear that we must find an African solution to our problems, and that this can only be found in African unity. Divided we are weak; united, Africa could become one of the greatest forces for good in the world.

Although most Africans are poor, our continent is potentially extremely rich. Our mineral resources, which are being exploited with foreign capital only to enrich foreign investors, range from gold and diamonds to uranium and petroleum. . . . Never before have a people had within their grasp so great an opportunity for developing a continent endowed with so much wealth. Individually, the independent states of Africa, some of them potentially rich, others poor, can do little for their people. Together, by mutual help, they can achieve much. . . . Only a strong political union can

Kwame Nkrumah. Kwame Nkrumah (1909–1972), the leader of African nationalism, who began campaigning for the independence of the Gold Coast from Britain in 1947, was imprisoned by the British in 1950, and was elected prime minister of the Gold Coast in 1952, in which position he led his country to independence in 1957 as the Republic of Ghana.

bring about full and effective development of our natural resources for the benefit of our people. . . .

There is a tide in the affairs of every people when the moment strikes for political action. Such was the moment in the history of the United States of America when the Founding Fathers saw beyond the petty wranglings of the separate states and created a Union. This is our chance. We must act now.

From Nkrumah, Kwame, *I Speak of Freedom: A Statement of African Ideology* (London: Heinman, 1961).

Question: Was Nkrumah being too idealistic in 1961, or was this a realistic dream for independence?

rejected the Schuman Plan, but France, West Germany, Italy, and the Benelux states (Belgium, the Netherlands, and Luxembourg) agreed to create the European Coal and Steel Community in 1951. Monnet, a strong advocate of a United States of Europe, became the first president of the Coal and Steel Community. Despite appeals by Schuman and Monnet, British conservatives still refused to join, so the six continental states chose "to create Europe without Britain."

The Common Market. The Paris Treaty of 1951 that created the Coal and Steel Community also contained

Jomo Kenyatta. Jomo Kenyatta (c. 1894–1978) became the first president of the Republic of Kenya in 1964, after an African nationalist career that began in 1922 when he led a campaign for the return of land that white settlers had taken from the Kikuyu people. Kenyatta served a decade in British prison as the leader of the Mau Mau rebellion, the violent anticolonialist resistance campaign of the 1950s. In this photograph, he takes the oath of office as president of Kenya.

The United Nations Declaration against Colonialism (1960)

The General Assembly, mindful of the determination proclaimed by the peoples of the world in the Charter of the United Nations to reaffirm faith in fundamental human rights, in the dignity and worth of the human person, in the equal rights of men and women and of nations large and small, and to promote social progress and better standards of life in larger freedom . . . declares that:

1. The subjection of peoples to alien subjugation, domination, and exploitation constitutes a denial of fundamental human rights, is contrary to the Charter of the United Nations and is an impediment to the promotion of world peace and cooperation.

2. All peoples have the right to self-determination; by virtue of that right they freely determine their political status and freely pursue their economic, social, and cultural development.

Ho Chi Minh. Ho Chi Minh, born Nguyen That Thanh (1890–1969), created and led the national liberation movement of the Vietnamese people and became the leader of revolutionary anticolonialism in Asia after World War II. As a colonial worker, Ho had joined in founding the French Communist Party in 1920, and he united communism with his nationalism during a 30-year war to drive the Japanese, the French, and then the Americans from Southeast Asia. Ho died before the American withdrawal in 1975 allowed the creation of an independent, united Vietnam.

3. Inadequacy of political, economic, social or educational preparedness should never serve as a pretext for delaying independence.

4. All armed action or repressive measures of all kinds directed against dependent peoples shall cease in order to enable them to exercise peacefully and freely their right to complete independence.

From United Nations, *Official Records of the General Assembly,* December 14, 1960. Resolution 1514. New York: United Nations.

Question: Why would Britain, France, and the United States vote against this document?

plans for a European Parliament to sit in Strasbourg, and the six members added other **supranational institutions.** One such institution was the European Court of Human Rights (1953), a dedication to human rights that would later become one of the hallmarks of European unity when other states sought to join. (Even if it were in Europe, the United States would be ineligible for membership because the death penalty in America violates the European standard of human rights.) When the Coal and Steel Community prospered, this persuaded "the Six," as its members were called, to begin to discuss a **common market** (a free trade zone) for all goods. The

Rome Treaties of 1957 then created the European Economic Community (the EEC)—often called the Common Market—in which the Six accepted the gradual elimination of tariffs (1959–1968) among themselves and a common tariff policy toward other countries.

Europe at Sixes and Sevens. The six members of the EEC enjoyed economic advantages during the recovery of the 1950s and the prosperity of the 1960s. Their success was so clear that seven other countries—Austria, Denmark, Norway, Portugal, Sweden, Switzerland, and a reluctant Britain—formed a similar organization, the European Free Trade Association (EFTA), in 1959. The EEC, however, moved more quickly to economic and political cooperation than the EFTA did, and by the early 1960s, EEC membership clearly was highly desirable. Greece obtained associate status in the EEC in 1961, with limited trade benefits, and Turkey followed in 1963. Britain, Ireland, and

Norway then applied for full membership in the EEC. President de Gaulle of France—who had never forgotten the British and America treatment of him during World War II and who believed that the British were unwilling to surrender any measure of sovereignty to a continental organization—vetoed British entry into the Common Market, and this led the EEC to table all applications. Instead of expanding, the EEC chose to tighten its internal unity, and the EEC, the European Coal and Steel Community, and other organizations linking the Six were merged to form the European Community (EC) in 1967.

Growth of the European Community. Charles de Gaulle remained an obstacle to expansion of the EC until his retirement in 1969, but the Six voted for expansion immediately after his departure. The EC accepted all four applications, but Norwegians rejected membership in a national referendum (53–47 percent), so the Six became the Nine. The British, whose relations with Europe had been troubled for a generation, reconsidered their membership and demanded new terms for entry into the EC. They joined in 1973, but domestic opinion still demanded concessions; after winning some agreements, the British supported membership in a national referendum in 1975. Most of non-Communist Europe then began to line up for entry into the EC.

THE COOLING DOWN OF THE COLD WAR: OSTPOLITIK AND DÉTENTE (1965–1975)

The cold war in Europe began to end in the mid-1960s, and both the Soviet and American alliance systems began to weaken. A growing rift between the USSR and China opened in the 1960s, and the USSR denounced Chinese policy as anti-Leninist and branded Mao a dictator. The chill between these countries worsened when the Chinese detonated their first hydrogen bomb in 1967, and frontier incidents became common in the late 1960s. Simultaneously, American alliances were strained by the protracted Vietnam War, which was widely denounced in Europe.

The diplomatic consequences of these events were enormous, and new policies emerged during the late 1960s and early

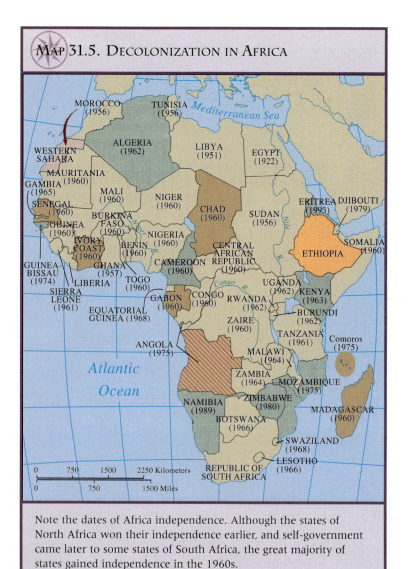

MAP 31.5. DECOLONIZATION IN AFRICA

Note the dates of Africa independence. Although the states of North Africa won their independence earlier, and self-government came later to some states of South Africa, the great majority of states gained independence in the 1960s.

1970s. President de Gaulle of France and Chancellor Willy Brandt of West Germany led Europe into this new era—de Gaulle by distancing France from the Western alliance in the late 1960s and Brandt by normalizing relations with Eastern Europe in the early 1970s. These changes initially discomfited American governments, but they helped change American policy. President Lyndon B. Johnson and Secretary Leonid Brezhnev cautiously accepted arms control negotiations in the late 1960s, and this produced a series of important treaties in the 1970s. The next president of the United States, Richard M. Nixon, carried this policy to dramatic lengths by improving relations with the USSR and Maoist China, despite his career-long image as a dedicated anti-Communist.

De Gaulle and French Independence.

Charles de Gaulle opened a decade of diplomatic change in 1966 with a dramatic announcement that France was quitting its role in the NATO alliance and that NATO must leave French soil. De Gaulle also had a vision behind his actions. He visited the USSR and eastern Europe in 1967 to promote his vision of "Europe to the Urals." This was not his most startling idea. The French tested their first atomic bomb in 1966 and their first hydrogen bomb in 1968, and de Gaulle then proclaimed an independent French *force de frappe* (nuclear striking force) that was aimed at *toutes azimuths* (all points of the compass).

Willy Brandt and Ostpolitik.

Willy Brandt's role in the diplomatic revolution had a more pacific tone. Brandt was shaped by his wartime experience as a refugee from Nazi Germany. He became famous as the mayor of West Berlin (1957–1966) at the height of the cold war, leading that isolated city during confrontations over the Berlin Wall. Brandt then became the head of the West German Socialist Party (SPD) and led it to electoral victory. As chancellor of West Germany, he introduced his own dramatic policy known as *Ostpolitik* (eastern policy). He improved relations between the two Germanys by visiting the DDR (*Deutshe Demokratische Republik;* the German Democratic Republic, or East Germany) in 1970 and shaking hands with the Communist prime minister. He signed treaties with both the Soviet Union and Poland, guaranteeing Germany's postwar frontiers, especially the Oder–Neisse Line that left much of prewar Germany inside Poland. He then negotiated a series of treaties between the two Germanys, culminating in a 1972 treaty permitting both states to enter the UN. Ostpolitik won Brandt the Nobel Peace Prize, but he resigned in 1974, when a spy scandal revealed that a member of his staff was an East German agent.

Arms Control and Détente.

These European changes encouraged the improvement in Soviet–American relations known as détente. **Arms control** negotiations with the USSR were controversial in the United States, and conservatives had fought against President John F. Kennedy's Test Ban Treaty (1963) in which both sides promised not to test nuclear weapons in the atmosphere, in outer space, or under the oceans. The French and Chinese nuclear explosions of 1967 persuaded Washington and Moscow to resume negotiations for the nuclear nonproliferation treaty of 1968, and this treaty encouraged the United States and the USSR to open larger Strategic Arms Limitation Talks (SALT) in 1969.

Summit Meetings and Arms Limitation Treaties.

Presidents of the United States and first secretaries of the Soviet Union had met face-to-face in a variety of **summit meetings** during the cold war, and hopes for arms limitation treaties improved after at summit in Glassboro, New Jersey, in 1967. Anti-Communist conservatives in America fought this policy, but it succeeded when a conservative anti-Communist adopted it. Richard Nixon, who placated anti-Communists by waging vigorous war in Asia, followed the left-wing policy of détente to new relations with the Soviet Union. Nixon and Brezhnev exchanged state visits for summit meetings in the early 1970s and signed a series of arms treaties, beginning with the SALT treaty of 1972, signed at the Moscow Summit meeting. A vivid symbol of the age of détente came in the summer of 1975, when American and Russian spacecrafts docked together in outer space, but Nixon provided an even more dramatic symbol in his Chinese policy. He accepted Communist Chinese membership in the UN, flew to Beijing to meet with Chairman Mao, agreed that Taiwan was part of China, and posed for photographs atop the Great Wall of China. The cold war was ending.

UNREST, VIOLENCE, AND TERRORISM (1968–1975)

Although the cold war was less heated in 1970 than it had been in the 1950s, Europe faced other violence. One of the foremost sources of this violence—and the origins of the era of terrorism—was the violence of imperialism and decolonization. Frantz Fanon, a French psychiatrist greatly influenced by the brutality of the Algerian War, summarized a simple lesson: "Violence is a cleansing force" (see Document 31.6).

The Vietnam War.

The war in Southeast Asia, which had been an enormously violent battleground for 30 years (the United States dropped more tons of explosives on Vietnam than all explosives used in World War II), led to widespread domestic violence from 1968 to 1975. Fighting in Vietnam reduced the global prestige of the United States to its lowest level since World War II. Student and left-wing demonstrations in the great

THE EUROPEAN COMMUNITY

Dreams of European unity, ranging from military conquest to idealistic cooperation, had existed for centuries, but it required the horrors of the two world wars (and some 75 million deaths) to convince Europeans to proceed to genuine efforts at closer unity. Under the leadership of statesmen such Jean Monnet of France, barely a decade passed between the end of the war in 1945 and the founding of the European Economic Community (the predecessor of the European Union) in the Treaty of Rome in 1957.

Jean Monnet on European Unity (1953)

Jean Monnet was the director of the French Planning Commissariat after World War II and earned much credit for the postwar economic recovery of France. Throughout that period he championed the idea of European unity, and in 1950, he was one of the primary authors of the plan for a European Coal and Steel Community, later known as the Schuman Plan for the French politician who implemented it. The plan dictated that such heavy industrial goods would circulate in Europe without tariffs or internal regulations, as if Europe were a single country. When such a community was created, Monnet served as its first president from 1952 to 1955—arguably as Europe's first president. He continued to champion European unity, as this speech of June 1953 shows.

In respect to coal and steel, the Community has set up a huge European market of more than 150 consumers, i.e., equal in number to the population of the United States of America. Under terms of the Treaty, customs duties and quota restrictions have been abolished between Germany, Belgium, France, Italy, and the Netherlands; the principal discriminations in respect of transport have been done away with. Coal and steel, iron-ore and scrap can now circulate freely, without restriction or discrimination, except for such transitional measure as have been taken for the purpose of avoiding too abrupt impacts, and facilitating the necessary readjustments.

Jean Monnet. Jean Monnet (1888–1979), the French economist who was one of the most important founding fathers of European unity.

At the risk of repeating myself—and I apologize for this to the members of the Common Assembly—I wish to say that the decisions of this first European Executive, which is the High Authority [the body of which Monnet was president], are being carried out in our six countries as if they were but one country. This is, indeed, one of the essential transformations which our enterprise has brought about, and is the test of its success. . . . The Court of Justice, which has had a number of appeals against the decisions of the High Authority laid before it, will be pronouncing final judgment.

The first Common Market, these first supranational institutions, are the beginnings of a united Europe. . . .

The attitude of the United States is well-known to you: . . . President Eisenhower reaffirmed that "the uniting of Europe is a necessity for the prosperity of Europeans and the peace of the whole world." He says "the Coal and Steel Community appears to

cities of Europe protested American militarism. Simultaneously, American military prestige suffered in 1968, when the Viet Cong's Tet (the lunar new year) Offensive overran American positions and took the fighting into the cities of South Vietnam. American moral leadership suffered when the U.S. army began a war crimes trial of American officers for killing 567 civilians in the village of My Lai in 1969, and the evidence led to the conviction of Lt. William Calley. Such events produced great turbulence in American society. The late 1960s and early 1970s witnessed vehement student protests on university campuses; race riots in American cities; a police riot in Chicago; an antiwar march on Washington, D.C.; the assassination of two American political leaders (the Reverend Dr. Martin Luther King, Jr., and Senator Robert F. Kennedy); and

me to be the most hopeful and constructive development so far toward the economic and political integration of Europe."

Our Community is an open Community. We want other countries to join on an equal footing with us. I would remind you here that on the very first day when, in the name of the French government, M. Robert Schuman made his statement of 9th May, 1950, he invited all the nations of Europe to join us, to give up the divisions of the past and, by pooling their coal and steel production, to ensure the establishment of common bases for economic development as the first stage towards the European federation.

From *Joint Meeting of the Members of the Consultative Assembly of the Council of Europe . . . Official Report,* 22 June 1953, pp. 8–12; reprinted in John W. Boyer and Jan Goldstein, eds., *Twentieth-Century Europe* (Chicago: University of Chicago Press, 1987, pp. 554–555).

Question: Which of the ideas and institutions that Monnet mentions seem more likely to lead to unity?

The Treaty of Rome, 1957

Preamble

[The governments of Belgium, France, Germany, Italy, Luxembourg, and the Netherlands,]

DETERMINED to establish the foundations of an ever closer union among the European peoples,

DECIDED to ensure the economic and social progress . . . by . . . eliminating the barriers which divide Europe,

DIRECTING their efforts to . . . constantly improving the living and working conditions of their peoples,

RECOGNIZING that the removal of existing obstacles calls for concerted action. . . .

ANXIOUS to strengthen the unity of their economies and to ensure their harmonious development by reducing the differences existing between the various regions and by mitigating the backwardness of the less favored,

DESIROUS of contributing by . . . common commercial policy to the . . . abolition of restrictions on international trade,

INTENDING to confirm the solidarity which binds Europe and overseas countries, and desiring to insure the development of their

prosperity, in accordance with the principles of the charter of the United Nations,

RESOLVED to strengthen the safeguards of peace and liberty by establishing this combination of resources. . . .

HAVE DECIDED to create a European Economic Community. . . .

Article One

By the present treaty, the High Contracting Parties establish among themselves a European Economic Community.

Article Two

It shall be the aim of the Community, by establishing a Common Market . . . to promote throughout the Community a harmonious development of economic activities, a continuous and balanced expansion, an increased stability, an accelerated raising of the standard of living, and closer relations between its Member States.

Article Three

. . . [T]he activities of the Community shall include. . . .

(a) the elimination, as between Member States, of customs duties and of quantitative restrictions in regard to the importation and exportation of goods. . . .

(b) the establishment of a common customs tariff . . . towards third countries;

(c) the abolition . . . of the obstacles to the free movement of persons, services, and capital;

(d) the inauguration of common agricultural policy;

(e) the inauguration of a common transport policy;

Article Four

The achievement of the tasks entrusted to the Community shall be ensured by: an Assembly, a Council, a Commission, a Court of Justice.

From Committee for the Common Market, *Treaty Establishing the European Economic Community* (Brussels: Secretariat of the Interim Committee, 1957).

Question: Which agreements seem the most important?

the use of armed troops against protesters, resulting in the killing of four students at Kent State University.

Soviet Suppression of Prague Spring. One consequence of these events for Europe was that the United States lost much of its authority to oppose the Soviet Union when a crisis occurred in Czechoslovakia. In January 1968, the Czech Communist Party selected a liberal reformer, Alexander Dubcek, for the leadership post of first secretary of the party. Dubček proposed political and economic liberties to humanize communist society. The enthusiastic Czech response to Dubček's brand of socialism led to an optimistic period known as the Prague Spring, but the reforms and the optimism were both short-lived. Brezhnev ordered an invasion of Czechoslovakia in August 1968. An occupying force of

VIOLENCE AND TERRORISM IN EUROPE

Although no European wars were fought during the age of the cold war, Europeans lived with frequent violence. In addition to fighting the global wars of decolonization and living with the fears of nuclear annihilation, Europeans experienced numerous rebellions (in East Germany in 1953, in Hungary in 1956, in Czechoslovakia and France in 1968), the proliferation of violent revolutionary groups (such as the Red Brigades in Italy and the Baader–Meinhof gang in West Germany), several movements of nationalist terrorism (such as the Basque independence movement in Spain and the Irish nationalist campaign in Britain), and repeated experiences of state violence (especially the Russian repression of rebellion in eastern Europe).

Rebellion in the Soviet Bloc. Throughout the cold war, the Soviet Union faced the problem of discontent in its satellite states in eastern Europe. Major uprisings in East Germany in 1953, Hungary in 1956, and Czechoslovakia in 1968 were put down by force. This photo shows a scene from the Soviet-led Warsaw Pact invasion of Czechoslovakia: a Soviet tank has come under attack and crashed into a building in central Prague.

200,000 Soviet and Warsaw Pact troops encountered Czech protests, and 650,000 soldiers were ultimately needed to end the demonstrations, oust Dubček, and install a pro-Moscow government.

Paris Student Rebellion of 1968. Militant student protests at European universities, the rise of European terrorist movements, and the rebirth of violent nationalist movements also characterized the era. The largest European student protest occurred in Paris in the spring of 1968. Demonstrations at the University of Paris (which had an enrollment of 160,000) were part of an international youth rebellion of the late 1960s that had produced major outbreaks from the University of California to the University in Berlin a few weeks earlier. Many issues angered students, but in most protests they denounced American imperialism in Asia and the autocratic administration of their campus. The demonstrations at Paris became a global symbol of a near-revolution sparked by students, as many of the revolutions of 1848 had been. They began with disputes on the suburban campus at

Nanterre, then closed the Sorbonne, and grew into riots in central Paris. Once again, barricades closed streets in Paris. On one night, an estimated 25,000 students fought the police. The events of May 1968 assumed greater importance when industrial workers called a general strike to support the students and paralyzed much of France. The strikes and riots soon ended, but they led to the resignation of President de Gaulle a few months later.

Terrorism in Europe. Student protests were not the most violent legacy of the late 1960s and early 1970s. More fearsome was the rebirth of terrorism in European politics, often with roots in the extreme left-wing politics of the era. The *Baader–Meinhof* gang in West Germany (also known as the Red Army Faction) brought together a violent group that terrorized Germany for a decade by actions such as setting bombs in a Frankfurt department store in 1968. The group was led by a radical revolutionary, Andreas Baader, and a sympathetic left-wing journalist, Ulrike Meinhof. The *Brigate Rosse* (Red Brigades) in Italy began in 1969 as a left-wing study group at the

Violence in the West. Despite the growing prosperity of western Europe and the continuation of European peace, the late 1960s and early 1970s witnessed a range of violent forms of protest in western Europe. Terrorist groups were active in both West Germany and Italy, and in France, a rebellion of students and workers took place in May 1968. In this photo, French riot police with helmets, goggles, and shields try to hold their phalanx against demonstrators.

IRA Bombing. The wreckage of businesses on the main shopping street in the English town of Coventry after the explosion of an IRA terrorist bomb, which killed five people. Nationalist terrorism was widespread in late twentieth-century Europe. Violence also characterized Basque movement in Spain and the Corsican movement in France.

University of Trent and grew into an underground organization of Marxist revolutionaries. The group assassinated prominent individuals (such as the president of Fiat motors and, in 1978, a prime minister of Italy) and terrorized more by **"kneecapping"** people—shooting them in the kneecap to leave them crippled.

Violence and the Middle East Question.
International politics, particularly the Middle Eastern question, was an important source of terrorism in Europe. Members of European terrorist groups obtained arms training in the Middle East, as the Baader–Meinhof gang did by joining Palestinian radicals in Jordan in 1970. More often, however, violence resulted from Middle Eastern terrorists taking action in Europe. In 1972 alone, international terrorists hijacked a German jetliner, attacked Jewish athletes at the Munich Olympic games, and sent letter bombs to businessmen in several countries.

Nationalist Terrorism.
A continuing part of the new violence in European politics was the escalation of nationalist terrorism. Basque nationalists sought independence for *Euskal Herria* (the Basque Homeland), a region straddling the western Pyrenees Mountains, although chiefly located in Spain. A Basque terrorist organization, known as ETA (standing for *Euskadi Ta Askatasuna,* or **Basque Country and Liberty**) was founded in 1959 to win independence through kidnappings (to raise funding), assassinations (such as the car-bombing death of Spanish premier Luis Carrero Blanco in 1973), and urban bombings. In the last decades of the twentieth century, ETA killed an estimated 800 Spanish officials. Similarly, Corsican nationalists founded a National Front for the Liberation of Corsica and fought for independence from France by bombing public buildings.

Violence in Northern Ireland.
The most uncompromising terrorist movement in Europe was that of the Irish. When the British government sent troops to Northern Ireland to maintain order, their action revived the Irish Republican Army (IRA), which hoped to drive the British out of Ulster and reunite Northern Ireland

FRANTZ FANON ON THE USE OF VIOLENCE

Frantz Fanon (1925–1961) was a French psychiatrist and revolutionary writer, born in Martinique but educated in France. He became a noted political theorist with the publication of *Black Skin, White Masks* in 1952, a book that analyzed the destructive impact of colonialism on both the colonizer and the colonized. Fanon served as the head of a psychiatric hospital in Algiers during the 1950s and became a strong supporter of the Algerian revolution for independence from France. His observations there led to the publication of Fanon's best-known work, *The Wretched of the Earth*, in 1961. In this work, he explored the violence at the root of western imperialism and concluded that violence must characterize its end.

. . . [D]ecolonization is always a violent phenomenon. At whatever level we study it, . . . decolonization is quite simply the replacing of a certain "species" of men by another "species" of men . . . The naked truth of decolonization evokes for us the searing bullets and the bloodstained knives which emanate from it. For if the last shall be first, this will only come to pass after a murderous and decisive struggle between the two protagonists. . . . The violence which has ruled over the ordering of the colonial world, which has ceaselessly drummed the rhythm for the destruction of native social forms and broken up without reserve the systems of reference of the economy, the customs of dress and external, that same violence will be claimed and taken over by the native. . . .

At the level of individuals, violence is a cleansing force. It frees the native from his inferiority complex and from his despair and inaction; it makes him fearless and restores his self-respect. Even if the armed struggle has been symbolic and the nation is demolished through a rapid movement of decolonization, the people have the time to see that the liberation has been the business of each and all of them and that the leader has no special merit. . . .

When the people have taken part in the national liberation, they will allow no one to set themselves up as "liberators". They show themselves to be jealous of the results of their action and take good care not to place their future, their destiny or the fate of their country in the hands of a living god. Yesterday they were completely irresponsible; today they mean to understand everything and make all decisions. Illuminated by violence, the consciousness of the people rebels against any pacification. From now on the demagogues, the opportunists and the magicians have a difficult task. The action which has thrown them into a hand-to-hand struggle confers on the masses a voracious taste for the concrete. The attempt at mystification becomes in the long run practically impossible.

From Fanon, Frantz, "Concerning Violence," in *The Wretched of the Earth* (New York: Grove Press, 1968, pp. 35–50).

Question: How convincing is Fanon's argument that the violence and terrorism of the colonial world is the direct product of the violence of Western imperialism?

---

with the Republic of Ireland. The British government, however, was intransigent. In 1971, the British proclaimed emergency powers of detention and arrest and curtailed civil rights; in early 1972, Britain suspended the government of Northern Ireland and established direct rule by London. Later in 1972, British troops fired upon Catholic rioters in Londonderry, killing thirteen people in the "Bloody Sunday Massacre." By early 1973, the IRA had opened the largest terrorist campaign in postwar European history. A series of pub bombings in Guildford and Birmingham shocked British opinion by killing nearly thirty people in 1974, but London became the favorite IRA target. Bombs exploded there in courts of law and at tourist attractions; later, the IRA bombed a major department store during Christmas shopping, launched a mortar assault on the prime minister's residence at 10 Downing Street, attempted to assassinate the prime minister with a hotel bomb during a party conference, and set off an enormous explosion in the financial district. The first 5 years

of public riots, sectarian assaults, vigilante justice, police and military repression, and terrorist attacks killed more than 1,000 people.

CONCLUSION

The era following World War II is recent enough that public memory and historical analysis still wrestle with its depiction. The period from 1945 to 1975 began in austerity for Europeans as they rebuilt their world. The entire era, even after economic recovery, was a period of international tension and threat of nuclear war, as the democratic states of western Europe and the communist states of eastern Europe confronted each other in a cold war. The two sides never directly combated each other, but they fought constant small wars by proxy around the globe and a war of nerves and confrontation in Europe. Europeans watched the arms race and the subsequent space race produce devastating weapons and possibilities of destruction, knowing that they occupied the primary battlefield between the United States and the Soviet Union.

It is remarkable, therefore, that against this background western Europe achieved so much. France and Germany reached a historic reconciliation, led western Europe in restoring (or creating) working democracies, and simultaneously created welfare states that offered far-ranging benefits to their citizens. The continental states founded an economic union that produced both prosperity and tantalizing possibilities for a federated Europe. The old colonial empires of Europe were completely dismantled within a single generation, and Britain showed that this decolonization was possible with less global warfare than the cold war produced. Europeans took a leading role in the relaxation of cold war tensions. It was a generation of peace in Europe and considerable accomplishment globally.

Review Questions

- What were the origins of the cold war?
- How did the welfare state in postwar Britain originate?
- What explains the recovery of Germany and its acceptance into the Western alliance?
- How would you describe the ending of European colonial empires?
- What were the origins of European Economic Community?

For Further Study

Readings
Feis, Herbert, *From Trust to Terror: The Onset of the Cold War, 1945–1950* (New York: Norton, 1970). A detailed study by a distinguished diplomatic historian.

Hobsbawm, Eric, *The Age of Extremes: A History of the World, 1914–1991* (New York: Pantheon Books, 1994). A stimulating account of contemporary history by a leading British academic.

Mayne, Richard J., *The Recovery of Europe: From Devastation to Unity* (New York: Harper, 1970). A good introduction to postwar recovery.

Springhall, John, *Decolonizaton since 1945: The Collapse of European Overseas Empires* (London: Palgrave, 2001). A comprehensive account.

References
Chamberlain, Muriel, ed., *The Longman Companion to European Decolonization in the Twentieth Century* (London: Longman, 1998).

Cook, Chris, and Stevenson, John, eds., *The Longman Handbook of the Modern World: International History and Politics Since 1945* (London: Longman, 1998). Convenient reference for chronologies, biographies, and data.

InfoTrac College Edition
For additional reading, go to your online research library at *http://infotrac.thomsonlearning.com*.
Using Key Words, enter the search term: *decolonization*

Using the Subject Guide, enter the search terms
decolonization   *European Economic Community*
cold war

Web Sites
http://www.coldwar.org   The site of the Cold War Museum, an affiliate of the Smithsonian.
http://wwics.si.edu   The site of the Woodrow Wilson International Center for Scholars. Look under "Programs" for the Cold War Project.
http://www.fordham.edu/halsall/mod/modsbook51.html   A helpful Web site at Fordham University containing numerous primary sources on decolonization.

Visit the Western Civilization Companion Web Site for resources specific to this textbook:
http://history.wadsworth.com/hause02/

The CD in the back of this book and the Western Civilization Resource Center at *http://history.wadsworth.com/western/* offer a variety of tools to help you succeed in this course, including access to quizzes; images; documents; interactive simulations, maps, and timelines; movie explorations; and a wealth of other sources.

THE AGE OF THE COLD WAR, 1945–1975

1940	1945	1950	1955	1960	1965	1970	1975

THE EUROPEAN ECONOMIC COMMUNITY (EEC)

1948: Treaty Creates Benelux Customs Union

1948: Organization of European Economic Cooperation Links Non-Communist West

1949: Paul-Henri Spaak calls for European Political Institutions

1949: Council of Europe Founded

1950: Schumann Plan to Share Steel and Coal

1951: Paris Treaty Creates Coal and Steel Community in West

1951: Jean Monnet of France–First President of the Community

1953: European Court of Human Rights Founded

1957: Rome Treaties Create European Economic Union

1959: Competing European Free Trade Association Founded

1963: De Gaulle Blocks British Entry into EEC

1967: EEC and EFTA Merge as EC

1969: de Gaulle Retires

1973: Norway Rejects EC

1975: EC Expands to Nine

THE COLD WAR

Communist Takeover in Eastern Europe

1950–1953: Korean War

Beginning of Era of "Détente"

1944: Red Army Establishes Pro-Soviet Government in Poland

1945: Yalta and Potsdam Agreements Recognize Strong Soviet Position in Eastern Europe

1945: Managed Elections Create Communist Government in Yugoslavia

1946: Churchill's "Iron Curtain" speech

1946: Free Elections Make Communist Party Largest in Czechoslovakia

1946–1949: Greek Civil War Defeats Communist Coup d'état

1947: Truman Doctrine of Aid to Greece and Turkey in Resisting Communism

1947: Managed Elections Create Communist Government in Hungary

1947: Managed Elections Create Communist Poland

1948: Communist Coup d'état in Czechoslovakia

1948: Berlin Airlift Keeps Berlin from Communist Control

1948: U.S. Marshal Plan to Help Postwar Recovery

1948: United States and Western Europe Found NATO Alliance

1949: Communists Win Control of China

1949: USSR Detonates Atomic Bomb

1950: Sino-Soviet Alliance

1952: United States Detonates First Hydrogen Bomb

1953: United States Tests First Long-Range Missile for Nuclear Bombs

1953: Death of Stalin

1953: Anti-Communist Uprising in East Berlin Suppressed

1955: Reunited Germany (West) Joins NATO

1955: USSR and Eastern Europe Create Warsaw Pact

1956: Hungarian Uprising Suppressed

1957: USSR Launches First Space Satellite

1961: USSR Achieves First Manned Space Flight

1961: Construction of Berlin Wall

1962: Cuban Missile Crisis

1963: Partial Test Ban Treaty

1968: Nuclear Non-Proliferation Treaty

1972: SALT Treaty

Chapter 32

THE AGE OF EUROPEAN UNION SINCE 1975

FOCUS QUESTIONS

- What were the chief consequences of the Revolutions of 1989, and why did they happen?
- How did the cold war end and the Soviet Union break apart?
- What progress has European Union made since 1975, and how far does Europe remain from full union?
- How was the Thatcher revolution in Britain different from developments on the continent?
- What were the causes and results of the Yugoslav War?

During the late summer and early autumn of 1989, unusually large numbers of people began to attend church services in officially atheist East Germany, and nowhere was this trend more dramatic than in the Saxon city of Leipzig, where first thousands and soon tens of thousands of people suddenly began to attend Monday evening prayer services. Led by the historic Lutheran church of St. Nicholas, where Johann Sebastian Bach had been the cantor for more than a quarter of a century and composed many of his most famous works, the Monday evening prayers had become "Prayers for Peace," and they had been followed by demonstrations on the nearby central square of Leipzig, the Karl Marx Platz. By late September, the demonstrators, most of whom wanted the right to emigrate to the west, were estimated to number between 5,000 and 10,000, and the East German police had begun to beat both dissidents and bystanders with equal brutality. Yet on Monday, October 2, the crowds in Leipzig had doubled to nearly 20,000, and they perplexed the police by singing the Communist anthem, the Internationale, as their protest song. During the following week, the police used brutality—even by East German standards—to stop demonstrations. They prepared thoroughly for Monday, October 9, by calling out riot police, heavily equipped army units, and unofficial gangs of thugs, intending to clear away demonstrators with the same determination that the Chinese had shown in clearing protesters from Tiananmen Square in June. But the "Prayers for Peace" on October 9 brought more than 70,000 people into Karl Marx Platz, and their number included some of the most famous citizens of the city, such as Kurt Masur, who conducted the Leipzig symphonic orchestra, and three of the leaders of the Communist Party of Leipzig. The night passed without the anticipated violence, and Monday crowds soon grew into the hundreds of thousands, who quickly won not merely the right to travel but a new Germany. Exactly 1 month after the tense night of Monday, October 9, the Berlin Wall fell, in significant part due to the demonstrators in Leipzig.

Chapter 32 examines contemporary Europe since the mid-1970s, a period of remarkable change. Within a single generation, Europeans witnessed the end of the cold war that had divided the continent since 1945; the collapse and breakup of the Soviet Union, which had been the greatest military superpower on the continent; the revolutions of 1989, which freed the states of eastern Europe from Russian domination and led to the reunification of Germany; and the accelerating integration of Europe that produced the European Union (EU).

ECONOMIC PROGRESS AND THE WELFARE STATE SINCE 1975

An Era of Peace and Prosperity. One of the basic facts of late twentieth-century Europe was that the Western democracies experienced an unprecedented era of peace and prosperity. By the turn of the millennium, the West had experienced more than 50 years without a war anywhere in the region (although a near civil war raged in Northern Ireland, nationalist violence troubled many regions, and wars of decolonization continued)—a fact unequaled in any other period of modern European history. Western Europe had experienced 43 years of peace between the Franco-Prussian War and World War I, prompting many to consider that age the Belle Époque (and that, too, was an era of Balkan and colonial wars). The age of Metternich, which was punctuated by numerous revolutions and saw French, Austrian, and Russian armies march against such uprisings, lasted less than 33 years between the battle of Waterloo and the revolutions of 1848. In short, the economies of the states that founded the **Common Market** in 1957 had unprecedented opportunity to prosper.

Peace in Asia. During 1975, two dramatic events gave Europe even greater hopes for an age of peace. The first was the end of the Vietnam War. This conflict, the last stage of 30 years of fighting to drive Japanese, then French, and finally American armies out of Southeast Asia, ended in April 1975 with the evacuation of the last American officials from South Vietnam and the fall of the Saigon government. Although this long war ended in Communist expansion, it did not greatly exacerbate cold war relations; instead, it allowed them to improve, especially in Europe, where the war had been widely opposed.

Détente and the Helsinki Accords. The most hopeful sign of peace occurred in Europe. Despite the conflict in Southeast Asia, *détente* (an easing of tension) between east and west—which Chancellor Willy Brandt of West Germany had launched with his *Ostpolitik* (diplomatic overtures to eastern Europe) in the early 1970s—had grown, and the end of the war permitted even better relations among the United States, Western Europe, the USSR, and China. Détente culminated in the Helsinki Accords of 1975, in which thirty-five nations guaranteed the frontiers of 1945, renewed their support for the United Nations (UN) and the peaceful resolution of crises, swore respect for "the sovereign equality and individuality" of all states, expanded economic cooperation, renounced the threat or use of force, and pledged respect for human rights. The Helsinki Accords contained no mechanism to enforce its principles during crises, yet it still promoted hope,

like most idealistic treaties—such as the UN Declaration of Human Rights of 1946, the Geneva Conventions, the Kellogg–Briand Pact of 1928, the League of Nations Charter of 1920, and the Hague Treaties of 1899 and 1906. Westerners acclaimed a treaty that obliged the USSR to honor human rights; but Soviet leader Leonid Brezhnev believed that the document permitted actions such as the invasion of Afghanistan.

Détente in Outer Space. The ending of the Vietnam War and the signing of the Helsinki Accords were signs that the cold war was changing, but the best illustration of the new mood came from outer space. In July 1975, American astronauts aboard an Apollo spacecraft and Soviet cosmonauts aboard a Soyuz spacecraft docked their ships into a single orbiting craft, foreshadowing an age of Russian–American cooperation in space. The Russian and American commanders hooked hands through open hatches—much as American and Red Army soldiers had shaken hands at the Elbe River in 1945—in an exciting moment of mutual triumph that temporarily overshadowed differences. The path of détente from such moments in 1975 to end of the cold war in 1989 was not always calm, but it was sufficiently reassuring to Europeans that it provided an environment for economic integration and prosperity.

European Prosperity. By the late 1970s, western Europe had developed a booming economy, which created a standard of living comparable to that in the United States. Recovery from the devastation of World War II had been largely completed by the late 1950s, and thriving European economies began to catch up with the United States during the 1960s. West Germany had become the most prosperous country in Europe, with a gross national product (GNP) larger than that of France or Britain. The economic miracle of Ludwig Erhart and Konrad Adenauer created the fastest growing economy in German history. The **German model** of labor relations, in which labor, management, the government, and public opinion shared a strong consensus on supporting a welfare state and promising job security in return for strike- and strife-free production, resulted in a rapidly growing economy. German unemployment fell so low that foreign **guest workers** (*Gastarbeiter;* Gast'-ar-buy-ter) from Turkey and other Mediterranean countries were needed to fill jobs. The German domestic market absorbed most of this production during the 1960s, but Germany increased exports by 1,300 percent during the 1970s. The other European Economic Community (EEC) states also began exporting more goods. French agriculture prospered so well that France became the world's second largest food exporter. By the end of the 1970s, the European Community (the predecessor of the European Union)

THE ERA OF DÉTENTE

The Helsinki Accords, 1975

The Conference on Security and Cooperation in Europe produced the most idealistic international agreement of the cold war. Thirty-five countries signed the Final Act of this conference, which became known as the Helsinki Accord.

The participating states will respect human rights and fundamental freedoms, including the freedom of thought, conscience, religion or belief, for all without distinction as to race, sex, language or religion.

They will promote and encourage the effective exercise of civil, political, economic, social, cultural, and other rights and freedoms all of which derive from the inherent dignity of the human person and are essential for his free and full development.

Within this framework the participating states will recognize and respect the freedom of the individual to profess and practice, alone or in community with others, religion or belief acting in accordance with the dictates of his own conscience.

The participating states on whose territory national minorities exist will respect the rights of persons belonging to such minorities to equality before the law, will afford them the full opportunity for the actual enjoyment of human rights and fundamental freedoms and will, in this manner, protect their legitimate interests in this sphere.

From *New York Times*, August 2, 1975.

Question: What makes this treaty an important step in the spirit of détente?

Willy Brandt. Willy Brandt, the chancellor of West Germany, was the most influential statesman in launching the age of détente in the 1970s. Brandt repeatedly made friendly overtures to the states of eastern Europe, especially to East Germany and Poland—a policy known as Ostpolitik. He not only negotiated treaties that improved relations but also made a series of symbolic gestures, as seen in this photo, taken during a state visit to Poland: Brandt is seen kneeling and silently contemplating a monument to the Jewish victims of the Warsaw ghetto, killed by Germans.

had become a major economic competitor of the United States. By 1990, GNP per capita in France ($16,000) and Germany ($18,500) neared that in the United States ($19,800), and four Scandinavian states (led by oil-rich Norway at $21,724) surpassed the U.S. GNP.

The European Social Model. The European prosperity of the 1970s encouraged the growth of a west European version of the **welfare state,** often called the **European social model.** The welfare state evolved slowly in Europe as a secular replacement for church-based assistance, for private philanthropic aid, or for the severity of such traditional institutions as the workhouse and the poorhouse. Discussions of state benefits for the elderly and the ill had been discussed in France

during the 1790s, early welfare legislation had been introduced in Germany by Bismarck in the 1880s, and such legislation was emulated in many states before World War I and expanded during the depression of the 1930s, but the comprehensive welfare state dates from 1945. The socialist government (the Labour Party) of Clement Attlee in Britain and the conservative government of General de Gaulle in France both nationalized sectors of the economy and raised taxes to fund more comprehensive systems of **social security.** Although the most advanced versions of the European welfare state were developed as socialist programs, such as Swedish state socialism, the success of the European welfare state rested on the fact that conservatives (such as Bismarck and de Gaulle) and socialists (such as Attlee or Léon Blum) agreed that the nation must devote a significant share of new wealth and production to public services and benefits. However, the left and the right always disagreed on the scope of the welfare state. In West Germany, both the socialist governments of Willy Brandt (1969–1974) and Helmut Schmidt (1974–1982) and the conservative government of Helmut Kohl (1982–1998) accepted high tax rates as the price of social cohesion. In France, the conservative administrations of Georges Pompidou, Valéry Giscard d'Estaing, and Jacques Chirac all expanded the welfare state.

Social Benefits. The benefits of European prosperity were large. Higher tax rates and lower military spending enabled Britain, France, and Germany to establish workweeks of less than 38 or 39 hours for full pay—led by a French workweek of 35 hours (which often meant a 4-day work week). Britain, France, Germany, and Italy all guaranteed workers a minimum of 5 to 6 weeks of paid vacation per year, compared with the 2 weeks standard in the United States and Japan. Adding a typical 20 days of assorted holidays per year, many Europeans effectively work for 10 months per year. German workers won the most exceptional treatment: a minimum of 58 paid days off (11.5 weeks) per year in combined vacation days and paid holidays. European governments simultaneously diverted a large portion of gross domestic product (GDP), taken in high taxes, to funding early retirement with state pensions. France and Italy established age 60 for retirement at full pay, with age 50 or 55 being the standard in some occupations. In 1996, Germans were guaranteed 52 weeks of unemployment compensation, or 128 weeks after age 54, at 60 percent of salary. All EU countries except Luxembourg granted pregnant women a minimum of 3 months of paid maternity leave, with Denmark granting 6 months. Many countries, led by France, granted free tuition to state universities to all students. And the entire EU is committed to free, or low cost, medical care for all; some states, led by Germany, include free nursing home care for the elderly.

Taxation. The price of European social benefits has been high taxation. European taxation has been so high that in the late 1980s it consumed 33 to 50 percent of the GNP in Britain, France, and Germany and more than 55 percent in Sweden. And it has been growing: French government spending grew from 44 percent in 1987 to 52 percent in 1995. Although most of the taxation that supports this social system comes from indirect taxes—especially a value-added tax (VAT) hidden in the cost of goods—Europeans do notice the cost of these benefits. The unemployment of German workers, for example, is supported by a 3.25 percent payroll deduction from workers' gross income, matched by a 3.25 percent payment by employers; the lesser benefit in the United States is supported by a 2.3 percent tax on pay-roll, paid by employers. European conservatives such as Helmut Kohl of Germany tried to reduce spending on social services during the late 1980s and the 1990s, but ultimately they accepted both the welfare state and the taxation needed to finance it. Even the socialist president of France, François Mitterrand (served 1981–1995), who defended the welfare commitment, faced hard fiscal decisions, and his government adopted many conservative policies. The French public, however, has been one of the staunchest constituencies for protecting the welfare state. When the conservative government proposed reduced services in 1997, French socialists under Lionel Jospin won an upset parliamentary victory.

The Welfare Crisis of the Twenty-First Century. The delicate balance between generous social benefits and high taxes succeeded in Europe throughout the prosperous late twentieth century, although its assumptions were sharply challenged by some conservatives, led by Prime Minister Margaret Thatcher of the United Kingdom. By the opening years of the twenty-first century, however, the combination of a tighter economy and the clearly visible impact of the **baby bust** (see *Taxation and the Welfare State at the End of the Twentieth Century*) meant that governments had to consider basic changes in the European social model: cutting the generous benefits or raising taxes sharply.

MARGARET THATCHER AND THE CONSERVATIVE REVOLUTION (1975–1990)

Women in Politics. The most vigorous critique of the European social model came from Britain. In February 1975, Britain's Conservative Party elected Margaret Thatcher, a former minister of education, to lead the party. That event was a landmark in European history for two reasons: (1) never in the history of parliamentary democracy had one of the great powers chosen a woman to lead them, and (2) the base of her policies was the first vigorous challenge to the growth of the welfare state. Dramatic changes began in 1979, when Thatcher became the first woman prime minister in British history, a post she held for the longest period of any modern prime minister. Her success began an era of women reaching the top in European politics. In 1980, Norway elected a woman prime minister, Iceland a woman president, and Portugal a woman prime minister. By the 1990s, even Ireland (1990), France (1991), and Turkey (1993) had elected women as either prime ministers or presidents. With the election of a woman prime minister in 2003, Finland had women in both of the highest offices in the land, after electing woman

Taxation and the Welfare State at the End of the Twentieth Century

Table 32.1 Taxation and Gross National Product in the 1980s

Country	Total Taxation as a Percentage of GNP
Britain	36.5
France	43.8
Germany	38.1
Italy	37.8
Sweden	56.7
United States	30.1

Swedish data (1987) from *New York Review of Books*, October 24, 1991, p. 7; all other data (1989) from *New York Times*, November 29, 1992.

Table 32.3 Retirees (Pensioners) and Workers

This table shows retirees aged 65 or older as a percentage of active workers.

Country	Percentage in 2000	Estimated Percentage in 2030
Britain	23	38
France	21	39
Germany	22	49
Italy	22	48
Poland	16	32
Sweden	27	39
United States	19	37

Source: Adapted from graphic data in *The Economist*, February 3, 2001, p. 54.

Question: What conclusions can be drawn from these data about policy differences between Europe and the United States?

Table 32.2 Sources of Tax Revenue, 1985–1989

This table shows the percentage of government revenue from different taxes.

Country	Corporate Taxes	Individual Income Taxes	Property Taxes	Consumption (Sales) Taxes
Britain	9.6%	38.8%	11.7%	27.2%
France	5.9%	53.9%	1.9%	29.4%
Germany (West)	7.3%	56.1%	2.1%	20.9%
Italy	6.6%	67.8%	1.9%	24.2%
Norway	11.6%	35.6%	1.8%	33.0%
Sweden	39.4%	13.5%	3.6%	21.0%
United States	7.0%	50.7%	8.7%	13.3%

Source: The Economist, *Book of Vital World Statistics* (London: Hutchinson, 1990, pp. 134–135).

heads for the national bank and the Ministry of Defense. Simultaneously, European women gained a larger share of political power at lower levels. No country, however, elected a parliament in which 50 percent of the representatives were women (or **"parity"** as women's rights leaders sought). Sweden, where women won 41 percent of the seats in Parliament in 1994, had the highest rate and Greece had the lowest

WOMEN IN EUROPEAN POLITICS IN THE LATE TWENTIETH CENTURY

The Conservative Revolution. Margaret Thatcher, the first woman to become prime minister of Britain, was one of the strongest and most successful prime ministers in British history. She was the driving force behind a conservative revolution that dismantled much of the welfare state and the nationalized economy created by the Labour government after World War II.

Edith Cresson. In 1991, France became the second major European state to have a woman head of government. Edith Cresson (b. 1934) had supported François Mitterrand at the start of her political career in 1965, and he supported her rise through the Socialist party. After serving in several cabinet posts, Cresson became premier (named by President Mitterrand) in 1991.

TABLE 32.4 THE POLITICAL RIGHTS OF WOMEN AFTER WORLD WAR II

1944	French government in exile adopts women's suffrage and women vote for National Assembly.	1949	Basic Law (Grundgesetz) of Federal Republic of Germany grants women's suffrage.
1945	Women's suffrage is proclaimed in Italy.	1970	Swiss parliament approves women's suffrage in federal elections.
1945–1946	Postwar elections are held in Belgium, Netherlands, Denmark, and Norway with restored universal suffrage, lost during German occupation, 1940–1944.	1971	Swiss referendum approves women's suffrage in federal elections, but local referendum continue to deny the local vote in some cantons.
1946	Women are allowed to vote in western zones of occupied Germany for first time since 1933.	1976	Women in Portugal obtain the vote on the same basis as men after unequal suffrage granted in 1931.
1946	Constitution of French Fourth Republic is adopted with women's suffrage.	1977	Women's suffrage is restored in Spain after 31-year suppression by Franco.
1947	Constitution of Italian Republic is adopted with women's suffrage.	1981	Switzerland adopts a constitutional amendment granting women equal rights.

percentage (5.3 percent), but seven European countries (mostly in Scandinavia) achieved the feminist target of 30 percent. Despite the presence of a woman at 10 Downing Street, Britain had been among the nations with a low percentage of women in Parliament during the Thatcher years. The landslide Labour victory of Tony Blair in 1997, however, included 102 women members of Parliament (M.P.s) in the new majority—far higher than the participation of women in France, Germany, or the United States.

The Rise of Margaret Thatcher. Margaret Thatcher was not born to the British political elite. She was born the daughter of a successful small-town gro-

TABLE 32.5 WOMEN IN POLITICAL LEADERSHIP IN EUROPE

1990	Russian women vote for local soviets in first free elections since 1917.
1991	Russian women vote in presidential election, the first general election in Russian history.
1974	Barbara Castle becomes Britain's first secretary of state for social security.
	Simone Veil becomes France's minister for health.
	Eva Kolstad becomes president of Norway's Liberal Party.
	Françoise Giroud becomes France's first minister for women's affairs.
1975	Margaret Thatcher becomes first woman to lead a major British political party.
1976	Mairead Corrigan and Betty Williams of Northern Ireland share Nobel Peace Prize.
	Françoise Giroud becomes France's minister of culture.
	Elena Bonner is cofounder of Helsinki Human Rights Group in the USSR
1979	Margaret Thatcher becomes first woman prime minister of Britain.
	Petra Kelly is cofounder of West Germany's environmentalist Green Party.
	Louise Weiss becomes senior member elected to the European Parliament.
1980	Maria de Lourdes Pintasilgo serves as Portugal's first woman prime minister.
	Vigdis Finnbogadottir elected first woman president of Iceland.
	Gro Brundtland becomes first woman prime minister of Norway.
1981	Karin Ahrland becomes Sweden's minister for public health.
	Shirley Williams is cofounder of Britain's Social Democratic Party.
1982	Gertrud Sigurdsen becomes Sweden's minister for public health.
	Anna-Greta Leijon becomes Sweden's minister of labor.
1983	Petra Kelly is elected Green Party member of West German Parliament.
1985	Melina Mercouri becomes Greece's minister of culture.
1986	Anita Gradin becomes Sweden's minister for foreign trade.
1987	Anna-Greta Leijon becomes Sweden's minister of justice.
	Margaret Thatcher is first modern prime minister to win three consecutive terms.
1990	Mary Robinson is elected first woman president of Ireland.
	Elisabeth Rehn of Finland becomes first woman defense minister in world.
1991	Edith Cresson becomes first woman premier of France.
1992	Betty Boothroyd becomes first woman Speaker of Britain's Parliament.
	Sirkka Hamalainen becomes first woman governor of Bank of Finland.
1993	Tansu Çiller becomes first woman prime minister of Turkey.
1995	Women achieve goal of 30 percent of seats in parliament in Denmark, Finland, Germany, Iceland, Netherlands, Norway, and Sweden.
1997	Labour landslide includes 102 women M.P.s.
2000	Angela Merkel is elected leader of the German Christian Democratic Union, the first woman to lead a major German party.
2003	Finnish parliament elects Anneli Jaatteenmaki as first woman prime minister.

cer who twice was elected mayor. Her father was also a Methodist lay preacher, and she was raised in strict family virtues drawn from religion as well as business. Although less typical of families in the 1930s, Thatcher's parents encouraged her to be ambitious and to develop her intelligence. She attended Oxford University as a scholarship student and chemistry ma-

jor during World War II, was drawn to British politics in the late 1940s, and soon studied law to advance that career. Elected to Parliament in 1959, she rose in Conservative Party ranks by becoming an expert on social issues, such as education and welfare, which, at the time, were often deemed the appropriate subjects for women in politics. When Edward Heath formed a

Conservative government in 1970, Margaret Thatcher became minister of education and science, the only woman in the Cabinet.

Thatcher as Political Leader.
Thatcher built her reputation during Heath's troubled Tory government. Conservatives struggled to restrict the power of the trade unions with only limited success. Strikes by tens of thousands of dockworkers, miners, and industrial workers protested plans to curb wages or union powers. Simultaneously, the Heath government faced a worsening of the Irish question. Sectarian riots, police battles, and terrorist bombings became commonplace in the early 1970s. The Conservative government responded by suspending the powers of the provincial government and Parliament in Northern Ireland, establishing direct British rule of the province, escalating the number of troops sent to maintain order, and finally governing under state of emergency decrees that suspended many civil liberties. Amidst these crises, the British public lost confidence in the government and Margaret Thatcher emerged as the strongest Tory leader.

Thatcher's Conservative Economic Program.
Thatcher had the strength to champion the conservative program of severe budget cuts even when they were immensely unpopular. As minister of education, she eliminated a national program of free milk at school for small children, dramatizing her opposition to the welfare state. In British popular culture, she became "Thatcher, Thatcher, Milk Snatcher," but in conservative circles, she became the leader of the future. She appealed to many conservatives because she embodied and defended their sense of Victorian virtues. As Thatcher put it, "I was brought up to work jolly hard. We were taught to live within our income, that cleanliness is next to godliness. We were taught self-respect. You were taught tremendous pride in your country." After Heath lost the parliamentary elections of 1974, Thatcher challenged him for the leadership of the Conservative Party in 1975 and won. She became prime minister in 1979, following a campaign in which she promised to restore many aspects of the nineteenth-century *laissez-faire* **liberal economics** of free enterprise. "Free choice is ultimately what life is about," she proclaimed. The cornerstones of her conservative economics would be a program of **privatization** (selling off government-owned sectors of the economy that had been **nationalized**), reduced taxes, limits on the growth of the welfare state, and reduction wherever practical (as a manifestation of a **socialist** economy).

The Thatcher Government.
The Thatcher government of 1979 to 1990 introduced Britain (and Europe) to strict fiscal conservatism. Thatcher championed **monetarist economics** that called for limiting the money supply to curb inflation. She coupled this with a promise to reduce taxes. The Conservative government honored this promise in one sense but violated it in another: It cut income taxes, but it raised indirect taxes, especially the national sales tax known as the VAT ("value-added tax"). Thatcher cut top income tax rates from 83 percent to 60 percent in 1979 and reduced them to 40 percent in 1979; the rate paid by average taxpayers fell from 33 percent to 30 percent and then to 25 percent. When she tried in 1990 to compensate for this huge loss of government revenue by instituting another regressive tax called the Poll Tax, antitax demonstrations drove her from office.

Reduction of the Welfare State.
This conservative revolution necessitated severe reductions in government spending, especially in the budgets that Thatcher knew well—education and welfare services. Thatcher asserted that the cradle-to-grave welfare state that had evolved out of the Beveridge Plan and the Attlee reforms of the 1940s cost more than the nation could pay. The demographic portrait of the nation—greater longevity, lower employment, and lower birthrates—meant that the costs of the welfare state, which stood at 25 percent of the budget in 1979 and rose to 31 percent by 1988 would continue to rise. (This situation arose chiefly because of retirement pensions and the high cost of benefits in a period of high unemployment.) The Thatcher government cut some benefits directly, chiefly housing benefits, and curtailed others by taxing them or not raising them to match inflation. Her monetarism and budget cuts lowered inflation (5 percent), increased unemployment (12.7 percent), reduced public services, and caused vehement public debate.

Privatization.
Simultaneously, Thatcher aimed to increase the private sector of the British economy by selling off some previously nationalized enterprises. (Ten percent of the British national economy was state-run in 1979.) This policy of privatization eliminated state monopolies in some areas and sold state-run enterprises in others. This extended a cycle in British history; the Labour Party had begun nationalizations in 1945. Conservatives in 1951 privatized two of the most controversial nationalizations (iron and steel), and a Labour government of 1967 made a few gestures toward the party's historic commitment. (Ironically, Thatcher's privatizations happened at the same time that François Mitterrand's socialist government in France was undertaking new nationalizations in 1981–1982.) Thatcher now sold nationalized coal, gas, oil, and steel interests such as the leading gasoline company, British Petroleum (BP).

Labor Unions.
Late twentieth-century Europe had developed three distinct patterns of **labor relations.** In

the Communist bloc of the Soviet Union and Eastern Europe, labor unions had been stripped of all power (such as the right to strike), and champions of freedom (especially in Poland) were seeking to assert the right of workers to organize. In a few states, labor relations followed the German model of consensus, in which labor and management worked well together and labor peace prevailed. But in some states, including Britain, France, and Italy, large and powerful labor unions clashed with the government over many policies and conducted frequent strikes. The Thatcher government adopted a tough policy in an attempt to break the power of the labor unions and public employees. Employment Acts in 1980, 1982, and 1988, as well as a Trade Union Act of 1984, changed labor relations in Britain and weakened trade unions. These laws continued a century-long battle over union powers, redefining the right to strike by requiring a membership ballot before a strike, restricting the right to picket, making unions liable for strike damages, and curtailing union monopolies known as **closed shops** (where all employees had to belong to the union). These restrictions were backed by the courts and grew stronger when unions became reluctant to strike.

Margaret Thatcher imposed her policies on a sometimes-nervous conservative government with a forceful, intransigent style of leadership that belied stereotypes about women leaders. Her tough policies and tougher style (especially in her dealings with the Soviet Union) earned her the nickname of "the Iron Lady." Thatcher also demonstrated her hard-line style during her chief foreign policy crisis. In the spring of 1982, Argentina invaded the Falkland Islands, a small British colony in the south Atlantic, claiming that the islands formed a historic part of the Argentine state. Against the strong opposition of the Labour Party and many members of her own party, Thatcher insisted on taking back the Falklands by war. One month after the Argentine occupation, British troops stormed the islands and reclaimed them after a 3-week land battle and several bloody encounters at sea. A year later, the Iron Lady was re-elected by an overwhelming majority.

DISCONTENT IN EASTERN EUROPE AND THE RISE OF SOLIDARITY (1975–1990)

Rebellions and the Brezhnev Doctrine. The peoples of eastern Europe demonstrated their hostility to Communist dictatorship on many occasions after 1945. Antigovernment demonstrations in East Berlin in 1953, an anti-Soviet rebellion in Hungary in 1956, and the Prague Spring reform movement in Czechoslovakia in 1968 were the most dramatic outbursts against the Soviet system. The frustration in eastern Europe grew from the desire for both Western freedoms and Western material conditions. The standard of living in the east was far below conditions in the west, so daily frustrations compounded the discontent. The Soviet Union had used force to suppress eastern European protest movements, asserting a right to intervene in neighboring states. This Soviet policy was known as the **Brezhnev Doctrine,** in analogy to the Monroe Doctrine by which the United States intervened in neighboring states of Latin America.

Charter 77. The Helsinki Agreement of 1975 contained a Soviet acceptance of human rights, and this inspired dissidents in several of the Soviet satellites. In January 1977, a group of 242 Czech intellectuals, led by the playwright Václav Havel, created a **civil rights movement** known as Charter 77. Their manifesto, widely published in the Western press, charged that the Czech government violated the human rights promised at Helsinki. Hundreds of other educated professionals soon joined the Charter 77 protest, and they gained some support from the Catholic Church—but the campaign was short-lived. The government proclaimed the Charter to be subversive. Havel, whose satirical plays had been banned since 1968, and five other civil rights activists were jailed in 1979 for this crime of subversion, and arrests and interrogations continued into the 1980s.

Solidarity. Poland witnessed the most successful challenge to Communist dictatorship in eastern Europe. The Poles had resisted in 1956; worker protests in Poznan led to more than 100 killings. Food riots were put down in 1970 and new strikes were suppressed in 1976, but Poland still became the home of sustained protests in the 1980s. Rising food prices in 1980 led workers in Gdansk to strike. The movement spread among Polish industries, building a network of unions known as the Solidarity movement (Solidarnosc), and by August 1980, more than 120,000 workers were out on strike. Solidarity was the first independent trade union in the Soviet bloc, and it grew to 10 million members. Under the leadership of Lech Walesa, a Gdansk shipyard electrician, Solidarity strikers issued a dramatic list of demands and won changes in government, increased wages, a 5-day and 41.5 hour workweek, and the right to form an independent labor union and to strike. Within a few months, however, a military government took power and banned the union, only to be faced with demands from farmers for a farmworkers' union.

Repression in Poland. The USSR warned Poland in 1981 to crack down on counterrevolution, and Poland was put under martial law with civil liberties suspended. Troops fired on strikers, killing seven. Walesa and thousands of strikers were imprisoned. Walesa won

THE SOLIDARITY MOVEMENT IN POLAND

Lech Walesa and the Solidarity Movement in Poland. The founder and president of the workers' movement known as *Solidarnosc* (Solidarity), which played a major role in the fall of the Communist government in Poland, was a 37-year-old electronics technician and electrical worker at the state shipyards in Gdansk named Lech Walesa. He expressed the grievances of shipbuilders so effectively that he became a national symbol of Solidarity's resistance to the government. Here, Walesa addresses dockworkers in Gdansk in 1980; 3 years later he won the Nobel Peace Prize.

Demands of the Solidarity Workers in Poland, 1980

Striking ship-workers at Gdansk confronted the Communist government with the following demands in August 1980.

1. Acceptance of free trade unions independent of the Communist Party.
2. A guarantee of the right to strike and of the security of strikes and those aiding them.
3. Compliance with the constitutional guarantee of freedom of speech, the press and publication.
4. A halt in repression of the individual because of personal conviction.
5. Guaranteed automatic increases in pay on the basis of increases in prices and the decline of real income.
6. A full supply of food products for the domestic market, with exports limited to surpluses.
7. The selection of management personnel on the basis of qualifications not party membership.
8. Privileges of the secret police, regular police and party apparatus are to be eliminated by equalizing family subsidies, abolishing special stores, etc.
9. Reduction in the age of retirement for women to 50 and for men to 55, or after 30 years of employment in Poland for women and 35 years for men, regardless of age.
10. Conformity of old-age pensions and annuities with what has actually been paid in.
11. Improvements in the working conditions of the health service to insure full medical care for workers.
12. Assurances of a reasonable number of places in daycare centers and kindergartens for the children of working mothers.
13. Paid maternity leave for three years.
14. A decrease in the waiting period for apartments.
15. A day of rest on Saturday.

From "Demands of the Solidarity Workers in Poland," *New York Times,* August 28, 1980.

Question: What is radical or revolutionary about this document?

---

international support, however, including a Nobel Peace Prize in 1983. The election of a Polish-born pope who supported Solidarity—John Paul II, the first non-Italian pope in 455 years—greatly strengthened the movement. Poland had remained strongly Catholic during the Communist regime, and Pope John Paul II's 1979 visit to Poland had strengthened the will to resist the government. In part because North Atlantic Treaty Organization (NATO) governments warned the Soviet Union that intervention in Poland under the Brezhnev Doctrine would end détente, the movement survived by a delicate compromise with the Communist regime during the 1980s.

Dissent in the USSR. The Soviet Union of the post-Stalin era had its own dissident movement. Khrushchev's **de-Stalinization** allowed enough freedom for dissident writers to risk criticism of the regime. In 1962, Aleksandr Solzhenitsyn was allowed to publish a novel entitled *A Day in the Life of Ivan Denisovitch,* which exposed conditions in the Soviet *gulag* (the Siberian network of prison camps) and led to the Western encouragement of a Nobel Prize for Literature. Solzhenitsyn's criticism of continuing censorship led to the banning of his subsequent books, which appeared in the West and circulated in the USSR in *samizdat* (clandestinely printed) form. His Nobel Prize for Literature gave Solzhenitsyn the stature to publish a massive history of Stalin's terror, *The Gulag Archipelago* (1973–1975), which led the frustrated Soviet regime to deport him to the West. Other distinguished dissidents included the physicist considered the father of the Russian hydrogen bomb, Andrey Sakharov, who championed international arms control and Soviet civil rights so persistently that he won the Nobel Peace Prize in 1975. Sakharov and his wife, Elena Bonner, then became persistent champions of the Helsinki Accords inside the USSR.

The Afghan War.

Discontent in the USSR worsened after the Red Army invaded neighboring Afghanistan in 1979. The Kremlin sought to prevent the establishment of a militant Islamic government on its southern border, adjacent to Soviet republics with large Islamic populations. A minor military campaign to install a friendly government in Kabul, however, soon grew into "the Soviet Union's Vietnam." Forty thousand troops were needed in the first month, because the Red Army encountered fierce resistance from Afghan rebels, the *mujahedeen*. As the war became a frustrating, no-win stalemate and Russian casualties sharply increased, the USSR met the same international hostility and domestic anger that the Vietnam War had caused the United States. A conference of thirty-six Islamic states condemned the Soviet Union. The UN voted on a resolution denouncing the war. A planned Soviet showcasing of Communist society, the 1980 Olympic Games, was boycotted by the United States, West Germany, and Japan. Internal dissent also increased. Sakharov and his wife, Elena Bonner, were so troublesome to the regime that they were exiled to a Russian city closed to foreigners.

Economic Failures.

Although Western governments (and intelligence agencies) badly misjudged the situation inside the USSR, the Communist regime was facing grave internal problems, especially economic problems, by the early 1980s. The dramatic economic growth and technological success of the 1950s and 1960s, typified by the spectacular Soviet success in the early days of the space race, had begun to fade in the 1970s, and serious problems had emerged in many economic sectors. A Russian shortage of consumer goods was the subject of Western humor, but the shortages (especially food shortages) were actually quite severe. Public dissatisfaction, worker demoralization (expressed in the world's highest alcoholism rate), bureaucratic bungling, failed economic planning, political corruption, production and distribution inefficiencies, environmental disasters (such as the explosion of an atomic power station at Chernobyl, in the farm belt of the Ukraine in 1986), unaffordable military and space program expenditures, and even energy shortages in a land of great natural richness all combined to create a desperate need for reform.

THE GORBACHEV REVOLUTION IN THE USSR (1985–1989)

The Rise of Mikhail Gorbachev.

The turning point for the USSR and eastern Europe came in 1985, when a youthful reformist and **Westernizer,** Mikhail Gorbachev (Gore'-bah-choff), became the head of the Soviet Union following a succession of ineffective, elderly, doctrinaire leaders. Gorbachev was the son of Russian peasants. He joined the Communist Party at age 21, rose to membership in the Supreme Soviet at 39, reached a cabinet post at 47, and in 1980 became the youngest member of the Politburo at 49. Gorbachev emerged as one of the energetic leaders of the Politburo during the rudderless period following the death of Leonid Brezhnev in 1982. The Soviet Union was widely considered a gerontocracy, and three aging heads of government died in quick succession between 1982 and 1985. The instability of this period encouraged the Politburo to accept the 54-year-old Gorbachev as first secretary.

The Arms Race.

Gorbachev had served as minister of agriculture from 1978 and knew that Soviet farming was failing. In 1981, Brezhnev had been forced to acknowledge the regime's economic failure before the Central Committee; food production had fallen to dangerously low levels for 3 consecutive years and stood at an embarrassing 30 percent of the planned harvest. The Soviet Union could not feed itself and imported 43 million tons of grain, much of it coming from the United States. Simultaneously, the war in Afghanistan was a great drain on Russian finances and morale. In 1982, the Politburo decided to seek economic stability by curtailing the enormously expensive arms race with the West. A few months later, however, President Ronald Reagan of the United States announced plans for an expensive new weapons system, the Strategic Defense Initiative, which would theoretically provide a missile shield for the United States. Reagan's plan, soon dubbed **star wars,** required vast new spending to develop antimissile technology. Reagan, who considered the USSR "the Evil Empire" and "the focus of all evil in the modern world," was willing to spend the United States deeply into debt to combat the Soviet Union. By 1985, the United States had become a debtor nation, but Mikhail Gorbachev came to power with another great concern to add to the human rights pressures, the antiwar mood, and the economic failures of the Soviet Union.

The Gorbachev Revolution.

In his first weeks in power, Gorbachev launched a liberalizing revolution. He retired older leaders and hard-liners while promoting reformers and Westernizers such as Eduard Shevardnadze, who replaced an old-line Communist,

THE GORBACHEV REVOLUTION

Mikhail Gorbachev. Mikhail Gorbachev, who became general secretary of the Communist Party of the Soviet Union in 1985, was the leading figure in the revolutions of 1989. His determined efforts to reform the USSR and eastern Europe created the environment in which Communist governments were toppled, and this made him enormously popular across Europe, as this 1987 photo of his state visit to Prague shows. Note the many smiling faces and the eagerness to shake Gorbachev's hand—a reaction to a Soviet leader that would have been unthinkable a few year earlier. Gorbachev won the Nobel Peace Prize for 1990.

Mikhail Gorbachev on Perestroika and Glasnost (1987)

What is perestroika? What prompted this idea of restructuring?

. . . Perestroika is no whim on the part of some ambitious individuals or a group of leaders. . . . Perestroika is an urgent necessity arising from the profound processes of development in our socialist society. This society is ripe for change. Any delay beginning perestroika could have led to an exacerbated internal situation in the near future. . . .

At some stage—this became particularly clear in the latter half of the seventies—something happened that was at first sight inex-

plicable. The country began to lose momentum. Economic failures became more frequent. Difficulties began to accumulate and deteriorate, and unresolved problems to multiply. . . .

The 27th Congress of the Communist Party of Soviet Union [1986] . . . was a courageous congress. We spoke openly about the short-comings, errors, and difficulties. We emphasized the untapped potential of socialism, and the Congress adopted a detailed long-term plan of action. It became a congress of strategic decisions. . . . Now we can see better and it is clear that we have to resolutely continue . . .

The main idea . . . was the development of democracy. It is the principal guarantee of the irreversibility of perestroika. The more socialist democracy there is, the more socialism we will have. This is our firm conviction, and we will not abandon it. We will promote democracy in the economy, in politics and within the Party itself. . . . Soviet society has been set in motion and there's no stopping it . . .

The greatest difficulty in our restructuring effort lies in our thinking, which has been molded over the past years. Everyone, from General Secretary [Gorbachev] to worker, has to alter this thinking. . . . We have to overcome our conservatism. . . .

The new atmosphere is, perhaps, most vividly manifest in glasnost. We want more openness about public affairs in every sphere of life. People should know what is good and what is bad too, in order to multiply the good and to combat the bad. . . . Truth is the main thing. Lenin said: More light! Let the Party know everything. . . . As never before, we need no dark corners where mold can reappear. Glasnost is a vivid example of a normal and favorable spiritual and moral atmosphere in society, which makes it possible for people to understand better what happened to us in the past, what is taking place now . . . and, on this basis of this understanding, to participate in the restructuring effort. . . .

From Gorbachev, Mikhail, *Perestroika: New Thinking for Our Country and the World* (New York: Harper & Row, 1987, pp. 17–19, 60–75, 177). Copyright © Mikhail Gorbachev. Reprinted by permission of HarperCollins Publishers, Inc.

Question: How does Gorbachev define *perestroika* and *glasnost?*

Andrey Gromyko, as foreign minister. Within 1 year, Gorbachev had changed 70 percent of all cabinet ministers and 50 percent of the higher administration. The Gorbachev revolution, outlined in his speech to the 1986 Communist Party Congress, was characterized by two objectives: *glasnost* (glaz'-nost; openness) and *perestroika* (pair'-es-troy-ka; restructuring). Glasnost meant a freer political and cultural life in which criticism of the party and state was possible. In June 1986, Glavlit, the government censorship office, was closed down and

its thousands of workers assigned to other jobs. Gorbachev even allowed television broadcasts depicting the quagmire in Afghanistan and its increasing casualty rate. Perestroika meant reforming political and economic structures to create more democracy and efficiency. In June 1987, Gorbachev persuaded the Supreme Soviet to approve the restructuring of the Soviet economy. In less than 2 years, he had made begun a remarkable series of reforms, but he had also awakened expectations for even faster change; in late

1987, Gorbachev fired the head of the Communist Party in Moscow, Boris Yeltsin, for his criticism of the slow pace of reform.

Reform and the Cold War.
Gorbachev's two doctrines also led to a **détente offensive** to persuade the West to curtail the cold war and its costly arms race. To prove his earnestness, he announced a unilateral freeze on medium-range missiles during his first month in office. In September 1985, the USSR offered a 50 percent cut in arms in return for a Western cut in the star wars program. Many Western leaders, led by Margaret Thatcher, were greatly impressed by this beginning, and European opinion soon strongly favored the curtailment of cold war military expenditures. In the fall of 1985, more than 100,000 people demonstrated in London to stop these ruinous expenses, and Gorbachev received popular greetings during visits to the West. Reagan and Gorbachev held 6 hours of face-to-face meetings in Geneva, but Reagan refused to back down from his star wars program, even when Gorbachev offered to eliminate all nuclear arms by the year 2000.

Glasnost and Freedom.
The Communist Party Congress of 1986 heard Gorbachev denounce the stagnation of the Brezhnev era (1964–1982), much as Nikita Khrushchev had attacked Stalin 30 years earlier. The congress endorsed Gorbachev's program, and for the next 4 years, an astonished world watched historic changes unfold. Gorbachev scored his first successes by responding to his human rights critics. During 1986, prominent dissidents such as Sakharov were gradually released from confinement. Anatoly Shcharansky was freed from his 13-year sentence to a prison camp for his campaign to help Russian Jews emigrate. In 1987, Gorbachev denounced Stalin's terror and praised Khrushchev's report on the crimes of the Stalin era; he truly shocked devout Communists by admitting that Lenin had relied on terror, too. A few months later, Gorbachev announced that the Soviet Union would withdraw its army of 120,000 men from Afghanistan. By early 1988, he was promising religious freedom.

Perestroika and Democratization.
Gorbachev's campaign for perestroika also stunned the Western world. In 1987, he unveiled a startling plan to dismantle the one-party political system by allowing multiple candidates and a secret ballot. He explained that the Communist Party bore much of the blame for Russian economic stagnation and that only greater democracy could revitalize the USSR. Soviet police even tolerated a few limited demonstrations, chiefly by Baltic and south Asian peoples. More surprisingly, Gorbachev told the nation—which was accustomed to policies defined by the tenets of Marxism-Leninism—that he wanted "socialism extricated from the slag heap of dogma." Gorbachev in-

creased the pace of democratization in 1988. A special congress of the Communist Party voted a remarkable agenda: the enlargement of glasnost and perestroika, the reform of the judicial system, a war on bureaucratic intransigence, greater rights for minority nationalities, and the rehabilitation of Stalin's opponents purged in the 1930s. Legislation began to transfer decision making from the central government to the local level while reducing government guarantees and financing.

Boris Yeltsin and the Fall of Gorbachev.
At this point, the speed of change began to exceed Gorbachev's control of it. A blunt-talking champion of reform, Boris Yeltsin, pushed Gorbachev to go further, faster. Yeltsin's criticism of Gorbachev had led to his dismissal as Moscow party head and then to Yeltsin's resignation of his Politburo membership. When Yeltsin called for a multiparty system of government, more than 10,000 people turned out in the streets of Moscow to support him. When Gorbachev created a new congress and held the first free elections in the history of the USSR in March 1989, Yeltsin, like Andrey Sakharov, was one of the first deputies elected to it. By early 1990, the Communist Party had lost its control of the state, multiparty politics had been legalized and a Russian presidency created. The Gorbachev revolution had gone beyond Gorbachev. He no longer had a strong constituency of supporters inside the Soviet Union. Ardent Communists began to detest him for destroying Communism, but ardent reformers wanted leaders who would go much further. Revolutions often consume individuals who stand between the extremes, and Gorbachev was now a centrist. On May Day 1990, he was publicly booed by thousands of demonstrators, chiefly hard-line Communists and staunch Russian Nationalists. Before the month was over, Yeltsin was elected to the presidency instead of Gorbachev.

THE END OF THE COLD WAR (1985–1989)

The Gorbachev revolution in the Soviet Union launched a series of dramatic and historic changes in Europe: it led directly to the end of the cold war with the West, to the collapse of the Soviet bloc in eastern Europe and the rise of democratic regimes there, to the reunification of East and West Germany, to the breakup of some states as smaller nation-states declared independence, and to a bitter war in the Balkans over the breakup of Yugoslavia.

Gorbachev–Reagan Summit Meetings.
Within weeks of being named party leader, Mikhail Gorbachev launched his "détente offensive" to improve relations with the West, in an effort to reduce the enormous bur-

The Fall of the Soviet Regime

Leonid Brezhnev (1906–1982), Head of the Soviet Government, 1964–1982.

Mikhail Gorbachev (b. 1931), Last Head of the Soviet Government, 1985–1990.

Boris Yeltsin (b. 1931), First President of the Russian Federation.

den of Russia's military expenses. His offer in September 1985 to cut Russian arms by 50 percent was rejected by a skeptical administration in Washington, but it won Gorbachev considerable support in Europe. His domestic reforms launched in 1985–1986 increased that support and his credibility. NATO and the Warsaw Pact nations then began talks on arms reductions. When Gorbachev and Reagan met at Reykjavik, Iceland, in 1986, the United States still insisted on building the new generation of star wars weapons. But when the two heads of state met in the Washington summit of 1987, Reagan agreed to cut nuclear arsenals and Gorbachev accepted unbalanced terms: over the following 3 years, the USSR would dismantle 1,752 missiles and the United States, 859.

Gorbachev's Arms Cuts. Gorbachev's followed his remarkable concession at the Washington summit with an announcement in May 1988 that he would withdraw all Russian troops from Afghanistan. Even the toughest conservative in Europe, Margaret Thatcher,

did not hesitate to say that she believed that the West could trust Gorbachev and deal with him when he then offered to reduce Soviet military expenditures and to end the arms race. Even Pope John Paul II signaled the changing Western attitude by welcoming talks with Gorbachev. With this encouragement from Europe, Gorbachev went to the UN in December 1988 and made a unilateral promise to reduce Red Army forces in Europe by 500,000 men and 10,000 tanks—a cut so deep that the commander-in-chief of those forces immediately resigned. (The total of Soviet forces stood at 5 million men.) Despite opposition from his military, Gorbachev kept cutting. In January 1989, he announced a 14.2 percent cut in military expenditures and a 12 percent cut in personnel. During 1989–1991, numerous arms reduction treaties and summit meetings underscored the conclusion that the age of the cold war was over.

The Malta Summit. Gorbachev's efforts led to a significant breakthrough in negotiations with the United

Brezhnev was born in the Ukraine, the son of a steelworker. He rose steadily in the Communist Party after joining Komsomol (the Communist Youth League) and working on the collectivization programs of the 1920s. His career was sponsored by the party chief in the Ukraine, Nikita Khrushchev, resulting in his appointment as chief of the new territory of Moldova, which was acquired after World War II. Brezhnev's success in Moldova pleased Stalin, who named him to a national leadership post on the Politburo. The Communist leadership saw him as a moderate in domestic and international affairs, leading to his selection to succeed Khrushchev as First Secretary of the Communist Party in 1964. He then led the Soviet during some of the tense years of the cold war, although declining health later led to criticism of him for weak leadership.

Gorbachev was the son of peasant farmers in the Caucasus whose brilliance in school led him to an education in law at the University of Moscow. His work for the Communist Party led to a regional appointment as agriculture secretary, a post in which he impressed the leadership of post-Brezhnev Russia, who named him as national Agriculture Secretary in 1978. It also led to an appointment to the Politburo in 1983, in which Gorbachev was charged with directing the Communist economy. Gorbachev concluded that the Communist economy was failing, and he introduced a team of young technocrats, rather than party ideaologues, to high posts. He became a leading critic of the hard-line policies of the cold war, setting the stage for his dramatic reform policies upon becoming First Secretary in 1985.

Yeltsin was the son of a construction worker in Sverdlovsk and began his career in the same occupation. After joining the Communist Party in 1961, he rose rapidly and attracted the attention of Mikhail Gorbachev, who was seeking the talents of a new generation. In 1985, Yeltsin became the party chief of Moscow and launched an anticorruption campaign, making him one of the most popular of Communist leaders. He became Chairman of the Russian Federation Supreme Soviet and used that post to criticize Gorbachev for being too slow in introducing reforms. This led to his election as president of Russia in 1991, a post that he had to defend with arms in 1993.

States and further nuclear arms reduction agreements. One of the clearest signs that the cold war was ending came in October 1989, when the foreign ministers of the Warsaw Pact nations renounced the Brezhnev Doctrine. On December 4, 1989, Gorbachev and U.S. President George H. Bush met on the Mediterranean island of Malta and issued a joint declaration that the half-century-long cold war was "at an end"—leading phrase makers to say that the cold war had lasted "from Yalta to Malta." A few months later, Mikhail Gorbachev won the Nobel Peace Prize for 1990.

THE REVOLUTIONS OF 1989 IN EASTERN EUROPE

The Gorbachev revolution in the USSR led directly to the breakup of the Communist bloc in Eastern Europe and to the dissolution of the Soviet Union itself. The Warsaw Pact had been renewed only a few weeks be-fore Gorbachev came to power in 1985. But 4 years later, the revolutions of 1989 ended the Soviet Empire in eastern Europe and redrew the map of Europe with few shots being fired. In 1991, the USSR itself dissolved into more than a dozen republics.

Poland. The revolutions of 1989 began in Poland and Hungary. The Solidarity movement, which had been struggling with the Communist government of Poland for nearly a decade, finally won legal recognition in January 1989. The union movement used that new status and its vast popularity to press the government to extend perestroika in Poland by liberalizing the political system. The government, whose only signals from Moscow were to accept restructuring, capitulated to Solidarity in a series of April meetings and agreed to free elections for the upper house of Parliament. Lech Walesa called those meetings "the beginning of the road to democracy." That agreement guaranteed the Communist Party a large block of seats whatever the outcome of the voting, but Polish voters gave Solidarity a landslide victory (80 percent of the vote) in June 1989. In the *Sejm*, the nonelected lower house of the Polish Parliament, the agreement gave the Communist Party 38 percent of the seats and Solidarity 35 percent.

The two houses would together elect the president of Poland. The Polish elections of 1989–1990 ended a generation of Communist government in Poland. Solidarity candidates won 96 percent of the seats in the upper house. In elections to the Sejm, many prominent Communists who were unopposed still could not win the 50 percent of the vote needed for election. Lech Walesa, the shipyard electrician and chief founder of Solidarity, won the presidency of Poland in 1990 with 75 percent of the vote. The new government immediately launched plans for the difficult transition to a market economy.

Hungary. The Hungarian revolution of 1989, in contrast, began among reformers within the Communist Party. The government announced in January that Hungarian perestroika would allow multiple political parties, and it backed that announcement with a new constitution ending the Communist Party's monopoly of political power. Communist reformers were so determined to end the postwar regime that they abolished their party in October 1989 and tried to reorganize themselves as a socialist party in hopes of surviving free elections. None of their decisions was more popular than the January 1990 Hungarian–Soviet agreement for the withdrawal of all Soviet troops stationed on Hungarian soil. None was a more powerful symbol than the June 1990 reopening of the Budapest Stock Exchange. But the most momentous decision of Hungarian reformers came in May 1989, when the government opened the border between Austria and Hungary, demolishing fortifications and removing barbed wire. This breech in the Iron Curtain allowed east Europeans free access to western Europe. Communist states slower to embrace change now faced the prospect that thousands of their citizens might flee to the west.

East Germany. The most dramatic of the revolutions of 1989 occurred in East Germany. The DDR remained a strict Communist dictatorship under Erich Honecker, the aging leader who had supervised the construction of the Berlin Wall a generation earlier. Honecker, the son of a militant coal miner in the Saar, had been a Communist since the Weimar Republic and had spent 10 years in Nazi prisons. He had been a leading organizer of the postwar Communist Party, who rose to become the head of state security in 1958, and had served as party leader since 1971. Honecker had followed a policy of severe domestic repression and strictly controlled economy. He was personally responsible for an order that border guards shoot to kill anyone seeking to flee to the west, and in February 1989, he had confi-

dently predicted that the Berlin Wall would remain standing for 100 years.

Erich Honecker vigorously resisted reform of the Communist regime and fought against the idea of perestroika. The tightly bottled-up discontent of East Germans became clear in the late summer of 1989, following the Hungarian decision to open their Austrian border. By West German law, all East Germans who came to West Germany received automatic citizenship, but the Iron Curtain had kept that number small. Suddenly, thousands of East Germans exploited Hungarian liberalization to visit there and then cross into West Germany; 7,000 people fled on the first night that the border was open, and 60,000 went to West Germany in the first month. The DDR was soon losing 300 citizens—chiefly the young, the skilled, and the educated—per hour. The Honecker government denounced Hungary and called for another Warsaw Pact invasion. As East German Communists tried to close this border, they soon faced demonstrations in favor of reform.

Leipzig, the Heldenstadt. Leipzig became known as the *Heldenstadt* (city of heroes) as thousands of people took to the streets, marching in defiance of a heavy military presence, standing up to the threat of tanks. Honecker seriously considered turning the army loose on the crowds. At that moment, Gorbachev visited East Berlin (October 1989) and was received by crowds chanting, "Gorby, Gorby, make us free." Gorbachev, who had already publicly reversed the Brezhnev Doctrine, told Honecker that the Warsaw Pact would not act against reformers, and he urged the East Germans to choose liberalization instead of civil war. When Honecker did not unleash the army, his regime collapsed. He was forced to resign as party leader, and he was later indicted for the crimes of the Communist era. In November, the East German Politburo was replaced and plans were announced for free elections. On midnight of November 9–10, the new government opened the border between East Berlin and West Berlin at the Brandenburg Gate. A carnival atmosphere enveloped Berlin—the symbolic city of the cold war—as thousands of people walked freely into West Germany, and others danced atop the Berlin Wall. Berlin thus provided the most symbolic moment of the revolutions of 1989, as German crowds began to tear down sections of the hated wall. In the new spirit of the free-market economy, the Berlin Wall ended its days broken into small fragments and sold as tourist souvenirs.

Czechoslovakia. The revolution of 1989 in Czechoslovakia became known as the **Velvet Revolution** because it, too, was a nonviolent transition, but it did not seem that way at the beginning. Encouraged by events in the Soviet Union, university students in Prague began demonstrations at the start of the school

THE FALL OF THE BERLIN WALL

The Fall of the Berlin Wall, November 1989

The following text is an eyewitness description of the opening of the Berlin wall in November 1989. The author is Timothy Garton Ash, a British journalist and contemporary historian who was deeply involved in the transformation of eastern Europe during the 1980s. Ash observed the momentous events of 1989, often from an inside vantage point.

Once upon a time, and a very bad time it was, there was a famous platform in West Berlin where distinguished visitors would be taken to stare at the Wall. American presidents from Kennedy to Reagan stood on that platform looking out over the no man's land beyond. They were told that this, the Potsdamer Platz, had once been Berlin's busiest square. . . . Their hosts pointed out a grassy mound on the far side: the remains of Hitler's bunker. East German border-guards watched impassively, or rode up and down the death strip on their army motorbikes.

On the morning of Sunday, 12 November I walked through the Wall and across that no man's land with a crowd of East Berliners, a watchtower to our left, Hitler's bunker to our right. Bewildered border-guards waved us through. (As recently as February their colleagues had shot dead a man trying to escape.) Vertical segments of the wall stood at ease where a crane had just dumped them, their multicolored graffiti facing east for the first time. A crowd of West Berliners applauded as we came through, and a man handed out free city plans. . . .

Everyone has seen the pictures of joyful celebration in West Berlin, the vast crowds stopping the traffic on the Kürfurstendamm, Sekt corks popping, strangers tearfully embracing—the greatest street-party in the history of the world. Yes, it was like that. But it was not only that. Most of the estimated two million East Germans who flooded into West Berlin over the weekend simply walked the streets in quiet family groups, often with toddlers in pushchairs. They queued up at a bank to collect the 100 Deutschmarks 'greeting money' [about $60] offered to visiting East Germans by the West German government, and then they went, very cautiously, shopping. Generally they bought one or two small items, perhaps some fresh fruit, a Western newspaper and toys for the children. Then, clasping their carrier-bags, they walked quietly back through the Wall, through the grey, deserted streets of East Berlin, home.

It is very difficult to describe the quality of this experience because what they actually did was so stunningly ordinary. . . . And

The End of the Berlin Wall. The Berlin wall, constructed in 1961, was the foremost symbol of the Iron Curtain separating East and West during the cold war. The opening of the Berlin Wall in November 1989—a delirious event to the crowds in this photo—quickly became the symbol of the revolutions of 1989 and the fall of Communism.

yet, what could be more fantastic? . . . Everyone looks the same as they make their way home . . . but everyone is inwardly changed, changed utterly.

From Ash, Timothy Garton, *The Magic Lantern* (New York: Random House, 1990).

Question: What was fantastic about doing ordinary things?

---

year in October. The Communist government initially felt secure and the first demonstrations were met with force and arrests. The Czech dissident movement had for a long time drawn its leaders from the intelligentsia who had supported the Prague Spring in 1968, drafted Charter 77 in 1977, and then grouped themselves together under the leadership of Václav Havel in the Civic Forum. After Gorbachev visited Prague in October

THE EUROPEAN REVOLUTIONS OF 1989

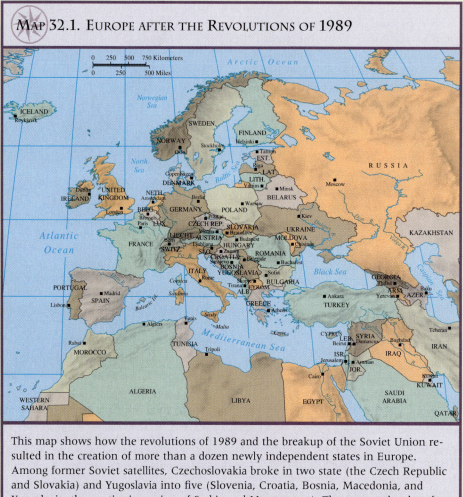

MAP 32.1. EUROPE AFTER THE REVOLUTIONS OF 1989

This map shows how the revolutions of 1989 and the breakup of the Soviet Union resulted in the creation of more than a dozen newly independent states in Europe. Among former Soviet satellites, Czechoslovakia broke in two state (the Czech Republic and Slovakia) and Yugoslavia into five (Slovenia, Croatia, Bosnia, Macedonia, and Yugoslavia, the continuing union of Serbia and Montenegro). The western border of the USSR yielded six independent states (Estonia, Latvia, Lithuania, Belarus, Ukraine, and Moldova), and the southwestern border along the Caucasus yielded three independent states, two of which aspired to be included in Europe (Georgia and Armenia).

1989, the Civic Forum resumed demonstrations, and this time they were backed by a widespread strike of workers. The Czechoslovak Communist Party initially agreed to surrender its monopoly on power and to include non-Communists in the government, but the tempest of perestroika could not be contained with such limited concessions. Negotiations with leaders of the Civic Forum produced an agreement to abolish controls on the press and television, release political prisoners, and end the Marxist control of universities. Demonstrations continued, however, and within a few weeks, the Communist government resigned.

TABLE 32.6 THE REVOLUTIONS OF 1989 IN EASTERN EUROPE

USSR

January	Coal miners in Ukraine defy government and strike.
February	Gorbachev withdraws last Soviet troops from Afghanistan.
March	Elections for new Parliament give landslide victory to reformers.
	Government admits that Nazi–Soviet Treaty of 1939 planned Baltic annexation.
	Estonia, Latvia, Lithuania, Armenia, Azerbaijan, Georgia, and Ukraine demand autonomy.
September	Azerbaijan becomes first republic of USSR to declare its independence.
December	Lithuania changes its constitution and abolishes Communist monopoly of power.
	Presidents Gorbachev and Bush meet in Malta and declare the cold war over.

Poland

January	Government legalizes Solidarity and multiple trade unions.
February	Solidarity enters negotiations for reform of Polish political system.
March	Government agrees to multiple party political system and calls elections.
June	First free Polish elections after World War II give sweeping victory to Solidarity.
August	Poland ends 40 years of Communist rule.
September	New Polish government launches plans for transition to market economy.

Hungary

January	Reforms permit multiple political parties.
March	Draft constitution ends dominance of Communist Party.
September	Government violates treaties and allows massive transit of East Germans to West.
October	Reformers abolish Communist Party and regroup as Socialist Party.
	Parliament democratizes constitution and calls elections.

East Germany

September	Hundreds of thousands of East Germans flee to West through Hungary.
October	Gorbachev visits East Germany and encourages liberalization.
	Mass demonstrations of New Forum in Leipzig and other cities.
	President Erich Honecker forced to resign amid growing demonstrations.
November	Government allows citizens to visit West without visas; thousands cross borders.
	Demonstrating crowds begin to demolish the Berlin Wall.
December	East German government resigns and free elections scheduled for early 1990.

Czechoslovakia

October	Government troops crush student demonstrations in Prague and arrest dissidents.
	Gorbachev urges Czech government to accept need for restructuring.
	Civic Forum leads demonstrations in Prague, demands resignation of government.
November	Entire Czech government resigns but demonstrations and strikes continue.
December	Non-Communist cabinet is installed in the Velvet Revolution.
	Czech Parliament approves Western-style democracy and names dissident president.
	Slovaks open question of cession to create separate state of Slovakia.

Romania

December	Secret police shoot demonstrators seeking ethnic and religious freedom in Timisoara.
	Units of army join demonstrators as National Salvation Front against Ceausescu dictatorship.
	Ceausescu arrested, tried, and executed by provisional government.

Question: Does any event on this list seem like a "turning-point"?

Václav Havel. The Czech Parliament hurriedly adopted a democratic system of government and scheduled elections; in the interim, it named Havel president of Czechoslovakia. Havel negotiated the withdrawal of the Soviet army and led Civic Forum to victory in the first free elections in June 1990. Like all of the states breaking away from their Communist past, Czechoslovakia faced great problems, and President Havel admitted them with a refreshing candor: "For forty years you have heard from the mouths of my predecessors . . . how our country is flourishing . . . how we are all happy . . . and what beautiful prospects are opening ahead of us. I assume that you have not named me to this office so that I, too, should lie to you. Our country is not flourishing." Havel faced one problem that was especially urgent: Slovakian leaders representing the eastern portion of the country asked for two separate states—a Czech state (the western provinces of Bohemia and Moravia) and a Slovak state.

Romania. Only in Romania did the revolution of 1989 result in a bloody conflict. The struggle began in the Transylvanian town of Timisoara, one of the centers of the Hungarian minority population, which numbered 2 million. A Hungarian Protestant clergyman in Timisoara, Lazlo Tökés, had become a champion of religious and ethnic freedom there. In December 1989, the government of dictator Nicolae Ceausescu (Chow'-ches-cue) ordered Tökés deported; when Tökés refused to leave, an attempt to arrest

MAP 32.2. THE BREAKUP OF THE SOVIET UNION, 1989–1991

Independent republics created from the former USSR

Provinces in rebellion, seeking independence

The era of glasnost and perestroika in the Soviet Union, followed by revolutions of 1989 in Eastern Europe, led to the breakup of the Soviet Union in the early 1990s. As this map shows, Soviet republics along the western and southern borders of the USSR won independence. Some regions, notably the Baltic States, insisted on total independence, while many others agreed to retain an association with Russia in a "Commonwealth of Independent States" created in 1991. In the region of Chechnia, Russia fought against independence, leading to violence continuing in the twenty-first century.

him precipitated a demonstration of 10,000 people in Timisoara. The Romanian security police fired on the demonstrating crowds, killing several hundred people. Romanians responded with anti-Ceausescu demonstrations in Bucharest, and the Romanian army refused to break them up. When Ceausescu declared martial law, units of the army joined the demonstrators. Two weeks of fighting between the army and the security police, who remained loyal to Ceausescu, killed an estimated 10,000 to 80,000. Ceausescu was caught, given a 2-hour trial, and executed that same day.

THE BREAKUP OF THE SOVIET UNION (1989–1991)

Nationalist unrest in the USSR had become open in the late 1980s. In the north, the Baltic states (Estonia, Latvia, and Lithuania) began to challenge Moscow. In 1988, the Estonians amended their constitution to permit a local veto of Soviet laws. When Gorbachev rejected this de-

gree of autonomy, 60 percent of the entire population of Estonia (a nation of only 1.5 million) signed a petition demanding self-rule. In the south, the neighboring Asian republics of Armenia and Azerbaijan quarreled over territory and the treatment of each other's minority population. Only an old-fashioned intervention by the Red Army in September 1988 prevented open war.

Declarations of Independence. The Soviet Union began to break up in 1989. Riots against the central government in Georgia broke out in April, the Lithuanian legislature voted for independence in May, workers struck for local self-government in the Ukraine in July, demonstrations in all of the Baltic states called for independence in August, and Azerbaijan delivered the first formal declaration of independence in September. By the end of the year, the Estonian government had adopted a Declaration of Sovereignty, and the Lithuanian legislature had disavowed their 1940 treaty of annexation and restored their 1938 constitution, thereby abolishing the Communist monopoly of power. In early 1990, all three Baltic republics formally proclaimed their independence.

Once again, revolutionary events were racing past Gorbachev's ability to manage them. He tried to block Baltic secession, but a new Lithuanian president—only recently a dissident professor of music—and a Lithuanian army of 1,500 men refused to back down. Gorbachev made a desperate attempt to stand against the breakup of the Soviet Union by ordering an army crackdown in the Baltic states. When the Red Army fired on a protesting crowd in Lithuania, 1,300 were killed; 100,000 then turned out in Moscow to protest, and Gorbachev was beaten by the openness he had fostered. Lithuania was allowed to hold a referendum in February 1991, and 91 percent of the electorate backed independence. The trend became so powerful that 2 months later a similar referendum was held in Georgia (Stalin's birthplace), and 90 percent voted for independence. Before the year had ended, fifteen of the Soviet republics had chosen self-rule. These included the Baltic states and the European republics of Belarus (a state of predominantly White Russian population located on the eastern border of Poland), Moldova (a largely Romanian population located on the Romanian border), and the Ukraine. These six newly independent states formed a solid belt stretching from the Baltic Sea to the Black Sea, separating Russia from Europe.

Collapse of the Communist Regime. While the Soviet Union broke apart, the traditional Communist regime of Russia itself also collapsed. Between late 1989 and early 1991, Russia experienced constant change. Gorbachev announced a new agricultural plan to break up the **collective farms** and a new economic plan that introduced television advertising. Unions were given the right to strike and promptly tried it. The KGB announced that it disavowed its previous terrorism. Gorbachev publicly abandoned the concept of **class struggle.** Shevardnadze acknowledged that the Soviet invasion of Afghanistan had been illegal. The Red Army withdrew from most of eastern Europe, slowed only by limited finances for housing them in the Soviet Union. After 100,000 public demonstrators demanded a multiparty democracy within Russia, the Communist Party agreed to end its monopoly on political power. In one of the bluntest rejections of Communism, the Russian Parliament voted in March 1990 to approve of **private property,** in September 1990 to allow religious freedom, and in May 1991 to give all Russian citizens freedom of travel, including abroad. The Soviet archives were opened and confessions poured out—from the calculation that Stalin's terror had killed 20 million people to the admission that the Soviet Union had been responsible for the Katyn Forest massacre of Polish officers during World War II. The city of Leningrad reverted to its historic name, St. Petersburg. Thousands of other institutions and towns simply took down the portrait, or pulled down the statue, of Lenin, or any other symbol of the regime.

The Fall of Gorbachev. The stunning collapse of the USSR provoked conservative, antiperestroika Communists to attempt a coup d'état in August 1991. Advocates of the old regime, including several leaders of the army and the KGB, held Mikhail Gorbachev under house arrest and tried to seize centers of power such as the Parliament building in Moscow. Reformers, such as Yeltsin and the mayor of St. Petersburg, resisted the coup and used the army (which did not support the conspiracy) to bombard the conspirators into submission. Boris Yeltsin, standing atop a tank and exhorting the crowd to stand up to the conspirators, became the leader of the new Russia. While the ruins of the Russian Parliament still smoldered, Yeltsin shut down all offices of the Communist Party, purged hard-liners from the government, and suspended newspapers that had been sympathetic to the coup, such as *Pravda.* Crowds in Moscow vandalized the KGB building with impunity. Less than 2 weeks later, in September 1991, Parliament voted the dissolution of the USSR. Gorbachev remained in office until resigning in December 1991, when Yeltsin replaced him in the presidency. His farewell speech did not regret his historic role. "The old system," he said, "fell apart." Yeltsin, however, proved better at demanding reform than at implementing it, and he too would soon be rejected.

HELMUT KOHL AND THE REUNIFICATION OF GERMANY (1989–1990)

Two dramatic consequences quickly flowed from the collapse of the Soviet bloc: (1) in October 1990, the two Germanys reunited, when the German Democratic Republic (East Germany) joined the Federal Republic of Germany, and (2) in December 1990, Yugoslavia began to break apart and fell into a decade of internecine civil war (1991–1999), which killed hundreds of thousands and left Yugoslavia divided into seven states.

The Dream of Reunification. The Bonn Constitution of West Germany, adopted in 1949, had encompassed the dream of **reunification** in which the two Germanies would be united. The preamble stated that "the entire German people is called upon to achieve by self-determination the unity and freedom of Germany." The cold war postponed the German dream of reunification to a distant future, a delay that did not dismay many European states. The USSR uncompromisingly opposed any possibility of a strong, unified Germany near its frontiers.

Many Westerners privately preferred the division of Germany; it had facilitated the postwar Franco-German rapprochement and the progress toward the **European Union** (EU). Most Germans had accepted the reality of two Germanys—West Germans helped by their prosperity and East Germans by their comparative success within the Eastern bloc. The formal recognition of division, the absence of a German problem on his frontier, and the successful arms negotiations of the age of détente had been essential factors in facilitating the Gorbachev revolution. The combination of these facts was as important as the victory of American technology and spending to win the arms race or the unyielding pressure for human rights and freedom from within.

Helmut Kohl.

When the revolutions of 1989 upended the long-standing political realities in central Europe, the chancellor of West Germany was given the unexpected opportunity to become the Bismarck of the twentieth century. Helmut Kohl was an unlikely man for this comparison, but he succeeded in the role with remarkable ease. Kohl, like Adenauer before him, came from a conservative Catholic family from the Rhineland. He was the first chancellor from the generation too young to have had an active role in World War II, being 15 when the war ended. Kohl had taken a Ph.D. in political science and immediately entered local politics as a pragmatic, rather than ideological, conservative. By 1976, he had become the leader of the German conservative party, the Christian Democratic Union (CDU). In 1982, he engineered the ouster of the socialist chancellor, Helmut Schmidt, by persuading a small third party, the Free Democrats, to abandon their coalition with Schmidt and form a new majority with Kohl and the CDU. Kohl promised "a government of the middle" and followed a moderate course. He embraced the German model for social peace and economic growth—requiring more concessions to labor and more support of the welfare state than British or American conservatives would accept. In European policy, he was one of the chief advocates of the EU and, in foreign policy, one of the chief defenders of NATO and close ties to the United States. By 1989, he had achieved a long tenure as chancellor, but he had not given any signs that he would preside over one of the most important accomplishments of twentieth-century German history.

The Kohl Plan.

When the events of October–November 1989 reopened the German question, Helmut Kohl seized the opportunity with surprising speed. On the night that the DDR opened the Berlin Wall and joyous Berliners celebrated in the streets, Kohl made a simple speech nearby: "We are, and we remain, one nation." Kohl promptly produced, and the Bundestag ratified, a Ten-Point Plan for German Unity in November 1989. Point ten was clear: "We are working for a state of peace in Europe in which the German nation can recover its unity in free self-determination." The speed of Kohl's action surprised many, but he argued that something must be done to slow the torrent of East Germans migrating to

West Germany—500,000 immigrants arrived in November alone. World leaders could only respond as the surprised George H. Bush did: "We're pleased." A few weeks later, in January 1990, Gorbachev acknowledged that reunification was probable.

East German Acceptance of Union.

The East German government initially hesitated, and the prime minister of the DDR spoke of plans for a commission to study the possibilities, but the sentiment of public opinion was overwhelming. Demonstrations in East Germany denounced the old regime—especially after revelations of the activities of the Stasi, the former secret police—and hard-liners were forced to resign. East German elections of March 1990 settled the question. No party received an absolute majority, but 48 percent voted for a party backing immediate unification and nearly 70 percent voted for parties favoring some form of unification. The Communist Party received 16 percent of the vote. This election led directly to negotiations for unification. Helmut Kohl pressed for immediate action, and within a few weeks, the two Germanys had agreed on a common currency and economic policy, although this typically meant that West German standards had prevailed or difficult problems had been postponed. More than 8,000 state-run businesses in the DDR would be privatized. Institutions in East Germany would be transformed; universities, for example, were given West German administrators who closed most programs in Marxism-Leninism and reduced programs in Russian language and studies.

The German Treaties of 1990.

The negotiations between the Federal Republic and the DDR were expanded into the "two-plus-four negotiations" in May 1990, bringing together the two Germanys and the four powers that had divided Germany in 1945 (Britain, France, Russia, and the United States). In these talks, the four powers accepted German reassurances about the international aspects of the new Germany. A Russo-German Treaty of July 1990 and a Treaty of Final Settlement on Germany in September 1990 stated the terms: Germany could unite and remain within NATO, but the German government must (1) reduce its standing army to fewer than 400,000 troops; (2) renounce all nuclear, chemical, and biological weaponry; and (3) provide financial assistance to Russia for the repatriation of the Soviet army. While those details were still being worked out, the two Germanys formed an economic merger based on the West German mark. Then, in October 1990, 45 years after the postwar partition, a unified Germany with a population of nearly 8 million was created by the DDR joining the Federal Republic. The first all-German elections in nearly 60 years followed in December 1990, with Helmut Kohl becoming the first chancellor of the new state. The Bundestag voted in 1991, by a narrow margin, to return the capital of Germany to Berlin in a 12-year transition.

THE YUGOSLAV WARS (1991–1999)

Yugoslavia. While Germans were celebrating their union to the tune of Beethoven's "Ode to Joy," Yugoslavia was fragmenting in an internecine war. Yugoslavia had been created at the Paris Peace Conference of 1919, according to the principle of "the national self-determination of peoples," by merging the independent states of Serbia and Montenegro with provinces taken from the defeated Austro-Hungarian Empire. Although Yugoslavia ("the land of the southern Slavs") had been a dream of Slavic Nationalists, it had always been a delicate federation of several different peoples, chiefly Slovenes, Croatians, Bosnians, Serbs, Albanians, and Macedonians. These peoples practiced several different religions—chiefly Roman Catholicism in Slovenia and Croatia, Islam in Bosnia and Kosovo, and Orthodox Christianity in the other regions—and spoke languages different enough to require different alphabets.

Nationalism. Yugoslavia and the western Balkans had long been a powder keg of bitter nationalist and religious rivalries, many of which had been exacerbated by questions of collaboration with the Nazis during World War II. The forceful personality of President Tito—a Croatian who had been the leader of the predominantly Serbian resistance to Nazism—had held Yugoslavia together as a federation of equals. His refusal to follow Moscow as a satellite of the Soviet Union had earned Yugoslavia massive Western assistance, which helped sustain his regime. His successors were less able to follow these policies. Regional nationalism increased after Tito's death in 1980, despite Yugoslavia's rotating presidency, which gave each major ethnic group a turn at leadership. The Albanian minority, concentrated in the region of Kosovo, rioted in 1981, seeking independence. Widespread unrest was evident among the Muslim population of Bosnia in 1983. Croatian terrorists conducted a bombing campaign in 1985.

The Revolution of 1989. The collapse of the Yugoslav Communist Party in the revolution of 1989 worsened the federation's crisis of nationalist regionalism. Without the strong central authority that had held the federated republics together, political power passed to local authorities during 1990. The two most westernized republics, Slovenia and Croatia, held free elections in the spring of 1990. Slovenia, the most prosperous portion of Yugoslavia, adopted a declaration of sovereignty a few weeks later, and by the end of the year, a public referendum had approved secession from Yugoslavia. Croatia meanwhile prepared a new constitution that asserted the right to secede. Stimulated by these developments, the Serbian minority population in the non-Serbian republics of Croatia and Bosnia formed separatist groups that claimed the right of self-government.

War in Croatia (1991–1992). The Yugoslav crisis became the Yugoslav War in 1991, and it would kill far more people during the 1990s than the four decades of the cold war had killed in Europe. Slovenia and Croatia each proclaimed their independence from Yugoslavia in July. The Serbian minority in Croatia (especially those concentrated in a region that the Serbs called Krajina) resisted this declaration and announced the secession of some districts that would join the neighboring republic of Bosnia. Serbia, the largest state of Yugoslavia, controlled the military and intervened on behalf of the Serbian minority. The Yugoslav air force bombed Zagreb, the capital of Croatia, in October 1991, and a few days later, the Yugoslav army besieged and shelled the picturesque Croatian town of Dubrovnik on the Adriatic Coast. In November, the Croatian city of Vukovar surrendered to Serbian forces; shortly thereafter, the first stories of war **atrocities**—the murder of Croatian civilians in Vukovar—began to reach the West. By the end of 1991, the president of Yugoslavia announced that the country had ceased to exist. In early 1992, the EU recognized the independence of Slovenia, Croatia, and Bosnia, and the UN accepted all three as members.

War in Bosnia (1992–1995). In 1992, the chief theater of the Yugoslav Wars became Bosnia. Bosnia was an ethnically mixed region composed chiefly of

ETHNIC GROUP	PERCENTAGE
Serbians	36
Croatians	20
Bosnians (Muslim)	9
Slovenes	8
Albanians	8
Macedonians	6
Montenegrins	3
Hungarians	2
Others	8

TABLE 32.7 THE ETHNIC COMPOSITION OF YUGOSLAVIA IN 1991

Question: Is the ethnic division of a country into so many groups an obstacle to a unified national identity?

FIGURE 32.1 *War Crimes.* The Yugoslav Wars of the 1990s were bitterly contested and resulted in numerous accusations of war crimes, especially against civilian populations. Evidence of the "ethnic cleansing" of areas by removing all members of a minority population, the widespread policy of mass rape, and the mass murder of civilians led to Europe's first war crimes trials since the Nuremberg Trials. The Hague Tribunal has tried and convicted Serbs, Croatians, and Bosnian Muslims of war crimes, although the most prominent cases have involved charges against Serbia. In this illustration, a forensic investigator examines the skeletons in a mass grave in Croatia.

Bosnian Muslims (more than 40 percent), Serbian Orthodox Christians (more than 30 percent), and Croatian Catholics (less than 20 percent). The capital of Bosnia, Sarajevo, had been considered a model city of different peoples living together harmoniously when it hosted the winter Olympic Games in 1984. The Bosnian declaration of independence, however, had prompted a furious offensive—often centered on the siege and bombardment of Sarajevo—by the Bosnian Serbs, who proclaimed their own government led by a militant Serbian Nationalist, Radovan Karadzic. For the next 3 years, the Bosnian Serbs, with support from Serbia, conquered most of Bosnia in fighting so ferocious that it shocked the rest of the world. The Bosnian Serb army, commanded by General Ratko Mladic, devastated the city of Sarajevo in constant bombardments. In the villages of Bosnia, Mladic imposed a policy of **"ethnic cleansing"**—driving all non-Serbs from an area.

War Crimes. As the policy of ethnic cleansing suggests, the war in Bosnia produced the worst atrocities in Europe since World War II. By late 1992, accusations of extreme abuses in Serbian detention camps, including the execution of 3,000 people in one camp, reached the West. They were followed by a litany of horrors—from the intentional mass rape of Bosnian women as an instrument of policy to the mass execution of all Bosnian Muslim men taken captive. International opinion became so outraged at the continuing atrocities in the Balkans that the UN established the first international war crimes tribunal since the Nuremberg Trials of 1945–1946. The Hague Tribunal returned indictments against Croatians and Bosnian Muslims as well as Serbs, but most of the indictments and the gravest accusations were against Bosnian Serbs, whose head of state (Karadzic) and military leader (Mladic) were both indicted in absentia. (Mladic had made a public statement in 1994 calling for the extermination of Bosnian Muslims.) The worst atrocity of the Bosnian War occurred in July 1995 at the town of Srebrenica in eastern Bosnia, in a so-called safe zone under UN protection. In a coldly organized massacre reminiscent of Nazi atrocities, Bosnia Serbs rounded up between 7,000 and 8,000 Croatian and Bosnian Muslim men and murdered them; war crime investigators found nearly 5,000 bodies in a single mass grave.

The Dayton Accords (1995). The first effective cease-fire of the Yugoslav War produced a delicate peace agreement in 1995. The gradual arming of Croatia had produced significant military victories against the Serbs, an international Islamic coalition had begun to support Bosnia, and the United States had even bombed Serbian positions. In November 1995, the presidents of Serbia, Croatia, and Bosnia met in Dayton, Ohio, and signed a peace agreement brokered by the United States. Bosnian Serbs served in the Serbian delegation, but Radovan Karadzic could not negotiate alongside the other heads of government because the Bosnian Serbs were not recognized as an independent government and Karadzic remained under indictment for war crimes. The Dayton Accords dealt chiefly with Bosnia: it would remain a single state within its previous borders, but it would contain two entities—a Bosnian–Croatian federation and a Bosnian Serb republic. To maintain this unusual arrangement, NATO agreed to send 60,000 peacekeeping troops to Bosnia for 1 year.

The War in Kosovo (1998–1999). By 1998, the war had shifted to Kosovo, where Albanians and Serbs had been fighting since the early 1980s. (A Kosovo

Liberation Army [KLA] had been active since 1993.) Kosovo was a region of great patriotic importance to Serbs (it was the scene of an historic battle), but it was populated by an overwhelming majority (more than 90 percent) of Albanian Muslims. When the KLA attacked Serbian forces in 1998, President Slobodan Milosevic (Mill-osh'-eh-vich) of Serbia, who had revoked Kosovo's autonomy in 1989, ordered massive retaliation. NATO officials estimated that the Serbian army killed more than 10,000 civilians in 2 months and drove more than 600,000 (approximately one-third of the population) to flee to Albania and Macedonia and another 700,000 to flee internally. When evidence of new massacres was found, the Western powers did not hesitate as they had in Bosnia. After Serbia rejected peace proposals, NATO intervened to protect the Kosovar Albanians. In a 78-day air-war, NATO forced the Serbian army to withdraw and bombed Belgrade.

Continuing Instability. The Balkan Wars of the 1990s displaced more than 3 million people and killed more than 300,000. The war crimes were so severe that President Milosevic himself was arrested in 2001 and sent to the war crimes tribunal in the Hague to stand trial for crimes against humanity committed in Croatia (1991–1992), genocide in Bosnia (1992–1995), and war crimes in Kosovo (1998–1999), following the standards of the Nuremberg Trials and the Geneva Conventions on war. By 2003, twenty-nine others (eighteen Serbs, nine Croats, and two Bosnian Muslims) had already been convicted. Many of the early trials focused on the Serbian army's rape of an estimated 50,000 women, often in forced army brothels. But stability eluded Serbia, where two other presidents, including the president who extradited Milosevic, were assassinated. And several of the Balkan states, from Bosnia to Macedonia remained unstable.

THE EUROPEAN UNION SINCE 1975

Despite the enormous importance of such events as the ending of the cold war, the breakup of the Soviet Union, and the reunification of Germany, the most important development in recent European history has probably been the continuing integration of Europe into a closer and closer union. From the six founding states of the Common Market in 1957, through a European Union of fifteen independent states with close economic integration and often a single currency (the **Euro**) at the start of the twenty-first century, to a planned expansion (beginning in 2004) to a union of twenty-five countries with a population of more than 450 million and an increasingly integrated military ca-

pacity, Europe has begun an historic process of integration and union.

Evolution of the European Union. The mid-1970s witnessed an important turning point in the expansion of European **economic integration.** The European Community (EC), the association that grew out of the EEC in 1967 and that increased the cooperation of France, West Germany, Italy, and the Benelux countries, was the highest degree of European integration ever achieved. Negotiations to expand the EC revived in the 1970s, and plans were drafted for adding Britain, Ireland, Denmark, and Norway as the first step toward the economic union of all of non-Communist Europe. The most important (and sometimes the most troublesome) of these states, Britain, finally joined the EC in 1973. In several cases, membership treaties were submitted for public approval in a referendum. A negative vote in Norway kept that country out of the EC, but British membership was reaffirmed in a public vote in 1975, encouraging a generation of EC growth. The death of General Franco (1975) and the subsequent election of a democratic government in Spain (1977), plus free elections in Portugal (1975) that freed Iberia from the authoritarian governments of the 1930s, allowed the EC to accept both Iberian states, bringing membership to twelve.

Jacques Delors and the European Union. Under the leadership of Jacques Delors, Europe moved steadily toward a federal unity. Delors had an exceptional opportunity to act because he enjoyed the strong support of both Chancellor Helmut Kohl of Germany and President François Mitterrand of France, both of whom retained office in a period of rare stability. Delors was a Christian–Socialist idealist and a financial expert who had served in Monnet's Planning Commissariat and as the French Minister of Finance. Elected to the European Parliament in 1979, Delors was chosen to preside over the **European Commission** (the executive branch of the integrated government) in Brussels for an unprecedented period of 10 years (1985–1995), which gave him time to achieve much of his goal: "ever closer union." Under his leadership, the Schengen Agreement of 1985 removed all border controls between member states (although Britain and Ireland declined to implement this policy), making it possible to drive from Scandinavia to Spain without a passport or customs inspection. The Single European Act, adopted in 1986 with the approval of all twelve member states, implemented a single European market with **open frontiers,** encouraging the international flow of people, goods, services, and capital. Jacques Delors also presided over a European summit meeting held at Maastricht (the Netherlands) in 1991 that oversaw the transformation of the EC into the EU.

THE YUGOSLAV WARS OF THE 1990S

The Yugoslav Wars. The town of Mostar, the capital of the region of Herzegovina, was once one of the symbols of the ethnic diversity of the Yugoslav republic. It combined a largely Catholic, Croatian population with a Muslim, Bosnian population, linked by the sixteenth-century bridge (the *stari most*) that gave the town its name. During the Yugoslav civil war, Mostar also became a symbol of ethnic hatred as the two groups killed each other. In an act symbolic of the destruction of the war and of the separation of populations, Croatian shelling destroyed the bridge in 1993.

A Child's Experiences during the Siege of Sarajevo (1992)

Zlata Filipovic began a diary at age 10. Her father was a lawyer, and Zlata enjoyed a middle-class life in Sarajevo. Zlata liked American pop music, skiing in the mountains surrounding Sarajevo, and vacations in Italy. When school began in September 1991, Zlata was in high spirits, writing about the music on MTV and her favorite pizza. War had begun in neighboring Croatia, but life in Bosnia was calm. These excerpts from Zlata's diary are from April 1992. Serbian artillery on the ski slopes above Sarajevo began to shell Zlata's home in May, and the family moved into the inner rooms and slept on the floor. Zlata's diary became of record of death and destruction. Instead of MTV and pizza she wrote of "more blood on the streets of Sarajevo. Another massacre."

April 3, 1992: Daddy came back . . . all upset. He says there are terrible crowds at the train and bus stations. People are leaving Sarajevo.

April 4, 1992: There aren't many people in the streets. I guess it's fear of the stories about Sarajevo being bombed. But there's no bombing. . . .

April 5, 1992: I'm trying hard to concentrate so I can do my homework (reading), but I simply can't. Something is going on in town. You can hear gunfire from the hills.

The Euro. In 1988, a document known as the Delors Plan outlined the next steps to closer economic unity, including a **common currency,** the Euro. The dream of a common currency dated back to the Treaty of Rome (1957) and the founding days of European unity. A single currency had been championed for a generation by Pierre Werner, who served for 20 years as the prime minister of Luxembourg, and the outlines for a common currency, known naturally as the Werner Plan, had been adopted in 1971. Although he had left the presidency of the commission, Delors helped complete this work by drafting another document in 1998, "the Delors Report," which resulted in the creation of a European Central Bank at Frankfurt. This permitted the adoption of the Euro as Europe's common currency in 1999 and its public circulation in 2002—abolishing such historic currencies as the Italian Lira (versions of which had circulated since the Renaissance) and the Greek drachma (which predated Christianity). By 2003, the Euro had surpassed the dollar as the strongest currency on Earth. Once again, however, Britain declined to accept the common policy, retaining the pound sterling.

European Union Expansion. The economic and institutional progress of the 1980s and 1990s led to an expansion of the EU to fifteen members with the addition of Sweden, Finland, and Austria. The revolutions of 1989 and the collapse of the Soviet empire led to a wave of applications from Eastern Europe, and by 1997, plans were in place for the eventual membership of several formerly Communist states, led by the comparatively prosperous ones—Estonia, Poland, the Czech Republic,

April 6, 1992: Now they're shooting from the Holiday Inn, killing people in front of the parliament. . . . Maybe we'll go to the cellar . . .

April 9, 1992: I'm not going to school. All the schools in Sarajevo are closed. . . .

April 14, 1992: People are leaving Sarajevo. The airport, train and bus stations are packed. . . .

April 18, 1992: There's shooting, shells are falling. This really is WAR. Mommy and Daddy are worried, they sit up late at night, talking. They're wondering what to do, but it's hard to know. . . . Mommy can't make up her mind—she's constantly in tears. She tries to hide it from me, but I see everything.

April 21, 1992: It's horrible in Sarajevo today. Shells falling, people and children getting killed, shooting. We will probably spend the night in the cellar.

April 26, 1992: We spent Thursday night with the Bobars again. The next day we had no electricity. We had no bread, so for the first time in her life Mommy baked some.

April 28, 1992: SNIFFLE! Everybody has gone. I'm left with no friends.

April 29, 1992: I'd write to you much more about the war if only I could. But I simply don't want to remember all these horrible things.

From Filipovic, Zlata, *Zlata's Diary: A Child's Life in Sarajevo*, trans. Christina Pribichevich-Zovic (New York: Viking, 1994).

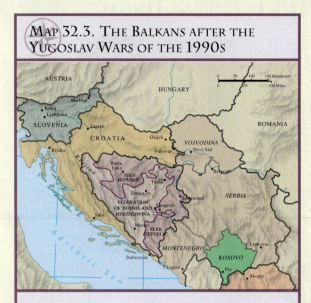

MAP 32.3. THE BALKANS AFTER THE YUGOSLAV WARS OF THE 1990S

The map shows the still-contested division of Yugoslavia. In the northwest, Slovenia and Croatia have become relatively secure independent states. In the center, the complex state of Bosnia created by the Dayton Accords of 1995 remains divided between a largely Muslim "Federation of Bosnia and Herzegovina" and a still defiant "Serb Republic of Bosnia," where some of the people most sought by the War Crimes Tribunal still find sanctuary. In the south, the federation of Yugoslavia saw the province of Kosovo break away and relations between Montenegro and Serbia strained to the point of breakup.

Hungary, and Slovenia. The EU held another summit meeting, at Nice (France) in 2000, to adopt guidelines for expansion in southern and eastern Europe; 2 years later, another summit meeting voted to accept ten new members, beginning in 2004. These members included the Baltic states of Estonia, Latvia, and Lithuania (all formerly part of the USSR); five states from the Soviet bloc (Poland, the Czech Republic, Slovakia, Hungary, and Slovenia); and two Mediterranean island nations, Malta and Cyprus. Referenda in candidate states approved membership, usually by a large margin (77 percent in Poland, 79 percent in the Czech Republic, nearly 90 percent in Slovenia). An EU of twenty-five members would have a population of more than 450 million people, compared with the U.S. population of just less than 290 million, and a gross domestic product of approximately the same size. (The fifteen-member EU had a GDP of $7.8 trillion in 2002, compared with the American GDP of $9.9 trillion for the same year.) The governments of Romania, Bulgaria, and Turkey all desired to increase the EU population, but they remained on a slower track to membership until the economy or human rights record drew closer to EU standards. Switzerland and Norway chose to remain outside the EU.

Opposition and Doubt. The closer federation of Europe was controversial in many places. Governments often held referenda to gain public approval of controversial treaties, such as the Maastricht Treaty. In France, long a leader in the drive toward greater unity, a referendum of September 1992 approved of Maastricht only by the narrow margin of 51 to 49 percent. Danes re-

THE EUROPEAN UNION

Jacques Delors (b. 1925), President of the European Commission (1985–1994), who presided over negotiations for the Schengen Agreement, the Maastricht Treaty, and the preparation for the Euro.

MAP 32.4. THE EUROPEAN UNION AT THE START OF THE TWENTY-FIRST CENTURY

Member of the European Union in 2003

New Members Entering in 2004

Applicants with Longterm Hopes of Economic Union Membership

€   Euro Symbol

This map depicts the growth of the European Union (EU) at the start of the twenty-first century. It highlights the newest members to join the EU (in 2004) and the applicants for future membership. Note also the inner membership of the EU indicated by those states that had adopted the Euro as their common currency.

jected the treaty by a narrow margin but negotiated "opt-out clauses" that convinced public opinion to ratify the treaty on the second try. Prime Minister Thatcher of Britain was the leading critic of the EU. She attacked the Brussels bureaucracy of **"Eurocrats";** the plans for a common currency; the Union's common social policy, which she denounced as a backdoor route for socialism into Britain; the increasing role of the European Parliament at Strasbourg (at the expense of Britain's Parliament); and the apparent birth of a European **"superstate."** "During my lifetime, Lady

Thatcher wrote, "most of the problems the world has faced have come, in one fashion or another, from mainland Europe."

European Institutions. Despite such opposition and the delays it produced, the federal institutions of the EU grew steadily. The first direct elections for the **European Parliament,** to meet in Strasbourg, were held in 1979, and a woman, Simone Veil of France, was chosen as its first president. The parliament was allowed only partial legislative powers: legislation

TABLE 32.8 THE GROWTH OF THE EUROPEAN UNION SINCE 1975

1975	British referendum accepts European Community (EC) membership.
	Greece, Spain, and Portugal apply for EC membership.
1979	First direct elections to the European Parliament in Strasbourg.
	Simone Veil elected first president of the European Parliament.
	The EC creates the European Monetary System (EMS).
1981	Greece begins 5-year phased entry into the EC as tenth member.
1983	Governments of the ten EC members sign the Solemn Declaration on unity.
1984	European Parliament adopts treaty on creating the European Union (EU).
1985	Spain and Portugal accepted into the EC as eleventh and twelfth members.
	Schengen Agreement removes border controls between EU members.
	Single European Act sets 1992 as date for open frontiers and single market.
1986	Single European Act adopted in parliaments of all twelve member states.
1987	Turkey applies for membership in the EC.
1988	Delors Plan outlines closer economic unity and a common currency (the Euro).
1989	EC adopts draft Charter of Fundamental Social Rights.
	Austria applies for membership in the EC.
1990	Cyprus and Malta apply for EC membership.
1991	Sweden applies for membership in the EC.
1992	Single European Act and Maastricht Treaty create open frontiers and single market: EC becomes the EU.
	Norway and Finland apply for EU membership.
	Twelve members of the EU agree to negotiations to expand to sixteen members.
	Switzerland applies for EU membership.
1994	Sweden, Finland, and Austria reach agreements to join the EU.
1995	Norwegian national referendum again rejects EU membership.
1998	Delors Report outlines plan for monetary union.
	European Central Bank established at Frankfurt.
1999	Euro becomes the official currency of eleven of fifteen EU members.
2000	Nice summit adopts plan for EU expansion in eastern and southern Europe.
	Brussels conference adopts plan for EU Rapid Reaction Force of 100,000 soldiers.
2002	Copenhagen summit accepts ten new members in EU, beginning in 2004.
	Denmark rejects Euro in national referendum.
2003	Draft of EU constitution submitted to members.

Question: Does any event on this list seem like a "turning point"?

would originate with the president of the commission, then be discussed and approved by the parliament, finally going through an elaborate bureaucratic procedure before it could become European law. Nonetheless, several dramatic programs won adoption. The European Convention on Human Rights quickly became an important part of the EU, and all potential members were required to subscribe to it and accept the jurisdiction of the European Court of Human Rights. The strict human rights standards for membership create an obstacle to joining the EU for several countries—laws allowing capital punishment or evidence of the use of torture can exclude a country. A conference of defense ministers held at Brussels in 2000 and the Nice Summit of that year launched the union on the creation of a European military force, distinct from the forces of NATO. Initial plans called for a Rapid Deployment Force of 60,000 soldiers within 60 days, with a reserve of an additional 40,000 troops. The first EU troops, wearing the EU badge of twelve yellow stars on a blue background, went on peacekeeping duty in Macedonia in 2003.

THE CHARTER OF FUNDAMENTAL RIGHTS OF THE UNION

The European Union has had a strong Bill of Rights throughout its evolution. An initial statement on human rights was drafted at Rome in 1950, and a full convention became mandatory throughout the EC in 1970, being expanded and amended by several subsequent protocols. The newest draft of the European Bill of Rights, known as The Charter of Fundamental Rights of the Union, was adopted at the European convention in July 2003 and forms Part Two of the Treaty Establishing a Constitution for Europe. The full text of this statement of rights contains fifty-four basic rights stated in seven different categories of rights; the opening sections, covering freedom is reproduced here. Other basic rights follow in sections on equality (such as "equality before the law"), solidarity (such as "right of collective bargaining"), citizen's rights (such as "to vote"), and justice (such as "presumption of innocence").

Article 1. **Human Dignity.** *Human Dignity is inviolable. It must be respected and protected.*

Article 2. **Right to Life.** *Everyone has the right to life. No one shall be condemned to the death penalty, or executed.*

Article 3. **Right to the Integrity of the Person.** *Everyone has the right to respect for his or her physical and mental integrity. In the fields of medicine and biology, the following must be respected in particular: (a) the free and informed consent of the person con-*

cerned. . . . (b) the prohibition of eugenic practices, in particular those aiming at the selection of persons, (c) the prohibition on making the human body and its parts as such a source of financial gain, (d) the prohibition of the reproductive cloning of human beings.

Article 4. **Prohibition of Torture and Inhuman or Degrading Treatment or Punishment. . . .**

Article 5. **Prohibition of Slavery and Forced Labor.** *No one shall be held in slavery or servitude. No one shall be required to perform forced or compulsory labor. Trafficking in human beings is prohibited.*

Article 6. **Right to Liberty and Security.** *Everyone has the right to liberty and security of the person.*

Article 7. **Respect for Private and Family Life.** *Everyone has the right to respect for his or her private and family life, home and communications.*

Article 8. **Protection of Personal Data.** *Everyone has the right to the protection of personal data concerning him or her. Such data must be processed fairly for specified purposes and on the basis of the consent of the person concerned. . . . Everyone has the right of access to data which has been collected concerning him or her, and the right to have it rectified. Compliance with these rules shall be subject to control by an independent authority.*

Article 9. **Right to Marry and Right to Found a Family.** *The right to marry and the right to found a family shall be guar-*

The European Constitution. The EU took its most dramatic step in 2003, when a convention under the presidency of Valéry Giscard d'Estaing (a former president of France) submitted its proposal for the constitution of a federal Europe. The draft constitution, which must be approved by all member states, would streamline the European bureaucracy, enhance the powers of the president of the Commission, eliminate the veto power of member states, and require instead approval by deputies representing 60 percent of EU population. If approved, however, it would mark the beginning of a federal government of Europe.

CONCLUSION

Europe has reached the beginning of the twenty-first century in an age of peace and prosperity—a new "belle époque" longer than the comparable age before World War I. The economies linked together in the European Union have produced a period of such development that it has created the highest standard of living in European history. That prosperity has sustained a comprehensive welfare state promising cradle-to-grave security and sharing such benefits of daily life as long vacations and early retirement. Europeans, in turn, learned to live with higher taxation as the price of benefits. Those benefits, however, were challenged and rethought in the 1970s and 1980s by the Thatcher revolution, and they face a new challenge at the start of the twenty-first century from demography—a reduced number of taxpayers confronting larger burdens of payment. The next generation of Europeans will undoubtedly be forced to rethink the nature of this prosperity, and the political costs may be high.

The peace of the new belle époque grew steadily after 1975, as the spirit of détente led to the Gorbachev revolution and the end of the cold war. The end of the Soviet empire after 1989 mean Russian troop withdrawals, reduced military concerns for the European

anteed in accordance with the national laws governing the exercise of these rights.

Article 10. **Freedom of Thought, Conscience, and Religion. . . .** This right includes freedom to change religion or belief and freedom, either alone or in community with others and in public or in private, to manifest religion or belief, in worship, teaching, practice and observance. The right to conscientious objection is recognized, in accordance with the national laws governing the exercise of this right.

Article 11. **Freedom of Expression and Information . . .** This right shall include freedom to hold opinions and to receive and impart information and ideas without interference by public authority and regardless of frontiers.

Article 12. **Freedom of Assembly and of Association.** Everyone has the right to freedom of peaceful assembly and to freedom of association at all levels, in particular in political, trade union, and civic matters, which implies the right of everyone to form and to join trade unions for the protection of his or her interests. . . .

Article 13. **Freedom of the Arts and Sciences.** The arts and scientific research shall be free of constraint. Academic freedom shall be respected.

Article 14. **Right to Education.** Everyone has the right to education and to have access to vocational and continuing training. This right includes the possibility to receive free compulsory education. The freedom to found educational establishments with due

respect for democratic principles and the right of parents to ensure the education and teaching of their children in conformity with their religious, philosophical and pedagogical convictions shall be respected, in accordance with the national laws governing the exercise of such freedom and right.

Article 15. **Freedom to Choose An Occupation and Right to Engage in Work. . . . .** Nationals of third countries who are authorized to work in the territories of the Member States are entitled to working conditions equivalent to those of citizens of the Union.

Article 16. **Freedom to Conduct a Business. . . .**

Article 17. **Right to Property.** Everyone has the right to own, use, dispose of and bequeath his or her lawfully acquired possessions. No one may be deprived of his or her possessions, except in the public interest and in the cases and under the conditions provided for by law, subject to fair compensation being paid in good time for their loss. The use of property may be regulated by law insofar as is necessary for the general interest. Intellectual property shall be protected.

Article 18. **Right to Asylum.** The right to asylum shall be guaranteed with due respect for the rules of the Geneva Convention . . . relating to the status of refugees. . . .

From The European Union. Posted at *http://europa.eu.int.*

Question: How does this Bill of Rights compare to other famous bills of rights?

Union, and significantly reduced European dependence on the United States. In the early years of the twenty-first century, the European Union began to plan its own military force and to develop a more independent voice in international relations. The next generation of Europeans will undoubtedly be forced to rethink the diplomatic and military roles of Europe in the world too.

Review Questions

- What were the central elements of Margaret Thatcher's critique of the welfare state?
- How did the Gorbachev revolution happen in the Soviet Union?
- What led to the end of the cold war?
- Why was it possible for the two Germanys to unite in 1990?
- What are the most important achievements of the European Union?

For Further Study

Readings

Ash, Timothy Garton, *The Magic Lantern: the Revolutions of '89 Witnessed in Warsaw, Budapest, Berlin, and Prague* (New York: Random House, 1990). An excellent blend of journalism and current history that conveys a vivid picture of the revolutions.

Ash, Timothy Garton, *History of the Present: Essays, Sketches, and Dispatches from Europe in the 1990s* (London: Allen Lane, 1999).

Ference, Gregory C., ed., *Chronology of 20th-Century Eastern European History* (Detroit: Gale, 1994). Although published in the middle of the Yugoslav wars, it is nonetheless a valuable reference for the cold war, the revolutions of 1989, and the Yugoslav wars.

Gillingham, John, *European Integration, 1950–2003: Superstate or New Market Economy?* (Cambridge: Cambridge University Press, 2003). The first comprehensive history of European integration.

THE GROWTH OF THE EUROPEAN UNION

1975	1980	1985	1990	1995	2000

1967–1992: The European Community (EC)

1992– : The European Union (EU)

1975: British Referendum Accepts EC Membership
1975: Greece, Spain, and Portugal Apply for EC Membership
1979: First Direct Elections to the European Parliament (Strasbourg)
1979: Simone Veil Elected President of the European Parliament
1979: EC Creates the European Currency Unit (ECU)
1981: Greece Begins 5-Year Phased Entry into EC
1983: The 10 EC Members Sign a Solemn Declaration on Unity
1984: European Treaty on Creating the European Union
1984: Margaret Thatcher Negotiates a Special Rebate for Britain
1985: Spain and Portugal Join the EC
1985: Jacques Delors Becomes President of the EC
1985: Single European Act Sets 1992 Date for Open Frontiers
1986: Single European Act Passed by All 12 Members
1986: Spain and Portugal Join the EC
1987: Turkey Applies for EC Membership
1988: Delors Plan Outlines Closer Economic Unity
1988: Thatcher Denounces EC "Superstate"
1989: EC Charter of Social Rights
1989: Austria Applies for EC Membership
1990: Thatcher Denounces EC Centralization
1990: Cyprus and Malta Apply for Membership
1990: Unification of Germany Adds East Germany to EC
1991: Sweden Applies for EC Membership
1992: Maastricht Treaty Creates EU
1992: Single Market Agreements
1992: Norway, Finland, and Switzerland Apply
1992: Swiss Vote to Remain outside the EU
1993: Danish Second Vote Accepts Maastricht
1994: Sweden, Finland, and Austria Join
1994: Poland and Hungary Apply to Join EU
1995: Norway Rejects EU Membership
1995: Estonia, Latvia, Lithuania, Bulgaria, Romania, and Slovakia Apply
1996: Czech Republic and Slovenia Apply
1997: EU Plan to Add 5 East European States
1998: 11 Countries Accept "Single" Currency
1999: Euro Launched
2000: Nice Treaty
2002: Euro Circulates

Photo Credits

Chapter 14

Page 322: Luther before the Diet of Worms (Charles V in the foreground), engraving from *Pictorial History of the World* by J. D. McCabe (Boston: Desmond Publishing Co., 1894)/private collection; 324: © Gail Mooney/CORBIS; 328: trade card (after Leffing) Germany, 1920/private Collection; 329: © David Lees/CORBIS; 330: trade card (after Titian) Germany, 1920/private collection; 331: National Museet, Copenhagen, © Archivo Iconografico, S.A./CORBIS; 333: engraving from *Great Men and Women* (New York: Selmar Hess, 1894)/private collection; 334t: trade card (after Holbein) Germany, 1920/private collection; 334b: trade card, England, 1919/private collection; 335l: trade card (after Holbein), England, 1919/private collection; 335r: National Portrait Gallery, London, UK/Bridgeman Art Library; 336t: trade card (after Moro) Germany, 1920/private collection; 336b: Lambeth Palace Library, London, UK/Bridgeman Art Library; 337: Louvre, Paris, France/Lauros/Giraudon/Bridgeman Art Library; 339: Prado, Madrid, Spain/Giraudon/Bridgeman Art Library; 340: Kunsthistorisches Museum, Vienna, Austria/Bridgeman Art Library

Chapter 15

Page 343: Detail from *Neptune Offering Gifts to Venice*, Giovanni Battista Tiepolo (1696-1770)/Palazzo Ducale, Venice, Italy/ Bridgeman Art Library; 344: Private Collection/Index/Bridgeman Art Library; 345l: Private Collection/Bridgeman Art Library; 345r: Villa Farnese, Caprarola, Lazio, Italy/Bridgeman Art Library; 346: Drawing © Joseph Wheatley, from *Historic Sail*, by Joseph Wheatley and Stephen Howarth, (London: Greenhill Books, 2000); 347tlr: courtesy Smithsonian Institution; 347br–48: engraving from *Great Men and Women* (New York: Selmar Hess, 1894)/private collection; 349: photograph © William J. Duiker; 350t: Bibliotheque Nationale, Paris, France/Lauros/Giraudon/ Bridgeman Art Library; 350b: William L. Clements Library, University of Michigan; 353: © The British Museum; 354: Musee du Temps, Besancon, France/Lauros/Giraudon/Bridgeman Art Library; 356t: engraving by Franz Hogenberg, October, 1567/ private collection; 357t: engraving (after, from left to right, Holbein, F. Zucchero, and Garrard the Elder), London: G. Barrie & Son, 1904/private collection; 357b: © National Maritime Museum, London; 358: engraving by T Woolnoth (after Porbus) from *The Gallery of Portraits* (London: Charles Knight, 1833)/private collection; 359: Private Collection/Bridgeman Art Library; 360: trade card (after Vandyke) Germany, 1920/private collection; 362t: trade card (chromolithograph after Walker) English, 1919/private collection; 362b: engraving by H. Bourne (after Kneller) from Becket and Loggan, *Contemporary Engravings* (London: Blackie & Son, 1860)/private collection; 364: engraving by Franz Hogenberg, July 14, 1578/private collection; 366tl: © Archivo Iconografico, S.A./CORBIS; 366tr: trade card (chromolithograph after Faithorne) English, 1919/private collection; trade card (chromolithograph) English, 1919/private collection

Chapter 16

Page 369: *The Burning of "The Royal James"* at the Battle of Sole Bank, 6th June 1672, Willem van de Velde, the Younger (1633-1707)/Rafael Valls Gallery, London, UK/Bridgeman Art Library; 371l: engraving from *Great Men and Women* (New York: Selmar Hess, 1894)/private collection.; 371tr: engraving from *Great Men and Women* (New York: Selmar Hess, 1894)/private collection.; 371br: trade card (chromolithograph), Germany, 1920/private collection; 372t: engraving by Robert Hart (after Ramsay) from *The Gallery of Portraits* (London: Charles Knight, 1833)/private collection; 372b: Louvre, Paris, France/Peter Willi/Bridgeman Art Library; 373: engraving by W. Holl (after Hals) from *The Gallery of Portraits* (London: Charles Knight, 1833)/private collection; 374: National Gallery, London, UK/Bridgeman Art Library; 375tb: engraving from *Great Men and Women* (New York: Selmar Hess, 1894)/private collection; 376l: New York Academy of Medicine; 376r: trade card (chromolithograph, after Hondius) English, 1919/private collection; 378: © Bettmann/CORBIS; 379t: © New-York Historical Society, New York, USA/Bridgeman Art Library; 379b: Johnny van Haeften Gallery, London, UK/Bridgeman Art Library; 380l: National Gallery of Ireland, Dublin; 380r: Rijksmuseum, Amsterdam, Holland/Bridgeman Art Library; 381: engraving from *Pictorial History of the World* by J. D. McCabe (Boston: Desmond Publishing Co., 1894)/private collection; 382: © Archivo Iconografico, S.A./CORBIS; 385: Hermitage, St. Petersburg, Russia/Bridgeman Art Library; 388: engraving by W. Holl (after Mignard) from *The Gallery of Portraits* (London: Charles Knight, 1833)/private collection; 390: Fine Arts Museums of San Francisco, CA, USA/Giraudon/Bridgeman Art Library; 391: Rijksmuseum, Amsterdam (SK-C-150); 392: Private Collection/ Rafael Valls Gallery, London, UK/Bridgeman Art Library

Chapter 17

Page 396: Custom House from the River Thames from R Ackermann's *Repository of Arts, Literature, Commerce, Manufacture, Fashion and Politics* (London: 1809-28)/engraved by John Bluck, 1808 (aquatint), after T. Rowlandson & A.C. Pugin/private collection; 399: Cheltenham Art Gallery & Museums, Gloucestershire, UK/Bridgeman Art Library; 400: Lady Lever Art Gallery, Port Sunlight, Merseyside, UK/National Museums Liverpool/Bridgeman Art Library; 401: Frans Hals Museum, Haarlem, The Netherlands/Index/Bridgeman Art Library; 406: Musee Lambinet, Versailles, France/Lauros/Giraudon/Bridgeman Art Library; 407: Louvre, Paris, France/Lauros/Giraudon/Bridgeman Art Library; 409: State Russian Museum, St. Petersburg, Russia/ Bridgeman Art Library; 410: Bibliotheque Nationale, Paris, France/Bridgeman Art Library; 411l: Spink & Son Ltd., London, UK/Bridgeman Art Library; 411r: Hospital de Tavera, Toledo, Spain/Giraudon/Bridgeman Art Library; 413: Philadelphia Museum of Art: The John H. McFadden Collection; 414: Hermitage, St. Petersburg, Russia/Peter Willi/Bridgeman Art Library; 417: Gathering the Cane, engraving (anonymous, 19th c)/private collection

Chapter 18

Page 420: Portrait of Johann Sebastian Bach c.1715 by Johann Ernst Reutsch/Stadtische Museum, Erfurt, Germany/Bridgeman Art Library; 421: Bibliotheque Nationale, Paris, France/Archives Charmet/Bridgeman Art Library; 426: engraving from *Great Men and Women* (New York: Selmar Hess, 1894)/private collection; 427: Lincolnshire County Council, Usher Gallery, Lincoln, UK/Bridgeman Art Library; 428l: Civico Museo Bibliografico Musicale, Bologna, Italy/Bridgeman Art Library; 428r: Royal College of Surgeons, London, UK/Bridgeman Art Library; 429: Bibliotheque Nationale, Paris, France/Archives Charmet/Bridgeman Art Library; 432: Bibliotheque Nationale, Paris, France/Archives Charmet/Bridgeman Art Library; 433: British Museum, London, UK/Bridgeman Art Library; 435: Private Collection/The Stapleton Collection/Bridgeman Art Library; 438: © Bettmann/CORBIS; 439: Coram Foundation, Foundling Museum, London, UK/Bridgeman Art Library; 441: Yale Center for British Art, Paul Mellon Collection/Bridgeman Art Library; 444: Bibliotheque Nationale, Paris, France/Archives Charmet/Bridgeman Art Library

Chapter 19

Page 448: Portrait of Maria Theresa of Austria/© Arte & Immagini srl/CORBIS; 452: © Copyright The British Museum; 453: Courtesy of the Trustees of Sir John Soane's Museum, London/Bridgeman Art Library; 454: Houses of Parliament, Westminster, London, UK/Bridgeman Art Library; 455l: Mary Evans Picture Library; 455r: engraving by W. Wallis (after Shepherd) London: Jones & Co., 1828/private collection; 458: The Granger Collection, New York; 459: Louvre, Paris, France/Giraudon/Bridgeman Art Library; 461: Chateau de Versailles, France/Bridgeman Art Library; 464: Magyar Nemzeti Galeria, Budapest, Hungary/Bridgeman Art Library; 465: Scala/Art Resource, NY; 470: engraving by E. Scriven (after Vanloo) from *The Gallery of Portraits* (London: Charles Knight, 1833)/private collection; 471: photogravure Hanfstaenl (after Warthmüller) from *Great Men and Women* (New York: Selmar Hess, 1894)/private collection; 473: Tretyakov Gallery, Moscow, Russia/Bridgeman Art Library; 474: Bibliotheque des Arts Decoratifs, Paris, France/Archives Charmet/Bridgeman Art Library

Chapter 20

Page 478: The Questioning, 1722 (engraving) by Bernard Picart/Bibliotheque des Arts Decoratifs, Paris, France/Archives Charmet/Bridgeman Art Library; 479: Amalienburg, Schloss Nymphenburg, Munich, Germany/Paul Maeyaert/Bridgeman Art Library; 480l: Nimes, France/Lauros/Giraudon/Bridgeman Art Library; 480r: Place de la Madeleine, Paris, France/Paul Maeyaert/Bridgeman Art Library; 481: Mme. de Châtelet and Voltaire chromolithograph (after Leleux), London: G. Barrie & Son, 1907/private collection; 482: Fitzwilliam Museum, University of Cambridge, UK/Bridgeman Art Library; 484: Ottobeuren, Germany/Lauros/Giraudon/Bridgeman Art Library; 486: trade card (chromolithograph after Döbler), Germany, 1920/private collection; 490: engraving from *Encyclopedia of Trades and Industry*, Diderot, 1752/private collection; 491: engraving from *Great Men and Women* (New York: Selmar Hess, 1894)/private collection; 492: Louvre, Paris, France/Bridgeman Art Library; 494: photogravure by Ludovic Baschet (after Girardet) from *Great Men and Women* (New York: Selmar Hess, 1894)/private collection; 496: Chateau de Versailles, France/Lauros/Giraudon/Bridgeman Art Library; 497: Labour Society, London, UK/Bridgeman Art Library; 498: trade card (chromolithograph), Germany, 1920/private collection

Chapter 21

Page 503: detail from "Louis XVI with his Confessor Edgeworth an instant before his death" (p. 516)/private collection; 504l: engraving from *Pictorial History of the World* by J. D. McCabe (Boston: Desmond Publishing Co., 1894)/private collection; 504r: Musee de la Ville de Paris, Musee Carnavalet, Paris, France/Lauros/Giraudon/Bridgeman Art Library; 507: photogravure by Goupil & Co. (after Mélingue) from *Great Men and Women* (New York: Selmar Hess, 1894)/private collection.; 509t: Musee de la Revolution Francaise, Vizille, France/Visual Arts Library, London, UK/Bridgeman Art Library; 509b: trade card (chromolithograph), Germany, 1920/private collection; 510t: Bibliotheque Nationale, Paris, France/Lauros/Giraudon/Bridgeman Art Library; 510bl: Bibliotheque Nationale, Paris, France/Bridgeman Art Library; 510br: Private Collection/Roger-Viollet, Paris/Bridgeman Art Library; 512l: Musee de la Ville de Paris, Musee Carnavalet, Paris, France/Bridgeman Art Library; 512r: engraving after Roussin, 19th c/private collection; 516: hand-colored print (engraved by Cazenave after Benazech) *Louis XVI. Avec Confesseur Edgeworth, un instant avant sa mort, Fils de St. Louis montez au Ciel* ("Louis XVI with his Confessor Edgeworth an instant before his death, Son of St. Louis ascend to heaven"), Paris: Vente, 1793/private collection; 518: Musee de la Ville de Paris, Musee Carnavalet, Paris, France/Archives Charmet/Bridgeman Art Library; 521: Musee de la Ville de Paris, Musee Carnavalet, Paris, France/Lauros/Giraudon/Bridgeman Art Library; 521: engraving by Robert Graves (after Abbott) 1842, hand-colored/private collection; 528: oil print by George Baxter, 1850s/private collection; 530l: Louvre, Paris, France/Peter Willi/Bridgeman Art Library; 530r: Musee d'Orsay, Paris, France/Giraudon/Bridgeman Art Library

Chapter 22

Page 533: © Peabody Essex Museum, Salem, Massachusetts, USA/Bridgeman Art Library; 535: Interior of a mill, carding and drawing/Private Collection/Bridgeman Art Library; 541: © Bettmann/CORBIS; 543l: Bibliotheque des Arts Decoratifs, Paris, France/Archives Charmet/Bridgeman Art Library; 543r: Scottish National Portrait Gallery, Edinburgh, Scotland/Bridgeman Art Library; 544: Private Collection/Ken Welsh/Bridgeman Art Library; 547l: British Library, London, UK/Bridgeman Art Library; 547r: Private Collection/Bridgeman Art Library; 548: Bibliotheque des Arts Decoratifs, Paris, France/Archives Charmet/Bridgeman Art Library; 549: chromolithograph (anonymous), London, 1901/private collection; 551l: Conservatoire National des Arts et Metiers, Paris, France/Archives Charmet/Bridgeman Art Library; 551r: Musee de la Ville de Paris, Musee Carnavalet, Paris, France/Archives Charmet/Bridgeman Art Library; 553: Private Collection/Bridgeman Art Library; 558: Private Collection/Archives Charmet/Bridgeman Art Library

Chapter 23

Page 564: Fanny Burney (engraving after E. Burney) New York: Johnson, Wilson & Co., 19th c./private collection; 567: © Bettmann/CORBIS; 568: Guildhall Library, Corporation of London, UK/Bridgeman Art Library; 570: photogravure by Goupil & Co. (after Edelfelt) from *Great Men and Women* (New York: Selmar Hess, 1894)/private collection; 571t: © Bettmann/CORBIS; 571b: Philip Mould, Historical Portraits Ltd, London, UK/Bridgeman Art Library; 573: Private Collection/Lauros/Giraudon/Bridgeman Art Library; 576: © CORBIS; 578: Ordre National des Pharmaciens, Paris, France/Archives Charmet/Bridgeman Art Library; 579: © Bettmann/CORBIS; 586: Ministere de L'Education Nationale,

Index

Bentham, Jeremy, 497
Bentley, Elizabeth, 535
Berbice Slave Rebellion, 417
Beria, Lavrenty, 808
Berkeley, George, 492–493
Berlin
    airlift, 804
    bread riots, 627
    congress of, 687, 698
    decree of 1806, 527–528
    revolution (1848), 629
    Wall, 844, 845
Bernhardi, Friedrich von, 699
Bernstein, Edouard, 673–674
Besant, Annie, 580
Bethmann-Hollweg, Theobald von, 701
Beveridge Report, 808–809
Biarritz Agreement, 649
Bible
    Czech translation, 327
    on divorce, 334
    King James version, 361
    Luther and, 329
Big Four, 718
Biological exchanges, 350–351
Birthrate
    contraception and, 579–580
    European, 563
    falling (twentieth century),
        789
Bismarck, Otto von
    antisocialism, 656, 674
    Ausgleich, 650–651
    Biarritz agreement, 649
    career, 646
    constitutional crisis, 647–648
    defense of empire, 655
    diplomacy, 686–688
    dismissal, 696
    Ems Dispatch, 651
    German Confederation, 650
    influence, 812
    Iron and Blood speech, 650
    kulturkampf, 656
    Napoleon III, 633
    welfare state, 657
Bismarckian system, 686–688,
    696
Bizonia, 804
Blackstone, William, 441, 473,
    493–494
Blair, Tony, 834
Blanc, Louis, 604, 628–629
Blanco, Luis Carrero, 825
Blast furnaces, 548, 672
Blaurock, Georg, 332
Bleeding, 428, 429
Blenheim, battle of, 424
Blitzkrieg, 753
Blood, circulation, 377
Bluestockings, 480

Blum, Léon
    election, 750
    nationalization program, 810, 811
    popular front, 734
    social security, 831–832
Blum, Robert, 632
Bodichon, Barbara, 638
Boerhaave, Hermann, 427
Boer War, 566, 692
Bohemia, 327–328, 358–359
Boleyn, Anne, 334
Bolivar, Simon, 622
Bolivia, 350
Bolsheviks. *See also* Communist Party
    decree on peace, 712
    government, 712–713
    meaning, 711
    power seizure, 711–712
Bonald, Louis de, 599
Bonaparte, Joseph, 528
Bonaparte, Louis, 527
Bonaparte, Lucien, 524
Bonaparte, Napoleon. *See* Napoleon I
Boniface VIII, Pope, 323
Bonner, Elena, 839
Book of Common Prayer, 335, 362,
    366
Books of Martyrs, 336
Bosnia, 685
Bosnia war, 851
Bossuet, Jacques-Bénigne, 381
Botanical Gardens at Uppsala, 491
Boucher, François, 459
Boulanger, Georges, 659–660
Bourbons, 355, 612
Bourgeoisie
    comforts, 553
    definition, 412
    diet, 576
    industrial, 552
    monarchy, 614
    revolution, 504
    upper, 412–413
    urban, 552
Bowdler, Thomas, 599
Boxer Rebellion, 694
Boycott, Charles, 665
Boyle, Robert, 373
Boyne, battle of, 457–458
Bradlaugh, Charles, 580
Brandenburg-Prussia. *See* Prussia
Brandt, Willie, 820–821
Braun, Wernher von, 764
Brazil, 347
Brazzaville Conference, 813–814, 815
Bread, diet of, 430–431
Bread riots, 504, 627
Brecht, Bertolt, 741
Bressemer, Henry, 672
Brest-Litovsk, treaty of, 703, 713
Brethren of the Common Life, 326

Brezhnev, Leonid, 821, 837, 843
Brezhnev Doctrine, 837
Briand, Aristide, 728, 729, 749
Brigate Rosse, 824
Bright, John, 621, 639, 665
Britain, battle of, 457–458, 756–758
British Broadcasting Corporation,
    726–727, 810
British expeditionary force, 755
Brittain, Vera, 724
Bronstein, Lev, 711
The Brothers Karamazov, 680
Browning, Elizabeth Barrett, 578
Broz, Josip. *See* Tito
Brueghel, Pieter the Elder, 340
Brumaire coup, 524
Brunswick Manifesto, 513–514
Bubonic plague, 425
Bukharin, Nikolay, 745
Bull, papal, 323
Bülow, Bernhard von, 658
Burghers, 412
Burke, Edmund, 513
Burney, Fanny, 564, 572
Burschenschaften, 609
Butler, Josephine, 590

Cabinet system
    definition, 448
    rise of, England, 451–452
    royal, 450–451
Cabral, Pedro Alvares, 344
Cagoulard, 733
Cahiers, 402, 505
Calas, Jean, 492
Calley, William, 822
Calonne, Charles de, 462
Calvin, John, 333–334, 339, 390
Calvinism
    cuius regio, eius religio, 358
    in England, 357
    in France, 355
    geographical predominance, 482
    Netherlands, 355, 356
    origins, 333
    spread of, 333–336
    theology, 333
Cameralists, 403
Campeggio, Cardinal, 334
Candide, 489, 493
Canning, 575–576
Cano, Sebastian del, 345
Capitalism
    coinage, 557
    doctrine of, 415–416
    evolution, 602
    founders, 491
    Marx's view, 557
    physiocrats, 415
Caporetto, battle of, 703
Captain Swing Riots, 616

Christianity
culture (eighteenth century),
483–484
The Enlightenment, 491–493,
492–493
high culture, 483–484, 484
primacy of faith, 487
reformation
German, 329–331
radical, 330–331
Switzerland, 331–334
in schools, 583
science and, 370
socialist, 604
Western Church reforms, 323–328
Christian IV of Denmark, 359
Churches, established, 484
Churches-state separation, 658,
662–663
Churchill, John, 383
Churchill, Randolph, 590, 666, 752
Churchill, Winston
appeasement attacks, 752, 753
Balkans' crisis, 699–700
Casablanca Conference, 762
Dresden bombing, 765
eloquence, 757
FDR meeting, 758
Iron Curtain speech, 803, 804
maiden speech, 757–758
Middle East intervention, 704
Stalin meeting, 768
Tehran Conference, 767–768
vision, 749
Yalta conference, 768–769
Circulatory system, 375, 377
Cisneros, Cardinal Francisco Jiménez,
336
Cities. *See also* Urbanization
British, size, 539
chartered, 412
industrial, 550
migration to (1600s), 389–390
migration to (1700s), 412
Old Regime
cleanliness, 425
economic structure, 412–414
populations, 410–412
social structure, 412–414
unrest, 453, 455
urbanization, 549–550
urban renewal, 550–551
Citizens, 511
City-states, Italian, 344, 354
Civil Code. *See* Napoleonic code
Civil disobedience, 696, 736
Civil wars
American, 639
English, 360–362, 366
French, 517–520
Greece (1946–1949), 803

Russian (1917–1920), 713–714
Spanish, 734
Classicism, 486, 606
Class struggle, 635
Clausewitz, Karl von, 699
Cleanliness, 425
Clemenceau, Georges
French secularization, 659
labor ministry creation, 662
Paris Peace conference, 718–719
radical-democratic program, 663
retirement, 723
worker strikes, 673
Clement VII, Pope, 324, 334, 337
Clement XIII, Pope, 489
Clement XIV, Pope, 482
Clergy
civil constitution, 509–510
criticism of, 327
ignorance of, 326
laws against (1793), 519
nonjuring, 514
opposition to, 659
Clericis Laicos, 323
Clothing, class distinctions, 391–392
Coal production, 543, 545–546
Cobden, Richard, 621
Coen, Jan Pieterszoon, 378
Coercive Acts of 1774, 457
Coffee, 432
Coffeehouses, 432, 480–481
Coitus interruptus, 444, 579
Coke, Sir Edward, 361
Colbert, Jean-Baptiste, 375, 386,
387
Cold war
in Asia, 804–805
cooling down, 820–821
ending, 841–849
events, chronology, 805
origins, 801–804
Coligny, Gaspard de, 356
Collective security, 769
Colombian exchange, 433, 538
Colonialism
biological exchange, 350
cost of, 689
economic importance, 387–388
end of. *See* Decolonization
English, 376–377
French, 377
imperialism *vs.*, 688
Irish, 361
penal, 601
Portuguese, 346–347, 378
post WWI, 735–736
self-determination, 735
Spanish
cultural legacy, 350
Dutch seizure of, 378
establishment, 347–348

Indians, treatment of, 348–349, 350
moral issues, 348
Colt, Samuel, 639
Columbus, Christopher, 344–345, 348
Combination Acts, 634
Commentaries on the Laws of England,
441, 494
Committee of public safety, 518
Common market, 818–820
Common Sense, 496
Communication, 422
The Communist Manifesto, 635, 674
Communist Party. *See also* Bolsheviks
collapse, 849
congress 1956, 745–746
Eastern European coups, 803
establishment (Russia), 714–715
great terror, 745–746
purges, 745
Compagnonnages, 634
Companionate marriage, 339
Compass, introduction, 344
Concentration camps
first use, 692
Franco's, 734
Nazi, 765–766
Concerning Education, 487
Concordat of 1801, 525
The Condition of the English Working Class,
552
Condoms, 444, 579, 792
Condorcet, Antoine de, 488, 499
Conference diplomacy, 767–768
Confessional Division, 646
Confessions of an English Opium Eater,
578
Congress of Berlin, 687, 698
Congress of Vienna, 595, 596, 622
Congress system, 597
Conquistadores, 348, 349
Conrad, Joseph, 680
Conservatism
evolution, 602
French, 730–731
law, 599–601
Metternichian, 595
morality, 723–724
religious, 597–599
revival (post-WWI), 723–724
Spanish, 597–599
Conservative alliance, 597
Conservative revolution, 834–837
Constance, Council of, 325, 328
Constantine of Russia, 611
Constitutions
French (1791), 511
French (1799), 524
French (year I), 516–517
French (Year III), 520
government-based, 450
unwritten, 448

Haiti, 347
Hals, Frans, 380
Hamburg epidemic, 568
Handel, George Frideric, 484
Hanoverian kings, 445
Hapsburg Empire
    Austrian succession, 463–464
    Bohemian War, 359
    church-state relations, 466–467
    enlightened despotism, 464–465
    French influence, 383, 384
    Hungry rule, 353
    last of, 384
    monarchs, 463
    peasant emancipation, 464
    pragmatic sanction, 463–464
    reforms, 466–468
    Salic law, 563
    serfdom, 465–466
    Seven Years' War, 359
    size, 463
    -Valois rivalry, 354
    Versailles treaty, 719
Hardenberg, Karl von, 595
Hardie, Keir, 666–667
Hard Times, 552, 583
Hargrreave, James, 546
Harrington, James, 366
Harvey, William, 375, 377
Hasek, Jaroslav, 726
Haussmanization, 551
Haussmann, Georges, 551
Havana, 376
Havel, Václav, 837, 845, 847–848
Hawkins, Sir John, 357
Health, biological exchange, 350–351
Health, Old Regime, 425–426
Heath, Edward, 835–836
Hegel, George Wilhelm, 607, 635
Heine, Heinrich, 568–569
Heldenstadt, 844
Helsinki Accords, 830, 831, 837
Helvetius, Adrianus Engelhard, 387
Helvétius, Claude, 493
Henry Navarre, 358, 359
Henry of Guise, 358
Henry "the Navigator," 344
Henry III of England, 358
Henry VII of England, 334–335, 357, 390
Henry VIII of England
    demands of, 337
    divorces, 334
    improvidence of, 356
    monasteries, suppression of, 334–335
    monastic lands, 360
Herder, Gottfried von, 491
Hereros, 693
Heresies, 327–328
Hermitage Museum, 479
Herzl, Theodor, 662

Heydrick Reinhard, 766
Hidalgos, 388
Hilton, Walter, 326
Himmler, Heinrich, 741, 766, 769
Hindenburg, Paul von, 703, 706, 741
Hiroshima, 765
History of Bohemia, 608
History of the Decline and Fall of the
    Roman Empire, 598
The History of the World, 607
Hitler, Adolf
    Afrika Korps, 758
    anti-Semitism, 766
    assassination attempt, 763
    Beer Hall Putsch, 728
    chancellorship, 741
    death, 765
    Dunkirk withdrawal, 755
    France's surrender, 755
    political career, 738
    reign, 727
    rise of, 740–741
    two-front war, 758
    war on US, 762
Hobbes, Thomas, 366
Ho Chi Minh, 696, 736, 816
Hoess, Rudolf, 766, 767
Hogarth, William, 390, 453
Hogenberg, Franz, 356
Holbach, Paul, 499
Holocaust, 765–767
Holstein, Fritz von, 696
Holy Alliance, 597
Holy Roman Empire
    Congress of Vienna, 596
    Hapsburg rule, 463
    hostility toward, 383
    Joseph II rule, 465–466
    Protestant Reformation, 330
    Salic Law, 463
Home rule, 664, 665–667
Homosexuality
    illegality (eighteenth century), 443
    illegality (nineteenth century),
        590–591
    scandals, 591
Honecker, Erich, 844
Hooch, Pieter de, 391
Horse-Hoeing Husbandry, 399
Horthy, Miklós, 727
Hospitals
    disease, 570
    foundling, 437–438
    Old Regime, 428
Hossbach memorandum, 751
House of Orange, 381
Housing
    comfort, (1600s), 392
    heat (eighteenth century),
        425–426
    middle class (1665), 391

slums, 672
urban, 550
Hugo, Victor, 551, 607, 608
Huguenots
    characterization, 355–356
    protection, 358
    refugees, 482
Humanae vitae, 793
Humanism, 328, 371
Humanitarianism, 690
Humanity, crimes against, 769
Human Rights, 769
Human rights, European court of, 819
Hume, David, 491
Humoral theory, 570
The Hunchback of Norte Dame, 607
Hungarian Rhapsodies, 608
Hunger march, 730
Hungry
    attack on, 359
    autonomy, 629, 651
    communist coup, 803
    elections, 844
    magnate class, 463
    rebellion (1848), 629
    rebellion (1956), 837
Hus, Jan, 327–328
Hussites, 327–328
Hutton, James, 491
Hydrogen bomb, 806

Ibsen, Henrik, 679
Ideology, 639
Ignatius of Loyola, 337
Il Duce. *See* Mussolini, Benito
Illegitimacy
    eighteenth century, 444, 445
    nineteenth century, 581
    twentieth century, 790–791
Il Risorgimento, 643
Immigration. *See* Migrations
Immunization
    church opposition, 566
    discovery, 424–425
    smallpox, 425
Imperialism
    arms race, 698–699
    Asia, 693–696
    colonialism *vs.,* 688
    French, 689, 695
    global conquest, 688
    humanitarian, 690
    -militarism, relationship, 690
    -nationalism, relationship, 689–690
    new, 685
    origins, 690–691
    post WWI, 735–736
    resistance, 692–693
Impression: Sunrise, 679
Impressionism, 679
Incan Empire, 348

Smuggling, Caribbean, 377
Snow, John, 567, 568
Social classes
    conflict, 390–391, 673
    diet and, 576–577
    disease and, 568
    distinctions in, 391–392
    life expectancy, 565
    middle, 552
    opium use, 578
    structure (nineteenth century), 552–555
The Social Contract, 489, 497
Social Darwinism, 681, 690
Social insurance law, 731
Socialism
    Bismarck's opposition, 656
    British, 730
    democratic, 673
    evolutionary, 635, 636, 673–674
    industrialization, 555
    parties espousing, 674–675
    principles, 604
    revolutionary, 634–636, 673–674
    rise of, 633–636
    Second International, 674–675
    state, 635
    term coinage, 601
    Third International, 714
    utopian, 604
    values, 814
    varieties, 604, 634
Social life
    cooperative, 402
    Old Regime, 420
    Old regime, 412–412
    Quechua, 348
    responsibility, 814
    stratification, 388–389
Society of Friends
    abolitionist movement, 416–417
    antislavery movement, 622–623
    Emancipation Act, 619
    founding, 482
Society of Jesus, 337, 373
Sola scriptura, 328
Soldiers
    general staff, 647
    homosexuality, 591
    rank, 363
Solzhenitsyn, Alexsandr, 744, 838
Somaschi, 336
Somme, 706
Sophia, A Person of Quality, 499, 500
The Sorrows of Young Werther, 607
Southey, Robert, 550
South Seas Bubble, 451–452
Sovereignty, definition, 449
Sovereignty, forms of, 449–450

Soviet Union. *See* Union of Soviet
    Socialist Republics
Sovkhoz, 744
Sozzini, Fausto, 331
Sozzini, Laelio, 331
Spaak, Paul-Herni, 817
Space race, 763–764, 830
Spain
    Basque terrorist, 825
    Caribbean market, 376
    Charles V and, 354
    civil war, 734
    colonies
        cultural legacy, 350
        establishment, 347–348
        Indians, treatment of, 348–349, 350
        moral issues, 348
        system, 349–350
    conservative, 597–599
    decline of, 363–364
    Dutch truce, 358
    French war, 354
    Inquisition, 484
    Netherlands' revolt, 355–356
    papal dominance, 336
    trade monopoly, 350
    Treaty of Tordesillas, 345
    war of Succession, 383, 384, 387
Spanish Armada, 357–358
Spanish influenza, 707
Spanish Main, 377
Spanish Succession, War of, 455–456
Speransky, Michael, 610–611
Spheres of influence, 768
Spice trade, 378
Spinning jenny, 546
Spinning mule, 546
Spinoza, Baruch, 381
Spirit of the Laws, 496
The Spirit of the Laws, 487, 489
The Spiritual Exercises, 337
Splendid isolation, 686
Sputnik, 806
St. Bartholomew's Day Massacre, 356
St. Peter's Basilica, 329, 366
Stab-in-the-back myth, 728
Stadtholder, 356
Staël, Germaine de, 462, 525
Stakhanovites, 807
Stalin, Joseph
    Baltic states annexation, 754
    birth place, 849
    brutality, 743
    Churchill, meeting, 768
    death, 808
    dictatorship, 744, 808
    five year plans, 744–745
    great terror, 745–746
    name change, 712

Nazi-Soviet Pact, 753
    reign, 727
    Tehran Conference, 767–768
    Yalta conference, 768–769
Stalingrad, 763
Stamp Tax of 1765, 456
Standard of living, 555, 779
Ständestaat, 402
Stanley, Henry Morton, 690, 692
Star Chamber, 362
The State of the Poor, 555
State service, 406
State socialism, 635
Status quo, 639
Stauaffenberg, Claus von, 763
Stavisky, Alexandre, 733
Stavisky scandal, 732–733
Steam engine, 543
Steel, age of, 672
Stein, Frieherr von, 557
Stephens, James, 638
Stephenson, George, 543, 549
Stephenson's rocket, 549
Stesemann, Gustav, 749
Stolypin, Peter, 670–671
Stopes, Marie, 772, 791–792
Strachey, Lytton, 591
Straits of Magellan, 349
Stravinsky, Igor, 679
Stream of consciousness, 726
Stressemann, Gustav, 728–729
Stuart dynasty, 360–361
Student rebellions, 824
Sturdy beggars, 389–390
Sturmabteilungen, 741
Sturm un Drang, 607
Subsistence diet, 430
Substance economy, 400
Suez Canal, 758
Suez Crisis, 807
Suffrage
    campaign for, 677–678
    expansion, 727
    universal, 515
Sugar
    colonies, 377
    gin production, 351
    slavery and, 416
    trade, 622
Sukarno, Achmed, 816
Süleyman the Magnificent, 353
Sultans, 353
Summit meetings, 821, 841–843
Surrealism, 726
Suspects, law of, 519, 520, 633
Süssmilch, Johann, 491
Sweden, 359, 360, 364
Swift, Jonathan, 451–452
Swiss Confederation, 331–334
Syllabus of Errors, 655